CURRENT LAW YEAR BOOK 1978

AUSTRALIA
The Law Book Company Ltd.
Sydney : Melbourne : Brisbane

CANADA AND U.S.A.
The Carswell Company Ltd.
Agincourt, Ontario

INDIA
N. M. Tripathi Private Ltd.
Bombay

ISRAEL
Steimatzky's Agency Ltd.
Jerusalem : Tel Aviv : Haifa

MALAYSIA : SINGAPORE : BRUNEI
Malayan Law Journal (Pte.) Ltd.
Singapore

NEW ZEALAND
Sweet & Maxwell (N.Z.) Ltd.
Wellington

PAKISTAN
Pakistan Law House
Karachi

CURRENT LAW
YEAR BOOK
1978

Being a Comprehensive Statement of
the Law of 1978

General Editor
PETER ALLSOP, M.A.
Barrister

Assistant General Editor
CLAIRE BOOTH, LL.B.
Solicitor

Administration
SANDRA MENEAUD

346

Editors

English Cases :
D. A. BARTLETT, B.A., *Barrister*
G. R. BRETTEN, M.A., LL.B., *Barrister*
C. M. BUTLER, LL.B., *Barrister*
CAROL DODGSON, *Barrister*
J. ELVIDGE, *Barrister*
I. F. GOLDSWORTHY, *Barrister*
J. GROVE HULL, M.A., LL.B., *Barrister*
JERVIS KAY, LL.B., *Barrister*
EDMUND LAWSON, M.A., *Barrister*
ANTHONY PITTS, *Barrister*
CLARE RENTON, *Barrister*
ROBERT WEBB, LL.B., *Barrister*

Scots, Irish and Dominion Cases :
DAVID E. B. GRANT, B.A., LL.B., *Barrister*

European Communities :
V. E. HARTLEY BOOTH, LL.B., *Barrister*

Delegated Legislation :
W. J. TATE, LL.B., *Barrister*

Northern Ireland :
T. R. ERSKINE, LL.B., *Barrister*

Damages Awards :
DAVID KEMP, B.A., *Barrister*
DERRICK TURRIFF, *Barrister*

Articles :
P. C. T. STEWART, *Barrister*

LONDON
SWEET & MAXWELL LTD.   STEVENS & SONS LTD.
1979

The Mode of Citation

of the CURRENT LAW YEAR BOOK

is *e.g.*:

[1978] C.L.Y. 1270

SBN 421 25820 9

Published in 1979 by
Sweet & Maxwell Limited of
11 New Fetter Lane, London,
and printed in Great Britain
by The Eastern Press Limited
of London and Reading

PREFACE

THIS volume completes thirty-two years of Current Law publishing. It supersedes the monthly issues of *Current Law* for 1978 and covers the law from January 1 to December 31 of that year.

Citators

The Case Citator and the Statute Citator are contained in a separate volume, issued with this volume.

The *Current Law Citator* covers cases during the years 1977 and 1978 and statutes during the period 1972–78. There are permanent bound volumes covering cases during the period 1947–76 and statutes during 1947–71.

The present volume contains a table of cases digested and reported in 1978 and the usual tables covering 1978 Statutory Instruments and their effect on the orders of earlier years and a table of Northern Ireland Statutory Rules and Orders.

Articles

In continuation of the consolidated Index of Articles 1947–56 published in the *Current Law Year Book 1956* there is an alphabetical index of articles published during 1978 in the present volume. This index includes the full title and reference of an article and the name of its author.

Index

The Subject-matter Index in this volume has been compiled by Claire Booth, LL.B., Solicitor. Due to the ever-increasing size of the index it was decided to include in 1977 references from 1972 onwards only. This provides an overlap of five years in the index which covers in great detail the whole of the law decided, enacted, issued or published during the years 1972–78. In addition this index includes all statutes enacted since 1947. The full thirty-year Index from 1947–76 may be found in the 1976 *Year Book*.

Statutes and Orders

Fifty-nine Acts received the Royal Assent during the year, there were three Church Assembly Measures. A complete list of Statutes appears under the title STATUTES AND ORDERS.

The number of Statutory Instruments during 1978 was 1,977. Of these, 1,048 are general and 929 are local and, although numbered, only 1,448 of these were printed. The effect on the orders of 1947 to 1978 is shown in a table following the list for 1978.

Cases

The number of cases digested herein is 1951. This figure does not include the short reports showing what damages have been awarded in cases of injury or death. Sixty-three of these decisions have been collected and edited by Mr.

PREFACE

David Kemp and Mr. Derrick Turriff, and an alphabetical table of these decisions will be found on page 37 together with a list of sub-headings under which they are digested.

The *Year Book* again includes a selection of cases of persuasive force from the Scottish courts and the courts of the British Dominions and from the English county courts. It also includes a section on the law of the European Communities.

Court of Appeal

As a service to the profession *Current Law* this year continues the publication of brief notes of decisions of the Court of Appeal (Civil Division) which have not hitherto been reported but whose transcripts are available in the Supreme Court Library at the Royal Courts of Justice. *Current Law* is indebted to Mr. Avtar S. Virdi, Barrister, who has prepared the notes of the details of the cases. Transcripts of these cases were previously available in the Bar Library.

Northern Ireland

All Northern Irish Acts and Orders and the cases reported from the courts of Northern Ireland have been digested together with a selection of the cases reported from the courts of Eire. This work has been carried out by our editor in Northern Ireland, Mr. T. R. Erskine.

How to Use Current Law

Those who want to get the full benefit of the service offered are reminded that they should study " How to Use Current Law " which is always available from the publishers.

The General Editor thanks those who have pointed out errors and have sent in notes of interesting cases.

March 1979

P. A.

CONTENTS

CONTENTS

8

TABLE OF CASES

9

TABLE OF CASES

TABLE OF CASES

11

TABLE OF CASES

TABLE OF CASES

13

TABLE OF CASES

TABLE OF CASES

15

TABLE OF CASES

TABLE OF CASES

TABLE OF CASES

TABLE OF CASES

19

TABLE OF CASES

20

TABLE OF CASES

TABLE OF CASES

TABLE OF CASES

TABLE OF CASES

24

TABLE OF CASES

TABLE OF CASES

TABLE OF CASES

TABLE OF CASES

TABLE OF CASES

TABLE OF CASES

TABLE OF CASES

31

COURT OF APPEAL

(CIVIL DIVISION)

SUPREME COURT LIBRARY TRANSCRIPTS

Decisions of the Court of Appeal (Civil Division) during the period May 1977 to June 1978, of which transcripts have been lodged in the Supreme Court Library and which have not been reported elsewhere in this Yearbook. These transcripts were formerly lodged in the Bar Library.

33

DAMAGES FOR PERSONAL INJURIES OR DEATH

The cases listed below are digested under the following headings in descending order of the amount of damages awarded:

Injuries of Maximum Severity
Multiple Injuries
Brain and Skull
Face
Jaw and Teeth
Burns and Scars
Skin
Sight
Spine
Respiratory Organs
Reproductive and Excretory Organs

Sacrum, Pelvis and Hip
Arm
Wrist
Hand
Fingers and Thumb
Leg
Ankle
Foot
Hernia
Minor Injuries
Fatal Accidents

DAMAGES FOR PERSONAL INJURIES OR DEATH

TABLE OF STATUTORY INSTRUMENTS 1978

1978		C.L.Y.	1978		C.L.Y.
1		1952	83		678
2		1952	84		678
3		3070	85		678
4		3070	86		3070
5		3070	87		1860
6 (C.1)		2608	88		1860
7		2581	89		1860
10		1582	90		1860
11		124	91		75
12		2846	96 (S.4)		3125
15 (C.2)		2495	97		1493
16		2494	98		1494
17		78	99		2456
18		78	105		1491
19		3070	106 (S.5)		3572
20		1951	107		2764
21		2033	109		678
22		1559	110		678
24		7	111		678
25		3073	112 (S.6)		3709
26		3073	113 (S.7)		3335
27		3070	114 (S.8)		3336
28		1655	115 (S.9)		3343
30		535	116 (S.10)		3341
31		127	117 (S.11)		3593
32		79	123 (S.12)		3224
34		1585	124 (S.13)		3486
36		2747	125 (S.14)		3222
37		1524	126		2624
38		1528	127		2915
39		3070	128		1559
40		1946	129		1854
41		1946	132 (C.3)		418
43		1860	133		1494
44		1530	134		2282
45		1860	139 (C.4)		146
46		1860	140		128
47		1860	141		1636
48		1860	142		3070
49		1860	143		3070
50		1559	146 (L.1)		1908
51		3070	147 (L.2)		1931
52		3070	148		3574
53		1634	152		3706
54		2747	153		951
57		2934	154		1731
60		3070	155		678
61		3070	158		3415
62		74	159 (C.5) (S.18)		3598
63		1860	160 (S.19)		3642
68 (S.1)		3303	161 (S.20)		3572
69		1581	162 (S.21)		3690
70		2784	163		79
73		2935	164		1559
74		1478	165		1559
75 (S.2)		3375	166		3070
76 (S.3)		3372	171		2468
77		678	172 (C.6) (S.22)		3360
78		678	173 (S.23)		3362
79		1749	175 (S.24)		3415
81		678	176 (L.3)		381
82		678	177		1720

TABLE OF STATUTORY INSTRUMENTS

1978	C.L.Y.	1978	C.L.Y.
178	2661	260	2661
179	2231	257	38
180	1727	258	38
181	1728	259	49
182	2432	261	3070
183	1650	262	3070
184	1650	263	3070
185	2515	264	3070
186	102	265	3070
187	2239	266	2267
188	2757	267	1470
189	1946	268	3070
190	1946	269	1508
191	1479, 3356	270	1445
192	678	271	685
193	678	272	291
194	668	273	3037
195	1961	274	291
196	1961	275	1721
197	873	276	165
198	2130	277	1735
199	2759	278	2287
201	70	279	824
205 (S.25)	3305	280	1486
206 (S.26)	3113	281	1486
207 (S.27)	3113	282	1650
208 (S.28)	3768	283	1945
209	1500	284	124
210	2277, 3559	285	3069
211	2277	286	2443
213	3070	287	2455
214	1498	288	1479
215	67	289	2272
216	2257	293	2597
217	1586	294	67
218	2461	295	67
219	1559	296	67
222 (S.29)	3629	297	67
223	2934	298	67
224	2524	299	67
225	1740	300	67
226	1559	301	67
227	1559	302	67
228	2036	303	67
229 (S.30)	3678	304	67
230	1536	305	67
231	1860	306	67
232	2766	307	67
233	2934	308	67
237	678	309	1559
238	3076	310	1559
239	198	315 (S.32)	3488
240	1891	316	1856
241	128	317	128
242	2934	318	2460
243	1489	319	1752
244	51	320	71
245	128	321	2759
246	678	322	2923
247	1851	323 (S.33)	3175
248	1559	324 (S.34)	3750
250	2260	325	3069
251 (L.4)	416	326	1660
252 (S.31)	3632	327	2879, 3747
254	2542	328	1559
255	1965	329	1555
256 (C.7)	47	330	1555

1978	C.L.Y.	1978	C.L.Y.
331	2043	417 (L.7)	1970
332	2043	419 (S.43)	3507
333	1559	420	1559
334	1559	421	1559
335	1559	422	2284
336	1559	423	2784
337	1559	425 (S.44)	3556
338	1559	427	2743
339	2031	428	67
340	1559	429	951
341	1559	430	2764
342	1559	431 (S.45)	3415
343	1559	432	2934
344	1559	433	2775
345	1559	434	1644
346	1559	436	1467
347	1559	437	1860
348	1559	438	1486
349	1559	439 (L.8)	452
350	1559	440	1868
351	1559	443	3027
352	1559	444	38
353	1559	445	2529
354	1559	446	51
355	1559	447	45
356	1559	448	2934
359 (L.5)	2411	453	213a
360 (S.35)	3352	454	2661
361	1559	455	1450
362	2934	461	1564
363	2934	462	2733
367 (C.8)	2797	463	1500
369 (S.36)	3615	464	1559
370 (S.37)	3609	467	859
371 (S.38)	3622	468	2372
372 (S.39)	3294	469	1503
373	2671	470	2141
374	2264	471	2459
375	2278	472	1729
376	1559	473	1865
380	62	474	1929
381 (S.40)	3421	475	2791
382	2921	476	1559
383	2743	477	1559
384	2287	478	1559
387	2467	481	2535
389	58	482	1860
390	920	483	3011
391	2280	484	3077
392	2280	485 (C.10)	634
393	2280	486 (C.11)	130
394	2775	487	884
397 (L.6)	375	489	2031
398	1559	490	1479
401 (S.41)	3424	491 (S.46)	3224
402 (C.9) (S.42)	52, 3112	492 (S.47)	3368
403	3070	493	1559
404	3070	494	2512
405	3070	495	2508
406	3070	496	1526
407	2270	497	1559
408	2270	501	1559
409	2784	504 (S.48)	3297
410	2784	505	66
412	1559	506	1749
415	1960	507	2784
416	1960	508	2775

1978		C.L.Y.	1978		C.L.Y.
509		3070	623		1555
510		3070	627	(C.15)	2862
511		3070	628		3070
516		1492	629		855
520		3069	632		1559
523		2912	635		2292
524		2775	636		3070
525		1559	639		2928
527		825	640		678
528	(S.49)	3561	641		678
529		2775	644		1925
532		3033	645	(S.58)	3294
533	(C.12)	2659	646		1500
537		1559	647		2743
540		1464	651		1872
541		79	652		1929
542		124	653		3070
543		246	660	(S.60)	3476
544		152	661		1581
545		1492	662		1662
546		2934	663	(S.59)	3113
547		2934	664		2759
552		2262	665		1750
553		1561	666		3070
554		128	667		3070
556		2909	668		3070
557	(C.13)	2908	669		2583
558		1751	670	(S.61)	3548
559	(S.50)	3118	671		1925
560	(S.51)	3359	672		1952
561	(S.52)	3294	673		2661
564		2446	674		678
569	(L.9)	255	675		2934
570	(L.10)	145	682	(L.12)	374
572		3070	683		77
579	(L.11)	2411	685		2037
580		2936	688		2934
581		2523	689		79
582	(S.53)	3415	690	(S.62)	3572
583	(S.54)	3365	691		972
584	(S.55)	3483	692		1722
585	(S.56)	3483	693		128
586	(C.14)	2245	697		2583
594		79	698		678
595		3069	704	(L.13)	145
596		1559	705	(L.14)	255
597		79	707		2616
598		678	708		79
600		2741	711		1559
601		678	712	(C.16)	450
602		1893	720		1704
605		2658	721		1690
607		2276	722		1704
608		2775	723		185
610		1860	724		2907
611		2663	725	(C.17)	2908
612		2934	726		2907
613		2934	727	(C.18)	2908
614		1559	733		2661
615		2656	735		1965
616		2212	737		951
617		1408	738		1506
618		1408	739		1872
619		1408	741		3078
620		2434	742		46
621		2246	743		2791
622	(S.57)	3588	749		2541

TABLE OF STATUTORY INSTRUMENTS

1978		C.L.Y.	1978		C.L.Y.
940		2934	1028		1732
941		2743	1029		2661
943	(S.80)	3113	1030		162
944	(S.81)	3113	1031		162
945		685	1032		1408
946		1486	1033		1294
947	(S.82)	3335	1034		1735
948	(S.83)	3341	1035	(C.29)	1944
949		2283	1036	(N.I.6)	2184
950		2032	1037	(N.I.7)	2184
951		843	1038	(N.I.8)	2101
952		2459	1039	(N.I.9)	2133
954	(C.23)	2445	1040	(N.I.10)	2128
955	(S.84)	3572	1041	(N.I.11)	2184
957		2168	1042	(N.I.12)	2105
958		2170	1043	(N.I.13)	2149
959		862	1044	(N.I.14)	2151a
960		1498	1045	(N.I.15)	2127
962	(S.85)	3306	1046	(N.I.16)	2175
963	(S.86)	3306	1047	(N.I.17)	2112
964	(S.87)	3423	1048	(N.I.18)	2189
965	(S.88)	3417	1049	(N.I.19)	2180
966		1190	1050	(N.I.20)	2157
968		1559	1051	(N.I.21)	2185
969	(S.89)	3297	1052		1735
970	(C.24) (S.90)	3293	1053		1735
971		1493	1054		1735
972		3033	1055		2849
975		79	1056		1650
976		79	1057		2382
977	(S.91)	3558	1058		127
979		2764	1059		2733
982		866	1060		353
983		1559	1061		2764
986		3070	1062		2752
987		1953	1063	(C.28)	886
988		1955	1064		3047
989		1955	1065		238
990		1860	1066	(L.26)	2411
991		961	1069		2743
992		961, 3103	1070	(S.95)	3628
993		2473	1071	(S.96)	3126
996		124	1072		2045
997	(C.25)	1904	1073		2780
998	(S.92)	3295	1074		85
999	(S.93)	3560	1075		85
1000		2782	1078		1586
1001		1957	1079	(C.30)	2659
1002	(C.26)	68	1080		3074
1003	(C.27)	69	1081		3071
1004		1954	1082		2518
1005		1937	1083		2518
1006		1954	1084		3070
1007		970	1085	(S.97)	3294
1010		67	1086		60
1011	(S.94)	3422	1087		1559
1014		1506	1089		2285
1017		2536	1090		2044
1018		2588	1091		2439
1019		866	1092		2437
1020		1936	1093		2244
1021		2934	1096		856
1022		1477	1097		856
1024		2661	1098		856
1025		1866	1099	(S.98)	3605
1026		75	1101	(C.31)	2154
1027		162	1102		2210

1978		C.L.Y.
1103		1408
1104		1408
1105		1724
1106		1456
1107		200
1108		61
1109		2583
1110		2588
1111		2597
1112		2597
1115	(S.99)	3415
1116		1559
1117		1673
1118		397
1119		2459
1120		2984
1121		1939
1122		1273
1123		2775
1124		1925
1125		1751
1126		1461
1127		2187
1128		1938
1129		3040
1131		2791
1132		2934
1137		1465
1138		1942
1139		1942
1140		1942
1141		2931
1142		678
1143		678
1144		870
1145		870
1146		858
1147		678
1148		675
1150	(C.32)	3023
1151		2227
1152		1731
1153		2652
1154	(S.100)	3462
1155		212
1156		697
1157		2581
1158		1407
1159		1658
1160		1522
1161		2929
1162		1756
1163	(L.27)	1917
1166	(S.101)	3768
1167	(S.102)	3341
1168		1479
1169		2306
1170	(S.103)	3561
1171	(S.104)	3560
1172	(S.105)	3746
1173	(S.106)	3639
1174	(S.107)	3635
1175	(S.108)	3637
1176	(S.109	3634
1177	(S.110)	3638
1178	(S.111)	3640
1179	(S.112)	3421

1978		C.L.Y.
1180		2536
1183		1559
1184		3070
1185	(S.113)	3767
1186		671
1187	(C.33)	3023
1188		79
1190	(S.114)	3521
1191		2766
1192		1929
1193		3070
1194		3070
1195		1559
1196		1673
1197		79
1198		3070
1199		3070
1200		3070
1205		678
1206		1559
1207		1559, 3415
1209		1559
1210		3069
1213		2775
1219		685
1221		2878
1222		1555
1223		1555
1224	(L.28)	152
1225		2934
1226		866
1228		2266
1229		3070
1230		3070
1231		3070
1232		3070
1233		2536
1234		2536
1235		2536
1236		2597
1237		2597
1239		2297
1240		3070
1243	(L.29)	376
1244	(L.30)	2370
1245		882
1246		1860
1247		1860
1248		58
1249		3070
1256	(L.31)	805
1257		2259
1260		2597
1261		2595
1262		2595
1263		2536
1266		1417
1267		2849
1268		2849
1269		1559
1272		1559
1273	(S.115)	3124
1274		124
1275		1464
1276		3070
1277		1509
1278	(S.116)	3297

TABLE OF STATUTORY INSTRUMENTS

1978	C.L.Y.	1978	C.L.Y.
1279 (S.117)	3123	1381	3070
1280	81	1382	1503
1284 (S.118)	3502	1387	2437
1285	1486	1388	2441
1286	1486	1389	2293
1287	1486	1391	124
1288	1749	1392 (S.126)	3422
1289 (C.34)	3023	1393 (C.35)	1720
1290	3015	1394	1703
1294	3015	1395	1703
1295	2258	1399 (S.127)	3629
1296	1543	1400	1929
1297	2528	1403	1450
1298 (L.32)	2370	1404	2287
1299	1860	1405	2287
1300	1860	1406 (N.I.22)	2149
1301	862	1407 (N.I.23)	2112
1302	1586	1408	1650
1303	128	1409	866
1304	1704	1410	1950
1305	2934	1411	2661
1306	1559	1412 (C.36)	1577
1307	2643	1413	1486
1312	1636	1414	3070
1313	3009	1415	3070
1314	2880	1416	3070
1315	3017	1417	264, 3167
1316	2582	1418	264
1317	2536	1419	1965
1318	2597	1420	1495
1319	2597	1421	1956
1320	2597	1422	2284
1321	2597	1423 (S.128)	3343
1325 (S.119)	3603	1424 (S.129)	3336
1326 (S.120)	3358	1425 (S.130)	3215
1329	2990	1426	2287
1330	1203	1430 (C.37)	1973
1333 (S.121)	3420	1431	1970
1334	2531	1432	1970
1340	2775	1433 (C.38)	1980
1342	678	1434	1860
1343 (S.122)	3748	1435	1860
1344	2989	1436	1860
1345	2607	1437	1860
1346	2607	1438	1860
1347	2601	1439	1860
1348	2278	1440 (C.39) (S.131)	3145
1349	2266	1441 (S.132)	3142
1353	2268	1442 (S.133)	3142
1354	2915	1443	1949
1355	2272	1444	1559
1356	1860	1445 (C.40)	2918
1357 (L.33)	578	1447	3070
1358	2258	1448	3070
1364	2581	1453	1863
1365	1925	1454	2518
1366 (S.123)	3415	1456	1703
1368	2270	1457	1693
1369	3070	1458	1693
1370	1860	1459	2799
1371	1749	1460	3102
1372	2915	1461	1946
1373 (S.124)	3572	1462	2779
1374	1486	1463 (S.134)	3294
1378 (S.125)	3556	1464 (S.135)	3625
1379	1486	1465	1860
1380	3070	1466 (C.41)	2751

1978	C.L.Y.	1978	C.L.Y.
1653 (L.36)	145	1768	1860
1654	255	1769	1559
1655	1559	1770	1559
1660	56	1771	2208a
1664	1860	1772	1941
1665	1860	1773	866
1666	3070	1777	925a
1667	3070	1778	1057
1668 (S.150)	3415	1779	115a
1669	2784	1780	2276
1672	3070	1781	3415
1673	3070	1782	3070
1674	3070	1783	1860
1675	1559	1784	1559
1680	2850	1785	1575
1682	1919	1786	671
1683	2523	1787	1496
1684	2603	1790	1492
1685	1559	1791	3013
1686	3216	1792	1860
1689	2779	1793	1860
1690	1860	1794	3556
1691	2278	1795	1852
1692	2281	1796	1941
1694	1860	1797	125a
1695	2453	1798	125a
1698	2783	1799	128
1699	1582	1800	86a
1701	2468	1802	1965
1702	2448	1804	3572
1703	2784	1805	3709
1704	675	1806	1860
1705	1559	1807	1559
1715	1486	1808	2266a
1716	2939a	1809	1958
1717	1520	1810	2597
1718	2658	1811	2597
1722	1860	1812	685
1723	954	1813	1860
1724	3085	1814	1860
1725	675	1816	3494
1726	1559	1817	3588
1727	3351	1818	3588
1728	2625	1819	1750a
1729	1686	1820	1479
1738	2261	1821	1489a
1739	2267	1822	1485
1740	3070	1823	3070
1741	2864	1827	2260
1742	2864	1830	2934
1747	3303	1831	2597
1748	82	1832	2597
1749	1860	1833	1555
1750	1860	1836	213b
1751	1860	1837	2273
1752	194	1838	1636
1754	2747	1839	2657
1755	2747	1840	2784
1756	2747	1841	1860
1757	2764	1842	1860
1758	2764	1843	1860
1759 (L.37)	802	1844	1886
1760	3415	1846 (L.38)	578
1761	3492	1847	1529
1762	3523	1848	1534
1763	2258	1849	3070
1764	2286	1854	1480

TABLE OF STATUTORY INSTRUMENTS

1978		C.L.Y.	1978		C.L.Y.
1855		2531	1908 (N.I.27)		2112
1859		1860	1909 (N.I.28)		2187a
1860		1860	1910		1298
1861		1860	1911		877, 3324
1862		1860	1912		296
1863		1860	1913		3011
1864		1860	1914		2733
1865		2170	1915		298
1866		694	1917		1852
1867		2468	1919		415a
1868		2468	1920		1427
1869		2468	1921		3064a
1870		2597	1922		1559
1871		3626	1923		1559
1872		3126	1924		1559
1873		1479	1925		1559
1874		2747	1926		3556
1875		3113	1927		1501
1876		1508	1928 (C.48)		83
1877		2784	1929		1555
1878		2581	1930		3014
1879		3494	1931		3014
1880		2743	1932		3070
1881		2743	1933		675
1882		692a	1934		3485a
1883		692a	1935		1559
1884		1716	1936		1559
1885		2693	1937		2459
1886		1452	1938		2581
1887		1450	1939		81
1888		1450	1940		3070
1889		1450	1941		678
1890		1427	1942		2523
1891		1427	1943 (L.39)		374
1892		1427	1944		3197
1893		1728	1945		3069
1894		1735	1950		1479
1895		1735	1951		1964
1896		1735	1952		1925
1897		1735	1953		298
1898		1735	1954		1559
1899		174a	1955		3070
1900		174a	1961 (L.40)		2509
1901		174a	1962		3072
1902		2287	1969		1559
1903		877	1970		1559
1904		877	1974		1559
1905		1450	1975		1559
1906 (N.I.25)		2184	1977		1555
1907 (N.I.26)		2166	1978		1555

TABLE OF S.R. & O. AND S.I. 1948–78

AFFECTED BY

STATUTORY INSTRUMENTS OF 1978

1901
1018 revoked No. 893 § 1739
1019 revoked No. 893 § 1739

1907
918 amended No. 660 (S.60) § 3476

1925
1093 amended No. 1601 § 1760

1931
413 amended No. 796 § 685
1066 revoked No. 186 § 102

1932
674 revoked No. 186 § 102

1933
309 amended No. 583 (S.54) § 3365
479 amended No. 583 (S.54) § 3365
544 revoked No. 186 § 102

1934
703 amended No. 583 (S.54) § 3365
1268 revoked No. 1684 § 2603

1935
488 amended No. 928 (S.79) § 3344

1936
626 amended No. 682 (L.12) § 374
626 amended No. 794 (L.20) § 374
626 amended No. 1943 (L.39) § 374

1937
525 amended No. 796 § 685
683 revoked No. 893 § 1739

1938
661 amended No. 1120 § 2984
1183 revoked No. 1954 § 1559

1939
1451 revoked No. 779 § 1722

1941
94 revoked No. 1126 § 1461
2023 revoked No. 893 § 1739

1946
1467 revoked No. 1357 (L.33) § 578

1948
604 amended No. 1577 § 2266
1446 revoked No. 1739 § 2267
1462 revoked No. 425 (S.44) § 3556
1943 amended No. 444 § 38

1949
330 amended No. 543 § 246
2368 amended No. 907 § 2227
2368 amended No. 1151 § 2227

1950
228 revoked No. 1326 (S.120) § 3358
687 revoked No. 1848 § 1534
804 revoked No. 1093 § 2244
1172 revoked No. 1614 § 64
1287 amended No. 583 (S.54) § 3365
1724 amended No. 583 (S.54) § 3365
1987 revoked No. 1739 § 2267
2144 amended No. 117 (S.11) § 3593

1952
900 amended No. 1315 § 3017
944 amended No. 1577 § 2266
2035 revoked No. 186 § 102
2113 amended No. 544 § 152
2113 amended No. 1224 (L.28) § 152
2232 revoked No. 893 § 1739

1953
1555 revoked No. 186 § 102

1954
23 amended No. 806 § 685

1955
125 revoked No. 1739 § 2267
291 revoked No. 1267 § 2849
292 revoked No. 1267 § 2849
589 revoked No. 683 § 77
982 revoked No. 425 (S.44) § 3556

1956
1022 amended No. 1577 § 2266
1738 revoked No. 1269 § 1559
1758 amended No. 1648 § 1962
1760 amended No. 1648 § 1962
1761 amended No. 1648 § 1962
1765 amended No. 1648 § 1962
1766 amended No. 1648 § 1962
1768 amended No. 1648 § 1962
1771 amended No. 1648 § 1962
1773 amended No. 1648 § 1962
1782 amended No. 1648 § 1962
1942 amended No. 1648 § 1962
1943 amended No. 1648 § 1962

1957
348 revoked No. 1267 § 2849
349 revoked No. 1267 § 2849
700 revoked No. 1464 (S.135) § 3625
754 revoked No. 20 § 1951
1173 revoked No. 467 § 859
1353 revoked No. 1739 § 2267

1957—cont.
2051 amended No. 1062 § 2752
2224 amended No. 182 § 2432

1958
558 amended No. 17 § 78
1051 revoked No. 186 § 102
1923 amended No. 963 (S.86) § 3306
1924 amended No. 962 (S.85) § 3306
1990 amended No. 1919 § 415a
2262 revoked No. 1684 § 2603

1959
81 revoked No. 259 § 49
359 revoked No. 259 § 49
364 amended No. 1144 § 870
365 amended No. 1146 § 858
413 amended No. 173 (S.23) § 3362
1832 amended No. 1145 § 870

1960
69 amended No. 1648 § 1962
250 amended No. 254 § 2542
436 revoked No. 186 § 102
971 revoked No. 1881 § 2743
977 revoked No. 1914 § 2733
1395 amended No. 1566 (S.148) § 3588
1471 amended No. 1570 § 2393
2195 amended No. 622 (S.57) § 3588
2397 revoked No. 1684 § 2603

1961
225 revoked No. 1836 § 213b
854 amended No. 1648 § 1962
1214 amended No. 1443 § 1949
1398 amended No. 1508 (S.139) § 3557
1441 amended No. 1353 § 2268
1755 revoked No. 259 § 49

1962
1423 amended No. 1648 § 1962
2045 amended No. 1752 § 194

1963
813 revoked No. 1954 § 1559
1133 revoked No. 1240 § 3070
1223 revoked No. 1096 § 856
1357 revoked No. 893 § 1739
1374 revoked No. 215 § 67
1631 amended No. 1628 § 2747
1636 revoked No. 1881 § 2743
2001 amended No. 1273 (S.115) § 3124

1964
264 revoked No. 1880 § 2743
706 revoked No. 257 § 38
707 revoked No. 258 § 38
1107 amended No. 1163 (L.27) § 1917
1148 amended No. 1577 § 2266
1150 revoked No. 1483 § 79
1152 revoked No. 1485 (S.137) § 3113
1174 revoked No. 215 § 67
1223 revoked No. 215 § 67
2029 revoked No. 1093 § 2244

1965
170 revoked No. 852 § 2758
283 amended No. 1682 § 1919

1965—cont.
321 amended No. 106 (S.5) § 3572
321 amended No. 113 (S.7) § 3335
321 amended No. 161 (S.20) § 3572
321 amended No. 690 (S.62) § 3572
321 amended No. 799 (S.69) § 3572
321 amended No. 925 (S.76) § 3337
321 amended No. 947 (S.82) § 3335
321 amended No. 955 (S.84) § 3572
321 amended No. 1373 (S.124) § 3572
321 amended No. 1804 (S.159) § 3572
403 revoked No. 252 (S.31) § 3632
577 revoked No. 436 § 1467
586 revoked No. 186 § 102
679 revoked No. 602 § 1893
1000 amended No. 1248 § 58
1021 (S.36) amended No. 1248 § 58
1067 revoked No. 1543 § 2747
1105 amended No. 1874 § 2747
1184 revoked No. 505 § 66
1456 amended No. 215 § 67
1457 amended No. 215 § 67
1469 revoked No. 215 § 67
1470 revoked No. 215 § 67
1500 amended No. 750 (L.15) § 377
1532 revoked No. 1105 § 1724
1542 revoked No. 1177 (S.110) § 3638
1559 amended No. 1648 § 1962
1660 revoked No. 1739 § 2267
1776 amended No. 251 (L.4) § 416
1776 amended No. 359 (L.5) § 2411
1776 amended No. 579 (L.11) § 2411
1776 amended No. 1066 (L. 26) § 2411
1826 revoked No. 1779 § 115a
1869 revoked No. 1880 § 2743
1872 revoked No. 1881 § 2743
1992 revoked No. 560 (S.51) § 3359
1995 amended No. 1729 § 1686

1966
165 amended No. 1460 § 3102
735 revoked No. 1839 § 2657
1045 amended No. 1577 § 2266
1152 revoked No. 1844 § 1886
1387 revoked No. 1844 § 1886
1522 amended No. 1508 (S.139) § 3557

1967
82 amended No. 1648 § 1962
224 amended No. 1030 § 162
226 revoked No. 1027 § 162
229 revoked No. 1901 § 179a
395 amended No. 1809 § 1958
430 revoked No. 602 § 1893
1310 amended No. 1729 § 1686
1689 revoked No. 436 § 1467
1699 amended No. 1325 (S.119) § 3603
1865 revoked No. 1420 § 1495
1919 revoked No. 1880 § 2743
1919 amended No. 1881 § 2743

1968
25 amended No. 1239 § 2297
43 amended No. 1346 § 2607
170 amended No. 1387 § 2437
208 amended No. 999 (S.93) § 3560
208 amended No. 1171 (S.104) § 3560
248 amended No. 1545 (S.144) § 3604

S.R. & O. AND S.I. 1948–78 AFFECTED IN 1978

1968—*cont.*

332 revoked No. 1543 § 2747
357 amended No. 1128 § 1938
614 revoked No. 436 § 1467
892 amended No. 454 § 2661
892 amended No. 1024 § 2661
1077 amended No. 1092 § 2437
1163 amended No. 1257 § 2259
1262 amended No. 1118 § 397
1265 revoked No. 30 § 535
1314 amended No. 12 § 2846
1315 amended No. 1388 § 2441
1389 revoked No. 216 § 2257
1408 amended No. 721 § 1690
1452 amended No. 1544 (S.143) § 3607
1558 amended No. 1883 § 692a
1745 revoked No. 1727 (S.152) § 3351
1919 amended No. 146 (L.1) § 1908
1919 amended No. 757 (L.18) § 1908
1920 amended No. 147 (L.2) § 1931
1920 amended No. 758 (L.19) § 1922
2042 amended No. 647 § 2743
2077 amended No. 1649 § 65

1969

414 amended No. 481 § 2535
483 amended No. 959 § 862
483 amended No. 1301 § 862
554 revoked No. 1096 § 856
841 revoked No. 998 (S.92) § 3295
905 amended No. 198 § 2130
1021 revoked No. 294 § 67
1075 amended No. 1030 § 162
1179 revoked No. 1600 § 1758
1626 amended No. 1699 § 1582
1704 revoked No. 809 § 38

1970

16 amended No. 397 (L.6) § 375
16 amended No. 817 (L.21) § 375
102 revoked No. 436 § 1467
147 amended No. 782 § 1452
147 amended No. 1886 § 1452
231 amended No. 754 (L.17) § 1918
287 amended No. 1880 § 2743
287 amended No. 1881 § 2743
400 amended No. 646 § 1500
400 amended No. 1420 § 1495
548 amended No. 1680 § 2850
596 amended No. 1796 § 1941
781 amended No. 76 (S.3) § 3372
789 amended No. 756 § 2523
789 amended No. 1683 § 2523
799 amended No. 38 § 1528
955 revoked No. 216 § 2257
1002 amended No. 1833 § 1555
1123 revoked No. 1739 § 2267
1127 amended No. 927 (S.78) § 3363
1288 revoked No. 796 § 685
1288 amended No. 271 § 685
1288 amended No. 277 § 1735
1400 amended No. 468 § 2372
1536 amended No. 274 § 291
1538 revoked No. 1881 § 2743
1712 revoked No. 1962 § 3072
1792 amended No. 869 (L.23) § 1898
1792 amended No. 869 (L.23) § 1898
1806 revoked No. 229 (S.30) § 3678

1970—*cont.*

1880 amended No. 286 § 2443
1881 amended No. 287 § 2455
1919 revoked No. 275 § 1721
1933 revoked No. 1028 § 1732
1994 revoked No. 30 § 535
2020 revoked No. 796 § 685

1971

1 revoked No. 1388 § 2441
90 amended No. 948 (S.83) § 3341
90 amended No. 1167 (S.102) § 3341
113 revoked No. 796 § 685
131 amended No. 370 (S.37) § 3609
132 amended No. 369 (S.36) § 3615
145 amended No. 1577 § 2266
156 amended No. 1169 § 2306
175 revoked No. 1544 (S.143) § 3607
232 amended No. 1578 § 2278
340 revoked No. 950 § 2032
352 amended No. 867 § 2588
352 amended No. 1018 § 2588
398 revoked No. 692 § 1722
450 amended No. 1536 § 2606
571 revoked No. 207 (S.27) § 3113
592 amended No. 670 (S.61) § 3548
694 amended No. 1261 § 2595
714 revoked No. 1027 § 162
769 amended No. 607 § 2276
769 amended No. 1780 § 2276
827 revoked No. 1962 § 3072
974 amended No. 1140 § 1942
1094 revoked No. 294 § 67
1212 revoked No. 1178 (S.111) § 3640
1292 amended No. 439 (L.8) § 452
1450 amended No. 1139 § 1942
1537 amended No. 504 (S.48) § 3297
1537 amended No. 969 (S.89) § 3297
1537 amended No. 1278 (S.116) § 3297
1634 revoked No. 324 (S.34) § 3750
1686 revoked No. 1303 § 128
1752 amended No. 663 (S.59) § 3113
1752 revoked No. 1875 (S.164) § 3113
1861 amended No. 1266 § 1417
1879 revoked No. 425 (S.44) § 3556
1917 revoked No. 216 § 2257
1954 revoked No. 1759 (L.37) § 802
2089 amended No. 924 (S.75) § 3623
2102 amended No. 1887 § 1450
2103 amended No. 1889 § 1450
2124 amended No. 977 (S.91) § 3558
2125 amended No. 1791 § 3013
2144 revoked No. 207 (S.27) § 3113

1972

71 amended No. 1808 § 2266a
84 revoked No. 294 § 67
429 revoked No. 1772 § 1941
431 revoked No. 1303 § 128
574 revoked No. 1364 § 2581
640 amended No. 1139 § 1942
641 amended No. 788 § 2531
641 amended No. 1334 § 2531
641 amended No. 1855 § 2531
666 revoked No. 1543 § 2747
673 amended No. 1060 § 353
729 amended No. 707 § 2616

53

1972—cont.

738 revoked No. 1875 (S.164) § 3113
759 revoked No. 1875 (S.164) § 3113
760 revoked No. 1875 (S.164) § 3113
764 amended No. 888 § 2657
764 amended No. 1594 § 2657
765 amended No. 1297 § 2528
814 revoked No. 1483 § 79
825 revoked No. 1485 (S.137) § 3113
844 revoked No. 998 (S.92) § 3295
852 revoked No. 483 § 3011
864 revoked No. 809 § 38
918 amended No. 1756 § 2747
932 revoked No. 436 § 1467
938 revoked No. 796 § 685
971 amended No. 1913 § 3011
1072 amended No. 1042 (N.I.12) § 2105
1115 revoked No. 1177 (S.110) § 3638
1200 amended No. 1139 § 1942
1207 revoked No. 257 § 38
1219 revoked No. 1875 (S.164) § 3113
1234 amended No. 1141 § 2931
1263 amended No. 1040 (N.I.10) § 2128
1263 amended No. 1041 (N.I.11) § 2184
1263 amended No. 1050 (N.I.20) § 2157
1265 amended No. 1045 (N.I.15) § 2127
1265 amended No. 1907 (N.I.26) § 2166
1294 amended No. 1754 § 2747
1295 amended No. 107 § 2764
1295 amended No. 979 § 2764
1295 amended No. 1758 § 2764
1344 amended No. 273 § 3037
1413 revoked No. 32 § 79
1500 revoked No. 1483 § 79
1536 revoked No. 796 § 685
1538 revoked No. 1485 (S.137) § 3113
1539 revoked No. 1875 (S.164) § 3113
1588 revoked No. 1527 § 2792
1634 amended No. 1048 (N.I.18) § 2189
1700 amended No. 1757 § 2764
1741 revoked No. 483 § 3011
1746 revoked No. 1759 (L.37) § 802
1758 amended No. 24 § 7
1804 amended No. 230 § 1536
1871 amended No. 36 § 2747
1874 amended No. 1755 § 2747
1939 revoked No. 1 § 1952
1996 amended No. 1038 (N.I.8) § 2101
1998 amended No. 1050 (N.I.20) § 2157
1998 amended No. 1907 (N.I.26) § 2166
1998 amended No. 1041 (N.I.11) § 2184
1999 amended No. 1041 (N.I.11) § 2184

1973

15 amended No. 272 § 291
15 amended No. 1248 § 58
24 revoked No. 1017 § 2536
66 revoked No. 216 § 2257
70 amended No. 1049 (N.I.19) § 2180
100 amended No. 207 (S.27) § 3113
100 amended No. 943 (S.80) § 3113
100 revoked No. 1875 (S.164) § 3113
106 revoked No. 796 § 685
176 amended No. 495 § 2508
178 amended No. 53 § 1634
288 amended No. 1660 § 56
327 amended No. 273 § 3037
334 amended No. 326 § 1660

1973—cont.

334 amended No. 1196 § 1673
379 revoked No. 1157 § 2581
390 amended No. 1565 (S.147) § 3588
414 amended No. 1042 (N.I.12) § 2105
416 amended No. 1041 (N.I.11) § 2184
424 amended No. 1330 § 1203
428 amended No. 375 § 2278
428 amended No. 1348 § 2278
428 amended No. 1578 § 2278
450 amended No. 125 (S.14) § 3222
659 amended No. 1454 § 2518
756 revoked No. 1017 § 2536
966 amended No. 1228 § 2266
966 amended No. 1349 § 2266
966 amended No. 1577 § 2266
1033 revoked No. 796 § 685
1176 revoked No. 998 (S.92) § 3295
1178 revoked No. 1748 § 82
1199 amended No. 1112 § 2597
1199 amended No. 1236 § 2597
1199 amended No. 1832 § 2597
1229 amended No. 1051 (N.I.21) § 2185
1278 revoked No. 1759 (L.37) § 802
1340 amended No. 1787 § 1496
1341 revoked No. 861 § 56
1347 revoked No. 1017 § 2536
1468 amended No. 950 § 2032
1469 amended No. 1089 § 2285
1521 amended No. 1108 § 61
1539 amended No. 495 § 2508
1678 revoked No. 693 § 128
1706 revoked No. 1017 § 2536
1756 amended No. 1888 § 1450
1864 revoked No. 1017 § 2536
1888 revoked No. 281 § 1486
1890 amended No. 1881 § 2743
1928 revoked No. 1699 § 1582
1965 amended No. 380 § 62
1965 amended No. 768 § 62
1967 amended No. 1080 § 3074
2070 revoked No. 693 § 128
2163 amended No. 1041 (N.I.11) § 2184
2182 amended No. 943 (S.80) § 3113
2182 revoked No. 1875 (S.164) § 3113
2205 amended No. 272 § 291
2217 amended No. 21 § 2033

1974

9 revoked No. 331 § 2043
64 revoked No. 1017 § 2536
67 revoked No. 259 § 49
81 revoked No. 1 § 1952
186 amended No. 339 § 2031
213 revoked No. 796 § 685
284 amended No. 950 § 2032
285 amended No. 950 § 2032
287 amended No. 950 § 2032
391 revoked No. 884 § 1502
411 amended No. 387 § 2467
411 revoked No. 1504 § 2467
447 amended No. 1795 § 1852
447 amended No. 1917 § 1852
450 revoked No. 602 § 1893
494 amended No. 1090 § 2044
506 amended No. 1762 (S.155) § 3523
520 amended No. 266 § 2267
520 amended No. 822 § 2267

1974—*cont.*

520 amended No. 1738 § 2261
520 amended No. 1739 § 2267
529 amended No. 652 § 1929
529 amended No. 813 § 1929
529 amended No. 814 § 1929
529 amended No. 1192 § 1929
547 revoked No. 1844 § 1886
600 amended No. 222 (S.29) § 3629
600 amended No. 1399 (S.127) § 3629
633 revoked No. 1844 § 1886
648 amended No. 197 § 873
765 revoked No. 1017 § 2536
799 revoked No. 32 § 79
812 amended No. 425 (S.44) § 3556
812 amended No. 1378 (S.125) § 3556
812 amended No. 1794 (S.158) § 3556
812 amended No. 1926 (S.168) § 3556
839 revoked No. 1875 (S.164) § 3113
903 amended No. 1126 § 1461
908 amended No. 1122 § 1273
909 revoked No. 796 § 685
973 revoked No. 1017 § 2536
1004 revoked No. 1759 (L.37) § 802
1005 revoked No. 1699 § 1582
1047 amended No. 1353 § 2268
1120 revoked No. 105 § 1491
1144 revoked No. 554 § 128
1173 revoked No. 998 (S.92) § 3295
1175 revoked No. 861 § 56
1211 revoked No. 884 § 1502
1255 revoked No. 1105 § 1724
1262 revoked No. 783 § 178
1266 revoked No. 1906 (N.I.25) § 2184
1304 revoked No. 1162 § 1756
1339 revoked No. 492 (S.47) §
1357 amended No. 1508 (S.139) § 3557
1386 amended No. 991 § 961
1387 amended No. 992 § 961
1441 revoked No. 1257 § 2259
1552 revoked No. 1504 § 2467
1557 revoked No. 1 § 1952
1708 revoked No. 273 § 3037
1806 revoked No. 884 § 1502
1895 revoked No. 1026 § 75
1982 amended No. 965 (S.88) § 3417
2005 amended No. 1763 § 2258
2008 amended No. 433 § 2775
2008 revoked No. 1698 § 2783
2010 amended No. 508 § 2775
2059 amended No. 392 § 2280
2064 revoked No. 554 § 128
2142 revoked No. 1906 (N.I.25) § 2184
2189 revoked No. 796 § 685
2204 revoked No. 796 § 685

1975

11 revoked No. 809 § 38
64 revoked No. 30 § 535
95 revoked No. 32 § 79
149 revoked No. 796 § 685
154 amended No. 943 (S.80) § 3113
154 revoked No. 1875 (S.164) § 3113
186 revoked No. 1017 § 2536
205 amended No. 1717 § 1520
225 amended No. 91 § 75
238 revoked No. 1017 § 2536
245 amended No. 1262 § 2595

1975—*cont.*

292 revoked No. 861 § 56
327 revoked No. 1504 § 2467
330 amended No. 1598 § 1479
330 amended No. 1873 § 1479
357 revoked No. 17 § 78
382 revoked No. 222 (S.29) § 3629
416 revoked No. 1906 (N.I.25) § 2184
423 amended No. 279 § 824
492 amended No. 70 § 2784
492 amended No. 423 § 2784
492 amended No. 507 § 2784
492 amended No. 821 § 2784
492 amended No. 1669 § 2784
492 amended No. 1703 § 2784
492 amended No. 1877 § 2784
528 amended No. 1462 § 2779
528 revoked No. 1689 § 2779
536 amended No. 1344 § 2989
539 amended No. 1509 (S.140) § 3685
541 amended No. 495 § 2508
554 amended No. 433 § 2775
554 amended No. 524 § 2775
554 amended No. 1511 § 2775
556 amended No. 409 § 2784
557 revoked No. 393 § 2280
557 amended No. 1123 § 2775
559 amended No. 1123 § 2775
560 amended No. 433 § 2775
562 amended No. 508 § 2775
564 amended No. 394 § 2775
564 amended No. 608 § 2775
564 amended No. 1123 § 2775
564 amended No. 1213 § 2775
638 amended No. 425 (S.44) § 3556
638 amended No. 1378 (S.125) § 3556
641 revoked No. 1017 § 2536
649 amended No. 273 § 3037
660 amended No. 1070 (S.95) § 3628
686 amended No. 1816 (S.161) § 3494
686 amended No. 1879 (S.167) § 3494
807 revoked No. 783 § 178
808 amended No. 783 § 178
850 amended No. 205 (S.25) § 3305
891 revoked No. 216 § 2257
896 revoked No. 1266 § 1417
916 amended No. 1797 § 125a
917 amended No. 1798 § 125a
940 revoked No. 1096 § 856
959 revoked No. 722 § 1704
1002 revoked No. 1759 (L.37) § 802
1021 revoked No. 216 § 2257
1046 amended No. 1110 § 2588
1051 revoked No. 32 § 79
1058 amended No. 1123 § 2775
1058 amended No. 1340 § 2775
1058 amended No. 1698 § 2783
1075 revoked No. 1 § 1952
1212 revoked No. 1906 (N.I.25) § 2184
1132 amended No. 1882 § 692a
1170 amended No. 558 § 1751
1173 amended No. 25 § 3073
1173 amended No. 26 § 3073
1178 amended No. 1080 § 3074
1179 amended No. 1080 § 3074
1228 revoked No. 998 (S.92) § 3295
1240 revoked No. 1699 § 1582

1975—cont.
1261 revoked No. 252 (S.31) § 3632
1262 revoked No. 216 § 2257
1265 revoked No. 861 § 56
1308 amended No. 1041 (N.I.11) § 2184
1322 amended No. 1011 (S.94) § 3422
1328 amended No. 1243 (L.29) § 376
1332 revoked No. 1875 (S.164) § 3113
1333 revoked No. 1875 (S.164) § 3113
1334 amended No. 206 (S.26) § 3113
1334 amended No. 944 (S.81) § 3113
1334 revoked No. 1875 (S.164) § 3113
1343 amended No. 1244 (L.30) § 2370
1344 amended No. 1298 (L.32) § 2370
1346 amended No. 1256 (L.31) § 805
1350 amended No. 570 (L.10) § 145
1350 amended No. 1653 (L.36) § 145
1351 amended No. 569 (L.9) § 255
1351 amended No. 1654 § 255
1393 revoked No. 693 § 128
1433 amended No. 807 § 1960
1440 revoked No. 1151 § 2227
1450 revoked No. 1504 § 2467
1467 revoked No. 1093 § 2244
1475 amended No. 272 § 291
1487 amended No. 1420 § 1495
1491 amended No. 273 § 3037
1503 amended No. 1042 (N.I.12) § 2105
1510 revoked No. 783 § 178
1511 revoked No. 783 § 178
1532 revoked No. 1120 § 2984
1692 revoked No. 600 § 2741
1702 revoked No. 1875 (S.164) § 3113
1708 revoked No. 454 § 2661
1803 amended No. 751 (L.16) § 2372
1832 revoked No. 783 § 178
1869 revoked No. 1759 (L.37) § 802
1927 amended No. 250 § 2260
1927 amended No. 1827 § 2260
1945 revoked No. 950 § 2032
2063 amended No. 1763 § 2258
2071 revoked No. 554 § 128
2101 amended No. 250 § 2260
2101 amended No. 1089 § 2285
2158 revoked No. 273 § 3037
2176 revoked No. 1906 (N.I.25) § 2184
2192 amended No. 185 § 2515
2210 amended No. 272 § 291
2232 amended No. 1464 (S. 135) § 3625

1976

11 amended No. 27 § 3070
17 revoked No. 1759 (L.37) § 802
26 revoked No. 1303 § 128
32 revoked No. 32 § 79
42 revoked No. 1614 § 64
59 amended No. 1042 (N.I.12) § 2105
128 revoked No. 1064 § 3047
143 amended No. 250 § 2260
148 amended No. 27 § 3070
210 revoked No. 892 (S.73) § 3742
225 amended No. 1527 § 2792
232 revoked No. 224 § 2524
246 amended No. 247 § 1851
256 revoked No. 1483 § 79
257 revoked No. 1483 § 79
258 revoked No. 1485 (S.137) § 3113
259 revoked No. 1485 (S.137) § 3113

1976—cont.
304 amended No. 1820 § 1479
316 revoked No. 1832 § 2597
317 revoked No. 1017 § 2536
332 revoked No. 260 § 2661
347 revoked No. 1121 § 1939
403 revoked No. 1772 § 1941
404 revoked No. 1689 § 2779
409 amended No. 393 § 2280
409 amended No. 433 § 2775
409 amended No. 1698 § 2783
422 revoked No. 783 § 178
423 revoked No. 1906 (N.I.25) § 2184
431 amended No. 1080 § 3074
453 revoked No. 708 § 79
476 amended No. 112 (S.6) § 3709
476 amended No. 1805 (S.160) § 3709
501 amended No. 239 § 198
528 revoked No. 1017 § 2536
582 amended No. 1907 (N.I.26) § 2166
585 amended No. 384 § 2287
585 amended No. 1426 § 2287
613 revoked No. 1096 § 856
666 revoked No. 796 § 685
676 revoked No. 1759 (L.37) § 802
692 revoked No. 1747 (S.153) § 3303
713 revoked No. 390 § 920
738 amended No. 615 § 2656
818 revoked No. 809 § 38
824 revoked No. 1409 § 866
838 amended No. 1148 § 675
840 amended No. 1108 § 61
883 revoked No. 554 § 128
937 amended No. 293 § 2597
937 amended No. 1811 § 2597
937 amended No. 1237 § 2597
937 amended No. 1318 § 2597
937 amended No. 1319 § 2597
954 revoked No. 260 § 2661
962 amended No. 540 § 1464
964 amended No. 540 § 1464
965 amended No. 540 § 1464
965 amended No. 1275 § 1464
978 revoked No. 1 § 1952
988 revoked No. 1188 § 79
1008 revoked No. 1177 (S.110) § 3638
1061 revoked No. 947 (S.82) §
1062 revoked No. 1686 (S.151) § 3216
1073 amended No. 528 (S.49) § 3561
1073 amended No. 1170 (S.103) § 3561
1073 amended No. 1510 (S.141) § 3561
1076 amended No. 697 § 2583
1076 amended No. 1109 § 2583
1093 revoked No. 32 § 79
1104 revoked No. 998 (S.92) §
1104 revoked No. 998 (S.92) § 3295
1117 revoked No. 1875 (S.164) § 3113
1118 revoked No. 1875 (S.164) § 3113
1129 amended No. 929 § 2291
1135 amended No. 553 § 1561
1145 revoked No. 1121 § 1939
1210 revoked No. 1906 (N.I.25) § 2184
1212 amended No. 1041 (N.I.11) § 2184
1217 revoked No. 134 § 2282
1222 revoked No. 1759 (L.37) § 802
1223 amended No. 1725 § 675
1242 amended No. 1078 § 1586
1256 revoked No. 1017 § 2536

1977—*cont.*

947 revoked No. 1483 § 79
958 revoked No. 1875 (S.164) § 3113
962 revoked No. 1188 § 79
966 revoked No. 260 § 2661
982 amended No. 462 § 2733
982 amended No. 1059 § 2733
985 amended No. 1638 § 1747
989 revoked No. 1485 (S.137) § 3113
990 revoked No. 1485 (S.137) § 3113
1015 revoked No. 1689 § 2779
1035 revoked No. 260 § 2661
1043 amended No. 1316 § 2582
1044 revoked No. 54 § 2747
1049 revoked No. 1010 § 67
1056 revoked No. 1121 § 1939
1057 revoked No. 1389 § 2293
1069 revoked No. 1073 § 2780
1084 amended No. 772 § 1479
1084 amended No. 1651 § 1479
1102 revoked No. 331 § 2043
1103 amended No. 228 § 2036
1132 revoked No. 1875 (S.164) § 3113
1133 revoked No. 1875 (S.164) § 3113
1139 revoked No. 32 § 79
1141 amended No. 1459 § 2799
1143 amended No. 1160 § 1522
1144 amended No. 1161 § 2929
1150 revoked No. 998 (S.92) § 3295
1152 amended No. 430 § 2764
1188 amended No. 250 § 2260
1190 revoked No. 796 § 685
1229 amended No. 743 § 2791
1236 revoked No. 1885 § 2693
1245 amended No. 1039 (N.I.9) § 2133
1253 amended No. 1042 (N.I.12) § 2105
1254 amended No. 1042 (N.I.12) § 2105
1272 revoked No. 1082 § 2518
1281 revoked No. 1083 § 2518
1284 revoked No. 1480 § 79
1286 revoked No. 1680 § 2850
1289 amended No. 100 § 2782
1295 revoked No. 1102 § 2210
1303 amended No. 594 § 79
1304 amended No. 272 § 291
1307 revoked No. 1097 § 856
1308 revoked No. 1098 § 856
1309 amended No. 669 § 2583
1310 revoked No. 1011 (S.94) § 3422
1324 revoked No. 1137 § 1465
1325 revoked No. 912 § 2775
1336 revoked No. 1699 § 1582
1341 amended No. 1738 § 2261
1341 amended No. 1739 § 2267
1344 revoked No. 260 § 2661
1356 revoked No. 998 (S.92) § 3295
1359 revoked No. 1190 (S.114) § 3521
1360 amended No. 1507 (S.138) § 3559
1362 revoked No. 1123 § 2775
1374 revoked No. 1121 § 1939
1401 revoked No. 1017 § 2536
1402 revoked No. 1832 § 2597
1409 revoked No. 1097 § 856
1437 amended No. 317 § 128
1451 revoked No. 1243 (L.29) § 376
1466 revoked No. 255 § 1965
1489 amended No. 1108 § 61
1497 amended No. 1538 § 1486

1977—*cont.*

1500 revoked No. 1504 § 2467
1501 revoked No. 1409 § 866
1519 revoked No. 1 § 1952
1530 revoked No. 1747 (S.153) § 3303
1576 revoked No. 1399 (S.127) § 3629
1614 amended No. 1312 § 1636
1624 revoked No. 1759 (L.37) § 802
1627 amended No. 780 § 1723
1630 revoked No. 1525 § 2287
1639 revoked No. 1017 § 2536
1656 revoked No. 886 § 268
1657 revoked No. 887 § 268
1679 amended No. 433 § 2775
1708 amended No. 1931 § 3014
1709 amended No. 1930 § 3014
1724 revoked No. 1425 (S.130) § 3215
1745 amended No. 1795 § 1852
1745 amended No. 1917 § 1852
1751 revoked No. 1480 § 79
1756 amended No. 1379 § 1486
1757 revoked No. 381 (S.40) § 3421
1759 amended No. 273 § 3037
1759 amended No. 532 § 3033
1759 amended No. 972 § 3033
1776 revoked No. 1879 (S.167) § 3494
1777 amended No. 210 § 2277
1786 revoked No. 1064 § 3047
1787 revoked No. 1064 § 3047
1788 revoked No. 1064 § 3047
1789 revoked No. 1064 § 3047
1790 amended No. 273 § 3037
1791 revoked No. 1064 § 3047
1792 revoked No. 1064 § 3047
1793 revoked No. 1064 § 3047
1794 revoked No. 1064 § 3047
1796 amended No. 273 § 3037
1797 revoked No. 1064 § 3047
1849 revoked No. 1064 § 3047
1896 amended No. 211 § 2277
1905 revoked No. 1485 (S.137) § 3113
1906 revoked No. 1485 (S.137) § 3113
1908 revoked No. 1483 § 79
1909 revoked No. 1483 § 79
1929 revoked No. 516 § 1492
1933 revoked No. 1962 § 3072
1950 revoked No. 1772 § 1941
1957 revoked No. 1599 § 2523
1987 amended No. 1689 § 2779
2000 revoked No. 1752 § 194
2001 revoked No. 1717 § 1520
2022 revoked No. 1729 § 1686
2033 revoked No. 554 § 128
2048 amended No. 820 § 694
2049 revoked No. 600 § 2741
2054 amended No. 469 § 1503
2054 amended No. 1382 § 1503
2054 amended No. 1498 § 1503
2055 amended No. 470 § 2141
2055 amended No. 1491 § 2141
2056 amended No. 1593 § 675
2092 amended No. 273 § 3037
2092 revoked No. 1064 § 3047
2112 amended No. 272 § 291
2127 amended No. 189 § 1946
2127 amended No. 987 § 1953
2132 amended No. 989 § 1955
2133 amended No. 988 § 1955

NORTHERN IRELAND

TABLE OF STATUTORY RULES AND ORDERS 1977–78

1977	C.L.Y.
355	2140
356	2140
357	2194
358	2100
359	2163
364	2135
365	2135
366	2135
367	2135
368	2135
369	2135
370	2135
371	2135
372	2135
373	2135
375	2147
378	2188
379	2185
380	2188
381	2133
382	2185
383	2188

1978	C.L.Y.
2	2160
4	2184
6	2163
9	2160
10	2188
11 (C.1)	2163
12 (C.2)	2163
14	2187
15	2171
16	2171
17 (C.3)	2185
18	2185
20 (C.4)	2195
21	2166
22	2149
23	2181
24	2138
27	2134
28	2102
29	2151
30	2143
31	2151
32	2181
33	2099
35	2188
39	2111
40	2126
41	2188
42 (C.5)	2188
43	2187
45	2185
46	2194
47	2099
48	2099
49	2099

1978	C.L.Y.
50	2140
51	2187
52	2099
53	2128
54	2133
55	2185
56	2111
57	2160
58	2100
59	2102
60	2193
61	2185
64	2166
65	2185
66	2099
67	2099
68	2099
69	2135
70	2185
71	2184
72	2115
73	2173
74	2188
75	2147
76	2185
77	2188
78	2188
79	2135
80	2185
81 (C.6)	2188
83	2165
84	2165
85	2165
86	2188
87	2188
88	2135
89	2135
90	2188
91	2188
92	2173
93	2173
94	2135
95	2188
96	2188
97	2148
98	2140
99	2184
100	2138
101	2188
102	2188
103	2171
104	2146
105	2188
106	2137
107	2188
108	2188
111	2099
112	2141
113	2165

TABLE OF NORTHERN IRELAND S.R. & O. 1977–78

1978	C.L.Y.	1978	C.L.Y.
114	2188	201	2176
115	2140	202	2188
116	2195	203	2137
117	2171	204	2188
120	2188	205	2100
121	2171	206	2141
122	2195	207	2099
123	2185	208	2185
126	2195	209	2185
128	2174	210	2185
129	2128	211	2099
130	2142	212	2099
131	2151	213	2130
132	2151	214	2128
133	2099	215 (C.8)	2176
134 (C.7)	2183	216	2128
135	2111	217	2128
136	2172	218	2140
137	2164	219	2163
138	2135	220	2188
139	2185	222	2188
140	2185	226	2099
142	2184	227	2110
147	2128	228	2100
149	2188	230	2188
150	2185	231	2132
151	2111	232 (C.9)	2133
152	2185	233 (C.10)	2133
153	2128	234	2185
154	2135	235	2185
155	2099	236	2188
156	2185	237	2099
159	2134	238	2137
160	2134	239	2100
161	2134	240	2099
162	2134	241	2135
163	2134	242	2135
164	2100	243	2135
165	2100	245 (C.11)	2157
166	2135	247	2100
167	2135	248	2107
168	2163	249	2180
169	2171	250	2135
170	2134	251	2137
175	2128	252	2165
177	2110	253	2157
178	2149	254	2135
179	2193	255	2099
180	2174	256	2184
181	2174	257	2184
182	2128	258	2185
183	2134	259	2157
184	2134	260	2157
185	2140	261	2143
186	2176	262	2188
187	2176	263	2135
188	2176	264	2135
189	2099	265	2157
190	2110	266	2184
191	2176	267	2149
192	2155	268	2185
193	2161	269	2171
194	2161	270	2171
195	2111	271 (C.12)	2098
196	2111	272	2193
199	2144	273	2185
200	2176	274	2135

TABLE OF NORTHERN IRELAND S.R. & O. 1977–78

1978	C.L.Y.	1978	C.L.Y.
275	2188	307	2171
276 (C.13)	2127	308	2188
277	2140	309 (C.15)	2149
279	2128	310	2147
280	2173	311	2131
281	2173	312	2185
285	2143	315	2198
286	2140	316	2185
287	2174	318	2185
288	2185	319	2185
289	2185	321	2100
290	2185	324	2166
291	2185	326	2188
292	2166	329	2193
293	2137	335	2149
294	2128	336	2179
295	2185	337	2176
296	2133	338	2176
297	2181	339	2140
298	2184	340	2161
299	2161	341	2176
300	2099	342	2193
301	2166	343	2185
303	2097	346	2173
304	2097	347	2173
305	2097	349	2101
306	2136		

TABLE OF ABBREVIATIONS

A.B.L.R. = Australian Business Law Review.
A.C. = Appeal Cases (Law Reports).
A.J.I.L. = American Journal of International Law.
A.L.J. = Australian Law Journal.
A.L.J.R. = Australian Law Journal Reports.
A.L.R. = Argus Law Reports.
A.T.C. = Annotated Tax Cases.
A.T.R. = Australian Tax Review.
Acct. = Accountant.
Acct.Rec. = Accountants Record.
Accty. = Accountancy.
Air Law = Air Law.
All E.R. = All England Reports.
Anglo-Am. = Anglo-American Law Review.
Art. = Article.
Aus. = Australia.

B.J.A.L. = British Journal of Administrative Law.
B.L.R. = Business Law Report.
B.T.R. = British Tax Review.
Brit.J.Criminol. = British Journal of Criminology.
Business L.R. = Business Law Review.

c. = Chapter (of Act of Parliament).
C.A. = Court of Appeal.
C.C.A. = Court of Criminal Appeal.
C.I.L.J.S.A. = Comparative and International Law Journal of South Africa.
C.L. = Current Law.
C.L.B. = Commonwealth Law Bulletin.
C.L.C. = Current Law Consolidation.
C.L.J. = Cambridge Law Journal.
C.L.L.R. = City of London Law Review.
C.L.P. = Current Legal Problems.
C.L.R. = Commonwealth Law Reports.
C.L.Y. = Current Law Year Book.
C.M.L.R. = Common Market Law Reports.
C.M.L.Rev. = Common Market Law Review.
C.P.L. = Current Property Law.
C.R.N.S. = Criminal Reports.
Can. = Canada.
Can.Bar J. = Canadian Bar Journal.
Can.B.R. or Canadian B.R. = Canadian Bar Review.
Can.C.L. = Canadian Current Law.
Ch. = Chancery (Law Reports).
Chart.Sec. = Chartered Secretary.
Chart.Surv. = Chartered Surveyor.
Chart.Surv.R.Q. = Chartered Surveyor Rural Quarterly.
Chart.Surv.U.Q. = Chartered Surveyor Urban Quarterly.
Com.Cas. = Commercial Cases.
Commercial Acct. = Commercial Accountant.
Conv.(N.S.) (or Conv. or Conveyancer) = Conveyancer and Property Lawyer (New Series).
Court = Court.

Cox C.C. = Cox's Criminal Cases.
Cr.App.R. = Criminal Appeal Reports.
Crim.L.R. = Criminal Law Review.
Cts.-Martial App.Ct. = Courts-Martial Appeal Court.
Cty.Ct. = County Court.

D.C. = Divisional Court.
D.L.R. = Dominion Law Reports.

E. = England.
E.A.T. = Employment Appeal Tribunal.
E.C.R. = European Court Reports.
E.C.S.C. = European Coal and Steel Community.
E.E.C. = European Economic Community.
E.G. = Estates Gazette.
E.L.Rev. = European Law Review.
E.P.L. Leaflet = Excess Profits Levy Leaflet.
E.P.T. Leaflet = Excess Profits Tax Leaflet.

F.D. = Family Division.
F.L.R. = Federal Law Reports.
F.S.R. = Fleet Street Patent Law Reports.
Fam. = Family Division (Law Reports).
Fam.Law = Family Law.

H.L. = House of Lords.
Harv.L.R. or Harvard L.R. = Harvard Law Review.

I.C.L.Q. = International and Comparative Law Quarterly.
I.C.R. = Industrial Court Reports.
I.L.J. = Industrial Law Journal.
I.L.T. or Ir.L.T. = Irish Law Times.
I.L.T.R. = Irish Law Times Reports.
Imm.A.R. = Immigration Appeal Reports.
I.R. or Ir.R. = Irish Reports (Eire).
I.R.L.R. = Industrial Relations Law Reports.
Ir.Jur. = Irish Jurist.
Ir.Jur.(N.S.) = Irish Jurist (New Series).
Ir.Jur.Rep. = Irish Jurist Reports.
I.T.R. = Industrial Tribunal Reports.

J. and JJ. = Justice, Justices.
J.A.L. = Journal of African Law.
J.B.L. = Journal of Business Law.
J.C. = Justiciary Cases.
J.C.L. = Journal of Criminal Law.
J.C.L. & Crim. = Journal of Criminal Law and Criminology.
J.Crim.L., C. & P.S. = Journal of Criminal Law, Criminology and Police Science.
J.I.B. = Journal of the Institute of Bankers.
J.L.S. = Journal of the Law Society of Scotland.
J.P. = Justice of the Peace Reports.

65

TABLE OF ABBREVIATIONS

J.P.J. or J.P.N. = Justice of the Peace Journal.

J.P.L. = Journal of Planning and Environmental Law.

J.R. = Juridical Review.

J.S.P.T.L. = Journal of the Society of Public Teachers of Law.

Jam. = Jamaica.

K.B. = Kings' Bench (Law Reports).

K.I.R. = Knight's Industrial Reports.

L.A.G.Bul. = Legal Action Group Bulletin.

L.C. = Lord Chancellor.

L.C.J. or C.J. = Lord Chief Justice.

L.Exec. = Legal Executive.

L.G.C. = Local Government Chronicle.

L.G.R. = Local Government Reports.

L.G.Rev. = Local Government Review.

L.J. = Law Journal Newspaper.

L.J. and L.JJ. = Lord Justice, Lords Justices.

L.J.A.C.R. = Law Journal Annual Charities Review.

L.J.N.C.C.R. = Law Journal Newspaper County Court Reports.

L.J.R. = Law Journal Reports.

L.P. = Reference to denote Lands Tribunal decisions (transcripts available from the Lands Tribunal).

L.Q.R. = Law Quarterly Review.

L.R. = Law Reports.

L.R.R.P. = Reports of Restrictive Practices Cases.

L.S.Gaz. = Law Society Gazette.

L.T. = Law Times.

L.Teach. = Law Teacher.

L.T.J. = Law Times Journal.

L.V.App.Ct. = Lands Valuation Appeal Court (Scotland).

L.V.C. = Reference to denote Lands Tribunal decisions (transcripts available from the Lands Tribunal).

Ll.L.Rep. = Lloyd's List Reports (before 1951).

Ll.P.C. = Lloyd's Prize Cases.

Lloyd's M.C.L.Q. = Lloyd's Maritime and Commercial Law Quarterly.

Lloyd's Rep. = Lloyd's List Reports (1951 onwards).

M.L.J. = Malayan Law Journal.

M.L.R. = Modern Law Review.

M.P.R. = Maritime Provinces Report.

M.R. = Master of the Rolls.

McGill L.J. = McGill Law Journal.

Mag.Ct. = Magistrates' Court.

Mal. = Malaya.

Mal.L.R. = Malaya Law Review.

Man.Law = Managerial Law.

Med.Sci. & Law = Medicine, Science and the Law.

Melbourne Univ.L.R. = Melbourne University Law Review.

Mel.L.J. = Melanesian Law Journal.

NATO R. = NATO Review.

N.I. = Northern Ireland; Northern Ireland Reports.

N.I.L.Q.=Northern Ireland Legal Quarterly.

N.Z.L.R. = New Zealand Law Reports.

N.Z.U.L.R. = New Zealand Universities Law Review.

New L.J. = New Law Journal.

New L.R. = New Law Reports, Ceylon.

Nig.L.J. = Nigerian Law Journal.

Oklahoma L.R. = Oklahoma Law Review.

Ord. = Order.

Osgoode Hall L.J. = Osgoode Hall Law Journal.

P. = Probate, Divorce and Admiralty (Law Reports).

P. & C.R. = Property and Compensation Reports.

P.C. = Privy Council.

P.L. = Public Law.

P.Q. = Political Quarterly.

P.S. = Petty Sessions.

P.T. = Profits Tax Leaflet.

Pr.A.S.I.L. = Proceedings of the American Society of International Law.

Prof.Admin. = Professional Administration.

Q.B. = Queen's Bench (Law Reports).

Q.J.P.R. = Queensland Justice of the Peace Reports.

Q.L.R. = Queensland Law Reporter.

Q.S. = Quarter Sessions.

Q.S.R. = Queensland State Reports.

r. = Rule.

R.A. = Rating Appeals.

R. & I.T. = Rating and Income Tax.

R. & V. = Rating and Valuation.

R.C.N. = Rating Case Notes.

R.F.L. = Reports of Family Law (Canadian).

R.I.C.S. = Royal Institution of Chartered Surveyors, Scottish Lands Valuation Appeal Reports.

R.P.C. = Reports of Patent, Design and Trade Mark Cases.

R.P.Ct. = Restrictive Practices Court.

R.R.C. = Ryde's Rating Cases.

R.T.R. = Road Traffic Reports.

R.V.R. = Rating and Valuation Reporter.

reg. = Regulation.

Reg.Acct. = Registered Accountant.

s. = Section (of Act of Parliament).

S. or Scot. = Scotland.

S.A. = South Africa.

S.A.L.J. = South African Law Journal.

S.A.L.R. = South African Law Reports.

S.A.S.R. = South Australian State Reports.

S.C. = Session Cases.

S.C.(H.L.) = Session Cases (House of Lords).

S.C.(J.) = Session Cases (High Court of Justiciary).

SCOLAG Bul.=Scottish Legal Action Group Bulletin.

S.I. = Statutory Instruments.

S.J. = Solicitors' Journal.

S.J.Suppl. = Supplement to the Solicitors' Journal.

S.L.C.R. = Scottish Land Court Reports.

TABLE OF ABBREVIATIONS

S.L.C.R.App.=Scottish Land Court Report (appendix).

S.L.G. = Scottish Law Gazette.

S.L.R. = Scottish Law Reporter (Reports 1865–1925).

S.L.R. = Scottish Law Review (Articles 1912–63).

S.L.T. = Scots Law Times.

S.L.T.(Land Ct.) = Scots Law Times Land Court Reports.

S.L.T.(Lands Tr.)=Scots Law Times Lands Tribunal Reports.

S.L.T.(Lyon Ct.) = Scots Law Times Lyon Court Reports.

S.L.T.(Notes) = Scots Law Times Notes of Recent Decisions.

S.L.T.(Sh.Ct.) = Scots Law Times Sheriff Court Reports.

S.N. = Session Notes.

S.R. & O. = Statutory Rules and Orders.

S.T.C. = Simon's Tax Cases.

Sc.Jur. = Scottish Jurist.

Sec. = Secretary.

Sec.Chron. = Secretaries' Chronicle.

Sec.J.= Secretaries' Journal.

Sh.Ct.Rep. = Sheriff Court Reports (Scottish Law Review) (1885–1963).

Sol. = Solicitor.

Sydney L.R. = Sydney Law Review.

T.C. *or* Tax Cas. = Tax Cases.

T.C. Leaflet = Tax Case Leaflet.

T.L.R. = Times Law Reports.

T.R. = Taxation Reports.

Tas.S.R. = Tasmanian State Reports.

Tax. = Taxation.

Traff.Cas. = Railway, Canal and Road Traffic Cases.

Trib. = Tribunal.

Tulane L.R. = Tulane Law Review.

U.G.L.J. = University of Ghana Law Journal.

U.T.L.J. = University of Toronto Law Journal.

V.A.T.T.R. = Value Added Tax Tribunal Reports.

V.L.R. = Victorian Law Reports.

W.A.L.R. = West Australian Law Reports.

W.I.A.S. = West Indies Associated States.

W.I.R. = West Indian Reports.

W.L.R. = Weekly Law Reports.

W.N. = Weekly Notes (Law Reports).

W.W.R. = Western Weekly Reports.

Washington L.Q. = Washington Law Quarterly.

Yale L.J. = Yale Law Journal.

UNREPORTED CASES

COURT OF APPEAL (CIVIL DIVISION)

1. Administrative Law—immigration—detention—habeas corpus

Appellant fraudulently obtained leave to remain in the United Kingdom indefinitely under the "1974 amnesty," claiming to have been "smuggled" into the United Kingdom in 1971—in 1977 the appellant was detained in prison after the Secretary of State was satisfied on evidence before him that the appellant had in fact overstayed his temporary permission to enter the United Kingdom—appeal dismissed—detention of appellant valid—adequate evidence for conclusions reached by the Secretary of State—appellant not dealt with unfairly. May 11, 1978. R. *v.* SECRETARY OF STATE FOR HOME AFFAIRS, *ex p.* AHMED.

2. —— —— leave to enter—prospective marriage

On December 11, 1977, applicant, born on June 2, 1952, and now 15½ years old, arrived at Heathrow airport to marry a man settled in the U.K.—arranged marriage with no date set for it—applicant unable to marry under English law until she was 16 years old—immigration officer refused leave on basis that he was not satisfied that the marriage would take place within a reasonable time under rule 50 of the immigration regulations—whether 5½ months "within reasonable time"—application for leave to appeal refused. Appeal from Queen's Bench vacation judge. January 13, 1978. R. *v.* IMMIGRATION OFFICER, HEATHROW, *ex p.* JAURINDER KAUR.

3. Agency—broker—commission

Plaintiffs claimed moneys which had been received by the defendant in relation to insurance premiums collected by him as agent for the plaintiffs but not paid to them—the defendant admitted the plaintiffs' claim but counterclaimed for loss of commission and damages for loss of reputation alleged to have resulted from the plaintiffs' failure to carry out certain instructions of his—judge dismissed the counterclaim holding that the defendant had failed to establish his case on the evidence—defendant's appeal dismissed. February 31, 1978. ZURICH INSURANCE CO. *v.* TIPPET.

4. Agriculture—agricultural holdings—claim for rent—water supply

Plaintiff council accepted a tender submitted by the defendant in respect of grazing land for eatage which was offered to be let subject to a month's notice on either side—letter of acceptance of the tender made it plain that although there was a supply of water to the grazing land, the supply was controlled by a stranger who was not willing to sub-let it and that the licensee would be responsible for supplying his own water—defendant took possession but refused to pay rent after a few months claiming that the plaintiffs were in breach of contract in not supplying any water—the judge found in favour of the plaintiffs on their claim for rent, and dismissed the defendant's counterclaim for damages for breach of contract—defendant's appeal dismissed—judge correct on the evidence and in law. March 3, 1978. HAMBLETON DISTRICT COUNCIL *v.* TAYLOR.

5. —— —— existence of licence

Agricultural Holdings Act 1948—whether there was a finding by the judge that the first defendant had a licence in relation to a field as consideration for entering into the lease of a pig farm—whether such finding was sufficient to constitute an agricultural tenancy—*Goldsack* v. *Shore* (1950) C.L.C. 129 referred to—no legally binding arrangements between father and first defendant (his daughter) to give rise to either a licence or an agricultural tenancy—plaintiffs' appeal allowed. November 7, 1977. CAMBRIDGE AND ROLPH v. EUSTACE.

6. —— —— licence—intention of parties

The defendants, father and son, were farmers—in 1943 the father obtained permission from the plaintiff council to use certain land (acquired by the council for recreational purposes) for grazing—in 1949 more land was included in the land for grazing by agreement between the council and the father—a letter confirming the arrangement between the council and the father was written but never sent to the father by the council—in 1975 the council purported to terminate by notice the defendants' right to occupy the land and sought possession on the basis that the defendants were licensees of the land—the defendants claimed that a tenancy at will was created in 1949 and came to an end in 1950, and that after 12 years from that date, i.e. 1962, they had acquired a squatter's title to the land by virtue of the Limitation Act 1939—the judge gave judgment in favour of the plaintiff council, holding that in 1943 the original arrangement was a licence which continued as such in 1949—defendants' appeal dismissed—judge arrived at right conclusion—relevant (though not decisive) factor that land acquired by local authority for recreational purposes as throwing light on question of intention of parties. January 31, 1978. THREE RIVERS DISTRICT COUNCIL v. CHAPMAN.

7. —— —— possession—joint tenancies

Agricultural Holdings Act 1948—order for possession of field—validity of notice to quit—defendants were joint tenants of agricultural holding—notice addressed to the firm and not sent to several joint tenants or any of them—defendants' appeal dismissed. November 25, 1977. CARPENTER v. PHELPS BROTHERS.

8. Arbitration—appointment of arbitrator—extension of time

Claimants' application under s. 27 of the Arbitration Act 1950 for extension of time for the appointment of an arbitrator under a charterparty between the claimants and the respondents dismissed—claimants' appeal contending, inter alia, that (i) the amount of claim involved was a very large one, some U.S. $800,000; (ii) the very substantial delay beyond the contractual time in the appointing of an arbitrator was excusable in the circumstances of the case; and (iii) the delay had caused no prejudice—appeal dismissed—judge's exercise of discretion not wrong. Appeal from Donaldson J. February 17, 1978. CAST SHIPPING v. TRADAX EXPORT S.A. "HELLAS IN ETERNITY."

9. —— clause in contract—validity—arbitrator's jurisdiction

Defendants were granted an order for stay of the plaintiff's action—plaintiff was claiming damages for destruction of her goods, by fire, while in the possession of the defendants—whether contract included arbitration clause—an arbitrator cannot decide his own jurisdiction—*Heyman* v. *Darwins* [1942] A.C. 356 referred to—plaintiff's appeal allowed. Appeal from Griffiths J. November 4, 1977. WILLCOCK v. PICKFORD REMOVALS.

10. —— costs—discretion of arbitrator

Plaintiff builders claimed in arbitration (i) some £20,000 damages in being required to do work which fell outside their building contract with the defendants, and (ii) some £7,000 damages for undue delay as breach of contract on the defendants' part—arbitral award rejected first claim and gave £3,000 on second claim, and decided that there should be no order as to costs—whether arbitrator misconducted himself or acted unjudicially in making the order as to costs—defendants' application under s. 22 of the Arbitration Act 1950 dismissed—defendants' appeal dismissed—obiter, that leave to appeal required from High Court decision. Appeal from Kerr J. May 11, 1978. THYSSEN (G.B.) v. AFAN BOROUGH COUNCIL.

11. —— sale of foodstuffs—export licence

Contract for sale of 2,000 tons of soya bean meal of United States origin—the claimant buyers' motion to set aside an award, on grounds of lack of jurisdiction, dismissed—decision of Board of Appeal in favour of the sellers upheld—whether wrong in law—arbitration rules 8, 10, 11 and 19 in the Grain and Feed Trade Association's standard form contract no. 125—effect upon a contract of a suspension of an export licence—delay in procedure of the Commercial Court—appeal of claimant buyers dismissed. Appeal from Mocatta J. December 14, 1977. WARINCO A.G. v. PROVIMI HELLAS A.E.

12. —— stay of proceedings—proceedings so far

S. 1 (1) of the Arbitration Act 1975—application by plaintiffs, as first fifth parties, for stay of first fifth party proceedings, refused—building contract for construction of a dam on Zambesi river—whether or not any step in proceedings had been taken—manner in which summons for directions was conducted by counsel for the plaintiffs—appeal of plaintiffs dismissed. November 8, 1977. KARIBA NORTH BANK CO. v. PRUDENTIAL ASSURANCE CO. AND EXCESS INSURANCE CO.

13. —— —— RIBA " green form " contract

In 1972, the plaintiffs were employed by the defendants as sub-contractors in the modernisation of a housing estate and their work was finished in 1974—in correspondence, defendants denied a contract between themselves and the plaintiffs on the basis of RIBA " green form "—plaintiffs issued a writ and later a statement of claim claiming £80,000 damages—defendants applied for stay on ground that matter ought to go to arbitration under terms of the arbitration clause in RIBA " green form "—judge reversed registrar's stay on basis that the defendants were not ready and willing to do all things necessary for the proper conduct of the arbitration under s. 4 of the Arbitration Act 1950—defendants' appeal dismissed. Appeal from Forbes J. February 3, 1978. G. DEW & CO. v. TARMAC CONSTRUCTION.

14. Banking—cheque—dishonour—confusion between brothers—no breach of contract

The plaintiff, having the same initials as his brother, brought an action against the defendants for damages for breach of contract in dishonouring certain cheques drawn by him in favour of " K. K. Arora "—the plaintiff's brother, on the same day as the plaintiff had done, also drew at a different branch of the defendant bank, cheques in favour of " K. K. Arora "—cheques dishonoured by the defendants because of suspicion of " cross-firing "—no agreement between the plaintiff and the defendants for overdrawing—defendants within their strict rights in refusing to honour cheques because, uncleared effects not being taken into account, plaintiff had not enough credit to meet the cheques—plaintiff's appeal was without merit and dismissed. June 6, 1978. ARORA v. BARCLAYS BANK.

15. Bankruptcy—property of bankrupt—possession of house—agreement with trustee

Trustee in bankruptcy obtained against the appellant defendant, who was adjudicated bankrupt in March 1973, an order for possession of his house—execution of the order for possession was suspended by an arrangement between the appellant and the trustee for so long as the appellant paid £60 a month—appellant discharged from bankruptcy in 1976 and ceased to pay the £60 a month after 11 instalments of £60 a month had been paid—trustee applied for a warrant of execution to enforce the order for possession—matter transferred to ordinary county court jurisdiction—warrant granted—appeal allowed—matter never really fully explored and doubt whether true position of arrangement relating to the house really revealed—appellant given leave to go back to county court to start afresh. May 2, 1978. KNIGHT v. BINSTEAD.

16. —— —— rights of action—appeal

Plaintiff's application out of time for leave to appeal against order giving defendants leave to appeal—also for leave to appeal against order that there should be no stay, and against order that the plaintiff should be restrained from taking further steps without leave—whether claim came within exception to general rule that rights of action constituting the property of a bankrupt vest in his trustees in bankruptcy—*Re Kavanagh,* C.L.C. 702, a special case, applied as to onus of proof—plaintiff's appeals dismissed, with variation of second order, and application to extend time for leave to appeal against order of Stocker J. refused. November 9, 1977. PALLANT v. ALLEN.

17. Bills of Exchange—cheque—conditional delivery

Plaintiff brought an action on a promissory note claiming money loaned to the first and second defendants and guaranteed by the third defendant—agreement that if third defendant paid by cheque, plaintiff would have his solicitors acknowledge such payment as being in full and final satisfaction of his claim—post-dated cheque paid but no acknowledgement by solicitors, and therefore third defendant stopped his cheque—third defendant given conditional leave to defend, condition being that he pay into court the amount of the cheque—third defendant's appeal allowed—condition precedent for presentation of cheque not satisfied—third defendant given unconditional leave to defend. Appeal from Park J. February 23, 1978. DROUBY v. WASSIF.

18. —— promissory note—defence—collateral agreement—condition

Plaintiff made a promissory note in favour of a Jersey company, described as a " dustbin company " of an advocate, Mr. Labesse, practising in Jersey and being the plaintiff's advisor in relation to his setting up a practice as a solicitor in Jersey—the third defendants, a company used by a firm of solicitors practising in Jersey, were the transferees of the promissory note which was undated and expressed to be payable on demand—the plaintiff brought an action against the defendant for, inter alia, conspiracy, fraud and false imprisonment—a defence was filed, and a counterclaim made by the third defendants on the promissory note—the judge gave judgment in favour of the third defendants on the promissory note—plaintiff's appeal allowed—a defence emerged for the first time in the Court of Appeal that there was a collateral agreement between the plaintiff and Mr. Labesse that the promissory note was not to be enforced unless the prospect of the plaintiff being able to occupy certain premises and practise from there was fulfilled—plaintiff given conditional leave to defend. Appeal from Donaldson J. March 14, 1978. MYERSON v. MARTIN.

19. —— —— non est factum

Plaintiffs given judgment on a claim on a promissory note signed by the defendant—defendant's plea of non est factum, i.e. that although he signed the document, he misunderstood the nature of it and did not even read it, was accepted by the judge—defendant's appeal dismissed. February 28, 1978. BRITISH MEDICAL FINANCE *v.* GHOSH.

20. Building and Engineering, Architects and Surveyors—failure to complete work—damages

Plaintiffs, small jobbing builders, did building work for the defendants on their house over a period of time under three separate agreements—plaintiffs claimed balance of £280 under the contracts, and the defendants served a defence and counterclaim alleging that work was done improperly—judge found for the defendants and gave them damages of £150, holding that the plaintiffs were entitled to recover nothing—letter sent by judge to the Court of Appeal for the purposes of the appeal stated that the plaintiffs were " entitled to a very modest amount but failed to prove what amount (if any)"—plaintiffs' appeal allowed—error by judge—where builder carries out work of a quality or quantity which is less than it should have been, the failure to complete the work properly does not disentitle the builder from payment altogether—new trial ordered in the circumstances. March 3, 1978. SULLIVAN BROTHERS *v.* MORRIS.

21. Charities—trustees—removal—appeal

Appeal of the plaintiff against three orders made under s. 20 of the Charities Act 1960, after an inquiry had been ordered by the Charity Commissioners under s. 6—plaintiff was trustee of charity registered as " Sanctuary "— appeal dismissed—admissibility of evidence on appeal under Charities Act 1970— *Jones* v. *Att.-Gen.* [1973] C.L.Y. 312 referred to—plaintiff's appeal dismissed. December 14, 1977. JONES *v.* ATT.-GEN.

22. Company Law—security agreement—construction of undertaking—release

Purchase price of a company take-over by plaintiffs secured by a debenture and security agreement made in favour of the defendants—plaintiffs undertook " not to dissipate in any way the assets of the first plaintiffs . . ."—plaintiffs applied for a release from their undertaking so that assets of a certain company, of which the plaintiffs were the controlling shareholders, could be sold on the basis that the company was insolvent and that it was in the best interests of the company and its shareholders that those assets should be sold—defendants contended that the disposal of the assets would be " dissipation " under the plaintiffs undertaking—plaintiffs' application refused on basis that having regard to the context in which the undertaking was given and in particular the inclusion of the words " in any way," " dissipate " must be taken to mean any disposal of assets of relevant companies save in the normal course of trading, and that in all the circumstances the release should not be granted—plaintiffs' application for leave to appeal dismissed—judge's reasoning absolutely right— plaintiffs over-anxious to dispose of assets as quickly as possible. Appeal from Boreham J. May 24, 1978. SWIFTERVEND *v.* BOWMAN.

23. —— winding up—deadlock—just and equitable

A company was incorporated in January 1971 to take over the business of the Indian Social Club with an authorised capital of £15,000, divided into 15,000 shares of £1 each, of which only 140 were ever issued and were fully paid up—70 shares were issued to the petitioning creditor, 35 to N and 35 to G —in December 1971, G transferred his 35 shares to N—from 1972 onward N carried on as if the business were his own, claiming that the petitioner walked out and abandoned the business to him—petitioner claimed that he was excluded from business by N—the judge found for the petitioner and directed the compulsory winding up of the company—petition presented in April 1975 alleged it was just and equitable to wind up the company on the ground of deadlock— N's appeal dismissed—no misdirection of himself by judge in holding that the valuation, based on the assumption that the company continued in existence, demonstrated that on its compulsory liquidation, there would prima facie be a surplus for the contributories—judge carefully reviewed facts and weighed them up and arrived at right conclusion—ample evidence for findings of judge—not unreasonable for the petitioner to seek a winding-up order rather than an order under s. 210 of the Companies Act 1948. May 10, 1978. *Re* THE INDIAN SOCIAL CLUB (COVENTRY).

24. Compulsory Purchase—compensation—assessment

The claimant and her brother, personal representatives of their father who died in 1974, claimed compensation in the sum of £63,785 for the freehold of certain premises, the goodwill of the premises and the business carried on there, and disturbance—the properties in question had been acquired by the father in 1920—in 1970 the area in question was approved as a development area and a compulsory purchase order was submitted in 1972 and confirmed in 1974 and a notice to treat served on the father in March 1974—the tribunal assessed compensation at £36,800—claimants' appeal by way of case stated dismissed— assessment approached correctly in law by tribunal. March 15, 1978. VIAZZANI *v.* AFAN BOROUGH COUNCIL.

25. Conflict of Laws—forum conveniens—discovery—legitimate juridical advantage—shipping guarantee

Plaintiffs, Greek shipowners, agreed to carry 9,000 tons of cement from Alicante to Lagos on one of their vessels under a voyage charterparty, the charterers being a Spanish company—charterparty provided for arbitration in London according to British law—defendants, an international concern having a registered office and carrying on business in London, gave a letter of guarantee in Madrid covering demurrage if vessel held up—plaintiffs incurred substantial demurrage charges upon being detained over 100 days outside Lagos before being discharged and brought an action in London against the defendants on their guarantee—defendants applied to have action stayed on the ground that they ought to be sued in Spain and not in England—plaintiffs having a legitimate juridical advantage in going on with proceedings in England on grounds, inter alia, that there was full and ample machinery in England for discovery of documents, likely to be of the utmost importance in the case, relating to all the issues in the case, whereas there was no similar availability of discovery in Spain—undertaking by defendants to effect discovery in the Spanish proceedings to the same standard as discovery in England not a satisfactory solution because impossible for English court to supervise discovery in the Spanish courts—plaintiffs not to be deprived of legitimate juridical advantage in proceeding in the English courts—burden on the defendants to show that the case should not go on in England—burden not satisfied—stay of proceedings to be refused—plaintiffs' appeal allowed. Appeal from Donaldson J. May 26, 1978. INTERSEAS SHIPPING CO. S.A. *v.* BANCO DE BILBAO.

26. —— jurisdiction—stay of proceedings—negligence

Plaintiff, a Somali, brought an action in negligence for severe injuries suffered by him during the course of his employment in Abu Dhabi, Oman, by the defendants, an English company—plaintiff issued writ while receiving medical treatment in England—defendants denied negligence and applied to stay the action contending that matter ought to proceed in Oman—judge refused stay on ground that plaintiff would be deprived of a substantial and legitimate juridical advantage in the form of damages if action was stayed—defendants' appeal dismissed—observations on *Boys* v. *Chaplin* [1969] C.L.Y. 469. Appeal from Lawson J. May 11, 1978. SIYAD v. GEORGE WIMPEY & CO.

27. Contract—building

Plaintiff claimed £229·24 for building work carried out to a kitchen—judgment for £180 based on three weeks' work—defendant's counterclaim of £800 dismissed—judgment could not be supported—only way to do justice between parties was to order a new trial—defendant's appeal allowed. November 18, 1977. PLOWRIGHT v. WINDOW.

28. —— —— quantum meruit

Preliminary issues arising from builders' contract—plaintiffs claimed payment on a *quantum meruit* basis for work done—defence were contending for completion for about £11,000 and counterclaimed that the work had been badly done—whether the parties had entered into a binding contract and, if so, on what terms—judgment for the defendants—*Courtney and Fairbairn* v. *Tolaini Bros.* (*Hotels*) [1975] C.L.Y. 409, distinguished—plaintiffs' appeal allowed in part. December 7, 1977. JOHN TWINAME v. JOHN BRYSON (KESWICK).

29. —— cancellation—dishonoured cheque—issues not pleaded

Cancellation by two defendants of a holiday booked with plaintiff company—Bills of Exchange Act 1882—judgment for plaintiffs for £168·10 on a cheque dishonoured because second defendant countermanded payment—no question of notice of dishonour can or should have been raised—judge reached his conclusion of the facts as found—two distinct contracts, the first being an oral agreement between the plaintiffs and the defendants to arrange an inclusive holiday on a Greek island—the second was the cheque between the second defendant and the plaintiffs and the second defendant's plea of waiver or estoppel could not avail her here—*Fielding and Platt* v. *Najjar* [1969] C.L.Y. 173 was of no assistance—whether amount of cheque should be reduced pro tanto in accordance with services for which it was given but were not in fact rendered—latitude is not given in the Court of Appeal to raise issues in argument which have not been pleaded—the pleadings should be amended to cover the issues between the parties—appeal of second defendant dismissed. December 21, 1977. TRAVEL WORKSHOP v. FINLAY.

30. —— for services—performance—not in breach

Plaintiff brought action against the defendants claiming damages for defective workmanship on the defendants' part in installing double glazing in his premises—judge satisfied that defendants performed a good workmanlike job in accordance with their contract, using high quality materials, and gave judgment for the defendants—plaintiff's appeal dismissed—no question of law involved on appeal, and judge's decision on facts not wrong. May 2, 1978. TILL v. KENT AND SUSSEX WINDOW COMPANY.

31. —— guarantee—memorandum—evidence

Summary judgment awarded to plaintiffs on their claim for £24,045·67—alleged oral agreement with defendants guaranteeing repayment of deposits and loans—Statute of Frauds 1677—whether evidence of agreement fulfilled statutory requirement—whether link-up would constitute sufficient note of memorandum—*Timmins* v. *Moreland Street Property Co.* [1957] C.L.Y. 3638—appeal of first and second defendants allowed. October 4, 1977. JAY v. GAINSFORD.

32. —— money due—judge's discretion as to costs

Claim for money due for architect's services—judgment for plaintiffs £222·50 plus costs and judgment for plaintiffs on counterclaim—no signed notes of judgment—judge's unfavourable view of defendant's evidence—judge's exercise of discretion as to costs—seven grounds of appeal—judge considered referring case to the D.P.P.—defendant's appeal dismissed. October 12, 1977. KINGHAM KNIGHT ASSOCIATES v. OKEKEAURU.

33. —— restraint of trade—restrictive covenant—validity

The plaintiff had been employed by the defendant company since 1957—in 1974 he was made a director with special responsibility for the dry-cleaning division, and given a written agreement determinable on 12 months' notice on either side—the agreement contained a clause that he would not, for a period of 12 months from the termination of his employment, engage in any part of the U.K. in any business similar to dry cleaning—in 1976 the defendant company came under new management—the plaintiff was unhappy with this change and wanted to accept an offer of a job with another dry-cleaning company, and himself issued a writ claiming a declaration that the restrictive clause was invalid—the defendants claimed that the clause was valid and sought an injunction to restrain the plaintiff—judge declared that clause was invalid and refused the injunction—defendants' appeal dismissed—clause geographically too wide. Appeal from Fox J. February 22, 1978. GREER v. SKETCHLEY.

34. —— whether binding

Plaintiff's claim was for £100, the cost of keeping a horse—claim dismissed—no evidence that the defendant gave authority to bind himself to pay the plaintiff's bill—unsigned proof of witness inadmissible under the Civil Evidence Act 1968—judge refused an adjournment—whether a denial of justice—defendant since the trial adjudicated bankrupt—no ground for interfering with judge's discretion—plaintiff's appeal dismissed. November 30, 1977. GREAVES v. MIKHAIL.

35. Copyright—infringement—order for destruction

Injunction restraining defendants from infringing copyright in two drawings for drawers used in furniture—order for destruction suspended pending appeal—plaintiffs' drawers marketed under name " Sheerglide "—whether it would appear to the notional non-expert that the three-dimensional object is a reproduction of the two-dimensional artistic work—defendants' appeal allowed. Appeal from Whitford J. October 26, 1977. L.B. PLASTICS v. SWISH PRODUCTS.

36. County court practice—appeal—jurisdiction—discretion of judge

Plaintiffs' claim was in relation to the construction of a garage—appeal in the matter of costs—whether Court of Appeal had jurisdiction to deal with appeal, when neither it, nor the County Court judge had given leave to appeal—County Court Rules (S.I. 1936 No. 626 (as amended)) Ord. 47, r. 5 (4)—whether a question of law—County Courts Act 1959, s. 108—discretion of judge—*Donald Campbell & Co.* v. *Pollak* [1927] A.C. 732 referred to—whether judge correct in certifying under r. 13 that a question of fact of exceptional complexity had arisen—judge made an error in law—defendant's appeal allowed. December 19, 1977. HAYWARD AND WALKER v. CAMPBELL.

37. —— —— right of plaintiff in person

Plaintiff obtained judgment for £85 in county court—defendant to pay judgment debt by instalments of £4 a week—plaintiff appealed—right to appeal assumed in favour of plaintiff appearing in person—no ground for interfering with order—plaintiff's appeal dismissed. January 13, 1978. ANYANWU v. MUNHUMUTURA.

38. —— application for new trial—exercise of discretion

Plaintiff appearing in person, applied in the county court for a county court judgment given against him to be set aside and a new trial to be ordered— application dismissed—plaintiff appealed on various grounds against his application for a new trial being dismissed—appeal dismissed—exercise of discretion not wrong in any way. March 3, 1978. BATTEN v. BIRMINGHAM TRAINING GROUP.

39. —— orders—appeal—appropriate tribunal

The plaintiff (in person) applied for leave to appeal against two county court orders which were as follows: (i) that the trial of the county court action be fixed for February 10, and (ii) that the plaintiff's application to add a third party to his counterclaim be dismissed—applications misconceived —appropriate tribunal to consider (i) whether or not the hearing should be adjourned, and (ii) a further application to add the third party, was the county court—applications refused. February 9, 1978. GANN v. MARSHALL.

40. —— striking out proceedings—action for damages—whether frivolous, vexatious and abuse of process

Plaintiff brought an action for damages against the defendants, legal personnel who had acted for the plaintiff's employers in an action the plaintiff had brought against the employers, alleging negligence or breach of duty, conspiracy and fraud, and breaches of the rules of court—substance of the plaintiff's complaint was that there had been delay during a certain period of time in giving him inspection of certain documents, and that if he had known of the contents of those documents at the proper time, he would have dropped a preliminary issue raised by his pleadings in the action against his employers—the defendants applied to strike out the action—whether pleadings disclosed no reasonable cause of action—whether action frivolous, vexatious and an abuse of process— defendants' appeal allowed—County Court Rules, Ord. 13, r. 6. January 27, 1978. TURNER v. MOORFOOT.

41. Damages—accident—allocation of blame between parties

Plaintiffs claimed £845, plus interest, for damage to their tanker, sustained in head-on collision with defendants' cattle truck—plaintiffs appealed against finding of 90 per cent. blame attributable to them—cross-appeal of defendants against their 10 per cent. culpability—whether blame attached to defendants' driver—whether 10 per cent. apportionment unreasonably high—*Mulligan* v. *Holmes* [1971] C.L.Y. 7762 referred to—defendants' driver negligent in that he collided with a stationary vehicle which could plainly be seen ahead—no effective effort to reduce speed until too late—prime cause of accident was, however, plaintiffs' vehicle which protruded across the centre of road—appeal and cross appeal dismissed. November 24, 1977. CALOR GROUP v. VARNHAM (MRS. A.) & SONS.

42. —— apportionment between defendants

Plaintiff was a welder who sustained burns in a gas explosion—judgment for £6,000 in his favour (including interest)—sixth defendants' liability assessed at 40 per cent.—second defendants', 30 per cent.—first defendants', 30 per cent.—accident was in April 1969—indemnity as to proceeding—review of apportionment undertaken in exceptional circumstances—whether first defendants did have authority from second defendants, or were entitled to assume such, to carry out the work—appeal of sixth and second defendants allowed; liability adjusted to 60 per cent. and nil respectively. Appeal from Thesiger J. November 23, 1977. GREENSTREET v. TURIFF CONSTRUCTION CORP.

43. —— assessment—breach of building contract—deduction of tax

Plaintiff, a labour-only sub-contractor, was awarded £195 damages against the defendants for breach of contract relating to building work—£195 damages assessed by deducting from a gross sum of £900 which the plaintiff would have earned if he had been allowed to complete his contract with the defendants, a gross sum of £600 earned by the plaintiff elsewhere during the relevant time, and by deducting from the remainder of the £300 income tax at the standard rate of 35 per cent.—whether defendants entitled to deduct tax—plaintiff's appeal allowed—wrong in principle to deduct tax. February 27, 1978. PAYNE v. GEE WALKER & SLATER.

44. —— detention—nominal only

Value of motor car—plaintiff's appeal against judgment for the plaintiff on defendant's negligence and detention—damages awarded were based on car's value at date of judgment, £1,000—cost of hire of another vehicle, £72 —damages for detention, £50—principle in *The Mediana* [1900] A.C. 113 confirmed that damages for the invasion of a right were nominal only— evidence of vintage car's reputation—no evidence of probability that vehicle would be exhibited in the United States—plaintiff's conduct in relation to the car was wholly unreasonable—plaintiff's appeal dismissed. Appeal from Croom-Johnson J. November 25, 1977. DEANE v. MORGAN.

45. —— exemplary damages—libel

Plaintiff, a member of the Privy Council, who had held some of the highest offices in the state, sought exemplary damages alleging that the defendants had published a defamatory article about him " calculated to make a profit which may well exceed the compensation payable "—judge dismissed defendants' application to strike out the claim for exemplary damages—defendants' appeal dismissed. Appeal from May J. March 17, 1978. MAUDLING v. STOTT.

46. —— industrial injury—quantum affected by unreasonable behaviour of employee

Plaintiff had been machine operator for 49 years—loss of tip of middle finger of right hand—issue was quantum only—total award of £3,005—defendants appealed against £2,000 for pain and suffering and loss of amenity and £400 for loss of earning capacity—whether £2,000 above scale which is properly applicable—plaintiff unreasonable in leaving defendants' employment—possibility of losing employment—*Moeliker* v. *Reyrolle & Co.* [1976] C.L.Y. 1881 referred to—defendants' appeal allowed—£1,500 for pain and suffering substituted, and £400 for loss of earning capacity set aside. Appeal from Brown J. October 14, 1977. ADAMSON v. GRUNDFOS MANUFACTURING.

47. —— measure—breach of service contract

Plaintiff awarded damages for defendant's failure to repair plaintiff's car properly—£484·45 awarded as damages, because plaintiff had lost £600 as the price which he had agreed with a purchaser of the car, less £115·55 that the plaintiff would have had to pay if car had been properly repaired—defendant's appeal allowed—proper measure of damages was the difference between the value the car would have as properly repaired and the value as it was, not having been properly repaired—new trial ordered. February 20, 1978. SELA v. BHAI.

48. —— personal injuries—loss of earnings—amendment to claim

In January 1973 the plaintiff, a steel erector, was injured whilst driving his car by an accident admittedly caused by the defendant and in September 1975 brought an action in the county court, his claim being limited to £1,000—in June 1977, he sought leave to amend his statement of claim to include damages of £16,000 for loss of earnings from December 1974 onwards—the judge allowed the amendment—defendant's appeal dismissed—as plaintiff was seeking general damages for pain, suffering and so on, the whole history of his injury and its effect on his ability to do his work would have to be gone into on the medical evidence, and it was therefore illogical not to allow the amendment. Appeal from Payne J. March 6, 1978. WOODRUFF v. PETTITT.

49. —— —— quantum—facial injuries

Defendants admitted liability for road accident—plaintiff accepted that his failure to wear a seat-belt would result in a 25 per cent. reduction to damages —plaintiff had sustained injuries to his face causing him some embarrassment —effect of injury to the cornea upon plaintiff's vision—judgment for £3,425·08 damages—whether judge should have itemised each injury, and added up what resulted—danger of duplication—judge's assessment plainly wrong—defendants' appeal allowed, total damages reduced to £2,080·20, with liberty to apply regarding interest. Appeal from Wien J. December 20, 1977. CRYAN v. GEORGE WIMPEY & CO.

50. Plaintiff, a single man in his early forties, was awarded £800 general damages for injuries, pain and suffering, sustained in a motor accident for which the defendant admitted liability—injuries fell mainly into two groups, scarring to the face, and concussion and its effects—whether award of damages excessive—defendant's appeal dismissed. March 8, 1978. NOLAN v. DOVE.

51. —— —— —— hip injury

Plaintiff, a married man aged 41 with two young boys and a girl, and leading an active life, injured in car accident in 1970 caused by defendant's negligence —injuries including, inter alia, a head injury and a hip joint injury leaving plaintiff with instability and limitation of movement and osteoarthritic pain—plaintiff's left leg shortened by osteotomy operation by half an inch to relieve pain—plaintiff off work for five months and returning to work in less remunerative and responsible job than before, with earnings reduced by £540 a year—plaintiff made redundant in 1977 and now working as a publican with loss of earnings above £540 a year—possibility of plaintiff being made redundant considered by judge—plaintiff awarded, inter alia, general damages of £6,000 for pain and suffering and loss of amenities, and special damages of £2,500 for future loss of fringe benefit of use of company car—award of damages too low—awards increased to £9,500 and £7,700 respectively—plaintiff's appeal allowed. Appeal from Lawson J. January 13, 1978. GORDON v. WINDLE.

52. —— —— reproductive organs

Plaintiff, a young man, was awarded, inter alia, £20,000 general damages for personal injuries suffered by him when the defendant driver ran him down in a mini-van—defendant appealed against liability and, inter alia, the £20,000 general damages—little dispute as to facts—appeal against liability dismissed —very serious injuries suffered by plaintiff, including loss of scrotum and testicles, leaving him sterile but not impotent, and scarring of his remaining genitals—unpleasant consequences—appeal against quantum dismissed—award in no way excessive. Appeal from Melford Stevenson J. February 13, 1978. WALSH v. HOUGHTON.

53. —— —— —— sight

Plaintiff, 53 years old at time of accident, fell on a wet patch in a school kitchen and suffered injuries for which the defendants were found liable— injuries were bilateral retinal detachment leaving her totally and permanently blind; and as a result of her falling down some stairs, certain fractures likely to lead to arthritis in later life left her unable to use the blind person's white stick in her right hand, she being right handed—judge awarded, inter alia, £35,000 damages for paid and suffering and loss of amenities, and £12,000 for further care and attention—whether £35,000 damages excessive—whether plaintiff entitled to the full cost of such attendance as proved to be necessary —whether plaintiff's attendance allowance of £12·20 a week, payable under s. 35 of the Social Security Act 1975, deductible from the £12,000 damages— defendants' appeal dismissed—*Bowker* v. *Rose* [1978] C.L.Y. 720 followed. Appeal from Cantley J. April 26, 1978. GOHERY v. DURHAM COUNTY COUNCIL.

54. Divorce and Matrimonial Causes—ancillary relief

Wife petitioner given custody of children, and husband excluded from matrimonial home—parties married in 1967—matrimonial home in joint names of parties—wife presenting petition for divorce in 1977 on grounds of unreasonable behaviour—application by wife for custody and for order excluding husband from matrimonial home—husband giving notice of similar application—both parties submitting that presence of other in matrimonial home represented an " impossible situation "—wife suffering from depressive mental illnesss, but there was medical evidence that, in the absence of stress, wife looked after children well, and was fit enough to look after children on her own—judge of opinion that children were of age when they should be with mother if she was capable of looking after them—on balance, the risk of damage was greater if husband was alone in matrimonial home than if wife there alone with children—husband's appeal that he be allowed to return to matrimonial home—appeal dismissed—impossible to say that judge came to wrong conclusion. January 31, 1978. RUSSELL v. RUSSELL.

55. Parties married in April 1969 when father was 23 and mother 20—two children, now aged four and three years—in March 1977, mother filed petition on ground of unreasonable behaviour, including violence, and was granted decree nisi by the special procedure in January 1978—in August 1977, father had left the matrimonial home—no plans to remarry by either party—judge ordered, inter alia, (i) that the children should be in the joint custody of the parents but with care and control to the mother and reasonable access to the father; and (ii) that the mother should continue to pay the mortgage repayments on the house, but on the sale of the house such payments should be credited to the father in the equal distribution of the proceeds of the sale— mother's appeal on point (i) dismissed, on point (ii) allowed. April 11, 1978. PHILLIPS v. PHILLIPS.

56. —— —— affidavit of means

Maintenance agreement made between parties in 1962—marriage dissolved in the 1940s—wife applied for detailed particulars of husband's income and property—registrar ordered husband to file affidavit setting out information relating to certain matters—order far too wide and oppressive—order set aside by judge who ordered that matter should proceed to hearing, husband knowing the questions to be asked—wife's appeal allowed—not satisfactory for matter to go to judge on that basis because matter would, as it stood, take an immensely long time and it would be impossible for wife's counsel to conduct the cross-examination of the husband properly—husband's duty to file affidavit containing full particulars of property and income—husband ordered to do accordingly—Matrimonial Causes Rules 1977 (S.I. 1977 No. 344), r. 100 (5); Matrimonial Causes Act 1973 (c. 18), s. 35—wife's appeal allowed. Appeal from Reeve J. June 9, 1978. SMITH v. SMITH.

57. —— —— school fees

Wife given £3,418 and husband £7,348 out of proceeds of matrimonial home, and husband ordered to pay £40 per week maintenance for wife and £10 per week for child, a boy now aged 14—boy originally sleeping in grandmother's home but now in boarding school with fees just over £2,000—whether such sum could be raised out of the joint resources of husband and wife—husband now remarried with new wife expecting child—husband's reasonable offer to undertake to pay boy's school fees if maintenance payments very significantly reduced not accepted by wife—wife's appeal dismissed. May 25, 1978. WOODGATE v. WOODGATE.

58. —— decree absolute—retrial

Wife's application for leave to extend time for applying for a retrial of divorce suit, dismissed—issue of whether the court had had jurisdiction to grant the divorce—wife sought to re-open the question of husband's intention to acquire a domicile of choice in South Africa—burden of establishing a change of domicile is on the party asserting it—no merits in admissible evidence—application of wife dismissed. December 13, 1977. CARRITT v. CARRITT.

59. —— decree nisi—behaviour of respondent

Judge granted wife petitioner decree nisi because of husband's behaviour—husband appealing on various grounds—impossible to say that judge wrong—appeal dismissed. Appeal from Arnold J. January 30, 1978. NDIRITY v. NDIRITY.

60. —— —— evidence

Decree nisi granted to wife under s. 1 (2) (b) of the Matrimonial Causes Act 1973 (c. 18)—whether judge placed too much weight on letter sent by husband to wife—husband's appeal dismissed. November 4, 1977. BARNES v. BARNES.

61. —— —— five years' separation—financial position

Husband applying for divorce on basis of five years' separation—wife not opposing divorce decree but indicating intention of having her financial position considered under s. 10 of the Matrimonial Causes Act 1973—decree nisi granted to husband—financial position of parties—husband refused to disclose certain aspects—wife's solicitors asking for various directions to be agreed by husband—husband's solicitors refusing to agree—hearing of s. 10 application intended to be limited to directions sought by wife's solicitors but no appropriate notice given—registrar refusing directions and proceeding with hearing—husband not liable to make any financial provision for wife—decree made absolute—judge upholding registrar and holding he had no discretion to set aside the decree absolute, and that if he had, he would not have exercised it in the circumstances —judge exercised his discretion correctly—wife's appeal allowed to the extent of varying judge's order so as to grant wife leave to apply for maintenance under s. 23 of the Matrimonial Causes Act 1973. January 16, 1978. QUINTON v. QUINTON.

62. —— —— stay of proceedings

Decree nisi granted to husband—wife had applied for adjournment of the hearing of the petition, to which she had filed no answer—unable to find £100 towards her Legal Aid costs in obtaining advice from an American lawyer—appeal misconceived—whether proceedings ought to be stayed pending the outcome of proceedings in Missouri which had not been brought at the time this matter was before the judge—circumstances in which a stay is appropriate—wife's appeal dismissed. December 2, 1977. TAYLOR v. TAYLOR.

63. —— financial provision—conduct

Order that wife transfer to husband her interest in a cottage—wife to receive £9,500 from proceeds of sale of former matrimonial home—husband to make periodical payments to wife of £65 per month—two crucial questions on appeal were whether the judge was right in reducing wife's maintenance by reason of her conduct, and whether he applied the correct test in arriving at the figure—wife's appeal allowed to the extent that maintenance pending suit was increased to £108 per month. November 29, 1977. COOKSON v. COOKSON.

64. —— —— conflict between case law and statute

Registrar's order that £1,500 be paid to wife by husband, increased by judge to £3,000—wife in similar financial position to formerly—husband worse-off than he was before the break-down of the marriage—when conflict arises between *Wachtel* v. *Wachtel* [1973] C.L.Y. 923, and the Matrimonial Causes Act 1973, it is the latter which must prevail—husband's appeal allowed. December 21, 1977. EVANS v. EVANS.

65. —— —— costs

Claim of wife for financial provision disposed of by agreement, except as to costs—order of judge that husband should pay £500 towards wife's costs —Court of Appeal's remarks as to a judge considering costs when he has not heard the cause—whether judge departed from Ord. 62, r. 3 (2)—it was part of the terms of the compromise that a judge should fix costs—wife's appeal dismissed. December 7, 1977. DENNE v. DENNE.

66. —— —— lump sum

Wife granted leave to appeal out of time against Registrar's order dismissing her application for a lump sum payment—her unchallenged evidence—husband had recently received money from sale of shares—husband had not filed any evidence in court below—husband's appeal dismissed. December 15, 1977. CLIFF v. CLIFF.

67. —— —— —— instalments

Parties, husband, now 43 and wife 40 years old, married in 1960—three children, 15, 13 and nine respectively—marriage dissolved in 1977—husband earned £14,000 per year and wife £5,500 per year—husband paying periodical payments of £1,000 to wife and £1,500 per year to each child—wife having small equity in matrimonial home—judge ordered husband to pay lump sum of £2,000 to wife, £1,000 to be paid in four months' time and the balance by equal monthly instalments thereafter—husband's appeal allowed—£500 to be paid to wife immediately, balance thereafter in equal monthly instalments, to stop further applications by husband and further dissipation of the assets. Appeal from Rees J. March 1, 1978. WILSON v. WILSON.

68. —— —— —— whether fair to wife

Parties married in 1969—two children, both girls now seven and five years old—in 1976 wife left, taking children with her, to live with another man whom she hoped to marry—husband now lived in matrimonial home together with another woman whom he hoped to marry—value of matrimonial home now £13,000, with equity about £10,000—husband paying £6 a week for each child—wife living in a " very good way "—judge gave wife lump sum of £3,330—wife's appeal dismissed—order by judge " almost more than fair " to wife. January 16, 1978. WINFIELD v. WINFIELD.

69. —— —— retired army officer

Judge's order that the husband should transfer their house to the wife, in accordance with his undertaking, and should make periodical payments to her of £5 per week—also pay half the costs of the application—difficulties of financial provision for an army officer's family when his marriage breaks down after an early retirement—husband's appeal allowed in part. May 25, 1977. GROOM v. GROOM.

70. —— irretrievable breakdown—five years' separation—" living apart "

Parties married in 1957 and had no children—they separated in February 1970, but the husband visited the wife frequently with sexual intercourse taking place—apart from these visits, during the five years from February 1970 the parties lived together continuously for four and a half months—quality of relationship between parties—whether relationship broken down—" visits " by husband did not mean the parties were " living together "—husband entitled to decree on basis of five years' separation—wife's appeal dismissed—Matrimonial Causes Act 1973, ss. 1 (2) (e), 2 (5) (b). February 23, 1978. PIPER v. PIPER.

71. —— petition—hearing—wife's absence

The parties had separated and their marriage had broken down—husband admitted having committed adultery in 1974 and filed a petition for divorce in June 1975—protracted negotiations between parties—no issue about children or about finance—matter came before judge in November 1977 when husband flew to England from Malaysia, where parties lived and where husband was a medical practitioner, but wife not present—judge granted decree on husband's petition—wife's appeal that a new trial be ordered, so that cross-decrees by consent be granted, dismissed. Appeal from Faulks J. March 16, 1978. WILLIAMS v. WILLIAMS.

72. —— wife's applications

Decree nisi granted to husband, based on unreasonable behaviour of wife —wife's prayer rejected—78 grounds of her appeal—wife's application for extension of time for leave to appeal against the part of the order which excluded her from the matrimonial home—also applied for adjournment of appeal against financial and property arrangements—appeal of wife against decree nisi, her application for adjournment, and her appeal against excluding order, all refused. November 16, 1977. LONGINOTTI v. LONGINOTTI.

73. Easements and Prescription—injunction—refusal

Plaintiff's claim to an easement and right of way over defendants' property going to and from refuse disposal bin—injunction refused—not an appropriate case for interlocutory relief—plaintiff's appeal dismissed. October 14, 1977. SCHMIDT v. MARZELL INVESTMENTS.

74. Employment—contract—construction of clause

Defendant was manager of plaintiffs' off-licence shop—plaintiffs claimed £631·63 after stocktaking which disclosed a deficiency—case dismissed—construction of clause in contract of service—whether burden rests on plaintiffs to establish a physical loss of goods before they can prove liability of defendant to pay sum claimed—inequality of bargaining power—perfectly legitimate clause to protect employers, while not unfairly unloaded against employee who accepts the contract—plaintiffs' appeal allowed. November 15, 1977. ARTHUR COOPER (WINE MERCHANT) v. McLAREN.

75. —— dismissal—suspension without pay—appropriate procedure

Plaintiff employed as fireman with the London Fire Brigade—on strike with other firemen—alternative work done by plaintiff (amongst other firemen) at a factory for extra money during the strike—theft from factory—plaintiff pleading guilty to the theft and fined £100 but no sentence of imprisonment passed by magistrates—plaintiff given notice of dismissal at end of strike and suspended from duty without pay—whether sentence of imprisonment essential for suspension without pay—plaintiff's appeal dismissed—correct code followed to suspend plaintiff without pay. Appeal from Jupp J. February 6, 1978. EDWARDS v. DARBY AND GREATER LONDON COUNCIL.

76. —— trade union—membership

Trade Union and Labour Relations (Amendment) Act 1976 (c. 7), s. 5 (1)—declaration that applicant was entitled on condition to be a member of the National Graphical Association reversed—whether applicant unreasonably discriminated against—rules of trade union—" closed shop "—Nagle v. Fielden [1966] C.L.Y. 12099—decision at authoritative level—meaning of unqualified person—appeal of applicant allowed. October 18, 1977. SIEVEWRIGHT v. NATIONAL GRAPHICAL ASSOCIATION.

77. —— unfair dismissal

Plaintiff's appeal from Employment Appeal Tribunal—whether tribunal was wrong in law in holding that a failure to observe the code of practice was not fatal to the defendants' case—Lewis Shops Group v. Wiggins [1973] C.L.Y. 1162 referred to—alleged serious misconduct and no written final warning was given—invitation by tribunal to put appeal on alternative basis —whether tribunal addressed its mind properly to the consideration in para. 6, sub-para. 8, of Sched. I to the Trade Union and Labour Relations Act 1974 —no error of law which could enable the Court of Appeal to find in favour of the appellant—plaintiff's appeal dismissed. December 20, 1977. JONES v. BRENT LONDON BOROUGH.

78. ———— terminatory letter

Plaintiff's claim for wrongful dismissal rejected—letter purporting to terminate plaintiff's employment or inviting him to retire—whether sent by proprietor or defendant company—plaintiff's appeal dismissed. December 2, 1977. HAWKINS v. N. R. GREEN.

79. Evidence—case insufficiently made out—new trial

Plaintiffs claimed £2,617 as money due for inland carriage charges and container service charge—judgment for plaintiffs on what might be called circumstantial evidence—judge did not say he disbelieved the defendant—failure of plaintiffs to call a witness or produce a vital document—only way justice can be done to both sides is to order a new trial—defendant's appeal allowed. November 9, 1977. SEA-LAND CONTAINER-SHIPS v. McCARRICK.

80. —— loan—conflict between parties—plaintiff failed to make out case

Plaintiff's claim was for £1,000 owing to him—alleged loan to defendant in 1971 for investment purposes—denial of loan by defendant—conflict of evidence—judge's reasoning for finding in plaintiff's favour was unsatisfactory—plaintiff failed to prove his case—defendant's appeal allowed. November 16, 1977. SURI v. NISCHAL.

81. —— on commission—" necessary for the purposes of justice "

Contract for supply and shipment of formic acid to Nigeria—order that evidence was to be taken on commission—such evidence could be given under the Civil Evidence Act 1972, and procedure should be as laid down in R.S.C., Ord. 38, rr. 22–25—Ord 39, r. 1 states "where it appears necessary for the purposes of justice"—court should not interfere with judge's discretion—contract was between a firm in Liverpool and a firm in Germany—evidence of custom of Sapela in Nigeria cannot be of primary importance—whether essential witnesses as to facts in favour of the defendants' case were involved—plaintiffs' appeal allowed. Appeal from Hollings J. November 28, 1977. JOHN A. MASON v. UNITED COMMERCIAL AGENCIES.

82. Executors and Administrators—probate—provision for widow—breach of trust

The first defendant, C, a solicitor, and the second defendant, M, were the executors and trustees under the will of Mr. ALC who died in November 1975—the plaintiff was the wife of the deceased but had separated from him in 1973, and divorce proceedings were pending—she was left a legacy of £50,000 on trust, but applied for further provision under the Inheritance (Family Provision) Act 1938 to be made for her from the deceased's substantial estate—in 1977, M retired as executor and the existing grant of probate was revoked and C applied for a new grant in his own name, with steps to be taken afterwards to appoint another executor with him—plaintiff applied for an injunction to restrain C from acting in connection with the administration of the estate pending the determination of a summons she intended to issue under s. 162 of the Supreme Court of Judicature Act 1925, to have C replaced as executor by some other person to be designated as administrator, C being alleged to have acted in breach of trust in relation to the trust funds—the judge granted the order sought by the plaintiff, and ordered that the costs to the plaintiff of the motion were to be borne personally by C—C's appeal dismissed—plaintiff's cross-appeal that C should also be ordered to pay personally his own costs of the motion allowed. Appeal from Goulding J. February 24, 1978. COISY v. CUTNER.

83. Factories—safe place of work—obligation to make and keep safe so far as reasonably practicable

Factories Act 1961 (c. 34), s. 29 (1)—plaintiff employed by defendants as safety officer—plaintiff injured by falling crate while inspecting conveyor belt in course of duties—plaintiff's case that his place of work not safe and that the defendants had not, so far as reasonably practicable, made and kept the place safe for him—defendants' answer that first, the place of work was safe, and secondly, even if the place of work was not safe, the plaintiff himself was solely to blame for the accident, being in breach of his duty as safety officer—defendants held not liable even if assumption that defendants liable for breach of statutory duty—plaintiff's appeal dismissed. Appeal from Mais J. January 12, 1978. OLNEY v. ROCKWARE GLASS.

84. Fraud, Misrepresentation and Undue Influence—misrepresentation—sale of car

Plaintiff was awarded damages of £635 for misrepresentation in the sale of a Jensen car to him on the basis that the plaintiff entered into the contract by reason of and after the defendant's representations, inter alia, that the motorcar was registered in 1971—defence was that no such representation was ever made, either by statement or by implication—defendant's appeal allowed both as to liability and damages—note of evidence plus the very short note of judge's judgment leading to conclusion that judgment unsatisfactory—new trial ordered. March 6, 1978. MANSFIELD v. RICE.

85. Guarantee and Indemnity—co-sureties—contribution—formula for contribution

The plaintiff, a director of A Ltd. with two others, L and B—bank required directors to guarantee on standard form A Ltd.'s indebtedness to the bank—guarantee signed by plaintiff and B but not signed by L—L resigned from board of A Ltd.—plaintiff lodged securities with bank in support of guarantee—defendant joined board of A Ltd. as financial director and signed a guarantee agreement with same bank guaranteeing all moneys and liabilities of A Ltd. subject to limit of £10,000—A Ltd. became insolvent and went into liquidation—B denied liability under guarantee—defendant paying £7,400 into bank under his guaranteee—plaintiff claimed contribution of £2,600 from defendant as being moneys paid to bank by plaintiff as surety—defendant delivered defence and counterclaim, claiming, inter alia, that the bank owed a duty to B to ascertain his attitude to continuing liability under the guarantee having regard to L's defection; that the bank having failed to do so, B was discharged from liability; and consequently the defendant was discharged from liability as co-guarantor—bank under no duty as alleged—defendant's guarantee an independent guarantee—defendant's appeal dismissed—parties' respective contributions to be assessable on the " independent liability " formula. Appeal from Goulding J. February 7, 1978. NAUMANN v. NORTHCOTE.

86. —— plea of non est factum

Plaintiffs obtained judgment against the second defendant on a guarantee signed by him—second defendant raised plea of non est factum contending that he signed thinking that he was giving a reference for the first defendant, a young man employed by him, to enable him to buy a motor-cycle—judge held second defendant was an educated man who must have known what he was signing—second defendant's appeal dismissed. April 14, 1978. UNITED DOMINIONS v. CLARKE.

87. Highways and Bridges—public paths—right of way—evidence

Bridle road running over defendants' land a public right of way since Inclosure Award of 1806—plaintiff owned land on same side of right of way and also on opposite side of it—width of right of way—master decided that plaintiff had right of way over the bridle road given in the Inclosure Award of 1806 which appointed and allotted the right of way with a width of 20 ft. measured from an iron fence which defined certain boundaries—position of iron fence—

new trial ordered—principles for new trial satisfied—hearing before master taking "wrong turns"—judgment not taking into account documents and evidence of "great if not decisive" importance—may need to be considered whether delineation, width and position of bridle road, as shown in OS 1912 map, was conclusive—National Parks and Access to the Countryside Act 1949, s. 32 (4)—defendants' appeal allowed. January 19, 1978. COLLEDGE v. CROSSLEY.

88. Hire Purchase—loan agreement—false particulars—default of purchaser—liability of vendor to finance company

Defendants, in order to obtain money from the plaintiffs, a finance company, to cover the price of a second-hand car that the defendants were selling to S, filled in a form which formed the basis of the loan agreement and which was signed by S who thereby undertook to pay the plaintiffs £14·50 per month— the form as filled in was false in material particulars—S defaulted in making the payments and the plaintiffs brought an action against the defendants claiming the amount of the loan—judgment for the plaintiffs after certain findings and inferences from the evidence that, inter alia, the plaintiffs relied on an inaccurate statement as to deposit in the form in making the loan to S—defendants' appeal dismissed—judge entitled to draw the inference that he did in the circumstances of the case on the material before him. May 9, 1978. WHITEWAY LAIDLAW & CO. v. CENTRAL GARAGE (LOW FELL).

89. Husband and Wife—financial provision

Order that husband should pay £250 to wife—leave granted to wife to appeal out of time—*Wachtel* v. *Wachtel* [1973] C.L.Y. 923, referred to—no basis on which conclusion of trial judge could be faulted on such inadequate evidence— considerable wastage of public money over litigation—wife's appeal dismissed. November 3, 1977. CRADDOCK v. CRADDOCK.

90. —— —— charges on property—application for discharge

The husband applied to have certain charges on the matrimonial home and another property (made to secure financial provision orders made in favour of the wife) discharged on the basis that his overall financial position was very bad and that certain prior charges on the two properties could not be satisfied on a sale of the properties—application dismissed—husband's appeal dismissed —no documentary evidence produced by husband in support of his contentions —wrong to deprive wife of security. Appeal from Payne J. February 17, 1978. LINDSEY v. LINDSEY.

91. —— —— fresh information

Order that husband pay £10 a week to wife—no order for lump sum payment —leave to appeal out of time granted to wife—allegations in wife's affidavit in relation to information which came to light since hearing—right course to set aside judge's order and remit case—wife's appeal allowed. November 10, 1977. SARKHEL v. SARKHEL.

92. —— —— periodical payments—variation of order

The husband applied for a variation of an order for periodical payments of £3,000 per annum for the wife and two children of the family on the ground, inter alia, that he had an income for the purpose of assessing periodical payments far below £6,000 per annum upon which the order for periodical payments was based—application dismissed—husband's appeal dismissed—no document to show state of husband's income, and husband totally failed to persuade court. Appeal from Dunn J. February 17, 1978. BROOMFIELD v. BROOMFIELD.

93. —— —— unappealable order

Equitable execution—appointment of receiver to enforce charging order upon husband's interest in property—leave to appeal—alleged earlier orders were obtained fraudulently—Court of Appeal refused leave to appeal against the order of a registrar, affirmed by a judge, that the husband should pay the wife the sum of £10,000, and also periodical payments—incompetent appeal by husband to House of Lords—Practice Direction issued by House of Lords on May 18, 1976 ([1976] C.L.Y. 2105), para. 1 (b), referred to—whether judge was exercising High Court or county court jurisdiction—judge exercised his discretion—order unappealable—husband's appeal dismissed. November 1, 1977, LAMB v. LAMB.

94. —— —— whether originally by consent

Husband ordered to pay, inter alia, £1,000 per annum as maintenance for three children—expressed to be " by consent," but order was subsequently varied—husband's application for leave to appeal against original order refused—husband's appeal on ground that original order was not a consent order, as he had been deceived or deluded—too late to set aside original order on a ground already adjudicated upon, and leave to appeal refused. November 28, 1977. McLAREN v. McLAREN.

95. —— —— wilful neglect

Order that husband should discharge the mortgage repayment of £720 per annum, and pay to his wife, to include these sums, payments totalling £2,202 a year—also £390 per year for the youngest child until he attained 17 —whether it was open to the judge to find wilful neglect to maintain on the basis of a matter which occurred only after the wife had issued her originating summons—whether judge wrong in finding wife unfit to work—whether order excessive—husband's appeal dismissed. December 2, 1977. TORESEN v. TORESEN.

96. —— injunction—ex parte application

On wife's ex parte application, injunction restraining husband from interfering with wife, or her parents, or from communicating with them, issued—liberty to husband to apply—whether judge should have attached to order a return date for inter partes hearing—Ansah v. Ansah [1976] C.L.Y. 1391 distinguished—whether wrong not to stipulate expiry date—jurisdiction of Court of Appeal in such matters—husband's appeal dismissed. November 14, 1977. BURGOYNE v. BURGOYNE.

97. —— —— power of county court

Domestic Violence and Matrimonial Proceedings Act 1976 (c. 50)—power of county court to grant injunctions—this case had wider importance than that to the parties concerned—injunction restraining plaintiff from molesting the defendant, and excluding party from the property—man and woman living together in the same household as husband and wife—no ground for interfering with judge's order—defendant's appeal dismissed. HILLS v. BUSHBY.

98. —— matrimonial home

Registrar ordered that husband should pay £7 per week for wife's maintenance and £8 per week for their child—house was to be sold when child attained 18, and proceeds of sale divided in the ratio of two-thirds to husband, one-third to wife—affirmed by judge—not within basis suggested in Wachtel v. Wachtel [1973] C.L.Y. 923—the falling value of money—dicta in Hector

88

v. *Hector* [1973] C.L.Y. 1625—court restricted by the paramount consideration of the children's welfare—case within the half-and-half basis—wife's
appeal allowed, order varied to strike out £7 per week maintenance. November
15, 1977. PERRY v. PERRY.

99. —— —— charge

Order of registrar for immediate lump sum payment of £9,000—amended
by judge so that wife was to give husband a charge on house in the same sum
—not to be realised till youngest child attained 17—cases like *Calder* v. *Calder*
[1976] C.L.Y. 776 have no application to this case—above £9,000 a wrong
interference with registrar's assessment—wife's appeal allowed. November 8,
1977. CECIL-WRIGHT v. CECIL-WRIGHT.

100. —— —— domestic violence—attaching power of arrest to injunction

Husband restrained by injunction from molesting wife—husband alleged to
be frequently drunk and that when he had had too much drink he would, inter
alia, assault wife and threaten to assault her—husband punching wife in breach
of court order and arrested and tried and made subject to conditional discharge
order—wife leaving home—husband trying to commit suicide—wife's application that power of arrest be attached to the molestation injunction refused but
a committal warrant, not to be executed without leave of the court, issued—
wife's appeal supported by affidavit that on one night husband came to door
of house in unpleasant mood and began to bang on it shouting occasionally at
the wife—wife's appeal dismissed—no finding by judge that husband likely
to again cause actual bodily harm—condition for power of arrest thus not
satisfied—impossible to say that judge wrong in his assessment on the evidence
—Domestic Violence and Matrimonial Proceedings Act 1976, s. 2 (1). January
31, 1978. DANTER v. DANTER.

101. —— —— —— injunction

Parties married in 1963—three children aged 13, 10 and seven—wife presented
petition for divorce based on unreasonable behaviour in 1977—husband, suffering from disabilities in his vision and having an arthrodoesed hip, filed answer
denying unreasonable behaviour and alleging unreasonable behaviour on the
wife's part—wife's application for injunction against molestation of wife or
children and order requiring husband to vacate matrimonial home refused—
alleged violence after wife had refused husband sexual intercourse in 1975—
demands for sexual intercourse by husband said by wife to be excessive—no
violence alleged before 1976—judge heard evidence from both parties and
satisfied that husband presented no danger to wife—wife's appeal dismissed—
no question here that husband should leave matrimonial home and therefore
no reason to consider the Housing (Homeless Persons) Act 1977. February 9,
1978. ROE v. ROE.

102. —— —— exclusion of husband—accommodation problem

Parties married in 1969 and had one child, a boy, now aged seven years—
wife alleged violence against the husband, and left the matrimonial home to
live in accommodation for homeless families—divorce and custody hearings
were pending—husband lived in matrimonial home with his illegitimate daughter
aged 14 years—wife's application to exclude husband from matrimonial home
refused on ground that it would not be unreasonable to expect wife and child
to return to matrimonial home on terms that the husband was confined to certain parts of the house—wife's appeal dismissed—problem essentially one of
housing—judge's conclusion justified by evidence. February 14, 1978. COFIE v.
COFIE.

103. —— —— —— **evidence**

Husband ordered to be restrained from, inter alia, entering or attempting to enter the matrimonial home save for purposes of access—power of arrest attached to order—husband's appeal that wife was not telling the truth—appeal dismissed—impossible to say that judge wrong in accepting evidence of wife and not accepting evidence of husband, both parties being seen and heard by judge in the witness box. January 23, 1978. R.D. *v.* T.D.

104. —— —— —— **ex parte grant of injunction exceptional**

Wife alleged, inter alia, violence on the part of the husband and claimed that she and her daughter, 15, would suffer mental breakdown—husband, a diabetic, also accused of drunkenness—judge made ex parte order on wife's application, and at inter partes hearing, ordered husband, inter alia, to vacate the matrimonial home, judge having believed the wife—husband's appeal dismissed—observations that ex parte injunctions to expel a husband from the matrimonial home only to be made in the most exceptional and extreme circumstances. April 12, 1978. ASHTON *v.* ASHTON.

105. —— —— —— **injunction**

Parties married in 1976 and had one child now 11 months old—wife petitioned for judicial separation on the basis of unreasonable behaviour and applied, inter alia, for order against molestation and that husband vacate matrimonial home—judge adjourned her application for injunction first, because the tenancy of the matrimonial home was in the husband's name, and secondly, because of conflicting decisions of the Court of Appeal, including *Davis* v. *Johnson* [1977] C.L.Y. 1527 (which had since been taken on appeal to the House of Lords). The judge took the view that those decisions had cut down the pre-existing powers in cases concerning husband and wife—wife's appeal—the decisions had in no way cut down the pre-existing jurisdiction to make the kind of order asked for as between husband and wife—jurisdiction could be exercised without awaiting a formal claim by wife for a transfer of property order—new trial ordered—wife's appeal allowed. February 10, 1978. ENRIGHT *v.* ENRIGHT.

106. —— —— —— **no sufficient evidence of cruelty**

Husband restrained from, inter alia, entering matrimonial home—parties married in 1972—wife filed petition for divorce in 1973 alleging cruelty but petition not served on husband—parties thrice reconciled and moving to a council house on joint tenancy—judge excluded husband from matrimonial home in order to ensure safety of wife and children—allegations of cruelty against husband were the not uncommon ones of slapping wife in the face, etc. —husband's appeal allowed—no medical evidence of injury to wife nor anything of that nature to say that wife's safety threatened to extent of excluding husband from the home—no ground upon which judge's order could be upheld—new trial ordered. January 27, 1978. MILLER *v.* MILLER.

107. —— —— **order to vacate**

Order that husband must vacate matrimonial home—intolerable delay—husband's appeal dismissed. May 24, 1977. POSNER *v.* POSNER.

108. Order that husband vacate the matrimonial home, and be restrained from going within a 50 yard radius of it, save for purposes of agreed access—no substance in any of his grounds of appeal—husband's appeal dismissed. October 19, 1977. MITCHELL *v.* MITCHELL.

109. Injunction restraining husband from molesting wife, and excluding him from the matrimonial home, issued—part of order excluding husband from matrimonial home stayed—case remitted. November 11, 1977. LANGRIDGE *v.* LANGRIDGE.

110. —— —— —— contempt of court—committal—validity

Parties married in 1953 and divorced in 1971—wife living in council flat with daughter, husband in matrimonial home—eventually, wife awarded one-quarter share and husband three quarters, and husband ordered to vacate house so that it could be sold—order of possession made against husband—husband in breach of orders and committed for contempt for two months—Official Solicitor's appeal (on behalf of husband) allowed—committal invalid because (i) there was no service of penal notice on husband, (ii) ground not specified on which committal order made—practical and convenient way of dealing with recalcitrant husbands suggested. February 2, 1978. KAVANAGH *v.* KAVANAGH.

111. —— —— ownership

Matrimonial home let to wife—wife as tenant then offered the house by owner—husband claimed to be real tenant and that wife obtained house by the trick of inserting her own name on rent book instead of his—registrar and judge found against husband—impossible to say that judge came to wrong conclusion —application to adduce fresh evidence—no reason why evidence could not with due diligence have been adduced before judge—wrong to allow evidence to be adduced for purposes of appeal—husband's appeal dismissed—Married Women's Property Act 1882, referred to. January 11, 1978. TINSLEY *v.* TINSLEY.

112. —— —— respective shares

Husband and wife married in 1954 when husband was 28 and wife 22 years old—three children, two boys now grown up, and a girl now 12 years old —matrimonial home bought on mortgage through proceeds of compensation received by husband for an industrial injury—husband in secure employment as bus driver, earning £46 a week plus £5 a week disability pension—wife's total income £27 a week, including £6 a week periodical payments from husband—marriage had been dissolved in 1977—wife lived in matrimonial home with daughter, while husband lived in bed-sitting room—judge ordered, inter alia, that house be transferred to husband and wife jointly in equal shares, on basis that wife would have right to occupy it until daughter attained age of 17 years or ceased to be in full-time education—wife's appeal allowed— two-thirds share to wife and one-third to husband, to give wife better chance of obtaining accommodation when daughter attains 17 years. April 4, 1978. CAWKWELL *v.* CAWKWELL.

113. Income Tax—consent judgment

In wholly exceptional circumstances, the defendant appellant in person was allowed to make a return of income, and accepted a final figure of assessment of income tax, plus interest—by consent, the judgment of the county court amended—defendant to pay costs awarded in the county court—case had no precedent. December 21, 1977, and February 2, 1978. MANNING *v.* ELIZABETH.

114. Landlord and Tenant—business tenancy—notice to quit—validity

In 1969, the Borough of Woodstock leased business premises to S for seven years—in 1974 S assigned the lease to the defendant—in 1972 the Local Government Act 1972 had created two authorities in place of the single borough, the Woodstock Town Council and the West Oxfordshire District Council—in

September 1975 the West Oxfordshire District Council served a notice under
s. 25 of the Landlord and Tenant Act 1954, purporting to determine the defendant's tenancy in March 1976, when the seven-year term ran out, and opposed
the grant of a new tenancy to him—in December 1975, pursuant to a notice
under art. 39 of the Local Authorities (England) (Property, etc.) Order 1973
(1973 S.I. No. 1861), the premises in question were held to be "historic"
properties and vested in the Woodstock Town Council as from April 1, 1974—
in December 1975 the Woodstock Town Council served a fresh notice (in the
same terms as before, mutatis mutandis) on the defendant under s. 25 of the
1954 Act—the defendant applied for a new tenancy in time from the second
notice but out of time from the first notice—whether the West Oxfordshire
District Council were landlords at date of first notice—whether the two
notices creating an estoppel stopping the plaintiffs relying on the first notice—
plaintiffs granted possession—defendant's appeal dismissed. February 27, 1978.
WOODSTOCK TOWN COUNCIL v. SHU MAN TSE.

115. —— —— termination—notice

Notice served under s. 25 of the Landlord and Tenant Act 1954—addressed
to "the secretary, Bernabo and Co."—whether valid, as no particular person
performed the duties of secretary to the tenant company—to say notice was
invalid would be to introduce a mischievous technicality into the law of
landlord and tenant—finding of judge that a counter notice in a letter was
sent through ordinary post but not received by landlords—applicants' appeal
dismissed. December 20, 1977. BENABO (L. V.) (TRADING AS BENABO & CO.) v.
SECRETARY OF STATE FOR THE ENVIRONMENT.

116. —— caravan site

Injunction restraining respondents to originating summons from entering and
occupying premises owned by the council—jurisdiction—appeal by sixth and
seventh respondents—"gypsies" as defined in the Caravan Sites Act 1968—
whether injunction bad in law—uncontradicted evidence of appellants before
judge—justice required that there should be a new trial—jurisdiction of judge
—R.S.C., Ord. 113, and County Court Rules, Ord. 26—matter should remain
for the moment undecided by the Court of Appeal—appeal of sixth and
seventh respondents allowed. November 8, 1977. SWANSEA CITY COUNCIL v.
BERRY.

117. —— lease—construction of clause

Construction of clause in lease—whether clause restricted user of premises
"for the purposes of the Council for Professions Supplementary to Medicine"
—whether premises could only be occupied by defendants, and whether there
could be an increase in rent—Packaging Centre v. Poland Street Estate [1961]
C.L.Y. 4738 referred to—plaintiffs' appeal dismissed. Appeal from Goulding J.
LONDON SCOTTISH PROPERTIES v. COUNCIL OF PROFESSIONS SUPPLEMENTARY TO
MEDICINE.

118. —— —— whether holiday letting—breach of covenant of quiet enjoyment

Action by plaintiffs contending, inter alia, that the defendants, in breach
of covenant and in breach of statutory duty under the Rent Act 1965, wrongly
deprived the plaintiffs of premises alleged to be let to first plaintiff by the
defendants for three months at £20·00 per week rent—defence and counterclaim served by defendants alleged, inter alia, that the letting was a holiday
letting only and denying substantially all of the other allegations—the judge
believed the evidence of the plaintiffs and of the witnesses called on their
behalf, and disbelieved the evidence of the defendants and their witnesses

where it conflicted with the evidence of the plaintiffs—judgment for the plaintiffs—defendants' counterclaim dismissed—defendants' appeal dismissed—plaintiffs' solicitors' note of judge's judgment, not having been agreed, and counsel not having been present at delivery of judgment and judge now being dead, accepted by Court of Appeal—" hopeless " appeal with hopeless grounds of appeal. April 26, 1978. DOE AND JAJI v. AKANEZI.

119. —— licence to occupy premises—agreement

In 1965, the defendants, after a discussion with the plaintiff, moved out of their flat, the tenancy of which was protected, to live with and look after the plaintiff's aged mother in a house conveyed by deed of gift by the plaintiff's mother to the plaintiff—defendants alleged that they were given an assurance that if they so moved out, they would be allowed to stay in the house for the rest of their lives, paying no rent—plaintiff's mother died in 1977 at age 88—plaintiff served notice to quit on defendants immediately afterwards, claiming possession—defendants claimed to be entitled to a licence of the whole of the house for the rest of their lives—judgment for defendants for, inter alia, possession of two rooms in the house—defendants' appeal allowed and plaintiff's cross-appeal dismissed—agreement between plaintiff and defendants that on their doing that which they did, they would get certain benefits—defendants acquired an irrevocable licence to occupy whole house rent free for the rest of their lives after plaintiff's mother's death. May 19, 1978. PIQUET v. TYLER.

120. —— —— employee's occupation of premises ancillary to employment

Defendant occupying premises, a flat, freehold of which belonging to his employers, the plaintiffs—flat required to be occupied by employee under terms of contract of employment—defendant terminating contract of employment—licence to occupy flat, being ancillary to the employment, also terminated—plaintiffs' appeal allowed—plaintiffs given possession—claim for mesne profits to go to county court. January 31, 1978. GOUGH BROTHERS v. IVES.

121. —— —— possession—evidence of tenancy

Judgment for possession of home made against defendants—second defendant occupied bedroom and was allowed to use kitchen, bathroom, etc. while paying £4 a week—" rent book " found by judge to be no more than a receipt book—conversation between plaintiff, sole surviving trustee of property, and second defendant that a tenancy never offered, the most being said was that if house was not sold, it might be possible to let property to her—second defendant's appeal dismissed—no evidence of tenancy—evidence entirely against second defendant's claim that she had become a tenant. May 18, 1978. VERRAN v. ARMITAGE.

122. —— —— service occupancy—intention behind agreement

Plaintiffs, proprietors of restaurant immediately under the premises in question, brought an action for possession against the defendants alleging that they occupied these premises under a service occupancy—alleged written agreement and an oral agreement pointing to, inter alia, the first defendant's failure to start work as agreed—first defendant denied that he had ever worked for the plaintiffs or had received an offer of employment from them—judgment given for defendants—no intention to have a service occupancy—written agreement a sham—oral agreement never proved—plaintiffs' appeal dismissed. May 17, 1978. LEE v. LAM.

123. —— mesne profits—tenant ceased occupation before accrual

Order that defendant pay £203·46, the balance of a claim for mesne profits in respect of a dwelling-house, and for damage to its contents—defendant a married soldier in occupancy of married quarters—whether first defendant responsible for the second defendant's (wife's) continued occupation after expiry of notice addressed to her—whether damage and deficiencies, and electricity charges, had arisen before first defendant went out of occupation —judge erred in attributing any liability to first defendant in the circumstances revealed by the evidence—appeal of first defendant allowed. December 15, 1977. MINISTRY OF DEFENCE v. GRAHAM.

124. —— possession—alternative accommodation—suitability

Order for possession of flat—judge's conclusion of fact as to the suitability of alternative accommodation—whether present action was res judicata, having regard to earlier decision—alleged by defendant's husband that a note, approved by judge as " substantially correct," was " a sham," and that the judge's examination of the premises was inadequate to enable him to form a proper conclusion about whether the accommodation was " suitable "—appeal of defendant dismissed. November 11, 1977. MAYOR, ALDERMEN AND BURGESSES OF THE LONDON BOROUGH OF HOUNSLOW v. PERERA.

125. Defendant, aged in her sixties, had occupied for about 40 years now, a detached dwelling-house surrounded by about two-thirds of an acre of garden and thus had free access all round the house from front to rear—plaintiff landlords sought an order for possession, offering alternative accommodation to the defendant at the same house but with a less substantial part of the garden, the plaintiffs having obtained planning permission for its development—possession order refused (under s. 98 of the Rent Act 1977) on basis that alternative accommodation offered was unsuitable because the proposed development would mean the defendant had no access to the rear of the premises except by going through the house—plaintiffs' appeal allowed—matter sent back for rehearing— judge may have allowed certain considerations about which he may have been mistaken to affect the view he took. May 4, 1978. G. A. EDWARDS (FOUR OAKS) v. GIBSON.

126. —— business premises—tenant or licensee

Plaintiff claimed possession of shop and its premises, together with mesne profits—in particulars of claim, plaintiff referred to defendant as being " a licensee of the plaintiff under an agreement whereby the defendant managed or conducted the plaintiff's business at the said shop "—defence referred to an agreement in writing, undated—defence also contended that the relevant agreement was partly oral—reliance upon, inter alia, s. 24 of the Landlord and Tenant Act 1954—whether relationship between parties was that of licensor and licensee, or landlord and tenant—whether a letter was properly to be construed as a surrender of the lease by the defendant, and the plaintiff to be treated as having accepted it—plaintiff's appeal dismissed. December 2, 1977. ASLAM v. GUJARAM.

127. —— expedited action—harassment

Action started by plaintiff landlord to eject defendant tenant from premises —judge refused to grant defendant tenant various injunctions to restrain the plaintiff landlord from harassing him, and ordering her to give him access to the premises from which he was forced out and kept out by her—defendant appealed—plaintiff burnt defendant's bedding, etc., for allegedly good reasons —no order on appeal, on undertakings given by plaintiff who had taken the law into her own hands—possession action should be expedited. April 21, 1978. HADLEY v. HALSALL.

128. —— —— grounds of appeal—prejudice

Order for possession of flat under the Rent Act 1968, s. 10—30 grounds of appeal by defendant—including service of summons being contrary to County Court Rules—service not amounting to personal service under Ord. 8, r. 8 (1) (*a*)—particulars allegedly defective within Ord. 7, r. 3 (*b*)—nothing to justify allegations that judge was prejudiced against defendant—appeal wholly misconceived—appeal of defendant dismissed. November 14, 1977. SUTTON v. TINGEY.

129. —— —— misrepresentations—equity in defendant's favour

Order for possession of house against defendant, the mother of the second plaintiff and personal representative of the deceased's mother—plaintiffs were executors of the deceased—plaintiffs contended defendant was merely a licensee, and served notice purporting to determine the licence—whether conduct of parties had raised an equity in favour of the defendant—*Inwards* v. *Baker* [1965] C.L.Y. 1487 referred to—three main issues to be determined—*Crabb* v. *Arun District Council* [1975] C.L.Y. 1191 and *Dodsworth* v. *Dodsworth* [1974] C.L.Y. 3144 discussed—best and fairest way to secure protection for a person who had been misled by representations made and subsequently repudiated—defendant's appeal allowed. December 6, 1977. GRIFFITHS v. WILLIAMS.

130. —— —— notice to quit—invalid

" Fully furnished " letting—value of furniture £460—order for possession of two rooms, arrears of £98, and £10 costs, to be paid by defendant—stay of order pending appeal—note of reasons not before the Court of Appeal—plaintiff claimed overcrowding of two room under s. 17 of the Rent Act 1968—defendant's original tenancy varied by plaintiff—conceded that defendant occupied one room only—notice to quit possession of two rooms therefore invalid—a relevant point in the case, and if brought to light could have directed judge's decision in one way only—namely to dismiss possession action —discussion of motion to accept fresh evidence—appeal of defendant allowed. November 25, 1977. JANKOVITCH v. PETROVITCH.

131. —— —— sale of lease—conditions not complied with

Plaintiff landlords obtained possession against defendant tenant for non-payment of rent—plaintiffs then agreed to lease tenanted premises to defendant —possession order suspended—s. 100 of the Rent Act 1977—plaintiffs not complying with the contract conditions of sale—notice to complete invalid—condition 7 of The Law Society's General Conditions of Sale, 1973, required vendors to " carry out roof repairs . . . to the reasonable satisfaction of the purchaser's surveyor prior to completion. . ."—plaintiffs' solicitors wrote directly to defendant's surveyors to have site meeting with plaintiffs' builders—surveyors charged a fee—not acting as " purchaser's surveyors "—plaintiffs' appeal dismissed—defendant's cross-appeal to have possession order set aside allowed. February 3, 1978. EUROMAP DEVELOPMENTS v. POWELL.

132. —— —— tenant not in personal occupation—alternative accommodation available

Plaintiffs' action for possession of a flat leased to the first defendant—first defendant held over at the expiry of the lease and claimed the benefit of the

Rent Acts—plaintiffs' case was that first defendant never resided at the flat which had in fact been occupied by the second defendant, an employee of the first defendant, rent free, presumably as part of her remuneration—judge came to conclusion that first defendant, who claimed to reside in the flat, was not residing in the flat to a sufficient degree to entitle him to the protection of the Rent Acts—further, on the facts, it was reasonable to make an order for possession, there being reasonable alternative accommodation available for the first defendant—defendants' appeal dismissed—court could not possibly interfere with judge's findings and conclusion—judge amply justified in coming to the conclusion that it was reasonable on the facts to make an order for possession. May 19, 1978. LONDON CITY AND WESTCLIFF PROPERTIES v. GOODMAN AND NIXON.

133. —— —— unsubstantiated counterclaim for non-repair of defects

The plaintiff landlords, a housing association, obtained an order for possession of premises let to the defendant tenant, and an order in respect of arrears of rent and mesne profits—defendant's counterclaim for damages for non-repair of defects to premises dismissed—defendant's appeal dismissed —no evidence of any contractual undertaking to do the repairs—no miscarriage of justice. February 6, 1978. FAMILY HOUSING ASSOCIATION (MANCHESTER) v. UZONWANNE.

134. —— —— whether house " reasonably required " for occupation by landlord

The plaintiff, a married lady with three young children, became owner of house by gift from her father, and sought possession against the defendant, who had been living in the house for 35 years with his wife, on the ground that she " reasonably required " the house for occupation by herself and her family—judge found that she had not established that she reasonably required the house for her occupation—plaintiff's appeal dismissed—impossible to say that conclusion reached by judge, who saw and heard the witnesses, was such that no reasonable tribunal, on the basis of the evidence before it, could have arrived at that conclusion. February 13, 1978. BARTHELL v. HARRIS.

135. —— rent—arrears—business premises

Arrears of rent—premises let to defendant by oral agreement at £5 a week rent from January 1, 1975—rent increased by agreement to £15 a week from January 1, 1976—no rent paid in 1975—considerable arrears of rent built up in 1976 under new agreement—landlord's action for rent—defendant claiming that new rent was agreed on basis that landlord should do much-needed repairs —no counterclaim by defendant nor any evidence from witness box in support of his claim—no evidence that defendant suffering damage from failure to do the repairs—judge found for the defendant and held that no increased rent was recoverable by landlord as repairs were never done—judge came to wrong conclusion on the law—landlord's appeal allowed. January 18, 1978. VIC KETTLE PRINT v. PEREIRA.

136. —— —— review clause—relevant considerations in determining rent—rôle of arbitrator

Rent review clause in lease—judge had fixed on £515,000—assumptions to be made by arbitrator in determining " the full yearly market rent "—on failure to reach agreement, and possibility of going elsewhere, certain other relevant factors—but weight to be attached to these was a matter for the arbitrator—impossible to say the judgment was wrong or might have misled the arbitrator

—tenants' appeal dismissed. November 11, 1977. ENGLISH ELECTRIC Co. v.
F. R. EVANS (LEEDS).

137. —— surrender of tenancy—surrender by operation of law

Plaintiffs, personal representatives of Mrs. W, deceased, claimed possession
against defendant who was in occupation of premises in question—premises
originally let by Mrs. W to a Mrs. G-B and on Mrs. G-B's death to the
defendant's mother at rent of £14·70 per quarter—will made by Mrs. W
putting property on trust for sale but directing that so long as defendant's
mother wished to reside on premises and did so reside there the trustees " shall
postpone the sale thereof and shall permit her to reside there rent free "—
defendant's mother continued to live on premises but stopped paying rent—
whether tenancy surrendered by defendant's mother—question of fact—whether
an effective, genuine transaction—defendant's appeal dismissed—tenancy surrendered and therefore defendant not entitled to Rent Act protection. February
8, 1978. STRACHAN AND CURRIE v. IRELAND.

138. Libel and Slander—consolidation of actions

Order consolidating three actions in respect of libel, slander and defamatory
libel in article in the " Voice of Fareham "—Ord. 4, r. 10—no note of judgment
—whether error in principle or in law—appeal of plaintiff in first action and of
defendant in second and third actions allowed. October 18, 1977, CHAMBERLAIN
v. SMITH.

139. —— damages—compensatory damages—assessment

" Vilest libels and slanders " suffered by plaintiff, a married lady—defendant
admitted liability—12 libels to neighbours, five libels to public at large, and
four slanders, all agreed to be dealt with by single award for totality of
damage suffered—distress and depression suffered—master awarding £1,250 for
damage suffered—plaintiff's appeal allowed—award increased to £4,000 with no
certainty " that this may not be on the low side." February 8, 1978. PERRY v.
STEVENS.

140. —— justification—no interim injunction to restrain publication

Plaintiff sought an interim injunction in an action for libel to restrain the
first defendant from publishing what was in effect an assertion that the plaintiff
was not the chairman of the English National Party but that the first defendant
was the chairman—defence pleaded was justification—judge refused injunction
—plaintiff's application dismissed—ordinary rule that injunctions not available
to restrain publication of defamatory matter where plea of justification is
applicable. Appeal from Griffiths J. April 5, 1978. ATKINSON v. HANSFORD-
MILLER.

141. —— malice—particulars

Words complained of were contained in a letter—R.S.C., Ord. 82, r. 3 (3)—
order striking out particulars of malice given by plaintiff, on second defendant's application to limit particulars of malice—no reason to interfere with
judge's decision—application of plaintiff dismissed. Appeal from Chapman J.
October 24, 1977. SHEKERDEMIAN v. A. O. WAKEFIELD.

142. Markets and Fairs—Sunday trading—retail trading elsewhere than in shop

The first defendants organised Sunday markets in the plaintiffs' local
government district—long history of regular promotion of Sunday markets by

the first defendants on a variety of sites for quite long periods—considerable scale of operations on the markets—whether sites upon which market operations conducted " places where any retail trade or business is carried on "—whether requisite degree of permanence present—Shops Act 1950, ss. 47, 58—plaintiffs granted interlocutory injunctions to restrain defendants—first defendants' appeal dismissed. Appeal from Templeman J. March 14, 1978. NEWARK DISTRICT COUNCIL v. E. & A. MARKET PROMOTIONS.

143. Minors—access

One girl, one boy—access by father to children refused—whether in children's best interests that they should at present see their father again—dismissal of father's appeal will not preclude a further application at a later date—father's appeal dismissed. October 31, 1977. HEPBIR v. HEPBIR.

144. Girls aged 13 and 10—order no access to father—hopeless appeal—unknown for Court of Appeal to interfere with the decision (relating to access) of a judge who has seen and talked to the children—no use appealing to Court of Appeal against a refusal of access if efforts to induce children or parent to comply have failed—father's appeal dismissed. November 4, 1977. MONK v. MONK.

145. Boy aged 14, girl aged 12—order for access by father refused—hopeless appeal—*Monk* v. *Monk* (supra) referred to—Official Solicitor's report—father's appeal dismissed. Appeal from Lane J. November 4, 1977. WILLIAMS v. WILLIAMS.

146. Boy aged six—order for father to have access to child once a month for six months—judge properly weighed the considerations which arose, and arrived at a correct conclusion—mother's appeal dismissed. November 17, 1977. Y.A. v. A.J.A.

147. Boy aged 12—mother no longer granted access—welfare officer's report—quite impossible to say judge's decision was wrong—mother's appeal dismissed. November 18, 1977. MARSDEN v. BRADLEY.

148. Girls aged 11, nine and eight—discussions in open court—interim order for access made pending welfare officer's report—the balance of convenience—mother's appeal allowed. December 14, 1977. MABE v. MABE.

149. Girl aged seven—order that father should be allowed access in Italy—mother's appeal that if child were allowed to go to father in Italy, there was a grave danger that she would not be returned—father appealed on the ground that his application for the immediate handing over of the child was refused—child had been with her mother some five months—highly disruptive if she were now sent back to Italy and thereafter sent back to this country—urgency of this case—how the best solution can be at odds with a good solution—father's appeal dismissed, mother's appeal allowed. December 19, 1977. *Re* W. G. No. 665 OF 1977.

150. Two girls aged nine and eight—parents married in 1962 but finally separated in 1976, the mother leaving the matrimonial home and taking the girls with her—mother petitioned for divorce in 1977 on the ground of unreasonable behaviour by father, alleging, inter alia, physical violence—mother granted interim custody and an injunction against molestation on ex parte application

—father applied for supervised access—welfare report that mother should have care and control, but making no recommendation for access by father—father refused access—father's appeal dismissed—impossible to say that judge came to the wrong conclusion in all the circumstances. January 18, 1978. S.I. v. M.I.

151. —— —— arrangements

Girls aged nine and 13—father's application for joint custody dismissed— order that children be under supervision of probation officer, and direction that person having custody notify any change of address—order that father have access and staying access, by agreement of both parties, on advice of supervising officer, or until further order—judge did not come to wrong conclusion—words in access order "unless application made by mother" restored—father's appeal dismissed. Appeal from Rees J. November 21, 1977. HIGGINS v. HIGGINS.

152. —— —— interests of children

Girls aged seven and eight—order that father should not have access until further order—whether or not it was in best interests of children that access should not take place—conclusion of judge right—father's appeal dismissed. November 17, 1977. PATTERSON v. PATTERSON.

153. —— —— interim order—pending conclusion of divorce proceedings

Parties married in January 1972 when father was 35 and mother 25—both previously married, father having three children by his former marriage—two children, a boy and a girl, now six and four—in March 1977, father gave undertaking to court not to molest wife or to return to matrimonial home, and interim custody was given to mother, with reasonable access to father— mother's petition for divorce, based on unreasonable behaviour, filed in March 1977, but proceeding extremely slowly—difficulties with access, and divorce issues interfering with welfare of children—in February 1978, judge refused father all access pending conclusion of divorce proceedings—father's appeal dismissed—harsh conclusion by judge but impossible to say that it was wrong. April 4, 1978. PERRYMAN v. PERRYMAN.

154. —— —— no order—delay

Serious breach of injunction by husband—order for his committal stayed pending appeal—delay—no order for father to have access to three children actually made—husband should forthwith take out an application for an order for access. October 28, 1977. HATJOULLIS v. HATJOULLIS.

155. —— —— no supervision—disciplinary reasons

Parties married in January 1965 and separated in July 1976 when father left the matrimonial home—two children, a girl and a boy, 12 and nine years old respectively—regular access by father after he left—in May 1977 mother obtained decree nisi of divorce on ground of unreasonable conduct and applied for custody—during access in July 1977, father found it necessary to chastise the girl and unintentionally caused her injury—mother then refused father all access—judge granted father staying access—children being spoilt and needed correction—no supervision, father to "do no more than chastise the children reasonably in accordance with their deserts"—mother's appeal dismissed. March 1, 1978. BLACK v. BLACK.

156. —— —— terms of order

Parties, father now aged 52 and mother 47, married in 1953—daughter, subject matter of appeal, aged seven years—father left in 1974, and in 1975 went to work in Saudi Arabia—he returned in August 1976, started living in lodgings, but not employed in remunerative work—no contact between father and daughter from 1974 until August 1976, when three short periods of supervised access were arranged—parties unable to agree access—girl's attitude against access—father (whose future wholly unsettled) refused access—access stirring up bitterness between parties and forcing it on girl—father's appeal dismissed—as regards form of order, access not to be refused in perpetuity but only until further order. February 20, 1978. MURDOCH v. MURDOCH.

157. —— —— visiting or staying—agreement

Father and mother married in July 1974 when they were aged 19 and 17 respectively—boy, now aged three and a half years, born December 1974—before custody hearing parties had a discussion outside court as a result of which the mother offered the father access once a week on Saturday or Sunday and the father abandoned his claim for custody of the boy but still claimed staying access—custody given to mother, with visiting access once a fortnight on Saturday or Sunday to the father; staying access refused—father's appeal dismissed—although the mother may have offered the father access once a week, the father did not accept that agreement, submitting the matter to the judge—judge exercised discretion correctly. May 25, 1978. Re " 7709442 " (A MINOR).

158. —— adoption

Applicant's application for adoption refused—further material, now before Court of Appeal, ought to be considered by judge—appeal allowed to extent of remitting case for retrial. November 14, 1977. Re K. M. (AN INFANT).

159. Boy aged five—order for natural father to have custody—whether judge placed too much emphasis on the blood tie—Re C [1966] C.L.Y. 6213 referred to—whether judge properly exercised his discretion—no grounds for interfering with the decision the judge made—adopters' appeal dismissed. November 15, 1977. Re W.G. 77/00952.

160. Boy aged eight—application of would-be adopters refused—failure of the guardian ad litem to comply with one of the duties imposed by the County Court Rules was not a sine qua non of an adoption order—s. 3 of the Children Act 1975 discussed—appeal of would-be adopters allowed. November 24, 1977. Re AN APPLICATION ORDER.

161. Order for interim custody of child to be awarded to prospective adopters wrong in principle—interests of proposed adopters should be further investigated—appointment of Official Solicitor as guardian ad litem—case transferred to High Court and should be heard as soon as reasonably possible after inquiries, December 5, 1977. J. P. O. AND L. O. v. M. (AN INFANT).

162. —— —— dispensing with consent of parent

Father and mother of boy married in April 1973 and separated three months later when the mother was pregnant by father—mother left because of father's cruelty and in January 1974 a finding of constructive desertion was made against the father in the magistrates' court and, inter alia, custody of boy was given to the mother—marriage dissolved in August 1976 and in the same month mother married a Mr. G—boy lived with the mother and Mr. G, Mr. G having been " on the scene " from the time the boy was six months old—in July 1977 the mother and Mr. G had a child of their own—father of boy had had no contact with boy. at all throughout his life except for one very brief visit three weeks after the boy was born—mother and Mr. G applied for adoption order—father refused consent to the adoption —whether adoption order in best interests of boy—whether father unreasonably withholding consent—mother's and Mr. G's appeal allowed—Children Act 1975 (c. 72), s. 1 (3). May 15, 1978. *Re* " S " (A MINOR).

163. —— care and control

Five boys, aged 10, nine, eight, seven and six—custody awarded to mother— care and control of three youngest boys to mother—care and control of eldest boy to father—care and control of second eldest boy to foster-parents—father's appeal dismissed. Date for further appeal fixed. May 20, 1977. RAMSDEN *v.* SPENCE.

164. Girls aged eight, six and four—joint custody to father and mother—care and control to mother—since judge's order, father had had weekend access to children—judge's reasoning convincing—father's appeal dismissed. July 15, 1977. BAX *v.* DAVIES.

165. —— —— appeal to be expedited

Order under Domestic Violence and Matrimonial Proceedings Act 1976— father must vacate the matrimonial home within 14 days—care and control of children granted to him during this 14 days, thereafter to mother— mother to have custody—supervision of a welfare officer also ordered—father's application for stay of order pending his appeal—whether desirable to leave children with him during this period, or whether judge's order should take effect immediately—desirable for appeal to be heard as soon as possible—application of father granted. September 26, 1977. BOND *v.* BOND.

166. —— —— foster mother—child's physical and emotional needs

The parents, who were from Sierra Leone, had been divorced, with the father now being in Sierra Leone, and the mother, now aged 38, living in England—mother wanted to return to her native country with three of her children, including a girl, the subject of the appeal, now aged five and living with a foster mother—the girl had been put with the foster mother when she was a month old, shortly after the mother returned to England after her marriage had broken up—foster mother was the only mother of the child for all practical purposes throughout the five years, with some visits from the natural mother—child suffered from sickle cell anaemia and needed constant attention—judge gave leave to the natural mother to take child with her— foster mother's appeal allowed—emotionally dangerous for child to be separated from foster mother—also dangerous from the sickness point of view —not practicable for child to be cut off from foster mother. Appeal from Comyn J. March 21, 1978. *Re* A MINOR.

167. —— —— interim order

Girl aged seven living with father—order for mother to have interim care and control—another girl aged four already living with mother—order that children should not be removed from the jurisdiction till they attained 18 years of age—judge applied the correct principles—father's appeal dismissed. October 27, 1977. HINE *v.* HINE.

168. —— —— local authority—grandfather's appeal

Parents married in July 1962—two children, a boy and a girl, now aged 13 and six respectively—maternal grandfather, a highly successful business man, disapproved of his daughter's choice of husband—daughter's (mother's) history sad and difficult—conflict between parties—grandfather made children wards of court, making mother the defendant—in February 1977, father left mother and mother went back to live with her father—in December, grandfather's business premises were burnt down and mother was put on remand charged with arson—children lived with grandparents and were going to school—judge placed the children in the care of the local authority—grandfather's appeal dismissed. Appeal from Mrs. Jane J. February 16, 1978. *Re* A MINOR.

169. —— **custody**

Girl aged 10, boy aged five—order for children to remain in custody, care and control of mother—access to father—common ground that children should continue to live in the matrimonial home—stay of order refused—granted by Court of Appeal—whether judge was wrong in altering the status quo—whether order in best interests of children—mother should return to matrimonial home—support for judge's view in welfare report—hopeless appeal—father's appeal dismissed. Appeal from Purchas J. October 14, 1977. HUTTON v. HUTTON.

170. Boy aged seven—mother's application for custody dismissed—liberty to father to take him for a holiday in Australia—whether father paid undue attention to the status quo—nothing wrong in approach, nor conclusion, of judge—mother's appeal dismissed. October 18, 1977. DOLLAR v. HUMPHREY.

171. Boy aged six—custody awarded to mother—fashionable forensic sin of presumption that small children are better off with their mothers—status quo argument—best interests of child—appeal of father dismissed. November 2, 1977. BARKER v. BARKER.

172. Girl aged 13, boy aged seven—earlier order, that custody should be transferred from mother to father, varied—whether, in interests of boy, he should be sent back to his father on his own—mother's appeal allowed. November 9, 1977. FELL v. FELL.

173. Boys aged nine and 10, girl aged seven—custody, care and control awarded to mother, who was living with father of children—" status quo " argument—judge followed advice of welfare officer as to where best interests of children lay—statements taken from children—appeal of father dismissed. November 9, 1977. HUTCHINGS v. HUTCHINGS.

174. Decree nisi of divorce made absolute—parties continued to live in matrimonial home with children—girl aged 16, boy nearly 14—custody to wife—what is best for children—not right to accede to father's wish that he should have joint custody—access also discussed—husband's appeal dismissed. November 10, 1977. WHITTAKER v. WHITTAKER.

175. Girls aged three and five—residing with father—order for custody to father—whether judge gave sufficient weight to advantages to children of such tender age being brought up with their mother—new circumstances, on balance, did not alter merits of case—what is best for children—appeal of mother dismissed. November 15, 1977. LYON v. LYON.

176. Boy aged nine, girl aged seven—order for custody to be awarded to mother—subsequent order refusing to vary original order—application for

leave to stay execution of order of March 26, 1976—hopeless appeal of father in person—appeal dismissed. December 6, 1977. DITCHFIELD *v.* DITCHFIELD.

177. Girl aged three—order for custody to father—significance of welfare officer's report—mother's appeal dismissed, save for amending existing order to an interim order. December 7, 1977. DREWERY *v.* DREWERY.

178. Order for custody of two children to mother—appeal of father not properly prepared—father's application for adjournment—whether children should be brought up in Kenya—on merits, if they had been argued, father would have had no possible chance of success in his appeal—father's application for adjournment refused, and appeal dismissed. Appeal from Arnold J. December 7, 1977. OMERRI *v.* OMERRI.

179. Custody of eight-year-old girl to father, and four-year-old girl to mother—appeal of father, cross-appeal of mother—children must stay together—no correct solution to a problem such as this—question of access—appeal of father allowed, cross-appeal of mother dismissed. December 12, 1977. BELLAMY *v.* BELLAMY.

180. Boy aged five, girl aged three—custody awarded to father—whether welfare officer misled the court or had misapprehended the true situation—normally speaking, children of this age should be with their mother—meaning of words like "care and control" in orders of this kind—mother's appeal allowed. December 14, 1977. MASKELL *v.* MASKELL.

181. Boy aged 10, girl aged seven—order for custody to mother—father had looked after the boy alone for almost three years previously—whether status quo should be upset—judge correct—father's appeal dismissed. Appeal from Latey J. December 15, 1977. TAYLOR *v.* TAYLOR.

182. Girls aged 11 and 12—judge ordered father to have custody, and girls to spend part of their holidays in Germany with their mother—law quite plain—court required to make its decision on the best interests of the children and on nothing else—there was no advantage to these children in disturbing the judge's order—mother's appeal dismissed. December 20, 1977. STAINER *v.* STAINER.

183. Children, brought up in Ireland, ages ranging from 14 downwards, ordered to be sent back to Ireland to father without hearing mother's evidence—judge accepting everything said on behalf of mother by counsel—mother's application for stay of execution refused—future of children ought to be dealt with by Irish court. Appeal from Comyn J. January 13, 1978. *Re* S. (MINORS).

184. Two girls aged six and two—father given interim custody on understanding that children should be looked after by his parents and that the mother be given the right of access at all times, including staying access—mother's appeal that she be given interim custody with reasonable access to father—impossible to say that judge came to wrong conclusion—welfare report ought now to be obtained as a matter of urgency for matter to be finally settled as soon as possible. January 19, 1978. M.R. *v.* D.R.

185. Parents married in 1962 and had three children, all boys, S, P and M aged 15, 13 and seven years respectively—mother formed attachment to A and in September 1976 found herself pregnant by him—in November 1976 she left the matrimonial home taking M with her and went to live with A—father

applied for custody of M before the magistrates, and custody was given to him—mother's appeal to the Divisional Court allowed—father's appeal dismissed—mother offering a normal, warm home as opposed to father's one-parent family—inevitable that boy of seven will be given to custody of mother. Appeal from Latey and Mrs. Lane JJ. February 13, 1978. *Re* M (A MINOR).

186. Father and mother, both in their early thirties, married in 1971—one child, a boy, now five years old—in July 1976 father left, taking child with him to live in his mother's house—divorce proceedings pending—father wished boy to remain with his family (father's mother, aged 52 years, well qualified to look after boy), and mother wished child to be with her and her family—judge concluded that on the whole, the present situation should remain, *i.e.* that the child should be with father and father's mother for the time being at least, but that access should be extended if possible—mother's appeal dismissed. February 23, 1978. *Re* J. W. (A MINOR).

187. Father and mother, now aged 29 and 32 respectively, married in 1968—four children, three girls and a boy all aged under 10 years—they lived in a council house and both parties went out to work—in May 1977 mother started an association with D, and in August went to live with him—father arranged for a young lady housekeeper to look after himself and the children—mother given custody—father's appeal that judge wrong to risk making order while the relationship between mother and D was subject to considerable doubt—appeal dismissed—important question was who was to look after the children—father's arrangements more risky than mother's. February 24, 1978. PRATT *v.* PRATT.

188. Parties married in 1970—two children, a boy and a girl now five and four years old respectively—in January 1977, the mother left and went to live with another man—in February the father presented a petition for divorce, and in May the marriage was dissolved—father lived with the children in the matrimonial home whilst the mother lived with the co-respondent and his two children in a council house which was not too far away from the matrimonial home and into which they had recently moved—children suffered from a congenital heart disease—judge decided that children would be better off with father—mother's appeal allowed—children should be with mother but should spend as much time as could be arranged with the father, as that preserved for them the best of both worlds. February 27, 1978. HEDGES *v.* HEDGES.

189. Parties married in 1959 and separated in 1970—three children, the youngest being a girl now 14 years old—father went to live with another woman and in 1971 applied in the magistrates' court for custody—custody given to mother—mother filed petition for divorce in March 1977—from about October 1976 the girl expressed desire to move from mother to father, and the father applied for variation of the custody order in his favour in respect of the girl—judge saw and heard the parties and saw the girl and dismissed application of the father who appeared in person—father's appeal dismissed—court unable to interfere with conclusion reached by judge. March 2, 1978. HARRIS *v.* HARRIS.

190. Two children, a girl and a boy, nine and 12 years old respectively—the mother carried on an affair with the co-respondent, to whom she was now married, behind the father's back for two and a half years—matter came to light when mother found herself unexpectedly pregnant by the co-respondent and left to live with him—father employed a housekeeper and was now going

to marry her—custody given to father in a "not easy" case—mother's appeal dismissed. Appeal from Baker P. March 7, 1978. WEST *v*. WEST AND CARPENTER.

191. Father and mother married in February 1972 when they were 22 and 17 years old respectively—one child, a girl, now four and a half years old—"stormy" marriage with husband being violent and having had at least one adulterous affair—in summer 1976 the mother left finally and went to live in a caravan with the first of her lovers—both sets of grandparents looked after child who remained with father when marriage broke up but in February 1977 went to the mother—divorce proceedings started—father now living with mistress and intending to marry her—mother, having had three lovers since the break up of the marriage, each relationship being temporary, never neglected child—custody given to father—mother's appeal allowed—nothing said against mother's caring of the child—custody to mother with supervision order. March 10, 1978. LONG *v*. LONG.

192. Two children, boys, now 10 and seven—American father, serving in the U.S. army, stationed in Georgia and employed as an instructor—mother was English and had two children, girls, now aged 15 and 13, from a previous marriage—mother became restless living with her husband and returned to England and lived in a council house with the four children with a standard of living lower than she would have in America with the father—no divorce proceedings—both parents fond of the children and willing, able and eager to bring them up—magistrates gave custody to the mother, and the Divisional Court of the Family Division allowed the father's appeal—mother's appeal allowed; undertakings given that children will be enabled to maintain contact, as far as geography and practicalities permitted, with both parents. Appeal from Sir George Baker P. and Comyn J. March 10, 1978. *Re* MINORS.

193. Parents married in 1955; two children, a girl, now 17 years old and working, and a boy, subject matter of the appeal, now aged 13 years—mother obtained decree of divorce in 1970 on the ground of cruelty—custody of the boy, then five, was committed to her—both parties remarried, and mother had another child born in January 1973—father had two children, a girl aged three and a boy aged two, by his new wife, and had moved to Guernsey—father did not press his claim to access because mother said that child did not wish to see him—children complained of mother's new husband's behaviour alleging that he frequently beat them—in August 1975 girl alleged to have run away because of problems in the mother's household, and went to live with maternal grandmother—mother's new husband had left her recently—mother a paranoid schizophrenic—boy suffered from asthma—custody given to father—mother's appeal dismissed, there to be no access until the summer unless the official solicitor advises that there should be. March 13, 1978. WARWICK *v*. WARWICK.

194. Father, a Maltese Roman Catholic, and mother, English, married in Malta in 1967—two children, both girls, now aged nine and five respectively—in 1969 the family returned to England—in February 1974 the mother formed an attachment with another man, C, and started living with him, and in March 1974 father took both children to Malta—children put out to be fostered and lived in separate foster homes immediately opposite the father's home—older child deaf but able to lip read in Maltese—in 1975 the mother, who had seen the children only twice since her departure, and who now had a child by C, applied for custody—judge gave custody to mother—father's appeal allowed—disastrous to uproot children from Malta now. March 15, 1978. MUSCAT *v*. MUSCAT.

195. Parties married in 1967—two children, both girls, now five and four respectively—about March 1977, mother started an affair with a married man, H —in September her affair was discovered, and she left to live with H—judge gave custody to father on basis that mother's future was too uncertain, making it unwise to transfer children from the home they had always lived in and the environment they had always been used to—mother's appeal dismissed. Appeal from Latey J. March 20, 1978. *Re* A MINOR.

196. Parties married in February 1966—two children, a boy and a girl now five and four years old respectively—in December 1977 the mother left the matrimonial home, and in March 1978 she presented a petition for divorce based on behaviour—father gave up job after mother left to look after the children— both parties living on social security—judge satisfied that marriage had broken down, and gave custody to mother pending a welfare officer's report, and ordered that the father leave the matrimonial home—father's appeal dismissed —judgment below wholly satisfactory. March 22, 1978. BOWMAN *v.* BOWMAN.

197. Parties married in July 1967—three children, the eldest, subject matter of the appeal, a boy now nine years old—in October 1976, father left and took boy with him to live with father's mother and step-father—marriage dissolved in November 1977 on wife's petition on grounds of unreasonable behaviour —mother living with E and his daughter—father living with A in her house with her three children, boys aged two to seven—regular access by mother— welfare reports present—in February 1978, judge granted custody to father with reasonable access to mother, subject to a supervision order—mother's appeal dismissed. April 5, 1978. PALMER *v.* PALMER.

198. Parties married in October 1966—two children, a boy and a girl now 10 and three years old respectively—in May 1966, mother left taking girl with her, but not the boy because father would not agree to that, and went to live with M (a married man separated from his wife) whom she intended to marry —father's parents moved in to live in matrimonial home with father and the boy—judge found, inter alia, that the relationship between mother and M was stable, and that boy was mainly being looked after by father's mother, aged 69 and a diabetic—custody of both children given to mother—father's appeal as regards the boy only dismissed. Appeal from Latey J. April 6, 1977. BOSWELL *v.* BOSWELL.

199. —— —— **adjournment of hearing**

Parents married in 1971 and had one child, a boy now aged 16 months old —in January 1978, the mother left the matrimonial home leaving the child behind, and went to live with another man together with his 13-year-old son from his marriage—no complaint made against father or mother—no welfare report—judge ordered welfare report and adjourned custody, mother leaving child with father pending the welfare report and hearing thereafter—mother's appeal allowed—" toddler " not to be separated from mother for a moment longer. March 2, 1978. SOUTHGATE *v.* SOUTHGATE.

200. —— —— **admirable but absent father—difficulty over access**

Parents married in March 1973 when the father was aged 19 and the mother 16—one child, a girl, born in October 1973 and now aged four and a half—mother left in June 1977, taking child with her, and went to live at her parents' house—father was in the army but planned to get out as soon as he could in about 18 months' time—difficulties with access—judge impressed with father—custody given to father—mother's appeal allowed—however admirable the father may be, he could not perform the functions which a mother performs by nature in relation to a little girl—if difficulties with access arise, appropriate court orders are available. February 15, 1978. M. v. M.

201. —— —— appeal—stay of judge's order

Girl aged two—living with father—custody granted to mother—reasonable access to father—stay of order for 14 days pending an appeal, and thereafter until hearing of appeal—Court of Appeal emphasised the urgency of their request in relation to the granting of a stay in infant cases—a judge should only grant a stay long enough for the party to apply to the Court of Appeal, for that court to gain seisin of the matter, and to give directions that will ensure an early hearing to the appeal—judge was correct in the reasons he had given for his judgment—father's appeal dismissed. December 20, 1977. FALCONER v. FALCONER.

202. —— —— care and control

Children removed from custody, care and control of mother, and custody, care and control awarded to father—whether Court of Appeal should order a new trial—judge reached the right conclusion—mother's appeal dismissed. November 2, 1977. MAGSON v. MAGSON.

203. —— —— character of mother

Father and mother married in March 1973 when father was 18 years old and the mother 16—two children, a girl, now aged four, and a boy, now aged two—marriage broke down in March 1977—father lived with his half-sister, Mrs. C, and her three children from her first marriage, and his own two children—mother living with Mr. C—custody given to father on basis that mother abandoned her role of mother—mother's appeal allowed—mother now asserting her role—unfair criticism of mother to which no significance to be attached. February 21, 1978. P. v. P. AND C.

204. —— —— character of stepmother

Mother and father, both previously married, had married in April 1971 and had two children, a girl aged eight and a boy aged four—the mother had two boys aged 13 and 11, from her previous marriage—in November 1975, the mother left the matrimonial home and went to live with another man, H, after the father had formed an association with another woman, M, who had then moved into the matrimonial home against the mother's objections—the two elder children moved in to live with the mother and H—custody of the two younger children was given to the father, the judge forming a good opinion of M in particular—mother's appeal allowed—wrong to award a child to the care of the stepmother because stepmother was thought more of than the mother—impossible to separate all the children—custody given to the mother. February 6, 1978. CLARKE v. CLARKE.

205. —— —— consent order—breach

Parties married in March 1969—three children, two boys now aged 10 and five, and a girl now aged three—in July 1976, mother left home and went to live with a pen friend, C, and presented a petition for divorce alleging unreasonable behaviour, including violence—in April 1977, a consent order was made committing custody to father—in autumn, mother disobeyed order by removing children and taking them with her to live in a battered wives' home—order made that mother in contempt of court and warrant of arrest issued—mother's appeal allowed—order committing mother for contempt of court and writ of attachment discharged—proper course to make another application for a new order—Official Solicitor to represent children in future proceedings, which would be heard by a High Court judge of the Family Division. April 7, 1978. WILLIAMS v. WILLIAMS.

206. —— —— expedited appeal

Mother's application to set aside stay of execution and that appeal be expedited—father having interim custody of children—father willing for boy to be with mother if boy expressed that wish—boy's views—order that appeal be expedited—stay of execution to be maintained—welfare officer to submit supplementary report for Court of Appeal—boy to be told of order—mother's application dismissed. January 3, 1978. A.M.P. v. E.P.

207. —— —— fresh medical evidence

Girl aged 11, boy aged nine—mother's application to vary original order awarding custody to father—appeal quite unarguable—father's desire to move —children's interest—welfare officer's report—no justification for saying judge wrong in refusing to see children—perfectly proper exercise of discretion— as to fresh evidence of a consultant psychiatrist, utterly wrong for parties, between the trial and the appeal, to try to get doctors to see children—mother's appeal dismissed. November 10, 1977. MYERS v. SOUTHWELL.

208. —— —— improper influence of earlier case

Father, a bricklayer, aged 38, and mother, 37, married in October 1961— one child, a boy born in November 1971 and now six years old—close bond between mother and child—in 1974, father started an adulterous association with A and in February 1975, finally left and went to live with A who was aged 42 and had two children, a married daughter, and a boy of 14 living with her—marriage dissolved in 1975—in early 1976 mother met and later married a Mr. White, aged 37, who had three children from a previous marriage, a girl of 15, and two boys, 15 and 13—in March 1978 judge gave custody of boy, who had been in the custody of his mother for the whole of his life, to father—whether judge wrong—whether judge wrongly relied on recollection of a case White v. White, which had taken place before him in 1976, when he had formed a very adverse view of the character of Mr. White —mother's appeal allowed—supervision order made—no access for three months to allow situation to " cool down "—further proceedings to be heard by High Court judge of the Family Division. April 17, 1978. WHITE (FORMERLY COPSEY) v. COPSEY.

209. —— —— interests of children

Father, a Roman Catholic, and mother, an Anglican, married in 1964— two children, both girls, now aged 12 and 10 respectively—in December 1976, mother left, formed an association with the co-respondent who had also left his own spouse, and started living with him—father filed petition for divorce in March 1977 and decree nisi was pronounced in July 1977—custody given to father on basis that children had already stayed with him for over a year and would gain nothing by " another upheaval "—mother's appeal allowed —real question was whether an upheaval now was better in the long-term interests of children—father's arrangements inevitably unsatisfactory—mother offered a more ordinary background for children—custody given to mother, with supervision to provide source of information for future about children. February 24, 1978. B. v. B AND P.

210. —— —— interim order

Girl aged four—custody awarded to mother pending full custody proceedings—balance of convenience—judge made the right order—father's appeal dismissed. December 20, 1977. GOBLE v. GOBLE.

211. Parties married in 1970—one child, a girl, born in 1971—in January 1978, the wife left and applied, inter alia, for interim custody of the child, alleging violence and that she left the child behind because the husband threatened to kill her if she took the child with her—the husband denied almost everything alleged by the wife, and made counter-allegations of drunkenness—judge believed the wife, and disbelieved the husband, and made orders, inter alia, giving interim custody to the wife—husband's appeal dismissed. March 15, 1978. KEENAN v. KEENAN.

212. —— —— —— **inquiries by Official Solicitor**

Parties married in February 1972—four children, a girl now 11 years old, and three boys, now six, four and three—in January 1978 the mother left, taking the children with her, and went to live with her parents in a council flat, but was in the process of moving to her own council accommodation— in February, father filed petition for divorce, alleging adultery, and obtained an order ex parte committing the custody of the children to him until further notice—whether ex parte order justified—in March, judge made a holding order in that he appointed Official Solicitor to represent children, and gave custody to the mother pending inquiries by the Official Solicitor, without having read all the affidavits (taking the view that it could be premature to do so) and without hearing oral evidence—father's appeal dismissed. April 13, 1978. WELTERS v. WELTERS.

213. —— —— —— **unsatisfactory**

As an interim measure, the judge in a custody matter made an order to preserve the situation as it was, *i.e.* that the children should remain with the father—mother's appeal allowed—judge's decision involved putting off a decision as to what might be called the permanent future of the children for an indefinite and, perhaps, prolonged time—arrangements ought to have been made for a hearing of the matter which was longer than half a day— a decision for the foreseeable future was preferable—new trial ordered. February 7, 1978. DAVIS v. DAVIS.

214. —— —— **long-term decision**

Girl aged 10 was youngest of four daughters—subject of wardship proceedings—leave granted to father to take her to Australia—mother's application to have custody, care and control—child's feelings very important—judge had seen child—wrong at this point of time to take what is a long-term decision that child's future lies with mother—welfare officers' reports—mother's appeal dismissed, father undertaking to give access. November 7, 1977. MONAGHAN v. MONAGHAN.

215. —— —— **older child's wishes**

Parties married in July 1966—two children, both girls, now 10 and eight— the parties separated in 1974 and the father went to live with his present wife and her illegitimate daughter, now 11 years old—the marriage was dissolved, and custody of both girls given to mother by consent with access (kept infrequently) to father—elder daughter struck up a close friendship with her step-sister and expressed desire to be with father—custody of elder daughter given to father (with reasonable supervised access to mother) because damaging to her emotional development to ignore her desire—mother's appeal dismissed. February 23, 1978. STEPHENS v. STEPHENS.

216. Parties married in November 1964—two children, girls, now 13 and 10—in August 1976, mother left taking children with her to live with A and his parents, alleging that she had no family life and hoped to find it with A—on same day, elder girl went back with father and remained with him in the matrimonial home and refused to see mother in A's home, A's parents having left leaving their business to A and mother—access arrangements unsatisfactory—judge ordered custody of both girls to be with mother—father's appeal as regards the older girl allowed—settled determination, manifested over a period of 16 months, of elder girl not to go to mother in A's house, not to be ignored—best for present time that elder child remain with father—reasonable access to mother. April 5, 1978. BROWN v. BROWN.

217. —— —— out-of-date order

Parents married in 1964 and had two children, boys now aged nine and six years respectively—custody given to father—mother's appeal allowed—change of circumstances making custody order in favour of father out of date—case sent back for retrial. February 14, 1978. COAKLEY v. COAKLEY.

218. —— —— rehearing

Custody of boy aged nine given to father—boy cared for by paternal grandparents " virtually all his life " and happy and reasonably well looked after—father had had practically no contact with boy for long time and not exercising any custodial control—father failing to appear in or contact court—interim order giving care and control to grandparents jointly, with direction that matter be reheard with grandparents as parties, to consider whether boy should be reconstituted with his mother and two sisters—appeal of mother allowed. January 17, 1978. G. v. G.

219. —— —— stay pending appeal

Mother ordered to have custody of boys aged five and one—stay pending father's appeal—what is best for these two children at the moment—whether elder boy should be treated in isolation—judge reached the right answer—when a stay pending appeal should be granted—father's appeal dismissed. December 8, 1977. S. v. S.

220. —— —— unsuitable mother

Parties married in 1970 when father was 42 and mother 25 years old—two children, a boy and a girl now six and 10 respectively—the girl was born to the mother before the marriage and adopted by parties, husband not being her natural father—marriage dissolved in 1977—thereafter, father lived in matrimonial home in reasonably affluent circumstances, while mother lived in a caravan—custody given to father—mother not sufficiently stable person and not sufficiently competent mother to be entrusted with custody—mother's appeal dismissed. February 16, 1978. HENDERSON v. HENDERSON.

221. —— —— welfare officer's report not followed

Parents married in May 1971 and had one child, a boy, now aged five—mother thought that marriage was unhappy and went to live with or near the co-respondent in the divorce proceedings—magistrates gave custody to the father, the mother having just left and her future being in a highly uncertain state—in time the mother's position became settled, and she proposed getting married to the co-respondent when free to do so—father, finding it difficult to cope with the child by himself, went to live with his parents—grandmother the only female influence in the child's life on a day-to-day basis, but father proposing to marry a young lady—custody given to mother—welfare officer's view not followed—father's appeal dismissed—judge came to the right conclusion in all the circumstances of the case. February 15, 1978. J. *v.* J.

222. —— interim custody—evidence

Boy aged six—parents married in 1968, mother having been previously married—father employed as paint sprayer and mother having various part-time jobs—mother had been seriously ill and had been admitted to a psychiatric hospital—father alleging that mother had a drink problem—mother alleging physical violence by father—child, aged three, admitted to hospital following the onset of uncontrollable screaming—request by a community physician in December 1976 that child be taken into care and child so received on a voluntary basis—child discharged from care in January 1977 on father's request and taken to his grandparents' home—interim custody granted to mother—welfare report—no indication of alleged drink problem of mother—boy missing his mother—psychiatrist's report that mother " a capable able woman who presented no psychiatric problems "—mother not unfit to have care of the boy—father's appeal dismissed—judge considered whole of evidence before him and it was impossible to fault the conclusion he arrived at. January 24, 1978. D.B. *v.* C.B.

223. —— removal from jurisdiction

Boy aged six—leave to mother to remove child out of the jurisdiction not before December 31, 1977, on mother's undertaking—best interests of child—father's appeal dismissed. October 31, 1977. BLEVINS *v.* DIDSBURY.

224. Elder of two girls, aged 10, living with father—application of mother for custody, care and control, and leave to take child to Northern Ireland refused—status quo not right test—best interests of child—mother's appeal allowed. November 1, 1977. SEXTON *v.* BUNTING.

225. —— wardship

Order that boy remain a ward of court and transferred to care and control of father with leave to take to Northern Ireland—stay pending appeal refused—s. 2 resolution passed by Council—applicant's appeal dismissed. November 1, 1977. *Re* W. G. 129/1977.

226. Girl aged three—wardship proceedings—normally High Court will not assume jurisdiction—no order as to access by father—warnings to mother—cost of transcript of proceedings—appeal of father allowed to extent of amending the order. November 3, 1977. *Re* W. G. 76/2886.

227. Mortgages—security—business transfer agents

Plaintiff finance company made loan to defendant for purchase of business premises—security was a legal charge in favour of business transfer agents, transferred to plaintiffs—form of wording stating the agreed charges—turnover and profit of business were much less than defendant had understood they were going to be—failure to pay instalments, and abandonment of premises—power of sale had arisen and become exercisable—judgment for the plaintiffs, amounting to the balance of the shortfall on realising the security of £3,576—counterclaim of misrepresentation stood over pending appeal against judgment—no answer to plaintiff's claim on short-fall on re-sale—whether judgment should be stayed pending the hearing of the counterclaim—whether business transfer agents were acting as agents of the plaintiffs, and whether any misrepresentations they made were within the scope of their agency—defendant's legal advice before commencing action—defendant's appeal and counterclaim dismissed. December 16, 1977. INDEPENDENT FINANCE CO. *v.* MEYER.

228. Negligence—accident—obstruction—breach of statutory duty

Lady aged 58, postal sorting worker—fell over box—Offices, Shops and Railway Premises Act 1963 (c. 41), s. 16—judgment for plaintiff, but finding of 50 per cent. contributory negligence—evidence of plaintiff as to place where she had fallen rejected—significant or reasonably foreseeable risk—" obstruction "—*Jenkins* v. *Allied Ironfounders* [1970] C.L.Y. 1076 referred to—whether judge wrong in law upon basis of a factual case not pleaded—whether on facts accepted by judge there was no " obstruction " and therefore no breach by defendants of s. 16—defendants' appeal dismissed. November 4, 1977. HUGHES *v.* BRITISH AIRWAYS.

229. —— causation—evidence

Plaintiff employed by defendants at factory as guillotine operator cutting steel sheets into pieces of given dimensions—back injury suffered by plaintiff in course of work—injury alleged to be caused by defendants' negligence—action taking many years to come on for hearing—judgment for plaintiff for £13,947 damages including £675 interest—defendants' appeal denying liability and disputing granting of interest—appeal as to the interest adjourned to await decision of House of Lords—plaintiff's injury alleged to be caused when he was feeding a heavy sheet of metal, weighing 5 cwt., size 6 ft. $\times$ 4 ft. $\times$ $\frac{1}{2}$ in., into guillotine machine the lower blades of which had been incorrectly adjusted thereby requiring extra effort on the plaintiff's part—plaintiff's back then gave with severe pain—defendants admitting liability if lower blades wrongly adjusted as alleged but alleging inherent improbability of plaintiff's version—judge accepted plaintiff's evidence—defendants' " formidable submissions " rejected without full reasons—defendants' appeal dismissed—no basis for suggesting that there had been any miscarriage of justice, that the judge had failed in any way in his duty in the terms in which he delivered his judgment, or that the Court of Appeal could either enter judgment for the defendants or order a new trial. Appeal from Michael Davies J. February 8, 1978. McMANUS *v.* PAINTER BROTHERS.

230. —— damages—third party—contractual indemnity

Plasterer working on platform of Jensen tower which collapsed—agreed plaintiff entitled to damages of £2,500 and costs—whether defendants entitled to a contractual indemnity from third party—construction of written agreement—whether indemnity applicable—appeal of third party dismissed. October 11, 1977. MISKELLY *v.* PINEWOOD STUDIOS.

231. —— duty of care—discharged by employers—drill operator

Plaintiff, emloyed by the defendants as a machine setter for over seven years, injured his back when drilling jig used for his job slipped out and fell from his hands when he was putting the jig away and claimed damages in negligence—the defendants denied negligence, saying that the accident was wholly the fault of the plaintiff—plaintiff was unable to show any clear reason why object slipped out of his hands—judge found for the defendants that there was no failure on their part to take reasonable care for the safety of their employees—plaintiff's appeal dismissed—res ipsa loquitur not applicable

—judge reached right conclusion on evidence. March 3, 1978. GIBBONS *v.* WOODS OF COLCHESTER.

232. —— liability—contributory negligence

First defendants provided eight buses to take the second defendants' men from a factory compound to a car park—plaintiff, in his mid-forties, employed by the second defendants, run over by bus driven by a servant of the first defendants when leaving work at the end of the day—chaotic and disorderly conditions of boarding buses some weeks before accident—plaintiff's action in negligence against both defendants—judge held that plaintiff himself was 80 per cent. to blame for the accident and his injuries, first defendants were not negligent at all, and second defendants 20 per cent. responsible, and awarded the plaintiff £15,000 against the second defendants—plaintiff's appeal dismissed—second defendants' cross-appeal allowed—judgment for both defendants against the plaintiff. Appeal from Watkins J. April 13, 1978. JAMIESON *v.* GEORGE WIMPEY & CO.

233. —— —— whether action should be stayed

Order pursuant to s. 41 of the Supreme Court of Judicature (Consolidation) Act 1925, staying action against second, third and fourth defendants—order reversed—*Shackleton* v. *Swift* [1913] 2 K.B. 304 referred to—plaintiffs had a contract with the first defendants in respect of an exhibition of Sèvres vases at Grosvenor House Antiques Fair—cl. 27 of the " Conditions of the Fair " protected the first defendants from the consequences of negligence—*Gore* v. *Van der Lann* [1967] C.L.Y. 399 discussed—one vase broken while being examined by the advisory committee, the appellants—whether or not an arguable issue—undertaking given by appellants—whether there was an implied promise by the plaintiffs not to sue—appeal of second, third and fourth defendants dismissed. Appeal from Gibson J. December 16, 1977. ANTIQUE PORCELAIN CO. *v.* TRUST HOUSES FORTE.

234. —— master and servant—duty of care—no breach

Plaintiff, aged 50, skilled or semi-skilled in his trade, was employed by the defendants to drill holes in flywheels—the flywheels had to be lifted two feet onto a table, by lifting contrivance provided, as part of the operation—a flywheel fell on plaintiff's big toe and he claimed damages—judge found that plaintiff did not screw in certain bolts, which had now become worn, as tightly as he ought to have done—whether defendants in breach of s. 26 of the Factories Act 1961—plaintiff's appeal dismissed—definition of " lifting tackle " in s. 26 (3) expressly limited to objects specified—no breach of duty under statute or common law by the defendants. Appeal from Robert Goff J. January 16, 1978. ROBBINS *v.* PEAK ENGINEERING CO.

235. —— —— liability—milk van dangerous in wet weather

Employer's liability to employees—plaintiff employed as milk roundsman by defendants—plaintiff slipping and falling and injuring himself on wet deck made of steel plates in use since 1960 while loading his milk van at defendants' premises—plaintiff alleging that deck surface should have been of different material rendering the wet deck less hazardous—evidence of two previous accidents from wet deck—expert evidence—whether defendants liable in not taking reasonable care in all the circumstances of the case—defendants held not liable—plaintiff's appeal dismissed. Appeal from Michael Davies J. January 13, 1978. LEWIS *v.* THE WALSALL AND DISTRICT CO-OPERATIVE SOCIETY.

236. —— road accident

Plaintiffs had compromised the action by payment of £20,000 to deceased's personal representatives—whether finding of judge that defendant was 20 per cent. to blame, and that £4,000 plus interest should be awarded to the plaintiffs, was wrong on the evidence—defendant pulled out to the right to pass a parked car having shown right indicator light, then making a left turn at about five m.p.h.—plaintiffs' lorry became out of control—numerous decisions of the Court of Appeal have held that one is not entitled to assume that there will be no negligence on the part of other drivers—first plaintiff was solely to blame—defendant's appeal allowed. Appeal from Kilner Brown J. November 10, 1977. MAGEE AND NORWICH ENTERPRISES v. SMITH.

237. —— vicarious liability

Plaintiff claimed damages for a hernia sustained while changing tyres on a heavy vehicle—alleged unsafe system of work—whether injury sustained in course of employment—impossible to overturn judge's finding of fact—whether it is proper conduct for a county court judge after giving an oral judgment, to indicate some correction or amplification of that judgment—plaintiff's appeal dismissed. November 9, 1977. THOMPSON v. CLARK EQUIPMENT.

238. Nuisance—injunction

Plaintiff's claim as owner/occupier of flat—defendants engaged in building work—interlocutory judgment for plaintiff, and injunction restraining nuisance granted—principles in *American Cyanamid Co.* v. *Ethicon* [1975] C.L.Y. 2640 —plaintiff's appeal on ground that injunction too narrow—whether Court of Appeal entitled to review position on evidence and consider new evidence— judge did not exercise his discretion wrongly nor too narrowly in favour of plaintiff—appeal of defendants dismissed. October 24, 1977. LAWSON v. HARRY NEAL.

239. —— land used for car parking—whether " uncompensatable damage " caused—injunction

Plaintiff was granted an injunction to restrain defendants from using, or causing or permitting to be used, their land, situated just outside plaintiff's bungalow and land, as a car parking area—whether a nuisance was being created and whether it posed a threat to health—" uncompensatable damage "—test of *American Cyanamid* v. *Ethicon* [1975] C.L.Y. 2640 applied—wrong to interfere with judge's discretion by discharging the injunction—defendants' appeal dismissed. Appeal from Nield J. July 28, 1977. DUNDAS v. OLIVER.

240. Partnership—accounts—retiring partner's share—appeal

Plaintiffs and the defendant, who were in partnership together, agreed upon the defendant's retirement from the partnership in September 1968, that the defendant would be credited with the full share of the general assets and goodwill of the partnership, but also that he would for his own purposes take over a certain branch practice and should be debited with the value of that branch of the practice—disputes arose because parties unable to agree figures, and therefore action started and the taking of necessary accounts referred to Official Referee—Official Referee ordered defendant to pay £17,857 to plaintiffs —defendant appealed, contending, inter alia, that plaintiffs wilfully and knowingly included in their accounts items which were not due—appeal dismissed —claim (even if well founded) did not come within R.S.C., Ord. 58, r. 5, which dealt with cases where the issue between the parties was one of fraud. March 8, 1978. DIAS v. LINDSEY.

241. —— —— whether prepared negligently

In July 1972, the defendant, an accountant, went into partnership with H and S, and in September 1973 the partnership was dissolved—the plaintiffs, accountants and auditors of H when he was in business alone and of the partnership when it was in existence, prepared accounts for the partnership until the time when it was dissolved and sent a bill for their fees for £480·60—the defendant paid £220·50 of that amount and the plaintiffs sued him for the balance—the defendant alleged that there had been delay and errors in the preparation and presentation of the accounts, as a result of which he had suffered damage—the judge held that there were implied duties on the plaintiffs to prepare the accounts with reasonable expedition and with reasonable care and skill as professional men, but found that the defendant had suffered no damage—defendant's appeal allowed only to the extent of reducing the amount claimed by the plaintiffs by £81·00, that being the amount of fees incurred by H personally and not for the partnership. February 2, 1978. R. NEEDS AND CO. v. SHAW.

242. —— partnership by estoppel—conduct of apparent partner—textile retailers

In 1972, the first defendant H began to trade as a retailer in textiles which the plaintiffs were to supply, and registered the name of his business with himself as sole proprietor—he kept the business stock in his house and in his van, and carried on business from certain market stalls—the second defendant, Mrs. H, whom H married in 1969, helped in the business but was not in fact or law a partner within s. 1 of the Partnership Act 1890—in 1975 Mr. and Mrs. H were divorced—the plaintiffs obtained judgment against H for the price of goods sold and delivered on credit between September 1974 and February 1976—same judgment given against Mrs. H as an apparent partner in the business—whether Mrs. H by her conduct held herself out, or knowingly permitted herself to be held out, as a partner in the business, and whether the plaintiffs gave credit on the faith of any such representation by conduct —Mrs. H's appeal allowed—Partnership Act 1890, s. 14 (1). Appeal from Melford Stevenson J. February 24, 1978. LATIN AMERICAN ARTS & CRAFTS v. HICKLING.

243. Patents and Designs—application—opposition—priority

Conflict between two separate applications for a convention patent in respect of similar inventions, one made by a Japanese company, F Ltd., and the other by an American company, O-I Inc., each opposing the grant to the other— invention claimed by each party related to gas discharge display devices— F Ltd.'s convention document was dated June 12, 1968 but O-I Inc. claimed an earlier priority date, November 24, 1967, under their convention document —Patents Appeal Tribunal held that O-I Inc. was entitled in respect of claim 9 in their English Complete Specification No. 1254114 to their claimed priority date—F Ltd.'s appeal dismissed—documents correctly construed. Appeal from Whitfield J. January 27, 1978. Re APPLICATIONS BY FUJITSU AND OWENS-ILLINOIS INC.

244. —— infringement—costs of action

Patent on a workbench known as "Workmate"—leave to the Black and Decker Manufacturing Company of the United States to be added as a plaintiff—alleged infringement of the " Multiplex " order made in first action to restrain any infringement of the patent—inquiry as to damages ordered, and defendant to pay those—delivery up of infringing workbenches ordered —court certified upon the trial of the action and the counterclaim, and the counterclaim being dismissed, that the defendant should pay the costs of the action and the counterclaim, including the costs of the present order—order in second action to same effect—appeal of defendants dismissed. Appeal from Graham J. December 13, 1977. HICKMAN v. ANDREWS.

245. —— —— injunction—balance of convenience

Infringement of patent—plaintiff company applying to restrain various alleged infringements of their patent by parties including the first defendant—defendant making a diving suit conceived by plaintiff to constitute an infringement of patent—judge refusing interlocutory relief on basis that no arguable case for infringement on true construction of claim—arguable that upon a consideration of text of claim, without deciding how it should be construed, that defendants' device constitutes an infringement of the claim—also arguable that first defendant had taken " pith and marrow " of patented invention—plaintiff's appeal allowed. Appeal from Whitford J. January 26, 1978. POSEIDON INDUSTRI A.B. v. R. J. WILLIAMS (DIVING PRODUCTS).

246. Practice—adjournment—discretion of trial judge

Refusal of judge to grant an adjournment—plaintiff's claim was for £386·90, in relation to the purchase of a colour television—defendants were willing to consent to plaintiff's application for an adjournment—whether the defendant appellants were precluded from putting their case properly—discretion of judge—*Dick* v. *Piller* [1943] K.B. 497, referred to—no miscarriage of justice —new trial would be a waste of time—defendants' appeal dismissed. October 7, 1977. SMITH v. BAKER AND COCKLING.

247. —— appeal—adjournment

Defendant ordered by county court judge in January 1976 to give up possession of flat to the plaintiff—order to be stayed provided defendant paid £700 by monthly instalments of £100 starting February 1976—defendant's notice of appeal, dated March 3, 1976, that order be set aside and judgment be entered in her favour—nothing in grounds of appeal to show any basis for appeal to be entertained by Court of Appeal—long series of adjournments of the appeal—defendant to appear in person—numerous communications that defendant too ill to attend court—duty of court to say that plaintiff, respondent to appeal, entitled to have appeal determined—appeal determined in plaintiff's favour in absence of defendant (appellant)—no arguable ground in notice of appeal. January 26, 1978. A. PEACHEY AND CO. v. SHASHA.

248. —— —— application for leave—extension of time

Defendant in person applied for an extension of time for leave to appeal against two judgments, contending, inter alia, that he was busy with other litigation—no merit in the appeals—applications dismissed—every single point raised by defendant " is the driest technical point." Appeal from Ackner J. and from Browne-Wilkinson J. April 18, 1978. BOWMAKER (COMMERCIAL) v. DE VRIES.

249. —— —— dismissal—non-appearance

Long series of instances of failure by defendant appellant to comply with the provisions of the rules, and of failure to appear when matters were listed for hearing—verbal message that appellant was suffering from influenza and that a medical certificate would follow—no medical certificate received—appeal dismissed. February 14, 1978. WILLIAMS *v.* HAYWOOD.

250. —— —— fresh evidence

Plaintiff, a builder, claimed against defendant the sum of £557 as the balance of the cost of work done and materials supplied—defendant claimed this was excessive, and counterclaimed, alleging that plaintiff failed to do work properly—judgment for plaintiff—no note of judgment, but defendant's (in person) version heard—defendant's appeal raised fresh evidence—grounds for admitting fresh evidence was satisfied—nothing to suggest that judge wrong—defendant's appeal dismissed. January 17, 1978. GOSTELOW *v.* BLINSTON.

251. —— —— insufficient documents—appellant not present

Plaintiff appellant failed to supply court with judge's notes of the evidence nor the reasons for the judgment—appellant notified of appeal but failed to appear—only course open to court was to dismiss the appeal—appeal dismissed with costs. January 27, 1978. OLISO-EMOSINGOIT *v.* PANCHAL.

252. —— —— out of time

Judge refused application for leave to appeal out of time against the order of a registrar—appeal allowed. December 5, 1977. DAVIES *v.* DAVIES.

253. —— —— striking out—notification—illness of appellants

Defendants' appeal that judge had wrongly refused adjournment of hearing on basis that defendants were too ill to attend court—judgment appealed against later set aside on basis that there had been no proper service of claim—one of the appellants too ill to attend—appeal put into list and effort made to contact respondent but without success—order that appeal be struck out. January 27, 1978. BELLVILLE *v.* LYON.

254. —— —— vexatious litigant

No appearance by appellant and not represented—order declaring appellant a vexatious litigant—nothing in notice of appeal to suggest any valid ground of appeal from the order against which it would seem the appellant was seeking to appeal—Court of Appeal had no alternative but to dismiss the appeal. December 6, 1977. *Re* JACK AUBURN (ORSE. HERBERT MORTON).

255. —— application or appeal—type of order

Wife's application for appealing against a registrar's order refusing to award her periodical payments—application refused—parties agreed to treat application to Court of Appeal as the appeal itself—judge refused to exercise his discretion to extend time by five days—whether difference existed between an order dismissing an application and an order making no order on an application—leave to appeal granted—wife's appeal allowed. November 28, 1977. CROXTON *v.* CROXTON.

256. —— compromise of action—enforcement of terms—jurisdiction of court

An action started by the plaintiffs in October 1965 was compromised and embodied as a rule of court in a court order of May 1970—by the compromise, the defendant agreed to repair the damage caused to the ceilings of the plaintiffs' library, any dispute arising to be referred to arbitration—compromise order included clause " liberty to restore "—dispute arose as to the repairs to be done by the defendants, and the matter was referred to arbitration—defendant failed to carry out repairs under the terms of the arbitral award, and eventually the plaintiffs themselves carried out the repairs and applied for a direction under R.S.C., Ord. 45, r. 8 that the defendant pay the costs of the repairs to the plaintiffs—whether court had jurisdiction to make such orders—R.S.C., Ord. 59, r. 10. Appeal from Jupp J. March 10, 1978. THE ROYAL SOCIETY OF LITERATURE v. LOWENTHAL.

257. —— contempt—breach of injunction—burden of proof—passing off

Plaintiff company alleged that the defendant and others conspired in various ways to damage the business of the plaintiffs by, amongst other ways, passing off whisky not of the plaintiffs' manufacture, as being their whisky by the use of bottles and labels bearing a close resemblance to the type of bottles and labels used by the plaintiffs in their business—on June 22, 1977, the plaintiffs obtained an injunction restraining the defendant, until judgment in the action or further order, from, inter alia, " conspiring with or enabling or procuring others to pass off any beverage or liquid, not being the Scotch whisky of the plaintiffs, as and for the plaintiffs' Scotch whisky "—plaintiffs' action commenced by writ on June 23, 1977—on June 21, 1977, the defendant was arrested and charged with conspiracy to defraud the plaintiff company—in August 1977, documents found by the police in a brief-case belonging to the defendant included a letter (dated July 25, 1977, and relating to the printing of certain labels), together with a sample of a label bearing a marked similarity to the labels used by the plaintiffs upon their whiskies—whether defendant in breach of injunction—defendant's appeal allowed—insufficient evidence to commit defendant—committal proceedings of quasi-criminal character with onus on plaintiffs of a higher quality than the ordinary civil standard of balance of probabilities, i.e. evidence must convince beyond reasonable doubt—presumption of continuance of a course of action was not evidence of a kind which would satisfy the burden of proof required here. Appeal from Walton J. February 6, 1978. JOHN WALKER & SONS v. BROADWAY.

258. —— —— committal

Plaintiffs obtained judgment for £3,000 against the defendant—their summons to obtain a committal order against him for contempt of court by both an assault and the failure to obey the order to appear for examination as a debtor before the district registrar, was refused—s. 13 (3) of the Administration of Justice Act 1960—whether the judge was wrong in refusing to decide an issue of fact—unsworn statements made to judge—plaintiffs' appeal allowed, with costs. Appeal from Wien J. December 21, 1977. ROBERT WEBSTER (FOLKESTONE) v. GRIFFIN.

259. —— —— —— breach of undertaking

Plaintiffs started proceedings against the defendants, seeking interlocutory relief to restrain them from interfering with a contract made between the first plaintiff and a Dutch company and relating to alleged sole selling rights of certain machines made by the Dutch company—before adjudication, the parties arrived at an arrangement under which the defendants undertook, inter alia, that until judgment or further order, they would not deal with the Dutch company in any way inconsistent with the contract stated—defendants exhibited machinery in question at a trade exhibition and the plaintiffs applied to commit for contempt of court by breach of the undertaking—judge refused the application because he was not satisfied on the facts that the defendants were dealing with the Dutch company in a manner inconsistent with the contract stated, the judge having found the first defendant an honest witness—plaintiffs' appeal dismissed—*obiter,* a distinction was to be drawn between a man doing an act which was in fact a breach, intending to do that act but not appreciating that it was a breach, and a man doing an act which upon its face did not appear to be a breach at all but which for some reason unknown to him involved a breach; no contempt in latter case. Appeal from Blackett-Ord V.-C. March 3, 1978. COLTOFF v. HOLLIER.

260. —— costs—court's discretion

Defendant appealing against order that he should pay costs of action—plaintiff's application to strike out notice of appeal—such an appeal cannot be brought without leave—s. 31 (1) (*h*) of the Judicature Act 1925—discretionary nature of court's jurisdiction in ordering costs—not a competent appeal—plaintiff's application allowed. Appeal from Dunn J. November 7, 1977. SWEET v. HULL.

261. —— —— discretion—supplier of hire-purchase vehicle

The defendant, a taxi driver, wished to acquire a Chrysler motorcar, and went to the fourth party who were in a position to supply it—the fourth party being unable to make the necessary financial arrangements, sold the car to the third party and the third party sold the car to the plaintiffs, a finance company, who then entered into a hire-purchase agreement with the defendant —the car gave trouble, and the defendant ceased to pay the hire-purchase instalments—the plaintiffs sued for those instalments—the defendant counterclaimed on the ground that the car was not of merchantable quality—the plaintiffs delivered a reply to the counterclaim relying on, inter alia, an exclusion clause, and joined the third party—the third party joined the fourth party—at the trial, the third and the fourth parties were represented by one counsel instructed by one firm of solicitors, counsel stating that there was no conflict of interest between them—judgment given for the plaintiffs on the claim and on the counterclaim with costs—third party claim dismissed with costs against the plaintiffs—no order made on the fourth party proceedings—whether fourth party entitled to costs—appeal by fourth party allowed—judge failed to exercise discretion. February 7, 1978. RATHMINES MIDLAND FINANCE CO. v. ROBSON.

262. —— —— scale

County court claim arising out of road accident—whether *Hobbs* v. *Marlowe* [1976] C.L.Y. 2127, distinguishable—no question of any claim in respect of loss of a no-claims bonus, actual or potential—whether judge wrongly exercised his discretion under R.S.C., Ord. 17 r. 1 in awarding the plaintiff costs under Scale 1—plaintiff's appeal dismissed. November 18, 1977. ATLEE v. BUTCHER.

263. —— —— security—counterclaim going beyond original action

Plaintiffs' application for security of costs on a counterclaim—plaintiffs claimed £2,475 as fees and expenses of architects' services—whether the counterclaim went so far beyond original claim as to constitute a fresh action—whether the plaintiffs' case was overloaded as a result of the counterclaim—no reason for disagreeing with the judge's exercise of his discretion—plaintiffs' appeal dismissed. June 22, 1977. FRY AND HUGHES (A FIRM) v. CHESGLEN.

264. —— discovery of documents

Plaintiff employed defendant surveyors in connection with a dispute between himself and certain builders—builders sued plaintiff for cost of certain conversion work carried out to plaintiff's premises—action by builders transferred to Official Referee—plaintiff alleging defects in work by builders—schedule of alleged defects to be prepared by plaintiff—defendant surveyors instructed to supply schedule but failing to do so—builders obtaining judgment for full amount of claim against plaintiff—defendants submitting to judgment in favour of plaintiff—case to Official Referee for assessment of damages—plaintiff ordered to serve original Official Referee's schedule with observations thereon —whether defendants should be required to complete schedule—plaintiff's appeal dismissed as misconceived—plaintiff to prepare schedule—proper course to seek discovery by discovery of documents against defendants for such preparation. February 10, 1978. FUTERMAN v. CULLEN PERKINS AND CALDER (A FIRM).

265. —— dismissal of action—failure to supply documents

Action dismissed for failure by plaintiffs to comply with orders to supply further and better list of documents, and further and better particulars of statement of claim—plaintiffs' claim was for damages for professional negligence in relation to the sale of leasehold interests—*Birkett* v. *James* [1977] C.L.Y. 2410 not applicable—plaintiffs' appeal dismissed. Appeal from Wien J. November 1, 1977. MULTISPAN (CARDIFF) v. W. CLEDWYN MORGAN & SON.

266. —— execution—garnishee order—construction of businessmen's agreement

Appeal of first judgment creditor to set aside a garnishee order absolute in favour of second judgment creditor—whether first creditor had an equitable right, arising from a document signed by both creditors, to share in certain proceeds with the second creditor—an advantage taken by a businessman does not necessarily mean there has been a breach of any arrangement between the parties—application of first creditor for the court to give directions on the ultimate destination of available funds—there was nothing in the case to displace the ordinary rules applicable to garnishee proceedings—appeal of first judgment creditor dismissed. July 21, 1977. H. & E. SHARPE (PLUMBERS) v. BRIGGS.

267. ——fieri facias—claim to goods by third party

Claimants' application for leave to appeal against an order dismissing their claim to goods of which the sheriff was in possession under a writ of fieri facias —unfortunate circumstances attaching to the claimants' solicitor's non-appearance before the master—solicitor willing to give an indemnity to the judgment creditors for costs thrown away to date—proper case for claim to be investigated by the master—leave to appeal granted, and claimants' appeal allowed. December 21, 1977. LEADA v. WESTVIEW PLANT HIRE.

268. —— garnishee order

Plaintiff awarded judgment in default of appearance—order that garnishee should pay £1,200 to judgment creditor—purchase of flat in Spain—whether judgment well-founded and judgment creditor entitled to execution—master was right to make the order absolute in the way he did—appeal of garnishee dismissed. July 21, 1977. CRAWLEY v. INDESA S.A.

269. —— indemnity—issue of fact—transfer to master

Hiring agreement—construction—failure to pay rental under lease—plaintiff finance company claimed loss was recoverable, and was recoverable from defendants under an indemnity—written agreement—*Sterling Industrial Facilities* v. *Lydiate Textiles* [1962] C.L.Y. 1398, referred to—R.S.C., Ord. 36, r. 9 —action not particularly suited to such procedures—plaintiffs' appeal dismissed. November 23, 1977. ACKERS JARRETT v. BAGLEY.

270. —— injunction—form

Injunction restraining the respondent " by himself, his agents or servants or invitees or licensees from . . . "—respondent's uncle and aunt in matrimonial home of parties as invitees or licensees if not as agents—order varied to include clearly uncle and aunt—order varied to make plain judge's original intention— wife's appeal allowed. January 12, 20, 1978. McGARRITY v. McGARRITY.

271. —— —— impossibility of performance

Mandatory injunction that second defendants should take all necessary steps to transport forthwith a trailer from Italy to Ghammas, and proceed with due expedition—whether injunction was clear—principle of lex non cognit ad impossibilia—whether possible to persuade Italian customs authorities to release the trailer—whether the court's order could be enforced without also enforcing the payment of a bribe—second defendants were subcontracting without the plaintiffs' knowledge—appeal of second defendants allowed. Appeal from Milmo J. July 29, 1977. MESPED v. ANCHOR GLOBAL TRANSPORT.

272. —— —— judge's discretion

The plaintiff claimed an injunction to restrain the second defendants from transferring the proceeds of sale to the first defendants—no order on plaintiff's motion—no order on undertaking of second defendants in lieu, and substantially in terms of an injunction which had issued ex parte—whether money in account of solicitors was held by them as the builders' agents, and whether they, as the builders' solicitors, owed no legal duty to the plaintiff—whether there existed a serious issue to be tried—fresh evidence was not before judge—Court of Appeal must not interfere with exercise of judge's discretion—*American Cyanamid* v. *Ethicon* [1975] C.L.Y. 2640—appeals of first and second defendants dismissed. Appeal from Griffiths J. November 18, 1977. WOLF v. HOSIER AND DICKINSON.

273. —— —— " sordid and suspicious " arrangement

History of the matter being very unusual, and certain aspects being " sordid and suspicious," the judge took a medial line and set aside an injunction obtained ex parte by the plaintiff, substituting one in more limited terms— matter relating to a bill of sale assigning chattels which formed the stock in trade of the defendant's shop to the plaintiff ostensibly in discharge of an obligation to pay him £5,000, said to have been lent by him to the defendant— defendant's version that a collusive arrangement made between them to pretend that those assets belonged to the plaintiff and not the defendant to keep them out of reach of the defendant's wife (with whom he was having matrimonial problems) should she succeed in obtaining a decree of divorce—plaintiff's appeal dismissed. Appeal from Bristow J. March 3, 1978. FOY (TRADING AS STAFF SPECIALISTS) v. LOWTHER-HARRIS.

274. —— —— to restrain grant of probate—misconceived

Plaintiff brought an action for defamation, conspiracy to defraud and conspiracy to pervert the course of justice against, inter alia, M—M died after the writ was served—M's executors sought probate of M's will and the plaintiff sought an injunction to restrain grant of probate—plaintiff not beneficially interested in the estate of M, nor a creditor unless and until he could establish his claim—plaintiff's action for an injunction thus self defeating because it disabled him to pursue his claim against M's estate—plaintiff's action for injunction struck out—plaintiff's application for leave to appeal dismissed—injunction relief sought by plaintiff misconceived. Appeal from Oliver J. May 22, 1978. PALLANT v. ROYSTON.

275. —— judge's order

Applications of first and second defendants for leave to appeal against order varying earlier order—claim in relation to agency agreement—whether judge made order that in effect shut out counterclaim—plausible and not frivolous —judge fully justified in order made—applications of first and second defendants dismissed. November 16, 1977. CONTSHIP S.A. v. C. T. O. INTERNATIONAL.

276. —— judgment—consent judgment—no real consent

An order introduced by the words " by consent " was made whereby the matrimonial home was settled upon trust for sale—two doctor's evidence of husband's very bad health was heard by judge who indicated to counsel in his private room that the case must be settled—counsel unable to get instructions from wife to settle—judge then said he would consent on behalf of the wife and made the order " by consent "— wife's appeal allowed—injustice done— new trial ordered. March 8, 1978. WOODHEAD v. WOODHEAD.

277. —— —— execution—stay of execution

The plaintiffs, building contractors, entered into two contracts with the defendants relating to building work to be done on two different sites respectively—the first contract was performed and completed but a dispute arose over the pricing of the work and the plaintiff issued a writ for work done and material supplied claiming £18,840—in Ord. 14 proceedings, the defendants agreed to submit to judgment by consent in the sum of £12,000 and were given leave to defend, and an order was made staying execution upon the judgment pending the trial of the defence and a counterclaim by the defendants in relation to the second contract which had been partly performed by the plaintiffs —on appeal the judge removed the stay of execution on the judgment and ordered that the costs of this application and of proceedings in the court below be taxed and paid by the defendants to the plaintiffs—the defendants appealed—no connection between the first and the second contract to make it just and equitable for the plaintiffs to be kept out of the money for which they had obtained judgment pending determination of the dispute arising out of the second contract—not appropriate for judge to vary order as to costs made below in Ord. 14 proceedings before registrar—appeal allowed to that extent only. Appeal from Forbes J. February 22, 1978. A B CONTRACTORS v. FLAHERTY BROTHERS.

278. —— —— in default of appearance

Both parties failed to appear or to be represented—judgment for the plaintiff in the sum of £153—judgment for defendant on counterclaim of £83—order that defendant should pay the balance of £70 to the plaintiff—the only possible course for the Court of Appeal to take in such a case, is to dismiss the appeal —defendant's appeal dismissed. December 1, 1977. GHOLAM REZA MASSOMIAM TABRIZI v. RYZEWSKA.

279. —— —— —— setting aside—terms

In May 1977, the plaintiff obtained judgment in default of appearance on a promissory note made by the defendant in June 1973 in the plaintiff's favour for £11,000—on the defendant's application, the judgment was set aside and leave to defend was given on terms that the £11,000 claimed in the action be paid into court, plus a sum in respect of costs up to the time of the order— defence affidavits making various allegations, including fraud, considered by judge to be without merit—defendant's appeal dismissed with costs. Appeal from Watkins J. March 15, 1978. KOHLI v. HAYER.

280. —— —— leave to set aside—delay

The second defendant applied to set aside in part a judgment given against him in March 1971—arguable point raised by defendant—judge refused application because deliberate and unreasonable delay in making appliction by second defendant—second defendant's appeal dismissed. Appeal from Griffiths J. February 2, 1978. REYNOLDS PORTER & CO. (A FIRM) v. PERESTRELLO & COMPANHIA.

281. —— jurisdiction—appeal from order of judge in chambers—procedure under R.S.C., Ord. 113.

Refusal of judge in chambers to grant an order under R.S.C., Ord. 113— plaintiffs applied for leave to appeal—Court of Appeal's jurisdiction to hear an appeal from an order of a judge in chambers—whatever may have been the position in affidavits put in by the four remaining defendants in the possession action, these matters would only have provided an answer to Ord. 113 procedure if they had been followed up by further evidence—the deponents of these affidavits, and others, had since agreed not to oppose the order—plaintiffs granted leave to appeal, and their appeal allowed. Appeal from Cusack J. December 19, 1977. HILTWEND v. COOK.

282. —— leave to appeal—application out of time

Application for leave to appeal out of time—reasons given in notice of appeal would preclude Court of Appeal from interfering with judge's decision —application dismissed. November 7, 1977. SHIRLEY-SMITH v. TINGEY.

283. Practice—new trial

Plaintiff obtained judgment in the county court to recover the sum of £752 on his claim, against which was to be set off the sum of £75 which the defendant was held entitled to recover on his counterclaim—defendant's appeal against the judgment on the plaintiff's claim allowed—certain aspects of the case would appear were not fully before, or may not have been fully or accurately understood by, the judge in giving his judgment—new trial ordered. May 18, 1978. LOVING v. NIELD.

284. —— Order 14—bills of exchange—alleged fraud

Summary judgment for plaintiffs in the sum of £39,000 due upon two cheques plus interest—leave to defend refused to defendants—stay on £12,295·77 pending a hopeless appeal—liberty to apply—purchaser of tokens at defendants' casino—Barclays Bank v. Aschaffenburger Zellstoffwerke A.G. [1967] C.L.Y. 209 referred to—alleged fraudulent misrepresentation by defendants against purchaser of tokens—cheques crossed "not negotiable," unendorsed—s. 81, Bills of Exchange Act 1882—whether defendants entitled to set up against plaintiff a subsequent equity which arose between defendants and the purchaser of tokens—defendants' appeal dismissed. Appeal from

Donaldson J. November 24, 1978. BANK OF CREDIT AND COMMERCE INTER-
NATIONAL (OVERSEAS) v. LADUP.

285. —— —— conditional leave to defend

Order directing that judgment against second defendant be set aside on terms
that the second defendant should pay £610 into court—plaintiffs' claim was
under a guarantee, and judgment had been awarded in default of defence—
whether exercise of the judge's discretion had been plainly wrong—second
defendant's appeal dismissed. Appeal from Melford Stevenson J. ARROWLINE
COACHES v. DOLPHIN ARTISTS.

286. —— —— indemnity

Summary judgment for plaintiffs of £85,821·64, and an inquiry ordered as
to amount of interest—claim arose under an indemnity—first defendant was
refused leave to defend—whether upon true construction of a letter, an obligation to give counter indemnity was an immediate obligation or a future
obligation—appeal of first defendant dismissed. Appeal from Whitford J.
July 27, 1977. UNITED DOMINIONS TRUST v. HAMMERSON.

287. —— —— independent agreement

Judgment for the plaintiffs of £25,000—defendant's appeal against judgment,
and for unconditional leave to defend—defendant's undertaking to procure
payment of £25,000 in an agreement made to compromise the action—whether
agreements were interdependent—no reason for interfering with judge's decision—Appeal of defendant dismissed. Appeal from Donaldson J. November
30, 1977. PALADEN ESTABLISHMENT S.A. v. SCRUTON.

288. —— —— leave to defend—defence of quantum meruit

Defendant given leave to defend, conditional upon paying £750 into court
and £50 costs, notwithstanding earlier order for judgment in default of defence
—plaintiffs, firm of architects, suing for professional fees of £2,295—writ issued
August 26, 1975—defendant claimed that plaintiffs should only be paid on a
quantum meruit basis, and the £500 paid by defendant on judgment was a
proper sum—list of documents served with further and better particulars still
defective—wholly wrong to interfere with discretion of Official Referee—
defendant's appeal dismissed. November 11, 1977. JAMES BATH ASSOCIATES
v. GRANT.

289. —— —— —— unconditional

Plaintiffs' claims were for arrears of instalments and damages in relation to
hire purchase of organs—unconditional leave to defend refused to defendants
on plaintiffs' application for summary judgment—defendants lodged interlocutory appeals—whether contracts were void for mutual mistake—whether
estoppel arose by reason of signatures—discretion of the court—case came
within R.S.C., Ord. 14, r. 3 (1)—very sound reasons why court should not
refuse leave to defend nor enter summary judgment—injustice in other cases
—appeals of defendants allowed. Appeals from Caulfield J. November 11, 1977.
PROGRESSIVE SUPPLY CO. v. ROSE; PROGRESSIVE SUPPLY CO. v. CHASE.

290. —— —— no defence to action under Statute of Limitations

Money lent by plaintiff company to defendant, a company director—plaintiffs
obtained summary judgment for £8,854·30, including interest—defendant given
leave to defend as to £1,586·80—whether defendant should be granted leave to
defend as to entire sum—whether claim was based on alleged fraud within

124

R.S.C., Ord. 14, r. 1 (2) (*b*)—whether a triable issue existed within Ord. 14, r. 3 —s. 19 (1) (*b*) of the Limitation Act 1939 applied, since the defendant, as a director, was under a continuous duty towards the plaintiffs, as beneficiaries, with regard to trust property—*Soar* v. *Ashwell* [1893] 2 Q.B. 390 applied— defendant's appeal dismissed. October 27, 1977. GORDON BARRIER *v.* BARRIER.

291. —— Order 14 proceedings—" shadowy " defence

Plaintiff claimed £5,000 on a guarantee given by defendant—defendant signed guarantee on perfectly clear arrangement—no defence disclosed by documents—defendant given leave to defend in Ord. 14 proceedings, conditional upon payment into court of £5,000 on basis that defence at best " shadowy "— defendant's appeal dismissed. Appeal from Drake J. April 7, 1978, THORP *v.* O'GORMAN.

292. —— originating summons—affidavit evidence

On an originating summons, the plaintiffs claimed money arising from legal charges—the mere presence of a disputed issue of fact does not mean that a matter cannot be satisfactorily dealt with by affidavit evidence—whether the judge was justified in the exercise of his discretion, under R.S.C., Ord. 28, r. 4, in holding that the plaintiffs' claim was made out—not suggested that *Heald* v. *O'Connor* [1971] C.L.Y. 1259, was wrong—whether entire transaction was vitiated by the Companies Act 1948, s. 54—appeal of first and second defendants dismissed, appeal of third defendant allowed. Appeal from Megarry V.-C. December 4, 1977. FOUR MILLBANK NOMINEES *v.* FREDERICK.

293. —— pleadings—amendment

In May 1974, plaintiffs brought an action against the defendants for damages of $1½ million for breach of contract, alleging that in July 1973 the defendants, owners of a ship called " Pacific Satellite," agreed to charter that ship to the plaintiffs—in October 1973, the plaintiffs threatened to arrest that ship and an agreement was made whereby the defendants produced a bank guarantee for $1½ million and the parties agreed to submit the matter to English arbitration or to the jurisdiction of the English courts—defendants denied the agreement to charter the ship, and counterclaimed for damages in the form of interest and other expenses relating to the guarantee—pleadings deemed closed in November 1974—in May 1977 plaintiffs gave notice of intention to proceed, and applied for leave to amend their points of claim—judge refused application, because amendments raised entirely new case which, if raised originally, might not have led the defendants to agree to submit to English jurisdiction at all—plaintiffs' application for leave to appeal dismissed. Appeal from Kerr J. February 10, 1978. KOCH MARINE INC. *v.* PACIFIC TANKERS INC.

294. —— —— —— at late stage of trial

Plaintiff brought an action against her employers, the defendants, for injuries suffered from an accident during the course of her work—accident happened when a drum became jammed while she was working on line 123—the defendants denied liability and alleged that the accident happened because, when the plaintiff ought never to have done so, she was endeavouring to remove a jammed drum from line 124—in the course of the defendants' final speech the judge indicated that whilst he was proposing to accept the defendants' evidence rather than the plaintiff's evidence, nonetheless, had the plaintiff originally pleaded the defendants' case, she might have been entitled to recover on that basis—amendment of that stage to plaintiff's statement of claim disallowed by judge—plaintiff's appeal dismissed—discretion of judge correctly exercised as a matter of principle and otherwise. Appeal from Forbes J. January 27, 1978. SMITH v. F. FRANCIS AND SONS.

295. —— —— —— at trial

Plaintiffs, stockbrokers, brought a claim against the defendant, who had been employed by them as an assistant analyst, alleging breach of his contract of employment in that he failed to abide by certain rules in the conduct of business by him—the defendant raised a defence and counterclaim based on various matters—at the trial, which started in the afternoon, the plaintiffs' counsel occupied the first day with the background of the case rather than the merits—on the second day at the conclusion of the opening, counsel for the defendant objected that matters not raised by the plaintiffs' pleadings had been canvassed in the opening as part of the plaintiffs' case—judge disapproved of counsel taking objection on second day as opposed to the first day, and gave leave to the plaintiffs to amend pleadings, adjourned the hearing and reserved the costs of the adjournment to the trial judge, and put defendant on terms—defendant's appeal allowed—order of judge set aside, leave to amend refused, costs occasioned by amendment and incidental thereto, and of the adjournment, to the defendant's costs in any event, and conditions on defendant removed. Appeal from Kenneth Jones J. March 22, 1978. FOSTER v. JONES.

296. —— —— further and better particulars

In June 1977, the plaintiffs, a shipping company, served a writ on the defendants claiming a large sum of money for having stored, out of the usual line of business, horse tic beans for the defendants—in July they obtained judgment in default of defence—judgment set aside and payments into court made by defendants—defence served by defendants—plaintiffs asked for further and better particulars, and when there were not forthcoming, obtained a peremptory order, and defendants were at risk of being barred altogether from defending unless request complied with by October 20—particulars served by defendants in the form of an amended defence and counterclaim, and plaintiffs applied that the defendants be debarred from defending and that judgment be entered forthwith for the plaintiffs on basis that their request for particulars had not been complied with in substance—judgment entered for the plaintiffs —defendants' appeal allowed—no material default in particulars supplied. Appeal from Melford Stevenson J. April 4, 1978. LOWESTOFT STORAGE & SHIPPING CO. v. R. D. HARBOTTLE (MERCANTILE).

297. —— —— no cause of action disclosed

Plaintiff brought an action for the return of two caskets containing the remains of two cats buried in 1956 and 1960 or for damages to detinue and/or conversion—action struck out on basis that statement of claim disclosed no reasonable cause of action and that claim was vexatious—plaintiff's application for leave to appeal dismissed. Appeal from Talbot J. April 13, 1978. ASHER v. STYAN.

298. —— —— —— copyright in drawings

Plaintiffs sought a copyright action against the defendants, who denied the plaintiffs' title to the copyright—the statement of claim alleged, inter alia, that the plaintiffs were the authors of, and owners of the copyright in a number of drawings—whether, on facts pleaded statement of claim disclosed any ownership of the copyright in law or in equity—whether plaintiffs ought to have leave to amend—judge struck out the statement of claim in relation to two sets of drawings, and gave leave to amend a claim for copyright in another set

of drawings—plaintiffs' appeal dismissed—defendants' cross-appeal allowed
—statement of claims, as particularised, disclosed no cause of action in respect
of any of the drawings—s. 53 (1) (c) of the Law of Property Act 1925 relevant
in respect of claim which was the subject matter of the cross-appeal—amendments refused because no cure thereby to the defect in title. Appeal from
Whitford J. March 1, 1978. ROBAN JIG & TOOL CO. (U.K.) v. TAYLOR (T/A
HILLCREST DESIGN TOOL & MOULD).

299. —— R.S.C., Ord. 13, r. 3—judgment set aside upon condition—effect of condition

Plaintiff was awarded judgment in default of appearance by the defendant,
with the defendant to make good the plaintiff's claim to property—set aside
upon condition—defendant's appeal that condition should be removed—
whether the defendant under indebtedness to plaintiff in respect of property—
possible risk that the condition was one which must of necessity preclude
defendant from putting forward an answer—risk justifiable—defendant's appeal
dismissed. November 15, 1977. SANDHU v. CHOPRA.

300. —— service of writ—substituted service—personal injuries

Plaintiffs suffered personal injuries in a road accident involving a motor
cycle ridden by man who gave his name as " David Vedel," and brought an
action against him—Vedel alleged to have stolen motor cycle, had disappeared
and could not be traced—substituted service orders made to enable Vedel to
be served at the address of the Motor Bureau—Bureau entered conditional
appearance for Vedel—conditional appearance later set aside, but Bureau
entered as co-defendant—orders for substituted service set aside on appeal
by Bureau—whether right—plaintiffs' appeal dismissed—Untraced Drivers
Agreement applicable—R.S.C., Ord. 65, r. 4. Appeal from Jupp J. May 16,
1978. CLARKE v. VEDEL AND THE MOTOR INSURERS' BUREAU.

301. —— specific performance

Conditional leave to defend for second defendants in respect of part of
a claim for $43,000—" mutuality " in respect of obtaining a decree of specific
performance—dicta in Price v. Strange [1977] C.L.Y. 2306, to the effect that
" for considerations of mutuality, go to discretion rather than jurisdiction,"
applied—appeal of second defendants dismissed. Appeal from Donaldson J.
November 28, 1977. UNDERGROUND LOCATION SERVICES v. MCELHANNEY OFF-
SHORE SURVEYING AND ENGINEERING.

302. —— striking out—action to set aside consent judgment

Defendant obtained consent judgment for £450 against plaintiff for breach
of contract to supply an air ticket resulting, inter alia, in the defendant
being unable to be called to Bar of Ceylon within a certain time—third
party and plaintiff also consented to pay £100 to the defendant, plus some
costs, the order stating that the third party proceedings by the plaintiff against
the third party be dismissed with no order as to costs—plaintiff's action to
set aside consent judgment on ground of mistake, in that consent would not
have been given had the fact been known that on the basis of the relevant
rules operative in Ceylon, the defendant could not in any event have been
called to the Bar of Ceylon within the certain time alleged—plaintiff alleged
that he was induced by a false representation to enter into the compromise—
whether plaintiff's action vexatious—whether action should be struck out as
disclosing no reasonable cause of action—defendant's appeal dismissed—third
party to be joined in proceedings to set aside consent judgment. January 20,
1978. RANASINGHAM v. COORAY.

303. —— —— whether action oppressive to defendants—action stayed pending concurrent libel proceedings

Plaintiffs brought an action for damages against the defendants, three police officers, the statement of claim alleging a conspiracy on the part of all three defendants to injure the plaintiffs by writing, and causing to be disseminated, a certain report—conspiracy alleged also indictable as a criminal conspiracy—whether pleading disclosed no reasonable cause of action—an action for libel was also brought by the plaintiffs against the Metropolitan Police Commissioner who was alleged to be vocariously liable for the report written by the three defendants—whether plaintiffs' action against the defendants vexatious or oppressive or an abuse of the process of the court as being oppressive and harrassing of the defendants in being allowed to proceed concurrently with the plaintiffs' libel action—defendant's appeal allowed—plaintiffs' action allowed to go on, but stayed temporarily until final determination of the plaintiffs' libel action or further order—s. 43 of the Supreme Court of Judicature (Consolidation) Act 1925 applied. Appeal from Cusack J. March 21, 1978. CHURCH OF SCIENTOLOGY OF CALIFORNIA v. PRICE.

304. —— summary judgment—conditional leave to defend—expedited hearing

In a motion under R.S.C., Ord. 14, it was ordered by the master that the plaintiffs should have possession of 14 Beauchamp Place against the defendants —on appeal the judge in chambers upheld the order—defendants' appeal allowed—conditional leave to defend granted, condition being that the defendants shall make payment into court within 14 days in respect of the potential future rent of the premises over the rest of the year in the sum of £2,500— desirable that action should be heard at earliest possible date having regard to the circumstances of the case and to the past history. Appeal from Griffiths J. May 10, 1978. REMOND v. 15, BEAUCHAMP PLACE.

305. —— —— stay of execution

Plaintiffs' claim for rent and mesne profits—whether defendant ought to have conditional leave to defend, or whether judgment should be entered for plaintiffs—execution stayed on grounds of a cross-action for rectification and for conspiracy to injure defendant—whether defendant entitled to an equitable set-off—*Morgan & Son* v. *Martin Johnson & Co.* (1948) C.L.C. 7744, distinguished—defendant's appeal dismissed. Appeal from Whitford J. November 11, 1977. INTERNATIONAL ORIENTAL CARPET CENTRE v. NORRELL.

306. —— time to appeal—action dismissed for want of prosecution

Plaintiff's application for extension of time to appeal refused—claim was professional negligence against firm of solicitors who had conducted plaintiff's divorce proceedings—writ was issued June 11, 1973, six years after alleged wrong advice—action was dismissed, for want of prosecution, on October 13, 1976—change in the law—whether *Birkett* v. *James* [1977] C.L.Y. 2410 applicable—*Re Berkeley* [1968] C.L.Y. 116, referred to—plaintiff's appeal dismissed. Appeal from Davies J. October 31, 1977. JONES v. TRAFFORD ALDRED HOLFORD.

307. —— transfer of action

Plaintiff's action for damages for assault, unlawful imprisonment, and malicious prosecution for loitering with intent—application to transfer action from county court to High Court refused—*Stiffel* v. *Industrial Dwelling Society* [1973] C.L.Y. 459, referred to—judge properly ignored fact that action had been set down in county court—whether reasonable to suppose amount recoverable to be in excess of amount recoverable in county court—no medical report to support application—plaintiff's appeal dismissed. October 24, 1977. JOHNSON v. CHIEF CONSTABLE OF THE WEST MIDLANDS POLICE.

308. —— trial—further evidence

Third party was held liable to the plaintiff and the defendants, building contractors, in an action by the plaintiff claiming he had been induced to buy a house by misrepresentation—third party applied for a new trial on basis of fresh evidence by the defendants' former site supervisor, Q—fresh evidence given in the form of signed statement appended to an affidavit by his solicitors, Q not being present—application dismissed on basis, inter alia, that evidence not credible—third party's appeal dismissed. March 22, 1978. MONTE v. KASS HOMES.

309. Defendant in person applied, inter alia, for a new trial with fresh evidence in relation to a claim by the plaintiff—extremely doubtful whether evidence would in any event be forthcoming should leave be given—applications dismissed. April 17, 1978. ECONOMIC FORESTRY v. ROSEN.

310. —— want of prosecution

In July 1972, the plaintiff started an action by writ claiming damages against the defendants, insurance brokers, for negligent advice given to her in October 1968—in August 1973 she delivered a statement of claim, and in August 1974 asked for further and better particulars of the defence delivered in November 1973—in September 1975, a summons for directions was drafted by the plaintiff's solicitors but was not issued or served—in April 1977 the plaintiff sought to revive the action, and in July the defendants applied to dismiss the action for want of prosecution—inordinate and inexcusable delay—whether prejudice caused to the defendants—plaintiff's action dismissed for want of prosecution—plaintiff's appeal dismissed—*Birkett* v. *James* [1977] C.L.Y. 2410 applied. Appeal from Ackner J. March 10, 1978. CLAY v. STEVENS WARREN HASTINGS & CO.

311. Legally aided plaintiff brought action against the defendants in July 1976 claiming, inter alia, that the defendants had unlawfully evicted her from her room in June 1976—defendants denied all claims made against them—in August, plaintiff applied for hearing to be speeded up and hearing date was fixed originally for November, but then for February 1977 because the court was unable to fit in the hearing in November—in January 1977, the action was adjourned generally with liberty to apply on the plaintiff's application which was opposed by the defendants—nothing else was done by the plaintiff until January 20, 1978, when she amended her particulars of claim—on January 27, 1978, the defendants applied to strike out the action for want of prosecution relying on the inactivity between February 1977 and January 1978—application granted and action struck out for want of prosecution—plaintiff's appeal allowed—although delay inordinate and inexcusable and it was prejudicial to the defendants for the action to proceed, discretion of judge wrongly exercised because the six-year period of limitation relevant to the plaintiff's action had not expired when striking out order made—case no exception to the general rule—*Birkett* v. *James* [1977] C.L.Y. 2410 followed. May 5, 1978. PERVAIZ v. SYED.

312. —— —— no special hardship to defendant

Action started in May 1970—plaintiff claiming certain remuneration and expenses for having acted on behalf of the defendant and others—action

" incredibly protracted " and it was found by judge that there was inordinate and inexcusable delay—whether requisite prejudice present—little oral evidence necessary, case would have to be decided on the documents—whether special hardship to the defendant, man aged 73, to have this litigation hanging over his head for long time—judge allowing action to proceed—defendant's appeal dismissed—particular hardship not sufficient to justify barring the plaintiff from going on with action—judge did not exercise discretion wrongly. Appeal from Lawson J. May 26, 1978. MEHTA v. ADAMS.

313. —— —— whether action should be dismissed

Application of three defendants to dismiss actions for want of prosecution, refused—plaintiffs alleged breach of a building contract; and/or negligence in construction against first defendants, and in design or architects' services against second defendants—also negligence against defendant engineers in a second action—power of Court of Appeal to interfere with exercise of judge's discretion—*Birkett* v. *James* [1977] C.L.Y. 2410 referred to—whether plaintiffs' delay was excusable—all defendants' appeals dismissed. Appeals from Griffiths J. December 20, 1977. OLDHAM ESTATE CO. (ST. PETERS) v. WIMPEY (GEORGE) & CO.

314. —— writ—service—extension of period

In September 1972 the plaintiff suffered serious injuries to his left hand because of the admitted negligence of the defendant in driving his car—on May 15, 1975, the plaintiff's writ was issued—between April and May 1976 the plaintiff's solicitors made unsuccessful attempts to serve the writ on the defendant—in May 1976 the writ was renewed for another year and on May 11, 1977, the plaintiff's solicitors succeeded in serving the writ on the defendant—a conditional appearance was entered by the defendant, and in June the writ was set aside—limitation period for the action expired—whether exceptional circumstances to justify extension of validity of writ—whether solicitor's failure to serve writ in June in all the circumstances a sufficient reason for extension—plaintiff's appeal dismissed. Appeal from Bristow J. March 16, 1978. INGRAM v. WILSON.

315. —— —— service out of the jurisdiction—action on contract governed by English law

The plaintiffs, a company incorporated in Scotland with a branch carrying on business in England, entered into a contract in England, in the English language, with the defendants, an Israeli company carrying on business in Israel—contract granting defendants option to purchase shares in a certain company—clause that agreement to be " governed by and construed in accordance with the laws of England, save that all acts that need to be performed in accordance with Israeli law shall be governed by Israeli law "—defendants exercised option to purchase shares in January 1975—plaintiffs called for completion of sale in March 1975 —defendants refused, claiming that plaintiffs were in fundamental breach of contract by permitting certain acts and activities of certain disaffected directors and shareholders of the company in question, thereby gravely reducing the value of the shares in question—plaintiffs not accepting that they were in breach and claiming that defendants wrongfully and unequivocally renounced their obligations under contract—plaintiffs given leave ex parte to serve notice of writ outside jurisdiction claiming damages for breach of contract—defendants entered conditional appearance to set aside order granting leave—application before master—plaintiffs' appeal to High Court judge allowed, granting plaintiffs leave —whether judge wrong in principle in holding that leave should be granted—

defendants' interlocutory appeal dismissed—R.S.C., Ord. 11, r. 1 (*f*). Appeal from Chapman J. January 25, 1978. JAMES SCOTT ENGINEERING GROUP *v.* ELCO.

316. —— writ and statement of claim—striking out

Plaintiff's application for leave to appeal from the order of a High Court judge which upheld an order by a master to strike out the plaintiff's writ and statement of claim under R.S.C., Ord. 18, r. 19—plaintiff's claim for himself personally, in respect of cottages, had been sufficiently covered by other proceedings—plaintiff's claim concerning the third defendant, a company, in respect of matters referred to, were not matters which went to ultra vires—there was no proper or sufficient allegation of fraud here, and *Russell* v. *Wakefield Waterworks Co.* (1875) L.R. 20 Eq. 474 had no application—plaintiff's application dismissed. Appeal from Wien J. December 5, 1977. FLETCHER *v.* COUTTS & CO.

317. Rating and Valuation—matters to be taken into account

The local valuation court reduced the assessment of the hereditament in question (leased to the appellant for 14 years for use as a launderette) to a G.V. of £625 and R.V. of £492, and amended the description in the valuation list to read " shop, store and premises "—lands tribunal affirmed the decision —appeal, by way of case stated, that tribunal paid no due regard to, inter alia, s. 31 of the Greater London Council (General Powers) Act 1973—appeal dismissed—restriction on user of premises irrelevant. April 4, 1978. BYRNE *v.* PARKER (VALUATION OFFICER).

318. Real Property and Conveyancing—adverse possession—discontinuance of possession

Single parcel of land, on which stood a house and a cottage, severed after 1954 when cottage sold separately from house—boundary between " house land " and " cottage land " marked by a wattle fence—plaintiffs bought house and planted parallel to, but about three feet away from the wattle fence, a hawthorne hedge—wattle fence gradually collapsed—plaintiffs never did anything to hedge on the cottage side nor anything to the disputed land on the cottage side of the hedge except lop a branch of the acacia tree—cottage owners did not do a great deal on the cottage side of the hedge except cut the grass and trim the hedge (the land being rough grass)—whether plaintiffs discontinued possession of the disputed land—whether defendants acquired disputed land by virtue of adverse possession—plaintiffs' appeal dismissed. February 19, 1978. MCCURDY *v.* LAING.

319. —— —— evidence

Defendant's claim to adverse possession based on testimony of a number of persons familiar with the situation during the relevant time—judge found in favour of defendant on basis that acts of possession, *i.e.* " position of hedges and fences, the planting of daffodils, the storage of machinery and its use as a sheep pen,'" for appropriate period destroyed plaintiff's title to land—plaintiff's appeal that no evidence to justify finding of judge and that defendant encroached onto land by taking advantage of his tenancy of adjoining land—sufficient evidence to justify finding of judge—plaintiff's appeal dismissed. January 19, 1978. CHORLEY MEAT CO. *v.* HAWES.

320. —— possession—whether charge existed on legal estate by virtue of an equitable interest under a will

Plaintiff had obtained order for possession against defendant—evidence sought to be adduced as to who paid for building of the house—onus of proof upon defendant to show that plaintiff's legal estate was burdened with an equitable interest in defendant's favour—any such interest arising out of residuary legacy of his mother—judge correct in his findings of fact—defendant's appeal dismissed. November 14, 1977. WALKER v. LANE.

321. —— profit à prendre—grant by licence agreement

By a tenancy agreement dated July 20, 1970, the plaintiffs became agricultural tenants of a farm which was part of the free estate of Lord Derby, the other parts of the estate being in settlement—the plaintiffs claimed to be entitled to compensation arising out of the extraction of sand and gravel from some fields on their farm by the defendant company under a " licence," dated April 5, 1967, entered into between Lord Derby of the first part, the defendant company of the second part, and the trustees of the settlement of the estate of the third part—whether benefit obtained by defendant company under the " licence agreement " was of contractual nature only, or whether intended to be a legal profit à prendre—construction of " licence agreement "—defendant company's appeals allowed—" licence agreement " created a legal profit à prendre of the kind described in the agreement—" licence agreement " being of earlier date than the tenancy, and creating a prior legal estate in the land, that estate must override the rights of the plaintiffs as tenants under the later tenancy agreement—under the " licence agreement," defendant company was under no obligation to pay compensation to anyone—consequently, plaintiffs' originating summons was misconceived, and should be struck out. Appeals from Blackett-Ord V.-C. February 15, 1978. HEYES v. PILKINGTON BROTHERS.

322. —— title—beneficial interest

Ownership of dwelling—plaintiff, the deceased's mistress and surviving joint tenant, claimed the beneficial interest in the property and a lien on its value for mortgage moneys paid out—the defendant, the deceased's widow, counterclaimed for possession and, damages for use and occupation—judge's order assessed the plaintiff's beneficial interest at three-quarters—whether property held in equal beneficial shares—defendant's counterclaim adjourned—maxim " equality is equity " cited from *Gissing* v. *Gissing* [1970] C.L.Y. 1243—conclusion of judge was fully justified—defendant's appeal dismissed. December 15, 1977. BURGESS v. BURGESS.

323. —— —— declaration

Ownership of piece of land on Canvey Island—declaration that land was vested in plaintiff, in fee simple, as beneficial owner and free from any estate right or interest in favour of defendants, refused—ancillary relief refused—possessory title of plaintiff's predecessors in title—adverse possession by plaintiff—plaintiff's appeal allowed. November 9, 1977. COOK v. CONNOR.

324. —— —— renunciation

Ownership of cottage—plaintiff claimed title to property—whether two wills ineffective as a result of an intestacy—whether judge entitled to draw inference of deliberate renunciation of right to property from an agreement—question should properly be treated as an issue of law—appeal of plaintiff dismissed. November 17, 1977. BARNES v. CLARKE.

325. —— trusteeship—evidence

Plaintiff sought declaration that the defendant held beneficial interest in property as a trustee for the plaintiff—land certificate and title deeds delivered

up, and agreed repayment of purchase price of £19,000 was made with interest
—judgment for defendant—whether decision was against the weight of the
evidence—judge's finding was consistent with the only reliable evidence that
he had available—plaintiff's appeal dismissed. Appeal from Whitford J. November 15, 1977. COHEN v. COHEN.

326. Rent Restriction—furnished letting—amount of rent attributable to furniture

Plaintiff tenant took a furnished tenancy of a basement flat from the
defendant landlord in June 1975 and prepared, but never filed, an application
for registration of a fair rent of £15 per week—in 1967 the flat was let
unfurnished and was registered at a rent of £2·40 per week—the landlord
asserted that the furniture provided by him at the commencement of the
tenancy was new or practically new and had cost about £800—tenant's
evidence that quality of furniture poor—judge assuming that furniture provided
worth about £100 and thus not forming a substantial part of the rent
and accordingly tenant entitled to declarations, inter alia, that the rent limit
in respect of the flat was £2·40 per week—defendant landlord's appeal regrettably dismissed, because of events taking place after case—judge's decision
in essence a decision of fact made on evidence justifying the findings.
February 14, 1978. ROWLANDS v. ONYEKWERE.

327. —— registered rent—not reviewable

Plaintiff landlords leased a flat to the defendant tenant who agreed to pay
a " yearly sum of £830 or such greater rent as shall for the time be registered
as the rent for the flat under the Rent Act 1965 "—an increase was registered
by the rent officer who noted that a specified sum in respect of services was
included in the rent which he had found—the defendant objected to the
increase and the county court judge made an interlocutory order that the
plaintiffs should give extensive and far-reaching discovery to the defendant in
support of his allegations that certain increases authorised by the rent officer
had been improperly arrived at—plaintiffs' appeal allowed—finding of rent
officer as to amount of rent conclusive, and the rent registered becomes the
rent payable by the defendant tenant under his lease—s. 90 of the Housing
Finance Act 1972 not relevant where rent determined by rent officer—inappropriate exercise of jurisdiction of county court—result would have been to
review rent conclusively determined by the rent officer. March 16, 1978. LEGAL
AND GENERAL ASSURANCE SOCIETY v. KEANE.

328. Road Traffic—accident—contributory negligence

Plaintiff, a police motor-cyclist, suffered damages when his motor-cycle
collided with the defendant's car on a wet and greasy road—judge found that
the accident happened because the defendant pulled out too suddenly to avoid
a stationary car when the plaintiff's motor-cycle was too close behind her, but
that an equal contributory cause of the accident was the plaintiff's failure to
anticipate such a movement on the defendant's part—plaintiff's appeal dismissed—nothing wrong with the judge's findings or apportionment for the
appeal court to interfere. February 21, 1978. SMITH v. MITCHELL.

329. —— —— liability—conflict of evidence

Road accident between two cars driven by plaintiff and defendant respectively—plaintiff's claim dismissed—judgment for defendant on counterclaim of
£121·92—whether car which plaintiff was driving was stationary behind parked
cars, or pulled out and caused the accident—the only issue was whose evidence
the judge accepted—the appellant coming to the Court of Appeal could not

give his evidence afresh as he gave it in the court below—plaintiff's appeal dismissed. November 25, 1977. B.L.D.A.-P.C.A.A.W. (TRADING AS ANIMAL WELFARE) v. LATHAM.

330. —— collision

Collision at road junction—experimental roundabout—findings of fact by judge amounted to a stationary vehicle suddenly pulling out into the path of another vehicle—judge accepted evidence of defendant's witness in preference to that of the plaintiff's biased witness—no case of negligence made out against defendant—plaintiff's appeal dismissed. November 30, 1977. BOND v. JAMES.

331. —— —— contributory negligence—apportionment of liability

Plaintiff, aged 18, was injured when his motor bicycle, which he had been riding for two months only on a provisional licence, collided with a big tanker driven by the first defendant (and owned by the second defendants) on an icy and slippery road 30 feet wide—collision occurred whilst the tanker driver was turning across a road which had no speed limit into a side turning on his right hand side—having found the primary facts, the judge inferred that it was not only the defendant driver whose look-out was at fault, but also that the plaintiff was not keeping a proper look-out—had plaintiff been keeping a proper look-out, he " should have, and must have, observed the manoeuvre which was being executed by this slow moving tanker "—plaintiff held to be 70 per cent. to blame and the tanker driver 30 per cent.—plaintiff's appeal allowed—tanker driver not less but more to blame for the collision in the negligence of his look-out than the plaintiff because he had the higher duty when exercising this " notoriously dangerous manoeuvre "—defendant driver 60 per cent. to blame and the plaintiff 40 per cent. Appeal from Reeve J. May 26, 1978. HORTON v. MORGAN AND HEAVY TRANSPORT (EEC).

332. Sale of Goods—conditional sale agreement—pleadings

Plaintiffs' action claiming that defendant in breach of conditional sale agreement in writing in respect of a motor car, the plaintiffs having provided the finance for the car—defence denied the agreement alleged, admitting that first defendant wrote certain personal particulars with signature on a form for a future sale agreement with the plaintiffs, but denying writing other particulars, averring that those other particulars were written by his step-father-in-law, employed by second defendants, without the first defendant's knowledge or authority, and that he did not submit, or authorise the second defendant to submit, that form—first defendant had left form with his step-father-in-law pending his decision whether or not to buy motor car on conditional sale basis—first defendant then decided not to buy on conditional sale basis but bought the car directly from his stepfather-in-law—plaintiffs provided finance on a conditional sale basis because of fraud of stepfather-in-law—plaintiffs sent, inter alia, a copy of the conditional sale agreement to the first defendant who, having realised that the agreement related to his motor car, phoned stepfather-in-law and got explanation that the form had been sent to the plaintiffs in error and that stepfather-in-law would sort matter out—first defendant thereupon left it to his stepfather-in-law to deal with matter without himself communicating with the plaintiffs—first defendant negligent in so acting—first defendant's appeal allowed—plaintiffs' pleadings amended to incorporate the negligence—no loss shown to flow from the negligence to the plaintiffs. COMMERCIAL BANK OF WALES v. ILLINGWORTH AND MEALBANK MOTORS (A FIRM).

333. —— delivery—whether agency existed

Plaintiffs' claim of £340·61 for goods sold and delivered—judgment in their favour—whether plaintiffs established that on the relevant date they had become, by a contract of re-sale, the owners of the goods, the property in which was being passed upon that day—plaintiffs cannot sue for the price of goods sold and delivered by them through people whom they claim were their agents to the defendants on the relevant date—plaintiffs could not rely upon clear notice having been given as to the precise role of the alleged agents—defendants' appeal allowed. December 1, 1977. BY APPOINTMENT (SALES) *v.* HARRODS (TRADING AS RACKHAMS).

334. —— terms—no additional warranty—evidence

Plaintiffs bought from defendants a weedkiller for the half-acre garden of their house—the garden had been part of a field prior to the building of the house—plaintiffs used weedkiller in September 1974 and in May 1975, after the ground had been prepared and levelled, sowed grass seed which grew well at first but died by July 1975—plaintiffs' evidence that they had told defendants: "We have a half-acre plot, originally a field, and wanted to kill off the weeds, and we wanted to lay a lawn in six to eight weeks' time"—defendants denied plaintiffs' evidence—judge came to conclusion that nothing was said about the minimum time which was required to elapse before re-sowing took place—plaintiffs' appeal dismissed—judge perfectly entitled to come to conclusion that he did—no specific duty on the defendants to give some particular and additional warning about a package (with words on it describing the contents) when judge found that the emphasis was on a weedkiller which would kill all the weeds—s. 14 of the Sale of Goods Act 1893 inapplicable. May 4, 1978. COWLEY *v.* FARM SUPPLY (THIRSK).

335. Shipping and Marine Insurance—charterparty—demurrage claim—arbitration clause

Charterparty—claim for demurrage of 340,000 U.S. dollars—whether charterparty provided for claim to be decided by arbitration in London—construction of clause—*Union of India* v. *E. B. Aaby's Rederi A/S* [1974] C.L.Y. 3550, referred to—plaintiffs' appeal dismissed. Appeal from Kerr J. November 2, 1977. TRANSAMERICAN OCEAN CONTRACTORS, INC. *v.* TRANSCHEMICAL ROTTERDAM B.V.

336. Social Security—benefit—increase for " householder "

Local council let premises to W at rent of £400 p.a. with usual clause that he would not assign or underlet or part with possession of the premises—W divided premises up and granted " sub-tenancies " to the two applicants, charging £8 a week rent each—applicants, unemployed and receiving ordinary social security benefits, claimed in addition increased benefits on ground that they were " householders "—claim rejected—applicants' application for leave to appeal dismissed—no clear error of law for appeal court to interfere—applicants had no households of their own and so not householders—meaning of " householder " a matter of common sense for tribunal concerned—Supplementary Benefits Acts 1966–1976. Application for leave to appeal dismissed. May 23, 1978. R. *v.* SOUTH LONDON SUPPLEMENTARY BENEFITS APPEAL TRIBUNAL, *ex p.* HOLLAND AND SZCZELKUN.

337. Solicitors—authority—evidence

Ex parte application for leave to appeal or set aside order on ground, inter alia, that instructions to solicitors and counsel were withdrawn before hearing day—solicitors still on record on hearing day—insufficient evidence that solicitors acting without authority—defendant's appeal dismissed. Appeal from Slynn J. January 3, 1978. SOUTH WESTERN MANAGEMENTS v. RYAN.

338. Plaintiff had instructed defendant solicitors to pursue claim for damages of £750 against two defendants—payment into court of £350 by second defendant in full satisfaction of claim—defendant solicitors accepting payment into court in settlement—whether acceptance without authority—conflict of evidence —judge accepted evidence of defendant solicitors that authority for acceptance received from plaintiff by telephone although no record made of it—" notes of judgment " considered de bene esse and accepted by Court of Appeal—no grounds for holding that judge came to wrong conclusion—plaintiff's appeal dismissed. January 17, 1978. ROBERTS v. S. GOODMAN (TRADING AS BOWLING & CO.).

339. —— claim for professional costs

Plaintiff claimed balance of costs alleged due to her from the defendant, in her professional capacity as solicitor acting for the defendant in connection with his separation agreement from his wife—judgment for the plaintiff on her claim of £796·31—judgment for the defendant on his counterclaim of £1,200 relating to building work done by him—also sums in relation to costs unnecessarily incurred, and a lump sum in connection with his wife's claim for ancillary relief—total judgment for defendant of £2,000, plus £75 costs —finding of negligence against plaintiff—plaintiff's appeal allowed to limited extent; new trial ordered as to quantum of damages. November 16, 1977. MULLANEY v. WILLIAMSON.

340. —— negligence—failure to make inquiries

Plaintiffs instructed a local solicitor, a senior partner in the defendant firm of solicitors, in the purchase of a house—solicitor did not make two supplementary inquiries which it was the common practice for local solicitors to include on searches—plaintiffs bought the house which later became included in a clearance area and was the subject of a proposed compulsory purchase— plaintiffs denied damages in negligence—judge dismissed claim, holding that the solicitor had not failed in his duty of care and was entitled to use his local knowledge, and that even if he had been negligent in not asking the two supplementary questions, the questions would not have revealed the relevant matter which would have stopped the plaintiffs buying the house—plaintiffs' (in person) application to adduce fresh evidence refused—plaintiffs' appeal dismissed. Appeal from Thompson J. March 7, 1978. HUGHES v. BARROW & COOK (A FIRM).

341. Tort—assault and wrongful arrest

Plaintiff claimed damages for assault, unlawful arrest and being kept in custody by a police officer—defendant's vicarious liability involved—acute conflict as to what transpired—court not concerned with emotional reaction of parties—police officer exposed as an untruthful witness—plaintiff an unreliable witness as to assault—plaintiff had to show his case was a good one on a balance of probabilities—plaintiff's appeal dismissed. November 25, 1977. IRWIN v. CHIEF CONSTABLE OF THE NORTHUMBRIA POLICE AUTHORITY.

342. —— damage to chattels, and trespass—evidence

In first action, plaintiffs alleged that the defendants had destroyed storage radiator, broken padlocks on gas-meters, and refused plaintiffs, as landlords, access—defendants' counterclaims relating to gas having been turned off— second action claiming first defendant had broken padlock on electricity meter, stolen money, appropriated padlock and trespassed—application for leave to execute possession and to commit first defendant for assault—judgment for defendants on claims and counterclaims—two actions consolidated—deplorable delay in bringing appeal—application for new trial on grounds, inter alia, of fresh evidence, refused—whether the judge wrongly rejected evidence proffered by the plaintiffs on the ground that, although relevant, it would be prejudicial —plaintiffs' appeal dismissed. October 20, 1977. HAMID v. SUTTON-CLARKE.

343. Town and Country Planning—betterment levy—when payable

The plaintiffs held two leases, running for about 12 years and 10 years respectively, relating to offices on the second floor and the penthouse floor in 8 Hanover Square, London W.1—by agreement, they surrendered the two leases to their landlords and in consideration of the surrenders, they were paid £30,000, and part of the consideration was an agreement by the landlords to grant them an underlease of two floors in different premises at 20 and 21 Princes Street, London W.1—notice of assessment of betterment levy served on the plaintiffs in the sum of £7,749—whether betterment levy payable— whether plaintiffs' transaction exempt—whether levy payable only when grant of new tenancy relates to *any* premises or only when grant of new tenancy relates to premises surrendered—Land Commission Act 1967, s. 85 (3) (*a*). February 22, 1978. BIRKETT & LYLE v. SECRETARY OF STATE FOR THE ENVIRONMENT.

344. Trade and Industry—restrictive trade practices—separate trials—discovery

The plaintiffs, a subsidiary of a large American corporation, had employed seven individual defendants since at least 1971—between 1973 and June 1974, the individual defendants became unemployed from the plaintiff company and set up, through the medium of the three defendant companies, a business alleged to be in direct competition with and similar to the one carried on by the plaintiffs—the plaintiffs' main claim, inter alia, against the defendants was that, from 1971, certain of the defendants wrongfully conspired and agreed together, and/or with other persons, to injure the plaintiffs by setting up the rival business and "filching" their customers and employees—the plaintiffs applied for discovery under R.S.C., Ord. 24, and the defendants objected to certain points and matters asked for in discovery, and applied for separate trials of the issues of liability and damages under R.S.C., Ord. 33 —the judge refused the order for separate trials, and made an order for discovery—defendants' appeal allowed—convenient in case for there to be the separate trials—order for discovery amended. Appeal from Templeman J. March 15, 1978. GAMLEN CHEMICAL CO. (U.K.) v. ROCHEM.

345. Vendor and Purchaser—completion—refusal—fraudulent misrepresentation

Plaintiff company entered into a contract with the defendant for the sale to the latter of a property, a service station, for £165,000—the defendant refused to complete the sale as agreed, and the plaintiffs brought an action and applied for summary judgment—the defendant alleged as a defence, inter alia, misrepresentation made to him by the plaintiff company's estate agent and one of its directors that the property could be resold immediately for £200,000 to certain companies—collateral arrangements agreed constituted a fraud on the plaintiff company—summary judgment obtained by plaintiff company—defendant's appeal dismissed—defendant could not be allowed to rely on his own wrongful act. Appeal from Megarry V.-C. March 17, 1978. FORTCLIFF INVESTMENTS v. GARRETT.

346. —— contract—breach—damages

On May 25, 1974, the plaintiffs agreed to sell to the defendant a house for £55,000 subject to the Law Society's General Conditions of Sale (1973 Revision), the rate of interest payable under General Condition 16 being 15 per cent. per annum and the date fixed for completion being July 28, 1974—in August the plaintiffs served a notice to complete under General Condition 19 and in September refused the defendant an extension of time and forfeited the defendant's deposit of £5,500—the house was put back onto the market and resold for £51,000—the plaintiffs brought an action for breach of contract claiming damages under various heads, and the defendant admitted breach of contract —whether plaintiffs entitled to recover additional damages over and above the liquidated damages to which they were entitled under General Condition 19— defendant's appeal allowed—" liquidated damages " under General Condition 19 conclusive where seller chooses (as here) to exercise his rights and remedies under that Condition—General Condition 16 not applicable where there has been a resale of the property. Appeal from Melford Stevenson J. February 8, 1978. TALLEY v. WOLSEY-NEECH.

347. —— —— —— sub-sale—whether completion possible—injunction

In October 1973, the plaintiff company entered into a contract of sale with the defendant company, owned and controlled by the second defendant, in respect of certain properties, the contract containing a clause, inter alia, that from the date of the contract, the purchaser would be responsible for the day-to-day management of the properties and would be entitled to the rents and profits therefrom, and would indemnify the vendor against all costs and expenses of whatever nature arising therefrom—contractual completion date fixed for October 1974—in December 1973, same parties entered into another contract of sale relating to certain other leasehold properties, completion being fixed for October 1974 but the sale taking effect from October 1973—in December 1973 the defendant company entered into a contract of sub-sale with the reversioner of the leasehold properties for the sale to the reversioner of all the subject-matter of the December 1973 contract—in December 1974 the defendant company brought an action against the plaintiff company relating to the October 1973 contract, alleging that at the date of the expiry of the notice to complete, there were trespassers in occupation of part of the premises in question so that completion was not possible, and in the circumstances the plaintiff company had repudiated the agreement, and the defendant company claimed recission and repayment of their deposit—defence served by plaintiff company claimed, inter alia, that under the contract the defendant company was to manage the property and was responsible for the day-to-day management, and if trespassers entered the property as alleged, the defendant company was responsible for their entry and was not entitled to rely on their presence in the property as a ground for treating the contract as repudiated—in June 1974 the defendant company brought an action relating to the December 1973 contract alleging that the property concerned was transferred by the plaintiff company to the reversioner in breach of contract— defence served was that, inter alia, the effect of the December 1973 contract was to operate as a legal assignment of the contract by the defendant company to the reversioner, alternatively it operated as an equitable assignment—winding up proceedings theatened against plaintiff company by the defendant company—money alleged to be owed because of the contracts— plaintiff company claimed an injunction to restrain the defendant company from, inter alia, presenting or causing or permitting to be presented a petition to wind-up the plaintiff company—judge granted an injunction in respect of the October 1973 contract claim until judgment or further order and, although he was not minded to grant an injunction in respect of the December 1973 contract claim, an injunction pending appeal in respect of that claim on intimation by counsel that an appeal would be taken—plaintiff company's appeal allowed on basis that there was an arguable case that all the rights and obligations under the December 1973 contract were assigned by a sub-sale contract to the reversioner—further evidence allowed to be adduced on appeal —defendant company's cross-appeal dismissed on basis that under the October 1973 contract there were grounds for thinking that there was a genuine and substantial dispute as to whether the defendant company could assert that the plaintiff company was unable to complete the contract at the relevant time and therefore whether the defendant company was entitled to assert that the plaintiff company had repudiated the contract. Appeals from Walton J. May 5, 1978. SOPHISTICATED DEVELOPMENTS v. STELADEAN AND MOSCHI.

348. —— —— whether cause of action existed

Defendants' application to strike out writ and statement of claim on ground that the pleadings disclosed no reasonable cause of action, or alternatively, that the action was frivolous/vexatious/an abuse of process—whether offer was capable of leading to contractual acceptance—whether case was not governed by s. 40 of the Law of Property Act 1925—importance of sworn evidence to the case—*Daulia* v. *Four Millbank Nominees* [1977] C.L.Y. 2505 referred to—common understanding in conveyancing practice when negotiation is subject to contract—defendants' appeal allowed. Appeal from Graham J. December 20, 1977. CREDIT SUISSE WHITE WELD v. DAVIS AND MORRIS.

349. Wills—family provision

Inheritance (Family Provision) Act 1938—widow's application for lump sum—death of husband on December 5, 1970, after 22 years of happy marriage —this was second marriage of deceased—financial situation at death different from that supposed when deceased made his will—whether deceased " failed to make reasonable provision "—widow ought to have absolutely the matrimonial home, to take effect in priority to interests of the grown-up, well-established children of deceased's first marriage—claim by eighth defendant for maintenance until she completed her school education—appeal of plaintiff allowed. December 9, 1977. BAYLISS v. LLOYDS BANK.

350. —— revocation—marriage

Plaintiff seeking grant of letters of administration of deceased husband's estate on ground that he died intestate—deceased made will in 1973 benefiting defendant—deceased married plaintiff in 1974 and died in 1976—defendant alleging that deceased unable to give valid consent to marriage because of mental subnormality—whether marriage ineffective—whether will revoked— Matrimonial Causes Act 1973, s. 12; Wills Act 1837, s. 18. Appeal from Walton J. January 12, 1978. ROBERTS v. ROBERTS.

351. —— validity—testamentary capacity

Testamentary capacity of deceased called in question—*Banks* v. *Goodfellow* (1870) L.R. 5 Q.B. 549 referred to—judge was right in holding evidence did not point to a mental imbalance at the time the will was made—defendant's appeal dismissed. Appeal from Walton J. November 21, 1977. *Re* BROOKE (DECD); GREEN v. BROOKE.

DATES OF COMMENCEMENT

Statutes

(in alphabetical order)

ADMINISTRATION OF JUSTICE ACT 1977—February 1, 1978: [1977] C.L.Y. 429. Ss. 14, 17 (1), 19 (1), 27.
July 3, 1978: [1978] C.L.Y. 367. S. 19 (2) (3) (5).

ADOPTION ACT 1968—October 23, 1978: [1978] C.L.Y. 1973. Ss. 5–7, 8 (1), 9.

AGRICULTURAL HOLDINGS (NOTICES TO QUIT) ACT 1977—April 7, 1978: [1978] C.L.Y. 47.

AGRICULTURE (MISCELLANEOUS PROVISIONS) ACT 1976—April 7, 1978: [1978] C.L.Y. 52. Ss. 13, 14 as respects Scotland.

BAIL ACT 1976—April 17, 1978: [1978] C.L.Y. 418.

CHILDREN ACT 1975—October 23, 1978: [1978] C.L.Y. 1980. S. 24.

CIVIL AVIATION ACT 1978—March 23, 1978: [1978] C.L.Y. 130. Ss. 1 (1) (3)–(5), 2, 3, 13, 16.
April 1, 1978: [1978] C.L.Y. 130. S. 1 (2).
May 1, 1978: [1978] C.L.Y. 130. Remaining provisions.

COMMONWEALTH DEVELOPMENT CORPORATION ACT 1978—April 23, 1978: [1978] C.L.Y. 161.

CONSOLIDATED FUND ACT 1978—March 23, 1978: [1978] C.L.Y. 2516.

CONSOLIDATED FUND (NO. 2) ACT 1978—December 14, 1978: [1978] C.L.Y. 2517.

CONSUMER CREDIT ACT 1974—July 1, 1978: [1977] C.L.Y. 2657. Sched. 3, paras. 44–46.

CONSUMER SAFETYACT 1978—November 1, 1978: [1978] C.L.Y. 2918. All provisions save for s. 10 (1), Sched. 3.

CONTROL OF POLLUTION ACT 1974—July 1, 1978: [1977] C.L.Y. 2431. S. 2.
August 1, 1978: [1978] C.L.Y. 2445. S. 13 (3) (5)–(7) (8).

CO-OPERATIVE DEVELOPMENT AGENCY ACT 1978—June 30, 1978: [1978] C.L.Y. 2919.

CRIMINAL JUSTICE ACT 1967—February 1, 1978: [1977] C.L.Y. 496a. S. 91, Sched. 7 (part).

CRIMINAL LAW ACT 1977—June 19, 1978: [1978] C.L.Y. 450. S. 62.
July 17, 1978: [1978] C.L.Y. 450. Ss. 14–32, 34–37, 41, 42, 45, 46, 58, 61 and 64; Scheds. 1–5, 8, 12 (part), 13 (part).

DOMESTIC PROCEEDINGS AND MAGISTRATES' COURTS ACT 1978—July 18, 1978: [1978] C.L.Y. 1904. Ss. 86, 88 (5), 89 (except subs. (2) (a)), 90, Scheds. 1, 3 (part).
November 20, 1978: [1978] C.L.Y. 1904. Ss. 73, 74, 87, 89 (2) (a), Scheds. 2, paras. 17, 18, 19 (b) (c), 45 (b), 49–53, 3 (part).

DATES OF COMMENCEMENT

EDUCATION (NORTHERN IRELAND) ACT 1978—May 25, 1978: [1978] C.L.Y. 2129.

EMPLOYMENT PROTECTION (CONSOLIDATION) ACT—November 1, 1978: [1978] C.L.Y. 928.

EMPLOYMENT SUBSIDIES ACT 1978—March 23, 1978: [1978] C.L.Y. 929.

EUROPEAN ASSEMBLY ELECTIONS ACT 1978—May 5, 1978: [1978] C.L.Y. 1275.

EXPORT GUARANTEES AND OVERSEAS INVESTMENT ACT 1978—July 30, 1978: [1978] C.L.Y. 2924.

GUN BARREL PROOF ACT 1978—December 1, 1978: [1978] C.L.Y. 1472. Ss. 2–7, 8 (1) (part) (2), 9, Sched. 3 (part), Sched. 4.

HOME PURCHASE ASSISTANCE AND HOUSING CORPORATION GUARANTEE ACT 1978—June 30, 1978: [1978] C.L.Y. 1576. Ss. 4–6.
December 1, 1978: [1978] C.L.Y. 1577. Ss. 1–3.

HOUSE OF COMMONS (ADMINISTRATION) ACT 1978—July 20, 1978: [1978] C.L.Y. 2208. Ss. 1, 3–5, Sched. 2, paras. 1, 2.
January 1, 1979: [1978] C.L.Y. 2208. S. 2, Sched. 2, paras. 3–5.

HOUSING (FINANCIAL PROVISIONS) (SCOTLAND) ACT 1978—April 1, 1978: [1978] C.L.Y. 1580. S. 11, Sched. 2, paras. 31, 35, 36, Sched. 3 (part).
June 25, 1978: [1978] C.L.Y. 1580. Remainder.

IMPORT OF LIVE FISH (SCOTLAND) ACT 1978—July 20, 1978: [1978] C.L.Y. 1481.

INDUSTRIAL AND PROVIDENT SOCIETIES ACT 1978—August 20, 1978: [1978] C.L.Y. 1687.

INSOLVENCY ACT 1976—March 1, 1978: [1978] C.L.Y. 146. Ss. 12, 14 (4) (part), Sched. 3 (part), 17.

INSURANCE BROKERS (REGISTRATION) ACT 1977—October 20, 1978: [1978] C.L.Y. 1720. Ss. 2–5, 9, 13–18, 19 (1)–(3), 20.

INTERPRETATION ACT 1978—January 1, 1979: [1978] C.L.Y. 2841.

IRON AND STEEL (AMENDMENT) ACT 1978—July 20, 1978: [1978] C.L.Y. 2935a.

JUDICATURE (NORTHERN IRELAND) ACT 1978, August 21, 1978: [1978] C.L.Y. 2154. Ss. 52, 53, 54 (2) (3) (4) (6), 55 (3), 56 (1) (2) (3), 99, 107, 116, 118–121, 122 (1) (part) (2) (part), 123, Scheds. 5 (part), 6, paras. 7, 10 (part), 7 (part).

LOCAL GOVERNMENT ACT 1974—April 1, 1979: [1978] C.L.Y. 1869. Sched. 8 (part).

LOCAL GOVERNMENT ACT 1978—July 20, 1978: [1978] C.L.Y. 1870.

LOCAL GOVERNMENT (SCOTLAND) ACT 1978—March 23, 1978: [1978] C.L.Y. 1871.
January 1, 1979: [1978] C.L.Y. 1871. Sched. 1, para. 2.

MEDICAL ACT 1978—May 5, 1978: [1978] C.L.Y. 1943. Ss. 4, 17, 32.
August 23, 1978: [1978] C.L.Y. 1944. Ss. 1 (part), 2, 30, 31 (part).
December 1, 1978: [1978] C.L.Y. 1944. S. 29.
February 15, 1979: [1978] C.L.Y. 1944. Ss. 22–28, 31 (part).

DATES OF COMMENCEMENT

MEDICINES ACT 1968—February 1, 1978: [1977] C.L.Y. 1895.

MERCHANT SHIPPING ACT 1970—July 1, 1978: [1978] C.L.Y. 2750. S. 100 (3) (part), Sched. 5 (part).

MERCHANT SHIPPING ACT 1974—October 16, 1978: [1978] C.L.Y. 2757. Ss. 1, 2, 4–8.

NATIONAL HEALTH SERVICE (SCOTLAND) ACT 1978—January 1, 1979: [1978] C.L.Y. 2039.

NORTHERN IRELAND (EMERGENCY PROVISIONS) ACT 1978—June 1, 1978: [1978] C.L.Y. 2169.

NUCLEAR SAFEGUARDS AND ELECTRICITY (FINANCE) ACT 1978—June 30, 1978: [1978] C.L.Y. 116.

OATHS ACT 1978—July 30, 1978: [1978] C.L.Y. 1430.

PARTICIPATION AGREEMENTS ACT 1978—February 23, 1978: [1978] C.L.Y. 2939.

PATENTS ACT 1977—June 1, 1977: [1978] C.L.Y. 2245. Ss. 1–52, 53 (part), 54–59, 60 (part), 61–76, 77 (part), 78 (part), 79–83, 89–113, 115–129, 131, 132 (part), Scheds. 1–5, 6 (part).

PENSIONERS PAYMENTS ACT 1978—November 23, 1978: [1978] C.L.Y. 2275.

PLANT VARIETIES AND SEEDS ACT 1964—July 1, 1978: [1978] C.L.Y. 68. S. 31 (1).

PROTECTION OF CHILDREN ACT 1978—August 20, 1978: [1978] C.L.Y. 583.

RATING (DISABLED PERSONS) ACT 1978—April 1, 1979: [1978] C.L.Y. 2470a.

REFUSE DISPOSAL (AMENITY) ACT 1978—April 23, 1978: [1978] C.L.Y. 1881.

RENTCHARGES ACT 1977—February 1, 1978: [1978] C.L.Y. 2495. (Remainder).

REPRESENTATION OF THE PEOPLE ACT 1978—July 20, 1978: [1978] C.L.Y. 877a.

ROAD TRAFFIC (DRIVERS' AGES AND HOURS OF WORK) ACT 1976—January 26, 1978: [1978] C.L.Y. 2608. S. 2.

SEXUAL OFFENCES (AMENDMENT) ACT 1976—April 22, 1978: [1978] C.L.Y. 634. Ss. 5 (1) (b), 6 (4) (b).

SHIPBUILDING (REDUNDANCY PAYMENTS) ACT 1978—May 5, 1978: [1978] C.L.Y. 2768.

SOCIAL SECURITY PENSIONS ACT 1975—June 7, 1978: [1978] C.L.Y. 2797. Ss. 22, 65 (1) (part), Sched. 4, paras. 47, 49, 51–53, in so far as they relate to mobility allowance for certain persons.
September 20, 1978: [1978] C.L.Y. 2797. Ss. 22, 65 (1) (part), Sched. 4, paras. 47, 49, 51–53 in so far as they relate to mobility allowance for certain persons.

SOLOMON ISLANDS ACT 1978—July 7, 1978: [1978] C.L.Y. 179.

STATE IMMUNITY ACT 1978—November 22, 1978: [1978] C.L.Y. 1738.

SUPPRESSION OF TERRORISM ACT 1978—August 21, 1978: [1978] C.L.Y. 886.

THEATRES TRUST (SCOTLAND) ACT 1978—June 30, 1978: [1978] C.L.Y. 2442.

DATES OF COMMENCEMENT

THEFT ACT 1978—October 20, 1978: [1978] C.L.Y. 642.

TORTS (INTERFERENCE WITH GOODS) ACT 1977—June 1, 1978: [1978] C.L.Y. 2862. Remaining provisions.

TOWN AND COUNTRY PLANNING ACT 1971—May 23, 1978: [1978] C.L.Y. 2908. S. 20, Sched. 23, Pt. I (part).
June 28, 1978: [1978] C.L.Y. 2908. S. 20, Sched. 23, Pt. I (part) (applicable only to East Sussex).
June 28, 1978: [1978] C.L.Y. 2908. S. 20, Sched. 23, Pt. I (part) (applicable only to the West Midlands).

TRANSPORT ACT 1978—August 4, 1978: [1978] C.L.Y. 3023. Ss. 15, 17, 18, 21, 23, 24 (part), Sched. 4 (part).
September 1, 1978: [1978] C.L.Y. 3023. Ss. 1–4, 7, 8 (part), 10–14, 16, 22, 24 (4) (part); Scheds. 1, 2 (part), 4 (part).
October 1, 1978: [1978] C.L.Y. 3023. Ss. 19 and 20.
November 1, 1978: [1978] C.L.Y. 3023. Ss. 5, 6, 8 (part), 9, 24 (4) (part); Scheds. 2 (part), 3, 4 (part).

TRUSTEE SAVINGS BANKS ACT 1976—April 28, 1978: [1978] C.L.Y. 2659. S. 10 (1) (3), Sched. 6 (part).

TRUSTEE SAVINGS BANK ACT 1978—June 30, 1978: [1978] C.L.Y. 2660.
August 18, 1978: [1978] C.L.Y. 2659. Ss. 12 (3), 36 (1) (2), Scheds. 5, para. 15 (a), Sched. 6 (part).

TUVALU ACT 1978—June 30, 1978: [1978] C.L.Y. 181.

CURRENT LAW YEAR BOOK

1978

ADMINISTRATIVE LAW

1. British nationality. See ALIENS.

2. By-laws—apprehended breach of criminal law—injunction

Although the court will not intervene by way of injunction to restrain individual breaches of the criminal law, it may do so where there has been a breach of the law by a group of people and there appears to be an intention by the defendants to continue the breach.

The local authority made new by-laws prohibiting meetings, processions or dogs in the pleasure grounds, and provided a penalty of £20. The seven defendants organised a protest march of 200 to 300 people and an unspecified number of dogs, which proceeded through the prohibited area. There were no prosecutions, but the council refused to bow to further protests and withdraw the by-laws. The defendants notified the council of their intention to hold another protest walk. The council sought an injunction restraining the defendants from organising meetings or processions or entering the pleasure grounds or inciting others to enter with dogs. *Held*, granting the injunction, that there was a plain breach of the by-laws, which the defendants intended to repeat, and the relief sought would be granted. (*Stafford Borough Council* v. *Elkenford* [1977] C.L.Y. 2824 applied.)

BURNLEY BOROUGH COUNCIL v. ENGLAND (1978) 76 L.G.R. 393, Slade J.
[See also § 2206.]

3. Certiorari—employment classification—whether board required to act judicially or fairly

[Can.] [Public Service Act, R.S.A. 1970, c. 298, ss. 10, 11 and 12.] Equipment operators had their positions reclassified from grade three to grade two. They appealed to the Alberta Classification Appeal Board. The Board denied the appeal. They applied for an order of certiorari to quash the Board's order. The only issue argued was whether the Board was a body whose decisions were amenable to certiorari. *Held*, allowing the appeal, that (1) it is first necessary to determine whether the decision of the Board affects the rights of public servants, which it did; (2) even though the Board is not required to hold a hearing, it is required to act judicially; (3) even if the Board's functions were characterised as only administrative in nature, and not judicial, the doctrine of fairness applied to the Board. (*Cooper* v. *Wandsworth Board of Works* (1863) 14 C.B.(N.S.) 180; 143 E.R. 414 and *Local Government Board* v. *Arlidge* [1915] A.C. 120 considered): Re ALBERTA UNION OF PROVINCIAL EMPLOYEES AND ALBERTA CLASSIFICATION APPEAL BOARD (1978) 81 D.L.R. 184, Alberta Sup.Ct.

4. Council on Tribunals

The nineteenth annual report of the Council on Tribunals, the body which keeps under review the constitution and working of many different types of tribunals, has been published. It covers the period August 1, 1977, to July 31, 1978, and includes the work of the Scottish Committee. The report is available from HMSO (H.C. No. 74) [£1·00].

5. Deportation order—petition to European Commission of Human Rights

[Convention for Protection of Human Rights and Fundamental Freedoms 1951, art. 25.] An Indian married couple, against whom deportation orders were made, applied for a declaration that they should not be deported pending the determination of their petition to the European Commission for Human

Rights, and that they should not be separated from their children born in England while H and W were living illegally in the U.K. having overstayed their original leave by nine and three years respectively. Art. 25 of the Treaty imposes on countries recognising the competency of the Commission, an undertaking not to hinder in any way the effective exercise of the right to petition. *Held*, dismissing the application, a declaration would not be granted. Art. 25 did not have the force of law, but in this instance there had been no hindrance to the applicant's right to petition. It was a case of wrongdoers seeking to enforce the strict observance by the Home Office of the petitioners' rights: UPPAL *v.* HOME OFFICE, *The Times,* October 21, 1978, Sir Robert Megarry, V.-C.

6. Habeas corpus—hospital patient—next friend

Mrs. Farr was suffering from the terminal stages of multiple sclerosis in a home. Her husband wanted to take her home, but the health authority refused because of the state of her health. The husband applied for a writ of habeas corpus to the Divisional Court, who adjourned the application so that the Official Solicitor could report on whether Mrs. Farr wanted to go home and was in a mental state to go. The husband appealed, and it was *held* that the Court of Appeal had no original jurisdiction to grant a writ of habeas corpus; the original decision to adjourn was correct. On seeing the Official Solicitor's report, the case was referred back to the Divisional Court. The Court of Appeal stated that Mr. Farr was not in any event in the circumstances the proper person to act as next friend to his wife: FARR *v.* SOUTH EAST THAMES REGIONAL HEALTH AUTHORITY, *The Times,* April 27 and May 13, 1978, C.A.

7. Immigration

IMMIGRATION (REGISTRATION WITH POLICE) (AMENDMENT) REGULATIONS 1978 (No. 24) [10p], made under the Immigration Act 1971 (c. 77), s. 4 (3); operative on March 1, 1978; increase the fees payable where aliens (other than EEC nationals) are required to register with the police.

8. —— appeal—whether defence to staying after expiration of leave

[Immigration Act 1971 (c. 77), ss. 14 (1), 24 (1) (*b*) (i).] Defendant (a nonpatrial) overstayed his leave to remain in the U.K. and was convicted of an offence against s. 24 (1) (*b*) (i) of the Immigration Act 1971. *Held*, dismissing his appeal, that his purported appeal to an adjudicator under s. 14 (1) of the Act, made in respect of a further determination of the Secretary of State after his leave had expired, was invalid and could not provide a defence to the charge. (*Suthendran* v. *Immigration Appeal Tribunal* [1977] C.L.Y. 2026 applied): R. *v.* HAMID, *The Times,* October 19, 1978, C.A.

9. —— deportation—Commonwealth citizen—order made after five years' ordinary residence—decision notified within five years

[Immigration Act 1971 (c. 77), s. 7.] U, a Commonwealth citizen, was notified of the Secretary of State's decision to deport him within five years of U becoming ordinarily resident in the U.K. The deportation order was not made until after U had been ordinarily resident in the U.K. for five years. *Held*, that although s. 7 of the 1971 Act provided that Commonwealth citizens who had been resident in the U.K. for five years were not liable to deportation, U could not rely on s. 7 as the Secretary of State had decided to make the order within the five-year period: R. *v.* SECRETARY OF STATE FOR THE HOME OFFICE, *ex p.* UWABOR [1978] Crim.L.R. 360, D.C.

10. —— —— five years ordinary residence—how time to run

[Immigration Act 1971 (c. 77), s. 7.] The Home Secretary issued a deportation order on M before he had been five years in the country. M sought to appeal against the decision. *Held*, as the decision was made before M had been ordinarily resident for five years, M was not protected by s. 7 of the Act and could not appeal against it, although the order was made after he had been resident for five years: MEHMET *v.* SECRETARY OF STATE FOR THE HOME DEPARTMENT [1977] Imm.A.R. 68, C.A.

11. —— entry—indefinite leave—authority of officer

[Immigration Act 1971 (c. 77).] Where an immigration officer by mistake gives an entrant to the U.K. leave to remain indefinitely, and there is no evidence of fraud or similar default on either part, it cannot be said that he is acting without authority so that the leave is void ab initio. The Minister has therefore no power to detain the entrant nor to give directions for his removal. The applicant was accordingly granted a writ of habeas corpus: R. *v.* SECRETARY OF STATE FOR HOME AFFAIRS, *ex p.* RAM, *The Times,* August 3, 1978, D.C.

12. —— leave to enter—deception, misrepresentation or fraud
   [Immigration Act 1971 (c. 77), s. 33, Sched. 2, para. 10.]
   Where the Secretary of State has reasonable grounds for belief that leave to enter the United Kingdom has been obtained by deception, the court will not enquire further into those grounds.
   C, a Pakistani, had his passport stamped with an indefinite leave to enter the U.K. When his wife applied for entry clearance from Pakistan, enquiries were made which led the authorities to believe that the passport had been so stamped as a result of deception by C who had no right to live in the U.K. They took C into custody pending his deportation. *Held,* dismissing his appeal against the refusal of the court to issue a writ of habeas corpus, that the stamping of the passport must have been done with want of authority so that its purported permission was valueless, and as the Secretary of State had reasonable grounds for concluding that C was unlawfully here, the court would not interfere by entertaining an application for a writ of habeas corpus. *Per* Lord Denning M.R.: where an order for detention is prima facie good, it is for the applicant to challenge its validity by establishing a lawful authority to live in the U.K.
   R. *v.* SECRETARY OF STATE FOR THE HOME DEPARTMENT, *ex p.* CHOUDHARY [1978] 1 W.L.R. 1177, C.A.

13.   [Immigration Act 1971 (c. 77), Sched. 2, para. 16.]
   Where a person is detained by virtue of Sched. 2, para. 16, to the Act the court will not interfere if it is ratified that the Secretary of State had reasonable grounds for concluding that the detainee was in the country illegally.
   In 1970 the applicant entered the United Kingdom and produced to the immigration officer a passport in the name I.L. He was granted leave to stay for two months. He remained illegally. In 1972 he obtained a passport from the Pakistani authorities in the name S.H. In 1974 he went to Germany for three days. When he returned that passport was stamped " Given leave to enter the United Kingdom for an indefinite period." In 1976 he was arrested by the immigration officer pursuant to Sched. 2, para. 16, to the Act as a preliminary step to returning him to Pakistan. The applicant sought a writ of habeas corpus. He deposed to the fact that he had always been known as S.H. and that he had been brought to this country by a relative who had physical possession of his passport. There was no doubt that I.L. and S.H. were the same person. The Divisional Court was satisfied that the applicant was I.L. and that there was evidence on which the Secretary of State could find that there had been fraudulent use of the passport. The application was refused. The applicant appealed and brought fresh evidence before the court including a birth certificate which indicated that there was a possibility that the applicant was S.H. *Held,* dismissing the appeal, that (1) the court would not interfere despite there being a prima facie case that the applicant had permission to stay indefinitely if the Secretary of State had acted on reasonable grounds; (2) since in 1974 the applicant must have made a false statement to the immigration officer about his original entry the permission to stay was obtained by fraud or misrepresentation and was of no effect; (3) even if the applicant was I.L. the passport he produced in 1974 was not a valid passport to the applicant's knowledge so that the leave to enter was ineffective for the same reason. (*R. v. Secretary of State for the Home Department, ex p. Badaike* [1977] C.L.Y. 11 considered; decision of the Divisional Court affirmed on different grounds).
   R. *v.* SECRETARY OF STATE FOR THE HOME DEPARTMENT, *ex p.* HUSSAIN [1978] 1 W.L.R. 700, C.A.

14. —— —— **overstaying—charges proved.** See R. *v.* TZANATOS, § 523.

15. —— **meaning of " already in the United Kingdom "**
[Statement of Immigration Rules for Control on Entry; Commonwealth Citizens (1973) H.C. 79, para. 39.]
To be " already in the United Kingdom and settled here," a person must be physically present in this country.
M applied for permanent settlement in the United Kingdom on the grounds that his mother was " already in the United Kingdom and settled here." His mother had settled in the United Kingdom but had returned to Kenya in 1972 and died there in 1973. *Held,* allowing an appeal by the Immigration Appeal Tribunal, that to be within the meaning of that expression as used in para. 39 of the Statement of Immigration Rules for Control on Entry; Commonwealth Citizens, a person must not only be settled here but also physically present in this country at the date of application for admission.
R. *v.* IMMIGRATION APPEAL TRIBUNAL, *ex p.* MANEK [1978] 1 W.L.R. 1190, C.A.

16. —— **refusal of admission—whether " whole family " settled in England**
An Indian father came to England in 1969 and in due course his wife and two daughters followed him; the applicant, a son, stayed behind and so did an older son who managed the family farm. *Held,* that although the applicant was an unmarried and dependent son, it could not be said that " the whole family " were settled in England within para. 44 of the Control on Entry Rules, the older son being part of the family unit; accordingly, the applicant was rightly refused leave to enter the U.K. *Secus* if the older brother had left home and married and had his own family: HARMAIL SINGH *v.* VICE-PRESIDENT OF THE IMMIGRATION APPEAL TRIBUNAL, *The Times,* July 12, 1978, C.A.

17. —— **registration—false passport**
[Immigration Act 1971 (c. 77).] Where a person uses a passport which is not his own to obtain registration as a British citizen under s. 5A of the British Nationality Act 1948, that registration is a nullity, and such a person is therefore subject to the immigration control provisions of Schedule 2 to the Immigration Act 1971, and the provisions as to deprivation of citizenship under s. 20 do not apply. Habeas corpus for the applicant was refused: R. *v.* SECRETARY OF STATE FOR THE HOME DEPARTMENT, *ex p.* SULTAN MAHMOOD, *The Times,* August 2, 1978, C.A.

18. —— —— **when leave to remain has expired**
[Immigration (Registration with Police) Regulations 1972 (S.I. 1972 No. 1758).] The Immigration (Registration with Police) Regulations 1972 do not apply to an alien who remains in the United Kingdom after his leave to remain has expired: R. *v.* NAIK, *The Times,* July 26, 1978, C.A.

19. **Immigration Appeal Tribunal decisions**
ARSHAD *v.* IMMIGRATION OFFICER, LONDON (HEATHROW) AIRPORT [1977] Imm.A.R. 19 (entry clearance to join their parents was given to two Pakistani boys. Their mother had already returned to Pakistan when it was issued. Refusal of entry was *held* justified as both parents had to be settled and " in " the United Kingdom according to para. 38 (*a*), H.C. 81.)
O'CONNOR *v.* SECRETARY OF STATE FOR THE HOME DEPARTMENT [1977] Imm. A.R. 29 [Immigration Act 1971 (c. 77), ss. 7, 33.] (O entered in breach of a deportation order made in 1970. He committed burglary offences and was convicted in 1974 and 1975. In 1976 the Secretary of State made a deportation order on him as " conducive to the public good." It was *held,* that as he had remained in breach of the immigration laws until his deportation was revoked in 1974, O could not claim to have become ordinarily resident on January 1, 1973, so as to be protected by s. 33 of the Act from deportation. As he had been a year out of the country between 1970 and 1971, s. 7 did not help him as he had not remained, in breach of the immigration laws, in the country.)
SECRETARY OF STATE FOR THE HOME DEPARTMENT *v.* TWO CITIZENS OF CHILE [1977] Imm.A.R. 36 (in considering political asylum applications it was *held,* that the authority had to abide by the provisions of the Immigration Act 1971

and the rules made thereunder, although the Convention and Universal Declaration of Human Rights may well help in determining how they are to be applied.)

SINGH *v.* ENTRY CLEARANCE OFFICER, NEW DELHI [1977] Imm.A.R. 1 (the admission of a Sikh priest was held to be discretionary rather than mandatory under para. 29 (*a*) of H.C. 79 which permits ministers of religion permit free entry to the U.K. As in this case work as a priest was ancillary to the appellant's main reason for seeking entry, refusal of permission was a correct application of the discretion.)

TANEJA *v.* ENTRY CLEARANCE OFFICER, CHICAGO [1977] Imm.A.R. 9 [Immigration Act 1971 (c. 77), s. 2 (1).] (when the Act came into force T was in the U.S.A. studying. He visited the U.K. in 1972 for one week, and in 1974 he obtained, but did not use, a " returning resident " entry certificate. His application for a further such certificate was refused. He applied for the time limit of two years to be extended under a discretion afforded by para. 51 of H.C. 79. *Held*, there was no such discretion thereby afforded. As T was not in the U.K. when the Act came into force he was not given indefinite leave to enter or remain in the United Kingdom. (*R.* v. *Secretary of State for the Home Department, ex p. Mughal* [1973] C.L.Y. 3 applied.))

20. Lands Tribunal. See RATING AND VALUATION.

21. Natural justice—application for licence refused—boxing manager

In an application, as distinct from the forfeiture category of case, which involves no imputations of dishonesty or deprivation of statutory right, the courts will not normally require the observance of natural justice in the determination of the application.

Per curiam: The courts must be slow to allow any implied obligation to be fair to be used as a means of bringing before the courts honest decisions of bodies exercising jurisdiction over sporting and other activities.

The plaintiff had at times held various licences in relation to boxing and its promotion. All his licences were withdrawn in 1973. Five subsequent applications for a manager's licence were refused. The plaintiff sought a declaration that the board had acted in breach of natural justice in failing to inform him of the case against him or to grant an oral hearing. *Held*, the board was under a duty to reach an honest, unbiased conclusion. This case was in the application rather than forfeiture or even expectation class, not involving any slur on character, and the board therefore were not under an obligation to give reasons or grant an oral hearing.

MCINNES *v.* ONSLOW FANE [1978] 3 All E.R. 211, Megarry V.-C.

22. —— public inquiry—failure to give party an opportunity to deal with matters on which decision might be based

It is in breach of the rules of natural justice for a tribunal to act on evidence with which a party has had no opportunity to deal.

S Co., gravel extractors, applied for planning permission to extract gravel from grade 1 agricultural land. The application was refused on the ground that the agricultural quality and productivity of the land would be seriously reduced. At the inquiry, S Co. were at pains to show that they could restore the land. At the end of his re-examination in answer to the inspector, the Ministry witness raised for the first time the point that the gravel was necessary to supply water through capillary attraction to the topsoil, and without it the land could not be restored. No questions had been put to S Co.'s witnesses on the point, and it had at no time formed part of the case of the planning authority or the Ministry. However, it was on that point that the inspector decided against S Co. and the Secretary of State accepted that recommendation to dismiss the appeal. On S Co.'s application for an order to quash the decision, *held*, granting the order, that there had been nothing to put S Co. on notice that the question might be an important one, and the Secretary of State had been in breach of the rules of natural justice in acting on it without giving S Co. an opportunity of dealing with it.

H. SABEY & CO. *v.* SECRETARY OF STATE FOR THE ENVIRONMENT [1978] 1 All E.R. 586, Willis J.

23. —— —— refusal to allow objector to cross-examine

An inspector's refusal at a public inquiry to allow an objector to cross-examine witnesses may amount to a breach of natural justice.

At a public inquiry into a proposal for open-cast mining the applicant objector was prevented by the inspector from cross-examining witnesses called by various local authorities who also objected to the scheme. The inspector's recommendation to authorise the scheme was accepted by the Secretary of State. *Held*, allowing an application to quash, that natural justice entitled the applicant to cross-examine the witnesses, there being no reason for concluding that such cross-examination would have been irrelevant or repetitive. (*Hibernian Property Co.* v. *Secretary of State for the Environment* [1974] C.L.Y. 379 applied.)

NICHOLSON v. SECRETARY OF STATE FOR ENERGY (1977) 76 L.G.R. 693, Sir Douglas Frank, Q.C.

24. —— restraint of trade—domestic tribunal refusing professional boxer's licence

[N.Z.] P was a professional boxer, who obtained a licence as such from the New Zealand Boxing Association. In May 1968, the NZBA wrote to P in terms of its rules, giving details of several complaints it had received against P, and calling on him to show cause why his licence should not be cancelled. P's solicitors wrote to the NZBA, containing P's explanations of the complaints. In July 1968, the NZBA advised P that they were taking no action with regard to the complaints. The NZBA had however considered other complaints of which P had not been given notice and had decided—instead of cancelling P's licence—to allow it to expire and consider further action if P thereafter applied for a further licence. P so applied in May 1969: the NZBA refused the application without advising P of the date of the meeting or giving him any warning an adverse decision might be made. It gave no reasons for its decision. Further applications by P in 1969, 1970, 1972 and 1973 were all refused. P commenced an action claiming damages and a declaration that the NZBA had wrongfully refused to hear his application for a licence. *Held*, (1) as P had not claimed an injunction he could not be awarded damages in lieu thereof, and semble the Chancery Amendment Act 1958 (Lord Cairns's Act) should not be invoked to award damages in cases of invalid decisions of domestic tribunals. (*Hoffmann-La Roche* v. *The Secretary of State for Trade and Industry* [1974] C.L.Y. 3801; *Sutcliffe* v. *Thackrah* [1974] C.L.Y. 2552 referred to); (2) a refusal by the NZBA of a licence application for misconduct without giving P any opportunity of answering the charge is capable of being an unreasonable restraint of trade and a breach of natural justice (*Weinberger* v. *Inglis* [1919] A.C. 606; *Faramus* v. *Film Artistes' Association* [1964] C.L.Y. 3699; *Nagle* v. *Feilden* [1966] C.L.Y. 12099; *Dickson* v. *Pharmaceutical Society of Great Britain* [1968] C.L.Y. 3880 referred to): STININATO v. AUCKLAND BOXING ASSOCIATION [1978] 1 N.Z.L.R. 1, N.Z.C.A.

25. Public service appeal boards—obligation to provide written transcript of evidence recorded at hearing before board

[Can.] [Public Service Act, R.S.A. 1970, c. 298.] The applicant sought to quash the decision of the Public Service Grievance Board by way of certiorari. The Board, as required by the Alberta Rules of Court, filed the record with the clerk of the court and included the tapes of the hearing but did not include a written transcript of the contents of the tapes. On an application for advice and direction in which the court was asked to determine whether the Board was obliged to provide a written transcript of the tapes and, if so, who should bear the cost of producing the same, *held*, the Board was not obliged to provide a written transcript of the tapes. Further, it was not necessary to lay down any rule as to who should bear the cost of producing such a transcript. (*R.* v. *Medical Appeal Tribunal, ex p. Gilmore* [1957] C.L.Y. 2269 applied): ALBERTA UNION OF PROVINCIAL EMPLOYEES v. QUEEN IN RIGHT OF ALBERTA [1978] 3 W.W.R. 63, Alta.Sup.Ct.

26. Race relations—advertisement—whether act of discrimination—construction
[Race Relations Act 1968 (c. 71), s. 6 (1).]
Whether an advertisement is taken as indicating an intention to do an act of racial discrimination depends upon whether a reasonable person would draw such an inference from reading it.

The defendants published in their newspaper an advertisement for nursing staff to work in South Africa, the advertisement referring to the conditions of employment and including the words " all white patients." The Commission sought a declaration that the advertisement was unlawful as it could reasonably be taken to indicate an intention not to employ coloured nurses. The judge sitting with assessors dismissed the action. *Held*, dismissing the Commission's appeal, that the court would not reverse the finding of fact reached by the county court judge with the assistance of assessors experienced in the problems of race relations, since it had not been shown that the judge had erred in reaching such a conclusion.

COMMISSION FOR RACIAL EQUALITY *v*. ASSOCIATED NEWSPAPERS GROUP [1978] 1 W.L.R. 905, C.A.

27. —— discrimination—employment. See JOHNSON *v*. TIMBER TAILORS (MIDLANDS), § 983.

28. —— local authority dispersing schoolchildren—particulars to be given. See COMMISSION FOR RACIAL EQUALITY *v*. EALING LONDON BOROUGH COUNCIL, § 2408.

29. —— transitional provisions in Acts—inference of racial discrimination
[Race Relations Act 1976 (c. 74), Sched. 2, para. 3.] C1 and C2 were of Indian origin and came from the West Indies. They alleged that on September 4, 1976, on account of their colour or race or ethnic or national origins, they had been ordered by the defendants' manager, M, to leave a public-house owned by the defendants. A complaint under ss. 2 (1) and 15 (1) of the Race Relations Act 1968 was made to the Race Relations Board on October 21, 1976. The complaint was investigated under s. 15 (2) (*a*) by a conciliation committee of the Board, who on March 9, 1977, reported to the Board under s. 15 (5) of their failure to achieve conciliation. On April 28, 1977, the Board determined under s. 15 (5) to bring proceedings under s. 19 (1). The 1968 Act was repealed by the Race Relations Act 1976 with effect from June 13, 1977. Proceedings were commenced by the Commission for Racial Equality, as successors to the Board, under the transitional provisions contained in Sched. 2 to the 1976 Act, on August 30, 1977. The defendants contended that (1) there was a lacuna in Sched. 2, since para. 3 applied to " pending proceedings " at the date of repeal, which the instant proceedings were not; and para. 4 applied only to a complaint which had not been " disposed of " by the repeal date, whereas the instant complaint had been " disposed of " by the Board's determination on April 28, 1977, to bring proceedings, since if a complaint were " disposed of " subsequently, para. 3 would be unnecessary; (2) C2 had assaulted M, causing M to refuse further drinks to C2; when C1 ordered a further drink for C2, service was refused, whereupon C1 and C2 left. *Held*, (1) para. 4 of Sched. 2 to the 1976 Act applied, since a complaint under the 1968 Act was not " disposed of " by a determination to bring proceedings: the 1968 Act contemplated (a) investigation and conciliation and (b) enforcement, and a complaint was not " disposed of " until either there was a determination not to attempt enforcement, or until enforcement proceedings ended in success or failure at court; (2) on the facts, M's evidence of an assault by C2 was not credible: that reason for refusal to serve C1 and C2 being rejected, the court had to ask if there was any other reason. None had been suggested. In a case where two coloured people were refused service, and no reasonable or credible explanation was put forward, there was material on which could be drawn an inference of colour prejudice; and the court drew that inference: COMMISSION FOR RACIAL EQUALITY *v*. IND COOPE, May 9, 1978, Judge Ruttle, Westminster County Ct. (*Ex rel. Peter Susman, Esq., Barrister.*)

ARTICLES. See *post*, p. [11].

AGENCY

30. Authority—ratification—agent operating fraudulent resale system

[Can.] An employee of R Ltd., C, was held out by them to A Ltd. as authorised to deal in platinum on their behalf. C told A Ltd. that he was acting for R Ltd. in facilitating the supply of platinum to G, a scientist, and later the resale of it back to A Ltd. In fact, G was a fictitious creation of C, who was purchasing it from A Ltd. with R Ltd.'s money, and reselling it to A Ltd. under an assumed name. Enquiries by A Ltd. of R Ltd. concerning these fraudulent transactions, were referred to, and dealt with by, C. R Ltd. sued A Ltd. in respect of the fraudulent transactions, relying on the conversion by C and his consequent inability to give a good title to the platinum. *Held*, R Ltd. had set up C as having complete control over their platinum transactions. It was not open to them to ratify some of his actions and deny others. Their claim therefore failed: CANADIAN LABORATORY SUPPLIES *v.* ENGLEHARD INDUSTRIES OF CANADA (1977) 78 D.L.R. 232, Ontario C.A.

31. Capacity—call options—whether brokers acting as principal or agent

H, whose head office was in New York, were overseas members of the London Cocoa Terminal Market Association (" the association ") and members of the International Commodities Clearing House Ltd. (" the clearing house "), with branches in Amsterdam (HA) and London (HL). In early 1973, P, who were also overseas members of the association, instructed HA to grant call options in 64 lots of July cocoa. The order was passed to HL, who, in accordance with the market procedure, instructed a trading member of the association to conclude the contracts for the options. The concluded contracts were registered with the clearing house in H's name. HA informed P that the options had been sold " for your account." All the options were exercised by the dates stipulated in the contracts, and the declarations pursuant to the clearing house regulations were made to the clearing house, which in turn notified HL of the exercise of the options. A informed P that declarations had been made in the case of 20 call options only, and on July 12 P instructed HA to "liquidate this long position." Later, HA confirmed that 44 lots had been sold for P's account. H then advised HA that the 44 options had been declared. HA advised P that they were 44 lots short which P denied. On July 23, without P's authority, H purported to purchase 44 lots of July cocoa for P's account. P stated that the contract was not authorised and returned the contract note sent to them by H. H contended that they acted as P's agents procuring the conclusion of the options and when the options were exercised, P were bound whether or not they were informed. P argued that their relationship with H was principal to principal and since H had failed to give notice in relation to 44 options, the options were deemed to be abandoned and P were 44 lots long on July 12 when they instructed D to liquidate their position. On a special case stated, *held*, (1) H acted as principals when dealing with P; (2) H were obliged to give notice of the declarations by the time stipulated in the contract: LIMAKO BV *v.* HENTZ & Co. INC. [1978] 1 Lloyd's Rep. 400, Ackner J.

32. Commission—settlement of sale—meaning of " sale "

[Aus.] The respondents were entitled to commission in respect of the settlement of a sale which they had brought about as agents for the appellants. As consent to the transfer of the land was refused the sale went off. The purchaser's proposal that the appellants should transfer the land to a company for a consideration effectively the same as the original purchase price was accepted. The respondents claimed to be entitled to their originally agreed commission. *Held,* they were so entitled. As, at the time of the original contract for sale, it was within the contemplation of the parties that, consent being refused, the purchaser could propose a nominee, a transfer to such nominee constituted a sale. Further, the respondents were entitled to their commission once the appellants had accepted a satisfactory purchaser. This entitlement did not cease if the parties to the sale then varied its terms: LORD *v.* TRIPPE (1977) 5 A.L.J.R. 574, High Ct. of Aus.

33. —— whether payable—no binding commitment—mortgage broker

[Can.] D hired P to obtain $80,000 in mortgage funds and agreed to pay P's commission " upon a binding commitment letter " from an investor being given. P received a letter from a potential investor setting the terms as " all monies will be at 17 per cent. interest over a two year period, interest only." The investor did not go through with the deal, and P sued for its commission. *Held*, the action was dismissed. The letter did not constitute a binding commitment as it contained uncertainties such as the time when funds were to be advanced and what guarantees were required. (*Peter Long* v. *Burns* [1956] C.L.Y. 57 considered): GREENBRIER MORTGAGE INVESTMENTS v. J. E. ONGMAN & SONS [1978] 5 W.W.R. 309, Brit.Col.Sup.Ct.

34. Estate agents—commission—agreement with potential purchaser

N, now deceased, instructed HS, a firm of estate agents, to sell two houses in Horsham, it being agreed that the eventual purchasers would indemnify the vendors in respect of commission payable on completion. Two property companies, Sheraton and Mountjoy, competed for the houses but, unknown to N, HS reached an agreement with Mountjoy giving them an interest in Mountjoy acquiring the property. Owing to the intervention of N's solicitor, Sheraton were successful as the purchaser, making a higher offer than Mountjoy. HS claimed commission on the sale from M, N's personal representative. *Held*, dismissing the claim, (1) the agreement with Mountjoy was inconsistent with HS's duty to N; (2) HS's negotiations were not an effective cause of the sale: HENRY SMITH & SONS v. MUSKETT (1977) 246 E.G. 655, Mackenna J.

35. —— —— when payable—incomplete transaction

[Can.] An owner of land agreed to pay a commission to an estate agent " on any sale . . . howsoever effected during the currency of this authority." The agreement further provided that " a sale shall be deemed to include entering into an agreement to exchange this property or the granting of an option to purchase this property during the currency of this listing if said exchange or option is subsequently completed." A conditional agreement of sale with a prospective purchaser having fallen through because of non-satisfaction of the condition, the estate agent brought an action for a commission. *Held*, dismissing the action, the reference to subsequent completion of exchanges or options showed that the word " sale " contemplated not a mere agreement, but a transaction that was ultimately completed. The failure to close was not attributable to the fault of the vendor, and the agents had not obtained a purchaser who, at any relevant time, was ready, willing and able to complete the purchase: C. AND S. REALTIES OF OTTAWA v. McCUTCHEON (1978) 84 D.L.R. (3d) 584, Ontario High Ct.

36. General agency—lease—service of notices. See TOWNSEND CARRIERS v. PFIZER, § 1790.

37. Undisclosed agent—building contract—personal liability

A chartered civil engineer who made a contract with a building company on behalf of the owners of a property was held personally liable since he had not made it clear that he was acting as an agent. It was not enough that he had signed the letters constituting the contract with his professional qualification: SIKA CONTRACTS v. GILL, *The Times*, April 27, 1978, Kerr J.

ARTICLES. See *post*, p. [11].

AGRICULTURE

38. Agricultural holdings

AGRICULTURAL HOLDINGS (ARBITRATION ON NOTICES) ORDER 1978 (No. 257) [25p], made under the Agricultural Holdings (Notices to Quit) Act 1977 (c. 12), ss. 5, 11 (6), and the Tribunals and Inquiries Act 1971 (c. 62), s. 10; operative on April 7, 1978; consolidates S.I. 1964 No. 706 with amendments necessitated by s. 5 (1) (*f*) (i) of the 1977 Act.

AGRICULTURE (FORMS OF NOTICES TO REMEDY) REGULATIONS 1978 (No. 258) [25p], made under the Agricultural Holdings (Notices to Quit) Act 1977, s. 2 (6); operative on April 7, 1978: revoke and re-enact S.I. 1964 No. 707.

AGRICULTURAL HOLDINGS (ENGLAND AND WALES) (AMENDMENT) RULES 1978

(No. 444) [10p], made under the Agricultural Holdings Act 1948 (c. 63), Sched. 6, para. 27; operative on April 19, 1978; amend S.R. & O. 1948 No. 1943 by substituting for the word " acres " in Forms B and C set out in Sched. 2 the word " hectares."

AGRICULTURE (CALCULATION OF VALUE FOR COMPENSATION) REGULATIONS 1978 (No. 809) [60p], made under the Agricultural Holdings Act 1948, ss. 51 (1), 79, as read with S.I. 1978 No. 272; operative on July 1, 1978; make provision for calculating the value of compensation payable to the outgoing tenant of an agricultural holding in respect of short-term improvements and other matters set out in the Fourth Sched. to the 1948 Act as amended.

39. —— applications for tenancy succession

[Agriculture (Miscellaneous Provisions) Act 1976 (c. 55), ss. 18, 20, 22.] The widow and son of a deceased tenant applied for the Agricultural Land Tribunal's direction entitling them to a tenancy of the holding. The landlords applied for the tribunal's consent to notices to quit. *Held*, dismissing the landlords' application, and that of the widow, but allowing the son's application, (1) neither the widow nor the son was ineligible by virtue of occupation of a commercial unit, since their occupation arose only after the tenant's death; (2) the widow was ineligible as her principal source of livelihood was not derived from agricultural work but from her marital relationship with the deceased tenant; (3) having carefully considered the evidence, the tribunal found the son a suitable tenant despite the landlords' criticism of his financial standing; (4) the landlords' application failed because their intention was to sell the farm and assist their tax position not to farm and manage the land (*National Coal Board* v. *Naylor* [1972] C.L.Y. 52 applied): HULME v. EARL OF AYLESFORD AND TRUSTEES OF EARL OF AYLESFORD'S SETTLEMENT (1965) (1978) 245 E.G. 851, Agricultural Lands Tribunal.

40. —— existence of tenancy—grazing for part of year

[Agricultural Holdings Act 1948 (c. 63), s. 2 (1).] For many years there was an " amicable arrangement " between M's father and S's predecessor in title (both now dead) that three fields now owned by S could be used by M's father at a rent of £30 per annum payable in advance. S removed M's agricultural machinery and cattle from the fields. S appealed against the judge's finding that the arrangement constituted a tenancy from year to year and that consequently S's actions amounted to trespass. *Held*, dismissing the appeal, all the evidence supported the judge's finding. S's submission that the proviso to s. 2 (1) of the 1948 Act applied as the agreement was for grazing or mowing only during some specified period of the year also failed, and his submission that M's right of occupation was not exclusive had not been taken in the court below: MIDGLEY v. STOTT (1977) 244 E.G. 883, C.A.

41. —— licence—tenancy from year to year

[Agricultural Holdings Act 1948 (c. 63), s. 2 (1).] J claimed possession of pasture land used by L for grazing his sheep pursuant to an agreement the nature of which was subject to dispute. The county court judge dismissed J's claim holding that on balance the true construction of the agreement was the grant of a tenancy for seven years to L. *Held*, dismissing J's appeal, the evidence did not disclose a tenancy for seven years as there was no commencement date and the rent was varied in the third year. J had granted L a licence to occupy the land for use as agricultural land which, by operation of s. 2 (1) of the 1948 Act, resulted in the creation of a tenancy from year to year. The proviso to s. 2 (1) did not apply because the judge found that no specified period short of a year was mentioned in the grant. (*Scene Estates* v. *Amos* [1957] C.L.Y. 46 applied): JAMES v. LOCK (1977) 246 E.G. 395, C.A.

42. —— prohibition against serving counter-notice—whether clause enforceable

[Agricultural Holdings Act 1948 (c. 63), s. 24 (1).]

A covenant in the lease of an agricultural holding purporting to prevent a tenant from serving a counter-notice to a notice to terminate under s. 24 (1) of the Agricultural Holdings Act 1948 will be invalid as being contrary to public policy.

L granted T a lease of a farm for a term of 10 years. T covenanted to give up possession immediately on termination of the tenancy, and not to serve a

counter-notice under s. 24 (1) of the Agricultural Holdings Act 1948. L
served a notice terminating the tenancy on the appointed date. T served a
counter-notice under s. 24 (1). L contended that the counter-notice was invalid
since the Act did not prohibit parties from contracting out of s. 24 (1), and
a party might renounce a right which existed solely for his own benefit. *Held,*
despite the absence of express prohibitory words, the right afforded by s. 24 (1)
was not merely private but a matter of public interest, because Parliament's
policy had been to encourage good husbandry by conferring security of tenure
on tenant farmers. The covenant in the lease was an attempt to oust the
agricultural land tribunal's jurisdiction under s. 24 (1), and was invalid as
being contrary to public policy.
    JOHNSON *v.* MORETON [1978] 3 All E.R. 37, H.L.

43. —— rents
    The Ministry of Agriculture, Fisheries and Food has published the results of
the 1978 Annual Rent Enquiry, conducted jointly by the Land Service of the
Agricultural Development and Advisory Service and the Ministry's Economics
and Statistics Group. This shows an average increase in agricultural rents,
between October 1977 and October 1978, of 18·5 per cent., compared with an
increase of 18·8 per cent. during the previous year.

44. —— —— payment by post
    [Agricultural Holdings Act 1948 (c. 63), s. 24 (2).] A tenant habitually paid
his rent by putting a cheque in the post. After a default, the landlords' agent
served a notice to pay within two months under the provisions of the Agricultural Holdings Act 1948. On the last day, the tenant posted a cheque to
one of the landlords. *Held,* that although on general principles the landlord
should have the rent in cash in his hands by the due date, there was a course
of dealing which showed that posting the cheque was accepted as payment,
and accordingly payment had been effected as required by s. 24 (2) of the
Act: BEEVERS *v.* MASON, *The Times,* July 19, 1978, C.A.

45. Agricultural Holdings Act 1948—amendment
    AGRICULTURAL HOLDINGS ACT 1948 (AMENDMENT) REGULATIONS 1978 (No.
447) [10p], made under the Agriculture (Miscellaneous Provisions) Act 1976
(c. 55), s. 7 (1) (2) (*a*) (5); operative on April 19, 1978; amends the 1948 Act
by substituting for references to areas expressed in imperial units references to
areas expressed in metric units.

46. —— variation
    AGRICULTURAL HOLDINGS ACT 1948 (VARIATION OF FOURTH SCHEDULE)
ORDER 1978 (No. 742) [20p], made under the Agricultural Holdings Act 1948
(c. 63), s. 78 (1); operative on July 1, 1978; varies the Fourth Schedule to the
1948 Act which lists those improvements and other matters for which a tenant
of an agricultural holding may be entitled to compensation from a landlord at
the termination of the tenancy without requiring the consent of the landlord
before the improvements are made.

47. Agricultural Holdings (Notices to Quit) Act 1977—commencement
    AGRICULTURAL HOLDINGS (NOTICES TO QUIT) ACT 1977 (COMMENCEMENT)
ORDER 1978 (No. 256 (C. 7)) [10p], made under the Agricultural Holdings
(Notices to Quit) Act 1977 (c. 12), s. 15 (2); operative on April 7, 1978; brings
into force the provisions of the 1977 Act which consolidate ss. 23–33 of the
Agricultural Holdings Act 1948, and certain other enactments relating to notices
to quit agricultural holdings in England and Wales.

48. Agricultural land and buildings—rating and valuation. See § 2460.

49. Agricultural land tribunals
    AGRICULTURAL LAND TRIBUNALS (RULES) ORDER 1978 (No. 259) [75p],
made under the Agriculture Act 1947 (c. 48), s. 73 (3) (4), as amended, the
Agricultural Holdings Act 1948 (c. 63), s. 50 (3), as amended, and the Agriculture (Miscellaneous Provisions) Act 1954 (c. 39), s. 6 (4) (6), and the Tribunals
and Inquiries Act 1971 (c. 62), s. 10; operative on April 7, 1978; consolidates
the instruments relating to rules of procedure for Agricultural Land Tribunals.

50. Agricultural wages—foreign students
The Agricultural Wages Board have issued the Agricultural Wages (Foreign Students) Order 1978 (1978 AWB No. 2), made under the Agricultural Wages Act 1948 (c. 47), ss. 3, 7. This became operative on June 2, 1978. It contains certain modifications to the Agricultural Wages Order 1978 (1978 AWB No. 1) in its application to foreign students, as defined, and supersedes the Agricultural Wages Board (Foreign Students) Order 1977 (1977 AWB No. 3).

51. Agriculture Act 1967—amendment
AGRICULTURE ACT 1967 (AMENDMENT) REGULATIONS 1978 (No. 244) [10p], made under Agriculture (Miscellaneous Provisions) Act 1976 (c. 55), s. 7 (1) (2) (*a*); operative on April 1, 1978; amend s. 51 (7) (*a*) of the 1967 Act by substituting for the word " acreage " the word " acre " and amend s. 52 (2) (*d*) of the 1967 Act by substituting references to areas expressed in imperial units for references to areas expressed in metric units.
AGRICULTURE ACT 1947 (AMENDMENT) REGULATIONS 1978 (No. 446) [10p], made under the Agriculture (Miscellaneous Provisions) Act 1976, ss. 7 (1) (2) (*a*); operative on April 19, 1978; amend the 1947 Act by substituting for references to areas expressed in imperial units references to areas expressed in metric units.

52. Agriculture (Miscellaneous Provisions) Act 1976—commencement
AGRICULTURE (MISCELLANEOUS PROVISIONS) ACT 1976 (COMMENCEMENT No. 2) ORDER 1978 (No. 402 (C. 49) (S. 42)) [10p], made under the Agriculture (Miscellaneous Provisions) Act 1976 (c. 55), s. 27 (3); operative on April 7, 1978; brings into force ss. 13, 14 as respects Scotland.

53. Animals. See ANIMALS.

54. Cattle. See ANIMALS.

55. Cereals
HOME-GROWN CEREALS AUTHORITY (RATE OF LEVY) ORDER 1978 (No. 883) [20p], made under the Cereals Marketing Act 1965 (c. 14), s. 13; operative on August 1, 1978; specifies the rate of levy to be raised for the year beginning August 1, 1978, in respect of home-grown wheat, home-grown barley and home-grown oats.

56. Common agricultural policy
COMMON AGRICULTURAL POLICY (WINE) REGULATIONS 1978 (No. 861) [40p], made under the European Communities Act 1972 (c. 68), s. 2 (2); operative on July 24, 1978; provide for the enforcement of EEC Regulations concerned with the production and marketing of wine and related products.
COMMON AGRICULTURAL POLICY (AGRICULTURAL PRODUCE) (PROTECTION OF COMMUNITY ARRANGEMENTS) (AMENDMENT) ORDER 1978 (No. 1660) [20p], made under the Agriculture Act 1957 (c. 57), ss. 5 and 35 (3); operative on November 23, 1978; art. 3 of S.I. 1973 No. 288 empowers the Intervention Board for Agricultural Produce to require any person engaged in the purchasing, selling or using of any commodity specified in the Schedule to that Order to keep, and produce on demand, records relating to those activities. Art. 5 of that Order empowers authorised officers to require any person engaged in the production, storage, grading, packing, slaughter or sale of any such commodity to produce books, accounts or records relating to those activities. This Order provides that the above-mentioned requirements apply to any person engaged in the relevant activities whether engaged as principal or agent.

57. Development
The Ministry of Agriculture's Annual Report on Research and Development 1976 has been published. The report shows the progress of the commissioning of research, the conclusions of reviews of commissioned research, and the funds made available by the Ministry during 1976/77 for research and development in various areas. The report is available from HMSO [£1·50.]

58. Eggs
EGGS AUTHORITY (RATES OF LEVY) ORDER 1978 (No. 389) [15p], made under the Agriculture Act 1970 (c. 40), ss. 2, 10, 13 (1); operative on April 1, 1978;

specifies the rate of levy to be raised in respect of the period ending on March 31, 1979, to finance the functions of the Eggs Authority.

EGGS (MARKETING STANDARDS) (AMENDMENT) REGULATIONS 1978 (No. 1248) [20p], made under the European Communities Act 1972 (c. 68), s. 2 (2); operative on September 20, 1978; amend S.I. 1973 No. 15.

59. European Communities. See EUROPEAN COMMUNITIES.

60. Farm improvements

FARM AND HORTICULTURE DEVELOPMENT REGULATIONS 1978 (No. 1086) [40p], made under the European Communities Act 1972 (c. 68), s. 2 (2); operative on September 4, 1978; implement in the U.K. the provisions of Directive No. 72/159/EEC on the modernisation of farms and Directive No. 75/268/EEC on mountain and hill farming in certain less-favoured areas. They supersede S.I. 1973 No. 2205.

61. Fertilisers

FERTILISERS (SAMPLING AND ANALYSIS) REGULATIONS 1978 (No. 1108) [£1·85], made under the Agriculture Act 1970 (c. 40), ss. 66 (1), 67 (5), 74A, 75 (1), 76 (1), 77, 78 (2) (4) (6), 79 (1) (2) (9), 84 (s. 74A having been inserted by the European Communities Act 1972 (c. 68), s. 4 (1) and Sched. 4, para. (6) as read with S.I. 1978 No. 272; operative on September 6, 1978; supersede in part S.I. 1973 No. 1521 and S.I. 1976 No. 840 by providing a new sampling procedure for solid fertilisers and additional methods of analysis.

62. Grants

FARM CAPITAL GRANT (VARIATION) SCHEME 1978 (No. 380) [15p], made under the Agriculture Act 1970 (c. 40), ss. 28, 29; operative on March 16, 1978; varies S.I. 1973 No. 1965 in order to provide for grant at the rate of 50 per cent. of expenditure incurred in cases where a programme of work is considered necessary to restore the productivity of land affected by flooding.

FARM CAPITAL GRANT (VARIATION) (NO. 2) SCHEME 1978 (No. 768) [20p], made under the Agriculture Act 1970, ss. 28, 29; operative on June 7, 1978; varies S.I. 1973 No. 1965 so as to provide grants at a higher rate than that currently provided to facilitate repair or replacement of buildings or other facilities damaged by severe weather conditions between October 1, 1977, and March 31, 1978.

63. Northern Ireland. See NORTHERN IRELAND.

64. Pest control

PREVENTION OF DAMAGE BY PESTS (THRESHING AND DISMANTLING OF RICKS) (REVOCATION) REGULATIONS 1978 (No. 1614) [10p], made under the Prevention of Damage by Pests Act 1949 (c. 55), s. 8 (1) (2) as read with S.I. 1978 No. 272; operative on January 1, 1979; revokes S.I. 1950 No. 1172 as amended.

65. Plant breeders

PLANT BREEDERS' RIGHTS (APPLICATIONS IN DESIGNATED COUNTRIES) (AMENDMENT) ORDER 1978 (No. 1649) [10p], made under the Plant Varieties and Seeds Act 1964 (c. 14), Sched. 2, Pt. I, para. 2 (7) as amended by S.I. 1964 No. 1574 and S.I. 1969 No. 1829; operative on November 20, 1978; amends S.I. 1968 No. 2077 by the substitution of a new Sched. 2, Pt. I, para. 2, art. 2 to the 1964 Act which enables an application for a grant of plant breeders' rights made in a country to which the paragraph applies to be treated as if made in the U.K.

66. Plant health

PROGRESSIVE WILT DISEASE OF HOPS ORDER 1978 (No. 505) [25p], made under the Plant Health Act 1967 (c. 8), s. 3 (1) (2) (4), as amended by the Criminal Justice Act 1967 (c. 80), s. 92 (2), Sched. 3, Pt. II, and by the European Communities Act 1972 (c. 68), s. 4 (1), Sched. 4, para. 8, as read with the Agriculture (Miscellaneous Provisions) Act 1972 (c. 62), s. 20; operative on April 28, 1978; supersede S.I. 1965 No. 1184, and requires occupiers and certain other persons to give to the Minister of Agriculture, Fisheries and Food notice of the presence, or suspected presence, on their farms of progressive wilt disease of hops and to destroy dead or dying bines and leaves of hop plants on infected farms.

67. Plant varieties and seeds

SEED POTATOES REGULATIONS 1978 (No. 215) [45p], made under the Seeds Act 1920 (c. 54), s. 7 (1), and the Plant Varieties and Seeds Act 1964 (c. 14), ss. 16 (1)–(5) (8), 36, as amended by the European Communities Act 1972 (c. 68), s. 4 (1), Sched. 4, para. 5 (1)–(3); operative on March 22, 1978; revoke S.I. 1963 Nos. 1374 and 1590 which are replaced and give effect to Directive 66/403/EEC regulating the marketing of seed potatoes in Great Britain.

PLANT BREEDERS' RIGHTS REGULATIONS 1978 (No. 294) [60p], made under the Plant Varieties and Seeds Act 1964, ss. 3 (6), 5 (1) (4), 9 (1)–(5), 10 (5), 36, Sched. 2, Pt. I, para. 3, as amended by the Agriculture (Miscellaneous Provisions) Act 1968 (c. 34), s. 43, Sched. 7, as extended to Northern Ireland by S.I. 1964 No. 1574; operative on April 1, 1978; prescribe the form and manner in which applications are to be made for grants of plant breeders' rights.

PLANT BREEDERS' RIGHTS (FEES) REGULATIONS 1978 (No. 295) [25p], made under the Plant Varieties and Seeds Act 1964, ss. 9 (1), 36, as extended by S.I. 1964 No. 1574 and S.I. 1969 No. 1829; operative on April 1, 1978; supersede S.I. 1977 No. 359 and make similar provisions.

SEEDS (NATIONAL LISTS OF VARIETIES) (FEES) REGULATIONS 1978 (No. 296) [25p], made under the Plant Varieties and Seeds Act 1964, s. 16 (1) (1A) (e) (8), as amended by the European Communities Act 1972, s. 4 (1), Sched. 4, para. 5 (1)–(3), as extended by S.I. 1964 No. 1574 and S.I. 1973 No. 609; operative on April 1, 1978; supersede S.I. 1977 No. 358 and prescribe the fees payable in certain specified circumstances in respect of matters arising under S.I. 1973 No. 994.

SEED POTATOES (FEES) REGULATIONS 1978 (No. 428) [10p], made under the Plant Varieties and Seeds Act 1964, s. 16 (1A) (e) (5) (a) (8), as amended by the European Communities Act 1972, s. 4 (1), Sched. 4, para. 5 (1)–(3); operative on April 13, 1978; prescribe fees in respect of matters arising under S.I. 1978 No. 215.

SEEDS (FEES) REGULATIONS 1978 (No. 1010) [30p], made under the Plant Varieties and Seeds Act 1964, s. 16 (1) (1A) (e) (5) (a) (8), as amended by the European Communities Act 1972, s. 4 (1), Sched. 4, para. 5 (1)–(3), and S.I. 1978 No. 272; operative on August 1, 1978; prescribes fees in respect of matters arising under specified statutory instruments.

Orders made under the Plant Varieties and Seeds Act 1964, ss. 1 (1) (5), 3 (1), 5 (7), as extended by S.I. 1964 No. 1574 and S.I. 1969 No. 1829:

S.I. 1978 Nos. 297 (broad beans and field beans) [10p]; 298 (brussel sprouts) [15p]; 299 (cabbages) [15p]; 300 (celery—including celeriac) [10p]; 301 (fenugreek) [10p]; 302 (lupins) [15p]; 303 (maize) [10p]; 304 (marrows) [15p]; 305 (red fescue—including chewings fescue) [15p]; 306 (turnips) [15p]; 307 (velvet bent, red top, creeping bent, and brown top) [15p]; 308 (wood meadow-grass, swamp meadow-grass, smooth stalked meadow-grass, rough stalked meadow-grass) [15p].

68. Plant Varieties and Seeds Act 1964—commencement

PLANT VARIETIES AND SEEDS ACT 1964 (COMMENCEMENT NO. 4) ORDER 1978 (No. 1002 (C. 26)) [10p], made under the Plant Varieties and Seeds Act 1964 (c. 14), s. 41 (2); operative on July 1, 1978; brings into force s. 31 (1) of the 1964 Act which repeals the Seeds Act 1920 and certain other specified obsolete enactments.

69. —— repeals

PLANT VARIETIES AND SEEDS ACT 1964 (REPEALS) (APPOINTED DAY) ORDER 1978 (No. 1003 (C. 27)) [10p], made under the European Communities Act 1972 (c. 68), s. 4, Sched. 3, Pt. III; operative on September 1, 1978; appoints a day for the repeal of certain provisions of the 1964 Act and the Trade Descriptions Act 1968 which are not compatible with the U.K.'s obligations to the EEC.

70. Poultry

SLAUGHTER OF POULTRY ACT 1967 EXTENSION ORDER 1978 (No. 201) [10p], made under the Slaughter of Poultry Act 1967 (c. 24), s. 7 (1); operative on

March 1, 1978; extends the Act to the slaughter of guinea-fowl, ducks and geese kept in captivity.

71. Sugar beet

SUGAR BEET (RESEARCH AND EDUCATION) ORDER 1978 (No. 320) [15p], made under the Sugar Act 1956 (c. 48), s. 18 (1) and (2); operative on April 1, 1978; provides for the assessment and collection of contributions for the year beginning on April 1, 1978, from the British Sugar Corporation and from growers of home-grown beet towards the programme of research and education set out in the Schedule.

72. Tenancy—qualifying worker—meaning of " engaged whole time in agriculture " —pheasants for sport

[Rent (Agriculture) Act 1976 (c. 80), s. 1.]

A gamekeeper employed to rear pheasants for sport is not an agricultural worker entitled to security of tenure within the Rent (Agriculture) Act 1976.

As a term of the defendant's employment as a gamekeeper he was provided with a rent-free cottage. His wages were paid by the employer's farm manager and were decided according to agricultural rates, but he did not work on the farm itself. After termination of his employment, the defendant resisted his employer's claim for possession of the cottage, claiming the protection afforded to agricultural workers under the 1976 Act. The county court judge determined that since the defendant's employment was for the purpose of rearing game for sport and not food, he was not engaged in " agriculture." *Held*, dismissing the defendant's appeal, that " agriculture " in the 1976 Act does not embrace every rural activity, and that the defendant's employment was excluded therefrom.

LORD GLENDYNE *v.* RAPLEY [1978] 1 W.L.R. 601, C.A.

73. The defendant had been employed as gamekeeper by the plaintiff. He occupied, as licensee, a cottage on the estate. It was conceded that the licence was " a relevant licence " within the meaning of the Rent (Agriculture) Act 1976. The defendant was dismissed, and the plaintiff sought possession of the cottage. The defendant defended the proceedings on the grounds that he was a " qualifying worker " within the meaning of the Act, and in the circumstances was entitled to a statutory tenancy. The only matter at issue was whether the defendant was " engaged whole time in agriculture." The evidence was that part of the defendant's time was spent controlling rabbits. It was conceded that this was agricultural work as defined in the Act since this work was done solely to control crop damage, and the defendant was therefore assisting in the production of " consumable produce." The majority of the defendant's time was spent in rearing, feeding and preserving pheasants. *Held*, (1) that although he was " keeping " the pheasants within the meaning of the Act, the pheasants were not " livestock " within the meaning of the Act, since " livestock " is defined as animals (including birds) which are kept " for the production of food "; (2) the pheasants were kept for the purpose of sport, and the fact that they were ultimately sold and eaten was purely ancillary and a by-product of the sporting activity, and they could not be said to be kept " for the production of food." The plaintiff's claim for possession therefore succeeded: REEVE *v.* ATTERBY, February 7, 1978, Judge Hutchinson, Skegness County Ct. (*Ex rel. J. S. Hodgson, Esq., Solicitor.*)

74. Tractors

AGRICULTURAL OR FORESTRY TRACTORS (TYPE APPROVAL) (FEES) (AMENDMENT) REGULATIONS 1978 (No. 62) [15p], made under the Finance Act 1973 (c. 51), s. 56 (1) and (2); operative on February 16, 1978; provide for an increase in all fees payable under S.I. 1976 No. 1701.

BOOKS AND ARTICLES. See *post*, pp. [1], [11].

ALIENS

75. British nationality

BRITISH NATIONALITY (AMENDMENT) REGULATIONS 1978 (No. 91) [15p], made under the British Nationality Act 1948 (c. 56), s. 29 (1), as extended and amended by the Cyprus Act 1960 (c. 52), s. 4 (7), the British Nationality (No. 2)

Act 1964 (c. 54), s. 6 (2), and the British Nationality Act 1965 (c. 34), s. 5 (2); operative on March 1, 1978; increase the fees payable under S.I. 1975 No. 225 in respect of the conferment of citizenship of the United Kingdom and Colonies on adults by registration or naturalisation.

BRITISH PROTECTORATES, PROTECTED STATES AND PROTECTED PERSONS ORDER 1978 (No. 1026) [25p], made under the British Nationality Act 1948, ss. 29 (5), 30, 32 (1) and the British Nationality (No. 2) Act 1964, s. 5; operative on August 16, 1978; defines who are to be British protected persons for the purposes of the 1948 Act by virtue of their connection with the former Solomon Islands protectorate, other than under the Solomon Islands Act 1978, or by virtue of their connection with any other former protectorate, any former Arabian protectorate or any former trust territory or Brunei. Also provides for the registration as British protected persons of certain categories of persons who are stateless. The Order supersedes S.I. 1974 No. 1895.

76. Immigration. See ADMINISTRATIVE LAW.

ANIMALS

77. Bees

IMPORTATION OF BEES ORDER 1978 (No. 683) [20p], made under the Agriculture (Miscellaneous Provisions) Act 1954 (c. 39), s. 10, and S.I. 1978 No. 272; operative on July 1, 1978; supersedes S.I. 1955 No. 589 and prohibits the importation into Great Britain of bees in fixed-comb hives and bees that have not been certified as being free of disease.

78. Cattle

BEEF PREMIUMS (PROTECTION OF PAYMENTS) ORDER 1978 (No. 17) [25p], made under the Agriculture Act 1957 (c. 57), ss. 5, 6, 35 (3) as read with S.I. 1969 No. 388 and applied by the European Communities Act 1972 (c. 68), s. 6 (3); art. 13 operative on January 16, 1978; the remainder operative on February 1, 1978; re-enact with modifications the provisions previously made for the protection of premium payments under Community arrangements for the regulation of the market in beef.

BEEF PREMIUMS (RECOVERY POWERS) REGULATIONS 1978 (No. 18) [10p], made under the European Communities Act 1972, s. 2 (2); operative on February 1, 1978; enables the recovery of a beef premium payment if the animal in respect of which it was paid is used contrary to S.I. 1978 No. 17.

79. Diseases

DISEASES OF ANIMALS (APPROVED DISINFECTANTS) ORDER 1978 (No. 32) [35p], made under the Diseases of Animals Act 1950 (c. 36), ss. 1 (1), 20 (viii) and (ix), 85 (1); operative on January 31, 1978; provides for the testing of disinfectants for approval and for the marking of disinfectant containers. The Order also gives power to inspectors to take samples, and makes the false marking of a disinfectant container an offence against the 1950 Act.

DESIGNATION OF LOCAL AUTHORITY (SOUTHAMPTON PORT HEALTH DISTRICT) ORDER 1978 (No. 163) [10p], made under the Diseases of Animals Act 1950, s. 59 (4), as extended by the Agriculture (Miscellaneous Provisions) Act 1954 (c. 39), s. 11; operative on April 1, 1978; makes the Southampton District Council the local authority in respect of the Southampton Port Health District for the purposes of the 1950 Act.

BRUCELLOSIS (ENGLAND AND WALES) (AMENDMENT) ORDER 1978 (No. 541) [25p], made under the Diseases of Animals Act 1950, ss. 1, 5, 85 (1) as read with S.I. 1971 No. 531 and as extended by the Agriculture Act 1970 (c. 40), s. 106 (3); operative on April 18, 1978, save for art. 4 (2) which is operative on November 1, 1978; amends S.I. 1977 No. 1284 by declaring new eradication areas; consolidating parts of that Order and making provision in respect of certain livestock markets.

BRUCELLOSIS INCENTIVE PAYMENTS (AMENDMENT) SCHEME 1978 (No. 594) [10p], made under the Agriculture Act 1970, ss. 106 (1), (9) and (10); operative on May 18, 1978; amends art. 8 of S.I. 1977 No. 1303 by providing for the recovery of incentive payments only if it is established as a fact that they have been wrongly made.

DISEASES OF ANIMALS (EXPORT HEALTH CERTIFICATES) ORDER 1978 (No. 597) [25p], made under the Diseases of Animals Act 1950, s. 36A as extended by S.I. 1952 No. 1236 as adapted by the Agriculture (Miscellaneous Provisions) Act 1954, s. 11 as amended by the European Communities Act 1972 (c. 68), s. 4 (1), Sched. 4, para. 7 (3); operative on May 9, 1978; makes the exportation of bovine animals, swine, fresh meat and fresh poultry meat from Britain to other EEC countries subject to specified exception, conditional upon the existence of an appropriate health certificate.

BRUCELLOSIS (ENGLAND AND WALES) (AMENDMENT) (No. 2) ORDER 1978 (No. 689) [20p], made under the Diseases of Animals Act 1950, ss. 1, 5, 85 (1), as read with S.I. 1971 No. 531 and as extended by the Agriculture Act 1970, s. 106 (3); operative on May 26, 1978; amends S.I. 1977 No. 1284 in order to implement provisions of Council Directive 78/52/EEC which relate to the accelerated eradication of brucellosis.

DISEASES OF ANIMALS (FEES FOR THE TESTING OF DISINFECTANTS) ORDER 1978 (No. 708) [10p], made under the Agriculture (Miscellaneous Provisions) Act 1963 (c. 11), s. 16 (1) (5); operative on June 13, 1978; revises the fees payable for the testing of disinfectants for the purposes of determining their suitability for listing as approved disinfectants in S.I. 1978 No. 32.

DISEASES OF ANIMALS (APPROVED DISINFECTANTS) (AMENDMENT) ORDER 1978 (No. 934) [40p], made under the Diseases of Animals Act 1950, ss. 1 (1), 11 (vi) (vii), 20 (viii) (ix), 50 (1), 85 (1); operative on July 25, 1978; revokes and re-enacts with amendments the list of disinfectants contained in S.I. 1978 No. 32.

ENZOOTIC BOVINE LEUKOSIS ORDER 1978 (No. 975) [10p], made under the Diseases of Animals Act 1950, ss. 1 (1) (*a*), 17 (2), 77 (3); operative on July 15, 1978; applies s. 17 of the 1950 Act to enzootic bovine leukosis and prescribes the notice to be served on the owner of the bovine animal which is intended to be slaughtered.

ENZOOTIC BOVINE LEUKOSIS (COMPENSATION) ORDER 1978 (No. 976) [20p], made under the Diseases of Animals Act 1950, ss. 17 (3) and 19 (7); operative on July 15, 1978; provides that the amount of compensation which has to be paid under s. 17 (3) of the 1950 Act in respect of a bovine animal slaughtered due to enzootic bovine leukosis shall be an amount equal to its market value, ascertained in accordance with art. 3.

DISEASES OF ANIMALS (MISCELLANEOUS FEES) ORDER 1978 (No. 1188) [30p], made under the Agriculture (Miscellaneous Provisions) Act 1963, s. 16 (1) (5); operative on September 1, 1978; revokes and re-enacts S.I. 1976 No. 988 and increases most of the fees payable thereunder.

WARBLE FLY (ENGLAND AND WALES) ORDER 1978 (No. 1197) [25p], made under the Diseases of Animals Act 1950, ss. 1, 20, 84 (3); operative on September 1, 1978; makes the infestation of cattle with the larva of the warble fly a disease for most purposes of the 1950 Act.

BRUCELLOSIS (ENGLAND AND WALES) ORDER 1978 (No. 1480) [40p], made under the Diseases of Animals Act 1950 (c. 36), ss. 1, 5, 17 (2), 19 (7), 85 (1), as read with S.I. 1971 No. 531 and extended by the Agriculture Act 1970 (c. 40), s. 106 (3); operative on November 1, 1978; consolidates existing Orders relating to eradication areas and attested areas.

BRUCELLOSIS AND TUBERCULOSIS (ENGLAND AND WALES) COMPENSATION ORDER 1978 (No. 1483) [25p], made under the Diseases of Animals Act 1950, ss. 17 (3), 19 (7), 85 (1), S.I. 1978 No. 1480 and S.I. 1964 No. 1151; operative on November 8, 1978; revokes and substantially re-enacts, with some amendments, S.I. 1964 No. 1150 and S.I. 1972 No. 1500.

80. Dogs—control of guard dogs—whether handler must be present

[Guard Dogs Act 1975 (c. 50), s. 1 (1).]

On a true construction of s. 1 (1) of the Act a person may lawfully use a guard dog without a handler being present on the premises provided that the dog is properly secured.

G used three guard dogs at his premises without a handler present. They were chained on chains 12, 12 and 13 feet long respectively so that they could not reach the gates or go into every part of the premises. He was charged with three offences against s. 1 (1) of the Act. The justices found that the dogs were secured within the meaning of the section and dismissed the informations on the ground that in those circumstances it was not necessary for a handler to be on the premises. The prosecutor appealed. *Held*, dismissing the appeal, that (1) s. 1 (1) of the Act was ambiguous but since it was penal it should be construed in favour of the subject; (2) whether a dog on a 12-foot chain was "not at liberty to go freely about the premises" within the meaning of the section depended on the circumstances of the case bearing in mind that the purpose of it is to enable a person, even though he may be a trespasser or burglar, to remove himself from the dog's range.

HOBSON *v.* GLEDHILL [1978] 1 W.L.R. 215, D.C.

81. Endangered Species (Import and Export) Act 1976—modification

ENDANGERED SPECIES (IMPORT AND EXPORT) ACT 1976 (MODIFICATION) ORDER 1978 (No. 1280) [10p], made under the Endangered Species (Import and Export) Act 1976 (c. 72), s. 3; operative on September 29, 1978; modifies the Schedules to the 1976 Act.

ENDANGERED SPECIES (IMPORT AND EXPORT) ACT 1976 (MODIFICATION) (No. 2) ORDER 1978 (No. 1939) [25p], made under the Endangered Species (Import and Export) Act 1976, ss. 3, 11; operative on January 19, 1979; modifies the Schedules to the 1976 Act. The additions bring under control international trade in certain parts.

82. Export

EXPORT OF HORSES AND PONIES (INCREASE OF MINIMUM VALUE) ORDER 1978 (No. 1748) [10p], made under the Diseases of Animals Act 1950 (c. 36), ss. 37 (3), 37 (4A), 85 (1) as amended by the Ponies Act 1969 (c. 28), s. 1 (*a*); operative on December 27, 1978; increases the minimum value of certain horses and ponies for the purposes of the 1950 Act, s. 37 (3) (4A).

83. Farriers (Registration) Act 1975—commencement

FARRIERS (REGISTRATION) ACT 1975 (COMMENCEMENT No. 2) ORDER 1978 (No. 1928 (C. 48)) [10p]; made under the Farriers (Registration) Act 1975 (c. 35), s. 19 (3); operative on June 1, 1979; brings into force s. 16 of the 1975 Act regarding offences by unregistered persons.

84. Northern Ireland. See NORTHERN IRELAND.

85. Protection of birds

WILD BIRDS (COQUET ISLAND SANCTUARY) ORDER 1978 (No. 1074) [10p], made under the Protection of Birds Act 1954 (c. 30), s. 3 (1); operative on August 14, 1978; establishes the land leased by the Royal Society for the Protection of Birds on Coquet Island, Northumberland as a bird sanctuary.

WILD BIRDS (HANNINGFIELD RESERVOIR SANCTUARY) ORDER 1978 (No. 1075) [10p], made under the Protection of Birds Act 1954, s. 3 (1); operative on August 14, 1978; establishes the Hanningfield Reservoir in Essex as a bird sanctuary.

86. Veterinary surgeons. See MEDICINE.

86a. Welfare of animals

WELFARE OF LIVESTOCK (INTENSIVE UNITS) REGULATIONS 1978 (No. 1800) [20p], made under the Agriculture (Miscellaneous Provisions) Act 1968 (c. 34), s. 2; operative on January 1, 1979; makes provision for the welfare of agricultural livestock kept in intensive units.

BOOKS AND ARTICLES. See *post,* pp. [1], [11].

ARBITRATION

87. Action containing claim in tort—whether action should be stayed

[Arbitration Act 1975 (c. 3), s. 1.] The plaintiffs brought an action alleging that the defendants had induced the Government of Rhodesia to declare U.D.I. in November 1965 by assurances that oil would continue to be supplied even if the Beira pipeline could not be used, and that in consequence, the defendants were in breach of a contract, " the Shippers Agreement," providing for the construction and operation of the pipeline, and were guilty of the tort of conspiracy. The defendants applied for a stay of the action pursuant to s. 1 of the 1975 Act, on the ground that the claims ought to be decided by arbitration. *Held*, (1) assuming that the allegations of fact could be made out, the claim in tort had a close connection with the Shippers Agreement and so came within the arbitration clause therein. It was beyond argument that the claim in contract came within it; (2) s. 1 gave the court no discretion as to whether a claim within a non-domestic arbitration agreement should be arbitrated or litigated. Unless the court was satisfied that the arbitration clause was null and void, inoperative or incapable of being performed, or that there was not in fact any dispute between the parties, the action had to be stayed. The Shippers Agreement arbitration clause could not be said to be inoperative on the ground that the same issues would arise in the action for conspiracy as in the claim in contract if separately arbitrated, and that arbitration would therefore be a sterile duplication of proceedings. The action would be stayed: LONRHO *v.* SHELL PETROLEUM CO., *The Times,* February 1, 1978, Brightman J.

88. Agricultural holdings. See AGRICULTURE.

89. Appeal—procedure—deposit of award moneys—extension of time
By a contract dated May 24, 1973, in GAFTA form 119, S sold to P 2,000 m.t. 10 per cent. more or less at P's option, of soya bean meal at $370 per m.t. f.o.b. Piraeus. Cl. 18 provided, inter alia, that in the event of prohibition of export preventing fulfilment of the contract, the contract should be cancelled. The contract provided for disputes under the contract to be arbitrated in London pursuant to the Arbitration Rules no. 125 of GAFTA, which stated, inter alia, that if, on appeal from the arbitrators, either party requested a special case to be stated, the Board of Appeal could in its absolute discretion direct that any money payable under the arbitration award should be deposited with the Association (r. 8). The rules further provided that if the appellant failed to make the requisite deposit, the appeal would be deemed to be withdrawn, with a proviso (r. 10) that if he were precluded by currency regulations from making such payment, he could be granted an extension of up to 35 days. R. 19 provided that in the event of non-compliance with r. 8, the Board could in its absolute discretion extend or dispense with the time for compliance. On June 7, the export licence obtained by S was revoked, and no meal was loaded. P claimed that S were in breach of contract. S contended that cl. 18 applied. The dispute was referred to arbitration, and on March 13, 1974, an umpire awarded P $260,000 damages. S appealed to the Board of Appeal and an application for a special case to be stated was granted. S was ordered to deposit $260,000 pending the appeal. S's application for exchange control permission to transfer currency for the deposit was refused and S asked for an extension of time under r. 10. An extension was granted, and on November 28, a further extension expiring on January 2, 1975, was granted. On December 23, 1974, S applied for a third extension but this was not granted. The hearing was on February 3, 1975, and the Board made an award in favour of S and stated a special case. P applied for an order that the special case be set aside on the ground that (1) the Board had no jurisdiction to make the award, since the appeal was barred under r. 8, for only one extension was possible under r. 10; (2) S could not rely on r. 19 as they had not taken steps to get the licence restored. *Held*, on appeal, (1) r. 19 permitted the Board to dispense with the necessity for complying with the order to deposit $260,000 not later than October 11, 1974, and with the two later extensions; they were entitled to determine the appeal as if all the conditions in r. 19 had been complied with, notwithstanding that the time for complying with them had expired; (2) P were not entitled to damages for non-fulfilment of the contract: PROVIMI HELLAS A.E. *v.* WARINCO A.G. [1978] 1 Lloyd's Rep. 373, C.A.

90. Arbitration clause—building contract—summary judgment for part of claim.
See ELLIS MECHANICAL SERVICES *v.* WATES CONSTRUCTION, § 183.

91. Award—burden of proof—principles of Mareva injunction

Where a charterparty contains an arbitration clause, there is a difference between the choice of forum and the right to security, so that security may be ensured pending the arbitration.

The R was arrested, then released on terms that, if the plaintiffs had been entitled to hold it, they could retain a letter of undertaking given on behalf of the shipowners. If not, they were to return the letter. An arbitration clause was held to be incorporated into the charterparty and the defendants entitled to a stay pursuant to it, since it was not "incapable of being performed" although the defendants might not be able to satisfy an award made under it. Further *held* that there was a distinction between the choice of forum and the right to security and that the latter should be recognised by releasing the ship, if at all, only on terms.

THE RENA K. [1978] 3 W.L.R. 431, Brandon J.

92. —— enforceability of foreign award—guarantee by foreign bank—whether arbitrator able to decide whether he had jurisdiction

In July 1962, P, an Indian public company, agreed to sell to M two cement factories in Pakistan in consideration, principally, for the delivery by M to P of an annual quantity of 75,000 tons of cement over a period of three years. D, a Pakistani bank with branches in Calcutta and London, guaranteed performance by M by undertaking to pay 94 Pakistani rupees for every ton that delivery should fall short of the contract quantity. The guarantee further provided that all disputes arising in connection with the guarantee were to be settled by arbitration under the rules of the International Chamber of Commerce, questions arising from such arbitration to be governed by Indian law. No cement was ever delivered, and in March 1971 the arbitrator appointed by the I.C.C. made two awards amounting to £2,980,298·75, with interest from specified dates "until the date of actual payment." In an action brought by P to enforce the awards, *held*, on appeal, that (1) the I.C.C. rules covered a case where, as here, the arbitrator's jurisdiction was attacked on the basis that a once-binding agreement has ceased to be so by subsequent illegality; (2) there was no difference in principle between such an agreement and one which was void ab initio, and Indian law would not allow the arbitrator finally to determine his own jurisdiction; (3) accordingly there was no reason why this action should not be resisted on the ground that the arbitrator had no jurisdiction because the arbitration agreement had been abrogated by subsequent illegality; (4) but on the facts, the guarantee and the arbitration agreement had not been abrogated by the war or external aggression between India and Pakistan in 1965 and 1971; (5) it was not contrary to English public policy to enforce an award in favour of a national of one friendly state against a national of another friendly state, even though those states were enemies of one another; (6) the court would not interfere with the arbitrator's provisions relating to interest, even if it had discretion to do so, since the parties, by their arbitral agreement, had left the matter for the arbitrator to decide: DALMIA DAIRY INDUSTRIES v. NATIONAL BANK OF PAKISTAN [1978] 2 Lloyd's Rep. 223, C.A.

93. —— misconduct of arbitrators—whether absence of opportunity a serious procedural mishap—whether charterers had waived right to remit award

By a charterparty dated June 16, 1976, O, the owners of the A, time chartered the vessel to C. On May 4, 1977, O claimed from C hire and bunkers amounting to U.S. $30,821.72. On June 6, 1977, C counterclaimed for U.S. $12,718.99 in respect of a total interruption of discharge in Anneba, Algeria, from August 6 to August 27, 1976. The arbitrators found that the interruption was caused by a quality dispute between the receivers and the suppliers, as alleged by O, and not by damage to the cargo or due to "an accident hindering or preventing the working of the vessel" within cl. 11A (the off-hire clause), as contended for by C. The award was published, and on September 12, 1977, C paid the arbitrators' fees and took up the award, by which C was to pay O U.S. $27,529.88. On C's notice of motion to remit the award, *held*, that (1) it was entirely reasonable for C to take up the award to see whether it was adverse or not, and their conduct in so doing should not be held to be a waiver of any right of remission; (2) the application should be allowed to be heard out of time since there was no unreasonable or culpable delay on the part of C or their legal representative, and the case was sufficiently arguable to justify its being heard; (3) given the course and stage of the proceedings, the arbitrators were free to conclude, that the cases were closed and to make an award, and were not guilty of misconduct in not informing C of the date and place of the adjudication or of a date by which any further evidence or submissions should be received; (4) the loss by C of the opportunity of putting before the arbitrators further material on the cause of the interruption to discharge could fairly be described as a procedural mishap; (5) C had not shown that the procedural mishap caused or might well have caused injustice to them; (6) C had not established good grounds for the remission of the award and the application had to be dismissed. (*G.K.N. Centrax Gears* v. *Matbro* [1976] C.L.Y. 95 applied): THE AROS [1978] 1 Lloyd's Rep. 456, Brandon J.

94. —— right of remission

It is reasonable for a party to an arbitration to pay the arbitrator's fees and take up the award to see whether it was adverse, and in doing so he does not impliedly waive any right of remission he would have if the decision turns out to be adverse: ROKOPOULAS v. ESPERIA SPA, *The Times*, February 8, 1978, Brandon J.

95. —— special cases—form

The following statement was made by Donaldson J. on February 22, 1978:

One of the main criticisms of the special case procedure is that it delays the moment when the successful party is able to enforce the award. It seems that in part this criticism is based upon a mistaken belief that an award in the form of a special case is not enforceable if there is a pending appeal. This is not correct. In some cases the questions of law will be answered in a way which makes it necessary to remit the award to the tribunal. However, in the majority of cases the answers will be such that one of various alternative final awards can take effect. The obligation to comply with the terms of a final award is not suspended by the giving of notice of appeal to the Court of Appeal. It is only suspended by an order of the Commercial Court or of the Court of Appeal staying execution on the award. The judges of the Commercial Court wish it to be known that applications for such orders are not granted as a matter of course, but are considered strictly on their merits. In the event of a successful appeal, any overpayment which has been made by the appellant will be repayable forthwith.

The Times, March 3, 1978.

96. V tendered bills of lading to P in respect of a shipment of oats c.i.f. Rotterdam. P refused to take up or pay for the bills of lading on the grounds that they contained a misdescription in that the goods shipped were " clipped oats," and accordingly not contractual goods. The umpire found for V, and P's application to the G.A.F.T.A. Board of Appeal to state its award in the form of a special case was refused on the grounds that the dispute " involved the question " whether the goods shipped were within the contract description. On P's application for an order that the G.A.F.T.A. Board of Appeal state its award in the form of a special case, *held* that (1) had the board indicated that the goods shipped were within the contract description, the application would have been refused, as this was eminently a question of fact; (2) since the dispute " involved the question " it was not necessarily resolved by the answer, and P could argue that the board intended to answer in the negative, and then hold that as a matter of law P were debarred from a remedy through having wrongfully rejected the documents. Application granted: TRADAX EXPORT S.A. v. ANDRE & CIE S.A. [1978] 1 Lloyd's Rep. 639, Donaldson J.

97. Central Arbitration Committee—reference by Secretary of State—alleged non-compliance with fair wages resolution

[Fair Wages Resolution 1946, para. 3; Arbitration Act 1950 (c. 27), ss. 21, 32.] The AUEW complained to the Secretary of State for Employment that I.M.I. Co. were failing to comply with the Fair Wages Resolution concerning training instructors at a certain site, and the Secretary of State referred the question to the C.A.C. under para. 3 of the Resolution. I.M.I. Co. asked the

C.A.C. to make an award on their claim that the Resolution did not apply, since the instructors did not work at a place where the government contract was being performed, in the form of a special case under s. 21 of the 1950 Act for review by the High Court. *Held*, that (1) a reference to the C.A.C. under the Resolution is not a reference to arbitration, but merely machinery for investigating, reporting and advising on a complaint of alleged non-compliance with the Resolution. The C.A.C. could not make an award binding on or affecting the rights of anyone; (2) accordingly, the C.A.C. had no obligation to state its award in the form of a special case for review; (3) in any event, even if the C.A.C. were acting as arbitrators, a reference under para. 3 of the Resolution was not a reference to arbitration under an arbitration agreement within s. 32 of the 1950 Act, and the High Court could not, therefore, order a special case to be stated: IMPERIAL METAL INDUSTRIES (KYNOCH) *v.* AMALGAMATED UNION OF ENGINEERING WORKERS (TECHNICAL, ADMINISTRATIVE AND SUPERVISORY SECTION) AND SINGLETON [1978] I.R.L.R. 407, C.A.

98. Costs—appeal—leave of court required

An appeal against an award of costs in an arbitration was an interlocutory appeal and so required the leave of the High Court judge or of the Court of Appeal. Although the question was obiter in the particular case it was understandable that the matter should be left in doubt: THYSSEN (G.B.) *v.* AFAN BOROUGH COUNCIL, *The Times,* May 17, 1978, C.A.

99. —— discretion—relevance of prior offer in settlement

A successful claimant in arbitration proceedings is not necessarily to be deprived of his costs by reason of the award being less than a prior offer in settlement where such offer was expressed to be full and final, making no allowance for costs or interest.

Per curiam: Amendment of the Rules of the Supreme Court may be desirable to enable a payment into court to include interest as well as capital.

In arbitration proceedings between the parties to a charterparty, the claimants at the end of the first two days' of the hearing (" the first hearing ") amended their claim to include a claim for rectification. During the long subsequent adjournment, the respondents made an offer of $6,000 in full and final settlement, stating that they did not " contemplate " any payment in respect of interest or costs. The offer was not accepted. At the adjourned hearing lasting two days (" the second hearing "), the claimants were awarded some 36 per cent. of their claim and the respondents 52 per cent. of their counterclaim the net award to the claimants being some $2,700. The costs were awarded to the respondents on the grounds, inter alia, that the respondents had been proportionately more successful than the claimants, that the costs of the second hearing were occasioned by the claimant's amendment which had not increased the amount of the award and that the respondents were " protected " in respect of the costs of the second hearing by their offer in settlement. *Held,* allowing the claimants' appeal and remitting the award of costs for reconsideration, that (1) prima facie, the claimants were entitled to their costs of the first hearing, the claim having been properly brought; (2) it was wrong to award costs on the grounds of proportionate success unless the original claim was unreasonably inflated; (3) although it was material to award costs in respect of the second hearing upon the basis that the same had been occasioned by the claimants' (as it proved, fruitless) amendment, it was incorrect to compare the award with the offer in settlement since there was no comparison of " like with like " where the offer made no allowance for interest or costs. *Jefford* v. *Gee* [1970] C.L.Y. 603 distinguished.)

TRAMOUNTANA ARMADORA S.A. *v.* ATLANTIC SHIPPING CO. S.A. [1978] 2 All E.R. 870, Donaldson J.

100. Extension of time—appointment of arbitrator—effect of Hague Rules

[Arbitration Act 1950 (c. 27), s. 27.]

The fact that a party's liability is apparently discharged by the application of the Hague Rules is no bar to an extension of time to appoint an arbitrator being given to the other party.

A dispute arose under a charterparty made subject to the Hague Rules in that the plaintiffs claimed that the cargo was short when discharged in January

1976. The plaintiffs made a written claim and were given a three-month extension of time, expiring in April 1977, by the defendants whose insurers indicated that the claim was under investigation. Negotiations ceased in May 1977. No arbitrator had previously been appointed and in September 1977 the plaintiffs made such appointment applying then to the court for an extension of time under s. 27 of the 1950 Act. Donaldson J. refused their application. *Held*, allowing the plaintiffs' appeal, that although the Hague Rules limitation destroyed the plaintiffs' right of action, an extension could, and in the court's discretion would, be granted. (*Aries Tanker Corp.* v. *Total Transport* [1977] C.L.Y. 2741 considered.)

CONSOLIDATED INVESTMENT & CONTRACTING v. SAPONARIA SHIPPING; THE VIRGO [1978] 1 W.L.R. 986, C.A.

101. —— court's power—rent review

[Arbitration Act 1950 (c. 27), s. 27.]

Where a lessor fails to appoint an arbitrator to determine a new rent within the time limits in the lease because he is misled by the lessee, the time for making such appointment may be extended under s. 27 of the Arbitration Act 1950.

A lease provided that in the absence of agreement as to a new rent after the review date, the lessor might appoint an arbitrator, the appointment to be made within two quarters prior to the review date. The lessors began negotiations six months prior to the review date and although the lessees contended that the new rent sought was excessive they said that they had appointed surveyors to deal with the negotiations. In reliance thereon the lessors did not appoint an arbitrator prior to the review date. Thereafter the lessees discontinued negotiations contending that since no arbitrator had been appointed in accordance with the lease the rent remained as it had been before. The lessors sought an extension of time to appoint an arbitrator under s. 27 of the 1950 Act. *Held*, granting the application, that since the lessors had been misled by the lessees, undue hardship within the meaning of s. 27 of the Act would result if no extension was allowed. (*International Tank and Pipe S.A.K.* v. *Kuwait Aviation Fuelling Co.* [1975] C.L.Y. 356 and *Nea Agrex S.A.* v. *Baltic Shipping Co.* [1976] C.L.Y. 2534 applied.)

S.I. PENSION TRUSTEES v. WILLIAM HUDSON (1977) 35 P. & C.R. 54, Forbes J.

102. Foreign awards

ARBITRATION (FOREIGN AWARDS) ORDER 1978 (No. 186) [15p], made under the Arbitration Act 1950 (c. 27), s. 35 (1); operative on March 2, 1978; specifies States which are parties to the 1927 Geneva Convention on the Execution of Foreign Arbitral Awards and which have satisfied Her Majesty that they have made reciprocal provisions.

103. Interim award—technical misconduct of arbitrator—whether to set aside or remit award

A dispute between R, a contractor, and S, a local authority, concerning payment due under a building contract was referred to arbitration, the issues being confined to (a) the extent to which the works had been varied, and (b) the work having stopped, which party had repudiated the contract. On S's notice of motion to remit or set aside the award, *held* that (1) although the arbitrator made no finding under (a), this was not misconduct, as, being an interim award, where it reached findings it was final, but where it did not the issues were still open; (2) the catalogue of faults in the award could only serve as the reasons for the crucial findings; (3) the reasons could be classified as (i) fault of S; (ii) fault of S's independent architect acting as S's agent; (iii) fault of the architect acting otherwise than as agent, of which (i) and (ii) were legitimate factors in deciding who had repudiated the contract, but (iii) was not, and in so doing the arbitrator had fallen into an error of law which appeared on the face of the award; (4) this was a case for setting aside the award under the court's inherent jurisdiction and under s. 23 of the Arbitration Act 1950: STOCKPORT METROPOLITAN BOROUGH COUNCIL v. O'REILLY [1978] 1 Lloyd's Rep. 595, Judge Edgar Fay Q.C.

104. Jurisdiction—balance of convenience

[Can.] In or about October 31, 1976, a cargo of grain belonging to B was loaded at Toledo, Ohio, on the A, owned by O and time chartered by T, for carriage to Leith, Scotland. B sold the cargo to P. The bill of lading provided, by cl. 8, that, in the event of disputes arising out of the bill of lading such disputes were to be arbitrated in London and governed by English law. On December 22, 1976, the A ran aground. She was refloated and towed to a berth in the harbour of Quebec City. The cargo was inspected and found to be damaged. P brought an action in rem against the A and in personam against O and T. The defendants (O and T) applied for leave to file a conditional appearance or to have P's action suspended or dismissed because of the arbitration clause. P contended that the voyage was abandoned in Canada and that the grounding of the A occurred while the vessel was in Canada, and thus the principal evidence would be there. *Held*, (1) the arbitration clause did not deprive the court of jurisdiction; (2) full effect should be given to an arbitration clause unless, on the balance of convenience, it was better that the matter should be decided in the court in which the action was brought; on the facts, the balance of convenience was in favour of the proceedings being continued in Canada. (*Le Syndicat de Normandin Lumber* v. *The Angelic Power* [1971] F.C. 263, applied): THE AGELOS RAPHAEL [1978] 1 Lloyd's Rep. 105, Canadian Fed.Ct., Trial Division.

105. —— —— forum conveniens

An agreement between a Pakistan corporation and a Singapore company provided for arbitration in London. The Singapore company contended that the agreement was made without authority. *Held*, that it was a proper case for the grant of an injunction to restrain reference to arbitration, and for service of proceedings out of the jurisdiction for that purpose; the forum conveniens for the resolution of the dispute was the High Court of Singapore. (*Kitts* v. *Moore* [1895] 1 Q.B. 253, 260 applied): BEN & CO. v. PAKISTAN EDIBLE OILS CORP., *The Times*, July 13, 1978, C.A.

106. Practice—claim for damages—whether should have been raised at same time as issue of liability

P bought sugar from V under two contracts, each containing an arbitration agreement. There was short delivery of part of the sugar and non-delivery of the rest, V contending to be protected by a force majeure clause in the contracts. P referred the dispute to arbitration, limited to the issue of liability. The arbitrators found in favour of P, who submitted a debit note to V. V refused payment, and P referred the claim for damages to arbitration. On a special case stated, *held*, that (1) the rule in litigation against serial claims for damages arising out of the same cause of action applied also to arbitration; but P had not made two claims for damages; (2) in litigation, the first cause would have been confined to the alleged breach and the second to remedies for that breach; and the second would not have merged in the first since the question of damages would not have been before the court; (3) in this case, the only dispute referred concerned the force majeure clause and the arbitrators could not have made an award of damages; (4) accordingly, P were not estopped from referring their claim for damages to arbitration: COMPAGNIE GRAINIÈR S.A. v. FRITZ KOPP A.G. [1978] 1 Lloyd's Rep. 511, Donaldson J.

107. Stay of proceedings—infringement of patent

On February 3, 1964, A, an American company and patentees of an organic compound and a number of derivatives, entered into an agreement with P which, by cl. 1, gave P the option to take an exclusive licence to use the organic compound throughout the world, except in the U.S. and territories under its jurisdiction and control. Cl. 12 provided for arbitration in the event of disputes arising out of the agreement. On December 7, 1966, P exercised the option. P marketed the compound in various countries. In 1976, the derivative was introduced into the U.K. by A. P started proceedings for the infringement of the U.K. patent against A and B, a wholly-owned subsidiary of A which sold and distributed A's products in the U.K. The writ was served on B only. P applied for an interlocutory injunction and B resisted the application which was refused. On January 20, 1977, A entered an unconditional appearance to the writ and both A and B applied for an order that all further proceedings be stayed pursuant to s. 1 of the Arbitration Act 1975, or under the court's inherent jurisdiction. P contended that B's action in resisting the injunction amounted to a step in the action within the meaning of s. 1 of the 1975 Act. *Held*, (1) a stay of the action against both companies would be granted in the exercise of the court's inherent jurisdiction; there was no difference between their respective positions; (2) on the facts, it would be right to hold that B was within the scope of the arbitration clause on the basis that it was " claiming " through or under the parent to do what it was doing; (3) on the facts, B had not taken any step in the action so as to debar them from relief by way of stay. (*The Atlantic Star* [1973] C.L.Y. 2702, referred to): ROUSSEL-UCLAF v. G. D. SEARLE & Co. [1978] 1 Lloyd's Rep. 225, Graham J.

108. —— **validity of arbitration clause—re-insurance treaty.** See EAGLE STAR INSURANCE CO. v. YUVAL INSURANCE CO., § 1710.

109. —— **wrongful repudiation—charterparty—damages.** See ASSOCIATED BULK CARRIERS v. KOCH SHIPPING INC.; THE FUOHSAN MARU, § 2690.

ARTICLES. See *post,* p. [11].

ARMED FORCES

110. National insurance. See NATIONAL INSURANCE.

ARTICLES. See *post,* p. [11].

ARREST

111. Obstruction—power of police. See WERSHOF v. METROPOLITAN POLICE COMMISSIONER, § 2303.

112. Power of—misuse of drugs—reasonable suspicion of possession. See R. v. LITTLEFORD, § 553.

113. Reasonable force—inquest—alternative counts
[Criminal Law Act 1967 (c. 58), s. 3.] While T was being arrested he suffered an injury from which he later died. The police evidence was that the injury was caused accidentally when a constable fell on T's abdomen. *Held*, that although the coroner had correctly directed the jury that the constable was entitled to use reasonable force, under s. 3 of the Criminal Law Act 1967, the true alternatives were verdicts of murder, manslaughter or accidental death; accordingly a verdict of justifiable homicide would be quashed and a new inquest ordered: R. v. CORONER FOR DURHAM COUNTY, *ex p.* ATT.-GEN., *The Times,* June 29, 1978, D.C.

114. Validity—breath test—already arrested for assault. See R. v. HATTON (FRANCIS), § 2553.

115. —— **failure to give reasons—stopping driver for breath test.** See R. v. SULLIVAN, § 2554.

ATOMIC ENERGY

115a. Nuclear installations
NUCLEAR INSTALLATIONS (EXCEPTED MATTER) REGULATIONS 1978 (No. 1779) [25p], made under the Nuclear Installations Act 1965 (c. 57), s. 26 (1); operative on January 1, 1979; prescribe certain specified quantities and forms of nuclear matter and supersede S.I. 1965 No. 1826.

116. Nuclear Safeguards and Electricity (Finance) Act 1978 (c. 25)
This Act provides for giving effect to an International Agreement for the application of safeguards in the U.K. in connection with the Treaty on the Non-Proliferation of Nuclear Weapons; it also authorises contributions to expenditure by the CEGB in connection with the construction of Drax Generating Station.
S. 1 enables effect to be given to the Agreement made on September 6, 1976, for the application of Safeguards in the U.K. (" the Safeguards Agreement ");

s. 2 deals with the right of inspectors of the International Atomic Energy Agency to enter civil nuclear installations; s. 3 empowers the Secretary of State to make regulations giving effect to certain provisions of the Safeguards Agreement; s. 4 relates to offences committed by corporate bodies; s. 5 authorises the Secretary of State to make contributions towards expenditure in connection with stage two of Drax Generating Station; s. 6 gives the short title. The Act extends to Northern Ireland.

The Act received the Royal Assent on June 30, 1978, and came into force on that date.

117. Nuclear waste

NUCLEAR INSTALLATIONS (GUERNSEY) ORDER 1978 (No. 1528) [25p], made under the Nuclear Installations Act 1965 (c. 57), s. 28 (1); operative on October 25, 1978; extends to Guernsey the provisions of the 1965 Act with certain adaptations, exceptions and modifications, which relate to the duty in respect of carriage of nuclear waste and compensation for breach of that duty.

118. Windscale—special development order. See § 2912.

ARTICLES. See *post*, p. [11].

AUCTIONEERS AND VALUERS

119. Conversion—title to goods—bailee only. See UNION TRANSPORT FINANCE *v.* BRITISH CAR AUCTIONS, § 1563.

120. Liability—exclusion clause—whether applicable to private sale after auction. See D. & M. TRAILERS (HALIFAX) *v.* STIRLING, § 2621.

121. —— seller having no title—provisional bid procedure

The rule that an auctioneer, however innocent, is liable to the true owner in conversion where he sells under the hammer goods to which the seller has no title, also extends to cases where sale is under the auctioneer's " provisional bid " procedure.

P Co., car dealers, let a car to X on H.P., the car to remain the property of P Co. until the sale price of £625 was paid. X paid a deposit of £350, then took the car to D Co., auctioneers, to sell, placing on it a reserve of £450. The highest bid was £410. The car was then sold by D Co.'s " provisional bid " procedure; *i.e.* they asked the highest bidder whether he was prepared to stand upon his bid, then arranged a sale at that price with X. X was then bankrupted and no payments were made on the car. The purchaser could not be traced. *Held,* that such a sale was indistinguishable from a sale under the hammer. (*Hollins* v. *Fowler* (1875) L.R. 7 H.L. 757, *Barker* v. *Furlong* [1891] 2 Ch. 172, and *Consolidated Co.* v. *Curtis & Son* [1892] 1 Q.B. 495 applied; *National Mercantile Bank* v. *Rymill* (1881) 44 L.T.N.S. 767 C.A. and *Turner* v. *Hockey* (1887) 56 L.J.Q.B. 301 D.C. doubted.)

R. H. WILLIS AND SON *v.* BRITISH CAR AUCTIONS [1978] 1 W.L.R. 438, C.A.

122. Mock auction—competitive bidding

[Mock Auctions Act 1961 (c. 47), ss. 1, 3 (1).]

The expression " competitive bidding " includes a situation where the chance of being a successful bidder depends on being selected by the vendor.

D was charged with conducting mock auctions by offering goods for sale by way of competitive bidding. He had asked a fixed price for an article, then, when several potential purchasers raised their hands, sold it to one such purchaser for less than that price. *Held,* allowing P's appeal, that there was " competitive bidding," within the meaning of the Mock Auctions Act 1961, where a purchaser had a chance, as against other potential purchasers, of raising his hand first, or of being selected by the vendor.

ALLEN *v.* SIMMONS [1978] 1 W.L.R. 79, D.C.

123. —— —— articles offered at fixed prices—limited number of purchasers

[Mock Auctions Act 1961 (c. 47), ss. 1 (3), 3 (1).]

The phrase " competitive bidding " within s. 3 (1) of the 1961 Act includes any mode of sale whereby prospective purchasers are enabled to compete for the purchase of articles in any way.

The defendant held a sale of household goods where lots were offered at a fraction of their real value. The price was fixed, and the buyers chosen by the defendant nominating those who first raised their hands. The defendant's appeal against conviction by the magistrates for conducting a mock auction was allowed. On the prosecution's appeal, *held*, allowing the appeal, that competitive bidding included any mode of sale in which prospective purchasers competed in any way. Here there had been an element of competition in the selection of the purchasers and hence " competitive bidding."

CLEMENTS *v.* RYDEHEARD [1978] 1 All E.R. 658, D.C.

AVIATION

124. Air navigation

AIR NAVIGATION (RESTRICTION OF FLYING) (KEMBLE AIRFIELD) REGULATIONS 1978 (No. 11) [10p], made under S.I. 1976, No. 1783 Art. 64; operative on February 1, 1978; restricts flying on specified occasions in the vicinity of Kemble Airfield.

AIR NAVIGATION (THIRD AMENDMENT) ORDER 1978 (No. 284) [15p], made under the Civil Aviation Act 1949 (c. 67), ss. 8, 57 and amended by the Civil Aviation Act 1971 (c. 75), s. 62 (1); operative on April 1, 1978; amends S.I. 1976 No. 1783.

AIR NAVIGATION (RESTRICTION OF FLYING) (EXHIBITION OF FLYING) REGULATIONS 1978 (No. 542) [10p], made under S.I. 1976 No. 1783; operative on May 15, 1978; restricts flying in specified areas on specified dates.

AIR NAVIGATION (RESTRICTION OF FLYING) (SECURITY ESTABLISHMENTS) (AMENDMENT) REGULATIONS 1978 (No. 838) [10p], made under S.I. 1976 No. 1783, art. 64; operative on July 10, 1978; amend S.I. 1976 No. 1985.

AIR NAVIGATION (RESTRICTION OF FLYING) (FARNBOROUGH) REGULATIONS 1978 (No. 996) [10p], made under S.I. 1976 No. 1783; operative on August 29, 1978; prohibits flying at specified areas on specified dates during the holding of the Farnborough Air Show.

AIR NAVIGATION (RESTRICTION OF FLYING) (SECURITY ESTABLISHMENTS) (SECOND AMENDMENT) REGULATIONS 1978 (No. 1274) [10p], made under S.I. 1976 No. 1783; operative on September 18, 1978; further amends S.I. 1976 No. 1985. An aircraft may now fly for the purposes of landing at or taking off from Enniskillen aerodrome if the aerodrome flight information unit at the aerodrome is accordingly notified.

RULES OF THE AIR AND AIR TRAFFIC CONTROL (FOURTH AMENDMENT) REGULATIONS 1978 (No. 1391) [10p], made under S.I. 1976 No. 1783, art. 60 (1) as amended; operative on November 2, 1978; further amend S.I. 1976 No. 1983. Introduces special rules to apply to aircraft flying above 6,000 feet above sea level within the Scottish Terminal Control Area.

AIR NAVIGATION (FOURTH AMENDMENT) ORDER 1978 (No. 1627) [30p], made under the Civil Aviation Act 1949, ss. 8, 57, 59 as amended by the Civil Aviation Act 1968 (c 61), s. 20, the Mineral Workings (Offshore Installations) Act 1971 (c. 61), s. 8 (4) and the Civil Aviation Act 1971 (c. 75), s. 62 (1); operative on January 1, 1979, save for art. 3 (2) (12) which is operative on April 1, 1979; further amends S.I. 1976 No. 1783 and makes provision relating to emergency exits from aircraft, flights in the vicinity of offshore installations, radio communication used to facilitate landing, equipment to be carried by helicopters, radar equipment and pilots of helicopters.

125. Air traffic—control. See § 669.

125a. Aircraft engine noise

GATWICK AIRPORT—LONDON NOISE INSULATION GRANTS (SECOND AMENDMENT) SCHEME 1978 (No. 1797) [10p], made under the Civil Aviation Act 1971 (c. 75), ss. 29, 29A the latter inserted by the Airports Authority Act 1975 (c. 78), s. 25 (1), Sched. 5 as amended by the Civil Aviation Act 1978 (c. 8), Sched. 1, para. 6 (8); operative on December 31, 1978; varies S.I. 1975 No. 916 by extending the time allowed for the completion of insulation work in respect of which a grant has been made.

HEATHROW AIRPORT—LONDON NOISE INSULATION GRANTS (SECOND AMEND-

MENT) SCHEME 1978 (No. 1798) [10p], made under the Civil Aviation Act 1971, ss. 29, 29A the latter inserted by the Airports Authority Act 1975, s. 25 (1), Sched. 5 and as amended by the Civil Aviation Act 1978, Sched. 1, para. 6 (8); operative on December 31, 1978; varies S.I. 1975 No. 917 by extending the time allowed for the completion of insulation work in respect of which a grant has been made.

126. Airports—control of stores. See § 670.

127. Carriage by air

CARRIAGE BY AIR (STERLING EQUIVALENTS) ORDER 1978 (No. 31) [10p], made under the Carriage by Air Act 1961 (c. 27), s. 4 (4); operative on February 1, 1978; specifies the sterling equivalents of amounts, expressed in gold francs, as the limit of the air carrier's liability under the Warsaw Convention of 1929, and under that Convention as amended by the Hague Protocol of 1955, as well as under corresponding provisions applying to carriage by air to which the Convention and Protocol do not apply.

CARRIAGE BY AIR (PARTIES TO CONVENTION) (SUPPLEMENTARY) ORDER 1978 (No. 1058) [10p], made under the Carriage by Air Act 1961, s. 2 (1) as applied by S.I. 1967 No. 480, Art. 5; certifies additional High Contracting Parties to the Warsaw Convention on international carriage by air.

128. Civil Aviation

RULES OF THE AIR AND AIR TRAFFIC CONTROL (SECOND AMENDMENT) REGULATIONS 1978 (No. 140) [10p], made under S.I. 1976 No. 1783; operative on March 1, 1978; amend S.I. 1976 No. 1983.

CIVIL AVIATION (ROUTE CHARGES FOR NAVIGATION SERVICES) (FOURTH AMENDMENT) REGULATIONS 1978 (No. 241) [15p], made under the Civil Aviation (Eurocontrol) Act 1962 (c. 8), ss. 4, 7 (1), the Civil Aviation Act 1968 (c. 61), s. 15 (3) and the Civil Aviation Act 1971 (c. 75), Sched. 10, para. 6; amends S.I. 1973 No. 2070 by making provision for certain new tariffs.

CIVIL AVIATION (CANADIAN NAVIGATION SERVICES) (AMENDMENT) REGULATIONS 1978 (No. 245) [10p], made under the Civil Aviation (Eurocontrol) Act 1962, ss. 4, 7 as amended by the Civil Aviation Act 1968, s. 15 and by the Civil Aviation Act 1971, Sched. 10, paras. 6, 7; operative on April 1, 1978; amends S.I. 1977 No. 314 by increasing the charge for air navigation services provided by the Government of Canada in the Gander Flight Information Region.

CIVIL AVIATION (NAVIGATION SERVICES CHARGES) (AMENDMENT) REGULATIONS 1978 (No. 317) [15p], made under the Civil Aviation (Eurocontrol) Act 1962, ss. 4, 7 as amended by the Civil Aviation Act 1971, Sched. 10, paras. 6, 7 and the Civil Aviation Act 1968, s. 15; operative on April 1, 1978; makes provision for charges in respect of certain specified navigation services within the United Kingdom by amending S.I. 1977 No. 1437.

CIVIL AVIATION (JOINT FINANCING) REGULATIONS 1978 (No. 554) [25p], made under the Civil Aviation (Eurocontrol) Act 1962, ss. 4, 7, as amended by the Civil Aviation Act 1968, s. 15, and Civil Aviation Act 1971, Sched. 10, paras. 6, 7; operative on May 10, 1978; consolidate, with minor and drafting amendments, S.I. 1974 No. 1144, as amended.

CIVIL AVIATION (ROUTE CHARGES FOR NAVIGATION SERVICES) REGULATIONS 1978 (No. 693) [20p], made under the Civil Aviation (Eurocontrol) Act 1962 (c. 8), ss. 4, 7 (1), the Civil Aviation Act 1968, s. 15 (3) and the Civil Aviation Act 1971, Sched. 10, para. 6; operative on June 12, 1978; consolidate with minor amendments S.I. 1973 No. 1678 as amended.

CIVIL AVIATION (ROUTE CHARGES FOR NAVIGATION SERVICES) (AMENDMENT) REGULATIONS 1978 (No. 837) [10p], made under the Civil Aviation (Eurocontrol) Act 1962, ss. 4, 7 (1), the Civil Aviation Act 1968, s. 15 (3), and the Civil Aviation Act 1971 (c. 75), Sched. 10, para. 6; operative on June 12, 1978; correct clerical errors in S.I. 1978 No. 693.

AIR NAVIGATION (GENERAL) (SECOND AMENDMENT) REGULATIONS 1978 (No. 873) [10p], made under S.I. 1976 No. 1783, art. 27 (1) (c); operative on July 17, 1978; amend S.I. 1976 No. 1982.

RULES OF THE AIR AND AIR TRAFFIC CONTROL (THIRD AMENDMENT) REGULA-

TIONS 1978 (No. 877) [25p], made under S.I. 1976 No. 1783, art. 60 (1); operative on July 1, 1978; amend S.I. 1976 No. 1983.

CIVIL AVIATION (NOTICES) REGULATIONS 1978 (No. 1303) [10p], made under the Civil Aviation Act 1971, s. 29 (1) (3) (3A) (4) as amended by the Civil Aviation Act 1978 (c. 8), Sched. 1, para. 6 (4) (5); operative on October 1, 1978; prescribe the manner of publishing and giving notices under s. 29 of the 1971 Act as amended by the 1978 Act.

AIR NAVIGATION (OVERSEAS TERRITORIES) (SECOND AMENDMENT) ORDER 1978 (No. 1520) [40p], made under the Civil Aviation Act 1949 (c. 67), and S.I. 1969 No. 592, as amended by S.I. 1976 No. 1912; operative on November 22, 1978; amends S.I. 1977 No. 820.

TOKYO CONVENTION (CERTIFICATION OF COUNTRIES) (SUPPLEMENTARY) ORDER 1978 (No. 1534) [10p], made under the Tokyo Convention Act 1967 (c. 52), s. 7 (1); certifies additional countries in which the Convention on Offences and certain other Acts Committed on board Aircraft, signed in Tokyo on September 14, 1963 is for the time being in force.

AIR NAVIGATION (INTERCHANGE OF CONCORDE) REGULATIONS 1978 (No. 1631) [10p], made under S.I. 1976 No. 1783; operative on December 1, 1978; facilitate temporary transfer of the registry of Concorde aircraft by enabling such transfer to be done by the commander of the aircraft at a point outside the U.K.

CIVIL AVIATION AUTHORITY (CHARGES) (REVOCATION) REGULATIONS 1978 (No. 1633) [10p], made under the Civil Aviation Act 1971, s. 9 (3); operative on January 1, 1979, revokes S.I. 1976 No. 1396: The charges payable under these Regulations have now been incorporated in a Scheme of Charges made by the Authority under s. 9 (1) of the 1971 Act.

CIVIL AVIATION (JOINT FINANCING) (AMENDMENT) REGULATIONS 1978 (No. 1799) [10p], made under the Civil Aviation (Eurocontrol) Act 1962, ss. 4, 7 as amended by the Civil Aviation Act 1968, s. 15 and the Civil Aviation Act 1971, Sched. 10, paras. 6, 7; operative on January 1, 1979; amend S.I. 1978 No. 554 by increasing the charges payable by operators of aircraft to the Civil Aviation Authority in respect of crossings between Europe and North America.

129. Civil Aviation Act 1978 (c. 8)

This Act establishes a fund from which payments may be made in respect of expenses incurred for the purpose of protecting aircraft, aerodromes or air navigation installations against acts of violence or in connection with the policing of airports; amends the law relating to the Civil Aviation Authority and the British Airways Board; amends the law relating to noise, vibration and atmospheric pollution caused by aircraft; and otherwise amends the law relating to aerodromes, aircraft and civil aviation.

S. 1 provides for the establishment of the Aviation Security Fund under the management and control of the Secretary of State, from which certain payments under s. 23 of the Protection of Aircraft Act 1973 (c. 47), and s. 7 of the Policing of Airports Act 1974 (c. 41), shall be made; s. 2 empowers the Secretary of State to make regulations governing contributions to the Fund from aerodrome authorities; s. 3 deals with the financing of the Fund, including borrowings by the Secretary of State; s. 4 confers powers of winding up the Fund upon the Secretary of State; s. 5 amends the financial borrowing powers of the Civil Aviation Authority and the British Airways Board; s. 6 provides means to control the capital expenditure and the hire of equipment by the Civil Aviation Authority; s. 7 grants the Authority power to charge for air navigation services in pursuance of an agreement; s. 8 extends certain powers to the making of byelaws regulating noise, vibration and pollution caused by aircraft near aerodromes; s. 9 permits the fixing of charges by aerodrome authorities by reference to noise factors; s. 10 enables the Secretary of State to give general directions to the Civil Aviation Authority in the interests of national security; s. 11 amends the existing offence of contravening an air transport licence; s. 12 relates to the pensions of British Airways Board staff; s. 13 lays down the procedure for making orders and regulations under the Act; s. 14 makes certain minor and consequential amendments, and contains certain repeals; s. 15 is the interpretation section; s. 16 contains the short title, and extends the Act to Northern Ireland.

The Act received the Royal Assent on March 23, 1978. Ss. 1 (1) (3)–(5), 2, 3, 13 and 16 came into force on March 23, 1978; s. 1 (2) came into force on April 1, 1978; the remaining provisions came into force on May 1, 1978.

130. —— commencement

CIVIL AVIATION ACT 1978 (COMMENCEMENT) ORDER 1978 (No. 486 (C. 11)) [10p], made under the Civil Aviation Act 1978 (c. 8), s. 16 (2); brings into force ss. 1 (1) (3)–(5), 2, 3, 13 and 16 of the 1978 Act on March 23, 1978, s. 1 (2) on April 1, 1978, and the remainder of the Act on May 1, 1978.

131. Commonwealth Air Transport Council

The tenth meeting of the Commonwealth Air Transport Council, established in 1945 as a consultative organisation to discuss civil aviation matters of mutual interest to Commonwealth countries, and to serve as an advisory body thereon, took place in London during September.

132. Discounted air fares

The Department of Trade have published the report of the Working Party on Discounted Air Fares. The Working Party was set up in February 1978 to look into the extent and development of unauthorised discounting, its effects on airlines, the travel trade and the traveller, and any possible measures against its harmful effects. The report is available from Room 550, Department of Trade, 1 Victoria Street, London SW1H OET.

133. Northern Ireland. See NORTHERN IRELAND.

134. Protection of aircraft

AVIATION SECURITY FUND REGULATIONS 1978 (No. 769) [20p], made under the Civil Aviation Act 1978 (c. 8), s. 2; operative on May 31, 1978; require certain aerodrome authorities to pay contributions to an Aviation Security Fund, out of which payments are defrayed that fall to be made under the Protection of Aircraft Act 1973, s. 23, and the Policing of Airports Act 1974, s. 7.

ARTICLES. See *post*, p. [11].

BAILMENTS

135. Bailee—deviation from agreement —liability

[Can.] D agreed to tow P's caravan trailer slowly behind his truck so that P could follow closely and observe it. D drove too fast, lost P, and the trailer inexplicably caught fire. *Held*, D was liable as a bailee, his obligation being to take reasonable care of the goods bailed. The onus was on D to show he was not negligent. Even after discharging this burden, he was still liable as a bailee who had deviated from the express terms of his bailment: ENGLAND v. HEIMBECKER (1977) 78 D.L.R. 117, Halvorson D.C.J.

136. —— loss of goods—burden of proof

[Contracts (Malay States) Ordinance (No. 14 of 1950), ss. 104, 105; Port Swettenham Authority Bye-Laws 1965, bye-law 91 (1); Port Authorities Act 1963 (No. 21 of 1963), s. 29.]

Where goods in the custody of a bailee are lost, the burden is upon the bailee to establish that such loss was not occasioned by this negligence.

93 cases of goods were shipped to Port Swettenham, the plaintiffs being the consignees under the bills of lading. The defendant port authority took charge of the goods (their charges being included in the port dues) and while the cases were in their warehouse, 64 disappeared. At the trial of the plaintiffs' claim, the defendants adduced evidence as to the system adopted by them but called no evidence as to the care taken by them of these particular cases. The trial judge, upheld by the Federal Court, held that the defendants had failed to discharge the evidential burden of proving that the loss had not been occasioned by their negligence. On appeal the defendants contended, inter alia, that their liability was limited to loss caused " solely " by their negligence or misconduct, as provided by bye-law 91 (1) of the 1965 Bye-Laws made under the 1963 Act. *Held*, dismissing the appeal, that both under the Contracts Ordinance and at

common law, the onus rests on a bailee to adduce evidence negativing negligence where goods have been lost whilst in his custody; and that bye-law 91 (1) was ultra vires the powers conferred under s. 29 (1) of the Act which powers permitted limitation of liability only in respect of loss occurring without the actual fault or privity of the port authority: bye-law 91 (1) clearly purported to limit liability which arose *with* the fault of the authority. (*Giblin v. McMuller* (1868) L.R. 2 P.C. 317, *Cheshire* v. *Bailey* [1905] 1 K.B. 237 and dictum of Sir Walter Phillimore in *Dwaska Nath* v. *River Steam Navigation Co.*, A.I.R. (1917) P.C. at 175, disapproved; *Morris* v. *C. W. Martin & Sons* [1965] C.L.Y. 178, approved.)

PORT SWETTENHAM AUTHORITY *v.* T. W. WU AND CO. (M.) SDN. BHD. [1978] 3 W.L.R. 530, P.C.

137. Gratuitous bailment—lawful demand—theft of goods—liability of bailee

A gratuitous bailee holds goods at his peril if he fails to return them after a lawful demand, and becomes insurer of them.

P, a squatter, was lawfully evicted from premises owned by D. D in order to assist P offered to act as gratuitous bailees and store her property. The goods were taken and stored in a lock-up garage. P's husband made a lawful demand for their return, but due to a misunderstanding on that date by D he did not collect the goods. Some four weeks later when P went to the premises to collect her possessions, they had been stolen by persons unknown. P alleged failure to take reasonable care. D admitted failure to deliver up, denied negligence and pleaded that the theft was due to circumstances beyond their control. *Held*, as gratuitous bailees, D were under a duty to take reasonable care and to deliver up when asked. Although they had taken reasonable care in storage, after their negligent failure to return goods when demanded, they held them at their peril and became insurers of them. (*Shaw & Co.* v. *Symmons & Sons* [1917] 1 K.B. 799 applied.)

MITCHELL *v.* EALING LONDON BOROUGH COUNCIL [1978] 2 W.L.R. 999, O'Connor J.

138. Negligence—exclusion clause—representation as to application of exclusion clause

[Can.] The defendants hired out storage space which they represented as being so secure that the plaintiffs need not insure their deposited goods. The contract contained exclusion clauses, which the defendants said they would not rely upon. The defendants negligently allowed stored goods to be stolen; when sued, they relied upon the exclusion clause. *Held*, they were not entitled to do so, first, because their negligence was a fundamental breach of contract, so that, having so broken the contract they could not plead its terms; secondly, their representations that they would not rely upon the exclusion clause bound them not to do so: DAVIDSON *v.* THE THREE SPRUCES REALTY [1977] 6 W.W.R. 460, Brit.Col.Sup.Ct.

ARTICLES. See *post*, p. [12].

BANKING

139. Cheques. See BILLS OF EXCHANGE.

140. Exchange control—breach of conditions—priority of security

In January 1973, Israel Financial Trust (IFT) purchased certain foreign securities, namely shares in the recently formed First International Bank of Israel (FIBI), with money borrowed from Swiss Bank and held initially by IFT's parent company, Triumph Investment Trust (Triumph) in accordance with Bank of England exchange control conditions including, inter alia, that the FIBI securities be kept in a separate account. On September 4, 1974, Swiss Bank drew Triumph's attention to the Bank of England conditions and asked that the FIBI securities be lodged with them as authorised depositary. That was refused and the FIBI securities were transferred as security for advances to Lloyd's Bank, IFT executing on October 24 a charge in favour of Lloyds Bank on all stocks and shares lodged with them. Triumph subsequently went into receivership and Swiss Bank, in December 1974, demanded payment of the principal. Attempts at compromise failed. To avoid a further call on the shares, IFT with Lloyds Bank's approval but without the knowledge or consent of Swiss Bank, sold the FIBI securities and the proceeds were converted into sterling. *Held,* Swiss Bank had an equitable interest in the FIBI securities by virtue of the combined effect of the loan arrangement and the Bank of England conditions, which being prior in time took priority over Lloyds Bank's subsequent charge. This charge was therefore void; if a contract bound a party to pay a debt out of specific property, such a contract was enforceable and created an equitable interest whether or not the parties knew or intended that legal consequence to follow. Further, Lloyds Bank were liable for damages in tort for converting the FIBI securities, once sold, into sterling in that by so doing they were knowingly interfering with Swiss Bank's contractual right, which could be insisted upon, to have the FIBI securities applied in repayment of their loan: SWISS BANK CORP. *v.* LLOYDS BANK, *The Times,* May 15, 1978, Browne Wilkinson J.

141. Guarantee—return of deposit—sale of goods—injunction

On January 15, 1976, S, manufacturers, entered into a contract with P, a Polish company, for the sale and delivery of certain equipment for £500,000. The contract provided for arbitration in Zurich. The contract also provided that £25,000 was payable in advance within 45 days of the signing of the contract on presentation of a guarantee by S's bank (guaranteeing, inter alia, a refund of the advance payment in case of non-delivery of the goods by March 31, 1977), and that £50,000 was to be paid by an irrevocable, unconfirmed letter of credit opened upon notification that the goods were ready for shipment. The guarantee was given by S's bank (upon taking a counter-indemnity from S), and S received the advance payment. P did not open the letter of credit. S completed the manufacture of the goods and in due course received a sum of money on account of the final instalment. P claimed repayment of £25,000 under the guarantee on the ground that delivery had not been made by March 31, 1977. S applied for an injunction to restrain P from claiming under the guarantee (*i.e.* to prevent the £25,000 from being taken out of the jurisdiction) unless and until the question of the second instalment had been arbitrated. *Held,* on appeal, that (1) the bank was in principle in a similar position to a bank which had opened a confirmed irrevocable letter of credit; the bank's obligation under the contract did not depend on the resolution of a dispute as to the sufficiency of performance under the contract; (2) the court would not interfere with P's right under the guarantee and the balance of convenience was against the grant of an injunction. (*American Cyanamid and Co.* v. *Ethicon* [1975] C.L.Y. 2640 applied): HOWE RICHARDSON SCALE CO. *v.* POLIMEX-CEKOP [1978] 1 Lloyd's Rep. 161, C.A.

142. Liability—fiduciary duty—knowledge that account held on trust

Bankers dealing with money deposited by a person for the benefit of third parties have a fiduciary duty to them. Where they purport to hold money in trust accounts, they are consequently liable for any misappropriation of funds.

On Friday July 14, 1967, M, the grandmother of the then four infant plaintiffs, deposited four cheques with the defendant bank B. Two uncles of the plaintiffs had accounts at the bank; neither M nor the children held accounts there, although the grandmother was well known. Four days later, a trust account was opened in the names of the uncles. M died six days later. One uncle, A, used all the money for his own purposes. On October 9, 1974, P issued a writ. On the question whether the bank were liable on a constructive or express trust, *held,* they had received the cheque in their capacity of banker; (2) in opening and operating the trust account, B owed P a fiduciary duty, and they had not acted as reasonably prudent bankers. (*Quistclose Investments* v. *Rolls Razor* (*in liquidation*) [1967] C.L.Y. 514 distinguished; *Re Gross, ex p. Kingston* (1871) L.R. 6 Ch.App. 632 and *Karak Rubber Co.* v. *Burden* (*No. 2*) [1972] C.L.Y. 206 applied.)

ROWLANDSON *v.* NATIONAL WESTMINSTER BANK [1978] 1 W.L.R. 798, John Mills, Q.C.

BOOKS. See *post,* p. [1].

BANKRUPTCY

143. Appeals from county courts

The following Practice Direction was issued by the Chancery Division on July 24, 1978:

1. It has been the practice hitherto for appeals from county courts in bankruptcy matters to be heard by Divisional Courts of the Chancery Division sitting on alternate Mondays, when required, throughout each term. This occasions disruption of the judge's work and interruption of the continuity of trials of other cases.

2. From the commencement of Hilary Term 1979, such appeals will normally be heard continuously during the second fortnight of each term (counting Easter Term and Trinity Term as a single term) or for such part of that fortnight as may be needed.

3. The Chief Clerk in Bankruptcy will during the last week of each term settle a list of the appeals to be heard during the following term. This will include all unheard appeals set down by that time. Any appeals set down between the settling of the list and the commencement of the sitting of the Divisional Court may be added to the list if time allows and the parties inform the Chief Clerk that they are ready.

4. The Chief Clerk will send a copy of the list to the solicitors to all parties to listed appeals (or to the parties themselves, if in person) not later than the first day of each term or, if appeals are added to the list pursuant to para. 3 above, forthwith on the inclusion of the appeal in the list.

5. Interlocutory applications may, while the Divisional Court is sitting, be made to that court instead of to the single judge pursuant to r. 133 of the Bankruptcy Rules 1952 (S.I. No. 2113).

6. If a sufficient case of urgency is made out, a Divisional Court may be convened to hear an appeal at any time.

7. Motions and other bankruptcy matters in the High Court requiring to be heard by a single judge will continue to be heard on Mondays, when required, throughout each term, except when the Divisional Court is sitting. If a sufficient case of urgency is made out for the hearing of any such motion or matter during the sitting of the Divisional Court, it will be heard by one of the judges of that court.

[1978] 1 W.L.R. 1060; [1978] 3 All E.R. 64.

144. Criminal bankruptcy—sentence—taking other offences into consideration. See D.P.P. v. ANDERSON, § 628.

145. Fees

BANKRUPTCY FEES (AMENDMENT) ORDER 1978 (No. 570 (L. 10)) [10p], made under the Bankruptcy Act 1914 (c. 59), s. 133, and the Public Offices Fees Act 1879 (c. 58), ss. 2, 3; operative on May 9, 1978; adds to Table A Fee 37 which is payable when a receiving order is made under the Insolvency Act 1976, s. 11; substitutes for Fees No. 18 and 19 in Table B an ad valorem fee payable by every trustee in bankruptcy on the submission of accounts of receipts and payments under s. 92 of the 1914 Act; increases to £3·75 the fee for insertion in the *London Gazette* of a notice authorised by the Act or the Bankruptcy Rules 1952.

BANKRUPTCY FEES (AMENDMENT No. 2) ORDER 1978 (No. 704 (L. 13)) [10p], made under the Bankruptcy Act 1914, s. 133 and the Public Offices Fees Act 1879, ss. 2, 3; operative on June 1, 1978; provides for the payment of VAT in addition to the amount of fee provided for in Table B in the Sched. to S.I. 1975 No. 1350 where the tax is chargeable in respect of the service to which that fee relates.

BANKRUPTCY FEES (AMENDMENT No. 3) ORDER 1978 (No. 1653 (L.36)) [10p], made under the Bankruptcy Act 1914, s. 133, and the Public Offices Fees Act 1879 ss. 2, 3; operative on December 1, 1978, amends S.I. 1975 No. 1350 by increasing certain fees taken by the Department of Trade in bankruptcy proceedings.

146. Insolvency Act 1976—commencement

INSOLVENCY ACT 1976 (COMMENCEMENT No. 4) ORDER 1978 (No. 139 (C. 4)) [10p], made under the Insolvency Act 1976 (c. 60), s. 14 (5); operative on

March 1, 1978; brings into force s. 12, 14 (4) in part and Sched. 3 in part of the 1976 Act.

147. Payment into court—attached earnings
[Bankruptcy Act 1914 (c. 59), s. 40; Attachment of Earnings Act 1971 (c. 32), s. 13 (1).] Money deducted by an employer from an employee's earnings pursuant to a consolidated attachment of earnings order, belonged, as from the date of payment into court, to the judgment creditors in whose favour the order was made, and did not vest in the employee's trustee in bankruptcy: *Re* GREEN (A BANKRUPT), *ex p.* OFFICIAL RECEIVER *v.* CUTTING, *The Times,* July 9, 1978, Walton J.

148. Petition—whether " abuse of process "—to defeat order in respect of matrimonial home
[Aust.] On December 8, 1975, in matrimonial proceedings, it was ordered that the matrimonial home was to be sold by P as agent of R, and for P to use the proceeds of sale to purchase another home for herself and the children of the marriage. On December 18, 1975, R presented his own petition in bankruptcy and was made bankrupt on December 19, 1975. The matrimonial home was not sold, and in February 1976, a meeting of creditors authorised the Official Receiver to join with P in accepting an offer of $85,000 for it. The sale realised $53,000 net, of which half was credited to R's estate. P argued that the bankruptcy should be annulled as R was solvent, and that his petition was presented solely to defeat the order of December 8, 1975, and to prevent P from ever obtaining R's half-interest in the former home. *Held,* that (1) P was a " person aggrieved " and a " person interested " in the bankruptcy. (*Att.-Gen (Gambia)* v. *N'Jie* [1961] C.L.Y. 6792, and *Ex p. Beesley* [1975] C.L.Y. 167 referred to); (2) where a man who is insolvent, or reasonably believes he is, presents a petition against himself and does not thereby commit a fraud on his creditors, his bankruptcy will not be annulled merely because his motive was " to protect himself from evils which he might otherwise suffer " (*Ex p. Painter* [1895] 1 Q.B. 85; *Re Hancock* [1904] 1 K.B. 585; *Re Dunn* (1949) C.L.C. 646; *Re a Debtor* [1971] C.L.Y. 602 referred to): *Re* MOTTEE; *ex p.* MOTTEE (1977) 29 F.L.R. 406, Fed.Ct.

149. Receiving order—debtor's own evidence insufficient to prevent
[Bankruptcy Act 1914 (c. 59), s. 5 (3).]
A court will not refuse to make a receiving order on the grounds that a debtor has no assets and no prospects where the only evidence comes from the debtor himself.
In January 1977, a deputy registrar refused a debtor's application for an adjournment and made a receiving order against him. In February 1977, the debtor swore a statement of affairs showing a deficiency of £1,000 and no assets. *Held,* dismissing his appeal against the making of the receiving order, that the court would not exercise its discretion to refuse such an order on the grounds that a debtor had no assets and no prospects where the only evidence of that came from him. A man may be too poor to be made bankrupt but the burden of proof on him is heavy.
Re FIELD (A DEBTOR) [1977] 3 W.L.R. 937, D.C.

150. —— payment to sheriff
R obtained a judgment against the debtor, and in due course filed a bankruptcy petition. Eight days before the receiving order was made, R levied execution and the sheriff received a sum on R's account which reduced the debt to a sum less than the minimum of £200 required for the presentation of a petition under s. 4 (1) (*a*) of the Bankruptcy Act 1914, as amended. The debtor appealed against the registrar's refusal to rescind the receiving order, on the ground that the court had no jurisdiction to make the order as the debt had been reduced to less than £200 before the making of the order. *Held,* dismissing the appeal, the payment to the sheriff only constituted payment to the judgment creditor when the creditor was in a position to maintain an action against the sheriff for money had and received, *i.e.* after 14 days following payment to the sheriff without notice by him of a bankruptcy notice or the making of a receiving order: *Re* A DEBTOR No. 2 OF 1977, *ex p.* THE DEBTOR *v.* GOACHER (1977) 122 S.J. 78, D.C.

151. —— unpaid income tax—refusal to rescind

[Bankruptcy Act 1914 (c. 59), s. 5 (3).] In 1973 the Inland Revenue obtained judgment against the taxpayer in the sum of £889·25, in respect of income tax unpaid during eight years ending April 5, 1970. In a counter-claim to bankruptcy proceedings founded on that debt, the taxpayer claimed £1,200 relief in respect of mortgage interest. In 1974 a bankruptcy petition was presented based upon the judgment and a further £173·25 indebtedness for the year 1970/71. The registrar decided that £708·15 of the judgment debt was indisputably due, and adjourned the hearing of the petition to allow the taxpayer to make payment of that sum. The sum was not paid, and in 1975 a receiving order was made, against which the taxpayer appealed. Subsequently, the financial position of the taxpayer improved. *Held,* that the receiving order was properly made, and that the registrar was justified in refusing to rescind it: ORAKPO *v.* I.R.C. [1977] T.R. 235, C.A.

152. Rules

BANKRUPTCY (AMENDMENT) RULES 1978 (No. 544) [10p], made under the Bankruptcy Act 1964 (c. 59), s. 132, and the Insolvency Act 1976 (c. 60), s. 10; operative on May 2, 1978; amends S.I. 1952 No. 2113.

BANKRUPTCY (AMENDMENT No. 2) RULES 1978 (No. 1224 (L. 28)) [20p], made under the Bankruptcy Act 1914 (c. 59), s. 132 and the Insolvency Act 1976, s. 10; operative on October 1, 1978; amend S.I. 1952 No. 2113 by revising the scale of allowances to auctioneers and brokers.

153. Set-off—taxation—company. See *Re* D. H. CURTIS (BUILDERS), § 261.

BOOKS AND ARTICLES. See *post,* pp. [1], [12].

BILLS OF EXCHANGE

154. Discounted bills—profits—when taxable profit accrues. See WILLINGALE *v.* INTERNATIONAL COMMERCIAL BANK, § 365.

155. Dishonour—drawer entitled to sue as holder in due course

[Bills of Exchange Act 1882 (c. 61), s. 29 (3).]

The drawer of a bill of exchange who then derives title from a holder in due course is a holder in due course, and his rights lie to be determined as such and not as drawer.

P Co. drew a bill of exchange on D Co. as the price of the first two consignments of steel. The bill was discounted by P Co. to their bank, then transferred to the Midland Bank. It was accepted by D Co., but dishonoured because of a dispute about the quality of the steel. The bill was then sent back to the discounting bank who returned it to P Co. after debiting their account. P Co. claimed the amount of the dishonoured bill. *Held,* that although P Co. were the drawers of the bill, they were also holders in due course, and by s. 29 (3) of the Bills of Exchange Act 1882, their rights fell to be determined as such. JADE INTERNATIONAL STEEL STAHL UND EISEN G.M.B.H. & Co. KG *v.* ROBERT NICHOLAS (STEELS) [1978] 3 W.L.R. 39, C.A.

ARTICLES. See *post,* p. [12].

BRITISH COMMONWEALTH

156. Australia—aborigines—right to share of mining profits—existence of trust

[Aus.] Some 24,000 aborigines inhabited the state of Queensland. Of these, 700 lived in a reserve at Aurukun. Bauxite was discovered on the reserve and P, as trustee of the reserve, entered into an agreement with three mining companies to approve the grant of a mining lease to them by the Crown. One agreed term was that P would be paid, on behalf of aborigines, three per cent. of the net profits. D, an aborigine living on the reserve, claimed that P was a trustee for aborigines residing on the reserve and that such a term on behalf of all aborigines was in breach of trust. P submitted that there was no trust enforceable in equity and none of the acts complained of was a breach of trust. *Held,* that ss. 29 and 30 of the Aborigines Act 1971 constituted statutory authority for the acts complained of: s. 30 (2) could not be read as creating mutually exclusive classes between which P had to choose. The aborigines on the reserve had no exclusive right to a share in the profits: DIRECTOR OF ABORIGINAL AND ISLANDERS ADVANCEMENT CORP. *v.* PEINKINNA, *The Times*, January 28, 1978, P.C.

157. Barbados—powers of Federal Supreme Court

[British Caribbean (Appeals to Privy Council) Order in Council 1962 (S.I. 1962 No. 1087), s. 3 *b*; Federal Supreme Court Regulations 1958 (Laws of West Indies), reg. 22 (2).]

The Court of Appeal of Barbados has an unfettered discretion under reg. 22 (2) of the Federal Supreme Court Regulations to order a new trial in a criminal matter, and such an order is not wrong merely because there has been a lapse of nearly two years before deciding the appeal, nor because it may appear that certain important evidence may be inadmissible.

D was charged with murdering his wife between September 1 and September 4, 1974. L, a witness, gave evidence that he had heard the wife at about 11.20 p.m. on September 1, just after she was last seen alive, shouting "murder, murder, I beg you D, don't kill me, Lord have mercy! " Later, the Crown's medical expert put the earliest time of death as 3 p.m. on September 2. D had not objected to the admissibility of L's evidence. D was convicted. In December 1976, the Court of Appeal of Barbados allowed D's appeal and ordered a new trial under reg. 22 (2) of the Federal Supreme Court Regulations 1958. The Court of Appeal of Barbados gave leave to appeal to the Privy Council against the order for a new trial under s. 3 *b* of the British Caribbean (Appeal to the Privy Council) Order in Council 1962. D also lodged a petition to the Privy Council for special leave to appeal. *Held*, (1) the Court of Appeal of Barbados had no power to grant leave to appeal to the Privy Council under s. 3 *b*, and the order purporting to do so was a nullity; (2) on hearing D's petition for special leave to appeal, there was no ground granting leave; reg. 22 (2) did not fetter the courts' discretion, and the lapse of time and possible inadmissibility of evidence were merely matters for the court to consider in the exercise of that discretion. (*Chung Chuck* v. *R.* [1930] A.C. 244, P.C. followed; *R. v. Saunders* [1974] C.L.Y. 517 considered.)

HOLDER *v.* R. [1978] 3 W.L.R. 817, P.C.

158. —— Privy Council. See § 2434.

159. British Honduras—insurance—third party—limitation of liability. See HARKER *v.* CALEDONIAN INSURANCE CO., § 2593.

160. British nationality. See ALIENS.

161. Commonwealth Development Corporation Act 1978 (c. 2)

This Act consolidates the enactments relating to the Commonwealth Development Corporation with corrections and minor amendments made under the Consolidation of Enactments (Procedure) Act 1949.

S. 1 lays down the constitution of the Commonwealth Development Corporation; s. 2 deals with its purpose, and its powers; s. 3 particularises enterprises to which these powers relate; s. 4 makes supplemental provisions to ss. 2 and 3; s. 5 empowers the Minister of Overseas Development to give to the Corporation directions as to the exercise and performance of its functions; s. 6 deals with the annual report of the Corporation, and other information and returns concerning its activities which it shall make to the Minister; s. 7 directs the Corporation to take all practicable steps to secure the interests of its employees; s. 8 makes special provisions as to the Corporation's activities in dependent territories; s. 9 delimits the borrowing powers of the Corporation; s. 10 empowers the Minister to make advances to the Corporation; s. 11 empowers made under the Bankruptcy Act 1914 (c. 59), s. 133 and the Public Offices Fees Act 1879 (c. 58), ss. 2, 3; operative on June 1, 1978; provides for the pay- the Treasury to guarantee the repayment of the principal and interest of any authorised borrowing; s. 12 deals with the Corporation's repayment of advances, and interest thereon, made under s. 10; s. 13 enables the Minister to remit certain debts of the Corporation; s. 14 makes provision with respect to the reserve fund of the Corporation; s. 15 adumbrates the Corporation's financial duty and directs the application of its surplus revenue; s. 16 regulates the accounts and audit of the Corporation; s. 17 is the interpretation section; s. 18 deals with repeals, savings and transitional provisions; s. 19 contains the short title.

The Act received the Royal Assent on March 23, 1978, and came into force on April 23, 1978.

162. Dominica

COMMONWEALTH OF DOMINICA CONSTITUTION ORDER 1978 (No. 1027) [£1·75], made under the West Indies Act 1967 (c. 4), s. 5 (4); operative on November 3, 1978; provides a new constitution for Dominica as a sovereign democratic republic within the Commonwealth, styled the Commonwealth of Dominica, to come into effect on November 3, 1978, upon the termination of the status of association of Dominica with the U.K. under the Act.

DOMINICA MODIFICATION OF ENACTMENTS ORDER 1978 (No. 1030) [25p], made under the West Indies Act 1967, ss. 13 (2), 14; operative on November 3, 1978; the status of association of Dominica with the U.K. ends on November 3, 1978. This Order effects amendments and modifications to certain Acts that appear to Her Majesty to be necessary in consequence thereof.

DOMINICA TERMINATION OF ASSOCIATION ORDER 1978 (No. 1031) [10p], made under the West Indies Act 1967, s. 17; operative on November 3, 1978; terminates the status of association of Dominica with the U.K., and provides that Dominica shall cease to be part of Her Majesty's dominions.

COMMONWEALTH OF DOMINICA CONSTITUTION (AMENDMENT) ORDER 1978 (No. 1521) [20p], made under the West Indies Act 1967, s. 5 (4); operative on November 3, 1978; amends the constitution of Dominica established by S.I. 1978 No. 1027 so as to effect various textual corrections.

DOMINICA MODIFICATION OF INSTRUMENTS (AMENDMENT) ORDER 1978 (No. 1622) [10p], made under the West Indies Act 1967, ss. 13 (2), 15 (2), 17 (6); operative on December 15, 1978; makes certain corrections to S.I. 1978 No. 1030.

163. Enforcement of judgments

The Legal Division of the Commonwealth Secretariat has published two reports entitled " The Recognition and Enforcement of Judgments and Orders and the Service of Process within the Commonwealth." The reports deal with arrangements for co-operation in these areas of law within the Commonwealth, and are available, free of charge, from the Commonwealth Secretariat, Marlborough House, Pall Mall, London SW1Y 5HX.

164. Fugitive offenders. See EXTRADITION.

165. Gibraltar

GIBRALTAR SUPREME COURT (ADMIRALTY PRACTICE) RULES ORDER 1978 (No. 276) [15p], made under the Colonial Courts of Admiralty Act 1890 (c. 27), s. 7; approves Rules of Court regulating court fees and allowances to be taken and paid in the Supreme Court of Gibraltar in the exercise of the jurisdiction conferred by the 1890 Act.

166. Immigration. See ADMINISTRATIVE LAW.

167. Jamaica—title to land—earlier possession proceedings. See PATRICK *v.* BEVERLEY GARDENS DEVELOPMENT CO., § 1198.

168. Malaysia—anti-corruption law

[Mal.] [Prevention of Corruption Act (Malaysia), s. 30.]

S. 30 of the Prevention of Corruption Act (Malaysia) enables a principal either to recover the amount of the bribe from his agent as money had and received, or compensation for actual loss through the transaction as damages for fraud, but not both. He must elect between the two.

A, the agent of a housing society, arranged with M that M should purchase cheap land that happened to be on the market; A then recommended the housing society to buy it at a greater price. M bought the land for $456,000 and spent $45,000 evicting squatters. The housing society paid $944,000, leaving M a profit of $443,000, of which he paid $122,000 to A as a bribe. A was convicted of corruption. The housing society brought proceedings against A for the amount of the bribe and for damages for the amount of their loss. The trial judge ordered that the housing society could only recover the amount of the bribe. The Federal Court held that it could recover both amounts, *i.e.* the $122,000 plus the $443,000. On appeal by A, *held,* allowing the appeal, that the housing society had to elect between the two claims at the time at which judgment was entered. (*United Australia* v. *Barclays Bank* [1941] A.C. 1, H.L.(E.) applied; dictum in *Salford Corporation* v. *Lever* [1891] 1 Q.B. 168, C.A. and *Hovenden and Sons* v. *Millhoff* (1900) 83 L.T. 41, C.A. not followed.)

T. MAHESAN S/O THAMBIAH v. MALAYSIA GOVERNMENT OFFICERS' CO-OPERATIVE HOUSING SOCIETY [1978] 2 W.L.R. 444, P.C.

169. **New Zealand—appeal—jurisdiction of Privy Council.** See THOMAS v. THE QUEEN, § 2433.

170. —— **option to purchase land—declaration procedure.** See ROSS v. HENDERSON, § 3057.

171. **Northern Ireland.** See NORTHERN IRELAND.

172. **Pakistan.** See INTERNATIONAL LAW.

173. **Rhodesia—sanctions—promoting emigration—encouraging " members of the public generally "**
[Southern Rhodesia (United Nations' Sanctions) (No. 2) Order 1968 (S.I. No. 1020), art. 14 (1) (*b*).]
The soliciting of a particular member of the general public to emigrate to Rhodesia is illegal as an act relating to " members of the public generally."
The defendant was indicted upon a number of specimen counts each alleging that he solicited or encouraged a named member of the public to emigrate to Rhodesia contrary to art. 14 (1) (*b*) of the 1968 Order, the defendant having been engaged in interviewing and supplying application forms to applicants seeking work in Rhodesia. The trial judge directed an acquittal upon all counts on the grounds that art. 14 (1) (*b*) referred to the doing of an act relating to " members of the public generally," which expression excluded from the prohibition an act relating to one particular member of the public. Upon a reference being made by the Att.-Gen., *held,* that the persons named in the particular counts were approached as " members of the public generally " and that accordingly the offence was made out.
ATT.-GEN.'S REFERENCE (NO. 2 OF 1977) [1978] 1 W.L.R. 29, C.A.

174. —— **Southern Rhodesia Act 1965—continuation**
SOUTHERN RHODESIA ACT 1965 (CONTINUATION) ORDER 1978 (No. 1625) [10p], made under the Southern Rhodesia Act 1965 (c. 76), s. 3 (2); operative on November 16, 1978; continues in force for a further year the powers conferred by s. 2 of the 1965 Act to make Orders in Council in relation to Southern Rhodesia.

174a. **St. Lucia**
SAINT LUCIA MODIFICATION OF ENACTMENTS ORDER 1978 (No. 1899) [25p], made under the West Indies Act 1967 (c. 4), ss. 13 (2) (3), 14; operative on February 22, 1979; effects amendments and modifications to certain enactments that are necessary in consequence of the termination of the status of association of St. Lucia with the U.K.
SAINT LUCIA TERMINATION OF ASSOCIATION ORDER 1978 (No. 1900) [10p], made under the West Indies Act 1967 (c. 4), s. 17 (2); operative on February 22, 1979; terminates the status of association of Saint Lucia with the U.K.
SAINT LUCIA CONSTITUTION ORDER 1978 (No. 1901) [£2·00], made under the West Indies Act 1967 (c. 4), s. 5 (4); operative on February 22, 1979; provides a new constitution for St. Lucia.

175. **Singapore—appeal to Privy Council—solicitor—disciplinary proceedings**
[Legal Profession Act (Statutes of the Republic of Singapore, 1970 rev., c. 217), ss. 84, 88 (1) (*b*), 89 (1); Supreme Court of Judicature Act (1970 rev., c. 15), s. 29.]
An order of a High Court judge on an originating summons in a case of disciplinary proceedings is a judgment or order of the High Court in a civil matter within s. 29 of the Supreme Court of Judicature Act 1970 and the Court of Appeal has jurisdiction to determine the advocate's appeal.
The Court of Appeal of Singapore refused to reopen an appeal on H's

application to hear fresh evidence. H accused the court of setting the seal upon dishonesty, and later repeated the accusation in writing. The Law Society found that behaviour to be improper and fined H $250 under s. 89 (1) of the Legal Profession Act 1970, though they found under s. 88 (1) (*b*) that no cause of sufficient gravity existed for a formal investigation. H applied by originating summons to the High Court to set the order aside on the ground that where the inquiry committee was proceeding under ss. 88 (1) (*b*) and 89 (1), the conduct complained of had to fall under the heads enumerated in s. 84 (2). The application was dismissed. The Court of Appeal upheld the High Court's decision, and held, in the alternative, that there was no right of appeal from such an order of the High Court. On appeal by H, *held*, that the Court of Appeal had jurisdiction to determine the appeal. However, the heads enumerated in s. 84 (2) were not exhaustive of cases of misconduct with which the Law Society can deal under ss. 88 (1) (*b*) and 89, and the Law Society's order was justified.

HILBORNE *v.* LAW SOCIETY OF SINGAPORE [1978] 1 W.L.R. 841, P.C.

176. —— **by-law—exclusion of liability of port authority.** See KARUPPAN BHOOMIDAS *v.* PORT OF SINGAPORE AUTHORITY, § 2075.

177. —— **defence—not raised at first instance.** See MOHAMAD KUNJO S/O RAMALAN *v.* PUBLIC PROSECUTOR, § 457.

178. **Solomon Islands**

SOLOMON ISLANDS INDEPENDENCE ORDER 1978 (No. 783) [£1·75], made under the Foreign Jurisdiction Act 1890 (c. 37); operative on July 7, 1978; makes provision for a Constitution for Solomon Islands to come into effect on independence.

179. **Solomon Islands Act 1978 (c. 15)**

This Act makes provision for, and in connection with, the attainment by Solomon Islands of independence within the Commonwealth.

S. 1 states that, on and after July 7, 1978 (" Independence Day "), the Solomon Islands shall be independent, and their territories no longer the responsibility of Her Majesty's Government; s. 2 deals with the effects of this independence upon British nationality; s. 3 defines those persons having a " connection with Solomon Islands "; s. 4 makes provisions with respect to British protected persons; s. 5 relates to the position of married women; s. 6 lays down rules of construction for the nationality provisions of the Act; s. 7 contains consequential amendments of law; s. 8 confers upon Her Majesty a discretion in dealing with pending appeals to the Privy Council where leave to appeal has been granted before Independence Day; s. 9 is the interpretation section; s. 10 directs the method of citing the Act.

The Act received the Royal Assent on May 25, 1978, and came into force on July 7, 1978.

180. **Trinidad and Tobago—jurisdiction—deprivation of liberty.** See MAHARAJ *v.* ATT.-GEN. OF TRINIDAD AND TOBAGO (No. 2), § 2340.

181. **Tuvalu Act 1978 (c. 20)**

This Act provides for the attainment of Tuvalu of independence within the Commonwealth.

S. 1 states that on and after October 1, 1978, the U.K. Government shall have no responsibility for the government of Tuvalu; s. 2 contains consequential modifications of British Nationality Acts; s. 3 provides for the retention of U.K. citizenship by certain citizens of Tuvalu; s. 4 contains consequential modifications of other enactments; s. 5 contains definitions; s. 6 gives the short title.

The Act received the Royal Assent on June 30, 1978, and came into force on that date.

BOOKS AND ARTICLES. See *post*, pp. [1], [12].

BUILDING AND ENGINEERING, ARCHITECTS AND SURVEYORS

182. **Amendment to R.I.C.S. chartered designation—whether valid**

Plaintiff members claimed alterations to charter designations in the institutions by-laws were unreasonable, consideration of them by the Privy Council as provided for under the charter, being postponed pending the outcome of these proceedings. *Held*, the institution's charter enabled by-laws to be so altered by special resolution. The court could only interfere if the institution had conducted itself in such a way as to make it inequitable for it to exercise its powers under the charter: MERRILLS *v.* ROYAL INSTITUTE OF CHARTERED SURVEYORS, *The Times*, November 1, 1978, Templeman J.

183. **Building contract—arbitration clause—summary judgment for part of claim**
The G.L.C. employed W Co. as main contractors for the development of an area of land. W Co. employed as sub-contractors E Co. to provide all mechanical services required. Cl. 21 of the sub-contract stated that if the main contract was determined, then the sub-contract should also determine and the sub-contractors be entitled to be paid. The contract also contained a general arbitration clause. On February 22, 1974, the contract between W Co. and the G.L.C. was repudiated; therefore under cl. 21, E Co. were entitled to be paid for all work and materials up to that date. The last interim certificate, dated January 25, 1974, had retained £52,437 as retention money. E Co. claimed that this sum was now due, and they calculated that W Co. also owed a further £135,000 for work to February 22, 1974. A writ was issued for the full amount and, under R.S.C., Ord. 14, judgment was given for the £52,437 and W Co. were given leave to defend as to the balance, but by consent it was to go to arbitration. W Co. appealed against that order, and Kilner-Brown J. set aside the judgment for £52,000, and referred the whole matter to arbitration. E Co. appealed. *Held*, that as there was no evidence that the sum of £52,000 was not owing, there should be judgment for that sum and the rest of the matters in dispute should go to arbitration: ELLIS MECHANICAL SERVICES *v.* WATES CONSTRUCTION [1978] 1 Lloyd's Rep. 33, C.A.

184. —— **express terms—obligation to supply at appropriate time.** See FISCHBACH AND MOORE OF CANADA *v.* NORANDA MINES, § 311.

185. **Building regulations**
BUILDING (FIRST AMENDMENT) REGULATIONS 1978 (No. 723) [60p], made under the Public Health Act 1936 (c. 49), ss. 61, 62, as substituted by the Health and Safety at Work etc. Act 1974 (c. 37), s. 61 (1), the Public Health Act 1961 (c. 64), s. 4 (2) (5) as amended by s. 61 (3), Sched. 6, Pt. I, para. 4 to the 1974 Act and s. 9 (3) of the 1961 Act amended by s. 61 (3) of Sched. 6 Pt. I, para. 8 to the 1974 Act; operative on June 1, 1978; amend S.I. 1976 No. 1676 by introducing provisions for the furthering of the conservation of fuel and power.

186. **Channel tunnel.** See HIGHWAYS AND BRIDGES.

187. **Dangerous premises.** See NEGLIGENCE.

188. **Factories.** See FACTORIES.

189. **Housing.** See HOUSING.

190. **Mortgages.** See MORTGAGES.

191. **Negligence—land subject to subsidence—failure to inspect properly—liability in tort and contract.** See BATTY *v.* METROPOLITAN PROPERTY REALISATIONS, § 2067.

192. —— **surveyor's report—no mention of dry-rot—measure of damages.** See UPSTONE *v.* G. D. W. CARNEGIE & Co., § 2071.

193. **Northern Ireland.** See NORTHERN IRELAND.

BOOKS. See *post*, p. [2].

BUILDING SOCIETIES

194. **Fees**
BUILDING SOCIETIES (FEES) REGULATIONS 1978 (No. 1752) [20p], made under the Building Societies Act 1962 (c. 37), s. 123 (1); operative on January 1, 1979; increases the fees payable in connection with the exercise by the Central Office and the Chief Registrar of their functions under the 1962 Act. They supersede S.I. 1977 No. 2000.

195. Home Purchase Assistance and Housing Corporation Guarantee Act 1978 (c. 27).
See § 1576.

196. Mortgages. See MORTGAGES.

197. Powers—losses incurred by another society—arrangement to compensate investors—whether intra vires
[Building Societies Act 1962 (c. 37), s. 43 (1).]
An arrangement in which building societies mount a rescue operation for investors in one society purely to preserve public confidence in building societies, is an arrangement within s. 43 (1) of the Act.
In 1978, on the death of the chairman of a building society, a huge deficiency was discovered which would have severely affected investors in the society. In order to protect the reputation of building societies generally, various other societies mounted a rescue operation so that the investors would not suffer. The societies sought the determination of the court as to whether the proposed arrangement was intra vires. *Held*, on a true construction of s. 43, the section did not require mutuality, nor did it prevent provision being made for part losses. The arrangement was therefore intra vires.
HALIFAX BUILDING SOCIETY *v.* REGISTRAR OF FRIENDLY SOCIETIES [1978] 3 All E.R. 403, Templeman J.

BURIAL AND CREMATION

198. Fees
HUMAN REMAINS REMOVAL LICENCE (PRESCRIBED FEE) ORDER 1978 (No. 239) [10p], made under the Fees (Increase) Act 1923 (c. 4), s. 7 (1) as amended by S.I. 1977 No. 2140; operative on April 1, 1978; increases to £5 the prescribed fee for a licence issued under s. 25 of the Burial Act 1857 for the removal of human remains interred in a place of burial.

CAPITAL TAXATION

199. Capital gains tax. See INCOME TAX.

200. Double taxation relief
DOUBLE TAXATION RELIEF (TAXES ON ESTATES OF DECEASED PERSONS AND INHERITANCES AND ON GIFTS) (REPUBLIC OF IRELAND) ORDER 1978 (No. 1107) [30p], made under the Finance Act 1975 (c. 7), Sched. 7, para. 7; gives effect to a Double Taxation Convention with the Republic of Ireland.

201. Estate duty—exemption—members of armed forces—whether wound was a cause of death
[Finance Act 1952 (c. 33).] By s. 71 of the Finance Act 1952, estate duty is not chargeable in respect of a person who died from a wound inflicted when the deceased was a member of the armed forces, and on active service, as certified by the Defence Council. The court held that the Council ought to have granted a certificate that the fourth Duke of Westminster died in 1967 from such a wound. The wound was on the evidence a cause of the death: it did not have to be the only cause nor a direct pathological cause: BARTY-KING *v.* MINISTRY OF DEFENCE, *The Times*, October 13, 1978, May J.

202. Finance Act 1978 (c. 42)
Pt. IV (ss. 62–74) deals with capital transfer tax: s. 62 and Sched. 10 set out the rates of tax; s. 63 increases the exemption limit for transfers to non-domiciled spouses; s. 64 provides for further relief for business property; s. 65 provides for further relief for woodlands; s. 66 amends the definition of control of a company; s. 67 relates to employee trusts; s. 68 relates to the alteration of dispositions taking effect on death; s. 69 relates to the sale of interests under a settlement; s. 70 charges capital transfer tax on the termination of a discretionary trust; s. 71 relates to protective trusts; s. 72 deals with Government securities in foreign ownership; s. 73 relates to life policies and deferred annuity contracts; s. 74 relates to the increase in value of settled property by the omission to exercise a right.

ARTICLES. See *post*, p. [13].

CARRIERS

203. Carriage by road—C.M.R. convention—limitation of action between sub-contractor and contractor

[Carriage of Goods by Road Act 1965 (c. 37), s. 1, Sched; Convention on the Contract for the International Carriage of Goods by Road, arts. 32, paras. 1 (c), 2, 4, 39.]

The limitation period for a claim by a sub-contractor against a contractor failing to pay for carriage under a contract subject to the C.M.R. conditions is, by virtue of art. 32, para. 1 (c) of the Convention, one year from the expiry of three months after the making of the contract.

In July 1971 L Ltd. sub-contracted to M Ltd. the carriage of certain machinery from Northfleet in Kent to Le Mans in France. The contract was subject to the conditions set out in the Schedule to the 1965 Act, the C.M.R. conditions. By a writ issued in March 1973 M Ltd. claimed monies allegedly due under the contract. L Ltd. contended that the claim was time-barred by virtue of art. 32, para. 1 (c) of the Convention. M Ltd. relied, inter alia, upon art. 32, para. 2 and art. 39, para. 4 to support a construction of the Convention which provided for a later start to the period of limitation. *Held,* dismissing the claim, that the action was time-barred and could not be resuscitated by reference either to art. 39 or to art. 32 para. 2.

MULLER BATAVIER *v.* LAURENT TRANSPORT CO. [1977] R.T.R. 499, May J.

204. —— —— sub-contracted carriage—whether acceptance of consignment note

[Carriage of Goods by Road Act 1965 (c. 37), s. 1, Sched.; Convention on the Contract for the International Carriage of Goods by Road, arts. 3, 4, 34, 35, 36].

On a true construction the words " acceptance of the . . . consignment note " in art. 34 of the C.M.R. Convention are to be given their natural and ordinary meaning and a consignment note is accepted when it is taken over by the carrier with a view to carrying out the next part of the carriage.

S, as consignees, entered into a contract under the Convention scheduled to the Act (C.M.R. Convention) with G Ltd., as carriers, for the carriage of certain goods from Heathrow Airport to Catania in Italy. G Ltd. sub-contracted the carriage for the whole journey to B.R.S. who sub-contracted part of the journey to F who were outside the jurisdiction. F sub-contracted that part of the carriage to V who carried the goods together with a copy of the consignment note which did not comply with art. 35 of the C.M.R. Convention in that it did not bear V's name and address. The goods were damaged. S began an action for damages against G Ltd. and B.R.S. They obtained leave to issue a concurrent writ and serve notice of it on F outside the jurisdiction on the basis that they were party to the contract by virtue of art. 34 of the C.M.R. Convention and were liable as " last carrier " within art. 36. F sought an order setting aside that order on the ground that V was the last carrier. S contended that V could not be the last carrier since he had not accepted the consignment note within art. 34 because he had not complied with art. 35. By the time F's application was heard any claim against V was time-barred. The master refused the application. F appealed. *Held,* allowing the appeal, that a mere failure by a carrier to enter his name and address on a copy of a consignment note received with the goods could not mean that there had been no acceptance of it within art. 34 and in those circumstances S could not establish that F were the " last carrier " within art. 36, therefore F could not be liable under the C.M.R. Convention. (*Ulster-Swift* v. *Taunton Meat Haulage* (*Note*) [1977] C.L.Y. 2553a considered.)

SGS-ATES COMPONENTI ELETTRONICI S.P.A. *v.* GRAPPO [1977] R.T.R. 442, Goff J.

205. —— liability of carrier—consignor's duty to indemnify carriers—applicability of indemnity

[Road Haulage Association's Conditions of Carriage (1967 edition).]

The contractual indemnity to be given by a trader to a carrier under cl. 3 (4) of the Road Haulage Association's Conditions of Carriage does not extend to the carrier's liability to his employee for breach of employers' duties.

Traders contracted with carriers for the carriage by road of two large cold boxes. The boxes were loaded on to the carriers' lorry but on their journey the boxes struck an overhead gantry which fell on to the cab, injuring the carriers' driver. The driver claimed damages from both the traders and the carriers and judgment was given against the carriers, the traders being cleared of any blame. The carriers thereupon claimed an indemnity from the traders, relying upon cl. 3 (4) of the Conditions of Carriage, to which the contract was subject, which clause required that the trader indemnified the carrier " against all claims or demands whatsoever by whomsoever made." *Held*, dismissing the claim, that the conditions, including that containing the indemnity, were intended to regulate the carriage of goods and rights and liabilities arising out of such carriage; that the driver's claim fell outside the scope of such matters.

BOUGHEN v. FREDERICK ATTWOOD; CRYOPLANTS (THIRD PARTY) [1978] R.T.R. 313, Donaldson J.

206. Carriage by sea. See SHIPPING AND MARINE INSURANCE.

207. Sub-contractors—loss of goods—indemnity clause in bill of lading

By a contract of carriage contained in or evidenced by bills of lading dated June 2 and 9, 1974, N agreed to carry a containerised cargo belonging to C on the E from Hong Kong to Southampton, and to deliver it at Liverpool. The contract provided, by cl. 1, that " ' merchant ' includes the receiver of the goods, any person owning or entitled to the possession of the goods or this bill of lading," and, by cl. 4, that the " merchant " undertook that no claim would be made against, inter alia, any sub-contractor of the carrier which imposed or attempted to impose any liability whatsoever in connection with the goods, and, if any claim were made, to indemnify the carrier against all consequences thereof. N sub-contracted the carriage of the goods from Southampton to Liverpool to SC and while the goods were in the custody of SC some of the goods were stolen. I, indorsees of the bills of lading, contended that SC were liable in negligence and claimed £25,075·60 in respect of the lost goods. N applied under s. 41 of the Judicature Act 1925 for an order that all further proceedings be stayed on the ground that I had become a party to the bill of lading and were bound by cl. 4. *Held*, (1) SC, as bailees, were liable unless they could prove that the theft occurred notwithstanding their taking reasonable care of the goods; (2) the fact that N could point to a clear right being infringed, prima facie entitled them to the relief claimed under s. 41; (3) there was a possibility that if the claim was allowed to proceed, N would suffer financial loss; the discretion ought to be exercised in their favour; (4) the words " if such claim should nevertheless be made " merely provided in express terms for the remedy which ought to follow if there were a breach of undertaking; (5) N were entitled to the relief sought. (*Gore* v. *Van der Lann* [1967] C.L.Y. 399, applied): THE ELBE MARU [1978] 1 Lloyd's Rep. 206, Ackner J.

BOOKS AND ARTICLES. See *post*, pp. [2], [13].

CHARITIES

208. Charitable purposes—recreation—promotion of a specific game

[Charities Act 1960 (c. 58), s. 4; Recreational Charities Act 1958 (c. 17), s. 1.]

The mere encouragement of the playing of a sport is not a charitable purpose.

One of the purposes of the Football Association Youth Trust is to organise or provide facilities which will enable or encourage pupils of schools or universities in the United Kingdom to play association football, or other games or sports, and thereby to assist in ensuring that due attention is given to the physical education and development of such pupils as well as to the development and occupation of their minds. The Inland Revenue applied for a declaration that the trust was not entitled to be registered as a charity under s. 4 of the Charities Act 1960 on the grounds that this particular object was not exclusively charitable. *Held*, (1) since the object was not for the provision of general physical education for the pupils, but for the promotion of specific games without any necessary connection between the playing of those games and the education of the pupils as a whole, it was not charitable as being

for the advancement of education; (2) it was not charitable as being for the benefit of the community, or pursuant to the Recreational Charities Act 1958. (*Re Notage, Jones* v. *Palmer* [1895] 2 Ch. 649, distinguished.)
I.R.C. v. McMULLEN [1978] 1 All E.R. 230, Walton J.

209. —— relief of poverty—" working men's hostel "—meaning
Where money is left under a will for the purposes of a working men's hostel to be constructed there is sufficient connotation of poverty in such a concept as to enable such object to constitute a valid charitable trust.
The testator directed that the residue of his estate be held on trust to pay the same to the appropriate official in his home town in Cyprus for the purpose of the construction of a working men's hostel. The trustees sought a declaration as to whether a valid trust was created. *Held,* that " working men's hostel " connoted modest accommodation for those workers of low income and accordingly the trust was valid as being for the relief of poverty. (*Re Lucas* [1922] 2 Ch. 52 and *Guinness Trust (London Fund) Founded 1890, Registered 1902* v. *Green* [1955] C.L.Y. 2338, applied.)
Re NIYAZI'S WILL TRUSTS [1978] 1 W.L.R. 910, Megarry V.-C.

210. —— showground purposes—whether exclusively charitable—defence of res judicata
A trust for " showground, park and recreational purposes " falls within the fourth head of *Pemsel's* case and is exclusively charitable.
In 1938, in consideration of Brisbane County Council's discharging a debt of £450, the trustees of a society who organised a district annual show, conveyed 20 acres of land to the council on certain conditions: that the area be set aside permanently for showground, park and recreational purposes; the show-ring to be levelled off and the society to have exclusive use of the ground free of charge for two weeks each year for the district show. In 1970 the council contracted to sell the land to developers for use as a shopping centre. The relator S objected to such planning consent and his appeal reached the High Ct. of Australia. An action by the Att.-Gen. in 1971 for a declaration that the purported sale was ultra vires and void failed. The Att.-Gen. then sought a declaration that the land was subject to a valid and enforceable charitable trust. The declaration was granted but the council and developers appealed on the ground that the council did not hold the land as a trustee and there was no such trust; even if there was, the Att.-Gen. was precluded from asserting that fact since, inter alia, the existence of the trust should have been put forward in the previous litigation between the parties. The Sup. Ct. dismissed the appeal and it came to the Privy Council. *Held,* dismissing the defendants' appeal, that (1) the conditions upon which the land was originally conveyed showed a clear intention to create a trust and the council therefore acquired the land as trustee; (2) the trust was exclusively charitable (a trust for " showground purposes " promoting agriculture), and was unaffected by the condition permitting the land to be used by private individuals; (3) it was inappropriate to assert the existence of a trust in the previous actions and the issue in the present action did not amount to an abuse of process, therefore the defence of res judicata failed. (*Income Tax Special Purposes Commissioners* v. *Pemsel* [1891] A.C. 531, and *I.R.C.* v. *Yorkshire Agricultural Society* [1928] 1 K.B. 611, C.A., applied.)
BRISBANE CITY COUNCIL v. ATT.-GEN. FOR QUEENSLAND [1978] 3 W.L.R. 299, P.C.

211. Charity Commissioners' Report
The Charity Commissioners have published their annual report for 1977, commenting that 3,598 new charities were registered during the year—601 more than in 1976—bringing the total number registered to 12,908; and that a record number of 986 administrative schemes for altering trusts were drawn up. The Report is available from HMSO (H.C. 494) [£1·10].

212. Commissioners' scheme
CHARITIES (THE NEW COLLEGE OF COBHAM) ORDER 1978 (No. 1155) [25p], made under the Charities Act 1960 (c. 58), s. 19 (1); operative on August 17, 1978; gives effect to a scheme of the Charity Commissioners for the New Col-

lege of Cobham in Kent, an almshouse charity administered by a body corporate, incorporated by Act of Parliament in 1597.

213. Cy-près doctrine—general charitable intent

Where a testator takes pains to identify a particular charitable purpose which is capable of being carried out at the date of the will but not at the date of the death, the court will be slow to find a general charitable intention.

T, by her will, bequeathed her residuary estate on trust "to pay and divide equally between the Blind Home, Scott Sheer, Keighley and the Old Folks Home at Hillworth Lodge, Keighley for the benefit of the patients." There was no "Blind Home" as such, but there was the "Keighley and District Association for the Blind" which had been in Scott Sheer since before the making of the will, and which was frequently called "the Blind Home." However, Hill-worth Lodge which had been an old people's home at the date of the will, had now closed down and the premises turned into government offices. The old people of the area were now accommodated in various old people's homes. *Held*, (1) the first gift was for the benefit of the patients for the time being of the Blind Home, not for the general purposes of the association which ran the home; (2) in relation to the second gift, neither the first gift nor the circumstances showed any general charitable intention and the court would be slow to find one where a particular charitable purpose had been specified. The gift could not be applied cy-près, it therefore failed and would pass as on intestacy. (*Re Harwood* [1936] Ch. 285 applied; *Re Lucas* (1947) C.L.C. 1109 and *Re Knox* [1937] Ch. 109 distinguished.)

Re SPENCE (DECD.); OGDEN *v.* SHACKLETON [1978] 3 W.L.R. 483, Megarry V.-C.

213a. Exempt charities

EXEMPT CHARITIES ORDER 1978 (No. 453) [10p], made under the Charities Act 1960 (c. 58), Sched. 2, para. (*c*); operative on May 1, 1978; declares University College London to be an "exempt charity" within the meaning of the 1960 Act.

213b. Methodist Church

CHARITIES (METHODIST CHURCH) REGULATIONS 1978 (No. 1836) [10p], made under the Charities Act 1960 (c. 58), ss. 29 (4), 43 (1), 45 (6); operative on February 1, 1979; enable land held upon certain model trusts of the Methodist Church to be sold or otherwise disposed of without the necessity of the Court or the Charity Commissioners which would otherwise be required by s. 29 of the 1960 Act.

214. Northern Ireland. See NORTHERN IRELAND.

215. Rating. See RATING AND VALUATION.

216. Rating relief—licensee occupying house owned by charity

[General Rate Act 1967 (c. 9), s. 40 (1).] A charity applied for rate relief on a house it owned which was being used for charitable purposes, being occupied by a licensee. *Held*, "occupation" in rating statutes means actual not legal occupation (*Westminster Council* v. *Southern Railway Co.* [1936] A.C. 511 applied). The degree of control to determine who was in actual occupation must take into account both the degree of control exercised by the owner and the purpose for which the owner allowed the other person to reside in the house (*Soldiers, Sailors and Airmen's Families Association* v. *Merton London Borough Council* [1966] C.L.Y. 10256 followed). In applying these tests, the charity was in rateable occupation within s. 40 (1): FORCES HELP SOCIETY *v.* CANTERBURY CITY COUNCIL (1978) 122 S.J. 760, Slade J.

217. Registration—objects not exclusively charitable

[Charities Act 1960 (c. 58), s. 4.] The objects of the Football Association Youth Trust as set out in its trust deed were (a) to organise or provide facilities which will enable or encourage pupils of schools and universities in any part of the United Kingdom to play Association football or other games or sports; and (b) to organise or provide facilities for physical recreation in the interests of social welfare. *Held,* that the objects were not legally charitable or not exclusively legally charitable, so that the Trust was not entitled to be registered under Charities Act 1960, s. 4: I.R.C. *v.* SIR ANDREW STEPHEN, *The Times*, October 19, 1978, C.A.

218. Value added tax. See VALUE ADDED TAX.

ARTICLES. See *post*, p. [14].

CLUBS AND ASSOCIATIONS

219. Rules—political party—power of N.E.C. to intervene—natural justice

Although the national Labour Party and a constituency party are separate associations, cl. VIII (2) (*a*) and (*c*) of the Labour Party constitution gives the National Executive Committee power to suspend officers and committees of the local party and to appoint a national agent to act in their stead.

There was a struggle for power in the Newham North-East local constituency Labour Party between two factions over whether Reg Prentice, M.P., should be retained as parliamentary candidate. The struggle became so intense that the national party intervened through the National Executive Committee, by suspending all the officers and committees of the local party and taking over control itself. By cl. VIII (2) of the constitution and standing orders of the Labour Party, the N.E.C. had the power to: (a) ensure the establishment of and keep in active operation a constituency Labour Party in every constituency; (b) to enforce the Constitution, Standing Orders and Rules of the party and to take any action it deemed necessary for such purpose, whether by way of disaffiliation of an organisation or expulsion of an individual, or otherwise. By cl. II (2) (*e*), constituency Labour parties were affiliated members of the party. The N.E.C. also ordered an inquiry into the activities of the two plaintiffs, who were leading members of one faction, with their suspension from membership of the party pending the result of the inquiry. The plaintiffs claimed declarations that the N.E.C.'s resolutions were ultra vires and contrary to natural justice, and injunctions restraining them from implementing them. *Held*, that although the national party and constituency party were separate asociations, the N.E.C. had power to take the actions it had under cl. VIII (2) (*a*) and (*c*); a suspension pending an inquiry imposed solely as a matter of good administration did not require compliance with the rules of natural justice, though such a suspension might have been invalidated if the N.E.C. could have been shown to have the ulterior motive of promoting one faction over the other. (*Furnell* v. *Whangarei High Schools Board* [1973] C.L.Y. 17 applied; *American Cyanamid Co.* v. *Ethicon* [1975] C.L.Y. 2640 distinguished; dictum of Megarry J. in *John* v. *Rees* [1969] C.L.Y. 353 not applied.)

LEWIS *v.* HEFFER; MCCORMICK *v.* HEFFER [1978] 1 W.L.R. 1061, C.A.

ARTICLES. See *post*, p. [14].

COMMONS

220. Open spaces. See OPEN SPACES AND RECREATION GROUNDS.

221. Registration—customary rights—no express reservation in lease—evidence of use

[Law of Property Act 1925 (c. 20), s. 62 (1).]

Where tenements were formed out of the waste of a manor and leased as customary land, express mention in the lease of the customary rights of common is not necessary for such rights to be conferred.

In the seventeenth century a parcel of waste land of the manor was leased for 99 years with provision for renewal upon expiry in return, *inter alia*, for a covenant to do " personal suit and service to the court baron." The lease was twice renewed, and in 1878 a further 99 year lease was granted; in 1929 the freehold reversion was conveyed to the leaseholder of whom E was the successor. C owned a farm adjoining the common over which, on the evidence, a previous tenant had exercised grazing rights until 1926, but not thereafter, there being no reservation of such rights in subsequent conveyances. The owner of the common lodged objections to the registration by E and C of rights of common, both registrations being confirmed by the Chief Commons Commissioner. *Held*, on appeal by the owner of the common, that E's registration would stand, the passing of customary rights of common being inferred in the case of the lease of customary land; but that C's registration would be cancelled since it could not be inferred from the use of the common for grazing until 1926 that such rights continued at the time of the conveyance to C's predecessor in title in 1948.

Re BROXHEAD COMMON, WHITEHILL, HAMPSHIRE (1977) 33 P. & C.R. 451, Brightman J.

222. —— decisions of the Commons Commissioner

Re BROOKWOOD LYE, WOKING, SURREY (No. 1), Ref. No. 236 D/148 (the commissioner *held* that prescriptive rights of estovers and turbary were registrable rights in common, being the right to take the natural produce of the land of another person, whether or not that other partook of them also).

Re BURY FIELD, NEWPORT PAGNELL, MILTON KEYNES BOROUGH, BUCKS., Ref. nos. 203/D/7–8 (the commissioners *held*, (1) the word "objection" in the Commons Registration Act 1965 means objection to a registration, so unless the use to which land is put throws light on the validity of a registration he had no jurisdiction to consider it; (2) a person possessing a right of common could license some third person to enjoy it and receive payment in money or in kind for it (*Davies* v. *Davies* [1974] C.L.Y. 316 applied)).

Re CLIFFORD COMMON, CLIFFORD, HEREFORD AND WORCESTER (No. 4) Ref. No. 215/D/225 (M came to live in Clifford in 1964; since that time, with other commoners, he fished the River Wye from Clifford Common without let or hindrance. *Held*, that such a period is not long enough for M to have acquired a right by prescription; further his alternative claim as a villager failed, since there is no right in a fluctuating body of persons, such as the inhabitants of a village (*Gateward's Case* (1607) 6 Co.Rep. 59b applied)).

Re HIGHER PREDANNACK DOWNS, MULLION, CORNWALL (No. 2), Ref. No. 206/D/492 (*held*, that a muddy lane, along which cattle passed and occasionally ate grass, was not a highway and was not thereby excluded from the definition of "common land" in s. 22 (1) of the Commons Registration Act 1965).

Re LUSTLEIGH CLEAVE, DEVON (No. 1), Ref. No. 209/D/114–130. (The question was raised of whether "shooting rights" or "sporting rights" were rights of common, and thus capable of registration under the Commons Registration Act 1965. *Held*, a right of common is an incorporeal hereditament giving a right to take some part of the natural produce of the land over which it is exercisable. The kinds of produce are nowhere defined with precision. The right to go on land for shooting, and such a right coupled with a further right to take away the game, was distinguished in *Webber* v. *Lee* (1882) 9 Q.B.D. 315. The right to take away the game was held to be a profit à prendre. The mere right to shoot is not: it differs fundamentally from a right of common. Rights of common result from the same necessity as common of pasture, viz. for the maintenance and carrying on of husbandry. A right of shooting or sporting, even when coupled with a right to take game is exercised primarily for pleasure, the value of the game as food for the commoner's family being a secondary consideration. Registrations which include rights of shooting or sporting are not to be confirmed.)

Re NORTHAM BURROWS, NORTHAM, DEVON (No. 1) (the Manor of Northam was granted to the Abbey of St. Stephen in Caen by William the Conqueror; since his reign persons grazed animals on Northam Burrows in the purported exercise of a right so to do. These persons were variously described in a number of documents as inhabitants of the parish, inhabitants of Northam, tenants and inhabitants within the manor, the parishioners, the potboilers of the parish and the potwallopers of the manor. *Held*, it was necessary to decide whether these persons were acting as inhabitants of the manor or of the parish: here they were acting as inhabitants of the parish. The courts have long endeavoured to support claims by inhabitants; in some cases, a grant by the Crown to the inhabitants of the right in question has been presumed, but not if that is inconsistent with the past and present state of things, and there is no evidence of a corporation having existed. In other cases, a grant to a corporation in trust for the inhabitants has been presumed. It is also possible to make a further presumption in these circumstances that the original grant to the Abbey could have been made subject to a condition or proviso that the members of the parish should enjoy the right to graze their animals on the Burrows. There was no evidence of such a condition or proviso, but there was nothing inconsistent with such, and there was evidence consistent with such a presumption. On that basis, there was a charitable trust in favour of the inhabitants of the ancient parish of Northam (*Gateward's Case* (1607) 6 Co.Rep. 59b explained; *Goodman* v. *Mayor of Saltash* (1882) 7 App.Cas. 663 and *Lord Rivers* v. *Adams* (1878) 3 Ex.D. 361 applied).

Re THE VILLAGE GREEN AND HARGILL, REDMIRE, NORTH YORKSHIRE. Ref. No. 268/D/250. The Commons Commissioner *held* that a long-continued encroachment on a village green cannot deprive that site of its status as part of the green. The only way the encroachment can lawfully continue, or the green be put to another use, is by private Act of Parliament. (*New Windsor Corp.* v. *Mellor* [1975] C.L.Y. 288 applied.))

223. —— **description of land—necessity for accurate description**
[Commons Registration Act 1965 (c. 64), s. 7 (1); Commons Registration (Objections and Maps) Regulations 1968 (S.I. 1968 No. 989).]

It is essential where land is to be registered as common land, that a brief and accurate description of the land should be published.

Owners of land were ignorant of the fact that it had been provisionally registered as common land. The notice of registration referred to it as CL116 which was the unit of land in which it was contained, but described unit CL116 as being an addition to CL108, which geographically it was not. *Held*, that s. 7 of the Commons Registration Act 1965 did not operate to make the provisional registration final. No one seeing the notice would have reason to believe that the land concerned was included in the notice.

SMITH v. EAST SUSSEX COUNTY COUNCIL (1977) 76 L.G.R. 332, Templeman J.

224. —— **transfer of alleged rights—whether transferor a " person aggrieved "**
[Commons Registration Act 1965 (c. 64), s. 18 (1).]

A person who claimed an interest in and a right over land and had an interest in proceedings before the Commissioner is a " person aggrieved " within s. 18 (1) of the Act.

C was one of 98 persons who claimed commoners' rights over certain land owned by the lords of the manor. All 98 signed a deed purporting to transfer their rights to the parish council and expressing their intention that the parish council should apply for registration of those rights pursuant to the Commons Registration Act 1965. The rights were provisionally registered in the land section and the rights section of the county council register. The landowners objected to both registrations and the matter was referred to the Chief Commons Commissioner. At the hearing before the Commissioner the parish council was represented by counsel and C was called to give evidence. The Commissioner decided that there were no such rights. C applied as a " person aggrieved " to the Commissioner pursuant to s. 18 (1) of the Act to state a case for the decision of the High Court. The Commissioner refused on the ground that C was not a " person aggrieved " within s. 18 (1). C applied for an order of mandamus directing the Commissioner to state a case. *Held*, granting the order, that C had both claimed an interest in and a right over the land and had an interest in the proceedings before the Commissioner and the words " person aggrieved " should not be subjected to a restrictive interpretation. (*Att.-Gen.* (*Gambia*) v. *N'Jie* [1961] C.L.Y. 6792 applied.)

R. v. CHIEF COMMONS COMMISSIONER, *ex p.* CONSTABLE (1977) 76 L.G.R. 127, D.C.

225. —— **waste land of a manor—land must belong to manor at date of registration**
Land which had once belonged to a manor, but which had ceased to have any connection with the manor more than 50 years ago, was *held* not to be " waste land of a manor " within s. 22 (1) (*b*) of the Commons Registration Act 1965. To be registrable as common land, the land must belong to the manor at

the date of registration: BOX PARISH COUNCIL *v.* LACEY, *The Times*, May 26, 1978, C.A.

226. Search—failure to search—negligence of solicitors. See G. & K. LADENBAU (U.K.) *v.* CRAWLEY & DE REYA, § 2823.

ARTICLES. See *post*, p. [14].

COMPANY LAW

227. Appointment of inspectors—natural justice

[Companies Act 1948 (c. 38), s. 165 (*b*) (ii); Companies Act 1967 (c. 81), s. 109.]

The rules of natural justice do not apply to an appointment of inspectors by the Department of Trade, and such an appointment cannot be challenged so long as the Secretary of State acts in good faith and within the powers conferred by the Companies Acts.

The Department of Trade appointed two inspectors to investigate N Co.'s affairs. The directors objected on the ground that there was no reason for such an appointment, and demanded to know the Department's reasons. The Department refused the information. N Co. sought a declaration that the appointment was unlawful and ultra vires. On the Department's motion, the judge at first instance struck out N Co.'s motion as disclosing no reasonable cause of action. On appeal by N Co., *held*, dismissing the appeal, that the appointment of inspectors carried no implication that there was any case against the company, and could not be challenged so long as the Secretary of State acted bona fide and within his powers under the Companies Acts.

NORWEST HOLST *v.* SECRETARY OF STATE FOR TRADE [1978] 3 W.L.R. 73, C.A.

228. Companies Acts

The Department of Trade has published its annual report, "Companies in 1977." This gives details of the Department's administration of the Companies Acts 1948–76, and its work on company law reform and harmonisation of EEC company law. The report is available from HMSO [£1·50].

229. Companies Court—petitioner's attendance duty

The following Practice Statement has been made by Brightman J. on October 9, 1978:

After consultation with the Vice-Chancellor, I wish to remind all concerned of the importance of due compliance with r. 33 of the Companies (Winding Up) Rules 1949 (S.R. & O. 1949 No. 330) so that the work of the Companies Court can proceed efficiently. R. 33 requires the petitioner or his solicitor to attend before the registrar on the appointed day and to satisfy him that the papers are in order. That day is invariably the Monday before the petition is due to be heard. Under the current practice it is not less than five weeks after the petition has been presented. Too frequently the petitioner or his solicitor does not attend with the papers until after the appointed Monday; sometimes not until the Friday before the petition is due to be heard, so that the registrar has little time to check the papers; sometimes not until the day the petition is due to be heard, so that the registrar has no time at all. Such failure to comply with the rules increases the burden on the Companies Registry and impedes the work of the Companies Court. Attention was drawn to this problem by judges of the Companies Court in 1975 and 1977: see Palmer's *Company Law*, Vol. 3, paras. H1202 and H1205. At the present moment, there are not less than 780 winding-up petitions set down for hearing this term. Plainly there is no room for any avoidable non-compliance with the time scale laid down by the rules. The purpose of this statement is to remind all concerned once again that, save in exceptional circumstances, the penalty for failure to attend before the registrar as required by r. 33, with the papers substantially in proper order, is that the petition will be summarily struck out as required by the rule.

(1978) 122 S.J. 713.

230. —— **practice direction.** See § 2332.

231. Corporation tax. See CORPORATION TAX.

232. Directors—duty of care—take-over—fiduciary relationship—fraud—negligence
[N.Z.] R1 and R2, a son and father, were managing director and chairman respectively of an old established private company in which many of the shareholders were relatives. They were also directors of another company in which the family company owned a half share; it also owned properties and had a quantity of cash. R1 had only a small shareholding in the family company, and planned to acquire all its shares at $4.80 each; he would pay for them entirely out of the company's assets, by using the cash and selling the properties, thereby leaving him sole owner. The major shareholders included some family trusts of which R2 was a trustee. As a result of approaches by R1 and R2, the shares of these trusts were secured at $4.80; before the subsequent take-over offer they had consequently been transferred to R2's trust. Opposition from a minority was feared; R1 formed a new company of which he was sole owner. This enabled a take-over offer to be made to all the shareholders in the name of an offeror which, not already holding any shares, could expect to obtain acceptances from holders of nine-tenths of the shares for which offers were made, so making available the compulsory acquisition provisions of the Companies Act 1955, s. 208. The new company made such an offer. R1 and R2, as directors of the offeree company, recommended shareholders to accept. The appellants, who were minority shareholders, reluctantly accepted. R1 sold the properties, using the proceeds and the cash to pay for the shares. He made these resources available to himself by temporary loans from the company, followed by capital dividends. The appellants brought an action claiming fraud, breach of fiduciary duty, negligence and breach of the Companies Act 1955, s. 62. The action was dismissed; they appealed. *Held,* (1) R1 and R2 owed fiduciary duties to the shareholders, arising from the family character of the company, the position of R1 and R2 in both family and company, their high degree of inside knowledge, the way in which they went about the takeover and the persuasion of shareholders. They were obliged not to make deliberately or carelessly misleading statements on material matters to shareholders, nor to disclose material matters. (*Lloyds Bank* v. *Bundy* [1974] C.L.Y. 1691; *Re Bugle Press* [1960] C.L.Y. 435; *Gething* v. *Kilner* [1972] C.L.Y. 384, applied): (2) R1 and R2 were admittedly under a duty of care in recommending shareholders to accept the take-over offer. They were also in breach of that duty because the recommendation to sell at $4.80, with their knowledge as to asset-backing, was not made with reasonable care for the interests of the shareholders: COLEMAN v. MYERS [1977] 2 N.Z.L.R. 225, 298, N.Z. Sup.Ct.

233. —— **powers—appointment of receiver under debenture**
The appointment of a receiver under a debenture does not preclude the directors of the company from pursuing a right of action provided that the interests of the debenture-holders qua debenture-holders are not threatened.

N Ltd. entered into a property development scheme with C Bank whereby C Bank would provide the finance. The scheme ran into difficulties. C Bank withdrew their financial support and appointed a receiver of N Ltd. under a mortgage debenture creating a charge of their undertaking and property. N Ltd. issued proceedings claiming damages for breach of the contract to provide financial support for the scheme. C Bank applied to have the writ set aside on the ground that it was issued without the consent of the receiver, who alone was entitled to the proceeds of the action. Chapman J. reversed the decision of the registrar and set aside the writ. N Ltd. appealed. *Held,* allowing the appeal, that the action did not threaten the interests of the debenture-holders qua debenture-holders, and although the directors could not dispose of the assets subject to the charge, they had a duty to exploit them for the benefit of the company. (Decision of Chapman J. reversed.)

NEWHART DEVELOPMENTS v. CO-OPERATIVE COMMERCIAL BANK [1978] 2 W.L.R. 636, C.A.

234. —— **right to inspect books**
[Companies Act 1948 (c. 38), s. 147.]
A director has the right, not by s. 147 of the Companies Act 1948 but at common law, to inspect the company's books either at a meeting or elsewhere, so as to enable him to carry out his duties as director; such right determines upon his removal from office.

Two directors of X Co. attempted to inspect the company's books on the ground that they suspected misapplication of assets. The remaining directors prevented them through the power vested in one O, who effectively had control of the company, to appoint a special director with voting supremacy at board meetings. The two therefore instituted proceedings against X Co. and O for an order for production of the documents. The defendants claimed that the plaintiff's purpose was to give assistance to trade competitors, and that inspection should not be ordered, at least until after a forthcoming general meeting where the future of the two as directors was to be considered. *Held*, (1) although s. 147 of the Companies Act 1948 recognised the existence of a director's right to inspect the company's books, the purpose of the section was merely to impose sanctions if the books were not properly kept; (2) the right was conferred by the common law to enable a director to carry out his duties as director; (3) the right determined on removal from office; (4) the court had a discretion whether or not to order inspection. The court would restrain a director if it was satisfied that his intention was to abuse the confidence reposed in him as director; in the absence of clear proof the court would assume he was exercising his right for the company's benefit; (5) where misconduct was alleged against the director, the balance of convenience was against the making of an immediate order before a meeting had been held to consider the director's removal. There was no risk of damage to the plaintiffs, and the motion would be adjourned. (*Burn* v. *London and South Wales Coal Co. and Risca Investment Co.* (1890) 7 T.L.R. 118 and dictum of Street J. in *Edman* v. *Ross* (1922) 22 S.R.(N.S.W.) 351, 361 applied.)
    CONWAY v. PETRONIUS CLOTHING CO. [1978] 1 W.L.R. 72, Slade J.

234a. Factoring agreement—payments made to company—conversion by director
A factoring agreement provided that the plaintiffs should purchase all the book debts of a company, and that if any payment was made to the company in respect of an assigned debt, the company would hold it on trust for the plaintiffs. Four cheques sent to the company in payment of such assigned debts were paid into the company's account by the defendant, a director of the company. It was held that the plaintiffs had a sufficient proprietory right to sue in conversion on the cheques and could recover their face value. The defendant, as the wrongdoer, could not set up against the plaintiff's claim the contention that the plaintiff could call on the debtors to pay over again following notice of assignment to the debtors: INTERNATIONAL FACTORS v. RODRIGUEZ (1978) 122 S.J. 680, C.A.

235. Insurance companies. See INSURANCE.

236. Memorandum and articles—objects—whether carrying on a business—tax
[Malaysian Income Tax Act 1967, s. 43.] The company, which had abandoned its principal object of manufacturing cigarettes, started to let its factory premises, such letting being included among its other objects in its memorandum of association. It claimed that the rents were income from a business and that it was entitled to set off carried forward losses against assessments on the rents under s. 43 of the Malaysian Income Tax Act 1967. The claim was upheld by the commissioners; but the Revenue succeeded on appeal to the Federal Court of Malaysia. *Held*, allowing the company's appeal, that the commissioners had reached the only possible conclusion: AMERICAN LEAF BLENDING CO. SDN. BHD. v. DIRECTOR-GENERAL OF INLAND REVENUE [1978] S.T.C. 561, P.C.

237. Northern Ireland. See NORTHERN IRELAND.

238. Protection of depositors
PROTECTION OF DEPOSITORS (ACCOUNTS) (AMENDMENT) REGULATIONS 1978 (No. 1065) [10p], made under the Protection of Depositors Act 1963 (c. 16),

s. 13 (6); operative on September 1, 1978; amend S.I. 1976 No. 1954 to take account of amendments to the Companies Acts 1948 and 1967, made by the Companies Act 1976.

239. Register—duty to specify classes of members
[Companies Act 1948 (c. 38), ss. 110 (1), 113 (2).]

A company limited by guarantee does not have to disclose in its register of members the different categories of membership enjoyed by those shown in the register.

The society, a company limited by guarantee, had three classes of members. Only full members were allowed to vote. The register of members did not show which were full members. The applicant, a provisional associate member of the society, sought, by originating summons, an order that a list of full members be supplied to her. Such an order was granted. *Held,* allowing the appeal by the society, that (1) where membership of a company with no share capital was divided into categories, s. 110 (1) of the Companies Act 1948 did not require those categories to be shown in the register; and (2) the company could be ordered to supply only such parts of its register of members as could be identified without reference to anything other than the information contained in the register.

Re PERFORMING RIGHT SOCIETY [1978] 1 W.L.R. 1197, C.A.

240. Registration of title—entry of company numbers. See § 1759.

241. Shareholders—right of minority shareholders to sue
Minority shareholders can sue majority shareholders if the latter have been guilty of gross negligence and profited from that negligence notwithstanding the absence of fraud.

The plaintiffs who were minority shareholders brought an action against the company and two of its directors, who were the majority shareholders. They alleged that in 1970 the company, on the instructions of the two directors, had sold company land to one of the two, who was the wife of the other, for £4,250 when they knew or ought to have known that it was worth a great deal more. It was resold in 1974 for £120,000. The defendants applied to strike out the statement of claim as disclosing no reasonable cause of action. *Held,* dismissing the summons, that on the facts alleged, the minority shareholders had a cause of action. (*Foss* v. *Harbottle* (1843) 4 Hare 461, *Alexander* v. *Automatic Telephone Co.* [1900] 2 Ch. 56, C.A., *Cook* v. *Deeks* [1916] 1 A.C. 554, P.C. and dictum of Danckwerts J. in *Pavlides* v. *Jensen* [1956] C.L.Y. 1149 applied; *Turquand* v. *Marshall* (1869) L.R. 4 Ch.App. 376 distinguished.)

DANIELS v. DANIELS [1978] 2 W.L.R. 73, Templeman J.

242. Shares—illegal transaction involving directors—alleged conspiracy—whether company fixed with directors' knowledge
[Companies Act 1948 (c. 38), s. 54.]

If a company is the victim of a conspiracy by its directors and others to procure it, to its disadvantage, to give financial aid to purchase its own shares, it is not to be regarded as a party to the conspiracy by reason of the directors' knowledge.

Pursuant to the resolution of its directors, the plaintiff company purchased all the shares in M Ltd. for £500,000, the vendors on the same day purchasing all the plaintiff's shares from its sole shareholder for £489,000. Later the receiver of the plaintiff company issued proceedings against the directors and other parties to the transactions, alleging that M's shares had been worth only £60,000 and that the defendants were or ought to have been aware that the vendors could not have purchased the shares in the plaintiff company had not the value of M's shares been inflated, the plaintiff having thereby given financial assistance for the purchase of its own shares. The pleading alleged conspiracy in connection with the share transaction and misfeasance and breach of trust against the directors. Foster J. dismissed the claim on the grounds that the plaintiff company could not sue on a conspiracy to which it was a party and that in the absence of a pleaded allegation of fraud or dishonesty, no claim lay for breach of constructive trust. *Held,* allowing the company's appeal in part, that the company was the victim of the conspiracy and was not to be regarded as party thereto but that in the absence of an unequivocal plea that the defendants had knowledge of dishonesty, breach of constructive trust could not be alleged. (Leave was given to amend the Statement of Claim.) (*Churchill* v. *Walton* [1967] C.L.Y. 713 and *Wallersteiner* v. *Moir* [1974] C.L.Y. 2143 considered; *Barnes* v. *Addy* (1874) L.R. 9 Ch.App. 244 and *Selangor United Rubber Estates* v. *Cradock* [1964] C.L.Y. 2985 applied.)

BELMONT FINANCE CORP. *v.* WILLIAMS FURNITURE [1978] 3 W.L.R. 712, C.A.

243. —— transfer—restriction on transfer—takeover—limited release from restriction

[Companies Act 1948 (c. 38), s. 174 (2) (4).]

The court may remove restrictions upon dealings in shares imposed under s. 174 of the Companies Act 1948 to enable a takeover to be completed whilst continuing to impose restrictions upon the proceeds of such transfer being withheld from the transferor.

A Board of Trade investigation into the affairs of a company resulted in restrictions under s. 174 of the Act being imposed in respect of certain shares registered in the name of M, who were agents for a Swiss bank who declined to reveal their customer's name. Inter alia, the shares could not be transferred. A takeover bid for the company was hampered by such restriction since the bidding company was required to present to the company a transfer of the relevant shares executed by M together with the consideration therefore, some £98,000 which the company, under s. 209 of the Act, would hold in a separate account for the benefit of M. To enable the takeover to proceed, the company and the bidder applied for the restriction on transfer to be lifted with a proviso that the money paid to the company would not be paid to M without the leave of the court. M resisted the imposition of such a restriction upon the proceeds. *Held*, that under s. 174 (4) the court had power to so restrict payment out by the company of the price of the shares pending completion of the investigation, such price being a sum due from the company in respect of the restricted shares under s. 174 (2) (*d*); the order was made accordingly.

Re ASHBOURNE INVESTMENTS [1978] 2 All E.R. 418, Templeman J.

244. Stamp duty. See STAMP DUTIES.

245. Stock Exchange. See STOCK EXCHANGE.

246. Winding-up

COMPANIES (WINDING-UP) (AMENDMENT) RULES 1978 (No. 543) [10p], made under the Companies Act 1948 (c. 38), s. 365 (1), and the Insolvency Act 1976 (c. 60), s. 10; operative on May 2, 1978; amends S.I. 1949 No. 330, rr. 132 and 195.

247. —— corporation tax—whether disbursement

[Companies Act 1948 (c. 38), s. 267; Companies (Winding Up) Rules 1949 (S.I. 1949 No. 330), r. 195 (1).] Corporation tax charged on a capital gain arising during the winding up of a company, although not an expense incurred by the liquidator in realising the asset, is a necessary disbursement of the liquidator within r. 195 (1) and an expense incurred in the winding up process within s. 267: *Re* MESCO PROPERTIES, *The Times*, November 8, 1978, Brightman J.

248. —— costs—basis of taxation

[R.S.C., Ord. 62, rr. 28, 29.]

The normal basis of taxation of litigious and non-litigious costs of liquidation is the common fund basis but where costs are incurred in the course of actual proceedings the court has a discretion to direct a different basis of taxation.

The liquidator brought proceedings to determine certain issues in the liquidation of N Ltd. The case had been prepared expertly with the emphasis on achieving an early distribution of a large sum among numerous claimants rather than on saving costs. In view of the special circumstances the court ordered that the costs should be awarded and taxed on a transfer basis. The Department of Trade applied for a variation of the order. On the questions whether (1) the court had power to make such an order and (2) the taxing master, in the absence of a court order, had power to tax costs on a common fund basis rather than on a solicitor and own client basis, *held,* (1) that the court had such power and (2) that R.S.C., Ord. 62 did not change the rule established prior to changes in the categories of taxation made in 1958 that liquidation costs should be taxed on a common fund basis and the taxing master should tax costs on that basis in the absence of a court order.

Re NATION LIFE INSURANCE CO. (IN LIQUIDATION) [1978] 1 W.L.R. 45, Templeman J.

249. —— —— company having no assets—whether costs to be paid by director
At the time of the first hearing of the winding-up petition, R Co. was heavily indebted to X, the petitioner, and had been in receivership for about six months prior thereto. D, the sole director of R Co. was fully aware of these facts. R Co. had some cross-claims against X, but even given credit for these, it was still hopelessly insolvent. A winding-up order was made, and X asked that the court order that costs be paid personally by D and not out of the assets of R Co. *Held,* that the court had no such jurisdiction where the director was not a party. An order was made that costs of the petitioner should not be paid out of company assets until all unsecured creditors had been paid in full. (*Re Bathampton Properties* [1976] C.L.Y. 272 followed; dicta of Buckley L.J. in *Re Consolidated South Rand Mines Deep* [1909] W.N. 66 considered): *Re* REPROGRAPHIC EXPORTS (EUROMAT), March 14, 1978, Slade J. (*Ex rel. S. P. Drury, Esq., Barrister.*)

250. —— —— liquidator instructing solicitors—no prior sanction
[Companies Act 1948 (c. 38), s. 245 (1).]
The court has power to give a retrospective sanction in a proper case to action taken under s. 245 (1) of the Act without the prior sanction of the committee of inspection or of the court.

The liquidator of A Ltd., in a winding up by the court, instructed solicitors in January 1975 to issue proceedings and collect a debt due to the company. It was thought that the debtor might become insolvent and the matter was to be treated as urgent. The solicitors acted speedily and recovered £15,800. They submitted a bill for £124·60. In June 1976 the committee of inspection purported to sanction the appointment of the solicitors. The taxing master disallowed the bill of costs on the ground that, under s. 245 (1) of the Act, the liquidator could not appoint a solicitor without the prior sanction of the committee of inspection or of the court; accordingly their appointment before June 1976 was invalid. The liquidator applied for a review of that decision. *Held,* that by virtue of s. 245 (1) of the Act, the liquidator had acted in breach of his implied warranty of authority in appointing the solicitors without prior sanction and was personally liable for their bill; nevertheless, the appointment had resulted in benefit to the creditors and it was a proper case for the court to allow the liquidator to retain out of the assets of A Ltd. sums to indemnify him against the solicitors' claim.

Re ASSOCIATED TRAVEL LEISURE AND SERVICES (IN LIQUIDATION) [1978] 1 W.L.R. 547, Templeman J.

251. —— —— taxation—extension of time
The following Practice Direction was issued by the Supreme Court Taxing Office on October 24, 1978:

Where, at the time an order is made for winding up a company, there are insufficient funds to justify a taxation, the practice of the Masters is to grant a general extension of time for lodging the bill and papers, provided a reference has already been taken.

No formal application for an extension is necessary; a letter addressed to the Master of the chambers concerned, setting out the facts, is all that is necessary.
(1978) 122 S.J. 764.

252. —— creditor—whether secured
[Companies Act 1948 (c. 38), s. 231.] A creditor issued a writ against a ship owned by a company prior to its going into liquidation and entered a caveat in proceedings in rem commenced by another creditor, neither serving

the writ nor arresting the ship. The plaintiff applied for leave to continue its action started before the winding up, the basis for granting leave requiring that the plaintiff be a creditor who had obtained priority over the creditors. *Held*, to give the plaintiff leave to proceed despite the winding up would enable an unsecured creditor to perfect what at the day of the liquidation was imperfect. The plaintiff by virtue of starting an action in rem had not yet invoked the Admiralty jurisdiction and would only do so on serving his writ. It was therefore impossible to describe the plaintiff in any real sense as a secured creditor and leave would not be granted: *Re* ARO Co., *The Times,* June 17, 1978, Oliver J.

253. —— **distress—whether to be restrained on subsequent liquidation**
[Companies Act 1948 (c. 38), ss. 226, 319 (7); Taxes Management Act 1970 (c. 9), s. 61.]
In levying distress on the goods of a company in creditors' liquidation, the Inland Revenue need rely not on Crown Prerogative but on s. 61 of the Taxes Management Act 1970.
In January 1975 the Inland Revenue levied distress on the company's goods and took walking possession of them. The company went into creditors' voluntary liquidation. The liquidator sold the goods on terms that the commissioners should have the same rights against the proceeds of sale as they would have had against the goods. The liquidator sought an order that proceedings under the distress be stayed and a declaration that the goods were property of the company available for distribution by him among the creditors of the company. *Held*, dismissing the appeal, that the commissioners were relying not on any prerogative power but on s. 61 of the Taxes Management Act 1970, so that there would be no argument that the Crown was seeking by prerogative power to exercise a right not given to it by statute. S. 61 of the Act of 1970 was not repugnant to s. 319 of the Companies Act 1948. The behaviour of the Crown had not been unconscionable and the discretion of the lower courts would not be interfered with.
HERBERT BERRY ASSOCIATES *v.* I.R.C. [1977] 1 W.L.R. 1437, H.L.

254. —— **distribution of assets—unclaimed dividends—whether shareholders creditors**
[Companies Act 1948 (c. 38), s. 302; Companies (Winding-up) Rules 1949 (S.I. 1949 No. 330), r. 106.]
Where present or former shareholders of a company have not claimed their dividends, despite the appropriate advertisements, the liquidators are entitled to treat them as creditors for the purpose of winding up, rather than as members of the company.
A company incorporated in 1911 was wound up voluntarily in 1975 and joint liquidators appointed. They gave notice requiring claims to be made by a certain date and advertised the notices in the appropriate fashion. Nevertheless a substantial number of shareholders failed to claim and seemed to be untraceable. The liquidators took out a summons seeking the direction of the court as to how the potential claimants should be treated, and various other questions concerning limitation of claims. *Held*, that the liquidators were entitled to treat these shareholders as " creditors " for the purpose of winding up; that they were not entitled to make provision for untraced shareholders; and that the winding up did not make the money held by a company in respect of unclaimed dividends " trust " property.
Re COMPANIA DE ELECTRICIDAD DE LA PROVINCIA DE BUENOS AIRES [1978] 3 All E.R. 668, Slade J.

255. —— **fees**
COMPANIES (DEPARTMENT OF TRADE) FEES (AMENDMENT) ORDER 1978 (No. 569 (L. 9)) [10p], made under the Companies Act 1948 (c. 38), s. 365 (3), and the Public Offices Fees Act 1879 (c. 58), ss. 2, 3; operative on May 9, 1978; substitutes for Fees No. 7 and 10 (2) (iii) an ad valorem fee payable by every liquidator on the submission of accounts of their receipts and payments under s. 249 of the 1948 Act; increases to £3·75 the fee for insertion in the *London Gazette* of notices in proceedings for the winding up of companies.
COMPANIES (DEPARTMENT OF TRADE) FEES (AMENDMENT No. 2) ORDER 1978 (No. 705 (L. 14)) [10p], made under the Companies Act 1948, s. 365 (3)

and the Public Offices Fees Act 1879, ss. 2, 3: operative on June 1, 1978; provides for the payment of VAT in addition to the amount of any fee provided for in the Schedule to S.I. 1978 No. 1351 where the tax is chargeable in respect of the service to which that fee relates.

COMPANIES (DEPARTMENT OF TRADE) (AMENDMENT No. 3) ORDER 1978 (No. 1654) [20p], made under the Companies Act 1948 (c. 38), s. 365 (3) and the Public Offices Fees Act 1879 (c. 58), ss. 2 and 3; operative on December 1, 1978; increases certain fees taken by the Department of Trade in proceedings for the winding up of companies.

256. —— fraudulent trading—single transaction—creditor a party
[Companies Act 1948 (c. 38), s. 332 (i).]
If a single transaction can properly be described as a fraud on a creditor perpetuated in the course of carrying on business, proceedings alleging fraudulent trading will not be struck out because there is only one transaction and only one creditor defrauded. Another creditor who, knowing of the circumstances, accepts money thus obtained may be liable to repay it although he took no part in the fraudulent trading.

J Ltd. lent £150,000 to C Ltd. to enable it to produce indigo. The sum was insufficient and the venture failed. C Ltd. nonetheless persuaded H Ltd. to place an order for the supply of indigo and to pay some £125,698 in advance. C Ltd. then discharged the bulk of its debt to J Ltd. and went into liquidation. H Ltd. sought a declaration that J Ltd. and its directors were personally liable for C Ltd.'s debts on the ground that they had knowingly been parties to fraudulent trading. J Ltd., and its directors, failed on their summons to strike out the claim as disclosing no cause of action. *Held,* that it was immaterial that only one transaction was involved and one creditor defrauded. There was a cause of action against J Ltd. and its directors, because, although they had taken no part in the trading, they had accepted the money with knowledge of the circumstances in which it had been procured.
Re GERALD COOPER CHEMICALS [1978] 2 All E.R. 49, Templeman J.

257. —— inability to pay debts—meaning
[Companies Act 1948 (c. 38), s. 223; Insurance Companies Act 1974 (c. 49), s. 50.]
An insurance company claiming to be unable to pay its debts is in the same position as an ordinary company and can prove it not only by showing that its existing, contingent and prospective liabilities exceed its existing and probable assets, but also by any of the alternative methods open to a company under ss. 222 and 223 of the 1948 Act.

An authorised insurance company carried on the business of long-term insurance and in 1976 presented a winding-up petition to the court. The Policy Holders Protection Board then took out a summons seeking a reduction of the company's liabilities under s. 50 of the 1974 Act. Evidence adduced by the Board did not establish that the company's present and prospective liabilities exceeded its assets. The Board contended that the court had jurisdiction to make the order as the company was "unable to pay its debts," and that the court had power to reduce the contracts which had accrued due before the date of the order. *Held,* the court did not have jurisdiction because (1) although an insurance company was in the same position as an ordinary company, in this case the fact that the company did not have sufficient liquid assets to pay its present debts where repayment had not been demanded, did not prove its inability to pay its debts; and (2) the court's jurisdiction was limited to ordering a reduction of amounts prospectively payable under the policies. (*Re Great Britain Mutual Life Assurance Society* (1882) 20 Ch.D. 351 applied.)
Re CAPITAL ANNUITIES [1978] 3 All E.R. 704, Slade J.

258. —— order declared void—" abatement " of pending actions
The plaintiff company appealed against a High Court order that their action against the defendants should be stayed/dismissed. *Held,* dismissing the appeal, that on the voluntary winding up of the company, the pending action ceased absolutely and for all time, and could not be revived by an order under s. 352 of the Companies Act 1948, declaring the dissolution void: FOSTER YATES & THOM *v.* H. W. EDGEHILL EQUIPMENT, *The Times,* November 30, 1978, C.A.

259. —— **petition—by contributory—dispute as to whether petitioner bona fide shareholder**

[Companies Act 1948 (c. 38), s. 224 (1).]

Where there is a genuine dispute as to whether shares have been allotted to a petitioner petitioning as a contributory for winding up, the petition will be dismissed.

The petitioner petitioned to wind up a company as a contributory, she being the recipient of shares under a purported allotment signed by a director. She paid nothing for the shares and was not included in the register of members; when the company was being formed, it had not been intended that she should be a shareholder and she applied for none. The company denied that she was a shareholder. *Held,* dismissing the petition, that although an allottee who is not registered as a shareholder is a contributory entitled to petition under s. 224 of the Act, since the petitioner's status as a shareholder was in question the petition would be dismissed. (*Re Anglo-Austrian Printing and Publishing, Isaac's Case* [1892] 2 Ch. 158, and *Re Bayswater Trading Co.* [1970] C.L.Y. 289 applied.) *Re* JN 2 [1977] 3 All E.R. 1104, Brightman J.

260. —— —— **debt disputed—whether petitioner to be restrained**

[Companies Act 1948 (c. 38), ss. 223, 224.]

Presentation of a creditor's winding-up petition will not be restrained where the debt in question is alleged by the company to be a prospective debt not payable at the time of presentation of the petition.

The plaintiff company sought to restrain the defendants from presenting a winding-up petition in respect of an alleged debt of some £39,000 for which the defendants had made formal demand. The plaintiffs contended, inter alia, that some £20,000 of the alleged debt was not yet payable by virtue of a credit arrangement with the defendants. *Held,* refusing the order, that although there was a substantial dispute between the parties, the petition would not be restrained because even on the plaintiff's case, the defendants were prospective creditors and entitled as such to present a petition, although the Companies Court would decide whether winding-up was in those circumstances justified. (*Mann* v. *Goldstein* [1968] C.L.Y. 456 applied; *Bryanston Finance* v. *de Vries (No. 2)* [1975] C.L.Y. 319 considered.)

HOLT SOUTHEY v. CATNIC COMPONENTS [1978] 1 W.L.R. 630, Goulding J.

261. —— **set-off—money owed in respect of taxation**

[Bankruptcy Act 1914 (c. 59), s. 31.]

Set-off under s. 31 of the Bankruptcy Act 1914 is not restricted to mutual creditors, debts and other dealings arising out of contract.

In the insolvent liquidation of a company it transpired that the company owed to the Crown moneys in respect of taxation and social security contributions. Moneys were owing to the company by way of " input " value added tax. The Crown sought, under s. 31 of the Bankruptcy Act 1914, to set off the moneys owing to it against its obligation to repay value added tax. *Held,* that the set off should be allowed, as s. 31 ought not to be restricted to mutual credits, debts and other dealings arising out of contract (*Mathieson's Trustees* v. *Barrup, Mathieson and Co.* [1927] 1 Ch. 562, applied).

Re D. H. CURTIS (BUILDERS) [1978] 2 W.L.R. 28, Templeman J.

262. —— **unregistered foreign company—only asset within jurisdiction a right of action—whether necessary to show action bound to succeed**

In order to found jurisdiction for a winding-up order in the case of an unregistered foreign company with no assets in the U.K. other than a right of action, it is sufficient for the petitioners to show the action has a reasonable chance of success.

A, a Liberian company not registered in the U.K., owned a ship which was entered in the books of an indemnity association. In 1968 events occurred which gave the petitioners a claim against A. The petitioners subsequently obtained judgment against A, but A, though insured by the indemnity association, took no steps to claim from them. A had no assets, but its claim against the association was (if valid) a valuable asset. The petitioners applied for A to be wound up so that they could pursue A's claim against the association. The association opposed the petition. *Held,* the court had jurisdiction to make a winding-up order, for it was not necessary for the petitioners to show that the action was bound to succeed, only that it had a reasonable possibility of success; the onus was on the association to show that the action did not have a reasonable chance of success. (*Re Compania Merabello san Nicholas S.A.* [1972] C.L.Y. 388 applied.)

Re ALLOBROGIA STEAMSHIP CORP. [1978] 3 All E.R. 423, Slade J.

263. —— **validity of sale—receiver appointed under a debenture**

Although winding up deprives a receiver appointed under a debenture of power to bind the company personally by acting as its agent, it does not affect his powers given by the debenture to hold and dispose of the company's property charged thereunder.

S charged a property by way of legal mortgage to D Ltd. to secure a loan. D Ltd. created a debenture in favour of two banks charging its assets for the discharge on demand of all present and future indebtedness to them. Under cl. 7 of the deed, when the security became enforceable the banks were empowered to appoint a receiver to take possession of and get in the property charged. Cl. 11 gave the banks and their nominees power of attorney to execute the assurance required for the purposes of the security. The banks demanded payment and appointed a receiver who, under cl. 7 was empowered to get in the asset represented by the mortgage debt charged on the property by S. Subsequently D Ltd. went into liquidation. The receiver under the debenture contracted to sell the property. The vendor was stated to be D Ltd. acting by the receiver. A conveyance was executed expressed to be made by D Ltd. acting by its attorneys, the banks, at the request of the receiver and in exercise of the power of sale conferred on D Ltd. by the mortgage and by statute. The Land Registry would only register the purchaser as proprietor on the basis of a conveyance sealed by D Ltd. as mortgagee, in the presence of its liquidator. S sought to determine whether the contract made by the receiver was an effective exercise of the power of sale under the mortgage and if so, whether the conveyance after the date of winding up effectively completed the sale. *Held*, that (1) the receiver had effectively exercised the power of sale; (2) the conveyance effectively completed the sale because by it the debenture holders used their power of attorney to execute the assurance required and they did so in the name of the company by exercising its power of sale under the mortgage; (3) the power of attorney was not revoked by the winding up since it was an authority coupled with an interest and came within s. 4 (1) of the Powers of Attorney Act 1971. (*Gaskell* v. *Gosling* [1896] 1 Q.B. 669, C.A.; *Thomas* v. *Todd* [1926] 2 K.B. 511 and *Gough's Garages* v. *Pugsley* [1930] 1 K.B. 615, D.C. applied.)

SOWMAN v. DAVID SAMUEL TRUST (IN LIQUIDATION) [1978] 1 W.L.R. 22, Goulding J.

BOOKS AND ARTICLES. See *post,* pp. [2], [14].

COMPROMISES AND FAMILY ARRANGEMENTS

ARTICLES. See *post,* p. [14].

COMPULSORY PURCHASE

264. **Acquisition of land**

ACQUISITION OF LAND (RATE OF INTEREST AFTER ENTRY) (SCOTLAND) (NO. 2) REGULATIONS 1978 (No. 1417) [10p], made under the Land Compensation (Scotland) Act 1963 (c. 51), s. 40 (1); operative on October 25, 1978; increase to 12½ per cent. per annum the rate of interest payable where entry is made, before payment, of compensation, on land in Scotland.

ACQUISITION OF LAND (RATE OF INTEREST AFTER ENTRY) (NO. 2) REGULATIONS 1978 (No 1418) [10p], made under the Land Compensation Act 1961 (c. 33), s. 32 (1); operative on October 25, 1978; increase to 12½ per cent. per annum the rate of interest payable where entry is made, before the payment of compensation, on land in England and Wales which is being purchased compulsorily and revoke S.I. 1978 No. 886.

265. Acquisition of part or whole of unit—whether church is an " other building "

[Lands Clauses Consolidation Act 1845 (c. 18), s. 92.] The London Transport Executive under the London Transport Act 1915 wished to acquire compulsorily part of a church site; it did not seek to acquire the church or house but only the land behind. The church therefore claimed the benefit of s. 92 in asking London Transport to take the entire property. To do so, it had to show within s. 92 that the church was " a house or other building " and that the land to be taken was part of that " house or other building." *Held*, London Transport were not entitled to take only part of the property; their powers would have to be exercised so as to acquire the whole site, or not at all: LONDON TRANSPORT EXECUTIVE *v.* CONGREGATIONAL UNION OF ENGLAND AND WALES (INC.), *The Times,* June 15, 1978, Goulding J.

266. Clearance area—confirmation of order—relevant considerations for Minister

[Housing Act 1957 (c. 56), Pt. III.]

The Secretary of State need not take into account the availability of suitable alternative accommodation for persons displaced nor the sufficiency of the authority's resources to carry out a scheme when deciding whether or not to confirm a compulsory purchase order; he must, however, consider the question of comparative cost as between demolition and rebuilding, and repair and rehabilitation.

The authority made compulsory purchase orders in respect of a clearance area where P was an owner-occupier. A public local inquiry was held. The inspector's report to the Secretary of State contained a passage which sounded like a reference to documents which had not been made available to objectors. The Secretary of State confirmed the order. P applied under para. 2 of Sched. 4 to the Housing Act 1957 to quash the order, on the grounds of breach of natural justice. Phillips J. called the inspector to give evidence about the matter, and the inspector subsequently swore an affidavit which showed that there was no substance in P's complaint. Phillips J. dismissed the application. P appealed on the ground that evidence should not have been called in that way, that the judge had disregarded the question whether the authority's resources were sufficient to carry out the clearance and redevelopment, and also the relative cost of demolition and rebuilding as compared with repair and rehabilitation. *Held*, allowing the appeal, and quashing the order, that (1) the judge had been right in calling evidence; (2) alternative accommodation and the authority's resources were not matters to be taken into account by the Secretary of State; but, (3) the question of cost was a relevant factor, and the Secretary of State should have considered the relative costs of demolition and rebuilding as compared with repair and rehabilitation. (Dictum of Lord Denning M.R. in *Luke* v. *Minister of Housing and Local Government* [1967] C.L.Y. 3794 applied; *Re Enoch and Zaretzky, Bock & Co.'s Arbitration* [1910] 1 K.B. 327, C.A. and *Fallon* v. *Calvert* [1960] C.L.Y. 2461 distinguished; *J. Murphy and Sons* v. *Secretary of State for the Environment* [1973] C.L.Y. 3256, and *Sovmots Investments* v. *Secretary of State for the Environment* [1977] C.L.Y. 333 considered.)

ECKERSLEY *v.* SECRETARY OF STATE FOR THE ENVIRONMENT (1977) 34 P. & C.R. 124, C.A.

267. Coal mines. See MINING LAW.

268. Compensation

ACQUISITION OF LAND (RATE OF INTEREST AFTER ENTRY) REGULATIONS 1978 (No. 886) [10p], made under the Land Compensation Act 1961 (c. 33), s. 32 (1); operative on July 20, 1978; increase to 11½ per cent. per annum the rate of interest payable where entry is made, before payment, of land in England and Wales being purchased compulsorily.

ACQUISITION OF LAND (RATE OF INTEREST AFTER ENTRY) (SCOTLAND) REGULATIONS 1978 (No. 887) [10p], made under the Land Compensation (Scotland) Act 1963 (c. 51), s. 40 (1); operative on July 20, 1978; increase to 11½ per cent. per annum the rate of interest payable where entry is made, before payment, of land in Scotland being purchased compulsorily.

269. —— assessment—relevance of knowledge of resumption—whether sale price of adjoining land to be considered

The pointe gourde principle in relation to the assessment of compensation for compulsory purchase applies notwithstanding that the land owner had knowledge of the scheme of which the resumption formed a part at the time of acquiring the land.

A developer bought 37 acres of land in Brisbane in 1964; a scheme was already in existence whereby a strip running across the land, dividing it into north and south parts, was to be compulsorily acquired for the purpose of building an express way. In 1965, outline permission was granted in respect of the northern part for development as a shopping centre. (It was later accepted that, but for the express way proposal, such permission would have been granted in respect of the whole 37 acres.) In 1966, the northern part was sold at $40,000 per acre. The developer sought compensation for the strip and in respect of diminution in value due to severance of the southern part. The Land Court assessed compensation upon the basis that the 1965 planning permission and the 1966 sale were not relevant. The Supreme Court declined to interfere upon the grounds that any error in calculating compensation was one of fact. *Held*, allowing the developer's appeal, that, applying the pointe gourde principle, the southern part should have been valued as if it had the benefit of the 1965 planning permission, disregarding any diminution in value due to the scheme; that regard could properly be had to the sale of adjoining land occurring after the date of resumption; and that a failure to apply proper principles of assessment was an error of law, not of fact. (*Pointe Gourde Quarrying and Transport Co.* v. *Sub-Intendent of Crown Lands* [1947] A.C. 565, applied.)

MELWOOD UNITS PTY. v. COMMISSIONER OF MAIN ROADS [1978] 3 W.L.R. 520, P.C.

270. —— owner-occupier's supplement—occupation as private dwelling throughout qualifying period—whether broken by sale

[Housing Act 1969 (c. 33), s. 68, Sched. 5, para. 1.]

Occupation of premises as a dwelling-house for the purposes of s. 68 of and Sched. 5, para. 1 to the Housing Act 1969, will not be broken by a very short period between a vendor moving out and a purchaser moving in.

V, the vendor, who had occupied the house since before April 6, 1971, sold the house, plus some furniture, to P. V left the house which remained empty, except for some furniture, for 10 days. P redecorated it, and then moved in on November 25. On April 6, 1973, the house was made subject to a compulsory purchase order. P claimed that compensation should include not only site value but owner-occupier's supplement under s. 68 of and Sched. 5, para. 1, to the Housing Act 1969, in that the house had been used as a residence by successive owners throughout the two years from April 6, 1971. *Held*, although a very short intervening period would not break occupation, the house had not been occupied between October 27 and November 25. The presence of furniture, and the redecoration work did not alter the situation, and therefore the house had not been occupied throughout the qualifying period. (*Arbuckle Smith & Co.* v. *Greenock Corp.* [1960] C.L.Y. 2677 applied.)

LAUNDON v. HARTLEPOOL BOROUGH COUNCIL [1978] 2 W.L.R. 732, C.A.

271. —— owner's entitlement—corporate occupier

[Scot.] A retail shop selling clothing was compulsorily acquired in 1968. It was made up of different units of property all forming the one shop floor area. W owned some of the units, the remainder belonged to S, a company set up to transfer shares within W's family. The actual retail business was carried on for some time before 1968 by C, a company with its own name and 1,000 issued ordinary shares of which W owned 999 and his wife one. W devoted his whole time to the business: his wife was the company buyer. At the date of acquisition, there was no formal lease of the shop premises between company C and either W or company S, although such lease had at one time been contemplated. W and S subsequently lodged a joint claim with the lands tribunal for £80,000 as compensation for the value of the heritage and a further £95,000 in respect of disturbance. The Second Division, affirming the decision of the lands tribunal, found that the occupier was company C, which had a distinct legal persona from W, and that company C had not been a mere shell or façade but a company de facto engaged in business in accordance with its memorandum of association. W and company S appealed to the House of Lords. *Held,* on the facts there was no basis consonant with the principle upon which the corporate veil could be pierced to the effect of holding W to be the true owner of C's business or of the assets of S; the appeal was dismissed. (*Salomon* v. *Salomon & Co.* [1897] A.C. 22 applied; *D.H.N. Food Distributors* v. *Tower Hamlets L.B.C.* [1976] C.L.Y. 294, distinguished): WOOLFSON *v.* STRATHCLYDE REGIONAL COUNCIL, 1978 S.L.T. 159, H.L.

272. —— prior s. 17 certificate—severance of land

[Land Compensation Act 1961 (c. 33), ss. 5 (2), 17, 22 (1), 39 (2); Compulsory Purchase Act 1965 (c. 56), s. 7.]

In a subsequent valuation of parts of an area, a s. 17 certificate, granted in respect of the whole area in a different and prior compulsory purchase proposition, is irrelevant.

In 1970, a compulsory purchase proposition led the landowner to obtain a s. 17 certificate for alternative development of the whole area comprising " front " and " back " land. In 1972, planning permission was refused and the landowner served a notice requiring the district council to purchase the whole area. For administrative reasons, different purchasers were designated for the " front " and " back " lands. The landowner in 1974 applied for a further s. 17 certificate in relation to the front land, without prejudice to his claim that the 1970 s. 17 certificate still applied to the back land. His claim for compensation to the Lands Tribunal on the basis that the assumptions of the 1970 s. 17 certificate still applied and that the resultant valuation should be apportioned between the parts according to acreage was rejected, the tribunal holding that the 1970 s. 17 certificate was irrelevant and the two areas were to be valued separately. A sum was awarded for each part which, when added together, was much less than the sum which would have resulted for the whole area applying the 1970 s. 17 assumptions. On appeal against the award for the " back " land only, on the basis that some additional sum should have been awarded in respect of the back land under s. 7 of the 1965 Act, *held,* allowing the appeal in part, that (1) subject-matter to be valued was the back land only, without reference to the 1970 s. 17 certificate which was irrelevant, for the valuation of that part could not be determined by reference to a premises s. 17 certificate issued in relation to the whole area and a different compulsory purchase proposition; (2) that the deemed planning permission of the 1970 s. 17 certificate resulted in the whole area possessing a substantially increased value, the landowner therefore suffered damage when the back land was severed from the front. The loss had to be calculated with reference to the back land itself with an additional sum for extra loss suffered by him in respect of the severance, if it could be said that the severance was a substantial cause of the extra loss. The case would be remitted for further consideration. *Pilkington* v. *Secretary of State for Environment* [1973] C.L.Y. 3255 applied; *Lucas (F.) & Sons* v. *Dorking Rural District Council* [1964] C.L.Y. 3603 distinguished; *Horn* v. *Sunderland Corporation,* [1941] 2 K.B. 26, *Pointe Gourde Quarrying and Transport Co.* v. *Sub-Intendent of Crown Land* (1947) C.L.C. 1433 considered.)

HOVERINGHAM GRAVELS *v.* CHILTERN DISTRICT COUNCIL (1978) 35 P. & C.R. 295, C.A.

273. —— housing scheme—validity—part of land to be used for road

[Housing Act 1957 (c. 56) ss. 96, 107.]

A housing authority cannot validly include in a compulsory purchase order land to be used for building a new road unless the provision of the road is reasonably incidental to the provision of housing.

A compulsory purchase order was made under Pt. V of the 1957 Act pursuant to a proposal to build up to 600 houses. Part of the land was to be used for construction of a new road to provide a through route for traffic to the adjoining city. The inspector appointed to hold an inquiry recommended that the order be confirmed in part only since he found that the principal function of the proposed road was independent of the housing scheme. The Secretary of State, however, confirmed the original order. *Held*, quashing the order, that (1) the authority had no power under the 1957 Act to order acquisition of land for a road scheme unless provision of such a road was fairly and reasonably incidental to the housing scheme; (2) the Secretary of State had to the substantial prejudice of the land-owners failed to comply with the Compulsory Purchase by Local Authorities (Injuries Procedure) Rules 1962 (S.I. No. 1424), in differing from the inspector's finding of fact (*Galloway* v. *London Corporation* (1866) L.R. 1 H.L. 34 applied).

MERAVALE BUILDERS v. SECRETARY OF STATE FOR THE ENVIRONMENT (1978) 36 P. & C.R. 87, Willis J.

274. **Development areas—land required for securing the treatment as a whole of an area in which the land situated**

[Town and Country Planning Act 1971 (c. 78), s. 112 (1) (*a*).] Planning permission was granted for a theatre, subject to a condition that the land be not developed until access roads were complete. The land was part of an area planned for redevelopment. The access necessary would only serve the theatre. The Secretary of State found that the land was necessary to provide access from the theatre, and for the purposes of securing the treatment as a whole of the rest of the area. The objectors applied for the order confirming compulsory purchase to be quashed. *Held*, in assisting part of the scheme, the proposed access assisted the whole. If the acquiring authority found it desirable to acquire in order to secure the development of the land as a whole, acquisition did not have to be essential: COMPANY DEVELOPMENTS (PROPERTY) v. SECRETARY OF STATE FOR THE ENVIRONMENT AND SALISBURY DISTRICT COUNCIL [1978] J.P.L. 107, Sir Douglas Frank, Q.C.

275. **Housing—statutory duty of local authority—where houses uninhabitable.** See ATT.-GEN., *ex rel.* RIVERS-MOORE v. PORTSMOUTH CITY COUNCIL, § 1565.

276. —— **unfit for human habitation—use of dwelling by authority**

[Housing Act 1957 (c. 56), ss. 16 (4), 17 (2), 20 (1) (3).]

The power of a local authority to purchase a house which is unfit for human habitation, and cannot be rendered fit at reasonable expense for the purposes of demolition under s. 17 (2) of the Housing Act 1957, is limited to use as temporary accommodation in an unfit condition; it does not cover a case where the authority intends to make a permanent addition to its housing stock, by restoring the house properly, in which case the appropriate procedure is that under s. 12.

Per curiam: In deciding whether or not it was just to exercise a compulsory power of expropriation, the financial implications for the property owner must always be relevant.

V.S. Co. owned a house which was unfit for human habitation under s. 4 of the Housing Act 1957. In 1975, the council issued a notice under s. 9 requiring the execution of specified works to render the house fit; V.S. Co. appealed, and the county court set aside the s. 9 notice. In 1976, the council gave notice to V.S. Co. that they had determined to purchase the property under s. 17 (2) of the Act, so that they could carry out extensive works and bring the property up to a full standard with an expected life of not less than 30 years. On V.S. Co.'s appeal against the notice, the county court judge ruled that the local authority could only purchase property under s. 17 (2) for the purpose of using it temporarily pending demolition. On appeal by the council, *held,* dismissing the appeal, that the appropriate procedure was that under s. 12.

VICTORIA SQUARE PROPERTY CO. v. SOUTHWARK LONDON BOROUGH COUNCIL [1978] 1 W.L.R. 463, C.A.

277. **Inquiry—non-attendance for illness—failure to grant adjournment—breach of natural justice**

G objected to a compulsory purchase order under Pt. III of the Housing Act 1957, on the grounds that the property was not unfit for human habitation and was capable of being rehabilitated. G was taken ill just before the inquiry, and applied for an adjournment which the inspector refused. G was unable to instruct counsel or a solicitor, or to give evidence. G applied for the decision confirming the order to be quashed. *Held*, a breach of natural justice had occurred. The inspector had deprived the applicants of the opportunity to put forward their case, despite the fact that an adjournment would not prejudice the other parties to the hearing: GILL & CO. (LONDON) *v.* SECRETARY OF STATE FOR THE ENVIRONMENT [1978] J.P.L. 373, Mars-Jones J.

278. —— non-attendance on religious grounds—natural justice
[Compulsory Purchase by Local Authorities (Inquiries Procedure) Rules 1962 (S.I. 1962 No. 1424), r. 4 (2).]
While it is a basic principle of natural justice that every party or objector should be given a fair opportunity of being heard, the considerations applicable to adjourning judicial proceedings are different from those applicable to an administrative inquiry where arrangements have to be made well in advance.
A surveyor lodged an objection, on behalf of the appellant, to a compulsory purchase order. He was informed that the inquiry was to be held on April 21. On April 1 he wrote asking for a special hearing since his client was unable to attend on the day proposed, for religious reasons. He set out reasons why the property should not be acquired at site value. The Secretary of State refused to alter the date, but the inspector considered the written objections and inspected her properties. The Secretary of State confirmed the order. The appellant's application to quash the order was refused. On appeal, *held*, dismissing the appeal, that the Secretary of State had properly fixed the hearing, giving not less than 42 days' notice, the appellant was given an opportunity for representation, her written representations had been considered, and there was no want of natural justice.
OSTREICHER *v.* SECRETARY OF STATE FOR THE ENVIRONMENT [1978] 1 W.L.R. 810, C.A.

279. Lands Tribunal decisions
ALI *v.* SOUTHWARK LONDON BOROUGH COUNCIL (Ref./154/1976) (1977) 246 E.G. 633 (freehold dwelling-house encumbered by two protected tenancies, the tenants being close friends of claimant landlord. *Held*, landlord's understanding they would vacate if he wished to reoccupy of no relevance; value placed in hope of early possession of no significance in absence of evidence of tenants' ages; investment value approach supported by comparables the proper approach.)
ARROW *v.* BEXLEY LONDON BOROUGH COUNCIL (Ref. 281/1976) (reference was to determine the compensation payable upon the compulsory purchase of a house, workshop and yard. A scheme underlay the acquisition since 1970. The house was kept empty after the owner was rehoused, at the request of the council because it was a public health hazard. The house was vandalised by the date of valuation in 1974. *Held,* the claimant was entitled to compensation representing the value of the house in its actual condition; the *Pointe Gourde* principle did not apply as the vandalism was not entirely due to the scheme).
BLOOM (KOSHER) & SONS *v.* TOWER HAMLETS LONDON BOROUGH COUNCIL (Ref. No. 204/1975) (reference was to determine the amount of compensation payable for disturbance on compulsory acquisition of the claimants' factory. The claimants admitted that since 1955 they had been looking for factory premises in addition to their old factory. They bought a new factory in 1966 when they realised that the old factory would be acquired. The authority recommended the area as a clearance area in November 1967. Notice to treat was served in March 1970. *Held*, that (1) a loss incurred before acquisition was too remote to be the subject of compensation for disturbance, (2) losses incurred in reasonable mitigation are recoverable only where they are the direct and natural consequence of acquisition and cannot precede the date of notice to treat).
J. D. BRITTON & SONS *v.* HILLINGDON LONDON BOROUGH COUNCIL (1977) 245 E.G. 317 (acquisition of small area of land in Ickenham, Middlesex separating development site from road. At time of acquisition, planning consent for development site provided for access from another road, but access through the subject land would be substantially shorter and, if planning consent for that were granted, there would be a cost saving of £10,000. The acquiring authority's principle of compensation on existing use value (£200) was rejected and the claimant's principle of proportion of cost saving upheld;

but the proper proportion was held to be 25 per cent., not 75 per cent., and a figure of £2,500 awarded).

BRODERICK *v.* EREWASH BOROUGH COUNCIL (Ref./66/1976) (1977) 34 P. & C.R. 214 (reference was to determine the validity of an objection to a blight notice by the authority on the ground that no part of the land to which the notice related was comprised in land of a specified description. The claimant was unable to sell his property because the property was listed in a slum clearance scheme. *Held*, despite the amendments to s. 193 (1) (*d*) of the Town and Country Planning Act 1971, by the Land Compensation Act 1973, s. 77, and the addition of the words " likely to be comprised in land of any of the specified descriptions ", s. 77 did not enlarge the categories set out in s. 192 (1) (*a*)–(*j*) of the 1971 Act and the objection must be upheld).

HOLMES *v.* KNOWSLEY BOROUGH COUNCIL (Ref. No. 60/1977) (reference was to determine whether a blight notice was well-founded. The local authority served a counter-notice on the grounds that the claimant was not an owner-occupier within s. 203 (1). *Held*, the claimant had put his home on the market with vacant possession in 1975 and it was unoccupied for 12 months before the blight notice. Although for the purposes of the subsection preparation for residential occupation would have been enough in this case the claimant did not qualify as an owner-occupier).

IND COOPE (LONDON) *v.* ENFIELD L.B.C. (REF./182/1976) (1977) 245 E.G. 941 (claim for compensation for off-licence with tied tenancy in Enfield. Claimants' refusal of alternative accommodation a quarter of a mile away not unreasonable so no failure to mitigate loss. Valuation approach for off-licences now no different from that for other retail premises. Accepted that tied trade has more security than free one or than the goodwill of any other retail business).

LEAKE *v.* WIRRAL METROPOLITAN BOROUGH; ARGYLE MOTORS (BIRKENHEAD) *v.* SAME (1977) 244 E.G. 725 (the claimants sought compensation for injurious affection to the freehold and leasehold of premises in Birkenhead following the execution of works to relieve traffic congestion at the approaches to the Mersey Tunnel. The claimants' car showrooms and offices were virtually isolated from passing traffic. *Held*, the claimants should succeed, as the premises had become quite unsuitable for original purposes. They were entitled to compensation under the Compulsory Purchase Act 1965, s. 10, on the basis of the difference in valuations of the premises before and after the execution of the works).

NATIONAL CARRIERS *v.* SECRETARY OF STATE FOR TRANSPORT (Ref. 109/1977) (reference was to determine the amount of compensation payable upon acquisition of premises used for the servicing of road vehicles used by claimants, who were statutory undertakers. The question arose whether assessment should be on the basis set out in the Town and Country Planning Act 1971 (c. 78), s. 238, or on an open market basis. Had representations been made, a certificate would have been issued by the Minister under para. 10 of Sched. 1 to the Acquisition of Land (Authorisation Procedure) Act 1946. *Held*, since a certificate would have been issued, the open market basis must be applied).

SERVICE WELDING *v.* TYNE AND WEAR COUNTY COUNCIL (Ref. No. 124/1976) (1977) 34 P. & C.R. 228 (a preliminary point arose as to whether compensation under r. 6 of the Land Compensation Act 1961, s. 5, for bank interest should be paid. The claimants agreed to sell their factory to the acquiring authority. Notice to treat was deemed served in July 1973. Thereafter, the claimants built a similar factory. The project was financed by a bank loan. *Held*, (1) the claimants had mitigated their loss, since the authority was not obliged to pay for loss of goodwill on extinguishment of the business; (2) the bank interest was the direct result of the mitigation; (3) compensation for bank interest should be awarded).

SUCCAMORE *v.* NEWHAM LONDON BOROUGH COUNCIL (1977) 245 E.G. 403 (the claimant's disturbance claim was in respect of acquisition of a terraced house in Silvertown and a subsequent move to a bungalow 31 miles away. Applying the test of Romer L.J. in *Harvey* v. *Crawley Development Corp.* [1957] C.L.Y. 476, *held*, that the tribunal allowed in full (1) the solicitors' fees for both parties to the mortgage advance; (2) removal expenses as "reasonable consequences" of acquisition; (3) survey fees and search fee on the abortive purchase, although incurred before a building society advance was secured; (4) survey fee on the property purchased; (5) travelling expenses). SYLVESTER *v.* SOLON HOUSING ASSOCIATION (REF/235/1977) (1978) 246 E.G. 665 (the reasonableness of a claim for disturbance payment pursuant to ss. 37 and 38 of the Land Compensation Act 1973 was not disputed by the housing association but referred by them to the Lands Tribunal because the GLC, who would have to pay the claim, did not agree it. *Held,* such a referral was unnecessary and involved a misunderstanding of s. 38 (4) of the 1973 Act).

280. Local authority—housing needs—grounds for Minister's decision

[Housing Act 1957 (c. 56), Pt. V.] The council made a compulsory purchase order. An inquiry was held. The inspector reported that the land was unsuitable for housing and that, although housing was needed in London as a whole, there was no great present need in Hillingdon, and the order should not be confirmed. The Secretary of State decided that the immediate housing need in London as a whole overrode the inspector's objections, and confirmed the order. The owners applied for the decision to be quashed. *Held,* there was some evidence on which the Secretary could reasonably arrive at his decision. The decision regarding need was a matter of value judgment for the Secretary of State and the inspector. The application must be dismissed: LESTER AND BUTLER *v.* SECRETARY OF STATE FOR THE ENVIRONMENT AND HILLINGDON LONDON BOROUGH COUNCIL [1978] J.P.L. 308, Sir Douglas Frank, Q.C.

281. Northern Ireland. See NORTHERN IRELAND.

282. Notice—service on one of joint owners—substantial prejudice

A compulsory purchase order was made on May 8, 1978, advertised in a local paper and served on the applicant's husband, G. The applicant was joint owner of the house. At an inquiry G was represented by counsel. The Secretary of State confirmed the order. Mrs. G then issued a notice of motion asking for the order to be quashed. *Held,* (1) the applicant must have suffered substantial prejudice; (2) the applicant's evidence in cross-examination should not be admitted except in exceptional circumstances; (3) the loss of a chance of being better off constituted substantial prejudice. It was not necessary to show that the decision would have been different; (4) the order must be quashed in so far as it related to the applicant's interest in the property: GEORGE *v.* SECRETARY OF STATE FOR THE ENVIRONMENT AND GREENWICH LONDON BOROUGH [1978] J.P.L. 703, Sir Douglas Frank Q.C.

BOOKS AND ARTICLES. See *post,* pp. [3], [15].

CONFLICT OF LAWS

283. Enforcement of judgments—EEC—Brussels Convention. See BAVARIA FLUG-GESELLSCHAFT SCHWABE & CO. K.B. AND GERMANIAR BEDARFSLUFTFAHRT G.M.B.H. & CO. K.G. *v.* EUROCONTROL, § 1235.

284. Foreign judgments—enforcement—registration—defect in judgment

[Foreign Judgments (Reciprocal Enforcement) Act 1933 (c. 13), ss. 1 (2) (*b*), 2 (1) (*b*), (5), 4 (1) (*a*) (i) (v), 4 (2) (*a*) (i) (iii), 5 (1).]

The fact that the judgment of a French court does not, in accordance with the French Code of Civil Procedure, expressly state the steps taken to bring the summons to the knowledge of a defendant in England is a technical defect which does not make the judgment a nullity so that "it could not be enforced by execution" within s. 2 (1) (*b*) of the Act.

C G T, who had branches in Paris and Lille, sold clothing from both branches to S Ltd. in England. The invoices provided that disputes should be referred to courts in either Paris or Lille according to the branch involved. C G T claimed payment for goods from both branches. S Ltd. informed solicitors acting for C G T that the disputes should be brought before the Lille court. Accordingly C G T commenced proceedings in that court to recover the price of the goods sold and delivered and a further 10,000 francs as "résistance abusive," a head of damage awarded in France for unreasonably refusing to pay a plain claim. The writ was served on S Ltd. who ignored it

and the Lille court gave judgment in default of appearance. S Ltd. were given notice of the judgment but it did not comply with the French Code of Civil Procedure in that it did not state expressly the steps taken to bring the summons to the notice of S Ltd. C G T applied to the High Court to register the judgment under s. 2 (1) of the Act. Master Warren ordered that the judgment in respect of the goods from the Lille branch should be registered but not in respect of the goods from the Paris branch or the 10,000 francs résistance abusive. S Ltd. then issued proceedings in the Paris court against C G T claiming a sum of money in respect of goods sold by the Paris branch and applied for leave to appeal out of time against the Lille judgment. Parker J. allowed C G T's appeal and ordered that the whole of the Lille judgment be registered under the 1933 Act. S Ltd. appealed. *Held*, dismissing the appeal (Goff J. dissenting in part), that (1) the defect in the judgment did not allow S Ltd. to rely upon the proviso in s. 2 (1) (*b*) of the Act but only rendered it voidable pending the outcome of S Ltd.'s appeal; (2) S Ltd. had " submitted to the jurisdiction " of the Lille Court within s. 4 (2) (*a*) (i) of the Act and had " agreed to submit to the jurisdiction " of that court within s. 4 (2) (*a*) (iii) and accordingly the Lille court had jurisdiction to deal with the claims by C G T in respect of both branches; (3) the claim for 10,000 francs " résistance abusive " was not a " fine or other penalty " within s. 1 (2) (*b*) of the Act and was not " contrary to public policy " in England under s. 4 (1) (*a*) (v) since it was a compensatory claim; (4) in all the circumstances the court should not exercise its discretion under s. 5 (1) of the Act either to set aside the registration or to adjourn the application to set it aside pending the appeal by S Ltd. (*Rookes* v. *Barnard* [1964] C.L.Y. 3703 and *Broome* v. *Cassell & Co.* [1972] C.L.Y. 2745 considered; *Ferdinand Wagner* v. *Laubscher Bros. & Co.* [1970] C.L.Y. 2305 applied; decision of Parker J. [1977] C.L.Y. 336 affirmed.)
S. A. CONSORTIUM GENERAL TEXTILES *v.* SUN AND SAND AGENCIES [1978] 2 W.L.R. 1, C.A.

285. Jurisdiction—property abroad—equitable exception
Where there is an equity between parties, the court has jurisdiction to entertain actions for determination of title to possessions outside the jurisdiction and to give the appropriate ancillary relief.
P, an American company, believed that a debtor was transferring antiques away from them from New York to the flat of a friend in Paris. The debtor and the friend were American citizens and the debt was an American debt. On the arrival of the friend in England, where he had a flat, notice of motion and an ex parte injunction were served on him, restraining him from removing the contents of the Paris flat and seeking facilities for an inspection of it. On a preliminary application to stay the action for want of jurisdiction, alternatively because England was not the appropriate forum for the action, *held*, that (1) there was an equity between the debtor and the corporation and, if the friend had assisted the debtor, between the corporation and the debtor, so that the court had jurisdiction to entertain an action for the determination of the right to property as between them; (2) P could proceed with their interlocutory application, notwithstanding that England was not the appropriate forum. In view of the urgency of the matter it would not be right to order a stay on that ground.
COOK INDUSTRIES *v.* GALLIHER [1978] 3 W.L.R. 637, Templeman J.

286. —— trespass to foreign land and chattels—alleged conspiracy in England
The English courts have no jurisdiction to entertain an action for conspiracy to trespass upon land situated abroad but they may entertain a claim relating to chattels outside the jurisdiction.
The Cypriot plaintiffs owned hotels situated in the part of Cyprus occupied by Turks in the invasion of 1974. After the plaintiffs' evacuation the hotels were operated by Turkish Cypriots who circulated in England a brochure advertising holidays in such hotels. The plaintiffs issued proceedings against an English travel agent and a London representative of the " Turkish Federated State of Cyprus " (the publishers of the brochure) alleging conspiracy to trespass and obtained interim injunctions restraining further acts in furtherance of the alleged conspiracy. The Court of Appeal discharged the injunctions and struck

out the statement of claim including an amendment alleging conspiracy to trespass in respect of the contents of the hotels. *Held,* allowing the plaintiffs' appeal in part, that although no action could be maintained for trespass or conspiracy to trespass upon foreign land, the same did not apply to foreign chattels and accordingly the action in respect of the hotel contents could continue. (Decision of Court of Appeal [1977] C.L.Y. 341, reversed in part; *British South Africa Co.* v. *Compania de Mocambique* [1892] A.C. 602 followed; *The Totten* [1946] P. 135, approved.)

HESPERIDES HOTELS v. MUFTIZADE [1978] 3 W.L.R. 378, H.L.

287. Public international law. See INTERNATIONAL LAW.

288. Recognition—valid foreign title to sue

The plaintiff's brother had been missing since 1973 and the plaintiff had taken proceedings in Lebanon to have him declared absent and to have himself appointed as his judicial administrator. It was *held,* for the first time, that a valid foreign title to sue is not recognised by English courts and the plaintiff's claim was therefore dismissed: KAMOUH v. ASSOCIATED ELECTRICAL INDUSTRIES INTERNATIONAL, *The Times,* October 6, 1978, Parker J.

ARTICLES. See *post,* p. [15].

CONSTITUTIONAL LAW

289. British Commonwealth. See BRITISH COMMONWEALTH.

290. European Assembly Elections Act 1978 (c. 10). See § 1275.

291. Ministers, transfer of functions

TRANSFER OF FUNCTIONS (WALES) (No. 1) ORDER 1978 (No. 272) [25p], made under the Ministers of the Crown Act 1975 (c. 26), s. 1; operative on April 1, 1978; transfers certain functions relating to agriculture, fisheries, water resources, water supply and land drainage to the Secretary of State for Wales.

TRANSFER OF FUNCTIONS (WALES) (No. 2) ORDER 1978 (No. 274) [15p], made under the Ministers of the Crown Act 1975, s. 1; operative on April 1, 1978; enables the Secretary of State for Wales to exercise in relation to Wales the functions of the Secretary of State for Education and Science.

292. Northern Ireland. See NORTHERN IRELAND.

293. Parliament. See PARLIAMENT.

294. Pay policy—government sanctions

Plaintiffs, seeking an injunction to stop a strike, suggested that the Department of Employment was misusing its powers by threatening sanctions in respect of breaches of the pay policy; and that, accordingly, the plaintiffs were inhibited from implementing a pay rise which, the employees contended, had been agreed. The Att.-Gen. intervened to state that it had never been the Government's policy to cause a breach of contractual or other obligations. The application was then withdrawn: HOLLIDAY HALL v. CHAPPLE, *The Times,* February 7, 1978.

295. Scotland Act 1978 (c. 51)

This Act provides for changes in the government of Scotland and in the procedure of Parliament and in the constitution and functions of certain public bodies.

Pt. I (ss. 1–34) deals with the Scottish Assembly and Executive: s. 1 provides for the existence and composition of the Scottish Assembly; s. 2 states the time of election, and the term of office, of the members of the Assembly; s. 3 governs the dissolution of the Assembly; s. 4 provides for the method of elections to the Assembly; s. 5 relates to by-elections; s. 6 directs how vacancies among additional members should be filled; s. 7 makes the day, time and place of the first meeting of the Assembly a decision for the Secretary of State; s. 8 governs the procedure of the Assembly; s. 9 sets out reasons for disqualification from membership of the Assembly; s. 10 states certain exceptions to disqualification and confers upon the Assembly a power to grant relief from disqualification; s. 11 deals with the effects of disqualification; s. 12 relates to judicial proceedings concerning disqualification; s. 13 makes requisite for members an oath of allegiance; s. 14 concerns the resignation of his seat by a member; s. 15 confers subsidiary powers upon the Assembly; s. 16 relates to defamatory statements in the Assembly proceedings; s. 17 makes the Assembly a public body for the purposes of the Prevention of Corruption Acts 1889 to 1916; s. 18 deals with Scottish Assembly Acts; s. 19 defines the legislative competence of the Assembly; s. 20 provides for the scrutiny of Assembly Bills; s. 21 sets up the Scottish Executive; s. 22 confers the Executive's powers; s. 23 confers powers on the Executive in relation to the making of subordinate legislation; s. 24 makes certain provisions in respect of powers exercisable with the consent of, or concurrently with, another Minister; s. 25 relates to Crown interests and public records; s. 26 provides for preserving order in the Assembly's proceedings; s. 27 directs the making of standing orders governing the passage of bills; s. 28 is concerned with members' pecuniary interests; s. 29 relates to the appointment of committees; s. 30 deals with financial initiatives; s. 31 provides for members of the Assembly to act as additional Commissioners under the Private Legislation Procedure (Scotland) Act 1936 (c. 52); s. 32 sets out the Clerk, officers and servants of the Assembly; s. 33 states the application of employment legislation to the Clerk, officers and servants; s. 34 stipulates the remuneration of members.

Pt. II (ss. 35–42) concerns relations with United Kingdom authorities: s. 35 states certain agency arrangements and the provision of services; s. 36 relates to the provision of information; s. 37 confers power to make changes in law consequential upon the Scottish Assembly Acts; s. 38 confers a power to move rejection of certain Assembly bills; s. 39 gives the Secretary of State the power to prevent or require action; s. 40 contains a power to revoke subordinate instruments; s. 41 lays down certain industrial and economic guidelines; s. 42 requires the Minister's consent to the terms and conditions of service of certain persons.

Pt. III (ss. 43–62) contains financial provisions: s. 43 sets up the Scottish Consolidated Fund and the Scottish Loans Fund; s. 44 governs payments out of the Scottish Consolidated Fund; s. 45 directs the method of appropriation of sums forming part of the Scottish Consolidated Fund, and the destination of receipts; s. 46 deals with payments out of the Scottish Loans Fund; s. 47 governs payments into the Scottish Consolidated Fund out of moneys provided by Parliament; s. 48 relates to payments into the Scottish Loans Fund out of the National Loans Fund; s. 49 states the law on short term borrowing by the Scottish Executive; s. 50 permits a Treasury guarantee of such sums borrowed by the Scottish Executive; s. 51 contains a limitation on capital expenditure financed by borrowing; s. 52 states the rates of interest on certain loans from the Scottish Loans Fund; s. 53 creates the office of Scottish Comptroller and Auditor General; s. 54 arranges for a salary and pension to be payable to him; s. 55 gives him access to certain books and documents; s. 56 relates to appropriation and other accounts and audit; s. 57 provides for the appointment and functions of an Accounts Committee; s. 58 requires the publication of accounts and reports under ss. 56 and 57; s. 59 is a modification of enactments providing for payments into or out of the Consolidated Fund or authorising advances from the National Loans Fund; s. 60 relates to the existing debt; s. 61 concerns the preparation of accounts by the Secretary of State; s. 62 directs the method of putting forward proposals for powers to raise money.

Pt. IV (ss. 63–65) concerns devolved matters and the determination of questions relating thereto: s. 63 defines " devolved matters "; s. 64 contains reservations to this area; s. 65 sets out the legal proceedings involving devolution issues.

Pt. V (ss. 66–78) contains miscellaneous provisions: s. 66 deals with the voting powers of Scottish Members of Parliament; s. 67 relates to the Speaker's Conference; s. 68 defines the status and remuneration of certain officers and servants; s. 69 concerns rate support grants; s. 70 makes certain provisions in respect of public bodies; s. 71 alters the functions of the British Tourist Authority; s. 72 makes certain adjustments to planning law; s. 73 requires the transfer of property to the First Secretary; s. 74 relates to the acquisition and disposal of land by the First Secretary; s. 75 makes supplementary provisions as to this property's vesting; s. 76 permits certain exemptions from jury service; s. 77 is concerned with complaints of maladministration; s. 78 protects special interests of the Orkneys and Shetlands.

Pt. VI (ss. 79–89) is general and supplemental: s. 79 stipulates the method of reckoning time for certain purposes; s. 80 modifies enactments requiring the laying of reports before Parliament; s. 81 relates to secondary legislation under the Act; s. 82 provides for expenses; s. 83 is the interpretation section; s. 84 prescribes the construction and amendment of existing enactments; s. 85 concerns commencement of the Act; s. 86 makes special provisions for the Orkneys and the Shetlands; s. 87 governs the necessary referendum; s. 88 concerns the period between a general election and the referendum; s. 89 gives the short title.

The Act received the Royal Assent on July 31, 1978, and shall come into force on such day or days as the Secretary may by order appoint.

296. —— referendum

SCOTLAND ACT 1978 (REFERENDUM) ORDER 1978 (No. 1912) [40p], made under the Scotland Act 1978 (c. 51), Sched. 17, paras. 1, 4; operative on December 20, 1978; provides for the conduct of the referendum on devolution to be held in Scotland and specifies the date on which the poll is to be held.

297. Wales Act 1978 (c. 52)

This Act provides for changes in the government of Wales and in the constitution and functions of certain public bodies.

Pt. I (ss. 1–32) concerns the Welsh Assembly: s. 1 sets up the Welsh Assembly; s. 2 directs the time of election and term of office of members; s. 3 regulates electors and elections; s. 4 governs by-elections; s. 5 deals with grounds for disqualification from membership of the Assembly; s. 6 contains exceptions, and the power to grant relief from disqualification; s. 7 sets out the effects of disqualification; s. 8 directs certain judicial proceedings for disqualification; s. 9 stipulates the functions of the Assembly; s. 10 confers power to support cultural and recreative activities; s. 11 confers other non-statutory powers; s. 12 stipulates functions under local Acts; s. 13 relates to the first meeting of the Assembly; s. 14 provides for the procedure of the Assembly to be regulated by standing orders; s. 15 requires the disclosure of members' interests; s. 16 directs the appointment of subject committees; s. 17 provides for the setting up of an Executive Committee; s. 18 stipulates the method of taking any financial initiative; s. 19 directs the exercise of certain powers of subordinate legislation; s. 20 provides for the scrutiny of subordinate legislation; s. 21 relates to party balance within committees; s. 22 states the degree of privilege, for the purposes of defamation law, covering the Assembly's proceedings; s. 23 deals with staff appointments to the Assembly; s. 24 empowers the Assembly to institute inquiries; s. 25 empowers it to institute civil proceedings; s. 26 contains supplementary powers; s. 27 forbids the Assembly to conduct relations with any country outside the United Kingdom; s. 28 provides for the fulfilment of certain international obligations; s. 29 directs the swearing of an oath of allegiance by elected members of the Assembly; s. 30 relates to resignation by members; s. 31 provides for their remuneration; s. 32 exempts members from jury service.

Pt. II (ss. 33–38) determines relations with United Kingdom authorities: s. 33 empowers the Secretary of State to prevent or require action; s. 34 empowers the Secretary of State to revoke subordinate instruments; s. 35 requires the consent of a Minister of the Crown before the Assembly can exercise certain powers; s. 36 sets out industrial and economic guidelines; s. 37 contains arrangements for agency and the provision of services; s. 38 relates to the provision of information.

Pt. III (ss. 39–56) contains financial provisions: s. 39 sets up a Welsh Consolidated Fund and a Welsh Loans Fund; s. 40 governs payments out of the Welsh Consolidated Fund; s. 41 relates to the appropriation of sums forming part of the Welsh Consolidated Fund and destination of receipts; s. 42 deals with payments out of the Welsh Loans Fund; s. 43 provides for payments into the Welsh Consolidated Fund out of moneys provided by Parliament; s. 44 relates to payments into the Welsh Loans Fund from the National Loans Fund; s. 45

makes certain provisions in relation to short-term borrowing; s. 46 empowers the Treasury to guarantee sums borrowed by the Assembly; s. 47 limits the capital expenditure financed by borrowing; s. 48 creates the office of Welsh Comptroller and Auditor General; s. 49 provides for the salary and pension of the Welsh Comptroller and Auditor General; s. 50 confers access to the Assembly's books and documents upon the Welsh Comptroller and Auditor General; s. 51 relates to appropriation and other accounts and audit; s. 52 deals with the appointment of an Accounts Committee; s. 53 directs the publication of accounts and reports; s. 54 modifies enactments providing for payments into or out of the Consolidated Fund or authorising advances from the National Loans Fund; s. 55 relates to existing advances from the National Loans Fund; s. 56 concerns the preparation and certification of accounts.

Pt. IV (ss. 57–67) contains miscellaneous provisions: s. 57 deals with rate support and other grants; s. 58 confers power on a Minister of the Crown to make certain provisions as regards specified bodies; s. 59 relates to tourism; s. 60 sets up a Countryside Commission for Wales; s. 61 relates to water and land drainage; s. 62 relates to planning; s. 63 determines the status and remuneration of certain officers and servants; s. 64 provides for the transfer of certain property; s. 65 concerns stamp duty; s. 66 provides for the investigation of complaints of maladministration by the Assembly; s. 67 brings the Assembly within the scope of corrupt practices legislation.

Pt. V (ss. 68–80) is general and suplementary: s. 68 lays down the method of determination of issues as to the Assembly's powers; s. 69 directs the system of reckoning time for the purposes of ss. 33 and 34; s. 70 relates to subordinate legislation under the Act; s. 71 provides for expenses; s. 72 gives directions for the construction of references to Ministers, etc.; s. 73 deals with statutory references to Parliament in connection with subordinate legislation; s. 74 modifies certain enactments requiring the laying of reports before Parliament; s. 75 contains amendments; s. 76 is the interpretation section; s. 77 is the commencement provision; s. 78 provides for a referendum to decide whether effect is to be given to this Act; s. 79 relates to the period between a general election and the referendum; s. 80 gives the short title.

The Act received the Royal Assent on July 31, 1978, and shall come into force on such day or days as the Secretary of State may by order appoint.

298. —— referendum

WALES ACT 1978 (REFERENDUM) ORDER 1978 (No. 1915) [40p], made under the Wales Act 1978 (c. 52), Sched. 12, paras. 1, 4; operative on December 20, 1978; provides for the conduct of the referendum on devolution to be held in Wales and specifies the date on which the poll is to be held.

WALES ACT 1978 (REFERENDUM) (WELSH FORMS) ORDER 1978 (No. 1953) [30p], made under the Welsh Language Act 1967 (c. 66). s. 2 (1), as extended by the Wales Act 1978, Sched. 12, para. 10; operative on January 22, 1979; prescribes the form of the papers to be used in the referendum on devolution.

BOOKS AND ARTICLES. See *post*, pp. [3], [15].

CONTRACT

299. Acceptance—interpretation of phrase—different meanings

[Can.] P contracted to purchase supplies of propane from D in March 1973. In September and December 1973 P wrote to D and voluntarily offered to pay a higher price " on the understanding that they would be able to re-negotiate a new contract for the [following] year based on economic value at that time." D did not reply to P's letter, but did bill P at a higher price in accordance with P's offer. D refused to renew P's contract. P claimed for breach of contract and, in the alternative, that D received the excess payments in trust to the use of P. *Held*, no binding contract regarding the re-negotiation of the original contract ever came into existence. A fundamental term was found in the words " economic value " which had a different meaning to each party. Therefore there was no acceptance by D of P's offer. P was entitled to recover the amount of over-payment: HYDROGAS *v.* GREAT PLAINS DEVELOPMENT CO. OF CANADA [1978] 5 W.W.R. 22, Alta.Sup.Ct.

300. Agency. See AGENCY.

301. Arbitration. See ARBITRATION.

302. Assignment—benefit of debt—clause in contract forbidding assignment

A clause in a contract preventing a contractor from assigning " the contract or any part thereof or any benefit or interest therein or thereunder " will prevent assignment of a debt arising under the contract.

D council entered into a contract with X to carry out road-works. There was a clause preventing X from assigning " the contract or any part thereof or any benefit or interest therein or thereunder " without the written consent of the council. X assigned the amount alleged owing by the council to P, the plaintiff, without the council's consent. P contended that the clause did not prevent the assignment of debts arising under the contract. *Held*, the debt was a chose in action and " a benefit or interest " under the contract, and the purported assignment was invalid.

HELSTAN SECURITIES *v.* HERTFORDSHIRE COUNTY COUNCIL [1978] 3 All E.R. 262, Croom-Johnson J.

303. Breach—claim for compensation for expenditures—losses not a direct result of breach

[Can.] Parties entered into a contract whereby P would cut timber under D's timber sale, and D would be responsible for hauling timber away from site for sale. P claimed D was in breach of contract, as D had not supplied sufficient trucks to make P's operation, which was losing money, viable. P claimed not for loss of profits but for compensation for expenditures. D argued that P's operation lost money not because of a lack of trucks but because of P's inefficiency, and further, that even if D was in breach, P should not be awarded damages because its operation would have lost money in any case. *Held*, P was awarded nominal damages of $250. D was in breach by not supplying sufficient trucks, but had met the onus of showing that P's operation would have lost money even if sufficient trucks were supplied. Therefore, the expenses incurred were losses flowing from P entering into the contract, and not from D's breach. (*Anglia Television* v. *Reed* [1971] C.L.Y. 1735 distinguished; *Frederick Rose (London)* v. *William Pim & Co.* [1953] C.L.Y. 3291, *Cullinane* v. *British " Rema" Manufacturing Co.* [1953] C.L.Y. 935 applied): BOWLAY LOGGING *v.* DOMTAR [1978] 4 W.W.R. 105, Brit.Col.Sup.Ct.

304. —— damages—assessment on basis of a contractual termination rather than as a rescission by an accepted repudiation thereof

[Can.] D failed to load P's cargo as required by the terms of a contract of affreightment. P gave notice of cancellation pursuant to the terms of the contract and sued for damages. The question to be determined was whether the damages should be assessed up to the date of the notice of cancellation or up to the end of the contract period. *Held*, P was entitled to recover damages only for those breaches which occurred up to the date of cancellation. By electing to cancel the contract rather than assuming the responsibility of proving that D had in fact repudiated the contract, P surrendered its right to claim damages for subsequent breaches. (*Sweet & Maxwell* v. *Universal News Services* [1964] C.L.Y. 2073, *Heyman* v. *Darwins* [1942] A.C. 356, *Re A.B.C. Coupler and Engineering Co. (No. 3)* [1970] C.L.Y. 311, and *United Dominions Trust (Commercial)* v. *Ennis* [1967] C.L.Y. 1827 applied): CELGAR *v.* STAR BULK SHIPPING CO. [1978] 3 W.W.R. 20, Brit.Col.Sup.Ct.

305. —— —— mitigation of losses. See APECO OF CANADA *v.* WINDMILL PLACE, § 704a.

306. —— delivery service—inoperative limitation clause—measure of damages

The plaintiffs manufactured knitwear and used the defendant's delivery service which was subject to a limitation clause. The defendants were in breach of contract because of late delivery, and the plaintiffs were unable to find another purchaser when the original purchaser declined delivery. It was *held* that the limitation clause would limit damages on an ordinary contract but here there was a total breach of contract since the late delivery resulted in the loss of the sale, as was within the contemplation of the parties, and there was no other market available. The proper damages were the contract price less any sum actually obtained on disposal: JOHN CURRIE SON & CO. *v.* SECURICOR MOBILE (1978) 122 S.J. 294, Forbes J.

307. —— **employer not estopped from denying breach after a finding of unfair dismissal by industrial tribunal.** See TURNER *v.* LONDON TRANSPORT EXECUTIVE, § 902.

308. —— **liability—employee's arson—no reliance on exemption clause**
It is a fundamental breach of contract for a security guard to burn down a factory which his firm has been employed to protect against fire.

P contracted with D that D would patrol P's factory and protect it, inter alia, from fire and theft. The contract contained wide exemption clauses. An employee of D, while patrolling the factory, lit a fire which burned it down. *Held,* allowing P's appeal, that the exemption clauses could not protect D, either because the lighting of the fire was a fundamental breach discharging the contract or alternatively because the presumed intention of the parties would be that such an act should not be covered by the exclusion clauses nor would it be reasonable for D to rely on it.
PHOTO PRODUCTION *v.* SECURICOR TRANSPORT [1978] 1 W.L.R. 856, C.A.

309. —— —— **whether limited—condition not brought to party's attention at time contract made**
[Can.] P wished to buy a wooden-hulled boat, about which he was not knowledgeable. P contracted with D to have an expert survey done of the boat, which survey was performed by an employee of D, who reported the boat was in good general condition. Relying on the survey, P purchased the boat. Two months later P discovered dry-rot in the hull. P brought an action for the cost of repairs against D, who relied on a condition in the report that D's obligation was limited to providing a surveyor believed to be competent. *Held,* D was liable for breach of contract. The limiting condition did not assist D because P was not aware of it at the time the contract was made and because the evidence did not show D believed its employee to be competent. (*Olley* v. *Marlborough Court* (1949) C.L.C. 4933 applied): CAMPBELL *v.* IMAGE [1978] 2 W.W.R. 663, Br.Col.Co.Ct.

310. —— **specific damages—remoteness.** See H. PARSONS (LIVESTOCK) *v.* UTTLEY INGHAM & CO., § 789.

311. Building contract—express terms—obligation to supply at appropriate time
[Can.] A contract for the installation of mining equipment provided that the owner would deliver certain drawings to the contractor " as work progresses " and " from time to time as the work progresses." The owner also undertook to supply certain equipment. It was further provided in the contract that no implied obligation of any kind should arise to bind the owner. The owner failed to supply the drawings or the equipment in time for the contractor to complete by the agreed completion date, and the owner purported to terminate the agreement. The contractor succeeded at trial in an action for breach of contract, but the owner appealed on the ground that there was no breach of any express obligation and the contract itself excluded implied obligations. *Held,* the owner was bound by an express obligation to deliver the drawings from time to time as the work progressed, that is, at appropriate times in all the circumstances, taking into account the completion date. The obligation to supply was an obligation to supply at an appropriate time: FISCHBACH AND MOORE OF CANADA *v.* NORANDA MINES (1978) 84 D.L.R. (3d) 465, Sask.C.A.

312. Contract for services—whether binding on purchaser—novation—priority of estate in lease
[Can.] P had a business of placing and servicing washers and dryers in apartment buildings. P signed a five-year location contract with M Ltd., by which P was granted the exclusive right to install and maintain machines in a building owned by M. One of the terms of the agreement was that M's successors would be bound by it. M subsequently sold the building to D, and the location contract was attached to the sale agreement. P continued to maintain and service the machines until D contacted P with a view to negotiating a

contractual relationship. P was not interested, and D then seized, locked up and replaced the machines. P sued for damages on the ground that D was bound by the contract. *Held*, the action should succeed (1) as the incorporation of the location agreement into the sale agreement, coupled with the long period (10 months) of acquiescence by D, was sufficient to establish novation; (2) as the location agreement was a lease and D a subsequent purchaser with notice, P also succeeded on the ground of privity of estate. (*Scarf* v. *Jardine* (1882) 7 App.Cas. 315; *British Westinghouse* v. *Underground Electric Railways of London* [1912] A.C. 673 applied): PACIFIC WASH-A-MATIC *v*. R. O. BOOTH HOLDINGS [1978] 5 W.W.R. 525, Brit.Col.Sup.Ct.

313. Exemption clause—late delivery—meaning of " consequential damage "

V agreed to sell building materials to P. Cl. 4 of the contract of sale provided, inter alia: " (V) are not under any circumstances to be liable for any consequential loss or damage caused or arising by reason of late supply. . . ." P claimed from V, inter alia, an indemnity against a claim by sub-contractors regarding delay in their work caused by V's late delivery of materials. V contended that the damage was " consequential " upon the late delivery, and that accordingly their liability was excluded by cl. 4. *Held*, on appeal, that " consequential " did not cover any loss which directly and naturally resulted in the ordinary course of events from late delivery. Judgment for P. (*Millars Machinery Co.* v. *David Way & Son* (1934) 40 Com.Cas. 210 applied): CROUDACE CONSTRUCTION *v*. CAWOODS CONCRETE PRODUCTS [1978] 2 Lloyd's Rep. 55, C.A.

314. —— whether to be enforced—effect of fundamental breach

[Can.] It has been *held* that where an exemption clause expressly and clearly excludes liability it must be given full effect. The doctrine of fundamental breach is a doctrine of construction only, and must yield to a clear exclusion of liability. Thus, a clause in a building contract excluding the owner's liability in case of delay caused by his own default, and limiting his obligations to an equivalent extension of time to the builder is enforceable according to its terms. (*Suisse Atlantique Société D'Armement Maritime S.A.* v. *N.V. Rotterdamsche Kolen Centrale* [1966] C.L.Y. 1797 applied): WOOLLATT FUEL & LUMBER (LONDON) *v*. MATTHEWS GROUP (1978) 83 D.L.R. (3d) 137, Ontario H.C.J.

315. Frustration—force majeure—state intervention—whether state enterprise a separate legal entity

A state trading organisation operating a government monopoly of limited independence, can rely on a decree published by its own Government for the defence of force majeure under rr. 18 and 21 of the Refined Sugar Association, to a claim for non-performance of commercial contracts.

Under Polish economic policy, the majority of home produced sugar beet was sold domestically, the rest on the world market through a Polish state enterprise, Rolimpex. Under Polish law, Rolimpex has a separate legal entity and though subject to ministerial directions had considerable freedom of autonomy. In May and July 1974 as part of an export quota, it contracted to sell 200,000 metric tons of sugar to an English company. The rules of the Refined Sugar Association were incorporated into the contract. R. 18 (*a*) provided that if delivering was prevented by, inter alia, " government intervention beyond the seller's control " the contract would be void without penalty. The seller was made responsible for obtaining the requisite export licence under r. 21; failure to obtain such, not being " sufficient grounds for a claim of force majeure if the regulations in force . . . when the contract was made, called for such licences to be obtained." The 1974 crop was poor and the whole needed for domestic consumption. A ministerial resolution imposed an immediate ban on all sugar exports. On the same date a formal decree was issued giving legal effect to the ban though it did not in terms revoke the export licences already ordered in compliance with r. 21. In reliance on the force majeure clause Rolimpex informed the buyers the contract could not be fulfilled and the dispute was referred to arbitrators namely a panel of the Refined Sugar Association in London, who found in favour of Rolimpex relying on r. 18 (*a*). This was affirmed in the Court of

Appeal. The buyers appealed. *Held*, dismissing the appeal (Lord Salmon dissenting) that (1) the arbitrators had established the sellers were not an organ or a dependent of the Polish Government but an independent state organisation. The contract was therefore frustrated by "government intervention" within r. 18 (*a*) and the sellers were relieved of their liability under the contracts (*Crown Lands Commissioners* v. *Page* [1960] C.L.Y. 1719 considered); (2) the obligation under r. 21 to "obtain" the requisite export licence implied no obligation or warranty to maintain it in force; the sellers were not thereby precluded from relying on r. 18 (*a*).

CZARNIKOW v. CENTRALA HANDLU ZAGRANICZNEGO ROLIMPEX [1978] 3 W.L.R. 274, H.L.

316. —— —— strike—extension of shipment period. See THE KASTELLON, § 2628.

317. **Fundamental breach—completion of work—whether entitled to award on quantum meruit basis**

[Can.] In the course of performance of a contract to construct a power dam, the owner was in several important respects in breach of the contract. The trial judge found this to amount to a fundamental breach that would have justified termination by the contractor. However, the contractor continued the work and completed the project, claiming compensation for the owner's breach on a quantum meruit basis. The trial judge gave judgment for the contractor on that basis. On appeal, *held*, allowing the appeal, the contractor having elected to continue with the work in face of the owner's breach was limited to recovery under the contract. The award based on quantum meruit would be set aside and remitted for determination of the contractor's rights under the contract. Since the contractor had completed the work, and had an adequate remedy under the contract, there was no need for the law to fashion a restitutionary remedy. Nor would it be right for the contractor to obtain a possibly higher rate of compensation then that agreed under the contract. (*Heyman* v. *Darwins* [1942] A.C. 356, *Lodder* v. *Slowey* [1904] A.C. 442, *Luxor* (*Eastbourne*) v. *Cooper* [1941] A.C. 108, *United Australia* v. *Barclays Bank* [1941] A.C. 1, *Howard* v. *Pickford Tool Co.* (1951) C.L.C. 7644 and *Lakshmijit s/o Bhai Suchit* v. *Sherani* [1973] C.L.Y. 1963 referred to): MORRISON-KNUDSEN CO. INC. v. B.C. HYDRO & POWER AUTHORITY (1978) 85 D.L.R. (3d) 186, Brit.Col.C.A.

318. **Independent contractor—failure to execute performance bond—company not bound**

[Can.] D2 contracted to build an apartment block for P, and also contracted to obtain a performance bond. D1 prepared the bond and sent it to D2 for his signature and further delivery to P. D2 never signed or delivered it, but returned it to D1, falsely telling D1 it was not required and falsely telling P it was still awaiting the bond's arrival. D2 failed to complete the building, and P claimed D1 was liable on the bond. *Held*, D1 was not liable. D1 intended to be jointly and severally bound with D2 and was not so bound until D2 executed the bond. Further, the delivery of the bond was conditional on its being executed and re-delivered. (*Naas* v. *Westminster Bank* [1940] A.C. 366, *Luke* v. *South Kensington Hotel Co.* (1879) 11 Ch.D. 121 applied): HELM v. SIMCOE AND ERIE GENERAL INSURANCE CO. [1978] 4 W.W.R. 188, Alta.Sup.Ct.

319. **Mistake—void contract—purported seller of company assets acting ultra vires —return of deposit**

[Can.] S, the receiver-manager of C and related companies, advertised for a purchaser for the sale of the companies. F made an offer and paid a deposit of five per cent. Negotiations between S and F fell through, and it was agreed between them that F would forfeit $10,000 of his deposit. On an application to the court to approve a later offer to purchase, it was ruled that S, as receiver-manager, had power only to preserve the assets of the companies, not to dispose of them. F claimed that the $10,000 was paid under a mistake of law, as S had no legal right to enter into the original contract with F. *Held*, the deposit was ordered to be returned to F. The contract of sale was void ab initio, and it being the basis of the later compromise, the compromise, although not a nullity, at law was set aside in equity. (*Magee* v. *Pennine Insurance Co.* [1969] C.L.Y. 1819 applied): TORONTO DOMINION BANK *v.* FORTIN (1978) 5 W.W.R. 302, Brit.Col. Sup.Ct.

320. Money due—interest—law reform. See § 1824.

321. Negligent mis-statement—pre-contractual negotiations—capacity of barges. See HOWARD MARINE AND DREDGING CO. *v.* A. OGDEN & SONS (EXCAVATIONS), § 1516.

322. Offer and acceptance—whether contract concluded—subject to trial voyage. See JOHN S. DARBYSHIRE, THE, § 2725.

323. —— whether correspondence constituted a contract
D, the harbour authority at Weymouth, offered berthing facilities at the Weymouth ferry terminal to P, ferry operators. Correspondence between D and P followed, with a view to P operating a service from Weymouth to Cherbourg. D then informed P that the berthing facilities were withdrawn. P claimed damages from D on the ground that the correspondence constituted a contract which D had broken, and that D were in breach of the Harbours, Dock and Pier Clauses Act 1847, s. 33, which imposed on them a duty to ensure that the harbour should be open to all persons for shipping and unshipping of goods, and embarking and landing of passengers. *Held,* (1) the correspondence constituted a contract, and D were in breach of it; (2) D were not in breach of s. 33 of the 1847 Act, as D were not indicating that they would refuse to allow P to use the harbour on an ad hoc basis if a berth were available: THORENSEN CAR FERRIES *v.* WEYMOUTH PORTLAND BOROUGH COUNCIL [1977] 2 Lloyd's Rep. 614, Donaldson J.

324. Performance—whether impossible—prohibition clause—force majeure
By a contract dated November 9, 1973, V sold to P 5,000 tonnes of Argentine wheat at U.S.$230 per tonne f.o.b. Necochea. Cl. 14, the prohibition clause provided, inter alia, that the contract be cancelled should fulfilment be rendered impossible by any executive act in the country of origin of the goods. On the same day, V contracted to buy from A the same quantity of wheat at the same price on a back-to-back basis. On November 12 the Argentine wheat Junta extended its monopoly to the 1973/74 wheat crop, the effect of which was that wheat could only be obtained from the Junta at a price fixed by it. A was not prepared to buy on behalf of V for more than U.S.$230 per tonne, whereas the Junta refused to sell for less than U.S.$290 per tonne. *Held,* on appeal, that (1) on the basis of *Warinco* v. *Mauthner* [1978] C.L.Y. 334, V could not establish as a matter of law that on the present facts they were excused from performance; (2) they were not so excused, since they could have bought from another seller in the Argentine, albeit at a much higher price, and so were not within the terms of cl. 14: EXPORTELISA S.A. *v.* ROCCO GIUSEPPE & FIGLI SOC. COLL. [1978] 1 Lloyd's Rep. 433, C.A.

325. Price—valuation of shares—whether parties bound
P agreed to sell to D shares at a price to be agreed between the parties, or in default of agreement, at a price which the auditors of D ("acting as experts and not arbitrators") should certify in writing to be in their opinion the fair selling value. P alleged that the valuation certified by the auditors was vitiated by several fundamental errors, and was consequently substantially lower than the fair selling value of the shares; *Held,* on appeal by P, (1) the contract provided that the auditors should be considered to be acting as experts, and it would be wrong that P should be entitled to frustrate the agreement by alleging mistake in the expert's opinion; (2) on the proper construction of the valuation clause, P had agreed to accept the risk of the auditors making mistakes in the valuation; (3) P were bound by the valuation made honestly and in good faith. (*Campbell* v. *Edwards* [1976] C.L.Y. 1533, applied): BABER *v.* KENWOOD MANUFACTURING Co. [1978] 1 Lloyd's Rep. 175, C.A.

326. Repudiation—damages assessment—date from which to be assessed—Hong Kong. See TAI HING COTTON MILL *v.* KAMSING KNITTING FACTORY, § 2647.

327. —— effect—employment. See THOMAS MARSHALL (EXPORTS) *v.* GUINLE, § 916.

328. Rescission—non-disclosure of material facts—party in fiduciary relationship and under a duty to disclose—whether contract voidable

[Can.] P, an independent contractor, was engaged by D to organise and assemble construction projects. Up to March 1976 P was paid an agreed annual sum of $50,000. In February 1976 P negotiated a renewal of its contract at $50,000 per annum plus a share in the profits of certain projects including three apartment complexes which were underway. It was P's custom not to report to D during the course of a project, but only at the end. Thus P alone knew at the time of the negotiations the costs and profits that would be realised on the three complexes. P sued on the contract, claiming it was owed $600,000. D refused to pay on the ground that P was under a duty to disclose the knowledge of the costs, and that its intentional non-disclosure of those material facts made the contract voidable at D's option. *Held*, P was allowed $250,000 on a quantum meruit basis, plus $50,000 as its annual fee. There was a fiduciary relationship between the parties, and P was under a duty of disclosure of material facts to D. As P failed to disclose, D was entitled to treat the contract as voidable. But as, on the evidence, D's large profits were the results of P's talent and skill, P was awarded the $250,000 on the basis of quantum meruit. (*Phipps* v. *Boardman* [1966] C.L.Y. 11052 referred to): MIDA CONSTRUCTION v. IMPERIAL DEVELOPMENTS (1978) 5 W.W.R. 577, Manitoba C.A.

329. —— fraud inducing purchase of business premises—impossibility of restitutio in integrum not a bar

[Can.] By falsifying their accounts to show a fictional profit the defendants induced the plaintiff to buy their motel, which soon lost a lot of money. The plaintiff claimed, inter alia, rescission of the contract. *Held*, where the subject matter of a sale is a business concern, and it makes a continuing loss as the result of the vendor's deceit, the fact that complete restitution is impossible is no bar to rescission: WANDINGER v. LAKE (1977) 78 D.L.R. 305, Ontario High Ct. of Justice.

330. Restraint of trade—balance of convenience—solicitor

[Can.] The plaintiffs sought to restrain the defendant from practising as a solicitor within an 100 mile radius of his former practice for 10 years, as agreed in his agreement made when selling them his practice. *Held*, as the plaintiffs themselves had sent the defendant work to do, as had other clients, it would not be within the balance of convenience to grant an injunction restraining him from so practising pending the trial of the issue of the validity of such term. (*Texaco* v. *Mulberry Filling Station* [1972] C.L.Y. 513 applied): CRAMPTON AND BROWN v. ROBERTSON [1977] 6 W.W.R. 99, B.C.Sup.Ct.

331. —— penalty clause—actual damage greater than amount stipulated—whether amount stipulated limits recovery

[Can.] It has been *held* that where an employee covenants not to compete after leaving his employer's employment and on default to pay $1,000 as liquidated damages, the employer may obtain an injunction to restrain future breaches of the covenant together with damages in respect of past breaches. However, the damages must be limited to the $1,000 stipulated, whether or not the promise to pay it is characterised as a penalty clause. Penalty clauses are only to be struck down on the ground of oppression, and it is not oppressive to limit a party who stipulates for a penalty to the amount stipulated. (*Cellulose Acetate Silk Co.* v. *Widnes Foundry* [1933] A.C. 20 and *Imperial Tobacco Co.* v. *Parslay* [1936] 2 All E.R. 515 referred to): ELSLEY v. COLLINS INSURANCE AGENCIES (1978) 83 D.L.R. (3d) 1, Can.Sup.Ct.

332. —— restrictive covenant in articles of clerkship—validity

The defendant was articled as a solicitor's clerk to the plaintiff whose firm had three offices in the London Borough of Ealing. There was a restrictive covenant in his articles restraining him for three years from their expiration from working in the borough or taking as client any client of the plaintiff's firm. He was offered employment at the end of his articles with a firm within the borough and offered an undertaking not to solicit any clients from the plaintiff's firm save a dozen who were, he said, personal to him. This was not accepted. The court discharged an interim injunction against the defendant since the matter could go to speedy trial and each side could pay damages: RICHARDS v. LEVY (1978) 122 S.J. 713, C.A.

333. Sale of goods. See SALE OF GOODS.

334. —— non-delivery—prohibition on export
S agreed to sell to B U.S. soya bean meal c.i.f. Weser, shipment Mediterranean port between May 29 and June 15, 1973. Cl. 21 of the GAFTA terms provided that, in a case of prohibition of export, the contract shall be cancelled, S to notify B without delay and, if necessary, must produce proof to justify the claim for cancellation. S purchased the soya bean meal f.o.b. Piraeus from P, the holders of an export licence. S notified B that the contract would be performed. Before loading began, the export licence was suspended. S took all reasonable steps to have the suspension lifted, but in vain. B claimed damages for non-delivery. S contended that they were protected by cl. 21. *Held*, on appeal, when sellers undertook to supply goods shipped from one of a number of ports, they could not rely on an event included in an exception clause if that event happened, but affected only one of the ports, unless they could show they could not have shipped goods of the contractual description, and within the time for shipment, from any one of the other ports. S were not protected by cl. 21. (*Tradax Export S.A.* v. *André and Cie S.A.* [1976] C.L.Y. 2464 distinguished): WARINCO A.G. v. FRITZ MAUTHNER [1978] 1 Lloyd's Rep. 151, C.A.

335. Sale of real property—oral agreement—entry into possession—whether sufficient act of part performance. See REGENT v. MILLETT, § 3050.

336. Specific performance—whether contract concluded—sale of council house— correspondence and conduct of parties. See GIBSON v. MANCHESTER CITY COUNCIL, § 3062.

337. Terms—construction—perpetuity—water supply
A contract to supply goods or services " at all times hereafter " does not conclusively declare perpetuity, and the further words " during the subsistence of this agreement " may be implied.

In 1929, the water company entered into an agreement with a hospital to supply 5,000 gallons of water per day free and all the additional water it required at 7d. per 1,000 gallons, " at all times hereafter." In 1975, the water company gave notice that they intended to terminate the agreement in six months' time, and that thereafter, they proposed to supply the hospital with 5,000 gallons per day free, and to charge for any excess at the normal rate of 45p per 1,000 gallons, *i.e.* 15 times the old price. On an originating summons, by the hospital, the judge held that the 1929 agreement, by virtue of the words " at all times hereafter," had been made in perpetuity and the water company was bound by it. On appeal, *held*, allowing the appeal, that the court would infer a power to terminate on reasonable notice, and construe the words " at all times hereafter " as meaning " at all times hereafter during the subsistence of this agreement." (*Crediton Gas Co.* v. *Crediton Urban District Council* [1928] Ch. 447 and *Re Spenborough Urban District Council's Agreement* [1967] C.L.Y. 600 applied; *Llanelly Railway and Dock Co.* v. *London and North Western Railway Co.* (1875) L.R. 1 H.L. 550 and *Martin-Baker Aircraft Co.* v. *Canadian Flight Equipment* [1955] C.L.Y. 468 distinguished.)

STAFFORDSHIRE AREA HEALTH AUTHORITY v. SOUTH STAFFORDSHIRE WATERWORKS CO. [1978] 3 All E.R. 769, C.A.

338. —— description of goods—words of identification only
By a charterparty dated November 7, 1973, O, the owners of a vessel under construction, agreed to charter the vessel to C. The preamble to the charter provided, inter alia, " It is agreed between the owners of the good Newbuilding tank vessel known as Osaka Shipbuilding Co., Hull No. 352 until named. . . ." The charter provided, by cl. 41, " this charterparty is for a motor tank vessel to be built at Osaka Shipbuilding Co., Hull No. 352." The charter also provided that the contract was to be governed by English law, and gave English courts jurisdiction to deal with disputes. The vessel

was not built at Osaka, but at a yard at Oshima, 300 miles away. C sought to rescind the charter on the ground that the vessel chartered did not correspond to the contractual description. O claimed US $11,000,000 as damages, and took proceedings under R.S.C., Ord. 14, against C. *Held,* on appeal, (1) the words " good Newbuilding tank vessel known as Osaka Shipbuilding Co., Hull No. 352 until named " were only words of identification; (2) applying the principles in *The Diana Prosperity* [1976] C.L.Y. 2582, there were no words of contractual obligation requiring the owners to tender a vessel built at the Osaka Shipbuilding Co.'s yard at Osaka; O were entitled to tender the ship built at Oshima; (3) the case was one in which the court could properly give judgment for O for damages to be assessed under Ord. 14. (*The Diana Prosperity* [1976] C.L.Y. 2582, applied): SANKO STEAMSHIP CO. *v.* KANO TRADING [1978] 1 Lloyd's Rep. 156, C.A.

339. —— incorporation of standard conditions—indemnity clause—whether apt to include negligence of profferers

A reference in a contractual document to the contract being subject to general conditions " available on request " is sufficient to incorporate into the contract the terms contained in the current edition of such conditions.

The appellants regularly overhauled equipment at the respondents' factory. In 1970, the appellants having indicated their willingness to carry out such an overhaul in July, the respondents in May sent to the appellants a purchase note specifying the required services, which request was expressed to be subject to "our General Conditions Contract 24001, obtainable on request." The appellants acknowledged the order but did not request a copy of the conditions, although a copy of the 1969 edition of the conditions was sent to them. At the material time the 1969 edition had been superseded by a new edition, both such editions (and the original version) bearing the number 24001. Each version of such conditions included an indemnity clause whereunder the appellants were required to indemnify the respondents against " any liability, loss, claim or proceedings whatsoever . . . arising out of, or in the course of, the execution of the order." Whilst the work was in progress, an employee of the appellants was seriously injured and successfully sued the respondents, to whose negligence and breach of duty the accident was found to have been wholly attributable. In third party proceedings the respondents were held to be entitled to an indemnity from the appellants. *Held,* allowing the appeal, that the reference on the purchase note was sufficient to incorporate into the contract the latest edition of the respondents' general conditions, but that the indemnity clause was inapt to include liability occasioned by the respondents' own negligence, express words being necessary to confer such a right upon the respondents. (Dicta of Lord Greene M.R. in *Alderslade* v. *Hendon Laundry* [1945] 1 All E.R. 245 and of Lord Maxwell of Henryton in *Canada Steamship Lines* v. *R.* [1952] C.L.Y. 610, applied; dicta of Buckley and Orr L.JJ. in *Gillespie Brothers & Co.* v. *Roy Bowles Transport* [1973] C.L.Y. 407, disapproved.)
SMITH v. SOUTH WALES SWITCHGEAR [1978] 1 All E.R. 18, H.L.

340. —— unusual and onerous—whether signer bound

[Can.] D rented a motor car from P and elected to pay an additional premium for full insurance against damage. D signed the document without reading it. On the face of the document it provided that the cover should not apply if the vehicle was driven in violation of any of the provisions of the agreement. On the back, in fine and faint print, it was provided that the vehicle was not to be operated by anybody who had drunk any quantity of intoxicating liquor. The car was damaged while being driven by D who gave evidence, accepted at trial, that though he had consumed some alcohol, he was not intoxicated and was capable of controlling the vehicle. *Held,* a signature can only be relied on as manifesting assent to a document when it is reasonable for the party relying on the signed document to believe that the signer really did assent to its contents. In a transaction such as a car rental contract, where P emphasises in its advertising the speed and ease of the transaction, it can be held to know that its customers do not really assent to all the provisions of the documents they sign, and in such circumstances cannot rely on unusual and onerous printed terms not drawn to the customers' attention. (*L'Estrange* v. *Graucob* [1934] 2 K.B. 394 distinguished; *McCutcheon* v. *David MacBrayne* [1964] C.L.Y. 568, *Jaques* v. *Lloyd D. George & Partners* [1968] C.L.Y. 35, and *Neuchatel Asphalte* v. *Barnett* [1957] C.L.Y. 235 referred to): TILDEN RENT-A-CAR v. CLENDENNING (1978) 83 D.L.R. (3d) 400, Ont.C.A.

341. Warranty—breach—warranty that save as disclosed no material adverse change in net assets of company prior to completion date

On the reduction of a company's assets between balance sheet date and completion, disclosure generally of the causes of probable future losses, as opposed to disclosure of a quantified reduction in the net asset value or the actual rate of continuing losses, will not protect the vendors of the company from being in breach of a warranty that " save as disclosed there will have been no material adverse change in the overall value of the net assets of the company."

The plaintiffs were the shareholders of L Co., a fashion company, who marketed clothes designed by L, a well-known designer. L became ill and could not work, and L Co. began to run at a loss. The plaintiffs negotiated to sell L Co. to the defendants. They disclosed that no new collection had been designed, that L Co. was running at a loss and that it was in a traded down state they could not specify, because they did not know, how much money was being lost. The defendants agreed to buy L Co.'s assets for £44,000 and goodwill for £10,000. The agreement contained a warranty that " save as disclosed between balance sheet date and completion date there will have been no material adverse change in the overall net assets of the company allowing for normal trade fluctuations." When the defendants took over, they found an adverse change of £8,600. They refused to pay the full purchase price. *Held*, the defendants were entitled to damages for breach of the warranty. The reduction was entirely special to the company and had not happened before, and was not a " normal trade fluctuation "; it was a " material adverse change " which was not covered by the general disclosure of the cause of future losses and which had not been specifically disclosed for the purposes of the warranty. LEVISON v. FARIN [1978] 2 All E.R. 1149, Gibson J.

BOOKS AND ARTICLES. See *post*, pp. [3], [15].

COPYRIGHT

342. Infringement—architect's plans—damages an adequate remedy

[Copyright Act 1956 (c. 74), s. 17 (4).] The plaintiff drew plans for the rebuilding of an hotel. When part of the building was completed, the company was sold to the third defendants. The first defendants were appointed architects, and substantially modified the plaintiff's plans. On application for an interlocutory injunction, it was *held* that (1) the plaintiff had a prima facie case for breach of copyright; (2) there was a strongly arguable case that the company could use the plaintiff's plans as they wished; (3) damages were an adequate remedy, to be assessed as the sum payable if a licence to use the plans had been granted: HUNTER v. FITZROY ROBINSON AND PARTNERS [1978] F.S.R. 167, Oliver J.

343. —— co-authors of literary work—measure of damages

[Aust.] P., together with the two other co-authors of a book, entered into a publication agreement with L Co. relating to the book. Subsequently, P agreed with L Co. and H Co. to the publication of a cheaper edition of the book by H Co. Several years later, H Co. purported to authorise the publication, without the consent of P or either co-author, of excerpts of the book in a newspaper. P brought an action for breach of the publication agreement against L Co., and for infringement of copyright against H Co. and the printers and publishers of the newspaper. *Held*, (1) despite unequal contributions to a work, co-authors hold copyright as tenants in common. On the evidence, it was held in unequal shares, P holding 60 per cent.; (2) on an infringement, one co-owner may recover damages in respect of his proportion; (3) the measure of damages was the depreciation, in terms of loss of sales of the book or other saleable rights, caused by the infringement to the value of the copyright. (*Sutherland Publishing Co.* v. *Caxton Publishing Co.* [1936] Ch. 323 applied): PRIOR *v.* LANSDOWNE PRESS PTY. [1977] F.L.R. 59, Vict.Sup.Ct.

344. —— copies—conversion—knowledge
[Copyright Act 1968 (Com.), ss. 10, 102, 103, 116.]
The plaintiff, Y, had an exclusive licence to distribute Minos and Margaphone records, and the right to reproduce them. Y refused to supply recordings to the defendants, who obtained records by purchase and arrangements with other retail outlets. The plaintiff alleged that the sales constituted an infringement and conversion. *Held,* (1) two of the defendant companies had each sold a record which was an infringing copy; (2) for the summons to succeed, the infringing copy must have been made to the knowledge of the seller; (3) the plaintiff had failed to establish the defendants' knowledge; (4) the defendants' reasonable belief that they were not selling infringing copy afforded a defence to a claim for damages for conversion.
YOUNG *v.* ODEON MUSIC HOUSE PARTY [1978] R.P.C. 621, Sup.Ct. of New South Wales.

345. —— discovery—similar fact evidence
The third defendants, in an action for infringement, claimed copyright in film music, and had allegedly authorised infringements by the other defendants. The plaintiffs sought discovery in respect of documents relating to acts of infringement in previous legal actions, on the grounds that it would be admissible as similar fact evidence. *Held,* refusing discovery, the documents were not relevant to the issue in the present case, except as to the credit of the third defendants: E.G. MUSIC *v.* S.F. (FILM) DISTRIBUTORS [1978] F.S.R. 121, Whitford J.

346. —— importation and resale of books—no implied licence
[Aus.] The first plaintiff owned the exclusive right of publication and sale in Australia of books, the copyright of which was owned by the second plaintiff. The defendant was a bookseller in Sydney who ordered from a U.S. wholesaler books which were then sold at a lower price than those obtained through the first plaintiffs. The second plaintiffs sought a declaration as to title, and injunction to restrain infringement of rights of the first plaintiff. *Held,* (1) there was no implied licence to import the books nor a licence to resell them after importation; (2) there was no relevant analogy to resale of patented articles: TIME-LIFE INTERNATIONAL (NEDERLANDS) B.V. *v.* INTERSTATE PARCEL EXPRESS CO. PTY. [1978] F.S.R. 251, High Ct. of Australia.

347. —— interlocutory relief—undertakings by defendants
The plaintiffs sought interlocutory relief in an action for infringement of copyright and breach of confidence. The defendants gave extensive undertakings until the hearing of the motion. The plaintiff sought to stand the motion over until trial of the action. The defendants sought orders that their undertakings be discharged. *Held,* (1) the motion should be stood over to trial; (2) the court should not bind the defendants to their undertakings for a longer period than anticipated; (3) the plaintiff should pay the costs of the motion generally and of this application: WOODCOCK *v.* DENTON TACKLE [1978] F.S.R. 548, Megarry V.-C.

348. —— knowledge—publication—importations
[Copyright Act 1956 (c. 74), ss. 3, 5.] The plaintiffs designed a fabric P1, in which the defendant expressed interest but ultimately did not buy. R, an employee of the defendants, went to Hong Kong where he was shown a design identical to P1 which he ordered to be printed and made up, and shipped to England. It was agreed that knowledge should be imputed to the defendants after the plaintiffs wrote to them on March 5, 1975. The plaintiffs claimed damages for infringement of copyright. *Held,* (1) if R recognised the fabric, this would not necessarily seize him with knowledge that the design would infringe the plaintiffs' copyright; (2) R had no detailed recollection of the fabric; (3) the defendants could rely on s. 5 until March 5, 1975; (4) the defendants had not, by selling and distributing, issued copies in breach of s. 3 (5); (5) s. 5 must be construed so as to provide a defence to a claim in

conversion in the same way that it does under the head of infringement: INFABRICS v. JAYTEX SHIRT Co. [1978] F.S.R. 451, Whitford J.

349. —— photograph inspiring painting—whether copying

[Copyright Act 1911 (c. 46), ss. 1 (2), 5 (1).] The plaintiff's photograph of two cocks fighting was published in a magazine. The first defendant, an artist, saw the photograph and painted a picture in which the two cocks were in a similar position, but the colours heightened. The judge held that the effect of the painting was entirely different, and that the photograph was only an inspiration. The plaintiff appealed. *Held*, dismissing the appeal, that (1) the test applied by the judge was the correct one; (2) the relative position of the birds was a less important factor because the photographer merely chose the moment at which to photograph them: BAUMAN v. FUSSELL [1978] R.P.C. 485, C.A.

350. —— reversionary interests—mechanical rights—pre-1912 assignments—implied licence

[Copyright Act 1911 (c. 46), ss. 1, 5, 19, 24, 31, 33, 35; Copyright Act 1956 (c. 74), ss. 1, 18, 50.] The plaintiffs held the reversionary interests by assignment in numerous songs by 177 deceased song-writers. The plaintiffs sought an injunction to restrain the defendants, music publishers, from exploiting these songs. The defendants and other publishers claimed declarations as to title and sought an injunction and damages for slander of title. At the hearing of a consolidated test action, it was *held* that in respect of title, (1) pre-1912 assignments by authors to the defendants operated to assign substituted copyrights; (2) although no specific reference to the new substituted copyright was necessary, on a proper construction, the agreements did not transfer the substituted copyright of pre-1912 work assigned to the publisher after the entry into force of the 1911 Act; (3) a song in which the music was written by one person and the lyrics by another was a collective work; (4) similar rules for the construction of agreements were applied by New York courts and English courts; furthermore, in respect of infringement, (1) where the defendants had paid royalties after mechanical rights came into existence, first to authors and then to their estates beyond 25 years after death, the defendants were impliedly authorised to act as agents and look after mechanical rights; (2) there was not sufficient evidence from which to infer an implied licence as to copyright: REDWOOD MUSIC v. FRANCIS, DAY & HUNTER [1978] R.P.C. 429, Goff J.

351. —— steel lintels

The plaintiffs, C Ltd., manufactured steel lintels. The defendants had obtained C's brochure, and had a copy of a drawing of an experimental lintel by an employee of C. The defendants produced a lintel. The plaintiffs amended their pleadings to include allegations of infringement of copyright in drawings disclosed in their patent specification, but without disclosed dimensions. *Held*, that (1) the defendants' initial drawings were not copied; (2) the defendants had copied the drawing insufficiently to amount to an infringement of copyright; (3) on publication of a patent specification, the patentee abandoned copyright; (4) the defendants' lintels were both infringements of the plaintiffs' claims: CATNIC COMPONENTS v. HILL AND SMITH [1978] F.S.R. 405, Whitford J.

352. —— test whether substantial use made of plaintiffs' work—interlocutory relief

The plaintiffs owned copyright in paintings of views of London. The defendants, picture postcard manufacturers, employed an artist to paint the same views, and showed her copies of the plaintiffs' paintings. The defendants' paintings were not slavish copies and had individual characteristics. *Held*, (1) although a prima facie case was established, interlocutory relief should not be granted since damages were an adequate remedy; (2) infringement of copyright occurs only if some substantial use has been made of the work of the person whose work it is alleged has been infringed. In a painting of a well-known subject, the copyright generally consists in the choice of viewpoint, the balance of foreground, features in middle ground, and figures introduced. In these choices the artist makes his original contribution: KRISARTS S.A. v. BRIARFINE (TRADING AS LENTON PUBLICATIONS) [1977] F.S.R. 557, Whitford J.

353. International arrangements
  COPYRIGHT (INTERNATIONAL CONVENTIONS) (AMENDMENT) ORDER 1978 (No. 1060) [10p], made under the Copyright Act 1956 (c. 74), ss. 31, 32 and 47; operative on August 23, 1978; further amends S.I. 1972 No. 673, to take into account the accession of Costa Rica to the Berne Copyright Convention and the accession of Norway to the International Convention for the Protection of Performers, Producers of Phonograms and Broadcasting Organisations.

ARTICLES. See *post,* p. [15].

CORONERS

354. Northern Ireland. See NORTHERN IRELAND.

355. Pensions. See § 2264.

ARTICLES. See *post,* p. [15].

CORPORATION TAX

356. Accounting basis—profits of trade—change from on-costs to accrued profit method
  A surplus arising from a change in accounting basis is chargeable to corporation tax.
  In consequence of a change in the character of its business, the taxpayer company decided to adopt a new basis for its final accounts by anticipating a proportion of the final gross profits of long-term contracts in the annual valuation of work-in-progress. The result was an increase in the figure attributable to work-in-progress, and in the 1969 accounts this increase was described as " surplus arising on change in accounting basis." The taxpayer company contended that this surplus was not a profit of the period and was not assessable to corporation tax. *Held,* affirming the decision of Templeman J., that the surplus resulting from the re-valuation was a profit of the 1969 accounting period, and attracted corporation tax accordingly.
  PEARCE *v.* WOODALL DUCKHAM [1978] 1 W.L.R. 832, C.A.

357. Capital allowances—provision of machinery or plant
  [Finance Act 1971 (c. 68), s. 41.]
  Commitment fees and interest payments charged on a company's capital for the purpose of procuring finance for the purchase of machinery, are not expenditure incurred on the provision of machinery or plant.
  In 1969 the taxpayer company incurred expenditure of approximately £500,000 by way of commitment fees and interest in procuring finance for the construction of a drilling rig. The expenditure was charged to capital in the company's accounts. The company claimed that the expenditure qualified for capital allowances under F.A. 1971, s. 41. *Held,* that the expenditure did not qualify for capital allowances as it was not incurred " on the provision " of machinery or plant (*Sherritt Gordon Mines* v. *Minister of National Revenue* [1968] Ex.C.R. 459, distinguished).
  BEN-ODECO *v.* POWLSON [1978] 1 W.L.R. 1093, H.L.

358. Capital gains—apportionment
  [Finance Act 1965 (c. 25), Sched. 6, para. 21 (4).] R Ltd. was a wholly owned subsidiary of the taxpayer company (the shares having cost the taxpayer company £114,024), and was indebted to the taxpayer company for £500,000 on simple contract debts. W Ltd. agreed to purchase the whole of the share capital of R Ltd. on terms requiring the taxpayer company to waive the debt of £500,000. The taxpayer company was assessed to corporation tax on a chargeable gain of £135,976 in respect of the disposal of the shares. It appealed, contending, inter alia, that the sum of £250,000 paid by the purchaser was paid for both the shares and the waiver of the debt, and should be apportioned accordingly. *Held,* allowing the appeal in part and varying the decision of the Court of Session, that on the true construction of the contract the sum of £250,000 was paid not only for the transfer of the shares but also for the waiver of the debt. The case should be remitted to the Special Commissioners

to make an apportionment under F.A. 1965, Sched. 6, para. 21 (4): ABERDEEN
CONSTRUCTION GROUP *v.* I.R.C. [1978] S.T.C. 127, H.L.

359. —— chargeable gains—loans—debt on security
[Finance Act 1965 (c. 25), Sched. 7, paras. 5, 11.]
The essential characteristic of a " debt on a security " is the issue of a
marketable or convertible document.
The taxpayer company acquired 68 shares in C Ltd. at a premium of £2,719
per share. On the same day it made two loans (L1 and L2) to C Ltd., each of
£218,750 for 30 and 31 years respectively, carrying interest at 11 per cent. The
loan agreements were varied by reducing the rate of interest on L1 to nil, and
increasing that on L2 to 22 per cent. L2 was then sold at its market value of
£391,481. Subsequently, L2 was repaid at a premium, and L1 at par. The result
was to reduce the value of C Ltd., and to cause a loss on the taxpayer company's shares in C Ltd. The Inland Revenue claimed that L2 was a debt on a
security, so that the profit on the sale of L2 was a chargeable gain. *Held*, following *Aberdeen Construction Group* v. *I.R.C.* [1978] C.L.Y. 358, that L2 lacked
the essential features of a debt on a security, so that the gain on disposal was
not a chargeable gain.
W. T. RAMSAY *v.* I.R.C. [1978] 2 All E.R. 321, Goulding J.

360. —— groups of companies—beneficial ownership
[Income and Corporation Taxes Act 1970 (c. 10), ss. 272, 273, 526 (5).] H &
B Co. wished to sell its shares in OBD Co. to Seagrams without incurring liability
for corporation tax on chargeable gains. To this end, the following transactions
were effected: (1) V Ltd. was formed with 76 participating preference shares
being allotted to H & B Co. and 24 ordinary shares being allotted to Seagrams,
(ii) Z Ltd. was incorporated as the wholly-owned subsidiary of V Ltd., (iii) with
moneys provided by Seagrams Z Ltd. purchased the shares in OBD Co. from
H & B Ltd., (iv) V Ltd. was wound up, £76 being repaid to H & B Co. and the
shares in Z Ltd. being distributed to Seagrams. The scheme depended upon
ICTA 1970, s. 274 (1), applying on the sale of shares, by H & B Co. to Z Ltd.
The Revenue contended that H & B Co. was never the beneficial owner of the
76 participating preference shares in V Ltd., so that the section could not apply.
Held, dismissing the Crown's appeal, that the intention to liquidate V Ltd. did
not prevent H & B Co. being the beneficial owner of the preference shares in that
company: BURMAN *v.* HEDGES & BUTLER, *The Times*, November 9, 1978,
Walton J.

361. Close company—shortfall in distributions—restriction not imposed by law
[Income and Corporation Taxes Act 1970 (c. 10), s. 290.]
Restrictions contained in a company's articles of association are not
restrictions imposed by law.
The taxpayer company was a close company carrying on an investment
business. The company's articles of association restricted the amount which it
could distribute by way of dividend. The company appealed against a shortfall
assessment, the ground of appeal being that it was unable under its articles to
make the required distribution. *Held*, allowing the Revenue's appeal from the
decision of the General Commissioners, that the restriction in the company's
articles of association was not a restriction imposed by law which prevented
apportionment of income under the shortfall provisions.
NOBLE *v.* LAYGATE INVESTMENTS [1978] 2 All E.R. 1067, Oliver J.

362. Finance Act 1978 (c. 42)
Pt. III (ss. 15–17) deals with corporation tax: s. 15 charges corporation tax
for the financial year 1977; s. 16 provides that the rate of corporation tax for
1978 shall be thirty-three sixty-sevenths; s. 17 relates to other rates of
corporation tax.

**363. Losses—computation—sale of shares—assessment of value upon acquisition—
bargain not at arm's length**
[Finance Act 1965 (c. 25), s. 22 (4).]
For the purposes of assessing an allowable loss in respect of corporation
tax, the acquisition value of newly issued loan stock acquired under a bargain

not made at arm's length will be deemed to be the market value thereof, as opposed to any higher price actually paid.

The taxpayer company's liability for corporation tax was assessed upon the basis that the allowable loss which it was entitled to claim upon the sale by it of shares and loan stock in T Co. was the difference between the sale price, £40,000, and the market value of such shares and stock at the time of acquisition, £72,500, notwithstanding that the taxpayer had paid some £223,000 upon such acquisition. The taxpayer had purchased the shares for £13,000 from N, its subsidiary, and in addition subscribed to £210,000 of loan stock newly created by T Co., the £210,000 thereby subscribed being employed by T Co. in extinguishing its liability for loan made by N. On appeal against the assessment, *held*, dismissing the taxpayer's appeal, that in a bargain not made at arm's length, it was clear that the market value was to be taken as the acquisition value, although there had been no " disposal " prior to " acquisition " within the meaning of s. 22 (4) of the Act.

HARRISON *v.* NAIRN WILLIAMSON [1978] 1 W.L.R. 145, C.A.

364. Profits—computation—contingent liability—capital or revenue expenditure
The taxpayer company carried on business in Bengal, and under the laws of that state it became liable to pay gratuities to certain lower-paid employees on their leaving its employment for any reason other than gross misconduct. The amount to which any employee would be entitled had to be calculated by reference to his remuneration and length of service. The taxpayer company decided to make annual provision against its contingent liability, rather than charge actual liabilities as they accrued. It took actuarial advice, and in its accounts for the year ended December 31, 1971, it debited the sum of £221,619 under the heading " Current liabilities—Provision for Retirement Gratuities." Of this sum, £23,547 related to service during 1971. The Inland Revenue claimed that the portion of £221,619 which was related to service for years prior to 1971, was a capital provision and was not, in any event, a proper debit to be charged in computing profits for 1971. *Held*, that the whole amount of the provision was a revenue and not a capital item, and was properly charged in computing profits for 1971 (*Southern Railway of Peru v. Owen* [1956] C.L.Y. 4172, applied): I.R.C. *v.* TITAGHUR JUTE FACTORY Co. [1978] S.T.C. 166, Ct. of Session, First Division.

365. —— —— unrealised bills of exchange
[Income and Corporation Taxes Act 1970 (c. 10), s. 108.]
The general principle that profit is not to be taxed until it is realised is applicable to discounted bills of exchange, no taxable profit arising until maturity or sale of such bills.

The business of the taxpayer bank included that of discounting bills of exchange, some of which were sold by the bank but most of which were held until maturity. In its annual accounts, the bank included in its profits a fractional part of the anticipated profits from such bills. The Revenue claimed that such anticipated profits were subject to corporation tax. The bank successfully appealed against such assessment, and the decision of the Commissioners was upheld by Walton J. and the Court of Appeal. *Held*, dismissing the Revenue's appeal (Lords Diplock and Russell of Killowen dissenting), that no taxable profit accrued until maturity of the bills or their prior realisation.

WILLINGALE *v.* INTERNATIONAL COMMERCIAL BANK [1978] 2 W.L.R. 452, H.L.

ARTICLES. See *post,* p. [17].

CORPORATIONS

366. Municipal corporations—city commissioners entering into irregular contract—court's powers of review
[Can.] P made an unsuccessful bid to be granted a towing contract by the defendant city. It claimed that the contract made with the company whose tender was successful was irregular as the tender did not completely comply with the invitation to tender and as the city had not passed the necessary by-law to enter into the contract. *Held*, the action was dismissed. The court had no authority to review a matter relating to the internal management of the city

where what was alleged was a mere irregularity in the exercise of the city's powers, particularly where the contract did not involve an interference with P's private rights, and where P had not suffered special damages peculiar to him from an interference with a public right (*Boyce* v. *Paddington Borough Council* [1906] A.C. 1 referred to; *Foss* v. *Harbottle* (1843) 2 Hare 461 applied): CLIFF'S TOWING SERVICE *v.* EDMONTON [1978] 5 W.W.R. 31, Alta. Sup. Ct.

COUNTY COURT PRACTICE

367. Administration of Justice Act 1977—commencement

ADMINISTRATION OF JUSTICE ACT 1977 (COMMENCEMENT NO. 5) ORDER 1978 (No. 810 (C. 20)) [10p], made under the Administration of Justice Act 1977 (c. 38), s. 32 (6); operative on July 3, 1978; brings into force s. 19 (2) (3) (5) of the 1977 Act.

368. Adoption. See MINORS.

369. Appeal—notice of evidence taken by counsel—submission to judge. See PITMAN *v.* SOUTHERN ELECTRICITY BOARD, § 2054.

370. Contempt—order not served on father

[R.S.C. Ord. 45, r. 7 (7).] On the morning of August 30, 1978, the county court judge made an order that the father, who was present, should return a child to the mother that afternoon. He did not do so and deliberately disappeared. The formal order was sent to his solicitors on September 4. On September 8, the judge made an order for the father's arrest. Subsequently he surrendered voluntarily to the police and when he came before the judge on September 12, he indicated where the child could be found. The judge committed him to prison for one month for contempt in disobeying the order of August 30, 1978. The father appealed against the orders for arrest and committal, contending that the original order of August 30 had not been served on him or his solicitors that day. *Held,* allowing the father's appeal to the extent of releasing him immediately, this was a proper case for dispensing with service of the original order. In the absence of an express provision in the C.C.R., R.S.C., Ord. 45, r. 7 (7) could be followed (dicta of Cotton L.J. in *Hyde* v. *Hyde* (1888) 13 P.D. 166, 171 followed: *Gordon* v. *Gordon* [1949] P. 99 distinguished): TURNER *v.* TURNER (1978) 122 S.J. 696, C.A.

371. Costs—basis on which taxed

[County Court Rules, Ord. 47, r. 1.] Under the provisions of Ord. 47, r. 1, the county court judge, like a High Court judge, has a discretion to order an unsuccessful litigant to pay the other party's costs on a solicitor and own client basis. Pleadings in either court must be signed by solicitor or counsel, or else by the litigant in person; no other person should be permitted to sign a pleading: GREENHOUSE *v.* HETHERINGTON (1977) 122 S.J. 47, C.A.

372. —— claim for damages for personal injuries exceeding £5—whether claim must be admitted or established

Plaintiff's county court action included a claim for personal injuries not exceeding £5. The defendants paid a sum into court but in covering letters to the plaintiff's solicitors stated they did not admit that the plaintiff had suffered any personal injuries and said the payment included nothing in respect of that part of the claim. The plaintiff's solicitor said the plaintiff, while prepared to accept the offered payment, could not accept the contention accompanying it and so a hearing was fixed where the plaintiff asked for leave to take the money out of court. The plaintiff successfully appealed against the Registrar's award of costs. She was entitled to her solicitor's costs on scale 2 under C.C.R., Ord. 47, r. 5 (4) since she claimed damages for personal injuries exceeding £5. The defendants appealed. *Held,* " claim " in Ord. 47 was not to be interpreted as one which had been duly confirmed either by admission or judicial decision but which had simply been made by the plaintiff: VARLEY *v.* TARMAC (1978) 122 S.J. 540, C.A.

373. —— matrimonial causes. See § 797.

374. County Court rules

COUNTY COURT (AMENDMENT) RULES 1978 (No. 682) (L. 12)) [20p], made under the County Courts Act 1959 (c. 22), s. 102; operative on June 2, 1978; amend the Rules to take into account the provisions of the Torts (Interference with Goods) Act 1977. They also enable an application for an injunction under s. 1 of the Domestic Violence and Matrimonial Proceedings Act 1977 to be served at least four days before the return date and to be heard in chambers. Increases the amount of an unexecuted warrant in respect of which fortnightly returns must be made to £50.

COUNTY COURT (AMENDMENT No. 2) RULES 1978 (No. 794 (L.20)) [10p], made under the County Courts Act 1959, s. 102; operative on July 3, 1978; amend the Rules so as to raise to £200 the amount of a claim on which no solicitor's costs are generally allowable but give the court power in appropriate circumstances to direct this restriction shall not apply when the claim exceeds £100.

COUNTY COURT (AMENDMENT No. 3) RULES 1978 (No. 911) [10p], made under the County Courts Act 1959, s. 102; operative on July 3, 1978; provide that the restrictions on the allowances of costs imposed by S.I. 1978 No. 794 in cases involving sums between £100 and £200 shall not apply to proceedings commenced before the coming into operation of those Rules.

COUNTY COURT (AMENDMENT No. 4) RULES 1978 (No. 1943 (L. 39)) [25p], made under the County Courts Act 1959, s. 102; operative as to rr. 1–3, 6, 7 on February 5, 1979, and as to rr. 4 and 5 on March 12, 1979; makes various minor amendments to the Rules.

375. Districts

COUNTY COURT DISTRICTS (DEVIZES) ORDER 1978 (No. 397 (L. 6)) [15p], made under the County Courts Act 1959 (c. 22), s. 2; operative on April 1, 1978; closes the Devizes County Court and the district of the court is divided between those of neighbouring courts. Also provides for the sitting of the Trowbridge County Court to be held at Devizes.

COUNTY COURT DISTRICTS (WARMINSTER) ORDER 1978 (No. 817 (L. 21)) [10p], made under the County Courts Act 1959, s. 2; operative on July 1, 1978; closes the Warminster County Court and divides its district between neighbouring courts.

376. Fees

COUNTY COURT FEES ORDER 1978 (No. 1243 (L. 29)), made under the County Courts Act 1959 (c. 22), s. 177, the Public Offices Fees Act 1879 (c. 58), s. 2 and the Companies Act 1948 (c. 38), s. 365 (3); operative on October 2, 1978; replaces S.I. 1975 No. 1328 as amended. It amalgamates a large number of fees and deletes a number which are no longer considered relevant.

377. Funds

COUNTY COURT FUNDS (AMENDMENT) RULES 1978 (No. 750 (L.15)) [20p], made under the County Courts Act 1959 (c. 22), s. 168 as amended by the Administration of Justice Act 1965 (c. 2), s. 9; operative on July 3, 1978; transfer to the chief clerk of the county court the administrative functions of the registrar in relation to funds in court.

378. Hearing—adjournment—whether justified. See R. v. A CIRCUIT JUDGE (SITTING AS NORWICH COUNTY COURT), *ex p.* WATHEN, § 1780.

379. Injunction—power to grant—whether ancillary to damages claim
[County Courts Act 1959 (c. 22), s. 74 (1).]

A county court judge need not weigh the importance of a claim for an injunction as against the importance of a claim for specific relief in order to decide whether the one is ancillary to the other.

P Co., hairdressers, took proceedings against D, an ex-employee, for breach of a restrictive covenant not to work within one mile of P Co. for one year after her apprenticeship. They sought an injunction against her, and damages for breach of contract limited to £1 since D could not pay substantial damages. D resisted an application for an interlocutory injunction, contending that the injunction was the substantial remedy sought and that therefore it could not be ancillary to the claim for damages. The county court judge granted the injunction. On appeal by D, *held*, dismissing the appeal, that the claim for £1 damages was a proper claim, and the judge did not need to weigh it before deciding whether the claim for an injunction was ancillary to it.

HATT & CO. (BATH) *v.* PEARCE [1978] 2 All E.R. 474, C.A.

380. Internationally Protected Persons Act 1978 (c. 17). See § 1730.

381. Jurisdiction

COUNTY COURTS JURISDICTION (INHERITANCE—PROVISION FOR FAMILY AND DEPENDANTS) ORDER 1978 (No. 176 (L. 3)) [10p], made under the Inheritance (Provision for Family and Dependants) Act 1975 (c. 63), s. 22 (1); operative on March 1, 1978; increases the jurisdiction of the county courts in proceedings relating to a claim on a deceased person's estate by a relative or dependant under s. 2 of the 1975 Act.

382. —— time for service of default summons—extension

[County Court Rules (S.I. 1956 No. 471), Ord. 8, r. 35; Ord. 13, r. 5; Ord. 40, r. 8 (1A).]

The words of C.C.R., Ord. 8, r. 35, are not of sufficiently mandatory nature to oust the jurisdiction of the court to grant an extension under Ord. 13.

In April 1976 the landlords of business premises gave L notice to terminate the tenancy. On August 23, L issued an application in the county court for a new lease of the premises, giving as the landlords' address for service that which appeared on the landlords' notice. The landlords had moved and the court was unable to effect service. L's solicitors at once attempted to ascertain the new address but, through no fault on their part, were not supplied with it until September 29. The court was notified, and the application was served. The landlords applied to strike out the application on the ground that it had not been served within one month of being made, as required by Ord. 8, r. 35, as applied by Ord. 40, r. 8 (1A); and that the provisions of Ord. 8, r. 35, were mandatory, and therefore deprived the court of jurisdiction under Ord. 13, r. 5, to extend the time for service. The judge dismissed the application to strike out and granted L an extension of time for service of the original application. The landlords appealed. *Held*, dismissing the appeal, that the court had jurisdiction, and in the circumstances the case was a proper one in which to grant an extension of time.

LEWIS *v.* WOLKING PROPERTIES [1978] 1 All E.R. 427, C.A.

383. —— writ of restitution—contempt—refusal to give possession

On September 21, 1977, the plaintiff society obtained an unfettered order for possession by reason of the defendant's default of his obligations under a mortgage. Possession was delivered up to the plaintiffs under a warrant for possession and thereupon secured against re-entry. The defendant went back into possession without consent and failed to comply with written demands to restore possession to the plaintiffs. The plaintiffs applied to the registrar *ex parte* on affidavit for the issue of a writ of restitution. The affidavit set out the facts above and further recited that a warrant of possession had also been issued and executed pursuant to an order of a Divorce Court dated April 25, 1977, in proceedings brought by the defendant's wife, and that in that case also, after the warrant had been executed, the defendant had re-entered the premises and changed the locks. The Registrar refused the plaintiff society's application on the grounds that " a writ of restitution is not applicable in the County Court." The plaintiff society appealed against the Registrar's decision, and also applied for the committal of the defendant for contempt in failing to comply with the order for possession (notices in Forms 140 and 194 having been served upon him). *Held*, notwithstanding the note in the 1978 County Court Practice at p. 83, the judge construed s. 74 of the County Courts Act 1959 as giving him jurisdiction on the plain words of subss. (1) and (2) and in particular para. (*a*) of subs. (1). The appeal was therefore allowed by issue of a writ of restitution. He was also satisfied that the defendant was in contempt, and that it was an appropriate case to commit the defendant to prison for seven days. (*Alliance Building Society* v. *Austin* (1951) C.L.C. 7549 referred to): ABBEY

NATIONAL BUILDING SOCIETY *v.* MORRIS, July 27, 1978, Judge Barr, Uxbridge County Ct. (*Ex rel. Messrs. Tucker, Turner & Co., Solicitors.*)

384. Northern Ireland. See NORTHERN IRELAND.

385. Order 26—power of court to suspend order. See SWORDHEATH PROPERTIES *v.* FLOYDD, § 1803a.

386. Possession—deferment of enforcement—failure of tenant to comply with agreement—whether further extension justifiable. See BRISTOL CITY COUNCIL *v.* RAWLINS, § 1584.

387. —— summary proceedings—whether appropriate—evidence of tenancy
The applicants, who purchased the premises in November 1977, commenced proceedings under Ord. 26 of the County Court Rules claiming possession. They filed an affidavit alleging that the respondent P was a mere licensee of a statutory tenant who had vacated the premises. P's affidavit asserted that he was a tenant. He had taken over from the previous tenant the task of collecting rent from the other occupiers and forwarding it to the former owner, D. In July 1977, he had informed D of the new arrangement, and D had offered no objection. In August 1977, D had written to P asking for rent arrears to be paid. P further alleged that the applicants had accepted rent after proceedings had been commenced. P submitted that that was strong evidence that he was a tenant and that summary proceedings under Ord. 26 were not appropriate where, as here, there was a triable issue, following *Islamic Republic of Pakistan v. Ghani* [1977] C.L.Y. 1738. *Held,* directions would be given that the affidavits filed for the applicants and the respondent should stand as particulars of claim and defence; that the applicants should have leave to file an affidavit in reply, and that there should be discovery and trial of the action in due course: PHSEROWSKY & STANTON *v.* PHILLIPS, March 22, 1978, Judge McDonnell, Lambeth County Court. (*Ex rel. A. Brunner, Esq., Barrister and A. Waite, Esq., Solicitor.*)

388. Procedure—rent control. See § 2508.

389. Right of audience—extension
The Lord Chancellor has made a Direction that any Fellow of the Institute of Legal Executives whose employment consists of or includes giving assistance in the conduct of litigation to a solicitor, whether in private practice or not, may address a county court in certain kinds of proceedings in which that solicitor is acting: the County Courts (Right of Audience) Direction 1978, operative on April 1, 1978.

390. Transfer of proceedings to High Court—minors—adoption and guardianship. See PRACTICE NOTE, § 1971.

BOOKS AND ARTICLES. See *post,* pp. [3], [17].

CRIMINAL LAW

391. Abstracting electricity—dishonesty—intention and reasonable belief of ability to pay
[Theft Act 1968 (c. 60), s. 13.]
Whether, in abstracting electricity without consent, a defendant is acting honestly is a question of fact which must be answered subjectively.
D, whose electricity supply had been cut off, informed the electricity board of his intention to reconnect it to the mains, which he did. The Crown Court allowed his appeal against a conviction under s. 13 of the Theft Act 1968 after finding that his state of mind at the time was not dishonest. *Held,* dismissing P's appeal, that the question as to whether or not D had acted dishonestly was not decided merely by his failure to obtain the consent of the electricity board but was a question of fact and was a subjective test with the application of which the Divisional Court would not interfere.
BOGGELN *v.* WILLIAMS [1978] 1 W.L.R. 873, D.C.

392. Accomplice—evidence—corroboration. See R. *v.* THORNE, § 476.

393. Affray—cautions—application of Judges' Rules

Although the prosecution must adduce all its evidence before the end of its case, that does not apply to evidence which is available, but goes only to the credit of the defendant. After an affray, it is quite fanciful to think that the police should consider whether to caution each person involved before taking a statement from him; such a caution need only be given under the Judges' Rules when it becomes clear that there is evidence against the witness: R. *v.* HALFORD, *The Times*, April 12, 1978, C.A.

394. Aiding and abetting—mens rea—intention

Knowledge of the actual offence committed need not be shown before a person can be convicted of aiding and abetting; it is sufficient to show that he knew the type of offence to be committed or the essential matters constituting the offence.

Per curiam. Although aiders and abettors, counsellors and procurers, can be charged as principals, the particulars of the offence in the indictment should make clear the nature of the case against a defendant.

D was a member of the Ulster Volunteer Force which used firearms and bombs to attack Catholics. He was told by the organisation to guide a number of strangers in a following car to an inn, who then attempted to bomb the inn, D was convicted of unlawfully and maliciously doing an act with intent to cause an explosion likely to endanger life, contrary to s. 3 (*a*) of the Explosive Substances Act 1883 and possession of the bomb contrary to s. 3 (*b*). The Court of Appeal of Northern Ireland dismissed his appeal, but certified the following question as one involving a point of law of general public importance: if the crime committed by the principal, and actually assisted by the accused, is one of a number of offences, one of which the accused knows the principal will probably commit, is the guilty mind which must be proved against an accomplice thereby proved against the accused? On D's appeal, *held*, dismissing the appeal, that an aider and abettor need only know the type of offence to be committed or the essential matters constituting the offence. D was a member of the organisation which carried out such attacks, he knew when he acted as guide that he was taking part in such an attack, and that the weapons must be in the following car. D therefore knew the essential matters constituting the offences, and had rightly been convicted. (Dictum of Lord Goddard C.J. in *Johnson* v. *Youden* (1950) C.L.C. 978 and *R.* v. *Bainbridge* [1959] C.L.Y. 629 applied.)

D.P.P. FOR NORTHERN IRELAND *v.* MAXWELL [1978] 1 W.L.R. 1350, H.L.

395. —— presence alone insufficient

To be guilty of aiding and abetting an assault there must be some actual encouragement given. Mere presence is not enough.

The appellants, who were present at the scene of a street fight, were charged with aiding and abetting an assault. The jury were directed that if by their presence they were encouraging what was going on, they should be convicted. *Held*, allowing their appeal, that mere presence was not enough, even if it did encourage the assault. It must be shown that there was an intention to encourage and some wilful encouragement of the crime committed.

R. *v.* JONES AND MIRRLESS (1977) 65 Cr.App.R. 250, C.A.

396. Alibi—defence of self-defence concurrently—jury may be directed on both matters

It is possible for self-defence to become an issue where a concurrent defence is alibi, but it would need to be fairly cogent evidence to have this effect.

B's defence at his trial for unlawful wounding was one of alibi. The defence submitted that self-defence was also an issue, but the judge ruled against that submission and did not leave the question to the jury. On appeal, *held*, dismissing the appeal, that a judge has the duty to leave to the jury any fit issue raised by the evidence. This can include self-defence in an alibi case if the evidence is sufficiently strong to raise a prima facie case, but it would need to be fairly cogent evidence, where the best witness dissociates himself

from it by his alibi. (*R.* v. *Walker* [1974] C.L.Y. 711 applied; *Palmer* v. *R.* [1971] C.L.Y. 2509 considered.)
R. *v.* BONNICK (1977) 66 Cr.App.R. 266, C.A.

397. Appeal
CRIMINAL APPEAL (AMENDMENT) RULES 1978 (No. 1118) [25p], made under the Supreme Court of Judicature (Consolidation) Act 1925 (c. 49), s. 99, the Criminal Appeal Act 1968 (c. 19), s. 46, as amended by the Courts Act 1971 (c. 23), s. 56 (1) and Sched. 8, para. 57 (2), and the Bail Act 1976 (c. 63), ss. 5 (1) and 8 (4); operative on October 2, 1978; amend S.I. 1968 No. 1262 in consequence of the Bail Act 1976.

398. —— **abandonment—fresh evidence**
[Criminal Appeal Act 1968 (c. 19), s. 17.] G and N were jointly indicted. N failed to appear to stand trial and G was convicted of theft. He was refused leave to appeal by the single judge and on his solicitors' advice abandoned his appeal. N subsequently pleaded guilty to theft and made a statement supporting G's defence that G had not been involved. *Held*, rejecting an application for G's abandonment of appeal to be treated as a nullity and for leave to appeal, that as G's mind had gone with his act of abandonment the court had no discretion to exercise in his favour. The proper procedure was to refer the case to the Home Secretary for him to consider referring it to the court under the Criminal Appeal Act 1968, s. 17: R. *v.* GRAVES [1978] Crim.L.R. 216, C.A.

399. —— **after guilty plea—exceptional circumstances**
[Criminal Appeal Act 1968 (c. 19), s. 2 (1) (*a*); Criminal Law Act 1977 (c. 45), s. 44.] Under s. 2 (1) (*a*) of the Criminal Appeal Act 1968, as substituted by s. 44 of the Criminal Law Act 1977, the Court of Appeal has power to allow an appeal against conviction notwithstanding that the defendant pleaded guilty, but will do so only in an exceptional case. In particular, not everyone who pleads guilty on advice, albeit on a mistaken view of the law, can succeed on appeal. However, sound advice to plead guilty, followed by a new reported decision which shows that in fact a defendant had a defence, may lead to a successful appeal. (*R.* v. *Carver* [1978] C.L.Y. 546 and *Bocking* v. *Roberts* [1973] C.L.Y. 513 considered): R. *v.* LIDIARD (1978) 122 S.J. 743, C.A.

400. —— **correct test for court—proviso**
The defendant was convicted of murder in Grenada and appealed to the Court of Appeal there. That court held that there had been a misdirection by the trial judge, but applied the proviso under the relevant Grenada Act (based on the Criminal Appeal Act 1968), and considered whether there was evidence on which a reasonable jury could convict. The Privy Council said that the court should have asked themselves whether the verdict was unsafe or unsatisfactory. The Privy Council therefore themselves considered whether the proviso should be applied in the exceptional circumstances, and dismissed the appeal: FERGUSON *v.* R. (1978) 122 S.J. 696, P.C.

401. —— **fresh evidence**
Three men were convicted of offences very largely on the scientific evidence that a shoe found in the appellant's house had been worn during the offences. Fresh evidence cast doubt on this scientific evidence, and the Court of Appeal accordingly allowed their appeals against conviction: R. *v.* MORGAN, BROWN & COWLEY, *The Times*, June 9, 1978, C.A.

402. —— **grounds—new evidence**
[Criminal Appeal Act 1968 (c. 19), ss. 17 (1) (*b*), 23 (2).] The Secretary of State sought the opinion of the Court of Appeal under s. 17 (1) (*b*) of the Criminal Appeal Act 1968, with regard to M's conviction for murder in 1970. *Held*, that fresh alibi evidence should be rejected as "not likely to be credible" within s. 23 (2) of the Act: R. *v.* McMAHON, *The Times*, April 12, 1978, C.A.

403. —— **leave to appeal—renewal of application—time-limit**
Upon G's application to renew his application for leave to appeal after expiration of the 14-day period, the court re-iterated that it is settled practice that the 14-day period would only be enlarged in the most exceptional circumstances: R. *v.* GALLAGHER [1978] Crim.L.R. 216, C.A.

404. Notification that M had been refused leave to appeal against a two-year sentence of imprisonment did not reach M in prison because he had absconded. About five months later he applied for an extension of time for renewing his application, having been recaptured. He had absconded because his wife needed to go to hospital for treatment for a suspected malignant disease. *Held*, refusing an extension, that this application was impudent: R. *v.* MARSHALL [1978] Crim.L.R. 424, C.A.

405. —— **miscarriage of justice—ground for allowing appeal**

[Scot.] [Criminal Procedure (Scotland) Act 1975 (c. 21), s. 254 (1) (c).] The High Court, on an appeal, shall allow the appeal if they think that on any ground there was a miscarriage of justice. B pleaded guilty to an indictment for assault and robbery. Subsequently, he applied out of time for leave to appeal and for an extension of time in which to do so. *Held*, " on any ground " was wide enough to cover an appeal where B had pleaded guilty. As the Crown accepted he was not guilty, he would be allowed an extension of time and leave to appeal, and his appeal would succeed: BOYLE *v.* H.M. ADVOCATE, 1976 J.C. 32, High Ct. of Justiciary.

406. —— **time-limits**

C's notice of renewal of his application for leave to appeal against sentence following refusal of leave by the single judge was put in over five weeks out of time because a newly qualified, inexperienced solicitor dealt with his case. *Held*, that an extension of time should be granted as, unlike those in custody, C had not been made aware of the time-limits. Any firm undertaking criminal work should apprise itself of the time-limits. They were to be complied with: R. *v.* CODY [1978] Crim.L.R. 550, C.A.

407. —— **transcript—practice where inaccuracies alleged**

In this case, the Court of Appeal emphasised that where it is suggested that a transcript is inaccurate, the Registrar should be informed and he will then take the matter up with shorthand writers and, if necessary, with the judge: R. *v.* BRILL [1978] Crim.L.R. 550, C.A.

408. Arson—evidence of propensity

The fact that one defendant has a propensity to commit wanton arson is not admissible to support an allegation by a co-defendant that the original defendant acted alone.

The appellant's defence to a charge of arson was that, although he had been with B, it was B who had started the fire. His application to adduce evidence that B had previously started fires in similar circumstances was refused by the trial judge. *Held*, dismissing his appeal, that it had been rightly refused. The fact that B had a propensity to commit arson was a *non sequitur* to the defence of the appellant.

R. *v.* NEALE (1977) 65 Cr.App.R. 304, C.A.

409. —— **statutory defence—whether act done " in order to protect property belonging to another "**

[Criminal Damage Act 1971 (c. 48), s. 5 (2).] H, believing that the council had been informed that fire alarms in a block of old people's flats did not work but had done nothing, set fire to a bed in a fairly isolated part of the block, told his wife to get the people out, summoned the fire brigade and broke the alarm to show it was not working. The judge withdrew the statutory defence under s. 5 (2) of the 1971 Act from the jury. *Held*, dismissing H's appeal against conviction of arson, that the test of whether an act was done " in order to protect property belonging to another " within s. 5 (2) was objective. H's act was not one which did or could in itself protect property: R. *v.* HUNT [1977] Crim.L.R. 740, C.A.

410. Assault—actual bodily harm—proof

Justices found D to have struck X in the face and that the blow must have caused bruising and injury to X. *Held*, dismissing D's appeal against conviction of assault occasioning actual bodily harm, that the justices were entitled to infer that X sustained some bodily harm, however slight, without direct evidence of such harm: TAYLOR *v.* GRANVILLE [1978] Crim.L.R. 482, D.C.

411. —— consent—lawful sport

B punched G in the face during a rugby match in an off-the-ball incident, fracturing G's jaw. Evidence was given by a former Welsh International Rugby player that punching was now the rule in rugby rather than the exception. The trial judge directed the jury that (i) rugby players are deemed to have consented to force of a kind which could reasonably be expected to happen during a game; but (ii) there must be some cases which cross the line of that to which players are deemed to consent; and (iii) a decisive distinction may be that between force in and outside the course of play. B was convicted of assault occasioning grievous bodily harm: R. v. BILLINGHURST [1978] Crim.L.R. 553, Newport Crown Court.

412. —— not an alternative verdict to causing grievous bodily harm—common assault

[Offences against the Person Act 1861 (c. 100), s. 18; Criminal Law Act 1967 (c. 58), s. 6 (3).]

On a count charging attempting to cause, or causing grievous bodily harm to a person, without setting out the particulars relied upon, common assault is not a possible alternative verdict.

D disapproved of his son-in-law because he was not a Roman Catholic. He therefore drove his car at him. The son-in-law escaped by jumping over some railings. D was charged with attempting to cause grievous bodily harm with intent, without setting out particulars. In evidence, D said, " I thought it would cause him to think that I was being violent towards him." The judge directed the jury that if they found him not guilty of the offence charged, they could and should find him guilty of common assault on his own evidence. They did so. On appeal by D, *held*, allowing the appeal, that the lesser offence, in order to be a possible alternative offence, had to be a necessary step towards the commission of the greater offence. As it was possible to cause grievous bodily harm without committing any assault, D could not be convicted of common assault (*R.* v. *Austin* [1974] C.L.Y. 644, *R.* v. *Springfield* [1969] C.L.Y. 813, *R.* v. *Lillis* [1972] C.L.Y. 666, applied; *R.* v. *Walkden* (1845) 1 Cox C.C. 282 considered).

R. v. LAMBERT (1976) 65 Cr.App.R. 12, C.A.

413. —— on constable—whether " in course of duty "—no powers of entry to effect arrest

D was charged with assault on a police constable in the execution of his duty, contrary to s. 51 (1) of the Police Act 1964; M was charged, inter alia, with assault on the same constable with intent to resist and prevent the lawful apprehension of D, contrary to s. 38 of the Offences against the Person Act 1861. D was seen by three police constables in a public street and was suspected to be soliciting or loitering for the purpose of prostitution, contrary to s. 1 of the Street Offences Act 1959. She was followed to her flat where one constable, P1, attempted to arrest her on the front steps; but D unlocked the door, burst into the hallway, and as P1 was holding her wrist, a scuffle ensued inside the hallway. M came out of D's flat and became involved in the struggle. The two other constables intervened, subdued M and arrested him. The defence submitted there was no case to answer. *Held*, allowing the submission, that (1) the arrest was effected inside the building: see *Alderson* v. *Booth* [1969] C.L.Y. 2750; (2) the Street Offences Act 1959 gave the police a power of arrest, but not a power of entry to effect an arrest; (3) s. 2 of the Criminal Law Act 1967 gave a power of entry to effect an arrest if the offence was an " arrestable offence "; (4) an offence under s. 1 of the Street Offences Act 1959 was not an " arrestable offence " within the meaning of the Criminal Law Act 1967; (5) the common law gave the police no right to enter premises save in certain restricted circumstances, *i.e.* to prevent a breach of the peace; (6) accordingly, P1 had no right of entry and was trespassing when the arrest was effected, and was not therefore acting in the execution of his duty. That being so, and as all the other counts of the indictment rested on the lawfulness of the arrest, the jury were directed to return verdicts of not guilty on all counts on the indictment against both defendants: R. *v.* McKenzie and Davis, December 13, 1978, Mr. Recorder Hollis, Q.C., Bristol Crown Ct. (*Ex rel. T. Alun Jenkins, Esq., Barrister.*)

414. Attempt—inciting perjury—inciting another to incite perjury

C was alleged to have sent a letter to B, asking B whether he could get B's wife to " go bent " as her statement was the only real evidence against C and B of burglary. C was subsequently tried on a count in which the statement of offence was " attempting to incite perjury " but the particulars of offence alleged an attempt to incite B to " procure perjury." The judge told the jury that if C sent B a note telling him he wanted B's wife put up to telling a pack of lies, that was attempting to incite perjury. Later he told them: " Say the prosecution, what can that lettter possibly mean but an attempt to get B to get his wife to tell lies on oath? " *Held,* allowing C's appeal against conviction, that (1) the question whether C's act was sufficiently proximate to constitute an attempt should have been left to the jury; (2) the confusion between the statement and particulars of offence was sufficient reason to allow the appeal: R. *v.* Cromack [1978] Crim.L.R. 217, C.A.

415. —— theft—intention

It cannot be said that one who has it in mind to steal only if what he finds is worth stealing has a present intention to steal.

A and B were seen tampering with the back door of a van which contained a holdall which in turn contained valuable goods. They were charged with attempted theft. Their defence was that they were curious, not felonious. At first instance, the judge directed the jury on the question of intention, that they could infer that A and B were about to look into the holdall and, if its contents were valuables, to steal it. On appeal, *held,* allowing the appeal, that that direction was the exact contrary of the correct one. There had to be a step taken to constitute an attempt, and there was. There had also to be a present intention to steal, at the time that step was taken, not merely an intention to deprive the owner of such property as proved worth taking. There was a misdirection on an essential part of the Crown's case, and the conviction must be quashed. (*R.* v. *Stark* (unreported) October 5, 1967 considered.)

R. *v.* Husseyn (1978) 67 Cr.App.R. 131, C.A.

415a. Attendance centres

Attendance Centre (Amendment) Rules 1978 (No. 1919 [10p], made under the Criminal Justice Act 1948 (c. 58), s. 52 (1); operative on January 1, 1979; amend S.I. 1958 No. 1990 so as to make provision for the attendance at attendance centres of female persons.

416. Bail

Rules of the Supreme Court (Amendment) (Bail) 1978 (No. 251 (L.4)) [25p], made under the Supreme Court of Judicature (Consolidation) Act 1925 (c. 49), s. 99 (4) and the Bail Act 1976 (c. 63), ss. 5 (1), 8 (4); operative on April 17, 1978; amends Ord. 79, r. 9 of the Rules of the Supreme Court and the related forms of Appendix A in consequence of the Bail Act 1976, in particular the manner in which records of bail decisions are to be made under s. 5 of that Act.

417. —— surety seeking release—failure of accused to appear—whether forfeiture of whole recognisance correct

[Magistrates' Courts Act 1952 (c. 55), s. 96 (1) (3).]

Where an accused fails to appear and a surety stands to be forfeited, the court has a duty to inquire into the circumstances of the case. But where this has been done, and a conclusion reached which was open to a reasonable bench, properly instructed, the Divisional Court will not interfere by certiorari.

R stood as surety for his son in the sum of £1,000. His son left home, and R attempted to obtain release from his suretyship, without success. The justices directed that the whole sum should be forfeited. On an application for certiorari, *held,* dismissing the application, that the culpability of the surety is a factor to which the court must have regard in assessing the question of forfeiture of recognisance, but that provided the bench came to a conclusion which was properly open to them, the Divisional Court had no power to interfere by certiorari. (*R.* v. *Southampton Justices, ex p. Green* [1975] C.L.Y. 2038, *R.* v. *Horseferry Road Stipendiary Magistrate, ex p. Pearson* [1976] C.L.Y. 1674 and *Bracegirdle* v. *Oxley* (1947) C.L.C. 9026 applied.)

R. *v.* TOTTENHAM MAGISTRATES' COURT, *ex p.* RICCARDI (1977) 66 Cr.App.R. 150, D.C.

418. Bail Act 1976—commencement

BAIL ACT 1976 (COMMENCEMENT) ORDER 1978 (No. 132 (C. 3)) [10p], made under the Bail Act 1976 (c. 63), s. 13 (2); operative on April 17, 1978; brings the whole of the Act into force.

419. Betting and gambling. See GAMING AND WAGERING.

420. Blasphemous libel—mens rea—subjective intent to commit blasphemy not required

The offence of blasphemous libel is made out without proof that the publisher intended the publication to be blasphemous.

The defendants were convicted of blasphemous libel in respect of a poem and drawing published by them in which acts of fellatio and sodomy were described as occurring to Christ's body immediately after his crucifixion. They appealed on the grounds, inter alia, that the judge erred in directing the jury that an intent to blaspheme was not an essential ingredient and that it was not necessary for an attack upon Christ or the Christian religion to be proved. *Held*, dismissing the appeals, that (1) an intention to blaspheme was not required; and (2) the offence was committed by some immoderate insulting or vilifying and offensive reference to the Deity or the Christian religion, the jury deciding such issue by reference to the contemporary opinion of society. (Dictum of Lord Denman C.J. in *R.* v. *Hetherington* (1841) 4 St.Tr.N.S. at 593 applied.)

R. *v.* LEMON; R. *v.* GAY NEWS [1978] 3 W.L.R. 404, C.A.

421. Breach of the peace—discharge of shotgun to disperse participants—whether an offence

[Scot.] Whilst a breach of the peace was occurring outside his house, the appellant, hoping to stop it, fired a shotgun in the air, though without the desired effect. He was convicted of a breach of the peace. *Held*, discharging a gun was likely to put people in fear. It did not matter that they were undesirables. Further, it is not lawful to commit one breach of the peace to stop another : PALAZZO *v.* COPELAND, 1976 J.C. 52, High Ct. of Justiciary.

422. Burglary—intention to steal—trespasser looking for something worth stealing

B was charged, inter alia, with burglary with intent to steal. He had been seen leaving a flat which he had had no lawful authority to enter. Nothing had been stolen or disturbed inside. B first claimed to have lost his way and then to have been too drunk to have known what he was doing. *Held*, allowing a submission of no case to answer, that as there was no evidence sufficient to provide a proper basis for the inference that B intended to deprive the occupiers of the flat of any item of property, whether he did not know what he was doing or whether he intended to steal anything worth stealing, the offence could not be proved. (*R.* v. *Easom* [1971] C.L.Y. 2816; *R.* v. *Husseyn* [1978] C.L.Y. 415, and *D.P.P.* v. *Nock* [1978] C.L.Y. 430 applied): R. *v.* BOZICKOVIC [1978] Crim.L.R. 686, Nottingham Crown Ct.

423. Certiorari—witness statements—prosecutor's failure to disclose

H was convicted of driving without due care and attention. He then heard that the police had taken statements from two witnesses who had not been called. *Held*, quashing the conviction, that (1) to deprive H of the elementary right to be notified about witnesses known to the police was a denial of natural justice; (2) the appropriate remedy was certiorari: R. *v.* LEYLAND JUSTICES, *ex p.* HAWTHORN [1978] Crim.L.R. 627, D.C.

424. Committal proceedings—validity—duty of legal advisor to consider statements

[Criminal Justice Act 1967 (c. 80), ss. 1 (1), 2 (1), (2).]

A committal without consideration of the evidence will not be invalidated if statements put before the court contain matters which are inadmissible or irrelevant nor if the statements are not considered by a defendant's advisor.

Written statements were put before justices which contained no reference to D. They were not considered by D's legal advisor. Statements subsequently served did show a case against D. *Held,* dismissing D's appeal, that there had been a valid committal, notwithstanding those omissions. D's legal advisor should have considered the statements, but his failure to do so did not render the committal invalid.

R. *v.* BROOKER (1977) 65 Cr.App.R. 181, C.A.

425. Community Service by Offenders (Scotland) Act 1978 (c. 49)

This Act provides for the performance of unpaid work by persons convicted or placed on probation in Scotland.

S. 1 defines a community service order, and places certain restrictions upon the imposition of such an order by a court; s. 2 contains further provisions about such orders; s. 3 states the obligations of persons subject to community service orders; s. 4 sets out penalties for failure to comply with such an order; s. 5 deals with the amendment and revocation of community service orders, and the substitution of other sentences; s. 6 provides for community service orders relating to persons residing in England and Wales; s. 7 inserts into the Criminal Procedure (Scotland) Act 1975 (c. 21), a provision empowering courts to order probationers to perform unpaid work; s. 8 enables the making of a community service order after failure to comply with the requirements of a probation order; s. 9 empowers the Secretary of State to make grants in respect of community service facilities; s. 10 enables the Secretary of State to make rules regulating the performance of community service work; s. 11 is the interpretation section; s. 12 makes financial provisions; s. 13 contains certain minor and consequential amendments; s. 14 contains the short title. With the exception of s. 6 (3) and paras. 2, 3 and 5 of Sched. 1, the Act extends to Scotland only.

The Act received the Royal Assent on July 31, 1978, and shall come into force on such day or days as the Secretary of State shall, by statutory instrument, appoint.

426. Compensation—enforcement—guidelines

[Powers of Criminal Courts Act 1973 (c. 62), ss. 34–38; Administration of Justice Act 1970 (c. 31), s. 41 (1) (8), Sched. 9, Pt. I (as amended); Magistrates' Courts Act 1952 (c. 55), ss. 63, 107.]

The Court of Appeal has laid down guidelines for Crown Court judges in connection with the exercise of their powers relating to compensation orders and imprisonment in default.

On conviction on two counts of theft, the defendant was ordered to pay compensation within 28 days with a period of nine months' imprisonment in default consecutive to other terms of imprisonment. The compensation was, in fact, paid. On appeal, *held*, that the periods of payment in default would be set aside. The following guidelines to Crown Court judges were laid down: (1) the court may allow time for payment or payment by instalments; (2) a compensation order made by the court is enforceable as a sum adjudged to be paid on conviction by a magistrates' court; (3) the court may specify a period of imprisonment in default not exceeding 12 months if it considers the magistrates' courts powers insufficient; (4) on default, the court may issue either a warrant of distress or a warrant committing the defaulter to prison; (5) the minimum period of imprisonment is five days and there is no power to imprison a defaulter under the age of 17. The court also drew attention to the Court Business Circular No. 10 of 1977, dated July 22, 1977.

R. *v.* BUNCE (1977) 66 Cr.App.R. 109, C.A.

427. —— order—financial position of payor—imprisonment in default not appropriate

[Powers of Criminal Courts Act 1973 (c. 62), s. 35; Administration of Justice Act 1970 (c. 31), s. 41 (8).]

The court must have regard to the means of the payor when fixing a sum for compensation, and a period of imprisonment in default is normally inappropriate.

DC was ordered to pay the sum of £2,069 compensation, that sum being an arithmetical calculation of loss suffered. He was given four years to pay with 12 months in default. There was only shadowy evidence to suggest he might be able to pay it. On appeal against the compensation order, *held*, allowing the appeal, that the court must have regard to the financial means of the person to pay, and to make an excessive order was counter-productive. To fix a period in default was not an appropriate course, except where required by s. 41 (8) of the Administration of Justice Act 1970. Order reduced to £500, and £250 in O'Donoghue's case.

R. *v.* O'DONOGHUE AND DALLAS-COPE (1974) 66 Cr.App.R. 116. C.A.

428. Conspiracy—agreement to steal—whether conspiracy at common law—effect of 1977 Act
[Criminal Law Act 1977 (c. 45), s. 1.] Q and others were charged with conspiracy to steal, contrary to s. 1 of the 1977 Act, and conspiracy to steal contrary to common law. *Held*, that common law conspiracy to defraud includes a conspiracy to steal and is therefore preserved by the Act and is not governed by s. 1. Accordingly the proper charge was at common law. It would be equally in order to state the offence as conspiracy to defraud by conspiring to steal or simply as conspiracy to steal: R. *v.* QUINN [1978] Crim. L.R. 750, Nottingham Crown Ct.

429. —— impossible offence—burden of proof
The position of the prosecution in cases of common law conspiracy was (a) the burden of proof rested with the prosecution; (b) if evidence was available to the prosecution which might show that at the time the agreement was made, the carrying out of it was impossible, it was their duty to call that evidence or make it available to the defence; (c) if there was no such evidence the evidential burden of proving impossibility shifts to the defence; (d) the probative burden remains with the prosecution and any remaining questions of impossibility should be left to the jury with appropriate directions; (e) if there was no evidence of impossibility the jury need not be directed about it. There was a fundamental distinction between an agreement which, when made, could never if carried out result in the commission of the offence alleged because the result was physically or legally impossible (*D.P.P.* v. *Nock* [1978] C.L.Y. 430; *Haughton* v. *Smith* (*R. D.*) [1974] C.L.Y. 637 applied) and an agreement which would, if carried out in accordance with the parties' intentions, result in the commission of an offence but which cannot be carried out because a person not a party to the agreement lets the parties down, or through incompetency, or the unassailable defence of the victim (*R.* v. *Mulcahy* [1868] L.R. 3 H.L. 306, and *R.* v. *Aspinal* (1876) 2 Q.B.D. 48 applied): R. *v.* BENNETT, WILFRED AND WEST, *The Times*, August 11, 1978, C.A.

430. —— impossibility of implementation—manufacture of controlled drug
When two or more persons agree upon a course of conduct with the object of committing a criminal offence, but, unknown to them, it is impossible to achieve that object by that course of conduct, they do not commit the crime of conspiracy.

A and B agreed to produce cocaine by separating from a powder which they thought was a mixture of cocaine and lignocaine. In fact it contained no cocaine and therefore it was impossible to produce it. They were convicted of conspiracy to produce cocaine, and the conviction was upheld on appeal. On appeal to the House of Lords, *held*, allowing the appeal, that the agreement could not possibly have led to the completion of the offence, and therefore there was no conspiracy. (*R.* v. *Smith* (*Roger*) [1974] C.L.Y. 637 applied; *R.* v. *Green* (*Harry*) [1975] C.L.Y. 504 considered; *Haggard* v. *Mason* [1976] C.L.Y. 508 distinguished.)

D.P.P. *v.* NOCK AND ALSFORD [1978] 3 W.L.R. 57. H.L.

431. —— to obstruct the course of justice—agreeing to be indemnified as sureties
J was granted bail in his own recognisance with two sureties, each in the sum of £2,500. H1, H2 and B entered into an agreement that H1 and H2 should stand as sureties for J, on the basis that they would be indemnified, in

order that J could be admitted to bail. H1 and H2 then entered into sureties for J, who was admitted to bail. *Held,* dismissing the appeals of H1 and H2 against convictions of conspiracy to obstruct public justice, that it was not necessary to show an intent to obstruct justice in such a way that J would not surrender to his bail, to make out the offence. The essence of the decision to grant bail was that two persons were sufficiently sure of being able to see that J surrendered to his bail to stake £2,500. Thus there had been an obstruction to the course of public justice. (*R. v. Porter* [1910] 1 K.B. 369, applied): R. *v.* HEAD [1978] Crim.L.R. 427, C.A.

432. Contempt—employer dismissing juror before jury service—procedure
   A juror was dismissed from his job shortly before serving on the jury and complained at the court of trial that he had been dismissed through his jury service. The judge caused the employer to be brought before him and fined him for contempt. *Held,* that (1) there was insufficient evidence to show contempt beyond reasonable doubt; and (2) the matter should not have been dealt with by the judge acting as both prosecutor and judge, but by motion to the Divisional Court. (*Balogh* v. *St. Albans Crown Court* [1974] C.L.Y. 2912 distinguished): ROONEY *v.* SNARESBROOK CROWN COURT, *The Times,* June 17, 1978, C.A.

433. —— litigant in person
   A litigant in person is entitled to apply to a judge of the Q.B.D. for a committal order for contempt of court; the practice should be the same as in the Chancery Division. (*Bevan* v. *Hastings Jones* [1978] C.L.Y. 2336 applied): DE VRIES *v.* KAY, *The Times,* October 7, 1978, O'Connor J.

434. —— reporting of pleas of guilty taken in jury's absence
   [R.S.C., Ord. 52, r. 9.] Newspaper and television reports during X's trial referred to four counts to which he had pleaded guilty before the trial in the jury's absence. The judge discharged the jury and ordered a retrial. *Held,* granting the Att.-Gen.'s applications for orders under Ord. 52, r. 9, alleging contempt of court, that the charges of contempt were proved. Every reporter should know that publishing information about offences, other than those charged, which an accused has or is alleged to have committed and publishing material which has deliberately been kept from the jury's ears, were contempts of court: R. *v.* BORDER TELEVISION, *ex p.* ATT.-GEN.; R. *v.* NEWCASTLE CHRONICLE AND JOURNAL, *ex p.* ATT.-GEN. [1978] Crim.L.R. 221, D.C.

435. Corruption—police procedures
   New police procedures for dealing with allegations of corruption in public life have been announced by the Government. The procedures implement Recommendations 33–35 of the Royal Commission on Standards of Conduct in Public Life (Cmnd. 6524). The new procedures are set out in Home Office Circular 92/1978.

436. —— recovery of bribe—damages for fraud—Malaysia. See T. MAHESAN S/O THAMBIAH *v.* MALAYSIA GOVERNMENT OFFICERS' CO-OPERATIVE HOUSING SOCIETY, § 168.

437. —— taking bribes
   [Prevention of Corruption Act 1906 (c. 34).] A person who accepts a gift knowing that it is intended as a bribe enters into a corrupt bargain even if he makes a private mental reservation not to carry out his side of the bargain. However, if the money was received in order to entrap the giver or to provide evidence for police listening and the acceptor did not intend to keep it, it would not be corrupt: R. *v.* MILLS, *The Times,* June 14, 1978, C.A.

438. Costs—central funds—case stated—respondent's application nine months after hearing
   [Costs in Criminal Cases Act 1973 (c. 14), s. 5 (1).]
   Under s. 5 (1) of the Act, the Divisional Court may order the payment out of central funds of the costs of any party to criminal proceedings before the Divisional Court even where the application is made many months after the hearing.
   H, a police inspector, was the successful respondent to a motorist's appeal

by case stated. He applied nine months after the hearing of the appeal for an order that his costs be paid out of central funds. *Held,* that the order would be made.

CANNINGS v. HOUGHTON (No. 2) [1977] R.T.R. 507, D.C.

439. —— convicted persons—upper limit—whether necessary

M and K were ordered to pay prosecution costs, a fine, compensation and a legal aid contribution, no upper limit being placed on the prosecution costs. *Held,* that although it was generally preferable to put a limit on the costs paid by convicted persons, particularly where a financial penalty is imposed, this practice need not necessarily be followed in all cases: R. *v.* MOUNTAIN AND KILMINSTER [1978] Crim.L.R. 550, C.A.

440. —— determination of sum

When a defendant in criminal proceedings is ordered to pay costs, the order should be for payment of a fixed sum or of costs to be taxed not exceeding a fixed sum. (*R. v. Hier* [1976] C.L.Y. 419 applied): R. *v.* SMITH (WILLIAM AUGUSTUS), *The Times,* April 12, 1978, C.A.

441. —— moneys paid to an informer

[Costs in Criminal Cases Act 1973 (c. 14), s. 7 (4).]

Moneys paid to an informer will not normally be regarded as " costs properly incurred . . . in an appeal " for the purposes of taxation.

The applicant paid £2,000 reward to an informer whose information was of material assistance in quashing his conviction. On his application to have this sum included in the costs awarded to him out of central funds, *held,* dismissing his application, that this sum was not within the meaning of the words " costs properly incurred by the applicant in his appeal."

R. *v.* WHITBY (1977) 65 Cr.App.R. 257, C.A.

442. Counterfeit money—meaning of " utter "

[Coinage Offences Act 1936 (c. 16), ss. 5 (1), 17 (*b*).]

The word " utter " in s. 5 (1) of the Coinage Offences Act includes selling coins; it is not restricted to putting coins into circulation.

A, B and C were convicted of conspiring to utter counterfeit coins. The coins had once been legal tender but were no longer so. They were, however, deemed to be " current coin of the realm " within s. 5 (1) of the Coinage Offences Act 1936, by reason of s. 17 (*b*). A, B and C appealed, contending that " uttering " within s. 5 (1) was restricted to putting counterfeit coins into circulation. *Held,* dismissing the appeal, that " uttering " counterfeit coins means passing them off as genuine, and included selling them. (*Selby* v. *D.P.P.* [1971] C.L.Y. 2357 applied, and dictum of Lord Cross of Chelsea approved; R. *v. McMahon* (1894) 15 N.S.W.L.R. 131 explained and distinguished.)

R. *v.* WALMSLEY, DEREYA AND JACKSON (1978) 67 Cr.App.R. 30, C.A.

443. Courts-martial. See ARMED FORCES.

444. Criminal damage—compensation—spitting on police officer's raincoat

A was alleged to have spat on a police officer's raincoat. The raincoat was produced at the hearing and a faint mark could be seen on it in the general area where the spittle was said to have landed. The prosecution said the coat therefore needed dry cleaning. *Held,* allowing A's appeal against conviction, that there was no case to answer. As no attempt had been made to clean the coat, there was no likelihood that if wiped with a damp cloth there would be any mark left. The coat had thus not been damaged since it had not been rendered imperfect or inoperative: " A " (A JUVENILE) *v.* THE QUEEN [1978] Crim.L.R. 689, Kent Crown Ct.

445. —— information against wife—damaging husband's property—whether consent of Director of Public Prosecutions required

[Theft Act 1968 (c. 60), s. 30 (4).] W obtained an injunction in divorce proceedings restraining H from molesting her and debarring him from the matrimonial home. Justices thereafter held that they had no jurisdiction to hear H's information against W, alleging criminal damage to H's property, without the D.P.P.'s consent since s. 30 (4) of the 1968 proceedings between married couples for criminal damage required the D.P.P.'s consent. _Held,_ that the justices had erred since the injunction was a judicial order which removed the obligation on W and H to cohabit. Accordingly, s. 30 (4) did not apply: WOODLEY _v._ WOODLEY [1978] Crim.L.R. 629, D.C.

446. Criminal injuries compensation—award—persons entitled to receive award— assessment of compensation

The aunts of three children whose father had strangled their mother were awarded sums in compensation by the Criminal Injuries Compensation Board. The aunts had given up work to look after these children and the Board assessed compensation by deducting a boarding-out allowance, given to the aunts for the children by the local authority, from the aunts' lost salaries. _Held,_ granting an order of certiorari to quash the Board's decision, that (1) any award could only be made to the children, not the aunts, although the Board could direct that the money be paid to the aunts; (2) the matter would be remitted to the Board for reassessment, bearing in mind that only that part of the boarding-out allowance attributable to material services, as opposed to payment for outgoings, should be deducted from the aunts' lost salaries: R. _v._ CRIMINAL INJURIES COMPENSATION BOARD, _ex p._ MCGUFFIE [1978] Crim.L.R. 161, D.C.

447. —— gang member—whether undue fettering of discretion

Upon R.J.C.'s application for compensation the Criminal Injuries Compensation Board found that he was a member of a gang and was injured in the course of a gang fight. Accordingly they made no award in line with a policy document which the Board had issued stating that compensation would not be awarded to such applicants. _Held,_ granting R.J.C.'s application for certiorari, that the policy document sought to deprive the Board of its discretion under para. 17 of the scheme to make a restricted award even if the facts were found against the applicant. As the Board's decision was based only on the gang aspect it would be quashed and the case remitted for reconsideration by the Board. The Board were exercising a judicial function until it was decided whether and if so, how much, compensation should be paid: R. _v._ CRIMINAL INJURIES COMPENSATION BOARD, _ex p._ R.J.C. (AN INFANT) [1978] Crim.L.R. 220, D.C.

448. —— review

The report of an interdepartmental working party who have had under review the operation of the Criminal Injuries Compensation scheme, has been published by HMSO. The report contains 52 recommendations for change to the scope and operation of the scheme. [£2·00.]

449. Criminal Injuries Compensation Board

The Criminal Injuries Compensation Board have published their Fourteenth Report, a review of the year 1977–78. This gives details of the increase since the previous year of compensation paid to victims of violent crime, and also the increase in applications. The Report is available from HMSO (Cmnd. 7396) [£1·00].

450. Criminal Law Act 1977—commencement

CRIMINAL LAW ACT 1977 (COMMENCEMENT NO. 5) ORDER 1978 (No. 712 (C. 16)) [20p], made under the Criminal Law Act 1977 (c. 45), s. 65 (7); operative as to part on June 19, 1978, and as to the rest on July 17, 1978; brings into force on June 19, 1978, s. 62 of the 1977 Act, and brings into force on July 17, 1978, ss. 14–32, 34–37, 41, 42, 45, 46, 58, 61 and 64 of and Scheds. 1–5, 8, 12 (part), and 13 (part) to the 1977 Act.

451. Criminal statistics

The Home Office have issued the annual volume " Criminal Statistics, England and Wales, 1977." It includes historical tables showing changes over the last 10 years, and has a new chapter on the use of remand by the police and the courts. The report is available from HMSO (Cmnd. 7289) [£7·75].

452. Crown Court

CROWN COURT (AMENDMENT) RULES 1978 (No. 439 (L.8)) [25p], made under the Courts Act 1971 (c. 23), ss. 13 (5), 14 (1) (2), 15, and the Bail Act

1976 (c. 63), ss. 5 (1), 8 (4); operative on April 17, 1978; amend the Crown Court Rules 1971 (S.I. 1971 No. 1292) in consequence of the Bail Act 1976.

453. —— business

The following Practice Direction was issued by Lord Widgery L.C.J. on June 30, 1978:

With the concurrence of the Lord Chancellor and pursuant to s. 4 (5) of the Courts Act 1971 I direct that, with effect from July 17, 1978, the following amendments shall be made to the directions on the distribution of Crown Court business given by me on October 14, 1971 [1971] C.L.Y. 9159 as amended:

1. In para. 1 delete from " Class 3 " to the end and substitute:

" *Class 3.* All offences triable only on indictment other than those in Classes 1, 2 and 4. They may be listed for trial by a High Court judge or by a Circuit judge or by a recorder.

Class 4. (a) Wounding or causing grievous bodily harm with intent (Offences Against the Person Act 1861, s. 18).

(b) Robbery or assault with intent to rob (Theft Act 1968, s. 8).

(c) Offences under para. (a) of s. 2 (2) of the Forgery Act 1913 where the amount of money or the value of goods exceeds £1,000.

(d) Offences under para. (a) of s. 7 of the Forgery Act 1913 where the amount of money or the value of the property exceeds £1,000.

(e) Incitement or attempt to commit any of the above offences.

(f) Conspiracy at common law or conspiracy to commit any offence other than one included in Classes 1 and 2.

(g) All offences triable either way and any offence in Class 3, if included in Class 4 in accordance with directions, which may be either general or particular, given by a presiding judge or on his authority.

When tried on indictment offences in Class 4 may be tried by a High Court judge, Circuit judge or recorder but will normally be listed for trial by a Circuit judge or recorder."

2. In para. 5 (3) delete " s. 16 of the Criminal Justice Act 1972 " and substitute " s. 15 of the Powers of Criminal Courts Act 1973."

3. For para. 12 (iii) there shall be substituted:

" (iii) Class 4 offences shall be listed for trial by a Circuit judge or recorder unless, bearing in mind the considerations set out in para. 2 above and the views, if any, put forward by justices, the officer responsible for listing decides that the case should be tried by a High Court judge.

Such a decision shall be taken only after consultation with a presiding judge (or a judge acting for him) or in accordance with directions, either general or particular, given by a presiding judge including, in the case of any specified offence, directions relating to further considerations to be borne in mind by the officer responsible for listing."

[1978] 1 W.L.R. 926; [1978] 2 All E.R. 912.

454. —— cases stated

The following Practice Direction was issued by Widgery L.C.J. on December 4, 1978:

It is desirable that there should be uniformity in cases stated by the Crown Court.

Pending any amendment of the relevant rules, the content of any such case should comply with r. 68 of the Magistrates' Courts Rules 1968 (S.I. 1968 No. 1920) and the form with form 148 of the Magistrates' Courts (Forms) Rules 1968 (S.I. No. 1919), with necessary amendments only.

122 S.J. 848.

455. Cruelty to children—meaning of " expose "

[Children and Young Persons Act 1933 (c. 12), s. 1 (1).] G took six young boys across a deep, disused semi-stagnant stretch of water on the London Docks on a baulk of timber. It was alleged that the situation was dangerous although no harm came to the children. G was charged with cruelty to a child in that he had wilfully exposed six children in a manner likely to cause them unnecessary suffering or injury to health. *Held,* directing the jury to acquit, that "expose" in the Children and Young Persons Act 1933, s. 1 (1), did not include "expose to risk." The section was aimed at cruelty to children, which was not proved here. (*R.* v. *Hayles* [1968] C.L.Y. 1947 applied): R. *v.* GIBBINS [1977] Crim.L.R. 741, Woodford Crown Ct.

456. Dangerous drugs. See MEDICINE.

457. Defence—not raised at prior instance—Singapore
[Singapore General Code (C103, 1970 rev.), s. 300 (*c*), exception 4.]
The Privy Council will consider on appeal a defence not raised at first instance if there was evidence upon which a reasonable tribunal could have found the defence made out.
D had an argument with a friend when both of them were drunk. D hit his friend a number of times, mostly whilst he was on the ground, with an exhaust pipe. The friend died, and D was charged with murder contrary to s. 300 of the Penal Code of Singapore. The case was heard by two judges whose decision had to be unanimous since the charge carried the death penalty. They held unanimously that D was not so drunk as to be unable to form the intention of inflicting the blows and that D was therefore guilty of murder. D's appeal to the Court of Criminal Appeal was dismissed. D then raised before the Privy Council the defence of sudden fight, exception 4 to s. 300, which was a defence to a charge of murder. The defence had not been raised or considered by any judge at any prior stage. *Held*, dismissing the appeal, that the Privy Council should consider whether there was sufficient evidence on which a reasonable tribunal could have found the defence made out. To do so, D would have had to prove that he had "not taken undue advantage or acted in a cruel or unusual manner" in the terms of the exception. He could not have done so and the defence was not open to him.
MOHAMAD KUNJO S/O RAMALAN *v.* PUBLIC PROSECUTOR [1978] 2 W.L.R. 130, P.C.

458. Deprivation of property—right of police to retain—for use in evidence—not for payment of compensation
Police seized £7,000 in English banknotes and £3,000 in foreign currency from M's home. M was committed for trial on charges of conspiracy and handling, but no specific charge related to the money. *Held*, allowing an appeal against a mandatory injunction ordering the return of the money to M, that (i) its retention was justified as police witnesses might be handicapped or discredited in their evidence if unable to produce the actual notes; (ii) however, retention purely for the purpose of satisfying a possible restitution, compensation or forfeiture order would not have been justified: MALONE *v.* METROPOLITAN POLICE COMMISSIONERS [1978] Crim.L.R. 555, C.A.

459. Disclosure of offence—spent—insurance purposes—amendment of pleadings.
See REYNOLDS *v.* PHEONIX ASSURANCE SOCIETY, § 1708.

460. Drunkenness
The Home Office have issued a report entitled "Offences of Drunkenness 1977: England and Wales," which gives the statistics governing total numbers of criminal convictions, comparative rates of increase, and respective rates between the sexes, together with information about sentencing, police cautioning, detoxification centres and driving offences. The report is available from HMSO (Cmnd. 7317) [70p].

461. Evidence—admissibility—hearsay identification—whether part of res gestae—correct test
Where there is hearsay evidence of identification by the victim of an attack on a bystander, the correct test of admissibility is spontaneity, and the degree of risk of concoction, fabrication or error, rather than concentration on whether the statement was made as part of the res gestae.
L and N were in a car which collided with the vehicle in front, the driver of which was assaulted by either L or N. A police officer was told by the victim "that man (L) hit me in the face." N was in the driving seat of the rear car, and was breath and blood tested without demur. The judge commented on that fact in the summing up as being in support of the Crown case that N was the driver. On appeal against conviction on the grounds that the evidence

of identification was inadmissible and the judge had misdirected the jury on the second point, *held,* dismissing the appeal, that the evidence of identification was admissible as it was so spontaneous there was little room for concoction or error. The judge's direction that N's acquiescence to a blood test could support the Crown's case was a misdirection, but on the facts, did not render the verdict unsafe. (*Ratten* v. *R.* [1971] C.L.Y. 4587 applied.)

R. v. NYE AND LOAN (1977) 66 Cr.App.R. 252, C.A.

462. —— —— **obtained illegally—court's discretion to exclude.** See R. v. SMITH (BENJAMIN WALKER) § 2568.

463. —— —— **previous offences—statement of defendant**
[Criminal Evidence Act 1898 (c. 36), s. 1 (*e*), (*f*).] D1 was charged with demanding money with menaces. He gave evidence that his only conviction was for a driving offence. Prosecuting counsel cross-examined regarding D1's earlier trial for assault occasioning actual bodily harm at which D1 was bound over to keep the peace and the charge had been left on the file, and put the details of the charge to D1. *Held,* allowing D1's appeal against conviction and that of his co-accused, D2, that as D1 had not claimed never to have been charged with other offences the cross-examination was not permissible. D1's credibility may have been wrongly impaired and this may have rubbed off on to D2. (*R.* v. *Maxwell* [1935] A.C. 309 applied): R. v. MEEHAN AND MEEHAN [1978] Crim.L.R. 690, C.A.

464. —— —— **previous proceedings—issue estoppel—rape**
[Aust.] Accused charged with raping woman. Accused admitted having had sexual intercourse with the woman, but denied the use of force or threats, and said that the woman had consented. The Crown tendered evidence to show the accused had on a previous date been tried for rape upon the same woman and that he had been acquitted. The trial judge admitted the evidence, and directed the jury they were to draw no inferences for or against either the accused or the woman from the fact of the previous acquittal. The accused was convicted and appealed. *Held,* (1) the evidence relating to the previous charge and acquittal was admissible as being relevant to the question of consent by the woman; (2) the trial judge's exercise of his discretion not to exclude the evidence should not be interfered with; (3) as the acquittal of the accused on the previous charge was not being in any way impeached, the admission of the impugned evidence did not offend the rule against double jeopardy. (*R.* v. *Humphreys* [1976] C.L.Y. 488; *Sambasivam* v. *Public Prosecutor, Federation of Malaya* (1950) C.L.C. 1979 considered): R. v. GARRETT (1977) 15 S.A.S.R. 501, S.Aust.Sup.Ct.

464a. —— —— **standard of proof**
[Criminal Procedure Act 1865.] Where a judge in a criminal trial has to decide a question of admissibility, and the admissibility depends wholly on the Criminal Procedure Act 1865, he need only be satisfied of the genuineness of the disputed evidence on the civil standard, and not beyond reasonable doubt. This is because the 1865 Act merely applies the civil provisions of the Common Law Procedure Act 1854: R. v. ANGELI (1978) 122 S.J. 591, C.A.

465. —— —— **statement by non-compellable witness—reason for confession— whether voluntary**
The defendant was indicted for burglary. The burglar was disturbed by the householder, but there was insufficient evidence of identification. The defendant's car was found by the house and he returned for it some time after the incident, explaining that the radiator had got too hot. The main evidence against the defendant was a threefold confession to the police at the police station—oral, written and in reply to the charge. At the end of the prosecution case, the judge raised the problem of the introduction, in opening the prosecution case, of references to a statement which had been made by the defendant's wife and put to the defendant during the course of the interview at the police station and as a result of which the defendant made his confessions. Three points of law were canvassed: (a) whether a jury should know that a statement had been shown to the defendant having been made by a non-compellable

witness; (b) the voluntary nature of the confession; and (c) whether the remaining evidence was sufficient for a conviction—his lies, his journey home which would not generally have taken him past the burgled house, his " furtive " walking up and down the road before going to his car. It was recognised that this was not enough by itself to secure a conviction. *Held*, (a) it was not right that the jury should know of the wife's statement, for they might adversely presume its contents; (b) on the facts, after the showing to the defendant of his wife's statement, the prosecution failed to prove that the defendant's statement and reply to the charge was voluntary: R. *v*. EDWARDS, September 7, and 8, 1978, John Bailey, Esq., sitting as deputy circuit judge, Manchester Crown Ct. (*Ex rel. Miss Patricia Bailey, Barrister*).

466. —— —— statement implicating co-defendants—judge's duty to intervene

At the trial of Y, R and A, the judge ruled that statements made by Y and R were inadmissible. R's counsel, however, examined R about the circumstances in which the statement was made. Crown counsel carefully avoided reference to the contents of the statement but at the judge's instigation R's statement, which implicated Y and A, was put before the court after he had admitted signing it. The judge directed the jury that if the statement was obtained by duress it would be wrong to attach any weight to it whatsoever, and that it was only before them to test the truth of R's evidence in that regard, but no warning was given that the statement was not evidence against Y or A. *Held*, allowing appeals against conviction, that (1) despite the judge's earlier ruling, there was justification for admitting the statement, but a much clearer direction to the jury should have been given; (2) the judge should have intervened much earlier in R's interests to warn R's counsel of the dangers of his line of questioning of R; (3) the trial and verdict were unsatisfactory: R. *v*. YOUNG AND ROBINSON [1978] Crim.L.R. 163, C.A.

467. —— —— statements by defendant to police first put to him in cross-examination

Evidence which is capable of forming part of the affirmative case for the prosecution should generally be led by it in the course of its case.

After the close of the prosecution case, evidence was tendered, during the cross-examination of the defendant, of a conversation he had with a police officer after he was charged, but before his committal. *Held*, that that had led to a material irregularity in the course of the trial. There had been no opportunity to consider the admissibility of the conversation, so that the appeal would be allowed.

R. *v*. KANE (1977) 65 Cr.App.R. 270, C.A.

468. —— age—proof by admission

[Aus.] D was charged with running an unauthorised accommodation house for persons over 60. The informant asked the inmates their ages. Either they gave them in D's hearing or D told the informant their ages. D contended their ages had not been proved. *Held,* such evidence as to age was admissible as an exception to the hearsay rule and it was for the court to decide what weight to attach to it: STOCK *v*. ORCSIK [1977] V.R. 382, Sup.Ct. of Victoria.

469. —— antecedents—method of giving sentence—whether proper to see counsel in private

Evidence of antecedents must not be given by a police officer unless it is based on first-hand information about which the officer can be questioned.

Per curiam. The occasions when it is proper for a judge to see counsel in private are strictly limited. It is most improper for the judge to discuss sentence with prosecuting counsel, and ask for his views.

W was convicted of living on the earnings of prostitution, and before sentence a two-page antecedent history was produced, without prior notice to W. The document contained a mass of highly prejudicial hearsay material. W was sentenced to three and a half years' imprisonment. On appeal against sentence, *held*, allowing the appeal, that antecedents based on a précis of allegations in documentary form must never be given by an officer who has no first-hand knowledge of them and cannot answer questions on them, especially where the defendant is unrepresented. Sentence reduced to two years. (*R. v. Van Pelz*

(1944) 29 Cr.App.R. 10, and *R.* v. *Robinson* [1969] C.L.Y. 625 applied. *R.* v. *Crabtree* [1952] C.L.Y. 751 explained; *R.* v. *Coughlan*; *R.* v. *Young* [1976] C.L.Y. 414 considered.)
R. *v.* WILKINS (1977) 66 Cr.App.R. 49, C.A.

470. —— **assault—subsequent assault—whether subsequent assault part of res gestae**
[Aus.] H was charged with assault on a security officer, who called a policeman, whom H also assaulted. It was sought to admit the evidence of the second assault as part of the res gestae. *Held*, it was not admissible as part of the res gestae. The two assaults were sufficiently removed from each other in time that either could be understood without reference to the other: R. *v.* HEIDT (1976) 14 S.A.S.R., Sup.Ct.

471. —— **character—accused giving evidence " against " co-accused—whether charged with same offence**
[Criminal Evidence Act 1898 (c. 36), s. 1 (*f*) (iii).]
Two defendants charged on the same indictment with assaulting each other are not " charged with the same offence " for the purposes of s. 1 (*f*) (iii) of the Criminal Evidence Act 1898.
The appellant was convicted of an assault upon E who had been tried at the same time and acquitted upon a count alleging an assault upon the appellant. E gave evidence against the appellant who was refused leave to cross-examine E as to his previous convictions. *Held*, dismissing the appeal, that leave was properly refused since the appellant and E were not " charged with the same offence." (*R.* v. *Russell* (*George*) [1970] C.L.Y. 441 considered.)
R. *v.* LAUCHLAN (NOTE) [1978] R.T.R. 326, C.A.

472. —— —— **previous sexual experience—circumstances in which allowed**
[Sexual Offences (Amendment) Act 1976 (c. 82), s. 2.] Cross-examination of the complainant about her previous sexual experiences under s. 2 of the Sexual Offences (Amendment) Act 1976 is not to be permitted if it is designed to blacken her character, but only if it affects the trustworthiness of her evidence. Before permitting such cross-examination the judge should be satisfied on balance that it is likely to lead the jury to take a different view of the evidence: R. *v.* MILLS, *The Times,* November 21, 1978, C.A.

473. —— **confession—inducement**
The applicants claimed to have made confessions after being told that " it's in your own hands. If you make a statement admitting it I can get bail sorted out so that you will get bail." The trial judge said that he did not know what had been said to them but if the officer had said what they claimed, this was not an inducement but a statement of fact. *Held*, quashing the convictions, that the trial judge had admitted the evidence without applying the proper test: R. *v.* BAMFORD [1978] Crim.L.R. 752, C.A.

474. —— —— **whether voluntary—obtained by innocent misrepresentation**
P at first denied alleged offences of unlawful sexual intercourse and indecent assault. He admitted the offences after a police officer told him that forensic examination of clothing of the alleged victim would show it to be stained by P's semen. In fact there was no forensic evidence. *Held*, excluding the only evidence against P, namely verbal admissions and a written statement under caution, that although the suggestion to P was made in good faith, P had been misled and was under a material misapprehension as to the true facts when making the admissions. Such admissions could not be said to be voluntary: R. *v.* KWABENA POKU [1978] Crim.L.R. 488, Melford Stevenson J.

475. —— **co-accused's statement from dock—significance**
G sought leave to appeal against convictions for robbery and murder, on the ground, inter alia, that he had been unfairly prejudiced by a statement made from the dock by his co-defendant X, to the effect that G was the person behind the whole affair. *Held*, rejecting the application, that the situation was analogous to an out-of-court statement by an accused that damages a co-accused. In neither case can the accused be permitted to call evidence in rebuttal of the statement. Such statements should be put before the jury as being wholly ineffective to weigh in the scales against the defendant, and in

the present case, this had properly been done: R. *v.* GEORGE, *The Times,* October 31, 1978, C.A.

476. —— corroboration—accomplice—warning to jury

The fabrication of an alibi may, in certain circumstances, be of itself corroboration, but a jury may convict on the uncorroborated evidence of an accomplice provided adequate warning of the dangers is given.

Per curiam. The recent tendency to overload indictments must end. No more accused should be indicted together than absolutely necessary for the proper presentation of the prosecution case against the principal accused.

T and eight others were convicted on numerous counts of robbery and conspiracy to rob in a trial lasting 111 days. The main prosecution witness, O'M, was an informer and former accomplice of T. An application to cross-examine a police officer about previous trials in which O'M gave evidence which resulted in acquittals was refused. T appealed on the ground that the application was wrongly refused and that without corroboration it was unsafe to convict on O'M's evidence. *Held,* dismissing the appeal, that provided a judge gives adequate warning of the dangers of acting on the uncorroborated evidence of an accomplice, a jury may properly convict. Further, that fabrication of an alibi is itself capable of being corroboration provided the judge is satisfied that its falsity has not arisen from mistake or through panic or stupidity. The judge was correct in refusing the application to cross-examine the police officer. (*R. v. Turner* (*Bryan James*) [1975] C.L.Y. 559 explained.)

R. *v.* THORNE (1977) 66 Cr.App.R. 6, C.A.

477. —— —— hearsay

The Att.-Gen. had applied for a solicitor to be struck off the roll on the grounds that he had earlier lied to a court in which he was a defendant in saying that he had attended a meeting with X. X denied this, and the judge held this to be corroborated by the solicitor saying that another person said to be present had "no recollection" of the meeting. It was *held* that this latter was hearsay and not corroboration, and that it was not safe to convict the solicitor of the equivalent of perjury on the evidence of one witness alone: *Re* A SOLICITOR (1978) 122 S.J. 264, C.A.

478. —— —— sworn evidence of children aged 12 and 16—discretion of judge

It is not possible to state as a general proposition what is the age above which a warning as to the requirement for corroboration of a young person's evidence is unnecessary.

M was convicted of indecent assault on the evidence of the victim, aged 11, his brother aged 12, and a boy of 16. The jury were warned of the need for corroboration of the victim's evidence and of the possibility that the boys were lying, but not in terms about the possibility of collusion between the boys. *Held,* dismissing M's appeal, that the judge was guilty of an omission in not directing the jury as to the need for corroboration of the brother's evidence; as to the elder boy, the question of the need for a warning was a matter for the judge's discretion and that the omission amounted to no more than an irregularity which had given rise to no miscarriage of justice.

R. *v.* MORGAN (MICHAEL) [1978] 1 W.L.R. 735, C.A.

479. —— fingerprints—circumstances in which may be taken

[Magistrates' Courts Act 1952 (c. 55), s.40 (2).]

Where a magistrates' court orders that the fingerprints be taken of a person on bail, such fingerprints can only lawfully be taken in the court building.

When the driver of another car "jumped the queue" where the appellant driver was awaiting a parking place, the appellant drove towards it and collided with it causing minimal damage (costing £8 to repair). The appellant was arrested by an observing policeman and subsequently bailed. She refused to allow her fingerprints to be taken and the police obtained a magistrates' order authorising the taking thereof, under s. 40 (2) of the 1952 Act. The appellant, who was still on bail, was taken to the police station where she resisted attempts forcibly to take her fingerprints and during the struggle bit two police officers. She was later convicted of assaulting the officers, dangerous driving and causing criminal damage. *Held,* quashing all convictions, that (1) the officers were acting unlawfully in attempting to take fingerprints at the station and there was no evidence that the appellant had used more than reasonable force in resisting; (2) the offence of dangerous driving was totally inappropriate for such a " pettifogging incident; " and (3) the jury may have been influenced upon the criminal damage count by all the inadmissible evidence adduced as to the appellant's subsequent conduct.

R. v. JONES (YVONNE) [1978] R.T.R. 137, C.A.

480. —— identification—driver of car—whether man or woman driving
The requirement to give detailed directions to a jury as to the dangers of identification evidence is of minimal application in a driving case where the defence is that the defendant was not the driver but a passenger in a car driven by a woman.

At his trial for driving with excess alcohol the defendant contended that he was a passenger in the car and that his female companion was the driver. After his conviction the defendant appealed complaining, inter alia, of the judge's failure to direct the jury in accordance with R. v. Turnbull [1976] C.L.Y. 451. Held, dismissing the appeal, that upon its facts this was not a case to which R. v. Turnbull applied.

R. v. HEWETT [1978] R.T.R. 174, C.A.

481. —— —— no warning given
The Court of Appeal has quashed a conviction because the jury were not given the proper warning about identification evidence, notwithstanding that the prosecution evidence was " circumstantially strong." (R. v. Turnbull [1976] C.L.Y. 451 applied): R. v. RAPHAEL, The Times, October 13, 1978, C.A.

482. —— —— relevance of false alibi
A jury may only rely on a false alibi as supporting an identification if they are satisfied that the sole reason for the fabrication was to deceive them on the issue of identification.

The appellant was convicted on the identification evidence of his victim. The evidence of identification had strengths, but also weaknesses which did not emerge with clarity in the summing up. One particular defect was the omission of the judge to tell the jury in the summing-up that a false alibi could only support an identification if the jury were satisfied that it was solely to mislead them on that issue that the alibi was presented. Held, allowing the appeal, that the judge must clearly warn the jury of the dangers of convicting on unsupported identification evidence. (R. v. Turnbull [1976] C.L.Y. 451 considered.)

R. v. KEANE (1977) 65 Cr.App.R. 247, C.A.

483. —— —— single witness giving evidence of identification before trial—admissibility—jury directed that corroboration necessary
[Scot.] D was charged with assault on M. At an identification parade, M and two others identified D as the attacker, though they failed to identify him in court. A police sergeant gave evidence of their identification at the parade. D claimed the sergeant was not competent to do so, and consequently such evidence was inadmissible. Held, as the jury had been directed that the sergeant's evidence required corroboration of a circumstantial kind, rather than that the evidence of the sergeant and the three witnesses was sufficient in law, the evidence was admissible and the sergeant was competent: BENNETT v. H.M. ADVOCATE, 1976 J.C. 1, High Ct. of Justiciary.

484. —— —— witness informed defendant had record
On a charge of shoplifting the prosecution case was based on the evidence of a store detective. Notice of alibi had been served. The officer in charge of the case handed to defence counsel at court the antecedent form saying " I've just added another one to the previous convictions " in such circumstances that the store detective may have heard the comment. Held, that since the case relied upon identification evidence there may be an element of prejudice if the witness had any knowledge of the defendant's previous convictions. Although the identification was strong and might stand alone the prosecution were invited to offer no evidence and a verdict of not guilty was directed: R. v. WADE [1978] Crim.L.R. 378, Canterbury Crown Ct.

485. —— imputation on character of prosecution witness—cross-examination on previous convictions

[Criminal Evidence Act 1898 (c. 36), s. 1, proviso (f) (ii).]

It is for the trial judge to use his discretion on the facts of the case as to where to draw the line between a mere denial of the prosecution case and allegations that constitute an imputation on character.

T denied making certain admissions to police and parts of other interviews, his counsel merely suggesting the police were mistaken. In cross-examination he agreed with the suggestion that he was saying that the police evidence was a complete invention. The judge allowed cross-examination about his previous convictions. On appeal on the grounds that this discretion was wrongly exercised, *held*, dismissing the appeal, that a distinction must be drawn between merely denying the evidence of a prosecution witness and making a specific allegation of serious impropriety. It is for the trial judge to decide where to draw the line, and his discretion would only be interfered with on very limited grounds. (*R.* v. *Cook* [1959] C.L.Y. 674, and *Selvey* v. *D.P.P.* [1968] C.L.Y. 687 considered and applied.)

R. v. TANNER (1977) 66 Cr.App.R. 56, C.A.

486. —— medical evidence—whether jury must accept it

A jury must act on medical evidence, and where there is no evidence that disputes it, they must accept it.

At B's trial three doctors were called to substantiate B's plea of diminished responsibility, and all agreed that he was suffering from an abnormality of mind induced by disease. No evidence was called in rebuttal. The jury rejected the evidence and convicted of murder. On appeal, *held*, allowing the appeal, that though juries are not bound by what medical witnesses say, they must act on evidence, and if there is nothing that throws doubt on that evidence, they must accept it. (*R.* v. *Matheson* [1958] C.L.Y. 754 applied.)

R. v. BAILEY (1977) 66 Cr.App.R. 31 (Note), C.A.

487. —— night poaching—proof of time of sunset—whether almanac admissible

[Night Poaching Act 1828 (c. 69), s. 2.] D was charged with assaulting a gamekeeper, contrary to the 1828 Act, s. 2. It was necessary for the prosecution to prove the assault to have taken place at night, night being defined as commencing one hour after sunset. *Held*, that an almanac was not admissible evidence of the time of sunset. The prosecution therefore called an astronomer: R. v. CRUSH [1978] Crim.L.R. 357, Croydon Crown Ct.

488. —— previous convictions—cross-examination of co-defendant—whether co-accused " charged with same offence "

[Criminal Evidence Act 1898 (c. 36), s. 1 (f) (iii).]

For the purposes of cross-examining as to a co-accused's previous convictions, co-accuseds are only " charged with the same offence " within s. 1 (f) (iii) of the Criminal Evidence Act 1898 offence, if they are alleged to have been pursuing the same enterprise, not where the essence of the case is that each has committed an offence against the other.

There was a fight between A and B. In the result, A was charged with assault occasioning actual bodily harm against B, and B with the malicious wounding of A. A sought to cross-examine B as to his previous convictions on the ground that both were charged with the same offence, under s. 1 (f) (iii) of the Criminal Evidence Act 1898. Leave was refused, and A was convicted of common assault. On appeal, *held*, dismissing the appeal, that where A and B were charged with offences against each other, s. 1 (f) (iii) was inapplicable. (*R.* v. *Russell* [1970] C.L.Y. 441 distinguished.)

R. v. ROCKMAN (1978) 67 Cr.App.R. 171, C.A.

489. —— —— imputation on character of prosecution witness

[Criminal Evidence Act 1898, s. 1 (f).] M assaulted L in a café. In chief, L admitted making to take off his coat as if to start a fight, and that he had been drinking heavily. He denied a suggestion, put to him in cross-examination, that he had also been swearing. The trial judge allowed cross-examination of M as to his previous convictions on the basis that the defence had resulted in imputations of bad character against L. *Held*, allowing M's appeal against conviction, that allegations of intoxication or swearing did not amount to the kind of imputations of character upon which s. 1 (f) was based: R. v. McLEAN [1978] Crim.L.R. 430, C.A.

490. —— —— judge's discretion

[Criminal Evidence Act 1898 (c. 36), s. 1 (f) (ii).] On defendant's trial for shoplifting, his defence involved imputations on the character of prosecution witnesses. At the time of the offence, the defendant bore a good character, but before his trial he had pleaded guilty to other offences of dishonesty. The judge permitted cross-examination on these matters under s. 1 (f) (ii) of the Criminal Evidence Act 1898. Held, that the judge had appreciated that the matter was one of discretion and there was material on which he was entitled to exercise his discretion in the way he did: the defendant's appeal against conviction would be dismissed: R. v. COLTRESS, The Times, October 27, 1978, C.A.

491. —— —— whether defendant being proceeded against for any offence other than handling

[Theft Act 1968 (c. 60), s. 27 (3).] A was charged in an indictment with counts of conspiracy to defraud and handling. The judge allowed an application for severance of the indictment and the handling counts were then tried alone. A opposed an application to adduce evidence under s. 27 (3) of the 1968 Act of three convictions of handling stolen goods, made within the five years preceding the date of the offence charged. Held, allowing proof of the previous convictions, that A was not a person " being proceeded against for any offence other than handling stolen goods." The phrase " is being proceeded against " indicates the proceedings before the court. Accordingly, the notice of intention to prove the convictions was valid: R. v. ANDERSON [1978] Crim.L.R. 223, Newcastle-upon-Tyne Crown Ct.

492. —— privilege—written communication between counsel and client—extent of privilege

A note from a defendant to his counsel is not privileged against being used by prosecution counsel if it comes into his possession by whatever means.

D was accused of handling a stolen stereo set. X identified it as his by its having a loose button. D denied that it had ever been loose, and demonstrated that it was not. However, during an adjournment, a representative of the prosecuting solicitors picked up from the floor of the court a note from D to his counsel, saying that the button had been loose and that he had stuck it on with Airfix. Counsel for the Crown put the note to D in cross-examination and asked him if he still stuck to his previous answer. He did not. He was convicted. Held, dismissing his appeal, that D had convicted himself from his own mouth. There was no breach of natural justice—natural justice demanded D's exposure. Counsel for the Crown's behaviour was perfectly proper, and no irregularities, material or otherwise, had occurred. (Butler v. Board of Trade [1970] C.L.Y. 1039, R. v. Yousry (1925) 11 Cr.App.R. 13, dictum of Lord Goddard C.J. in Kuruma, Son of Kanui v. R. [1955] C.L.Y. 573 and of Winn J. in R. v. Rice [1963] C.L.Y. 677 applied; R. v. Smith (Winston) [1975] C.L.Y. 741 distinguished.)

R. v. TOMPKINS (1978) 67 Cr.App.R. 181, C.A.

493. —— records of a business—bill of lading and cargo manifest

[Criminal Evidence Act 1965 (c. 20), s. 1 (1).]

A single document setting out the history of one transaction may be a " record " within s. 1 (1) of the Act although it is no more permanent than commercial necessity demands.

J and S ran a transport business. They were charged with conspiracy to steal from containers. One of the containers broken into had been packed in Hong Kong and shipped to Southampton. The prosecution put in evidence under s. 1 (1) of the Act a bill of lading and a cargo manifest, both made out in Hong Kong, being the " record " of a trade or business made by a person beyond the seas, for the purpose of proving the content of the container. J and S were convicted and appealed on the ground, inter alia, that the documents were not a " record " within the meaning of the subsection.

Held, dismissing the appeal, that s. 1 (1) of the Act did not mention terri-
toriality and did not require that the document was compiled in this country
and since the documents contained a carefully compiled history of the transaction for the information of the recipient they were records within the
meaning of the subsection. (Dictum of Lord Parker C.J. in *R.* v. *Gwilliam*
[1968] C.L.Y. 3427 not followed.)

R. *v.* JONES (BENJAMIN) [1978] 1 W.L.R. 195, C.A.

494. ―― ―― medical records

[Criminal Evidence Act 1965 (c. 20), s. 1 (1) (4).]

Medical records of a National Health Service hospital are not " business
records " within the meaning of s. 1 of the Criminal Evidence Act 1965.

At the appellant's trial, the prosecution were permitted to produce in
evidence medical records of a health service hospital in order to rebut the
appellant's allegation that alleged admissions attributed to him had been obtained
by the use of physical violence by the police. The appellant appealed against
his subsequent conviction. *Held,* allowing the appeal, that " business records "
within the meaning of the 1965 Act were records relating to some commercial
function and that since a National Health Service hospital was not a commercial organisation, the records were improperly admitted in evidence. (*Town
Investments* v. *Department of the Environment* [1977] C.L.Y. 2516, *Rolls* v.
Miller (1884) 27 Ch.D. 71 and *Bramwell* v. *Lacey* (1879) 10 Ch.D. 691
distinguished.)

R. *v.* CRAYDEN [1978] 1 W.L.R. 604, C.A.

495. ―― similar fact

The mere speculative possibility that witnesses who corroborate each other
may have put their heads together to give false evidence is insufficient grounds
for severance of an indictment.

D was charged with buggery and indecency with five boys aged 14 and 15,
having accosted each of them in amusement arcades. D applied to sever the
indictment in relation to each boy, on the grounds of no striking similarities,
and that the boys knew one another and there was a real chance of a false
story having been concocted. The judge refused the application, and D was
convicted on all counts. On appeal by D, *held,* dismissing the appeal, that
there were striking similarities, and the evidence of each boy was admissible
to corroborate the other; there was no more than a speculative possibility
that they had put their heads together, which was not a ground for severance.
(*D.P.P.* v. *Kilbourne* [1973] C.L.Y. 524 applied; *Selvey* v. *D.P.P.* [1968] C.L.Y.
687 and *Boardman* v. *D.P.P.* [1974] C.L.Y. 753 considered.)

R. *v.* JOHANSSEN (1977) 65 Cr.App.R. 101, C.A.

496. ―― ―― admissibility

[Criminal Evidence Act 1898 (c. 36), s. 1 (*f*).] N and three others were
charged with affray. N was also charged with wounding with intent. N had
stabbed another with a knife. His defence was that he had first seen the knife
on the ground when he was fighting and had then seized it and used it in self-
defence. The trial judge allowed counsel for a co-accused to ask a police
officer questions concerning N's previous convictions of having an offensive
weapon, once a knife and once a broken bottle. *Held,* allowing N's appeal
against conviction of affray and malicious wounding, that s. 1 (*f*) of the 1898
Act was not relevant, and the evidence of N's previous convictions was clearly
inadmissible: R. *v.* NIGHTINGALE [1977] Crim.L.R. 744, C.A.

497. ―― ―― homosexual offences with boys

Similar fact evidence should only be admitted as corroboration of accomplices in homosexual cases if it shows conduct of a uniquely and strikingly
similar nature.

Four defendants were charged with a variety of homosexual offences which
had been committed at the Playland Amusement Arcade, Piccadilly Circus,
including conspiracy to procure acts of gross indecency by male persons with
themselves, living off the earnings of male prostitution, importuning in a public
place for immoral purposes, and specific offences of gross indecency. The evidence consisted first, of evidence of observation by police; secondly, of ten

youths as to acts of indecency between themselves and the accused; and thirdly, of police interviews. The judge directed the jury that in order for the boys' evidence to be corroborative of one another, there must be some striking similarity each with the other. He did not, however, give the jury any direction as to what evidence on the conspiracy they could look to as providing corroboration on the specific offences, nor did he tell them to ignore the conspiracy evidence on the specific counts. On appeal, *held*, allowing the appeals in part, that although the judge's direction as to specific counts was impeccable, the absence of direction in relation to conspiracy evidence could not be disregarded. (*Boardman* v. *D.P.P.* [1974] C.L.Y. 753 and *R.* v. *Sims* (1946) C.L.C. 2082 considered)

R. *v.* NOVAC (1977) 65 Cr.App.R. 197, C.A.

498. —— —— identity

A previous attempt at theft or deception may be admitted as similar fact evidence on a charge of subsequent theft or deception as being probative, despite any prejudicial effect it may have.

M was alleged to have bought about £20 worth of meat from each of two frozen-food shops on the same day, using a stolen Barclaycard and forging the signature. The issue was identification. The evidence was strong. The Crown adduced evidence that M loaded a trolley with about £20 worth of meat in another frozen-food shop three months earlier and had abandoned it and left when he saw he was being observed. The person who observed him together with two shop-assistants and other witnesses from the subsequent incidents identified him at trial. He was a man of striking appearance. Evidence was also allowed that a stolen Access card had been found at M's home a week after the offences and M admitted that he had been copying the signature on it. M was convicted. On appeal, *held*, dismissing the appeal, that the evidence was admissible as similar facts. (*R.* v. *Reading* [1966] C.L.Y. 2280 applied; *Boardman* v. *D.P.P.* [1974] C.L.Y. 753 considered.)

R. *v.* MUSTAFA (1976) 65 Cr.App.R. 26, C.A.

499. —— —— propensity

Evidence should not be called against an alleged rapist which goes merely to show that he has a propensity to invite strange women into his car for sexual purposes.

T was charged with raping A. A charge of raping was dismissed at committal. At the trial there was forensic evidence linking A and B. The judge gave leave for B to be called to give similar fact evidence. B had failed to identify T on an identification parade. At trial, however, she unexpectedly identified T in the dock. The judge also gave leave for the prosecution to call C and D to give evidence that they had been persistently approached by a man of similar appearance to T in the same city at about the same time, and offered lifts in his car. C had taken the number of the car which coincided, except for one figure, with that of T's car. T was convicted. On appeal, *held*, allowing the appeal, that (1) the judge had wrongly failed to warn the jury of the dangers of dock identification; (2) B's evidence was of facts uniquely and strikingly similar and was prima facie admissible; (3) the evidence of C and D showed only a propensity towards a particular type of crime, which was inadmissible. (Dictum of Salmon L.J. in *Boardman* v. *D.P.P.* [1974] C.L.Y. 753 applied.)

R. *v.* TRICOGLUS (1976) 65 Cr.App.R. 16, C.A.

500. —— —— sexual offences

Similar fact evidence is admissible only if it goes beyond showing a tendency to commit crimes of that particular kind, and is positively probative in regard to the crime charged.

D was charged with one offence of buggery and seven of indecent assault, in relation to six boys who lived in the same vicinity as D. D alleged that the evidence of one boy was faked. The judge therefore ruled that character was in issue, and allowed the Crown to put D's numerous previous convictions for similar offences to him. Further, Crown's case was that the various crimes alleged at the trial was evidence of similar facts in relation to one another, within the rules in *D.P.P.* v. *Boardman.* D was convicted. On appeal, *held,* allowing the appeal, that (1) although the judge had not erred in allowing evidence of D's previous bad character, the jury had not received proper guidance to treat it as going to credit only, as opposed to amounting to similar fact evidence; (2) the evidence allowed in as similar facts was not positively probative of the crime charged; it was merely the stock in trade of the seducer of small boys; in such cases, the judge should rule it out firmly if not completely satisfied of its admissibility. (*D.P.P.* v. *Boardman* [1974] C.L.Y. 753, *R.* v. *Scarrott* [1977] C.L.Y. 553 and dictum of Lord Widgery C.J. *R.* v. *Rance and Herron* [1976] C.L.Y. 461 applied.)

    R. *v.* INDER (1978) 67 Cr.App.R. 143. C.A.

501. —— spouse as victim—not a compellable prosecution witness

Where a husband is charged with inflicting injury upon his wife, the wife is a competent but not a compellable witness for the Crown.

H was charged with wounding W, his wife, with intent to do grievous bodily harm. H married W after the alleged offence, two days before his trial. At the trial, W indicated that she was unwilling to give evidence, but the judge compelled her to do so, and H was convicted. H's appeal was dismissed by the Court of Appeal. On appeal to the House of Lords, *held* (Edmund-Davies L.J. dissenting) that W was not compellable, and H's conviction could not stand. (*R.* v. *Lapworth* [1931] 1 K.B. 117 overruled; dicta in *Leach* v. *R.* [1912] A.C. 305 applied.)

HOSKYN *v.* METROPOLITAN POLICE COMMISSIONER [1978] 2 W.L.R. 695, H.L.

502. —— thefts irrelevant to defendant's guilt—purpose to explain setting of trap—summing-up

A judge allowed the prosecution to call evidence of a series of thefts from a changing room to explain the setting of a trap by police officers. L was convicted of theft from the changing room. *Held,* dismissing L's appeal, that the judge had failed and declined to explain to the jury precisely the limits of the evidence of the previous thefts but the proviso would be applied as the jury would have reached the same conclusion if properly directed: R. *v.* LARGE [1978] Crim. L.R. 222, C.A.

503. —— value to be attached to documents—accomplice's diaries

V was convicted of two offences of corruptly receiving money and one offence of conspiracy. The evidence against V was almost wholly that of accomplices, one of whom was permitted to refresh his memory from diary entries, copies of which were before the jury. *Held,* allowing V's appeals against conviction, that there was a risk that the diaries had achieved an unwarranted importance. The trial judge referred to them as " the most important documents in the case " and " powerful evidence pointing to a corrupt relationship." Although the direction on corroboration was impeccable, the jury should have been told of the diaries' very limited value, they being no more than a means for the witness to give accurate dates, chapter and verse for the incidents about which he gave evidence which required corroboration: R. *v.* VIRGO [1978] Crim.L.R. 557, C.A.

504. —— witness—called after close of defence case—for purpose of corroboration only

[Can.] In a trial for assault, the judge called a witness after the close of the defence case. The witness, who had been in court during the trial, only corroborated other prosecution witnesses' evidence, as the judge knew he would before he called him. *Held,* calling a witness in such circumstances, not to rebut ex improviso evidence but to shore up the prosecution case, was a material irregularity; the resultant conviction would therefore be quashed (*R.* v. *Liddle* (1928) 21 Cr.App.R. 3 applied): R. *v.* MORIN [1977] 6 W.W.R. 229, Saskatchewan Dist.Ct.

505. —— witness refreshing memory—notes of another policeman

[Aust.] At trial, a constable gave evidence that she had a conversation with the accused and that, shortly afterwards, she had made written notes of the conversation. A second constable, who was present at the conversation, had not made any notes of it. When called as a witness, the second constable said he could not recall the conversation accurately and in detail without refreshing his memory from the notes made by the first constable. *Held*, the second constable should not be permitted to use the notes to refresh his memory: R. *v.* SINGH (1977) 15 S.A.S.R. 591, S.Aust.Sup.Ct.

506. Extradition. See EXTRADITION.

507. False accounting—meaning of " material particular "

[Theft Act 1968 (c. 60), s. 17 (1) (*b*).]

On a charge of furnishing false information contrary to s. 17 (1) (*b*) of the Theft Act 1968, the prosecution need not show that the false " material particular " is material to an accounting purpose, so long as the document itself is for an accounting purpose.

D, a car dealer, made out a hire-purchase agreement form, which stated falsely that the purchaser had been a director of a named company for eight years. The sale was therefore financed by the finance company. D was convicted of dishonestly and with a view to gain for himself producing a document for an accounting purpose which to his knowledge was misleading or false in a material particular. D appealed, contending that the false statement had to be of a particular which was material for an accounting purpose. *Held*, dismissing the appeal, that only the document itself need be shown to be made or required for an accounting purpose.

R. *v.* MALLETT [1978] 1 W.L.R. 820, C.A.

508. False trade description. See also SALE OF GOODS.

509. —— whether mere puff—meaning of " showroom condition "

[Trade Descriptions Act 1968 (c. 29), s. 1 (1) (*b*).] D, a secondhand car dealer, advertised a 1968 car as being in " showroom condition throughout." In fact, the car had many defects. *Held*, dismissing D's appeal against conviction of supplying a car to which a false trade description was applied, contrary to s. 1 (1) (*b*) of the 1968 Act, that the words used were not " mere puff." *Obiter*: the words " showroom condition," even without " throughout," referred to the exterior, interior and mechanical condition of the vehicle: HAWKINS *v.* SMITH [1978] Crim.L.R. 578, Portsmouth Crown Ct.

510. Firearms—possession—whether antique—burden of proof. See R. *v.* BURKE, § 1476.

511. Food and drugs. See FOOD AND DRUGS.

512. Forfeiture order—when appropriate

[Powers of Criminal Courts Act 1973 (c. 62), s. 43 (1); Criminal Appeal Act 1968 (c. 19), ss. 4 (3), 11 (3).]

It is inappropriate to make a forfeiture order of a car used in an insurance swindle where the defendant is not in possession or control of the vehicle and has repaid the insurance company.

Per curiam. To increase a prison sentence because it is suspended is a misuse of the power to suspend.

T participated in a swindle of his insurance company by falsely pretending that his vehicle had been stolen. The car was not in his possession and he had repaid the insurance company. He was given a 15 month suspended sentence and ordered to forfeit the vehicle. T appealed against sentence. *Held*, allowing the appeal, that an immediate custodial sentence of nine months was appropriate, but the court was precluded by s. 4 (3) of the Criminal Appeal Act 1968 from imposing that sentence. It was inappropriate to make a forfeiture order where the car was not in T's possession and he had repaid the swindled money.

R. *v.* THOMPSON (1978) 66 Cr.App.R. 130, C.A.

513. Fugitive offenders. See EXTRADITION.

514. Going equipped to cheat—obtaining by deception—hotel waiter selling his own goods

[Theft Act 1968 (c. 60), ss. 15 and 25.]

A waiter in possession of wines and spirits, which he dishonestly intended to sell to hotel guests without revealing their true ownership, may properly be convicted of going equipped to cheat.

The defendant wine waiter was found in possession of a number of bottles of wines and spirits, which, according to an alleged confession evidently believed by the jury, he intended to sell to hotel guests without revealing that the liquor was not the hotel's property or that he was intending to keep the proceeds of sale. He was convicted of having the wine and spirits in the course of or in connection with a cheat contrary to s. 25 of the 1968 Act. *Held,* dismissing his appeal, that the defendant's guilt depended essentially upon the prosecution making out the various ingredients of the offence of obtaining property by deception and that such offence was made out since it must be assumed that no reasonably honest customer would have purchased the liquor had he known it not to belong to the hotel. (*R.* v. *Rashid* [1977] C.L.Y. 468, considered.)

R. v. DOUKAS [1978] 1 W.L.R. 372, C.A.

515. Habeas corpus—backing warrant—whether application for bona fide purposes
[Backing of Warrants (Republic of Ireland) Act 1965 (c. 45), s. 1 (1) (*a*), 2 (2).]
The court is entitled to look behind an application to ensure that it is made for a bona fide purpose, and with no ulterior motive.

L was convicted of a minor offence by a Dublin court in 1972, but failed to appear for sentence. He subsequently gave evidence for the prosecution at a murder trial, then at a retrial but refused to attend the third trial. Upon arrest in England on a warrant backed by English justices, he applied for habeas corpus. *Held,* granting the motion, that the Divisional Court was entitled to look at the purpose of an application under the Act, to ensure that it was for a bona fide purpose and not made with an ulterior motive as here, viz. the return of L to Ireland.

Re LAWLOR (1977) 66 Cr.App.R. 75, D.C.

516. Handling—knowledge or belief
S was accused of handling stolen jewellery. In directing the jury as to the ingredient of knowledge the judge said that an objective standard should be applied. *Held,* allowing S's appeal against conviction, that the test to be applied was subjective. (*Atwal* v. *Mussey* [1971] C.L.Y. 2822, *R.* v. *Grainge* [1974] C.L.Y. 639 and *R.* v. *Griffiths* [1975] C.L.Y. 595 applied): R. v. STAGG [1978] Crim.L.R. 227, C.A.

517. —— mental element—correct test
[Theft Act 1968 (c. 60), s. 22 (1).]
On a charge of handling stolen goods, the correct test is not whether, on a balance of probabilities, the defendant thought the goods were more likely stolen than not, but whether he actually believed they were stolen.

Per curiam. Where simple words are used such as " belief," it is undesirable for the judge to explain what those words mean.

In R's trial for handling, the judge directed the jury on the legal definition of " belief," indicating that belief meant that R thought it more likely than not that the goods were stolen. *Held,* on appeal, that that direction was a misdirection. It is not sufficient that a defendant believes goods are probably stolen; he must believe they are stolen as required by the section. (*R.* v. *Grainge* [1974] C.L.Y. 639 considered.)

R. v. READER (1977) 66 Cr.App.R. 33, C.A.

518. —— proof of theft—whether defendant's belief evidence
H told police that he thought that a " music centre " and a radio which he had bought for £130 and £60 from someone in a public-house were " probably bent " because they were worth £250–£300 and £100 respectively. There was no other evidence that the goods were stolen. *Held,* that there was no case for H to answer on a charge of handling stolen goods because, as no expert evidence of the true value of the goods had been adduced, the defendant's admissions could not be evidence that the goods were stolen: R. v. HACK [1978] Crim.L.R. 359, Inner London Crown Ct.

519. —— whether goods stolen—relevance of defendant's belief
O told the police he knew 17 cigarette lighters which he bought were stolen because they were worth at least five times what he had paid for them. The trial judge told the jury to ask themselves whether they agreed with O and

whether they were sure that the lighters were stolen. *Held*, dismissing O's appeal against conviction of handling stolen goods, that O's belief was irrelevant to the question of whether the lighters were stolen. However, the judge was really only saying that there was material on the admitted facts to found the conclusion that they were stolen. If necessary the proviso would be applied: R. *v*. OVERINGTON [1978] Crim.L.R. 692, C.A.

520. —— whether receipt " in course of stealing "
[Theft Act 1968 (c. 60), s. 22 (1).]
Once a dishonest appropriation has been completed, subsequent dealing with the goods will not be " in the course of stealing " within s. 22 (1) of the Theft Act 1968.

M's friend, X, was sent to prison. M therefore decided to steal all X's furniture. He offered it to A and B who went to X's house and bought it very cheaply. M, A and B went to collect the furniture in a furniture van. M was convicted of burglary, and A and B of handling the goods. They appealed on the ground that the handling was in the course of stealing, and therefore not within the ambit of s. 22 (1) of the Theft Act 1968. *Held*, dismissing the appeal, that M had assumed the rights of the owner when he had invited A and B to buy the furniture which was a dishonest appropriation amounting to theft. A and B's subsequent involvement therefore amounted to handling otherwise than in the course of stealing.
R. *v*. PITHAM; R. *v*. HEHL (1976) 65 Cr.App.R. 45, C.A.

521. Identification parades
New guidance for police on the conduct of identification parades have been issued by the Home Office, following the recommendations of the Devlin Committee. In future, all suspects will be given a leaflet describing the purpose and nature of an identification parade, their rights in respect of it and the consequences if they refuse to take part. The guidance also contains material on other matters, including the showing of photographs to witnesses, the use of Photofit and Identikit pictures, and parades involving juveniles.
HOME OFFICE CIRCULAR No. 109/1978.

522. Illegal immigration—detention order—wrong ground given—no prejudice to applicant—habeas corpus refused
[Habeas Corpus Act 1816 (c. 100), ss. 3, 4; Immigration Act 1971 (c. 77), Sched. 2, para. 16 (1) (2).]
On an application for habeas corpus, the court can inquire into the true state of the facts and determine whether good grounds for detention exist notwithstanding defects in the detention document.

X was arrested pursuant to a detention order as an illegal immigrant. Two alternative grounds for detention were specified in the detention order: " pending his further examination under the Act " and " pending the completion of arrangements for dealing with him under the Act." The second ground was the proper ground for X's detention, but the immigration officer deleted that ground by mistake. X applied for a writ of habeas corpus on the ground that the detention was invalidated by the error in the order. *Held*, (Boreham J. dissenting) refusing the application, that the court could consider whether good grounds for detention did in fact exist, and on the facts X's detention was amply justified. X had not been prejudiced by the error and the application would be dismissed. (R. *v*. *Secretary of State for the Home Department, ex p. Hussain* [1978] C.L.Y. 13 followed.)
Re SHAHID IQBAL [1978] 3 W.L.R. 884, D.C.

523. —— remaining after permit's expiry—indictment—within two dates
[Immigration Act 1971 (c. 77), s. 24 (1) (*b*) (i).] The appellant, a non-patrial, was convicted on an indictment charging that " on a day between September 30, 1976 and February 18, 1977 " he knowingly remained in the U.K. beyond the time limited by his leave. The trial judge refused an application to quash. *Held*, on appeal, the indictment was not defective, notwithstanding that the offence is not a continuing one (*Gurdev Singh* v. *The Queen* [1973] C.L.Y. 9 referred to.) The prosecution had proved that the material date lay within the two dates in the indictment: R. *v*. TZANATOS, March 17, 1978, C.A. (*Ex rel. R. W. Spon-Smith, Esq., Barrister.*)

524. —— —— **meaning of " knowingly "**

[Immigration Act 1971 (c. 77), s. 24 (1) (*b*) (i).] B was charged with knowingly remaining in the U.K. after expiry of his permit, contrary to s. 24 (1) (*b*) (i) of the 1971 Act. His defence was that he was so upset by news of his mother's death in Nigeria that at the relevant time he did not know he was in the U.K. after his permit's expiry. *Held*, dismissing B's appeal against conviction, that (i) the trial judge should not have ruled that the defence was not available in law. This should be done only very rarely; (ii) the proviso would be applied, as a conviction was inevitable since in law a person could not be said not to have " known " of something if he had the capacity for reviving the recollection of it from his memory: R. *v.* BELLO [1978] Crim.L.R. 551, C.A.

525. Indictment—effect of charging wrong statute

It is an absolute requirement that, where a statutory offence is charged, the correct statute shall be named in the indictment, and if the wrong one is named, the subsequent proceedings are a nullity.

D was convicted before Judge Solomon on July 18, 1973, of causing death by dangerous driving contrary to s. 2 (1) of the Road Traffic Act 1960. At the time, that section of that Act no longer existed, having been repealed and replaced by s. 1 (1) of the Road Traffic Act 1972. On appeal by D, *held*, allowing the appeal, that the indictment had to charge the correct statute. The wrong statute had been charged, and the mere fact that it had been repealed and re-enacted in a later statute could not save the subsequent proceedings from being a nullity. (*R. v. Taylor* (1924) 18 Cr.App.R. 105, and dictum of Lord Goddard C.J. in *Meek* v. *Powell* [1952] C.L.Y. 2101 applied.)

R. *v.* CROOK (1977) 65 Cr.App.R. 66, C.A. (Note).

526. —— **failure to name statute in statement of offence**

Where the statement of offence in a count in an indictment fails to specify the relevant statute, the indictment is defective, but not to the extent of rendering the proceedings a nullity.

Per curiam: The Court of Appeal has no power to amend an indictment on appeal.

D was charged with possessing an offensive weapon. The statement of offence failed to specify that the offence was in contravention of s. 1 (1) of the Prevention of Crime Act 1952. At the end of the trial D moved to arrest judgment on the ground that due to the defect, the proceedings were a nullity. The judge refused this motion, did not allow an amendment and sentenced D. On appeal by D, *held*, that the indictment was not a nullity, but merely defective, and there were no grounds on that basis for quashing the conviction. *R.* v. *Crook* was wrongly decided. (Dicta of Lord Goddard C.J. in *Meek* v. *Powell* [1952] C.L.Y. 2101, and of Lord Diplock in *D.P.P.* v. *Merriman* [1972] C.L.Y. 664 considered; *R.* v. *McVitie* [1960] C.L.Y. 1250 applied; *R.* v. *Crook* [1978] C.L.Y. 525 disapproved.)

R. *v.* NELSON (1977) 65 Cr.App.R. 119, C.A.

527. —— **false statutory declaration charged as perjury—whether indictment defective—proviso**

[Perjury Act (c. 6), ss. 1 (1), 5 (*a*); Criminal Justice Act 1967 (c. 80), s. 24 (3); Indictment Rules 1971 (S.I. 1971 No. 1253), rr. 5, 6.]

An indictment referring to the correct section of the Perjury Act 1911, with a correct statement of the particulars of offence, but incorrectly referring to the offence as perjury instead of making a false declaration not on oath, is defective; but a conviction on that defective indictment need not be quashed where there has been no slightest miscarriage of justice.

P was convicted on various road traffic summons in his absence. He later made a statutory declaration that he had never received the summons. He was charged with an offence of perjury, contrary to s. 5 (*a*) of the Perjury Act, the particulars of which were that he had made a false statement in a statutory declaration. After conviction for perjury, it became clear that there had been a failure to comply with r. 5 of the Indictment Rules 1971, in that the wrong offence had been alleged. On appeal, *held,* dismissing the appeal, that though there had been a material irregularity in that r. 5 had not been complied with, it was clear that r. 6 had, and that as there had not been the slightest miscarriage of justice the proviso would be applied. (*R.* v. *McVitie* [1960] C.L.Y. 1250 and *R.* v. *Nelson* [1978] C.L.Y. 526 considered.)

R. *v.* Power (1977) 66 Cr.App.R. 159, C.A.

528. —— greater offence includes only the lesser—authority to appeal

[Offences against the Person Act 1861 (c. 100), s. 18; Criminal Law Act 1967 (c. 58), s. 6 (3).]

Solicitors have no implied authority to appeal against a court order. Neither common assault nor unlawful wounding are necessarily incorporated in the offence of causing grievous bodily harm.

M and H, charged with causing grievous bodily harm were convicted, one of common assault, other of unlawful wounding. A co-defendant, similarly charged, was convicted of common assault. On application for leave to appeal, *held* that (1) as solicitors for the co-defendant were without express instructions to appeal they had no implied authority to do so; but (2) that the applications, and the appeals, of M and H would be allowed. The power of the court to accept a verdict for a lesser offence when a greater is charged can be exercised only if the particulars of the lesser offence are necessarily comprised in the greater. In the case of common assault and unlawful wounding then, if the charge is causing grievous bodily harm this is not the case.

R. *v.* McCready; R. *v.* Hurd [1978] 1 W.L.R. 1376, C.A.

529. —— separate counts—" same offence "—accused giving evidence against co-accused

[Criminal Evidence Act 1898 (c. 36), s. 1 (*f*) (iii).]

For offences to be regarded as " the same offence " for the purposes of the Criminal Evidence Act 1898, they must be the same in all material respects, including the time at which they were committed.

H was charged in one count, and L in another, with causing death by dangerous driving. H gave evidence against L, L was acquitted, and H convicted after L's application to cross-examine him as to his character had succeeded. *Held*, allowing H's appeal from the dismissal of his appeal by the Court of Appeal, that for the offences charged to be the same, for the purposes of the Criminal Evidence Act 1898, they must be the same in all material respects as if there was an interval of time between them, no matter how short, they could not be said to be " the same." Where defendants are separately charged, the test of whether they are charged with the same offence is to ask whether they could have been jointly charged with it. Here they could not.

R. *v.* Hills [1978] 3 W.L.R. 423, H.L.

530. Insanity—fitness to plead—direction to jury

[Criminal Procedure (Insanity) Act 1964 (c. 84), s. 4 (4).]

Where fitness to plead is an issue, the jury must be directed as to the matters upon which to base their findings.

B was found unfit to plead by a jury which had heard medical evidence that B was a paranoid schizophrenic, and had heard B himself give evidence. The judge did not give directions to the jury as to the matters which they should consider. *Held*, allowing the appeal, the trial judge must give clear directions to the jury that they must consider a defendant's ability to challenge jurors, to instruct counsel, to understand the evidence and give evidence himself. A state of high abnormality is not necessarily conclusive of unfitness. (*R.* v. *Pritchard* (1836) 7 C. & P. 303; and *R.* v. *Robertson* [1968] C.L.Y. 758 applied.)

R. *v.* Berry (1977) 66 Cr.App.R. 156, C.A.

531. Judges' Rules

The Home Secretary, with the agreement of the Lord Chief Justice, has reissued the Judges' Rules, which guide the police on questioning members of the public, together with the related Administrative Directions to the police, amended to take account of relevant Home Office circulars issued since 1964. The Rules and Directions are available from HMSO (Home Office Circular No. 89/1978) [30p].

532. —— accused's right to telephone solicitor

At K's trial for burglary the only evidence was alleged admissions during an interview. K claimed to have refused to answer questions because his requests to telephone a certain solicitor were denied. The interviewing officer denied the alleged requests but admitted not telling K that he could telephone a solicitor before answering questions. *Held*, that the Judges' Rules 1964, Appendix B, para. 7, placed no obligation on a police officer to inform a person before questioning him about an offence that he may first speak to a solicitor of his choice unless the person has first raised the matter: R. *v.* KING (STEPHEN) [1978] Crim.L.R. 632, Inner London Crown Ct.

533. Juries. See JURIES.

534. Kidnapping—carrying away—extent of

The offence of kidnapping is made out if there is some carrying away of the victim albeit a relatively short distance and not to the kidnapper's intended destination.

The defendant approached the victim and her boyfriend in the street and by falsely pretending to be a policeman looking for drugs persuaded her to accompany him, he having sent the boyfriend away. Believing the defendant's claim, the victim walked about 100 yards with the defendant to a car which he told her to get into. The boyfriend and others returned and removed the girl from the car, whereupon the defendant drove off. He appealed against his conviction for kidnapping on the grounds that it had not been proved that he had carried the girl to his intended destination. *Held*, dismissing the appeal, that all that was required to prove the offence was deprivation of liberty and the carrying away of the victim to a place he would not otherwise wish to be. (*R.* v. *Reid* [1972] C.L.Y. 1679 applied.)

R. *v.* WELLARD [1978] 1 W.L.R. 921, C.A.

535. Legal aid

LEGAL AID IN CRIMINAL PROCEEDINGS (ASSESSMENT OF RESOURCES) REGULATIONS 1978 (No. 30) [25p], made under the Legal Aid Act 1974 (c. 4), s. 34; operative on March 1, 1978; provide for the assessment of the resources of any person concerned when a court is considering whether to make a legal aid order in criminal proceedings or a contribution order under ss. 28 and 32, respectively, of the 1974 Act.

536. —— taxation

[Legal Aid in Criminal Proceedings (Fees and Expenses) Regulations 1968 (S.I. 1968 No. 1230), regs. 7 (6) (as substituted by the Legal Aid in Criminal Proceedings (Fees and Expenses) (Amendment) Regulations 1977 (S.I. 1977 No. 875), s. 10 (4)).]

On the true construction of reg. 7 (6) of the Legal Aid in Criminal Proceedings Regulations 1968, exceptional circumstances which will justify taxation of solicitors' or counsels' fees above the limitations imposed by the regulations must be exceptional to the particular case, and do not include inflation.

Three firms of solicitors appealed against the review of the taxing master of the review of the taxing authority of assessments made by the taxing authority of the fees and expenses payable to the firms of solicitors in respect of work done in criminal proceedings. All the stages of taxation had been completed, and the appeal had come on for hearing, but not been heard by June 20, 1977, when the Legal Aid in Criminal Proceedings (Fees and Expenses) (Amendment) Regulations 1977 came into force. Those regulations amended reg. 7 (6) of the 1968 regulations, so that the limitation on sums payable was not applicable where the nature, importance, complexity or difficulty of the work done was such that the sums payable would not provide fair remuneration. *Held*, (1) the appeal was to be determined as if all of it had been heard after June 20, but the court could not give effect to reg. 7 (6) as amended, since the review had to be decided on the representations put forward to the taxing authority at the commencement of the taxation, and the court's powers on appeal was the same as those of the taxing authority; (2) on the true construction of the original reg. 7 (6), exceptional circumstances allowing payment beyond the limitation could not include inflation; (3) the 1972 guidelines did not have statutory force, and if inflation prevented the sums payable thereunder less than a fair remuneration, the taxing authority could remunerate by reference to the 1968 regulations; (4) in relation to travelling time, a reduction of a third was not obligatory. The matter should be decided by reference to all the circumstances; (5) if the case in court justified a partner or senior person being present, the fee should reflect that fact, though it might not be the same as that allowed for preparatory work; (6) there was no rule that charges allowable in criminal proceedings should be less than in other types of work. (Dicta of Pollock C.B. in *Wright* v. *Hale* (1860) 6 H. & N. at 230, and of Lord Wright in *New Brunswick Railway Co.* v. *British and French Trust Corp.* [1938] 4 All E.R. at 763, applied.)

R. *v.* DUNWOODIE [1978] 1 All E.R. 923, Slynn J.

537. Magisterial law. See MAGISTERIAL LAW.

538. Manslaughter—criminal negligence—test to be applied

[Aus.] N appealed against his conviction for manslaughter. He had burned a woman to death whilst setting fire to himself. *Held,* allowing the appeal, that in order to establish manslaughter by criminal negligence, the prosecution must establish that the act which caused the death was done by the accused consciously and voluntarily, and although without any intention of causing death or grievous bodily harm, in circumstances which involved such a great falling short of the standard of care which a reasonable man would have exercised, and such a high risk that death or grievous bodily harm would follow, that the doing of the act merited criminal punishment. (*D.P.P.* v. *Newbury* [1976] C.L.Y. 496, applied): NYDAM *v.* R. [1977] V.R. 430, Sup.Ct. of Victoria.

539. Mens rea—meaning of " evade "—breach of export and import controls. See R. *v.* HURFORD-JONES, § 606.

540. Misuse of drugs

The Home Office has published statistics of the misuse of drugs in the United Kingdom during 1977. These include, inter alia, figures of those found guilty of offences involving controlled drugs, offences of unlawful import and export, and numbers of addicts in the United Kingdom notified to the Home Office.

541. —— cannabis—conspiracy to supply

Defendant, charged with conspiracy to supply cannabis, gave evidence that she only discovered the nature of her co-accused's activity after she had been helping him for some time; thereafter she gave no further help, although she admitted that she would have done so had the occasion arisen. The jury were directed that even on her own version she was guilty of conspiracy. *Held,* that her conviction must be quashed: R. *v.* SCOTT, *The Times,* July 4, 1978, C.A.

542. —— —— " knowingly concerned in the management of premises "

[Misuse of Drugs Act 1971 (c. 38), s. 8.]

A person can be concerned in the " management of premises " even if he has no legal title to be on them.

The appellants, who were squatters or trespassers in a building, ran a card school there. Cannabis was found on a man in the house when they were present, and they were convicted of " being concerned in the management of premises " in that they knowingly permitted cannabis to be smoked thereon. *Held,* dismissing their appeal, that they could be so concerned although they had no legal right to be there.

R. *v.* JOSEPHS (1977) 65 Cr.App.R. 253, C.A.

542a. —— forfeiture of money—validity of forfeiture order

[Misuse of Drugs Act 1971 (c. 38), s. 27; Courts Act 1971 (c. 23), s. 11.]

A forfeiture order made under s. 27 of the Misuse of Drugs Act 1971 is not a sentence or other order made within s. 11 of the Courts Act 1971 and accordingly it can be made at any time after sentence.

The appellant pleaded guilty to being knowingly concerned in a fraudulent evasion of the prohibition on the importation of cocaine. More than three months after being sentenced, a forfeiture order was made for moneys found upon her on her arrest. *Held,* dismissing the appeal, an order forfeiting a drug smuggler's money made under s. 27 of the Misuse of Drugs Act 1971 is not a sentence or other order made by the Crown Court within s. 11 of the Courts Act 1971 and accordingly it can be made at any time after sentence.

R. *v.* MENOCAL [1978] 3 W.L.R. 602, C.A.

543. —— intention to supply

[Misuse of Drugs Act 1971 (c. 38), s. 5 (3).] K gave evidence that it was his habit, when friends visited him, to make a " reefer " cigarette from his own supply of herbal cannabis, to smoke some of it and then pass it on to his friends. Expert evidence was given that such practice was routine when persons smoked cannabis together. K was being tried for possessing cannabis with intent to supply it to another, contrary to s. 5 (3) of the 1971 Act. *Held,* that (1) s. 5 (3) required a real intent to supply, a willingness to do what is referred to and a real likelihood that this will be done; (2) the control over a cigarette exercised by an individual within a circle of smokers as described by K was not such that there was a " supply " by K within s. 5 (3): R. *v.* KING [1978] Crim.L.R. 228, Maidstone Crown Ct.

544. —— offer to supply—extent of offence

[Misuse of Drugs Act 1971 (c. 38), s. 4 (3) (*c*).] S. 4 (3) (*c*) of the Misuse of Drugs Act 1971, which prohibits being concerned in the making to another of an offer to supply a controlled drug, is widely drawn and includes those who make an arrangement with a third party to go out and tout for business: R. *v.* BLAKE; R. *v.* O'CONNOR, *The Times,* May 4, 1978, C.A.

545. —— possession—cannabis—fruiting or flowering tops—difficulty of extracting resin

[Misuse of Drugs Act 1971 (c. 38), s. 37 (1).] The fruiting or flowering tops of the cannabis plant are " cannabis " within s. 37 (1) of the Misuse of Drugs Act 1971 if they contain resin, even if the resin can only be extracted from them with difficulty. (*R. v. Mitchell* [1977] C.L.Y. 596 distinguished): R. *v.* MALCOLM, *The Times,* May 6, 1978, C.A.

546. —— —— —— minute quantities

[Misuse of Drugs Act 1971 (c. 38), s. 5 (2).]

A conviction for possession of a drug will not be justified where the quantity is so minute that it is unusable in any manner intended to be prohibited by the Misuse of Drugs Act 1971.

Per curiam: It was only rarely that such evidence alone would justify the prosecution bringing a charge of possession of a greater quantity at an earlier time.

D admitted to having been in possession of a roach end and a wooden box which was found, by scraping, to contain two milligrammes of cannabis resin. The roach end was found on analysis to contain not less than twenty microgrammes of cannabis resin. Neither quantity could have been used in any manner intended to be prohibited by the misuse of drugs legislation. A was convicted. On appeal by D, *held,* allowing the appeal, that D had not been shown to be in unlawful possession of cannabis resin, because the amount was too small to be usable in any manner which the Misuse of Drugs Act 1971 was designed to prohibit. (*Bocking* v. *Roberts* [1973] C.L.Y. 513 explained; *R.* v. *Worsell* [1969] C.L.Y. 2212 and *R.* v. *Graham (Christopher)* [1969] C.L.Y. 2213 considered.)

R. *v.* CARVER [1978] 2 W.L.R. 872, C.A.

547. —— —— —— —— separate pieces—whether two offences

Evidence indicated that two pieces of cannabis resin of 0.011 and 0.083 grams respectively had been found separately in the communal living-room where the defendants and another lived. *Held,* that there was no case to answer on charges of possessing and supplying cannabis resin since there was no evidence that the defendants were in possession of a " usable quantity." In any event the counts were bad for duplicity since it was not permissible for the Crown to add the two amounts together in the same count: R. *v.* BAYLISS AND OLIVER [1978] Crim.L.R. 361, Coventry Crown Ct.

548. —— —— **cannabis leaves and stalk**

[Misuse of Drugs Act 1971 (c. 38), s. 37 (1), Sched. 2, Pt. IV.]

Possession of cannabis leaves and stalk does not amount to possession of cannabis, of cannabis resin, or of a cannabinol derivative.

D admitted possession of cannabis leaves and stalk. He was convicted of unlawful possession of cannabis, and charges of possession of cannabis resin and of a cannabinol derivative were directed to lie on the file. D's conviction for possession of cannabis was quashed by the Court of Appeal, on the ground that leaves and stalk were not cannabis. D was then tried again for unlawful possession of a cannabinol derivative, and, on the judge's ruling, pleaded guilty. On appeal by D, the Court of Appeal held that D was in possession of vegetable matter containing a cannabinol derivative, namely, tetrahydrocannabinol, and that he was therefore guilty of the offence. On the Attorney-General's reference, the court held that D had not committed the offence of possession of cannabis resin within the meaning of s. 37 (1) of the Misuse of Drugs Act 1971. On appeal by D to the House of Lords, *held,* allowing the appeal, that possession of naturally occurring leaf and stalk of which the cannabinol derivative was an unseparated constituent could not be charged as possession of a " cannabinol derivative."

D.P.P. *v.* GOODCHILD [1978] 1 W.L.R. 578, H.L.

549. —— —— **cannabis resin—minute quantity**

Police officers found three reefer ends on the floor of H's van. He admitted they were his, and two contained at least 20 micrograms of resin and the other 1 milligram. 20 micrograms would be invisible. Burning of any part of a cannabis plant would leave invisible traces of resin. *Held,* there was no case of possession of cannabis resin on the day of finding of the reefers for H to answer, as the prosecution had not adduced evidence that H knew the reefers still contained cannabis. Furthermore, the principle of de minimis might be applicable: R. *v.* HIEOROWSKI [1978] Crim.L.R. 563, Lancaster Crown Ct.

550. —— —— **knowledge—burden of proof**

[Misuse of Drugs Act 1971 (c. 38), ss. 5 (1), 28.]

For the purposes of s. 5 (1) of the Misuse of Drugs Act 1971, proof of possession of a drug entails proof of knowledge, and the onus remains upon the prosecution to show this.

D was found by police asleep in his car. When his car was searched, in the driver's door pocket there was found a reefer which contained 200 mg. of cannabis resin. D claimed that it was not his. He was convicted of possession of a controlled drug, contrary to s. 5 (1) of the Misuse of Drugs Act 1971. The judge directed the jury that if the prosecution had proved possession beyond reasonable doubt, then the defendant could avail himself of a defence under s. 28 (1) of the Act by proving on a balance of probabilities that he did not know it was there, and that it was a controlled drug. On appeal by D, *held,* allowing the appeal, that knowledge of the presence of the thing in question was an essential prerequisite to possession and the usual burden was on the prosecution to prove it. (*Warner* v. *Metropolitan Police Commissioner* [1968] C.L.Y. 2439 applied; dictum of MacKenna J. in R. v. *Wright* [1976] C.L.Y. 509, approved.)

R. *v.* ASHTON-RICKHARDT (1977) 65 Cr.App.R. 67, C.A.

551. —— —— **uncertain form of cannabis**

[Misuse of Drugs Act 1971 (c. 38), s. 5 (1).] Pieces of brass which together formed a pipe and contained at least 20 microgrammes of cannabis as debris were found in D's flat. On D's appeal to the Crown Court against conviction of possessing cannabis resin, it was found that the 20 microgrammes were the debris of a larger amount of cannabis resin or herbal cannabis. *Held,* allowing D's appeal, that as the Crown Court could not decide whether D had possessed cannabis resin or herbal cannabis, it could not be said that the case against D, as charged, had been proved: MUIR *v.* SMITH [1978] Crim.L.R. 293, D.C.

552. —— —— **urine sample taken without caution—admissibility**

On a possession of drugs charge, where a urine sample is taken without caution, the admissibility of the analysis of that sample is for the discretion of the trial judge on the facts of the case.

B pleaded guilty to two counts of possession of amphetamines after the judge ruled admissible evidence of the analysis of a urine sample taken from him. B was " required " to provide the sample and there was some doubt about having been cautioned. On appeal, *held,* dismissing the appeal, that the admissibility of such evidence is a matter for the discretion of the trial judge on the particular facts of the case. No analogy should be drawn with road traffic cases where the issues are different. (*R.* v. *Payne* [1963] C.L.Y. 3051 distinguished.)

R. *v.* BEET (1977) 66 Cr.App.R. 188, C.A.

553. —— power of arrest—reasonable suspicion of possession—whether reasonable suspicion that drug in defendant's car sufficient

[Misuse of Drugs Act 1971, s. 23.] A police officer reasonably believed that L's car had been involved in drug trafficking. He searched the vehicle and found cannabis resin. *Held,* that s. 23 of the 1971 Act gave police power to search any person or vehicle when they had reasonable grounds to suspect that the *person* was in possession of a controlled drug. Here the vehicle was suspected, not L. However, as the officer's actions were understandable, the evidence would be admitted although illegally obtained : R. *v.* LITTLEFORD [1978] Crim.L.R. 48, Doncaster Crown Ct.

554. Mock auction—competitive bidding. See ALLEN *v.* SIMMONS, § 122.

555. Murder—diminished responsibility—abnormality of mind
[Homicide Act 1957 (c. 11), s. 2 (1).]

It is for the jury to decide whether abnormality of mind within the meaning of the Homicide Act 1957, or some other factor, is the main cause of a killing.

The appellant killed a man with whom he had been out drinking. It was admitted that he had abnormality of mind arising from its retarded development. The issue left for the jury was whether the drink or the abnormality was the main factor in the killing. *Held,* dismissing the appeal, that that was the correct test to apply and there was no evidence that the jury had not applied it correctly.

R. *v.* TURNBULL (1977) 65 Cr.App.R. 242, C.A.

556. —— manslaughter—alternative verdict

The prosecution in a Jamaican case appealed to the Judicial Committee after the defendants had had the verdict of constructive manslaughter entered against them quashed by the Court of Appeal. The defendants had successfully contended that it was wrong for prosecuting counsel to have first raised the possibility of this alternative verdict on a charge of murder in his closing speech to the jury. *Held,* reversing the Jamaican Court of Appeal, that on an indictment charging murder, it was open to the jury to return a verdict of manslaughter wherever the facts and the evidence supported it. The trial judge had, in this case, adequately and clearly directed the jury on all such verdicts as were available to them on the evidence, and had correctly left the issues to them : D.P.P. *v.* DALEY AND MCGIE (1978) 122 S.J. 861, P.C.

557. —— mens rea—direction to jury
[Homicide Act 1957 (c. 11), s. 1 (1).]

A direction that a person accused of murder must have had an intention to kill or cause grievous bodily harm is a proper direction and that intention can be established by showing that the accused knew that his act would have such consequences whatever his actual motive.

Two drunken soldiers, A and B, asked an old man for a light. When he could not oblige them, A battered him to death whilst B kept watch. On their being tried for murder, the jury was directed that there must have been a specific harmful intention, namely either to kill, or cause some really serious injury. A and B were convicted. On appeal, *held,* dismissing the appeal, that direction was correct. (*R.* v. *Vickers* [1957] C.L.Y. 818 followed, as explained in *D.P.P.* v. *Smith* [1960] C.L.Y. 739 and *Hyam* v. *D.P.P.* [1974] C.L.Y. 657.)

R. *v.* WILLIAMSON AND ELLERTON (1978) 67 Cr.App.R. 63, C.A.

558. —— provocation—nature of " reasonable man " test

[Homicide Act 1957 (c. 11), s. 3.]

When considering, on a charge of murder, whether a reasonable man would have been provoked to lose his self-control under s. 3 of the Homicide Act 1957, the jury should be told that the reasonable man in question is a person having the power of self-control to be expected of an ordinary person of the sex and age of the accused, but in other respects sharing such of the accused's characteristics as they think would affect the gravity of the provocation to him.

D, aged 15, killed K by splitting his skull with a chapati pan. At D's trial for murder, he claimed provocation on the ground that K had buggered him in spite of his resistance and then laughed at him. Counsel for the defence addressed the jury on the basis that the test for provocation was not the reaction of a reasonable adult, but a reasonable boy of 15. The judge directed the jury that that was wrong, and that the test was objective, *i.e.* the reaction of a reasonable man. D was convicted of murder. His appeal to the Court of Appeal was allowed, and a verdict of manslaughter substituted. On appeal by the D.P.P. to the House of Lords, *held,* dismissing the appeal, that the judge had erred in instructing the jury to pay no attention to D's age. They should have taken into consideration those factors, including D's age and physical characteristics, which in their opinion would have affected the gravity of the provocation offered, and the conviction for murder had been rightly quashed. (*Bedder* v. *D.P.P.* [1954] C.L.Y. 769 not followed.)

R. v. CAMPLIN [1978] 2 W.L.R. 679, H.L.

559. —— —— no evidence of loss of self control—direction to jury—majority verdicts

[Homicide Act 1957 (c. 11), s. 3; Criminal Appeal Act 1968 (c. 19), s. 2 (1) proviso.]

If there is evidence on which a jury could find provocation sufficient to cause loss of self-control, the issue must be left to the jury, even though the judge believes that no reasonable jury could possibly come to that conclusion.

Per curiam: Although Practice Directions do not have the force of law, High Court judges should set an example by observing them.

G quarrelled with the victim about money matters arising from a job they had done together. G struck the victim with a knife, but when questioned later by police remained silent about the facts leading up to the incident. At trial, he raised the issues of self-defence and provocation for the first time. The judge left the issue of provocation to the jury, and gave directions on provocation, self-defence, and majority verdicts. On appeal against conviction, *held*, dismissing the appeal and applying the proviso, that as there was nothing to suggest G had suffered loss of self-control when stabbing his victim, the issue of provocation should not have been left to the jury. Further, the judge's failure to comply with the Practice Direction on majority verdicts was no ground for impugning the validity of the jury's verdict. (Dicta of Viscount Simon in *Holmes* v. *D.P.P.* (1946) 31 Cr.App.R. 123 and of Lord Devlin in *Lee Chun-Chuen* [1962] C.L.Y. 700 considered.)

R. v. GILBERT (1977) 66 Cr.App.R. 237, C.A.

560. Northern Ireland. See NORTHERN IRELAND.

561. Oaths Act 1978 (c. 19). See § 1430.

562. Obscene publications—import—EEC treaty

[Customs Consolidation Act 1876 (c. 36), s. 42; Customs and Excise Act 1952 (c. 44), s. 304; EEC Treaty (Cmnd. 5179–II), Arts. 30, 36, 177.]

Art. 30 of the EEC Treaty deals with quantitative, not total, prohibitions on importation; and art. 36, which allows prohibitions which are " justified " on grounds of public morality, is not to be read as meaning " necessary."

H was convicted of fraudulently evading a prohibition on the importation of obscene articles. He sought to argue that that offence, created by the Customs Consolidation Act 1876 and the Customs and Excise Act 1952, had ceased to exist by reason of the provisions of art. 30 of the EEC Treaty which prohibited quantitative restrictions on imports and that, although art. 36 did not preclude prohibitions on imports which were justified on the grounds of public morality or public policy, " justified " should be read as meaning " necessary." *Held*, dismissing his appeal, that the offence imposed a total restriction on imports. Art. 30 dealt with only quantitative restrictions and did not apply to it. In art. 36 the word " justified " meant " justified " and not " necessary," so that no question as to what was the meaning of " public morality " need be referred to the European Court of Justice.

R. *v.* HENN; R. *v.* DARBY [1978] 1 W.L.R. 1031, C.A.

563. —— " public good " defence—meaning of " learning "—admissibility of expert evidence

[Obscene Publications Act 1964 (c. 74), ss. 1 (1), 4.]

In the context of s. 4 (1) of the Obscene Publications Act 1964, " learning " means " a product of scholarship."

At a trial of alleged offences of having obscene articles for gain, the defence relied upon the statutory defence, under s. 4 (1) of the Act, that publication was justified as being for the public good and called expert evidence that publication was in the interests of " learning," the books in question being a means of sex education. Upon the Attorney-General's reference, *held*, that (1) the trial judge erred in not defining " learning " to the jury, such word meaning " product of scholarship "; (2) expert evidence adduced under s. 4 (2) is not admissible upon the issue as to whether the publication is obscene and a jury should be so directed. (Dictum of Lord Wilberforce in R. v. *Jordan* [1977] C.L.Y. 615, applied.)

ATT.-GEN.'S REFERENCE (No. 3 OF 1977) [1978] 1 W.L.R. 1123, C.A.

564. Obtaining by deception—squatter—whether entitled to let premises—whether an " adverse possessor "

E, a squatter in G.L.C. property, was alleged to have purported to let part of the premises to X. E eventually left but continued accepting " rent " from X. The G.L.C. had known that E was living there as she had paid towards the rates. *Held*, that (1) E had never become an " adverse possessor," as opposed to a trespasser, if there was any distinction; (2) trespassers could exclude others or lawfully charge them an entrance fee but could not lawfully let; (3) E's conviction of obtaining by the deception that it was lawful for her to let the premises and collect rent would be reduced to an offence of attempt on another ground: R. *v.* EDWARDS [1978] Crim.L.R. 49, C.A.

565. —— standard of proof

A doctor was charged with dishonestly submitting N.H.S. claim forms for expenses which had not in fact been incurred. There was a mass of prosecution evidence. *Held*, it was not necessary for each juror to take the same view about the details of the evidence as every other juror: it was sufficient if they had agreed that the charge or charges were proved. The judge had not erred in omitting to direct the jury that in respect of each event they all had to be agreed about at least one of the pieces of evidence relied on by the prosecution. R. *v.* AGBIM, *The Times*, October 24, 1978, C.A.

566. Offensive weapons—sheath knife—question of fact

[Prevention of Crime Act 1953 (c. 14), s. 1 (1), (4).]

Whether an article is an offensive weapon for the purposes of s. 1 of the Prevention of Crime Act 1953 is a question of fact for the jury.

D pleaded not guilty to possessing an offensive weapon, a sheath knife, in a public place, contrary to s. 1 (1) of the Prevention of Crime Act 1953. On the judge's ruling that the knife was an offensive weapon *per se*, D changed his plea to guilty. On appeal, *held*, allowing the appeal, that the question was for the jury to decide.

R. *v.* WILLIAMSON (1978) 67 Cr.App.R. 35, C.A.

567. Perverting course of justice—assisting another to avoid lawful arrest

Doing an act calculated to assist another to avoid lawful arrest by the police amounts to the offence of perverting or attempting to pervert the administration of public justice. (R. v. *Vreones* [1891] 1 Q.B. 360 and R. v. *Bailey* [1956] C.L.Y. 2069 applied): R. *v.* THOMAS; R. *v.* FERGUSON, *The Times*, November 9, 1978, C.A.

568. —— attempt—false allegation

The making of a false allegation of crime to the police resulting in an innocent person facing the risk of arrest amounts to the common law offence of attempting to pervert the course of justice.

The appellant complained to the police that one T had robbed him at pistol point. As a result, T was arrested, charged and held in custody for five days. The charge then being withdrawn upon the appellant retracting his statement made pursuant to the complaint, he explaining it as " a joke which got out of hand." Thereafter the appellant procured a colleague to search the venue of the commission of the alleged offence, such colleague finding an imitation gun which, as the appellant later admitted, had been planted by him to lend substance to his story. The appellant appealed against his conviction for attempting to pervert the course of justice on the grounds, inter alia, that such single-handed conduct did not in law amount to the offence charged. *Held*, dismissing the appeal, that the offence was properly charged, the appellant having committed an act or series of acts which had a tendency, and were intended, to pervert the course of justice. (*R.* v. *Vreones* [1891] Q.B. 360 and *R.* v. *Bailey* [1956] C.L.Y. 2069 applied).

R. *v*. ROWELL [1978] 1 W.L.R. 132, C.A.

569. Picketing. See NUISANCE; TRADE UNIONS.

570. Poaching—taking rabbits by night—not having any gun, net, etc.

[Night Poaching Act 1828 (c. 69), s. 1.] D was charged with unlawfully taking or destroying rabbits by night in land occupied by X. Justices found no case to answer on the ground that D did not have with him any gun, net, engine or other instrument for the purpose of taking or destroying game. *Held*, allowing the prosecutor's appeal, that s. 1 of the 1828 Act created two separate offences: (1) unlawfully taking or destroying any game or rabbits and (2) unlawfully entering or being on land with any gun, net, etc., for the purpose of taking or destroying game: JONES *v.* EVANS [1978] Crim.L.R. 230, D.C.

571. Practice—appeal—leave—application direct to High Court Judge

Forms applying for leave to appeal against L's conviction and sentence were sent to the Registrar of Criminal Appeals. Simultaneously, application for leave was made locally to a High Court Judge who gave leave to appeal against sentence only because insufficient information was before him to decide the question of leave to appeal against conviction. *Held*, granting leave to appeal against conviction, that the procedure adopted was not to be encouraged: R. *v.* LAMBERT [1977] Crim.L.R. 736, C.A.

572. —— —— costs of unsuccessful application

B abandoned his appeal against sentence and was refused leave to appeal against conviction. He applied to renew his application for leave to appeal six weeks out of time. *Held*, that there were no possible grounds for leave to appeal and B would pay £20 towards the costs of preparing documents, including the transcript, for the court: R. *v.* BERRY [1977] Crim.L.R. 736, C.A.

573. —— indication as to sentence—pre-trial review—seeing the judge

The rules as to seeing the judge, and the judge giving indications as to sentence as laid down in *R.* v. *Turner*, still represent the correct practice today. A judge should not indicate at a pre-trial review that his sentence may depend on the defendant's plea.

At a pre-trial review of D's case on a charge of handling, the judge said to counsel on hearing that the plea would be one of not guilty, " I do not see any reason why he should go to prison for this. Have a word with him. If he decides on your advice—and on the strict understanding that he only pleads guilty if he is guilty—to change his plea, we can dispose of it all today. But he must only plead guilty if he is guilty." D fought the case and lost. He was sentenced to six months' imprisonment. During mitigation, the judge alluded to his previous comments, then continued, " But he has not pleaded guilty, has he? A man who is found guilty, having denied it, is in a far different position, is he not? " Then, prior to sentencing, the judge said to the defendant, " If you had pleaded guilty it would have shown me that at least you regretted what you had done; but I am unable to reduce your sentence on that account.

You have chosen, which was your right, to contest the matter to the end." On appeal, *held,* allowing the appeal, that what the judge had done could very well have given the impression that there was a bargain, or that pressure was being exerted upon D to plead guilty. That was so damaging to the face of justice that the sentence must be quashed. There was no rule that there must never be any communication outside trial, either openly or privately, between judge and counsel. There was no doubt that *R.* v. *Turner* [1973] C.L.Y. 579 still represented the correct practice, and any conflict with *R.* v. *Cain* [1975] C.L.Y. 1412 was resolved by the *Practice Direction* (*Crime: Inconsistent Decisions*) [1976] C.L.Y. 539, which ruled that in case of inconsistency *R.* v. *Turner* should prevail.

R. *v.* ATKINSON [1978] 1 W.L.R. 425, C.A.

574. —— late sittings

Late sittings should be avoided where humanly possible, very long hours making people tired, so that they ceased to be at their best, notwithstanding that, there might well have been a good reason for a trial at Chester Crown Ct. in August 1976, that commenced at 4 p.m. and went on till 7.45 p.m. Thus *held* the Court of Appeal, dismissing the appeals against sentence of eight men, jointly indicted on 16 counts, who had pleaded guilty; although two of them objected to offences to be taken into consideration, and had been sentenced in November by another judge: R. *v.* HARRIES, *The Times,* April 28, 1978, C.A.

575. —— sentence—offences committed by gangs—disparity criterion

Where a gang is involved it is desirable that all of them should appear at the same court and at the same time. Save in the most exceptional circumstances, the disparity argument on sentence only arises in relation to sentences passed at the same time.

D was a member of a group who obtained a van worth £1,000 by hiring it in a false name with a bogus driving licence and filling in a hire-form to that effect. The van was then disposed of. For the various offences entailed in obtaining the van, D was sentenced to a total of nine months' imprisonment, plus three months consecutive for breach of probation, plus six months consecutive for breach of a suspended sentence, making a total of 18 months' imprisonment. The other men, except for one, received similar sentences. The one exception, however, appeared at a different court and at the end of a deferred sentence, was put on probation. D appealed against sentence on the ground of disparity. *Held,* that (1) disparity was normally only relevant to sentences passed at the same time; (2) merely because one glaringly inadequate sentence had been passed was not grounds for passing a second glaringly inadequate sentence. (Dictum of Lord Widgery C.J. in *R.* v. *Brown* (unreported) November 28, 1974, applied.)

R. *v.* STROUD (1977) 65 Cr.App.R. 150, C.A.

576. Prisons. See PRISONS.

577. Probation. See MAGISTERIAL LAW.

578. Prosecution of offences

PROSECUTION OF OFFENCES REGULATIONS 1978 (No. 1357 (L. 33)) [20p], made under the Prosecution of Offences Act 1879 (c. 22), ss. 2, 5 and 8, the Prosecution of Offences Act 1908 (c. 3), s. 2, and the Administration of Justice Act 1965 (c. 2), s. 27; operative on January 1, 1979; replace S.I. 1946 No. 1467; provides for the D.P.P. to conduct certain criminal proceedings, to advise on criminal matters and to be supplied with information relating to criminal offences by chief officers of police and clerks to justices.

PROSECUTION OF OFFENCES (AMENDMENT) REGULATIONS 1978 (No. 1846 (L. 38)) [10p], made under the Prosecution of Offences Act 1879, ss. 2, 5, 8 as amended by the Prosecution of Offences Act 1884 (c. 58), s. 3, the Prosecution of Offences Act 1908, s. 2, and the Administration of Justice Act 1965, s. 27; operative on January 1, 1979; amend S.I. 1978 No. 1357 by deleting reg. 6 (1) (9).

579. —— promise of immunity—discretion of D.P.P.

[Prosecution of Offences Acts 1879 (c. 22) and 1908 (c. 3); Prosecution of Offences Regulations 1946 (S.I. 1946 No. 1467.] At T's trial S gave evidence for the prosecution having received an undertaking from the D.P.P. that S would not be prosecuted for his part in the offence. In addressing the jury prosecuting counsel said that S risked a private prosecution despite the undertaking. T was convicted and brought a private prosecution against S. The D.P.P. sought to intervene with a view to offering no evidence. T sought declarations that the D.P.P.'s action was unlawful and ultra vires and that he was estopped from intervening by prosecuting counsel's statement in T's trial. *Held*, striking out T's statement of claim and dismissing his action, that (1) in view of the wide powers of the D.P.P. under the 1879 and 1908 Acts and the 1946 Regulations, his action could not be said to be unlawful or ultra vires; (2) there could be no estoppel as (a) the statement relied upon was a statement of law, not fact, and (b) estoppel could not be raised to prevent performance of a statutory duty and the 1946 Regulations imposed a duty on the D.P.P. to intervene in these circumstances; (3) there should be no preliminary trial as to whether the D.P.P. had exercised his discretion properly as his powers were very wide, it was no longer suggested that he had acted in bad faith and he had acted in the public interest in complying with his undertaking to S having regard to the possible consequences to S and the effect of future criminal inquiries and prosecutions if he did not intervene: TURNER *v*. D.P.P. [1978] Crim.L.R. 754, Mars-Jones J.

580. —— right to prosecute—health inspector—proof of appointment

[Health and Safety at Work etc. Act 1974 (c. 37), s. 38, Sched. 2, para. 20 (3).]

An inspector appointed under the Health and Safety at Work etc. Act 1974 does not need, in the absence of evidence to the contrary, to prove his appointment by written instrument as a condition precedent to prosecuting a case in a magistrates' court.

An inspector of the Health and Safety executive brought proceedings against the respondents under the 1974 Act. The respondents challenged his competence to prosecute. The inspector produced written evidence of his appointment, but such written instrument did not specifically refer to the inspector's right to prosecute under s. 38 of the Act. The magistrates dismissed the information on that ground. *Held*, allowing the inspector's appeal, that it was not necessary for s. 38 to be specifically mentioned in the appointment; that in any event the maxim omnia praesumuntur rite esse acta applied to his appointment in the absence of rebutting evidence adduced by the respondents. CAMPBELL *v*. WALLSEND SLIPWAY AND ENGINEERING CO. [1978] I.C.R. 1015, D.C.

581. —— time-limit—sexual offences

[Sexual Offences Act 1967 (c. 60), s. 7 (1).] On a charge of gross indecency, the defendant is entitled to be acquitted if the evidence is that the offence was committed, or might have been committed, more than 12 months before the commencement of the proceedings, so that the time-limit provided by s. 7 of the Sexual Offences Act 1967 has not been complied with. It is not necessary for the judge to direct the jury in every case that they must be sure that the offence was committed within the prescribed period; such a direction is only required if the defence raises the issue, or if the evidence shows that the time-limit may not have been complied with: R. *v*. LEWIS, *The Times*, November 11, 1978, C.A.

582. Prostitution—living on earnings of prostitute—burden of proof

[Sexual Offences Act 1956 (c. 69), s. 30 (2).] B was seen fairly frequently in the company of a prostitute, T. The evidence was such that it was almost an inevitable inference that B knew of T's "pitches" for plying for trade and observed her being picked up by lorry-drivers. The trial judge directed the jury that the fact that B was frequently in T's company gave rise to a conclusion that B was living on T's earnings. *Held*, dismissing B's appeal against conviction, that it would have been better if the jury had been properly directed as to the consequences of B being seen in the company of T. However, the jury were entitled to reject B's defence, which was a total denial of an association with T in circumstances of living on her earnings. If the judge had erred in failing to explain the different burdens of proof, both on the prosecution to prove the habitual company and on the defence thereafter to negative the presumption of knowingly living on T's earnings, the proviso would be applied: R. *v.* BELL [1978] Crim.L.R. 233, C.A.

583. Protection of Children Act 1978 (c. 37)

This Act prevents the exploitation of children by making indecent photographs of them, and penalises the distribution, showing and advertisement of such indecent photographs.

S. 1 makes it an offence to take indecent photographs of a child, or to distribute such photographs, or to possess or publish such photographs; s. 2 relates to evidence for offences under s. 1; s. 3 deals with offences by corporate bodies; s. 4 empowers a justice of the peace to issue warrants for entry, search and seizure of premises where he reasonably suspects there are indecent photographs of children; s. 5 relates to the forfeiture of articles seized under s. 4; s. 6 sets out the punishments for offences under this Act; s. 7 relates to interpretation; s. 8 provides for similar legislation to be made in Northern Ireland; s. 9 gives the short title. The Act does not extend to Scotland or Northern Ireland.

The Act received the Royal Assent on July 20, 1978, and came into force on August 20, 1978.

584. Public nuisance—obscene phone calls—class of people affected

N made over 600 threatening and obscene telephone calls to nearly 500 women resident in Norfolk between July 1972 and November 1976. He was indicted for public nuisance. *Held*, that this was the very kind of series of acts which the public has an interest in condemning and a right to vindicate, and constituted a public nuisance: R. *v.* NORBURY [1978] Crim.L.R. 435, Norwich Crown Ct.

585. Public order—fighting in public place—whether threatening behaviour

[Public Order Act 1936 (c. 6), s. 5 (as substituted by Race Relations Act 1965 (c. 73), s. 7).]

A person fighting in the street may be guilty of using threatening behaviour contrary to s. 5 of the Act whether or not he could have been charged with another offence such as affray.

O was seen by a police officer fighting with others in the street. He was arrested and charged with a number of offences including using threatening behaviour contrary to s. 5 of the Act. O was convicted and appealed on the ground, inter alia, that an offence under s. 5 was not committed since at the relevant time he was committing a substantive breach of the peace. *Held*, dismissing the appeal, that the jury were entitled to convict on the evidence before them.

R. *v.* OAKWELL [1978] 1 W.L.R. 32, C.A.

586. —— insulting words—one of alternative modes of behaviour sufficient

[Public Order Act 1936 (c. 6), s. 5, as amended by Race Relations Act 1965 (c. 73), s. 7.]

For the purposes of s. 5 of the Public Order Act 1936 as amended, the offence is committed if the words or behaviour are alternatively threatening, abusive or insulting.

R was one of a disorderly group of people whom the police were trying to move on after a dance. R, on being requested to go home, replied " fuck off " to a police officer. He was convicted, and appealed by way of case stated. *Held*, dismissing the appeal, that the prosecution need prove only one of the alternative modes of conduct laid down by the Act. This expression shouted at an officer attempting to control a disorderly crowd was insulting, and likely in those circumstances to cause a breach of the peace.

SIMCOCK *v.* RHODES (1977) 66 Cr.App.R. 192, D.C.

587. —— " public place "—front gardens not within definition

[Public Order Act 1936 (c. 6), s. 5.] E and R were convicted of an offence under s. 5 of the 1936 Act. The trial judge had directed the jury that W's front garden, where the relevant incident occurred, was a public place on the basis of implied permission for the public to approach W's house via the garden. *Held,* allowing appeals against conviction, that " public place " could not include front gardens of private premises on this basis: R. *v.* EDWARDS AND ROBERTS [1978] Crim.L.R. 564, C.A.

588. —— —— village hall hired for private party

D was charged with threatening behaviour at a village hall. The hall was available for hire to the public. It was hired for a private party and 200 tickets were sold to friends of the hirers. D was alleged to be a gatecrasher. There was evidence that steps were taken to check tickets and to vet any non-ticket holders before being allowed entry but D had not been so screened as he had arrived late. *Held,* the village hall and its environs were not, at the material time, a public place and the counts of threatening behaviour were therefore withdrawn from the jury. (*R.* v. *Kane* [1965] C.L.Y. 719 applied): R. *v.* COLEMAN, May 18, 1978, Exeter Crown Ct., Judge Goodall. (*Ex rel. G. J. C. Still, Esq., Barrister.*)

589. Rape—by husband of wife—consent—effect of non-molestation undertaking given to court

Where a husband and wife are living apart, an undertaking given to the court by the husband not to molest the wife has the same effect as an injunction, namely of eliminating the wife's matrimonial consent to intercourse.

W, who was living apart from H, sought an injunction to prevent him from approaching or molesting her. The application was adjourned on H's undertaking not to do so. Subsequently, in breach of that undertaking, H forced W to have intercourse with him. He was convicted of rape. On appeal by D, *held,* that the undertaking was the equivalent of an injunction, which eliminated W's matrimonial consent to intercourse. (*R.* v. *Clarke* (1949) C.L.C. 2271, *R.* v. *Miller* [1954] C.L.Y. 786 and *R.* v. *O'Brien* [1975] C.L.Y. 613 considered and distinguished).

R. *v.* STEELE (1976) 65 Cr.App.R. 22, C.A.

590. Removing articles from places open to public—meaning of " access in order to view "—meaning of " displayed "

[Theft Act 1968 (c. 60), s. 11.] At B's trial for removing from a church a cross and ewer displayed to the public and to which the public had access to view, contrary to s. 11 of the 1968 Act, the vicar gave evidence that although persons visited the church to look around it, it was only open for devotional purposes in the widest sense and the cross and ewer were placed there to complete the church's furnishings and as aids to devotion. *Held,* that there was no case for B to answer since whether the public " have access to a building in order to view " depended on the purposes of those giving access, not those actually visiting, and " displayed " meant " exhibited," as in an art gallery: R. *v.* BARR [1978] Crim.L.R. 244, Bristol Crown Ct.

591. Sentence

The Home Office has published the third edition of its handbook " The Sentence of the Court," a guide for courts on the treatment of offenders. The revisions to this publication take account of changes in this area of the law since 1969, including changes shortly to be brought into force under the Criminal Law Act 1977, and an entirely new section on juveniles. The handbook is available from HMSO. [£2.00]

592. —— administering noxious thing—19 year old—whether maximum sentence appropriate

[Offences against the Person Act 1861 (c. 100), s. 23.]

In a bad case, the maximum sentence is not wrong for a 19-year old, if he is a psychopath and a danger to others.

S. aged 19, had forced his stepmother, 60, to swallow quantities of digoxin tablets against some considerable resistance from her. After further threats he left her tied and locked in her room. She narrowly escaped death. Medical reports suggested he was psychopathic but not mentally ill. On appeal against sentence, *held,* dismissing the appeal, that this case was within the worst band for this type of case, and though S was only 19, and not suffering from mental illness, he was a psychopath and a potential danger to others.

R. *v.* SHOLANKE (1977) 66 Cr.App.R. 127, C.A.

593. —— appeal—each case to be treated individually
[Criminal Justice Act 1961 (c. 39), s. 3.]
Where judges are used to dealing with cases of a particular kind, they must treat each case on its individual merits, and not allow themselves to become mere rubber-stamps.

H, a student of 20, and of previous good character, pleaded guilty to possessing cannabis with intent to supply. He received a sentence of three years' imprisonment, which was the same sentence imposed on other defendants in the same city by the same judge. On appeal against sentence, *held*, allowing the appeal, that although it is inevitable that a judge's sentences will become stereo-typed, he must remind himself to treat each case on its merits and look at every case afresh. A two-year sentence was appropriate, but as the court was precluded from passing this sentence by s. 3 of the Criminal Justice Act 1961, Borstal training would be substituted.

R. *v.* HARNDEN (1978) 66 Cr.App.R. 281, C.A.

594. —— —— effects of changes in legislation—accidents caused by drunken driving
[Criminal Law Act 1977 (c. 45), s. 50 (1).]
The sentencing to imprisonment of drunken drivers who cause accidents resulting in injury or death, remains proper sentencing policy despite the changes brought about by s. 50 (1) of the Criminal Law Act 1977.

E pleaded guilty to causing death by dangerous driving and was given a six-month prison sentence, a £500 fine and was disqualified for three years. His blood alcohol reading was above the prescribed limit. He appealed against sentence. Held, allowing the appeal, that although the court had to consider current sentencing policy in the light of the changes brought about by s. 50 (1) of the Criminal Law Act 1977, it concluded that drunken drivers who cause accidents must nevertheless expect to lose their liberty unless there are exceptional mitigating circumstances. In this case, the prison sentence would be reduced to three months, and the disqualification period to two years.

R. *v.* EADIE (1978) 66 Cr.App.R. 234, C.A.

595. —— appeals
Assault occasioning actual bodily harm
R. *v.* GUNSTONE, HUGHES, MORSE AND UFFINDELL [1978] Crim.L.R. 176 (unprovoked attack on two people walking home at 11 p.m.—U attacked a police officer—no relevant previous convictions—G, H and U: nine months' imprisonment; A: six months' imprisonment; U: three months' concurrent for assaulting constable—upheld).
Assault on mental patient
R. *v.* GUDDOY [1978] Crim.L.R. 366 (in charge of 21 subnormal boys—convicted on six counts of ill-treating patient by elementary assaults ranging from slaps on buttocks to pulling boys by hair—no previous convictions—three years' imprisonment in all reduced to eighteen months).
Assault on public servant
R. *v.* HOWE [1978] Crim.L.R. 50 (in temper pushed two Underground ticket collectors about and struck member of public in face and knocked him to ground and kicked him—no previous convictions—16 months between offence and trial—three months' imprisonment reduced to allow immediate release—one month appropriate but immediate release because of delay).
Assault with intent to resist arrest
R. *v.* O'KEEFE [1977] Crim.L.R. 756 (threatened police officer with carving knife when officer went to O'K's home to execute bench warrant—arrested—at police station certified unfit to be detained—two previous convictions for minor dishonesty: fined—nine months' imprisonment reduced to three).
Attempted murder
R. *v.* DE VERE TAYLOR [1978] Crim.L.R. 236 (T put seconal in C's coffee after C had left T to return to C's husband; hoped thereby to reduce C's resistance and then to kill her; C did not drink coffee but T then unsuccessfully tried to strangle her—no previous convictions—no mental illness; acted in despair; intended to kill self also—nine years' imprisonment reduced to four).

Attempted robbery—voluntary confession—credit

R. v. WILLS [1978] Crim.L.R. 636 (used replica P.38 automatic pistol in attempted robbery of newsagent; struck owner of shop on head twice with gun, cutting him, but threw gun at dog when dog was called and ran away —later surrendered to police and made full confession—no previous convictions—W had just had all his money stolen, had been drinking and had been given gun by friend—five years' imprisonment reduced to three in view of surrender to police when no other evidence against him).

Bail Act 1976—court's powers

R. v. SINGH [1978] Crim.L.R. 756 (during the course of the trial of S and X, S failed to surrender to his bail on a Monday morning being incapable of doing so as a result of excessive drinking on the previous day. He appeared at two o'clock. Bail was not renewed. The jury were eventually discharged, being in disagreement. The judge sentenced S to three months' imprisonment for failing to surrender to his bail contrary to s. 6 (1) of the Bail Act 1976, which S admitted. *Held,* that by virtue of s. 6 (5) there were alternative ways of dealing with an offender under s. 6 either by way of proceedings for a summary offence or by way of committal for what was to be treated as a criminal contempt of court without the necessity for more elaborate proceedings. The judge had acted perfectly properly in dealing with S as if he had committed a criminal contempt of court).

Bail pending appeal—relevance

R. v. LANCASTLE [1978] Crim.L.R. 367 (L was granted bail pending her appeal against a twelve-month prison sentence—appeal dismissed as sentence proper and court could not be influenced by fact L had been at liberty pending appeal).

Blackmail

R. v. MULLALLY AND CURLEY [1977] Crim.L.R. 756 (threatened by letters and telephone calls, between February and April 1975, to introduce poisons into Cadbury Schweppes' products to be distributed to the public unless paid £80,000. C stole poisons, M handled them. C's defence: duress from organisation such as I.R.A.—previous convictions: M: office-breaking, robbery, attempted theft; C: robbery with M: imprisoned—12 years' imprisonment upheld).

Breach of parole

R. v. KENT [1978] Crim.L.R. 440 (burgled cottage two weeks after release on parole from sentence for, inter alia, burglary—sentenced to three years' imprisonment and parole licence revoked—on appeal, three years' probation with condition of residence substituted—could then be helped not to fall back into dishonesty on release—due to be released from earlier sentence in four months if parole not renewed—court would not comment on whether K's application for restoration of parole licence should be successful, as matter was for Parole Board).

Buggery

R. v. HORNBY [1978] Crim.L.R. 298 (H found E asleep with H's wife. He struck E across the face with a bottle, dragged wife upstairs, committed buggery with her by force, knowing her to have piles, " because I know it will hurt you "—several previous convictions, including two for actual bodily harm: fines—sentence: three years' imprisonment for wounding E with intent to do grievous bodily harm, reduced to two years on appeal; five years concurrent for buggery, reduced to three in view of the provocation).

R. v. NEVILLE [1978] Crim.L.R. 368 (aged 63, pleaded guilty to six offences of buggery of his two sub-normal sons when they were aged 11 and 15—N's wife had died when sons very young—one son in care; other lived with N in squalid conditions where there was only one bed—offences against one son two or three times per month; against other two or three times per week—no previous convictions—five years' imprisonment upheld).

R. v. ROSS [1978] Crim.L.R. 297 (pleaded guilty to buggery of one boy, X, who had had previous homosexual relationships; met outside public lavatory;

X stayed at R's flat for two-and-a-half weeks when he should have been at reform school—also pleaded guilty to two counts of buggery of Y, who was under supervision and had approached R for work; R took Y touring instead of meeting case against himself in respect of X—previous convictions: sodomy, indecency; sentence: three years' imprisonment for the offence against X; five years for each offence against Y, to run concurrently, but consecutive to the three years—on appeal, reduced to three and three consecutive, as no especially aggravating features although R had deprived Y's parents of him for four months).

Burglary—multiplicity of offences

R. v. DAWSON [1978] Crim.L.R. 437 (burgled two dwelling-houses on one night—86 offences taken into consideration: 38 of obtaining by deception, remainder burglaries—total property involved £5,400 in value—previous convictions also burglaries: had been through Borstal and imprisonment—out of trouble May 1974 to August 1976; mother had recently died; co-operative with police—five years' imprisonment upheld).

Causing death by dangerous driving

R. v. CHAPMAN [1978] Crim.L.R. 172 (drove, with double the blood-alcohol concentration limit, along narrow, winding city road; took approaching bend at 30 to 40 m.p.h. in area of 30 m.p.h. limit; swerved into lamp-post to avoid oncoming van, and killed passenger—nine months' imprisonment upheld; eight-year disqualification reduced to two).

R. v. OLSSON [1978] Crim.L.R. 633 (Swedish visitor shortly after landing in England drove nearly a mile on wrong side of road, collided head on with other car, killing passenger—O's net annual income £2,000; remorseful—£1,000 fine and five-year disqualification reduced to £250 and two years').

R. v. TURNER [1978] Crim.L.R. 438 (T, aged 25, failed to see cyclist in middle of wide road; drove into cyclist, killing him—previous convictions: making false statements to obtain use of hire car and dangerous driving, resulting in fines and disqualifications—12 months' imprisonment and six-year disqualification upheld).

Community service—powers of court on failure to comply with order

R. v. CORBETT [1978] Crim.L.R. 51 (failed to comply with community service order imposed by magistrates—sentenced to nine months' imprisonment by Crown Court after committal for sentence—reduced to six months as sentencing court's powers were restricted by Powers of Criminal Courts Act 1973, s. 16, to those of court making community service order).

—— *recommendation not followed*

R. v. HATHERALL [1977] Crim.L.R. 755 (pleaded guilty to three counts of shoplifting; seven offences taken into consideration—sentence adjourned for assessment for community service—three weeks later sentenced to 30 months' imprisonment by differently constituted court despite strong recommendation for community service—appeal dismissed; no proper analogy with deferred sentences; possibility only mentioned on first occasion).

Compensation

R. v. McGEE [1978] Crim.L.R. 370 (sentenced to fifteen months' imprisonment suspended and ordered to pay £519·45 compensation at £10 per week—later sentenced to three months' imprisonment and suspended sentence activated consecutively. None of compensation had been paid—extension of time and leave to appeal against compensation order granted as M could not pay whilst in custody—rate of payment altered to £5 per week, first payment to be six months after M's release).

—— *imprisonment in default*

R. v. BRUCE [1978] Crim.L.R. 236 (imprisoned and ordered to pay £1,010 compensation with nine months' imprisonment in default—order for imprisonment in default quashed as inappropriate—only appropriate where, under Administration of Justice Act 1970, judge wishes to extend maximum term under Magistrates' Courts Act for committal for failure to pay).

Confiscation order—whether can be combined with absolute discharge
R. v. HUNT [1978] Crim.L.R. 697 (H allowed friends to put stolen calcu-
lators in the boot of his car—sentence: absolute discharge; order depriving
him of his car—confiscation order quashed as could not be combined with
absolute discharge).

Consecutive sentences
R. v. AGBOGUN [1978] Crim.L.R. 371 (sentenced to six months' imprisonment for 1973 burglary, twelve months' consecutive for each of two 1977
attempted burglaries and one 1977 burglary which were part of series of burglaries and attempts, and six months' consecutive for going equipped for theft
(total four years)—*held*: fresh offences should be treated as whole and not
as separate offences: twelve-month sentences altered to two-and-a-half years
concurrent; sentence for 1973 offence made concurrent as offence stale; sentence
for going equipped made concurrent as part of one of the attempted burglaries).

—— *formula for judge*
R. v. RICE [1978] Crim.L.R. 301 (whilst serving the first of two consecutive
sentences, each of 18 months' imprisonment, R assaulted another inmate
—sentence: 18 months' imprisonment " consecutive to your present term "—
on appeal, upheld—judge had failed to use the formula in the *Practice
Direction (C.C.A.) (Sentence)* [1959] C.L.Y. 92, but the judge's words overall
showed he intended the sentence to be consecutive to the total three years R
had then been serving).

Conspiring to pervert the course of justice
R. v. SULTANA [1978] Crim.L.R. 300 (E, an American national, was brought
to England to testify for the prosecution at the trial of S and M for murder
—S put him in touch with people who would bribe him with sums of money
to return to America, which he did—sentence: five years' imprisonment—on
appeal, reduced to three years, as five years seemed to be out of line with
current sentencing policy, although the court was by no means certain that
it was inappropriately severe in this instance. People convicted of conspiring
to pervert the course of justice, especially where grave charges were being
investigated, must expect severe sentences).

Corruption—guilty plea discount
R. v. TILBROOK AND SIVALINGAM [1978] Crim.L.R. 172 (S convicted of
receiving corrupt payments from A Ltd. for accepting their tenders; T was
paid by S and A Ltd. for keeping quiet; between 1966–1974, when in other
employment, T was paid £9,000 in bribes; S received much more and was the
dominant figure; T disclosed all to authorities and gave evidence for Crown—
sentences: T: four years' imprisonment for each of eight offences of
corruption, concurrent as to first seven, consecutive on eighth; S: five years',
plus £5,000 fine for conspiracy to defraud, two years' concurrent on each of
eight offences of corruption—previous convictions: T: none; S: aiding and
abetting exchange control offences—S refused leave to appeal; T's sentence
reduced to three years' in view of plea).

Cultivating cannabis
R. v. ANDERSON [1977] Crim.L.R. 757 (pleaded guilty to cultivating cannabis
and possessing cannabis resin—no previous convictions—twelve months'
imprisonment, on basis that quantity was such that it must have been intended
to supply to others, upheld, although not charged with possession with intent
to supply to others—had there been an offence of growing cannabis with
intent to supply which had *not* been charged, it could have been argued
strongly that the punishment should not reflect the intention to supply).

Dangerous driving
R. v. ADENIYI [1978] Crim.L.R. 634 (took car without authority, chased by
police reaching 65 m.p.h., went wrong way round roundabout and passed two
" keep left " signs on wrong side—at least one previous conviction: theft:
fined—Nigerian, due to sit " A " levels in June 1979—Borstal and two-year
disqualification upheld).

Deferment

R. *v.* LATIMER [1978] Crim.L.R. 51 (in November 1976, sentence for August 1976 offences deferred four months for investigation of possibilities of day training centre placement; in January 1977, sentenced by different judge to 18 months' imprisonment for July 1976 offences—upheld: second judge entitled to sentence as he thought fit).

Deportation recommendation

R. *v.* WALTERS [1978] Crim.L.R. 175 (aged 17; convicted of three thefts: two pick-pocketing, one shoplifting—several previous convictions including one theft from person—came to England when 14 to join parents; parents now in America; only grandparents now in Jamaica; could return to home in England where uncle and two sisters now living—sentence: Borstal and deportation recommendation—excellent Borstal reports—recommendation set aside).

Deterrent sentence

R. *v.* ALEXANDER [1978] Crim.L.R. 372 (obtained social security payments totalling £616·50 by deception that unemployed—seventeen offences September to October 1976 and March to May 1977—in fact self-employed as painter and decorator with ten employees and contract with local authority to paint council houses—offences committed to tide over business during difficult time— fifteen previous convictions, mainly driving, some larceny: fined; imprisoned 1976 for failing to provide laboratory specimen—twelve months' imprisonment upheld as a deterrent sentence justified on its facts: Crown Court would have knowledge of local conditions).

Disparity

R. *v.* BURN [1978] Crim.L.R. 569 (B and his brother, X, attacked some youths, each breaking the jaw of a youth. B was sentenced to 18 months' imprisonment—X had been dealt with summarily and fined £25 by a different bench—sentence reduced to nine months to allow immediate release in view of degree of disparity, although normally unsuitably lenient sentencing of co-accused was no good reason to reduce a proper sentence).

—— *appropriate time for sentencing jointly charged defendants*

R. *v.* HAIR AND SINGH [1978] Crim.L.R. 698 (three pleaded guilty to conspiracy to utter forged documents—one, M, was sentenced to nine months' imprisonment suspended for two years and fined £200 on basis that a less important participant—during trial of H and S, became clear M was ringleader —sentences: H, 18 months' imprisonment; S, two years' imprisonment plus activation of suspended sentence consecutively—upheld).

Dispute of fact following guilty plea

R. *v.* GRAVELL [1978] Crim.L.R. 438 (pleaded guilty to assault occasioning actual bodily harm—G's version of facts differed widely from prosecution's— with counsel's consent, judge heard evidence with cross-examination—no previous convictions—*held*, no general rule pronounced, but in this case procedure could not be criticised).

Drugs—current sentencing policy

R. *v.* REES [1978] Crim.L.R. 298 (R was a party to fitting a container with concealed compartments used to smuggle 217·3 kilogrammes of cannabis resin, valued at £250,000, from Turkey to England—others involved were not convicted—R expected to gain £15,000—no previous convictions—court refused to allow counsel to cite comparable cases, as keeping sentences in check was for judges, not counsel—sentence: nine years' imprisonment, reduced to six on appeal).

Extended sentence—parole

R. *v.* GLEASE [1978] Crim.L.R. 372 (when being considered for pre-release employment scheme completed form giving reason for application that wanted to shoot his wife, the man she was living with, the children and anyone who tried to stop him; then wrote to probation officer making threats to attack wife and anyone who interfered—sentence for sending letter threatening murder: eighteen months' imprisonment concurrent with existing sentence certified as extended sentence—numerous previous convictions, no violence—not violent, unlikely to carry out threats—18 months upheld but not as extended sentence although incorrect to say extended sentence always wrong if sentence so short; judge unwise to discuss parole and how and when G might be released on parole: sentencing courts should not discuss parole at all).

Family circumstances

R. v. IVORY [1978] Crim.L.R. 374 (sentenced to six months' imprisonment for forgery, obtaining by deception and two burglaries—previous convictions: theft as servant, false representation to obtain social security payments: probation; conditional discharge—had three children, one nearly blind, one with spinal affliction, one severely retarded and husband in bad health—sentence upheld: in normal circumstances would be extremely lenient in view of gravity of offences and numbers taken into consideration; tragic home circumstances do not provide licence to plunder).

Fraud—by solicitor

R. v. WOODING [1978] Crim.L.R. 701 (solicitor party to very large fraud whereby C obtained bridging loans on security of supposed bona fide contracts for sale of land—contracts in fact at grossly inflated prices to companies owned by W—loans totalling £20,000 granted on W's undertaking to hold title deeds or proceeds of sale until bridging loan repaid—four such deals—no previous convictions; adjudged bankrupt in 1968 as result of guarantees given on behalf of client and thus could only work for firm on commission basis—30 months' imprisonment reduced to 18 in view of W's misfortunes in life).

Grievous bodily harm

R. v. LYNCH [1977] Crim.L.R. 757 (police called to scene of domestic quarrel between L and mistress—L lunged at officer with knife—two other officers broke in to arrest L. L threw axe at one, missing only because officer ducked. L used knife in ensuing melée, cutting both officers—previous convictions: many, three for violence; borstal, imprisonment—total of 10 years' imprisonment reduced to seven).

R. v. HONOUR [1978] Crim.L.R. 369 (following an earlier altercation H and M, at C's instigation, attacked K and R. H hit K with a mallet on head at least twice causing depressed fracture as result of which K unable to speak for weeks; M hit R on head with hammer causing broken nose and head wound; windscreen of R's car smashed—on arrest H threatened officers with carving knife causing one to fall backwards—five previous convictions, including possessing offensive weapon and assault occasioning actual bodily harm: conditional discharge, fine—seven years' imprisonment in all reduced to five).

Handling

R. v. ATKINS [1977] Crim.L.R. 758 (£5,000's worth of frying pans delivered to A's warehouse—following day discovered they had been stolen and covered them up—also received goods dishonestly acquired in public-house over some months for competition—no previous convictions—18 months' imprisonment upheld, although retained frying pans in fear of thieves, and his business and family in ruin as result of sentence).

—— *relevant facts—criminal bankruptcy—whether offence caused relevant loss*

R. v. DE POIX [1978] Crim.L.R. 634 (acquitted of robbery—pleaded guilty to handling parts of proceeds of a robbery and a burglary of an hotel—previous convictions: minor dishonesty 1966 and 1971—eight and 10 years concurrent and criminal bankruptcy reduced to three years each concurrent as trial judge wrongly sentenced on basis D a professional receiver; bankruptcy order a nullity as, though victims of robbery and burglary lost over £15,000, no evidence that D's offences caused such loss. Thus no jurisdiction to order bankruptcy).

Importing cannabis

R. v. HANCOCK AND HOLDGATE [1978] Crim.L.R. 174 (D2 recruited D1: system for fraudulently evading prohibition on importing cannabis from Colombo to Toronto via London and New York; D2 collected the cannabis; labels on case to be switched in London so seeming to originate in London; D1 booked same flights London–New York–Toronto; D2 was to receive £2,000, D1 £1,500—both treated as of good character—both on bottom rung of drug smuggling ladder—D2 recruited in India by man who saved him from addiction—D2: five years' imprisonment; D1: four years'; upheld).

Imprisonment in default of paying compensation

R. *v.* BRYAN [1978] Crim.L.R. 572 (sentenced to nine months' imprisonment suspended for two years, and ordered to pay £226 compensation at £7·50 per week with nine months' imprisonment in default of payment—subsequently sentenced in November 1976 to nine months' imprisonment with suspended sentence activated consecutively—in February 1977, warrant of commitment issued by magistrates' court for further nine months' imprisonment for default in paying compensation—appeal allowed as wrong for B to suffer imprisonment in default when it was outside his power to pay).

Incest

R. *v.* MELLOR [1978] Crim.L.R. 570 (lived with wife and six children in depths of country—had committed incest with second daughter for some years since she was thirteen, until she became pregnant—she said they were very fond of each other—six years' imprisonment reduced to four).

Indication of sentence before plea

R. *v.* HOWELL [1978] Crim.L.R. 239 (pleaded guilty to bigamy—acquitted of obtaining by deception—before trial judge said to counsel in his room that he proposed suspended sentence for bigamy and deception if convicted and that if bigamous wife, X, gave evidence his view might change for or against H—no previous convictions—sentence: nine months' imprisonment, judge having formed good impression of X—immediate release ordered on appeal: judge's course could be interpreted as pressure to plead guilty to deception; in view of previous indication, immediate sentence could be regarded as unfair).

Life imprisonment—arson

R. *v.* RYAN [1978] Crim.L.R. 700 (set fire to curtains in friend's house and watched; then told neighbour who called fire brigade—had almost completed probation order for similar offence made in 1975—no appropriate medical treatment: time the only healer—more likely to want to behave acceptably with determinate sentence—three years' imprisonment substituted as her behaviour did not present such a threat as to merit life sentence).

Living on earnings of prostitution

R. *v.* SAVILLE [1977] Crim.L.R. 758 (prostitute befriended S and thereafter S allowed self to be kept in luxury on her earnings from particularly unsavoury form of prostitution—several previous convictions: fined, except one similar offence in respect of same prostitute for which four months' suspended sentence imposed—20 months' imprisonment reduced to eight—consecutive activation of suspended sentence upheld).

Manslaughter—diminished responsibility—young adult

R. *v.* HANDOLL [1978] Crim.L.R. 637 (age 18—hit boy aged 14 with iron bar in fight, killing him—convicted manslaughter: diminished responsibility—father a hardened criminal: background of crime, violence and depravity impaired H's mind so much as to cause diminished responsibility—15 years' imprisonment reduced to 10: proper sentence life imprisonment as indeterminate but Court of Appeal could not impose because must be regarded as more serious than fixed term).

Perjury

R. *v.* KAYODE [1978] Crim.L.R. 302 (during his trial for theft and false accounting, K falsely gave evidence of a credit entry in his bank account, and the next day produced a false receipt and called a witness in support—pleas of guilty to perjury and attempting to pervert the course of justice—at time of sentence, K was on parole for original offences—sentence: 18 months on each count, concurrent, but to run consecutive to another sentence he was then serving—on appeal, the court upheld the sentences as completely justified. Perjury was easy to commit but hard to prove, and when proven, an offender must expect severe punishment).

R. *v.* LAL [1978] Crim.L.R. 52 (in county court action for non-payment for goods supplied, falsely testified that had bought some of the goods elsewhere—no previous convictions—nine months' imprisonment upheld—irrelevant that county court judge not deceived).

Permitting premises to be used for smoking cannabis

R. v. DWYER [1977] Crim.L.R. 759 (convicted of permitting premises to be used for smoking cannabis, acquitted of supplying cannabis—two American Air Force members entered D's house and left after some time with much cannabis—four found in house smoking reefer—also £500 and $200 cash in house—no previous convictions for drug offences—six months' imprisonment suspended quashed, £200 fine upheld).

Plea bargaining—judge's duties

R. v. ECCLES [1978] Crim.L.R. 757 (charged with three pairs alternative counts burglary with intent to rape/indecent assault and one burglary; pleaded guilty two indecent assaults, and burglary; prosecution not satisfied although judge indicated on two occasions he thought pleas should be accepted; on subsequent occasion, judge discussed policy regarding pleas not acceptable to prosecution and way in which E's case should be dealt with with prosecuting solicitor and assistant—thereafter E pleaded guilty to further common assault —accepted by prosecution—although no great harm done, as E had suffered no prejudice, extremely important that judges should avoid situation in which it might be thought they were engaging in plea-bargaining or some kind of interference—justice to be seen to be done—total sentence reduced from 60 months' imprisonment to 45 in view of irregularity and fact sentence too high as no guilty plea to burglary with intent to rape).

Reckless driving

R. v. PHELAN [1978] Crim.L.R. 303 (annoyed with the driving of a van, P pursued it by car, stopped it, kicked and rocked it; pursued it again when van was driven off and repeated the attack; pursued it again, driving alongside so that the vehicles touched. P's passenger shattered van's window with a brick and injured the van's passenger so that the van driver lost control, collided with lamp, and went into shop window—P had minor previous road traffic convictions including one for criminal damage—fined £250, disqualified three years—appeal against disqualification dismissed).

Restitution

R. v. POPE [1978] Crim.L.R. 303 (post office worker stole £600 from package; when case adjourned for report, judge said whether P in position to pay restitution when sentenced may affect whether immediate custodial sentence imposed—by the time for sentence, P, in grave financial difficulties, had sold car and paid £250 restitution which had been accepted; prosecuting counsel then disclosed that the remainder of the packet from which £600 had been taken, and which had contained £9,000 in all, had later disappeared —judge adjourned sentence to discover effect on P's employment, saying a custodial sentence was inevitable in view of the breach of trust and the fact of the package having disappeared; but he would suspend it if he could— sentence: nine months' imprisonment—on appeal, suspended for two years, although a proper sentence, in view of the judge's comments—not appropriate to put a defendant in the position of trying to buy his way out of a custodial sentence).

Robbery

R. v. BROOK [1978] Crim.L.R. 441 (B, aged 20, and X visited home of W, a woman aged 72, to investigate damp. On subsequent occasion, B returned to burgle W's flat. W surprised him and began screaming. B put hand over W's nose and mouth with such force W thought she was dying. Took five rings valued at £281, leaving W in hysterical state with scratched face and bleeding nose and mouth—no previous convictions for violence—B expressed remorse and said he attacked W in panic—seven years' imprisonment upheld).

—— *spontaneous confession—credit*

R. v. WIGLEY [1978] Crim.L.R. 635 (pleaded guilty to planned robbery with sawn-off shotgun taking a hostage, and a similar attempted robbery and other offences—when interviewed by police about another matter, voluntarily confessed to three offences, saying wanted to start afresh—numerous previous convictions: imprisonment—12 years' imprisonment reduced to seven as insufficient credit given for remorse and repentance—voluntary disclosure of offences is mitigating factor much greater than guilty plea).

Shoplifting

R. *v.* BAILEY [1978] Crim.L.R. 53 (shoplifting expedition with others—stole anorak in one shop and toys in another—one previous conviction shoplifting three months before—three months' imprisonment upheld).

R. *v.* FINNIGAN [1978] Crim.L.R. 441 (F and X transferred goods from shop shelves into holdall whilst S kept watch—F and S ran off when challenged and X aimed blows at store manager and employee—F had one previous conviction for handling and fraudulently using vehicle excise licence—F and S surrendered to police on reading reports indicating offence was planned robbery; X not traced, S acquitted—F sentenced to nine months' imprisonment, reduced to three).

Supplying heroin—guilty plea discount

R. *v.* NG AND DHALAI [1978] Crim.L.R. 176 (half-pound heroin left with D as security for loan; two years later agreed to sell it to G for £4,000—G, a police officer posing as prospective heroin purchaser, had approached C and T; G, C and T then approached N, who put them in contact with D—no previous convictions—C and T sentenced to six years' imprisonment—D: eight years' upheld (gave evidence for Crown after changing plea)—N: five years', reduced to four to give more credit for guilty plea and assisting Crown from outset).

Suspended sentence—activation

R. *v.* BISHOP [1978] Crim.L.R. 573 (took vehicle from workshop where he was supposed to have worked on it; returned it later—numerous previous convictions, including violence and dishonesty—three months' imprisonment, and 12 months' suspended sentence for wounding activated consecutively—upheld).

R. *v.* GARTLAND [1978] Crim.L.R. 53 (18 months' suspended for two years for burglary; one year later fined for theft of lead from roofs; five months later again fined for attempted theft and brought before Crown Court for breach of suspended sentence—activated with reduced period of twelve months—appeal on ground fresh offences " trivial " and time since original imposition of suspended sentence very long dismissed: during much of time G had been working on oil rig off Scottish coast).

Suspended sentence plus fine

R. *v.* SCARLETT [1978] Crim.L.R. 241 (sentence: 18 months in all suspended for two years plus fines totalling £1,950, half to be paid within six months, half within further six months; nine months' imprisonment in default—unemployed and no savings—fines held unrealistic and reduced to £750 total to be paid at £10 per week (offered by S) with six months' imprisonment in default).

——— *term in default*

R. *v.* GRANT [1978] Crim.L.R. 240 (suggestion that wrong to impose period of imprisonment in default of fine imposed at same time as suspended sentence because defendant might then serve a sentence of imprisonment whilst subject to suspended sentence held misconceived—term in default of payment of fine must be fixed).

Theft—breach of trust

R. *v.* EDWARDS [1978] Crim.L.R. 374 (teacher collected £145 in 1973 from 20 pupils for school trip—after trip cancelled refunded £79 and kept £66; obtained £120 from school funds by deception that £120 not returned by travel agents after trip cancelled; in 1974 collected £395 for school trip to Wales, kept £191 and obtained £50 cheque from school by deception that required for refund—lost job; jury said hoped previous good character and pressures of work would be taken into account—two years' imprisonment reduced to one as E muddled in way he kept money and was tempted from time to time).

Theft of growing crop

R. *v.* RENNISON AND ELLIOTT [1977] Crim.L.R. 760 (went in R's van to farm and dug up one and a half cwt. potatoes, value £12—previous convictions: R, one receiving, fined; E, one theft, fined—potatoes recovered, not taken for resale, led to commit offences by fact others there who escaped—deterrent sentence right, but 14 days' imprisonment quashed and £25 fine substituted—already spent four days in prison—12-month driving disqualification upheld).

Threatening behaviour—racial attack

R. *v.* CUSHEN AND SPRATLEY [1978] Crim.L.R. 571 (C, S and others shouted at R, a coloured man, crossing a bridge alone, " let's get the black bastard " and " let's throw him in the river," and chased him until he reached a restaurant—three months' imprisonment upheld).

Trade descriptions

R. *v.* EDELSON [1978] Crim.L.R. 759 (offences over 12-month period in father's carpet business; sold and advertised for sale to public substandard carpets as first-class goods; gave false or misleading prices falsely indicating prices less than recommended price; made false statements about manufacturers' guarantees, firm's credit interest rate, etc.—10 sample counts—no previous convictions—no prosecution of father as in extremely bad health—12 months' imprisonment in all, £500 fine each count, £1,000 prosecution costs—imprisonment not appropriate: sentence varied to allow immediate release, fines halved as E had served equivalent of six-month sentence, prosecution costs £500 or taxed, whichever less).

Unemployment benefit fraud

R. *v.* STRINGER [1978] Crim.L.R. 698 (obtained £118 unemployment benefit without disclosing earnings of £60 per week—no previous convictions since 1966—nine months' imprisonment upheld).

Young Offender

R. *v.* HAYES [1978] Crim.L.R. 574 (age: 20—numerous offences of theft, taking vehicles and burglary—previous convictions included two burglaries: borstal—subnormal to an extent—nuisance and menace—total of five years' imprisonment upheld).

R. *v.* WOODBRIDGE [1978] Crim.L.R. 376 (aged 15; when 14 robbed small general store with others aged 20 and 16; W threatened proprietor's wife and daughter with knife, another restrained proprietor—W said others suggested burglary and provided knife—only took £21—over 100 previous offences including those taken into consideration, including robbery, burglary, aggravated burglary, dishonesty, motoring offences and possessing weapons: care, conditional discharge, detention—confidence, maturity and intelligence of much older person—seven years' detention under Children and Young Persons Act 1933, s. 53 (2) reduced to five).

—— *robberies*

R. *v.* THOMAS [1977] Crim.L.R. 760 (age 17—with his gang, took motorcycle from 17-year-old and rode it—also pleaded guilty to five robberies from children in Wolverhampton area—amount about 10p each occasion—hit or kicked those children who did not co-operate—40 other robberies and five shopliftings taken into consideration—one previous conviction for being drunk and disorderly—three years' imprisonment upheld).

—— *where intermediate length sentence would be appropriate*

R. *v.* RAMMELI DJEMAL AND MOURAT DJEMAL [1978] Crim.L.R. 54 (mother and son aged 20 handled proceeds of serious crime over long period—both sentenced to three years' imprisonment—no previous convictions—MD's sentence based on judge's belief he was too educated and sophisticated to benefit from Borstal—sentence reduced to Borstal for MD as judge made fundamental error in approach; RD's sentence reduced to 18 months to reflect plea and assistance).

596. —— **arson**

Sentences of around three and a half years are appropriate for sentences of violence which include arson.

H, 37, paid a visit to the house of a man who had deceived him in a transaction, and getting no reply to his banging on the door, stuffed fish and chip papers through the letter box and set fire to them. They in turn set fire to curtains in the house. No one was injured. H had 14 previous convictions, none for a similar offence. On appeal against a three year sentence. *Held,* dismissing the appeal, that a sentence in this band was appropriate for an offence of violence, which includes arson, despite the lack of previous convictions for a similar offence.

R. *v.* HOGAN (1977) 66 Cr.App.R. 120, C.A.

597. —— attempted robbery—discount for decade of good behaviour

S pleaded guilty to attempted robbery with violence in 1968. He had discharged a sawn-off shotgun into the ceiling of a bank, and when challenged, had hit the bank guard and fled empty-handed. He had had a bad record for dishonesty for 10 years prior to the offence, but afterwards had assumed a new name and identity and lived an honest and industrious life for the next 10 years. He was sentenced to three years' imprisonment: R. *v.* SESSIONS, July 10, 1978, Dunn J., Winchester Crown Ct. (*Ex rel. Geoffrey Still, Esq., Barrister.*)

598. —— —— use of firearms

For a young man of 21 years, a total of 10 years' imprisonment, account being taken of every feature of the gravity of several charges, is somewhat excessive.

The appellant, aged 21, in conjunction with another, drove a motorcar, without the owner's consent, to a post office where they demanded money at gun point. The appellant's revolver was loaded, he had no firearm certificate, and he subsequently used the weapon to resist arrest by a police officer. He had a bad criminal record as a juvenile, and this had of late shown a shift towards violence. On his appeal against a sentence of 10 years' imprisonment, *held*, that the sentence of five years imposed by the trial judge for the attempted robbery was exactly right; but that the overall period of imprisonment was somewhat excessive and the concurrent sentences on two less serious counts would be reduced by two years, to run consecutively to the five years, making a total of eight years' imprisonment in all.

R. *v.* HALL (1977) 65 Cr.App.R. 311, C.A.

599. —— Borstal training—burglary—unrealistic social inquiry reports

Persons, including adolescents, who burgle houses, must expect to lose their liberty, even though they may be persons of good character.

Per curiam: Probation officers' reports are not likely to be of much value to the court if they are not realistic.

A and B, aged 18 and 19, who had both been in trouble before for offences of dishonesty, burgled a house and turned it upside down. One of them said they believed the occupants had loads of money and they had ransacked the place for a bit of a laugh. They were sentenced to Borstal training. On appeal against sentence, *held*, dismissing the appeal, that whilst detention might have been called for in the case of first offenders, in the present cases, a long period of discipline and training was appropriate. The probation officer in recommending a fine might have been concerned about the future of one of the appellants; the court was concerned about the security of citizens' houses, and courts would have to decide what should be done in this class of case with regard to that object.

R. *v.* SMITH AND WOOLLARD (1978) 67 Cr.App.R. 211, C.A.

600. —— —— subsequent to detention centre

There is no absolute or rigid rule that a defendant who has just completed a sentence of detention should not serve a Borstal sentence; each case must be looked at in all the circumstances.

While awaiting trial on a charge of assault occasioning actual bodily harm, the appellant had, alongside others, become involved in an affray, and caused serious head injuries to a victim whom he struck with a piece of metal. He was sentenced to three months at a detention centre for the original offence, and having served this, came up for trial on the charges arising from the affray. He was found guilty of assault occasioning actual bodily harm, and sentenced to Borstal training. Applying to the Court of Appeal for leave to appeal, he contended that it was wrong in principal to pass such a sentence on a person who had just completed a sentence of detention, and furthermore that the court had had no opportunity to evaluate whether the defendant had benefited by the original sentence. *Held*, refusing the application, that on the facts, the sentence of Borstal training for the affray and the vicious attack was clearly the correct one; it could not possibly be said to be wrong in principle. (*R.* v. *Bingham* [1968] C.L.Y. 820 and *R.* v. *McWilliams* [1971] C.L.Y. 2605, applied.)

R. v. SIMPSON (1977) 65 Cr.App.R. 308, C.A.

601. —— burglary—young offenders

The public interest requires that young men who commit burglary and similar crimes should receive condign punishment.

In one day two young men, aged 19 and 20, led by another man, obtained entry to two houses by smashing windows, and stole property to the value of £260. The next day they committed a further burglary, where they obtained £400, which was taken into consideration on sentencing. Neither of them had a previous criminal record. They were both sentenced to six months' detention centre. Dismissing the appeal against this sentence, *held,* that the public interest would be served by making it clear that crimes of that sort would receive condign punishment, and the correct disposal had been made.

R. v. CORDAROY; R. v. PRING (1977) 65 Cr.App.R. 158, C.A.

602. —— case remitted—whether plea was equivocal

M appealed to the Crown Court against his sentence for burglary and assault occasioning actual bodily harm. M's counsel repeated the mitigation put forward by M's solicitor in the magistrates' court that M had only pushed a conductor to shove him out of the way and had not entered the flat which was burgled. The deputy circuit judge inquired into the original proceedings, obtained evidence from the justices' clerk and remitted the case to the justices for pleas of not guilty to be entered on the ground that the original pleas of guilty were equivocal. The justices refused to rehear the case on the ground that they were functi officio. *Held*, allowing the prosecutor's application for an order of certiorari to quash the Crown Court decision, that the Crown Court ought not to inquire into the question of whether justices should have exercised their discretion to allow a change of plea unless there was prima facie evidence to suggest that they should have done so. Here there was no evidence that the justices should even have considered exercising their discretion: R. v. COVENTRY CROWN COURT, *ex p.* MANSON [1978] Crim.L.R. 356, D.C.

603. —— compensation order—financial loss—whether appropriate to award interest

[Power of Criminal Courts Act 1973 (c. 62), s. 35 (1).]

A court may, in a case of compensating for financial loss, make an order which includes a sum by way of interest.

S was convicted on charges of deception and theft and ordered to pay compensation which included a sum by way of interest. On application to vary the order by omitting the interest, *held,* dismissing the application, that " loss " in s. 35 (1) means any kind of loss. Where this is financial loss, the court may, in a straightforward case, include a sum by way of interest equivalent to that the victim would be likely to recover if he pursued his claim in the civil courts.

R. v. SCHOFIELD [1978] 2 All E.R. 705, C.A.

604. —— —— in favour of innocent buyer of stolen goods

[Powers of Criminal Courts Act 1973 (c. 62), s. 35 (1), (4).]

When a handler sells stolen goods to an innocent buyer who returns them to the owner, the court has jurisdiction to make a compensation order in favour of the innocent buyer.

H pleaded guilty to various counts of handling, and in addition to receiving a prison sentence was ordered to pay compensation to the innocent buyer of the stolen goods who had returned the goods to the rightful owner. On appeal against the compensation order, *held,* dismissing the appeal, that a wide meaning should be given to the words " resulting from an offence " in s. 35 (1) of the Act. Accordingly, the trial judge has jurisdiction to make an order in favour of the innocent buyer. (*R.* v. *Thompson Holidays* [1973] C.L.Y. 3278 applied).

R. v. HOWELL (1978) 66 Cr.App.R. 179, C.A.

605. —— —— sum neither agreed nor proven

[Powers of Criminal Courts Act 1973 (c. 62), s. 35.] The appellant pleaded guilty to a number of offences, including two of taking and driving away a motor vehicle without authority, for which he was sentenced to nine months' imprisonment, disqualification for 12 months, and ordered to pay £100 compensation in respect of damage to a car with which he collided in attempting to escape. The only evidence of the damage was a statement by the car owner to the effect that he had received an estimate for repairs amounting to £209. The estimate was disputed. *Held*, an order for compensation could not be made unless the figure was agreed or proved. The order would be quashed: R. *v.* VIVIAN, *The Times*, August 24, 1978, C.A.

606. —— conspiracy to defraud—fiduciaries

Where bank employees are convicted of offences involving breach of trust, such as conspiracies resulting in the obtaining of stolen cheques from a bank and obtaining money on forged cheques, it is in the public interest that sentences of deterrent value should be passed.

The appellant, of previously good record, had been employed as a part-time typist/telephonist at the Newington Green branch of the Midland Bank for six years, when she was convicted together with other defendants, of conspiracy to defraud, conspiracy to obtain property on a forged instrument, handling stolen goods, and theft. The first conspiracy arose out of the impersonation of the bank's customers, resulting in a total of £5,570 being withdrawn dishonestly from an account; the second conspiracy was one where stolen cheque books were obtained and forged cheques from these books were passed at banks and shops to obtain cash and goods. Evidence showed that the appellant had actually participated in obtaining such cheque books and other documents, and in using her direct knowledge of confidential banking procedures. She was sentenced to 21 months' imprisonment in all. On her appeal against sentence, her counsel adduced details of her difficult family circumstances, and drew the court's attention to undue influence that may have been brought to bear upon her by one of her more culpable co-defendants. *Held*, dismissing the appeal, that these were serious offences where the public interest was involved. Even difficult personal circumstances, affecting her two children, did not itself permit the court to exercise leniency in this case.

R. *v.* TUNBRIDGE (1977) 65 Cr.App.R. 314, C.A.

607. —— criticism by another judge

A judge at first instance should only in very rare circumstances find it necessary to comment on a sentence passed by another judge of equal standing. Where the circumstances did exist, the comment should be made temperately and not be such as to embarrass the Court of Appeal: R. *v.* BAILEY, *The Times*, June 22, 1978, C.A.

608. —— death by dangerous driving—disqualification—period of

Momentary inadvertence by a driver, causing the death of another roaduser, may not warrant a long period of disqualification.

The appellant bus driver failed properly to negotiate a bend and collided head-on with an oncoming car, killing its driver. He was convicted of causing death by dangerous driving; he was aged 27, regarded as of good character and had held a driving licence for only some 10 weeks prior to the accident. The trial judge disqualified him for 10 years. *Held*, allowing his appeal, that the accident could reasonably be attributed to a momentary lapse as opposed to seriously reprehensible driving; and that in those circumstances disqualification for two years with a condition that the appellant should retake a driving test was appropriate.

R. *v.* HESLOP [1978] R.T.R. 441, C.A.

609. —— —— deferment—whether better to adjourn

[Powers of Criminal Courts Act 1973 (c. 62), s. 1.] A crown court which is minded to adjourn a case to another crown court for sentence should not defer sentence before ordering the adjournment, for deferment entitles the defendant to suppose that if he commits no further offences he cannot be given a custodial sentence. The C.A. has allowed an appeal against imprisonment imposed by the court to which such a case was adjourned, with "great reluctance," and has commented that judges are tending to overlook the fact that the power to defer sentence has not taken away the power to adjourn: R. v. ROBERTS, *The Times*, January 19, 1978, C.A.

610. —— drunken driving—imprisonment—disqualification

Substantial imprisonment and disqualification is warranted where an offender commits repeated offences of drunken driving.

The appellant, aged 47, was convicted of two offences of driving with excess alcohol, one of driving whilst unfit through drink and one of refusing a laboratory specimen, relating to three incidents in the course of two months. His blood contained 229 and 319 milligrammes of alcohol per 100 millilitres on the two occasions when a specimen was provided. On one occasion, an elderly man was knocked over and on another stationary vehicles were damaged. Medical evidence indicated that the appellant would not accept that he had a drink problem. He had previous convictions for drunken driving. *Held*, that imprisonment totalling 30 months and 20 years' disqualification was not excessive.

R. v. McLAUGHLIN [1978] R.T.R. 452, C.A.

611. —— duty of counsel

It is the duty of counsel to acquaint themselves with the maximum sentences that a court can impose and to see that they are not exceeded.

The applicant was committed to the Crown Court pursuant to the provisions of the Magistrates' Courts Act 1952, s. 28, with a view to Borstal training. She was sentenced to six months' imprisonment. The maximum allowable sentence was three months. *Held*, allowing the appeal, and reducing the sentence to three months, that it is the duty of counsel to acquaint themselves with the maximum sentences which the court can impose and to see that they are not exceeded.

R. v. O'NEIL (1977) 65 Cr.App.R. 318, C.A.

612. —— fines—not to be too large

The Court of Appeal, reducing a fine for stealing a car from £1,500 to £500, has observed that large fines are not to be encouraged: R. v. MERCER, *The Times*, April 14, 1978, C.A.

613. —— football hooliganism

Young persons who commit offences of violence on the occasion of football matches are liable to custodial sentences, however good their previous character.

D, aged 18, left a football match with three friends. They got into a car and proceeded to tour the town looking for opposing supporters to beat up. They found some and D attacked one of them in the mouth with a hammer, fracturing his jaw, splitting his mouth and breaking six teeth. They all then kicked this man. D was convicted of causing grievous bodily harm with intent, conrary to s. 18 of the Offences against the Person Act 1861, and sentenced to three years' imprisonment. On appeal against sentence, *held*, dismissing the appeal, that despite D's age and previous good character, there were no grounds whatsoever for interfering with the sentence.

R. v. BRUCE (1977) 65 Cr.App.R. 148, C.A.

614. —— —— likelihood of custodial sentence

Football hooligans who commit offences of violence or damage property should expect to lose their liberty unless there are exceptional mitigating circumstances.

M was one of a group of football supporters travelling home in a coach after a match. Two vehicles were struck by missiles thrown from the coach, their windscreens shattered and both drivers were injured. M was convicted on four counts, two of actual bodily harm and two of criminal damage. M was from a good home, had a good work record and only minor previous convictions. He appealed against a sentence of Borstal training. *Held*, dismissing the appeal, that unless there are exceptional mitigating circumstances, hooligans of 17 and over should not expect to return home for some

considerable period; and that even for offenders of 14–17 years, the courts
should consider the possibility of a detention centre.

R. *v.* MOTLEY (1978) 66 Cr.App.R. 274, C.A.

615. —— forfeiture of car—application for return by owner—powers of Crown Court

[Police (Property) Act 1897 (c. 30), s. 1 (1); Powers of Criminal Courts Act 1973 (c. 62), s. 43.]

A court's order under s. 43 of the Powers of Criminal Courts Act 1973 depriving an offender of rights in property in his possession at the time of his arrest is not definitive of rights of ownership in such property and a third party claimant may seek its return.

Upon the applicant's husband being convicted on indictment, the judge made an order under s. 43 of the 1973 Act depriving him of his rights in a car used to facilitate the commission of offences and the car was accordingly taken into police possession. The applicant claimed that the car was her own and attempted unsuccessfully to persuade the judge to vary the order. She thereafter applied to justices under s. 1 (1) of the 1897 Act for delivery up of the car to herself, but the justices refused to hear the application on the grounds that the matter was res judicata in view of the Crown court decision. *Held*, granting mandamus directing the justices to hear the application, that an order under s. 43 does not determine ownership of property but simply deprives an offender of his rights, if any, in it.

R. *v.* CHESTER JUSTICES, *ex p.* SMITH [1978] R.T.R. 373, D.C.

616. —— illegal importation of drugs

In sentencing an international drug smuggler, the fact that he was merely in transit and the drugs were not to be distributed in the U.K. are not mitigating factors: R. *v.* KENCE, *The Times*, April 15, 1978, C.A.

617. —— informer—whether credit to be given

Substantial credit should be given to informers who have pleaded guilty, where their information can be acted upon by the police.

After his arrest, L made statements admitting a vast number of offences, and implicating many other people. The only evidence against L was contained in his confessions. As a result of his statements, quantities of stolen goods were recovered and many arrests made. L was sentenced to a total of 11 years imprisonment. On appeal, *held*, allowing the appeal, that it was in the public interest to encourage those involved in gang activities to come forward and give information to the police. Accordingly, substantial credit should be given in such cases. Sentence reduced to five years.

R. *v.* LOWE (1977) 66 Cr.App.R. 122, C.A.

618. —— insurance fraud—imprisonment appropriate

An attempted commission of a fraud upon an insurance company merits immediate imprisonment.

The applicant agreed with B and an insurance broker to make a fraudulent claim upon an insurance policy by claiming that B had been injured in an accident involving the applicant's car during the currency of the insurance. In fact B had been injured in an accident not involving that car and in any event prior to the insurance cover taking effect. The broker received £100 for his assistance. The applicant later tried to withdraw the fraudulent claim. During the applicant's (legitimate) absence abroad, B and the broker were convicted and sentenced each to twelve months' imprisonment. Upon his return to the country the applicant was charged with and admitted attempting to obtain property by deception and corruption (making payments to the broker). He was sentenced to 12 months' imprisonment. *Held*, refusing leave to appeal, that although the applicant was to be treated as of good character, the offence was serious and no doubt the applicant would have received the same sentence had he stood trial with his accomplices.

R. *v.* HALEWOOD [1978] R.T.R. 341, C.A.

619. —— judge's powers—counsel's duty to remind judge

The Court of Appeal in this case stated that it was important that in all cases counsel should bear in mind the limitations on a judge's powers of sentencing and invite his attention to any slip he makes: R. v. DEARDEN [1978] Crim.L.R. 287, C.A.

620. —— **murder—reduced to manslaughter—finding of provocation by jury**

The court must, when sentencing, take into account that the jury by their verdict had accepted the provocation to be of sufficient gravity to reduce the charge of murder to manslaughter; but nevertheless, 10 years' imprisonment may be a proper sentence.

W married in 1970 and his wife bore a child in 1976. Their marriage was stormy with outbreaks of violence. W eventually bought a shotgun with the intention of killing the whole family. An argument later developed and W produced the gun, but was only provoked into using it when he was told that the child was not his. He was convicted of manslaughter by a majority, and sentenced to 10 years' imprisonment. On appeal against sentence, *held*, dismissing the appeal, that the court must give effect to the verdict of the jury, but the scene was set before the words of provocation were uttered, and the trial judge was in the best position to assess the various factors involved.

R. v. WELLS (1978) 66 Cr.App.R. 271, C.A.

621. —— **plea bargaining—counsel seeing judge**

A judge should not conduct any discussion with counsel in private about sentencing in a case beyond the limits laid down in *R. v. Turner*.

D was charged with conspiracy to steal. Before arraignment, the judge invited counsel into his room to hear how the defendants proposed to plead, and to decide how they were to be tried. At the time, he indicated that he considered D to be the ring-leader, and that a plea of guilty would be regarded favourably. On that basis, D was advised to plead guilty. He dismissed his counsel and solicitors and refused to take any further part in the trial, being of the opinion that he could not get a fair trial in the circumstances. He was convicted, and sentenced. On appeal, *held*, allowing the appeal, that there was no justification in the judge sending for counsel. Such matters should have been dealt with in a pre-trial review, or, at least, in open court. The judge's comments had gone beyond the guidelines contained in *R. v. Turner*, justice had not been seen to be done, and the conviction would be quashed. (*R. v. Turner* [1970] C.L.Y. 479 applied; *R. v. Grice* [1978] C.L.Y. 625, *R. v. Bird (Note)* [1978] C.L.Y. 623, *R. v. Atkinson* [1978] C.L.Y. 573, and *R. v. Ryan* [1978] C.L.Y. 622 considered.)

R. v. LLEWELLYN (1978) 67 Cr.App.R. 149, C.A.

622.

The cases in which a judge should mention a sentence to counsel are very rare indeed, and only occur where he knows positively what type of sentence he will pass whatever happens, and being in possession of all the facts.

Counsel persuaded D, who wished to plead not guilty, to allow him to see the judge to ascertain what sentence the judge had in mind. The judge told counsel that on a plea of guilty at that stage he would consider probation or a bind-over with a condition of hospital treatment. Counsel told R that a non-custodial sentence was likely if he admitted his guilt. D changed his plea to guilty. Additional evidence came to light, and the judge passed a custodial sentence. D appealed on the ground that his pleas were a nullity, in that he had been induced to plead guilty under pressure. *Held*, allowing the appeal, and ordering a venire de novo, that the trial judge should only have given an indication if he was in possession of all the facts, and knew what sentence he was going to pass in any event. (*R. v. Turner* [1970] C.L.Y. 479 and *R. v. Inns* [1975] C.L.Y. 669 applied.)

R. v. RYAN (1978) 67 Cr.App.R. 177, C.A.

623. —— —— **counsel's duty**

If a judge offers a more lenient sentence for a plea of guilty to counsel in private, then it is part of counsel's duty to his client to mention the matter in mitigation.

D was charged with theft of £2,000 from his employer. Twice during the case the deputy judge sent for counsel, and indicated that if D fought the case to the end, there would be an immediate sentence of imprisonment, whereas if he pleaded guilty, there would be a suspended sentence. D fought the case, and was convicted. The deputy judge indicated to counsel that what had been said in his room was strictly private. Counsel indicated that nevertheless he proposed to rely on it in mitigation. He then argued in open court that if justice required a suspended sentence, the requirements of justice could not be different if D exercised his right of putting the prosecution to proof. D had given evidence, denying the offence, but the deputy judge said that in sentencing he was not punishing D for being no respecter of truth. He then sentenced him to an immediate sentence of imprisonment. On appeal by D, *held*, that it appeared to everyone who knew what had happened, including D, that that was precisely what was being done. Although the sentence would have been amply justified under different circumstances, justice had not been seen to be done, and the sentence would be suspended. Counsel had been right to raise, in open court in the interests of his client, what ought not to have been said at all in private; he would have been wrong to do otherwise. (*R.* v. *Cain* [1975] C.L.Y. 1412 and *Practice Direction* [1976] C.L.Y. 539 considered.)

    R. *v.* BIRD (1978) 67 Cr.App.R. 203, C.A.

624. —— —— **private discussions between counsel and judge**
The C.A. has again deprecated unnecessary discussions in private during a criminal trial between counsel and the judge. Such discussions should take place in open court in the jury's absence so that a shorthand note can be taken of them: R. *v.* WINTERFLOOD, *The Times,* November 21, 1978, C.A.

625. —— —— **sentence subsequently increased on breach of undertaking**
[Courts Act 1971 (c. 23), s. 11.]
The occasions when a judge should discuss sentence with counsel should be extremely rare, and the utmost care should be taken to comply with the directions in *R.* v. *Turner.*
G was charged with unlawful sexual intercourse with his adopted daughter and was induced to change his plea by an indication from the recorder that in sparing the girl giving evidence and on undertaking not to see her again, he would not impose an immediate custodial sentence. He received two years' imprisonment suspended for two years, but on breach of the undertaking was brought back to court some days later and the sentence was varied to one of immediate imprisonment. On appeal against sentence, *held*, allowing the appeal, that the recorder had disregarded the directions as to plea bargaining, and further, that it was only in exceptional circumstances that the judge should use his powers under s. 11 (2) of the Courts Act 1971 to increase sentence. The subsection was there to enable errors to be corrected. (Dictum of Lord Parker C.J. in *R.* v. *Turner* [1970] C.L.Y. 479 applied).

    R. *v.* GRICE (1977) 66 Cr.App.167, C.A.

626. —— **powers of Court of Appeal—judicial review of magistrates' decisions.** See R. *v.* BILLERICAY JUSTICES, *ex p.* RUMSEY, § 1932.

627. —— **printing and distributing obscene literature**
Persons who conspire to publish and send through the post obscene articles for gain, and thereby derive huge profits, must expect as well as prison sentences, fines which will take the profit out of their trade.
E was convicted of conspiracy to publish obscene articles for gain, and conspiracy to send postal packets containing indecent or obscene articles. He was sentenced to 12 months' imprisonment on the first count, a fine of £4,000 on the second count, with six months' imprisonment consecutive in default, plus an order for £8,000 towards prosecution costs, plus an order for up to £8,000 towards his legal aid costs. The evidence showed the distribution of pornography on a very large scale and very large profits from it. On appeal against sentence, *held,* that a prison sentence was appropriate as a warning to others, and that a large fine or other financial penalty was appropriate to take the profit out of a very profitable trade.

    R. *v.* EMMERSON (1977) 65 Cr.App.R. 154, C.A.

628. —— **procedure—taking other offences into consideration—indictment containing sample counts—criminal bankruptcy order**
[Powers of Criminal Courts Act 1973 (c. 62), s. 39 (1) (2).]

Further offences which have not been charged may only be taken into consideration when sentencing if the defendant has been informed explicitly of, and explicitly admitted each offence, and expressed his desire to have them taken into consideration; this rule applies to all offences which are not charged on an indictment containing merely sample counts.

D was convicted on an indictment containing 13 counts of obtaining money by deception from his employers to the value of £7,112. Those counts were merely sample counts, and a schedule to the indictment set out a further 20 offences amounting to £19,600 which were not proceeded with by the Crown. Evidence of those offences was however adduced at the trial without D's consent. The judge took the further 20 offences into consideration when passing sentences. Also, by adding the two figures together, and reaching a sum greater than the statutory minimum of £15,000 under s. 39 (1) (b) of the Powers of Criminal Courts Act 1973, the judge made a criminal bankruptcy order against D under the section. The Court of Appeal upheld the order. On appeal by D, held, allowing the appeal, that the only basis upon which the order could have been made was if D had had the opportunity to consider the schedule after the verdict, and explicitly asked for enough offences to be taken into consideration to bring the figures above the statutory £15,000. Accordingly the bankruptcy order would be set aside. (R. v. Syres (1908) 1 Cr.App.R. 172 considered.)

D.P.P. v. ANDERSON [1978] 2 All E.R. 512, H.L.

629. —— recommendation for deportation—national of EEC country—when appropriate.

[EEC Treaty, art. 48—Directive No. 64/221, art. 3.]

A court's recommendation for deportation of an offender from an EEC country is subject to the EEC restrictions upon interference with the free movement of workers.

When a French national working in England appeared at court for his second conviction for possessing dangerous drugs, the magistrate indicated that he was minded to make a recommendation for deportation. The defendant contended that such a course would offend against the EEC Treaty, art. 48. The magistrate sought the ruling of the European Court upon the contentions raised. Held, (1) that a recommendation for deportation was an action restricting the right to freedom of movement and was a " measure " within Directive 64/221; (2) that by virtue of art. 3 (2) of the Directive, previous criminal convictions do not by themselves justify such a recommendation although they might be some evidence that a defendant's continued presence represents a present threat to public policy, the threat not being simply that occasioned by the commission of the particular offence.

R. v. BOUCHEREAU [1978] 2 W.L.R. 251, European Ct.

630. —— retributive and deterrent elements—solicitor using clients' money in breach of trust

Where a solicitor uses clients' money in breach of trust to bolster-up other business interests, ordinarily the retributive and deterrent elements have to be considered, and hardship to the solicitor's family will be ignored.

D, aged 55, a solicitor of 15 years' experience, started taking his clients' money to bolster-up some failing business in which he had become involved. He then became involved, using clients' money, in a number of unsuccessful building speculations, using considerable skill and ingenuity in covering his tracks. Over three years, his defalcations amounted to £260,000. It was urged upon the court that D had ruined himself, that he had co-operated with police and pleaded guilty. It was further argued before the Court of Appeal, on appeal against a sentence of four years' imprisonment, that D's wife had been severely afflicted by his imprisonment, and that she had developed suicidal tendencies which would continue so long as D was in prison. Held, dismissing the appeal, that such matters as that could not normally be taken into consideration in such a case. The factors that should be considered were retribution (which had in the past not been considered fashionable as part of sentencing policy), and the deterrent element, for being in breach of trust.

R. v. DAVIES (1978) 67 Cr.App.R. 207, C.A.

631. —— **review of maximum penalties.** See § 1826.

632. —— **variation—within 28 days—scope of possible variation**
[Courts Act 1971 (c. 23), ss. 11 (2), 57 (1).]
The scope of the variation of sentence under s. 11 (2) is very wide, and includes the power to vary not only the length but also the nature of the sentence.
S fired an air rifle at a group of people outside his flat, slightly wounding a woman in the head. Convicted of malicious wounding, he was given a six months' prison sentence. It became clear in prison that he was mentally disturbed and was brought back to court within 28 days. A psychiatrist concluded that S had a paranoid psychosis. Sentence was varied to a hospital order under s. 60 of the Mental Health Act 1959, with a s. 65 restriction. On appeal, *held*, dismissing the appeal, that the word " varied " in s. 11 (2) of the Courts Act 1971 had a very wide meaning which enabled a judge not only to vary the length but also the nature of a sentence.
R. *v*. SODHI (1978) 66 Cr.App.R. 260, C.A.

633. —— **young offenders**
The Government has published a Green Paper entitled " Youth Custody and Supervision: a New Sentence," which contains proposals for a new sentence of " youth custody " for offenders in England and Wales aged between 17 and 21. This would replace existing custodial sentences for the age group, such as detention centres, Borstal training and imprisonment. The Green Paper is available from H.M.S.O. (Cmnd. 7282) [£1·50].

634. Sexual Offences (Amendment) Act 1976—commencement
SEXUAL OFFENCES (AMENDMENT) ACT 1976 (COMMENCEMENT) ORDER 1978 (No. 485 (C. 10)) [10p], made under the Sexual Offences (Amendment) Act 1976 (c. 82), s. 7 (4); operative on April 22, 1978; brings into force ss. 5 (1) (*b*), 6 (4) (*b*) (which relate to the anonymity of the complainant and the accused in rape cases tried by court-martial in Northern Ireland.

635. Soliciting—kerb crawling—young girls—whether offence
[Sexual Offences Act 1956 (c. 69), ss. 6 (1), 32.]
The soliciting for sex of girls under 16 while kerb-crawling is immoral and an offence under s. 6 of the Act.
D several times drove past three 14-year old girls, inviting them to have sex with him. On appeal against conviction, *held*, dismissing the appeal, that soliciting of girls of this age was not only immoral but also a criminal offence under s. 6 (1) of the 1956 Act, and that an offence under s. 32 had therefore been made out. (*Crooke* v. *Edmondson* [1966] C.L.Y. 12325 distinguished.)
R. *v*. DODD (1977) 66 Cr.App.R. 87, C.A.

636. Suicide—aiding and abetting—whether an offence
[Suicide Act 1961 (c. 60), s. 2 (1); Offences against the Person Act 1861 (c. 100), s. 23.]
Every attempt to commit an offence is an offence at common law even where the crime in question is itself in the nature of an attempt. Consent cannot render innocent an otherwise dangerous act.
M visited her mother, who had previously threatened suicide, in a convalescent home, pinned nembutal tablets in her clothing, and discussed suicide with her, encouraging her to get it right this time. *Held*, dismissing her appeal against conviction, that any attempt to commit an offence was an offence at common law even though the crime defined in s. 2 (1) of the Suicide Act 1961 was itself in the nature of an attempt; that consent could not render innocent what was in fact a dangerous act, namely the administration of a noxious substance for the purpose of suicide. (*R.* v. *Coney* (1882) 8 Q.B. 534 considered.)
R. *v*. McSHANE (1977) 66 Cr.App.R. 97, C.A.

637. Suppression of terrorism—extradition. See § 1456.

638. Taking conveyance without consent—horse—whether a conveyance
[Theft Act 1968 (c. 60), s. 12 (1) (7) (*a*).]
S. 12 of the Theft Act is directed towards artefacts rather than animals, which consequently are not within the ambit of the section.

The defendants took three horses from a field, attaching bridles to them in order to ride them away. The justices did not consider a horse to be a "conveyance," nor attaching a bridle to be "adapting" it for carriage. On the prosecutor's appeal, *held*, dismissing the appeal, that a horse was not a conveyance for the purpose of the Act, nor did putting a bridle on a horse constitute "adapting" it.

NEAL v. GRIBBLE [1978] R.T.R. 409, D.C.

638a. Theft—attempt—entering a car

A defendant who enters a car with the intention of stealing anything which seems worth taking is not guilty of attempted theft, although he may be convicted of loitering with intent or of going equipped for theft. (*R.* v. *Easom* [1971] C.L.Y. 2816 applied): R. v. HECTOR, *The Times*, January 19, 1978, C.A.

639. —— joint enterprise

[Theft Act 1968 (c. 60), ss. 1 (1), 16 (1).]
Where a cashier "under-rings" goods which a shopper then removes from a shop, both may be guilty of theft.

The appellant cashier underpriced goods for a shopper, whom she knew, by "under-ringing" them on the till. Both were charged with, and convicted of, theft. *Held*, dismissing the cashier's appeal, that there had been an appropriation of the goods, by putting them in the basket and taking them from the shop, and that, as there was a joint enterprise, both were guilty of theft.

R. v. BHACHU (1977) 65 Cr.App.R. 261, C.A.

640. —— obtaining by deception—blatant dishonesty

[Theft Act 1968 (c. 60).] The Court of Appeal considered further the difficulties caused by ss. 15 and 16 of the Theft Act 1968, in reluctantly quashing convictions "resulting from blatant dishonesty": R. v. CLOW, *The Times*, August 9, 1978, C.A.

641. —— when property passes—formation of dishonest intent—non-payment in supermarket

D was given fruit in a supermarket after it had been weighed, bagged and priced. Instead of paying at the exit, she then left with the goods without paying. The justices found there was no case to answer, on the ground that property in the goods had passed to D when she received them and there was no evidence of a dishonest intent before then. *Held*, allowing the prosecutor's appeal, that property in goods in a supermarket does not pass until the goods are paid for. The situation might have been different if the assistant concerned had been in a managerial or other special category: DAVIES v. LEIGHTON [1978] Crim.L.R. 575, D.C.

642. Theft Act 1978 (c. 31)

This Act replaces s. 16 (2) (*a*) of the Theft Act 1968.

S. 1 makes it an offence dishonestly to obtain services from another by deception; s. 2 makes it an offence to evade liability by deception; s. 3 creates the offence of dishonestly making off without payment; s. 4 sets out the punishments for offences under ss. 1–4; s. 5 contains supplementary provisions; s. 6 relates to the enactment of the same provisions for Northern Ireland; s. 7 gives the short title. The Act does not extend to Scotland or Northern Ireland.

The Act received the Royal Assent on July 20, 1978, and came into force on October 20, 1978.

643. Trial—alternative verdicts

[Criminal Law Act 1967 (c. 58), s. 6 (3); Offences Against the Person Act 1861 (c. 100), ss. 18, 20, 47.] N was indicted for causing grievous bodily harm with intent contrary to s. 18 of the 1861 Act. The judge directed the jury that they could alternatively convict of causing grievous bodily harm, contrary to s. 20 or assault occasioning actual bodily harm contrary to s. 47. *Held*, allowing N's appeal against conviction of assault occasioning actual bodily harm, that s. 47 was not, under the Criminal Law Act 1967, s. 6 (3), an alternative verdict on a charge of s. 18: R. v. NICHOLLS [1978] Crim.L.R. 247, C.A.

644. —— **application for retrial—discretion of judge—extent of prosecution's duty to disclose information to defence**

During M's trial for handling, his counsel applied for a retrial on the ground that prosecuting counsel had failed to disclose to the defence that it was a co-defendant who had told the police that the stolen property was hidden at M's premises. *Held*, refusing leave to appeal against conviction on the ground that a retrial should have been ordered, that (1) the granting of a retrial was a matter of discretion for the trial judge; (2) in general, there was no duty on the prosecution to reveal to the defence the line of attack on the credibility of a defence witness. The prosecution could use any material available to attack the credibility of a witness the defence chose to call: R. *v.* MADGE [1978] Crim.L.R. 305, C.A.

645. —— **autrefois acquit—where no trial on merits**

Magistrates refused an adjournment when the prosecution were not ready to proceed on a charge of theft. As no evidence was available at court the case was dismissed. *Held*, allowing a plea of autrefois acquit and quashing an indictment alleging the same theft, that references to " trial on the merits " were concerned with res judicata and were not appropriate in cases concerned with autrefois acquit or convict where it is the acquittal or conviction itself which is a bar to subsequent proceedings: R. *v.* PRESSICK [1978] Crim.L.R. 377, Chester Crown Ct.

646. —— **costs—payable by defendant—sum to be specified or limited**

[Costs in Criminal Cases Act 1973 (c. 14), s. 4 (1).]

When a defendant is ordered to pay prosecution costs, the amount payable must either be specified or be limited to a particular sum.

The defendant was convicted of a driving offence and by way of sentence ordered, inter alia, to pay the costs of the prosecution (which in the event amounted to £150). *Held*, allowing his appeal, that the order for costs would be limited to £75.

R. *v.* NEWLOVE [1978] R.T.R. 150, C.A.

647. —— **defendant dispensing with counsel—discretion of judge to hear defendant**

In the course of a criminal trial, the defendant applied to dispense with the services of his counsel. The judge refused to hear the defendant and, having ascertained that counsel was not forensically embarrassed, refused the application. *Held*, that the judge had acted within his discretion, though normally the defendant would be allowed to give his reasons: R. *v.* LYONS, *The Times*, July 13, 1978, C.A.

648. —— **defendant " not represented by counsel "—solicitor not having practising certificate**

[Criminal Justice Act 1967 (c. 80), s. 1 (1).] At committal proceedings the defendant was represented by counsel, and he was duly committed without consideration of the witness statements pursuant to s. 1 (1) of the Criminal Justice Act 1967. In due course he was convicted at the Crown Court. It was discovered that the solicitor who instructed counsel did not have a practising certificate, and was, accordingly, not qualified to act as a solicitor. *Held*, that this did not mean that the defendant was " not represented by counsel " within s. 1 of the Act of 1967; accordingly, the committal and conviction were good: R. *v.* SCOTT, *The Times*, June 29, 1978, C.A.

649. —— **judge—bias—same witness**

[Can.] Eight charges were laid against six accused, all arising out of the same labour dispute. Two of the accused were tried and found guilty; the third of the six accused was then tried: his trial was adjourned at the conclusion of the Crown's evidence. After the adjournment a further information was laid against another accused, relating to similar subject matter. Application for prohibition founded on bias. *Held*, judges cannot be insulated from the world in which they live. The fact a judge disbelieves a witness in one case does not necessarily mean that he will disbelieve the same witness in another case. (*R.* v. *Grimsby Borough Quarter Sessions, ex p. Fuller* [1955] C.L.Y. 1627 and *R.* v. *Camborne Justices, ex p. Pearce* [1954] C.L.Y. 2011 referred to): HUZIAK *v.* ANDRYCHUK (1977) 1 C.R.N.S. 132, Sask. Q.B.

650. —— **jury convicting on all of alternative counts—judge's duty to repeat direction**
A was indicted on three alternative counts. The judge directed the jury that they need not consider the second and third counts if satisfied of A's guilt on the first since they were alternative counts. The jury convicted on all three counts. *Held*, quashing all three convictions, that the judge should have repeated the direction and sent the jury out again to decide of which of the three offences A should be convicted: R. *v.* ALI [1978] Crim.L.R. 245, C.A.

651. —— **order for new trial—principles**
In setting down guidelines for when a new trial should be ordered, pursuant to s. 14 (2) of Jamaica's Judicature (Appellate Jurisdiction) Act, after a verdict has been quashed, the Privy Council *held* that, while the list of factors to be considered was not exhaustive and had to take account of the circumstances of each case, and while the Committee refrained from giving any one factor more importance than another, considerations such as the seriousness and prevalence of the offence; the expense and duration of a new trial; the second ordeal to be undergone by the defendant; the effects on the evidence of any great time-lapse since the alleged offence; and, most notably, the weight of the prosecution evidence, all demanded attention: REID *v.* R. (1978) 122 S.J. 861, P.C.

652. —— **procedure—defendant not giving evidence—prosecution's right to closing address**
Prosecuting counsel has the right to make a closing speech where a represented defendant has called no evidence, but such right should be exercised sparingly.
At their trial the applicants who were represented by counsel neither gave nor called evidence. Their co-defendant called evidence which could have affected the credibility of a prosecution witness. Prosecuting counsel made a closing speech in which he commented, inter alia, upon the cases of the applicants. They sought leave to appeal against their subsequent convictions upon the grounds that the Crown was not entitled to a final speech and/or to comment upon the case against them. *Held*, refusing leave, that in such circumstances prosecuting counsel was entitled to make a closing speech, and that in the opinion of the court such right should only rarely be exercised, such as in long and complex cases, and should be exercised briefly. (*R.* v. *Gardner* [1899] 1 Q.B. 150 and *R.* v. *Trevelli* (1882) 15 Cox C.C. 289 applied; *R.* v. *Baggott* (1927) 20 Cr.App.R. 92 distinguished.)
R. *v.* BRYANT; R. *v.* OXLEY [1978] 2 W.L.R. 589, C.A.

653. —— **refusal of adjournment for defence expert to complete analysis**
D was charged with trafficking more than 30 gms. of morphine, an offence carrying a mandatory death penalty in Singapore. An application for an adjournment at the close of cross-examination by the prosecution to enable the defence chemist to complete his analysis was refused. *Held*, dismissing D's appeal against conviction, that on detailed examination of the evidence and since there had been no basis for suggesting that the prosecution chemist's analyses were incorrect or that any relevant evidence could become available as a result of the defence analysis the refusal of an adjournment was justified and D had suffered no injustice: TEO HOOK SENG *v.* PUBLIC PROSECUTOR [1978] Crim. L.R. 378, P.C.

654. —— **summing up—burden of proof—self-defence**
The trial judge summed up in such a way that the jury may have thought it was for F to establish his defence of self-defence. *Held*, applying the proviso, that a judge must be very careful indeed not to leave a jury with the impression that it was for the defence to establish this defence: R. *v.* FOLLEY [1978] Crim.L.R. 557, C.A.

655. —— —— **comment on likelihood of police officer manufacturing evidence**
W's defence involved suggesting that a police officer's evidence was a pack of lies. The issue for the jury was whether the officer was telling the truth. The judge adjourned the case near the end of his summing-up. In the few remaining sentences the following morning the judge said: " You may wonder if this officer would be so stupid as to risk his career in manufacturing evidence

of the sort that this defendant says he has." *Held,* dismissing W's appeal, that there was no material irregularity, although the deputy judge had made a slip. It was desirable to avoid comments of this kind (*R.* v. *Culbertson* [1970] C.L.Y. 544 distinguished): R. *v.* WELLWOOD-KERR [1978] Crim.L.R. 760, C.A.

656. Unlawful sexual intercourse—parties in same age group—provocation—whether custodial sentence appropriate

[Sexual Offences Act (c. 69), s. 60.]

Where an offender is charged with unlawful sexual intercourse with a girl under 16 who is willing, and the parties are of the same age-group, it is normal to impose a moderate sentence.

O'G received suggestive letters from a 14-year-old girl, succumbed to her advances, and eventually had intercourse with her. O'G was of the same age-group as the girl. O'G appealed against a sentence of three months at a detention centre. *Held,* allowing the appeal, that where the parties are in the same age-group, and both willing, and having regard to the current standards of sexual behaviour, it was wrong to impose a penalty of loss of liberty.

R. *v.* O'GRADY (1978) 66 Cr.App.R. 279, C.A.

657. Vandalism

The Central Policy Review Staff have published a report entitled " Vandalism," which is particularly relevant to a national conference on that subject called on October 31, 1978. The report recommends that a dossier of practical, cost-conscious preventative measures should be prepared and kept under review by local authorities and other agencies; and concludes that effective combative methods are those which involve a sense of individual and collective responsibility. The report is available from H.M.S.O. [£1·75].

658. Verdict—inconsistency—whether necessarily a ground for quashing

D was convicted of having a firearm in a public place, but acquitted of possessing a firearm without a certificate. Both counts related to the same incident. D had acquired a pistol when drunk at a social club and later produced it and used it. *Held,* dismissing D's appeal, that inconsistency of verdicts brought in by the same jury at one trial tended to show that the jury were confused and that the verdict was unsafe. In this case, so far as having the firearm in a public place was concerned, D had had it in his hand. But the jury may have thought it unrealistic to charge possession without a certificate as he had possibly only possessed the firearm for an hour or two. Thus the verdicts could have been reached without confusion and the inconsistency was not sufficiently fundamental to go to the root of the conviction. The court would not speculate on the reason for the jury's verdict: R. *v.* DAWES [1978] Crim.L.R. 503, C.A.

659. —— reached late in evening—whether unsafe or unsatisfactory

G brought a private prosecution for assault occasioning actual bodily harm against S and M, police officers. The issue was who struck the first blow. It was desirable for " important considerations " that the trial should end on the second day, a Friday. The jury retired at 7.44 p.m., having been asked whether they wished to retire that evening or the following morning. A majority direction was given at 10.05 p.m. and majority verdicts of guilty in each case were returned at 10.30 p.m. *Held,* allowing the appeal, that a verdict reached at 10.30 p.m. must be open to challenge as unsafe or unsatisfactory: R. *v.* SUTTON AND MOORE [1978] Crim.L.R. 442, C.A.

660. Vicarious liability—employers—unknown and unauthorised act of employee—child labour for milkround

[Children and Young Persons Act 1933 (c. 12), s. 21.] A milkman employed by the P.I.M.C.S. employed a boy aged 10 to help him at a time when employment of children was prohibited by by-laws made under s. 21 of the 1933 Act. The by-laws also prohibited employment of children under 14. *Held,* allowing the P.I.M.C.S.'s appeal against conviction of contravention of the by-laws, that it was not liable for the unknown and unauthorised act of its milk roundsman. (*Robinson* v. *Hill* [1910] 1 K.B. 94 followed): PORTSEA ISLAND MUTUAL CO-OPERATIVE SOCIETY *v.* LEYLAND [1978] Crim.L.R. 554, C.A.

661. Witness—immunity from prosecution—application for judicial review
On the prosecution of Mr. Jeremy Thorpe and others for conspiracy to murder, the D.P.P. offered a prosecution witness resident abroad immunity from prosecution if he came to England for the purpose of giving evidence. Mr. Thorpe applied for a judicial review, contending that the immunity would extend to perjury committed by the witness; that contention was rejected on behalf of the D.P.P. *Held*, that the application was refused: *Re* THORPE, *The Times*, November 17, 1978, D.C.

662. —— intimidation—solicitor's professional misconduct. See *Re* A SOLICITOR, § 2831.

663. —— judge's powers
At a criminal trial, the judge is not entitled to insist that the prosecution call a witness. The judge's own power to call the witness should be sparingly exercised: R. *v.* BALDWIN, *The Times*, May 3, 1978, C.A.

BOOKS AND ARTICLES. See *post*, pp. [3], [17].

CROWN PRACTICE

664. Crown proceedings. See PRACTICE.

665. Government policy—no power to suspend operation of law
[Can.] The respondent, an Indian, claimed that because it was government policy not to prosecute Indians under the Migratory Birds Convention Act, it was an abuse to seek to prosecute him under that Act. *Held*, the Crown has no power to direct that the operation of a duly enacted law be suspended or dispensed with, either generally, or with respect to any group or individual. Accordingly, the executive was not fettered by its policy, and the prosecution was not an abuse of process: R. *v.* CATAGAS [1978] 1 W.W.R. 282, Manitoba C.A.

666. Licensing. See INTOXICATING LIQUORS.

667. State Immunity Act 1978 (c. 33). See § 1737.

ARTICLES. See *post*, p. [20].

CUSTOMS AND EXCISE

668. Agricultural products
AGRICULTURE LEVY RELIEFS (FROZEN BEEF AND VEAL) ORDER 1978 (No. 194), [15p], made under the Import Duties Act 1958 (c. 6), s. 5 (4); operative on February 14, 1978; requires the Minister of Agriculture, Fisheries and Food to allocate the U.K.'s share of a quota for the levy-free import of frozen beef and veal under the provisions of Council Reg. 2861/77.

669. Air traffic
H.M. Customs and Excise have issued Notice No. 29 (January 1978): Customs control of air traffic.

670. Airports
H.M. Customs and Excise have issued Notice No. 124 (January 1978): Control of stores and store floors at customs airports.

671. Beer, wines and spirits
BEER (AMENDMENT) REGULATIONS 1978 (No. 1186) [10p], made under the Customs and Excise Act 1952 (c. 44), ss. 127, 171 and 250; operative on September 1, 1978; amend S.I. 1978 No. 893 by substituting a new Reg. 46 and associated Sched. 10. They are made to avoid any possibility that the Schedule as worded in S.I. 1978 No. 893 might be considered to give the Commissioners of Customs and Excise a discretion under the regulations which is not conferred upon them by the enabling provision.
EXCISE DUTY (RELIEF ON ALCOHOLIC INGREDIENTS) REGULATIONS 1978 (No. 1786) [25p], made under the Finance Act 1978 (c. 42), s. 2, the Finance Act 1976 (c. 40), s. 2 (5) (*d*), and the Customs and Excise Act 1952, s. 140 (1) (*e*), as substituted and amended by the Finance (No. 2) Act 1975 (c. 45), Sched. 3,

para. 27; operative on January 1, 1979; set out the conditions governing the repayment of the excise duty paid in respect of bear, cider, made-wine and wine used as an ingredient in the production of beverages and other articles of a low alcohol content.

672. Coins—prohibition of imports and exports—meaning of " capital "—referral to European Court

J and others were convicted of offences based upon the prohibitions on importation of gold coins and exportation of U.K. coins of silver alloy minted before 1947, made under the Import of Goods (Control) Order 1954 and the Export of Goods (Control) Order 1970 respectively. The relevant imports and exports were to and from West Germany. The Crown Court held that (1) these prohibitions were not in conflict with arts. 30 to 37 of the EEC Treaty, by reason of " public policy "; (2) the coins concerned were not " goods " within Title I of the Treaty, but " capital " within Title III, even though used as commodities by the defendants. On appeal by the defendants, *held*, several questions would be referred under art. 177 EEC to the European Court, notably whether this term includes (1) gold coins produced in non-Member States; (2) silver alloy coins which are legal tender in a Member State; and (3) similar coins which, although not legal tender, are protected in a Member State from destruction. Also referred was the question of whether their manner of sale (in casu: sale of their metal content) could deprive them of the status of inclusion in this term.

R. *v.* JOHNSON, THOMPSON AND WOODIWISS [1978] 1 C.M.L.R. 390, C.A.

673. Community transit

H.M. Customs and Excise have published Notice No. 753 (January 1978): the simplified procedure for goods carried by rail.

674. CUSTOMS AND EXCISE (COMMUNITY TRANSIT GOODS) REGULATIONS 1978 (No. 1602) [20p], made under the European Communities Act 1972 (c. 68), s. 2 (2); operative on December 8, 1978; amend the Customs and Excise Act 1952, ss. 28, 47, 49 and 307, and the Finance Act 1971, Sched. 1, by excluding from their scope goods in transit through the U.K. under cover of Community transit documents issued under Council Regulation 222/77.

675. Customs duties

CUSTOMS DUTIES (QUOTA RELIEF) ORDER 1978 (No. 878) [10p], made under the Import Duties Act 1958 (c. 6), ss. 5 (4), 13, as amended by the European Communities Act 1972 (c. 68), s. 5 and Sched. 4, para. 1; operative on July 1, 1978; provides for the administration of the U.K. tariff quota.

CUSTOMS DUTIES (INWARD AND OUTWARD PROCESSING RELIEF) REGULATIONS 1978 (No. 1148) [20p], made under the European Communities Act 1972, s. 5 (6); operative on September 1, 1978; amend the Import Duties Act 1958; S.I. 1976 No. 838 and S.I. 1977 No. 910 by omitting certain words from s. 5 (4) of that Act, and by the revocation of certain transitional provisions of S.I. 1976 No. 838.

CUSTOMS DUTIES (GREECE) ORDER 1978 (No. 1593) [10p], made under the European Communities Act 1972, s. 5 (2), (3); operative on January 1, 1979; amends S.I. 1977 No. 2056 by altering the reference to degree of alcohol to the symbol " % vol." in the description of made wine, cider and perry originating in Greece.

CUSTOMS DUTIES RELIEF REGULATIONS 1978 (No. 1704) [10p], made under the European Communities Act 1972, s. 5 (6); operative on April 1, 1979; repeal the Import Duties Act 1958, Sched. 4, para. 3, and thereby remove from the list of articles which qualify for relief from custom duties under s. 6 of that Act articles intended to be used in scientific research, or for a purpose connected with the advancement of learning or art or with promotion of sport.

CUSTOMS DUTIES (DEFERRED PAYMENT) (AMENDMENT) REGULATIONS 1978 (No. 1725) [10p], made under the Finance Act 1976 (c. 40), s. 15; operative on January 1, 1979; amend S.I. 1976 No. 1223 in order to implement the obligations contained in Council Directive 78/453 on duty deferment.

CUSTOMS DUTIES (ECSC) (QUOTA AND OTHER RELIEFS) ORDER 1978 (No. 1933) [25p], made under the Import Duties Act 1958, s. 5, Sched. 3, para. 3 (2), as amended by the European Communities Act 1972, s. 5 (3), Sched. 4, para. 1, and by S.I. 1976 No. 2130; operative on January 1, 1979; provides for reliefs from customs duty on certain iron and steel products originating in the developing countries specified in Sched. 2, in accordance with two decisions of the representatives of the governments of the Member States of the ECSC meeting in council of December 19, 1978.

676. —— **EEC—charges having equivalent effect.** See FRATELLI CUCCHI *v.* AVEZ S.P.A. § 1260.

677. —— **levy—processing of precious metals—EEC.** See STATENS KONTROL MED AEDLE METALLER *v.* PREBEN LARSEN AND FLEMMING KJERULFF, § 1261.

678. **Dumping**

ANTI-DUMPING AND COUNTERVAILING DUTIES (POSTPONEMENT OF COLLECTION) REGULATIONS 1978 (No. 77) [15p], made under the European Communities Act 1972 (c. 68), s. 2 (2); operative on January 23, 1978; makes provision concerning the implementation of recommendations made in pursuance of Commission Recommendation 77/329/ECSC and provides that the collection of duty imposed by an order under s. 5 (1) of the 1972 Act may be postponed if the importer gives security for the payment of the duty charged and so long as the charge of duty continues.

CUSTOMS DUTIES (ECSC) ANTI-DUMPING (No. 1) ORDER 1978 (No. 78) [10p], made under the European Communities Act 1972, s. 5 (1) (3); operative on January 24, 1978; imposes an anti-dumping duty on iron or steel coils for re-rolling originating in Czechoslovakia or the Republic of Korea; and postpones the duty in accordance with S.I. 1978 No. 77.

CUSTOMS DUTIES (ECSC) ANTI-DUMPING (No. 2) ORDER 1978 (No. 81) [10p], made under the European Communities Act 1972, s. 5 (1) (3), operative on January 25, 1978; imposes an anti-dumping duty on the import of certain sheets and plates of iron or steel originating in Bulgaria, Czechoslovakia or Japan and postpones the duty in accordance with S.I. 1978 No. 77.

CUSTOMS DUTIES (ECSC) ANTI-DUMPING (No. 3) ORDER 1978 (No. 82) [15p], made under the European Communities Act 1972, s. 5 (1) (3); operative on January 25, 1978; imposes an anti-dumping duty on imports of certain haematite pig iron and cast iron originating in Canada and postpones the duty in accordance with S.I. 1978 No. 77.

CUSTOMS DUTIES (ECSC) ANTI-DUMPING (No. 4) ORDER 1978 (No. 83) [10p], made under the European Communities Act 1972, s. 5 (1) (3), operative on January 25, 1978; imposes an anti-dumping duty on imports of certain sheets and plates of iron or steel originating in Czechoslovakia and postpones the duty in accordance with S.I. 1978 No. 77.

CUSTOMS DUTIES (ECSC) ANTI-DUMPING (No. 5) ORDER 1978 (No. 84) [10p], made under the European Communities Act 1972, s. 5 (1) (3), operative on January 25, 1978; imposes an anti-dumping duty on imports of certain wire rod of iron or steel originating in Czechoslovakia and postpones the duty in accordance with S.I. 1978 No. 77.

CUSTOMS DUTIES (ECSC) ANTI-DUMPING (No. 6) ORDER 1978 (No. 85) [10p], made under the European Communities Act 1972, s. 5 (1) (3), operative on January 25, 1978; imposes an anti-dumping duty on imports of certain zinc-coated sheets and plates of iron or steel originating in Poland or Spain and postpones the duty in accordance with S.I. 1978 No. 77.

CUSTOMS DUTIES (ECSC) ANTI-DUMPING (No. 7) ORDER 1978 (No. 109) [10p], made under the European Communities Act 1972, s. 5 (1) (3), operative on January 30, 1978; imposes an anti-dumping duty on imports of certain angles, shapes and sections of iron or steel originating in Spain and postpones the duty in accordance with S.I. 1978 No. 77.

CUSTOMS DUTIES (ECSC) ANTI-DUMPING (No. 8) ORDER 1978 (No. 110) [10p], made under the European Communities Act 1972, s. 5 (1) (3), operative on January 30, 1978; imposes an anti-dumping duty on imports of certain sheets and plates of iron or steel originating in the GDR, East Berlin, Roumania or Spain and postpones the duty in accordance with S.I. 1978 No. 77.

CUSTOMS DUTIES (ECSC) ANTI-DUMPING (No. 9) ORDER 1978 (No. 111) [10p], made under the European Communities Act 1972, s. 5 (1) (3), operative on January 30, 1978; imposes an anti-dumping duty on imports of certain sheets and plates of iron or steel originating in Japan and postpones the duty in accordance with S.I. 1978 No. 77.

CUSTOMS DUTIES (ECSC) ANTI-DUMPING (No. 10) ORDER 1978 (No. 155) [10p], made under the European Communities Act 1972, s. 5 (1) and (3); operative on February 6, 1978; imposes an anti-dumping duty on imports of iron or steel coils for re-rolling, originating in Bulgaria or Japan. Collection of the duty charged is postponed in accordance with S.I. 1978 No. 77.

CUSTOMS DUTIES (ECSC) ANTI-DUMPING (No. 11) ORDER 1978 (No. 192) [10p], made under the European Communities Act 1972, s. 5 (1) and (3); operative on February 9, 1978; imposes an anti-dumping duty on imports of certain angles, shapes and sections of iron or steel originating in Japan. Collection of the duty is postponed in accordance with S.I. 1978 No. 77.

CUSTOMS DUTIES (ECSC) ANTI-DUMPING (No. 12) ORDER 1978 (No. 193) [10p], made under the European Communities Act 1972, s. 5 (1), (3); operative on February 9, 1978; imposes an anti-dumping duty on imports of certain sheets and plates of iron or steel, originating in Poland, at a rate equal to the amount by which the price paid by the importer for the goods inclusive of insurance and freight and the duty under the ECSC unified tariff is lower than the price published by the ECC. Collection of the duty charged by the Order is postponed in accordance with S.I. 1978 No. 77.

CUSTOMS DUTIES (ECSC) ANTI-DUMPING (No. 13) ORDER 1978 (No. 237) [15p], made under the European Communities Act 1972 s. 5 (1) (3); operative on February 21, 1978; imposes an anti-dumping duty on imports of iron or steel coils for re-rolling originating in Australia and postpones the duty in accordance with S.I. 1978 No. 77.

CUSTOMS DUTIES (ECSC) ANTI-DUMPING (No. 14) ORDER 1978 (No. 246) [15p] made under the European Communities Act 1972, s. 5 (1) (3); operative on February 22, 1978; imposes an anti-dumping duty on imports of certain zinc-coated sheets and plates of iron or steel originating in the GDR, East Berlin or Japan and postpones the duty in accordance with S.I. 1978 No. 77.

ANTI-DUMPING AND COUNTERVAILING DUTIES (POSTPONEMENT OF COLLECTION) (AMENDMENT) REGULATIONS 1978 (No. 598) [10p], made under the European Communities Act 1972, s. 2 (2); operative on April 21, 1978; amends S.I. 1978 No. 77 by providing that where any charge of anti-dumping or countervailing duty on iron and steel products imported into the United Kingdom by virtue of any order imposing a provisional duty ceases to have effect with respect to some of the products, the postponement of the collection of duty charged on the products comes to an end and in future such goods may be imported without the payment of any duty or having to give any security for such duty.

CUSTOMS DUTY (ECSC) ANTI-DUMPING (AMENDMENT) ORDER 1978 (No. 601) [10p], made under the European Communities Act 1972, s. 5 (1) (3); operative on April 21, 1978; provides that no anti-dumping duties shall be charged on imports of certain iron or steel originating in Japan where such duties were imposed by specified Order.

CUSTOMS DUTIES (ECSC) ANTI-DUMPING (REVOCATION) (No. 1) ORDER 1978 (No. 640) [10p] made under the European Communities Act 1972, s. 5 (1) (3); operative on April 29, 1978; revokes S.I. 1978 No. 82.

CUSTOMS DUTIES (ECSC) ANTI-DUMPING (No. 15) ORDER 1978 (No. 641) [20p], made under the European Communities Act 1972, s. 5 (1) (3); operative on April 29, 1978; imposes an anti-dumping duty in respect of imports of iron or steel coils for re-rolling originating in the Republic of Korea, certain sheets and plates of iron or steel originating in Bulgaria, the German Democratic Republic, East Berlin or Rumania. The Order replaces S.I. 1978 Nos. 78, 81, 110, in so far as those Orders relate to goods originating in the Republic of Korea, Bulgaria, the German Democratic Republic, East Berlin or Rumania. The effect of S.I. 1978 No. 77 in relation to those Orders and the duty is accordingly payable.

CUSTOMS DUTIES (ECSC) ANTI-DUMPING (AMENDMENT No. 2) ORDER 1978 (No. 674) [10p], made under the European Communities Act 1972, s. 5 (1) (3);

operative on May 6, 1978; provides that no anti-dumping duties shall be charged on imports of certain iron and steel products originating in Czechoslovakia or Spain where such duties were imposed by specified Orders.

CUSTOMS DUTIES (ECSC) ANTI-DUMPING (No. 16) ORDER 1978 (No. 698) [20p], made under the European Communities Act 1972, s. 5 (1) (3); operative on May 12, 1978; imposes an anti-dumping duty on imports of iron or steel coils for re-rolling originating in Bulgaria. The Order replaces S.I. 1978 No. 155 and the duty imposed by that Order is now payable, S.I. 1978 No. 77 having ended in respect of goods originating in Bulgaria.

CUSTOMS DUTIES (ECSC) ANTI-DUMPING (No. 17) ORDER 1978 (No. 765) [20p], made under the European Communities Act 1972, s. 5 (1) (3); operative on May 27, 1978; imposes an anti-dumping duty on imports of certain zinc-coated sheets and plates of iron or steel originating in the G.D.R. and East Berlin. It also replaces S.I. 1978 No. 246 in so far as that Order relates to goods originating in the G.D.R. and East Berlin, and brings to an end S.I. 1978 No. 77 and the duty on the goods is now payable.

CUSTOMS DUTIES (ECSC) ANTI-DUMPING (AMENDMENT No. 3) ORDER 1978 (No. 909) [10p], made under the European Communities Act 1972, s. 5 (1) (3); operative on June 30, 1978; provides that no anti-dumping duty shall be charged after the coming into operation of this Order on imports of certain iron and steel products originating in Romania where such duty was imposed by S.I. 1978 No. 641.

CUSTOMS DUTIES (ECSC) ANTI-DUMPING (No. 18) ORDER 1978 (No. 1142) [25p], made under the European Communities Act 1972, s. 5 (1) (3); operative on August 4, 1978; imposes an anti-dumping duty on imports of certain zinc-coated sheets and plates of iron and steel originating in Japan, Spain, Czechoslovakia and Poland which may be reduced in certain circumstances, and replaces a number of specified Orders.

CUSTOMS DUTIES (ECSC) ANTI-DUMPING (AMENDMENT No. 4) ORDER 1978 (No. 1143) [10p], made under the European Communities Act 1972, s. 5 (1) (3); operative on August 4, 1978; provides that no anti-dumping duty shall be charged after the coming into operation of this Order on imports of certain iron and steel products originating in Australia, Czechoslovakia, Japan, Poland, or Spain where such a duty was imposed by S.I. 1978 Nos. 237 and 1142.

ANTI-DUMPING AND COUNTERVAILING DUTIES ORDER 1978 (No. 1147) [20p], made under the Finance Act 1978 (c. 42), s. 6 (1) (2); operative on August 31, 1978; implements in U.K. law the Community obligations of the U.K. under arts. 15–19 of Recommendation 77/329/ECSC of the Commission of European Communities, on protection against dumping or the granting of bounties or subsidies by non-member countries in respect of products covered by the ECSC Treaty.

CUSTOMS DUTIES (ECSC) ANTI-DUMPING (REVOCATION) (No. 2) ORDER 1978 (No. 1205) [20p], made under the European Communities Act 1972, s. 5 (1) (3); operative on August 12, 1978; revoke a number of specified orders which, inter alia, imposed anti-dumping duties on imports of certain iron and steel products originating in, Czechoslovakia, Japan, Spain or Poland.

CUSTOMS DUTIES (ECSC) ANTI-DUMPING (REVOCATION) (No. 3) ORDER 1978 (No. 1342) [10p], made under the European Communities Act 1972, s. 5 (1) (3); operative on September 14, 1978; revokes S.I. 1978 No. 237. Collection of duty under that Order was postponed and any security given will be released in accordance with the provisions of S.I. 1978 No. 77.

ANTI-DUMPING (AMENDMENT) ORDER 1978 (No. 1497) [10p], made under the Customs Duties (Dumping and Subsidies) Act 1969 (c. 16), s. 15 (4), and the Finance Act 1978 (c. 42), s. 6 (7); operative on November 19, 1978; amends S.I. 1977 No. 716 by amending the description of certain stainless steel originating in Spain which is subject to duty according to its metallurgical composition at the rate of 8 per cent.

CUSTOMS DUTIES (ECSC) (ANTI-DUMPING) (AMENDMENT No. 5) ORDER 1978 (No. 1941) [20p], made under the European Communities Act 1972, s. 5 (1) (3); operative on December 29, 1978; provides that no anti-dumping duty shall be charged on imports of certain iron and steel products originating in Korea.

679. Duty

H.M. Customs and Excise have published Notice No. 101 (April 1978): duty deferment.

680. EEC—common customs tariff—compensatory amounts for traders—liability of Commission for sudden changes. See MERKUR ASSENHANDEL G.M.B.H. & CO. KG *v.* E.C. COMMISSION, § 1245.

681. —— customs levies—national rule of natural justice—applicability to Community law. See BALKAN-IMPORT-EXPORT G.M.B.H. *v.* HAUPTZOLLAMT BERLIN-PACKHOF, § 1259a.

682. EEC preferences—rules of origin. See § 1282.

683. Exchange control. See REVENUE AND FINANCE.

684. Excise duty—beer. See § 1739.

685. Export and import controls

EXPORT OF GOODS (CONTROL) (AMENDMENT) ORDER 1978 (No. 271) [10p], made under the Import, Export and Customs Powers (Defence) Act 1939 (c. 69), s. 1; operative on March 24, 1978; further amends S.I. 1970 No. 1288 by including in Group 1 of Sched. 1 certain equipment suitable for riot control purposes and armour plate among the goods of which the export is controlled.

EXPORT OF GOODS (CONTROL) ORDER 1978 (No. 796) [£1·25], made under the Import, Export and Customs Powers (Defence) Act 1939, s. 1; operative on July 3, 1978; revokes and replaces S.I. 1970 No. 1288.

IMPORT OF GOODS (CONTROL) (AMENDMENT) ORDER 1978 (No. 806) [10p], made under the Import, Export and Customs Powers (Defence) Act 1939, s. 1; operative on July 3, 1978; further amends S.I. 1954 No. 23 by making it clear that an import licence for transit or transhipment can be granted on condition that the goods are exported to a specified destination or within a specified time and provides that if any such condition imposed is contravened or not complied with the goods will be liable to forfeiture.

EXPORT OF GOODS (CONTROL) ORDER 1978 (AMENDMENT) ORDER 1978 (No. 945) [10p], made under the Import, Export and Customs Powers (Defence) Act 1939, s. 1; operative on July 10, 1978; amends S.I. 1978 No. 796 by including certain iron and steel products among the goods of which the export is controlled to Austria, Finland, Norway, Portugal or Sweden.

EXPORT OF GOODS (CONTROL) ORDER 1978 (AMENDMENT NO. 2) ORDER 1978 (No. 1219) [10p], made under the Import, Export and Customs Powers (Defence) Act 1939, s. 1; operative on September 14, 1978; amends S.I. 1978 No. 796 by including cobalt waste and depleted uranium among the goods the export of which is controlled.

EXPORT OF GOODS (CONTROL) ORDER 1978 (AMENDMENT NO. 3) ORDER 1978 (No. 1496) [10p], made under the Import, Export and Customs Powers (Defence) Act 1939, s. 1; operative on November 9, 1978; further amends S.I. 1978 No. 796 by adding to the category of goods of which export to South Africa or Namibia is controlled.

EXPORT OF GOODS (CONTROL) ORDER 1978 (AMENDMENT NO. 4) ORDER 1978 (No. 1812) [10p], made under the Import, Export and Customs Powers (Defence) Act 1939, s. 1; operative on December 13, 1978; amends S.I. 1978 No. 796. It removes certain iron and steel products from goods of which export is controlled to Austria, Finland, Norway, Portugal or Sweden.

686. —— meaning of "evade"

[Customs and Excise Act 1952 (c. 44), s. 56 (2).]

It is not a defence to a charge of breaching the statutory prohibition in s. 56 (2) of the Customs and Excise Act 1952, that D had an honest mind and that he did not believe he was breaking the law.

The word "evade" in s. 56 (2) of the Customs and Excise Act 1952 has its normal English meaning of "get around" or "avoid" and does not carry the connotation of fraud, as the word "avoid" does in income tax law. It does not matter that a defendant acted with an honest mind, that he was unaware that he was breaking the law or that no injury was caused to the public.

R. *v.* HURFORD-JONES [1977] 65 Cr.App.R. 263, C.A.

687. Films

H.M. Customs and Excise have issued Notice No. 210 (November 1977): temporary importation of films and similar goods for copying, printing, etc., to fulfil export orders.

688. Finance Act 1978 (c. 42)

Pt. I (ss. 1–10) deals with customs and excise: s. 1 increases tobacco products duty; s. 2 provides for the repayment of excise duty on beer, s. 3 relates to warehousing regulations; s. 4 deals with the control of movement of goods; s. 5 imposes a penalty on the removal of seals, locks or marks; s. 6 authorises the Secretary of State to make provision for anti-dumping measures on ECSC products; s. 7 relates to gaming licence duty in Scotland; s. 8 exempts disabled persons from paying vehicle excise duty; s. 9 exempts disabled persons in Northern Ireland from paying vehicle excise duty; s. 10 continues in force powers under the Finance Act 1961, s. 9.

689. Hydrocarbon oil

H.M. Customs and Excise have issued Notices Nos. 171 (January, 1978): hydrocation oil: customs duty; 179 (January, 1978): excise duty on hydrocarbon oil—bonded installations, and 179M (Supplement) (February 1978): Meters at bonded oil installations.

690. Imports—indecent or obscene articles—jurisdiction. See R. *v.* HENN; R. *v.* DARBY, § 562.

691. Inward processing relief

H.M. Customs and Excise have issued Notice No. 221 (January 1978): inward processing relief.

692. Outward processing relief

H.M. Customs and Excise have issued Notice No. 235 (May 1978): outward processing relief EEC 1976.

692a. Personal reliefs

CUSTOMS DUTY (PERSONAL RELIEFS) (NO. 1) ORDER 1975 (AMENDMENT) ORDER 1978 (No. 1882) [10p], made under the Finance Act 1968 (c. 44), s. 7 as amended by the Finance Act 1972 (c. 41), s. 55 (2) (3); operative on January 1, 1979; increases to £70 the total value of goods on which an aggregate rate may be charged. The increase is in accordance with the provisions of Reg. (EEC) No. 2780/78.

CUSTOMS DUTY (PERSONAL RELIEFS) (NO. 1) ORDER 1968 (AMENDMENT) ORDER 1978 (No. 1883) [20p], made under the Finance Act 1968, s. 7 as amended by the Finance Act 1972, s. 55 (2) (3); operative on January 1, 1979; places on a legislative footing the higher scale of duty free allowances provided by Council Directive 69/169/EEC as amended for goods obtained duty and tax paid in the EEC.

693. Public notices

H.M. Customs and Excise have issued Notice No. 1000 (April 1978): Public notices obtainable from H.M. Customs and Excise.

694. Quota relief

CUSTOMS DUTIES (QUOTA RELIEF) (PAPER, PAPERBOARD AND PRINTED PRODUCTS) (AMENDMENT) ORDER 1978 (No. 820) [10p], made under the Import Duties Act 1958 (c. 6), ss. 5, 13, Sched. 3, para. 8 (2) as amended by the European Communities Act 1972 (c. 68), s. 5 (3), Sched. 4, para. 1 and S.I. 1976 No. 2130; operative on July 1, 1978; amends S.I. 1977 No. 2048 in relation to nine duty-free tariff quotas agreed between the EEC and Switzerland for certain paper and paperboard products.

CUSTOMS DUTIES (QUOTA RELIEF) (PAPER, PAPERBOARD AND PRINTED PRODUCTS ORDER 1978 (No. 1866) [40p], made under the Import Duties Act 1958, s. 5; operative on January 1, 1979; provides for the opening during 1979 of duty-free tariff quotas for paper, paperboard and printed products originating in certain specified contries.

695. Returned goods relief

H.M. Customs and Excise have issued Notice No. 236 (August 1977): relief from customs duties, CAP charges, excise duties and VAT.

696. Surcharge

H.M. Customs and Excise have published Notice No. 20 (April 1978): the economic regulator: administration of Customs and Excise special surcharge or rebate.

697. Tobacco

TOBACCO PRODUCTS (HIGHER TAR CIGARETTES) REGULATIONS 1978 (No. 1156) [20p], made under the Finance Act 1978 (c. 42), s. 1, and the Finance Act 1976 (c. 40) s. 4, as amended by the Finance Act 1977 (c. 36), s. 3 (5); operative on September 4, 1978; prescribe how tar yield is to be determined for the purpose of s. 1 of the 1978 Act (additional duty charged on cigarettes with a tar yield of not less than 20 mg.).

698. Valuation of goods

H.M. Customs and Excise have issued Notice No. 252 (November 1978): Valuation of imported goods for customs purposes, VAT and trade statistics.

699. Vehicles. See ROAD TRAFFIC; TRANSPORT.

700. Warehouses

CUSTOMS AND EXCISE (WAREHOUSES) REGULATIONS 1978 (No. 1603) [25p], made under the European Communities Act 1972 (c. 68), s. 2 (2); operative on December 8, 1978; amend the Customs and Excise Act 1952 and related Acts to provide for warehouses to be defined as either customs warehouses or excise warehouses so that different procedures may be applied to each type of warehouse.

ARTICLES. See *post,* p. [20].

DAMAGES

701. Assessment—evidence—value of car—award below unchallenged expert assessment

In assessing the pre-accident replacement value of a car, a judge is not entitled to reach a figure substantially below that supported by uncontradicted evidence.

The plaintiff's car was damaged beyond economical repair by the defendant's admitted negligence. The plaintiff gave evidence that he could not obtain a similar car for less than £875 and called an expert who assessed the car's retail value at £795, less, possibly, a small discount at a garage. No contrary evidence was called by the defendant. The judge assessed the value of the car at £700. The plaintiff appealed on the grounds that on the evidence the judge could not have concluded that the car was valued at less than £775. *Held,* allowing the appeal, that the damages would be increased by £75.

THATCHER *v.* LITTLEJOHN [1978] R.T.R. 369, C.A.

702. —— future loss of earnings—deduction as motherhood likely—loss of opportunity of marriage

In assessing damages for loss of further earnings in the case of a young woman, a reduction in the conventional multiplier is appropriate to allow for the likelihood that she would have ceased work at least temporarily to have children; but such reduction may be compensated by damages for loss of the opportunity of marriage.

The female plaintiff was aged 20 at the time of an accident in 1973 as a result of which she became paraplegic and was confined to a wheelchair for the rest of her life. By consent, damages were to be reduced by 12½ per cent. *Held,* that the appropriate multiplier for use in computing loss of future earnings was 11, as opposed to 15 as would be used for a male, since it was likely that the plaintiff would have married and not worked, at least for a period, whilst bringing up children; accordingly such damages would be reduced from £27,500 to £20,000; but that she was entitled to a further £7,500 damages in compensation for the lost opportunity of marriage. (*Harris* v. *Harris* [1973] C.L.Y. 741, applied.)

MORIARTY *v.* MCCARTHY [1978] 1 W.L.R. 155, O'Connor J.

703. Awards—special cases—form. See § 95.

704. Breach of contract—mitigation of losses—actions not arising out of consequences of breach

The defendant had repudiated an agreement to lease. About six months later, at a time when the building was mostly vacant, the plaintiff landlord entered into a lease with a third party. The point in issue was whether the rental received by the landlord under the lease should be deducted from the damages awarded to him, as mitigation of his losses. *Held,* it should not be deducted, since the lease to the third party was not a transaction arising out of the consequences of the defendant's repudiation of the lease agreement. The concept of mitigation of damages in breach of contract includes the general principle that a plaintiff cannot recover for any part of his loss which has been successfully avoided by subsequent action. However, for subsequent action to be taken into account, it must arise directly out of the consequences of the breach, and in the ordinary course of business. (*British Westinghouse Electric & Manufacturing Co.* v. *Underground Electric Ry. of London* [1912] A.C. 673 applied): APECO OF CANADA v. WINDMILL PLACE (1978) 82 D.L.R. (3d) 1 Can.Sup.Ct.

705. Death of wife—compensation for lack of housekeeper—basis

[Fatal Accidents Act 1976 (c. 30).] After the loss of his wife, the plaintiff, a night porter, gave up his job in order to look after his young family. He claimed damages under the Fatal Accidents Acts on the basis of compensation for lack of a housekeeper. The salary of a housekeeper would have exceeded his loss of earnings. *Held,* that the measure of his damages should be his own loss of earnings: BAILEY v. BARKING AND HAVERING AREA HEALTH AUTHORITY, *The Times,* July 22, 1978, Pain J.

706. Economic loss—remoteness of damage—not reasonably foreseeable by defendants

[Can.] The plaintiffs were the only users of a railway bridge, spanning a river, owned by the Crown. As a result of the defendant ship's negligent collision with the bridge, they had to re-route their trains for eight days while repairs were effected, at some considerable cost. The plaintiffs had a contractual right to use the bridge for their operations. *Held,* damages for economic loss ought only to follow when it was a direct and reasonably foreseeable consequence of negligence. Here the plaintiffs were not persons who would be in the defendant's contemplation as affected by damage to the bridge and their loss was therefore too remote to be recoverable, especially in view of their lacking any easement in respect of the bridge (*Re Ellenborough Park* [1955] C.L.Y. 882, considered; *Spartan Steel & Alloys* v. *Martin & Co.* (*Contractors*) [1972] C.L.Y. 2341, disapproved; *Rivtow Marine* v. *Washington Iron Works* (1974) C.L.Y. 2585, applied): GYPSUM CARRIER INC. v. THE QUEEN (1978) 78 D.L.R. 175, Fed. Ct., Collier J.

707. Exemplary damages—unlawful eviction—not specifically claimed. See DRANE v. EVANGELOU, § 1822.

708. Fatal accident—claim—death caused by negligence of one dependant against another

[Fatal Accidents Act 1846 (c. 93), s. 2.]

The Fatal Accidents Acts give remedies to dependants individually, not as a group, and one dependant can claim for negligence against another.

H died when W was driving. Negligence was admitted. There was one child, a boy aged eight. The administrators claimed under the Fatal Accidents Acts 1846–1959. *Held,* each dependant was a separate plaintiff for the purposes of the Acts, and the validity of the son's claim was not affected by the fact that another dependant was responsible for the death of the deceased. (*Mullholland* v. *McCrea* [1962] C.L.Y. 2128, *Hay* v. *Hughes* [1975] C.L.Y. 772, *K.* v. *J.M.P. Co.* [1975] C.L.Y. 785 and *Cookson* v. *Knowles* [1978] C.L.Y. 713 applied; *Jenner* v. *Allen West & Co.* [1959] C.L.Y. 872 and *Howitt* v. *Heads* [1972] C.L.Y. 813 considered.)

DODDS v. DODDS [1978] 2 W.L.R. 434, Balcombe J.

709. —— loss of dependency—future inflation

In assessing damages for future dependancy in a fatal accidents case, Bristow J. has taken into consideration the likelihood of future inflation at not less than 7 per cent. per annum. (*Mallett* v. *Mcmonagle* [1969] C.L.Y. 898 not followed; *Taylor* v. *O'Connor* [1971] C.L.Y. 3122 considered): DOYLE *v.* NICHOLLS, *The Times,* May 20, 1978, Bristow J.

710. Foreign currency—restitutio in integrum—expenditure incurred in foreign currency

The court may award damages for negligence or for breach of contract in the currency that best expresses the plaintiff's loss.

In the first case, the D and the E collided. The owners of the D agreed to pay the owners of the E 85 per cent. of the damage, the expense of which had arisen in several currencies, bought in the currency of the plaintiffs' business. The Court of Appeal held that there was jurisdiction to award damages in tort in a foreign currency, and that in these circumstances, the appropriate currency was the plaintiffs' currency rather than the currency of the expenditure. In the second case, C Co., a French company, chartered a vessel from O Co., a Swedish company, to ship onions to Brazil. The cargo arrived damaged. C Co. settled the claim against them in Brazilian cruzeiros which they bought with French francs, the currency of their business. The hire was payable in U.S. dollars. O Co. admitted liability to C Co. for the damage to the cargo, but they claimed that payment should be made in cruzeiros which was now worth half of what it had been against the French franc. The Court of Appeal held that the proper currency of the award was the currency of C Co.'s business. On appeal to the House of Lords, *held,* dismissing both appeals, that (1) it was reasonably foreseeable that a plaintiff who conducted his business in a certain currency would use that currency to purchase the currency required to put right the damage caused by the defendant's tort, and, applying the principle of restitutio in integrum, that was the currency in which damages should be awarded; (2) where the terms of the contract did not expressly or by implication show that the parties had intended that payment arising from breach should be paid in a specific currency, the court should give judgment in the currency which best expressed the party's loss. That, in this case, was French francs, the currency of C Co.'s business. (*Milangos* v. *George Frank (Textiles)* [1975] 2657 applied; *S.S. Celia (Owners)* v. *S.S. Volturno (Owners); The Volturno* [1921] 2 A.C. 544, H.L.(E.), and *The Canadian Transport* (1932) 43 Ll.L.Rep. 409, C.A. distinguished; *Di Ferdinando* v. *Simon, Smits & Co.* [1920] 3 K.B. 409, C.A. overruled; *Jugoslavenska Oceanska Plovidba* v. *Castle Investment Co. Inc.* [1973] C.L.Y. 101 and *Jean Kraut A.G.* v. *Albany Fabrics* [1977] C.L.Y. 2334 approved.)

SERVICES EUROPE ATLANTIQUE SUD (SEAS) OF PARIS *v.* STOCKHOLMS REDERIAKTIEBOLAG SVEA OF STOCKHOLM, THE DESPINA R [1978] 3 W.L.R. 804, H.L.

711. Inconvenience factor—sale of car—unroadworthy condition

A second-hand car was sold in breach of an implied condition as to road-worthiness, to the plaintiff. The judge found that the car had been bought for pleasure use, but had given nothing but trouble because of its unroadworthy condition. The plaintiff's pregnant wife had to use other more reliable transport on her visits to hospital, the car had broken down on several occasions, and expense involving bus and taxi fares had been incurred. The plaintiff was awarded £75 damages for "inconvenience and frustration": GASCOIGNE *v.* BRITISH CREDIT TRUST, June 20, 1978, Judge Suddards, Bradford County Ct. (*Ex rel. Paul Worsley, Esq., Barrister.*)

712. Interest—claim after judgment

[Scot.] [Interest on Damages (Scotland) Act 1971 (c. 31), s. 1 (1).] P applied for interest on damages for personal injuries to accrue from the date of the injuries, or such date as the court should deem proper, relying on s. 1 (1) of the Act. *Held,* the sum P had sued for must be deemed to have included interest. It would not be proper, therefore, to add it to those damages already awarded: ORR *v.* METCALFE, 1973 S.C. 57, First Division.

713. —— Fatal Accidents Acts—guidelines for assessment

[Fatal Accidents Acts 1846–1959; Law Reform (Miscellaneous Provisions) Act 1934 (c. 41).]

In fatal accident cases, damages ought to be split into two parts, pre-trial loss and future loss. The former will attract interest at half the normal rates, but the latter will attract neither interest nor an allowance for inflation.

Per curiam. It is proper for an appellate court to lay down guidelines for the exercise of judicial discretion, but it is not expounding a rule of law from which the judge is precluded from departing.

The plaintiff, widow of the deceased, claimed damages against the defendant for negligence. Liability was admitted. At trial, the judge took the combined earnings of both parties as they would have been at date of trial, the dependency at two-thirds of that figure, and a multiplier of 11. He gave 9 per cent. interest on that figure from the date of death to the date of trial. The defendant appealed to the Court of Appeal, and both parties appealed thence to the House of Lords. *Held,* affirming the decision of the Court of Appeal, that (1) damages in fatal accidents cases should be split into pre-trial loss and future loss; (2) interest should be awarded on the former from death to trial at half short-term interest rates. In assessing the multiplicand, the figure used should be the estimated annual dependency at the date of trial, and that no interest should be awarded on future loss nor allowance made for inflation. (*Mallet* v. *McMonagle* [1969] C.L.Y. 898, *Jefford* v. *Gee* [1970] C.L.Y. 603, and *Taylor* v. *O'Connor* [1971] C.L.Y. 3122 considered.)

COOKSON v. KNOWLES [1978] 2 W.L.R. 978, H.L.

714. Loss of earnings—wife's claim for husband's injuries—no duty owed to victim's spouse—remoteness of damage

[Scot.] H received injuries, as a result of which W was obliged to give up her job in order to look after him. W claimed damages for this loss of income and for expenses incurred in visiting H in hospital. H claimed the loss of the benefit of W's income to him. *Held,* although W could recover solatium if H died, she was unable to recover in respect of loss of earnings and travelling expenses as no duty to take reasonable care of one spouse is owed to the other. However, if it could be shown that the loss of the benefit of W's earnings was not too remote, H could recover them: JACK v. ALEXANDER M'DOUGALL & CO. (ENGINEERS), 1973 S.C. 13, Outer House.

715. Mitigation—set off of benefits arising from defendants' negligence

It is a question of fact whether a benefit accruing to a plaintiff relates sufficiently closely to a head of damage for it to be appropriate to set off that benefit.

D, a firm of solicitors, served a bad notice under the Landlord and Tenant Act 1954. That meant that P had to pay compensation to a tenant of premises, but that they did get vacant possession of those premises. *Held,* that the question of whether it was appropriate to set off a particular benefit was one of fact. If it were established that a benefit had accrued to P from having vacant possession of the premises, that was a benefit which ought to be set off.

NADREPH v. WILLMETT & CO. (A FIRM) [1978] 1 All E.R. 746, Whitford J.

716. Negligence—economic loss—remoteness—multiple test to be applied. See YUMEROVSKI v. DANI, § 2074.

717. Pearson Report

The report of the Royal Commission on Civil Liability and Compensation for Personal Injury, chaired by Lord Pearson, has been published. The Commission recommend that (1) a " no-fault " compensation scheme for motor vehicle accidents should be established, funded by a levy of about 1p a gallon on petrol; (2) there should be an improved industrial injuries scheme extended to cover the self-employed, commuters and more cases of occupational disease; (3) severely handicapped children should all receive a new benefit of £4 a week, tax free, as an addition to child benefit. The Commission also recommend various changes in the tort system, including the introduction of strict liability for, among others, vaccine damage, defective products and rail transport. The Report is available from H.M.S.O. Cmnd. 7054 [Vol. 1 £7·60; Vol. 2 £3·60; Vol. 3 £3·60.]

718. Personal injuries—employer's liability—supervening heart disease

In September 1971 P, who was right-handed, suffered injuries to his left hand in the course of his employment by D. The injuries resulted in the amputation of his ring, middle and index fingers; continued risk of infection; loss of pleasure of physical activity with his children; and loss of his hobby of racing-pigeons. In 1974, liability was agreed at 70 per cent. In mid-1976 a serious heart condition developed, as a result of which P became unfit for work, and his expectation of life was agreed at 7½ years from the date of trial. *Held*, (1) D were not liable for P's loss of earnings after mid-1976, since the heart disease was a supervening, non-tortious act; (2) the agreed special damages up to mid-1976 of £5,000 with interest at 4½ per cent. would be awarded; (3) £11,500 would be awarded in respect of the injury and its consequences, of which P would be entitled to 70 per cent. without interest. (*Cookson* v. *Knowles* [1978] C.L.Y. 713; *Jones* v. *National Coal Board* (December 13, 1976, unreported) applied; *Baker* v. *Willoughby* [1970] C.L.Y. 1862 distinguished): HODGSON v. GENERAL ELECTRICITY Co. [1978] 2 Lloyd's Rep. 210, Latey J.

719. —— quantum of damages—enforced early retirement—whether pension benefits should be deducted from assessment of future earnings

[Can.] On appeal against an assessment of damages for personal injuries, *held*, that where a plaintiff is forced to take an early retirement because of injuries suffered, his pension benefits should be taken into account to reduce the amount of general damages for loss of future earnings. The pension benefits are really part of his wages or salary: the pension is really a reduced salary. (*Parry* v. *Cleaver* [1969] C.L.Y. 906 disapproved): TRIZEC EQUITIES v. GUY (1978) 85 D.L.R. (3d) 634, Nova Scotia Sup.Ct.

720. —— —— no deduction by reason of mobility or attendance allowances

The Court of Appeal decided, following its decision in *Daish* v. *Wauton* [1972] C.L.Y. 836, that payment of a mobility allowance and an attendance allowance made to a plaintiff under the Social Security Pensions Act 1975 and the Social Security Act 1975, were not to be brought into account so as to reduce the damages payable to him in respect of a motor accident as a result of which he had become a tetraplegic. Leave to appeal to the House of Lords was granted: BOWKER v. ROSE, *The Times*, February 3, 1978, C.A.

720a. —— shortened life expectation—" lost years "

The House of Lords has overruled the Court of Appeal decision in *Oliver* v. *Ashman* [1961] C.L.Y. 2311 which prevented the award to persons who suffer injury or disease which shortens their lives, of damages for loss of what they might have earned during the " lost years." They remitted the action to the High Court to assess the relevant damages: PICKETT v. BRITISH RAIL ENGINEERING, *The Times*, November 4, 1978, H.L.

721. —— special damages—provision of nursing care by daughter—whether recoverable in absence of contract

[Can.] P claimed damages for personal injuries caused by D's negligence. Among the special damages claimed was a claim for the provision of nursing services which her daughter, a qualified nurse, had provided without a contract to recompense her. D claimed it was not recoverable. *Held*, as the injuries required nursing care, it mattered not whether they had been provided under a contract. P had required such care as a result of D's negligence, and therefore could recover for it. (*Donnelly* v. *Joyce* [1973] C.L.Y. 727 followed): HASSON v. HAMEL (1978) 78 D.L.R. 573, Zalev Cty.Ct.J.

Personal injuries or death—quantum of damages

Details have been received of the following cases in which damages for personal injuries or death were awarded. The classification and sequence of the classified awards follows that adopted in *Kemp and Kemp on the Quantum of Damages*, 4th ed., Vol. 2. Unless there is some statement to the contrary the age of the applicant is his age at the time of the court hearing. The damages are stated on the basis of full liability, *i.e.* ignoring any reduction made for contributory negligence. The sum is the amount of the general damages awarded unless otherwise stated.

Injuries of Maximum Severity

722. CRUTCHETT *v.* BUCKINGHAMSHIRE AREA HEALTH AUTHORITY (March 10, 1978; Melford Stevenson J.) The infant plaintiff was born in April 1964 and was the only child of the adult plaintiffs who were aged 52 and 48 (the wife). The infant plaintiff was a gifted child who would have gone on to grammar school and university and would possibly have qualified as a teacher. On June 17, 1975, she went into hospital for a minor operation and following a respiratory arrest followed by a cardiac arrest in the recovery room she suffered irreversible cerebral damage. As a result she lost most of her motor activity. She was unable to speak. She was incontinent and needed to be turned every two hours in the night. She had minimal perception although she expressed apparent pleasure and displeasure. She was able to eat only mashed food. Her vision was excellent and she was responsive to music, laughing and smiling. She had marked contractures of the limbs, particularly on the left. The arms were firmly adducted to the trunk with the elbows flexed acutely and the wrist and fingers semi-flexed with thumbs firmly pressed against the index. Her left lower limb was flexed at the hip and knee with inversion of the foot, the right lower limb moved quite a lot voluntarily but the ankle joint was firmly flexed. At the time of trial she spent 3–4 days a week at hospital and extended week-ends at home. The intention was to bring her home to live permanently and extensions to the house had been made accordingly. She needed full time attention in addition to her mother, who also had to look after the house. A special motor caravan had been purchased. Melford Stevenson J. on March 10, 1978, approved an overall settlement by consent of £150,000, split as to £110,000 for the infant and £40,000 for the parents. The £110,000 for the infant was broken down approx. as to £25,000 for general damages, £70,000 for future nursing costs on the basis of 8 hours during the day and 8 hours at night, 7 days a week. This was also on the basis that the life expectancy of the child was likely to be similar to that of the mother (29½ years) and a multiplier of 12 was taken for this purpose. A further £15,000 was taken into account for future loss of earnings on the basis that the infant plaintiff was bright and would have qualified. The £40,000 for the parents was calculated approximately as to £24,000 for nursing attendance by both of them for 12 years at £2,000 per annum and £16,000 for such nursing attendance from the date of the injury to date plus the cost of extensions to the home and the purchase of the motor caravan for taking the child out for trips and holidays. (*Ex rel. Neil Kaplan, Barrister.*)

723. BUCKINGHAM *v.* SYMONS-D'SOUZA (April 28, 1978; Jupp J.). Male, aged 19. At the date of accident in April 1975, was at grammar school and was hoping to became commercial artist. Almost totally quaddraplegic; paralysed from sixth cervical vertebra down, with only slight movement of arms and left wrist. Because of lack of movement, had to be kept at constant temperature day and night. Life expectancy between 20 and 25 years. No prospect of future remunerative employment. Damages for loss of life expectancy assessed at £500, for future nursing expenses at £44,500, for loss of future earnings at £40,000 and for pain and suffering and loss of amenities at £30,000. *Agreed special damages*: £19,115. *Total general damages*: £115,000.

BOULTON *v.* SANKEY BUILDING SUPPLIERS (October 17, 1978; Michael Davies J). Male, aged 55. Unmarried. Former warehouseman. As a result of accident in 1975 suffered fractured spine causing paraplegia. Permanently paralysed from waist down. Life expectancy about 12 years. Loss of future earnings assessed at £10,900 cost of future care at Star and Garter Homes assessed at £49,777, and pain and suffering and loss of amenities assessed at £22,250. *Special damages*: £12,960. *Total general damages*: £82,927

725. ANDERSON *v.* LAMBETH LONDON BOROUGH (*The Times*, July 20, 1978; Caulfield J.). Male, aged 13 at date of accident and 17 at date of hearing. Injured when jumped from disused building (which it was alleged defendant council should have boarded up) on to mattresses and landed on neck—a game often played by local boys. Now quadraplegic. Contributory negligence of between

50 per cent. and 60 per cent. allowed for in compromise of claim. *Agreed damages*: £60,000.

Multiple Injuries

726. DREYER *v.* UNIGATE FOODS (January 30, 1978; Talbot J.). Married woman, aged 34, with 2 year old child. Former R.A.C. patrol woman earning £16 a week plus commission. By date of hearing, but for accident, would have been earning £44 a week including commission. Had considered taking up fashion modelling. Before accident in 1974 she and her husband had led active, happy sex life. Fractures of both legs and left elbow as result of which she suffered thrombosis in legs and developed stones in her kidneys. Left knee cap removed. Now had constant pain in her legs and tenderness in elbow and had to walk with stick. Had regularly to take pain-killing tablets and sleeping pills. Had been prescribed stronger drugs but did not take them because they made her " unaware of the realities of life," which was important in relation to her looking after her child. Had to do household and gardening chores sitting down, as she could not stand for long. Because of sedentary life she was forced to lead her weight had increased from 9 to 14 stones. Now depressed and concerned about her marriage. Sexual side of married life had almost ceased. However, judge concluded that her depression and concern might not be lasting because her husband was a good man who said he was going to stand by her. Now unfit for pre-accident job and would no longer be able to take up fashion modelling. But for accident would have continued to work. Loss of future earnings assessed at £10,000. Pain and suffering and loss of amenities assessed at £11,000. *Agreed special damages*: £1,618. *Total general damages*: £21,000.

Brain and Skull

727. LAWSON *v.* RAMSDEN (February 21, 1978; Lawson J.). Boy, aged 5 at date of accident in June 1972 and 11 at date of hearing. Severe concussion and brain damage and fractures to arm, leg and several ribs. Unconscious for about six weeks. Now mentally retarded and gap between chronological age and mental age would widen as he became older. Right leg now shorter than left. Would need sheltered accommodation from age of about 19. Loss of future earnings and earning capacity assessed at £35,000, cost of future nursing care at £15,000 and pain and suffering and loss of amenities at £25,000. No special damage. *Total general damages*: £75,000.

Face

728. SKELTON *v.* STATE (May 10, 1978; Kilner Brown J., Leeds). Female, aged 20. Thrown through windscreen of car in November 1975. Multiple lacerations of face resulting in permanent scarring. Very unsightly for nearly two years; three operations wrought great improvement so that now not unattractive; but no further improvement expected. Scars had caused overlay of psychological trauma, namely impaired ability to cope with social situations, personality change, depression. Would recover altogether from this in another four to five years. Awarded £3,000 for direct physical result; £2,000 for psychological aspects. *Per curiam*: damage to facial appearance in an attractive young woman is devastating. *Total general damages*: £5,000 (*Ex rel. J. Scott Wolstenholme, Esq., Barrister.*)

729. JEARRARD *v.* HERTFORDSHIRE AREA HEALTH AUTHORITY (*The Times*, November 18, 1978; Jupp J.). Girl, aged 3. Whilst here mother was undergoing caesarian section operation during her birth surgeon inadvertently cut plaintiff's left cheek. As a result of failure to stitch or attempt to seal wound two-inch scar resulted which might be removed by plastic surgery in due course. Any residual disfigurement would not affect her marriage prospects. *Damages*: £1,750. *Per* Jupp J. There was no comparable case and the assessment of damages was difficult. Because there was no known pain or suffering, the only criterion was the effect, physically and mentally, on the child in the future.

Jaw and Teeth

730. HOLMES v. GREEN (May 24, 1978; Judge Lymbery, Q.C.). Female aged 26. Shop assistant at time of accident, now security officer. Unmarried and "not unattractive." Knocked off moped, landed on face. Lost three middle teeth on upper jaw; also small scar on chin which could be covered up by make-up, and slight pain and swelling on upper shins but not a major factor. Main injury was loss of teeth. Off work three weeks, had not overplayed injury. Now wore temporary bridge which caused some discomfort. *Special damages*: £105·35. *Total general damages*: £1,930, made up of £1,350 for pain and suffering and loss of amenity, and £580 for future dental treatment. (*Ex rel. Richard Robinson, Esq., Barrister.*)

731. DUBBINS v. WALKER (October 30, 1978; Deputy Judge Lowry; Frome County Court). Male, aged 59, pedal cyclist. Collided with side of car when car unexpectedly left car park onto main road in front of him and plaintiff lost control of cycle attempting to take evasive action. Landed on face on road and came to rest beneath car. Fracture of nose, fractures of two upper molar teeth, extensive lacerations within the mouth and on upper and lower lips, abrasions to right side of face, chin and knees. General shock. Treated in Casualty Department of local hospital. Lacerations took a considerable time to settle down. Nose still slightly displaced. Slight osteo-arthritis in knee joint. Permanent dental disability necessitating a denture and some residual sensory loss in right upper lip. Ten days off work. *General damages*: £1,400. *Agreed special damages*: £240·06. *Interest on special damages*: £9·00. (*Ex rel. Richard Snow, Solicitor.*)

Skin

732. COWAN v. DURHAM COUNTY COUNCIL (October 12, 1978; Judge Johnson; Newcastle upon Tyne High Ct.) The plaintiff was aged 39 years. From 1966, worked as a labourer with the defendants on road-laying machinery, which brought his skin into contact with diesel, an admitted substance likely to cause dermatitis. In October 1976, a rash broke out on both hands and spread to both wrists, his stomach and thighs. He continued this work until dermatitis was eventually diagnosed in May 1977 and attributed to this contact with diesel. By this time he had also become sensitised to the nickel because of the continuation at work while he had this dermatitic condition. The evidence showed that the dermatitis had only been accelerated by four or five years, and would have occurred apart from the negligence and breach of Reg. 12 (1) of the Construction (Health and Welfare) Regulations 1966 (S.I. 1966 No. 95) which were found proved; but it was *held*, that the nickel sensitivity that had set in could have been prevented altogether. The nickel sensitivity now prevented him coming into contact with almost any metal because of the wide-spread prevalence of nickel. He had to use wooden handled implements. Permanently unfit for previous employment, and a loss of earnings continuing at £3,172 per annum. The defendants fully liable because of inadequate instruction, advice and warnings of the dangers concerning diesel, and inadequate provision of washing facilities, despite provision of various protective gloves, barrier cream and cleansing gel. Plaintiff awarded £600, being £50 per annum with a multiplier of 12, because no longer able to maintain his own motor car and to do painting work on his house; £10,000 future loss of earnings, judge starting with a multiplier of 12 on the annual continuing loss, divided by three because of the prospect of the plaintiff obtaining some work which would probably be paid at the same rate, with a further reduction because the plaintiff would have had to give up this work permanently in any event, because of the inevitability of dermatitis. *Agreed special damages*: £359·54. *General damages for pain and suffering and loss of amenity*: £2,500. (*Ex rel. Roger Thorn, Esq., Barrister.*)

Burns and Scars

733. NEAL v. FAULKNER ENGINEERING (July 5, 1978; Thompson J.). Male, aged 27. Severely burned over 35 per cent. of his body in April 1975 when chemical salt bath exploded at work. Had burns to the face, scalp, back of neck, both arms and both sides of his trunk. Spent 10 weeks in hospital and underwent skin graft operations. Injuries healed well, but leaving scars. Plaintiff now assessed at 3 per cent. disabled but working in another job for same employers with no loss of earnings. *General damages for pain and suffering and loss of amenity*: £7,500. *Agreed special damages*: £13.

734. BROMLEY v. REED PAPER AND BOARD (U.K.) (January 12, 1978; Judge Laughton-Scott Q.C.). Male, aged 23. Unmarried. Paper mill worker. Suffered friction burns and other minor injuries to right hand, forearm and shoulder in accident in September 1975. Attended hospital for out-patient treatment on day of accident and returned three days later as in-patient for skin grafting operations to shoulder. On discharge returned to pre-accident work. Left with permanent scarring on forearm and at back of shoulder and some limitation of movement of arm. Scarring on shoulder raised, and judge (who examined plaintiff) said it was no exaggeration to describe site as " grotesquely defaced." Plaintiff found scarring caused him considerable difficulty in his social life, particularly with members of opposite sex. He tried to cover it at all times. He wore shirt when on beach during holidays. Although he removed shirt when bathing, he walked backwards into sea to hide scars from onlookers. He also complained that scarring affected his sexual life. Before accident had had considerable success with opposite sex. Only girl with whom he had had sexual intercourse since accident " nearly had a fit " when she felt scars. Not a person who could approach his difficulties by making light of them so that effect of scarring on him had been much greater than it would have been on more robust or resilient personality. Functioning of shoulder sufficiently impaired to deprive him of enjoyment of pre-accident hobbies of playing squash and badminton and doing weight-lifting. No loss of earning capacity. No special damages. *General damages*: £6,000.

735. BRAND v. WOODLEY TOWN COUNCIL (September 27, 1978; Master Ritchie) West Indian female, aged 15 at date of accident in March 1976; school girl, a keen and proficient netball player before accident. Fell through glass door in sports centre. 1 in. laceration of right forehead which has now almost disappeared; 3 in. laceration of left palm exposing muscles; laceration of left midfinger; 4 in. laceration of left thigh, and 4 in. curved laceration on right lower leg extending into the deep fascia. All scars except for the one on forehead are quite visible and unsightly and embarrassing. Slight loss of sensation and limited flexion in left hand. Master Ritchie approved an overall settlement by consent of £3,500. (*Ex rel. Jonathan Sofer, Esq., Barrister.*)

Sight

736. QUAYSON v. CITY AND EAST LONDON AREA HEALTH AUTHORITY (*The Times*, July 18, 1978; Croom-Johnson J.). Male, aged 48. While undergoing treatment at hospital for groin complaint became totally blind. *Agreed damages*: £65,000.

737. DENT v. LEVI STRAUSS (U.K.) (April 21, 1978; Latey J.; Leeds). Female, aged 20 at date of accident in January 1975 and 23 at date of trial. Very attractive with cheerful disposition. Had married soon after accident and at date of trial had child aged two and was expecting second child in August. Former sewing machine operator in clothes manufacturing factory in which which work she was skilled and qualified. Whilst operating machine, needle broke and point became embedded in left eye creating traumatic cataract. In March 1975 underwent operation for removal of lens which still had point of needle in it. There followed a somewhat protracted convalescence and then up to point eye settled down, but divergent squint developed. Contact lens tried, but plaintiff's eye would not tolerate it. For all practical purposes had total loss of vision in left eye. Now had to wear spectacles to improve vision in right eye, *e.g.* when watching television or reading, which she did not have to do before accident. Unable accurately to judge distance so that, *e.g.* she often missed a cup when pouring liquids and used to misjudge distance when laying baby in cradle or cot, a difficulty which she had since overcome by having hand underneath baby so that she could lower it by feel. Could no longer play tennis or swim in pool because chemicals in water hurt her eye. Pupil of left eye noticeably up-drawn and divergent squint very noticeable: cosmetic surgery likely to be necessary in hope of correcting latter. Although had made best of her misfortune could not help being conscious of resulting extreme disfigurement. Possibility of glaucoma and detachment of retina later in life. Unable to return to her pre-accident work or to do any work calling for good vision and accurate visual judgment with result that field of potential employment substantially narrowed. She anticipated that when children were at school she would want to work. It would be some time before she would be able to start work and when she did it was likely to be part-time for some years. Pain and suffering and loss of amenities assessed at £7,750 on basis of decision of Court of Appeal in *Cookson* v. *Knowles* [1977] 5 C.L. 370a, *viz.* that no interest was to be awarded in respect of that head of damage, but that in assessing it account should be taken of inflation. Damages for reduced competitiveness in labour market in future assessed at £500. No special damages. *Total general damages*: £8,250. (*Ex rel. J. H. Mitner and Son, Solicitors.*)

738. CONDON v. CONDON (December 8, 1977; Bristow J.). Married woman, aged 53. At time of accident in October 1974 was due to start work as secretary at Easter 1975. Penetrating injury to right eye which destroyed part of iris. Laceration from nose to right eyelid which had left permanent scar which could be covered by make-up. Plastic surgery to left eyelid had balanced its appearance well with damaged eyelid. Lacerations to forehead which had left two modest scars. Fracture of left wrist and other lacerations which had healed well. Developed cataract in right eye which was removed by operation in August 1975. Early in 1977 cysts were removed from right eyelid. Eye now had outward squint of 20°, pupil was missing and it was practically useless. Visual function now permanently limited to 30 per cent. unless she underwent further surgery—which she did not want to do—to enable her to wear contact lens and thus restore very limited amount of useful vision. Had to wear dark glasses because abnormal amount of light admitted by damaged eye caused discomfort. Good eye became tired during reading or sewing. Loss of binocular vision spoiled her enjoyment of tennis and was real handicap in domestic activities. Now doing part-time job with Royal School of Music with continuing loss of earnings of £710 p.a. Multiplier of four applied, giving total of £2,840 for loss of future earnings. Pain and suffering and loss of amenities assessed at £6,500. *Special damages*: £1,750 (consisting of £500 agreed damages and £1,250 in respect of loss of earnings to date of hearing). *Total general damages*: £9,340. *Per* Bristow J. Figure of £6,500 for pain and suffering and loss of amenities was awarded "as at today" and did not carry interest under law as it now stood following *Cookson* v. *Knowles* [1978] C.L.Y. 713. But for that decision he could have awarded £6,000 plus interest.

739. JONES v. NIDUM PRECISION TOOLING (June 15, 1978; Balcombe J.; Cardiff). Male, aged 20 at date of accident in May 1971, and about 27 at date of trial. Apprentice toolmaker. Keen and promising Rugby Union football player. Suffered penetrating injury to left eye when metal chip thrown out from machine which he was operating and entered eye. In hospital initially for three weeks. Underwent operation for removal of chip from eye. Two weeks after discharge from hospital suffered detachment of lower half of retina and was re-admitted to hospital for a month. Underwent further operation for re-attachment of retina. As result of injury to lens, had experienced gradually deteriorating vision in eye due to developing cataract. Cataract removed surgically in June 1975, and contact lens prescribed and fitted in October 1975, but neither resulted in any improvement in vision in eye, and plaintiff had ceased to wear contact lens. Vision continued to deteriorate so that by date of trial, he was for all practical purposes a one-eyed man. By then, left eye possessed only peripheral field of vision which would serve to warn him of large objects outside field of vision of good right eye. No improvement possible, and it was probable that vision would deteriorate further, leading ultimately to total loss. Had suffered considerable discomfort. Still suffered from headaches as result of which was unable to watch television for more than half an hour at a time, and was unable to go to cinema. Had ceased to play rugby football. *Agreed special damages*: £400. *General damages*: £6,250. (*Ex rel. G. R. L. George, Esq., Barrister.*)

740.   PALMER *v.* WHITE & SONS (*The Times*, June 13, 1978; Thompson J.) Married woman, aged 17. Blinded in one eye when bottle of Pepsi-Cola exploded in her face in 1972. *Agreed damages*: £6,000.

741.   NORRIS *v.* WALTHAM FOREST LONDON BOROUGH (December 12, 1977; Moccatta J.). Girl, aged 9. Nice looking. Loss of eye as result of stone being thrown up by mower cutting grass at her school in May 1974. Had adapted most ably to her misfortune. There would be cosmetic disadvantage. Might have difficulty in getting certain jobs when she grew up. *Per curiam*: More attention should be paid to cosmetic aspect in case of girl than in case of boy. No special damages. *General damages*: £5,250.

742.   WHITE *v.* VEREY (March 3, 1978; Melford Stevenson J.). Male, aged 43. As result of being hit by shot gun pellets in January 1970 lost sight in one eye. No special damages. *General damages*: £5,000.

Spine

743.   MULCRONE *v.* DUNLOP RUBBER CO. (April 24, 1978; Waterhouse J.; Liverpool). Male, aged 31 at date of accident, 36 at date of trial. Had been employed as a government-trained fitter with prospects of advancement. Suffered a fracture of the spine resulting in paraplegia below the waist. All functions below the waist paralysed, sexual intercourse became impossible but with some control over urinary and excretory functions. Subsequent calcification of the hips giving regular but infrequent stabbing pains with occasional aching. Since accident, has lived with his mother who at 81 will soon become incapable of looking after him; his sister, a trained nurse but who may wish to live an independent life; his daughter of 13, and a brother. The plaintiff was living in totally unsuitable accommodation for a paraplegic. He was awarded £13,500 for adaptations to his house; the cost of nursing services to the date of trial were assessed at £3,500, and at £25,000 for nursing and domestic services thereafter; future loss of earnings assessed at £50,000 on the basis of a 12½ years' purchase at £4,000 p.a.; loss of earnings to date of trial: £9,500; miscellaneous losses and expenses: £1,000; damages for pain and suffering and loss of amenity: £27,500. *Special damages*: £17,000, including £3,000 interest. *Total general damages*: £116,000. (*Ex rel. Messrs. Brian Thompson, Solicitors.*)

744.   BONNEY *v.* MINISTRY OF DEFENCE (June 23, 1978; Lawson J.; Exeter). Plaintiff, aged 40 at date of trial. Painter. Had stepped into open manhole in February 1975. Lumber disc prolapse. Disc removed at operation in March 1976 after unsuccessful treatment by way of manipulations and injections. There was a pre-existing degeneration of the spine. Plaintiff wears a spinal support and will never return to pre-accident work. Permanently limited to light work. Persistent aching pain. Restriction of movement. Unable to have sexual intercourse but improvement expected at conclusion of litigation. *Damages for pain, suffering and loss of amenity* (*but excluding future loss and labour market*): £8,500. *Total damages* (*including future loss and special damage*): £26,000. (*Ex rel.*)

745.   GRAY *v.* HUMPHREYS AND GLASGOW (October 4, 1978; Wien J.). Male, aged 39. In February 1974 he sustained twisting back injury causing stiffness and pain in back, with flexion reduced to one-third of normal, and pins and needles in left leg. Returned to work after 10 days, but during following 18 months was off work five or six times for up to two weeks due to back pain. In June 1975 he underwent heat treatment and traction followed by operation for removal of intervertebral disc. Now had pain in back, buttocks and thigh and was unable to do heavy lifting. Found gardening tedious and could no longer play football or cricket. No future loss of earnings. No special damages. *General damages*: £3,250.

746. HURRAN *v.* SIR ROBERT MCALPINE AND SONS (June 6, 1978; Talbot J.). Male, aged 75 at time of accident in 1976. Employed as messenger before and after accident. Sustained fracture to fourth lumbar vertebra. Six weeks' absence from work. Continued to have moderately severe discomfort, controlled by regular analgesics. Wears a corset all day but not at night and this is sometimes uncomfortable in hot weather. Not easy to bend or do anything strenuous; intermittent nagging pain in bed in certain positions. Damages reduced because of his age. *Special damages*: £300·46. *Total general damages*: £1,250. (*Ex rel. J. Sofer, Esq., Barrister.*)

Respiratory organs

747. CROSSMAN *v.* BRITISH RAIL ENGINEERING (March 21, 1978; May J.). Male, aged 61. Married. Keen pedal cyclist who had formerly been able to manage round trips of up to 20 miles. As result of many years' exposure to " blue " asbestos dust in course of his employment he developed asbestosis in 1969. In about 1974 or 1975 he was awarded a disability pension assessed on basis of 10 per cent. disability. He was awaiting a further assessment. By time of hearing he was diagnosed as suffering from asbestosis of moderate severity and judge accepted that from objective clinical viewpoint existing assessment of his disability was low. However, in contrast to other sufferers from asbestosis of moderate severity plaintiff was still at work, could keep up with his job without too much difficulty and anticipated that he could be able to go on working until normal retirement age of 65, though he was becoming shorter of breath as time passed, particularly if he extended himself. He was still able to cycle for pleasure, but could now only manage round trip of about six miles. He could walk about a mile, then needed a rest. He did not suffer from anxiety, as was commonly the case with sufferers from his disease, and suffered subjectively less than most if not all asbestosis patients, though medical evidence suggested that this might be due to strength of character. As time passed he would develop more and more symptoms attributable to his lungs being increasingly affected by the disease. He would be able to be looked after at home until last few weeks or months of his life, when he would have to go into hospital. Towards end of that period he would have to have most things done for him. Taking account of the asbestosis alone judge considered that plaintiff had 50/50 chance of living out his normal life span of 14½ years. However, in consequence of the disease there was a risk of his developing lung cancer and another malignant condition, mesothelemia, both of which might strike at any time and with very little warning. Medical evidence was that risk of his life being cut short by lung cancer was of order of 50 per cent., though it might be higher because he was a smoker, and by mesothelemia of between 7 per cent. and 10 per cent. After considering, *inter alia*, the awards in *Smith* v. *Central Asbestos Co.* [1972] C.L.Y. 2035 and *Shaw* v. *Cape Insulation* [1977] C.L.Y. 781 and *Buick* v. *Cape Insulation* (reported only in Kemp and Kemp, *The Quantum of Damages*, Vol. 2, para. 7–017/1), judge assessed damages for him and suffering and loss of amenities at £9,000 and damages for loss of expectation of life at £300. *Total general damages*: £9,300. *per* May J.: The award in *Buick's* case was difficult to reconcile with the awards in *Smith's* case and *Shaw's* case, particularly bearing in mind the fall in the value of the pound since 1970. If " the appropriate inflation factor " was applied to the awards in *Smith's* case, they would now be the equivalent of £15,000 to £20,000. (*Ex rel. Messrs. Pattinson and Brewer, Solicitors.*)

748. HEMBRY *v.* MINISTRY OF DEFENCE (June 30, 1978; Lawson J.; Exeter). Male aged 64 at date of trial, no dependants. Engaged in work involving exposure to asbestos and its dust (including blue asbestos from 1948–1951) for over 20 years. First complained of chest symptoms in 1967, slight asbestosis diagnosed in 1975. In 1975 he was taken off his normal duties and given outdoor work. Able to work until normal retirement age of 65. The asbestosis had hardly progressed over the last three years but the plaintiff's genuine symptoms of anxiety and hyperventilation aggravated his condition. His condition was likely to deteriorate gradually but his life expectancy of 10–15 years could not be said to have been reduced by the disease unless he contracted lung cancer or mesothelioma in which case his symptoms would be more painful but he would not have to suffer as long. Likely to need domestic/nursing assistance in the last six to 12 months of his life. *Special damages (to include future loss up to retirement)*: £541·61. *General damages*: £9,500. (*Ex rel. Messrs. Rowleys & Blewitts, Solicitors.*)

Sacrum and Pelvis

749. JOBBER v. CAMMELL LAIRD (December 7, 1976; Purchas J.; Liverpool). Married man, aged 27 at the date of trial. He had been crushed between two cranes resulting in a fractured pelvis and a wrenching injury to the left sacro-iliac joint. He also had an abrasion over the right thigh and some unascertained damage to the knees. He was confined to bed for one month and returned to light duties at work two months after his accident. By the time of trial, one-and-a-quarter years later, he still had occasional stiffness in the left leg, numbness on top of the left foot, and once or twice a week, had pain and tenderness in the left groin, that pain sometimes being sharp. The fracture of his pelvis had healed and was unlikely to give rise to any increased symptoms. He had returned to his normal work but there was a chance that the cartilage of the hip joint had been injured and whilst this in itself was not disabling at the time of trial, it was possible that the injury could lead to an earlier onset of arthritis in the future than if the accident had not occurred. The judge held that there was only a fairly remote chance that in 20–30 years time osteo-arthritis might develop but if it did the plaintiff would have 10 years or so of considerable pain and discomfort, followed by a major operation after which he would be relieved of pain and would then be able to return to heavy work. In the early stages the plaintiff suffered a lot of pain and he was to be compensated for that and for the continuing condition in which, once or twice a week, he gets pain (not crippling pain or pain requiring him to stop work but pain which made it less of a pleasure to get home in the evening). He was also to be compensated for the remoter danger of a serious disability arising, with major surgery involved. *Special damages*: £600·45. *General damages*: £3,750. (*Ex rel. Messrs. Brian Thompson, Solicitors.*)

Reproductive and Excretory Organs

750. HODGSON v. HARRISON (November 28, 1977; Caulfield J.; Carlisle). Male, now aged 46. Former mental nurse. Married with three children (no plans for any more). Sustained the accident April 1973. Fractured pelvis and right acetabulum. Damage to pelvic nerve. Rupture of urethra and perineum involving rectum and anal canal. Minor injuries included fractured rib, and bruising of ankles and legs. Was an in-patient 11 weeks, and underwent four major operations. Present condition permanent. Total impotence and loss of libido. Frequent micturition ($\frac{3}{4}$ hour to $1\frac{1}{2}$ hour intervals). Sleep interrupted four times nightly. Dilatation operation needed every three months—each followed by painful sequelae for about two days. Portable urinal worn permanently. Occasional faecal incontinence. He was a cheerful, extrovert, happily-married man, but is now embarrassed socially, and his condition has severely affected his wife. The contentment of the home has been disrupted. Not totally employable, and probable that eventually he would obtain work of some kind. But his various disabilities will make it difficult. Twenty job applications to date had failed. Not possible for him to return to nursing. *Special damages*: £9,358. General damages: £13,000 for pain and suffering and loss of amenities; £24,000 for future loss of earnings. *Total general damages*: £37,000. (*Ex rel. Julian Hall, Esq., Barrister.*)

751. CHAPMAN v. BRITISH LEYLAND U.K. (January 18, 1978; Preston). The plaintiff, a 44 year old storeman at the time of trial, sustained a right inguinal hernia in an accident at work on January 15, 1976, having sustained a previous such hernia in 1951. A repair operation was carried out on September 28, 1976, and thereafter the plaintiff was off work for six weeks. At the time of the accident, the plaintiff was employed as a pipe tester by the defendants, which entailed repetitive bending and lifting. In January 1977 the plaintiff successfully applied for the lighter work of storeman with the defendants, for fear of a further occurrence of the hernia, and thereby incurred partial loss of earnings of £513 per annum after tax. The judge accepted the plaintiff's medical evidence that it was reasonable for him to seek such alternative lighter work, and that under normal circumstances there was at least a 10 per cent. chance of a further recurrence of the hernia. The judge awarded £1,600 for pain, suffering and loss of amenity, £5,643 for future loss of earnings (having applied a multiplier of 11), and £500 for loss of earning capacity. *Agreed special damages*: £680. *Total general damages*: £8,423. (*Ex rel. Messrs. Brian Thompson, Solicitors.*)

752. ABBOTT *v.* JORDANOU (April 23, 1978; Chapman J.). Male, aged 57. Shot in groin in November 1973. At time of shooting, wife aged 40 and he had before him expectation of reasonable period of continued sexual activity. Had to have one testicle and part of penis removed. Not rendered physically incapable of sex act, but since accident had been unable to obtain erection or have sexual intercourse. *Agreed special damages*: £68·75. *General damages*: £5,000.

Arm

753. CLARE *v.* LAMBETH SOUTHWARK AND LEWISHAM AREA HEALTH AUTHORITY (February 23, 1978; Donaldson J.). Boy, aged 8 at date of negligent treatment in May 1973 and 13 at date of hearing. Had suffered left arm fracture which was incorrectly treated in hospital. As result he was left with mutilated, stiff and almost useless left forearm and hand which was reduced almost to a club. Due to skin grafts to arm, body was scarred at donor site or sites. Schoolfellows taunted him as a " spastic " and at his age he was not able to cope with this. Was severely disturbed by his injuries and, after missing two school terms, was now attending special school. Pain and suffering and loss of amenities assessed at £15,000 and loss of earning capacity at £13,000. *Agreed special damages*: £75. *Total general damages*: £28,000.

754. INGRAM *v.* J. HESKETH (A FIRM) (March 10, 1978; Hollings J.; High Court at Preston). Male aged 29. Employed as welder/fitter by small family firm. Right handed. Fracture dislocation of the left elbow joint with consequential subluxation of radio ulnar joint at wrist. Fracture of pelvis which united without complication. Permanent disability consisted of 20 degrees' loss of straightening and 10 degrees' loss of rotation of left forearm. Some aching and pain at work and at end of day. Osteo-arthritic changes likely over period of 15–20 years in left elbow and wrist joints. Required help at work with heavy tasks such as lifting or digging. Some restriction in pastime of swimming. A valued employee who would be retained for so long as he could continue with some assistance to do his work. No loss of earnings which were approximately £50 per week net. General damages for pain, suffering and loss of amenities assessed at £5,500 and loss of earning capacity at £3,000. *Agreed special damages*: £1,200. *Total general damages*: £8,500. (*Ex rel. Victor Watts, Barrister.*)

Wrist

755. CRITCHER *v.* SAMUEL ELLIOTT AND SONS (February 1, 1978; Judge Laughton-Scott Q.C.). Male, aged 35. Former lorry driver. Injured in accident in September 1973. Right wrist injury. In May 1974 underwent operation for removal of cartilage. Wrist movement now permanently restricted. Could no longer lift anything heavy and wrist was painful under pressure. Now unable to play snooker or darts and required help in digging his garden. Had been forced to give up his pre-accident job and was now in less remunerative employment as a postman. Future loss of earnings assessed at £3,120 and pain and suffering and loss of amenities at £3,000. *Agreed special damages*: £1,018. *Total general damages*: £6,120.

756. SMITH *v.* PEL (December 1, 1977; O'Connor J.; Birmingham). Female, aged 50 years, sustained injuries on September 7, 1976, whilst at work. The injury was diagnosed as a fracture of the scaphoid bone of the right wrist and treated conventionally for such injury. The forearm was in plaster for some 12 weeks. In the early part of 1977 it was noticed a ganglion had developed on the inner-side of the wrist. The operation was performed in October 1977. Degenerative changes in the right wrist pre-existed injury. It was common ground that the plaintiff had a pain-free wrist until September 7, 1976, and since that time it had been a painful one. The plaintiff was off work until the date of trial but the defendants offered employment that the plaintiff could perform at the trial at her pre-accident rate of pay. It was possible that the wrist would settle down; it may be that plaintiff would have to have it fixed. There would be some risk on the labour market if the plaintiff ever lost her job. *Agreed special damages*: £1,440. *General damages*: £4,000. (*Ex rel. Messrs. Rowleys and Blewitts, Solicitors.*)

Hand

757.   BUNTING *v.* THAMES SERVICES (MARINE) (July 10, 1978; O'Connor J.; High Court at Norwich). Male, aged 53 at date of accident in November 1973, employed as a buoy man by a Conservancy Board. Right-handed. Deep laceration in palm of left hand severing some muscles and nerves. Fracture of left radius with dislocation of radio-ulnar joint. Fracture required plating. Residual disabilities: movements of left wrist restricted by about 50 per cent.; grip to left hand reduced to less than one-third of that of right hand; clumsiness of fine movements of left fingers and thumb; some aching in left wrist, particularly in wet weather, and some tenderness over scars. Confined to light duties at work with consequential loss of earnings of £1,018 per annum. Would expect to retire at 65. Estimated reduction in future pension due to lower earnings: £625 per annum. Awarded £4,000 for pain, suffering and loss of amenities. £4,072 for loss of future earnings, on a four years' purchase. £2,750 for future loss of pension. *Total general damages*: £10,822. (*Ex rel. Victor Watts, Esq., Barrister.*)

Fingers and Thumb

758.   GOODCHILD *v.* HENLEY FORKLIFT CO. (April 10, 1978; Comyn J.; Cardiff). Male, aged 33 at date of hearing. Fabrication operator. Right handed. Traumatic amputation of greater part of terminal phalanx of left index finger. Loss of ¾-inch of finger. The stump had healed but was a little deformed and somewhat tender particularly in cold weather and when knocked. Returned to work doing full pre-accident job after 10 weeks. Pain and suffering and loss of amenities assessed at £1,600 and loss of employability, £500. *Agreed special damages*: £406. *Total general damages*: £2,100. (*Ex rel. Messrs. Brian Thompson, Solicitors.*)

759.   MUKTA PUJARA *v.* JENSON BOOK CO. (July 27, 1978; Park J.). Female, aged 45. Right-handed. Injured during course of her work on book-binding and sewing machine. Sustained a compound fracture of the proximal phalanx of the right index finger involving lacerations and crushing of the tissue. Off work for 15 weeks. Residual stiffness in joints, extending into arm and shoulder. Slightly restricted grip, flexion, etc. Not able to work at her previous speed. Award of £750 for her future risk in the open labour market. *Agreed special damages*: £162·57. *General damages*: £2,000. (*Ex rel. Messrs. Robin Thompson & Partners, Solicitors.*)

760.   WEBBER *v.* GRAMADA DEVELOPMENTS (SUFFOLK) (July 21, 1978; Judge Edgar Fay Q.C.). Man, aged 25 at time of accident in September 1973. Director and site engineer for small building firm. Right handed; injured left hand falling on to chain saw. *Held*, no liability, but quantum considered. Cut tendons on main and little fingers of left hand. Two days in hospital with numerous attendances thereafter. Little finger useless and a nuisance, subsequently amputated. Competent cosmetic job. Difficult to manipulate ring finger and could only clench fist by hooking middle finger around it. Unable to play piano to previous high standard—clearly lost great pleasure; also some disadvantage at golf. No continuing disability at work or loss of earnings. Taking into account age, not leading hand, general damages for pain and suffering would have been £2,000. (*Ex rel. Richard Robinson, Esq., Barrister.*)

761. BRENT *v.* F. MCNEIL & CO. (December 5, 1978; Judge Freeman). Male, aged 42. Married with four children. Right-handed. Right hand caught in wrapping machine. Suffered compound fracture of terminal phalanx of right ring finger, laceration of nail bed and palmar surfaces of right ring finger, bruising of right middle finger and shock. After initial suturing, he required a second operation for avulsion of the fingernail. He wore a splint for a week, sutures for a further two weeks and bandages for a total of seven weeks. He returned to his normal pre-accident work after four weeks. Plaintiff had no permanent disability except that he was left with 10 degree loss of flexion in the end joint, slight thickening of affected finger, 1½-inch scar extending through the nail bed and around the inside of the finger, and a deformed nail which would probably continue to grow in two sections, causing slight inconvenience and embarrassment. *Agreed special damages:* £15·64. *Total general damages:* £750. [*Ex. rel. Alexander Layton, Esq., Barrister*]

Leg

762. MARSDEN *v.* CARRIGAN AND ENVIROCOR (March 17, 1978; Jupp J.; Sheffield.) Male, aged 29 at date of trial. Metal fabrication worker. Injured in accident in August 1974. Concussion, lacerations to face and right index finger, comminuted compound fracture of right femur, fracture of lower end of left radius. In hospital for three months and then allowed home in plaster. In early 1975 readmitted to hospital for bone-grafting operation on leg and detained in hospital for six weeks. In plaster until May 1975; thereafter attended hospital for physiotherapy until November 1975 when discharged from further attendance. Resumed light work in May 1976. Two-inch shortening of leg with slight limitation of rotation at hip and 25° loss of flexion at knee. Agility impaired. Walking more than two miles resulted in pain and aching in leg; ability to squat limited and could not walk over rough ground or do climbing work. Also ability to lift heavy weights with left hand impaired. Left with minor facial scarring and unpleasant scarring to hip which judge did not regard as serious cosmetic disability. Small risk of osteo-arthritis in wrist in later life. Before accident had been keen amateur footballer; captain of local team and played football in both summer and winter and trained regularly. Also played tennis, swam and went dancing. Since accident unable to follow these pursuits. Awarded £7,800 for future loss of earnings (multiplier of 15 years), £500 for handicap in labour market, £5,000 for pain and suffering and loss of amenities. *Agreed special damages*: £4,636. *Total general damages*: £13,300. (*Ex rel. D. R. Bentley, Esq., Barrister.*)

763. MCCUSKER *v.* W. & C. FRENCH (CONSTRUCTION) (October 3 and 4, 1978; O'Connor J.) Male aged 50 at date of trial. Batching plant operator at time of accident. Injured in March 1973 when fell approximately 20 ft. from vertical ladder. Sustained compound fracture of left femur, a crack fracture through left patella, and laceration to scalp. Kürtcher nail inserted in left femur. In hospital for six weeks; at rehabilitation centre for further three months. On crutches until end of July 1973; thereafter used two sticks for walking and one stick until March 1974. Resumed light work in April 1974. Permanent loss of movement in left knee, and pain in left knee and left femur; osteo-arthritic changes in left knee had already developed; unable to walk any great distance, and tendency for left knee to creak. Unable to do work involving climbing or heavy lifting. At date of trial, employed on light duties as janitor. Finding of one-third contributory negligence. Awarded £7,000 for loss of future earning capacity, and £5,000 for pain and suffering and loss of amenity. *Special damages*: £9,000. *Total general damages*: £12,000. (*Ex rel. Frank R. Moat, Esq., Barrister.*)

WADSWORTH *v.* GILLESPIE (November 8, 1978; Sir Basil Nield, Leeds). Plaintiff male, 19 years at date of accident in 1976, 21 years at date of trial. Apprentice engineer at date of accident. Qualified in December 1977 and now working in mill as maintenance engineer. Suffered compound fracture dislocation of left knee in road accident. Surgery on knee, five screws inserted. Development of arthritis inevitable in 10–15 years after accident at which time he would require knee replacement operation. Would require possibly two or three operations of this nature during his life because of need to renew artificial joints of knee periodically. Cannot kneel and can squat only with great difficulty. Difficulty in working at a low level on machines in course of work. Had to request a colleague to carry out doing work in a low place but his job was secure and there was no indication that was likely to lose job in ordinary course of events. Suffers continuous pain in knee. Prognosis that condition would get worse. Twelve-inch scar on medial aspect of left leg and two-inch scar on right of his left knee. Very obvious scars but he was not embarrassed by them. Had been a junior table tennis champion but had had to give up table tennis. Difficulty now in climbing ladders and stairs. On basis that no real evidence of future loss of earning capacity, £500 under that head. *Agreed special damages*: £653·09. *General damages for pain and suffering and loss of amenity*: £6,000 (on basis of full liability). (*Ex rel. Robert S. Smith, Esq., Barrister.*)

765. CHAMBERS *v.* AMEY ROADSTONE CORP. (October 3, 1978; Forbes J.). Male plant operator, aged 52. As result of accident in June 1974 he sustained fracture of right tibia and fibula and thrombosis in left calf. Now almost completely recovered. No future loss of earnings. *Agreed special damages*: £565. *General damages*: £3,000.

766. LEVY *v.* ATTE INVESTMENT CO. (March 10, 1978; Wien J.). Widow, aged 72. Injured in accident in October 1971. Completely displaced sub-capital fracture of left femur. Prosthesis was cemented in which gave good results, although left leg now shortened by ¾ inch. Had made remarkable recovery for person of her age. Now walked with slight limp. Could walk half a mile with aid of walking stick and managed stairs without difficulty. No special damage. *General damages*: £2,500.

767. BOOTH *v.* SUCHOPAREK (May 17, 1978; Judge Lauriston, Q.C.; Sheffield). Male, aged 38 at date of accident, 42 at date of trial. Accountant with building company. Laceration to forehead, bruising to backs of both hands, 1 in. laceration of right knee with lateral dislocation of patella. Allowed home in plaster. Plaster removed after one month. Off work for 10 weeks. Knee continued to give pain for which doctors could find no cause. Ultimately transpired that he had developed mild osteo-arthritis in knee. Still suffering some discomfort in the knee which tended to swell up after heavy work. Able to drive and to play squash and golf, but would have to give up squash within five years and golf by age of 55. Since his job did not involve heavy physical work progress of osteoarthritic condition in knee would be slow. Would not require arthrodesis. *General damages*: £2,500. (*Ex rel. D. R. Bentley, Esq., Barrister.*)

768. ELGOOD *v.* MINISTRY OF AGRICULTURE FISHERIES AND FOOD (November 21, 1978; Judge Stockdale; Westminster County Ct.). The plaintiff was a lady aged 56 at the time of accident on August 9, 1976, and 58 at the date of trial. She was employed by the defendants as a messenger, and slipped on some polished linoleum She suffered a sprain of the left knee and bruising of the right elbow. She was in considerable pain, but was only off work for one week after the accident. She had stayed at work ever since, although she had changed her job and now followed a more sedentary occupation. The bruising of the elbow had recovered satisfactorily. As far as the knee was concerned, the accident had caused discomfort, pain and inconvenience to the knee ever since, as a result of the aggravation of pre-existing symptom-free osteoarthritis of the knee. It was common ground between the medical experts that the accident had caused an acceleration of four to five years in the onset of symptoms of osteoarthritis which would probably not have been felt by the plaintiff until she was about 61 years of age. The result of this acceleration of the onset of symptoms was that the plaintiff was handicapped in a number of respects. It was difficult for her to go downstairs, she had to descend crabwise and she wakes up with a stiff knee. She gets pain if she has to walk any long distance. The knee gets stiff when at rest, and she cannot kneel to do her housework. The plaintiff was a widow who looks after her house and has a son to look after as well.

Booth v. *Suchoparek* [1978] C.L.Y. 767 and *Britz* v. *Safranek* (reported in Kemp and Kemp, *The Quantum of Damages*, Vol. 2, para. 10–473/5) referred to. *Agreed special damages*: £16. *General damages*: £1,100, plus interest, at 9 per cent. since date of accident, of £230·67. (*Ex rel. R. P. Glancy, Esq., Barrister.*)

Ankle

769. HOGARTH v. GEORGE BLAIR & Co. (November 24, 1978; Eastham J.: Newcastle). Male, aged 34 at date of accident on December 31, 1975. Chargehand setter in car works. Sustained a chip fracture of the anterior margin of the articular surface of the right tibia. Soundly united with slight deformity. Scars of three minor lacerations over the external malleous. Further scar of 2" × 1" laceration just below and in front of the medial malleous. Soft tissue injury around the joint. Ankle movement limited; dorsi-flexion just below neutral; plantar flexion almost full; inversion and eversion of the foot full. Resumed work as a labourer (sweeping) on September 13, 1976. Could stand on tip-toe but some pain over the anterior aspect of the ankle joint. Unable to lift heavy weights. No risk of arthritis. Before accident had been keen amateur footballer, cricketer and basketball player. Since accident unable to follow these pursuits or take children ice-skating or play football with them. Awarded £5,772 for future loss of earnings (multiplier of 12 years); £2,000 for handicap in the labour market; £4,000 for pain and suffering and loss of amenities. *Agreed special damages*: £750. *Total general damages*: £11,772. (*Ex rel. William Birtles, Esq., Barrister.*)

770. PARKER v. KENT AREA HEALTH AUTHORITY (July 28, 1978; Thesiger J.). Male, aged 38. In accident in November 1970, broke both ankles and fractured his spine. Left with a gait which was peculiar and troublesome. Before the accident was paranoid schizophrenic and had not worked for some time. Judge found that even without his physical injuries it was unlikely the plaintiff would have been able to live in the community and earn his living. Plaintiff in fact lived in hospital. *General damages for pain and suffering and loss of amenity*: £8,500.

771. THWAITES v. SMITHS DOCK Co. (March 10, 1978; Boreham J.; Teesside). Male aged 25 at date of accident. Welder, engaged in work on board ships. Sustained a comminuted fracture of left os calsis, involving sub-talar joint. Permanent loss of inversion and eversion movements of left foot, together with stiffness in ankle and loss of agility. Due to his determined attitude had returned to pre-accident work, although the climbing involved caused him discomfort which was considerable at times. Arthritis was likely to develop in the sub-talar joint, but would probably not increase his disability. Unable to play football or " romp about " with his young children. Judge found there was no likelihood of his losing his present job. No award for possible future handicap on labour market. *Total general damages*: £5,000. (*Ex rel. T. S. A. Hawkesworth, Esq., Barrister.*)

Foot

772. BATE v. HALTON BOROUGH COUNCIL (July 25, 1978; Hollings J.; Liverpool). Male, aged 44 at date of trial. Plumber. Injured in accident in October 1976 when fell from ladder in course of employment by the defendants. Fracture of right os calcis. The fracture extended into the subtaloid joint. Complete loss of inversion and eversion of the foot. 10 degree loss of plantar flexion in the ankle. Plaintiff has pain when walking over rough ground because of involuntary twisting of the foot. Foot aches after walking more than four to five miles. He cannot run or engage in athletic activities, except that his pre-accident hobby of cycling is not seriously affected because plaintiff pedals with front of his foot. Plaintiff unable to climb ladders and this incapacity and inability to crouch hampers him in his work. Plaintiff had returned to his pre-accident employment with the defendants, who provided another man to climb ladders in the plaintiff's place. No award for loss of earning capacity because plaintiff's employment was secure and because of demand for plumbers. General damage awarded only for pain, suffering and loss of amenity. *Agreed special damages*: £923·28. *Total general damages*: £4,500. (*Ex rel. Marilyn Mornington, Barrister.*)

773. BUSH *v.* GLANMORFA (February 1, 1978; Judge Jones; Swansea). Male, profile cutter, aged 53. Fell 10 ft. from a steel structure in July 1975. Fracture of the right os calcis. Out patient for three months, then discharged to G.P.'s care. Fracture united, but with a little broadening of the heel and a slight valgus deformity, leaving him with a slightly flat footed gait. He returned to pre-accident work on December 1, 1975, but was away for a further six weeks in February 1977 after he had undertaken work which involved heavy lifting, pulling and pushing which left his foot painful. He regained full range of movement in all joints of the limb, except for the subastragaloid and mid tarsal joints where he was likely to develop osteo-arthritic changes as a late complication which was unlikely to require surgical treatment. Likely to have recurrences of pain in the foot from time to time if he had to do anything particularly heavy in the course of his work. It was possible that he would be unable to work on Sundays because of the five-mile walk to work when no public transport was available. Plaintiff was awarded £100 for the purchase of a bicycle to travel to work on a Sunday. *Agreed special damages*: £1,017·49. *Total general damages*: £2,500. (*Ex rel. Messrs. Brian Thompson, Solicitors.*)

Hernia

774. HARPER *v.* JOHN HARPER & Co. (April 14, 1978, C.A.). Male, aged 59. On June 12, 1975, wrenched himself at work resulting in left inguinal hernia. He was eight months in a truss, with occasional discomfort in working hours. He underwent an operation in February 1976. Nine weeks off work, and for about six months suffered discomfort; thereafter made a complete recovery. Apart from accident, the chance of a hernia was no higher than 5 per cent. Judge Skinner, Q.C. found that the condition the plaintiff suffered was very definitely at the lower end of the scale of seriousness, and awarded £700 general damages for pain and suffering. The Court of Appeal declined to intervene. *Per* Ormrod L.J., "the award was absolutely right." *Total general damages*: £700. (*Ex rel. Anthony Barker, Esq., Barrister.*)

Minor injuries

775. JAREK *v.* BRITISH RAILWAYS BOARD (March 21, 1978; O'Connor J.). Male, aged 67. Fractures of 3rd and 4th metatarsals of left foot and blow on head resulting in headaches for 3 months. Off work 18 weeks. *Agreed special damages*: £320. *General damages*: £1,500.

776. MASON *v.* LONDON BRICK Co. (October 1978; Jones J.). Male, aged 20, suffered undisplaced fracture of the medial malleolus when the wheel of a bogie struck and ran over his left ankle whilst carrying out his duties as a brick setter at the defendant's premises. Below knee walking plaster applied which was removed after six weeks. Plaintiff off work for three months and returned to pre-accident employment. He made a full recovery. The judge considered the pain suffered by the plaintiff to be similar to "the classic fractured leg case." *Agreed special damages*: £261·28. *General damages*: £1,200). (*Ex rel. Messrs. Whiteman, Bretherton & Co., Solicitors.*)

777. TYSON *v.* GREATER LONDON COUNCIL (October 20, 1978; Judge Lipfriend); First plaintiff was a boy aged 11 at the time of accident on February 26, 1976, and 14 at the date of trial. Walking along pavement when a wall 5′ 6″ high and 13″ thick fell on him. He was 4′ 11″ tall. He was trapped. He extricated himself and got home. He was found by his father who heard a noise at the front door. He was in a state of terror. His face and hair were matted with blood and sweat and blood seeped through his torn clothing. He was taken to hospital but not detained. Injuries consisted of: (1) heavy bruising and small abrasion of the left shoulder which cleared up in six weeks; (2) severe bruising of left anterior and lateral thigh which cleared up in six weeks; (3) laceration above left knee and knee intermittently gave way for 12 months thereafter, then cleared up; (4) strain of left lower back muscles, necessitating carrying him upright for two weeks, completely recovered by June 1976; (5) emotional shock causing recurrence of enuresis, a complaint suffered since infancy and cleared up completely 18 months before accident. This lasted with continued progress until September 1977, *i.e.* 18 months. The second plaintiff, father, (head of one-parent family consisting of himself and three sons, of which first plaintiff was youngest), woke boy four times nightly at first, then three times nightly to ensure dry bed. Father's claim based in part upon nursing services and in part upon inconvenience. First plaintiff award *general damages*: £900. Second plaintiff's *general damages*: £250, plus *agreed special damages*: £26. (*Ex rel. C. J. M. Tyrer, Esquire, Barrister*).

778. THOMA *v.* OSMAN (April 6, 1978; Judge Fay Q.C.). Male aged 45, self-employed grocer. Fracture of one rib in road accident, but no other injuries. This was painful during the course of one week, during which he was unable to attend his shop at all. During the next two to three weeks, he was able to supervise two friends who were running the shop without payment; and within four weeks, he had made a complete recovery. No special damages, except damage to his motorcar, were claimed; 15 per cent. reduction to award of general damages, for failing to wear a seat belt. *General damages*: £450. (*Ex rel. J. Sofer, Esq., Barrister.*)

779. HUGHES *v.* J. BROWNE CONSTRUCTION CO. (October 13, 1978; Judge Graham-Hall, Croydon Cty.Ct.) Male aged 53, labourer. In August 1976 suffered comminuted, but not compound, fractures of distal phalanges of fourth and fifth toes of left foot when a lamp-post fell from a dumper truck. In considerable pain at time of accident and for some time afterwards. Treated as an out patient at hospital; immobilised for two weeks; off work for eight weeks. Full recovery made with no limitation in movement; only a lack of " spring " in left foot and some slight discomfort in cold weather. *Agreed special damages*: £316. *General damages*: £400. (*Ex rel. Charles Bird, Esq., Barrister.*)

780. SMITH *v.* BATCHELOR FOODS (March 22, 1978; Judge William Stabb Q.C.). Male, factory worker. Suffered injuries to left arm and shoulder when struck by 4 cwt. trolley of food in December 1973. No broken bones, but was off work for several months. Still complained of pains in arm and shoulder and weakness in left hand, but judge accepted medical evidence that this was due to hysteria and tension caused by his personal problems and not to accident. *Special damages*: £518. *General damages*: £250.

781. McHARDY *v.* BENNETT (September 19, 1978; Judge Peter Fallon, Q.C., Bristol County Court). Male, aged 19, motor cyclist. Collided with rear of car when car made unexpected right turn and plaintiff attempted to take avoiding action. Thrown over handlebars, landed on head, and thrown over from right shoulder onto back. No head injuries; multiple bruises and some abrasions. Some injury to left little toe and residual inability to bend it, but of little effect on him. No broken bones. One and a half days in hospital; nine days off work. 25 per cent. reduction for contributory negligence. *Agreed special damages*: £691·22. *Total general damages*: £250. (*Ex rel. Messrs. Robert Boyd & Co., Solicitors.*)

782. LINDLEY *v.* HICKSON & WELCH (September 14, 1978; Judge Chapman, Q.C. Pontefract County Ct.). Male, aged 35. Suffered steam " scald " to right forearm in region elbow. Area affected 6 in. by 2¼ in. No treatment required other than dressings. Dressings retained for three weeks. Injury said to be very painful for one week and thereafter uncomfortable for several weeks. Lost no time off work. A few weeks interference with hobbies of golf and badminton. Redness completely disappeared by date of hearing (*i.e.* within eight months). Judge commented that injury was of a minor nature but that it was important to keep pace with decline in value of money. *General damages*: £200. (*Ex rel. Benjamin Nolan, Esq., Barrister.*)

783. WALKER *v.* HICKSON & WELCH (September 14, 1978; Judge Chapman, Q.C., Pontefract County Ct.). Male, aged 36. " Barked " shin on metal plinth causing bruise and some superficial skin loss. Injury dressed by plaintiff's own doctor. Lost no time off work. Leg healed completely within two months. Thereafter some tenderness at site of injury but only affected him when banged or knocked. Slight scarring but only just visible at date of trial (eight months later). Judge commented that injury was described in the medical report as " completely unimportant " and he regarded it as such. Nevertheless, it was necessary to keep pace with the declining value of money: *General damages*: £200. (*Ex rel. Benjamin Nolan, Esq., Barrister.*)

Fatal Accidents

784.   PANDIAN *v.* FRENCH (*The Times*, February 22, 1978; Goff J.). Deceased, male, aged 42. Senior hospital registrar. Died in road accident in April 1972. Left widow aged 45, son aged 14 and daughter aged 11. *Agreed damages*: £137,500.

785.   ROBERT *v.* EVANS (March 6, 1978; Mais J.). Deceased was male, aged 34 at time of death in September 1976. Dairyman earning £2,073 net per annum at time of death. This would have risen to £2,200 per annum by date of trial. Did home decorating, vegetable gardening, and got 21 pints free milk per week. Gave all wages to wife. Left widow aged 28, two daughters aged 6 and 4, son aged 2. Judge awarded £2,950 plus interest for loss of dependency to date of trial (72 weeks). Applied multiplier of 13 and 32/52 (making 15 years in all) for future loss. He valued the multiplicand for future loss at £2,430 per annum. This sum included the value of benefits in kind and work in house and garden (valued at £230 p.a.). *Law Reform Act award*: £750. *Fatal Accidents Acts award*: £33,758. (*Ex rel. J. Sofer, Esq., Barrister.*)

786. Quantum—car not of merchantable quality—fair market price

In assessing damages in respect of goods not of merchantable quality, regard should be had to what would have been the fair market value of the goods had the defects been known at the time of contracting.

The plaintiff agreed to the hire-purchase of a car with the defendant finance company, arranging the purchase through car dealers, who were told by the plaintiff prior to completion of the transaction of his intention to use the car for a family holiday abroad. Soon after delivery the car exhibited a wide variety of defects, some serious, which the dealers attempted to rectify, but the defects continued to occur during the holiday and, according to the plaintiff, spoilt the family holiday. Some six months after the contract the plaintiff stopped paying the hire-purchase instalments and claimed a " refund " of the purchase price; the defendants counterclaimed for outstanding hire-purchase instalments. A county court judge found that the car was not of merchantable quality and/or fit for purpose, and awarded £200 damages in respect thereof together with £75 for the spoilt holiday. *Held,* allowing the plaintiff's appeal, that the damages were inadequate; regard should have been had to what would have been the market value of the car at the time of contracting had the defects been known. An appropriate global figure for damages was £500.

JACKSON *v.* CHRYSLER ACCEPTANCES; MINORIES GARAGES (THIRD PARTY) [1978] R.T.R. 474, C.A.

787. —— **failure to replant land—part-ownership of plots**

On the basis of *rusticum judicium*, Megarry V.-C. has awarded the sum of A$75 per acre as damages for failure to replant land.

The parties having failed to agree on the quantum of damage, Megarry V.-C. awarded damages in respect of the breaches by the British Phosphate Commissioners, deciding the point in exercise of a *rusticum judicium*, at A$75 an acre. He made appropriate award to plaintiffs who had proved part ownership of relevant plot of land. He directed an inquiry in respect of those plaintiffs who had proved such part ownership but who had not proved its extent. He made no order for costs.

TITO *v.* WADDELL (No. 2); TITO *v.* ATT.-GEN. [1977] 3 W.L.R. 972 (Note), Megarry V.-C.

[For substantive issue, see [1977] C.L.Y. 2709.]

788. —— **plaintiff on supplementary benefits—whether credit should be given**

In a running-down case, the only issue between the parties was as to damages and whether the plaintiff should give credit to the defendant for the supplementary benefits payments he received. The plaintiff had made insufficient National Insurance contributions to qualify for sickness benefit. The plaintiff relied, in his contention that credit should not be given, on *Parry* v. *Cleaver* [1969] C.L.Y. 906, or *Daish* v. *Wauton* [1972] C.L.Y. 836, and on *Bowker*

v. *Rose* [1978] C.L.Y. 720. The defendant contended that the latter two cases were distinguishable from the present case, in that they were related to mobility allowances and other allowances for specific services, whereas supplementary benefit is cash for those in need, and is not discretionary. If credit was not afforded the defendant, the plaintiff would be paid these sums twice over. *Held*, that the supplementary benefit payments made to the plaintiff were deductible in full from damages awarded. (*Bowker* v. *Rose* distinguished in accordance with the defendant's contention; *Cackett* v. *Earl* [1976] C.L.Y. 666 followed): SANGER *v.* KENT AND CALLOW, November 3, 1978, Milmo J., Winchester Crown Ct. (*Ex rel. R. Hay, Esq., Barrister.*)

789. Remoteness—foreseeability—pig food unfit for consumption

Where parties contemplate the type of consequence which may follow a breach of contract, they will be liable for specific damage of that type, even where the specific damage was not foreseeable.

The defendants sold a pig-food hopper to the plaintiffs. It was defective. The nuts in it went mouldy. 254 pigs died as a result of eating mouldy nuts. At the time of the contract it was found, as a fact, that the parties could not have foreseen serious illness arising as a result of the consumption of mouldy nuts. *Held*, dismissing D's appeal, that while P could not recover for his loss of profit on the pigs, it would have been in the contemplation of the parties that there was a real possibility of harm coming to the pigs if their food was made unfit by reason of the condition of the hopper. The fact that they could not foresee the extent of the harm was immaterial and P could recover the cost of his pigs.

H. PARSONS (LIVESTOCK) *v.* UTTLEY INGHAM & CO. [1977] 3 W.L.R. 990, C.A.

790. Solicitors' negligence—assessment. See RUMSEY *v.* OWEN, WHITE AND CATLIN, § 2821.

ARTICLES. See *post*, p. [20].

DEATH DUTIES

791. Estate duty—discretionary trust—power to accumulate

[Finance Act 1894 (c. 30), s. 2 (1) (*b*) (iv) (as substituted by Finance Act 1969 (c. 32), s. 36 (2)); Trusts (Scotland) Act 1961 (c. 57), s. 5.] Under the trusts of a discretionary trust, the trustees had a power to accumulate for a specified period which had not expired when the truster died. The Inland Revenue claimed estate duty under F.A. 1894, s. 2 (1) (*b*) (iv), on the ground that under the Trusts (Scotland) Act 1961, s. 5, the power to accumulate terminated on the truster's death. *Held*, that a discretionary power to accumulate income was caught by the 1961 Act, and the effect of that Act being to cause the power to accumulate to terminate on the truster's death, estate duty was properly exigible: BAIRD *v.* LORD ADVOCATE [1978] S.T.C. 282, I.H., 2nd Div.

792. —— shares—whether situated in Great Britain or abroad

[Finance Act 1949 (c. 47), s. 28 (2).]

For the purposes of estate duty, shares in foreign companies which nevertheless keep registers in Great Britain, and the certificates of which are deposited in British banks, are capable of being property situate outside Great Britain if the deceased owner could, or would in practice, have dealt with the shares only from outside Great Britain.

The testatrix, who had been born in England, but who had been resident in Southern Rhodesia since 1951, and was domiciled there at her death, held shares in two companies, the Charter Group and the Gold Fields Group. The shares were registered in South Africa, and dividends were paid there. Gold Fields kept a branch register in England, and the Charter Group kept a duplicate register there. After 1962 the testatrix, being anxious about the political situation in South Africa, deposited the share certificates with a bank in England. On the death of the testatrix, the question arose whether the shares were property situate out of Great Britain. *Held*, the shares were property situate out of Great Britain, because (1) the Charter Group's registers in England were not branch registers where title to the shares could be dealt with; and (2) although the shares in the Gold Fields Group could have been dealt with in England or South Africa, it appeared that in practice the testatrix would not have dealt with the shares otherwise than in South Africa. (*Brassard* v. *Smith* [1925] A.C. 371; *Treasurer for Ontario* v. *Blonde* [1947] A.C. 24, applied.)

STANDARD CHARTERED BANK v. I.R.C. [1978] 1 W.L.R. 1160, Goulding J.

ARTICLES. See *post*, p. [20].

DEEDS AND BONDS

793. Construction—no seal or wafer affixed—signature across circle marked " L.S." —whether due execution

A document intended to serve as a deed may be duly executed notwithstanding that no seal or wafer is affixed thereto, in particular when the promissor signs across the space marked for the affixing of the seal and when the signature is duly attested.

The plaintiffs claimed possession of mortgaged property and arrears in respect of repayment of a loan advanced by plaintiffs upon the security of a legal charge of the property. The legal charge was described as a " deed " and at its conclusion it was stated to be " signed, sealed and delivered " by the mortgagor. A printed circle containing the letters " L.S." (locus sigilli) was alongside. No seal was affixed thereto, but the mortgagor signed across the circle and the signature was duly witnessed. The county court registrar and judge both dismissed the plaintiffs' action upon the grounds that the charge was not made under seal. Held, allowing the plaintiffs' appeal, that the printed circle was nowadays itself often regarded as a substitute for a seal and that the defendant's attested signature across such circle was sufficient evidence of execution of the document as his deed. (*Re Sandilands* (1871) L.R. 6 C.P. 411 and dictum of Danckwerts J. in *Stromdale & Ball* v. *Burden* (1951) C.L.C. 5559 applied; *National Provincial Bank of England* v. *Jackson* (1886) 33 Ch.D. 1 distinguished.)

FIRST NATIONAL SECURITIES v. JONES [1978] 2 W.L.R. 475, C.A.

794. Validity—rules—legal charge on land

P were a bank, holding a legal charge over D's property. D had defaulted in repayments under the charge, and possession proceedings were initiated. The charge was duly signed and attested, but displayed no waifer seal or " LS " mark. The question was whether the charge was valid as a deed. *Held*, (1) the underlying principles are as follows: (a) for a document to be a deed, the cardinal rule is that the signatory must intend to deliver it as his deed; (b) the intention must appear from the attestation clause or the physical appearance of the deed, *i.e.* it must be manifest to the witness that the signatory intends to deliver the document as his deed; (c) manifestation of the necessary intention may be either by a seal itself, but a verbal formula may serve the same purpose, *e.g.* if a witness cannot read or see, then if the signatory says: " I deliver this as my act and deed," that is sufficient; (d) from the authorities, it is established that the words " Signed, sealed and delivered " perform the same function as the seal or verbal formula, assuming the witness can read or is told of the words. If one has this, nothing more is necessary; (2) if this last principle is indeed the rule, it makes sense nowadays since, time and again, deeds are signed without any red adhesive paper or the " magic words "; (3) in the present case, both intention and manifestation are present; (4) the legal charge is valid on this basis, and P is entitled to judgment and possession. (*Re Sandilands* (1871) 6 L.R.C.P. 411; *Stromdale and Ball* v. *Burden* (1951) C.L.C. 5559, and *First National Securities* v. *Jones* [1978] C.L.Y. 793 applied): COMMERCIAL CREDIT SERVICES v. KNOWLES, February 28, 1978, Judge Kershaw, Stockport County Ct. (*Ex rel. Messrs. Blakeney, Greene & Pride, Solicitors.*)

ARTICLES. See *post*, p. [20].

DIVORCE AND MATRIMONIAL CAUSES

795. Appeals—single judge—weekly payments cases

The following Practice Direction was issued by the Principal Registry of the Family Division on May 22, 1978:

With effect from June 1, 1978, R.S.C., Ord. 90, r. 16 is amended. Unless the President otherwise directs, an appeal under the Matrimonial Proceedings (Magistrates' Courts) Act 1960 (c. 48) to the Family Division of the High Court may be determined by a single judge, instead of by a Divisional Court in cases where the appeal relates only to the amount of any weekly payment ordered to be made. The President may also direct that such an appeal be heard and determined by a single judge at " a divorce town," within the meaning of the Matrimonial Causes Rules (S.I. 1977 No. 344 (L.6)). Consequential amendments are made to Ord. 90, r. 16 concerning the number of copy documents required to be lodged where the appeal is to quantum only.

The practice to be followed in respect of any such appeal to a single judge of the Family Division will be that contained in Practice Direction, May 11, 1977 (Divisional Court: simplification of procedure) [1977] 5 C.L. 257, subject to the following modifications: —

(i) one copy only of the various documents in support of the appeal need be lodged, unless the President directs that an appeal which has been listed before a single judge shall instead be heard by a Divisional Court when the Clerk of the Rules will notify the appellant's solicitor (or the appellant if acting in person) and request that he do lodge the additional copies required by R.S.C., Ord. 90, r. 16 and Practice Direction dated May 11, 1977, prior to the date fixed for the hearing;

(ii) any request to fix an appeal for hearing by a single judge at a place other than at the Royal Courts of Justice should be made in writing to the Clerk of the Rules;

(iii) where the President directs that the appeal be heard at a divorce town, as defined by the Matrimonial Causes Rules, the Clerk of the Rules will inform the appellant of the relevant town and will refer the papers to the listing officer of the appropriate circuit office for a date of hearing to be fixed and notified to the appellant.

It should be noted that every appeal under the Matrimonial Proceedings (Magistrates' Courts) Act 1960 must continue to be entered in the Principal Registry.

Registrar's Direction dated December 16, 1971 (Divisional Court Appeal: date of hearing) [1971] C.L.Y. 3658, is hereby cancelled.

[1978] 1 W.L.R. 797; [1978] 2 All E.R. 432.

796. Conflict of laws. See CONFLICT OF LAWS.

797. Costs

MATRIMONIAL CAUSES (COSTS) (AMENDMENT) RULES 1978 (No. 922 (L. 25)) [10p], made under the Matrimonial Causes Act 1973 (c. 18), s. 50; operative on July 31, 1978; amend S.I. 1977 No. 345 by increasing the fixed costs and the prescribed sums to be allowed in average cases under the divorce scale applicable to matrimonial proceedings in divorce county courts.

798. Cruelty—insanity of respondent—whether a defence

[Can.] *Held*, that in a petition for divorce based upon cruelty, the insanity of the respondent at the time of the alleged acts is no defence to the action. (*Williams* v. *Williams* [1963] C.L.Y. 1048 considered and distinguished): MACKAY v. MACKAY (1978) 1 R.F.L. (2d) 80, Prince Edward Island Sup.Ct.

799. Declaration of satisfaction as to children—child maintained by social security—whether relevant

[Matrimonial Causes Act 1973 (c. 18), s. 41 (1).]

The fact that a child is being supported by social security is not a relevant factor in determining whether to make a declaration under s. 41 (1) of the Matrimonial Causes Act 1973 unless there is reason to suppose that funds in excess of the supplementary benefits payment could be obtained.

In granting a decree nisi on divorce the judge declined to make a declaration under s. 41 (1) of the 1973 Act that he was satisfied as to the arrangements for the child of the family on the grounds that although the wife had obtained previously a maintenance order for the child and herself, such sums were collected by the D.H.S.S. who in turn supported the wife and child with social security payments; the judge ruled, inter alia, that it was in neither the public nor the child's interest that it should be supported on social security. *Held*, allowing the wife's appeal, that since there was no reason to suppose that the maintenance order could be varied so as to provide more than the amount of social security and other welfare payments currently being made, the judge had taken into account an irrelevant consideration.

COOK *v.* COOK [1978] 1 W.L.R. 994, C.A.

800. Decree absolute—voidable

[Matrimonial Causes Act 1973 (c. 18), s. 10.] The parties separated in 1971, W returning to the Isle of Man with the two children. H maintained W and the two children by a voluntary allowance. In 1976, H filed a divorce petition based on five years' separation. W intended not to oppose the grant of a decree nisi but to apply for financial provision under s. 10 of the 1973 Act as she would be entitled to a police widow's pension on H's death. W's English solicitors were not on the record but had applied for Legal Aid which was granted on December 10, 1976. On December 1, 1976, H was granted a decree nisi. As the woman he intended to marry was suffering from a severe liver complaint, H's application for expedition of decree absolute was granted and the decree made absolute on December 10, 1976. H remarried. W's application to have the decree absolute set aside was transferred to the High Court. *Held*, failure to comply with *Practice Note* (*Fam.Div.*) (*Divorce: decree absolute*) [1972] C.L.Y. 1029, made the decree absolute voidable, not void (*Dryden v. Dryden* [1973] C.L.Y. 892 applied). As H gave satisfactory undertakings to W this decree would not be set aside : BRIDGE *v.* BRIDGE (1977) 122 S.J. 95, Balcombe J.

801. Desertion—maintenance—short marriage

The parties married when both were aged 45. W gave up her employment, pension rights and widow's pension to look after H whose hours were irregular. The parties lived with W's father who died five days after the marriage, leaving W a rent-free life occupancy of the property. After 12 weeks, H left W, her complaint of desertion was proved, and she was awarded £20 per week maintenance. H appealed, contending that W should get a nominal order. *Held*, dismissing the appeal, the financial consequences of the marriage had been more severe on W than on H, who had a gross income of £85 per week, and the justices had not erred in principle: ABDUREMAN *v.* ABDUREMAN (1978) 122 S.J. 663, Balcombe J.

802. Divorce County Courts

DIVORCE COUNTY COURTS (AMENDMENT) ORDER 1978 (No. 818 (L. 22)) [10p], made under the Matrimonial Causes Act 1967 (c. 56), s. 1 (1); operative on July 1, 1978; amends S.I. 1971 No. 1954 by designating the Altrincham, Bishop Auckland, Gateshead, Llanelli, Macclesfield, North Shields, Rotherham, Runcorn, Skipton, South Shields and Welshpool County Courts as divorce county courts.

DIVORCE COUNTY COURTS ORDER 1978 (No. (No. 1759 (L.37)) [20p], made under the Matrimonial Causes Act 1967, s. 1 (1); operative on January 2, 1979; supersedes S.I. 1971 No. 1954 and subsequent amending orders. Designates the divorce county courts in which matrimonial causes may be commenced and those at which undefended matrimonial causes may be tried.

803. Domestic Proceedings and Magistrates' Courts Act 1978 (c. 22). See § 1903.

804. Domicile. See CONFLICT OF LAWS.

805. Fees

MATRIMONIAL CAUSES FEES (AMENDMENT) ORDER 1978 (No. 1256 (L. 31)) made under the Matrimonial Causes Act 1973 (c. 18), s. 51 and the Public Offices Fees Act 1879 (c. 58), ss. 2, 3; amends S.I. 1975 No. 1346 by increasing the fees payable on the presentation of a petition to £20. Also makes consequential amendments in other fees to take into account the changes made by the County Court Fees Order 1978 and the Supreme Court Fees (Amendment) Order 1978.

806. **Financial provision—agreement—duty of court to review**
[Matrimonial Causes Act 1973 (c. 18), s. 25.]

A court, in performing its duty under s. 25 of the 1973 Act, also owes a duty to uphold agreements especially when made between parties at arm's length negotiated by legal advisers, where the circumstances remain the same and which are not against public policy; that a registrar has approved the agreement does not relieve the judge from his primary responsibility of consideration under s. 25.

The parties were married in 1965 and there were two children of the marriage. Following negotiation between the respective solicitors an agreement was reached as to W's financial provision. Minutes of the agreement were signed with a view to incorporation in an order made on decree nisi. H filed a petition under s. 1 (2) (*a*) of the 1973 Act. Shortly after signing the agreement W changed her mind and wished to withdraw from the agreement. *Held*, in considering financial provision under the 1973 Act the court has a discretion to be exercised at the time of decree or later, with a duty under s. 25 to consider whether the arrangements agreed by the parties were reasonable. It is a matter of public policy that the court should retain jurisdiction over matters of maintenance, although collusion was no longer a bar to divorce. (*Bennett* v. *Bennett* [1952] C.L.Y. 1058 applied.)

DEAN v. DEAN [1978] 3 W.L.R. 288, Bush J.

807. —— —— **whether effective**
[Matrimonial Causes Act 1973 (c. 18), ss. 23, 34.]

In 1969 both parties filed divorce petitions which were defended. In 1972, after negotiations, H filed a fresh petition pursuant to s. 1 (2) (*d*) of the 1973 Act, with W's consent. The petition contained an agreement concerning financial provision preceded by the preamble " neither the petitioner nor the respondent make or pursue any financial claims against the other save. . . ." In November 1977, H obtained a declaration that W was not entitled to proceed with applications under ss. 23 and 24 of the 1973 Act. *Held*, dismissing W's appeal, the preamble clearly precluded future as well as immediate financial claims and the order should have said so: SAUNDERS v. SAUNDERS (1978) 8 Fam. Law 206, C.A.

808. —— **amendment of acknowledgment of service—whether permissible after remarriage**
[Matrimonial Causes Act 1973 (c. 18), s. 28 (3).]

After remarriage a wife is not entitled to apply to amend the acknowledgment of service to comply with the wording specified in notice of application for ancillary relief (Form 11).

H and W married in 1945. H petitioned under s. 1 (2) (*a*) of the Matrimonial Causes Act 1973. W filed an acknowledgment of service (Form 6) notifying intention to apply for a lump sum and a settlement and/or transfer of property. Decree nisi was granted on October 30, 1975, decree absolute on December 15, 1975, and W remarried on July 31, 1976. On December 7, 1976, W's solicitors sent H a Form 11 dated November 26, 1976, claiming a lump sum. H's solicitors replied stating they would rely on s. 28 (3) of the 1973 Act. It was suggested on behalf of W that the Form 6 was filed as an application in substance if not in form and the filing of Form 11 was simply done to correct the form. *Held*, (1) affirmative replies to questions relating to ancillary relief on the acknowledgment of service are merely an expression of intention to apply at some future date; (2) the court has no jurisdiction to amend the acknowledgment to comply with the wording on Form 11 in favour of a wife who has remarried. (*Dryden* v. *Dryden* [1973] C.L.Y. 892 and *Marsden* v. *Marsden* [1972] C.L.Y. 2686 considered.)

HARGOOD (FORMERLY JENKINS) v. JENKINS [1978] 2 W.L.R. 969, Wood J.

809. —— **discovery of documents—company director—custody, possession or power**
[Rules of Supreme Court, Ord. 24.]

Where a company is not merely the alter ego of a spouse, the court may order discovery only of such documents as are in the possession, custody or power of a spouse and not those over which he merely has a right of inspection.

A husband held 51 per cent. of the shares in a company which owned 75 per cent. of the shares of the operating company of which he was chairman. The registrar, on application by his wife, made an order for discovery of documents of the operating company. *Held*, allowing his appeal in part, that the court's discretionary power to order disclosure and production of documents extended only to those in the husband's possession, custody or power. Company documents which were within his actual custody or physical possession must be disclosed, but not so in the cases where, the company not being merely an alter ego of the husband, he had only a right of inspection of the documents.

B. *v.* B. [1978] 3 W.L.R. 624, Dunn J.

810. —— lump sum

The parties married in 1950, separated in 1969 and divorced in 1973. There was one son now aged over 20. In 1974 H remarried W2 and two children, aged 7 and 3, were born of that union. In 1975 W2 died and thereafter H looked after the children in the flat over his shop, with help from their paternal grandmother. The premises had a net equity of £11,300 and H had an insurance policy with surrender value of £1,400 but no other capital assets. W1 lived on state benefits in council accommodation. The registrar's order, confirmed by the judge, was that H pay a lump sum of £3,500 to W within six months. On appeal H adduced evidence, which the judge refused to admit, that he could only raise £3,500 by selling the premises, not by further mortgage. *Held*, allowing H's appeal, and ordering him to pay £1,400 to W, it would be wrong to order payment of a sum involving either sale or even an increase in mortgage on this property: PORTER *v.* PORTER [1978] Fam. Law 143, C.A.

811. —— —— children—whether leave required for application

[Matrimonial Causes Rules 1977 (S.I. 1977 No. 344), rr. 68, 69.]

A petitioner is not a person entitled to make an application for ancillary relief for children under r. 69 of the Matrimonial Causes Rules 1977.

The parties were divorced in 1970, custody of the children being awarded to the petitioning wife; her petition sought, inter alia, " child maintenance, a lump sum and/or secured provision." The court approved an agreement whereby the husband was to make certain periodical payments, and transferred property to the wife in full and final satisfaction of her claim for lump sum maintenance. The wife thereafter went to Australia and remarried, the husband continuing to make periodical payments for the children. After the breakdown of her second marriage, the wife in 1976 applied for lump sum provision for the children. (The courts had no power to order such provision prior to 1971.) On the preliminary question as to whether the wife was entitled to make such application and/or required leave therefor, *held*, that (1) the wife was not a person entitled to make application under r. 69 of the 1977 Rules; (2) the wife's petition failed to comply with r. 68, since the prayer therein for " a lump sum " could not be construed to include lump sum provision for children because at that time the court had no power to award the same; and (3) accordingly leave was required, and that in the circumstances leave would be refused. (*Chaterjee* v. *Chaterjee* [1976] C.L.Y. 783, applied.)

McKay (FORMERLY CHAPMAN) *v.* CHAPMAN [1978] 1 W.L.R. 620, Lionel Swift, Q.C.

812. —— —— transfer of property

The parties married in 1937 and divorced in 1975. All five children were independent of the parties at divorce. H worked in Nigeria from 1951 to 1960 when he returned home to find W had left to live with B-W by whom she had three girls, two of whom were invalids. The former matrimonial home, now valued at £14,000, was purchased in joint names in 1956 by borrowing from H's employers and family and a mortgage paid off by H in 1972. In

1974 B-W transferred his house, now having a net equity of £9,000 into W's sole name. B-W had debts of £7,000 being paid at £85 per month leaving him and W only £138 per month to live on. H was retired living on state benefits with £300 savings. The judge ordered H to make a lump sum payment of £4,500 whereupon W would transfer her interest in the home to H. *Held*, allowing H's appeal, W should be given a one-third interest in the property not to be realised until H should die or voluntarily cease to reside in the house. W had a roof over her head and had not suffered financial loss from the marital breakdown: DALLIMER *v.* DALLIMER [1978] Fam. Law 142, C.A.

813. —— —— wife owning property
[Matrimonial Causes Act 1973 (c. 18), s. 25 (1).]
Upon a husband's application for lump sum maintenance where the wife owns property upon which she and the children rely for income, regard must be had to the amount which the wife can reasonably raise and the amount necessary to enable the husband to obtain accommodation.
After the parties' marriage in 1964 the wife's father bought and conveyed to the wife a farm whereupon they lived and upon which the husband worked hard in order to improve it and to produce a successful farming business. After their separation and divorce the wife continued living at the farm together with the three children of the marriage. The husband, who had no other means, applied, inter alia, for a lump sum and for a transfer of property order. The farm, contents and stock were valued at £102,000 and the husband's share of stock and contents at £8,000. The husband appealed against the judge's award to him of £15,000 payable in three instalments over one year. *Held*, dismissing his appeal, that since the wife had only a nominal award of maintenance against the husband, she needed to retain the farm to provide income for herself and the children and that in all the circumstances £15,000 was appropriate since she could not reasonably raise more than that and such a sum sufficed to provide the husband with an alternative home. (Dictum of Scarman L.J. in *Calderbank* v. *Calderbank* [1975] C.L.Y. 693, applied; *O'D.* v. *O'D.* [1975] C.L.Y. 983, considered.)
P. *v.* P. (FINANCIAL PROVISION: LUMP SUM) [1978] 1 W.L.R. 483, C.A.

814. —— maintenance pending suit—arrears
On November 26, 1976, H was ordered to pay W maintenance pending suit of £42·47 less tax. On December 1, 1976, W obtained a decree nisi of divorce which was made absolute on July 20, 1977. H fell into arrears and on May 4, 1977, the judge ordered that he be committed for 28 days but suspended execution of the order on terms. On June 21, 1977, H applied for variation of the order of May; the judge ordered that H should pay maintenance of £35 per week less tax, the committal order being further suspended on terms. On October 26, 1977, the judge activated the committal order of May 4, but this was again suspended on October 28 on H's undertaking to pay arrears of £819 into a joint bank account and to serve notice of appeal against the order of June 21. *Held*, allowing H's appeal, the proper order was for H to pay W the sum of £675·80 arrears and provide a certificate of deduction of tax in respect of the grossed up figure: BEAUMONT *v.* BEAUMONT [1978] 8 Fam. Law 111, C.A.

815. —— one-third rule—husband's standard of living to be considered
When ordering periodic payments where the incomes are low, and the dominating feature is provision for the children, the one-third rule is of no assistance.
H and W were married in 1969 and separated in 1976. There were three children, the youngest being four at the time of hearing. The matrimonial home was purchased in H's name for £3,800. H and W both contributed to the deposit, and H paid the instalments. W had £2,000 capital, and H an income of £3,400 a year. On their separation H moved into lodgings at £11 a week, and W remained in the matrimonial home with the children. The registrar ordered H to pay £6 a week in respect of each child, and £11 a week for W; he also ordered that a trust for sale of the house, now worth £7,000, be set up on terms that the wife and children should remain there until the youngest was 18, when the proceeds of sale should be divided as to 60 per cent. to H, and 40 per cent. to W. On appeal by H, *held*, allowing the appeal in part, that (1) the matrimonial home

must first be appropriated for the use of the children and the party responsible for their upbringing, and the order would be affirmed; (2) the one-third rule was of no assistance in such a case; the court should take into account the reality of the situation, which was that H's standard of living could not be compared with that of W and the children. Accordingly, the payment would be reduced by £6 a week.

SCOTT *v.* SCOTT [1978] 1 W.L.R. 723, C.A.

816. —— **periodical payments—application time-barred**
[Matrimonial Causes Act 1973 (c. 18), s. 28 (3).]
A party to a marriage who has made no application for a financial provision order before remarriage is not entitled to make such an application subsequently.

W indicated in her acknowledgment of service that she intended to apply for ancillary relief. She did not file an answer, but made a Form 11 application for periodical payments for her children. W remarried and was ganted leave to amend Form 11 to include an application for financial provision for herself. On H's application for a declaration that W was barred by s. 28 (3) of the Act from so doing, *held*, granting the declaration, that the Form 11 application for the children could not be construed as an application for the wife's benefit, and accordingly she was barred from making such an application by s. 28 (3) of the 1973 Act. (*Doherty* v. *Doherty* [1975] C.L.Y. 978 distinguished; *Wilson* v. *Wilson* [1975] C.L.Y. 980 considered).

NIXON *v.* FOX [1978] 3 W.L.R. 565, Dunn J.

817. —— —— **subsistence level**
H appealed against a registrar's order that he pay W £10 per week increasing to £15 per week after one year and that he pay £10 per week to the child until the age of 17. After other necessary payments H would be left with slightly less than the minimum subsistence for a single man. *Held*, allowing the appeal and reducing the payments to W to £8 per week, the rent and rate rebates which W would receive were " financial resources which [W was] likely to have in the foreseeable future " within s. 25 of the 1973 Act (*Reiterbund* v. *Reiterbund* [1975] C.L.Y. 973 applied). The proper order was one which neither depressed H below subsistence level nor promoted him above it. (*Williams* (*L. A.*) v. *Williams* (*E. M.*) [1974] C.L.Y. 1050 applied): WALKER *v.* WALKER [1978] 8 Fam. Law 107, Purchas J.

818. —— —— **supplementary benefit scale**
A larger figure may be ordered as a periodical payment than that produced by reference to the supplementary benefit scale, so long as it does not bring the payer spouse's income below subsistence level.

H was earning £62·44 per week. The county court judge ordered him to pay £30·50 per week for the maintenance of W and their two children. Although H was left with less than the supplementary benefit scale, the judge held that he could afford the amount ordered, and that W needed it. On appeal by H, *held*, dismissing the appeal, that the supplementary benefit scale was altogether different from the subsistence level. Had the supplementary benefit scale been applied, H would have been left with £15 per week above subsistence level, whilst W would have been left with about £2 per week below. (*Smethurst* v. *Smethurst* [1977] C.L.Y. 1541 and *Ashley* v. *Ashley* [1965] C.L.Y. 1297 considered.)

SHALLOW *v.* SHALLOW [1978] 2 W.L.R. 583, C.A.

819. —— **sale of farm—wife's contributions—only source of income**
Two years after marriage in 1966, H and W acquired a farm (with house), for £36,000. W contributed £6,000 towards the purchase, given by W's parents, although the property was conveyed into the sole name of H. W had also contributed indirectly by helping on the farm. After divorce in 1976, the farm was valued at £120,000. The husband's liabilities amounted to some £29,000, leaving a net sum of £91,000. The Registrar followed the one-third approach (*Wachtel* v. *Wachtel* [1973] C.L.Y. 923) and awarded W a lump sum of £30,000. W was awarded custody of the two children plus £15 per week in respect of each child. On appeal by H, W again called evidence stating that part of the farm could be sold without substantially affecting H's income from

the farm, and that the sale value of the farm had increased to £134,000. *Held*, on appeal, that the lump sum be reduced to £26,000 to avoid the necessity of selling the farm (the only source of H's income). The maintenance for each child was reduced to £8 per week, though H was required to pay to W £10,000 by 10 annual instalments of £1,000 for the education of the children. *P. v. P.* [1977] C.L.Y. 1565 considered and distinguished: F. *v.* F., July 12, 1978, Comyn J., Bristol. (*Ex rel. Messrs. Rickerby's, Solicitors.*)

820. —— short marriage

H, a widower aged 61, met W, a 51-year-old divorcee, in December 1970. They married in July 1971, W giving up a council tenancy in consequence, but by November 1971 the marriage had broken down and justices found H's complaint of W's cruelty proved. In ancillary proceedings H contended that he should make no financial provision because of W's conduct and the short duration of the marriage. *Held*, H's contentions were well-founded but he was comparatively well-off and W lived on social security. He should pay £1,000 in full and final settlement: WARDER *v.* WARDER (1978) 122 S.J. 713, Purchas J.

821. —— variation—finality

[Matrimonial Causes Act 1973 (c. 18), s. 23 (1).] In January 1973, the court made a consent order giving effect to a comprehensive settlement of all financial and property issues agreed between husband and wife which included maintenance of 5p a year to the wife until the completion of a conveyance of the husband's share on the matrimonial home to the wife. The husband complied with the terms of the order and maintenance payments duly ceased. Subsequently, W applied for an order " varying " the periodical payments payable under the January 1973 order. *Held*, on the true construction of s. 23 (1), the court had no jurisdiction to entertain a new application (*L.* v. *L.* [1961] C.L.Y. 2729 applied). As a matter of public policy the courts would encourage " a clean break " between the parties so that the resolution of their financial disputes by final orders, by consent or otherwise, achieved the desirable objective of finality: MINTON *v.* MINTON, *The Times*, November 24, 1978, H.L.

822. —— —— notice

In June 1977 the justices ordered H to pay £220 per month to W and £50 per month to his son. H resigned his position as company secretary because of ill-health and in November 1977 the order was reduced to £10 per week for W and £5 per week for the boy. W appealed contending (i) H had given evidence of his resignation resulting from anger at the June decision; and (ii) the justices had paid too little attention to H's earning capacity and too much to her earning capacity. *Held*, remitting the case for a rehearing, W should have had notice in the variation complaint of the suggestion she should seek work giving her an opportunity to rebut it as she had not worked during the marriage: ADAMS *v.* ADAMS [1978] Fam. Law 141, D.C.

823. —— wealthy father—settlement for children

H, a millionaire, petitioned for divorce in 1967. He made various settlements for W, and in addition agreed to provide £30,000 for the school fees of their two daughters. The divorce was granted in 1969, and both H and W remarried. In 1973 it was ordered that H pay £1,320 per annum for each child until that child attained 18; in 1971 W applied to vary that order, and Payne J. ordered that H should pay the children's school fees and should settle £25,009 on each of them for life. He was also ordered to pay £1,812 for each child until she had reached 18. H appealed against the order regarding school fes and the settlements of £25,000. *Held*, allowing the appeal, there should not be one rule for millionaires and another for less wealthy fathers. H had already set up a trust for the fees and it would be unjust to place a primary liability on him for them. As to the settlements, the court would not be justified in ordering H to provide an income for his children for life: L. *v.* G. (1978) 122 S.J. 433, C.A.

824. Maintenance

RECOVERY ABROAD OF MAINTENANCE (CONVENTION COUNTRIES) ORDER 1978 (No. 279) [10p], made under Maintenance Orders (Reciprocal Enforcement) Act 1972 (c. 18), ss. 25 (1), 45 (1); operative on March 23, 1978; declares that Switzerland is a convention country for the purposes of Pt. II of the 1972 Act.

825. Matrimonial Causes Rules
MATRIMONIAL CAUSES (AMENDMENT) RULES 1978 (No. 527) [15p], made under the Matrimonial Causes Act 1973 (c. 18), s. 50; operative on May 2, 1978, save for rr. 5, 8, 9, which are operative on June 6, 1978; enables the registrar in a defended cause to treat a request for directions for trial as a summons for directions under Ord. 25 of the R.S.C. The Rules also facilitate disposal of causes in the special procedure list where there is an objection to paying any costs for which the petitioner prays, and where there are children of the family.

826. Matrimonial home. See HUSBAND AND WIFE.

827. Nullity—fraud—lack of intention to enter a real marriage
[Can.] D told P he would go through a religious ceremony after the civil marriage and make her his wife according to their religious customs. In fact he had no intentions of doing so and was marrying her in order to be allowed to reside permanently in the country. *Held,* such deceit constitutes fraud which rendered the marriage void: KALYAN (NARSIH) (LAL) *v.* LAL (1976) 28 R.F.L. 229, B.Col.Sup.Ct.

828. —— voidable marriage—effect on will. See *Re* ROBERTS (DECD.), § 3082.

829. Petition—irretrievable breakdown—petitioner's own adultery
[Matrimonial Causes Act 1973 (c. 18), s. 1 (2) (*b*).] W filed a petition under s. 1 (2) (*b*) of the 1973 Act; H did not cross-pray. W had committed adultery in 1972 which H discovered in 1974. W agreed to end the affair but it resumed at the end of 1974 and was still continuing. W's petition complained of H's sulkiness at the infrequency of the parties' intercourse. *Held,* W's petition would be dismissed. The marital breakdown was not necessarily irretrievable, but had been brought about by W's passion for the other man, not by H's behaviour. H was right not to cross-pray if he did not wish to do so: WELFARE *v.* WELFARE [1978] Fam. Law 55, Bush J.

830. —— within three years of marriage—exceptional hardship and depravity
[Matrimonial Causes Act 1973 (c. 18), s. 2 (3).] After her marriage, which followed three years of a heterosexual relationship between the parties, W discovered that H was having homosexual relations with at least one man and seemed incapable of maintaining a heterosexual relationship with her. *Held,* allowing her appeal from the judge's refusal to give leave to file a divorce petition within three years of the marriage, W had shown that she had suffered exceptional hardship as a result of H's conduct, but had not shown that his conduct amounted to exceptional depravity by present standards: C. *v.* C., *The Times,* November 24, 1978, C.A.

831. Polygamous marriage—effect on decree nisi
H married W1 in Nigeria in 1962. There were five children of the marriage born in England between 1965 and 1972. The marriage became polygamous in 1972 when H married W2, again in Nigeria. There were two children of that union and both families lived together in England, W1 raising no objection. Later W1 petitioned for divorce alleging the marriage had become monogamous and thus H had committed adultery with W2 or alternatively H's behaviour was unreasonable. *Held,* dismissing the petition for adultery but granting W1 a decree because of H's behaviour, it was artificial to find adultery proved in this case: ONABRAUCHE *v.* ONABRAUCHE [1978] 8 Fam. Law. 107, Comyn J.

832. Practice—defended cases—pre-trial review. See PRACTICE DIRECTION, § 2368.

833. —— proceedings in two countries—judge's discretion to stay English proceedings—exercise
[Domicile and Matrimonial Proceedings Act 1973 (c. 45), Sched. 1, para 9.] H and W married in England, then lived in Geneva. When the marriage broke down, H induced W and the children to return to England and bought them a house here. W petitioned for divorce in England; H petitioned in Geneva and applied for a stay of the English proceedings, which the judge refused. *Held,* he was exercising his discretion in so doing. He had not exercised it improperly as, on the balance of fairness, it was just that W be

given English ancillary relief, especially as the Swiss court could not make an effective order about the house: MYTTON v. MYTTON [1977] Fam. Law 244, C.A.

834. Recognition—Khula divorce

[Recognition of Divorces and Legal Separations Act 1971 (c. 53), ss. 2, 6.] H petitioned the English court for a declaration that his marriage to W was dissolved by a Khula divorce in Bangkok in 1968 or, alternatively, by a Talaq divorce pronounced in Karachi in 1974. W sought a decree of nullity, alternatively a declaration that neither the Khula nor the Talaq was entitled to recognition, alternatively the return of her dowry if either had dissolved the marriage. *Held*, s. 2 of the 1971 Act covered recognition of divorces by " judicial or other proceedings " and the Talaq fell within the latter category. The Khula did not, but would be declared to have dissolved the marriage at common law pursuant to s. 6 of the Act. W had had her dowry back: QUAZI v. QUAZI (1978) 8 Fam. Law 203, Wood J.

835. Separation—sexual intercourse during separation—whether cohabitation

[Can.] Parties ceased residing together in November 1971; in 1976 the wife presented a petition based on three years' separation. She admitted at trial that four or five acts of sexual intercourse had taken place during the period of separation, but without any intention to be reconciled or resume cohabitation. *Held*, the act of sexual intercourse between a husband and a wife is cohabitation even if they do not share the same house; they cannot be said to be living separate and apart. (*Wheatley* v. *Wheatley* (1949) C.L.C. 3106 applied): BOECHLER v. BOECHLER (1976) 30 R.F.L. 118, Sask.Q.B.

836. Undefended cases—no application for hearing—striking out of lists

The following Practice Direction was issued by the Principal Registry of the Family Division on March 22, 1978:

In order to clear the lists of undefended cases which have been set down for trial for some time but in respect of which no application for a hearing date has been made or, as regards special procedure cases, the date fixed by the court for pronouncement of the decree has been vacated, the following listed causes have now been struck out of the respective lists.

County Court Hearing List
Causes numbered 1 to 5,000 with the prefix " L."

Special Procedure List
Causes listed prior to the introduction of the prefix " A."

Causes struck out of the lists under this direction may be restored to the current lists on application being made to Divorce Registry.

837. Unreasonable behaviour—husband's low sexual drive

[Matrimonial Causes Act 1973 (c. 18), s. 1 (2) (*b*).] W's petition under s. 1 (2) (*b*) of the 1973 Act was undefended. In it she alleged that H's behaviour was unreasonable because intercourse was infrequent and unsatisfactory when it did take place. The judge dismissed the petition as W had failed to establish the fact on which she relied. *Held*, dismissing W's appeal, H's low sexual drive undoubtedly made W unhappy but did not in itself amount to unreasonable behaviour. (*Stringfellow* v. *Stringfellow* [1976] C.L.Y. 809 applied): DOWDEN v. DOWDEN [1977] 8 Fam. Law 106, C.A.

838. Welfare officer's report—extent and admissibility of matters covered—practice.

See *Re* HOGUE AND HAINES (FORMERLY HOGUE), § 1989.

BOOKS AND ARTICLES. See *post,* pp. [4], [21].

EASEMENTS AND PRESCRIPTION

839. Easements—Lands Tribunal decisions

KEITH v. TEXACO (Ref. No. LTS/APP/1/151) (1977) 34 P. & C.R. 249 (the applicant developer was given a right of access over the objectors' land. Application was to discharge a land obligation restricting use and requiring erection of a dwelling. The dominant owners sought compensation in the event of discharge. *Held,* (1) the intention had been to provide access to the applicant's house and grounds and could not be used for access to a housing estate; (2) the changed character of the area rendered the restrictions unreasonable and inappropriate; (3) the objectors had shown no financial detriment; (4) the increase in value to the servient land must not be assessed on development value because the tax for which the developer would be liable and the price of a new access must be taken into account).

WILSONS BREWERY v. WEST YORKSHIRE METROPOLITAN COUNTY COUNCIL (Ref. No. 35/1977) (1977) 34 P. & C.R. 224 (reference was to determine a claim for compensation for injurious affection caused by loss of right of support for a wall. The preliminary issue arose as to whether such right existed. In 1922, the conveyance showed that gable wall of the claimants and that of the adjoining premises as a common wall. The adjacent premises were rebuilt in 1938 with a nine-inch cavity wall. In 1973, the authority acquired and demolished the adjacent premises. *Held*, there was no unequivocal evidence of intention by the dominant owners to abandon the easement existing in 1938. The right of support still subsisted in 1976).

840. Limitation of actions. See LIMITATION OF ACTIONS.

841. Right of way—grant—whether a " tenancy." See LAND RECLAMATION v. BASILDON DISTRICT COUNCIL, § 1774.

842. —— wording of conveyances

[Can.] [Land Registry Act R.S.B.C. 1960; Municipal Act R.S.B.C. 1960, s. 407 (2).]

Following a tax sale, R became the registered owner of four parcels of land, on which it proposed to construct a building. The land lay between the shoreward boundary of A's land and the waters of the bay, and the building would interfere with her view and with her access to the foreshore. A's title was rooted in the deposit in the registry office of the original plan of development, and the subsequent conveyance of one of the lots to her predecessor. The deed recited that the foreshore reserves were to be held by the grantor for the purpose of giving free access to the shore to purchasers of the lots. The title to the foreshore reserves originated in the deposit in the registry office in 1912 of the original plan; in 1917 the development company conveyed all the unsold lots and reserves to a trustee; the deed stated that all conveyances made by the trustee were to be subject to the restrictive covenants and conditions used in the sale of properties already sold; there was no provision for either the dedication or maintenance of the reserves. *Held*, (1) an easement had been granted in favour of A to cross over and use the reserves by the words of the original conveyance of A's lot, and in the words of conveyance to the trustee. (*Re Ellenborough Park*; *Re Davies*; *Powell* v. *Maddison* [1955] C.L.Y. 882 applied): DUKART v. SURREY [1978] 4 W.W.R. 1, Can.Sup.Ct.

BOOKS AND ARTICLES. See *post*, pp. [4], [21].

ECCLESIASTICAL LAW

843. Benefices

VACATION OF BENEFICES (LEGAL AID) RULES 1978 (No. 951) [20p], made under the Incumbents (Vacation of Benefices) Measure 1977 (No. 1), s. 15 (3); operative on September 1, 1978; provides that an incumbent of a benefice and certain other persons are entitled to have costs incurred by them at inquiry under Pt. I of the 1977 Measure refunded to them.

844. Church—partial demolition—whether crypt " part of church left standing "—planning consent for listed building

A crypt, even though existing in a hole in the ground, is a " part of a church left standing."

The vicar and churchwardens of a church sought a faculty authorising the demolition of a parish church to three feet above ground for the purpose of reconstruction. On the petition, it was *held* that there was power to grant such a faculty (and that such a faculty would be granted) because there was to be a " part of the church left standing " as required by s. 2 (3) of the

Faculty Jurisdiction Measure 1964, that part being the crypt, although it existed only underground. As the demolition was only to be partial demolition, listed building consent would not be required.

Re ST. LUKE'S, CHEETHAM [1977] 3 W.L.R. 969, Const.Ct.

845. Church of England (Miscellaneous Provisions) Measure 1978 (No. 3)

This Measure makes further provision respecting the special majorities required for the approval of certain Measures; it also makes other miscellaneous provisions.

S. 1 amends art. 8 of the Constitution of the General Synod relating to special majorities required for certain measures; s. 2 provides for certain persons in office at the commencement of the Ecclesiastical Offices (Age Limit) Measure 1975; s. 3 alters the financial year of the Church Commissioners; s. 4 amends Sched. 1 to the Church Commissioners Measure 1947 relating to the constitution of the Church Commissioners; s. 5 provides for the diocesan member of the Central Land Board of Finance to be entitled to vote at meetings; s. 6 restricts the power to charge fees for searches of certain registers; s. 7 extends the power to dispose of land no longer required; s. 8 states that in certain circumstances where the fee simple is in abeyance, a church is to be vested in the Church Commissioners; s. 9 empowers a bishop to extend the Inspection of Churches Measure 1955; s. 10 relates to the vacation of office by non-residentiary canons in Christ Church Cathedral; s. 11 makes a correction to the Endowments and Glebe Measure 1976; s. 12 abolishes the requirement to enrol certain deeds in the High Court; s. 13 contains the short title.

The Measure received the Royal Assent on June 30, 1978, and came into force on July 30, 1978.

846. Clergy pensions

CLERGY PENSIONS (CHANNEL ISLANDS) ORDER 1978 (No. 784) [10p], made under the Channel Islands (Church Legislation) Measure 1931 (No. 4), s. 2, Sched. 1, as amended by the Channel Islands (Church Legislation) Measure 1931 (Amendment) Measure 1957 (No. 1), ss. 1, 2, and the Clergy Pensions Measure 1961 (No. 3), s. 49, the Clergy Pensions (Amendment) Measure 1969 (No. 1), and the Clergy Pensions (Amendment) Measure 1972 (No. 5), s. 7 (2); operative on July 1, 1978; applies the 1969 and 1972 Measures to the Channel Islands.

847. Dioceses Measure 1978 (No. 1)

This Measure makes provision for enabling alterations to be made in the diocesan structure of the provinces of Canterbury and York and for the discharge of functions of certain diocesan bodies and for enabling certain functions of diocesan bishops to be discharged by suffragan bishops: it abolishes the power to commission suffragan bishops, and makes further provisions for their nomination, and provides for constituting separate synods for areas of a diocese.

S. 1 deals with the appointment of a Dioceses Commission by the Standing Committee of the General Synod; s. 2 lays down the advisory functions of the Commission in respect of diocesan structure of Canterbury and York and the episcopal administration of any diocese; s. 3 allocates to the Commission the preparation, etc., of " reorganisation schemes "; s. 4 deals with procedures for proposing schemes to the commission; s. 5 relates to the Commission's preparation of draft schemes; s. 6 provides for the approval by the General Synod of such schemes; s. 7 deals with the confirmation of such schemes by Order of Her Majesty in Council; s. 8 makes supplementary provisions in respect of reorganisation schemes; s. 9 confers power on the General Synod to make temporary provision in respect of membership of certain Convocations; s. 10 provides for the temporary delegation, by a diocesan bishop, of certain functions to a suffragan bishop; s. 11 instigates permanent schemes for the discharge of episcopal functions within each area of a diocese; s. 12 lays down procedures for submission of such schemes to the Commission; s. 13 relates to variations of such schemes; s. 14 makes special provision as regards rights of collation; s. 15 abolishes the power to commission a suffragan bishop; s. 16 makes provision with respect to Acts and Measures conferring functions on diocesan bishops; s. 17 deals with the creation of area synods for episcopal areas; s. 18 relates to the creation or revival of suffragan sees; s. 19 instigates schemes for the discharge of functions of diocesan bodies corporate; s. 20 makes further provision with respect to these schemes; s. 21 empowers the Commission to pay stipends to certain bishops; s. 22 relates to cathedral churches of new dioceses created by the aforesaid schemes; s. 23 permits amendment of reorganisation schemes by other schemes; s. 24 contains definitions; s. 25 contains the short title, and deals with commencement and extent.

The Measure received the Royal Assent on February 2, 1978, and came into force on May 2, 1978.

848. Faculty—memorial tablet—principles of entitlement

The grant of a faculty to erect a memorial tablet is a special privilege reserved for exceptional cases.

On an application for an entitlement to erect a memorial tablet in the church of St. Nicholas, Brockenhurst, representations were made by the Bowden-Smith family for a tablet to the two last male members of that family. *Held,* that the faculty would be granted. Although the two members concerned had had only a tenuous connection with the church and the grant of such a faculty was an exceptional privilege, there was no risk of setting a precedent for future applications, the look of the church would not be affected and the tablets commemorating previous members of the Bowden-Smith family in the church provided an interesting family historical monument.

Re St. Nicholas, Brockenhurst [1977] 3 All E.R. 1027, Const.Ct.

849. —— work undertaken before grant—reconstruction of organ—effect of retrospective faculty

Work undertaken after a petition has been filed requesting a grant of faculty to carry out such work, but before the faculty has been granted, is a breach of the law.

Per curiam: A confirmatory faculty of the kind the petition had been amended to include in its requests, protects a party for the future, but does not have retrospective effect to legalise actions committed before a faculty is obtained, for which the perpetrators remain personally liable.

In June 1976, the churchwardens and other members of the congregation of a parish church filed a petition for the reconstruction of the church organ, an instrument made by Hill about 100 years previously. The organist considered it to be inadequate to the church's needs; but the diocesan advisory committee on receiving the petition, felt unable to recommend the reconstruction scheme to the chancellor. Shortly after the petition was filed, but before a faculty was obtained, the organ builder employed by the petitioners dismantled the Hill organ, and introduced other components into the church for the organ's reconstruction. The petitioners became aware from the intervention of the archdeacon and correspondence with the diocesan advisory committee that the work was illegal, but continued with it. The registrar of the consistory also warned them that the work should cease pending a grant of faculty. At the hearing, where the petition was opposed by the archdeacon who also cross-petitioned for the organ to be restored to its status quo, *held,* dismissing the petition, that (1) the petitioners had acted in flagrant breach of the law by causing the existing organ to be dismantled before a faculty had been granted for this purpose; (2) the organ should be restored as far as possible and advisable, with such improvements as might be indicated by expert advice.

Re St. Mary's, Balham [1978] 1 All E.R. 993, Southwark Consistory Ct.

850. Marriage. See Divorce and Matrimonial Causes; Husband and Wife.

851. Parochial Registers and Records Measure 1978 (No. 2)

This Measure consolidates with amendments certain enactments relating to the registration of baptisms and burials and repeals some of those enactments; it also makes fresh provision with respect to diocesan record offices.

S. 1 states that every parish shall have a register book of public and private baptisms, and sets out the format of such book; s. 2 provides for the registration of baptisms in the register book; s. 3 provides for the registration of burials in the register book; s. 4 gives the procedure to be followed when errors are discovered in the register book of baptisms or burials; s. 5 applies ss. 1–4 to cathedrals and collegiate churches, and other non-parochial churches; s. 6 states that the incumbent of the benefice shall have custody of the register books of baptisms, confirmations, banns of marriage, marriage, burials or services provided for any church in his parish; s. 7 deals with the provision of diocescan record offices; s. 8 states that a diocesan record office may be used as a place of deposit for manorial documents; s. 9 provides for the periodic inspection of register books and records in parochial custody; s. 10 sets out the circumstances in which register books should be deposited in the diocesan record office; s. 11 deals with the safe-keeping, care and preservation of register books and records in parochial custody; s. 12 empowers the bishop to make an order for the deposit of register books in the diocesan record office; s. 13 relates to the return to parochial custody of register books deposited in the diocesan record office; s. 14 states that the chief officer of a diocesan record office shall have custody of any register books or records deposited in that office; s. 15 provides for the transfer of certain books and records from one record office to another; s. 16 states that register books and records may be deposited in a diocesan record office or other suitable safe place for the purpose of exhibition or research; s. 17 provides for certain records and register books in diocesan record offices to be made available for exhibition or research; s. 18 sets out provisions ancillary to ss. 16 and 17; s. 19 provides for the disposal of register books and records on the dissolution of a parish; s. 20 relates to searches of certain register books; s. 21 empowers the bishop of a diocese to apply to the county court for an order that an unauthorised person do return register books in his possession; s. 22 makes special provision as to marriage registers; s. 23 applies s. 3 of the Church of England (Miscellaneous Provisions) Measure 1976 to the functions of a diocesan bishop in relation to matters arising under this Measure; s. 24 relates to the service of notices and orders; s. 25 contains definitions; s. 26 contains amendments, repeals and transitional provisions; s. 27 gives the short title and extent.

The Measure received the Royal Assent on February 2, 1978, and shall come into force on such day as the Archbishops of Canterbury and York may jointly appoint.

852. Rating—rateable valuation. See RATING AND VALUATION.

853. Registration of births, deaths and marriages. See REGISTRATION OF BIRTHS, DEATHS AND MARRIAGES.

EDUCATION

854. Admissions policy—where there is a duty to act fairly

An educational institution is under no duty to act judicially in considering applications for admissions to courses, in that it need not grant a hearing or give reasons for refusal of admission. But if an interview is granted, the institution may have an obligation to act fairly. In the present case, there was such an obligation because (1) the educational institution (the North East London Polytechnic was publicly funded; (2) the applicant's professional career would be seriously jeopardised by a refusal; and (3) details of the polytechnic's selection procedures had been published, and a copy sent to the applicant: CENTRAL COUNCIL FOR EDUCATION AND TRAINING IN SOCIAL WORK v. EDWARDS, *The Times*, May 5, 1978, Slade J.

855. Approved schools

CESSATION OF APPROVED INSTITUTIONS (ST. EDWARD'S SCHOOL) ORDER 1978 (No. 629) [20p], made under the Children and Young Persons Acts 1969 (c. 54), s. 46, operative on June 1, 1978; makes provision for the cessation as an approved institution of St. Edward's School.

856. Awards

STATE AWARDS REGULATIONS 1978 (No. 1096) [25p], made under the Education Act 1962 (c. 12), ss. 3 (*b*), (*c*) and (*d*) and 4 (2), as amended by the

Education Act 1975 (c. 2), s. 2; operative on September 1, 1978; consolidate, with amendments, the scheduled regulations relating to state studentships, bursaries and scholarships for mature students.

LOCAL EDUCATION AUTHORITY AWARDS REGULATIONS 1978 (No. 1097) [70p], made under the Education Act 1962, ss. 1, 4 (2), Sched. 1, paras. 3, 4, as amended by the Education Act 1975, s. 1, and the Education Act 1976 (c. 81), s. 8; operative on September 1, 1978; consolidate with amendments S.I. 1977 No. 1307, the principal amendments relate to residence in local education authority areas; they also increase awards and relax means tests.

STUDENTS' DEPENDANTS ALLOWANCES REGULATIONS 1978 (No. 1098) [25p], made under the Education Act 1973 (c. 16), s. 3; operative on September 1, 1978; consolidate with amendments S.I. 1977 No. 1308 the principal changes are that the Regs. are drafted with reference to S.I. 1978 No. 1097 and that the means test for an allowance is relaxed so far as it concerns the students' scholarship and similar income and the earned income of his spouse.

857. Dismissal of staff—power delegated to board of governors—whether exercisable by local authority

If governors are unable to exercise a delegated power of dismissal, the local education authority has a residual power to do so.

A college of further education's articles of government empowered the governors to dismiss full-time members of the teaching staff subject to confirmation by the authority. Charges were made against P, the plaintiff, a head of department, and X, the principal. A committee of governors heard the charges against X. It was thereafter felt that the charges against P should be heard by a different committee, and it was impossible to form one from the eligible governors. The local authority was therefore asked to establish a committee instead. P brought an action against the local authority and the governors for a declaration that the authority were acting ultra vires by exercising the governors' rights, and the governors were acting ultra vires in purporting to delegate them. A deputy High Court judge granted the declaration and injunctions. On appeal, *held*, allowing the appeal, (1) there was no "delegation" of the governors' powers to dismiss P, since the governing body would still be free to accept or reject the committee's recommendations; (2) in any case, the authority had residual power to take action to dismiss the plaintiff.

WINDER *v.* CAMBRIDGESHIRE COUNTY COUNCIL (1978) 76 L.G.R. 549, C.A.

858. Handicapped pupils

HANDICAPPED PUPILS AND SPECIAL SCHOOLS (AMENDMENT) REGULATIONS 1978 (No. 1146) [10p], made the Education Act 1944 (c. 31), s. 33; operative on September 1, 1978; amend S.I. 1959 No. 365 so as to take account of amendments to the Schools Regulations 1959 by S.I. 1978 No. 1144.

859. Independent schools

INDEPENDENT SCHOOLS (EXEMPTION FROM REGISTRATION) ORDER 1978 (No. 467) [10p], made under the Education Act 1944 (c. 31), ss. 70 (2), 111; operative on May 1, 1978; revokes S.I. 1957 No. 1173 but provides that a school exempt under that order shall continue to be so unless otherwise notified.

860. Industrial training. See TRADE AND INDUSTRY.

861. Local education authorities—duty—policy of exclusively comprehensive system
[Education Act 1944, ss. 1 (1), 8 (1).]

The word " character " in s. 8 (1) of the Act means the intangible attributes of a school rather than its size and method of selection; and local education authorities are entitled under ss. 1 (1) and 8 (1) of the Act to implement the comprehensive policy and apply it to a particular school, provided they listen to all objections and consider whether or not the policy should be applied.

The policy of the local education authority was to provide secondary education exclusively in comprehensive schools and to eliminate schools which selected pupils according to ability. The authority proposed to implement that policy by phasing out an old-established boys' grammar school. Before submitting their proposals to the Secretary of State, they considered objections

and alternative proposals put forward by parents, and a report by the education officer which recommended that the authority cease to maintain the grammar school. The Secretary of State approved the proposals. The parents' association claimed a declaration that the proposals were unlawful under the 1944 Act and an injunction restraining the authority from implementing them. On a motion for an interlocutory injunction the parents contended that the duty of the authority under ss. 1 (1) and 8 of the Act to provide secondary schools for an area which were " sufficient . . . in character " required them to ensure that there were schools where pupils were selected according to ability or schools which were smaller as regards numbers than comprehensive schools. The judge granted interlocutory injunctions restraining the authority from implementing the proposals and ordering them to cancel or reverse any implementation of them already carried out. The authority appealed. *Held,* allowing the appeal and discharging the injunctions, that (1) the courts were entitled to interfere where the authority had exceeded or misused its powers, had misdirected itself in fact or in law, or had exercised its discretion wrongly or for no good reason, but since the authority had considered the report of their education officer and the objections of the parents, they had acted properly and the court was not entitled to interfere with the implementation of the proposals; (2) a local authority should not be restrained from exercising its statutory powers by interlocutory injunction unless the plaintiff shows that there is a real prospect of his succeeding at the trial, and in these circumstances there was no real prospect of the parents succeeding in their claims at the trial. (*Wood* v. *Ealing London Borough* [1966] C.L.Y. 4256, *British Oxygen Co.* v. *Ministry of Technology* [1970] C.L.Y. 2809, *Cummings* v. *Birkenhead Corporation* [1971] C.L.Y. 3831, *American Cyanamid Co.* v. *Ethicon* [1975] C.L.Y. 2640, and dicta of Lord Diplock in *Secretary of State for Education and Science* v. *Tameside Metropolitan Borough* [1976] C.L.Y. 829 applied.)
SMITH *v.* INNER LONDON EDUCATION AUTHORITY [1978] 1 All E.R. 411, C.A.

862. Meals

PROVISION OF MILK AND MEALS (AMENDMENT) REGULATIONS 1978 (No. 959) [20p], made under the Education Act 1944 (c. 31), s. 49, as read with the Education (Milk) Act 1971 (c. 74), s. 1, and as amended by the Education Act 1976 (c. 81), s. 9; operative on August 1, 1978; amend S.I. 1969 No. 483 with regard to the provision of free school milk.

PROVISION OF MILK AND MEALS (AMENDMENT) (No. 2) REGULATIONS 1978 (No. 1301) [10p], made under the Education Act 1944, s. 49 read with the Education (Milk) Act 1971, s. 1 as amended by the Education Act 1976, s. 9; operatice on November 13, 1978; amend S.I. 1969 No. 483 and raise the level of net weekly income below which a parent qualifies for remission of charges for school meals and increase the amount which may be deducted from net income in respect of any special diet prescribed by a registered medical practitioner.

863. Minister's powers—submission of proposals—form of comprehensive schooling to be adopted

[Education Act 1976 (c. 5), s. 2 (4).] The Secretary of State for Education and Science had power under the 1976 Act to compel a local authority to submit fresh proposals for a single comprehensive school in place of the original plan, favoured by the local authority, for the retention of two smaller separate schools to be run on a comprehensive basis. The powers under the 1976 Act reversed the position in *Secretary of State for Education and Science* v. *Tameside Metropolitan Borough Council* [1976] C.L.Y. 829, in so far as there is a difference in policy between central and local government: NORTH YORKSHIRE COUNTY COUNCIL *v.* SECRETARY OF STATE FOR EDUCATION AND SCIENCE, *The Times,* October 20, 1978, Browne-Wilkinson J.

864. Northern Ireland. See NORTHERN IRELAND.

865. Racial discrimination—local authority dispersing schoolchildren of ethnic minority—particulars to be given. See COMMISSION FOR RACIAL EQUALITY *v.* EALING LONDON BOROUGH COUNCIL, § 2408.

866. Remuneration of teachers

REMUNERATION OF TEACHERS (PRIMARY AND SECONDARY SCHOOLS) (AMENDMENT) ORDER 1978 (No. 982) [10p], made under the Remuneration of Teachers Act 1965 (c. 3), ss. 2 (6), 7 (3); operative on July 17, 1978; gives effect to the agreed remuneration of teachers and restores to their position on the incremental scale teachers who suffered loss or diminution of an increment by reason of their salary exceeding £8,500 per annum.

REMUNERATION OF TEACHERS (PRIMARY AND SECONDARY SCHOOLS) (No. 2) ORDER 1978 (No. 1019) [10p], made under the Remuneration of Teachers Act 1965, ss. 1, 2 (2)–(4), 7 (2) (3); operative on July 28, 1978; brings into operation the scales and other provisions relating to remuneration of teachers previously recommended.

REMUNERATION OF TEACHERS (FURTHER EDUCATION) (AMENDMENT) ORDER 1978 (No. 1226) [20p], made under the Remuneration of Teachers Act 1965, s. 1; operative on August 25, 1978; gives effect to recommendations for the remuneration of teachers in establishments of further education.

REMUNERATION OF TEACHERS (FURTHER EDUCATION) ORDER 1978 (No. 1409) [20p], made under the Remuneration of Teachers Act 1965, s. 1; operative on September 28, 1978; brings into operation the scales and other provisions relating to the remuneration of full-time teachers in all establishments of further education maintained by local education authorities and of other such further education teachers on the staff of such authorities.

REMUNERATION OF TEACHERS (FURTHER EDUCATION) (AMENDMENT No. 2) ORDER 1978 (No. 1773) [20p], made under Remmuneration of Teachers Act 1965, ss. 1, 2, 7 (3); operative on December 14, 1978; gives effect to recommendations for the remuneration of teachers in establishments of further education and other further education teachers on the staff of local education authorities.

867. School—attendance—failure to secure attendance—reasonable excuse—onus of proof

[Scot.] [Education (Scotland) Act 1962 (c. 47), s. 35.] A's son failed to attend school regularly. At A's trial for failure to secure his attendance, a certificate of non-attendance was produced. A gave no evidence to establish any, or any reasonable, excuse. The sheriff found A not guilty. *Held*, the onus of proving reasonable excuse was on A. He had done nothing to discharge this onus. A conviction would therefore be directed. (*Kennedy* v. *Clark* [1970] C.L.Y. 3133 followed): LANARKSHIRE COUNTY CLERK v. VINCENT 1976 J.C. 5, High Ct. of Justiciary.

868. —— —— —— whether absence " with leave "

[Education Act 1944 (c. 31), s. 39 (1) (2).]

A child is not absent from school " with leave " if he is suspended because of his parents' refusal to return him to the school.

A pupil ran away from school to escape caning. His father, who held views against corporal punishment, refused to return the pupil, who was suspended and absent from school for the rest of the term. The father was convicted of an offence under s. 39 of the Education Act 1944 by reason of the pupil's failure to attend the school. *Held*, dismissing his appeal, that the pupil was not absent " with leave " within the meaning of that section. Suspension did not constitute such leave.

HAPPE v. LAY (1977) 76 L.G.R. 313, D.C.

869. —— choice—suitability of education

[Education Act 1944 (c. 31), ss. 8, 36, 76.] While parents are under a duty to cause their child to be educated suitably for his age and ability, and the local education authority are similarly obliged to provide such education, that authority is not obliged to keep the child at a school preferred by the parents if the school does not provide education suitable for that child. The general principle, laid down in s. 76, that children are, so far as it is possible, to be educated according to their parents wishes, does not apply when the parents choice of school is unsuitable for the child: WINWARD v. CHESHIRE COUNTY COUNCIL, *The Times*, July 21, 1978, Judge Mervyn Davies, Q.C.

870. Teachers

SCHOOLS (AMENDMENT) REGULATIONS 1978 (No. 1144) [10p], made under the Local Government Act 1974 (c. 7), s. 5 (2); operative on September 1, 1978; amend S.I. 1959 No. 364 to relax the requirement that a person on first appointment as a teacher shall satisfy the Secretary of State of his health and physical capacity for teaching to allowing the question to be determined by the local education authority.

DIRECT GRANT SCHOOLS (AMENDMENT) REGULATIONS 1978 (No. 1145) [10p], made under the Education Act 1944 (c. 31), s. 100; operative on September 1, 1978; amend S.I. 1959 No. 1832 and make provision for the Secretary of State to be satisfied of a teacher's health on first appointment.

871. —— extent of duties—unfair dismissal. See REDBRIDGE LONDON BOROUGH COUNCIL *v.* FISHMAN, § 1125.

872. Universities. See UNIVERSITIES.

ARTICLES. See *post,* p. [21].

ELECTION LAW

873. Electoral registration

REPRESENTATION OF THE PEOPLE (AMENDMENT) REGULATIONS 1978 (No. 197) [10p], made under the Representation of the People Act 1949 (c. 68), ss. 42, 171 (5); operative on February 15, 1978; increase the fee payable for copies of the register of electors prepared in accordance with S.I. 1974 No. 648.

874. European Assembly Elections Act 1978 (c. 10). See § 1275.

875. Northern Ireland. See NORTHERN IRELAND.

876. Offences—relief from liability to prosecution—whether offences arose from inadvertence

[Representation of the People Act 1949 (c. 68), ss. 95, 145.] B, a local government election candidate who admitted having caused election leaflets to be printed without accurate names and addresses of the printer and publisher contrary to s. 95 of the 1949 Act, applied to the High Court for relief from liability to prosecution under s. 145 on the ground that the offence arose from inadvertence and not want of good faith. *Held*, refusing the application, that as B had twice before been warned about alleged election offences and his affidavit was less than frank, the court was not satisfied that the offence arose inadvertently and in good faith: *Re* BERRY [1978] Crim.L.R. 357, D.C.

877. Representation of the people

EUROPEAN ASSEMBLY CONSTITUENCIES (ENGLAND) ORDER 1978 (No. 1903) [40p], made under the European Assembly Elections Act 1978 (c. 10), Sched 2, para. 1; operative on January 3, 1979. provides for the division of England into constituencies for the European Assembly elections.

EUROPEAN ASSEMBLY CONSTITUENCIES (WALES) ORDER 1978 (No. 1904) [10p], made under the European Assembly Elections Act 1978, Sched. 2, para. 1; operative on January 3, 1979; provides for the division of Wales into constituencies for the European Assembly elections.

EUROPEAN ASSEMBLY CONSTITUENCIES (SCOTLAND) ORDER 1978 (No. 1911) [20p], made under the European Assembly Elections Act 1978, Scheds. 1, para. 1 (2), 2, Pt. II, para. 4 and the House of Commons (Redistribution of Seats) Act 1949 (c. 66), s. 3; operative on January 3, 1979; sets out the Scottish constituencies for the European Assembly.

877a. Representation of the People Act 1978 (c. 32)

This Act increases the limits on candidates' election expenses at parliamentary elections.

S. 1 amends s. 64 (2) (*a*) of the Representation of the People Act 1949 so as to increase the limits on election candidates' expenses; s. 2 empowers the Secretary of State to vary the maximum amounts specified in ss. 64 (2) (*a*) (*b*) and 167 (4) (5) of the 1949 Act; s. 3 contains supplementary provisions; s. 4 gives the short title.

The Act received the Royal Assent on July 20, 1978, and came into force on that date.

878. Validity—discrepancy in statutory notices—no likelihood that result affected

[Representation of the People Act 1949 (c. 68); Local Elections (Principal Areas) Rules 1973 (S.I. 1973 No. 79), r. 35 (5) (6).]

A local election will not be declared void notwithstanding the existence of a discrepancy in the publication of the requisite statutory notices where it is conducted substantially in accordance with the law and where there is no real likelihood that the discrepancy affected the result.

At a local government election notices were displayed in accordance with the Local Elections (Principal Areas) Rules 1973. The notices were inconsistent. One said that only one candidate could be voted for, the other said that two could be. *Held,* dismissing a petition which sought a declaration that the election was void, that the election had been conducted substantially in accordance with the law, and that there was no real likelihood that the result of the election had been affected.

JAMES *v.* DAVIES (1977) 76 L.G.R. 189, D.C.

ARTICLES. See *post*, p. [21].

ELECTRICITY

879. Control

FUEL AND ELECTRICITY (CONTROL) ACT 1973 (CONTINUATION) (JERSEY AND ISLE OF MAN) ORDER 1978 (No. 1626) [10p], made under the Fuel and Electricity (Control) Act 1973 (c. 67), s. 10 (3); operative on November 15, 1978; continues in force for one year the 1973 Act.

880. Northern Ireland. See NORTHERN IRELAND.

EMERGENCY LAWS

881. Northern Ireland. See NORTHERN IRELAND.

882. Prevention of terrorism

SUPPRESSION OF TERRORISM ACT 1978 (DESIGNATION OF COUNTRIES) ORDER 1978 (No. 1245) [10p], made under the Suppression of Terrorism Act 1978 (c. 26), s. 8; operative on October 25, 1978; designates certain countries for the purposes of the 1978 Act so that they become convention countries.

SUPPRESSION OF TERRORISM ACT 1978 (GUERNSEY) ORDER 1978 (No. 1529) [10p], made under the Suppression of Terrorism Act 1978, s. 7 (2); operative on October 25, 1978; specifies the exceptions, adaptations and modifications in the 1978 Act as it has effect in the Bailiwick of Guernsey.

SUPPRESSION OF TERRORISM ACT 1978 (ISLE OF MAN) ORDER 1978 (No. 1530) [20p], made under the Suppression of Terrorism Act 1978, s. 7 (2); operative on October 25, 1978; specifies the exceptions, adaptations and modifications of the 1978 Act as it has effect in the Isle of Man.

SUPPRESSION OF TERRORISM ACT 1978 (JERSEY) ORDER 1978 (No. 1531) [10p], made under the Suppression of Terrorism Act 1978, s. 7 (2); operative on October 25, 1978; specifies the exceptions, adaptations and modifications in the 1978 Act as it has effect in Jersey.

883. The Home Office has published a " Review of the Operation of the Prevention of Terrorism (Temporary Provisions) Act 1974 and 1976," undertaken by the Rt. Hon. Lord Shackleton, K.G., O.B.E. The review was set up within the following terms of reference: " Accepting the continuing need for legislation against terrorism, to assess the operation of (this legislation) with particular regard to (its) effectiveness and to its effect on the liberties of the subject." The review is available from H.M.S.O. (Cmnd. 7324) [£1·75].

884. Prevention of Terrorism (Temporary Provisions) Act 1976—continuance

PREVENTION OF TERRORISM (TEMPORARY PROVISIONS) ACT 1976 (CONTINUANCE) ORDER 1978 (No. 487) [10p], made under the Prevention of Terrorism (Temporary Provisions) Act 1976 (c. 8), s. 17 (2) (*a*); operative on March 25, 1978; continues in force the provisions of the 1976 Act for a further twelve months.

885. Suppression of Terrorism Act 1978 (c. 26)

This Act gives effect to the European Convention on the Suppression of Terrorism; it also amends the law relating to extradition and the obtaining of evidence for criminal proceedings outside the U.K.; it confers jurisdiction in respect of certain offences committed outside the U.K.

S. 1 sets out cases in which certain offences are not to be regarded as of a political character; s. 2 imposes restrictions on the return of a fugitive criminal under the Extradition Act 1870; s. 3 adds certain offences to the list of extraditable offences; s. 4 confers jurisdiction in respect of offences committed outside the U.K.; s. 5 empowers the Secretary of State to apply the provisions of this Act to non-convention countries; s. 6 amends the Criminal Jurisdiction Act 1975, Sched. 3, para. 2 (2); s. 7 extends the Act to the Channel Islands, the Isle of Man and other countries; s. 8 contains definitions; s. 9 gives the short title and repeals.

The Act received the Royal Assent on June 30, 1978, and came into force on August 21, 1978.

886. —— commencement

SUPPRESSION OF TERRORISM ACT 1978 (COMMENCEMENT) ORDER 1978 (No. 1063 (C. 28)) [10p], made under the Suppression of Terrorism Act 1978 (c. 26), s. 9 (3); operative on August 21, 1978; brings into force the whole of the 1978 Act.

ARTICLES. See *post,* p. [21].

EMPLOYMENT

887. Advisory, Conciliation and Arbitration Service—officers—importance of impartiality

[Trade Union and Labour Relations Act 1974 (c. 52), Sched. 1, paras. 26, 32.] The importance of maintaining the strict impartiality of conciliation officers of the Advisory, Conciliation and Arbitration Service in their role in the settlement of disputes between employer and employee, was stressed. An officer must never get involved in the merits of an agreement or be put in a position where he seemed to favour one side of industry against another: DUPORT FURNITURE PRODUCTS *v.* MOORE, *The Times,* October 18, 1978, E.A.T.

888. Appeal—review pending appeal

An application for review of a tribunal decision may continue notwithstanding the fact that an appeal from that decision is pending.

B appealed from the finding of an industrial tribunal and from its refusal to review its decision. *Held,* that an application for review can be heard notwithstanding the existence of a pending appeal. The proper course for the tribunal is to consult the Registrar of the Appeal Tribunal as to the most convenient course.

BLACKPOLE FURNITURE *v.* SULLIVAN [1978] I.C.R. 558, E.A.T.

889. —— time limit—when time begins to run

Where an industrial tribunal reaches a decision on the issue of liability and adjourns the question of remedies, the time for appealing against that decision runs from the date on which it is entered on the register and not from the date of a subsequent decision on compensation.

An industrial tribunal found that C had been unfairly dismissed by F Ltd. They made a recommendation of reinstatement, and adjourned the question of remedies. The decision was entered on the register on June 16, 1976. On October 28, a different industrial tribunal assessed compensation at £1,000. That decision was entered on December 15. On January 20, 1977, within 42 days of the second hearing, F Ltd. sought leave to appeal against the finding of unfair dismissal, the recommendation of reinstatement, and the award of compensation. The registrar of the appeal tribunal dismissed the application for an extension of time for appealing against the first decision entered. F Ltd.'s appeal was heard by a fully constituted division of the appeal tribunal. *Held,* allowing the appeal, that (1) since the notice of appeal against the finding of unfair dismissal was substantially out of time, the time for appealing would not be extended; (2) although the time for appealing against the recommendation of reinstatement was also out of time, the reasons of the industrial tribunal could be read as meaning that they had not reached a final decision on that issue at the first hearing, and F Ltd. should be permitted to make further submissions on that part of the case. Accordingly, they would be granted a further 14 days to enter notice of appeal. (*Jowett* v. *Earl of Bradford* [1977] C.L.Y. 1010 applied.)

FIRESTONE TYRE AND RUBBER CO. *v.* CHALLONER [1978] I.C.R. 175, E.A.T.

890. Baking and sausage making

BAKING AND SAUSAGE MAKING (CHRISTMAS AND NEW YEAR) REGULATIONS 1978 (No. 1516) [10p], made under the Health and Safety at Work etc. Act 1974 (c. 37), ss. 11 (2) (*d*), 15 (1) (5) (*a*), 50 (3), as amended by the Employment Protection Act 1975 (c. 71), s. 116, Sched. 15, para. 6; operative on November 27, 1978; enable women who have attained the age of 18 to be employed on specified Saturday afternoons and Sundays in December 1978 and January 1979 in the manufacture of meat pies, sausages, cooked meats, packaging of bacon and the manufacture of bread or flour confectionery.

891. Constructive dismissal—basic award—calculation—whether "tips" to be included

[Trade Union and Labour Relations Act 1974 (c. 52), Sched. 1, para. 5 (2) (*c*); Employment Protection Act 1975 (c. 71), Sched. 4, Pt. II, para. 3.]

Calculation of compensation for unfair dismissal of an employee who had enjoyed a share in tips left by customers should disregard such tips in assessing his pre-dismissal earnings.

The employee barman was sworn at by the manager and told that he could leave if he did not like such language; he left. An industrial tribunal found that he had been unfairly dismissed and in assessing compensation took account not only of the employee's salary of £30 per week, but also of the £60 to £80 per week which he received as his share of tips left by customers. *Held*, allowing the employers' appeal in part, that (1) there were no grounds for interfering with the finding of constructive dismissal; but (2) the tribunal had erred in taking account of tips since the employee's share therein was not remuneration payable by the employers. (*Western Excavating (E.C.C.)* v. *Sharp* [1978] C.L.Y. 900 applied.)

PALMANOR *v.* CEDRON [1978] I.C.R. 1008, E.A.T.

892. —— breach of necessary mutual trust and confidence—burden of proof

A false accusation of dishonesty which is unreasonably made against an employee may amount to a repudiation of the contract of employment.

E, a man of good character, had worked for many years for D Co. He was falsely accused of theft by them and the police were called. E resigned. He was promised a written apology, but did not get it, and so he resigned again. He applied for compensation for unfair dismissal, but the industrial tribunal held that E had failed to prove that D Co.'s action was such as to terminate the contract of employment. On appeal by E, *held*, that such a situation could amount to repudiation of a contract of employment, and the burden was on the employer to show some background knowledge to justify the steps they had taken. Accordingly, the case would be remitted to another tribunal for rehearing.

ROBINSON *v.* CROMPTON PARKINSON [1978] I.C.R. 401, E.A.T.

893. —— employer's conduct—obligation to act reasonably in dealing with complaints—safety matters

[Trade Union and Labour Relations Act 1974 (c. 52), Sched. 1, para. 5 (2) (*c*).] In November 1978, B.A.C.'s safety officer, following a complaint by A that she could not wear eye protectors provided for her work because she had to wear spectacles, approached management to see whether they would pay for special protectors fitted with A's spectacles. A resigned in May 1977, as she had heard no more of the matter. *Held*, dismissing B.A.C. Co.'s appeal, that A was entitled to resign and claim constructive dismissal under the test of reasonableness applied by the tribunal or the contractual test which had since become law, since B.A.C. had been in fundamental breach of A's contract of employment in failing to investigate her complaint. B.A.C. were in breach of their obligation to act reasonably in dealing with complaints of lack of safety. Obiter: It is ordinarily an implied term of a contract of employment that the employers will not behave in any way which is intolerable or with which employees cannot be expected to put up (*Western Excavating (E.C.C.)* v. *Sharp* [1978] C.L.Y. 900 applied.)

BRITISH AIRCRAFT CORP. v. AUSTIN [1978] I.R.L.R. 322, E.A.T.

894. —— **enforced change in duties during period of notice**

F, a sales manager, gave three months' notice of resignation following a disagreement. M.T. Co. thereupon directed him to undertake only estimating work, to vacate his office and not to have any contact with any files with which he had dealt. F therefore left. *Held*, dismissing M.T. Co.'s appeal, that the tribunal were entitled to find that M.T. Co. had repudiated the contract of employment, entitling F to leave and claim constructive dismissal. The dismissal was unfair: MILTHORN TOLEMAN v. FORD [1978] I.R.L.R. 307, E.A.T.

895. —— **Industrial Tribunal decision**

Employer encouraging lesbian relationship

WOOD v. FREELOADER [1977] I.R.L.R. 455 (W, aged 18, was employed to look after Mr. and Mrs. C's two children. On Mrs. C's instigation, a lesbian relationship developed between her and W. W was willing but resigned after her parents discovered the situation. *Held*, that W had been constructively dismissed since Mrs. C had brought about an intolerable situation.)

896. —— **refusal to give employee time-off—employee's son sick**

[Trade Union and Labour Relations Act 1974 (c. 52), Sched. 1, para. 5 (2) (c).] W, a shop assistant, was refused permission to take a day or half-day off to supervise her son's insulin injection and give him the right food on his first day out of hospital after he was found to be diabetic. W resigned and claimed constructive dismissal. *Held*, that the tribunal had correctly decided that W had not been dismissed. B.S. were a small business and it could not therefore be an implied term of W's contract that there should be reasonable time off in emergency: WARNER v. BARBERS STORES [1978] I.R.L.R. 109, E.A.T.

897. —— **remuneration—implied terms in contract of employment**

B resigned because she had not received a pay increase for two years whereas other employees had. *Held,* allowing an appeal against a finding of constructive dismissal, that (1) it was unclear whether, in saying that B had been victimised, the tribunal meant more than that she had a grievance; (2) in most cases it is reasonable to infer a term that an employer will not treat employees arbitrarily, capriciously or inequitably in matters of remuneration; (3) if there was evidence of such deliberate conduct, a finding of constructive dismissal may be justified; (4) the case would be remitted for consideration of G Co.'s conduct in the light of what the contract expressly or impliedly required. (*George Wimpey & Co.* v. *Cooper* [1977] C.L.Y. 945 and *Western Excavating (E.C.C.)* v. *Sharp* [1978] C.L.Y. 900 considered): F. C. GARDNER v. BERESFORD [1978] I.R.L.R. 63, E.A.T.

898. —— **terms of employment—employer's breach—change in hours of work**

S, a toolmaker, was employed in 1969, when his written particulars gave his hours of work as 7.30 a.m. to 4.30 p.m. In April 1972, he began working on the night shift pursuant to an informal agreement with the chargehand and works manager. In August 1976, when D.S. Co. ordered him to work on days, he did so for two weeks but wrote saying he would only do so for a normal night shift premium. D.S. Co. refused to pay him the night shift premium and he therefore left in April 1977. *Held*, allowing S's appeal, that (1) the tribunal had erred in finding that S's contract had never been varied from day work to night work, although his written particulars were never altered. In attempting unilaterally to change S's hours of work from nights to days D.S. Co. had repudiated S's contract, and S had been constructively dismissed; (2) by working the day shift for two weeks, S had not accepted the situation as he had made his standpoint clear in writing: SIMMONDS v. DOWTY SEALS [1978] I.R.L.R. 211, E.A.T.

899. —— **test to apply**

[Trade Union and Labour Relations Act 1974 (c. 52), Sched. 1, para. 5 (2) (c).]

In assessing the employer's conduct within the meaning of para. 5 (2) (c) of Sched. 1 to the Act, an industrial tribunal should guide itself by similar criteria to those which it is required to apply in deciding whether a dismissal has been fair or unfair.

For over five years S worked satisfactorily for A Ltd. in the machine shop as a radial driller. As a result of a disagreement between S and a trade union, A Ltd. had offered S a job in the stores in order to avoid a strike in the machine shop. It was made clear to him that A Ltd. hoped that the job could be temporary, pending a more satisfactory permanent solution. S agreed to start work in the stores the following day, but changed his mind over-night and asked for his cards. He complained to an industrial tribunal that he had been unfairly dismissed on the basis that A Ltd. had repudiated the contract to employ him as a radial driller. The tribunal held that A Ltd. had not repudiated the contract by asking S to work in the stores temporarily, and S was not entitled to treat their conduct as a dismissal under para. 5 (2) (c) of Sched. 1 to the Act. S appealed. *Held,* dismissing the appeal, that there was no fundamental breach of the contract, and A Ltd. had acted reasonably in attempting to make temporary arrangements, thus their conduct could not be a dismissal within para. 5 (2) (c) of Sched. 1 to the Act. (Dictum of Megaw L.J. in *Turner* v. *London Transport Executive* [1978] C.L.Y. 902 followed; *Wetherall (Bond St.)* v. *Lynn* [1978] C.L.Y. 901 explained.)

SCOTT *v.* AVELING BARFORD [1978] 1 W.L.R. 208, E.A.T.

900. [Trade Union and Labour Relations Act 1974 (c. 52), Sched 1, para. 5 (2) (c).]

The question of whether or not there has been a constructive dismissal within the meaning of para. 5 (2) (c) to Sched. 1 to the Act, should be determined in accordance with the law of contract and not by applying a test of unreasonableness to the employer's conduct.

S was suspended from work by W Ltd. for five days without pay, after taking time off contrary to instructions. He was short of money, and when his requests for an advance of holiday pay and for a loan were refused he terminated his employment in order to obtain his accrued holiday pay. He made a complaint of unfair dismissal. The industrial tribunal held that S had been justified by his employer's conduct in terminating his employment pursuant to para. 5 (2) (c) of Sched. 1 to the Act. The Employment Appeal Tribunal dismissed an appeal by W Ltd. on the ground that the tribunal had neither erred in law, nor reached a conclusion to which no reasonable tribunal could have come. W Ltd. appealed. *Held,* allowing the appeal, that there had been no breach or repudiation of the contract of employment by W Ltd., and S could not be treated as having been dismissed. (*Wetherall (Bond St.)* v. *Lynn* [1978] C.L.Y. 901 approved; *Scott* v. *Aveling Barford* [1978] C.L.Y. 899 considered; dictum of Megaw L.J. in *Turner* v. *London Transport Executive* [1978] C.L.Y. 902 not followed; decision of E.A.T. reversed.)

WESTERN EXCAVATING (E.C.C.) *v.* SHARP [1978] 2 W.L.R. 344, C.A.

901. [Trade Union and Labour Relations Act 1974 (c. 52), Sched 1, para. 5 (2) (c).]

In deciding whether or not an employee has been constructively dismissed within the meaning of para. 5 (2) (c) of Sched. 1 to the Act, an industrial tribunal should consider the employer's conduct, and whether he had repudiated the contract of employment by showing an intention not to be bound by its terms.

After working for W Ltd. as assistant area manager for one year, L was transferred to head office to be retail stock controller. Three months later, following a dispute over a holiday and criticisms of his work by a director of the company, L received an official warning letter from that director accusing him of negligence and inefficiency. He was absent from work for 17 weeks suffering from a nervous breakdown, during which period he made repeated requests for an interview with the director concerned, all of which were refused. He then resigned from the company, and complained to an industrial tribunal that he had been constructively dismissed by W Ltd. and that the dismissal was unfair. The tribunal held that W Ltd. had acted unreasonably, and that L was entitled to terminate his contract within the meaning of para. 5 (2) (*c*) of Sched. 1 to the Act. W Ltd. appealed. *Held*, dismissing the appeal, that in the circumstances it was clear that W Ltd. had repudiated the contract and that he had been constructively dismissed; since W Ltd. had acted unreasonably within the meaning of para. 6 (8) of Sched. 1 to the Act, the dismissal was unfair. (*Gilbert* v. *Goldstone* [1977] C.L.Y. 1176 and *Logabax* v. *Titherley* [1977] C.L.Y. 943 explained.)

WETHERALL (BOND ST.) *v.* LYNN [1978] 1 W.L.R. 200, E.A.T.

902. —— tribunal's finding—estoppel

Where an employee is found by an industrial tribunal to have been unfairly dismissed, his employer is not in the absence of a clear finding by the tribunal, estopped from denying breach of contract in subsequent civil proceedings.

The plaintiff after some 20 years in the defendants' employ resigned when he was not short-listed for interview for promotion. An industrial tribunal ruled that the plaintiff had been unfairly dismissed and awarded compensation of £5,200. Thereafter the plaintiff issued county court proceedings for breach of contract claiming damages for, inter alia, the emotional distress occasioned by his dismissal. The plaintiff unsuccessfully contended as a preliminary issue that the defendants were estopped by the tribunal's finding from denying breach of contract. *Held*, dismissing his appeal, that the tribunal's reasons for finding that the plaintiff was unfairly dismissed were too obscure for it to be said that an identical issue was here to be determined; and that it is not necessary for an industrial tribunal to find that there has been a breach of contract in order to conclude that a dismissal is unfair.

TURNER *v.* LONDON TRANSPORT EXECUTIVE [1977] I.C.R. 952, C.A.

903. —— union membership agreement—non-membership—failure to comply with terms of agreement

[Trade Union and Labour Relations Act 1974 (c. 52), Sched. 1, para. 6 (5) (8).] When LSE Co. had almost reached a closed shop agreement with APEX they suspended J on April 30, 1976, on full pay for refusing to join the union. On August 16, 1976, a union membership agreement which set out a procedure for dealing with non-members was signed. Thereafter, when it was clear that the union would not relax its attitude concerning J's non-membership, but before all stages of the agreed procedure had been gone through, J was dismissed. *Held*, allowing J's appeal, that (1) even if J's suspension on April 30, 1976, was repudiatory conduct by LSE Co., it could not be said that dismissal took place before the union membership agreement when the separation between J and LSE Co. took place so long after the suspension; (2) the tribunal had erred in finding the dismissal fair in accordance with para. 6 (5) of Sched. 1 to the 1974 Act since before employers can rely on para. 6 (5) they must establish strict compliance with the terms of the union membership agreement. Accordingly the case would be remitted for rehearing as the fairness of the dismissal fell to be decided under para. 6 (8): JEFFREY *v.* LAURENCE SCOTT & ELECTROMOTORS [1977] I.R.L.R. 466, E.A.T.

904. —— whether employers had evinced an intention not to be bound by contract —whether employee need give reasons for leaving

[Trade Union and Labour Relations Act 1974 (c. 52), Sched. 1, para. 5 (2) (*c*).]

The correct test of whether an employer has repudiated a contract entitling an employee to consider himself constructively dismissed is whether the employer's conduct amounts to a significant breach going to the root of the contract of employment.

W was employed for five years as a manager, but following the appointment of an assistant manager without consultation, and various other demeaning matters, he resigned. The Tribunal found that applying the " contract " rather than " industrial " test, W was not constructively dismissed. *Held*, dismissing the employee's appeal that the correct test was the " contract " test, and the employers had not shown they no longer intended to be bound by an essential term of the contract. In those circumstances, W ought to have indicated that he regarded their conduct as a repudiation of the contract (*Western Excavating E.C.C.* v. *Sharp* [1978] C.L.Y. 900; *Logabax* v. *Titherley* [1977] C.L.Y. 943 applied).

WALKER v. JOSIAH WEDGWOOD AND SONS [1978] I.C.R. 744, E.A.T.

905. Contract of employment—collateral agreement—whether incorporated into individual contract

BL Co. entered an agreement with unions about the discontinuation of a department in Glasgow whereby affected employees would be interviewed and lists would be drawn up of those who wished to be made redundant and those who wished to be retrained. In January 1977 BL Co. later changed their policy and the employees were given the choice of being transferred to Bathgate or Preston or possible retraining. In August 1977 M resigned because of uncertainty about his future. *Held*, allowing BL Co.'s appeal against a finding of constructive dismissal, that the tribunal had erred (1) in finding the terms of the company/union collective agreement to have been incorporated in M's individual contract; and (2) in any event, in finding that breach of the agreement was a significant breach going to the root of the contract and entitling M to terminate his contract. Mere uncertainty as to the future does not amount to actual or constructive dismissal. (*Western Excavating (E.C.C.)* v. *Sharp* [1948] C.L.Y. 900; *Morton Sundour Fabrics* v. *Shaw* [1967] C.L.Y. 1448 and *Devon County Council* v. *Cook* [1977] C.L.Y. 934 applied): BRITISH LEYLAND (U.K.) v. McQUILKEN [1978] I.R.L.R. 245, E.A.T.

906. —— continuity of employment—absence due to sickness or injury following dismissal

[Contracts of Employment Act 1972 (c. 53), Sched. 1, para. 5 (1) (*a*).] S was dismissed on July 6, 1977, following a period of absence without explanation. He was re-engaged on August 1, 1977, but again dismissed on August 23, 1977. *Held*, that the tribunal had erred in holding that S's period of continuous employment ran only from August 1. S's service could be deemed to have continued between July 6 and August 1 by virtue of the 1972 Act, Sched. 1, para. 5 (1) (*a*) because he was incapable of work due to sickness or injury, even though he had been dismissed. It would be otherwise if the dismissal had been for reasons unconnected with the sickness. (*Fitzgerald* v. *Hall Russell & Co.* [1969] C.L.Y. 1281 considered): SCARLETT v. GODFREY ABBOTT GROUP [1978] I.R.L.R. 456, E.A.T.

907. —— transfer of business—absence through sickness

[Contracts of Employment Act 1972 (c. 53), Sched. 1, para. 9 (2).] It is not necessary to show that the transferred part of the business was carried on entirely separately in order to establish continuity of employment; it is sufficient if it is a recognisable and identifiable part of the whole business.

In 1966 G was employed by a company which carried out gas fitting and plumbing contracts. In 1973 he fell ill and was off work for a year. In the meantime the gas fitting part of the business was transferred. On his return, G sought a declaration as to the commencment date and continuity of his employment. The tribunal held that there was no continuity. *Held*, allowing the appeal, that it was only necessary to show that an identifiable and recognisable part of the business had been transferred, which had been done in this case, and accordingly employment was continuous since 1966.

GREEN v. WAVERTREE HEATING AND PLUMBING CO. [1978] I.C.R. 928, E.A.T.

908. —— voluntary resignation—temporary employment with same employer

[Redundancy Payments Act 1965 (c. 62), ss. 8 (2), 9 (2) (*a*); Contracts of Employment Act 1972 (c. 53), s. 13, Sched. I.] Unless one of the exceptions to continuity of employment contained in the provisions of Sched. 1 to the 1972 Act applies, there is no break in the employment.

W entered the service of a local authority in 1972 on a temporary basis, but was employed on a permanent basis from 1973–1975. In 1975 he voluntarily resigned to take up once again his temporary post with the same authority.

He was subsequently made redundant, and both the tribunal and the Employment Appeal Tribunal held that he had broken his continuity of employment. On W's appeal, *held*, allowing the appeal, that unless one of the exceptions contained in the 1972 Act applied, there was no break in employment, and that as none of them applied here the employers had failed to rebut the presumption of continuity contained in the 1965 Act.

WOOD *v.* YORK CITY COUNCIL [1978] I.C.R. 840, C.A.

909. —— dismissal—employee's election to treat contract as subsisting—employee's entitlement to bonus payments

Where an employer refuses to fulfil his obligations under a contract, the employee is entitled to repudiate the contract or to treat it as still subsisting without prejudicing his eventual legal rights to enforce performance of the obligations.

L was promoted in 1974 with the offer of a bonus in addition to his salary. Only one bonus payment was made. He was dismissed as redundant in 1977 and claimed unfair dismissal. The tribual rejected the complaint, but held that L was entitled to the missing bonus payments. On the employer's appeal on this point, *held*, dismissing the appeal, that the employers' refusal to fulfil their obligations entitled L to repudiate, or to treat the contract as subsisting and continue working. As he had taken the second course, he was entitled to bonus payments until the date of dismissal. (Dictum of Winn L.J. in *Denmark Productions* v. *Boscobel Productions* [1977] C.L.Y. 1999 considered).

W.P.M. RETAIL *v.* LANG [1978] I.C.R. 787, E.A.T.

910. —— hiving-down agreement—employees subcontracted to subsidiary company —objective test

The correct test of whether employees are transferred in a hiving-down agreement is an objective one, depending on the general circumstances, the documents and what was said and done.

Per curiam. The secrecy of negotiations in such transactions does not preclude the necessity for consultations, nor can the practice of hiving-down be used as an excuse to avoid such consultation.

B Ltd., in financial difficulties, acquired a subsidiary company and entered into a hiving-down agreement where the subsidiary bought the whole business, less employees. The employees were subcontracted to the subsidiary for four weeks, and when the beneficial ownership was acquired by L Ltd., dismissed. The tribunal found that B Ltd. was the employer in all cases, and found that the dismissals were unfair although only the case of P was actually argued. On the employees' appeals, *held*, allowing the appeals, that in the case of P alone, as B Ltd. had retained a business activity and had not disposed of all the business, the hiving-down agreement did not of itself terminate P's employment; the test was an objective one. However, because of incompleteness of documents, case remitted to another tribunal for rehearing (*Re Foster Clark Indenture Trust* [1966] C.L.Y. 1358 distinguished).

PAMBAKIAN *v.* BRENTFORD NYLONS [1978] I.C.R. 665, E.A.T.

911. —— hours worked—part-time worker

[Contracts of Employment Act 1972 (c. 53), Sched. 1, para. 4A.] The computation of the period of time required to be worked by a part-time employee meant 16 hours a week worked regularly within para. 4A, and not on average. A normal working week differs from an average working week, otherwise by putting a few weeks extra long hours a part-time employee could qualify for an adjudication by an industrial tribunal: OPIE *v.* JOHN GUBBINS (INSURANCE BROKERS), *The Times,* November 1, 1978, E.A.T.

912. —— illegal contract—whether statutory rights for unfair dismissal and redundancy apply

Statutory rights to compensation will not be enforced where the contract of employment on which they are based is illegal.

T was paid, *inter alia,* £15 weekly from petty cash. She and her employer knew that income tax was thereby avoided. On her claim for unfair dismissal and a redundancy payment, the tribunal dismissed her application. *Held,* dismissing her appeal, that although her rights not to be unfairly dismissed and the redundancy payments were statutory rights, they would not be enforced where they depended on a contract of employment which was illegal.

TOMLINSON *v.* DICK EVANS "U" DRIVE [1978] I.C.R. 639, E.A.T.

913. —— jurisdiction of tribunal—amendments to contract to clarify terms
[Contracts of Employment Act 1972 (c. 53), s. 8 (2) (5).]

The power of an industrial tribunal to substitute or amend particulars in a contract of employment may be exercised only where there has been an omission from such a contract.

In a dispute between employer and employee as to what his basic salary was, the employee sought an amendment to his contract of employment, pursuant to s. 8 (2) and (5) of the Contracts of Employment Act 1972. The statement of the contract provided by his employers contained all the particulars of the employment required by that statute. The tribunal amended that statement to resolve the dispute in favour of the employee. *Held,* allowing the employer's appeal, that there was no power to do so, there having been no " omission " in the employer's original statement.

LEIGHTON *v.* CONSTRUCTION INDUSTRY TRAINING BOARD [1978] I.C.R. 577; [1978] 2 All E.R. 723, E.A.T.

914. —— misrepresentation—defendants' knowledge of plaintiff's lack of experience.
See MCNALLY *v.* WELLTRADE INTERNATIONAL, § 1512.

915. —— reorganisation of business—change from employee to self-employed—whether right of appeal from Secretary of State's ruling

It is perfectly proper for parties to enter into an arrangement expressly to alter the status of an employee to that of independent contractor, provided there are no provisions in the contract inconsistent with the new status.

In a business reorganisation by B.S.M., T's contract of service as a driving instructor was terminated, and he was engaged under a new written contract as an independent contractor. None of the terms of the contract were actually inconsistent with the latter status, though they could equally have pointed to his status as an employee. On an inquiry by T as to his status for national insurance purposes, the Secretary of State ruled that he was an employed person. *Held,* on appeal, allowing the appeal, that the question was one of law and accordingly an appeal lay from the Secretary's ruling that it was proper for the parties expressly to alter the status of an employee in this way, provided the provisions in the new contract were not inconsistent with the new status. (*Massey* v. *Crown Life Insurance* [1978] C.L.Y. 1116 followed.)

B.S.M. (1257) *v.* SECRETARY OF STATE FOR SOCIAL SERVICES [1978] I.C.R. 894, Sir Douglas Frank, Q.C.

916. —— repudiation by employee—whether contract automatically determined

An employee's unilateral repudiation of his contract of employment does not ipso facto determine the contract.

The plaintiffs appointed the defendant as managing director under a service agreement to run for 10 years from 1972, the agreement providing, inter alia, that during its currency the defendant would not without consent engage in other employment and that he would not disclose confidential information concerning the company nor use or disclose any confidential information concerning the company's suppliers or customers. Unbeknown to the company the defendant began trading in competition to the company and traded with suppliers and customers of the company. In 1977 the defendant purported to resign as managing director of the plaintiffs who thereafter brought proceedings against him and further sought interlocutory injunctions restraining the defendant from, inter alia, acting in breach of the 1972 agreement. *Held,* granting the injunction, that (1) the defendant could not unilaterally discharge himself from his contractual obligations; (2) the defendant would be restrained from dealing with the company's customers and suppliers in breach of his employee's obligations of fidelity and good faith; (3) the same obligations warranted his being restrained from using confidential information, although the contractual prohibition was limited to the disclosure of the same. (*Lumley* v. *Wagner* (1852) 1 De G.M. &

G. 604; *William Robinson & Co.* v. *Heller* [1898] 2 Ch. 451 and *Warner Brothers Pictures Inc.* v. *Nelson* [1937] 1 K.B. 209 applied.)

THOMAS MARSHALL (EXPORTS) v. GUINLE [1978] 3 W.L.R. 116, Megarry V.-C.

917. —— **whether implied—whether director an employee of company.** See PARSONS v. ALBERT J. PARSONS & SONS, § 1065.

918. Counter-inflation. See REVENUE AND FINANCE.

919. Employees' guide

The Department of Employment have published a quick-reference guide entitled " Individual Rights for Employees." This gives an easy-to-follow account of the various individual rights of employees under employment protection legislation (including the Employment Protection (Consolidation) Act 1978), and sets out the corresponding obligations upon employers. It also contains sections on racial and sex discrimination, industrial tribunals, contracts of employment, unfair dismissal and redundancy. The guide is available, free of charge, from Unemployment Benefit Offices, Jobcentres and Employment Offices.

920. Employment agencies

EMPLOYMENT AGENCIES AND EMPLOYMENT BUSINESSES LICENCE FEE REGULATIONS 1978 (No. 390) [10p], made under the Employment Agencies Act 1973 (c. 35), ss. 2 (2), 12 (1) and (3); operative on June 1, 1978; revoke S.I. 1976 No. 713 and prescribe the increased fees payable on the grant or renewal of a licence under the 1973 Act to carry on an employment agency or business.

EMPLOYMENT AGENCIES ACT 1973 (CHARGING FEES TO AU PAIRS) REGULATIONS 1978 (No. 805) [10p], made under the Employment Agencies Act 1973, ss. 5 (1), 6 (1), 12 (1)–(3); operative on July 10, 1978; provides that an employment agency may charge a fee to a person for finding that person employment as an au pair in a place outside the U.K. This is subject to certain special conditions.

921. Employment Appeal Tribunal—procedure—rules

The following Practice Direction was issued by the Employment Appeal Tribunal on March 3, 1978 :

1. The Employment Appeal Tribunal Rules 1976 (S.I. 1976 No. 322) (hereinafter called " the Rules ") came into operation on March 30, 1976.

2. By virtue of para. 15 (2) of Sched. 6 to the Employment Protection Act 1975, the Appeal Tribunal has power, subject to the Rules, to regulate its own procedure.

3. Where the Rules do not otherwise provide, the following procedure will be followed in all appeals to the Appeal Tribunal.

4. Appeals out of time

a. By virtue of Rule 3 (1) of the Rules, every appeal under s. 88 of the Employment Protection Act 1975 to the Employment Appeal Tribunal shall be instituted by serving on the Tribunal, within 42 days of the date on which the document recording the decision or order appealed from was sent to the appellant, a notice of appeal as prescribed in the Rules.

b. Every notice of appeal not delivered within 42 days of the date on which the document recording the decision or order appealed from was sent to the appellant must be accompanied by an application for an extension of time, setting out the reasons for the delay.

c. Applications for an extension of time for appealing cannot be considered until a notice of appeal has been presented.

d. Unless otherwise ordered, the application for extension of time will be heard and determined by the Registrar on a date appointed by him pursuant to Rule 9 of the Rules.

e. In determining whether to extend the time for appealing, particular attention will be paid to the guidance contained in *Marshall* v. *Harland & Wolff*

[1972] I.C.R. 97; [1972] C.L.Y. 1185, and to whether any excuse for the delay has been shown.

f. It is not necessarily a good excuse for delay in appealing that legal aid has been applied for, or that support is being sought, *e.g.* from the Equal Opportunities Commission, or from a trade union. In such cases the intending appellant should at the earliest possible moment, and at least within the time limited for appealing, inform the Registrar, and the other party, of his intentions, and seek the latter's agreement to an extension of time for appealing.

g. Time for appealing runs from the date on which the document recording the decision or order of the industrial tribunal was sent to the appellant, notwithstanding that the assessment of compensation has been adjourned, or an application has been made for a review.

h. In any case of doubt or difficulty, notice of appeal should be presented in time, and an application made to the Registrar for directions.

5. Institution of appeal

a. Subject to Rule 3 (2) of the Rules, if it appears to the Registrar that a notice of appeal gives insufficient particulars or lacks clarity either as to the question of law or the grounds of an appeal, the Registrar may postpone his decision under that Rule pending amplification or clarification of the notice of appeal, as regards the question of law or grounds of appeal, by the intended appellant.

b. Upon the hearing of an appeal an appellant will not ordinarily be allowed to contend that " the decision was contrary to the evidence " or that " there was no evidence to support the decision," or to advance similar contentions, unless full and sufficient particulars identifying the particular matters relied upon have been supplied to the Appeal Tribunal.

c. In any case where it appears to the Registrar that the questions raised by a notice of appeal, or the grounds of appeal stated therein and any further particulars given under (a) above, do not give the Appeal Tribunal jurisdiction to entertain the appeal, he will notify the appellant accordingly, informing him of the reasons for his decision.

d. Where the appellant, having been notified of the Registrar's decision under Rule 3 (2), serves a fresh notice of appeal under Rule 3 (2) within the time limited by that Rule, the Registrar may consider such fresh notice of appeal with regard to jurisdiction as though it were an original notice of appeal lodged pursuant to Rule 3 (1).

e. Where an appellant is dissatisfied with the reasons given by the Registrar for his opinion that the grounds of appeal stated in the notice of appeal do not give the Appeal Tribunal jurisdiction to entertain the appeal, the Registrar will place the papers before the President or a judge for his direction.

f. It will not be open to the parties to reserve a right to amend, alter or add to any pleading. Any such right is not inherent and may only be exercised if permitted by order for which an interlocutory application should be made as soon as the need for alteration is known.

6. New procedure

a. Where an appeal has not been rejected pursuant to Rule 3 (2) but nevertheless the Appeal Tribunal considers that it is doubtful whether the grounds of appeal disclose an arguable point of law, the President or a judge may direct that the matter be set down before a division of the Appeal Tribunal for hearing of a preliminary point to enable the appellant to show cause why the appeal should not be dismissed on the ground that it does not disclose an arguable point of law.

b. The respondent will be given notice of the hearing but since it will be limited to the preliminary point he will not be required to attend the hearing or permitted to take part in it.

c. If the appellant succeeds in showing cause, the hearing will be adjourned and the appeal will be set down for hearing before a different division of the Appeal Tribunal in the usual way.

d. If the appellant does not show cause, the appeal will be dismissed.

e. The decision as to whether this procedure will be adopted in any particular case will be in the discretion of the President or a judge.

7. Interlocutory applications

a. Every interlocutory application made to the Appeal Tribunal will be considered in the first place by the Registrar who will have regard to the just and economical disposal of the application, and to the expense which may be incurred by the parties in attending an oral hearing.

b. The Registrar will submit a copy of the application to the other side together with notice of the time appointed for the hearing, and will indicate in the notice of appointment that if it is not intended to oppose the application it may be unnecessary for the parties to be heard and that the appropriate order may be made in their absence. Where the application is opposed the Registrar will also in appropriate cases give the parties an opportunity of agreeing to the application being decided on the basis of written submissions.

c. Save where the President or a judge directs otherwise, every interlocutory application to strike out pleadings or to debar a party from taking any further part in the proceedings pursuant to Rules 9 or 15 will be heard on the day appointed for the hearing of the appeal, but immediately preceding the hearing thereof.

8. Meeting for directions

On every appeal from the decision of the Certification Officer, and, if necessary, on any other appeal, so soon as the answer is delivered, or if a cross-appeal, the reply, the Registrar will appoint a day when the parties shall meet on an appointment for directions and the Appeal Tribunal will give such directions, including a date for hearing, as it deems necessary.

9. Right to inspect the register and certain documents and to take copies

Where, pursuant to the direction dated March 31, 1976, a document filed at the Employment Appeal Tribunal has been inspected and a photographic copy of the document is bespoken, a copying fee of 25p for each page will be charged.

10. Listing of appeals
A. England and Wales

When the respondent's answer has been received and a copy served on the appellant both parties will be notified in writing of a date, between four and six weeks ahead, after which the hearing will take place. In the same letter the parties will be invited to apply for a date to be fixed for the hearing. For that purpose an application form will be enclosed, to be returned to the Listing Officer within 14 days on which solicitors (or if appropriate litigants in person) will be able to specify any dates they wish to be avoided. The date that has been fixed will then be notified to the parties with as much notice as possible.

If the application form is not returned to the Employment Appeal Tribunal within 14 days a party will have no right to ask for a fixed date. The case will in due course be listed for hearing (*i.e.* in the Warned List) and once this has been done it will be liable to be listed at a day's notice, though in practice it is hoped to be able to give much longer notice than that in the majority of cases. (Where either of the parties is appearing in person at least a week's notice will be given.) The Warned List will appear weekly in the Daily Cause List and it will also be displayed in Room 6 at the Royal Courts of Justice. The onus will be on solicitors' or counsels' clerks to watch the Warned List; no date will be able to be vacated except by formal application to the Tribunal.

The Warned List will accordingly contain:

    a. cases fixed for hearing during the coming week, with the date on which they are to be heard.

    b. cases where the " not before date " has passed, no application has been made for a fixed date, and the date of hearing has not yet been fixed.

Cases where the " not before date " has not yet been reached, or cases in which an application has been made for a fixed date but the date has not yet been fixed; and cases that have been fixed for hearing beyond the following week will not be included in the Warned List. Normally a case estimated to take half a day or less will be listed together with another of the same duration for one court in one day, and when two or more courts are sitting " floaters " will also be listed as appropriate.

B. Scotland

When the respondent's answer has been received and a copy served on the appellant both parties will be notified in writing that the appeal will be ready for hearing in approximately six weeks. The proposed date of hearing will be notified to the parties three or four weeks ahead. Any party who wishes to apply for a different date must do so within seven days of receipt of such notification. Thereafter a formal notice of the date fixed for the hearing will be issued not less than 14 days in advance. This will be a peremptory diet. It will not be discharged except by the judge on cause shown.

11. Admissibility of documents

a. Where, pursuant to Rules 9 or 13, an application is made by a party to an appeal to put in at the hearing of the appeal any document which was not before the Industrial Tribunal, including a note of evidence given before the Industrial Tribunal (other than the Chairman's Note), the application shall be submitted in writing with copies of the document(s) sought to be made admissible at the hearing.

b. The Registrar will forthwith communicate the nature of the application and of the document(s) sought to be made admissible to the other party and where appropriate, to the Chairman of the Industrial Tribunal, for comment.

c. A copy of the comment will be forwarded to the party making the application, by the Registrar who will either dispose of it in accordance with the Rules or refer it to the Appeal Tribunal for a ruling at the hearing. In the case of comments received from the Chairman of the Industrial Tribunal a copy will be sent to both parties.

12. Complaints of bias, etc.

a. The Appeal Tribunal will not normally consider complaints of bias or of the conduct of an industrial tribunal unless full and sufficient particulars are set out in the grounds of appeal.

b. In any such case the Registrar may inquire of the party making the complaint whether it is the intention to proceed with the complaint in which case the Registrar will give appropriate directions for the hearing.

c. Such directions may include the filing of affidavits dealing with the matters upon the basis of which the complaint is made or for the giving of further particulars of the complaint on which the party will seek to rely.

d. On compliance with any such direction the Registrar will communicate the complaint together with the matters relied on in support of the complaint to the Chairman of the Industrial Tribunal so that he may have an opportunity of commenting upon it.

e. No such complaint will be permitted to be developed upon the hearing of the appeal, unless the appropriate procedure has been followed.

f. A copy of any affidavit or direction for particulars to be delivered thereunder will be communicated to the other side.

13. Exhibits and documents for use at the hearing

a. The Appeal Tribunal will prepare copies of all documents for use of the judges and members at the hearing in addition to those which the Registrar is required to serve on the parties under the Rules. In Scotland a copy of the Chairman's Notes will not be supplied to the parties except on application to the Appeal Tribunal on cause shown.

b. There is no inherent right to a copy of the Chairman's Notes but in England and Wales copies will be sent to the parties as soon as they are available, unless, in the discretion of the Appeal Tribunal, all or part of such notes is considered to be unnecessary for the purposes of the appeal. A Chairman's Notes are supplied for the use of the Appeal Tribunal and not for the parties to embark on a " fishing " expedition to establish further grounds of appeal.

c. It will be the responsibility of the parties or their advisers to ensure that all exhibits and documents used before the Industrial Tribunal, and which are considered to be relevant to the appeal, are sent to the Appeal Tribunal immediately on request. This will enable the Appeal Tribunal to number and prepare sufficient copies, together with an index, for the judges and members at least a week before the day appointed for the hearing.

d. A copy of the index will be sent to the parties or their representatives prior to the hearing so that they may prepare their bundles in the same order.

The Practice Direction dated January 7, 1977 [1977] C.L.Y. 965, as amended on March 9, 1977 [1977] C.L.Y. 966, is hereby revoked.

[1978] 1 W.L.R. 573; [1978] 2 All E.R. 293.

922. —— **rules—absence of appellant—costs**

[Employment Appeal Tribunal Rules 1976 (S.I. 1976 No. 322), r. 21 (1).]

A party's failure to attend the hearing of an appeal to an appeal tribunal may be " unreasonable conduct in conducting the proceedings " within r. 21 (1) of the Employment Appeal Tribunal Rules, and he may accordingly be ordered to pay costs.

E appealed from the decision of an industrial tribunal that they had no jurisdiction to hear his complaint for unfair dismissal. He wrote to the appeal tribunal saying that he could not afford legal representation, that he would be abroad at the date of the hearing, and that the appeal tribunal should hear his appeal in his absence. He made written submissions to the tribunal. *Held*, dismissing the appeal, that that conduct was unreasonable and E would be ordered to pay £50 towards the employers' costs.

CROYDON *v.* GREENHAM (PLANT HIRE) [1978] I.C.R. 415, E.A.T.

923. —— **sittings, vacations and office hours 1979**

The following Practice Direction was issued by the President of the Employment Appeal Tribunal on October 9, 1978:

Pursuant to para. 12 of Sched. 6 to the Employment Protection Act 1975, and to the powers vested in me by r. 25 (1) of the Employment Appeal Tribunal Rules 1976 (S.I. No. 322) I direct that:

1 The sittings of the Employment Appeal Tribunal for the year 1979 shall be Thursday, January 11 to Wednesday, April 11, Monday April 23 to Thursday, May 24, Monday, June 4 to Tuesday, July 31, Monday, September 3 to Friday, September 28, Monday, October 1 to Friday, December 21.

2 The Central Office of the tribunal in London will be closed on the following days: Saturdays and Sundays, Monday, January 1, Easter, Friday, April 13 and Monday, April 16, May Day Bank Holiday, Friday, May 25 and Spring Bank Holiday May 28, Late Summer Holiday Monday, August 27, Christmas, Monday, Tuesday and Wednesday December 24, 25 and 26.

3 The Glasgow Office of the tribunal will be closed on the following days: Saturdays and Sundays, Monday and Tuesday January 1 and 2, Easter, Friday and Monday April 13 and 16, May Day Monday May 7, HM the Queen's Birthday Holiday Monday May 28, Summer Holiday Monday July 16, Autumn Holiday Monday September 24, Christmas, Tuesday and Wednesday December 25 and 26.

The hours during which the offices of the Employment Appeal Tribunal shall be open to the public shall, subject to paras. 2 and 3 above, be 10 a.m. until 4.30 p.m. except during the month of August when they shall be 10 a.m. until 2.30 p.m. (1978) 122 S.J. 732.

924. —— **withdrawal of appeal—costs**

The appellant company withdrew its appeal nine days before the hearing date. *Held*, parties should not be discouraged from withdrawing appeals but a reasonable time should be given before withdrawal. Here there had been unreasonable delay, and the company were ordered to pay part of respondent employee's costs: T.V.R. ENGINEERING *v.* JOHNSON, *The Times*, October 10, 1978, E.A.T.

925. Employment (Continental Shelf) Act 1978 (c. 46)

This Act makes provision for the application of certain enactments to employment connected with the exploration or exploitation of areas of the continental shelf adjacent to areas designated under the Continental Shelf Act 1964.

S. 1 extends the power to apply employment legislation contained in s. 127 of the Employment Protection Act 1975 to any activities connected with the exploration or exploitation, in a foreign sector of the continental shelf, of a cross-boundary petroleum field; s. 2 is the interpretation section; s. 3 gives the short title.

The Act received the Royal Assent on July 31, 1978, and came into force on that date.

925a. Employment protection

EMPLOYMENT PROTECTION (VARIATION OF LIMITS) ORDER 1978 (No. 1777) [20p], made under the Employment Protection (Consolidation) Act 1978 (c. 44), ss. 15, 122 (5) (6), 148, 154 (3), Sched. 14, para. 8 (1)–(4); operative on February 1, 1979; varies certain of the limits which are required to be reviewed annually by the Secretary of State under s. 148 of the 1978 Act. The limit of guarantee pay payable under s. 15 (1) of the Act in respect of any day is increased to £7·25. The limit on the amount for the purpose of calculating the sum payable by the Secretary of State under s. 122 in respect of a debt due to an employee whose employer becomes insolvent is increased to £110.

926. —— dismissal—written reasons—employers' unreasonable refusal

[Employment Protection Act 1975 (c. 71), s. 70.] DIB Co. failed to reply to I's request under s. 70 for written reasons for dismissal after he had been dismissed for theft of £1,700 from DIB Co., because the police had asked DIB Co. not to answer correspondence or deal with any matter relating to the police investigation of the company's records. *Held,* dismissing DIB Co.'s appeal, that the tribunal were entitled to hold that DIB Co. had unreasonably refused I's request within s. 70 (4), as a reasonable employer would have explained the position to the police and asked their advice: DAYNECOURT INSURANCE BROKERS v. ILES [1978] I.R.L.R. 335, E.A.T.

927. —— Industrial Tribunal decision

MILSOM v. LEICESTERSHIRE COUNTY COUNCIL [1978] I.R.L.R. 433 (the L.C.C. gave M £111·68 for expenses in taking a diploma, to be returned if M left the L.C.C. within a certain time. M gave in his notice within such time and the L.C.C. wrote making it clear that M should repay the money. M disagreed and wrote refusing to have the sum deducted from any payment due to him. The L.C.C. then issued a pay statement to M with a deduction of £111·68. The nature of the deduction was specified as code number 70 which, according to the key to the code on the back of the payslip, meant "miscellaneous deduction/payment." *Held,* that the pay statement was not an itemised pay statement within the Employment Protection Act 1975, s. 81, as insufficient particulars of the purposes of the deduction were given. Nor was the deduction made in accordance with a standing statement of fixed deductions under s. 82, which envisages regular deductions at specified times and that all standing deductions should be specified in one document. Although the county court had held the deduction not to be in breach of contract, an award of £25 would be made as s. 84 (5) (b) enabled a penalty to be imposed on an employer not complying with s. 81).

928. Employment Protection (Consolidation) Act 1978 (c. 44)

This Act consolidates certain enactments relating to rights of employees arising out of their employment; and certain enactments relating to the insolvency of employers; to industrial tribunals; to the recoupment of certain benefits; to conciliation officers; and to the Employment Appeal Tribunal.

Pt. I (ss. 1–11) relates to particulars of terms of employment: s. 1 sets out the requirements for written particulars of terms of employment; s. 2 contains supplementary provisions; s. 3 states that certain hours of employment are to be disregarded; s. 4 makes provision for changes in terms of employment; s. 5 excludes certain contracts in writing from ss. 1 and 4; s. 6 empowers the Secretary of State to require further particulars; s. 7 confers power to vary the number of weekly hours of employment necessary to qualify for these rights; s. 8 declares an employee's right to an itemised pay statement; s. 9 relates to standing statements of fixed deductions; s. 10 empowers the Secretary of State to amend ss. 8 and 9; s. 11 deals with references to industrial tribunals.

Pt. II (ss. 12–32) specifies certain rights arising in the course of employment: s. 12 confers the right to guarantee payments; s. 13 contains exceptions to s. 12; s. 14 directs the method of calculating guarantee payments; s. 15 sets out limits on the amount of and entitlement to a guarantee payment; s. 16 contains supplementary provisions in respect of guarantee payments; s. 17 provides for complaints to industrial tribunals; s. 18 defines exemption orders; s. 19 confers the right to remuneration on suspension on medical grounds; s. 20 contains general exclusions from this right; s. 21 directs the method of calculating this remuneration; s. 22 provides for complaints in this respect to an industrial tribunal; s. 23 states an employee's rights in connection with trade union membership and activities; s. 24 makes provision for complaints concerning these matters to an industrial tribunal; s. 25 contains supplementary provisions; s. 26 sets out the rules for assessing compensation on a complaint under s. 24; s. 27 permits time off for employees carrying out trade union duties; s. 28 permits time off for employees to engage in trade union activities; s. 29 permits time off for employees to perform certain public duties; s. 30 contains certain provisions for industrial tribunals hearing complaints about the preceding matters; s. 31 concerns time off for employees to look for work or make arrangements for training; s. 32 makes provisions supplementary to ss. 27–31.

Pt. III (ss. 33–48) deals with maternity: s. 33 confers rights on the employee in connection with pregnancy and confinement; s. 34 defines the extent of maternity pay; s. 35 directs the method of calculating maternity pay; s. 36 provides for complaint to an industrial tribunal; s. 37 relates to the Maternity Pay Fund; s. 38 permits the Treasury to make certain advances from the National Loans Fund to be paid into the Maternity Pay Fund; s. 39 defines maternity pay rebate; s. 40 governs payments to employees out of the Maternity Payment Fund; s. 41 is concerned with the unreasonable default of the employer; s. 42 makes supplementary provisions relating to an employer's insolvency; s. 43 relates to complaints and appeals to industrial tribunals; s. 44 deals with the obtaining of information when an application under s. 40 has been made; s. 45 confers on this group of employees the right to return to work; s. 46 provides for the enforcement of these rights; s. 47 sets out how the right of return shall be exercised; s. 48 resolves any conflict of this right with a contractual right to return to work.

Pt. IV (ss. 49–53) governs termination of employment: s. 49 sets out the respective rights of employer and employee to a minimum period of notice; s. 50 deals with the rights of the employee in the period of notice; s. 51 determines the measure of damages in proceedings against employers; s. 52 relates to statutory contracts; s. 53 entitles an employee to a written statement of reasons for dismissal.

Pt. V (ss. 54–80) relates to unfair dismissal: s. 54 states the right of an employee not to be unfairly dismissed; s. 55 defines " dismissal "; s. 56 sets out the circumstances in which a failure to permit a woman to return to work after confinement shall be treated as dismissal; s. 57 contains general provisions relating to the fairness of a dismissal; s. 58 deals with dismissals relating to trade union membership; s. 59 is concerned with dismissal on grounds of redundancy; s. 60 deals with dismissal on grounds of pregnancy; s. 61 relates to dismissal of replacements; s. 62 concerns dismissal in connection with a lock-out, strike or other industrial action; s. 63 lays down the principle of disregard for any pressure on an employer to dismiss unfairly; s. 64 states the qualifying period and upper age limit to operate in unfair dismissal claims; s. 65 relates to dismissal procedure agreements; s. 66 deals with revocation of orders under s. 65; s. 67 concerns complaints to an industrial tribunal for unfair dismissal; s. 68 sets out the remedies available to a complainant; s. 69 deals with re-engagement or reinstatement; s. 70 contains supplementary provisions; s. 71 concerns the enforcement of an order under s. 69 and compensation; s. 72 defines compensation; s. 73 directs the method of calculating the basic award; s. 74 directs the method of calculating the compensatory award; s. 75 places limits on compensation; s. 76 prescribes the compensation for acts which constitute sexual or racial discrimination (or both), as well as unfair dismissal;

s. 77 provides for interim relief pending determination of the complaint of unfair dismissal; s. 78 prescribes orders for continuation of a contract of employment; s. 79 contains supplementary provisions relating to interim relief; s. 80 makes special provision for teachers in aided schools.

Pt. VI (ss. 81–120) deals with redundancy payments: s. 81 makes general provision as to the right to redundancy payments; s. 82 contains general exclusions from the right to redundancy payments; s. 83 defines " dismissal "; s. 84 relates to renewal of a contract or re-engagement; s. 85 provides for the case where an employee anticipates the expiry of an employer's notice; s. 86 states that the failure to permit a woman to return to work after a confinement is to be treated as dismissal; s. 87 relates to lay-off and short-time; s. 88 confers in some circumstances a right to redundancy payment by reason of lay-off or short-time; s. 89 contains supplementary provisions in respect of s. 88; s. 90 defines " the relevant date " in relation to redundancy payments; s. 91 provides for reference of certain questions to a tribunal; s. 92 makes special provisions as to termination of contract in cases of misconduct or industrial dispute; s. 93 deals with implied or constructive termination of contract; s. 94 provides for a change of ownership of a business; s. 95 provides for transfers to Crown employment; s. 96 permits the making of orders of exemption from s. 81; s. 97 deals with claims as to extension of terms and conditions; s. 98 relates to the exclusion or reduction of redundancy payment on account of pension rights; s. 99 deems s. 81 inapplicable to public offices, etc.; s. 100 contains provisions affecting domestic servants; s. 101 sets out certain requirements for making redundancy payment claims; s. 102 directs the giving of written particulars of a redundancy payment; s. 103 continues in force the Redundancy Fund; s. 104 makes provision for redundancy rebates; s. 105 permits payments out of the fund to employers in other cases; s. 106 permits payments out of the fund to employees; s. 107 contains supplementary provisions for applications under s. 106; s. 108 governs references and appeals to a tribunal relating to payments out of the fund; s. 109 makes financial provisions relating to the fund; s. 110 applies in the case of a strike during the currency of an employer's notice to terminate a contract; s. 111 provides for payments equivalent to redundancy rebates in respect of civil servants, etc.; s. 112 deals with references to a tribunal relating to these equivalent payments; s. 113 contains provisions for employment under overseas governments; s. 114 defines " government of overseas territory "; s. 115 stipulates the application of this Part of the Act to employments not under contract; s. 116 is a provision for treating the termination of certain employments by statute as equivalent to dismissal; s. 117 relates to employees paid by a person other than the employer; s. 118 concerns statutory compensation schemes; s. 119 makes provisions as to notices; s. 120 creates certain offences.

Pt. VII (ss. 121–127) concerns the insolvency of employers: s. 121 states that certain debts or insolvency shall have priority; s. 122 sets out an employee's rights on the insolvency of his employer; s. 123 relates to the payment of unpaid contributions to an occupational pension scheme; s. 124 provides for complaints to an industrial tribunal; s. 125 directs the transfer to the Secretary of State of right and remedies in certain circumstances; s. 126 confers power on the Secretary of State to obtain information in connection with applications; s. 127 is the interpretation section for ss. 122–126.

Pt. VIII (ss. 127–136) is concerned with the resolution of disputes relating to employment: s. 128 provides for the maintenance of industrial tribunals; s. 129 makes the industrial tribunal the remedy for infringement of certain rights under this Act; s. 130 confers the jurisdiction of referees upon industrial tribunals; s. 131 confers upon the Minister power to give industrial tribunals jurisdiction in respect of damages, etc., for breach of contract of employment; s. 132 relates to the recoupment of unemployment benefit and supplementary benefit; s. 133 makes general provisions as to conciliation officers; s. 134 sets out the functions of conciliation officers on a complaint under s. 67; s. 135 continues in existence the Employment Appeal Tribunal; s. 136 deals with appeals to the tribunal from industrial tribunals and the certification officer.

Pt. IX (ss. 137–160) contains miscellaneous and supplemental matters: s. 137

grants power to extend employment protection legislation; s. 138 specifies the application of the Act to Crown employment; s. 139 makes provisions as to House of Commons staff; s. 140 restricts the ability to contract out of the Act's provisions; s. 141 relates to employment outside Great Britain; s. 142 concerns contracts for a fixed term; s. 143 sets out minimum periods of employment; s. 144 affects mariners; s. 145 relates to dock workers; s. 146 deals with other miscellaneous classes of employment; s. 147 applies ss. 1–4 to excluded employment; s. 148 requires the Secretary of State to review various limits imposed by the Act; s. 149 confers a general power to amend the Act; s. 150 provides for the death of an employee or employer; s. 151 relates to continuous employment; s. 152 directs the method of calculating normal working hours and a week's pay; s. 153 is the interpretation section; s. 154 provides for the making of rules, regulations and orders; s. 155 deals with offences by bodies corporate; s. 156 concerns payments into the Consolidated Fund; s. 157 makes arrangements for Northern Ireland; s. 158 provides for reciprocal arrangements with the Isle of Man; s. 159 contains transitional provisions, savings, consequential amendments and repeals; s. 160 deals with citation, commencement and extent. Except for ss. 137 and 157 and Sched. 16, paras. 12 and 28, the Act does not extend to Northern Ireland.

The Act received the Royal Assent on July 31, 1978, and came into force on November 1, 1978, except for s. 139 (2) to (9) and certain repeals contained in Sched. 17 which came into force on January 1, 1979.

929. Employment Subsidies Act 1978 (c. 6)

This Act authorises payments to employers as a means of contributing to the alleviation of unemployment.

S. 1 empowers the Secretary of State for Employment, and for Northern Ireland the Department of Manpower Services, to set up schemes for making payments to employers, enabling them to retain persons in employment who would or might otherwise become unemployed, to take on new employees, and generally to maintain or enlarge their work force; s. 2 provides for Parliamentary control of expenditure upon such schemes; s. 3 contains supplementary provisions; s. 4 gives the method of citation.

The Act received the Royal Assent on March 23, 1978, and came into force on that date.

930. Equal pay—contribution to pension scheme

[Equal Pay Act 1970 (c. 41), ss. 1, 6.] A pay scheme whereby male employees under 25 received more than their female counterparts, because the man had to contribute to the bank's pension scheme, contravened the equal pay code: WORRINGHAM *v.* LLOYDS BANK, *The Times*, November 10, 1978, E.A.T.

931. —— job evaluation study—breach of non-statutory pay policy required

[Sex Discrimination Act 1975 (c. 65), s. 6 (2) (*a*); Equal Pay Act 1970 (c. 41), s. 1 (2) (*b*) (5).]

The consequences of a proper job evaluation study should not be avoided merely because its implementation would contravene the Government's non-statutory pay policy.

A performance appraisal system was introduced by R for both men and women. The women had their salaries increased, but the men did not for fear that the Government's pay policy would be contravened. *Held*, allowing the male employees' appeals, that the men were entitled to equality of pay with the women notwithstanding the fact that there might be a breach of such a non-statutory policy.

HEBBES *v.* RANK PRECISION INDUSTRIES (TRADING AS RANK HILGER) [1978] I.C.R. 489, E.A.T.

932. —— —— satisfaction of requirements

[Equal Pay Act 1970 (c. 41), s. 1 (2) (*b*), (5).]

Where a claim is made under s. 1 (2) (*b*) of the Equal Pay Act 1970 relying on an evaluation study, the employee must show that the evaluation study satisfies the requirements of s. 1 (5).

The B Council carried out a job evaluation study of the staff's work. The scheme used was the "London Scheme," but varied so as to add points for

special factors. E's work was given the same number of points as two females under the basic scheme, but as a result of extra points for special factors the two women were graded higher and paid more. E claimed that he was employed either on like work, or on work rated as equivalent. The tribunal found that the work was not like work, and since the scheme had been modified the work had not been rated as equivalent. On appeal by E, *held*, dismissing the appeal, that the only evaluation study in force was the London Scheme as varied; that that study was the only one which could satisfy the requirements of s. 1 (5); and that E could not bring himself within s. 1 (2) by contending either that the London Scheme should have been adopted without variation, or that the scheme did not satisfy s. 1 (5).
ENGLAND *v.* BROMLEY LONDON BOROUGH COUNCIL [1978] I.C.R. 1, E.A.T.

933. —— —— **validity—where scheme not yet applied**
[Equal Pay Act 1970 (c. 41), ss. 1 (2) (*b*), 1 (5).] The applicants were given an equal rating with certain jobs done by men under a joint management/ union job evaluation scheme. They continued to be paid less than the men, although they had been told that their new job grades would have effect from April 26, 1976, and a merit assessment scheme was devised to determine where on the appropriate scale each employee would be, because of S-C Co.'s understanding of the Government's incomes policy. *Held*, allowing the applicants' appeal, that, inter alia, (1) the job evaluation was a valid study within the 1970 Act, ss. 1 (2) (*b*) and 1 (5). It is perfectly proper to declare an employee entitled to pay appropriate under a particular grade and leave the parties to determine where within that grade she is to be placed; (2) it is not necessary within the meaning of the Act for the job evaluation scheme to have been applied in the sense that the employees have been paid under it: O'BRIEN *v.* SIM-CHEM [1978] I.R.L.R. 399, E.A.T.

934. —— **like work**
Mrs. M was a packer who also did some clerical work. Mr. S was a packer who also undertook storeman's duties. Mrs. H and Mr. W were machine operators. Mr. W could set his own machine. *Held*, that (1) the tribunal had not erred in finding that, although M and S were employed on work of the same or broadly similar nature, there were differences in the work they did " of practical importance in relation to terms and conditions of employment." Generally, a part of work done by a man cannot be ignored, in applying the " like work " test, on the ground that his pay includes an additional element re that work. There might be exceptions where part of the work is in effect a separate and distinct job; (2) although W only spent about one hour per week setting his machine, this was sufficient to justify the tribunal in finding his job more responsible than H's and therefore that they were doing different jobs. If persons are not employed on like work it is irrelevant that the difference in their remuneration is not commensurate to the difference in their jobs. (*Dugdale* v. *Kraft Foods* (*No.* 2) [1977] C.L.Y. 975 not followed): MAID-MENT AND HARDACRE *v.* COOPER & CO. (BIRMINGHAM) [1978] I.R.L.R. 462, E.A.T.

935. —— —— **choice of representative for comparison**
Where one particular employee of several is selected for comparison purposes, he must be treated as representative of his group, even though he may not in fact be typical of the group.
The complainants, women, claimed equal pay with male employees in the same warehouse. The complainants themselves selected a male employee for job comparison. The tribunal found that the men were required to do, and in practice did, a wider variety of jobs and dismissed the applications. *Held*, dismissing the appeals, that where a representative was chosen for comparison, his duties must be examined on the basis that he was a representative, even though he might in fact be untypical; that it was necessary to look both at the contractual terms, and what was done in practice, to decide the question of " like work." (*Electrolux* v. *Hutchinson* [1977] C.L.Y. 977 and *Redland Roof Tiles* v. *Harper* [1977] C.L.Y. 978 considered.)
DANCE *v.* DOROTHY PERKINS [1978] I.C.R. 760, E.A.T.

936. ——— ——— comparison with previous employee

[Equal Pay Act 1970 (c. 41), s. 1 (1) (2) (4) (as amended by Sex Discrimination Act 1975 (c. 65), s. 8).]

An employee is entitled to compare his or her work with that done by a recent predecessor for the purpose of claiming equal pay. E was a stockroom manageress. She was employed on like work as the previous manager, and there was no material difference between her work and that of her predecessor. The industrial tribunal held that E was entitled to compare her work with that of her predecessor, and to claim equal pay. On appeal by the employers, *held*, dismissing the appeal, that that was correct so long as the interval was a short one. Where the interval was longer, however, a tribunal should proceed with caution, since a difference in treatment might well be due to reasons other than discrimination. (*Charles Early* v. *Marriott* (*Witney*) *& Smith* [1977] C.L.Y. 1257 considered.)

MACARTHYS v. SMITH [1978] 1 W.L.R. 849, E.A.T.

937. ——— ——— dispensing manager deputising for branch manager

F, a female dispensary manager in a chemist's shop, frequently deputised for X, the branch manager. *Held*, dismissing F's appeal against a finding that she was not employed on like work with X, that the tribunal had correctly taken a broad view of the differences between what was done by F and by X. It would be wrong only to consider the periods when F was deputising for X. Clearly the jobs of F and X were different: FORD v. R. WESTON (CHEMISTS) (1977) 12 I.T.R. 369, E.A.T.

938. ——— ——— genuine material difference

T.C.B. Co. admitted that the difference between the rates of pay of Mrs. B and Mr. C, time-keepers, was partly due to discrimination against women. T.C.B. Co. gave Mrs. B a £360 salary increase, claiming that the remaining difference of £300 per annum was due to a genuine material difference other than sex, namely C's longer service and protected rate as a result of former additional duties. *Held*, that the tribunal had correctly dismissed Mrs. B's application for equal pay, notwithstanding that T.C.B. Co. could not quantify precisely how they reached the figure of £360 as extinguishing the sex discriminatory element in the pay variation: BOYLE v. TENNENT CALEDONIAN BREWERIES [1978] I.R.L.R. 321, E.A.T.

939. ——— ——— ——— burden of proof

[Equal Pay Act 1970 (c. 41), s. 1 (3) (as amended by Sex Discrimination Act 1975 (c. 65), s. 8 (1).]

A scheme which grades employees according to their experience, capacity, skill and application will not be contrary to the Equal Pay Act 1970 if it is genuinely applied irrespective of sex.

Employees engaged on " like work " were graded according to various aspects of their ability. W complained that she was doing the same work, but getting a lower wage, than higher graded male employees. *Held*, allowing the employer's appeal that such a scheme was not contrary to the Equal Pay Act 1970, where it was applied irrespective of sex; that the standard of proof on the employer was on the balance of probability, a standard satisfied by the employer in this case.

NATIONAL VULCAN ENGINEERING INSURANCE GROUP v. WADE [1978] 3 W.L.R. 214, C.A.

940. ——— ——— ——— difference based upon past discrimination

[Equal Pay Act 1970 (c. 41), s. 1 (3).]

Where a change in a house purchase scheme could make a provision that eligible employees should include those women who should have received an allowance under the old scheme were it not for a debarring provision which is no longer continued, but fails to do so, the consequent variation in pay will not be due to a reason other than sex.

S operated a staff house purchase scheme. Under it male employees were entitled to an allowance if they had had one under a previous scheme. D would have been so entitled had she not been a married woman which debarred her under the former, but not under the current scheme. She was not otherwise entitled to an allowance under the current scheme. *Held*, dismissing the employer's appeal, that S had not shown that D's lack of entitlement to an allowance under the new scheme was due to a difference other than sex.

SUN ALLIANCE AND LONDON INSURANCE *v.* DUDMAN [1978] I.C.R. 551, E.A.T.

941. —— —— —— **differing experience**
[Equal Pay Act 1970 (c. 41), s. 1 (3).] A Co. claimed that the difference in remuneration between C, a female work study engineer, and X, who was employed on like work with C, was due to a material difference (other than that of sex) between C's case and X's, namely that X had much longer experience in that type of work. *Held*, dismissing A Co.'s appeal against a decision upholding C's application under the 1970 Act, that A Co. had failed to provide the necessary cogent evidence that C's work performance differed from X's and that X's level of remuneration was related under his contract to his experience: A.R.W. TRANSFORMERS *v.* CUPPLES (1977) 12 I.T.R. 355, E.A.T.

942. —— —— —— **night work**
[Equal Pay Act 1970 (c. 41), s. 1 (3), as amended by Sex Discrimination Act 1975 (c. 65), s. 8.]
Where a man and a woman do the same work, the mere fact that one works at night should be disregarded when considering whether they are employed on like work.
The complainant, S, and another were employed as canteeen workers on day shift. T, a male, was employed to do the same job on night shift at considerably better pay. The tribunal rejected the employers' argument that T was " red circled " and that variation in pay was genuinely due to a material difference between their cases. On the employers' appeal, *held*, dismissing the appeal, that if a man and a woman did the same work, the mere fact that they did it at different times should be disregarded in considering whether they did like work. S was entitled to equal pay save for an appropriate allowance for night work. (*Dugdale* v. *Kraft Foods* [1977] C.L.Y. 975 applied.)
NATIONAL COAL BOARD *v.* SHERWIN [1978] I.C.R. 700, E.A.T.

943. —— —— —— **not arising in performance of work**
[Equal Pay Act 1970 (c. 41) s. 1 (3) (4), as amended by the Sex Discrimination Act 1975 (c. 65), s. 8; EEC Treaty (Cmnd. 5179—II), art 119.
A difference in work is not of practical importance if the differences do not, in fact, arise during the actual performance of the work.
A female employee worked in a South London betting shop where she was paid less than male employees similarly so employed. The reason given by the employers was that men acted partly as security guards, as deterrents to trouble expected in that area and as carriers of cash. No such trouble had in fact been experienced by the employers in that particular shop. *Held*, dismissing the employers' appeal, that (1) the difference in the contractual obligations of the two sexes were irrelevant unless these led to actual (and not infrequent) differences in practice, which they did not; and (2) there were no differences in training of the two sexes, so that the employers could not succeed in an allegation that the differences in pay were due to a material difference other than sex. The differences found by the tribunal were all based on sex.
SHIELDS *v.* E. COOMES (HOLDINGS) [1978] 1 W.L.R. 1408, C.A.

944. —— —— —— **red-circling**
[Equal Pay Act 1970 (c. 41), s. 1 (3).] Y, a dayshift supervisor, claimed equal pay with five male nightshift supervisors employed on like work. U.B. Co. claimed the variation in pay to be due to the fact that when nightshift supervisors' pay was negotiated in January 1974 it contained a responsibility element and although that element had now gone, the nightshift rate was protected through a " red circle." *Held*, dismissing U.B. Co.'s appeal, that as U.B. Co. had led no evidence to show that considerations giving rise to the original red circle still applied when the latest of the male nightshift supervisors was employed in early 1975, the tribunal were entitled to find that U.B. Co. had failed to show the variation in pay to be due to genuine

material difference other than sex under s. 1 (3) of the 1970 Act: UNITED·
BISCUITS *v.* YOUNG [1978] I.R.L.R. 15, E.A.T.

945. —— —— —— wages in previous job

[Equal Pay Act 1970 (c. 41), s. 1 (3), as amended by the Sex Discrimination
Act 1975 (c. 65), s. 8 (i).]

In determining whether a variation in contracts of employment is due to a
material difference other than sex, regard should be had to the personal
equation between man and woman rather than to extrinsic circumstances.

A female employee sought equality of pay with a male colleague. The
reason for his increased rate of pay was that he would only have accepted
employment at the rate which had been paid in his former employment. The
employers were indifferent to his sex. *Held,* allowing the applicant's appeal,
that in determining whether pay difference was due to a material difference
other than sex, regard had to be had to the personal equations of the woman
and the man and not to any extrinsic factors, such as that in the instant case,
which might have led to the variation.

CLAY CROSS (QUARRY SERVICES) *v.* FLETCHER [1978] 1 W.L.R. 1429, C.A.

946. —— —— —— —— where initial difference has disappeared

[Equal Pay Act 1970 (c. 41), s. 1 (3) as amended by Sex Discrimination
Act 1975 (c. 65), s. 8 (1).]

Prolonged maintenance of a red-circle, especially if contrary to good industrial practice, may lead to an employer's failure to prove under s. 1 (3) of the
Equal Pay Act 1970 that a variation in a man's and a woman's contract is
genuinely due to a material difference other than sex.

W claimed she should be paid as much as M. The tribunal, without calling
on W to give evidence, found that after 1974 M and W had done like work,
owing to M's having become ill, although prior to 1974 M's work had not
been like work. They held that the employer was justified in not reducing M's
salary on humane grounds after 1974, but that the situation had continued
for too long, and that the employer had failed to prove that the variation in pay
was genuinely due to a material difference other than sex. On the employers'
appeal, *held,* allowing the appeal, that although the prolonged maintenance of
a red-circle might lead to a doubt as to whether there was genuine reason for
variation other than sex, the length of time which had elapsed in the present
case was not sufficient, and the case would be remitted to an industrial tribunal
to hear W's evidence. (*Snoxell* v. *Vauxhall Motor Co.* [1977] C.L.Y. 1257
explained.)

OUTLOOK SUPPLIES *v.* PARRY [1978] I.C.R. 388, E.A.T.

947. —— —— trainee and experienced worker

[Equal Pay Act 1970 (c. 41), s. 1 (4).]

Similar work may not be " like work " where one employee is a trainee and
the other experienced.

In 1970 the complainant was being given instruction by two senior women
employees in the trustee department of the employing bank. At the end of
1971 he moved to another department. He subsequently applied for equality of
pay with the two women employees. *Held,* dismissing his appeal, that (1) as
a trainee he was not engaged on " like work " with the more experienced
employees, although the work itself was similar; (2) the difference in pay was
due to a material difference other than sex, namely experience; and (3) as the
complainant was no longer employed with the two women on December 29,
1975 (when the Equal Pay Act 1970, came into force) the industrial tribunal
had no jurisdiction to hear his case.

DE BRITO *v.* STANDARD CHARTERED BANK [1978] I.C.R. 650, E.A.T.

948. —— —— whether differences of practical importance

[Equal Pay Act 1970 (c. 41), s. 1 (4).] Mrs. P and Mr. H were van drivers.
H was required on occasion to drive on the public highway whereas P was
only required to do so when H was away. Eventually H was transferred to
another section where he was paid much more for the same kind of work.
Held, that the tribunal had not erred in law in finding that P and H were
employed on like work. They were entitled to find that H's duties in driving

on occasion on public roads were not of practical importance in relation to their terms and conditions of employment within s. 1 (4) of the 1970 Act, the test being whether the differences were such as to put the two employments into different categories or grades in an evaluation study: BRITISH LEYLAND *v.* POWELL [1978] I.R.L.R. 57, E.A.T.

949. —— previous application—estoppel

Where one tribunal has found that a complainant is not engaged on " like work " with a male colleague, it is not open to her to make the same complaint about the same colleague to a different tribunal in the absence of changed circumstances.

A tribunal found that M was not engaged on " like work " with a male colleague. Her appeal was refused as being out of time. M made a further application in respect of the same colleague. *Held,* that the first adjudication had created an estoppel per rem judicatam and that, in the absence of changed circumstances, no further application could be made.

MCLOUGHLIN *v.* GORDONS (STOCKPORT) [1978] I.C.R. 561, E.A.T.

950. Factories. See FACTORIES.

951. Guarantee payments

GUARANTEE PAYMENTS (EXEMPTION) (NO. 15) ORDER 1978 (No. 153) [15p], made under the Employment Protection Act 1975 (c. 71), s. 28 (1); operative on March 14, 1978; excludes from the operation of s. 22 of the 1975 Act employees to whom the Agreement dated July 30, 1977, between the British Carton Association and the GMWU and SOGAT relates.

GUARANTEE PAYMENTS (EXEMPTION) (NO. 16) ORDER 1978 (No. 429) [15p], made under the Employment Protection Act 1975, s. 28 (1); operative on April 19, 1978; excludes from the operation of s. 22 of the 1975 Act employees to whom the agreements between Henry Wiggin and Co. Ltd. and the Electrical, Electronic and Telecommunications Union-Plumbing Trades Union and the A.U.E.W. relate.

GUARANTEE PAYMENTS (EXEMPTION) (NO. 17) ORDER 1978 (No. 737) [10p], made under the Employment Protection Act 1975, s. 28 (1); operative on June 27, 1978; excludes from the operation of s. 22 of the 1975 Act employees to whom the Scheme of Conditions of Service of the National Joint Council for Workshops for the Blind relates.

GUARANTEE PAYMENTS (EXEMPTION) (NO. 18) ORDER 1978 (No. 826) [20p], made under the Employment Protection Act 1975, ss. 22, 28 (1) (4); operative on July 13, 1978; excludes from the operation of s. 22 of the 1975 Act employees in the cord clothing industry, to whom one of three specified agreements relate.

952. —— casual worker—entitlement—number of hours worked

[Employment Protection Act 1975 (c. 71), s. 22 (1) (3); Contracts of Employment Act 1972 (c. 53), Sched. 1, paras. 3, 4.]

The average number of hours worked over a period of weeks may not be the test for what are the number of hours normally worked in a week. Where an employee does not have to work at all there may be no contract of employment.

W was a part time packer. She had no written contract of employment. She averaged more than 16 hours work a week from September 1974 to March 1977, when work ceased. For the four weeks preceding that cessation she averaged less than 16 hours. She did not have to work on a particular day if she did not wish to. The tribunal held that she was entitled to a guarantee payment from her employers. *Held,* allowing their appeal, that (1) there was no express contract of employment, and none was implied since she could refuse to work on any particular day; and (2) her claim was barred, in the alternative, by s. 22 (3) of the Employment Protection Act 1975 because during the four weeks prior to the cessation of work she had worked less than 16 hours a week.

MAILWAY (SOUTHERN) *v.* WILLSHER [1978] I.C.R. 511, E.A.T.

953. —— Industrial Tribunal decisions

Choice of hours worked

MILLER *v.* HARRY THORNTON (LOLLIES) [1978] I.R.L.R. 430 (H.T. employed women on the basis that they could choose the hours most convenient to them but after choosing those hours H.T. could call on them to work any weekday and could vary the number of hours worked. In September 1977 they were laid off because of threatened power cuts. They had been working 8.30 a.m. to 4.00 p.m. five days per week. *Held*, that the women were entitled to guarantee payments under s. 22 of the Employment Protection Act 1975. If it is contemplated that so many hours per week will be worked under a contract, there can be said to be normal working hours within s. 24 (1) even though the hours may sometimes be varied by mutual consent. An offer of work on days other than those on which the lay-off occurred could not be an offer of alternative work within s. 23 (2)).

Time off for Jewish holidays

NORTH *v.* PAVLEIGH; SKEET *v.* CARR MILLS CLOTHING CO. [1977] I.R.L.R. 461 (P Co. and CMC Co., both under the control of X, who strictly observed Jewish holidays and felt unable to allow non-Jewish employees to work for him on such days, posted notices setting out annual holidays, including under " unpaid holidays " the Jewish holidays. *Held*, dismissing employees' claims for guarantee payments, that (1) as the contracts of employment had not " contemplated " that the employees would not be required to work during Jewish holidays, the days in question were days on which they were " normally " required to work; (2) however, no guarantee payments were payable as the reason for work not being provided was neither a diminution in the companies' requirements for work within s. 22 (1) (*a*) of the Employment Protection Act nor an " occurrence " affecting the normal working of the employer's business in relation to work of the employee's kind within s. 22 (1) (*b*)).

Trade dispute affecting an associated company

THOMPSON *v.* PRIEST (LINDLEY) [1978] I.R.L.R. 99 (T claimed guaranteed pay in connection with a lay-off. *Held*, that he was not entitled to such pay as the lay-off was " in consequence of a trade dispute " affecting an associated company within s. 23 of the Employment Protection Act 1975. It was irrelevant that the trade dispute was not the sole cause of the lay-off if there would have been no lay-off but for such dispute).

Work during normal factory shutdown period

YORK AND REYNOLDS *v.* COLLEGE HOSIERY CO. [1978] I.R.L.R. 53 (CH Co.'s policy was to offer those who had been allowed to take holidays other than during their annual shutdown period, work during that period if available. If they did not work at that time they were not paid. Y and R wished to work during that period but no work was available for four of the relevant days. *Held*, that as these four days were not days during any part of which Y and R would normally be required to work in accordance with their contracts of employment, they were not entitled to guarantee payments under the Employment Protection Act 1975).

954. Health and safety at work

HEALTH AND SAFETY (GENETIC MANIPULATION) REGULATIONS 1978 (No. 752) [20p], made under the Health and Safety at Work etc. Act 1974 (c. 37), ss. 11 (2) (*d*), 15 (1) (2) (3) (*b*) (4) (*a*) (5) (*b*), 50 (3), 52 (2), 82 (3) (*a*), Sched. 3, para. 15 (1) as amended by the Employment Protection Act 1975 (c. 71), s. 116, Sched. 15, para. 6; operative on August 1, 1978; provide that no person shall carry out genetic manipulation unless he has given notice of his intention to do so to the appropriate authorities, and for the purposes of Pt. I of the 1974 Act, extends the meaning of the word " work " to include any activity involving genetic manipulation.

COMPRESSED ACETYLENE (IMPORTATION) REGULATIONS 1978 (No. 1723) [10p], made under the Health and Safety at Work etc. Act 1974, ss. 15 (1)–(3), 43 (2), 82 (3) (*a*) and Sched. 3, paras. 2 (1) and (4), as amended by the Employment Protection Act 1975, s. 116 and Sched. 15, para. 6; operative on

December 6, 1978; reg. 2 applies the provisions of s. 40 (9) (*a*)–(*e*) of the Explosives Act 1875 to acetylene at a pressure between 0·62 bar and 18·0 bar. Those provisions prohibit the importation of explosives into the U.K. except under licence issued by the Health and Safety Executive.

955. —— **coalmines—respirable dust.** See § 1960.

956. —— **improvement notice—decision on notice as preliminary point—whether proper without investigation of facts**
    [Health and Safety at Work etc. Act 1974 (c. 37), s. 24 (2).]
    It is inappropriate for a tribunal to decide on the validity of an improvement notice as a preliminary point without a prior investigation of the facts.
    After a fire at the company's factory, improvement notices were served on it under the 1974 Act. The company appealed against the notices as a preliminary point, alleging they were invalid as being imprecise and vague. The tribunal, without reviewing the facts, ruled the notices were valid. On appeal, *held*, dismissing the appeal that the appellate jurisdiction of the tribunal under s. 24 (2) of the Act envisaged an investigation of the facts; accordingly it was inappropriate for the tribunal to deal with the matter as a preliminary point without such investigation; the appeal was therefore premature.
    CHRYSLER UNITED KINGDOM *v.* McCARTHY [1978] I.C.R. 939, D.C.

957. Industrial injuries benefit. See SOCIAL SECURITY.

958. Industrial organisation and development. See TRADE AND INDUSTRY.

959. Industrial relations. See TRADE UNIONS.

960. Industrial training. See TRADE AND INDUSTRY.

961. Industrial tribunals
    INDUSTRIAL TRIBUNALS (LABOUR RELATIONS) (AMENDMENT) REGULATIONS 1978 (No. 991) [20p], made under the Trade Union and Labour Relations Act 1974 (c. 52), Sched. 1, Pt. III, para. 21; operative on August 21, 1978; amend S.I. 1974 No. 1386 so as to give power to a tribunal to require of its own notion a party to furnish further particulars, to review a decision of another tribunal, to strike out any originating application for want of prosecution.
    INDUSTRIAL TRIBUNALS (LABOUR RELATIONS) (SCOTLAND) (AMENDMENT) REGULATIONS 1978 (No. 992) [20p], made under the Trade Union and Labour Relations Act 1974, Sched. 1, Pt. III, para. 21; operative on August 21, 1978; amend S.I. 1974 No. 1387 so as to give power to a tribunal to require of its own motion a party to furnish further particulars, to review a decision of another tribunal, to strike out any application for excessive delay.

962. —— **adjournment—award of costs**
    [Industrial Tribunals (Labour Relations) Regulations 1974 (S.I. 1974 No. 1386) r. 10 (2) (*a*) (as amended by Industrial Tribunals (Labour Relations) (Amendment) Regulations 1976 (S.I. 1976 No. 661), reg. 6).]
    Where an adjournment of an industrial tribunal hearing is justified, and therefore granted, it should not be the subject of an order for costs.
    An employee sought an adjournment when new reasons to justify his dismissal were brought forward at the hearing. The adjournment was granted subject to the employee paying the costs. *Held,* allowing his appeal, that where the adjournment was justified it should not be made the subject of an order for costs.
    RAJGURU *v.* TOP ORDER [1978] I.C.R. 565, E.A.T.

963. —— **agreement to withdraw complaint—whether void**
    [Trade Union and Labour Relations Act 1974 (c. 52), Sched. 1, para. 32 (1) (*b*)].
    An employee will not be bound by an agreement to withdraw an application to an industrial tribunal.
    An employee complained to an industrial tribunal. Agreement was reached and a letter sent to the secretary to the tribunal saying that the employee no longer wished to proceed with his complaint. He subsequently changed his

mind. The tribunal held that his claim had been validly compromised by agreement. *Held*, allowing his appeal, that the provision in the agreement whereby the employee agreed to withdraw his complaint was void as being within the terms of para. 32 (1) (*b*) as an agreement preventing " the bringing of any proceedings before " a tribunal.

NAQVI *v*. STEPHENS JEWELLERS [1978] I.C.R. 631, E.A.T.

964. —— appeal—allegation of bias against chairman

Where an allegation of bias against the chairman of an industrial tribunal is relied on as a ground of appeal to the Employment Appeal Tribunal, the notice of appeal must give full particulars and the notice should be drawn to the attention of the chairman so that he may make comment or provide any necessary information. The convenient course is for the parties in such a case to communicate with the registrar who will ensure that all necessary steps are taken. B complained to an industrial tribunal that she had been unfairly dismissed. The case took four days when it might have taken half that time. B was represented at the hearing by her husband who was unqualified and whose inexperience led to the chairman warning him from time to time that he was attempting to bring in irrelevant evidence and pursue irrelevant cross-examination. The tribunal dismissed the complaint. B appealed on the ground, inter alia, that the chairman of the tribunal " appeared to be openly biased." *Held*, dismissing the appeal, that there was no real likelihood that the result would have been different if the chairman had been more lenient to B's husband.

BHARDWAJ *v*. POST OFFICE [1978] I.C.R. 144, E.A.T.

965. —— —— time limit to be strictly applied

In view of the need for speedy final determination, the 42 day time-limit for appealing from an industrial tribunal would be strictly applied: HEM *v*. SYKES AND SONS (SHEPLEY), *The Times*, October 25, 1978, E.A.T.

966. —— costs—frivolous or vexatious behaviour

[Industrial Tribunals (Labour Relations) Regulations 1974 (S.I. 1974 No. 1386).] L was dismissed without notice for rewarding staff for overtime with food from the canteen instead of cash. She was given no opportunity to explain and was threatened with a suit for damages if she took legal advice. CS Co. described L as " a criminal " in their notice of appearance. At the the hearing CS Co. called no evidence. The tribunal awarded compensation for unfair dismissal and costs against CS Co. on the basis that they were guilty of vexatious behaviour. *Held*, dismissing CS Co.'s appeal, that the tribunal were entitled to find CS Co. guilty of either frivolous or vexatious conduct in these circumstances under r. 10 of the 1974 Rules. Vexatiousness and frivolity which may result in costs being awarded are not confined to the institution of proceedings: CARTIERS SUPERFOODS *v*. LAWS [1978] I.R.L.R. 315, E.A.T.

967. —— jurisdiction—employee of Commonwealth Secretariat

G claimed compensation for unfair dismissal from the accounts department of the Commonwealth Secretariat. *Held*, dismissing G's appeal, that the industrial tribunal had no jurisdiction to hear the claim because the Commonwealth Secretariat is immune from any suit or legal process under the Commonwealth Secretariat Act 1966: GADHOK *v*. COMMONWEALTH SECRETARIAT (1977) 12 I.T.R. 440, C.A.

968. —— oral judgment—not complete until put in writing

After delivering an oral judgment but before putting it in writing, the chairman of an industrial tribunal acted within her powers in inviting the parties to return for further legal argument. Although industrial tribunals were the creation of statute, the civil practice that a decision was not complete until an order had been drawn up should be applied (*Jowett* v. *Earl of Bradford* [1977] C.L.Y. 1010 distinguished). The power should be used carefully and sparingly and only when an obvious mistake came to light after the hearing: HANKS *v*. ACE HIGH PRODUCTIONS, *The Times*, July 7, 1978, E.A.T.

969. —— practice—discovery—claim of racial discrimination

R, who claimed that the Commission in not appointing him for the post of Director of Community Affairs, had discriminated against him on racial grounds, applied for discovery of numerous documents. He appealed against refusal of discovery of some of these documents. *Held,* allowing the appeal in part, that R was entitled to discovery of documents which would enable him to make a comparative analysis between his own qualifications and history, and those of his competitors. These included all applications received from the nine short-listed candidates, their references and curricula vitae, and all documentary information relating to the nine candidates that was available to the Commissioners at the time of interview and before or at the time of shortlisting: RASUL *v.* COMMISSION FOR RACIAL EQUALITY [1978] I.R.L.R. 203, E.A.T.

970. Job Release Act 1977—continuation

JOB RELEASE ACT 1977 (CONTINUATION) ORDER 1978 (No. 1007) [10p], made under the Job Release Act 1977 (c. 8), s. 1 (4) (*b*) (5); operative on September 30, 1978; continues in force until September 29, 1979, s. 1 of the 1977 Act which would have otherwise ceased to have effect on September 29, 1978.

971. Labour Conventions

A White Paper has been published setting out certain Conventions and Recommendations agreed by the International Labour Organisation which concern occupational hazards arising from air pollution, noise and vibration, and also the general working conditions of nurses. The Government intends to ratify certain of these Conventions and Recommendations. The White Paper is available from HMSO (Cmnd. No. 7420) [80p].

972. Local employment

DERELICT LAND CLEARANCE AREAS ORDER 1978 (No. 691) [10p], made under the Local Employment Act 1972 (c. 25), ss. 8 (6), 18; operative on June 8, 1978; specifies as derelict land clearance areas the areas set out in the Sched. to this Order.

973. —— road schemes grants

Rules have been made by the Director of Transport and Highways under which grants may be made to local authorities or private developers under the Local Employment Act 1972 towards the cost of roads in development and intermediate areas. Expenditure is eligible for consideration for grant only where as a primary purpose of the roadworks there is a clear prospect of a positive contribution to industrial development, either by attracting new industry or by assisting the expansion of existing industry.

WELSH OFFICE CIRCULAR NO. 49/78.

974. Local government employee—loss of job—whether " attributable " to provisions of 1972 Act. See MALLETT *v.* RESTORMEL BOROUGH COUNCIL, § 1884, and WALSH *v.* ROTHER DISTRICT COUNCIL, § 1885.

975. Master and servant. See NEGLIGENCE.

976. Maternity pay—dates—contractual provision—limitation on statutory provision

[Employment Protection Act 1975 (c. 71).] A teacher was held entitled to start her six weeks paid maternity leave at any time after the eleventh week before the date of her expected confinement, despite the fact that she was contractually bound by her staff code that leave had to start at the beginning of the eleventh week. It was *held,* that the contractual provision was a limitation on the provisions of s. 36 of the Employment Protection Act 1975, which should prevail, and which gave the employee a free choice. Leave to appeal was granted: INNER LONDON EDUCATION AUTHORITY *v.* NASH, *The Times,* November 13, 1978, E.A.T.

977. —— Industrial Tribunal decision

Entitlement to rebate

J. WILLIAMS & CO. *v.* SECRETARY OF STATE FOR EMPLOYMENT [1978] I.R.L.R. 235 (G stopped work about 13 weeks before her expected week of confinement. W & Co. paid her six weeks' maternity pay. *Held,* dismissing W Co.'s appeal, that employers are only entitled under s. 42 (1) of the Employment

Protection Act 1975 to a rebate from the maternity fund in respect of payments they are liable to make under the Act. G was not entitled to any maternity pay under the Act because she had not worked up to the eleventh weeks before her expected week of confinement. Accordingly, W Co. were not entitled to any rebate).

978. National insurance. See NATIONAL INSURANCE.

979. Northern Ireland. See NORTHERN IRELAND.

980. Pay and incomes policy—C.A.C. award—appeal—principles and jurisdiction
[Employment Protection Act 1975 (c. 71), Sched. 11.] ASTMS claimed increased holidays under the general level provisions of Sched. 11 to the 1975 Act for Staff at TI Tube Division Services, Development Engineering Department. Held, dismissing TI's appeal against an award of certain increased holidays, that (1) Sched. 11 confers a wide discretion on the CAC; (2) certiorari or mandamus can only be applied for where the CAC have erred in law. Even then the court will only intervene if the CAC exceeded its jurisdiction, the rules of natural justice have been broken or there is an error of law apparent on the face of the record of proceedings; (3) the court cannot retry cases or receive fresh evidence: R. v. THE CENTRAL ARBITRATION COMMITTEE, *ex p.* T.I. TUBE DIVISION SERVICES [1978] I.R.L.R. 183, D.C.

981. Place of employment—whether ordinarily outside Great Britain
[Trade Union and Labour Relations Act 1974 (c. 52), Sched. 1, para. 9 (2).]
A person cannot be ordinarily working inside and outside Great Britain at the same time; where an employee " ordinarily works " cannot be determined purely by reference to what happened in fact. The correct approach is to look at the express or implied terms of the contract over the whole period. In the absence of special factors, an employee normally will be " ordinarily working " in the country where his base is.
W, a management consultant, was employed by a Swedish company which was part of an international group. The contract was silent as to W's place of work, but he was expected to work in any country where the company had contracts. He worked in Italy for 50 weeks and in Great Britain for 40 weeks. He was then dismissed. A tribunal held that he did not ordinarily work in Great Britain because he had worked longer under the contract outside Great Britain than inside, and that therefore there was no jurisdiction to hear his complaint of unfair dismissal. The E.A.T. dismissed his appeal. On appeal by W, *held*, allowing the appeal, that the tribunal should have looked at the whole period of the contract, not merely the period prior to dismissal, and ascertained where W's base was, examining all the relevant contractual terms, such as his headquarters, his projected travels, his private residence, the currency of payment and where national insurance was to be paid. (*Portec (U.K.)* v. *Mogensen* [1976] C.L.Y. 972 overruled.)
WILSON v. MAYNARD SHIPBUILDING CONSULTANTS A.B. [1978] 2 W.L.R. 466, C.A.

982. Police. See POLICE.

983. Racial discrimination—Industrial Tribunal decisions
JOHNSON v. TIMBER TAILORS (MIDLANDS) [1978] I.R.L.R. 146 (when J, a black Jamaican, applied for a job as a wood machinist, TT Co.'s work's manager, L, told J that he would contact him in a couple of days to let him know whether or not he was successful. J was not contacted and after repeated unsuccessful attempts to contact L, J was told the vacancy was filled. Another advertisement for wood machinists with TT Co. appeared the same night. J applied again for the job and was told the vacancy was filled. About a week later he applied again and was told the same although a further advertisement appeared for the job that day. *Held*, that the evidence established that J had been discriminated against on grounds of race).
VIRDEE v. E.C.C. QUARRIES [1978] I.R.L.R. 296 (V, a Sikh, applied for, but was not given, a job as a laboratory technician. At his interview, he was asked the nationality of his previous co-employees and whether he experienced trouble supervising white technicians. V was subsequently rejected for a post with E.E.C.Q. Co., as senior laboratory technician, being told that

he was too well-qualified for both posts and did not have suitable experience for the senior post. E.C.C.Q. Co. failed to answer all but one of nine questions put to them by V under s. 65 (1) of the Race Relations Act 1976. *Held*, that (1) E.E.C.Q. Co.'s manager had read and understood s. 65 before replying to V's questionnaire. Accordingly the failure to answer eight questions amounted to deliberately " evasive " reply under s. 65 (2) (*b*) from which the inference could be drawn that V had been discriminated against; (2) compensation was limited to £150, as there was no evidence that V would have been selected but for the discrimination; (3) s. 56 (1) (*b*) did not empower the tribunal to award costs against the respondents).

984. Redundancy—agreed selection procedure—whether unfair to dismissed employee
[Trade Union and Labour Relations Act 1974 (c. 52), Sched. 1, para. 6 (7) (8).]

Where an agreed selection procedure properly applied has the effect of being unfair to an individual employee, the tribunal must consider whether or not either the employers or the union have manipulated a situation unfair to him.

W, a labourer and fork-lift truck driver, was dismissed for redundancy. He claimed compensation for unfair dismissal on the ground that he had been unfairly selected within para. 6 (7) of Sched. 1 to the Act. The industrial tribunal found that the employers had failed to prove that they had operated an agreed selection procedure and since they had not compared W with other employees in similar work they had not acted reasonably within para. 6 (8) of Sched. 1, and the dismissal was unfair. The employers appealed. *Held*, allowing the appeal, that the finding that there was no agreed procedure for selecting for redundancy was contrary to the evidence and the case would be remitted for the tribunal to consider whether or not the procedure had been complied with and, if so, whether or not either side had manipulated a situation unfair to W.

WAILES DOVE BITUMASTIC *v*. WOOLCOCKS [1977] I.C.R. 817, E.A.T.

985. —— calculation of payment—normal working hours
[Contracts of Employment Act 1972 (c. 53), Sched. 2, para. 1 (1).]

An employee who is entitled to overtime when employed for more than a fixed number of hours in a week has normal working hours for the purposes of Sched. 2 of the Act even though he is not obliged to work a minimum number of hours per week.

F, an agricultural worker, was not obliged to work a specified number of hours per week but worked as many hours as the job demanded. His wages were regulated by the Agricultural Wages Order 1976 which provided that he was entitled to overtime for hours worked in excess of 40 in a week. He often worked 50 or 60 hours in a week. F was made redundant and claimed a redundancy payment. The industrial tribunal found that he had "normal working hours " within the meaning of Sched. 2 to the Act, namely 40 hours per week, and that his redundancy payment should not include overtime. F appealed on the ground that there were no fixed number of hours in excess of which he was entitled to overtime within Sched. 2, para. 1 (1) to the Act therefore he had no normal working hours so that his pay included overtime. *Held*, dismissing the appeal, that there was a fixed number of hours within Sched. 2, para. 1 (1) to the Act and therefore he had normal working hours and his overtime should not be included in calculating the amount of his redundancy payment. (*Tarmac Roadstone Holdings* v. *Peacock* [1973] C.L.Y. 1103 applied.)

FOX *v*. C. WRIGHT (FARMERS) [1978] I.C.R. 98, E.A.T.

986. —— cessation of business—retirement of immediate employer only
[Redundancy Payments Act 1965 (c. 62), s. 1 (2) (*a*).]

An employee whose employment determines upon his immediate employer giving up the business is entitled to a redundancy payment notwithstanding that the employer's own erstwhile employer continues in business.

An employee was employed by the sub-postmistress at a sub-post office until the employer retired and gave up running the business. The employee's claim for a redundancy payment on the grounds that her dismissal was due to her employer ceasing to carry on the business, within the meaning of s. 1 (2) (*a*) of the 1965 Act, was dismissed by an industrial tribunal who ruled that the " business " was that of the Post Office and that such business was continuing. *Held*, allowing the employee's appeal, that the tribunal had placed an unwarranted narrow interpretation upon s. 1 (2) (*a*), since it sufficed that the person in immediate control of the business ceased to carry it on.

THOMAS *v.* JONES [1978] I.C.R. 274, E.A.T.

987. —— **change in place of work—trial period—expiry**

L, a switchboard operator who was not " mobile " under her employment contract, agreed to move to her employers' new premises on a trial basis. She was never served notice of dismissal, but gave notice of resignation after two months at the new premises. *Held*, inter alia, that L was entitled to a redundancy payment and was not disentitled to such a payment by the four-week trial period introduced by the Redundancy Payments Act 1965, as amended, under which, in some cases, an employee shall be regarded as not having been dismissed by reason of the ending of his employment under a previous contract, since for those provisions to apply, the circumstances must be such that, without the provisions, the employee would be regarded as having been dismissed. In these circumstances, L had, by consent, merely postponed the decision whether to treat the contract as repudiated. The only time dismissal takes place is when the employee decides not to continue in the employment before expiry of a reasonable time. If the employers take no steps to inquire what the employee is going to do, the trial period continues until the employee decides or until it would be unreasonable to consider it to be continuing. (*Shields Furniture v. Goff* [1973] C.L.Y. 1095 referred to): AIR CANADA *v.* LEE [1978] I.R.L.R. 392, E.A.T.

988. —— **change of ownership of business**

[Redundancy Payments Act 1965 (c. 62), s. 13 (1).] H.P. Co. manufactured suits for their shops in factories at Dagenham and Blantyre. In January 1977 E.M. Co. took over H.P. Co.'s enterprise at Blantyre, taking over the lease, acquiring the fixtures, retaining the workforce on the same terms and taking over the work in progress and manufacturing for the same customers. *Held*, allowing H.P. Co.'s appeal against a finding that M and other employees were entitled to a redundancy payment, that the tribunal had erred in finding that there had not been a change in the ownership of H.P. Co.'s business within s. 13 (1) of the 1965 Act rather than a mere sale of certain of their assets. That E.M. Co. effectively took over the business as a going concern was a very strong factor indicating transfer: HECTOR POWE *v.* MELON [1978] I.R.L.R. 258, E.A.T.

989. —— **death of employer—employment by personal representative**

[Redundancy Payments Act 1965 (c. 62), Sched. 4, paras. 3, 4 (as amended by Employment Protection Act 1975 (c. 71), Sched. 16, Pt. I, para. 23).]

Provisions for entitlement to redundancy payments on the death of an employer apply only where the employees do not remain in the employment of the personal representatives.

An employer, R, died. His widow and personal representatives continued to employ and pay his employees for three months until his business was sold to a company, for whom his employees then worked. On their claim for redundancy payments, *held*, allowing the widow's appeal, that para. 4 of Sched. 4 to the Redundancy Payments Act 1965 applied only where employees did not remain in the employment of the personal representative and that the case should be remitted to the tribunal to determine whether there had in fact been a renewal of their contracts of employment or a re-engagement of the employees. It was not enough to show that the employees had worked for the widow for a short time after the death.

RANGER *v.* BROWN [1978] I.C.R. 603, E.A.T.

990. —— **dismissal—completion of apprenticeship—no entitlement to redundancy payment**

[Redundancy Payments Act 1965 (c. 62), s. 30.]

The due termination of an apprentice's contract operates as a dismissal due to non-re-engagement rather than redundancy, but there is no right to a redundancy payment on refusal of employment.

An apprentice was told just before the expiry of a four-year contract that he could not be employed as a fitter, and was given a redundancy payment. The employers then applied for a redundancy rebate to the Secretary of State, which was refused. A tribunal found the dismissal was not attributable to redundancy. *Held*, dismissing the employers' appeal, that the nature of the contract of apprenticeship was such that it was not renewable at the end of the fixed term. Dismissal was therefore attributable to non-re-employment with a fresh contract rather than redundancy, and the employers, not being obliged to make a redundancy payment, were not entitled to a rebate. (*Secretary of State for Employment* v. *Globe Elastic Thread* [1978] C.L.Y. 1016 distinguished.)

NORTH EAST COAST SHIPREPAIRERS v. SECETARY OF STATE FOR EMPLOYMENT [1978] I.C.R. 755, E.A.T.

991. —— —— **failure to consult trade union—before dismissal.** See BARLEY v. AMEY ROADSTONE CORP. (No. 2), § 1155.

992. —— —— **date when proposals made by a subsidiary company**
[Employment Protection Act 1975 (c. 71), s. 99 (3) (5).]
Proposals for redundancy are not necessarily made when a parent company notifies a subsidiary company of them.

The parent company notified a subsidiary that redundancies would be needed in its workforce. A meeting was fixed for the subsidiary with the workforce, for February 14, 1977, general discussions took place and a further meeting was fixed for February 21. On February 18 the trade union complained that there had been a failure to consult about the redundancies. The tribunal held that the complaint was premature. *Held*, dismissing the union's appeal, that the subsidiary company was not the same as the parent, so that the complaint was premature, the initial consultation having taken place only on February 14.

NATIONAL AND LOCAL GOVERNMENT OFFICERS ASSOCIATION v. NATIONAL TRAVEL (MIDLANDS) [1978] I.C.R. 598, E.A.T.

993. —— —— **further considerations—compensation**
Once it is established that an employee's selection for dismissal for redundancy was not unfair, an industrial tribunal, having considered whether there was adequate consultation or effort by the employers to find the employee alternative employment, should then go on to consider what would have been the result if the employers had acted properly.

B Co. ran out of money for research. They therefore made a number of managers, including C, redundant. The industrial tribunal found that C had been fairly selected for redundancy, but that there had been a failure of consultation and a failure to do all that B Co. might have done to find C alternative employment, and that therefore the dismissal was unfair. On appeal by B Co., *held*, allowing the appeal, that having reached that decision, the tribunal should have gone on to consider what would have been the result had B Co. acted properly, *i.e.* if the employee would still have been dismissed, and if so, would the dismissal have been unfair, and if so whether compensation should be awarded. The case would be remitted to the tribunal for further consideration.

BRITISH UNITED SHOE MACHINERY CO. v. CLARKE [1978] I.C.R. 70, E.A.T.

994. —— —— **only after individual notices issued—whether sufficient**
[Employment Protection Act 1975 (c. 71), s. 99.]
To comply with s. 99 of the Employment Protection Act 1975, the beginning of consultation with trade union representatives about a dismissal for redundancy must precede the giving of the notice of dismissal.

On October 28, 1976, the council's education committee authorised the immediate despatch of notices to part-time teachers terminating their contracts of employment in order to reduce expenditure. By a letter dated October 29, 1976, the council informed the teachers' trade union of the redundancies. A tribunal dismissed the union's complaint that the council had failed to comply with the consultation requirements under s. 99 of the Employment Protection

Act 1975. On appeal by the union, *held*, allowing the appeal, that the tribunal had erred, and that the council had failed to comply with s. 99. Accordingly, the case would be remitted to an industrial tribunal for re-hearing.

NATIONAL UNION OF TEACHERS *v.* AVON COUNTY COUNCIL (1978) 76 L.G.R. 403, E.A.T.

995. —— —— protective award—discretion

[Employment Protection Act 1975 (c. 71), ss. 99, 101 (5).] G.D. Co. went into receivership on August 16, 1977, and contacted the union regarding redundancies on August 23 or 24, 1977, and the receiver sent letters of immediate dismissal to all employees on August 26, 1977. The tribunal declared that G.D. Co. had contravened s. 99 of the 1975 Act in failing to comply with its redundancy consultation requirements, but declined to make a protective award since the default was not serious in consequence or degree as consultations could not have affected the receiver's inevitable decision. *Held,* that the tribunal had erred in concentrating upon whether the employer was at fault and in failing to assess the situation in the light of all the circumstances " having regard to the seriousness of the . . . default " and then to decide what is " just and equitable," as required by s. 101 (5). An important element is the great disruption created by immediate dismissal for redundancy: TRANSPORT AND GENERAL WORKERS UNION *v.* GAINSBOROUGH DISTRIBUTORS (U.K.) [1978] I.R.L.R. 460, E.A.T.

996. —— —— —— length of period

[Employment Protection Act 1975 (c. 71), s. 101.]

The primary consideration in determining the length of a protective period awarded under s. 101 (5) of the Employment Protection Act 1975 should be to compensate the employees rather than to penalise the employers for the latter's default.

Without prior consultation, the employers gave to their employees' trade union notice that two factories were to be closed and the employees made redundant, in one case the proposed closure being 14 days after the notice and in the other 64 days. An industrial Tribunal made a declaration that the employers had failed to consult the union as to the redundancies as required by s. 99 of the Act and made protective awards of 60 days' duration in favour of all the employees. On appeal, the employers challenged the length of the awards. *Held,* allowing the appeal in part, that although the seriousness of an employers' default was a relevant consideration, the primary object of such awards should be to compensate employees for their employers' default; and that since the employers should have given the union 60 days' notice and the employees a further 14 days' notice thereafter, in the case of the employees at the first factory the award was appropriate; but that in the case of the second factory the period would be reduced to 30 days (" on a broad equitable approach ") since they were in fact given substantial notice.

TALKE FASHIONS *v.* AMALGAMATED SOCIETY OF TEXTILE WORKERS AND KINDRED TRADES [1977] I.C.R. 833, E.A.T.

997. —— —— recognition

[Employment Protection Act 1975 (c. 71), s. 99 (1) (8).]

Where there is de facto recognition of a union by an employer, the requirements as to consultation before redundancy must be complied with.

On January 31, 1977, employees were told that the warehouse in which they worked would be closing on February 26. The union area organiser complained of lack of consultation. A protective award of 40 days was made. *Held,* dismissing the employers' appeal, that there was, in aggregate, clear evidence of recognition of the union by the employer, and that, as there were no special circumstances exempting the employer from the obligation of consultation, the award should stand.

JOSHUA WILSON AND BROS. *v.* UNION OF SHOP, DISTRIBUTIVE AND ALLIED WORKERS [1978] I.C.R. 614, E.A.T.

998. —— —— " special circumstances "

[Employment Protection Act 1975 (c. 71), s. 99.] K Co. were in financial difficulty in early 1977 and from the end of April sought a purchaser for the business as a going concern. The last prospective purchaser disappeared at the end of June when a receiver was appointed who immediately gave notice of redundancy to the whole workforce. *Held*, dismissing the union's appeal, that the tribunal were entitled to find special circumstances making it not reasonably practicable for K Co. to comply with the consultation provisions of s. 99 of the 1975 Act. K Co. were not " proposing " to make the workforce redundant, until the receiver was appointed. An employer only " proposed " to dismiss when he formed a view of the number of employees to be dismissed, when and how, although this does not entitle employers to shut their eyes to the obvious. Furthermore, compliance with s. 99 would have been fatal to the delicate negotiations for sale of the business even if K Co. had been " proposing " dismissal: ASSOCIATION OF PATTERNMAKERS AND ALLIED CRAFTSMEN *v.* KIRVIN [1978] I.R.L.R. 318, E.A.T.

999. ──── ──── **ignorance of provision**
[Employment Protection Act 1975 (c. 71), s. 99 (8).]
Ignorance of a statutory requirement to consult a union is not a " special circumstance " which makes it impractical to consult the union.
The employers wishing to dismiss an employee for redundancy consulted the D.O.E. and were wrongly told there was no need for prior consultation with the union. The union applied for a protective award, but the tribunal held that the misinformation to the employers was a " special circumstance " within the meaning of s. 99 (8) and that no protective award would be made. On the union's appeal, *held*, allowing the appeal, that the tribunal had erred in law, and that ignorance of a statutory requirement of consultation was not a special circumstance within the meaning of the 1975 Act.
UNION OF CONSTRUCTION, ALLIED TRADES AND TECHNICIANS *v.* H. ROOKE AND SON [1978] I.C.R. 818, E.A.T.

1000. ──── **insolvency**
[Employment Protection Act 1975 (c. 71), ss. 99 (8), 101 (2).]
" Special circumstances " for failure to give notification of pending redundancies means circumstances which are uncommon or out of the ordinary. Insolvency is not enough.
The employers were in financial difficulties. When their last money-raising attempt failed they closed, and declared redundancies on the same day. On the union's complaint that the requirements of consultation had not been observed, the employers contended that they had held a genuine hope of continuing trading such as to amount to " special circumstances " within the meaning of s. 99 (8) of the Employment Protection Act 1975. *Held*, allowing their appeal in part from an award of 49 days' pay, and allowing a cross-appeal by the union that " special circumstances " meant circumstances which were uncommon and out of the ordinary, so that insolvency alone was not " special circumstances " within the meaning of the section.
CLARKS OF HOVE *v.* BAKERS' UNION [1978] 1 W.L.R. 1207, C.A.

1001. ──── **Industrial Tribunal decisions**
Failure to consult union—earliest possible opportunity
TRANSPORT AND GENERAL WORKERS' UNION *v.* NATIONWIDE HAULAGE [1978] I.R.L.R. 143 (on May 8, 1977, NH Co. announced their intention to cease night trunking work from May 13, 1977. Five night workers refused offers of alternative employment with reduced pay and were dismissed on May 13. Proposals were then put to tramp drivers which led to some of them being made redundant on May 30. *Held*, that (1) the 60-day minimum period of consultation with the TGWU under the Employment Protection Act 1975, s. 99 (3) (*b*), did not apply because there was no intention to dismiss 10 or more employees at the time the first proposal was made; (2) NH Co. had failed to consult the union " at the earliest opportunity " about both sets of redundancies under s. 99 (3); (3) the fact that NH Co. proposed to dismiss employees at a date so near in the future that there was no time for consultation could not be said to have made it not reasonably practicable to begin consultations " at the earliest opportunity." Losses had been continuing for months previously; (4) it was unnecessary to consider individual circum-

stances in determining the protective award since only the potential rather than actual consequences for employees could be considered in practice).

Outworker having contract of service

D'AMBROGIO *v.* HYMAN JACOBS [1978] I.R.L.R. 236 (D'A, a machinist, worked at home from a date about three months after commencing employment. when the business was closed down, she was refused a redundancy payment on the ground that she was an outworker. *Held*, that D'A was an employee with a contract of service, as opposed to a contract for services, in view of the degree of control by HJ Co. to which she had been subject, which in this case was sufficient to create the relationship of master and servant. Accordingly, she was not disentitled from receiving a redundancy payment).

Selection—discrimination against unmarried person

PICKERING *v.* KINGSTON MOBILE UNITS [1978] I.R.L.R. 102 (KMU selected P for redundancy in preference to another with less service because P was a bachelor and the other was married with four children. *Held*, that the selection was unfair. It was unreasonable to discriminate against unmarried as opposed to married people).

1002. —— new post created—whether necessary—dismissal
[Redundancy Payments Act 1965 (c. 62), s. 1 (2) (*b*).]
Where there is no evidence to show that the creation of a new post was necessary, when the occupant of that post is subsequently dismissed, it cannot be said that he was dismissed for redundancy.

R was manager of a cash-and-carry business taken over by another company. A manager was appointed in his place and he was given the title of assistant manager. There was no evidence that an assistant manager was needed. In order to cut management costs, R was subsequently dismissed. A tribunal held him to be redundant and dismissed his claim. *Held*, allowing R's appeal, that tribunals should avoid the use of expressions like " redundancy situation " which tend to produce error, and stick to the words of the statute; that as there was no evidence to show that an assistant manager had ever been needed, it could not be said that R's dismissal was due to redundancy within the meaning of the Act. R's dismissal was therefore unfair.

RANSON *v.* G. & W. COLLINS [1978] I.C.R. 765, E.A.T.

1003. —— notice in writing of claim
[Redundancy Payments Act 1965 (c. 62), s. 21 (*b*).]
The test of whether there is sufficient notice in writing of a claim for redundancy payment for the purposes of s. 21 (*b*) of the Redundancy Payments Act 1965, is whether the writing relied on is of such a character that the recipient would reasonably understand in all the circumstances of the case that it is the employee's intention to seek a redundancy payment.

E Co. told A that his contract would not be renewed. There was an oral discussion about his entitlement to redundancy payment, and subsequently A's solicitors wrote to E Co.'s solicitors in a letter headed " without prejudice " saying that they had not heard from them " in respect of A's claim for a redundancy payment." No settlement was reached and A applied to an industrial tribunal. The tribunal declined to hear the matter for lack of jurisdiction on the ground that there was no written notice within s. 21 of the Redundancy Payments Act 1965. On appeal by A, *held*, allowing the appeal, that in the circumstances, the combined effect of the letter and the discussion was that E Co. should have understood that A was seeking a redundancy payment, and therefore the requirements of s. 21 (*b*) were fulfilled. (*Hetherington* v. *Dependable Products* [1971] C.L.Y. 4056 followed.)

PRICE *v.* SMITHFIELD & ZWANENBERG GROUP [1978] I.C.R. 93, E.A.T.

1004. —— offer of suitable alternative employment—refusal—whether unreasonable
[Redundancy Payments Act 1965 (c. 62), s. 2 (5).] F applied for a redundancy payment. He had been offered suitable alternative employment but claimed that he had reasonably refused such offer. The tribunal found F's refusal of the offer unreasonable and took into account that S.R.C. had offered the only type of alternative employment which they had power to

offer. *Held*, dismissing F's appeal, that there are many factors other than those personal to the employee which may properly be taken into account in deciding whether or not a refusal was unreasonable under s. 2 (5) of the 1965 Act and that the employers offered the only type of alternative employment available was not necessarily irrelevant: FORRESTER *v.* STRATHCLYDE REGIONAL COUNCIL (1977) 12 I.T.R. 424, E.A.T.

1005. —— protective award—tribunal's discretion to make award—qualifying notice
[Employment Protection Act 1975 (c. 71), ss. 99, 101 (3), 103; Employment Protection Act 1975 (Commencement No. 2) Order 1976 (S.I. 1976 No. 144 (C. 5)), art. 3 (1) (3).]

An industrial tribunal is not entitled to make a protective award without hearing argument and addressing their minds to the question of whether they would exercise their discretion under s. 101 (3) of the Act.

The employers gave provisional notice to 12 employees that they would be made redundant within 90 days. A few days later ss. 99 and 101 of the Act were brought into force by the 1976 Order. Art. 3 (1) provided that ss. 99 and 101 would not apply to any dismissal which, pursuant to a qualifying notice given before the commencement date, was to take effect before the expiry of 90 days. Subsequently the employees were given formal notice specifying the date of dismissal. They complained that the employers had failed to comply with s. 99 of the Act and the employees were entitled to a protective award. The industrial tribunal heard argument only on the question of validity of the first notice for the purpose of art. 3 (1) and held that it did not comply with the requirements of art. 3 (3). The tribunal made a protective award but left the length and amount to be determined in the future. The employers applied for a review of the decision on the ground that the tribunal had failed to consider whether or not to exercise their discretion under s. 101 (3) of the Act. The application was refused and the employers appealed. *Held*, that (1) to satisfy the requirements of art. 3 (3) of the commencement order a qualifying notice had to be a notice terminating the employees contract of employment and specifying the date of dismissal; thus the first notice did not comply with the requirements and the qualifying notice was given after s. 99 of the Act came into force; (2) the tribunal could not be said to have exercised their discretion under s. 101 (3) of the Act and the employers were entitled to argue that no protective award should be made. *Quaere*: Whether an industrial tribunal has jurisdiction to deal with the amount of a protective award unless there are complaints by individual employees under s. 103 of the Act.

SIR ALFRED MCALPINE & SON (NORTHERN) *v.* FOULKES [1977] I.C.R. 748, E.A.T.

1006. —— —— whether each site a separate establishment
[Employment Protection Act 1975 (c. 71), s. 99 (3).]

Where a building firm dismisses employees from a number of different building sites, it is a question of fact for the industrial tribunal whether each site constitutes a separate establishment for the purposes of the statutory requirement of trade union consultation.

Without duly consulting the relevant trade union, the appellant company, which employed men upon a number of different building sites, dismissed 24 employees from eight different sites due to a trade recession. Upon the union seeking a declaration and protective award under s. 99 of the Act, the company contended that each site was a separate establishment (each being in the charge of a site foreman but connected by telephone to the company's office) and that the dismissals were therefore outside the controls imposed by s. 99 (3) (*b*) of the Act. The tribunal found for the union. *Held*, dismissing the company's appeal, that the tribunal's factual decision could not be said to be unreasonable.

BARRATT DEVELOPMENTS (BRADFORD) *v.* UNION OF CONSTRUCTION, ALLIED TRADES AND TECHNICIANS [1978] I.C.R. 319, E.A.T.

1007. —— redundancy payment—appeal of employers—no constructive dismissal
B, a long-distance lorry driver employed by P Co. since 1969, began work on a particular job in 1975. When the job ended in March 1976, he tried out

alternative work offered by P Co. but left after six weeks because he was earning less and the work was inconvenient. *Held,* allowing P Co.'s appeal against the award of a redundancy payment, that the tribunal were not entitled on these facts to find that B had been dismissed: G. PRIESTNER v. BALL (1977) 12 I.T.R. 451, E.A.T.

1008. —— —— continuity of employment

[Contracts of Employment Act 1972 (c. 53), Sched. 1, paras. 4, 5 (1) (c).] M worked for B Co. from 1957 to 1976. In August 1976 she took another job and went on a training course following a dispute about holidays and two weeks off ill. In October 1976 B Co. re-employed her at her request. The managing director told her her old contract stood, her duties and wages were the same and she received the maximum holiday entitlement under the Wages Council Order, not that applicable to new employees. *Held,* dismissing M's appeal, that the tribunal had correctly decided that since M had clearly repudiated her contract by taking other employment, her contract had been terminated and between August and October 1976 her relationship with B Co. had not been governed by a contract of employment within the 1972 Act, Sched. 1, para. 4. Accordingly her continuity of employment had been broken. Nor was M regarded as by arrangement or custom as continuing in employment within para. 5 (1) (c) as para. 5 (1) (c) only applies when the arrangement exists at the time when the absence began: MURPHY v. BIRRELL & SONS [1978] I.R.L.R. 458, E.A.T.

1009. —— —— employee on call

[Contracts of Employment Act 1972 (c. 53), Sched. 1.] A part-time fireman required to reach the station within 4 minutes if summoned, during the 102½ hours per week he was on call came within the terms of the 1972 Act. He therefore qualified for redundancy payment and compensation for unfair dismissal although his employment did not require him to be an active duty for " 21 hours or more weekly ": BULLOCK v. MERSEYSIDE COUNTY COUNCIL, *The Times,* November 9, 1978, C.A.

1010. —— —— entitlement—fixed term contract

[Redundancy Payments Act 1965 (c. 62), s. 15 (2) (4); Trade Union and Labour Relations Act 1974 (c. 52), Sched. 1, para. 21 (4).]

When, in considering entitlements to redundancy payments, it falls to be considered whether an employee was employed under a contract for a fixed term of two years or more, it is the final contract of employment which falls to be considered.

T worked for a period of 18 months. Her employers then offered her a seven-month contract which was not subsequently renewed. She applied for a redundancy payment and was given one by the tribunal. She also made a complaint for unfair dismissal which was dismissed by the tribunal on the basis that it was out of time, T having been aware of her rights within the time limit. *Held,* dismissing her appeal, that that finding was one of fact with which the appellate tribunal would not interfere, and, dismissing the employers' appeal against the award of a redundancy payment, that she had not been employed for a fixed period of two years or more because the contract which fell to be considered, for redundancy purposes, was the last contract for a period of only seven months.

OPEN UNIVERSITY v. TRIESMAN [1978] I.C.R. 524, E.A.T.

1011. —— —— failure to consider offer of new employment

[Redundancy Payments Act 1965 (c. 62), ss. 2 (4), 13.]

An employee dismissed for redundancy who fails to consider or investigate an offer of new employment expressed to be open to negotiation is not entitled to a redundancy payment.

Whilst in the process of being taken over by B, the employers on April 30 notified the applicant employee that from the following week he would be transferred to B and should report for work to B. The applicant failed to so report and continued working for the employers. On May 29 B offered the applicant new terms of employment, which terms the applicant rejected as his present employment had not been terminated. The employers on June 9 informed the applicant that their business was being run down and that B would re-engage the applicant on substantially similar terms, except that the applicant might be required to work away from his home area. The applicants' solicitors indicated their view that the applicant had been dismissed and rejected B's offer. On June 27 B repeated their offer, stating that the terms were open to negotiation; such offer was again rejected by the solicitors and on July 4 The applicant left his employment. An industrial tribunal awarded the applicant a redundancy payment, holding, inter alia, that the letter of April 30 amounted to a notice terminating his employment. *Held,* allowing the employers' appeal, that (1) although the April 30 letter was an anticipatory breach by the employers, it was of no effect since the employers did not enforce compliance with it; (2) the employee had not been dismissed but merely warned of the likelihood of future redundancy; and (3) even if the employee was dismissed, his failure to investigate the offer of June 27 debarred him from recovering compensation by virtue of ss. 2 (4) and 13 of the Act.

M. S. ROSE (HEATING) *v.* EDGINGTON [1977] I.C.R. 844, E.A.T.

1012. —— —— notice excluding right—service of notice

[Redundancy Payments Pension Regulations 1965 (S.I. 1965 No. 1932), reg. 5 (1) (*a*).]

A notice excluding the right to a redundancy payment must be served within a reasonable time.

B was made redundant while off sick. In October 1976 he claimed a redundancy payment. In January 1977 his employers served on him a written notice claiming that his pension entitlement cancelled out his entitlement to a redundancy payment. The tribunal awarded him a redundancy payment, holding that the employer's notice was served too late, it being after the date of the dismissal. *Held*, dismissing their appeal, that where no period for serving a notice was laid down, it must be done within a reasonable time. The proper time to serve the notice would usually be when the situation had matured, namely at the moment of dismissal.

STOWE-WOODWARD B.T.R. *v.* BEYNON [1978] I.C.R. 609, E.A.T.

1013. —— —— part-time employee—reduction to allow for holiday periods

A part-time teacher who is made redundant is entitled to a redundancy payment calculated by reference to his hourly rate of pay without any deduction by reason of a proportion of such pay relating to holiday periods.

The employee was employed part-time as a teacher, being remunerated at an hourly rate. When she was made redundant, the employers, upheld by an industrial tribunal, made a redundancy payment calculated upon the basis of a reduced hourly rate to allow for the fact part of the rate of pay related to holiday periods. *Held*, allowing the employee's appeal, that, in the absence of an agreement to the contrary, the employee was entitled to a payment based upon her actual rate of pay without deduction.

COLE *v.* BIRMINGHAM DISTRICT COUNCIL [1978] I.C.R. 1004, E.A.T.

1014. —— —— regular bonus—whether " remuneration "

The factory where M was employed closed down. When it reopened M was re-employed and was asked to operate a press in addition to her regular duties, for a bonus of £10 per week. She did so until made redundant. *Held,* dismissing the employers' appeal that the £10 per week bonus had correctly been ranked as remuneration for the purpose of computing M's redundancy payment: A & B MARCUSFIELD *v.* MELHUISH [1977] I.R.L.R. 484, E.A.T.

1015. —— —— transfer of business—continuity of employment

[Redundancy Payments Act 1965 (c. 62), ss. 8 (1), 13 (1).]

For the purpose of assessing entitlement to a redundancy payment, a business is deemed to have been transferred when the new employer takes over a going concern and operates the business without interruption.

The employer company contracted with a firm to take over the running of the firm's canteen, previously operated by the firm, the agreement, after an initial trial period, being terminable upon notice. Although the firm were to provide the premises and equipment, the company had exclusive use thereof. The existing canteen employees were employed by the company who wrote to them indicating their willingness to " continue your present contract." Less than two years later, a number of employees were made redundant, but their claim for redundancy payments was rejected on the ground that there had been no change in the ownership of the business within s. 13 (1) of the Act and that, accordingly, they had not been employed for 104 weeks, as required by s. 8 (1). *Held,* allowing the employees' appeals that (1) the business of running the canteen had been transferred to the company within the meaning of s. 13 (1), and that therefore the employees were entitled to redundancy payments; (2) the employees' alternative argument that the company was estopped from denying continuity of employment by its letters, failed, since the company had not intended to convey such a meaning therein. (*Evenden* v. *Guildford City Association Football Club* [1975] C.L.Y. 1143 and *Kenmir* v. *Frizzell* [1968] C.L.Y. 1421 applied.)

RASTILL *v.* AUTOMATIC REFRESHMENT SERVICES [1978] I.C.R. 289, E.A.T.

1016. —— —— **whether rebate payable to employer**

[Redundancy Payments Act 1965 (c. 62), s. 30 (1).]

An employer who is estopped from denying an employee's entitlement to a redundancy payment may recover a rebate out of the redundancy fund.

An employee, who had worked for the same company since 1948, agreed in 1970 to a transfer to another employer who assured him that his employment would be regarded as continuous for the purposes of accrued redundancy entitlement. When the employee was made redundant in 1975, an industrial tribunal held that although he was not entitled under the Act to payment based upon service since 1948, his employers were estopped from denying his entitlement by reason of the 1970 assurance. Thereafter the employers applied successfully to a tribunal for a declaration of their entitlement to a rebate under s. 30 of the Act. *Held,* dismissing the Secretary of State's appeal, that the employers were entitled to a rebate notwithstanding that the employee's entitlement thereto arose from an assurance to which the Secretary of State was not party. (Decision of E.A.T. affirmed; *Evenden* v. *Guildford City Association Football Club* [1975] C.L.Y. 1147 applied.)

SECRETARY OF STATE FOR EMPLOYMENT *v.* GLOBE ELASTIC THREAD CO. [1978] 3 W.L.R. 679, C.A.

1017. —— **selection procedure—degree of consultation with union**

[Code of Practice, para. 46.] CP Co. reached a union/management agreement as to selection for redundancy whereby absenteeism, timekeeping, efficiency, etc., would be considered and then selection would be on the basis of seniority. *Held,* allowing CP Co.'s appeal against a finding of unfair selection, that the tribunal had erred in law in finding CP Co.'s failure to disclose to union representatives the points system used for assessing absenteeism, etc., to be a failure to consult sufficiently as required by the Code of Practice, para. 46. Employers need only show that selection for redundancy is fair in general terms: CLYDE PIPEWORKS *v.* FOSTER [1978] I.R.L.R. 313, E.A.T.

1018. —— —— **employers' decision, not that of tribunal**

Where employers operate an agreed redundancy system of " last in, first out, all other things being equal," it is for them, rather than for the tribunal, to decide whether such other things are equal.

S was 25. He was dismissed for redundancy. The employers, operating an agreed system of " last in, first out, all other things being equal " had to choose between him and another man of 65 who had been with them longer. They dismissed S. The tribunal held that all other things were not equal, in view of the age differential, and decided that the other employee should have been dismissed. *Held,* allowing the employers' appeal, that it was for them, and not for the tribunal to decide whether other things were equal.

CAMPER & NICHOLSON *v.* SHAW [1978] I.C.R. 520, E.A.T.

1019. —— —— **industrial action—failure to re-engage**

Striking employees were dismissed by F.I. Co. After the strike there was insufficient work to justify re-engagement of all the original employees. L was not selected for an offer of re-engagement because of his previous poor conduct. C, a supervisor, was selected for redundancy some time after the strike because, unlike some supervisors, she had not agreed to carry out work which she would ordinarily have supervised during the strike. *Held,* that the tribunal had erred (1) in finding F.I. Co.'s failure to offer re-engagement to L to have been fair, since the sole reason for the failure was L's previous conduct, not the lack of work; (2) in selecting C for redundancy since, although loyalty was a relevant consideration, in the absence of a customary arrangement or agreed redundancy procedure, it was unfair of F.I. Co. not to follow the normal practice of consulting with the union and candidates for redundancy: LAFFIN AND CALLAGHAN *v.* FASHION INDUSTRIES [1978] I.R.L.R. 448, E.A.T.

1020. —— —— no restriction on work-area

H, employed originally as a packer, was moved to other work making fittings. She was selected for redundancy when a redundancy situation arose in the fittings section. A tribunal found her dismissal unfair because others with less service in other departments, including packing, were retained. *Held,* dismissing T & BM Co.'s appeal, that it is not correct that an employer is restricted to selecting employees for redundancy from the section in which redundancies have been established: THOMAS & BETTS MANUFACTURING CO. *v.* HARDING [1978] I.R.L.R. 213, E.A.T.

1021. —— —— other employees in same situation not dismissed—whether employer acted reasonably

[Trade Union and Labour Relations Act 1974 (c. 52), Sched. 1, para. 6 (7) (8).]

If an industrial tribunal finds that there is no failure to apply an agreed procedure in circumstances constituting redundancy which apply equally to other employees within para. 6 (7) of Sched. 1 to the Trade Union and Labour Relations Act 1974, it should then go on to consider whether the employer acted reasonably in treating the redundancy as sufficient reason for dismissal under para. 6 (8).

E, having had a dispute with A, a fellow employee, over a union matter, was allowed to exchange duties with B, who had been employed for a shorter time than E. E was then made redundant and B was not. The industrial tribunal found that there was no failure to apply an agreed procedure in circumstances constituting redundancy which applied equally to B within para. 6 (7) of the Trade Union and Labour Relations Act 1974; but it also found that the dismissal was unfair within para. 6 (8) in that E had not been warned that unless he resolved his dispute with A, he risked being made redundant. On appeal by the employer, *held,* dismissing the appeal, that the industrial tribunal, having found that para. 6 (7) did not apply, was right then to consider para. 6 (8); it could not be said that the conclusion reached could not have been reached by a tribunal properly directing itself, and it therefore must be upheld. (*Bessenden Properties* v. *Corness* [1978] C.L.Y. 1156 applied; *Vickers* v. *Smith* [1977] C.L.Y. 1182 and *Wells* v. *Derwent Plastics* [1978] C.L.Y. 2838 considered.) EARL OF BRADFORD *v.* JOWETT (No. 2) [1978] I.C.R. 431, E.A.T.

1022. —— —— whether unreasonable

[Trade Union and Labour Relations Act 1974 (c. 52), Sched. 1, para. 6 (8).]

It is not reasonable for employers to select a long-serving and satisfactory employee for redundancy in preference to very recent employees.

The employee, an electrician, was employed by electrical contractors from July 1976 and he worked satisfactorily for them upon a number of different contracts. In March 1977 the employers engaged two further electricians to work on a contract upon which the employee had at one time been employed. The employers then purported to dismiss the employee for redundancy upon the basis that the particular contract upon which he was then working had come to an end. An industrial tribunal upheld a complaint of unfair dismissal. *Held,* dismissing the employers' appeal, that the employers had not acted with the fairness of reasonable employers in selecting the employee for redundancy; it was not reasonable for the employers to regard each contract upon which they worked as completely separate.

N. C. WATLING & CO. *v.* RICHARDSON [1978] I.C.R. 1049, E.A.T.

1023. —— strike—whether selection unfair

[Trade Union and Labour Relations Act 1974 (c. 52), Sched. 1, para. 6 (8).]

The fact that men have been absent from work because of a strike is a factor which an employer is entitled to take into account when selecting for redundancy.

H, a Newmarket trainer, employed a number of stable lads who were members of the T.G.W.U. In May 1975, six of the lads supported an official strike. By July 23, when the strike ended, the number of horses at H's establishment dropped and redundancies were necessary. H selected five of the lads who had been on strike and dismissed them for redundancy. The dismissed lads claimed compensation for unfair dismissal on the ground that they had been unfairly selected. The industrial tribunal dismissed the applications, holding that there was a genuine redundancy situation and that H's belief that he might lose the loyalty of the remaining lads if he dismissed any of those who did not strike was reasonable and the selection was not unfair. The dismissed lads appealed. *Held,* dismissing the appeals by a majority, that H's belief that selection of employees who had continued working during the strike would have caused friction was reasonable; that he was not obliged to consult the union before making his selection and therefore the decision of the tribunal that H had acted reasonably within para. 6 (8) of Sched. 1 of the Act was correct.

CRUICKSHANK *v.* HOBBS [1977] I.C.R. 725, E.A.T.

1024. —— time off to seek other employment—evidence of appointment—refusal of alternative employment

[Employment Protection Act 1975 (c. 71), s. 61 (7).]

It is not a condition precedent to an employee being allowed time off to seek alternative employment that he has, or should produce evidence of, an appointment for an interview.

After full consultation with all concerned, the employers asked the employee, a machinist, to move to another department on the same terms as a trainee capstan operator, there being a shortage of work for machinists. The employee refused. He was offered two weeks' redundancy pay and two weeks' notice. During such period the employee took time off to seek another job but the employers refused to pay him for such time off when he failed to produce evidence of an appointment. They further withdrew the offer of a redundancy payment. An industrial tribunal dismissed the employee's claims for unfair dismissal, a redundancy payment and, under s. 61 (7) of the 1975 Act, for payment in respect of the time off. *Held,* that (1) there were no grounds for interfering with the tribunal's findings of fact that the employee had been fairly selected for redundancy and had unreasonably refused the offer of alternative employment; (2) evidence of an appointment was relevant to a a claim under s. 61 (7) only inasmuch as it related to the reasonableness of the employers' conduct. (The employers undertook to pay half a day's pay to the employee.)

DUTTON *v.* HAWKER SIDDELEY AVIATION [1978] I.C.R. 1057, E.A.T.

1025. Restraint of trade—professional cricketers—exclusion from test and county cricket—inducing breach of contract

The International Cricket Conference and the Test and County Cricket Board, in excluding from test and county cricket respectively professional cricketers who had contracted to play for the private " Packer circus," acted unlawfully in restraint of trade and in inducing such cricketers to break their contracts.

The I.C.C., whose members consisted of the appointees of the cricketing governing bodies of test-match playing countries, arranged test matches to be played and controlled the qualifications of those permitted to play therein. The T.C.C.B. whose members were, principally, the English counties playing first-class cricket, regulated county cricket, its authority being conferred upon it by its members (who did not include the players). An Australian promoter signed contracts with a number of the world's leading players including the plaintiffs, three well-known English cricketers, whereby the plaintiffs undertook to be available to play in matches organised by the promoter between September and March, although the promoter did not expressly undertake that such matches

would take place. When news of such contracts became public in May 1977, the
I.C.C. met and resolved that any player who remained contracted to play in
such private matches by October 1977 would, subject to certain limitations,
be disqualified from playing in test matches. The T.C.C.B. made known that a
similar ban would apply to county matches and would apply for two years after
the last private match in which a cricketer played or for which he made himself
available. The plaintiff cricketers sought declarations against the I.C.C. and
the T.C.C.B. that, inter alia, their rulings were unlawful as in restraint of trade.
The promoter also claimed a declaration that both bodies had acted unlawfully
in inducing the players to act in breach of contract. The defendants contended,
inter alia, that the contracts with the promoter were void and further, or alternatively, that as " employers' associations " they were exempt from proceedings
in tort by reason of s. 28 (2) of the Trade Union and Labour Relations Act
1974. *Held*, that (1) the contracts were neither void nor voidable since there
was an implied term that the promoter would at least organise a cricketing tour
in Australia for which the players would be paid; (2) since the contracts were
enforceable and since the deferment of the change of rules for qualification to
play in test and county matches was clearly intended to put pressure on the
contracting players to withdraw from their contracts, the defendants had acted,
albeit in good faith, without justification in inducing a breach of contract;
(3) neither defendant had succeeded in showing that it had acted reasonably
in imposing a bar which was prima facie in restraint of trade; (4) under its constitution the I.C.C. was not an employers' association since its members were
regarded as being the member counties as opposed to the cricketing governing
body; and (5) the T.C.C.B. although largely composed of " employers " was not
an employers' association within the meaning of the Act since it did not regulate relations between employers and employees. (*Aspdin* v. *Austin* (1844) 5
Q.B. 671, *Devonald* v. *Rosser & Sons* [1906] 2 K.B. 728, *Rookes* v. *Barnard*
[1964] C.L.Y. 3703, *Torquay Hotel Co.* v. *Cousins* [1969] C.L.Y. 3574, *Nordenfelt* v. *Maxim Nordenfelt Guns and Ammunition Co.* [1894] A.C. 535 and
Eastham v. *Newcastle United Football Club* [1963] C.L.Y. 3459 applied.)
    GREIG *v.* INSOLE; WORLD SERIES CRICKET PTY. *v.* INSOLE [1978] 1 W.L.R.
302, Slade J.

1026. —— restrictive covenant—threat of breach. See LITTLEWOODS ORGANISATION
v. HARRIS, § 2941.

1027. Service agreement—restrictive undertaking—injunction to restrain breach. See
THOMAS MARSHALL (EXPORTS) *v.* GUINLE, § 916.

1028. Sex discrimination—age of retirement—fixture exempt under Act
    [Sex Discrimination Act 1975 (c. 65), ss. 1 (1) (*a*), 6 (2) (*b*) (4).]
    Provision in relation to death or retirement, which is exempted from the
Sex Discrimination Act 1975 by s. 6 (4), covers all arrangements relating to
retirement including the fixing of a retirement age.
    The area health authority's retirement ages were 60 for women and 65 for
men. W, a woman hospital worker was dismissed at 60. She claimed compensation for unlawful discrimination against her under s. 6 of the Sex Discrimination Act 1975, on the ground that a man would not have had to retire until he
was 65. The tribunal held that s. 6 (4) applied so as to exclude such a provision from being discriminatory, and they dismissed W's complaint. On appeal
by W. *held*, dismissing the appeal, that the fixing of a retirement age also
came within s. 6 (4) and was exempted.
    ROBERTS *v.* CLEVELAND AREA HEALTH AUTHORITY [1978] I.C.R. 370, E.A.T.

1029. —— appeal—grounds on which appeal lies against dismissal of complaint
    [Sex Discrimination Act 1975 (c. 65), s. 6 (2) (*b*).]
    On an appeal from an industrial tribunal's decision, the onus is on the
appellant to show that the tribunal had erred in law, or that there was no
evidence to support the finding or that no reasonable tribunal could have
reached the same conclusion.
    M, a female student, was dismissed from her part-time job at a university
hall of residence. She complained to an industrial tribunal that the employers
in dismissing her had unlawfully discriminated against her by reason of sex

within s. 6 (2) (*b*) of the Act. The tribunal found that there was no evidence of discrimination and dismissed the complaint. M appealed. *Held,* dismissing the appeal, that (1) where it was established that there had been an act of discrimination and that one party to the discrimination was male and the other party female a prima facie case of discrimination on the ground of sex was raised; (2) M had not discharged the onus of proof required of an appellant and the tribunal's decision could not be interfered with.

MOBERLY *v.* COMMONWEALTH HALL (UNIVERSITY OF LONDON) [1977] I.C.R. 791, E.A.T.

1030. —— applicants for employment—burden of proof—information to be supplied by employers
[Sex Discrimination Act 1975 (c. 65), ss. 6, 74.]
A complainant alleging unlawful sexual discrimination by employers in selecting employees bears the burden of proving such discrimination.

Per curiam: Only in exceptional or frivolous cases should an industrial tribunal dismiss a complaint of sexual discrimination at the close of a complainant's case.

The complainant was one of four male applicants who, together with 13 females, were interviewed for positions as clerical workers by the employers whose employees were mainly female. The complainant was unsuccessful: four women and one man were offered employment. The complainant, having made a complaint of sexual discrimination, sent to the employers a questionnaire (pursuant to s. 74 of the Act) demanding details of the sex, age, names and addresses of the selected applicants; he later asked for particulars of their qualifications. The employers supplied details of sex and age only. The tribunal dismissed his complaint. *Held,* dismissing his appeal, that the complainant had failed to prove discrimination; that although it was desirable that details of qualifications (but not names and addresses) be supplied, the complainant had not been prejudiced by the employers' failure to supply such details since all the applicants possessed the necessary minimum educational qualifications.

OXFORD *v.* DEPARTMENT OF HEALTH AND SOCIAL SECURITY [1977] I.C.R. 884, E.A.T.

1031. —— benefits continuing after retirement—whether provisions " in relation to retirement "
[Sex Discrimination Act 1975 (c. 65), s. 6 (2) (4).]
To provide concessionary travel for the families of male employees after their retirement but to provide concessionary travel only for retired female employees themselves and not their families, is unlawful.

B gave to male employees concessionary travel facilities for themselves and their families, continuing after their retirement. Female employees' concessions ended, in respect of their families, on their retirement. The tribunal found that the scheme was a " provision in relation to retirement " so as to prevent the applicant from claiming about the discrimination. *Held,* allowing her appeal, that she was not so prevented, and that there had been an unlawful discrimination. The access to benefits was a present one and was not part of a specific plan for retirement, even though the effects of the policy would not be felt by the applicant until after her retirement.

GARLAND *v.* BRITISH RAIL ENGINEERING [1978] I.C.R. 495, E.A.T.

1032. —— detriment—requirement to wear overalls
[Sex Discrimination Act 1975 (c. 65), s. 60.]
An employer is entitled to a large measure of discretion in controlling the image of his establishment, including the appearance of staff, and especially so when they come into contact with the public.

E Co. owned a bookshop. By the company's rules, female employees were not allowed to wear trousers and were obliged to wear overalls, and male employees were not allowed to wear tee-shirts. A, a female employee, persisted in wearing trousers and was dismissed. She complained to an industrial tribunal that the overall restriction was an unlawful " detriment " to her within s. 6 (2) (*b*) of the Sex Discrimination Act 1975 and that both restrictions were "less favourable treatment" within s. 1 (1) (*a*). The tribunal found that there was no discrimination. On appeal by A, *held*, dismissing the appeal that an employer had a large measure of discretion in such matters. The overall restriction was not serious enough to be a "detriment," and since there could be no such restriction as the trouser restriction in relation to men, there could not be said to be less favourable treatment; alternatively, in view of the tee-shirt restriction, both sexes were restricted as to clothing. Accordingly the complaint had been correctly dismissed. (*Peake* v. *Automotive Products* [1977] C.L.Y. 1077 applied.)

SCHMIDT v. AUSTICKS BOOKSHOPS [1978] I.C.R. 85, E.A.T.

1033. —— —— women not required to do certain work—power to order discontinuance

[Sex Discrimination Act 1975 (c. 65), ss. 6 (2) (*b*), 65.]

An industrial tribunal may declare a practice to contravene the Sex Discrimination Act 1975 but has no power to order its discontinuance.

Male and female employees were employed as quality examiners. Only the males were required periodically to work in a " dirty " shop, protective clothing and showers being provided. A higher rate was paid for work in such conditions. A male employee complained that the employers' practice contravened the Act. An industrial tribunal made a declaration accordingly and further ordered the employers to discontinue the practice, recommending the provision of separate showers for women employees. *Held*, that the practice amounted to unlawful discrimination notwithstanding that a higher rate of pay applied, but that the tribunal had no power to do other than make a declaration.

MINISTRY OF DEFENCE v. JEREMIAH [1978] I.C.R. 984, E.A.T.

1034. —— discovery—confidential documents

[County Court Rules, Ord. 14, rr. 1, 2; Industrial Tribunals (Labour Relations) Regulations 1974 (S.I. 1974 No. 1386), Sched., r. 4 (2) (*a*) (*b*).]

Orders for general discovery, *e.g.* of confidential reports on fellow employees, should not generally be made in discrimination cases and, if they are made, the documents should first be the subject of scrutiny by the chairman or judge.

In one case, a married woman trade unionist complained of discrimination. In the other, heard with it, an Asian made a similar claim. Both sought discovery of confidential reports on fellow employees who might have benefited from the alleged discrimination. On appeal from the industrial tribunal's decisions, the court had ordered the production of the reports. *Held*, allowing the employers' appeal, that general orders for discovery should not usually be made in such cases but specific documents might become discoverable if, after their scrutiny by the chairman (or by the judge in the county court) it was clear that the interests of justice demanded their disclosure.

SCIENCE RESEARCH COUNCIL v. NASSÉ; LEYLAND CARS v. VYAS [1978] 3 W.L.R. 754, C.A.

1035. —— —— principles to be applied

Dr. M and Ms B claimed to have been discriminated against in their applications to Reading and Essex Universities respectively for jobs. Dr. M obtained an order for discovery of references regarding other candidates taken up and any other documents submitted by other candidates. Ms B's application for discovery was rejected. *Held*, that (1) confidential reports, references or assessments by independent assessors to whom candidates' qualifications have been referred ought normally to be treated as sacrosanct; (2) in very rare circumstances it might be appropriate for the tribunal to inspect the documents concerned before giving a ruling; (3) the proper stage for an application for discovery of such documents is during the hearing if the point arises at which the complainant can say that in view of some of the answers given it is impossible for justice to be done without a sight of the documents; (4) accordingly the tribunal had wrongly ordered discovery in Dr. M's case and correctly excluded it in Ms B's case. (*Science Research Council* v. *Nassé*; *Leyland Cars* v. *Vyas* [1978] C.L.Y. 1034 applied): UNIVERSITY OF READING v. MACCORMACK; BUSFIELD v. UNIVERSITY OF ESSEX [1978] I.R.L.R. 491, E.A.T.

1036. —— failure to end discrimination after recommendation by tribunal
[Sex Discrimination Act 1975 (c. 65), s. 65 (1) (c), (3).] Women employees
were passed over for promotion, and in November 1976 their complaint to an
industrial tribunal on the ground of discrimination was upheld and a recommendation made under the 1975 Act that the employer should, within six
months, seriously consider each woman for promotion, disregarding their sex.
In November 1977, they complained of the failure to comply with this recommendation, and the tribunal considered the employer had reasonable grounds
for so doing and no compensation was ordered. *Held*, in dismissing the appeal,
it was the tribunal's discretion to award compensation under s. 65 (3) on the
particular facts of each case: NELSON *v.* TYNE AND WEAR PASSENGER TRANS-
PORT EXECUTIVE (1978) 122 S.J. 642, E.A.T.

1037. —— indirect—age limit of 28—fewer women able to apply
[Sex Discrimination Act 1975 (c. 65), s. 1 (1) (b).]
An imposition of an age limit of 28 may be discriminatory against women,
a large proportion of whom are occupied with children at that age.
The Civil Service advertised for applicants aged " at least 17½ and under 28
years of age." The applicant was 35. She complained that she had been
unlawfully discriminated against on the ground of sex. *Held*, allowing her
appeal, that the words " can comply with " [the age limitation] did not mean
theoretically possible, but practically possible. The case would be remitted to
the industrial tribunal to determine whether there was a substantially smaller
pool of women, perhaps drawn from a pool of qualified persons, than of men.
PRICE *v.* CIVIL SERVICE COMMISSION [1977] 1 W.L.R. 1417, E.A.T.
[For rehearing, see § 1038.]

1038. —— Industrial Tribunal decisions
Decency or privacy
WYLIE *v.* DEE & CO. (MENSWEAR) [1978] I.R.L.R. 103 (D & Co., men's
clothiers who already employed seven male sales assistants, refused to consider
W, a woman, to fill a vacancy for a sales assistant on the ground that the job
involved taking inside leg measurements. *Held*, that D & Co. had unlawfully
discriminated against W on grounds of sex. There was insufficient evidence that
the requirement to take inside leg measurements arose often and one of the
male assistants could take the measurement when necessary).

Maternity leave—right to return to work
EDGELL *v.* LLOYD'S REGISTER OF SHIPPING [1977] I.R.L.R. 463 (before
taking maternity leave E was employed as a book-keeper with authority to
sign cheques up to a certain amount, reporting direct to the manager, being
responsible for the accounts of LR Inspection and RTD British Division. When
she returned after the leave, she was offered a post as book-keeper on the same
grade dealing with LR Inspection alone, with no authority to sign cheques
and reporting to the supervisor. Her former part-time assistant was then
working full-time handling RTD British Division's accounts. E resigned after
one week. *Held*, that E's right to return to work after maternity leave had not
been contravened as the work offered was of the same nature and on the same
terms as her original job. The differences were not fundamental changes to her
contract of employment).

Maximum age limit of 28
PRICE *v.* CIVIL SERVICE COMMISSION [1978] I.R.L.R. 3 (the E.A.T. had
held that the upper age limit of 28 for candidates for entry into the Civil
Service as executive officers was " in practice " harder for women to comply
with than men and had remitted the case for consideration of whether the
limit was justifiable irrespective of candidates' sex and, if not, what was the
remedy. *Held*, that (1) as the limit was not necessary, it was not justifiable;
(2) it would not be just or equitable, in view of the difficulties of determining
proper conditions of entry into various grades of the Civil Service, to order
that P had the right to be considered for direct entry as executive officer;
(3) however, it would be recommended that the respondents jointly determine
by the 1980 competition year what other age limit, if any, should be applied).
[For decision of E.A.T. see § 1037.]

Pregnancy

REANEY *v.* KANDA JEAN PRODUCTS [1978] I.R.L.R. 427 (R was dismissed because she became pregnant. *Held,* that dismissal on grounds of pregnancy was not sex discrimination under the Sex Discrimination Act 1975, since, as a man could not become pregnant, there could be no comparison with men in the same relevant circumstances within s. 5 (3)).

1039. —— job application—questions asked at interview
[Sex Discrimination Act 1975 (c. 65), ss. 1 (1) (*a*), 6 (1) (*a*).]

It is doubtful whether the asking of questions at a job interview can constitute " arrangements " made for the purpose of determining who should be offered employment within s. 6 (1) of the Sex Discrimination Act 1975, though they may be evidence as to whether there has been discrimination.

A female golf professional applied for a job as a club professional. She was asked a number of questions about her ability, as a woman, to do the job. When she did not get the job, she complained to an industrial tribunal that the questions she had been asked amounted to sex discrimination in the " arrangements " made for the purpose of determining who should be offered employment within s. 6 (1) of the Sex Discrimination Act 1975. The industrial tribunal found against her on the facts. On appeal by the applicant, *held,* dismissing the appeal, that it was doubtful whether such questions could be " arrangements," but assuming they could be, the industrial tribunal's finding of fact that they were not unlawful was one with which the appeal tribunal had no jurisdiction to interfere.

SAUNDERS *v.* RICHMOND-UPON-THAMES LONDON BOROUGH COUNCIL [1978] I.C.R. 75, E.A.T.

1040. —— promotion on basis of seniority—women only employed permanently since 1975.
[Sex Discrimination Act 1975 (c. 65), ss. 1 (1) (*b*), 6 (2) (*a*).]

The Sex Discrimination Act 1975 does not operate retrospectively, but the Act will be applied to acts of discrimination of a continuing nature and as far as possible to the continuing effects of past discrimination.

The Post Office awarded postal walks according to seniority. Seniority was judged according to permanent status, and women had not been able to attain permanent status until 1975, even though many had been employed on a regular basis for many years. The complainant applied for a postal walk. She had been employed as a postwoman on a temporary basis since 1961 and had become permanently employed in 1975. The walk was given to a man whose total employment was shorter, but who had been of permanent status longer. *Held,* the Post Office had to show that the seniority requirement was justifiable in respect of the fact that the proportion of women who could comply with it was considerably smaller than the proportion of men; the case would be remitted to the industrial tribunal to consider the question and to consider whether or not this rule could be revised to give women credit for their temporary service.

STEEL *v.* UNION OF POST OFFICE WORKERS [1978] 1 W.L.R. 64, E.A.T

1041. —— redundancy payments for employees over 60—women compulsorily retired at 60
[Sex Discrimination Act 1975 (c. 65), ss. 1 (1) (*b*), 6 (2) (*a*).]

Where women have to retire at 60, it may be discriminatory to provide for a higher rate of redundancy pay for employees retiring above that age.

The employers' scheme for redundancy provided for higher rate of payment in respect of employees over 60. Women employees had to retire at 60. T complained of unlawful discrimination because she could never qualify for the higher rate of payment. The tribunal upheld her complaint. *Held,* dismissing the employers' appeal, Phillips J. dissenting, that there had been unlawful discrimination (relating to retirement) expressly made lawful by the Sex Discrimination Act 1975, s. 6 (4).

MACGREGOR WALLCOVERINGS *v.* TURTON [1978] I.C.R. 541, E.A.T.

1042. —— **rejection of complaint—failure to hear both sides**
[Sex Discrimination Act 1975 (c. 65), s. 6 (1).]
Where a complainant is better qualified and more experienced than a co-applicant for a job, then the respondents should usually be called on if the complaint is that the complainant's sex was the reason for her non-selection.

The complainant, a woman, was more experienced and better qualified for a teaching job than a male co-applicant to whom it was awarded. After hearing her complaint of unlawful discrimination the tribunal dismissed it without calling on the respondents. *Held*, allowing her appeal, that although the initial burden of proof was upon her, only in exceptional or frivolous cases would it be right to dismiss her case without calling on the respondents.

HUMPHREYS *v.* BOARD OF MANAGERS OF ST. GEORGE'S CHURCH OF ENGLAND (AIDED) PRIMARY SCHOOL [1978] I.C.R. 546, E.A.T.

1043. Shipbuilding (Redundancy Payments) Act 1978 (c. 11). See § 2768.

1044. Superannuation. See PENSIONS AND SUPERANNUATION.

1045. Teachers. See EDUCATION.

1046. Terms of employment—fixed pursuant to statute
[Employment Protection Act 1975 (c. 71), Sched. 11, para. 3.] N.U.P.E. made a Sched. 11 claim that the Regional Health Authority were observing terms and conditions of employment, concerning ambulancemen, less favourable than the "general level." *Held*, granting orders of certiorari quashing the Central Arbitration Committee's award and prohibition to prevent them from purporting to hear and determine the claim, that the claim could not be brought as it concerned workers whose remuneration or terms and conditions or minimum remuneration or terms and conditions are fixed (otherwise than by the employer) in pursuance of an enactment, within para. 3 of Sched. 11. The remuneration of ambulancemen was negotiated by the Whitley Council under the National Health Service Reorganisation Act 1973, and regulations made thereunder, and then the remuneration is approved and fixed by the Secretary of State under the regulations. Para. 3 is neither restricted to employees having an enforceable legal right parallel to Sched. 11 rights, nor to those whose remuneration of terms and conditions are directly affected by an enactment: R. *v.* THE CENTRAL ARBITRATION COMMITTEE, *ex p.* NORTH WESTERN REGIONAL HEALTH AUTHORITY [1978] I.R.L.R. 404, D.C.

1047. —— **Industrial Tribunal decision**
Safe place of work—duty of employer
KEYS *v.* SHOEFAYRE [1978] I.R.L.R. 476 (K, a part-time shop assistant, was told following a robbery at the shop where she worked that there was nothing that could be done to ensure staff safety. K therefore said she would look for another job and did not return to work following a second robbery at the shop less than three weeks later. *Held*, that it is a fundamental term of a contract of employment that the employer will take reasonable steps to operate a safe system of work and take reasonable care to have reasonably safe premises. S Co. were in breach of that term and K was entitled to treat that breach as conduct entitling her to resign and claim to have been dismissed within the Trade Union and Labour Relations Act 1974, Sched. 1, para. 5 (2) (*c*)).

1048. —— **public holidays—unilateral transfer to other dates**
B.L. Co. proposed transferring August Bank Holiday and the New Year's Holiday to December to give a week off between Monday, December 27 and Friday, December 31. At a meeting with the plaintiff members of the T.G.W.U., B.L. Co.'s industrial relations manager at Swindon gave a written assurance that statutory holidays would not be transferred except by mutual agreement between management and all unions represented in the plant. Later the works committee, which represented the majority of the relevant unions, agreed the new holiday arrangements. The plaintiffs made it clear that they intended to take the August and New Year's holidays at the usual time. They did not work on December 30 or 31, 1976. *Held*, that in the absence of express contractual provision or regular usage to the contrary, hourly paid employees are entitled to take recognised public holidays at the usual time without fear of dismissal and if entitled to a guaranteed minimum weekly wage are entitled

to be paid for the day without working extra hours during the week. Although there was a term that employees may be required to take public holidays in accordance with agreements with unions, this could not be relied upon against the plaintiffs in the light of the written assurance they had been given. Accordingly the plaintiffs were entitled to be paid for December 30 and 31, 1976: TUCKER v. BRITISH LEYLAND MOTOR CORP. [1978] I.R.L.R. 493, Swindon County Ct.

1049. Time off for public duties—Industrial Tribunal decisions

EMMERSON v. I.R.C. [1977] I.R.L.R. 458 (when E was elected leader of the opposition of Portsmouth Council he discovered that the 18 days' special paid leave for carrying out his public duties, under the Civil Service Staff Regulations were insufficient. He wrote asking for additional unpaid leave. The regulations provided that such leave may be granted. It was refused. *Held*, that the I.R.C. had failed to allow E reasonable time off in accordance with s. 59 of the Employment Protection Act to perform his public duties and a declaration to that effect would be made).

RATCLIFFE v. DORSET COUNTY COUNCIL [1978] I.R.L.R. 191 (R, a college lecturer, asked for time off to carry out public duties as a councillor. The Council reorganised his teaching timetable to enable him to attend Committee meetings in the afternoon, but expected him to continue performing his full functions, which meant his having to do some work at home at weekends and in the evenings. *Held*, that the Council had contravened R's right to time off during working hours to perform public duties under the Employment Protection Act 1975, s. 59. Swapping time around is not giving time off).

1050. —— powers of tribunal—tribunal imposing conditions

[Employment Protection Act 1975 (c. 71), s. 60 (2).]

Where a complaint is made regarding failure to give adequate time off for public duties, the tribunal does not have power to impose conditions on the parties as to the way in which time off shall be granted.

C complained that his employers had failed to give him adequate time off to fulfil his duties as a justice of the peace. The tribunal made a declaration as to the number of days off C should have and imposed conditions about unpaid days off. On appeal by C as to whether the tribunal had jurisdiction to impose the conditions, *held*, allowing the appeal, that on making a declaration under s. 60 (2) of the Act, the tribunal had no jurisdiction to impose conditions upon the parties.

CORNER v. BUCKINGHAMSHIRE COUNTY COUNCIL [1978] I.C.R. 836, E.A.T.

1051. Trades dispute—whether in contemplation or furtherance of—interlocutory injunction. See BEAVERBROOK NEWSPAPERS v. KEYS, § 3004.

1052. Trade unions. See TRADE UNIONS.

1053. Trade union activities—individual's right—"appropriate time" for such activities

[Employment Protection Act 1975 (c. 71), s. 53 (1) (*b*) (2) (*b*).]

In the absence of agreement by the employers, working hours may not be an "appropriate time" for pursuing union activities.

R's contract of employment, signed when he was not a union member, allowed him to take part in union activities at the appropriate time. That time was not specified. R later joined a union and pursued union activities with enthusiasm. His job was altered as a result. On his complaint that a penalty had been imposed on him for becoming a trade union member the tribunal and the appellate court found that as the penalty had to be imposed in respect of union activities carried on "at an appropriate time" before the tribunal could provide a remedy, then, as no appropriate time had been agreed with the employers, it could not be said that those activities, which had taken place during working hours, had taken place "at an appropriate time."

ROBB v. LEON MOTOR SERVICES [1978] I.C.R. 506, E.A.T.

1054. —— Industrial Tribunal decision

VINE v. D.R.G. (U.K.) [1978] I.R.L.R. 475 (V, a bag tackler, was refused paid time off as a member of the Bristol branch committee of NATSOPA, a union recognised by D.R.G. Co., to attend a course on the trade union movement. *Held*, that as V's duties as a member of the Bristol branch committee of NATSOPA were not concerned with industrial relations between D.R.G. Co. and their employees and were not such duties as were mentioned in the list of duties given as examples in the Code of Practice of the kind of duties for which paid time off should be given, V was not entitled to paid time off under s. 57 of the Employment Protection Act 1975).

1055. Trusts. See SETTLEMENT AND TRUSTS.

1056. Unemployment benefit. See SOCIAL SECURITY.

1057. Unfair dismissal

UNFAIR DISMISSAL (INCREASE OF COMPENSATION LIMIT) ORDER 1978 (No. 1778) [10p], made under the Employment Protection (Consolidation) Act 1978 (c. 44), s. 75 (2); operative on February 1, 1979; increases to £5,750 the limit on the amount of compensation which can be awarded by an industrial tribunal in claims for unfair dismissal.

1058. —— breach of trust by employee

Where there is a relationship between employer and employee involving mutual confidence and trust, a breach of that trust alone will justify the employer in dismissing the employee.

A and B, two of the managers in E Co.'s precision engineering company, started a similar company of their own without E Co.'s knowledge. E Co. found out and, suspecting A and B of dishonestly using their equipment, instituted a police investigation and suspended A and B. E Co. then invited A and B to attend a meeting to discuss their possible dismissals. A and B refused and were dismissed. An industrial tribunal found that they had been unfairly dismissed, in that it was unreasonable to expect them to attend such a meeting when they were suspended and under investigation. On appeal by E Co., *held*, allowing the appeal, that there had been a breach of trust by persons in a position of trust, and E Co. were entitled to dismiss A and B. E Co. had acted reasonably and had given A and B reasonable opportunity to state their case; accordingly the dismissals were not unfair.

MANSARD PRECISION ENGINEERING CO. *v.* TAYLOR [1978] I.C.R. 44, E.A.T.

1059. —— burden of proof—test

In deciding that M's dismissal was fair, a tribunal applied the test of whether the dismissal was so wrong that no sensible or reasonable management could have decided to dismiss, saying that " in effect the employer must be shown to have acted patently unreasonably." *Held*, allowing M's appeal, that such a test did not apply to unfair dismissal cases as opposed to unfair redundancy selection cases. Furthermore, the tribunal had erred in looking at whether M had in fact suffered injustice in deciding upon the fairness of the dismissal. (*W. Devis & Sons* v. *Atkins* [1977] C.L.Y. 1160 applied; *Vickers* v. *Smith* [1977] C.L.Y. 1182 distinguished): MITCHELL *v.* THE OLD HALL EXCHANGE AND PALATINE CLUB [1978] I.R.L.R. 160, E.A.T.

1060. —— capability—dismissal in breach of contract

F, an apprentice motor mechanic, was dismissed after a medical report confirmed that, as a result of defective eyesight, he could not be employed as a motor mechanic apprentice without undue danger to himself or to others. *Held*, dismissing F's appeal, that the dismissal was fair, though in breach of contract: FINCH *v.* BETABAKE (ANGLIA) [1977] I.R.L.R. 470, E.A.T.

1061. —— —— multiplicity of minor incidents—relevance of manager's results

M, an estate manager, was dismissed after about seven months' service by reason of seven small incidents which together led the respondents to think M incapable of performing the job adequately. He had been given a warning over three months before dismissal. *Held*, dismissing M's appeal against a finding that the dismissal was fair, that it is not wrong in law to add several minor incidents together to find a situation in which no confidence can be felt in the employee. A manager's results are an important element but are by no means the sole element: MILLER *v.* EXECUTORS OF JOHN C. GRAHAM [1978] I.R.L.R. 309, E.A.T.

1062. —— —— **warning—opportunity to state case**

B, secretary and personal assistant to H A Co.'s managing director, was dismissed for lethargy and lack of initiative and inability to work without supervision. Some three months previously she had been told that her work was unsatisfactory and particular areas for improvement were pointed out. *Held*, dismissing B's appeal, that the tribunal were entitled to find the dismissal fair although B had never been specifically warned that failure to improve would result in dismissal and had not specifically been given an opportunity to state her case. B's relationship with X had reached the stage at which X felt it could continue no longer: BROWN *v.* HALL ADVERTISING [1978] I.R.L.R. 246, E.A.T.

1063. B's work as an electrician was satisfactory until 1977. In August 1977 he was dismissed whilst on holiday, following several complaints from contractors. *Held*, dismissing S and G Co.'s appeal from a finding of unfair dismissal, that in cases of poor performance over which the employee has some control the employee should be warned, preferably several times and given plenty of opportunity to improve. If it becomes clear that the employee is incapable the employer is entitled to dismiss but should give the employee a final opportunity to explain: SUTTON AND GATES (LUTON) *v.* BOXALL [1978] I.R.L.R. 486, E.A.T.

1064. —— **company director—whether an employee**

A company director appointed by the company as managing director and paid a regular salary as such is to be regarded as an employee, notwithstanding the absence of a contract of employment or company resolution as to remuneration.

The Nigerian employee of a Nigerian company was appointed managing director of an English subsidiary company. Although he was appointed by resolution of the English company, no remuneration was resolved and no service contract entered. The employee carried out managerial functions for the English company, and was paid by it a salary equivalent to that previously earned in Nigeria. After a short time he was dismissed, and upon his complaining of unfair dismissal, the English company successfully contended that it was not his employer. *Held*, allowing the employee's appeal, that since he fulfilled the obligations of an employee and was paid as such, he was to be regarded as in the employ of the English company.

FOLAMI *v.* NIGERLINE (U.K.) [1978] I.C.R. 277, E.A.T.

1065. —— —— —— **jurisdiction of tribunal**

[Trade Union and Labour Relations Act 1974 (c. 52), s. 30.] An industrial tribunal has no jurisdiction to entertain a claim for unfair dismissal as there was no contract of service in existence and none could be implied on these facts. The applicant director was not an " employee " within s. 30 and was therefore not entitled to compensation for unfair dismissal. (*Trussed Steel Concrete Co.* v. *Green* [1946] Ch. 115, considered): PARSONS *v.* ALBERT J. PARSONS & SONS, *The Times*, November 14, 1978, C.A.

1066. —— **company in voluntary liquidation—reasonable retention of other employees**

On November 14, 1977, B was given written notice of redundancy as from February 15, 1978. On December 15, 1977, F.B. Co. was forced into voluntary liquidation and on December 19, 1977, B and others were dismissed forthwith although some employees were kept on to clear up and deal with outstanding orders. *Held*, allowing an appeal against a finding of unfair dismissal, that (1) it is doubtful whether there can ever be an unfair dismissal in the case of a properly conducted entry into voluntary liquidation, even where the dismissal is in breach of contract; (2) it did not follow from the fact that some employees were temporarily kept on that there had been an unfair selection for redundancy: FOX BROTHERS (CLOTHES) *v.* BRYANT [1978] I.R.L.R. 485, E.A.T.

1067. —— **company reorganisation—change in nature of job requirements—redundancy**

[Redundancy Payments Act 1965 (c. 62), s. 1 (2).]

An employee dismissed because his employer's reorganisation of work leaves no post involving work of the particular kind previously carried out by him, is not unfairly dismissed.

The appellant employee worked as an operations manager being responsible to a general manager. Upon his employer effecting a reorganisation, the two posts were merged, the resulting job being more complex than either of the previous jobs and requiring different qualities. The appellant was dismissed for alleged redundancy, but complained unsuccessfully to an industrial tribunal that his dismissal was unfair. *Held*, dismissing his appeal, that the employee's work was " of a particular kind " and the new post required work of a different kind, so that the appellant was redundant within the meaning of s. 1 (2) (*b*) of the 1965 Act.

ROBINSON *v*. BRITISH ISLAND AIRWAYS [1978] I.C.R. 304, E.A.T.

1068. —— compensation—continuity of employment—licensed premises
[Contracts of Employment Act 1972 (c. 53), Sched. 1, para. 9 (2).]
A surrender of the tenancy of a public-house amounts to the transfer of the business from one person to another for the purposes of continuity of employment of persons employed therein.

The applicant was employed by the tenant of hotel premises from 1958 to January 1976 when the tenant surrendered his tenancy, the business being thereafter carried on by a manager appointed by the owning brewery and the applicant being employed in the same capacity until his dismissal in October 1976. An industrial tribunal found the dismissal to have been unfair but calculated compensation ignoring the applicant's employment by the former tenant. *Held*, allowing the applicant's appeal, that compensation should be reassessed on the basis that the applicant had been continuously employed since 1958, for in the licensed trade the surrender of a tenancy would be unlikely to affect the nature of the business and should accordingly be regarded as a transfer of the business within the meaning of para. 9 (2) of Sched. 1 to the Act. (*Lloyd* v. *Brassey* [1969] C.L.Y. 1281 applied.)

YOUNG *v*. DANIEL THWAITES & CO. [1977] I.C.R. 877, E.A.T.

1069. —— —— duty to consider categories of compensatory awards—employee of poor intellect
In assessing the loss of earnings of an employee who has been unfairly dismissed, an industrial tribunal must assess subjectively his ability to find new employment.

G, a labourer of poor intellect, was dismissed by his employers. He claimed compensation for unfair dismissal. At the time of the hearing he had been out of work for three months. The industrial tribunal found that he had been unfairly dismissed and awarded compensation for loss of earnings up to the date of the hearing on the ground that he had had sufficient time to find new employment. G appealed. *Held,* allowing the appeal, that (1) the industrial tribunal's notes of evidence and reasons were inadequate in that they did not show whether the five different categories of compensatory awards had been considered, whether a subjective test had been applied to the question of G's ability to find new employment or whether the tribunal had found that G had not tried hard enough during the three-month period; (2) if G had tried to find new employment but had failed through lack of capacity he was entitled to more than three months' compensation and the case would be remitted to the tribunal for further consideration subject to any agreement between the parties. (*Tidman* v. *Aveling Marshall* [1977] C.L.Y. 1113 applied.)

GREEN *v*. J. WATERHOUSE & SONS [1977] I.C.R. 759, E.A.T.

1070. —— —— entitlement to basic award
[Employment Protection Act 1975 (c. 71), ss. 72 (5), 73.]
When an industrial tribunal finds that an employee has been unfairly dismissed, it is bound at least to make a basic award of compensation although it may conclude that no loss has been suffered.

The employee was dismissed after a long absence from work due to illness which continued after his dismissal. An industrial tribunal ruled that his dismissal was unfair, but declined to order any compensation on the grounds that the employee would not in any event have been fit to return to work.

Held, allowing the employee's appeal, that although a tribunal is empowered to make a reduced or nil compensatory award in such circumstances, it must make a basic award, which in these circumstances would be £280.

CADBURY v. DODDINGTON [1977] I.C.R. 982, E.A.T.

1071. —— —— **likelihood of redundancy situation**

The likelihood of a redundancy situation arising is a relevant consideration in calculating compensation for loss of future earnings where an employee has been unfairly dismissed.

In assessing compensation for unfair dismissal, an industrial tribunal having previously found that the employee would " probably " have been made redundant in any event, made no reduction in respect thereof when awarding compensation for loss of future earnings over a 12-month period. *Held*, allowing the employers' appeal, that the likelihood of redundancy was a relevant consideration; and that, by invitation of the parties, the tribunal would substitute its own finding, reducing the period for assessment of future loss to nine months.

YOUNG'S OF GOSPORT v. KENDELL [1977] I.C.R. 907, E.A.T.

1072. —— —— **loss of pension rights—employers' accrued contribution**

Compensation for unfair dismissal should include an element for the amount of the employers' contributions to a pension scheme made prior to dismissal.

The employee was unfairly dismissed after seven years' employment. He had belonged to the employers' contributory pension scheme under which he was entitled to withdraw the amount of his own contributions on leaving his employment. An industrial tribunal in awarding compensation made no allowance for the value of the employers' contributions to the scheme during the applicant's employment, namely £1,077. *Held*, allowing the employee's appeal, that compensation was due in respect of loss of interest in the pension scheme and that allowing for accelerated capital payment, £750 was the appropriate figure. (*Cawthorn & Sinclair* v. *Hedges* [1974] C.L.Y. 1299 and *Gill* v. *Harold Andrews Sheepbridge* [1974] C.L.Y. 1295 applied.)

HILL v. SABCO HOUSEWARE (U.K.) [1977] I.C.R. 888, E.A.T.

1073. —— —— **pension contributions**

An industrial tribunal having ruled that an employee of the defendant company had been unfairly dismissed, it made an award of compensation to the employee that included a sum for loss of pension rights. The employee had opted to take his past contributions to the pension fund immediately, rather than wait for a deferred pension that would be larger. On appeal by the employers, *held*, that the employee had indeed suffered a loss, but was under no legal duty to mitigate this by accepting a deferred pension: STURDY FINANCE v. BARDSLEY, *The Times*, November 21, 1978, E.A.T.

1074. —— —— **reduction due to employee's misconduct**

[Trade Union and Labour Relations Act 1974 (c. 52), Sched. 1, para. 19 (3).]

When considering a reduction in compensation under para. 19 (3) of Sched. 1 to the Trade Union and Labour Relations Act 1974, an industrial tribunal should consider the employee's conduct rather than his state of mind.

L Co. proposed to close down and sell a number of their betting shops. A and B made plans to buy two of the shops and run them whilst continuing to work for L Co. A and B did not realise they were acting wrongly, and maintained throughout that their plans had not been intended to remain secret. However, when L Co. found out, they suspected, wrongly, that A and B had formed a criminal conspiracy to sell the company's property at an undervalue, they took statements under caution from A and B, then summarily dismissed them. The industrial tribunal found that L Co. had not given A and B a reasonable opportunity to explain their conduct, and that therefore the dismissals were unfair. Then when they came to consider reducing compensation for the employees' own conduct, they reduced only by 20 and 25 per cent. on the ground that A and B had not realised that they were acting wrongly. On appeal by the employees, *held*, that the dismissals were unfair; however in assessing the reduction in compensation, the tribunal should have considered the employees' conduct, not their state of mind; the gravity of their breach of trust was such that a reduction of 50 per cent. in each case would be appropriate. (*Mansard Precision Engineering Co.* v. *Taylor* [1978] C.L.Y. 1058 considered.)

LADBROKE RACING v. MASON [1978] I.C.R. 49, E.A.T.

1075. R was dismissed for disobeying a proper order. A tribunal found the dismissal unfair because R had not been afforded the opportunity of an interview with his superior, but found that it was just and equitable to reduce compensation by 100 per cent. as R was 100 per cent. responsible for the dismissal. The award was thus the statutory minimum basic award only. *Held*, dismissing R's appeal, that it could not be said that the tribunal had not properly exercised their discretion (*Cooper* v. *British Steel Corp.* [1975] C.L.Y. 1164 and *Kemp* v. *Shipton Automation* [1976] C.L.Y. 974 distinguished): REDPATH v. DOMESTIC ELECTRIC RENTALS (1977) 12 I.T.R. 366, E.A.T.

1076. —— —— —— **considerations**
[Employment Protection Act 1975 (c. 71), s. 76 (6).]
On the question of an employee's contributing to his own dismissal, s. 76 (6) of the Employment Protection Act 1975 permits a broad consideration of the employee's conduct, including improper behaviour and lack of ability for the job.

After about five years of employment with E Co., A, a factory manager, admitted improperly having had bonuses paid to himself, as a recompense for the withdrawal of fringe benefits. He was interviewed, but then told he was to be summarily dismissed without any opportunity to explain his conduct. The industrial tribunal found that his dismissal was due, in reality, not to his dishonesty, but to his lack of ability for the job. They awarded him compensation for unfair dismissal, but deducted 10 per cent. for A's own conduct. On appeal by E. Co., *held*, allowing the appeal, that the dismissal had been unfair; but, that on the broad consideration of A's behaviour including both his improper behaviour and his lack of ability, his compensation should be reduced by a total of 20 per cent.

ROBERT WHITING DESIGNS v. LAMB [1978] I.C.R. 89, E.A.T.

1077. —— —— **tribunal excluding overtime and deducting unemployment benefits**
An employee who has been unfairly dismissed should be compensated according to the loss he has suffered.

M was dismissed from his employment with B Ltd. and applied for compensation for unfair dismissal. The industrial tribunal found that he had been unfairly dismissed. They assessed his loss of earnings on the basis of his weekly wage excluding overtime payments and deducted the amount of unemployment benefits he had received following his dismissal from the total compensation award. M appealed against the amount of the award. *Held*, allowing the appeal, that the tribunal were right to deduct any benefit received from the total loss but since he had regularly worked overtime prior to his dismissal the tribunal should have considered the sums M was likely to earn including probable overtime payments when calculating the compensation for loss of earnings.

MULLETT v. BRUSH ELECTRICAL MACHINES [1977] I.C.R. 829, E.A.T.

1078. —— —— **where employee suffers no loss**
[Employment Protection Act 1975 (c. 71), s. 64.]
On an application to the Secretary of State under s. 64 of the Act for payment for a period of notice, the employee must bring into account his earnings during the notice period.

W was dismissed by his employers without notice but started new employment almost immediately. The employers went into liquidation and W applied under s. 64 of the Act for payment for four weeks' notice to which he was entitled under the Contracts of Employment Act 1972. The industrial tribunal found that W was not obliged to give credit for money earned in the notice period and ordered the Secretary of State to make the appropriate payment. On appeal, *held*, allowing the appeal, that the general intention shown by the Contracts of Employment Act 1972 was to incorporate the provisions of the Act into the contract of employment. By s. 3 the employee's remedy against an employer's failure to give notice was to claim damages for breach of contract and his rights against the Secretary of State could be no better than his rights against an employer. Thus, since W had suffered no loss the Secretary of State was not bound to make any payment.

SECRETARY OF STATE FOR EMPLOYMENT *v.* WILSON [1978] I.C.R. 200, E.A.T.

1079. —— —— **whether overtime payments to be taken into account**
[Employment Protection Act 1975 (c. 71), ss. 74, 76.]
Normal overtime pay should not be included in calculating a compensatory award for unfair dismissal.

B was unfairly dismissed. The tribunal made him a basic award, excluding his normal overtime payments, and a compensatory award, from which they also excluded such payments. *Held,* allowing his appeal, that they were correct in relation to the basic award, but that likely net overtime payments should have been included in the compensatory award.

BROWNSON *v.* HIRE SERVICE SHOPS [1978] I.C.R. 517, E.A.T.

1080. —— —— **notice of appearance—whether grounds to be stated—review**
[Industrial Tribunals (Labour Relations) Regulations 1974 (S.I. 1974 No. 1386), Sched., reg. 3 (1).]
The requirement that a respondent to a complaint of unfair dismissal should include grounds in his notice of appearance is directory, not mandatory.

Employers entered a notice of appearance upon receipt of notification of a claim for unfair dismissal. No grounds were included in the notice, it being stated that grounds would follow. At the hearing, their solicitor indicated that he had insufficient instructions to proceed and that the employers' managing director was unable to attend through illness. The tribunal heard the complaint in the employer's absence and made an award against them. Subsequently the tribunal refused a review, inter alia, on the basis that no grounds had been stated in the notice of appearance. *Held,* allowing the employers' appeal and ordering a review, that the interests of justice required a review since the failure to specify grounds was not fatal and particularly since illness had prevented the employers attending the hearing. (*Howard* v. *Secretary of State for the Environment* [1974] C.L.Y. 3731 applied.)

SELDUN TRANSPORT SERVICES *v.* BAKER [1978] I.C.R. 1035, E.A.T.

1081. —— —— **time-limit**
K was dismissed on August 22, 1976. He knew of his right to claim compensation and of the time-limit but wrongly thought that his case was being dealt with because proceedings had been started to have the question of entitlement to unemployment benefit heard by a local tribunal. He realised on December 9, 1976, that this tribunal was not hearing his complaint and his unfair dismissal complaint was received by the Central Office of Industrial Tribunals on January 10, 1977. *Held,* dismissing W.M. Co.'s appeal, that the tribunal were entitled to find it not to have been reasonably practicable for K to present his claim in time and that he had presented his complaint within a reasonable time after the time-limit had expired. These were questions of fact for the tribunal. Reasonable ignorance or mistaken belief can be grounds for finding it not to have been practicable to present a complaint but not if it arises from the fault of the complainant in not making reasonable enquiries or from the fault of his professional advisers in not giving him all information which they reasonably should have: WALL'S MEAT CO. *v.* KHAN [1978] I.R.L.R. 499, C.A.

1082. —— —— —— **" reasonably practicable "**
[Trade Union and Labour Relations Act 1974 (c. 52), Sched. 1, para. 21 (4).]
There is no rule of law that ignorance of one's rights means that it is not " reasonably practicable " for a complaint to be presented within the time limit.

H resigned on December 31, 1976. His claim for compensation reached the tribunal on May 16, 1977. He claimed not to have known of the existence of tribunals until he read a newspaper article on April 28, 1977. *Held,* allowing an appeal by his employer, that in interpreting the words " reasonably practicable " one looks at the common sense of the matter and should not admit ignorance, however abysmal or unreasonable, as a universal excuse.

AVON COUNTY COUNCIL *v.* HAYWOOD-HICKS [1978] I.C.R. 646, E.A.T.

1083. M lodged an originating application claiming unfair dismissal compensation in August 1976 within the time-limit. However, he omitted to insert his own name and address on the form. In April 1977, having discovered the omission, M lodged a second application, out of time. *Held,* allowing an appeal, that (1) although the mere absence of an address need not automatically make an application invalid, in this case, the employer having been ignorant of the claim for eight months through M's fault, it could not be said that a properly completed application had been received within the time-limit; (2) nor had it been not reasonably practicable to present the complaint in time: HOPES *v.* MILLER (1977) 13 I.T.R. 64, E.A.T.

1084. [Trade Union and Labour Relations Act 1974 (c. 52), Sched. 1, para. 21 (4).]
An employee has to satisfy the industrial tribunal not only that he did not know of his rights throughout the period preceding the complaint and there was no reason why he should know, but also that there was no reason why he should make inquiries.

P was charged with theft in May 1976 and dismissed. He consulted solicitors and apprised them of the situation. In March 1977 the prosecution offered no evidence on the theft charge. P heard about unfair dismissal from someone else and in April 1977, made a complaint. The tribunal were not satisfied that it was not reasonably practical to have presented the complaint in time. P's appeal was dismissed by the E.A.T. *Held,* dismissing P's further appeal (Ormrod L.J. dissenting), that although the tribunal had not set out its reasons, they must, as must the E.A.T., have been satisfied that P ought to have known of his rights, and it was therefore reasonably practicable to have presented a complaint in time. (*Dedman* v. *British Building and Engineering Appliances* [1974] C.L.Y. 1316 applied.)

PORTER *v.* BANDRIDGE [1978] 1 W.L.R. 1145, C.A.

1085. ———— ———— ———— **skilled advice followed**
[Trade Union and Labour Relations Act 1974 (c. 52), Sched. 1, para. 21 (4).] Following incorrect advice from a Citizen's Advice Bureau, the applicant's complaint of unfair dismissal was presented outside the three-month time limit. *Held,* having " engaged " the bureau and their advice being at fault, the applicant had to accept its consequences. An industrial tribunal was not bound to join the bureau as a party, nor to hear evidence from them. (*Dedman* v. *British Building and Engineering Appliances* [1974] C.L.Y. 1316 applied): RILEY *v.* TESCO STORES, *The Times,* November 13, 1978, E.A.T.

1086. ———— **conduct—acquiescence by employers**
B, a chief nursing officer, entered into lengthy correspondence with R.R. Co. between October 13, 1975, and December 3, 1975, in which B complained that she was being demoted, made vague but serious allegations against the chief medical officer, and demanded that a full impartial inquiry should be held. She rejected R.R. Co.'s grievance procedure. On December 3, 1975, R.R. Co. required B to cease the correspondence and consider her position. B's solicitor then began negotiating with R.R. Co. but B was dismissed whilst B's solicitor was abroad. The tribunal found the dismissal unfair as discussions with B's solicitor had not been completed before dismissal but found B's conduct to have contributed 70 per cent. to the dismissal. *Held,* dismissing B's appeal, that B's conduct very largely contributed to her dismissal and there was nothing approaching acquiescence by R.R. Co. in B's conduct: BROWN *v.* ROLLS-ROYCE (1971) (1977) 12 I.T.R. 382, E.A.T.

1087. ———— ———— **apportionment of blame—nil compensation**
[Trade Union and Labour Relations Act 1974 (c. 52), Sched. 1, para. 19 (1) (3).]
In applying para. 19 of Sched. 1 to the Act, an industrial tribunal must deal with the requirements of para. 19 (1) as a separate operation before going on to consider any reduction of the assessment under para. 19 (3).

N, an assistant hatchery manager for poultry farmers, was dismissed for leaving the hatchery whilst on duty. He complained that he had been unfairly dismissed. The industrial tribunal found that his breach of duty was serious but that the employers had failed to warn him of the likely consequences of his conduct. Accordingly, they found that his dismissal was unfair but awarded him no compensation. N appealed against the finding of nil compensation. *Held*, allowing the appeal, that since the tribunal had not stated their reasoning clearly and might have combined the separate operations under para. 19 of Sched. 1 to the Act, the case would be remitted for them to reconsider their assessment. (*Kemp* v. *Shipton Automation* [1976] C.L.Y. 974 and *Trend* v. *Chiltern Hunt* [1977] C.L.Y. 1114 considered.)

NUDDS *v.* W. & J. B. EASTWOOD [1978] I.C.R. 171, E.A.T.

1088. —— —— **breach of company rules—effect of disciplinary agreement—opportunity to state case**

O, a till operator, breached the till procedure by failing to register £1·14 from a sale, failing to put the money in the till and failing to offer a receipt. By a company/union agreed disciplinary procedure, such a breach was regarded as gross misconduct, and gross misconduct normally was to result in dismissal. O was immediately suspended and later it was decided to dismiss her. Dishonesty was admittedly not involved. *Held*, dismissing L.S. Co.'s appeal against a finding of unfair dismissal, that even if the terms of the disciplinary procedure had been more mandatory the tribunal would have had to consider whether the employers had acted reasonably in imposing the extreme sanction of dismissal for an isolated, unexplained breach of till procedure. The tribunal were entitled to find O not to have been given sufficient opportunity to offer an explanation: LAWS STORE *v.* OLIPHANT [1978] I.R.L.R. 251, E.A.T.

1089. —— —— **dishonesty—employers' duty to make sufficient inquiries**

When challenged about having a watch which had been lost six months beforehand, H eventually admitted finding it in a yard. *Held*, dismissing J M M Co.'s appeal against a finding that H's dismissal was unfair, that the tribunal were entitled to make the finding in view of the facts that H had 15 years' unblemished service, investigations into the matter took only a few hours, the manager who had acted in a kind of appeal capacity had already discussed the matter and agreed that dismissal was appropriate before he dealt with the matter " on appeal," and a witness who H had said could have confirmed that H had mentioned finding the watch was not called. The gravity of stealing depends on all the circumstances, such as whether the theft was of employer's property, and stealing would not always justify dismissal: JOHNSON MATTHEY METALS *v.* HARDING [1978] I.R.L.R. 248, E.A.T.

1090. O Co. introduced a till roll in their cash register in October 1976 when the integrity of L, a shop assistant was questioned. In January 1977, O Co.'s proprietor saw L enter a transaction into a book without placing money in the till. L was dismissed the next day when no entry was found on the till roll. *Held*, allowing L's appeal, that the tribunal had erred in finding the dismissal fair. To justify dismissal for suspected dishonesty the employer must show reasonable grounds for the suspicions. Here there were various ways in which the money could have gone missing without dishonesty. It would have been reasonable for O Co. to try to contact the customer concerned. Further, the tribunal erred in finding O Co. to have given L a reasonable opportunity to explain her position since the tribunal had been unable to resolve a conflict of evidence as to what had happened when L was confronted prior to dismissal: LEES *v.* THE ORCHARD [1978] I.R.L.R. 20, E.A.T.

1091. —— —— —— **loss of pension rights**

H was suspended on full pay when investigations into allegations of dishonesty on his part were made. He was charged with five offences but, before his trial, a director of T.S. Co. discussed the subject of two of the charges with H, who admitted his default. H was then dismissed. He was ultimately acquitted of four charges and fined for the fifth. *Held*, that (1) having suspended H, T S Co. should have made better inquiries if they were to dismiss him before his trial. They had not warned him or made a real effort to find out his side of the story. Accordingly, the finding of unfair dismissal could not be reversed; (2) the tribunal had erred in calculating loss of pension rights by multiplying the pension payable at 65 by 4½ to give £6,358 since the cost of a single premium to provide such a pension would be £2,250; (3) the tribunal failed to consider sufficiently whether H might have been dismissed fairly following his trial: TESCO STORES *v.* HEAP (1977) 13 I.T.R. 17, E.A.T.

1092. —— —— —— —— **opportunity for employee to state case**

H was suspended when released on bail charged with theft, and was told that the decision was to continue the suspension. However, when it was apparent that, as H had elected trial by jury, his trial would not be heard for some time, he was dismissed. *Held*, that it is not always wrong to dismiss an employee before guilt or innocence of a criminal offence is established, as a serious breach of duty or discipline may be involved in any event; (2) the dismissal was unfair, applying the reasonableness test, because H (I) Co. had made insufficient prior inquiries; (3) it is proper for an employer considering dismissal of an employee charged with a criminal offence to seek to question him or his solicitor. The discussion needed is more in relation to the employer's proposed action than the alleged offence in itself; (4) by failing to do this, H (I) Co. had denied H the opportunity to state his case. (*Carr* v. *Alexander Russell* [1976] C.L.Y. 1007 overruled): HARRIS (IPSWICH) *v.* HARRISON [1978] I.R.L.R. 382, E.A.T.

1093. —— —— **standard of proof**

B was dismissed for acts of dishonesty with co-employees concerning staff purchases. She was implicated by a co-employee during the investigation. *Held*, allowing B.H.S. Co.'s appeal, that the tribunal had applied too strict a standard of proof to B.H.S. Co. The test was whether they entertained at the time of a dismissal reasonable suspicion, amounting to a belief, in the guilt of the employee of the misconduct in question: BRITISH HOME STORES *v.* BIRCHELL [1978] I.R.L.R. 379, E.A.T.

1094. —— —— **effect of subsequent misconduct on fairness of dismissal and on compensation**

[Trade Union and Labour Relations Act 1974 (c. 52), Sched. 1, para. 6 (8).] M, a farm manager, was dismissed with 10 weeks' notice but then dismissed summarily during that notice when his son was found poaching on M(F)'s waters. Following dismissal it was found that M had accepted dishonest payments for contracts placed by him on M(F)'s behalf. *Held*, that (1) following amendments by the Employment Protection Act 1975, it could be said that discovery of subsequent misconduct could make a dismissal reasonable having regard to equity and the substantial merits of the case; (2) however, knowledge subsequently acquired cannot make an unreasonable act of the employer reasonable; (3) M's dishonesty could not therefore affect the fairness of his dismissal, nor could it amount to conduct contributing to the dismissal; (4) it could, however, affect the discretionary compensatory award: D. G. MONCRIEFF (FARMERS) *v.* MACDONALD [1978] I.R.L.R. 112, E.A.T.

1095. —— —— **failure to use safety device**

M was dismissed for by-passing a safety device on an automatic lathe which prevented operation of the machine with one hand only. M admitted that he thought that neglect of safety devices would lead to dismissal. *Held*, dismissing M's appeal, that the tribunal were entitled to find the dismissal fair: MARTIN *v.* YORKSHIRE IMPERIAL METALS [1978] I.R.L.R. 440, E.A.T.

1096. —— —— **high degree of skill required—test to be applied—natural justice**

[Trade Union and Labour Relations Act 1974 (c. 52), Sched. 1, para. 6 (1) (8) (9) (*a*); Air Navigation Order 1974 (S.I. 1974 No. 1114), art. 26 (2).]

If an employee is dismissed for dishonesty or incompetence, it is sufficient for the employer to prove that he honestly believed on reasonable grounds that the employee was dishonest or incompetent; he need not prove that the employee was in fact dishonest or incompetent.

Per curiam: In activities where departure from a high standard of professional skill may be disastrous one failure in performance may justify dismissal.

E was a commercial airline pilot. He made a faulty landing in good conditions, and seriously damaged the aircraft. A board of inquiry was held at which E was represented and given an opportunity to explain. The board's conclusion was that the accident was due to lack of flying knowledge, and that there was no justification for it. E was dismissed. An industrial tribunal held that although E had been dismissed for an admissible reason, namely lack of capability, the company had not acted reasonably in relying on the conclusions of the board. The Employment Appeal Tribunal allowed the company's appeal. On appeal by E, *held*, dismissing the appeal, that an inquiry need not have been held in the first place. The company honestly believed on reasonable grounds that E lacked capability; it was their duty to be satisfied that he was competent, under art. 26 (2) of the Air Navigation Order 1974, and E had been properly dismissed.

ALIDAIR *v.* TAYLOR [1978] I.C.R. 445, C.A.

1097. —— —— **insubordination—warnings**

[Trade Union and Labour Relations Act 1974 (c. 52), Sched. 1, para. 6 (8).]

Where an employee has shown that he is determined to go his own way contrary to his employers' instructions, it may be reasonable to dismiss him without warning.

Per curiam. The Employment Appeal Tribunal cannot overrule an industrial tribunal merely because it would have decided the case differently. Normally a rehearing should be a full rehearing before a fresh tribunal.

E was a house-father in a home for mentally retarded adults. Residents were not required to work after 2 p.m. and could not, according to established practice, be punished. X, aged 34, but with a mental age of seven, was made by E to scrub floors at 9 p.m. for failing to work in the morning. The governing body pointed out the rules to E, who refused to accept them. He was therefore dismissed. The industrial tribunal held that the governing body had acted reasonably in treating that as a sufficient reason for his dismissal, but the Employment Appeal Tribunal overturned the decision, and, holding that 90 per cent. of the case had been decided, remitted the case to a fresh tribunal to consider the remaining 10 per cent. On appeal by the employers, *held*, allowing the appeal, that the tribunal had acted correctly, and their decision must be restored. (Dictum of Sir John Donaldson in *James* v. *Waltham Holy Cross U.D.C.* [1973] C.L.Y. 1129 considered.)

RETARDED CHILDREN'S AID SOCIETY *v.* DAY [1978] I.C.R. 437, C.A.

1098. —— —— **natural justice—employee's right to know what is being said against him**

M was dismissed following a fight between M and S. Each blamed the other. Witness statements were taken and the assistant personnel officer interviewed M and S separately. M's appeal was heard by the personnel officer and the financial controller who was not a director. B.E. Co.'s procedure provided for hearing of apeals by the director responsible for the department. *Held*, dismissing B.E. Co.'s appeal from a finding of unfair dismissal, that the tribunal had not erred in finding B.E. Co.'s failure to give M the written witness statements or the opportunity to hear and cross-examine the witnesses or S contravened natural justice and, coupled with the departure from B.E. Co.'s own disciplinary procedure, rendered the dismissal unfair. A man must know sufficiently what is said against him so that he can present his case properly. It is a question of degree in each case: BENTLEY ENGINEERING CO. *v.* MISTRY [1978] I.R.L.R. 436, E.A.T.

1099. —— —— **refusal to accept duties—lack of warning—compensation**

D was dismissed for refusing to accept his duties as Deputy Head of U.B. Co.'s Documentary Credit Department, U.B. Co. had previously sent him a letter stating that they " must insist that you undertake these responsibilities and duties forthwith if you are to continue in your present position. . . ." *Held*, inter alia, that (1) as the letter did not suggest that dismissal would follow refusal to undertake the duties and responsibilities involved, the tribunal had not erred in finding the dismissal unfair on the ground of lack of a warning in terms; (2) U.B. Co.'s appeal and D's cross-appeal against a finding of 50 per cent. contributory fault should both be dismissed. As D could change his conduct, lack of a specific warning was important but D's conduct was not trivial; (3) the tribunal had correctly deducted £3,156, given to D on his dismissal partly as pay in lieu of notice and partly by way of an ex gratia payment, from the compensatory award before reducing the award on grounds of contributory fault : UBAF BANK v. DAVIS [1978] I.R.L.R. 442, E.A.T.

1100. —— —— **school teacher—conviction of indecency not connected with work**
    B, a schoolteacher of 30 years' standing, was dismissed following his conviction of gross indecency with a man in a public lavatory. *Held*, allowing the N.C.C.'s appeal against a finding of unfair dismissal, that in this case, provided they approached the matter fairly and properly, the employers could have fairly dismissed B or not : NOTTINGHAMSHIRE COUNTY COUNCIL v. BOWLY [1978] I.R.L.R. 252, E.A.T.

1101. —— —— **violence towards co-employee—failure to follow grievance procedure**
    S, a technical manager, was dismissed after perpetrating a moderately serious and unprovoked assault upon a co-employee at a company social event outside working hours in the company's canteen. *Held*, dismissing S's appeal, that the tribunal were entitled to find the dismissal fair. That the grievance procedure had not been followed to the letter did not in these circumstances render the dismissal unfair. If the grievance procedure had been adhered to, no different result would have been reached. The fundamental question always remains whether the employers have acted reasonably : STEVENSON v. GOLDEN WONDER [1977] I.R.L.R. 474, E.A.T.

1102. —— —— —— **first breach of discipline**
    [I.R. Code of Practice, para. 133 (ii).] A tribunal found M's dismissal following a fight unfair in view of the I.R. Code of Practice, para. 133 (ii), which provides that no one should be dismissed for a first breach of discipline except in cases of gross misconduct. *Held*, that the tribunal had erred in law in deciding that gross misconduct meant something tantamount to virtual repudiation of contract and the dismissal was thus unfair although M's misconduct was " serious." The question was whether P Co. had acted reasonably. Whether or not to dismiss for fighting is essentially a matter for the employer to decide : C. A. PARSONS & Co. v. McLOUGHLIN [1978] I.R.L.R. 65, E.A.T.

1103. —— —— —— **reasonableness of summary dismissal**
    Following a fight between R and W at work, R was dismissed. *Held*, dismissing an appeal against a finding of unfair dismissal, that as there was no clear, direct, specific rule brought directly to all employees' attention that if they fight they will be dismissed (although there was a rule referring to " any assault or violent act ") and there was no evidence that the fighting was particularly dangerous, the tribunal was entitled to hold the dismissal unfair : MEYER DUNMORE INTERNATIONAL v. ROGERS [1978] I.R.L.R. 167, E.A.T.

1104. —— —— **warning—relevance of previous conduct not leading to warnings**
    W, a shop manager, was dismissed for swearing at a young female employee. *Held*, dismissing W's appeal against a finding that the dismissal was fair, that (1) the tribunal were entitled to take into account a prior warning although that was an unsatisfactory warning in that W had not been given an opportunity to state his case although he protested against the warning; (2) the tribunal had not erred in accepting evidence of previous similar incidents, although care should be taken in examining such evidence : WOOD v. KETTERING CO-OPERATIVE CHEMISTS [1978] I.R.L.R. 438, E.A.T.

1105. —— **continuous service minimum—associated companies—where several persons together control both companies**
    [Contracts of Employment Act 1972 (c. 53), Sched. 1, para. 10 (2).] Z and S were employed in B Co.'s canteen, at first by TS Co., who managed the canteen, and then by B Co. direct when they took over the canteen management themselves. A tribunal found that Z and S did not qualify to claim unfair dismissal compensation as they had not done 26 weeks' continuous service. *Held*, allowing an appeal, that the tribunal had erred in law in acting on the basis that if no one person controlled both companies they were not associated companies within Sched. 1, para. 10, to the 1972 Act, so that Z and S could not say that the two employments were continuous. " A third

person " in para. 10 (2) includes " persons." Where several persons hold more than 50 per cent. of the shares in two companies, whether they have control together of the companies depends upon what has happened in practice. The case should be remitted for reconsideration as in this case the two persons who held over 50 per cent. of the shares of both companies were related: ZARB AND SAMUELS *v.* BRITISH & BRAZILIAN PRODUCE CO. (SALES) [1978] I.R.L.R. 78, E.A.T.

1106. —— —— **computation of 26-week period**

[Trade Union and Labour Relations Act 1974 (c. 52), Sched. 1, para. 5 (as amended by Employment Protection Act 1975 (c. 71), Sched. 16, Pt. 111, para. 10).]

The words "notice required to be given by an employer" in para. 5 (6) of Sched. 1 to the 1974 Act refer to the minimum period of notice required by s. 1 (1) of the Contracts of Employment Act 1972 and not to the period of notice stated in the contract of employment.

J was employed under a contract of employment for 12 months from May 10, 1976, subject to one month's notice by either party. He was summarily dismissed and paid wages in lieu of notice. His employment terminated not later than October 15, 1976. J complained that he had been unfairly dismissed. The industrial tribunal, on the preliminary issue whether he had been continuously employed for the qualifying period of 26 weeks, found that by virtue of para. 5 (6) of Sched. 1 to the 1974 Act J could rely on the period of one month's notice to which he was contractually entitled. Thus his employment did not terminate until mid-November 1976 which was after the expiry of the 26-week period. F Ltd. appealed. *Held,* allowing the appeal, that the "notice required to be given" by the employer by para. 5 (6) of Sched. 1 was one week, accordingly J had not been employed for the qualifying period and the tribunal had no jurisdiction to hear the complaint.

FOX MAINTENANCE *v.* JACKSON [1978] I.C.R. 110, E.A.T.

1107. [Trade Union and Labour Relations Act 1974 (c. 52), Sched. 1, para. 10.]

In computing whether an employee has been employed for 26 weeks, the week during which he is dismissed is to be included.

On March 8 the employee was engaged to work for a trial period of five months. On July 21, the employers wrote to the employee stating that he would not be taken onto the permanent staff and gave one month's notice of dismissal, during which month the employee would not be required to work but would receive salary in lieu. The employers were subsequently wrongly advised that they could not dismiss the employee prior to August 31. They allowed the employee to work until August 13 and thereafter wrote confirming termination of his employment on August 31, offering salary in lieu of notice. On the employee's claim for unfair dismissal, the industrial tribunal ruled that the employee's date of dismissal was August 31 and that accordingly he had been continuously employed for 26 weeks, thereby conferring jurisdiction on the tribunal. *Held,* dismissing the employers' appeal, that the employers' subsequent conduct after the letter of July 21 was inconsistent with summary dismissal on that date. (*Coulson* v. *City of London Polytechnic* [1976] C.L.Y. 970 applied.)

I.P.C. BUSINESS PRESS *v.* GRAY [1977] I.C.R. 858, E.A.T.

1108. —— —— **transfer of business—insolvent company**

[Contracts of Employment Act 1972 (c. 53), Sched. 1, para. 9 (2).]

The fact that a company is insolvent and not a going concern at the time of transfer is relevant to the question of whether there was a transfer of business, but it is not the only criterion and other matters may be taken into consideration.

In 1975 C Ltd., an insolvent company, transferred its business assets and future contracts to another company. D was dismissed and re-employed by the new company on the same day. On his subsequent dismissal three days later he complained of unfair dismissal. The tribunal found for him and computed his period of employment from the date he commenced with C Ltd. On the employer's appeal, *held,* dismissing the appeal, that (1) the fact that a company was insolvent at the time of transfer did not necessarily mean there had been no transfer; (2) although D had been dismissed before the transfer, he had been re-engaged on the same day, and the gap of part of a day could be disregarded.

TEESSIDE TIMES *v.* DRURY [1978] I.C.R. 822, E.A.T.

1109. —— —— where employee appeals according to disciplinary procedure

S was summarily dismissed on February 21, 1978, for gross misconduct. He appealed in accordance with J.S. Co.'s disciplinary procedure. His appeal was dismissed on May 31, 1978, and he was so notified on June 1, 1978. *Held,* allowing J.S. Co.'s appeal, that the effective date of termination of S's employment was February 21, 1978. Accordingly, S did not have the requisite 26 weeks' continuous service to qualify him to present a complaint of unfair dismissal : J. SAINSBURY *v.* SAVAGE [1978] I.R.L.R. 479, E.A.T.

1110. —— —— work commenced on Saturday—whether preceding week included

[Trade Union and Labour Relations Act 1974 (c. 52), Sched. 1, paras. 10 (*a*), 30; Contracts of Employment Act 1972 (c. 53), Sched. 1, paras. 4, 11.]

If an employee begins working on a Saturday, then the preceding week, provided it was a week normally involving at least 16 hours' work can be included in calculating the qualifying period of employment.

W started work as a hairdresser on Saturday, January 15, 1977. On July 9 of that year she was dismissed and complained of unfair dismissal. On a preliminary point the tribunal held that the preceding week did not count and they had no jurisdiction. On appeal, *held,* allowing the appeal that " week " in the 1972 Act meant a week ending with Saturday, and the preceding week therefore was to be included in the qualifying period calculation. (*Coulson* v. *City of London Polytechnic* [1976] C.L.Y. 970 applied.)

WYNNE *v.* HAIR CONTROL [1978] I.C.R. 870, E.A.T.

1111. —— contributory fault—acts or omissions arising from traits of character can be relevant

M was dismissed for lack of capability. The tribunal found the dismissal unfair, but reduced M's compensation by 40 per cent. for contributory fault. *Held,* dismissing M's appeal against the 40 per cent. reduction, that it was not an absolute rule of law that an act or failing attributable to a defect of character or personality which it is not under the claimant's control to alter can never be material in deciding whether, or to what extent, he has contributed to the matters to which the complaint relates. (*Kraft Foods* v. *Fox* [1978] C.L.Y. 1118 distinguished): MONCUR *v.* INTERNATIONAL PAINT CO. [1978] I.R.L.R. 223, E.A.T.

1112. —— costs—frivolous or vexatious application

S, employed as partnership secretary by solicitors, declined to carry out an instruction, and gave one month's notice to determine her employment. She worked out her period of notice, and thereafter complained that she had been unfairly dismissed. She was required by the tribunal to give further and better particulars, from which it was apparent that she relied on one incident only when she claimed to have been wrongly reprimanded, and that she claimed to have been constructively dismissed. The hearing was fixed for Monday, February 13, 1978. On the afternoon of Friday, February 10, solicitors acting for S, who had acted on her behalf throughout the presentation of her complaint, informed the respondents and the tribunal that the application would be withdrawn. The respondents had instructed counsel. Both parties were represented before the tribunal, but S was not present. On the application of the respondents for costs against S, *held,* S could not have believed for any length of time that there was substance in her allegation of constructive dismissal; she should have withdrawn her complaint when required to give further and better particulars. Her conduct in pursuing the case thereafter was frivolous, and perhaps even vexatious. S was ordered to pay the respondents' costs, to be taxed on County Court Scale 3 : SEWELL *v.* REDMAYNE WYATT & KERSHAW, February 13, 1978, London North Industrial Tribunal. (*Ex rel. John Samuels, Barrister.*)

1113. —— disciplinary hearings—rules of natural justice

At a disciplinary hearing into the conduct of K, a midwifery staff nurse, following complaints by five patients, the patients were not called to give oral evidence and K did not ask for them to be called. Their written statements and a " statement of case " had been given to K's union representative at a disciplinary interview. *Held*, dismissing K's appeal against a finding that her dismissal was fair, that there are only three basic rules of natural justice to be complied with during a disciplinary inquiry, namely that (1) the employee should know the nature of the case against him; (2) he should be given an opportunity to state his case; and (3) the disciplinary tribunal should act in good faith. (*Byrne* v. *Kinematograph Renters Society* [1958] C.L.Y. 2778 applied): KHANUM v. MID-GLAMORGAN AREA HEALTH AUTHORITY [1978] I.R.L.R. 215, E.A.T.

1114. In striking, the plaintiff teachers argued that their action amounted to a fundamental breach of their contracts of employment, and that the I.L.E.A., in not immediately dismissing them, had waived the breach, so that their subsequent dismissal was unfair. Further, the disciplinary procedures followed by the I.L.E.A. were in breach of natural justice. *Held*, it was for the I.L.E.A. to decide whether to treat the strike as a matter for dismissal (*Morgan* v. *Fry* [1968] C.L.Y. 3954 applied). Despite the unsatisfactory dual role of the education officer in both prosecuting the plaintiffs and preparing the report to go before the disciplinary tribunal, the I.L.E.A. had acted fairly and justly, throughout; there had been no unfair dismissal: ELLIS v. INNER LONDON EDUCATION AUTHORITY, *The Times*, November 7, 1978, E.A.T.

1115. —— **dismissal or resignation—unambiguous words used by employee**
During a heated argument with the head of G Co.'s business, G said " I am leaving, I want my cards." *Held*, allowing G Co.'s appeal against a finding of unfair dismissal, that where words are used by an employee which contain no ambiguity and are understood by the employer as a resignation, it cannot be held that there was not a resignation because a reasonable employer objectively would not have so understood the words. (*Tanner* v. *Kean* [1978] C.L.Y. 1184 distinguished; *Chesham Shipping* v. *Rowe* [1977] C.L.Y. 1162 distinguished and discussed): B. G. GALE v. GILBERT [1978] I.R.L.R. 453, E.A.T.

1116. —— **" employee "—agreement to change to independent contractor**
Parties to a contract cannot alter the true nature of their relationship by attaching a different label to it.
Per curiam: When a situation is in doubt or ambiguous so that it can be brought under one relationship or the other, it is open to the parties by agreement to stipulate what the legal situation between them shall be.
From 1971 to 1973 M worked as manager of a branch office as an employee of C Co. who paid him wages and deducted tax. M also had a general agency agreement with C Co. In 1973, at his own request, M entered into an agreement with C Co. whereby he continued to do the same job but became self-employed. In 1975 C Co. terminated that agreement and M brought a complaint of unfair dismissal. The industrial tribunal held that he was not an employee for that purpose and dismissed the complaint. The Employment Appeal Tribunal upheld that decision. M appealed. *Held*, dismissing the appeal, that whatever the nature of the previous relationship, the agreement of 1973 established that M was an independent contractor and not an employee. (*Ferguson* v. *John Dawson & Partners* (*Contractors*) [1976] C.L.Y. 871 distinguished; dictum of MacKenna J. in *Ready Mixed Concrete* (*South East*) v. *Minister of Pensions and National Insurance* [1968] C.L.Y. 2550 approved.)
MASSEY v. CROWN LIFE INSURANCE CO. [1978] 1 W.L.R. 676, C.A.

1117. —— **employee carrying out work under dispute**
If an employee continues to carry out work even though his obligation to do so is under dispute, thus conveying to his employer that he has accepted it as part of his duties, then he may be fairly dismissed for failure to carry out the work.
In June 1975 there was a dispute between the E Council and the employee's, A's, union as to whether it was part of A's duties to paint lamp posts. The dispute was not resolved and A continued to paint lamp posts. In July 1976 A was informed that he was not painting sufficient lamp posts and asked to

give an undertaking that in future he would paint lamp posts when told to do so. He did not give the undertaking, and was dismissed. An industrial tribunal found that the dismissal was unfair. On appeal by the council, *held*, allowing the appeal, that it might be that A had given the council the impression that he had accepted painting lamp posts as part of his duties. As the tribunal had not considered that question, the case would be remitted to them to do so. (*Farelee Motors (Gosport)* v. *Winter* [1971] C.L.Y. 4049 applied.)

WEST YORKSHIRE METROPOLITAN DISTRICT COUNCIL *v.* PLATTS [1978] I.C.R. 33, E.A.T.

1118. —— employee doing his incompetent best—whether dismissal unfair

The dismissal of an employee who, whilst doing his best, is incapable of properly fulfilling his function, is not unfair.

The respondent employee was promoted to a post previously held by an efficient and skilled person; he proved incapable of carrying out his allotted tasks and was dismissed. An industrial tribunal found, in effect, that the employee had done his incompetent best, that his dismissal was unfair and that his incompetence warranted a 50 per cent. reduction in the award. *Held*, allowing the employers' appeal, that incompetence or incapacity on the part of an employee does not render his dismissal unfair.

KRAFT FOODS *v.* FOX [1978] I.C.R. 311, E.A.T.

1119. —— employee resigning—required to leave early—whether dismissed

An employee who resigns and desires to leave before the expiry of his notice period may nevertheless be " dismissed " if his employer requires him to leave by an earlier date to which he has not agreed.

L, a pilot, resigned and was required to give three months' notice. He asked if he could leave one month early. No agreement was reached but the employers found a replacement and required L to leave earlier than anticipated. The tribunal found him to have been unfairly dismissed. *Held*, dismissing the employers' appeal, that, as there was no binding agreement as to when L should leave, the employers dismissed him by requiring him to leave by a certain date. Further, that the engagement of a replacement was not " some other substantial reason " within the meaning of the 1974 Act.

BRITISH MIDLAND AIRWAYS *v.* LEWIS [1978] I.C.R. 782, E.A.T.

1120. —— employee seconded to subsidiary—which company is employer

Where an employee's contract of employment is varied to permit him to work for a subsidiary company, the parent company nevertheless remains his employer for unfair dismissal purposes at all times.

C was employed by RDL Ltd. but sent to work for BBB for a lengthy period, with variations to his contract to include BBB's terms and conditions. He was dismissed by BBB, returned to work for RDL, and was dismissed for redundancy by them. C complained of the first dismissal. The tribunal found unfair dismissal by BBB, but held they had no jurisdiction to hear the complaint against RDL. On cross-appeals, *held*, allowing both appeals, that although BBB had use of C's services, and in certain circumstances would have been vicariously liable for him, in the absence of express or implied transfer in the contract of employment, C remained throughout, for the purposes of unfair dismissal, the employee of RDL.

CROSS *v.* REDPATH DORMAN LONG [1978] I.C.R. 730, E.A.T.

1121. —— estoppel—denial of breach of contract in civil proceedings. See TURNER *v.* LONDON TRANSPORT EXECUTIVE, § 902.

1122. —— evidence—duty of tribunal to hear both parties

In an arguable case, industrial tribunals should hear the evidence of both parties.

B and R were dismissed from their employment with G Ltd. They complained that their dismissal was unfair. The industrial tribunal heard evidence that they had been found asleep or resting when they should have been working. Without calling upon them to give evidence, the tribunal found that B and R had been unfairly dismissed but reduced the compensatory awards by 30 per cent. because of their conduct. On appeal by G Ltd., and on the cross-appeal by the employees against the contributory award, *held*, allowing the appeal and the cross-appeal, that since the tribunal had misdirected itself in not hearing the evidence of the employees, the case would be remitted for a rehearing.

GEORGE A. PALMER *v.* BEEBY [1978] I.C.R. 196, E.A.T.

1123. —— —— **further and better particulars of application**

IC Co. dismissed W for submitting a fraudulent expense claim. The tribunal rejected IC Co.'s request for further and better particulars of W's claim that IC Co. had long condoned the same practice by other employees. *Held,* allowing IC Co.'s appeal, that they were entitled to the particulars: INTERNATIONAL COMPUTERS *v.* WHITLEY [1978] I.R.L.R. 318, E.A.T.

1124. —— **exclusions and qualifications—normal hours of work**

[Trade Union and Labour Relations Act 1974 (c. 52), Sched. 1, para. 9 (1) (*f*); Contracts of Employment Act 1972 (c. 53), Sched. 1, para. 4.]

The number of hours of work normally involved in an employee's contract of employment for the purposes of Sched. 1, para. 9 (1) (*f*) to the 1974 Act and Sched. 1, para. 4 to the 1972 Act is determined either from express terms in the contract or by inferring such terms from what happens in practice.

K was employed by ITT as a clerk under a contract specifying her normal hours of work as 20 hours per week with payment for overtime worked. After four years she was promoted to supervisor but continued to work a 20-hour week with an average of four hours' overtime. She was dismissed and applied for compensation for unfair dismissal. The industrial tribunal calculated the number of hours worked weekly by including the hours of overtime and decided as a preliminary point that she was employed under a contract normally involving at least 23 hours work a week. Accordingly she was not excluded from her claim by virtue of para. 9 (1) (*f*) of Sched. 1 to the 1974 Act. ITT appealed. *Held,* allowing the appeal, that however the hours normally worked under a contract of employment were determined, they did not include voluntary overtime and since the tribunal had not applied the correct test and K's contractual obligations might have been varied on her promotion, the case would be remitted to the industrial tribunal.

I.T.T. COMPONENTS GROUP (EUROPE) *v.* KOLAH [1977] I.C.R. 740, E.A.T.

1125. —— **extent of teacher's duties**

[Trade Union and Labour Relations Act 1974 (c. 52), Sched. 1, para. 6 (8).]

Although a teacher may be required to do work other than that for which he was engaged, that requirement must be reasonable according to the circumstances, the particular duties the teacher was engaged to undertake, and the custom and practice of the profession.

T, a teacher, was engaged to take charge of the school's resources centre, which included video-tapes, films, cassettes and other teaching aids. This was a virtually full-time occupation. A new head teacher, with more traditional ideas, who regarded the resources centre as the equivalent of a library rather than a central part of the teaching activities, asked T to teach 12 English periods a week. T agreed, but refused a request to teach a further six, on the ground that it would interfere with her conduct of the resources centre. She was dismissed. The industrial tribunal held that the dismissal was unfair. On appeal by the local authority, *held,* dismissing the appeal, that the local authority had acted unreasonably in treating her refusal as a sufficient reason for dismissal. Her teaching commitment was ancillary to her duties regarding the resources centre, and the dismissal was unfair.

REDBRIDGE LONDON BOROUGH COUNCIL *v.* FISHMAN (1978) 76 L.G.R. 408, E.A.T.

1126. —— **fixed term contract—termination**

[Trade Union and Labour Relations Act 1974 (c. 52), Sched. 1, paras. 5 (2) (*b*), 12.] In the context of the code for unfair dismissal laid down in the Act, " fixed-term " means a specified term, even though it may be terminable by notice within the term; otherwise by the mere insertion of a phrase like " determinable by one week's notice," an employer could evade the provisions of the Act (*British Broadcasting Corp.* v. *Ioannou* [1975] C.L.Y. 1091 disapproved):

DIXON v. BRITISH BROADCASTING CORP.; CONSTANTI v. BRITISH BROADCASTING CORP., *The Times,* October 6, 1978, C.A.

1127. —— —— where precise date of expiry unknown

[Trade Union and Labour Relations Act 1974 (c. 52), Sched. 1, para. 5 (2) (*b*).]

For the purposes of an unfair dismissal claim, a contract of employment is for a fixed term if its termination is fixed by specified external events.

As a part-time teacher, the employee entered into a new contract of employment for each academic year; she agreed to teach certain subjects on particular days and was paid only for those days. Her teaching sessions did not necessarily continue until the end of the academic year. When her contract was not renewed, she claimed unfair dismissal. An industrial tribunal ruled that it had jurisdiction to entertain the claim, her contract being for a fixed term within the meaning of para. 5 (2) (*b*) of Sched. 1 to the Act. *Held*, dismissing the employer's appeal, that since it was known that the employee's contract would terminate no later than the end of the academic year, it was for a fixed term. (*British Broadcasting Corp.* v. *Ioannou* [1975] C.L.Y. 1091, distinguished.)

WILTSHIRE COUNTY COUNCIL v. NATIONAL ASSOCIATION OF TEACHERS IN FURTHER AND HIGHER EDUCATION [1978] I.C.R. 968, E.A.T.

1128. —— guidelines of tribunal—construction of statutes. See WELLS v. DERWENT PLASTICS, § 2838.

1129. —— ill-health—lack of consultation

[Trade Union and Labour Relations Act 1974 (c. 52), Sched. 1, para. 6 (8).]

Before an employer dismisses an employee on the ground of ill-health, he should take all reasonable steps to ascertain the true medical position.

W commenced his employment as a cold metal handler with A Ltd. in October 1974. In January 1975, he suffered a slipped disc, and his doctors provided A Ltd. with certificates to show that he was incapacitated. On March 31, 1976, he informed A Ltd. that he was on the waiting list for admission to hospital, and that he hoped soon to be able to return to light work. On June 28, 1976, A Ltd. gave him notice of dismissal expiring on July 11. On June 30, there was a meeting between W and A Ltd. which resulted in his being seen by one of their doctors who advised against him doing anything but the lightest work. However, A Ltd. co-operated in expediting arrangements for him to see a specialist. The examination took place on July 12, the day after his dismissal became effective, when the specialist formed the opinion that W had made a spontaneous recovery and was fit to return to his former job. W claimed compensation for unfair dismissal. The industrial tribunal held that A Ltd. had acted reasonably within the meaning of para. 6 (8) of Sched. 1 to the 1974 Act. W appealed. *Held*, allowing the appeal, that there was no reason why W should not have been consulted before the decision to dismiss him, and A Ltd. should have discussed the matter with him; accordingly, the case would be remitted for rehearing. (*Spencer* v. *Paragon Wallpapers* [1977] C.L.Y. 1151 and *East Lindsey District Council* v. *Daubney* [1977] C.L.Y. 1142 applied.)

WILLIAMSON v. ALCAN (U.K.) [1978] I.C.R. 104, E.A.T.

1130. —— —— whether employer reasonable in relying upon medical opinion

E, a domestic assistant at a hospital, was dismissed as unfit to continue her duties on the basis of a medical report by a doctor of the medical advisory service. E appealed but her request for a further and better medical report was refused and her appeal was dismissed. A subsequent medical report contained a conclusion that E was fit for her work. *Held*, allowing an appeal against a finding of unfair dismissal, that an employer faced with a medical opinion is not required to evaluate it as a layman in terms of medical expertise unless it is clearly erroneous as to the facts or indicates that no proper examination has taken place. The tribunal had erred in finding that the expert opinion of the sister-in-charge for whom E worked should have been sought: LIVERPOOL AREA HEALTH AUTHORITY (TEACHING) CENTRAL & SOUTHERN DISTRICT v. EDWARDS [1977] I.R.L.R. 471, E.A.T.

1131. —— **inadmissible reason—trade union activities—appropriate time**
[Trade Union and Labour Relations Act 1974 (c. 52), Sched. 1, para. 6 (4A), as added by Employment Protection Act 1975 (c. 71), Sched. 16, Pt. III, para. 11.]
It is not necessary for there to be an express agreement between a union and employers permitting union activities during working hours, for such activities to be at an " appropriate time " within the meaning of the 1974 Act.
S, a shop steward, called a meeting with the employers over another employee's pay claim. At the meeting his status was challenged and he left to call a further meeting with other workers which stopped work for an hour. S was dismissed, and claimed unfair dismissal in that he was involved in trade union activities at an appropriate time. The tribunal found the dismissal unfair. On the employer's appeal, *held*, dismissing the appeal by a majority, that an express agreement permitting union activities during working hours was not necessary, and since convening a meeting during working hours accorded with accepted industrial practice, the activities were at an appropriate time. (*National Union of Gold, Silver and Allied Trades* v. *Albury Brothers* [1978] C.L.Y. 2998 referred to.)
MARLEY TILE CO. v. SHAW [1978] I.C.R. 828, E.A.T.

1132. —— —— —— **burden of proof—less than 26 weeks' service**
[Trade Union and Labour Relations Act 1974 (c. 52), Sched. 1, para. 11 (1).]
The burden of proving that dismissal was due to an inadmissible reason (trade union activities) under para. 11 (1) of Sched. 1 to the 1974 Act rests upon the employee.
In August 1976 the employee was engaged as part-time clerk to the council. In November he told two councillors of his application to join a trade union. In December he was dismissed after a council meeting had voted by six votes to five to so act; one councillor stated that he was against the employee because of his joining the union. By reason of his short period of employment, the employee could succeed in a complaint of unfair dismissal only if such dismissal was for the inadmissible reason of his joining the trade union. He failed in his application to the industrial tribunal and to the E.A.T. *Held*, dismissing his appeal (Lord Denning M.R. dissenting), that the employee had failed to discharge the burden upon him of proving that the principal reason for his dismissal was an inadmissible one.
SMITH v. HAYLE TOWN COUNCIL [1978] I.C.R. 996, C.A.

1133. —— **industrial tribunal—written statements admissible as evidence**
[Civil Evidence Act 1968 (c. 64), s. 2 (1); R.S.C., Ord. 38, r. 29.]
Proceedings for unfair dismissal are civil proceedings before a tribunal to which s. 2 (1) of the Civil Evidence Act 1968 applies, and written statements may be admitted so long as they comply with the provisions of the section and with R.S.C., Ord. 38.
E, a school cleaner, was permitted to take her four month old baby to work with her, because she had nowhere to leave him, so long as the baby did not interfere with her work. However, by the time the baby was two, he had become very active, and suffered two accidents on the premises. E was told to make other arrangements, she refused, and was dismissed. At the hearing of E's claim for compensation for unfair dismissal before an industrial tribunal, E's counsel tendered in evidence the statements of two witnesses who had failed to attend. The tribunal refused to admit them on the ground that the council's solicitor would thereby be deprived of an opportunity to cross-examine, then went on to find that E's dismissal was fair. On appeal by E, *held*, (1) that as the child was a distraction at work, the council was entitled to act as it had; (2) the statements could have been admissible, but as the provisions of s. 2 (1) of the Civil Evidence Act had not been complied with, the chairman of the tribunal had a discretion to exclude them, and he had exercised that discretion correctly so as to avoid injustice to the council.
LAWRENCE v. NEWHAM LONDON BOROUGH COUNCIL [1978] I.C.R. 10, E.A.T.

1134. —— Industrial Tribunal decisions

Complaint subsequent to settlement

NENSI *v.* VINOLA (KNITWEAR) MANUFACTURING CO. [1978] I.R.L.R. 297 (N's application for unfair dismissal was settled on terms that N should be re-employed on the terms and conditions under which he was employed prior to dismissal. The tribunal ordered that all further proceedings on the claim be adjourned generally until further order, with leave to either party to ask for further directions in the event of any default or difficulty in carrying out the agreed settlement. The following month, N was again dismissed for lack of capability. *Held,* that the tribunal had no power to deal with N's original application, as V Co. had complied with the terms of the settlement. No minimum period of re-employment could be implied; nor could continuity of employment be implied. In any event, breaches of the settlement were matters for the county court. The tribunal could not hear N's second application for compensation as he did not have the requisite 26 weeks' continuous service).

Discovery of documents

GOWANS *v.* U.B.M. MOTORS (1978) 13 I.T.R. 163 (following G's dismissal, police investigated his conduct, but did not prosecute. A tribunal granted U.B.M. Co. witness orders requiring a police officer to attend and produce documents, including a witness statement made to the police. *Held,* setting aside the orders, that (1) the document having been made after the dismissal, it could not be relevant to the fairness of the dismissal and could only be of use for cross-examination; (2) the minimal detriment to public interest in the judicial sphere arising from non-disclosure was outweighed by the substantial detriment in the administrative or executive side arising from disclosure).

Employer's onus of proof

SEALEY *v.* AVON ALUMINIUM CO. [1978] I.R.L.R. 285 (employees on strike in support of S were sent letters stating that their breach of contract in failing to attend for work was being taken to mean that their contracts of employment were terminated. *Held,* that (1) they had been dismissed. Fundamental breach does not terminate a contract without acceptance unless the breach is express termination of contract; (2) AA Co. had failed to discharge the onus on them under the Trade Union and Labour Relations Act 1974, Sched. 1, para. 6. As one of the strikers had subsequently been re-engaged, para. 7 applied, so that AA Co. had to show the principal reason for failing to re-engage the applicants rather than the principal reason for dismissal. This created an insoluble anomaly since the principal reason was that they had not applied for re-engagement, which was not a designated reason under para. 6 (2). Accordingly, the dismissal was unfair. Further anomalies were discussed in the decision).

Gross misconduct before employment commences

BELL *v.* THE DEVON & CORNWALL POLICE AUTHORITY [1978] I.R.L.R. 283 (B, a chef, was suspended on full pay following his statement to the police prior to his trial for two acts of gross indecency. He admitted being bi-sexual but was acquitted on technical grounds. Thereafter about a third of the police and civilian staff at the D.C.P.A. canteen were asked to make statements about B. Four said they had nothing against B but could not eat food prepared by him as they found what was described in the statements about B revolting. All the police officers said they would stop using the canteen. *Held,* that B's dismissal was unfair. The homosexual acts concerned took place before his employment commenced. Conduct before commencement of employment cannot be gross misconduct unless the employee makes a false statement in relation thereto before being employed. It was unfair to base the dismissal on the statements taken from one-third of staff without more inquiry and attempts to solve the problem by consultation, and without giving B an opportunity to comment on the statements).

Minimum period of service

RUSSELL *v.* JOHN GILL TRANSPORT [1978] I.R.L.R. 196 (R terminated his contract of employment during his 25th week of service, and claimed constructive dismissal. Para. 5 (6) of Sched. 1 to the Trade Union and Labour Relations Act 1974, under which the effective date of termination is deemed to be the date when the statutory minimum notice would have expired where the contract is terminated by the employer without the notice specified by the Contracts of Employment Act 1972, does not apply to cases of constructive dismissal. Accordingly, R did not have the requisite 26 weeks' service to bring an unfair dismissal claim).

Pregnancy—failure to offer suitable alternative job

MARTIN v. B.S.C. FOOTWEAR (SUPPLIES) [1978] I.R.L.R. 95 (M, a warehouse employee employed on " pulling and checking," was advised when she became pregnant that the " pulling " work was too heavy for her. B.S.C. decided it was not feasible to put her on full-time checking. When M refused to do pulling, she was given six weeks' notice during which she did various light jobs and a temporary vacancy in display packaging was filled by another employee. *Held*, that M had been unfairly dismissed on grounds of pregnancy contrary to s. 34 (2) of the Employment Protection Act. Although s. 34 (2) does not require an employer to modify a woman's existing job to meet her requirements resulting from pregnancy or to create a suitable job, it does require the employer to look for and offer to a woman incapable of performing her usual job, " any suitable vacancy." M should have been offered the vacancy in display packaging until the woman who usually did that job returned or M began her pregnancy leave of absence).

Refusal to join union

ASHBY AND BRIDGES v. COLEMAN [1978] I.R.L.R. 51 (A and B, painters normally employed on " outside work," agreed to work at a refinery site as an alternative to redundancy when " outside work " decreased. After two weeks they were returned to outside work. The following year they were dismissed after refusing a direction to work at the refinery again because they were no longer union members; by an arrangement all on the site had to be union members and A and B said they could not afford the subscription arrears involved in rejoining. *Held*, that notwithstanding that the respondents were not a party to the union membership agreement, A and B had been fairly dismissed for a reason within para. 6 (5), Sched. 1 to the 1974 Act).

Refusal to wear protective clothing

MAYHEW v. ANDERSON (STOKE NEWINGTON) [1978] I.R.L.R. 101 (M, a part-time sewing machinist, was dismissed for refusing to wear protective goggles bought by A Co. for 78p to fit over her spectacles. Following a number of minor injuries to M's eyes A Co.'s insurers had threatened to withdraw cover unless M wore protective eye pieces. Spectacles with optical lenses to suit M would cost £33 to £35 but A Co. said that to purchase those for M might create a precedent with other employees. *Held*, that the dismissal was unfair as A Co. should have bought M the more acceptable eye protectors).

Sleeping on job

AYUB v. VAUXHALL MOTORS [1978] I.R.L.R. 428 (A, a production manager, was dismissed for sleeping during his shift after he had finished the quota for his shift. *Held*, that dismissal was unfair because (1) no reasonable employer would regard such conduct as gross misconduct. Different considerations would apply if notices had been displayed advising employees that dismissal would follow sleeping on the job; (2) an employee dismissed three days earlier for the same offence had had his dismissal set aside on appeal and a three-day suspension substituted).

Union membership agreement

SCOTT v. E. & E. KAYE [1978] I.R.L.R. 193 (following a union membership agreement, the union concerned claimed that S was in arrears of dues. S claimed to have paid the arrears but agreed to have sufficient of the alleged arrears deducted at source for his membership not to lapse. There remained sufficient alleged arrears for S to be " out of compliance " so that under union rules he had no rights of representation. *Held*, that S's dismissal under the union membership agreement for refusing to pay the remaining alleged arrears was unfair. An out of compliance member of a union is not an employee who is " not a member of a specified union " within the Trade Union and Labour Relations Act 1974, Sched. 1, para, 6 (5)).

1135. —— **interim relief—whether complaint " likely " to succeed**

[Employment Protection Act 1975 (c. 74), s. 78.]

In order to qualify for interim relief, an employee alleging dismissal due to trade union activities must show that this allegation is likely to succeed, in that he has a " pretty good " chance of success.

The employee alleged that he had been unfairly dismissed because of his trade union activities. His application for interim relief was rejected on the grounds that he had not established that it was " likely " (under s. 78 (5) of the Act) that his allegation would succeed. The industrial tribunal chairman ruled that " likely " meant nearer to " certainty " as opposed to mere probability." *Held*, dismissing the employee's appeal (by a majority), that to be " likely " to succeed, an allegation had to have a " pretty good " chance of success, more than a 51 per cent. probability; the chairman had not in the result erred in law: TAPLIN v. C. SHIPPAM [1978] I.C.R. 1068, E.A.T.

1136. —— **jurisdiction—existence of contract of service—sales representative on commission—conduct and relationship**

[Contracts of Employment Act 1972 (c. 53), s. 11 (1).]

The question of whether or not a person is an employee depends not on labels but on the reality of the relationship to be inferred from the parties' conduct.

H was engaged as a sales representative, informed he was self-employed, paid Schedule D tax and was paid a commission. He was instructed when and where to work each week and was to apply the company sales techniques contained in the employers' manual. On a complaint of unfair dismissal, the tribunal decided on a preliminary issue that H had a contract of service and therefore the tribunal had jurisdiction. *Held*, dismissing the employers' appeal, that according to the definition of employee in s. 11 (1) of the Act, the question was whether there was contract of service; this question had to be answered, not by looking at labels, but by reference to the reality of the relationship and the parties' conduct. (*Ferguson* v. *John Dawson* [1976] C.L.Y. 871 applied; *Massey* v. *Crown Life Insurance* [1978] C.L.Y. 1116 considered.) TYNE AND CLYDE WAREHOUSES v. HAMERTON [1978] I.C.R. 661, E.A.T.

1137. —— —— **number of employees—complainant hired assistant as agent**

[Trade Union and Labour Relations Act 1974 (c. 52), Sched. 1, para. 9 (2) (*a*).] A, employed by a club as stewardess, was given an extra £11 with which to engage and pay an assistant or assistants. A engaged only X with the £11. The club employed only two others. A tribunal held that the club employed four employees and that there was accordingly jurisdiction to hear A's complaint of unfair dismissal. *Held*, dismissing the club's appeal, that the common understanding in such a situation was that, in employing X, A was acting as agent for the club. A was thus employed by the club: SHOTTON COLLIERY OFFICIALS CLUB v. AYRE (1977) 12 I.T.R. 433, E.A.T.

1138. —— —— **whether employee ordinarily works outside Britain—" base " test**

[Trade Union and Labour Relations Act 1974 (c. 52), Sched. 1, para. 9 (2).]

In deciding whether an employee " ordinarily " works outside Great Britain, the " base " test should be applied, regard being had to the location of the employee's work base.

The employee pilot was employed by an airline company for duties on international routes: later analysis proved that he spent some 53 per cent. of his flying days outside Great Britain. Upon his complaining of unfair dismissal, a preliminary question as to jurisdiction was tried (para. 9 (2) of Sched. 1 to the Act excluding jurisdiction in respect of employees " ordinarily " working outside Great Britain); an industrial tribunal, affirmed by the E.A.T., ruled against the employee. *Held*, allowing his appeal, that the contract of employment was not conclusive and that applying the " base " test formulated in *Wilson's* case, the employee's case fell within the jurisdiction since his working base had at all material times been in Great Britain. (*Wilson* v. *Maynard Ship-*

building Consultants A.B. [1978] C.L.Y. 981 applied; *Claisse* v. *Keydril* [1978] C.L.Y. 1140 not applied.)

TODD v. BRITISH MIDLAND AIRWAYS [1978] I.C.R. 959, C.A.

1139. —— —— whether four people employed—distinction between salary and honorarium

[Trade Union and Labour Relations Act 1974 (c. 52), Sched. 1, paras. 4, 9 (1) (*a*).]

A person who receives an honorarium is not an employee for the purposes of the 1974 Act.

Upon the hearing of a club steward's complaint of unfair dismissal the question arose as to whether the complaint was excluded by virtue of para. 9 (1) (*a*) of Sched. 1 to the Act, the employers contending that there were less than four employees. Resolution of the issue depended upon the status of the club secretary who under the club rules was selected but remained thereafter in office during the pleasure of the club and was liable to removal by the vote of two-thirds of the members. The rules provided that the secretary should receive such honorarium or such salary as might from time to time be determined. The secretary received £225 per annum which he regarded as an honorarium. The industrial tribunal ruled that the secretary was an employee for the purposes of para. 9 (1) (*a*). *Held*, allowing the employers' appeal, that the tribunal should reconsider the case to determine whether the £225 was an honorarium or a salary, since in the case of the former he would not be an employee.

102 SOCIAL CLUB AND INSTITUTE v. BICKERTON [1977] I.C.R. 911, E.A.T.

1140. —— —— whether work on oil rig is inside Great Britain—onus of proof

[Trade Union and Labour Relations Act 1974 (c. 52), Sched. 1, para. 9 (2).]

Since an employee on an oil rig moving constantly in and out of territorial waters cannot discharge his burden of proving that he ordinarily works inside Great Britain, the tribunal has no jurisdiction to hear his complaint.

C worked on an oil rig used in drilling operations in the North Sea which was moved as required to locations both inside and outside territorial waters. The tribunal held that it had no jurisdiction to hear the complaint. On appeal, *held*, dismissing the appeal, that since C worked both inside and outside Great Britain, he had not discharged the onus of proving he ordinarily worked inside Great Britain and accordingly the tribunal had no jurisdiction to hear the complaint. (*Wilson* v. *Maynard Shipbuilding Consultants* [1978] C.L.Y. 981 applied.)

CLAISSE v. KEYDRIL [1978] I.C.R. 812, E.A.T.

1141. —— lay-off—no notice given—whether dismissal

[Contract of Employment Act 1972 (c. 53), s. 1 (2), as amended by Employment Protection Act 1975 (c. 71).]

In the absence of an express or implied agreement to the contrary, an employer is not entitled to temporarily lay off employees without giving one week's notice of pay in lieu.

In October 1975 an employer anticipating cash-flow problems warned his small work-force that he might have to lay them off temporarily. On November 28, the employees were laid off without further notice. One, the applicant, forthwith consulted solicitors, notified the employer that his action amounted to dismissal and complained to an industrial tribunal of unfair dismissal and redundancy. The tribunal rejected his claim. *Held*, allowing the employee's appeal and remitting the case for rehearing, that since the tribunal had not appreciated that the employer could not in the absence of an agreement to the contrary, lay-off the employee without at least one week's notice, the tribunal must reconsider whether the employer's action, which amounted to a dismissal, was unfair or resulted from a redundancy situation. (*Devonald* v. *Rosser & Sons* [1906] 2 K.B. 728, applied.)

JOHNSON v. CROSS [1977] I.C.R. 872, E.A.T.

1142. —— maternity leave—right to return to work

[Employment Protection Act 1975 (c. 71), Sched. 3, para. 5.]

An employee, on returning to work after maternity leave, cannot take advantage of Sched. 3, para. 5 to the Employment Protection Act 1975 so as to combine the more favourable aspects of both her statutory and contractual rights.

B was employed as a full-time physiotherapist, Grade I. On her return from maternity leave she agreed to work part-time on the basic grade. Later B claimed she was entitled to work part-time on her original grade. The tribunal held she was not entitled to her old job back on a new basis. On appeal, *held*, dismissing the appeal, that an employee could not take advantage of the Act so as to combine the more favourable aspects of her statutory and contractual rights.

BOVEY v. BOARD OF GOVERNORS OF THE HOSPITAL FOR SICK CHILDREN [1978] I.C.R. 934, E.A.T.

1143. [Employment Protection Act 1975 (c. 71), s. 35 (1) (*b*).]

S. 35 of the Act applies to cases which can be made out in their entirety by reference to acts taking place after the date when the section came into operation.

H, employed by the area health authority as a higher clerical officer, became pregnant in October 1975. In January 1976 she informed her employers that the baby was due in July 1976 and that she would resign prior to that date and not return to work. In March 1976 another clerical officer was engaged and started training as H's replacement. Later that month H wrote to the employers asking to be granted maternity leave and indicating her intention of returning to work after the birth. On April 26 she left and was paid up to April 30. She received no payment in respect of maternity leave. On June 1, 1976, the relevant provisions of the Act came into force. H complained that she had a right to return to work by virtue of s. 35 (1) (*b*) of the Act. The industrial tribunal found that she had clearly resigned and had thereby forfeited her right to return to work. H appealed. *Held*, dismissing the appeal, that since a number of relevant acts took place before the commencement of the relevant part of the statute H was not entitled to relief under the Act. *Quaere*, where a woman, fully understanding her rights, resigns, it may be that it is only resignations taking effect before the 11th week before the expected date of confinement which are binding and irrevocable.

HUGHES v. GWYNEDD AREA HEALTH AUTHORITY [1978] I.C.R. 161, E.A.T.

1144. —— —— —— **notice**

[Employment Protection Act 1975 (c. 71), s. 35 (2) (*c*).] An employee who failed to give her employers notice at least three weeks before she left that she was pregnant and that she intended to return to work after the birth, was not entitled to have her job back. She knew her rights and clearly knew that notice had to be given, and had failed to show that it was not reasonably practicable to have given notice: NU-SWIFT INTERNATIONAL v. MALLINSON *The Times*, October 14, 1978, E.A.T.

1145. —— **normal retiring age—whether claim debarred**

[Trade Union and Labour Relations Act 1974 (c. 52), Sched. 1, para. 10 (*b*).]

An employee who has passed the " normal retiring age " for workers in the undertaking in which he is employed, may be debarred from complaining of unfair dismissal notwithstanding that his employers operate a scheme for re-employment of those passing such an age.

Upon reaching the age of 60, the appellant employee was re-engaged by the Post Office under a temporary contract pursuant to a scheme operated by the employers, whereby employees reaching such an age, whilst not being entitled to insist upon continuing employment, could retire with a pension, or, inter alia, be temporarily re-engaged. The employee was dismissed, and claimed compensation for unfair dismissal. An industrial tribunal found that 60 was the normal retiring age for such employees, and that this claim was therefore barred by virtue of para. 10 (*b*) of Sched. 1 to the Act. *Held*, dismissing the appeal, that there was no evidence to contradict the prima facie conclusion that the normal retiring age was 60. (*Ord* v. *Maidstone and District Hospital Management Committee* [1974] C.L.Y. 1328 distinguished.)

SMITH v. POST OFFICE [1978] I.C.R. 283, E.A.T.

1146. —— —— woman over 60

[Trade Union and Labour Relations Act 1974 (c. 52), Sched. 1, para. 10 (*b*).]

On a true construction of para. 10 (*b*) of Sched. 1 to the Trade Union and Labour Relations Act 1974, which removes the right to complain for unfair dismissal from an employee who has attained the normal retiring age, *i.e.* if a man 65, or if a woman 60, the normal retiring age in a particular profession is the age on which an employee must or should retire, and only in the absence of such a requirement will the restrictions of 65 and 60 apply.

A, a woman, was employed as a teacher under a contract of employment which provided for automatic retirement at the age of 65. She was dismissed at the age of 61, and she brought a complaint for unfair dismissal. The tribunal held that it had no jurisdiction to hear the complaint under para. 10 (*b*) of Sched. 1 to the Trade Union and Labour Relations Act 1974. The Employment Appeal Tribunal dismissed A's appeal, holding that para. 10 (*b*) presented a double barrier, and that although A had not reached normal retiring age, she was a woman and had reached 60. On appeal by E, *held*, allowing the appeal, that the age restrictions of 65 and 60 only came into operation where there was no normal retiring age to be considered. A had not reached that age, and therefore was not precluded from complaining for unfair dismissal.

NOTHMAN *v.* BARNET LONDON BOROUGH COUNCIL [1978] 1 W.L.R. 220, C.A.

1147. —— other substantial reason—business reorganisation—refusal to accept changes—onus of proof on employers

[Trade Union and Labour Relations Act (c. 52), Sched. 1, para. 6 (*b*), (8).]

It is sufficient, where an employer dismisses for refusal to accept reorganisation involving the employee's job, to show that the reorganisation was undertaken for a sound business reason, and proper prior consultation is not necessary.

The employers decided to reorganise their business in Cornwall. H objected to the reorganisation and the lack of consultation. H refused to sign a new contract and was dismissed. The tribunal held the dismissal to be fair. *Held*, allowing the appeal of H, that it was not necessary to show the proposed reorganisation was an alternative to disaster, only that it was for sound business reasons; nor was it necessary to show prior proper consultation. Here, however, the employers had not discharged their onus of showing they had acted reasonably. (*Ellis* v. *Brighton Co-op Society* [1977] C.L.Y. 1164 considered).

HOLLISTER *v.* NATIONAL FARMERS' UNION [1978] I.C.R. 712, E.A.T.

1148. —— —— pressure from employer's major customer

A cigarette lighter belonging to a naval officer to whose house P had been sent to pack his property, was found in P's pocket. P, a packer, reported the matter to S. Co. who decided to take no action unless an official report was received. A letter was subsequently received from the U.S. naval authorities, S. Co.'s major customer, indicating that P could no longer be accepted for work with the U.S. Government. *Held*, allowing S. Co.'s appeal against a finding that the company had failed to show the reason for P's dismissal, the fact that the company's major customer would not accept P on their work was "some other substantial reason" for his dismissal. A dismissal in such circumstances was not unreasonable even if the customer's motives for seeking the employee's removal were suspect: SCOTT PACKING & WAREHOUSING CO. *v.* PATERSON [1978] I.R.L.R. 166, E.A.T.

1149. —— pressure on employer to dismiss—test

[Trade Union and Labour Relations Act 1974 (c. 52), Sched. 1, para. 5.]

An employee need not show that pressure brought on an employer was pressure explicitly to dismiss if it was reasonably foreseeable that the pressure might lead to a dismissal.

Workers in a factory threatened to strike if particular workers were allowed to work in the old tool room of the factory. The employers dismissed those workers rather than allow them so to work and face a strike. The tribunal held that the dismissals were unfair, but failed to state the reason for them. *Held*, allowing the employers' appeal and remitting the case to a tribunal, that they should have found a reason for the dismissal; further, that it was not necessary for the employees to show that those exerting pressure on the employers expressly sought their dismissal if it was foreseeable that such pressure might result in their dismissal.

FORD MOTOR CO. *v.* HUDSON [1978] I.C.R. 482, E.A.T.

1150. —— procedure—failure to comply with contractual terms

C's contract of employment incorporated an agreed dismissal procedure under which a proposal to dismiss " shall be conveyed to the officer concerned by letter over the signature of the chief officer stating the grounds . . . ," and there was to be a right of appeal within seven days. C and other employees were charged by the police with conspiracy to assault a rent collector employed by the Council. At a meeting between C, his union representative and Council representatives, C admitted committing what the tribunal described as " a serious criminal charge." C was then suspended and his superior wrote asking him to attend a disciplinary interview. When, on advice, he refused to appear, the Council wrote dismissing him on the ground that there was reason to believe he had committed serious offences, and informing him of his right of appeal. *Held*, remitting the case to another tribunal, that (1) the tribunal had erred in finding the dismissal unfair because the Council had failed to comply with their own dismissal procedures which were terms of C's contract. The question was whether the exceptional nature of C's conduct overrode the necessity to comply with the Council's own procedure; (2) the tribunal's reduction of compensation by 50 per cent. was based upon a finding that C had admitted committing an act of dishonesty, which finding was unsupported by any of the evidence. (*Carr v. Alexander Russell* [1976] C.L.Y. 1007 and *Lowndes v. Specialist Heavy Engineering* [1976] C.L.Y. 986 applied): CARDIFF CITY COUNCIL *v.* CONDE [1978] I.R.L.R. 218, E.A.T.

1151. —— reasonableness—employee applying for job falsely stating no previous convictions

[Rehabilitation of Offenders Act 1974 (c. 53).]

An employer is under no duty to disregard spent convictions when engaging an employee to hold a position of trust.

When T applied for a job as a railway guard he falsely stated that he had no previous convictions. In fact he had been sentenced to terms of imprisonment for offences of dishonesty on two previous occasions. The employer's found out about the first offence and as a result he was prosecuted for dishonestly obtaining a pecuniary advantage by deception. He pleaded guilty and was conditionally discharged. T was dismissed but was offered alternative employment as a railman which he refused. His complaint that his dismissal was unfair in that the employers acted unreasonably was dismissed by the industrial tribunal. T appealed on the ground that although his previous convictions were not spent within the meaning of the 1974 Act, the employers ought to have regard to public policy in relation to rehabilitation of offenders and that it was unfair to dismiss him because of his previous convictions. *Held*, dismissing the appeal, that the employers were not obliged to pursue the social philosophy of disregarding spent convictions but it was their duty to act fairly having regard to the requirements of the job and the interest of the employee; that since this was a position of trust, T should have truthfully disclosed all relevant information when making his application and the employers had acted reasonably in dismissing him.

TORR *v.* BRITISH RAILWAYS BOARD [1977] I.C.R. 785, E.A.T.

1152. —— —— employee dismissed and replaced by employer's son

[Trade Union and Labour Relations Act 1974 (c. 52), Sched. 1, para. 6 (1) (*b*).]

The words " some other substantial reason " in para. 6 (1) (*b*) of Sched. 1 to the Act are not to be construed ejusdem generis with the reasons for dismissal specified in para. 6 (2).

P, a farm labourer, who was unable to operate or repair farm machinery was dismissed by D, his employer, so that his son could take over the work which was insufficient for two men. D's son had farming experience and was a competent mechanic. P knew when he commenced the employment that the son would eventually work on the farm. P complained that he had been unfairly dismissed. The industrial tribunal found that the reason for dismissal was " a substantial reason of a kind such as to justify the dismissal " within para. 6 (1) (*b*) of Sched. 1 to the Act and that the dismissal was fair. P appealed. *Held*, dismissing the appeal, that the tribunal should consider first whether the reason was a substantial reason within para. 6 (1) (*b*) and then whether the employer had acted reasonably in the circumstances within para. 6 (8) and the tribunal had not misdirected themselves in law.

PRIDDLE *v*. DIBBLE [1978] I.C.R. 149, E.A.T.

1153. —— —— policy of Africanisation

[Trade Union and Labour Relations Act 1974 (c. 52), Sched. 1. para. 6 (1) (*b*).]

Where employers operate a policy of employing only persons associated with the country controlling the company, the industrial tribunal hearing a complaint of unfair dismissal must decide whether that policy was a substantial reason of a kind to justify dismissal within para. 6 (1) (*b*) of Sched. 1 to the Act.

E Corp. introduced a policy of "Africanisation" and F, a white British citizen employed as a technical representative in the United Kingdom was dismissed. A citizen of one of the three controlling African countries was appointed in his place. F complained of unfair dismissal. The industrial tribunal rejected E Corp.'s contention that the policy was " some *other* substantial reason " of a kind to justify F's dismissal within para. 6 (1) (*b*) of Sched. 1 to the Act and found that the dismissal was unfair. E Corp. appealed. *Held*, allowing the appeal, that the tribunal were wrong in failing to consider the merits and details of the policy and the case would be remitted to a tribunal for consideration of whether E Corp. had acted reasonably.

EAST AFRICAN AIRWAYS CORP. *v*. FOOTE [1977] I.C.R. 776, E.A.T.

1154. —— —— probationary clerical worker—warnings of unsatisfactory work

In deciding whether or not the dismissal of an employee at the end of a probationary period is unfair, the industrial tribunal should consider whether the employer has made a proper assessment of the probationer's capabilities.

M was engaged as a trainee clerical officer for a probationary period of one year. She was given several warnings by the sales manager that her work was unsatisfactory and that she would be dismissed if it did not improve. During the tenth month of the probationary period M was told by her immediate superior that her clerical work was up to the required standard but that her telephone work was not. No further complaint was made after that date. At the end of the trial period the sales manager, who did not know that she had been told her clerical work was satisfactory, dismissed M on the ground that her work was not up to the standard of the permanent staff. M claimed compensation for unfair dismissal. The industrial tribunal found that the employers had acted unreasonably in treating her lack of ability as a sufficient reason for dismissing her. The employers appealed contending that a lesser degree of capability sufficed to justify dismissal during the probationary period than during permanent employment and it was for them to assess whether a probationer had reached the required standard at the end of the trial period. *Held*, dismissing the appeal, that question for the tribunal was whether the employers had maintained a proper appraisal of M's progress during her probation, giving guidance when necessary, and whether the final decision was based on a reasonable assessment; that although the procedure laid down by the employers was satisfactory, since M had been told that her clerical work was up to standard and had been given no subsequent warnings, the employers had acted unreasonably in dismissing her.

POST OFFICE *v*. MUGHAL [1977] I.C.R. 763, E.A.T.

1155. —— redundancy—failure to consult employees prior to dismissal—compensation

Where employees dismissed for redundancy without prior consultation would have been dismissed in any event they are entitled only to a basic award of compensation for unfair dismissal.

B was dismissed for redundancy without any prior consultation. On his complaint that the dismissal was unfair the industrial tribunal found that he had been unfairly dismissed but that, had the consultation taken place, he would still have been dismissed. Accordingly he was only entitled to a basic award of compensation. B appealed against the award. *Held,* dismissing the appeal, that the tribunal was justified in finding that B had not suffered any loss through lack of consultation and the award was correct.

BARLEY *v.* AMEY ROADSTONE CORP. (NO. 2) [1978] I.C.R. 190, E.A.T.

1156. —— —— **reasonableness—alternative grounds**
[Industrial Relations Act 1971 (c. 72), s. 24 (5) (6).]
Where a dismissal is not unfair by virtue of s. 24 (5) of the Act it is nevertheless open to an industrial tribunal to find that the dismissal was unfair under s. 24 (6).

C was the longest serving of three listing negotiators for B Ltd., estate agents. For economic reasons it became necessary for B Ltd. to reduce their staff. C was dismissed for redundancy and complained to an industrial tribunal. The tribunal found, inter alia, that, the dismissal was unfair by virtue of both s. 24 (5) and s. 24 (6) of the Act and awarded compensation. B Ltd. appealed to the National Industrial Relations Court which held that the tribunal was wrong in law in holding that the claim could be maintained under s. 24 (5) but upheld the alternative basis of claim under s. 24 (6). On appeal B Ltd. contended that if the dismissal was not unfair because there were no special reasons of a kind envisaged by s. 24 (5) there could be no question of unfair dismissal under s. 24 (6). *Held,* dismissing the appeal, that once subs. (5) was out of the way the matter was wholly at large under subs. (6) and the decision of the tribunal could not be interfered with since they had not erred in law.

BESSENDEN PROPERTIES *v.* CORNESS [1977] I.C.R. 821 (NOTE), C.A.

1157. —— —— —— **" other substantial reason "**
[Trade Union and Labour Relations Act 1974 (c. 52), Sched. 1, para. 6 (1) (*b*) (2) (*c*) (8).]
Having regard to the informal nature of pleadings before an industrial tribunal, an employer may argue that even if an employee was not redundant within s. 1 (2) (*b*) of the Redundancy Payments Act 1965, the reason for his dismissal was " some other substantial reason " within para. 6 (1) (*b*) of Sched. 1 to the Trade Union and Labour Relations Act 1974, even though that has not been pleaded.

E complained of unfair dismissal. The company claimed that he had been dismissed for redundancy. The tribunal upheld the company's contention, and held that it had acted reasonably in treating redundancy as a sufficient reason for dismissal within para. 6 (8) of Sched. 1 to the Trade Union and Labour Relations Act 1974. They did not set out clearly their finding of fact or their reasoning. On appeal by E, *held,* allowing the appeal, that the case should be remitted to the industrial tribunal for reconsideration on the evidence before them; but on that remission, although " some other substantial reason " within para. 6 (1) (*b*) of Sched. 1 to the Trade Union and Labour Relations Act 1974 was not pleaded, the employers would be entitled to argue it. (*Nelson* v. *British Broadcasting Corp.* [1977] C.L.Y. 1123 considered.)

GORMAN *v.* LONDON COMPUTER TRAINING CENTRE [1978] I.C.R. 394, E.A.T.

1158. —— —— **selection**
When work of a particular squad ran out, all its members were dismissed by F.C. Co., including K, a general labourer who was registered disabled and with long service. *Held,* that the tribunal had correctly found K's selection for redundancy, purely because he was a member of a particular squad of builders and ignoring his personal circumstances, to be unfair: FORMAN CONSTRUCTION *v.* KELLY [1977] I.R.L.R. 468, E.A.T.

1159. —— —— —— **employer's onus**
K, a credit control manager was dismissed as redundant. A tribunal found the dismissal unfair on grounds that BF Co. had not shown that they had looked for alternative employment within their group for K or helped him find work elsewhere although K had made no complaint re these matters. *Held,* allowing BF Co.'s appeal, that where it is shown that selection for redundancy is unfair, if there is no complaint of unfairness on some other ground, the employer's burden does not include rebutting grounds of unfairness in respect of which no complaint is made. (*British United Shoe Machinery Co.* v. *Clarke*

[1977] C.L.Y. 1045 applied): BARWORTH FLOCKTON *v.* KIRK [1978] I.R.L.R. 18, E.A.T.

1160. [Trade Union and Labour Relations Act 1974 (c. 52), Sched. 1, para. 6 (8).]

In order to discharge their burden in a redundancy situation, the employers must be prepared not only to deal with the why, by whom and the basis of selection points, but in outline with the redundancy situation generally and other general points of importance relating to an employee.

C had worked for the same employer for 25 years and was one of 385 selected for redundancy. C complained of vindictive selection for redundancy but not specifically of lack of effect to find him alternative employment. A company director gave evidence of the general redundancy situation and of the position as regards vacancies elsewhere. The tribunal found the dismissal fair. *Held*, dismissing the employer's appeal, that the onus was on the employer to deal with the criteria for selection and to outline the background to the redundancy situation; but where no specific complaint was made of failure to redeploy, it was sufficient for a senior man to explain the circumstances of redundancy and in general terms what was contemplated for an employee. (*Barworth Flockton* v. *Kirk* [1978] C.L.Y. 1159; *Bristol Channel Ship Repairers* v. *O'Keefe* [1978] C.L.Y. 1161 considered.)

COX *v.* WILDT MELLOR BROMLEY [1978] I.C.R. 736, E.A.T.

1161. —— —— —— **test cases**

[Trade Union and Labour Relations Act 1974 (c. 52), Sched. 1, para. 6 (1) (8).]

Where an employee is dismissed for redundancy, the employer must show how, by whom and on what basis the selection was made.

Per curiam: Where one case is taken as a test case for a number of applicants, great care should be taken to ensure that the interests of others are not prejudiced by a test case which is not truly identical.

O'K was one of 35 dismissed for redundancy. Although it became clear that the employers had considered the selection carefully no evidence was heard as to who had taken the decision or on what criteria he had relied. *Held*, dismissing the employer's appeal, that where there was a redundancy situation, the employers must show, how, by whom and on what basis the selection had been made, otherwise they failed to discharge their burden of proof.

BRISTOL CHANNEL SHIP REPAIRERS *v.* O'KEEFE [1978] I.C.R. 691, E.A.T.

1162. —— **refusal to work overtime**

A dismissal for refusal to work overtime may be fair, even though that refusal involves no breach of contract.

E worked as a driver for the council, collecting disabled people from their houses. He was employed to work a 40-hour week and there was no provision as to overtime. There was a union agreement recognising that drivers were regularly working overtime, and E did so for 10 years. He then decided not to work overtime any more, since his contract did not require it. After warning him, the council dismissed him. The industrial tribunal held that as he had worked overtime for so long, he was in breach of contract in refusing to do so, and that the breach of contract was sufficient ground for dismissal; alternatively, if there was no breach of contract, there was nevertheless sufficient ground for dismissal. On appeal by E, *held*, dismissing the appeal, that the evidence did not suport the conclusion that at the time E contracted it was necessary for business efficacy to imply a term that he would work overtime; however, the tribunal was entitled to reach the conclusion that the council had acted reasonably in dismissing E without there being a breach of contract.

HORRIGAN *v.* LEWISHAM LONDON BOROUGH COUNCIL [1978] I.C.R. 15, E.A.T.

1163. —— **re-instatement—whether order complied with—whether compliance practicable**

[Employment Protection Act 1975 (c. 71), s. 72 (2) (*b*).] Following a finding of unfair dismissal and an order that H and W, cooks, be reinstated not later than February 20, 1978, E Co. agreed to treat H and W as remaining in employment until February 20 but as from that date declared them redundant as there would be no requirement for cooks at least until April 1978. *Held*, dismissing E Co.'s appeal against additional awards for failure to comply with the order under s. 72 (2) of the 1975 Act, that as E Co. had made no serious, genuine attempt to comply with the order, it was open to the tribunal to decide that it would have been practicable to do so. Even if there was no work for H and W until April 1978 they could have done more to comply with the order. Obiter: it is not appropriate to order reinstatement where there must be a personal relationship, save in exceptional circumstances: ENESSY Co. S.A., T/A THE TULCAN ESTATE *v.* MINOPRIO [1978] I.R.L.R. 489, E.A.T.

1164. —— **" some other substantial reason "—employee's failure to obtain fidelity bond**

[Trade Union and Labour Relations Act 1974 (c. 52), Sched. 1, para. 6 (1) (b).] FTR Co. employed M from August 23, 1976, to February 28, 1977, when T Co. took over the business and offered M employment in the same position, with continuity of service but with a requirement that T Co.'s insurers should accept M for fidelity guarantee insurance. M was dismissed accordingly when his application for the fidelity bond was rejected. *Held*, dismissing M's appeal, that the tribunal were entitled to find the refusal of the bond " some other substantial reason " for dismissal within the 1974 Act, Sched. 1, para. 6 (1) (*b*), and to find the dismissal fair: MOODY *v.* TELEFUSION [1978] I.R.L.R. 311, E.A.T.

1165. —— **statutory prohibition on continued employment—probationary teacher— failure to consult**

S, a probationary teacher, was dismissed after the D.E.S. had found him unsuitable as a teacher after an extension to his probationary period. The tribunal held that it must be reasonable for employers to dismiss an employee if it would be unlawful to continue the employment. The Schools Regulations provide that a teacher shall not be further employed as a qualified teacher if the Secretary of State determines him to be unsuitable. *Held*, allowing S's appeal, that the fact that the Council could not have lawfully continued S's employment did not inevitably mean that the dismissal was fair. If S showed that he had never had a chance to prove himself and was treated unreasonably and discriminated against, then the law was being used as a device to get rid of him. Since the Council had unreasonably failed to discuss the matter with S or the D.E.S. to see whether what had gone wrong could be corrected, a finding of unfair dismissal might be made: SANDHU *v.* DEPARTMENT OF EDUCATION AND SCIENCE AND HILLINGDON LONDON BOROUGH [1978] I.R.L.R. 208, E.A.T.

1166. —— **strike—less than 26 weeks' service—intimation of withdrawal of labour**

[Trade Union and Labour Relations Act 1974 (c. 52), Sched. 1, paras. 6 (4), 7 (2).] W was dismissed after he intimated, after a strike had begun, that he would not work when he was due to be on duty the following day. *Held*, that (1) the tribunal had correctly decided that, since W had less than 26 weeks' continuous service, he could not rely upon the protections against victimisation of employees dismissed when on strike under para. 7 (2) of Sched. 1 to the 1974 Act, unless he could also show he had been dismissed for an inadmissible reason within para. 6 (4); (2) the tribunal had not erred in finding W to have been dismissed for taking part in a strike rather than trade union activities. When employees on shift work decide to stop work from the time of a meeting, those due to work the following shifts are taking part in a " strike or other industrial action " as soon as they intimate that their labour will be withdrawn when they are due to start work: WINNETT *v.* SEAMARKS BROTHERS [1978] I.R.L.R. 387, E.A.T.

1167. —— —— **return to work of some employees—dismissal of those remaining on strike**

[Trade Union and Labour Relations Act 1974 (c. 52), Sched. 1, para. 8 (2) (*b*).]

On a true construction of para. 8 (2) of Sched. 1 to the 1974 Act, " dismissal of employees who took part in a strike " does not mean " dismissal of

employees who at the date of dismissal were taking part in a strike ";
thus, dismissing all who took part in strike action will not be unfair; but
not dismissing or re-engaging those who went back to work will render the
dismissal of the others unfair if it is for an inadmissible reason.

A strike followed a dispute about union recognition. Some employees who
had been on strike returned to work before the end of the strike. Those who
remained on strike were dismissed. Phillips J. held that the dismissal was
unfair because those who had gone back to work had taken part in the strike
within the clear words of para. 8 (2) (*a*) of Sched. 1 to the Trade Union
and Labour Relations Act 1974, the Court of Appeal affirmed that decision.
On appeal to the House of Lords, *held*, dismissing the appeal, that failure
to dismiss those who had gone back to work had rendered the dismissal of
the rest unfair within the clear wording of para. 8 (2) (*a*). *Per* Viscount
Dilhorne and Lord Fraser of Tullybelton: when the language of a statute
is plain it is not open to the court to remedy a defect of drafting. *Per* Lord
Edmund-Davies: dislike of the effect of a statute is no reason for departing
from its plain language.

STOCK *v.* FRANK JONES (TIPTON) [1978] 1 W.L.R. 231, H.L.

1168. —— —— **where employer in fundamental breach**
[Trade Union and Labour Relations Act 1974 (c. 52), Sched. 1, para. 7.]
W and others, drivers, went on strike after complaining that they were being
required to drive overloaded lorries. *Held*, dismissing their appeals, that their
dismissals were automatically fair by virtue of para. 7, Sched. 1, to the 1974
Act. Even if C Co. had been in fundamental breach of contract, the act of
going on strike did not indicate that the employees concerned were regarding
the contract as ended by virtue of the breach: WILKINS *v.* CANTRELL AND
COCHRANE (G.B.) [1978] I.R.L.R. 483, E.A.T.

1169. —— **trade union activities—complaint about safety**
[Trade Union and Labour Relations Act 1974 (c. 52), Sched. 1, para. 6
(4) (*b*).]
The provision in the 1974 Act relating to unfair dismissal for taking part in
the activities of an independent trade union should be reasonably, and not too
restrictively, interpreted.

The employees, joiners in the construction industry, complained about the
inadequacy of safety equipment provided by the employers. After an argument
the employees left. They subsequently complained of constructive dismissal
which was unfair as it was for an inadmissible reason. The tribunal held that
" trade union activities " was to be strictly interpreted, and dismissed the complaints. On appeal, *held*, dismissing the appeal, that although the court disagreed with the tribunal's restrictive interpretation of the provisions, the
employees had failed to show that this was the principal reason for their
dismissal.

DIXON *v.* WEST ELLA DEVELOPMENTS [1978] I.C.R. 856, E.A.T.

1170. —— —— **" inappropriate time "**
[Trade Union and Labour Relations Act 1974 (c. 51), Sched. 1, para. 6 (4).]
Whilst operating her machine and in tea and lunch breaks, Z discussed union
matters and encouraged recruitment. She was dismissed for behaving in a
" disruptive manner " and engaging in union activities at an " inappropriate
time." *Held*, allowing Z's appeal, that the tribunal had erred (1) in finding
that Z's conversations whilst working could not be union activities in working
hours in accordance with arrangements agreed with or consent given by
A.J. Co. within para. 6 (4), Sched. 1 to the 1974 Act; consent or arrangements
could be implied from the fact that employees were allowed to converse upon
anything they wished during work; and (2) in concluding that Z's activities
during tea and meal breaks were not at an " appropriate time " within para.
6 (4) as she was being paid during those breaks. Merely because an employee
is on the employer's premises and is being paid does not mean he is necessarily
required to be at work or that the time is within working hours. (*Marley Tile
Co.* v. *Shaw* [1978] C.L.Y. 1131 and *Post Office* v. *Union of Post Office
Workers* [1974] C.L.Y. 3850 applied): ZUCKER *v.* ASTRID JEWELS [1978]
I.R.L.R. 385, E.A.T.

1171.   —— —— not activities of member of trade union
[Trade Union and Labour Relations Act 1974 (c. 52), Sched. 1, para. 6 (4) (*b*).]
An individual's independent activities as a trade unionist are not the same as the activities of an independent trade union.
C organised a petition complaining about the safety standards of some machinery. The Industrial Tribunal found on a fact that he was dismissed for organising that petition but held the same not to be a trade union activity within the meaning of para. 6 (4) (*b*) of Sched. 1 to the Trade Union and Labour Relations Act 1974. *Held*, dismissing C's appeal, that organising the petition was the activity of an independent trade unionist and not the activity of " an independent trade union " so that C had not been dismissed for an inadmissible reason.
CHANT *v.* AQUABOATS [1978] I.C.R. 643, E.A.T.

1172.   —— —— relevant only after commencement of employment
[Trade Union and Labour Relations Act 1974 (c. 52), Sched. 1, para. 6 (4) (*b*).]
Where an employee is dismissed for trade union activities carried out before the commencement of his employment, para. 6 (4) (*b*) of Sched. 1 to the Act does not render the dismissal unfair.
When B applied for employment as a bricklayer with the council he gave a false name because he believed that his previous trade union activities might prevent his being taken on. He was given the job but his deception was discovered and he was dismissed for misconduct. Subsequently he was taken on again under his real name but when the news reached the general manager he was dismissed immediately. The reason given was his deception on the previous occasion. B complained that he had been unfairly dismissed on the ground that he had been dismissed because of his trade union activities within para. 6 (4) (*b*) of Sched. 1 to the Act. The industrial tribunal found in his favour. The council appealed. *Held*, allowing the appeal, that such a claim could only be founded upon activities engaged in or proposed to be engaged in after the employment had commenced.
BIRMINGHAM CITY DISTRICT COUNCIL *v.* BEYER [1978] 1 All E.R. 910, E.A.T.

1173.   —— union membership—onus of proof on employers
[Trade Union and Labour Relations Act 1974 (c. 52), Sched. 1, para. 6 (1) (*b*), (2) (*a*), (5), as amended by Trade Union and Labour Relations (Amendment) Act 1976 (c. 7), s. 3 (5).]
The burden of proof lies firmly on the employer to prove an employee is not a member of the union, where the employer relies on a closed shop agreement to justify dismissal.
W was employed onshore by the appellants, and was not a registered seafarer. He was offered, and accepted, work at sea. After three voyages, a query was raised as to his union membership. After perfunctory enquiries, he was dismissed under para. 6 (5) of Sched. I of the 1974 Act, as not being a union member. At the hearing, the appellants attempted unsuccessfully to amend their grounds to rely on W's not being a registered seafarer as amounting to another substantial reason for dismissal. *Held*, dismissing the employer's appeal, that where the employer relies on a closed shop agreement to justify dismissal, the onus was on him to prove the employee was not a union member. Further, " qualification " means more than mere licence, permit or authorisation unless these are substantially concerned with aptitude. (*Nelson* v. *British Broadcasting Corp.* [1977] C.L.Y. 1123 considered.)
BLUE STAR SHIP MANAGEMENT *v.* WILLIAMS [1978] I.C.R. 770, E.A.T.

1174. [Trade Union and Labour Relations Act 1974 (c. 52), s. 30, Sched. 1, para. 6 (5).]
In deciding whether there was a union membership agreement within s. 30 of the Act, the industrial tribunal has to determine whether there was an agreement between the employers and the union that every employee's contract of employment required him to be a union member.
There was an agreement between J Ltd. and the T.G.W.U. that new employees would be told of the presence of the union and that union

representatives would be expecting them to join the union after the one-month trial period. G commenced his employment with J Ltd. in 1972 and became a paid-up member of the union. In 1974 he fell into arrears with his subscriptions and shop stewards told J Ltd. that he was no longer a union member and he was dismissed. G complained that he had been unfairly dismissed. At the hearing it was conceded that G was, and was entitled to be, a member of the union. The industrial tribunal found that there was a union membership agreement within s. 30 of the Act and held that the dismissal was fair by virtue of para. 6 (5) of Sched. 1 to the Act. G appealed. *Held,* dismissing the appeal, that (1) the court could not go behind the tribunal's decision that there was a " closed shop "; (2) para. 6 (5) of Sched. 1 to the Act did not require the employers to show that they were justified and had acted reasonably in dismissing G, and since J Ltd. genuinely believed that G was not a member of the union the dismissal was fair even though that belief was mistaken. (*Abernethy* v. *Mott, Hay and Anderson* [1974] C.L.Y. 1285 applied.)

GAYLE v. JOHN WILKINSON AND SONS (SALTLEY) [1978] I.C.R. 154, E.A.T.

1175.   [Trade Union and Labour Relations Act 1974 (c. 52), Sched. 1, para. 6 (5), as amended by Trade Union and Labour Relations (Amendment) Act 1976 (c. 7), s. 3 (5).]

When dismissing employees for non-membership of a specified union, an employer must show that almost all employees of that class belonged to that union.

The employers decided that their workforce of 60 should belong to a union. Initially, a free choice was given as to which union to join, but subsequently the employers signed an agreement with U.S.D.A.W., confirming by letter that membership of this union was to be a condition of employment. In the meantime, several employees had joined the T.G.W.U. At dismissal date, only 33 out of 42 belonged to the specified union. The tribunal held that the dismissal of the nine was fair. *Held,* allowing their appeal, that the mere posting on a notice board of the terms of union membership was not reasonable notice of the withdrawal of the previous freedom of choice; that when dismissing for non-membership of a union, it was necessary to show that almost all employees were members of that union. Normally, 33 out of 42 did not come within the meaning of " almost all." (*Home Counties Dairies* v. *Woods* [1977] C.L.Y. 3074; *Strover* v. *Chrysler U.K.* [1975] C.L.Y. 1171 considered.)

HIMPFEN v. ALLIED RECORDS [1978] I.C.R. 689, E.A.T.

1176. —— —— **prior rights to choose union**

[Trade Union and Labour Relations Act 1974 (c. 52), s. 30, Sched. 1, para. 6 (5) (*a*), (*b*).] An employee, first employed in 1974, was dismissed because of his refusal to join a union, contrary to a closed shop agreement imposed in 1976. *Held,* dismissing the appeal, the employee was fairly dismissed and could not rely on the legislation in force when he was first employed which then allowed a choice of union: BEAUMONT v. McNEILL, *The Times,* October 10, 1978, E.A.T.

1177. —— —— **reasonable belief of employers**

[Trade Union and Labour Relations Act 1974 (c. 52), Sched. 1, para. 6 (5) (*b*).]

Employers who genuinely believe an employee not to be a member of a trade union are not guilty of unfair dismissal when they dismiss him by reason of a closed shop agreement.

Employers who operate a closed shop dismissed the appellant after he had been expelled by his union. The appellant later obtained a declaration that he had been wrongly expelled and thereafter complained unsuccessfully to an industrial tribunal of unfair dismissal. *Held,* dismissing the appeal, that the employers' genuine belief at the time of dismissal that the appellant was no longer a union member rendered the dismissal fair under Sched. 1, para. 6 of the Act. (*Gayle* v. *John Wilkinson & Sons (Saltley)* [1978] C.L.Y. 1174 applied.)

LAKHANI v. HOOVER [1978] I.C.R. 1063, E.A.T.

1178. —— —— **refusal to join union or pay into charity**

[Trade Union and Labour Relations Act 1974 (c. 52), Sched. 1, para. 6 (1) (*b*) (5).]

A union membership agreement made membership of APEX a condition of employment but gave existing non-members the option of paying " an equal amount into a charity to be mutually agreed." R refused to join or pay into a charity. *Held*, dismissing R's appeal, that (1) R had been fairly dismissed for not being a member of the specified trade union in accordance with a union membership agreement within para. 6 (5), Sched. 1, to the 1974 Act; (2) in any event the reason for dismissal would have been " some other substantial reason " within para. 6 (1) (*b*) and would have been fair: RAWLINGS *v.* LIONWELD [1978] I.R.L.R. 481, E.A.T.

1179. —— —— **religious belief**

[Trade Union and Labour Relations Act 1974 (c. 52), Sched. 1, para. 6 (5).]

A tribunal accepted S's evidence that his reason for not joining a trade union specified in a union membership agreement was his conviction that with the growth of his faith he had become more convinced that he could not join a union, his conscience stemmed from his religion, his faith was showing him the way more clearly, there had been a continuous process of thought and a Christian could not be a trade unionist. Nevertheless, the tribunal held that S's objection was on more general grounds of conscience than religious belief. *Held*, allowing S's appeal, that no reasonable tribunal could have reached such a conclusion: SAGGERS *v.* BRITISH RAILWAYS BOARD (No. 2) [1978] I.R.L.R. 435, E.A.T.

1180. —— **victimisation—racial discrimination by employer against third parties**

[Race Relations Act 1976] (c. 74), ss. 1, 30, 54.] A barmaid who was dismissed for refusing to obey her employer's order not to serve coloured customers, was entitled to bring a complaint of race discrimination against her employer although she herself was not personally discriminated against. An industrial tribunal had jurisdiction to hear the plaintiff's complaint of victimisation (*Race Relations Board* v. *Applin* [1974] C.L.Y. 19 applied): ZARCZYNSKA *v.* LEVY, *The Times*, October 21, 1978, E.A.T.

1181. —— **warning—failure to give—unlikelihood of improvement if warning given—reduction of award for incapacity**

[Employment Protection Act 1975 (c. 71), ss. 75 (7), 76 (6).]

When an industrial trubunal making a compensatory award under s. 76 (1) of the Employment Protection Act 1975 reduces the award under s. 76 (6) on the ground of incapacity, it should avoid duplication by, on the one hand, failing to take into account any extra period during which the employee would have worked had he been given an adequate warning, and, on the other hand, reducing the award on the ground of the employee's own conduct.

E, who was manager of a bicycle shop, was dismissed for incompetence. An industrial tribunal found that he was clearly incapable of doing his job, but that his dismissal was unfair since he had not been warned. However, the tribunal also found that he was unlikely to have improved if he had been warned, and reduced his basic and his compensatory award by one-third. Both employers and employee appealed. *Held*, dismissing both appeals, that (1) whether a sufficient warning was given was a question of fact for the tribunal; (2) since the tribunal had considered that E's work would not improve even after a warning and no part of the compensatory award reflected that he might have been employed longer if he had been warned, the award had been calculated correctly; (3) the tribunal had been entitled to reduce the basic award on the ground of E's own contributory conduct.

BROWN'S CYCLES *v.* BRINDLEY [1978] I.C.R. 467, E.A.T.

1182. —— **whether dismissed—employee leaving before notice expired**

W was given seven weeks' notice terminating her employment. Thereafter she did not return to work. *Held*, dismissing W's appeal, that the tribunal had correctly found that W had terminated her employment and had not been dismissed: WALKER *v.* COTSWOLD CHINE HOME SCHOOL (1977) 12 I.T.R. 342, E.A.T.

1183. —— —— **termination of contract—agreement**

An employee whose employment terminates by virtue of some contractual provision is not to be regarded as dismissed.

The employers agreed to the employee taking five weeks' unpaid leave in order to visit his sick mother in Pakistan. The employee signed an agreement to the effect that should he fail to return to work at the end of the five-week period, his employment would automatically terminate. The employee failed to return on the due date, apparently due to his own sickness. The employers regarded his employment as terminated. *Held,* allowing their appeal against an industrial tribunal's finding of dismissal, that the employment had ended contractually and that accordingly the employee had not been dismissed.

BRITISH LEYLAND (U.K.) *v.* ASHRAF [1978] I.C.R. 979, E.A.T.

1184. —— —— **whether employer's words merely spoken in annoyance**

T was told not to use the company's van outside working hours and was lent £275 to buy a car. When he found that T was still using the van outside working hours, K, T's employer, said: "What's my fucking van doing outside; you're a tight bastard. I've just lent you £275 to buy a car and you are too tight to put juice in it. That's it, you're finished with me." *Held,* that the tribunal were entitled to find K's words to have been spoken in annoyance and not to have been a dismissal: TANNER *v.* KEAN [1978] I.R.L.R. 110, E.A.T.

1185. —— **whether employer's dissatisfaction evidence of manager's incapacity**

When responsible employers conclude over a reasonable period that a manager is incompetent, that is some evidence of his incapacity to perform his job.

Per curiam: It is important that the operation of the legislation in relation to unfair dismissal should not impede employers unreasonably in the efficient management of their business.

C became manager of one of T Ltd.'s wholesale food cash-and-carry depots. He had been employed as manager of another depot but had had no previous experience of the food side of the business. It became quickly apparent that he was not performing his job satisfactorily and despite warnings and advice he did not improve. He was offered the managership of another non-food depot at the same salary but refused. He was dismissed. On his application for compensation for unfair dismissal the tribunal found that there had been a fall in the depot's profits due to his poor management and that T Ltd. were justified in dismissing him. C appealed. *Held,* dismissing the appeal, that the test was whether T Ltd. had acted reasonably in treating C's lack of capacity as sufficient reason for dismissing him and having regard to the employers dissatisfaction and the loss of profits T Ltd. had acted reasonably in dismissing him.

COOK *v.* THOMAS LINNELL & SONS [1977] I.C.R. 770, E.A.T.

1186. —— **whether tribunal's decision was unreasonable—salesman submitting inaccurate reports**

M, a salesman, was dismissed for putting in inaccurate day-to-day reports. *Held,* dismissing B-M Co's appeal against a finding of unfair dismissal with compensation reduced by one third for contributory conduct, that M's conduct was serious but it could not be said that no reasonable tribunal could have reached the decision: BRISTOL-MYERS CO. *v.* MATLOCK (1978) 13 I.T.R. 158, E.A.T.

1187. —— **working hours per week—computation—additional preparation at home**

[Trade Union and Labour Relations Act 1974 (c. 52), Sched. I, para. 9 (1) (*f*).]

Where an employer is under a contractual obligation, albeit implied, to do work outside the place of work sufficient to ensure the satisfactory performance of duties, those additional hours may be included in the computation of hours worked.

L was employed as a teacher, on duty, according to her contract, for less than 21 hours per week. In addition, L spent several hours per week in preparation at home. The tribunal held that these additional hours could not be included in the computation of hours normally worked. *Held,* allowing her appeal that

L was under a contractual duty to do as much work outside school as necessary for the proper performance of her teaching duties. Accordingly, the additional hours of preparation could be included in the computation of hours normally worked.

LAKE *v.* ESSEX COUNTY COUNCIL [1978] I.C.R. 657, E.A.T.

1188. —— **written reasons for dismissal—whether delay constituting unreasonable refusal**

[Employment Protection Act 1975 (c. 71), s. 70 (1) (4).]

S. 70 of the Act should be strictly construed and only applied where the evidence clearly indicates that there has been an unreasonable refusal to provide the written statement required. A was dismissed by C Ltd. on November 5, 1976. On November 15 she wrote to the industrial tribunals referring to her complaint under s. 70 of the Act. A copy of that letter was sent to C Ltd. who received it on or about November 19. On December 10 C Ltd. wrote to A giving written reasons for dismissing her. The tribunal concluded that a request for those particulars had been made in the week following her dismissal and although there was no express refusal by C Ltd. their inaction constituted an unreasonable refusal within s. 70 (4). A was awarded two weeks pay. C Ltd. appealed. *Held,* allowing the appeal, that although C Ltd. had delayed in providing the written particulars requested, there was insufficient evidence to justify the finding of the tribunal that there had been an unreasonable refusal.

CHARLES LANG & SONS *v.* AUBREY [1978] I.C.R. 168, E.A.T.

1189. Wages—minimum wage—" recognised " level of basic pay

[Employment Protection Act 1975 (c. 71), Sched. 11, paras. 1, 2 (*a*) (*b*).]

A formal agreement acknowledging a minimum wage will not be tacitly altered by reason, *e.g.* of inflation, in the absence of further express agreement.

Unions and management fixed a general minimum wage of £42 weekly for a particular industry. Some years subsequently D, who were paying that wage, were alleged to be observing terms and conditions less favourable than the general level in the industry. C.A.C. decided that this was so. *Held*, granting an order of certiorari quashing their decision, that the formal wage agreement could only be altered by further formal agreement and that, in the absence of such an agreement, D could not be said not to be obeying a recognised condition within the industry.

R. *v.* CENTRAL ARBITRATION COMMITTEE, *ex p.* DELTAFLOW [1978] I.C.R. 534, D.C.

1190. Wages councils

S.I. 1978 No. 966 (Road Haulage Wages Council—abolition) [10p].

1191. Workmen's compensation. See WORKMEN'S COMPENSATION.

BOOKS AND ARTICLES. See *post,* pp. [4], [21].

EQUITY

1192. Doctrine of election—surrender of beneficial interest—whether appropriate

The equitable doctrine of election does not apply where the elector by electing against the will or other instrument would have no adequate beneficial interest remaining thereunder from which he could compensate the other beneficiaries..

The testatrix and her son were joint legal and beneficial owners of a house; accordingly upon her death, the house became the son's sole property. By her will, however, the testatrix in addition to making small bequests to the son, purported to devise the house to the bank trustee on trust for sale providing that the son was to live there rent-free and that after the son ceased residence, the house would be sold and added to residue. The residue was to be held on trust as to half for the son for life and as to the remainder for the son's two daughters, the trustee having a discretion, inter alia, in the son's case to determine the statutory protective trusts and pay the income to the son. The son elected against the will and sold the house; the value of the bequests to him was insufficient to compensate the other residuary beneficiaries. On a summons to determine the consequences of the election, if such it was, Goulding J. held that the trustee had power, but was not bound, to determine the son's interest under the protective trust in order to compensate the other beneficiaries. *Held*, allowing the son's appeal, that the doctrine of election did not apply as the son had no interest under the will out of which he could compensate the beneficiaries; the son was therefore not bound to elect. (*Re Hargrove* [1915] 1 Ch. 398 applied; *Brown* v. *Gregson* [1920] A.C. 860 considered; *McCaroger* v. *Whieldon* (1867) L.R. 3 Eq. 236 distinguished; *Carter* v. *Gilber* [1891] 3 Ch. 553 overruled.)

Re GORDON'S WILL TRUSTS; NATIONAL WESTMINSTER BANK v. GORDON [1978] 2 W.L.R. 754, C.A.

1193. Equitable licence—revocation—misconduct of licensee. See WILLIAMS v. STAITE, § 2487.

1194. Fiduciary relationship—purchaser of land acting as vendor's agent—duty to disclose. See ENGLISH v. DEDHAM VALE PROPERTIES, § 3060.

1195. Restitution—no unjust enrichment—prospective purchaser improving land—no contract for sale. See PREEPER v. PREEPER, § 3059.

BOOKS AND ARTICLES. See *post*, pp. [4], [22].

ESTOPPEL

1196. Issue estoppel—application for equal pay—previous application. See Mc-LOUGHLIN v. GORDONS (STOCKPORT), § 949.

1197. Representations by council—planning permission—existing use rights. See WESTERN FISH PRODUCTS v. PENWITH DISTRICT COUNCIL AND THE SECRETARY OF STATE FOR THE ENVIRONMENT, § 2901.

1198. Res judicata—title to land—earlier possession action
[Jam.] [Landlord and Tenant Law (Laws of Jamaica, 1953 rev., c. 206), s. 54, proviso 2.]
An order for possession made under s. 54 of the Landlord and Tenant Law of Jamaica, which relates to the recovery of possession of small tenements, cannot constitute res judicata on the issue of title to the land in subsequent proceedings.

A owned five acres of land in Jamaica, and was registered as owner in 1904. In the early 1940s X became occupier of the land. A died in 1946, and in 1960, B, her daughter, obtained a vesting order for the fee simple title. In 1962, B obtained a possession order against X under s. 54 of the Landlord and Tenant Law, which provides for the recovery of possession of small tenements. The order was not enforced, and in 1963 X took proceedings against B claiming entitlement to the fee simple on the basis of a purchase for value in the 1940s. Fox J. struck out the action on the basis that title had already been determined in 1962, and an appeal by X to the Court of Appeal was dismissed. B died in 1967 and the land was acquired by C, developers. X remained in occupation. In 1972 C sought possession of the land, and injunctions to restrain further building and to pull down existing buildings. X pleaded that they had been in possession since 1944 and that C's title was bad being derived from the vesting order of 1960 which was a nullity. Chambers J. held that the matter had been decided in the 1962 proceedings. X obtained a stay of execution pending appeal, but C moved in and pulled down the buildings. X claimed damages against C for trespass. Vanderpump J. ordered the action to be struck out as an abuse of the process on the grounds that the matter had been decided in the 1962 proceedings. The Court of Appeal upheld the decisions of both judges. *Held*, that the 1962 proceedings could not be raised as a bar by virtue of the second proviso to s. 54 of the Landlord and Tenant Law, because an order made in such proceedings could not amount to res judicata. Therefore all subsequent decisions, which depended on that of Fox J. were erroneous since Fox J.'s decision itself depended on res judicata in relation to the 1962 proceedings.

PATRICK *v.* BEVERLEY GARDENS DEVELOPMENT CO. [1978] 2 W.L.R. 423, P.C.

ARTICLES. See *post*, p. [22].

EUROPEAN COMMUNITIES

1199. Administrative law—import rules—force majeure

The European Court considered an application against the Commission under arts. 178 and 215 (second paragraph) for damages. The applicant was a German firm that had entered into a contract with a Romanian firm for the supply of certain meat. This was an import considered exempt from the EXIM rule concerning equivalent exports. The meat was delayed in Romania by " force majeure " and thereafter, because of Commission rules, in particular 2033/75, the import was less profitable or convenient. The company claimed that there should have been a further exemption for licence holders because the delay was caused by force majeure. *Held*, in these circumstances, the Commission are under no duty to provide a transitional protection for agreements made before the change of regulations, and that no rule of community law applies force majeure to all relations between individuals and the public administration, and it did not assist the applicant in this case.

INTERCONTINENTALE FLEISCHHANDELSGESELLSCHAFT M.B.H. & CO. KG (IFG) *v.* E.C. COMMISSION (No. 68/77) [1977] 2 C.M.L.R. 733, European Ct.

1200. —— inspection fees—abandonment of action

The Bundesverwaltungsgericht considered an appeal concerning illegal phyto-sanitary inspection fees on apples imported from France. These fees were imposed by the defendant, a plant inspection authority. *Held,* a plaintiff in an action, which is hopeless because the European Court in a reference upon a preliminary issue ruled against it, may not withdraw the action without the consent of the defendant and may be forced to continue and to bear the costs of such continuance. The action was time-barred from its commencement and the same rules applied as to time in both the Supreme Court and the European Court.

REWE-ZENTRALFINANZ EG AND REWE-ZENTRAL AG *v.* LANDWIRTSCHAFTS-KAMMER FÜR DAS SAARLAND [1978] 2 C.M.L.R. 594, Bundesverwaltungsgericht.

1201. —— regulations—validity—appeal by Member States

The Raad van State, Netherlands, considered an appeal against the refusal by the Dutch Minister of Agriculture to appeal to the European Court for nulli-fication of Reg. 1111/77 EEC. By virtue of art 173 (1), Member States may lodge within two months of a Regulation's publication, such an appeal. *Held,* the appeal by the applicant was inadmissible. The decision by a govern-ment department not to appeal was not a decision of legal consequence against an individual or corporate body because such an appeal is the challenge of a Community Regulation of general application by seeking its nullification.

KONINKLIJKE SCHOLTEN-HONIG NV *v.* THE MINISTER OF AGRICULTURE AND FISHERIES [1978] 3 C.M.L.R. 251, Raad van State.

1202. —— —— —— retroactive effect—currency fluctuation

The European Court considered a reference under art. 177 EEC by the Queen's Bench Division, Commercial Court, concerning Reg. 2424/76: whether it applied to certain contracts concluded prior to the date of its promulgation, and whether it is invalid in so far as it purports to apply to exports effected in execution by such contracts. *Held*, this Regulation was valid and was applicable to such exports. The Commission may, in times of rapid currency fluctuation, make regulations changing the monetary compensation amounts to deal with this situation. A trader should anticipate that, at such times, this may happen and cannot claim that the regulation so made is invalid.

BRITISH BEEF CO. *v.* INTERVENTION BOARD FOR AGRICULTURAL PRODUCE (No. 146/77) [1978] 3 C.M.L.R. 47, European Ct.

1203. Agriculture

COMMON AGRICULTURAL POLICY (PROTECTION OF COMMUNITY ARRANGEMENTS) (AMENDMENT) REGULATIONS 1978 (No. 1330) [10p], made under the European Communities Act 1972 (c. 68), s. 2 (2); operative on October 5, 1978; provide that the requirements set out in reg. 3 of S.I. 1973 No. 424 apply to any person engaged in any of the relevant activities whether he is so engaged as a principal or agent.

1204. —— adjustment of levy—threshold price

The College van Beroep voor het Bedrijfsleven of the Netherlands referred a question concerning the interpretation of Council Reg. No. 120/67/EEC, art. 15 (2), to the European Court for a preliminary ruling under art. 177 EEC. *Held*, this article of this Regulation, being one of the fundamental rules of the Community system, must be interpreted in the light of the objectives and principles governing the common agricultural policy as well as the wording of the article itself. A charge may properly be imposed by the community, namely, the Community levy, in order to prevent the fluctuating world agriculture prices affecting the stability of Community prices. The article so referred to must be interpreted as permitting a variation or adjustment of the "threshold price" between the date when application for certificate is lodged and the date of the threshold price fixed and valid in the month of importation of the goods in question.

N. G. J. SCHOUTEN B.V. *v.* HOOFDPRODUKTSCHAP VOOR AKKERBOUWPRODUK-TEN (No. 6/77) [1977] E.C.R. 1291, European Ct.

1205. —— agricultural holding—definition

The European Court considered a reference under art. 177 EEC from the Tribunale di Roma for a preliminary ruling on the interpretation of art. 38 (1) (3) and (4) EEC and regs. 70/66 and 91/66 EEC. A company that employed labour in connection with its business of raising poultry sought a declaration that it should be classified as an agricultural holding and thus have to pay only insurance contributions to the relevant State authority. *Held*, no treaty rules or secondary legislation set out a definition or assist in the application of the term "agricultural holding." Thus it is for the Community institutions to decide what they take to be included in this expression.

SOCIETÀ SANTA ANNA AZIENDA AVICOLA *v.* ISTITUTO NAZIONALE DELTA PREVIDENZA SOCIALE AND SERVIZIO CONTRIBUTI AGRICOLI UNIFICATO (No. 85/77) [1978] E.C.R. 527, European Ct.

1206. —— amending legislation—effect on pre-existing situations

The European Court considered a reference to it by the Tribunal d' Instance, Valenciennes for a preliminary ruling under art. 177 EEC concerning the validity of Reg. 101/77 (EEC) on the common organisation of the market in sugar. *Held*, this Regulation is valid. Amending legislation applies to future effects of situations arising under previous rules, except as is otherwise provided.

S.A. ANCIENNE MAISON MARCEL BAUCHE AND S.à.r.l. FRANÇOIS DELQUIGNIES *v.* ADMINISTRATION FRANÇAISE DES DOUANES (No. 96/77) [1978] E.C.R. 383, European Ct.

1207. —— common organisation—annual prices—starch refunds

The Finanzgericht at Münster referred several questions to the European Court under art. 177 EEC for a preliminary ruling on the validity of art. 1 (1) of Reg. 3113/74 and the interpretation of the second subparagraph of art. 40 (3) EEC and art. 1 of Reg. 231/75. *Held*, the council's general power expressly conferred on itself by arts. 11 (3) and 26 of Reg. 120/67 is not restricted by art. 2, Reg. 371/67 and art. 7, Reg. 1132/74. Annual fixing of agricultural prices is a basic feature of the common agricultural policy. Despite this, those fixed prices may be changed or adjusted in certain circumstances by the council. The production refund for potato starch and art. 1, Reg. 231/75, does not constitute discrimination against maize starch producers.

HOFFMANN'S STÄRKEFABRIKEN AG *v.* HAUPTZOLLAMT BIELEFELD (No. 2/77) E.C.R. 1375, European Ct.

1208. —— —— **conversion rate of aid for casein manufactured from skimmed milk**

The High Court of Ireland asked the European Court of Justice for a preliminary ruling under art. 177 EEC as to whether the amount of aid payable to a manufacturer of casein and caseinates from skimmed milk is to be calculated with reference to the rate of exchange between the Irish pound and the unit of account applicable on the date of manufacture or to the rate of exchange applicable on the date of marketing the casein. *Held*, art. 6 of Reg. No. 1134/68 of the Council of July 30, 1968, together with Reg. No. 756/70 of the Commission of April 24, 1970, must be taken to mean that the amount of aid for skimmed milk processed into casein before October 27, 1974, but marketed after that date is to be calculated by reference to the rate of conversion between the Irish pound and the unit of account applicable on the day of marketing.

NORTH KERRY MILK PRODUCTS *v.* MINISTER FOR AGRICULTURE AND FISHERIES (No. 80/76) [1977] E.C.R. 425, European Ct.

1209. —— —— **sugar**

The Pretura di Recco referred several questions for a preliminary ruling to the European Court of Justice under art. 177 EEC concerning the interpretation of art. 13 (2) of the EEC Treaty and of Council Regs. No. 1009/67 of December 18, 1967, and No. 3330/74 of December 19, 1974, on the common organisation of the market in sugar. *Held*, (1) authorisation under art. 38 of Reg. No. 3330/74 to grant the aids provided for therein cannot be taken to mean that any method of financing these aids is compatible with Community law; (2) the prohibitions in arts. 9 and 13 EEC are aimed at any tax demanded at the time of or by reason of importation and which, being imposed specifically on imported products to the exclusion of a similar national product results in the same restrictive consequences on the free movement of goods as a customs duty by altering the cost price of that product; (3) a duty falling within a general system of internal taxation applying to national and to imported products according to the same criteria can constitute a charge having an effect equivalent to a customs duty on imports only if it has the sole purpose of financing activities for the specific advantage of the taxed domestic product, if the taxed product and the domestic product benefiting from it are the same, and if the charges imposed on the domestic product are made good in full.

INTERZUCCHERI S.P.A. *v.* DITTA REZZANO E CAVASSA (No. 105/76) [1977] E.C.R. 1029, European Ct.

1210. —— **community production refund for starch-glucose**

The applicant, the most important EEC manufacturer of glucose with a high fructose content, applied to the European Court of Justice for the annulment of Reg. No. 1862/76 of the Council of July 27, 1976, and Reg. No. 2158/76 of the Commission of August 31, 1976, which provided for the reduction and abolition of the production refunds for starch used in the manufacture of glucose with a high fructose content. *Held*, (1) the application was inadmissible as the regulations were of general application and applied to objectively determined situations and produced legal effects with regard to categories of persons envisaged generally and in the abstract; (2) the legislative nature of a measure is not called in question by the possibility of determining more or less precisely the number or even the identity of the persons to whom it applies at a given time so long as it is established that it is applied by virtue of an objective legal or factual situation defined by the measure in relation to the objective of the latter; (3) to refuse to acknowledge the legislative nature of rules on production refunds only because they concern a specific product and to take the view that such rules affected the manufacture of that product by virtue of circumstances which differentiated them from all other persons, would widen the concept of a decision to such an extent as to jeopardise the system of the Treaty.

KONINKLIJKE SCHOLTEN HONIG N.V. *v.* E.C. COMMISSION (No. 101/76) [1977] E.C.R. 797, European Ct.

1211. —— **compensatory amounts—imports from third countries**
The Finanzgericht Hamburg referred several questions to the European Court under art. 177 EEC concerning the interpretation of Reg. 1380/75 EEC. The case involved a dispute concerning the charging of monetary compensatory amounts on a consignment of frozen beef imported from Argentina by the German undertaking Kühlhaus Zentrum, the plaintiff in the main action. *Held*, this Regulation is not to be interpreted in the sense that the monetary compensation should be reduced by multiplication by a monetary coefficient, where the import levy into a Member State from a third country has been fixed but suspended, and where the monetary compensation is charged.
KÜHLAUS ZENTRUM AG v. HAUPTZOLLAMT HAMBURG-HARBURG (No. 79/77) [1978] E.C.R. 611, European Ct.

1212. —— **cost distribution—skimmed milk**
The Landgericht Oldenburg referred a question to the European Court under art. 177 EEC for a preliminary ruling concerning the validity of a skimmed milk Regulation. *Held*, discriminatory distribution of costs between different agricultural production sectors imposed by any community rules or arrangements is not justified in achieving the objectives of the common agricultural policy. Under this ruling, Reg. Council No. 563/76 was declared null and void.
BELA-MÜHLE JOSEF BERGMANN KG v. GROWS-FARM GMBH & CO. KG (No. 114/76) [1977] E.C.R. 1211, European Ct.

1213. A similar question posed in Case No. 114/76 was referred to the European Court by the College van Beroep voor het Bedrijfsleven of the Netherlands with the same result (see § 1212).
GRANARIA B.V. v. HOOFDPRODUKTSCHAP VOOR AKKERBOUWPRODUKTEN (No. 116/76) [1977] E.C.R. 1247, European Ct.

1214. A similar question posed in Case No. 114/76 was referred to the European Court by the Finanzgericht Hamburg with the same result (see §§ 1212, 1213).
ÖLMÜHLE HAMBURG A.G. v. HAUPTZOLLAMT HAMBURG WALTERSHOF AND FIRMA KURT A. BECHER v. HAUPTZOLLAMPT BREMEN-NORD (NOS. 119 and 120/76) [1977] E.C.R. 1269, European Ct.

1215. —— **customs duties—incompatibile legislation**
The European Court considered several questions referred to it by the Tribunal d'Instance, Bowg-en-Bresse under art. 177 EEC on the interpretation and validity of art. 31 (2) of Reg. 816/70. The case involved a challenge by importers into France of wine from Italy to the French customs charges on Italian wines on the basis that the charges were equivalent to customs duty and that they amounted to a prohibited quantitative restriction not authorised by the rule as to avoidance of market disturbance. *Held*, elimination of customs duties and equivalent charges amount to a fundamental principle of the common market and any derogation must be clearly set out. Arts. 35–46 EEC do not authorise such charges of duty. Art. 31 (2) of Reg. 817/70, in so far as it purports to permit such charges or levy, conflicts with these treaty articles and art. 13 EEC, in particular paragraph (2).
SOCIÉTÉ DES COMMISSIONAIRES RÉUNIS S.à.r.l. v. RECEVEUR DES DOUANES; S.a.r.l. LES FILS de HENRI RAMEL v. RECEVEUR DES DOUANES (Joined Nos. 80–81/77) [1978] E.C.R. 927, European Ct.

1216. —— **EEC protective tax—uncertainties—potatoes**
The Finanzgericht at Hamburg referred several questions to the European Court under art. 177 EEC concerning the interpretation and validity of Regs. 348/76 EEC and 890/76 EEC. The case arose following Commission measures to cope with a drastic fall in potato production in Autumn 1975 and Spring 1976. *Held*, a prudent trader will forsee but not expect a strict community measure to deal with such problems. The Regulations referred to the court are valid. As the former contains tax uncertainties, particularly as to the exchange rates specified in Regs. 950/68 and 475/75, the one to be applied is the less onerous for the particular tax payer.
FIRMA JOHANN LÜHRS v. HAUPTZOLLAMT HAMBURG-JONAS [1978] E.C.R. 169, Finanzgericht, Hamburg.

1217. —— **export refunds—animal feed-stuffs**

The Hessisches Finanzgericht referred several questions to the European Court under art. 177 EEC concerning the interpretation and validity of Regulations No. 166/64 and 171/64. *Held*, under the latter Regulation, export refunds to third countries may be granted for compound animal feeding-stuffs containing cereals or milk products. An export refund for animal feeding-stuffs containing cereals can be granted under both these Regulations only if the cereals or the products referred to by Reg. 19/62 are contained in the mixture in significant amounts.

FIRMA PETER CREMER *v.* BUNDESANSTALT FÜR LANDWIRTSCHAFTLICHE MARKTORDNUNG (No. 125/76) [1977] E.C.R. 1593.

1218. —— **fixing of refunds—advance payments**

A number of applicants claimed damages under arts. 178 and 215 EEC against the Commission in respect of advance fixing of refunds under Reg. 413/76. *Held*, these refunds are fixed so that exporters can be certain of the refund when their export takes place in so far as they are carried out before the expiry of their licence. The system of advance payment refunding set up in Reg. 441/69 seeks to ensure equality of treatment with products originating in third countries who would otherwise be at an advantage. Regs. 441/69 and 413/76 pursue separate aims and do not merge. Despite holding an export licence which thus guarantees a refund, the holder does not have the right to have the system for advance payment of the refund applied to him in accordance with the rules in force on the day of issue of the licence. The licences are valid according to the relevant rules and can only be amended thereunder, not under the rules for the advance payment of refunds.

GROUPEMENT D'INTÉRÊT ECONOMIQUE " UNION MALT " *v.* E.C. COMMISSION [1978] E.C.R. 57, European Ct.

1218a. —— **frontier prices—imports—preferential treatment**

The European Court considered several questions referred to it by the Finanzgericht Berlin under art. 177 EEC concerning in particular art. 14 of Reg. 804/68 and arts. 2 to 7 of Reg. 1073/68 concerning the fixing of frontier prices for certain milk products. *Held*, the community must always maintain its freedom to determine the conditions of importation for agricultural products originating in third countries. This is so without prejudice to any undertakings into which it may have entered with these countries, paying due regard to the common organisation of the agricultural markets. An importer who has gained preferential treatment from time to time in the importation of certain agricultural products, gains no vested right to the maintenance of these advantages.

BALKAN IMPORT-EXPORT GMBH *v.* HAUPTZOLLAMT BERLIN-PACKHOF [1977] E.C.R. 2031, European Ct.

1219. —— **grant aids—dairy herd conversion**

The Ombudsman considered a complaint against a refusal by the Ministry of Agriculture, Fisheries and Food to give grant aid to a livestock farmer under the Dairy Herd Conversion Scheme. This scheme was introduced in 1973, when EEC beef and veal were scarce and there was a surplus of milk. The farmer had registered all his cows as beef cows to receive a beef cow subsidy. In his report, the Ombudsman said that, as they had been so registered, they could not be treated as dairy cows for grant aid purposes.

Re AID UNDER THE DAIRY HERD CONVERSION SCHEME [1978] 3 C.M.L.R. 61, Parliamentary Commissioner for Administration.

1220. —— **import restrictions—potatoes**

The High Court referred a question to the European Court under art. 177 EEC concerning the interpretation of arts. 9 and 60 (2) of the Act of Accession. The case concerned the legality of various restrictions contained in statutory instruments under the Import, Export and Customs Powers (Defence) Act 1939 (c. 69), imposed on the import of potatoes. *Held*, the question to be asked was whether such restrictions were permissible under art. 60 (2) of the former

Act in the light of art. 9 of this Act. Can they survive the transitional period which ended on December 31, 1977?

C. MEIJER B.V. v. THE DEPARTMENT OF TRADE, THE MINISTRY OF AGRI-CULTURE, FISHERIES AND FOOD AND THE COMMISSIONERS OF CUSTOMS AND EXCISE [1978] 2 C.M.L.R. 563, Donaldson J.

1221. —— intervention—national rules

The Bundesverfassungsgericht considered an appeal by four plaintiffs concerning the refusal of relief against a decision not to intervene to buy certain harvested wheat. This was a constitutional issue which challenged both the national intervention agency and a national regulation which restricted subsidies. In the spring of 1969, large quantities of cheap French grain flooded into the German grain market because of the devalued French franc. A very high proportion of German wheat was offered for intervention, but the E.C. Commission, by Decision 69/138, considerably restricted intervention buying retrospectively. *Held*, the German constitution does not prevent retrospective regulations. The power to pass such rules stems, by necessary implication, from the aim and purpose of the relevant statute. Under EEC Reg. 120/67, the right to intervene does fall within the " property guarantee " provisions of the German constitution. Except for its conversion into a right in the interest of good market organisation, it would only be a business opportunity.

Re INTERVENTION BUYING [1978] 2 C.M.L.R. 644, German Federal Constitutional Ct.

1222. —— national and community rules—compensatory amounts

The Tribunale di Genova referred several questions to the European Court under art. 177 EEC concerning Reg. 974/71, 1013/71, and 974/71. *Held*, Community Regulations that have direct application, apply and enter into force independently of national law. Member States must not impede and must carefully observe such Regulations. Where such a rule is difficult to interpret, the Member State may adopt detail rules to assist and clarify the rules. The above Regulations, as amended by Reg. 2887/71, do not permit Member States to legislate criteria as to applicability of compensatory amounts. Art. 4 (2) of Reg. 1013/71 is effective and must be interpreted so that the court's Member States should decide if certain contracts were executed. As to the application of this article, the question is whether the contract was executed under the conditions which would have existed in the absence of monetary measures which had led to the introduction of compensatory amounts. The day of import and export must be used to determine if conditions for applying compensatory amounts are fulfilled.

FRATELLI ZERBONE S.N.C. v. AMMINISTRAZIONE DELLE FINANZE DELLO STATO (No. 94/77) [1978] E.C.R. 99.

1223. —— poultry slaughtering

The Gerechtshof, Amsterdam, asked the European Court of Justice for a preliminary ruling under art. 177 EEC on the question whether the rules contained in the Verordening Produktie Slachtpluimveesector 1974 of the Produktschap voor Pluimvee en Eieren (restricting the slaughter of poultry by fixing quotas) were incompatible with Reg. No. 123/67 of the Council of June 13, 1967, on the common organisation of the market in poultrymeat or with arts. 30 to 37 of the EEC Treaty. *Held*, Reg. 123/67, especially arts. 2 and 13 thereof, must be interpreted to the effect that measures enacted by the national authorities to impose a quota on the slaughtering of poultry are incompatible with Reg. No. 123/67. In view of the above interpretation, it is unnecessary to give an interpretation of arts. 30 to 37 of the EEC Treaty.

OFFICIER VAN JUSTITIE v. BEERT VAN DEN HAZEL (No. 111/76) [1977] E.C.R. 901, European Ct.

1224. —— proceedings for damages—national authorities

The European Court considered an application made under art. 178 EEC and 215 EEC for damages by several companies concerning art. 1 of Reg. 1608/74 (EEC). These companies had suffered loss because the discretionary provision of monetary compensation amounts under this article was not applied to certain exports of sugar. *Held*, taking this Regulation as a whole, that it permits

Member States the discretion to grant or refuse the exemption from compensatory amounts. Where the complaint in the action is substantially directed against the national authority, then the conditions for proceedings to be brought under arts. 178 and 215 EEC are not fulfilled.

DE BAYSER S.A. *v.* E.C. COMMISSION (Nos. 12, 18 & 21/77) [1978] E.C.R. 553, European Ct.

1225. —— **processed products—discrimination**
The Finanzgericht referred several questions under art. 177 EEC to the European Court concerning the validity of art. 11 of Reg. 120/67 EEC of art. 1 of Reg. 1955/75 and, if necessary, of art. 11 of 2727/75. The case involved a product, Quellmehl, processed from maize and wheat or broken rice and pre-gelatinized starch. These two were in competition, particularly for use as leavening in rye bread. *Held,* art. 40 (3) does not refer clearly to the relations between different trade or industrial sectors in processed agricultural products. Prohibition of discrimination is a specific enunciation of the principle of equality which requires that similar situations or cases should not be treated differently without objective reasons. Art. 11 of Reg. 120/67 EEC and subsequent amendments and repetitions infringe this principle in that Quellmehl and pre-gelatinized starch are treated differently in respect of production refunds on maize used in these two products. As art. 5 of Reg. 1125/74 is thereby illegal and incompatible with the principle of equality, it does not render the whole Regulation invalid, and it is for the competent Community institutions to adopt measures to correct this incompatibility.

ALBERT RUCKDESCHEL & CO. AND HANSA-LAGERHAUS STRÖH & CO. *v.* HAUPTZOLLAMT HAMBURG; ST. ANNEN DIAMALT AG *v.* HAUPTZOLLAMT ITZEHOE (joined cases 117/76 and 16/77) [1977] E.C.R. 1753, European Ct.

1226. The Tribunal Administratif at Nancy referred several questions under art. 177 EEC to the European Court concerning the validity of Reg. 665/75 of the council amending Reg. 120/67 EEC and Reg. 2727/75 of the council. The case involved the manufacture of beer using malt, starch products from coarse-grained cereals, maize meal known as gritz, starch and starch products. There was competition between the maize industry which produced gritz and the starch industry and also the chemical industry which produced oil-based substitute products all of which were rival ingredients for the brewing industry. *Held,* the Court gave a similar judgment as in cases 117/76 and 16/77 (§ 1225) and art. 3 of Reg. 665/75 repeated in Reg. 2727/75 EEC with Reg. 1955/75 EEC and subsequent regulations were incompatible with the principle of equality in so far as there was a difference of treatment in respect of production refunds between maize groats and meal for the brewing industry and maize starch.

S.A. MOULINS ET HUILERIES DE PONT-À-MOUSSON *v.* OFFICE NATIONAL INTERPROFESSIONNEL DES CÉRÉALES; SOCIÉTÉ COOPÉRATIVE PROVIDENCE AGRICOLE DE LA CHAMPAGNE *v.* OFFICE NATIONAL INTERPROFESSIONNEL DES CÉRÉALES (joined cases 124/76 and 20/77) [1977] E.C.R. 1795, European Ct.

1227. —— **processing deposit—butter**
The Verwaltungsgericht of Frankfurt referred two questions to the European Court of Justice for a preliminary ruling under art. 177 EEC on the interpretation and validity of art. 18 of Reg. No. 1259/72 of the Commission of June 16, 1972, as amended by art. 3 of Reg. No. 1237/73 of the Commission of May 10, 1973, concerning the sale by tender of surplus butter at a reduced price to certain Community processing undertakings. *Held,* (1) art. 18 of Reg. No. 1259/72 as amended by Reg. No. 1237/73 must be interpreted as meaning that, even where the successful tenderer does not himself manufacture the processed products from the surplus butter, it still must be established that the processed products comply with the conditions laid down in art. 6 (1) (*c*) of the regulation and that they have been produced within the period therein prescribed before the deposit may be released; (2) the system regarding the processing deposit established by Reg. No. 1259/72 rests on a proper legal basis.

There is no factor of such a kind as to affect the validity of the second paragraph down to the end of indent (*a*) of art. 18 (2) of Reg. No. 1259/72.

N.V. ROOMBOTERFABRIEK ' DE BESTE BOTER ' AND FIRMA JOSEF HOCHE, BUTTERSCHMELZWERK *v.* BUNDESANSTALT FÜR LANDWIRTSCHAFTLICHE MARKTORDNUNG (Nos. 99 and 100/76) [1977] E.C.R. 861, European Ct.

1228. —— **regional marketing board—status**

The Armagh Magistrates' Court referred several questions to the European Court concerning the status of the plaintiff, the Pig Marketing Board, in EEC law. The court asked if the Board was an " undertaking " within the meaning of arts. 85 and 86 EEC, a " national market organisation " within the meaning of art. 2, reg. 26, or a " state monopoly of a commercial character " within the meaning of art. 36 EEC.

PIGS MARKETING BOARD (NORTHERN IRELAND) *v.* REDMOND [1978] 2 C.M.L.R. 697, Armagh Mags.Ct.

1229. —— **state aids to pig producers—interim measure**

By a decision of February 17, 1977, the Commission stated that the Government of the United Kingdom and Northern Ireland should forthwith terminate the provision of aid to its pig producers which it had been operating since January 31, 1977. However, the U.K. continued to keep the aid in force. The Commission referred the matter to the European Court of Justice under art. 93 (2) of the EEC Treaty. *Held,* as an interim measure the U.K. should cease forthwith to apply the pig aid measure. Arts. 92 and 93 EEC establish machinery for the review of the compatibility of State aids with the Common Market so that national measures instituting or altering any such aid shall be investigated by the Commission and that no such measures may be put into effect until the Commission has announced its decision. Even if a Member State was of the opinion that the aid measure was compatible with the Common Market and that the contrary decision of the Commission was vitiated by infringement of the rules of the Treaty, that would not entitle it to defy the clear provisions of art. 93 and to act as if the decision were non-existent in law.

E.C. COMMISSION *v.* UNITED KINGDOM OF GREAT BRITAIN AND NORTHERN IRELAND (Nos. 31/77R and 53/77R) [1977] E.C.R. 921, European Ct.

1230. —— **storage rules—validity of regulations**

The European Court considered the interpretation of Regs. 2498/74 and 2517/74 following a reference to it by the High Court of Ireland under art. 177 EEC. The case concerned aid given under Community Rules for the private storage of butter and cream produced in the Community. *Held,* Reg. 2517/74 concerns storage contracts agreed before the entry into force of Reg. 2498/74 as regards butter still stored since that date. The regulation may not be invalid for lack of reasons if these appear from the body of legislation of which it forms a part.

AN BORD BAINNE CO-OPERATIVE *v.* THE MINISTER FOR AGRICULTURE (No. 92/77) [1978] 2 C.M.L.R. 567, European Ct.

1231. —— **subsidy—butter.** See § 1498.

1232. —— **olive oil—producers**

The Corte Supreme di Cassazione of Italy referred several questions to the European Court under art. 177 ECC concerning the interpretation of Regs. 136/66 and 754/67 EEC on the establishment of a common organisation of the market in oils and fats and of olive oil subsidies. *Held,* as these regulations draw a clear line between the cultivation of olive trees and the production of olive oil, the term " producers of olive oil " in art. 10 of the former Regulation, and in the latter Regulation, must be interpreted as referring to the producers of the processed product, and the olive oil subsidy for the year 1967/68 should be granted to these producers.

AZIENDA DI STATO PER GLI INTERVENTI SUL MERCATO AGRICOLO *v.* ROCCO MICHELE GRECO [1977] E.C.R. 2059, European Ct.

1233. —— **sugar**

The applicant requested the European Court of Justice to partially annul Commission Reg. No. 1579/76 of June 30, 1976, laying down special detailed rules of application for sugar under Reg. No. 557/76 on the exchange rates to be applied in agriculture, in so far as it abolishes the right to cancel export licences certifying the refund fixed under the awards provided for by Reg. No. 2101/75, issued before March 15, 1976, and not yet issued on July 1, 1976. *Held,* (1) proceedings brought by natural or legal persons are admissible against a measure of an institution concerning them by reason of circumstances in which they are differentiated from all other persons and distinguished individually just as in the case of the person addressed; (2) however, proceedings brought by any natural or legal person against a measure (regulation) which is not applicable to the situation of the plaintiff are inadmissible for lack of legal interest.

SOCIÉTÉ POUR L'EXPORTATION DES SUCRES S.A. *v.* E.C. COMMISSION (No. 88/76) [1977] E.C.R. 709, European Ct.

1234. Aliens—residence formalities—EEC nationals

The European Court interpreted Dir. 360/68EEC on a reference from the Amstgericht Reutlingen. *Held,* (1) in implementing Dir. 360/68 (which concerns identity and residence formalities in the case of EEC nationals), a Member State may not take measures which derogate from the entry and residence rights throughout the Community guaranteed to EEC nationals by the EEC treaty—for example by assimilating nationals of another Member State to the position of other aliens (in respect of whom Member States have a complete discretion); (2) a Member State may not therefore require an EEC national to possess a residence permit which is different in scope from the special residence " permit " (or declaration of status) provided for in art. 4 (2) of Dir. 360/68; (3) a Member State can impose penalties for the infringement of measures it has adopted under the Directive, but it cannot increase those penalties solely by reason of the fact that there have been previous convictions of offences created by provisions not authorised by Community law; (4) penalties imposed by Member States for failure to hold a valid identity card can be greater in the case of nationals of other Member States than in that of local nationals, but they must not be so severe as to obstruct the freedom of entry and residence guaranteed by the Treaty.

REPUBLIC OF ITALY *v.* SAGULO [1977] 2 C.M.L.R. 585, European Ct.

1235. Brussels Convention—enforcement of judgments—bilateral agreements

The German Federal Court of Justice referred a question to the European Court under art. 3 of the Protocol of the 1968 Convention on Jurisdiction and the Enforcement of Judgments in Civil and Commercial Matters, namely whether under art. 56 of the Brussels Convention, the treaty and conventions referred to in art. 55 continue to have effect in respect of judgments which do not fall under the second paragraph of art. 1 of the Brussels Convention but are excluded from its scope. *Held,* all Member States are required by the principle of legal certainty and the objectives of the Brussels Convention to apply uniformly the legal concepts and classifications developed by the court in the context of the Brussels Convention. In enforcing the Brussels Convention, a national court must not apply it so as to recognise or enforce judgments which are excluded from its scope by the Court of Justice. However, the national court is not prevented from applying to such a judgment one of the special agreements in art. 55 of the Brussels Convention. The European Court only has jurisdiction under the above Protocol over the Brussels Convention and not these special agreements. Thus the same expression in the Brussels Convention interpreted one way by the European Court may be interpreted differently by a national court when it appears in a bilateral or special agreement.

BAVARIA FLUGGESELLSCHAFT SCHWABE & Co. K.B. AND GERMANIAR BEDARFS-LUFTFAHRT G.M.B.H. & Co. K.G. *v.* EUROCONTROL (Nos. 9 & 10/77) [1977] E.C.R. 1517, European Ct.

1236. Common customs tariff—classification—children's books

The European Court (Second Chamber) considered several questions referred (under art. 177 EEC) to it by the Oberfinanzdirektion concerning children's books which mostly consisted of illustrations but had short, simple captions and narrative. The problem was what tariff classification should be applied to such books. *Held,* if the principal method of communication is pictorial, not written, then such children's books will be classified as " children's picture books." CARLSEN VERLAG G.M.B.H. *v.* OBERFINANZDIREKTION KÖLN [1978] 3 C.M.L.R. 14, European Ct.

1237. —— —— electrical appliances

The Bundesfinanzhof asked the European Court of Justice for a preliminary ruling under art. 177 EEC as to whether certain electrical appliances were to be classified under tariff heading 85.17 of the CCT. *Held,* Note 2, together with Note 5 to s. XVI of the CCT, must be interpreted as meaning that individual electrical appliances which are suitable for use exclusively or principally with an electric sound or visual signalling apparatus within the meaning of tariff heading 85.17 are " parts " within the meaning of that note and must, in accordance therewith, be classified under tariff heading 85.17, even when imported without the cables linking the various parts, and without the acoustic or visual alarm signalling devices.

FRITZ FUSS KG *v.* OBERFINANZDIREKTION MUNCHEN (No. 60/77) [1977] E.C.R. 2453, European Ct.

1238. —— —— equipment for the support of mine tunnels

The Bundesfinanzhof referred two questions to the European Court of Justice for a preliminary ruling under art. 177 EEC concerning the interpretation of certain tariff headings in the CCT. *Held,* (1) the term " structure " in tariff heading 73.21 of the CCT may not be interpreted so as to include an article which is intended to render the mine face safe in mining; (2) the equipment in question is to be classified under tariff heading 84.23 of the CCT if it is directly attached to mining machinery for working the earth's crust; if this is not the case, it must be classified under sub-heading 84.59 E of the CCT. Whether or not the equipment in question fulfils these conditions is a matter of the application rather than the interpretation of the CCT and is for the national court to decide.

KLÖCKNER-FERROMATIK G.M.B.H. *v.* OBERFINANZDIREKTION MÜNCHEN (No. 108/76) [1977] E.C.R. 1047, European Ct.

1239. —— —— fats

The Bundesfinanzhof asked the European Court of Justice for a preliminary ruling under art. 177 EEC on the applicability of heading 15.13 of the CCT to certain mixtures of fats. *Held,* food preparations consisting mainly of milk fats are covered by tariff heading 21.07 of the CCT and thus cannot come under heading 15.13.

GERVAIS-DANONE A.G. *v.* HAUPTZOLLAMT MÜNCHEN-MITTE (No. 86/76) [1977] E.C.R. 619, European Ct.

1240. —— —— lead alloy scrap metal

The Finanzgericht Hamburg referred several questions to the European Court under art. 177 EEC for a preliminary ruling on the interpretation of tariff headings 78.01 and 78.02 of the Common Customs Tariff (CCT). The case concerned lead-based alloy metal bars imported from Denmark and the United States into Germany. The question was if this metal was included in the CCT. *Held,* the exception from customs tariff in part of the first of these headings (78.01B) concerning waste metal can only be claimed if the importer provides his goods for inspection and they can be readily recognised as waste or scrap. Heading 78.01A includes lead scrap bars if they are unusable as bars.

BLEIINDUSTRIE KG *v.* HAUPTZOLLAMT HAMBURG-WALTERSHOF (No. 111/77) [1978] E.C.R. 659, European Ct.

1241. —— —— paper

The Bundesfinanzhof asked the European Court of Justice for a preliminary ruling under art. 177 EEC as to whether tariff heading 48.15 of the CCT should be interpreted as including sets of sheets of different kinds of paper stuck together. *Held,* tariff heading 48.15 of the CCT must be interpreted as not covering goods consisting of a sheet of carbon paper and a sheet of flimsy paper stuck together. Such goods must be classified under tariff heading 48.18, as " other stationery of paper."

FIRMA LUDWIG POPPE v. OBERFINANZDIREKTION COLOGNE (No. 63/77) [1977] E.C.R. 2473, European Ct.

1242. —— —— waste and scrap

The Bundesfinanzhof referred several questions to the European Court under art. 177 EEC on the interpretation of the Common Custom Tariff (CCT) relating to its classification of unwrought aluminium and aluminium waste and scrap. *Held*, the European Court under such a reference can only decide the matter on the facts put before it by the national court and cannot verify those facts. The concepts of waste and scrap within subheading 76.01B (CCT) covers the metal fragments or parts left over from cutting, shaping or working of aluminium products or defective articles which are only fit for the recovery of the metal. Chopped aluminium wire should be put under subheading 76.01A (CCT) as it consists nearly entirely of aluminium.

FIRMA WOLFGANG OEHLSCHLÄGER v. HAUPTZOLLAMT EMMERICH (No. 104/77) [1978] E.C.R. 791, European Ct.

1243. —— —— works of art

The European Court considered a question referred to it by the Finanzgericht, Münster under art. 177 EEC concerning the interpretation of heads 49.11 and 99.02 of the Common Customs Tariff. *Held*, the distinction between works of art and similar articles, and printed books and similar items does not depend on artistic merit but on objective criteria adopted by the Common Customs Tariff. Artistic screen prints, despite the artist's signature, cannot be categorised as " original engravings, prints and lithographs " as they are produced by partly mechanical and photo-mechanical means.

WESTFÄLISCHER KUNSTVEREIN v. HAUPTZOLLAMT MÜNSTER (No. 23/77) [1978] 1 C.M.L.R. 373, European Ct.

1244. —— exemption—scientific apparatus

The European Court considered several questions referred to it by the Tariefcommissie, Amsterdam under art. 177 EEC concerning the interpretation of regs. 1798/75 and 3195/75. The Utrecht University Heart Clinic wished to import a " spectrophotometre " and applied for exemption from import duty. This was rejected and the clinic appealed. *Held*, the words " scientific instrument or apparatus " appearing in art. 3 (1) of reg. 1798/75 refer to an " instrument or apparatus possessing objective characteristics which make it particularly suitable for pure scientific research." However, the fact that such an instrument is used commercially does not necessarily mean it may not be of a scientific nature within this Regulation. Thus it may still be exempt from customs duties.

UNIVERSITEITSKLINIEK UTRECHT v. INSPECTEUR DER INVOERRECHTEN EN ACCIJNZEN UTRECHT (No. 72/77) [1978] E.C.R. 189, European Ct.

1245. —— monetary compensation for exporters—liability of commission for sudden changes

A German company claimed that, as a result of an EEC Regulation reducing the monetary compensation applicable to exports of certain goods, it had suffered loss in the performance of contracts relating to those goods. It applied for an order for the payment of damages by the Commission. *Held*, dismissing the application, that the Commission could only be liable if it modified or abolished compensatory amounts with immediate effect, without warning, in the absence of transitional measures and in such circumstances that the abolition or modification was not foreseeable by a prudent trader. The aim of the system of compensatory amounts was to encourage monetary stability in the common organisation of the markets rather than to protect the individual interests of traders.

MERKUR AUSSENHANDEL G.M.B.H. & CO. KG v. E.C. COMMISSION (No. 97/76) [1977] E.C.R. 1063, European Ct.

1246. Common fisheries policy—conservation orders—interim suspension

The Commission, supported by the Netherlands, applied to the European Court for the suspension of various measures taken by the Government of

Ireland concerning sea fisheries. *Held,* until judgment had been given in the main action, Ireland may, with the consent of the Commission, adopt in sea areas within its jurisdiction any measures, with the exception of those set out below, that are intended to ensure the protection of fish stocks which are in accordance with the provisions of Community Law and the objectives of the Common fisheries policy. Ireland must suspend their orders entitled Sea Fisheries (Conservation and Rational Exploitation) Order 1977 and Sea Fisheries (Conservation and Rational Exploitation) (No. 2) Order 1977, until judgment in the main action.

E.C. COMMISSION *v.* IRELAND (No. 61/77R) [1977] E.C.R. 1411, European Ct.

1247. Community and national law—dominant position—quantitative restrictions
The European Court considered several questions referred to it by the Belgian Cour de Cassation under art. 177 EEC concerning the interpretation of arts. 3 (*g*), 5 (2), 30, 86, 90 EEC and art. 5 of Dir. 72/464. *Held*, the provisions had the effect that price maintenance imposed by firms in a dominant position would not escape art. 86 EEC because such action was encouraged by national legislation. Further it is a question of fact and one which required a finding by the national court whether such a system was caught by art. 86. Each Member State may choose to control manufactured tobacco in its territory by its own fiscal methods; however a prohibition on retailers selling articles lower than that used for calculating the tax label is not justified. The EEC treaty precludes national law which hinders trade within the Community directly or indirectly, actually or potentially. Art. 86 imposes a duty on Member States to ensure that the article can be effective. Despite national legislation which might appear to encourage an abuse of a dominant position by one or more undertakings the latter remain bound to observe art. 86. Further, any national measure which does encourage such an abuse infringes arts. 30 and 34 EEC. National measures which hinder imports in any way have the same effect as a quantitative restriction. A maximum price applicable to domestic and imported products does not in itself form a measure equivalent to a quantitative restriction; it may have such an effect when it is fixed at a level where imports can only be sold with greater difficulty than domestic products.

G.B.-INNO-B.M. NV *v.* VERENIGING VAN DE KLEINHANDELAARS IN TABAK (No. 13/77) [1978] 1 C.M.L.R. 283, European Ct.

1248. —— incompatibility—criminal proceedings—conservation of sea fisheries
On February 16, 1977, the Irish Minister for Fisheries made two orders, the Sea Fisheries (Conservation & Rational Exploitation) Order 1977 and the Sea Fisheries (Conservation and Rational Exploitation) (No. 2) Order 1977, which prohibited fishing within the exclusive fishery limits of the Irish State by boats exceeding 33 metres in length or exceeding 1,100 brake horsepower. Ten Masters of Dutch trawlers were prosecuted in the Cork District Court for contravention of these orders. The court stayed the proceedings and asked the European Court of Justice for a preliminary ruling under art. 177, EEC, as to whether Community Law, in particular art. 7, EEC, arts. 2 & 4 of Council Reg. (EEC) 101/76 (the Reg. that lays down a common structural policy for the fishing industry), and arts. 100/103 of the Treaty of Accession, precluded Ireland from taking the measures set out in the orders and whether a conviction of these defendants would be incompatible with Community law. *Held*, (1) as the Community had not taken adequate conservation measures under art. 102 of the Act of Accession and art. 4 of Reg. 101/76, the Member States were, at the relevant time, entitled to take interim measures in relation to maritime waters coming within their jurisdiction, provided those measures are in accordance with Community law; (2) art. 7, EEC, art. 2 of Reg. 101/76 and arts. 100 and 101 of the Act of Accession preclude a Member State from adopting measures such as are set out in the orders in question; (3) where criminal proceedings are brought pursuant to a national legislative measure which is held to be contrary to Community law, a conviction in those proceedings is incompatible with that law.

E.C. COMMISSION *v.* REPUBLIC OF IRELAND; MINISTER FOR FISHERIES *v.* C. A. SCHOENBERG (No. 88/77) [1978] 2 C.M.L.R. 519, European Ct.

1249. —— —— national courts—health charges

The Pretore di Susa (Italy) referred several questions to the European Court under art. 177 EEC concerning the interpretation of art. 189 EEC. The case involved an apparent conflict between Community law and subsequent national law. A consignment of beef had been charged for veterinary and public health inspections at the frontier and questions arose from the issue whether these charges had an effect equivalent to quantitative restrictions within the meaning of art. 30 EEC and could be enforced by Italy. *Held,* reference under 177 EEC will be considered by the European Court providing a superior national court has not quashed the reference or the referring court has not withdrawn the matter. Where Community rules are directly applicable, they must be fully and uniformly enforced from the date of their entry into force. They are a direct source of rights and duties for all who are affected by them. Any conflicting national law is rendered inapplicable by the Community legislation, and precludes any subsequent national legislation which conflicts with it being valid. Similarly, subsequent national law may not encroach on Community law. National courts must apply community law even if it means refusing to apply conflicting national rules.

AMMINISTRAZIONE DELLE FINANZE DELLO STATO *v.* SIMMENTHAL S.P.A. (No. 106/77) [1978] E.C.R. 629, European Ct.

1250. —— restrictive practices—pleading—new torts

The Court of Appeal considered an appeal in an action in which the plaintiff sought damages for conspiracy and breaches of arts. 85 and 86 EEC. In particular, it was concerned with the contents of the statement of claim. *Held,* the appeal would be stood over to allow the plaintiff company to produce a new pleading, when it would be seen whether it adequately disclosed a cause of action. The conduct alleged to be in breach of these articles must be after British accession, and be specifically pleaded with particulars given. The implication of the continuance of pre-accession violations is not sufficient. It has not been settled whether breaches of these articles create new torts in British law. It was suggested in *Application des Gaz S.A.* v. *Falks Veritas* [1974] C.L.Y. 2889 by Lord Denning M.R., that new torts of undue restriction on competition within the Common Market, and abuse of a dominant position within the Common Market, may have been created, but it was pointed out that these remarks had not been reflected in the decision of the Court of Appeal in the earlier case.

VALOR INTERNATIONAL *v.* APPLICATION DES GAZ S.A. [1978] 3 C.M.L.R. 87, C.A.

1251. —— social security—migrant workers

The Arbeidsrechtbank, Antwerp, referred three questions to the European Court of Justice under art. 177 EEC for a preliminary ruling on the interpretation of art. 84 (4) of Council Reg. No. 1408/71 of June 14, 1971, on the application of social security schemes to employed persons and their families moving within the Community with reference to the rules governing the language to be used for the purposes of the regulation. *Held,* (1) art. 84 (4) of Reg. No. 1408/71 requires authorities, institutions and tribunals of Member States to accept, in spite of any provision of their national laws which may derogate therefrom or be contrary thereto, all claims and all other documents relating to the application of that regulation and written in an official language of another Member State. Member States are not permitted in this connection to create distinctions on the grounds of nationality or place of residence of the persons concerned; (2) it is impossible for the authority of Community Law to vary from one Member State to another through the effect of national laws, whatever their purpose, if the efficacy of Community Law and its uniform application throughout the Community are not to be jeopardised.

MARIS *v.* RIJKSDIENST VOOR WERKNEMERSPENSIONEN (No. 55/77) [1977] E.C.R. 2327, European Ct.

1252. —— —— —— declarations

The Arbeitsrechtbank of Hasselt referred several questions to the European Court under art. 177 EEC concerning the interpretation of art. 69 of Reg. 1408/71. *Held,* where a Member State has specified a law in its declaration under art. 5 of the Regulation, then this action must be accepted as proof that the benefits granted on the basis of that law are social security benefits within the meaning of this Regulation.

BEERENS v. RIJKSDIENST VOOR ARBEIDSVOORZIENING [1977] E.C.R. 2249, European Ct.

1253. —— —— **minimum benefit**

The Tribunal du Travail Liège referred several questions to the European Court under art. 177 EEC concerning the interpretation of art. 50 of Reg. 1408/71. *Held,* this article, concerning the application of social security schemes to employed persons and their families moving within the Community, is applicable only to cases in which provision is made in the legislation of a Member State in which the worker resides for minimum pension.

MARIO TORRI v. OFFICE NATIONAL DES PENSIONS POUR TRAVAILLEURS SALARIÉS [1977] E.C.R. 2299, European Ct.

1254. —— —— **unemployment benefit**

The Arbeidsrechtbank, Hasselt, asked the European Court of Justice for a preliminary ruling under art. 177 EEC on the compatibility of art. 124 of the Belgian Royal Decree of December 20, 1963 (concerning unemployment benefit rules in Belgium) with the relevant rules of Community Law on free movement of workers. *Held,* (1) although the court has no jurisdiction under art. 177 EEC to decide upon the compatibility of a national law with Community Law, it may nevertheless extract from the words of the national court's question those elements which come within the interpretation of Community Law; (2) for the purpose of granting unemployment benefits to former students who have never been employed, neither the EEC Treaty nor the provisions of Council Reg. No. 1408/71, relating to unemployment, may be interpreted as requiring the competent institution of a Member State to treat studies completed in another Member State as studies completed in an educational establishment which is established, recognised or subsidised by the competent state.

KUYKEN v. RIJKSDIENST VOOR ARBEIDSVOORZIENING (No. 66/77) [1977] E.C.R. 2311, European Ct.

1255. Community revenue—capacity to bring legal proceedings

The Pretore of Cento referred two questions to the European Court of Justice for a preliminary ruling on the interpretation of Council Decision of April 21, 1970, and of Council Reg. (EEC, Euratom, ECSC) No. 2/71 of January 2, 1971, concerning the replacement of financial contributions from Member States by the Communities' own resources. These questions arose out of criminal proceedings for a possible smuggling offence in respect of goods subject to the Common Customs Tariff and subject to agricultural levies. *Held,* only the Member States and their authorities are empowered to undertake prosecutions and proceedings before national courts for the purpose of claiming payment of Community revenue constituting own resources, such as duties under the CCT.

PRETORE OF CENTO v. A PERSON OR PERSONS UNKNOWN (No. 110/76) [1977] E.C.R. 851, European Ct.

1256. Community transit

H.M. Customs and Excise have isued Notice No. 750 (January, 1978): community transit.

1257. Competition—payment of fines

The applicants, pursuant to art. 40 of the Protocol on the Statute of the Court of Justice of the EEC and art. 102 of the Rules of Procedure, asked the European Court to interpret para. 3 (*b*) of the judgment of the Court of December 16, 1975, given in joined cases 40/73, to which the applicants were parties (see *Suiker Unie* v. *E.C. Commission* [1975] C.L.Y. 1240). In para. 3 (*b*) the court expressed the fines imposed on the applicants in units of account and indicated in brackets the value of the fine in the relevant national currency. *Held,* (1) since the u.a. is not a currency in which payment may be made, the Commission and the Court are of necessity bound to fix the amount of the fine in a national currency. The judgment must be understood to mean that the size of the debts arising out of the fines imposed under para. 3 (*b*) is to be determined by the amounts expressed in the national currency of each undertaking; in the case of the applicants, this is the sum expressed in French francs. The amounts expressed in u.a. were stated solely in order to check whether the prescribed limits within which the fines must fall have in fact been observed. Therefore, the commission was and is empowered to require the applicants to pay their debts in French francs; (2) there is no legal provision which prohibits the Commission from accepting payments made in a national currency of the Community other than that in which the debt has been determined; nevertheless, it is bound to ensure that the actual value of payments made in another currency corresponds to that of the sum fixed in national currency by the judgment of the Court, and the conversion between the two national currencies in question must be made at the free rate of exchange applicable on the day of payment.

SOCIÉTÉ ANONYME GÉNÉRALE SUCRIÈRE ET SOCIÉTÉ BÉGHIN SAY *v.* E.C. COMMISSION (Nos. 41, 43 & 44/73) [1977] E.C.R. 445, European Ct.

1258. Constitutional law—Community taxation directly enforceable—France
The French Constitutional Council *held* that the provisions of the Finance 1977 (Rectification) Bill relating to the collection of the EEC isoglucose levy imposed by Reg. 1111/77 of the E.C. Council of May 17, 1977, were not contrary to the French Constitution. In the case of the Regulation, Parliament was not required to intervene in the determination of the base and rate of the levy but solely to provide measures for its collection.

Re ISOGLUCOSE (No. 1) [1978] 2 C.M.L.R. 361, French Constitutional Council.

1259. —— Community taxation directly enforceable—France
The French Constitutional Council *held* that (1) the provisions of the Finance 1978 Bill relating to the collection of the EEC co-responsibility levy on milk imposed by Reg. 1079/77 of the E.C. Council of May 17, 1977, and Reg. 1822/77 of the E.C. Commission of August 5, 1977, were constitutional as the Regulations did not require the intervention of Parliament. Thus the Finance 1978 Bill, in not laying down any rule or any revenue or expenditure entry relating to the co-responsibility levy, did not conflict with the French Constitution; (2) the EEC levy on isoglucose imposed by EEC Reg. 1111/77 were not unconstitutional (see *Re Isoglucose* (*No.* 1) [1978] C.L.Y. 1258). The Bill did no more than list the product in question, which was not unconstitutional.

Re ISOGLUCOSE (No. 2) [1978] 2 C.M.L.R. 364, French Constitutional Council.

1259a. Customs and excise—national rules of natural justice—applicability in Community law
The Finanzgericht Berlin sought a ruling from the European Court on a number of questions concerning the role of natural justice in the context of Community customs levies. *Held*, (1) the customs authority of a Member State may not apply a national rule of natural justice to an application for exemption from charges due under Community law if so doing would alter the effect of the Community rules relating to the basis of assessment, the manner of imposition, or the amount of the charge; *sed aliter* when only the formalities of recovering the charge are concerned; (2) there is no provision in Community law for administrative action granting exception from charges introduced by Community law, on grounds of natural justice.

BALKAN-IMPORT-EXPORT G.M.B.H. *v.* HAUPTZOLLAMT BERLIN-PACKHOF (No. 118/76) [1977] E.C.R. 1177, European Ct.

1260. Customs duties—equivalent effect
The Pretore of Abbiategrasso referred several questions to the European Court of Justice under art. 177 EEC concerning the interpretation of arts. 1 to 8, 13 (2) and 38 to 43 of the EEC Treaty and of Council Reg. No. 1009/67 of December 18, 1967, and No. 3330/74 of December 19, 1974, on the common organisation of the market in sugar. *Held*, (1) a duty falling within a general system of internal taxation applying to domestic products as well as to imported products according to the same criteria can constitute a charge having an effect equivalent to a customs duty on imports only if its sole

purpose is to finance activities for the specific advantage of the taxed domestic product, if the taxed product and the domestic product benefiting from it are the same, and if the charges imposed on the domestic product are made good in full; (2) under Reg. No. 3330/74 the Community is, in the absence of express derogation, alone competent to adopt specific measures involving intervention in the machinery of price formation, in particular by limiting the effects of an alteration in the level of Community prices, whether this concerns intervention prices or the rate of exchange of the national currency in relation to the unit of account; an infringement in this respect of Reg. No. 3330/74 may be the subject of proceedings before the national courts brought by any natural or legal person whose stocks were subject to the national measure.

FRATELLI CUCCHI *v.* AVEZ S.P.A. (No. 77/76), [1977] E.C.R. 987, European Ct.

1261. —— —— precious metals

The Copenhagen City Court considered a case concerning the question whether levies imposed on un-hallmarked processing of precious metals in Denmark for export were equivalent to customs duties within art. 11 EEC or internal taxation within art. 95 EEC. Similar processing for a Danish customer only attracted the levy at the finished goods stage. *Held*, this question in respect of the interpretation of arts. 16 and 95 was referred under art. 177 EEC to the European Court for a preliminary ruling.

STATENS KONTROL MED AEDLE METALLER *v.* PREBEN LARSEN AND FLEMMING KJERULFF [1978] 2 C.M.L.R. 78, Copenhagen City Ct.

1262. —— price—warehousing—European Court's function

The Tarifcommissie, Amsterdam referred several questions to the European Court under art. 177 EEC concerning the interpretation of art. 10 (2) (*d*) of Directive 69/74 EEC. *Held*, the European Court cannot interpret national law, but can provide criteria enabling the national court to deal with an issue of incompatibility. Art. 10 (2) (*d*) of this Directive may be relied upon to verify whether national measures for its implementation accord with it. It must be interpreted to mean that if a price is taken as the basis in calculating the value of goods for customs, and if the cost of warehousing and storage are included that price must be adjusted in such a way as to exclude the latter factors.

ENKA B.V. *v.* INSPECTEUR DER INVOERRECHTEN EN ACCIJNZEN, ARNHEM [1977] E.C.R. 2203, European Ct.

1263. Damages—export refunds on butter

The applicant bought butter from the German Intervention Agency and obtained export certificates to export the butter to Morocco. The certificates fixed in advance export refunds on the butter. The competent German customs office reclaimed from the applicant the amount of refunds that had been paid to it on the ground that the applicant had not given proof of marketing the butter in Morocco. The applicant brought proceedings for damages against the Commission under the second paragraph of art. 215 of the EEC Treaty on the ground that, through its " communications," the Commission let it be assumed that payment of the refunds was dependent solely on the fact that the goods had arrived in Morocco. The action was also brought against the Council on the ground that it had failed to establish clearly the legal situation regarding export refunds. *Held*, the application would be dismissed as (1) there was no evidence that the Commission had led the applicant to believe that proof of marketing in the country of destination could not be required, nor was there any evidence that it had instilled doubts in the applicant as to the sort of proof required in connection with the payment of refunds; (2) the Council had not failed to establish clearly the legal situation regarding refunds in Reg. No. 876/86 of the Council of June 28, 1968.

MILCH- FETT- UND EIER-KONTOR G.M.B.H. *v.* E.C. COMMISSION (No. 44/76) [1977] E.C.R. 393, European Ct.

1263a. —— liability—invalid regulation

The plaintiffs claimed damages under para. 2 of art. 215 EEC for damage they alleged they had suffered due to an increase in the price of feeding stuffs resulting from the application of Council Reg. No. 563/76, which Reg. had subsequently been declared invalid. *Held*, the invalidity of the Reg. was insufficient in itself to make the Community liable for damages under art. 215 EEC. To have made the Community liable, it would have had to have been shown that the Community, in implementing part of its economic policy through this Reg., had acted in flagrant violation of its powers: BAYERISCHE HNL VERMEHRUNGSBETRIEBE GMBH AND CO. KG, GUT HEINRICHSRUH (GERMANY) *v*. E.C. COMMISSION, *The Times*, June 5, 1978, European Ct.

1264. —— —— monetary compensatory amounts—sugar exports
The applicant firm claimed damages against the European Community in respect of the damage it suffered when the system of monetary compensatory amounts was introduced into Italy by Reg. No. 2887/71 without the Commission having provided rules protecting export contracts, such as the applicant's, which had been concluded before December 19,1971. The applicant alleged that the Commission, by not protecting such export contracts, and thus not protecting the legitimate expectation of individuals, had committed a flagrant breach of a superior rule of law and had incurred the liability of the Community under the second para. of art. 215 EEC. Further, it was alleged that the Reg. exempted imports into Italy, pursuant to contracts made before December 19, 1971, from the compensatory amounts, but provided for no exemption for exports from one Member State to another and thus constituted an infringement of the principle of equality. *Held,* application dismissed, for (1) it was inherent in the system of monetary compensatory amounts that if Italy allowed the rate of exchange of its currency to fluctuate, monetary compensatory amounts might become applicable in Italy; (2) the previous Regs. of the Commission had never provided for rules giving exemption for exports, but only for imports. The principle of equality had not been infringed by this Reg.; (3) therefore, neither the application of the system of monetary compensation amounts to Italy, nor the absence of transitional rules protecting old export contracts, infringed the principle of the protection of the legitimate expectation of interested parties.
FIRMA GEBRÜDER DIETZ *v*. E.C. COMMISSION (No. 126/76) [1977] E.C.R. 2431, European Ct.

1265. —— sugar
The applicant sugar producers of Guadeloupe and Martinique brought proceedings before the European Court of Justice for damages against the Council and Commission under para. 2 of art. 215 EEC, in respect of loss which they claimed they suffered during the sugar marketing years 1971 to 1975. They asserted that the alleged loss resulted from the Community institutions failing to take into consideration, for the purpose of fixing the intervention prices for sugar, the discrepancy between the harvesting and selling periods for sugar in the European territory (July 1 to December 30) and the same periods in Guadeloupe and Martinique (January 1 to June 30). Thus, they claimed that the community was liable for the loss which the applicants allegedly suffered as a result of the implementation of council Reg. 1009/67 on the common organisation of the market in sugar. *Held*, since the disputed measure is legislative in character and was adopted in the sphere of economic policy, the Community cannot be liable under the second paragraph of art. 215 for any damage suffered by producers as a result of that measure, unless a flagrant violation of a superior rule of law for the protection of the individual has occurred. As, on the evidence no such flagrant violation had occurred, the applications would be dismissed.
COMPAGNIE INDUSTRIELLE ET AGRICOLE DU COMTÉ DE LOHEAC *v*. E.C. COMMISSION (Nos. 54 to 60/76) [1977] E.C.R. 645, European Ct.

1266. Directives, decisions and regulations

EEC, Euratom, ECSC

78/67/Euratom, ECSC, EEC:
Final adoption of the general budget of the European Communities for the financial year 1978. (O.J. 1978 L36/1.)

78/261/Euratom, ECSC, EEC:
Final adoption of amending budget No. 1 of the European Communities for the financial year 1978. (O.J. 1978 L71/1.)

78/339/Euratom, ECSC, EEC:
Final adoption of amending budget No. 2 of the European Communities for the financial year 1977 (O.J. 1978 L110/1.)

78/402/Euratom, ECSC, EEC:
Final adoption of amending and supplementary budget No. 2 of the European Communities for the financial year 1978. (O.J. 1978 L121/1.)

78/517/Euratom, ECSC, EEC:
Final adoption of supplementary budget No. 3 of the European Communities for the financial year 1978. (O.J. 1978 L162/1.)

78/639/Euratom, ECSC, EEC:
Council Decision of July 25, 1978, fixing the period for the first election of representatives of the European Parliament by direct universal suffrage. (O.J. 1978 L205/75.)

Council Regulation (EEC, Euratom, ECSC) No. 2859/77 of December 19, 1977, adjusting the remuneration and pensions of officials and other servants of the European Communities and the weightings applied thereto. (O.J. 1977 L330/1.)

Council Regulation (EEC, Euratom, ECSC) No. 2891/77 of December 19, 1977, implementing the decision of April 21, 1970, on the replacement of financial contributions from Member States by the Communities' own resources. (O.J. 1977 L336/1.)

Council Regulation (EEC, Euratom, ECSC) No. 2892/77 of December 19, 1977, implementing in respect of own resources accruing from value added tax the decision of April 21, 1970, on the replacement of financial contributions from Member States by the Communities' own resources. (O.J. 1977 L336/8.)

Council Regulation (Euratom, ECSC, EEC) No. 912/78 of May 2, 1978, amending the Staff Regulations of officials of the European Communities and the conditions of employment of other servants of the European Communities. (O.J. 1978 L119/1.)

Council Regulation (Euratom, ECSC, EEC) No. 913/78 of May 2, 1978, amending Regulation (EEC, Euratom, ECSC) No. 260/68 laying down the conditions and procedure for applying the tax for the benefit of the European Communities. (O.J. 1978 L119/7.)

Council Regulation (Euratom, ECSC, EEC) No. 914/78 of May 2, 1978, amending the Staff Regulations of officials of the European Communities as regards the allowance referred to in Article 4a of Annex VII to the Staff Regulations. (O.J. 1978 No. L119/8.)

Council Regulation (Euratom, ECSC, EEC) No. 1461/78 of June 26, 1978, adjusting the weightings applied to the remuneration and pensions of officials and other servants of the European Communities. (O.J. 1978 L176/1)

Council Regulation (Euratom, ECSC, EEC) No. 2711/78 of November 20, 1978, adjusting certain daily subsistence allowance rates for officials on mission laid down in Article 13 (9) of Annex VII to the Staff Regulations of officials of the European Communities. (O.J. 1978 L328/1.)

Euratom, EEC

1267. 78/70/Euratom, EEC:
Council Decision of January 23, 1978, appointing a member of the Economic and Social Committee. (O.J. 1978 L23/41.)

78/180/Euratom, EEC:
Council Decision of February 20, 1978, appointing a member of the Economic and Social Committee. (O.J. 1978 L54/31.)

78/181/Euratom, EEC:
Council Decision of February 20, 1978, appointing a member of the Economic and Social Committee. (O.J. 1978 L54/32.)

78/337/Euratom, EEC:
Council Decision of April 4, 1978, replacing a member of the Economic and Social Committee. (O.J. 1978 L98/18.)

78/807/Euratom, EEC:
Council Decision of September 19, 1978, appointing the members of the Economic and Social Committee for the period from September 19, 1978, to September 18, 1982. (O.J. 1978 L273/27.)

78/871/Euratom, EEC:
Council Decision of October 16, 1978, appointing a member of the Economic and Social Committee. (O.J. 1978 L298/11.)

Euratom

1268. 78/27/Euratom:
Council Decision of December 12, 1977, replacing a member of the Advisory Committee of the European Supply Agency. (O.J. 1978 L11/22.)

78/164/Euratom:
Agreement between the Kingdom of Belgium, the Kingdom of Denmark, the Federal Republic of Germany, Ireland, the Italian Republic, the Grand Duchy of Luxembourg, the Kingdom of the Netherlands, the European Atomic Energy Community and the International Atomic Energy Agency in implementation of art. III (1) and (4) of the Treaty on the non-proliferation of nuclear weapons. (O.J. 1978 L51/1.)

78/217/Euratom:
Amendment to the Agreement of October 6, 1959, in the form of an exchange of letters, between the European Atomic Energy Community (Euratom) and the Government of Canada for co-operation in the peaceful uses of atomic energy. (O.J. 1978 L65/16.)

78/264/Euratom:
Council Decision of March 6, 1978, adopting a programme of research and development for the European Atomic Energy Community on uranium exploration and extraction (indirect action). (O.J. 1978 L72/12.)

78/265/Euratom:
Council Decision of March 6, 1978, replacing a member of the Advisory Committee of the Euratom Supply Agency. (O.J. 1978 L72/14.)

78/470/Euratom:
Council Decision of May 30, 1978, amending Decision 76/345/Euratom adopting a research and training programme (1976 to 1980) of the European Atomic Energy Community in the field of fusion and plasma physics. (O.J. 1978 L151/8.)

78/471/Euratom:
Council Decision of May 30, 1978, on the establishment of the " Joint European Torus (JET), Joint Undertaking." (O.J. 1978 L151/11.)

78/472/Euratom:
Council Decision of May 30, 1978, on the conferment of advantages on the " Joint European Torus (JET), Joint Undertaking." (O.J. 1978 L151/23.)

78/568/Euratom:
Council Decision of June 26, 1978, replacing a member of the Advisory Committee of the Euratom Supply Agency. (O.J. 1978 L191/36.)

78/569/Euratom:
Council Decision of June 26, 1978, replacing a member of the Advisory Committee of the Euratom Supply Agency. (O.J. 1978 L191/37.)

78/730/Euratom:
Council Decision of August 11, 1978, approving the conclusion by the Commission of the Co-operation Agreement between the European Atomic Energy Community and the Swiss Confederation in the field of controlled thermonuclear fusion and plasma physics. (O.J. 1978 L242/1.)

78/843/Euratom:
Council Decision of October 10, 1978, amending Decision 74/642/Euratom adopting a research and training programme for the European Atomic Energy Community on plutonium recycling in light-water reactors (indirect under projects). (O.J. 1978 L291/17.)

EEC

1269. **Accession** of the Republic of Jibuti to the ACP—EEC Convention of Lomé (O.J. 1978 L147/36.)

Treaty amending certain financial provisions of the Treaties establishing the European Economic Communities and of the Treaty establishing a single Council of the European Communities.

Notice regarding the entry into force of the Treaty amending certain financial provisions of the Treaties establishing the European Communities and of the Treaty establishing a single Council and a single Commission of the European Communities, signed in Brussels on July 22, 1975.

Treaty amending certain provisions of the Protocol on the Statute of the European Investment Bank. (O.J. 1978 L91/1)

European Agreement concerning the work of crews of vehicles engaged in international road transport (AETR). (O.J. 1978 L95/1)

Opinion regarding the date of entry into force of the Act concerning the election of the representatives of the Assembly by direct universal suffrage, adopted by the Council Decision of September 20, 1976. (O.J. 1978 L173/30.)

77/770/EEC:
Council Decision of December 5, 1977, appointing a member of the Committee of Experts of the European Foundation for the Improvement of Living and Working Conditions. (O.J. 1977 L320/47.)

77/778/EEC:
Council Decision of November 21, 1977, adopting the annual report on the economic situation in the Community and laying down the economic policy guidelines for 1978. (O.J. 1977 L323/1.)

77/779/EEC:
Council Decision of December 12, 1977, amending Decision 75/458/EEC concerning a programme of pilot schemes and studies to combat poverty. (O.J. 1977 L322/28.)

77/780/EEC:
First Council Directive of December 12, 1977, on the co-ordination of the laws, regulations and administrative provisions relating to the taking up and pursuit of the business of credit institutions. (O.J. 1977 L322/30.)

77/781/EEC:
Commission Decision of November 23, 1977, relating to proceedings under Art. 85 of the EEC Treaty (IV/29.428: GEC-Weir Sodium Circulators). (O.J. 1977 L327/26.)

77/795/EEC:
Council Decision of December 12, 1977, establishing a common procedure for the exchange of information on the quality of surface fresh water in the Community. (O.J. 1977 L334/29.)

77/796/EEC:
Council Directive of December 12, 1977, aiming at the mutual recognition of diplomas, certificates and other evidence of formal qualifications for goods haulage operators and road passenger transport operators, including measures intended to encourage these operators effectively to exercise their right to freedom of establishment. (O.J. 1977 L334/37.)

77/799/EEC:
Council Directive of December 19, 1977, concerning mutual assistance by the competent authorities of the Member States in the field of direct taxation. (O.J. 1977 L336/15.)

77/800/EEC:
Council Directive of December 19, 1977, on a derogation accorded to the Kingdom of Denmark relating to the rules governing turnover tax and excise duty applicable in international travel. (O.J. L336/21.)

77/801/EEC:
Council Decision of December 20, 1977, amending Decision 71/66/EEC on the reform of the European Social Fund. (O.J. 1977 L337/8.)

77/802/EEC:
Council Decision of December 20, 1977, amending certain Decisions adopted pursuant to art. 4 of Decision 71/66/EEC on the reform of the European Social Fund. (O.J. 1977 L337/10.)

77/803/EEC:
Council Decision of December 20, 1977, on action by the European Social Fund for migrant workers. (O.J. 1977 L337/12.)

77/804/EEC:
Council Decision of December 20, 1977, on action by the European Social Fund for women. (O.J. 1977 L337/14.)

77/805/EEC:
Council Directive of December 19, 1977, amending Directive 72/464/EEC on taxes, other than turnover taxes, which affect the consumption of manufactured tobacco. (O.J. 1977 L338/22.)

77/806/EEC:
Council Decision of December 20, 1977, concerning the conclusion of the Protocol extending the arrangement regarding international trade in textiles. (O.J. 1977 L348/59.)

78/24/EEC:
Commission Decision of December 8, 1977, concerning an investigation to be made at the Vereinigung deutscher Freiformschmieden, Düsseldorf, pursuant to art. 14 (3) of Council Regulation No. 17 (Case IV AF 356.) (O.J. 1978 L10/32.)

78/25/EEC:
Council Directive of December 12, 1977, on the approximation of the laws of the Member States relating to the colouring matters which may be added to medicinal products. (O.J. 1978 L11/18.)

78/45/EEC:
Commission Decision of December 19, 1977, establishing a Scientific Committee on Cosmetology. (O.J. 1978 L13/24.)

78/49/EEC:
Council Decision of December 19, 1977, amending Decision 71/143/EEC setting up machinery for medium-term financial assistance. (O.J. 1978 L14/14.)

78/56/EEC:
Council Decision of December 19, 1977, appointing a member of the Advisory Committee on Safety, Hygiene and Health Protection at Work. (O.J. 1978 L16/30.)

78/57/EEC:
Council Decision of January 17, 1978, appointing two alternate members of the Advisory Committee on Safety, Hygiene and Health Protection at Work. (O.J. 1978 L18/6.)

78/59/EEC:
Commission Decision of December 2, 1977, relating to a proceeding under Art. 85 of the EEC Treaty (IV/147—Centraal Bureau voor de Rijwielhandel). (O.J. 1978 L20/18.)

78/68/EEC:
Commission Decision of December 8, 1977, relating to a proceeding under Art. 86 of the EEC Treaty (IV/29.132)—Hugin/Liptons). (O.J. 1978 /22/23.)

78/77/EEC:
Commission Directive of December 23, 1977, amending Directive 72/108/EEC fixing standard rates of yield for certain inward processing arrangements. (O.J. 1978 L25/52.)

78/85/EEC:
Commission Decision of December 21, 1977, authorising the United Kingdom of Great Britain and Northern Ireland to take measures in respect of national road transport involving exemptions from certain provisions of Council Regulation (EEC) No. 543/69 on the harmonisation of certain social legislation relating to road transport, as last amended by Council Regulation (EEC) No. 2827/77. (O.J. 1978 L33/8.)

78/139/EEC:
Council Decision of January 30, 1978, appointing an alternate member of the Advisory Committee on Vocational Training. (O.J. 1978 L44/12.)

78/140/EEC:
Council Decision of January 30, 1978, replacing a member of the Administrative Board of the European Foundation for the Improvement of Living and Working Conditions. (O.J. 1978 L44/13.)

78/141/EEC:
Council Decision of January 30, 1978, replacing two members and one alternate member of the Advisory Committee on Freedom of Movement for Workers. (O.J. 1978 L44/14.)

78/147/EEC:
Council Decision of January 30, 1978, authorising prolongation or tacit renewal of certain Trade Agreements concluded between the Member States and third countries. (O.J. 1978 L44/26.)

78/149/EEC:
Council Decision of February 7, 1978, appointing a member and an alternate member of the Advisory Committee on Vocational Training. (O.J. 1978 L45/23).

78/150/EEC:
Council Decision of February 7, 1978, adopting a European Economic Community concerted research project on the growth of large urban concentrations. (O.J. 1978 L45/24.)

78/154/EEC:
Commission Decision of December 22, 1977, authorising the United Kingdom to take certain protective measures under art. 108 (3) of the EEC Treaty and repealing Decision 75/487/EEC. (O.J. 1978 L45/30.)

78/155/EEC:
Commision Decision of December 23, 1977, relating to a proceeding under art. 85 of the EEC Treaty (IV/29.146—BWM Belgium NV and Belgian BMW dealers). (O.J. 1978 L46/33.)

78/156/EEC:
Commission Decision of December 20, 1977, relating to a proceeding under art. 85 of the EEC Treaty (IV/29.151—video cassette recorders). (O.J. 1978 L47/42.)

78/163/EEC:
Commission Decision of December 20, 1977, relating to proceedings under Art. 85 of the EEC Treaty (IV/28.282: The Distillers Company Limited, Conditions of Sale and Price Terms). (O.J. 1978 L50/16.)

78/165/EEC:
Council Decision of February 13, 1978, replacing an alternate member of the Committee of the European Social Fund. (O.J. 1978 L52/16.)

78/166/EEC:
Council Directive of February 13, 1978, concerning co-ordinated statistics on the business cycle in building and civil engineering. (O.J. 1978 L52/17.)

78/167/EEC:

Council Decision of February 13, 1978, adopting a concerted project of the European Economic Community in the field of registration of congenital abnormalities (medical and public health research). (O.J. 1978 L52/20.)

78/168/EEC:

Council Decision of February 13, 1978, adopting a concerted project of the European Economic Community in the field of cellular ageing and decreased functional capacity of organs (medical and public health research). (O.J. 1978 L52/24.)

78/169/EEC:

Council Decision of February 13, 1978, adopting a concerted project of the European Economic Community in the field of extracorporeal oxygenation (medical and public health research). (O.J. 1978 L52/28.)

78/170/EEC:

Council Directive of February 13, 1978, on the performance of heat generators for space heating and the production of hot water in new or existing non-industrial buildings and on the insulation of heat and domestic hot-water distribution in new non-industrial buildings. (O.J. 1978 L52/32.)

78/172/EEC:

Commission Decision of December 21, 1977, relating to a proceeding under art. 85 of the EEC Treaty (IV/29.418—spices). (O.J. 1978 L53/20.)

78/174/EEC:

Council Decision of February 20, 1978, instituting a consultation procedure and setting up a committee in the field of transport infrastructure. (O.J. 1978 L54/16.)

78/175/EEC:

Council Directive of February 20, 1978, amending the First Directive on the establishment of common rules for certain types of carriage of goods by road between Member States. (O.J. 1978 L54/18.)

78/176/EEC:

Council Directive of February 20, 1978, on waste from the titanium dioxide industry. (O.J. 1978 L54/19.)

78/177/EEC:

Council Decision of February 20, 1978, adopting a concerted action project of the European Economic Community on the effect of processing on the physical properties of foodstuffs. (O.J. 1978 L54/25.)

78/182/EEC:

Statement of revenue and expenditure of the European Centre for the Development of Vocational Training for the financial year 1978. (O.J. 1978 L55/1.)

78/183/EEC:

Statement of revenue and expenditure of the European Foundation for the Improvement of Living and Working Conditions for the financial year 1978. (O.J. 1978 L55/20.)

78/193/EEC:

Commission Decision of December 23, 1977, relating to a proceeding under art. 85 of the EEC Treaty (IV/29.246—Penneys). (O.J. 1978 L60/19.)

78/194/EEC:

Commission Decision of December 23, 1977, relating to a proceeding under art. 85 of the EEC Treaty (IV/26.437—Jaz-Peter). (O.J. 1978 L61/17.)

78/200/EEC:

Commission Decision of January 20, 1978, authorising Member States to permit temporarily the marketing of forestry reproductive material not complying with requirements of Council Directive 66/404/EEC. (O.J. 1978 L62/72.)

78/206/EEC:
Commission Directive of February 7, 1978, on the customs treatment of goods re-imported in the unaltered state under outward processing arrangements. (O.J. 1978 L62/40.)

78/227–230/EEC:
Commission Decisions of December 20, 1977, on aid from the Guidance Section on the EAGGF towards the expenditure of the Federal Republic of Germany on refunds on exports to non-member countries and intervention on the internal market in respect of the accounting periods 1967–68; 1968–69; second half-year of 1969; and 1970. (O.J. 1978 L70/3–9.)

78/231–234/EEC:
Commission Decisions of December 20, 1977, on aid from the Guidance Section of the EAGGF towards the expenditure of the Kingdom of Belgium on refunds on exports to non-member countries and intervention on the internal market in respect of the accounting periods 1967–68; 1968–69; 1969 (second half-year); and 1970. (O.J. 1978 L70/11–17.)

78/235–238/EEC:
Commission Decisions of December 20, 1977, on aid from the Guidance Section of the EAGGF towards the expenditure of the French Republic on refunds on exports to non-member countries and intervention on the internal market in respect of the accounting periods 1967–68; 1968–69; 1969 (second half-year); and 1970. (O.J. 1978 L70/19–25.)

78/239–242/EEC:
Commission Decisions of December 20, 1977, on aid from the Guidance Section of the EAGGF towards the expenditure of the Italian Republic on refunds on exports to non-member countries and intervention on the internal market in respect of the accounting periods 1967–68; 1968–69; 1969 (second half-year); and 1970. (O.J. 1978 L70/27–33.)

78/243–246/EEC:
Commission Decisions of December 20, 1977, on aid from the Guidance Section of the EAGGF towards the expenditure of the Grand Duchy of Luxembourg on refunds on exports to non-member countries and intervention on the internal market in respect of the accounting periods 1967–68; 1968–69; 1969 (second half-year); and 1970. (O.J. 1978 L70/35–39.)

78/247–250/EEC:
Commission Decisions of December 20, 1977, on aid from the Guidance Section of the EAGGF towards the expenditure of the Kingdom of the Netherlands on refunds on exports to non-member countries and intervention on the internal market in respect of the accounting periods 1967–68; 1968–69; 1969 (second half-year); and 1970. (O.J. 1978 L70/40–45.)

78/251/EEC:
Commission Decision of December 21, 1977, relating to a proceeding under art. 85 of the EEC Treaty (IV/29.236—Sopelem/Vickers). (O.J. 1978 L70/47.)

78/253/EEC:
Commission Decision of December 23, 1977, relating to proceedings under art. 85 of the EEC Treaty (IV/171, IV/856, IV/172, IV/117, IV/28.173—Campari). (O.J. 1978 L70/69.)

78/263/EEC:
Council Decision of March 6, 1978, adopting a multiannual research and development programme (1978 to 1981) for the European Economic Community in the field or primary raw materials (indirect action). (O.J. 1978 L72/9.)

78/267/EEC:
Council Decision of March 7, 1978, replacing an alternate member of the Advisory Committee on Freedom of Movement for Workers. (O.J. 1978 L72/16.)

78/268/EEC:
Council Decision of March 7, 1978, appointing a member of the Advisory Committee on Freedom of Movement for Workers. (O.J. 1978 L72/17.)

78/269/EEC:
Council Decision of March 7, 1978, replacing a member of the Administrative Board of the European Foundation for the Improvement of Living and Working Conditions. (O.J. 1978 L72/18.)

78/270/EEC:
Council Decision of March 7, 1978, replacing a member of the Advisory Committee on Freedom of Movement for Workers. (O.J. 1978 L72/19.)

78/271/EEC:
Council Decision of March 7, 1978, replacing a member of the Administrative Board of the European Foundation for the Improvement of Living and Working Conditions. (O.J. 1978 L72/20.)

78/272/EEC:
Commission Decision of February 16, 1978, replacing three members of the Waste Management Committee who have resigned. (O.J. 1978 L73/24.)

78/289/EEC:
Commission Decision of February 23, 1978, approving certain transfers of beef carried out by the Irish intervention agency between August 1 and December 31, 1977. (O.J. 1978 L74/33.)

78/294/EEC:
Commission Decision of February 28, 1978, excluding from admission free of Common Customs Tariff duties the scientific apparatus described as " Scorpio System 3000 multi-unibus disk-based multichannel analysing computer system." (O.J. 1978 L74/39.)

78/308/EEC:
Commission Decision of March 7, 1978, on the Advisory Committee on Cereals. (O.J. 1978 L76/45.)

78/315/EEC:
Council Directive of December 21, 1977, amending Directive 70/156/EEC on the approximation of the laws of the Member States relating to the type-approval of motorvehicles and their trailers. (O.J. 1978 L81/1.)

78/316/EEC:
Council Directive of December 21, 1977, on the approximation of the laws of the Member States relating to the interior fittings of motorvehicles (identification of controls, tell-tales and indicators). (O.J. 1978 L81/3.)

78/317/EEC:
Council Directive of December 21, 1977, on the approximation of the laws of the Member States relating to the defrosting and demisting systems of glazed surfaces of motorvehicles. (O.J. 1978 L81/27.)

78/318/EEC:
Council Directive of December 21, 1977, on the approximation of the laws of the Member States relating to the wiper and washer systems of motorvehicles. (O.J. 1978 L81/49.)

78/319/EEC:
Council Directive of March 20, 1978, on toxic and dangerous waste. (O.J. 1978 L84/43.)

78/328/EEC:
Commission Decision of March 16, 1978, extending Commission Decision 78/200/EEC of January 20, 1978, authorising Member States to permit temporarily the marketing of forestry reproductive material not complying with requirements of Council Directive 66/404/EEC. (O.J. 1978 L93/34.)

78/332/EEC:
Commission Decision of March 22, 1978, concerning the replacement of three members of the Advisory Committee on Customs Matters. (O.J. 1978 L93/40.)

78/336/EEC:
Council Decision of April 4, 1978, replacing a member of the Advisory Committee on Freedom of Movement for Workers. (O.J. 1978 L98/17.)

78/338/EEC:
Council Directive of April 4, 1978, on aid to shipbuilding. (O.J. 1978 L98/19.)

78/358/EEC:
Commission recommendation of March 29, 1978, to the Member States on the use of saccharin as a food ingredient and for sale as such in tablet form to the final consumer. (O.J. 1978 L193/32.)

78/365/EEC:
Commission Directive of March 31, 1978, adapting to technical progress for the second time Council Directive 71/318/EEC on the approximation of the laws of the Member States relating to gas volume meters. (O.J. 1978 L104/26.)

78/384/EEC:
Council Decision of April 17, 1978, adopting a multinational research and development programme (1978 to 1980) for the European Economic Community in the field of paper and board recycling (indirect action). (O.J. 1978 L107/12.)

78/385/EEC:
Council Decision of April 17, 1978, appointing the members and alternate members of the Committee of the European Social Fund. (O.J. 1978 L107/14.)

78/386/EEC:
First Commission Directive of April 18, 1978, amending the Annexes to Directive 66/401/EEC on the marketing of fodder plant seed. (O.J. 1978 L113/1.)

78/387/EEC:
First Commission Directive of April 18, 1978, amending the Annexes to Directive 66/402/EEC on the marketing of cereal seed. (O.J. 1978 L113/13.)

78/388/EEC:
First Commission Directive of April 18, 1978, amending the Annexes to Directive 69/208/EEC on the marketing of seed of oil and fibre plants. (O.J. 1978 L113/20.)

78/411/EEC:
Commission Decision of April 13, 1978, on the refusal to accept the scientific character of an apparatus described as "Tektronix logic analyzer, type 7 D01." (O.J. 1978 L120/35.)

78/415/EEC:
Commission Decision of April 14, 1978, authorising the Member States to restrict the marketing of forest reproductive material produced in Austria. (O.J. 1978 L120/39.)

78/420/EEC:
Council Directive of May 2, 1978, amending Second Directive 75/319/EEC on the approximation of provisions laid down by law, regulation or administrative action relating to proprietary medicinal products. (O.J. 1978 L123/26.)

78/453/EEC:
Council Directive of May 22, 1978, on the harmonisation of provisions laid down by law, regulation or administrative action concerning deferred payment of import duties or export duties. (O.J. 1978 L146/19.)

78/454/EEC:
Council Decision of May 22, 1978, appointing an alternate member of the Advisory Committee on Medical Training. (O.J. 1978 L146/22.)

78/464/EEC:
Council Decision of May 30, 1978, adjusting the amounts made available to the European Development Fund (1975) for the ACP States and for the overseas countries and territories and the French overseas departments. O.J. 1978 L147/37.)

78/465/EEC:
Council Decision of May 30, 1978, adjusting Decision 76/568/EEC on the association of the overseas countries and territories with the European Economic Community. (O.J. 1978 L147/39.)

78/473/EEC:
Council Directive of May 30, 1978, on the co-ordination of laws, regulations and administrative provisions relating to Community co-insurance. (O.J. 1978 L151/25.)

78/474/EEC:
Council Decision of May 30, 1978, replacing a member of the Advisory Committee on Freedom of Movement for Workers. (O.J. 1978 L152/15.)

78/475/EEC:
Council Decision of May 30, 1978, appointing an alternate member of the Advisory Committee on Social Security for Migrant Workers. (O.J. 1978 L152/16.)

78/476/EEC:
Council Decision of May 30, 1978, on the equivalence of checks on practices for the maintenance of varieties carried out in third countries. (O.J. 1978 L152/17.)

78/479/EEC:
Commission Decision of May 11, 1978, laying down the detailed rules for the financial compensation necessary under Article 131 of the Act of Accession. (O.J. 1978 L152/21.)

78/507/EEC:
Commission Directive of May 19, 1978, adapting to technical progress Council Directive 76/114/EEC on the approximation of the laws of the Member States relating to statutory plates and inscriptions for motor vehicles and their trailers, and their location and method of attachment. (O.J. 1978 L155/31.)

78/516/EEC:
Commission Decision of May 26, 1978, relating to a proceeding under art. 85 of the EEC Treaty (IV/29.559—RAI/UNITEL). (O.J. 1978 L157/39.)

78/518/EEC:
Council Decision of June 12, 1978, appointing a member of the Advisory Committee on Medical Training. (O.J. 1978 L159/36.)

78/528/EEC:
Council Decision of June 6, 1978, accepting on behalf of the Community three Annexes to the International Convention on the simplification and harmonisation of customs procedures. (O.J. 1978 L160/13.)

78/529/EEC:
Financial Regulation of June 6, 1978, concerning the Guarantee Section of the European Agricultural Guidance and Guarantee Fund for the 1967/68 to 1970 accounting periods. (O.J. 1978 L160/25.)

78/546/EEC:
Council Directive of June 12, 1978, on statistical returns in respect of carriage of goods as part of regional statistics. (O.J. 1978 L168/29.)

78/547/EEC:
Council Directive of June 12, 1978, amending Directive 70/156/EEC on the approximation of the laws of the Member States relating to the type-approval of motorvehicles and their trailers. (O.J. 1978 L168/39.)

78/548/EEC:
Council Directive of June 12, 1978, on the approximation of the laws of the Member States relating to heating systems for the passenger compartment of motorvehicles. (O.J. 1978 L168/40.)

78/549/EEC:
Council Directive of June 12, 1978, on the approximation of the laws of the Member States relating to the wheel guards of motorvehicles. (O.J. 1978 L168/45.)

78/557/EEC:
Council Decision of June 19, 1978, amending Annex II concerning the definition of the concept of " originating products " and methods of administrative co-operation, to Decision 76/568/EEC on the association of the overseas countries and territories with the European Economic Community. (O.J. 1978 L177/51.)

78/571/EEC:
Commission Decision of June 12, 1978, relating to a proceeding under art. 85 of the EEC Treaty (IV/29.453—SNPE-LEL). (O.J. 1978 L191/41.)

78/583/EEC:
Ninth Council Directive of June 26, 1978, on the harmonisation of the laws of the Member States relating to turnover taxes. (O.J. 1978 L194/16.)

78/584/EEC:
Council recommendation of June 26, 1978, on the ratification of Conventions on safety in shipping. (O.J. 1978 L194/17.)

78/609/EEC:
Council Directive of June 29, 1978, amending for the fifth time Directive 73/241/EEC on the approximation of the laws of the Member States relating to cocoa and chocolate products intended for human consumption. (O.J. 1978 L197/10.)

78/610/EEC:
Council Directive of June 29, 1978, on the approximation of the laws, regulations and administrative provisions of the Member States on the protection of the health of workers exposed to vinyl chloride monomer. (O.J. 1978 L197/12.)

78/611/EEC:
Council Directive of June 29, 1978, on the approximation of the laws of the Member States concerning the lead content of petrol. (O.J. 1978 L197/19.)

78/612/EEC:
Council Directive of June 29, 1978, amending for the first time Directive 74/329/EEC on the approximation of the laws of the Member States relating to emulsifiers, stabilisers, thickeners and gelling agents for use in foodstuffs. (O.J. 1978 L197/22.)

78//614/EEC:
Commission opinion of June 23, 1978, addressed to the Government of the United Kingdom concerning the provisions relating to certain measures in the field of working conditions in road transport. (O.J. 1978 L198/11.)

78/618//EEC:
Commission Decision of June 28, 1978, setting up a Scientific Advisory Committee to examine the toxicity and ecotoxicity of chemical compounds. (O.J. 1978 L198/17.)

78/619/EEC:
Commission opinion of June 28, 1978, pursuant to Art. 3 (2) of Council Regulation (EEC) No. 1463/70 of July 20, 1970, on the introduction of recording equipment in road transport (tachograph) on the exemption by Member States from this Regulation of vehicles constructed and equipped to carry not more than 15 persons including the driver. (O.J. 1978 L198/19.)

78/620/EEC:
Commission opinion of June 28, 1978, pursuant to Art. 14a (2) (a) of Council Regulation (EEC) No. 543/69 of March 25, 1969, on the harmonisation of opening tariff preferences for products covered by that Community and originating in Algeria. (O.J. 1978 L175/24.)

78/624/EEC:
Commission recommendation of June 29, 1978, concerning the general conditions for the application of the reference tariffs provided for in Art. 4 (3) of Council Regulation (EEC) No. 2831/77 on the fixing of rates for the carriage of goods by road between Member States. (O.J. 1978 L202/14)

78/628/EEC:
Council Directive of June 19, 1978, on a programme to accelerate drainage operations in the less-favoured areas of the west of Ireland. (O.J. 1978 L206/5)

78/629/EEC:
Council Directive of June 19, 1978, adapting to technical progress Directive 73/362/EEC on the approximation of the laws of the Member States relating to material measures of length. (O.J. 1978 L206/8)

78/632/EEC:
Commission Directive of May 19, 1978, adapting to technical progress Council Directive 74/60/EEC on the approximation of the laws of the Member States relating to the interior fittings of motor vehicles (interior parts of the passenger compartment other than the interior rear-view mirrors, layout of controls, the roof or opening roof, the backrest and rear part of the seats). (O.J. 1978 L206/26.)

78/634/EEC:
Council Decision of July 18, 1978, replacing a deputy member of the Administrative Islands, after becoming independent, of the arrangements provided for in Decision 76/568/EEC on the association of the overseas countries and territories with the European Economic Community. (O.J. 1978 L203/33.)

78/635/EEC:
Council Decision of July 18, 1978, replacing a deputy member of the Administrative Board of the European Foundation for the Improvement of Living and Working Conditions. (O.J. 1978 L203/35.)

78/636/EEC:
Commission Decision of June 29, 1978, establishing an Advisory Committee on Industrial Research and Development. (O.J. 1978 L203/36.)

78/637/EEC:
Commission opinion of June 30, 1978, concerning the exemptions from the Community Regulations on social matters relating to road transport proposed by the United Kingdom of Great Britain and Northern Ireland. (O.J. 1978 L203/38.)

78/638/EEC:
Commission Decision of June 30, 1978, authorising the United Kingdom of Great Britain and Northern Ireland to grant exemptions for national road transport operations from the Community Regulations on social matters relating to road transport. (O.J. 1978 L203/39.)

78/658/EEC:
Council Decision of July 24, 1978, on the adaptation of public budgets for 1978 and the preparation of public budgets for 1979 in the framework of the Community's concerted action. (O.J. 1978 L220/27.)

78/660/EEC:
Fourth Council Directive of July 25, 1978, based on Art. 54 (3) (*g*) of the Treaty on the annual accounts of certain types of companies. (O.J. 1978 L222/11.)

78/663/EEC:
Council Decision of July 25, 1978, laying down specific criteria of purity for emulsifiers, stabilisers, thickeners and gelling agents for use in foodstuffs. (O.J. 1978 L223/7.)

78/664/EEC:
Council Directive of July 25, 1978, laying down specific criteria of purity for anti-oxidants which may be used in foodstuffs intended for human consumption. (O.J. 1978 L223/30.)

78/665/EEC:
Commission Directive of July 14, 1978, adapting to technical progress Directive 70/220/EEC on the approximation of the laws of the Member States relating to measures to be taken against pollution of the air by gases from positive ignition engines installed in motor vehicles. (O.J. 1978 L223/48.)

78/666/EEC:
Council Decision of July 25, 1978, concerning the conclusion of the Financial Protocol between the European Economic Community and Greece. (O.J. 1978 L225/25.)

78/667/EEC:
Council Decision of July 25, 1978, authorising prolongation or tacit renewal of certain Trade Agreements concluded between the Member States and third countries. (O.J. 1978 L225/33.)

78/668/EEC:
Council Decision of July 25, 1978, on a research programme of the European Economic Community on forecasting and assessment in the field of science and technology (1978 to 1982). (O.J. 1978 L225/38.)

78/669/EEC:
Council Directive of August 2, 1978, amending Directive 71/305/EEC concerning the co-ordination of procedures for the award of public works contracts. (O.J. 1978 L225/41.)

78/670/EEC:
Commission Decision of July 20, 1978, relating to a proceeding under Art. 85 of the EEC Treaty (IV/28.852—GB-Inno-BM/Fedetab; IV/29.127—Mestdagh-Huyghebaert/Fedetab; IV/29.149—Fedetab recommendation). (O.J. 1978 L224/29.)

78/686/EEC:
Council Directive of July 25, 1978, concerning the mutual recognition of diplomas, certificates and other evidence of the formal qualifications of practitioners of dentistry, including measures to facilitate the effective exercise of the right of establishment and freedom to provide services. (O.J. 1978 L233/1.)

78/687/EEC:
Council Directive of July 25, 1978, concerning the co-ordination of provisions laid down by law, regulation or administrative action in respect of the activities of dental practitioners. (O.J. 1978 L233/10.)

78/688/EEC:
Council Decision of July 25, 1978, setting up an Advisory Committee on the Training of Dental Practitioners. (O.J. 1978 L233/15.)

78/689/EEC:
Council Decision of July 25, 1978, amending Decision 75/365/EEC setting up a Committee of Senior Officials on Public Health. (O.J. 1978 L233/17.)

78/696/EEC:
Commission Decision of July 28, 1978, relating to proceedings under Article 85 of the EEC Treaty (IV/29.440: Arthur Bell and Sons Ltd.—conditions of sale). (O.J. 1978 L235/15.)

78/697/EEC:
Commission Decision of July 28, 1978, relating to proceedings under Article 85 of the EEC Treaty (IV/28.859: Wm. Teacher and Sons Ltd.—conditions of sale). (O.J. 1978 L235/20.)

78/706/EEC:
Commission Decision of July 27, 1978, on certain administrative procedures for the operation of the European Social Fund. (O.J. 1978 L238/20.)

78/732/EEC:
Commission Decision of July 20, 1978, relating to a proceeding under Article 85 of the EEC Treaty (IV/26.186—Centraal Stikstof Verkoopkantoor). (O.J. 1978 L242/15.)

78/742/EEC:
Commission Decision of June 27, 1978, on the submission to the Commission of applications for assistance and claims for payment from the European Social Fund. (O.J. 1978 L248/1.)

78/765/EEC:
Commission Directive of September 7, 1978, amending Directive 76/447/EEC relating to the triangular system of the outward processing procedure. (O.J. 1978 L257/7.)

78/774/EEC:
Council Decision of September 19, 1978, concerning the activities of certain third countries in the field of cargo shipping. (O.J. 1978 L258/35.)

78/786/EEC:
Council Decision of September 19, 1978, replacing an alternate member of the Advisory Committee on Freedom of Movement for Workers. (O.J. 1978 L260/14.)

78/787/EEC:
Council Decision of September 19, 1978, replacing two alternates of the Administrative Board of the European Foundation for the Improvement of Living and Working Conditions. (O.J. 1978 L260/15.)

78/788/EEC:
Council Decision of September 19, 1978, replacing a member of the Committee of the European Social Fund. (O.J. 1978 L260/16.)

78/789/EEC:
Council Decision of September 19, 1978, appointing an alternate member of the Advisory Committee on Social Security for Migrant Workers. (O.J. 1978 L260/17.)

78/813/EEC:
Council Decision of September 25, 1978, appointing a member and an alternate member of the Advisory Committee on Medical Training. (O.J. 1978 L281/15.)

78/814/EEC:
Council Decision of September 25, 1978, replacing an alternate member of the Committee of the European Social Fund. (O.J. 1978 L281/16.)

78/815/EEC:
Council Decision of September 25, 1978, replacing an alternate member of the Committee of the European Social Fund. (O.J. 1978 L281/17.)

78/824/EEC:
Agreement amending the Internal Agreement on the financing and administration of Community aid signed on July 11, 1975. (O.J. 1978 L287/22.)

78/827/EEC:
Council Decision of October 10, 1978, on the provisional application to Tuvalu after its independence of the arrangements provided for in Decision 76/568/EEC. (O.J. 1978 L/287/32.)

78/842/EEC:
Council Directive of October 10, 1978, amending for the sixth time Directive 73/241/EEC on the approximation of the laws of the Member States relating to cocoa and chocolate products intended for human consumption (O.J. 1978 L291/15.)

78/855/EEC:
Third Council Directive of October 9, 1978, based on art. 54 (3) (g) of the Treaty concerning mergers of public limited liability companies. (O.J. 1978 L295/36.)

78/870/EEC:
Council Decision of October 16, 1978, empowering the Commission to contract loans for the purpose of promoting investment within the Community. (O.J. 1978 L298/9)

78/883/EEC:
Commission Decision of October 20, 1978, amending Decision 73/351/EEC setting up an Advisory Committee on Customs Matters. (O.J. 1978 L299/39.)

78/884/EEC:
Convention of Accession of October 9, 1978, of the Kingdom of Denmark, of Ireland and of the United Kingdom of Great Britain and Northern Ireland to the Convention on jurisdiction and enforcement of judgments in civil and commercial matters and to the Protocol on its interpretation by the Court of Justice. (O.J. 1978 L304/1.)

78/885/EEC:
Council Decision of October 16, 1978, appointing members and alternate members of the Advisory Committee on Vocational Training as laid down by the fourth principle of the Council Decision of April 2, 1963.

78/886/EEC:
Council Decision of October 16, 1978, on the signature of the Protocol of April 7, 1978, further extending the International Olive Oil Agreement 1963, and on the signature and deposit of the declaration of provisional application of that Protocol. (O.J. 1978 L306/29.)

78/887/EEC:
Council Decision of October 9, 1978, adopting a second three-year plan of action in the field of scientific and technical information and documentation. (O.J. 1978 L311/1.)

78/888/EEC:
Council Decision of October 9, 1978, adopting a European Economic Community concerted project in the field of analysis of organic micropollutants in water. (O.J. 1978 L311/6.)

78/889/EEC:
Council Decision of October 9, 1978, adopting a European Economic Community joint project in the field of physico-chemical behaviour of atmospheric pollutants. (O.J. 1978 L311/10.)

78/890/EEC:
Commission Decision of September 28, 1978, applying Council Decision 77/186/EEC on the exporting of crude oil and petroleum products from one Member State to another in the event of supply difficulties. (O.J. 1978 L311/13.)

78/891/EEC:
Commission Directive of September 28, 1978, adapting to technical progress the Annexes to Council Directives 75/106/EEC and 76/211/EEC on prepackaging. (O.J. 1978 L311/21.)

78/897/EEC:
Council Decision of October 30, 1978, concerning the conclusion of the Agreement in the form of an exchange of letters between the European Economic Community and the Bank for International Settlements concerning the mobilization of claims held by Member States under the medium-term financial assistance arrangements. (O.J. 1978 L316/21.)

78/898/EEC:
Council Decision of October 30, 1978, concerning the conclusion of the Agreement between the European Economic Community and Finland negotiated under Article XXVIII of GATT in respect of the bound products in Chapters 1 to 22 of the Finnish Customs Tariff. (O.J. 1978 L316/24.)

78/899/EEC:
Council Decision of October 30, 1978, giving a discharge to the Commission in respect of the implementation of the operations of the Development Fund for the overseas countries and territories (First Fund) for the financial year 1976. (O.J. 1978 L316/33.)

78/900/EEC:
Council Decision of October 30, 1978, giving a discharge to the Commission in respect of the implementation of the operations of the European Development Fund (1963) (Second EDF) for the financial year 1976. (O.J. 1978 L316/34.)

78/901/EEC:
Council Decision of October 30, 1978, giving a discharge to the Commission in respect of the implementation of the operations of the European Development Fund (1969) (Third EDF) for the financial year 1976. (O.J. 1978 L316/35.)

78/903/EEC:
Council Decision of October 30, 1978, replacing a member of the Advisory Committee on Freedom of Movement for Workers. (O.J. 1978 L318/66.)

78/904/EEC:
Council Decision of October 30, 1978, appointing an alternate member of the Advisory Committee on Medical Training. (O.J. 1978 L318/67.)

78/905/EEC:
Council Decision of October 30, 1978, appointing a member and an alternate member of the Advisory Committee on Vocational Training (O.J. 1978 L318/68.)

78/921/EEC:
Commission Decision of October 20, 1978, relating to a proceeding under Article 85 of the EEC Treaty (IV/29.133—WANO Schwarzpulver). (O.J. 1978 L/322/26.)

78/922/EEC:
Commission Decision of October 23, 1978, relating to a proceeding under Article 85 of the EEC Treaty (IV/1.576—Zanussi). (O.J. 1978 L322/36.)

78/932/EEC:
Council Directive of October 16, 1978, on the approximation of the laws of the Member States relating to head restraints of seats of motor vehicles. (O.J. 1978 L325/1.)

78/934/EEC:
Commission Decision of October 25, 1978, setting a time limit for the conclusion of the negotiations between professional organisations for the establishment of reference tariffs for the carriage of goods by road between Member States. (O.J. 1978 L326/8.)

78/956/EEC:
Commission Decision of November 6, 1978, nominating members of the Advisory Committee on Customs Matters. (O.J. 1978 L328/29.)

78/976/EEC:
Council Decision of November 20, 1978, on the provisional application to Dominica after its independence of the arrangements provided for in Decision 76/568/EEC:
Council Decision on the association of the overseas countries and territories with the European Economic Community. (O.J. 1978 L331/25.)

78/977/EEC:
Council Decision of November 20, 1978, replacing an alternate member of the Committee for the European Social Fund. (O.J. 1978 L331/27.)

78/978/EEC:
Council Decision of November 20, 1978, replacing an alternate member of the Advisory Committee on Social Security for migrant workers. (O.J. 1978 L331/28.)

78/979/EEC:
Council Decision of November 20, 1978, replacing an alternate member of the Advisory Committee on Vocational Training. (O.J. 1978 L331/29.)

78/1012/EEC:
Council Decision of November 23, 1978, replacing an alternate member of the Advisory Committee on Freedom of Movement for Workers. (O.J. 1978 L349/17.)

78/1013/EEC:
Council Decision of November 23, 1978, replacing an alternate member of the Advisory Committee on Social Security for Migrant Workers. (O.J. 1978 L349/18.)

78/1014/EEC:
Council Decision of November 23, 1978, appointing the members and alternate members of the Advisory Committee on Safety, Hygiene and Health Protection at Work. (O.J. 1978 L349/19.)

78/1015/EEC:
Council Directive of November 23, 1978, on the approximation of the laws of the Member States on the permissible sound level and exhaust system of motorcycles. (O.J. 1978 L349/21.)

78/1016/EEC:
Council Directive of November 23, 1978, amending Directive 76/135/EEC on reciprocal recognition of navigability licences for inland waterway vessels. (O.J. 1978 L349/31.)

78/1018/EEC:
Council Directive of November 27, 1978, on the harmonization of provisions laid down by law, regulation or administrative action in respect of standard exchange of goods exported for repair. (O.J. 1978 L349/33.)

78/1020/EEC:
Council Directive of December 5, 1978, amending Directives 66/401/EEC, 66/402/EEC and 69/208/EEC on the marketing of fodder plant seed, cereal seed of oil and fibre plants. (O.J. 1978 L350/27.)

78/1021/EEC:
Council Decision of December 5, 1978, appointing a member of the Advisory Committee on Medical Training. (O.J. 1978 L350/28.)

78/1022/EEC:
Council Decision of December 5, 1978, appointing an alternate member of the Advisory Committee on Medical Training. (O.J. 1978 L350/29.)

78/1023/EEC:
Council Decision of December 5, 1978, appointing an alternate member of the Advisory Committee on Medical Training. (O.J. 1978 L350/30.)

78/1024/EEC:
Council Decision of December 5, 1978, appointing a member of the Advisory Committee on Vocational Training. (O.J. 1978 L350/31.)

Commission Regulation (EEC) No. 2714/77 of December 7, 1977, amending the nomenclature of goods for the external trade statistics of the Community and statistics of trade between Member States (NIMEXE). (O.J. 1977 L325/1.)

Commission Regulation (EEC) No. 2826/77 of December 5, 1977, introducing a Community transit declaration form for use in an automatic or electronic data-processing system. (O.J. 1977 L333/1.)

Council Regulation (EEC) No. 2827/77 of December 12, 1977, amending Regulation (EEC) No. 543/69 on the harmonization of certain social legislation relating to road transport. (O.J. 1977 L334/1.)

Council Regulation (EEC) No. 2828/77 of December 12, 1977, amending Regulation (EEC) No. 1463/70 on the introduction of recording equipment in road transport. (O.J. 1977 L334/5.)

Council Regulation (EEC) No. 2829/77 of December 12, 1977, on the bringing into force of the European Agreement concerning the work of crews of vehicles engaged in international road transport (AETR). (O.J. 1977 L334/11.)

Council Regulation (EEC) No. 2830/77 of December 12, 1977, on the measures necessary to achieve comparability between the accounting systems and annual accounts of railway undertakings. (O.J. 1977 L334/13.)

Council Regulation (EEC) No. 2831/77 of December 12, 1977, on the fixing of rates for the carriage of goods by road between Member States. (O.J. 1977 L334/22.)

Council Regulation (EEC) No. 2840/77 of December 19, 1977, amending Regulation (EEC) No. 878/77 as regards the exchange rate for the French franc to be applied in agriculture. (O.J. 1977 L328/1.)

Council Regulation (EEC) No. 2844/77 of December 19, 1977, on the conclusion of the Agreement extending the Interim Agreement between the European Economic Community and the Portuguese Republic. (O.J. 1977 L329/1.)

Council Regulation (EEC) No. 2845/77 of December 19, 1977, amending Regulation (EEC) No. 1736/75 on the external trade statistics of the Community and statistics of trade between Member States. (O.J. 1977 L/329/3.)

Commission Regulation (EEC) No. 2854/77 of December 20, 1977, on the country nomenclature for the external trade statistics of the Community and statistics of trade between Member States. (O.J. 1977 L329/24.)

Commission Regulation (EEC) No. 2855/77 of December 21, 1977, amending Regulation No. 91/66/EEC as regards the number of returning holdings per division for the ' 1978 ' and subsequent accounting years. (O.J. 1977 L329/31.)

Council Regulation (EEC) No. 2893/77 of December 20, 1977, amending Regulation (EEC) No. 2396/71 implementing the Council Decision of February 1, 1971, on the reform of the European Social Fund. (O.J. 1977 L337/1.)

Council Regulation (EEC) No. 2894/77 of December 20, 1977, amending Regulation (EEC) No. 858/72 on certain administrative and financial procedures for the operation of the European Social Fund. (O.J. 1977 L337/5.)

Council Regulation (EEC) No. 2895/77 of December 20, 1977, concerning operations qualifying for a higher rate of intervention by the European Social Fund. (O.J. 1977 L337/7.)

Commission Regulation (EEC) No. 2903/77 of December 23, 1977, extending the period of validity of and amending Regulation (EEC) No. 2779/72 on the application of art. 85 (3) of the Treaty to categories of specialized agreements. (O.J. 1977 L338/14.)

Council Regulation (EEC) No. 2907/77 of December 20, 1977, on the conclusion of the Additional Protocol to the Agreement establishing an association between the European Economic Community and the Republic of Cyprus. (O.J. 1977 L339/1.)

Council Regulation (EEC) No. 2908/77 of December 19, 1977, on the conclusion of the Agreement in the form of an exchange of letters between the European Economic Community and the State of Israel concerning the import into the Community of preserved fruit salads originating in Israel. (O.J. 1977 L340/1.)

Council Regulation (EEC) No. 2909/77 of December 19, 1977, on the conclusion of the Agreement in the form of an exchange of letters between the European Economic Community and the People's Democratic Republic of Algeria concerning the import into the Community of preserved fruit salads originating in Algeria. (O.J. 1977 L340/4.)

Council Regulation (EEC) No. 2910/77 of December 19, 1977, on the conclusion of the Agreement in the form of an exchange of letters between the European Economic Community and the Kingdom of Morocco concerning the import into the Community of preserved fruit salads originating in Morocco. (O.J. 1977 L340/7.)

Council Regulation (EEC) No. 2911/77 of December 19, 1977, on the conclusion of the Agreement in the form of an exchange of letters between the European Economic Community and the Republic of Tunisia concerning the import into the Community of preserved fruit salads originating in Tunisia. (O.J. 1977 L340/10.)

Council Regulation (EEC) No. 2912/77 of December 19, 1977, on the conclusion of the Agreement in the form of an exchange of letters between the European Economic Community and the People's Democratic Republic of Algeria on the importation into the Community of tomato concentrates originating in Algeria. (O.J. 1977 L340/13.)

Council Regulation (EEC) No. 2913/77 of December 19, 1977, on the conclusion of the Agreement in the form of an exchange of letters between the European Economic Community and the Portuguese Republic regarding prepared or preserved tomatoes falling within subheading 20.02 C of the Common Customs Tariff. (O.J. 1977 L340/16.)

Council Regulation (EEC) No. 2914/77 of December 20, 1977, extending certain provisions of Regulation (EEC) No. 1641/77 as regards the arrangements applicable to trade with the Republic of Cyprus beyond the expiry of the first stage of the Association Agreement. (O.J. 1977 L340/19.)

Council Regulation (EEC) No. 2929/77 of December 19, 1977, implementing Decisions No. 2/77 and No. 3/77 of the Joint Committee set up under the Agreement between the European Economic Community and the Republic of Austria on the application of the rules on Community transit. (O.J. 1977 L341/1.)

Council Regulation (EEC No. 2930/77 of December 20, 1977, on the application of Decision No. 1/77 on the EEC-Austria Joint Committee supplementing and amending Protocol 3 concerning the definition of the concept of " originating products " and methods of administrative co-operation and replacing certain Decisions of the said Joint Committee. (O.J. 1977 L341/86.)

Council Regulation (EEC) No. 2931/77 of December 20, 1977, on the application of Decision No. 2/77 of the EEC-Austria Joint Committee derogating from the provisions of List A annexed to Protocol 3 concerning the definition of the concept of " originating products " and methods of administrative co-operation. (O.J. 1977 L341/86.)

Council Regulation (EEC) No. 2932/77 of December 19, 1977, implementing Decisions No. 2/77 and No. 3/77 of the Joint Committee set up under the Agreement between the European Economic Community and the Swiss Confederation on the application of the rules on Community transit. (O.J. 1977 L/342/1.)

Council Regulation (EEC) No. 2933/77 of December 20, 1977, on the application of Decision No. 1/77 of the EEC-Switzerland Joint Committee supplementing and amending Protocol 3 concerning the definition of the concept of " originating products " and methods of administrative co-operation and replacing certain Decisions of the said Joint Committee. (O.J. 1977 L342/27.)

Council Regulation (EEC) No. 2934/77 of December 20, 1977, on the application of Decision No. 2/77 of the EEC-Switzerland Joint Committee derogating from the provisions of List A annexed to Protocol 3 concerning the definition of the concept of " originating products " and methods of administrative co-operation. (O.J. 1977 L342/86.)

Council Regulation (EEC) No. 2935/77 of December 20, 1977, on the application of Decision No. 1/77 of the EEC–Finland Joint Committee supplementing and amending Protocol 3 concerning the definition of the concept of " originating products " and methods of administrative co-operation and replacing certain Decisions of the said Joint Committee. (O.J. 1977 L343/1.)

Council Regulation (EEC) No. 2936/77 of December 20, 1977, on the application of Decision No. 2/77 of the EEC–Finland Joint Committee derogating from the provisions of List A annexed to Protocol 3 concerning the definition of the concept of " originating products " and methods of administrative co-operation. (O.J. 1977 L343/60.)

Council Regulation (EEC) No. 2937/77 of December 20, 1977 on the application of Decision No. 1/77 of the EEC–Norway Joint Committee supplementing and amending Protocol 3 concerning the definition of the concept of " originating products " and methods of administrative co-operation and replacing certain Decisions of the said Joint Committee. (O.J. 1977 L344/1.)

Council Regulation (EEC) No. 2938/77 of December 20, 1977, on the application of Decision No. 2/77 of the EEC–Norway Joint Committee derogating from the provisions of List A annexed to Protocol 3 concerning the definition of the concept of " originating products " and methods of administrative co-operation. (O.J. 1977 L344/60.)

Council Regulation (EEC) No. 2941/77 of December 20, 1977, on the application of Decision No. 1/77 of the EEC-Iceland Joint Committee supplementing and amending Protocol 3 concerning the definition of the concept of "originating products" and methods of administrative co-operation and replacing certain Decisions of the said Joint Committee. (O.J. 1977 L346/1.)

Council Regulation (EEC) No. 2942/77 of December 20, 1977, on the application of Decision No. 2/77 of the EEC-Iceland Joint Committee derogating from the provisions of List A annexed to Protocol 3 concerning the definition of the concept of "originating products" and methods of administrative co-operation. (O.J. 1977 L346/60.)

Council Regulation (EEC) No. 2943/77 of December 20, 1977, on the application of Decision No. 1/77 of the EEC-Portugal Joint Committee supplementing and amending Protocol 3 concerning the definition of the concept of "originating products" and methods of administrative co-operation and replacing certain Decisions of the said Joint Committee. (O.J. 1977 L347/1.)

Council Regulation (EEC) No. 2944/77 of December 20, 1977, on the application of Decision No. 2/77 of the EEC-Portugal Joint Committee derogating from the provisions of List A annexed to Protocol 3 concerning the definition of the concept of "originating products" and methods of administrative co-operation. (O.J. 1977 L347/60.)

Commission Regulation (EEC) No. 2945/77 of December 22, 1977, amending Regulation (EEC) No. 938/77 fixing the monetary compensatory amounts, in view of the removal of "accession" compensatory amounts and of the amendments to the Tariff nomenclature from January 1, 1978. (O.J. 1977 L349/1.)

Council Regulation (EEC) No. 2946/77 of December 19, 1977, on the conclusion of the Agreement extending the Interim Agreement between the European Economic Community and the People's Democratic Republic of Algeria. (O.J. 1977 L348/1.)

Council Regulation (EEC) No. 2947/77 of December 19, 1977, on the conclusion of the Agreement extending the Interim Agreement between the European Economic Community and the Kingdom of Morocco. (O.J. 1977 L348/4.)

Council Regulation (EEC) No. 2948/77 of December 19, 1977, on the conclusion of the Agreement extending the Interim Agreement between the European Economic Community and the Republic of Tunisia. (O.J. 1977 L348/7.)

Council Regulation (EEC) No. 3014/77 of December 21, 1977, on the application of Decision No. 11/77 of the ACP-EEC Council of Ministers derogating from the concept of "originating products" to take account of the special situation of Mauritius with regard to certain products of the textile industry. (O.J. 1977 L355/34.)

Council Regulation (EEC) No. 3015/77 of December 21, 1977, on the application of Decision No. 12/77 of the ACP-EEC Council of Ministers derogating from the concept of "originating products" to take account of the special situation of Mauritius with regard to its production of canned tuna. (O.J. 1977 L355/36.)

Council Regulation (EEC) No. 3022/77 of December 20, 1977, amending Regulation (EEC) No. 517/72 on the introduction of common rules for regular and special regular services by coach and bus between Member States. (O.J. 1977 358/1.)

Council Regulation (EEC) No. 3024/77 of December 21, 1977, amending Regulation (EEC) No. 3164/76 on the Community quota for the carriage of goods by road between Member States. (O.J. 1977 L358/4.)

Commission Regulation (EEC) No. 3025/77 of December 23, 1977, applying Regulation (EEC) No. 1056/72 on notifying the Commission of investment projects of interest to the Community in the petroleum, natural gas and electricity sectors. (O.J. 1977 L358/12.)

Council Regulation (EEC) No. 3026/77 of November 28, 1977, on the conclusion of the Supplementary Protocol to the Association Agreement between the European Economic Community and Turkey consequent on the accession of new Member States to the Community. (O.J. 1977 L361/1.)

Council Regulation (EEC) No. 105/78 of January 17, 1978, on the conclusion of the Agreement between the European Economic Community and the Republic of India on trade in coir products. (O.J. 1978 L17/1.)

Council Regulation (EEC) No. 106/78 of January 17, 1978, concluding the Agreement between the European Economic Community and the Republic of India on trade and commercial co-operation in jute products. (O.J. 1978 L17/5.)

Commission Regulation (EEC) No. 243/78 of February 1, 1978, providing for the advance fixing of monetary compensatory amounts. (O.J. 1978 L37/5.)

Council Regulation (EEC) No. 494/78 of March 6, 1978, relating to the organisation of a survey of labour costs in industry, wholesale and retail distribution, banking and insurance. (O.J. 1978 L68/1.)

Council Regulation (EEC) No. 495/78 of March 6, 1978, relating to the organisation of a survey of earnings in industry, wholesale and retail distribution, banking and insurance. (O.J. 1978 L68/3.)

Commission Regulation (EEC) No. 525/78 of March 13, 1978, amending and consolidating the Annex to Regulation (EEC) No. 1687/76 laying down common detailed rules for verifying the use and/or destination of products from intervention. (O.J. 1978 L73/8.)

Council Regulation (EEC) No. 595/78 of March 20, 1978, extending Regulation (EEC) No. 744/77 on the advance implementation of certain provisions of the ACP-EEC Convention of Lomé relating to trade in respect of certain States that have signed Accession Agreements to that Convention. (O.J. 1978 L82/12.)

Commission Regulation (EEC) No. 607/78 of March 29, 1978, amending Regulation (EEC) No. 2826/77 introducing a Community transit declaration form for use in an automatic or electronic data-processing system. (O.J. 1978 L83/17.)

Commission Regulation (EEC) No. 609/78 of March 29, 1978, amending various common agricultural policy Regulations following the consolidation of provisions on the Community transit procedure. (O.J. 1978 L83/19.)

Commission Regulation (EEC) No. 651/78 of March 31, 1978, on the obligatory alterations to be made to monetary compensatory amounts fixed in advance. (O.J. 1978 L86/41.)

Commission Regulation (EEC) No. 724/78 of April 10, 1978, amending Regulation (EEC) No. 679/77 and fixing the coefficients for the 1978 financial year. (O.J. 1978 L98/9.)

Council Regulation (EEC) No. 850/78 of April 24, 1978, concerning the conclusion of the Agreement in the form of an exchange of letters amending Annex A to Protocol 1 to the Agreement between the European Economic Community and the Swiss Confederation. (O.J. 1978 L116/1.)

Council Regulation (EEC) No. 946/78 of May 2, 1978, concerning the conclusion of the Trade Agreement between the European Economic Community and the People's Republic of China. (O.J. 1978 L123/1.)

Council Regulation (EEC) No. 1245/78 of May 22, 1978, on the conclusion of the Additional Protocol to the Agreement establishing an Association between the European Economic Community and Greece consequent on the accession of new Member States to the Community. (O.J. 1978 L161/1.)

Council Regulation (EEC) No. 1300/78 of June 6, 1978, amending Regulation (EEC) No. 1703/72 laying down, inter alia, rules for the Community financing of expenditure arising from the implementation of the 1971 Food-Aid Convention. (O.J. 1978 L160/12.)

Council Regulation (EEC) No. 1301/78 of June 12, 1978, amending Regulation (EEC) No. 517/72 on the introduction of common rules for regular and special regular services by coach and bus between Member States. (O.J. 1978 L158/1.)

Council Regulation (EEC) No. 1302/78, on the granting of financial support for projects to exploit alternative energy sources. (O.J. 1978 L158/3.)

Council Regulation (EEC) No. 1303/78 of June 12, 1978, on the granting of financial support for demonstration projects in the field of energy-saving. (O.J. 1978 L158/6.)

Commission Regulation (EEC) No. 1392/78 of June 23, 1978, amending Regulation (EEC) No. 1380/75 laying down detailed rules for the application of monetary compensatory amounts. (O.J. 1978 L167/53.)

Council Regulation (EEC) No. 1431/78 of June 26, 1978, on the conclusion of the Supplementary Protocol to the Agreement establishing an Association between the European Economic Community and the Republic of Cyprus and the Protocol laying down certain provisions relating to trade in agricultural products between the European Economic Community and the Republic of Cyprus. (O.J. 1978 L172/1.)

Council Regulation (EEC) No. 1452/78 of June 19, 1978, on the application of Decisions No. 1/78 and No. 2/78 of the EEC–Austria Joint Committee— Community transit—on the amendment of the Appendices to the Agreement. (O.J. 1978 L174/1.)

Council Regulation (EEC) No. 1453/78 of June 19, 1978, on the application of Decisions No. 1/78 and No. 2/78 of the EEC–Switzerland Joint Committee—Community transit—on the amendment of the Appendices to the Agreement. (O.J. 1978 L174/21.)

Council Regulation (EEC) No. 1454/78 of June 26, 1978, on the conclusion of the Agreement extending the Interim Agreement between the European Economic Community and the People's Democratic Republic of Algeria. (O.J. 1975 L175/1.)

Council Regulation (EEC) No. 1455/78 of June 26, 1978, on the conclusion of the Agreement extending the Interim Agreement between the European Economic Community and the Kingdom of Morocco. (O.J. 1978 L175/7.)

Council Regulation (EEC) No. 1456/78 of June 26, 1978, on the conclusion of the Agreement extending the Interim Agreement between the European Economic Community and the Republic of Tunisia. (O.J. 1978 L175/11.)

Council Regulation (EEC) No. 1457/78 of June 26, 1978, on the conclusion of the Agreement extending the Interim Agreement between the European Economic Community and the Arab Republic of Eygpt. (O.J. 1978 L175/15.)

Council Regulation (EEC) No. 1458/78 of June 26, 1978, on the conclusion of the Agreement extending the Interim Agreement between the European Economic Community and the Hashemite Kingdom of Jordan. (O.J. 1978 L175/17.)

Council Regulation (EEC) No. 1459/78 of June 26, 1978, on the conclusion of the Agreement extending the Interim Agreement between the European Economic Community and the Lebanese Republic. (O.J. 1978 L175/19.)

Council Regulation (EEC) No. 1460/78 of June 26, 1978, on the conclusion of the Agreement extending the Interim Agreement between the European Economic Community and the Syrian Arab Republic. (O.J. 1978 L175/21.)

Commission Regulation (EEC) No. 1544/78 of July 4, 1978, amending Regulation (EEC) No. 243/78, in particular, as regards the adjustment of monetary compensatory amounts fixed in advance. (O.J. 1978 L182/7.)

Council Regulation (EEC) No. 1484/78 of June 19, 1978, concerning the application of Decision No. 1/78 of the ACP-EEC Council of Ministers amending Protocol 1 to the ACP-EEC Convention of Lomé concerning the definition of the concept of " originating products " and methods of administrative co-operation. (O.J. 1978 L177/1.)

Council Regulation (EEC) No. 1746/78 of July 24, 1978, on the conclusion of the Agreements in the form of exchanges of letters between the European Economic Community and Barbados, the People's Republic of the Congo, Fiji, the Cooperative Republic of Guyana, Jamaica, the Republic of Kenya, the Democratic Republic of Madagascar, the Republic of Malawi, Mauritius, the Republic of Surinam, the Kingdom of Swaziland, the United Republic of Tanzania, Trinidad and Tobago, the Republic of Uganda, and also the Republic of India, on the guaranteed prices for cane sugar for 1978/79. (O.J. 1978 L203/4.)

Council Regulation (EEC) No. 1760/78 of July 25, 1978, on a common measure to improve public amenities in certain rural areas. (O.J. 1978 L204/1.)

Council Regulation (EEC) No. 1814/78 of July 25, 1978, concerning the conclusion of the Agreement in the form of an exchange of letters rectifying Annex A to Protocol 1 to the Agreement between the European Economic Community and the Kingdom of Sweden. (O.J. 1978 L210/1.)

Commission Regulation (EEC) No. 1837/78 of July 31, 1978, defining the scope of Art. 4 (5) of Regulation (EEC) No. 1380/75 laying down detailed rules for the application of monetary compensatory amounts. (O.J. 1978 L210/51.)

Commission Regulation (EEC) No. 1907/78 of August 7, 1978, correcting Regulation (EEC) No. 1837/78 defining the scope of Art. 4 (5) of Regulation (EEC) No. 1380/75 laying down detailed rules for the application of monetary compensatory amounts. (O.J. 1978 L.217/13.)

Council Regulation (EEC) No. 1927/78 of July 25, 1978, concluding the Agreement between the European Economic Community and the People's Republic of Bangladesh on trade in jute products. (O.J. 1978 L225–15.)

Commission Regulation (EEC) No. 1947/78 of August 11, 1978, amending Regulation (EEC) No. 1380/75 laying down detailed rules for the application of monetary compensatory amounts. (O.J. 1978 L221/14.)

Council Regulation (EEC) No. 2112/78 of July 25, 1978, concerning the conclusion of the Customs Convention on the international transport of goods under cover of TIR carnets (TIR Convention) of November 14, 1975, at Geneva. (O.J. 1978 L252/1.)

Commission Regulation (EEC) No. 2116/78 of September 7, 1978, amending Regulation (EEC) No. 2598/70 specifying the items to be included under the various headings in the forms of accounts shown in Annex I to Council Regulation (EEC) No. 1108/70 of June 4, 1970. (O.J. 1978 L246/7.)

Commission Regulation (EEC) No. 2117/78 of September 7, 1978, amending Regulation (EEC) No. 1380/75 laying down detailed rules for the application of monetary compensatory amounts. (O.J. 1978 L246/9.)

Council Regulation (EEC) No. 2152/78 of July 18, 1978, on the application of Decision No. 1/78 of the EEC-Turkey Association Council amending Decision No. 5/72 on methods of administrative co-operation for implementation of Articles 2 and 3 of the Additional Protocol to the Ankara Agreement. (O.J. 1978 L253/1.)

Council Regulation (EEC) No. 2183/78 of September 19, 1978, laying down uniform costing principles for railway undertakings. (O.J. 1978 L258/1.)

Council Regulation (EEC) No. 2210/78 of September 26, 1978, concerning the conclusion of the Cooperation Agreement between the European Economic Community and the People's Democratic Republic of Algeria. (O.J. 1978 L263/1.)

Council Regulation (EEC) No. 2211/78 of September 26, 1978, concerning the conclusion of the Cooperation Agreement between the European Economic Community and the Kingdom of Morocco. (O.J. 1978 L/264/1.)

Council Regulation (EEC) No. 2212/78 of September 26, 1978, concerning the conclusion of the Cooperation Agreement between the European Economic Community and the Republic of Tunisia. (O.J. 1978 L265/1.)

Council Regulation (EEC) No. 2213/78 of September 26, 1978, on the conclusion of the Cooperation Agreement between the European Economic Community and the Arab Republic of Egypt. (O.J. 1978 L266/1.)

Council Regulation (EEC) No. 2214/78 of September 26, 1978, concerning the conclusion of the Cooperation Agreement between the European Economic Community and the Lebanese Republic. (O.J. 1978 L267/1.)

Council Regulation (EEC) No. 2215/78 of September 26, 1978, concerning the conclusion of the Cooperation Agreement between the European Economic Community and the Hashemite Kingdom of Jordan. (O.J. 1978 L268/1.)

Council Regulation (EEC) No. 2216/78 of September 26, 1978, concerning the conclusion of the Cooperation Agreement between the European Economic Community and the Syrian Arab Republic. (O.J. 1978 L269/1.)

Council Regulation (EEC) No. 2217/78 of September 26, 1978, concerning the conclusion of the Additional Protocol to the Agreement between the European Economic Community and the State of Israel, and of the Protocol relating to financial cooperation. (O.J. 1978 L270/1.)

Council Regulation (EEC) No. 2236/78 of September 25, 1978, concerning the conclusion of the Agreements on the accession of the Republic of Cape Verde, Papua New Guinea and the Democratic Republic of Sao Tome and Principe to the Lomé Convention. (O.J. 1978 L271/1.)

Council Regulation (EEC) No. 2237/78 of September 26, 1978, concerning the conclusion of the Financial Protocol and the Additional Protocol to the Agreement between the European Economic Community and the Portuguese Republic. (O.J. 1978 L274/1.)

Council Regulation (EEC) No. 2302/78 of September 29, 1978, on the application of Decision No. 3/78 of the EEC-Austria Joint Committee—Community transit—amending Annex II to the Agreement between the European Economic Community and the Republic of Austria on the simplification of formalities for trade in goods between the European Economic Community on the one hand and Greece and Turkey on the other, when the said goods are forwarded from Austria. (O.J. 1978 L276/2.)

Council Regulation (EEC) No. 2451/78 of September 19, 1978, concerning the conclusion of the Agreement in the form of an exchange of letters amending the Agreement between the European Economic Community and the Republic of Austria for the purpose of adjusting certain tariff specifications. (O.J. 1978 L302/1.)

Council Regulation (EEC) No. 2452/78 of September 19, 1978, concerning the conclusion of the Agreement in the form of an exchange of letters amending the Agreement between the European Economic Community and the Republic of Finland for the purpose of adjusting certain tariff specifications. (O.J. 1978 L302/13.)

Council Regulation (EEC) No. 2453/78 of September 19, 1978, concerning the conclusion of the Agreement in the form of an exchange of letters amending the Agreement between the European Economic Community and the Portuguese Republic for the purpose of adjusting certain tariff specifications. (O.J. 1978 L302/28.)

Council Regulation (EEC) No. 2454/78 of September 19, 1978, concerning the conclusion of the Agreement in the form of an exchange of letters amending the Agreement between the European Economic Community and the Kingdom of Norway for the purpose of adjusting certain tariff specifications. (O.J. 1978 L303/1.)

Council Regulation (EEC) No. 2455/78 of Sepember 19, 1978, concerning the conclusion of the Agreement in the form of an exchange of letters amending the Agreement between the European Economic Community and the Kingdom of Sweden for the purpose of adjusting certain tariff specifications. (O.J. 1978 L303/14.)

Council Regulation (EEC) No. 2456/78 of September 19, 1978, concerning the conclusion of the Agreement in the form of an exchange of letters amending the Agreement between the European Economic Community and the Swiss Confederation for the purpose of adjusting certain tariff specifications. (O.J. 1978 L303/25.)

Council Regulation (EEC) No. 2457/78 of October 16, 1978, concerning the conclusion of the Agreement in the form of an exchange of letters between the European Economic Community and the Republic of Tunisia concerning certain wines originating in Tunisia and entitled to a designation of origin. (O.J. 1978 L296/1.)

Council Regulation (EEC) No. 2573/78 of October 30, 1978, on the application of Decision No. 2/78 of the EEC-Turkey Council of Association relating to proof of origin for certain textile products exported by Turkey. (O.J. 1978 L309/1.)

Council Regulation (EEC) No. 2577/78 of October 30, 1978, amending Regulation (EEC) No. 1846/78 allocating catch quotas among the Member States for vessels fishing in Faroese waters. (O.J. 1978 L309/9.)

Council Regulation (EEC) No. 2607/78 of October 30, 1978, concerning the conclusion of the exchange of letters relating to Article 2 of Protocol 8 to the Agreement between the European Economic Community and the Portuguese Republic. (O.J. 1978 L.315/1.)

Council Regulation (EEC) No. 2779/78 of November 23, 1978, on the conclusion of the Financial Protocol between the European Economic Community and the Republic of Cyprus. (O.J. 1978 L332/1.)

Council Regulation (EEC) No. 2762/78 of November 23, 1978, on the conclusion of the Agreement in the form of an exchange of letters between the European Economic Community and the Republic of Tunisia fixing the additional amount to be deducted from the levy on imports into the Community of untreated olive oil, originating in Tunisia, for the period November 1, 1978, to October 31, 1979. (O.J. 1978 L332/14.)

Council Regulation (EEC) No. 2763/78 of November 23, 1978, on the conclusion of the Agreement in the form of an exchange of letters between the European Economic Community and the Kingdom of Morocco fixing the additional amount to be deducted from the levy on imports into the Community of untreated olive oil, originating in Morocco, for the period November 1, 1978, to October 31, 1979. (O.J. 1978 L332/17.)

Council Regulation (EEC) No. 2764/78 of November 23, 1978, on the conclusion of the Agreement in the form of an exchange of letters between the European Economic Community and the People's Democratic Republic of Algeria fixing the additional amount to be deducted from the levy on imports into the Community of untreated olive oil, originating in Algeria, for the period November 1, 1978 to October 31, 1979. (O.J. 1978 L332/20.)

Council Regulation (EEC) No. 2765/78 of November 23, 1978, on the conclusion of the Agreement in the form of an exchange of letters between the European Economic Community and Turkey fixing the additional amount to be deducted from the levy on imports into the Community of untreated olive oil, originating in Turkey, for the period November 1, 1978, to October 31, 1979. (O.J. 1978 L332/23.)

Council Regulation (EEC) No. 2778/78 of November 23, 1978, amending Regulation (EEC) No. 516/72 on the introduction of common rules for shuttle services by coach and bus between Member States. (O.J. 1978 L333/4.)

Council Regulation (EEC) No. 2760/78 of November 23, 1978, on the procedure for applying the European unit of account (EUA) to legal acts adopted in the customs sphere. (O.J. 1978 L333/5.)

Commission Regulation (EEC) No. 2788/78 of November 29, 1978, amending Regulation (EEC) No. 2695/77 determining the conditions under which goods for certain categories of aircraft and ships are eligible upon importation for a favourable tariff arrangement. (O.J. 1978 L333/25.)

Council Regulation (EEC) No. 2882/78 of December 5, 1978, on the conclusion of the Agreement in the form of an exchange of letters between the European Economic Community and the Portuguese Republic regarding prepared or preserved tomatoes falling within subheading 20.02 C of the Common Customs Tariff. (O.J. 1978 L344/1.)

Council Regulation (EEC) No. 2924/78 of December 12, 1978, concerning the conclusion of the Agreement in the form of an exchange of letters between the European Economic Community and the Republic of Cyprus on the correction of a clerical error in Article 2 (1) of the Protocol laying down certain provisions relating to trade in agricultural products between the European Economic Community and the Republic of Cyprus. (O.J. 1978 L350/1.)

ECSC

1270. 77/768/ECSC:
Decision of the representatives of the Governments of the Member States of the European Coal and Steel Community, meeting within the Council, of November 28, 1977, opening, allocating and providing for the administration of tariff quotas for certain steel products originating in developing countries. (O.J. 1977 L324/150.)

77/769/ECSC:
Decision of the representatives of the Governments of the Member States of the European Coal and Steel Community, meeting within the Council, of November 28, 1977, opening tariff preferences for certain steel products originating in developing countries. (O.J. 1977 L324/155.)

77/774/ECSC:
Commission Decision of November 23, 1977, authorising the formation of Framtek, a vehicle-springs manufacturing company. (O.J. 1977 L320/52.)

77/807/ECSC:
Amending ECSC operational budget for 1977. (O.J. 1977 L351/61.)

77/808/ECSC:
Commission recommendation of December 23, 1977, to the Governments of the Member States amending Commission recommendation 77/330/ECSC of April 15, 1977, establishing Community surveillance in respect of the importation into the Community of certain iron and steel products covered by the Treaty establishing the European Coal and Steel Community, originating in third countries. (O.J. 1977 L352/15.)

78/65/ECSC:
Council Decision of January 17, 1978, amending the Council Decision of February 16, 1976 on the granting of daily subsistence allowances and refunds of travel expenses to Members of the Consultative Committee of the European Coal and Steel Community. (O.J. 1978 L21/22.)

78/71/ECSC:
Council Decision of January 23, 1978, appointing a member of the Consultative Committee of the European Coal and Steel Community. (O.J. 1978 L23/42.)

78/148/ECSC:
Council Decision of February 7, 1978, appointing a member of the Consultative Committee of the European Coal and Steel Community. (O.J. 1978 L45/22.)

78/178/ECSC:
Council Decision of February 20, 1978, appointing a member of the Consultative Committee of the European Coal and Steel Community. (O.J. 1978 L54/29.)

78/179/ECSC:
Council Decision of February 20, 1978, appointing a member of the Consultative Committee of the European Coal and Steel Community. (O.J. 1978 L54/30.)

78/201/ECSC:
Commission Decision of January 24, 1978, derogating from High Authority recommendation 1/64 concerning an increase in the protective duty on iron and steel products at the external frontiers of the Community (93rd derogation). (O.J. 1978 L62/33.)

78/266/ECSC:
Council Decision of March 7, 1978, appointing a member of the Consultative Committee of the European Coal and Steel Community. (O.J. 1978 L72/15.)

78/282/ECSC:
Commission recommendation of March 9, 1978, to the Governments of the Member States amending Commission recommendation 77/330/ECSC of April 15, 1977, as last amended by recommendation 77/808/ECSC of December 23, 1977, establishing Community surveillance in respect of the importation into the Community of certain iron and steel products covered by the Treaty establishing the European Coal and Steel Community, originating in third countries. (O.J. 1978 L73/37.)

78/295/ECSC:
Commission Decision of March 1, 1978, approving aids from the French Republic to the coal-mining industry during the year 1977. (O.J. 1978 L75/13.)

78/351/ECSC:
Decision of the representatives of the Governments of the Member States of the European Coal and Steel Community, meeting within the Council, of March 20, 1978, establishing supervision for imports of certain products originating in Austria (1978). (O.J. 1978 L102/35.)

78/352/ECSC:
Decision of the representatives of the Governments of the Member States of the European Coal and Steel Community, meeeting within the Council, of March 20, 1978, establishing supervision for imports of certain products originating in Sweden (1978). (O.J. 1978 L102/37.)

78/375/ECSC:
Commission recommendation of April 17, 1978, to the Governments of the Member States amending Commission recommendation 77/330/ECSC of April 15, 1977, as last amended by recommendation 78/282/ECSC of April 9, 1978, establishing Community surveillance in respect of the importation into the Community of certain iron and steel products covered by the Treaty establishing the European Coal and Steel Community and originating in third countries. (O.J. 1978 L105/24.)

78/538/ECSC:
Commission Decision of June 6, 1978, authorising Arbed to acquire the whole of the capital of Neunkircher Eisenwerk AG, 25·09 per cent. of the capital of SA Métallurgique et Minière de Rodange-Athus, and to take over the management of the latter company. (O.J. 1978 L164/14.)

78/550/ECSC:
Decision of the Representatives of the Governments of the Member States of the European Coal and Steel Community, meeting within the Council of June 26, 1978, extending the period of validity of Decision 76/564/ECSC opening tariff preferences for products covered by that Community and originating in Tunisia. (O.J. 1978 L175/23.)

78/551/ECSC:
Decision of the Representatives of the Governments of the Member States of the European Coal and Steel Community, meeting within the Council of June 26, 1978, extending the period of validity of Decision 76/565/ECSC to imports of iron and steel coils for re-rolling originating in Australia. (O.J. 1978 L198/4.)

78/552/ECSC:
Decision of the Representatives of the Governments of the Member States of the European Coal and Steel Community, meeting within the Council of June 26, 1978, extending the period of validity of Decision 76/566/ECSC opening tariff preferences for products covered by that Community and originating in Morocco. (O.J. 1978 L175/25.)

78/553/ECSC:
Decision of the Representatives of the Governments of the Member States of the European Coal and Steel Community, meeting within the Council of June 26, 1978, extending the period of validity of Decision 77/419/ECSC opening tariff preferences for products covered by that Community and originating in Eygpt. (O.J. 1978 L175/26.)

78/554//ECSC:
Decision of the Representatives of the Governments of the Member States of the European Coal and Steel Community, meeting within the Council of June 26, 1978, extending the period of validity of Decision 77/420/ECSC opening tariff preferences for products covered by that Community and originating in Syria. (O.J. L175/27.)

78/555/ECSC:
Decision of the Representatives of the Governments of the Member States of the European Coal and Steel Community, meeting within the Council of June 26, 1978, extending the period of validity of Decision 77/421/ECSC opening tariff preferences for products covered by that Community and originating in Lebanon. (O.J. 1978 L175/28.)

78/556/ECSC:
Decision of the Representatives of the Governments of the Member States of the European Coal and Steel Community, meeting within the Council of June 26, 1978, extending the period of validity of Decision 77/422/ECSC opening tariff preferences for products covered by that Community and originating in Jordan. (O.J. 1978 L175/29.)

78/570/ECSC:
Commission Decision of June 7, 1978, authorising Ruhrkohle Handel GmbH, Düsseldorf, to acquire a 12·5 per cent. interest in Bayerischer Brennstoffhandel GmbH & Co. KG, coal wholesalers of Munich. (O.J. 1978 L191/38.)

78/617/ECSC
Commission recommendation of June 26, 1978, amending recommendation 77/330/ECSC establishing Community surveillance in respect of the importation into the Community of certain iron and steel products covered by the Treaty establishing the European Coal and Steel Community, originating in third countries. (O.J. 1978 L198/16.)

78/671/ECSC:
Council Decision of August 2, 1978, designating representative organizations required to draw up lists of candidates for the Consultative Committee of the European Coal and Steel Community. (O.J. 1978 L226/20.)

78/711/ECSC:
Commission Decision of July 28, 1978, authorising an agreement co-ordinating sales of concrete reinforcing bars and merchant bars by certain Italian steel undertakings (UCRO). (O.J. 1978 L238/28.)

78/731/ECSC:
Commission Decision of July 20, 1978, authorising specialisation agreements concerning stainless steel flats, squares, round bars and sections between Creusot-Loire SA and Ugine Aciers SA. (O.J. 1978 L242/10.)

78/798/ECSC:
Agreement between the Member States of the European Coal and Steel Community and the People's Democratic Republic of Algeria. (O.J. 1978 L2963/119.)

78/799/ECSC:
Agreement between the Member States of the European Coal and Steel Community and the Kingdom of Morocco. (O.J. 1978 L264/119.)

78/800/ECSC:
Agreement between the Member States of the European Coal and Steel Community and the Republic of Tunisia. (O.J. 1978 L265/119.)

78/892/ECSC:
Council Decision of October 16, 1978, designating four representative organisations required to draw up lists of candidates for the Consultative Committee of the European Coal and Steel Community. (O.J. 1978 L314/5.)

78/893/ECSC:
Council Decision of October 16, 1978, appointing the members of the Consultative Committee of the European Coal and Steel Community. (O.J. 1978 L314/6.)

78/924/ECSC:
Commission Decision of October 20, 1978, authorising the specialisation, joint-buying and joint-selling agreements between the Italian steel-producing undertakings Falck and Redaelli. (O.J. 1978 L324/26.)

78/943/ECSC:
Council Decision of November 16, 1978, appointing a member of the Consultative Committee of the European Coal and Steel Community. (O.J. 1978 L327/10.)

78/973/ECSC:
Commission Decision of November 16, 1978, extending the authorisation for the joint sale of fuels by the Belgian mining companies associated within the ' Comptoir belge des charbons, Société coopérative (Cobechar).' (O.J. 1978 L329/37.)

78/975/ECSC:
Commission Decision of November 16, 1978, on the authorisation of special Deutsche Bundesbahn tariffs in favour of coal and steel producers in the Saar (O.J. 1978 L330/34.)

78/1025/ECSC:
Council Decision of December 5, 1978, appointing a member of the Consultative Committee of the European Coal and Steel Community. (O.J. 1978 L350/32.)

Commission Decision No. 2996/77/ECSC of December 21, 1977, fixing the rate of the levies for the 1978 financial year and amending Decision No. 3/52/ECSC on the amount of and methods for applying the levies provided for in arts. 49 and 50 of the ECSC Treaty. (O.J. 1977 L351/53.)

Commission Decision No. 3000/77/ECSC of December 28, 1977, fixing minimum prices for hot-rolled wide strips, merchant bars and concrete reinforcing bars. (O.J. 1977 L352/1.)

Commission Decision No. 3001/77/ECSC of December 28, 1977, concerning the obligation on undertakings producing merchant bars, coils and concrete reinforcing bars to supply certain data on their deliveries of these products. (O.J. 1977 L352/4.)

Commission Decision No. 3002/77/ECSC of December 28, 1977, requiring dealers in iron and steel products to comply with pricing rules. (O.J. 1977 L352/8.)

Commission Decision No. 3003/77/ECSC of December 28, 1977, requiring undertakings in the iron and steel industry to issue certificates of conformity in respect of certain iron and steel products. (O.J. 1977 L352/11.)

Commission recommendation No. 3004/77/ECSC of December 28, 1977, modifying recommendation 77/329/ECSC on protection against dumping or the granting of bounties or subsidies by countries which are not members of the European Coal and Steel Community. (O.J. 1977 L352/13.)

Commission recommendation No. 112/78/ECSC of January 18, 1978, imposing a provisional anti-dumping duty on imports of iron or steel coils for re-rolling, originating in Czechoslovakia and South Korea. (O.J. 1978 L17/27.)

Commission recommendation No. 159/78/ECSC of January 27, 1978, imposing a provisional anti-dumping duty on certain angles, shapes and sections, of iron and steel, not further worked than hot-rolled or extruded, originating in Spain. (O.J. 1978 L23/31.)

Commission recommendation No. 160/78/ECSC of January 27, 1978, imposing a provisional anti-dumping duty on certain sheets and plates, of iron or steel, originating in the German Democratic Republic, Romania and Spain. (O.J. 1978 L23/33.)

Commission recommendation No. 161/78/ECSC of January 27, 1978, imposing a provisional anti-dumping duty on certain sheets and plates, of iron or steel, originating in Japan. (O.J. 1978 L23/35.)

Commission recommendation No. 245/78/ECSC of February 2, 1978, imposing a provisional anti-dumping duty on imports of iron or steel coils for re-rolling originating in Japan and Bulgaria. (O.J. 1978 L37/13.)

Commission recommendation No. 262/78/ECSC of February 7, 1978, imposing a provisional anti-dumping duty on certain sheets and plates, of iron or steel, originating in Poland. (O.J. 1978 L39/13.)

Commission recommendation No. 263/78/ECSC of February 7, 1978, imposing a provisional anti-dumping duty on certain angles, shapes and sections, of iron or steel, not further worked than hot-rolled or extruded, originating in Japan. (O.J. 1978 L39/15.)

Commission recommendation No. 359/78/ECSC of February 20, 1978, imposing a provisional anti-dumping duty on certain galvanised sheets and plates originating in the German Democratic Republic and Japan. (O.J. 1978 L50/13.)

Commission Decision No. 527/78/ECSC of March 14, 1978, prohibiting alignment on offers of iron and steel products originating in certain third countries. (O.J. 1978 L73/16.)

Commission recommendation No. 714/78/ECSC of April 6, 1978, providing for suspension of provisional anti-dumping duties established in relation to imports of steel products originating in Japan. (O.J. 1978 L94/21.)

Commission Decision No. 715/78/ECSC of April 6, 1978, concerning limitation periods in proceedings and the enforcement of sanctions under the Treaty establishing the European Coal and Steel Community. (O.J. 1978 L94/22.)

Commission recommendation No. 788/78/ECSC of April 19, 1978, extending the provisional anti-dumping measures established in relation to imports of steel products originating in Czechoslovakia. (O.J. 1978 L106/19.)

Commission recommendation No. 789/78/ECSC of April 19, 1978, extending the provisional anti-dumping measures established in relation to imports of steel products originating in Japan. (O.J. 1978 L106/20.)

Commission recommendation No. 790/78/ECSC of April 19, 1978, imposing a definitive anti-dumping duty on iron or steel coils for re-rolling originating in South Korea. (O.J. 1978 L196/21.)

Commission Decision No. 799/78/ECSC of April 19, 1978, amending Decision No. 527/78/ECSC prohibiting alignment on offers of iron and steel products originating in certain third countries. (O.J. 1978 L107/11.)

Commission recommendation No. 811/78/ECSC of April 21, 1978, imposing a definitive anti-dumping duty on certain sheets and plates, of iron or steel, originating in Bulgaria, the German Democratic Republic and Romania. (O.J. 1978 L108/26.)

Commission recommendation No. 812/78/ECSC of April 21, 1978, extending the provisional anti-dumping measures established in relation to imports of steel products originating in Poland and Spain. (O.J. 1978 L108/29.)

Commission Decision No. 849/78/ECSC of April 26, 1978, amending Decision No. 527/78/ECSC prohibiting alignment on offers of iron and steel products originating in certain third countries. (O.J. 1978 L115/45.)

Commission recommendation No. 859/78/ECSC of April 27, 1978, providing for the suspension of provisional anti-dumping duties established in relation to imports of steel products originating in Czechoslovakia. (O.J. 1978 L116/20.)

Commission recommendation No. 931/78/ECSC of April 28, 1978, providing for suspension of provisional anti-dumping duties established in relation to imports of steel products originating in Spain. (O.J. 1978 L120/21.)

Commission recommendation No. 932/78/ECSC of May 2, 1978, imposing a definitive anti-dumping duty on iron or steel coils for re-rolling originating in Bulgaria. (O.J. 1978 L120/22.)

Commission recommendation No. 933/78/ECSC of May 2, 1978, extending the provisional anti-dumping measures established in relation to imports of steel products originating in Poland. (O.J. 1978 L120/25.)

Commission Decision No. 960/78/ECSC of May 11, 1978, amending Decision No. 3001/77/ECSC concerning the obligation on undertakings producing merchant bars, coils and concrete reinforcing bars to supply certain data on their deliveries of these products. (O.J. 1978 L126/1.)

Commission Decision No. 961/78/ECSC of May 11, 1978, imposing the obligation on undertakings producing beams and wire rod to supply certain information concerning those products. (O.J. 1978 L126/3.)

Commission recommendation No. 962/78/ECSC of May 12, 1978, to the Governments of the Member States of the Community amending the list of products annexed to recommendations 77/330/ECSC and 77/518/ECSC, as last amended by recommendation 77/808/ECSC, establishing Community surveillance in respect of the import into the Community from third countries of certain iron and steel products covered by the Treaty establishing the European Coal and Steel Community. (O.J. 1978 L126/5.)

Commission recommendation No. 971/78/ECSC of May 11, 1978, extending the provisional anti-dumping measures established in relation to imports of steel products originating in Australia. (O.J. 1978 L125/20.)

Commission Decision No. 1005/78/ECSC of May 18, 1978, further amending Decision No. 527/78/ECSC prohibiting alignment on offers of iron and steel products originating in certain third countries. (O.J. 1978 L131/7.)

Commission recommendation No. 1006/78/ECSC of May 18, 1978, imposing a definitive anti-dumping duty on certain galvanised sheets and plates originating in the German Democratic Republic. (O.J. 1978 L131/8.)

Commission recommendation No. 1181/78/ECSC of May 31, 1978, extending the provisional anti-dumping measures established in relation to imports of steel products originating in Poland. (O.J. 1978 L145/45.)

Commission Decision No. 1209/78/ECSC of June 2, 1978, further amending Decision No. 527/78/ECSC prohibiting alignment on offers of iron and steel products originating in certain third countries. (O.J. 1978 L147/34.)

Commission recommendation No. 1235/78/ECSC of June 8, 1978, providing for suspension of the definitive anti-dumping duty established in relation to imports of steel products originating in Romania. (O.J. 1978 L153/19.)

Commission Decision No. 1395/78/ECSC of June 23, 1978, amending Decision No. 3002/77/ECSC requiring dealers in iron and steel products to comply with pricing rules. (O.J. 1978 L167/60.)

Commission Decision No. 1483/78/ECSC of June 14, 1978, adjusting the minimum prices for hot-rolled wide strips, merchant bars and concrete reinforcing bars. (O.J. 1978 L176/44.)

Commission Decision No. 1525/78/ECSC of June 30, 1978, establishing a system for the lodging of deposits in cases of the provisional establishment of an infringement of Commission Decisions fixing minimum prices for certain steel products. (O.J. 1978 L178/90.)

Commission recommendation No. 1535/78/ECSC of June 21, 1978, concerning the anti-dumping duties imposed on certain iron and steel products. (O.J. 1978 L183/1.)

Commission recommendation No. 1616/78/ECSC of July 10, 1978, amending recommendation 77/330/ECSC establishing Community surveillance in respect of the importation into the Community of certain iron and steel products covered by the Treaty establishing the European Coal and Steel Community, originating in third countries. (O.J. 1978 L189/12.)

Commission recommendation No. 1704/78/ECSC of July 19, 1978, imposing a definitive anti-dumping duty on certain sheets and plates, of iron or steel, originating in Czechoslovakia, Japan, Poland and Spain. (O.J. 1978 L195/17.)

Commission recommendation No. 1715/78/ECSC of July 20, 1978, imposing a definitive anti-dumping duty on certain galvanised sheets and plates originating in Japan. (O.J. 1978 L/198/1.)

Commission recommendation No. 1716/78/ECSC of July 20, 1978, providing for the suspension of the provisional anti-dumping duty established in relation certain social legislation relating to road transport and Art. 3 (2) of Council Regulation (EEC) No. 1463/70 of July 20, 1970, on the introduction of recording equipment in road transport (tachograph) on the exemption by Member States from these Regulations of vehicles constructed and equipped to carry not more than 15 persons including the driver. (O.J. 1978 L198/20.)

Commission recommendation No. 1758/78/ECSC of July 26, 1978, imposing a definitive anti-dumping duty on certain angles, shapes and sections of iron or steel, originating in Spain. (O.J. 1978 L203/28.)

Commission recommendation No. 1835/78/ECSC of July 25, 1978, amending the recommendation establishing Community surveillance in respect of the importation into the Community of certain iron and steel products covered by the Treaty establishing the European Coal and Steel Community and originating in third countries (O.J. 1978 L210/48.)

Commission recommendation No. 1905/78/ECSC of July 28, 1978, amending High Authority recommendation No. 1-64 to the Governments of the Member States concerning an increase in the protective duty on iron and steel products at the external frontiers of the Community. (O.J. 1978 L217/5.)

Commission Decision (EEC) No. 1981/78/ECSC of August 16, 1978, further amending Decision No. 527/78/ECSC prohibiting alignment on offers of iron and steel products originating in certain third countries. (O.J. 1978 L227/12.)

Commission recommendation No. 1999/78/ECSC of August 16, 1978, amending recommendation 77/330/ECSC establishing Community surveillance in respect of the importation into the Community of certain iron and steel products covered by the Treaty establishing the European Coal and Steel Community, originating in third countries. (O.J. 1978 L231/11.)

Commission Decision No. 2287/78/ECSC of September 29, 1978, amending Decision No. 3544/73/ECSC on coking coal and coke. (O.J. 1978 L275/78.)

Commission Decision No. 2292/78/ECSC of September 29, 1978, extending and amending Decision No. 1525/78/ECSC establishing a system for the lodging of deposits. (O.J. 1978 L275/90.)

Commission Decision (No. 2293/78/ECSC of September 29, 1978, further amending Decision No. 527/78/ECSC prohibiting alignment on offers of iron and steel products originating in certain third countries. (O.J. 1978 L275/92.)

Commission recommendation No. 2346/78/ECSC of October 5, 1978, amending the Annex to recommendation 78/282/ECSC. (O.T. 1978 L282/21.)

Commission Decision No. 2495/78/ECSC of October 20, 1978, amending Decision No. 25-67 of June 22, 1967, laying down in implementation of art. 66 (3) of the Treaty establishing the European Coal and Steel Community a Regulation concerning exemption from prior authorisation. (O.J. 1978 L300/21.)

Commission recommendation No. 2739/78/ECSC of November 23, 1978, providing for the suspension of the definitive anti-dumping duty established in relation to iron or steel coils for re-rolling originating in South Korea. (O.J. 1978 L330/13.)

Commission Decision No. 2869/78/ECSC of December 5, 1978, amending for the second time Decision No. 3002/77/ECSC requiring merchants of iron and steel products to comply with pricing rules. (O.J. 1978 L341/1.)

Commission Decision No. 2870/78/ECSC of December 5, 1978, amending Decision No. 3003/77/ECSC requiring undertakings in the iron and steel industry to issue certificates of conformity in respect of certain iron and steel products. (O.J. 1978 L341/5.)

Agriculture

1271. 77/771/EEC:
Commission Decision of November 23, 1977, on the implementation of the reform of agricultural structures in Ireland pursuant to Directive 72/159/EEC and to Titles III and IV of Directive 75/268/EEC. (O.J. 1977 L320/48.)

77/794/EEC:
Commission Directive of November 4, 1977, laying down detailed rules for implementing certain provisions of Directive 76/308/EEC on mutual assistance for the recovery of claims resulting from operations forming part of the system of financing the European Agricultural Guidance and Guarantee Fund, and of agricultural levies and customs duties. (O.J. 1977 L333/11.)

78/17/EEC:
Commission Decision of December 6, 1977, on the granting by the Guidance Section of the EAGGF to the United Kingdom of a payment on account in respect of expenditure incurred during 1976 on aids for the less-favoured farming areas. (O.J. 1978 L10/25.)

78/18/EEC:
Commission Decision of December 6, 1977, on the reimbursement by the Guidance Section of the EAGGF to the United Kingdom of expenditure incurred during 1974 on aids and premiums relating to the modernisation of farms. (O.J. 1978 L10/26.)

78/36/EEC:
Commission Decision of December 12, 1977, of the Advisory Committee for Wine. (O.J. 1978 L11/31.)

78/50/EEC:
Council Directive of December 13, 1977, supplementing, as regards the chilling process, Directive 71/118/EEC on health problems affecting trade in fresh poultrymeat. (O.J. 1978 L15/28.)

78/51/EEC:
Council Directive of December 13, 1977, prolonging certain derogation measures in respect of brucellosis and tuberculosis granted to Denmark, Ireland and the United Kingdom. (O.J. 1978 L15/32.)

78/52/EEC:
Council Directive of December 13, 1977, establishing the Community criteria for national plans for the accelerated eradication of brucellosis, tuberculosis and enzootic leukosis in cattle. (O.J. 1978 L15/34.)

78/54/EEC:
Council Directive of December 19, 1977, extending the derogations granted in respect of protection against swine fever to Denmark, Ireland and the United Kingdom. (O.J. 1978 L16/22.)

78/55/EEC:
Council Directive of December 19, 1977, amending Directives 66/400/EEC, 66/401/EEC, 66/402/EEC, 68/193/EEC, 69/208/EEC, 70/458/EEC and 70/457/EEC on the marketing of beet seed, fodder plant seed, cereal seed,

material for the vegetative propagation of the vine, seed of oil and fibre plants, vegetable seed and on the common catalogue of varieties of agricultural plant species. (O.J. 1978 L16/23.)

78/58/EEC:
20th Commission Directive of December 7, 1977, amending the Annexes to Council Directive 70/524/EEC concerning additives in feedingstuffs. (O.J. 1978 L18/7.)

78/66/EEC:
Commission Decision of December 2, 1977, relating to a proceeding under Art. 85 of the EEC Treaty (IV/28.948—Cauliflowers). (O.J. 1978 L21/23.)

78/73/EEC:
Commission Decision of December 20, 1977, laying down the standard code and the detailed rules for the transcription onto magnetic tape of the data of the survey on the structure of agricultural holdings for 1977. (O.J. 1978 L25/44.)

78/78/EEC:
Commission Decision of December 23, 1977, concerning certain detailed rules for Directive 64/432/EEC in respect of foot-and-mouth disease. (O.J. 1978 L25/58.)

78/82/EEC:
Commission Decision of December 21, 1977, on the granting by the Guidance Section of the EAGGF to the United Kingdom of a payment on account in respect of expenditure incurred during 1976 on aids relating to the provision of socio-economic guidance for and the acquisition of occupational skills by persons engaged in agriculture. (O.J. 1978 L33/7.)

78/84/EEC:
Commission Decision of December 21, 1977, on the reimbursement by the Guidance Section of the EAGGF to the United Kingdom of expenditure incurred during 1975 on aids for the less-favoured farming areas. (O.J. 1978 L33/7.)

78/93/EEC:
Commission Decision of December 22, 1977, on the final contribution of the Guidance Section of the EAGGF towards expenditure incurred by the United Kingdom on premiums paid during 1974 for the conversion of dairy herds to meat production. (O.J. 1978 L34/24.)

78/94/EEC:
Commission Decision of December 22, 1977, on the final contribution of the Guidance Section of the EAGGF towards expenditure incurred by the United Kingdom on premiums paid during 1975 for the conversion of dairy herds to meat production. (O.J. 1978 L34/25.)

78/109/EEC:
Commission Decision of December 23, 1977, on the reimbursement by the Guidance Section of the EAGGF to the United Kingdom of the expenditure incurred on the structures survey for 1975 as part of the programme of surveys on the structure of agricultural holdings. (O.J. 1978 L39/24.)

78/112/EEC:
Commission Decision of December 23, 1977, on the reimbursement by the Guidance Section of the EAGGF to the United Kingdom of expenditure incurred during 1973 on aids relating to the provision of socio-economic guidance for and the acquisition of occupational skills by persons engaged in agriculture. (O.J. 1978 L39/27.)

78/113/EEC:
Commission Decision of December 23, 1977, on the reimbursement by the Guidance Section of the EAGGF to the United Kingdom of expenditure incurred during 1974 on aids relating to the provision of socio-economic guidance for and the acquisition of occupational skills by persons engaged in agriculture. (O.J. 1978 L39/28.)

78/117/EEC:

Twenty-First Commission Directive of December 23, 1977, amending the Annexes to Council Directive 70/524/EEC concerning additives in feeding-stuffs. (O.J. 1978 L40/19.)

78/128/EEC:

Commission Decision of December 28, 1977, extending for the United Kingdom in respect of a certain number of varieties the period provided for in Art. 15 (1) of Directive 70/457/EEC. (O.J. 1978 L41/44.)

78/135/EEC:

Commission Decision of January 11, 1978, on the implementation of the reform of agricultural structures in the United Kingdom pursuant to Directives 72/159/EEC and 75/268/EEC. (O.J. 1978 L43/16.)

78/142/EEC:

Council Directive of January 30, 1978, on the approximation of the laws of the Member States relating to materials and articles which contain vinyl chloride monomer and are intended to come into contact with foodstuffs. (O.J. 1978 L44/15.)

78/143/EEC:

Council Directive of January 30, 1978, amending for the second time Directive 70/357/EEC on the approximation of the laws of the Member States concerning the antioxidants authorised for use in foodstuffs intended for human consumption. (O.J. 1978 L44/18.)

78/144/EEC:

Council Directive of January 30, 1978, amending for the sixth time the Council Directive of October 23, 1962, on the approximation of the laws of the Member States concerning the colouring matters authorised for use in foodstuffs intended for human consumption. (O.J. 1978 L44/20.)

78/145/EEC:

Council Directive of January 30, 1978, amending for the 13th time Directive 64/54/EEC on the approximation of the laws of the Member States concerning the preservatives authorised for use in foodstuffs intended for human consumption. (O.J. 1978 L44/23.)

78/192/EEC:

Commission Decision of February 2, 1978, on the Advisory Committee on Live Plants. (O.J. 1978 L58/46.)

78/200/EEC:

Commission Decision of January 20, 1978, authorising Member States to permit temporarily the marketing of forestry reproductive material not complying with requirements of Council Directive 66/404/EEC. (O.J. 1978 L62/27.)

78/254/EEC:

Commission Decision of February 13, 1978, on the implementation of the reform of agricultural structures in Italy (region of Basilicata) pursuant to Directives 72/159/EEC, 72/160/EEC and 75/268/EEC. (O.J. 1978 L69/27.)

78/255/EEC:

Commission Decision of February 13, 1978, on the implementation of the reform of agricultural structures in Italy (province of Trento) pursuant to Directives 72/159/EEC, 72/160/EEC, 72/161/EEC and 75/268/EEC. (O.J. 1978 L69/29.)

78/256/EEC:

Commission Decision of February 15, 1978, on the implementation of the reform of agricultural structures in Italy (region of Apulia) pursuant to Directives 72/159/EEC, 72/160/EEC and 72/161/EEC and Titles III and IV of Directive 75/268/EEC. (O.J. 1978 L69/31.)

78/262/EEC:

Council Decision of March 6, 1978, on the equivalence of forest reproductive material produced in Austria. (O.J. 1978 L72/5.)

78/284/EEC:
Commission Decision of February 20, 1978, on the reimbursement by the Guidance Section of the EAGGF to the United Kingdom of expenditure incurred during 1975 on aids relating to the provision of socio-economic guidance for and the acquisition of occupational skills by persons engaged in agriculture. (O.J. 1978 L74/28.)

78/301/EEC:
Commission Decision of March 1, 1978, amending the Annex to Fifth Council Decision 76/538/EEC on the equivalence of field inspections carried out in third countries on seed-producing crops. (O.J. 1978 L75/23.)

78/302/EEC:
Commission Decision of March 1, 1978, amending the Annex to Fifth Council Decision 76/539/EEC on the equivalence of seed produced in third countries. (O.J. 1978 L75/24.)

78/347/EEC:
Commission Decision of March 30, 1978, authorising the United Kingdom to restrict the marketing of seed of certain varieties of agricultural plant species. (O.J. 1978 L94/26.)

78/430/EEC:
Commission Decision of April 18, 1978, authorising the United Kingdom to permit as " certified seed " seeds which have been entered for certification as " basic seed." (O.J. 1978 L124/10.)

78/436/EEC:
Commission Decision of April 21, 1978, establishing a Scientific Committee for Pesticides. (O.J. 1978 L124/16.)

78/463/EEC:
Commission Decision of April 7, 1978, establishing a Community typology for agricultural holdings. (O.J. 1978 L148/1.)

78/480/EEC:
Commission Decision of May 11, 1978, approving the plan for the accelerated eradication of brucellosis put forward by the United Kingdom. (O.J. 1978 L152/22.)

78/511/EEC:
Commission Directive of May 24, 1978, amending Directive 74/268/EEC laying down special conditions concerning the presence of " Avena fatua " in fodder plant and cereal seed. (O.J. 1978 L157/34.)

78/512/EEC:
Commission Decision of May 24, 1978, amending Decision 74/269/EEC authorising certain Member States to make provisions which are more strict concerning the presence of " Avena fatua " in fodder plant and cereal seed. (O.J. 1978 L157/35.)

78/522/EEC:
Twenty-second Commission Directive of May 30, 1978, amending the Annexes to Council Directive 70/524/EEC concerning additives in feedingstuffs. (O.J. 1978 L159/43.)

78/544/EEC:
Council Decision of December 19, 1977, on the application by the European Economic Community, as a provisional measure, of the Protocol of March 23, 1973, for the extension of the 1963 International Olive Oil Agreement. (O.J. 1978 L169/1.)

78/582/EEC:
Commission Directive of June 28, 1978, amending Directive 77/16/EEC on the application of art. 31 of the Council Directive of March 4, 1969, on the harmonisation of provisions laid down by law, regulation of administrative action in respect of inward processing as regards certain cereal products. (O.J. 1978 L193/32.)

78/591/EEC:
Commission recommendation of June 30, 1978, relating to the directed herring fishing in maritime zones west of Ireland. (O.J. 1978 L194/28.)

78/592/EEC:
Commission Decision of June 16, 1978, setting out definitions relating to the list of characteristics for the 1979–80 survey of the structure of agricultural holdings. (O.J. 1978 L195/22.)

78/613/EEC:
Twenty-third Commission Directive of June 23, 1973, amending the Annexes to Council Directive 70/524/EEC concerning the additives in feedingstuffs. (O.J. 1978 L198/10.)

78/616/EEC:
Commission Decision of June 23, 1978, extending Commission Decision 78/200/EEC of January 20, 1978, authorising Member States to permit temporarily the marketing of forestry reproductive material not complying with requirements of Council Directive 66/404/EEC. (O.J. 1978 L198/13.)

78/627/EEC:
Council Directive of June 19, 1978, on the programme to accelerate the re-structuring and conversion of vineyards in certain Mediterranean regions in France (O.J. 1978 L206/1.)

78/630/EEC:
Council Directive of June 19, 1978, amending for the first time Directive 76/118/EEC on the approximation of the laws of the Member States relating to certain partly or wholly dehydrated preserved milk for human consumption. (O.J. 1978 L206/12.)

78/631/EEC:
Council Directive of June 26, 1978, on the approximation of the laws of the Member States relating to the classification, packaging and labelling of dangerous preparations (pesticides). (O.J. 1978 L206/13.)

78/633/EEC:
Eighth Commission Directive of June 15, 1978, establishing Community methods of analysis for the official control of feedingstuffs. (O.J. 1978 L206/43.)

78/640/EEC:
Council Decision of July 25, 1978, on financial participation by the Community in inspection and surveillance operations in the maritime waters of Denmark and Ireland. (O.J. 1978 L211/34.)

78/659/EEC:
Council Directive of July 18, 1978, on the quality of fresh waters needing protection or improvement in order to support fish life. (O.J. 1978 L222/1.)

78/661/EEC:
Council Decision of July 25, 1978, amending Fifth Decision 76/539/EEC on the equivalence of seed produced in third countries. (O.J. 1978 L223/1.)

78/662/EEC:
Council Decision of July 25, 1978, amending Fifth Decision 76/538/EEC on the equivalence of field inspections carried out in third countries on seed-producing crops. (O.J. 1978 L223/4.)

78/685/EEC:
Commission Decision of July 26, 1978, establishing a list of epizootic diseases in accordance with Directive 72/462/EEC. (O.J. 1978 L227/32.)

78/690/EEC:
Council Decision of May 12, 1978, concerning the signing and the deposit of a declaration of provisional application of the Protocols for the fourth extension of the Wheat Trading Convention and the Food Aid Convention constituting the International Wheat Agreement, 1971.

78/691/EEC:
Third Council Decision of July 25, 1978, on the equivalence of seed potatoes produced in third countries. (O.J. 1978 L236/10.)

78/692/EEC:
Council Directive of July 25, 1978, amending Directives 66/400/EEC, 66/401/EEC, 66/402/EEC, 66/403/EEC, 68/193/EEC, 69/208/EEC and 70/458/EEC on the marketing of beet seed, fodder plant seed, cereal seed, seed potatoes, material for the vegetative propagation of the vine, seed of oil and fibre plants and vegetable seed. (O.J. 1978 L236/13.)

78/743/EEC:
Twenty-Fourth Commission Directive of July 28, 1978, amending the the Annexes to Council Directive 70/524/EEC concerning additives in feedingstuffs. (O.J. 1978 L247/25.)

78/758/EEC:
Commission Decision of June 30, 1978, amending Decision 75/420/EEC setting up an Advisory Committee on Foodstuffs. (O.J. 1978 L251/18.)

78/764/EEC:
Council Directive of July 25, 1978, on the approximation of the laws of the Member States relating to the driver's seat on wheeled agricultural or forestry tractors. (O.J. 1978 L255/1.)

78/777/EEC:
Commission Decision of September 8, 1978, on the granting by the Guidance section of the EAGGF to the United Kingdom of a payment on account in respect of expenditure incurred during 1977 on aids for the less-favoured farming areas. (O.J. 1978 L259/24.)

78/778/EEC:
Commission Decision of September 11, 1978, on the reimbursement by the Guidance Section of the EAGGF to the United Kingdom of expenditure incurred during 1976 on annuities relating to measures to encourage the cessation of farming and the reallocation of utilized agricultural area for the purpose of structural improvement. (O.J. 1978 L259/25)

78/782/EEC:
Commission Decision of September 11, 1978, on the granting by the Guidance Section of the EAGGF to the United Kingdom of a payment on account in respect of expenditure incurred during 1977 on annuities relating to measures to encourage the cessation of farming and the reallocation of utilized agricultural area for the purpose of structural improvement. (O.J. 1978 L259/29)

78/816/EEC:
Council Directive of September 26, 1978, amending Directive 66/403/EEC on the marketing of seed potatoes. (O.J. 1978 L281/18)

78/823/EEC:
Commission Decision of September 21, 1978, relating to a proceeding under Article 85 of the EEC Treaty (IV/28.824—Breeders' rights—maize seed). (O.J. 1978 L286/23)

78/865/EEC:
Commission Decision of October 9, 1978, on the implementation of the reform of agricultural structures in the United Kingdom pursuant to Directive 72/159/EEC. (O.J. 1978 L297/22.)

78/902/EEC:
Council Decision of October 30, 1978, adopting joint research programmes for co-ordinating agricultural research. (O.J. 1978 L316/37.)

78/923/EEC:
Council Decision of June 19, 1978, concerning the conclusion of the European Convention for the protection of animals kept for farming purposes. (O.J. 1978 L323/12.)

78/927/EEC:

Commission Decision of October 24, 1978, on the reimbursement by the Guidance Section of the EAGGF to the United Kingdom of premiums paid during 1977 for the conversion of dairy herds to meat production. (O.J. 1978 L324/32.)

78/933/EEC:

Council Directive of October 17, 1978, on the approximation of the laws of the Member States relating to the installation of lighting and light-signalling devices on wheeled agricultural and forestry tractors. (O.J. 1978 L325/16.)

78/974/EEC:

Twenty-fifth Commission Directive of November 16, 1978, amending the Annexes to Council Directive 70/524/EEC concerning additives in feeding-stuffs. (O.J. 1978 L330/30.)

78/1017/EEC:

Council Directive of November 24, 1978, amending Directive 72/159/EEC on the modernisation of farms and Directive 73/131/EEC on the guidance premium provided for in Article 10 of the Directive of April 17, 1972, on the modernisation of farms. (O.J. 1978 L349/32.)

Council Regulation (EEC) No. 2970/77 of December 29, 1977, laying down certain interim measures for the conservation and management of fishery resources applicable to vessels flying the flag of Sweden. (O.J. 1977 L351/1.)

Council Regulation (EEC) No. 2971/77 of December 29, 1977, laying down certain interim measures for the conservation and management of fishery resources applicable to vessels flying the flags of certain non-member countries in the 200 nautical mile zone off the coast of the French department of Guyana. (O.J. 1977 L351/3.)

Council Regulation (EEC) No. 2972/77 of December 29, 1977, laying down certain interim measures for the conservation and management of fishery resources applicable to vessels flying the flag of Norway. (O.J. 1977 L351/4.)

Council Regulation (EEC) No. 3021/77 of December 30, 1977, laying down certain interim measures for the conservation and management of fishery resources applicable to vessels flying the flag of Spain. (O.J. 1977 L355/47.)

Council Regulation (EEC) No. 129/78 of January 24, 1978, on the exchange rates to be applied for the purposes of the common agricultural structures policy. (O.J. 1978 L20/16.)

Council Regulation (EEC) No. 179/78 of January 31, 1978, amending Regulation (EEC) No. 878/77 as regards the exchange rate for the pound sterling to be applied in agriculture. (O.J. 1978 L26/3.)

Council Regulation (EEC) No. 203/78 of January 31, 1978, laying down certain interim measures for the conservation and management of fishery resources applicable to vessels flying the flag of Sweden. (O.J. 1978 L29/1.)

Council Regulation (EEC) No. 204/78 of January 31, 1978, laying down certain interim measures for the conservation and management of fishery resources applicable to vessels flying the flag of Spain. (O.J. 1978 L29/3.)

Council Regulation (EEC) No. 205/78 of January 31, 1978, laying down certain interim measures for the conservation and management of fishery resources applicable to vessels flying the flag of certain non-member countries in the 200 nautical mile zone off the coast of the French department of Guyana. (O.J. 1978 L29/6.)

Council Regulation (EEC) No. 206/78 of January 31, 1978, laying down certain interim measures for the conservation and management of fishery resources applicable to vessels flying the flag of Norway. (O.J. 1978 L29/10.)

Commission Regulation (EEC) No. 215/78 of February 1, 1978, amending Regulation (EEC) No. 937/77 following the fixing of a new exchange rate to be applied in the United Kingdom in agriculture. (O.J. 1978 L31/13.)

Council Regulation (EEC) No. 218/78 of December 19, 1977, on the organisation of a survey on the structure of agricultural holdings for 1979/80. (O.J. 1978 L35/1.)

Council Regulation (EEC) No. 299/78 of February 13, 1978, amending Regulation (EEC) No. 2824/72 laying down general rules for the financing of interventions by the Guarantee Section of the European Agricultural Guidance and Guarantee Fund. (O.J. 1978 L45/3.)

Council Regulation (EEC) No. 310/78 of February 14, 1978, amending Regulation (EEC) No. 878/77 as regards the exchange rates to be applied for tomato concentrations and isoglucose. (O.J. 1978 L46/1.)

Council Regulation (EEC) No. 341/78 of February 20, 1978, laying down certain interim measures for the conservation and management of fishery resources applicable to vessels flying the flag of Spain, for the period February 21 to May 31, 1978. (O.J. 1978 L49/1.)

Council Regulation (EEC) No. 352/78 of February 20, 1978, on the crediting of securities, deposits and guarantees furnished under the common agricultural policy and subsequently forfeited. (O.J. 1978 L50/1.)

Commission Regulation (EEC) No. 547/78 of March 16, 1978, fixing the average world market price and the indicative yield for linseed for the 1977/78 marketing year. (O.J. 1978 L75/7.)

Council Regulation (EEC) No. 705/78 of April 4, 1978, amending Regulation (EEC) No. 3330/74 on the common organisation of the market in sugar. (O.J. L94/1.)

Council Regulation (EEC) No. 976/78 of May 12, 1978, amending Regulation (EEC) No. 878/77 as regards the exchange rates to be applied in agriculture for various currencies and concerning the effects of the fixing of new representative rates on existing rights and obligations. (O.J. 1978 (L125/32.)

Council Regulation (EEC) No. 1037/78 of May 22, 1978 amending the Annex to Regulation (EEC) No. 804/68 on the common organisation of the market in milk and milk products. (O.J. 1978 L134/1.)

Commission Regulation (EEC) No. 1054/78 of May 19, 1978, laying down detailed rules for the application of Regulation (EEC) No. 878/77 on the exchange rates to be applied in agriculture and replacing Regulation (EEC) No. 937/77. (O.J. 1978 L134/1.)

Council Regulation (EEC) No. 1117/78 of May 22, 1978 on the common organisation of the market in dried fodder. (O.J. 1978 L142/1.)

Council Regulation (EEC) No. 1125/78 of May 22, 1978, amending Regulation (EEC) No. 2727/75 on the common organisation of the market in cereals. (O.J. 1978 L142/21.)

Council Regulation (EEC) No. 1126/78 of May 22, 1978, amending Regulation (EEC) No. 1418/76 on the common organisation of the market in rice. (O.J. 1978 L142/23.)

Council Regulation (EEC) No. 1128/78 of May 22, 1978 concerning the conclusion of the Agreement in the form of two exchanges of letters amending the Agreement of June 5, 1970, between the European Economic Community and Spain on certain cheeses. (O.J. 1978 L142/26.)

Council Regulation (EEC) No. 1152/78 of May 30, 1978, amending Regulation (EEC) No. 516/77 on the common organisation of the market in products processed from fruit and vegetables. (O.J. 1978 L144/1.)

Council Regulation (EEC) No. 1157/78 of May 30, 1978, laying down certain interim measures for the conservation and management of fishery resources applicable to vessels flying the flag of certain non-member countries in the 200 nautical mile zone off the coast of the French department of Guyana, for the period June 1 to December 31, 1978. (O.J. 1978 L144/11.)

Council Regulation (EEC) No. 1158/78 of May 30, 1978, extending certain interim measures for the conservation and management of fishery resources applicable to vessels flying the flag of Spain, to June 24, 1978. (O.J. 1978 L144/14.)

Council Regulation (EEC) No. 1254/78 of June 12, 1978, amending Regulation (EEC) No. 2727/75 on the common organisation of the market in cereals. (O.J. 1978 L156/1.)

Council Regulation (EEC) No. 1346/78 of June 19, 1978, amending Regulation (EEC) No. 2358/71 on the common organisation of the market in seeds. (O.J. 1978 L165/1.)

Council Regulation (EEC) No. 1376/78 of June 21, 1978, extending certain interim measures for the conservation and management of fishery resources applicable to vessels flying the flag of Spain, to July 31, 1978. (O.J. 1978 L167/9.)

Council Regulation (EEC) No. 1396/78 of June 20, 1978, amending Regulation (EEC) No. 3330/74 on the common organisation of the market in sugar. (O.J. 1978 L170/1.)

Council Regulation (EEC) No. 1419/78 of June 20, 1978, amending Regulation No. 136/66/EEC on the establishment of a common organisation of the market in oils and fats. (O.J. 1978 L171/8.)

Council Regulation (EEC) No. 1421/78 of June 20, 1978, amending Regulation (EEC) No. 804/68 on the common organisation of the market in milk and milk products. (O.J. 1978 L171/12.)

Council Regulation (EEC) No. 1423/78 of June 20, 1978, amending Regulation (EEC) No. 2759/75 on the common organisation of the market in pigmeat. (O.J. 1978 L171/19.)

Commission Regulation (EEC) No. 1509/78 of June 30, 1978, amending Regulations (EEC) No. 937/77 and (EEC) No. 1054/78 laying down detailed rules for the application of Regulation (EEC) No. 878/77 on the exchange rates to be applied in agriculture. (O.J. 1978 L178/50.)

Council Regulation (EEC) No. 1562/78 of June 29, 1978, amending Regulation No. 136/66/EEC on the establishment of a common organisation of the market in oils and fats. (O.J. 1978 L185/1.)

Commission Regulation (EEC) No. 1685/78 of July 11, 1978, laying down detailed rules for the implementation of the decision by the Guidance Section of the EAGGF to grant aid for projects designed to improve conditions under which agricultural products are processed and marketed. (O.J. 1978 L197/1.)

Council Regulation (EEC) No. 1744/78 of July 24, 1978, extending certain interim measures for the conservation and management of fishery resources applicable to vessels flying the flag of Spain, to September 30, 1978. (O.J. 1978 L203/1.)

Council Regulation (EEC) No. 1761/78 of July 25, 1978, amending Regulation (EEC) No. 804/68 on the common organisation of the market in milk and milk products. (O.J. 1978 L204/6.)

Council Regulation (EEC) No. 1766/78 of July 25, 1978, amending Regulation (EEC) No. 1035/72 on the common organisation of the market in fruit and vegetables. (O.J. 1978 L204/12.)

Council Regulation (EEC) No. 1846/78 of July 25, 1978, allocating catch quotas between Member States for vessels fishing in Faroese waters. (O.J. 1978 L211/1.)

Council Regulation (EEC) No. 1847/78 of July 25, 1978, allocating certain catch quotas between Member States for vessels fishing in the Norwegian exclusive economic zone (O.J. 1978 L211/4.)

Council Regulation (EEC) No. 1848/78 of July 25, 1978, laying down certain measures for the conservation and management of fishery resources applicable to vessels registered in the Faroe Islands. (O.J. 1978 L211/6.)

Council Regulation (EEC) No. 1849/78 of July 25, 1978, laying down certain measures for the conservation and management of fishery resources applicable to vessels flying the flag of Norway. (O.J. 1978 L211/13.)

Council Regulation (EEC) No. 1850/78 of July 25, 1978, laying down certain measures for the conservation and management of fishery resources applicable to vessels flying the flag of Sweden. (O.J. 1978 L211/20.)

Council Regulation (EEC) No. 1851/78 of July 25, 1978, laying down certain conservation and management measures for common fishery resources off the West Greenland coast applicable in 1978 to vessels flying the flag of Canada. (O.J. 1978 L211/26.)

Council Regulation (EEC) No. 1852/78 of July 25, 1978, on an interim common measure for restructuring the inshore fishing industry. (O.J. 1978 L211/30.)

Council Regulation (EEC) No. 1883/78 of August 2, 1978, laying down general rules for the financing of interventions by the European Agricultural Guidance and Guarantee Fund, Guarantee Section. (O.J. 1978 L216/1.)

Council Regulation (EEC) No. 2084/78 of August 31, 1978, providing for certain technical adjustments to Regulations (EEC) No. 1849/78 and (EEC) No. 1848/78 laying down certain measures for the conservation and management of fishery resources applicable to vessels flying the flag of Norway and vessels registered in the Faroe Islands respectively. (O.J. 1978 L240/60.)

Council Regulation (EEC) No. 2175/78 of September 18, 1978, establishing the number of licences to be issued to vessels flying the flag of Canada fishing within the 200-mile fishing zones of the Member States off the west Greenland coast. (O.J. 1978 L256/1)

Council Regulation (EEC) No. 2327/78 of October 4, 1978, laying down certain measures for the conservation and management of fishery resources applicable to vessels flying the flag of Spain, for the period October 1, to December 31, 1978. (O.J. 1978 L280/16)

Council Regulation (EEC) No. 2301/78 of September 29, 1978, establishing the number of licences that may be issued to vessels flying the flag of Norway for fishing within the 200 mile fishing zones of the Member States. (O.J. 1978 L276/1)

Council Regulation (EEC) No. 2355/78 of October 9, 1978, providing for certain technical adjustments to Regulation (EEC) No. 1848/78 laying down certain measures for the conservation and management of fishery resources applicable to vessels registered in the Faroe Islands. (O.J. 1978 L285/1)

Council Regulation (EEC) No. 2356/78 of October 9, 1978, providing for certain technical adjustments to Regulation (EEC) No. 1850/78 laying down certain measures for the conservation and management of fishery resources applicable to vessels flying the flag of Sweden. (O.J. 1978 L285/3)

Commission Regulation (EEC) No. 2572/78 of October 26, 1978, on applications for aid from the Guidance Section of the European Agricultural Guidance and Guarantee Fund for projects in the inshore fishing industry as envisaged in Regulation (EEC) No. 1852/78. (O.J. 1978 L308/19.)

Council Regulation (EEC) No. 2575/78 of October 30, 1978, extending the area within which vessels flying the flag of Norway are permitted by Regulation (EEC) No. 1849/78 to fish for certain species. (O.J. 1978 L309/5.)

Council Regulation (EEC) No. 2576/78 of October 30, 1978, allocating among the Member States certain catch quotas for vessels fishing in the Norwegian exclusive economic zone. (O.J. 1978 L309/7.)

Council Regulation (EEC) No. 2578/78 of October 30, 1978, laying down the number of licences for vessels flying the flag of Sweden for fishing within the 200-mile fishing zones of the Member States. (O.J. 1978 L309/11.)

Council Regulation (EEC) No. 2579/78 of October 30, 1978, laying down the number of licences for vessels registered in the Faroe Islands for fishing within the 200-mile fishing zones of the Member States. (O.J. 1978 L309/12.)

Finance

1272. Financial Regulation of December 21, 1977, applicable to the general budget of the European Communities.

Decision of the Board of Governors of the European Investment Bank ot December 30, 1977, amending the Statute of the European Investment Bank to take account of the adoption of a new definition of the Bank's unit of account. (O.J. 1978 L199/1.)

Decision of the Board of Governors of the European Investment Bank of June 19, 1978, on the increase in the Bank's capital. (O.J. 1978 L199/3.)

1273. Employment benefits

EUROPEAN COMMUNITIES (IRON AND STEEL EMPLOYEES RE-ADAPTATION BENE-FITS SCHEME) (AMENDMENT) REGULATIONS 1978 (No. 1122) [20p], made under the European Communities Act 1972 (c. 68), s. 2 (2), and S.I. 1972 No. 1811; operative on August 27, 1978; further amend S.I. 1974 No. 908 by providing for a new method of calculation of payments based on previous earnings but with a deduction for income tax deducted from those earnings.

1274. European Assembly —constituencies. See § 877.

1275. European Assembly Elections Act 1978 (c. 10)

This Act makes provisions for, and in connection with, the election of representatives to the Assembly of the European Communities, and prevents any treaty providing for any increase in the powers of the Assembly from being ratified by the U.K. unless approved by Act of Parliament.

S. 1 states that representatives shall be elected in accordance with the provisions of this Act; s. 2 specifies the total number of representatives to the Assembly to be elected from the U.K., and how this number shall be made up between representatives from England, Scotland, Wales and Northern Ireland respectively; s. 3 deals with the method of election; s. 4 sets out certain offences of double voting; s. 5 exempts representatives to the Assembly from jury service; s. 6 provides that all treaties governing any increase in the powers of the Assembly must be approved by Parliament; s. 7 covers the meeting of consequential expenses out of the Consolidated Fund and money provided by Parliament; s. 8 is the interpretation section; s. 9 states the mode of citation, and confers powers of making subordinate legislation.

The Act received the Royal Assent on May 5, 1978, and came into force on that date.

1276. European Coal and Steel Community—merger control—national law

The Kammergericht considered a decision of the Federal German Cartel Office concerning a proposed merger between a British and a German company. The court examined the merger following the approval of the merger by the E.C. Commission under art. 66 ECSC. *Held,* such further consideration of a merger by a German court in respect of German legislation was lawful. Merger control had been removed from national jurisdiction by the ECSC only in so far as the activities of respective undertakings involved, and fell within, the coal and steel's area of concern, as defined by the Treaty. Activities outside this definition may be the subject of a prohibited merger under national legislation.

GUEST KEEN AND NETTLEFOLDS *v.* BUNDESKARTELLAMT [1978] 1 C.M.L.R. 66, Kammergericht.

1277. European Court—judgments—valuation of goods—patent process

The Finanzgericht Hamburg referred several questions under art. 177 to the European Court for a preliminary ruling concerning the interpretation of art. 3 (1) (*a*) of Reg. 803/68 EEC and of the judgment in case no. 1/77. The case involved the issue of whether the value of a patent for a process is to be included in the normal price of goods only if the process can be put into effect by the use of those goods or included in the normal price with other types of goods disregarding economic viability of the use of the process. *Held,* judgments given after a request under art. 177 ECC must be understood in the light of the grounds of the judgment. Art. 3 (1) (*a*) of Reg. 803/68 EEC should be interpreted to mean that the normal price of goods does include the value of a patent process where it is embodied in the goods. This is so where the process can only be economically used by the use of those goods.

ROBERT BOSCH GMBH *v.* HAUPTZOLLAMT HILDESHEIM (No. 135/77) [1978] E.C.R. 855, European Ct.

1278. —— procedure—intervention

The European Court considered an application by various manufacturers to intervene in an action for compensation put forward in pursuance of art. 178 EEC and second paragraph of art. 215 EEC for damages. *Held*, the applicants failed to prove a direct and present interest in any of the conclusions by one of the parties in the main action. The application was dismissed with costs.

G. R. AMYLUM N.V. *v.* E.C. COUNCIL AND COMMISSION (Nos. 116, 124 and 143/77) [1978] E.C.R. 893, European Ct.

1279. —— —— —— security

The European Court considered an application by a company who claimed the right to intervene in case 113/77. They claimed to have an interest in the result of the case. *Held*, such intervention would be allowed. The original parties should provide security for their performance of their obligation under art. 3, Reg. 1778/77 EEC. On this condition, the latter should be free from this obligation pending the final judgment in the case; this article being suspended for such period.

N.T.N. TOKYO BEARING CO. *v.* COUNCIL OF EUROPEAN COMMUNITIES (No. 113/77) [1977] E.C.R. 1721, European Ct.

1280. —— —— rectification

The European Court considered its judgment in Case 27/76 [1978] C.L.Y. 1344 in respect of clerical errors in calculation and clear slips in the judgment alleged to have been made. *Held*, two such errors would be rectified. This was permitted under art. 66 (1) of the Rules of Procedure of the European Court of Justice. This rule of procedure cannot alter a legal decision in a judgment.

UNITED BRANDS CO. AND UNITED BRANDS CONTINENTAL B.V. *v.* E.C. COMMISSION (RECTIFICATION) (No. 27/76) [1978] 3 C.M.L.R. 83, European Ct.

1281. EEC nationals—residence—employment

The Raad van State of the Netherlands considered a decision of the Secretary of State for the Ministry of Justice upholding a decision of the Chief of Police refusing to grant a further extension of the EEC residence permit issue to an Italian national. *Held*, the decision would be quashed. Residence cards issued to EEC nationals should issue for a period at at least five years on condition first that such EEC nationals are employed and secondly that their employment is expected to continue for at least one year. A one year card should be treated as valid for five.

S. A. SIMBULA *v.* STAATSSECRETARIS VAN JUSTITIE [1978] 2 C.M.L.R. 74, Raad van State of the Netherlands.

1282. EEC preferences

H.M. Customs and Excise have issued Notice No. 828 (January 1978): EEC preferences—rules of origin.

1283. Exports—export declarations—measures having an effect equivalent to a quantitative restriction

The Commission took proceedings pursuant to art. 169 EEC before the European Court of Justice for a declaration that the French Republic had failed to fulfil its obligations under the EEC Treaty, in particular under art. 34, in that it made exports of potatoes covered by subheading 07.01 A III (*b*) of the Common Customs Tariff, conditional from October 25, 1975, upon submission of an export declaration endorsed by the Fonds d'Orientation et de Régularisation des Marchés Agricoles (FORMA). *Held*, (1) apart from the exceptions provided for by Community law itself, arts. 30 and 34 EEC preclude the application to intra-Community trade of a national provision which requires, even as a formality, import or export licences or any other similar procedure. Even if, in connection with intra-Community trade, FORMA granted its endorsement without delay and for all quantities requested, and even if the object of the measure was merely to ascertain the intentions of exporters, it was a measure having an effect equivalent to a quantitative restriction on exports. In fact, the imposition of any special export formality constitutes an obstacle to trade by the delay which it involves and the dissuasive effect that it has upon importers; (2) from the end of the transitional period, the provisions of arts. 39 to 46 cannot be relied upon in justification of a unilateral derogation from the requirements of art. 34, even in respect of an agricultural product for which no common organisation of the market has yet been established; (3) therefore, by rendering exports to the other Member States of potatoes covered by subheading 07.01 A III (*b*) of the CCT, conditional since October 25, 1975, upon submission of an export declaration previously endorsed by FORMA, the French Republic failed to fulfil its obligations under art. 34.

E.C. COMMISSION *v.* FRENCH REPUBLIC (No. 68/76) [1977] E.C.R. 515, European Ct.

1284. —— monetary compensatory amounts—exchange rates—discrimination

The Tribunal Administratif de Paris referred several questions to the European Court under art. 177 EEC concerning the validity of Reg. 2042/73 involving a new system of "monetary compensatory amounts." *Held*, this regulation was not discriminatory against the plaintiff. It did not favour or affect exports or exporters prior to June 4, 1973. The plaintiff disclosed nothing affecting the validity of this regulation.

COMPAGNIE CARGILL *v.* OFFICE NATIONAL INTERPROFESSIONEL DE CÉRÉALES [1977] E.C.R. 1535, European Ct.

1285. Free movement of goods—charges having equivalent effect—phytosanitary inspections

The E.C. Commission applied to the European Court for a declaration that the kingdom of the Netherlands had failed to fulfil its obligations under arts. 12 and 16 EEC because it permitted the charging fees for phytosanitary inspections of plants exported to other member states. *Held,* these inspections were instituted by International Convention and were not unilateral measures. They were performed on a reciprocal basis by the exporting state and were designed to assist the free import of plants. Provided that the actual cost of the inspection is imposed, this does not amount to a charge having an equivalent effect to a customs duty. There is nothing to prevent institutions adopting a standard financing agreement for such inspections.

E.C. COMMISSION *v.* THE KINGDOM OF THE NETHERLANDS (No. 89/76) [1977] E.C.R. 1355, European Ct.

1286. —— trade marks—partitioning of market

The Arrondissementsrechtbank at Rotterdam referred several questions to the European Court under art. 177 EEC concerning the rules relating to the free movement of goods and art. 36 EEC. The case involved the purchase by the plaintiff, Centrafarm, of certain tablets from Britain which were marketed in the Netherlands under one of the trade marks of Centrafarm and different to that used in Britain. The question arose of whether this in the circumstances infringed EEC law. *Held*, the owner of a trade mark which is protected in a Member State is justified under art. 36 EEC (first sentence) in preventing the trade marked goods from being sold and marketed under this mark by a third party despite a previous lawful sale of the goods in another Member State under another mark also owned by the same proprietor. This may amount to a disguised restriction on trade between Member States within art. 36 (second sentence) if the object of this use of trademarks is to partition the market. The law concerning the names under which proprietary medicinal products are marketed do not affect this decision of the court: CENTRAFARM BV ROTTERDAM *v.* AMERICAN HOME PRODUCTS CORP. NEW YORK, *The Times*, October 16, 1978, European Ct.

1287. Freedom of movement—refusal of residence permit to EEC national—correct procedure

Two nationals of two different Member States of the EEC were refused French residence permits and were served with notices to leave France by the

Prefect of Alpes de Haute-Provence. They appealed on the basis that European Community law, in particular arts. 48 and 52, provided for freedom of movement within the Community by nationals of Member States, and that EEC Council Directive 64/221 of February 25, 1964, had been breached. The Directive was implemented by a French Decree of January 5, 1970. *Held*, the court would set aside the judgment of the administrative tribunal of Marseilles which dismissed the appeals against the decisions of the Prefect. S. 11 (2) of the Decree, implementing art. 6 of Directive 64/221, gives an EEC national who is refused permission to reside in France on grounds of public policy the right to state his case before a special commission. Such a person is also to be informed of the proposed refusal of a permit and the reasons for it. S. 11 (2) only provides for departure from such procedure in urgent cases. This case was not one of urgency and by omitting to inform the applicants of the proposed decisions to enable them to challenge the reasons for those decisions before the special commission, the Prefect acted in contravention of the obligations under the Decree and Directive.

Re HILL AND HOLZAPPEL [1978] 2 C.M.L.R. 554, French Conseil D'Etat.

1288. —— residence permits—identity documents

The Amstgericht, Reutlingen in the Federal Republic of Germany, referred several questions to the European Court under art. 177 EEC concerning the interpretation of arts. 7 and 48 EEC. The case arose from the fact that two Italians and one Frenchman had infringed Federal German municipal law in failing to have passports or residence documents in the case of the Italians, and failing to have a passport in the case of the Frenchman. *Held*, Member States may insist on a valid identity card and passport. This is provided for by arts. 2 and 4 of Directive 68/360. But it may not require that a person enjoying the protection of Community law should possess a " general residence permit." Where a conviction is imposed in breach of Community law the force of res judicata does not allow that conviction to be nullified; but where there is a second conviction which, unlike the first, was justified by Community law, the first conviction cannot be regarded as an aggravating circumstance. It is up to the Member State to punish those who infringe identity rules, but the penalties must not be disproportionate to the offence.

Re CONCETTA SAGULO, GENNARO BRENCA AND ADDELMADJID BAKHOUCHE (No. 8/77) [1977] E.C.R. 1495, European Ct.

1289. Harmonisation of laws—food additives

The European Court of Justice considered several questions referred to it by the Pretwa di Lodi, Italy, under art. 177 EEC, concerning the interpretation of art. 5 of Directive 74/63. *Held*, the court may not enquire into the reasons or relevance of such a reference. Even after the entry into force of this Directive, which concerns the harmonisation of the market in " Feedingstuffs (Undesirable Substances)," Member States may adopt measures against undesirable substances not in the annex, provided it is not imposed discriminatorily. Substances necessarily present in foodstuffs as a residue from previous manufacture, are to be regarded, where relevant, under the directive on undesirable substances, not under legislation on additives. Application of art. 100 EEC in respect of harmonisation of certain protective and health and safety legislation, means recourse to art. 36 EEC which is no longer necessary or justified.

CARLO TEDESCHI *v.* DENKAVIT COMMERCIALE S.R.L. [1978] 1 C.M.L.R. 1, European Ct.

1290. —— mandatory application—electrical equipment

The E.C. Commission applied to the European Court for a declaration that the Italian Republic had failed to fulfil its obligations under art. 13 of Directive 73/23/EEC concerning the harmonisation of the laws of Member States relating to electrical equipment. *Held*, Member States may not defer or postpone the implementation of a Council Directive when that Directive sets out a precise period for putting it into force within Member States.

E.C. COMMISSION *v.* ITALIAN REPUBLIC (No. 123/76) [1977] E.C.R. 1449, European Ct.

1291. Human rights—employment—discrimination

The European Court considered several questions referred to it by the Belgian Cour de Cassation under art. 177 EEC concerning the interpretation of art. 119 EEC. The case involved a rule imposed by the Belgian national airline that its air hostesses had to be compulsorily retired at the age of 40 whereas their male cabin staff performing similar duties were not treated in the same way. *Held*, art. 119 only has direct effect in respect of pay. Conditions of employment which have pecuniary consequences do not amount necessarily to remuneration. Although discrimination based on sex is prohibited by Community law and the court must ensure respect for this principle, it is covered by national employment law as regards the relationship between employee and employer. The protection of human rights that is part of Community law demands that Community law does not infringe such rights and that Community law must be interpreted so as to accord with these rights. Individuals may enforce directly effective Community legislation after time limits have expired. This includes Directive 76/207.

DEFRENNE *v.* SOCIÉTÉ ANONYME BELGE DE NAVIGATION AERIENNE (SABENA) (No. 149/77) [1978] 3 C.M.L.R. 312, European Ct.

1292. —— implied terms of EEC Treaty—forfeiture

The High Court considered an action involving the clandestine import into Britain of krugerrands from Germany and determined whether forfeiture under s. 44 (*f*) of the Customs and Excise Act 1952 was appropriate. *Held*, the European Convention on Human Rights, while being a relevant consideration, was not part of the EEC Treaty. There are no implied terms in this Treaty. There would be forfeiture and no reference under art. 177 EEC.

ALLGEMEINE GOLD UND SILBERSCHEIDEANSTALT *v.* CUSTOMS AND EXCISE COMMISSIONERS [1978] 2 C.M.L.R. 292, Donaldson J.

1293. Import quotas—licences—Taiwan

The British Ombudsman considered an accusation of maladministration alleged by a company that had an import licence for Taiwanese cloth that was not extended after the date when the licence expired. This company complained that this licence which represented an import quota allocation should have been extended to enable the cloth to be shipped from Taiwan. The Ombudsman did not uphold the complaint against the department but found that it was not unreasonable for the company to have expected that they could carry their unused quotas forward into 1977.

Re IMPORT OF TAIWANESE CLOTH [1978] 2 C.M.L.R. 587, Parliamentary Commissioner for Administration.

1294. Joint European Torus

EUROPEAN COMMUNITIES (PRIVILEGES OF THE JOINT EUROPEAN TORUS) ORDER 1978 (No. 1033) [10p], made under the European Communities Act 1972 (c. 68), s. 2 (2); operative on July 26, 1978; confers privileges on the Joint European Torus as required by Decision 78/472/Euratom of May 30, 1978.

1295. Judicial review—interest to bring proceedings—relator proceedings

The Arrondissementsrechtsbank of The Hague considered a request requiring the Government of the Netherlands to lodge an appeal with the Court of Justice for the annulment of Reg. 1111/77 EEC. *Held*, dismissing the application, that a Member State's right to appeal under art. 173 EEC against an EEC Regulation was motivated by general interest of either the EEC or that state, unlike an individual who acts in his own interest.

KONINKLIJKE SCHOLTEN-HONIG NV *v.* DER STAAT DER NEDERLANDER [1978] 2 C.M.L.R. 377, Arrondissementsrechtsbank, The Hague.

1296. Jurisdiction—appeal—enforcement of judgments

The European Court considered several questions referred to it by the Rechtbank van Eerste Aanleg, Antwerp, under the Full Faith and Credit Protocol 1971 concerning the interpretation of arts. 30 and 38 of the Brussels Convention on Jurisdiction 1968. *Held*, the phrase " ordinary appeal " contained in these articles should be interpreted to mean any appeal which is such that it may result in the annulment or the amendment of the judgment to be enforced and where there is a time limit for the appeal to be lodged. These articles should be determined by Community law, not the law of Member States.

INDUSTRIAL DIAMOND SUPPLIES *v.* RIVA (No. 43/77) [1978] 1 C.M.L.R. 349, European Ct.

1297. —— lex situs—business rental agreement

The European Court considered several questions posed by the Hoge Raad der Nederlanden under the Full Faith and Credit Protocol 1971 on the interpretation of art. 16 of the Brussels Convention on Jurisdiction 1968. *Held,* this provision grants exclusive jurisdiction in disputes relating to tenancies of immovable property to the courts of the state where the property is situated. Where the object of the tenancy agreement is the operation of a business this rule does not apply. The article does not include in the phrase " immovable property " reference to an agreement under Dutch law to rent under a usufructuary lease a retail business carried on in immovable property rented from a third party,

SANDERS *v.* VAN DER PUTTE (No. 73/77) [1978] 1 C.M.L.R. 331, European Ct.

1298. Lawyers

EUROPEAN COMMUNITIES (SERVICES OF LAWYERS) ORDER 1978 (No. 1910) [25p], made under the European Communities Act 1972 (c. 68), s. 2 (2); operative on March 1, 1979; gives effect to the EEC Council Directive of March 22, 1977, by enabling lawyers qualified in other EEC Member States to provide services in the United Kingdom.

1299. Legislation—direct applicability—subsequent national enactments

The Pretore at Susa requested the European Court of Justice to give a preliminary ruling under art. 177 EEC on the consequences of the direct applicability of Community law where the latter conflicts with national law enacted at a later date. *Held,* the national judge when applying Community law is obliged to ensure that it is put into effect fully while taking it upon himself, if necessary, not to apply any contrary provisions of national law, even where those provisions are subsequent to Community law: ITALIAN TAX AND REVENUE ADMINISTRATION *v.* S.A. SIMMENTHAL, *The Times, March* 13, 1978, European Ct.

1300. —— implementation by Member States—justification

The European Court considered an application under art. 169 EEC for a declaration that Italy had failed to fulfil its obligations under EEC Directives 71/316–318, 71/347, 349, 354, 360, 362 and 74/148 of the Council and Commission Directive 74/331 EEC. Italy put forward domestic difficulties as the explanation for this failure especially the premature end of the legislative period of the Italian Parliament. *Held,* domestic difficulties cannot justify such failure.

E.C. COMMISSION *v.* ITALIAN REPUBLIC (No. 100/77) [1978] E.C.R. 879, European Ct.

1301. The European Court considered an application under art. 169 EEC for a declaration that the Netherlands had failed to fulfil its treaty obligation by failing to put into force Directive No. 71/347/EEC. For various reasons the Netherlands had not put this Directive into force and argued that this failure had had no adverse effect on the functioning of the Common Market. *Held,* this argument cannot justify such failure.

E.C. COMMISSION *v.* KINGDOM OF THE NETHERLANDS (No. 95/77) [1978] E.C.R. 863, European Ct.

1302. The European Court considered an application under art. 169 EEC for a declaration that Italy had failed to fulfil its treaty obligation by failing to put into force Directive No. 73/23 EEC. Italy sought to justify such failure by the fact that the provisions of the Directive cannot be applied until certain community standards had been agreed and that there was no time-table for the implementation of the Directive or that existing national legislation substantially covered the subject-matter of the Directive. *Held*, none of these reasons amounted to a defence of such failure.

Re THE ELECTRICAL EQUIPMENT DIRECTIVE 1973; E.C. COMMISSION *v.* ITALY (No. 123/76) [1978] E.C.R. 460, European Ct.

1303. The European Court considered an application under art. 169 EEC for a declaration that Italy had failed to fulfil its treaty obligation by failing to put into force Directive No. 74/577 EEC and it was argued by Italy that earlier national legislation ensured the observance of the objectives of the Directive and that such failure had no adverse effect on the functioning of the Common Market. *Held*, this is no defence to failure to implement community legislation which is precise and absolute.

Re THE ANIMAL SLAUGHTER DIRECTIVE 1974; E.C. COMMISSION *v.* ITALY (No. 147/77) [1978] 3 C.M.L.R. 428, European Ct.

1304. —— **validity—retroactivity**

The European Court considered the validity of Regulation 101/77, following a reference to it by the Tribunal d'Instance, Valenciennes. The Regulation concerned monetary compensation amounts for exports from the EEC. In particular, the court was asked, inter alia, if this Regulation amended Reg. 3330/74, and whether the Commission was empowered or entitled to adopt the measure without express authorisation of the council. *Held*, Reg. 101/77 is valid. Amending legislation such as this applies to the future effects of situations arising under former law.

ANCIENNE MAISON MARCEL BAUCHE S.A. AND FRANCOISE DELINQUIGNIES S.A.R.L. *v.* ADMINISTRATION DES DOUANES (No. 96/77) [1978] 3 C.M.L.R. 133, European Ct.

1305. —— —— **locus standi—Italian imports**

A number of applicants who represented Italian traders who import motorcycles from Japan, applied to the European Court for the annulment of Reg. 1692/77 of the Council. This Regulation sets out certain transitional measures for the standardisation of import terms of Member States' imports from third countries. It included a quota for motor-cycles that might be authorised to be imported into Italy. This restriction was challenged by the applicants who claimed that it adversely affected rights they had previously acquired. *Held*, even though all the applicants might be refused an import authorisation under this Regulation, it does not give them the locus standi to challenge this law because they cannot be regarded as being individually concerned or directly addressed by the Regulation.

UNIONE NAZIONALE IMPORTATORI E COMMERCIANTI MOTOVEICOLI ESTERI *v.* COUNCIL (No. 123/77) [1978] E.C.R. 845, European Ct.

1306. National courts—bankruptcy—preferential claims—discrimination

The Court of Appeal of 's-Hertogenbosch heard the appeal of a French customs agent which had claimed in the bankruptcy of a Dutch company for sums paid to the French customs authorities on behalf of the bankrupt Dutch company. The lower Dutch court admitted the French agent's claim but denied it a right of priority as Dutch private international law did not recognise preferential rights of foreign states. The French agent argued that this constituted discrimination contrary to art. 7 EEC. *Held*, appeal dismissed. Art. 7 EEC had not been infringed. Dutch law does not give preferential rights to customs authorities of foreign states (or foreign agents subrogated to their rights) which wish to recover tax dues in the Netherlands from a bankrupt, irrespective of whether or not the foreign states have preferential rights under their fiscal laws. Nor can foreign states (or foreign agents subrogated to their rights) invoke in the Netherlands administrative rights of priority under Dutch fiscal laws since such priority rights are reserved solely to the Dutch State. Discrimination on the ground of nationality would only arise when a Dutch customs agent could invoke in the Netherlands a preferential right of the French fiscal authorities or a comparable Dutch fiscal right of priority in respect of taxes paid to the French Revenue on behalf of another party, but a French customs agent could not. This was not the case here.

KNUDEN RENOU S.A. *v.* W. J. A. BRAAT AND M. J. J. L. JANSSEN [1978] 2 C.M.L.R. 369, C.A. of 's-Hertogenbosch.

1307. —— judgment—action pending in English court—not inexcusable delay by parties. See AERO ZIPP FASTENERS *v.* YKK FASTENERS (U.K.), § 2421.

1308. —— —— registration—defect. See S.A. CONSORTIUM GENERAL TEXTILES *v.* SUN AND SAND AGENCIES, § 284.

1309. —— reference to European Court—trade names
The Bundesgerichtshof, considering an appeal from the Munich Oberlandes-gericht and applying a preliminary ruling of the European Court made follow-ing a reference under art. 177 EEC, was concerned with the use by an English defendant company of a trade name and the trade mark " Terrapin." *Held,* that this use of this word was capable of causing confusion with an established trade name and trade mark " Terranova" which belonged to a German plaintiff. Both parties were in the building manufacture industry. The former made prefabricated houses and the latter produced building materials. The court need not refer a question under art. 117 (3) EEC to the European Court where, in its judgment under an art. 177 EEC reference, it makes a ruling without expressly replying to the question asked. The mere fact that only only one alleged infringer of a trade mark is sued is irrelevant to the claim before the court, and is not arbitrary discrimination against the particular defendant.
TERRAPIN (OVERSEAS) *v.* TERRANOVA INDUSTRIE C.A. KAPFERER & Co. [1978] 3 C.M.L.R. 102, German Fed.Sup.Ct.

1310. National law—EEC Treaty—no retroactive effect
The Court of Appeal considered an appeal from a decision relieving the respondents in the appeal from the obligation to disclose certain documents relating to their position under EEC law. *Held,* the EEC Treaty has no retroactive effect to any period when Britain had not become a member. It is therefore not possible to plead the application of EEC law relating to such a period.
APPLICATION DES GAZ SA *v.* FALKS VERITAS [1978] 1 C.M.L.R. 383, C.A.

1311. Officials—accident compensation—default interest—delay
A former official of the E.C. Commission applied to the European Court for damages in respect of default interest on accident compensation paid to the applicant by the Commission 10 years after the accident. *Held,* in the circum-stances of the case, including various lengthy delays on the Commission's part, the latter must be ordered to pay default interest on the full amount of compensation paid to the applicant. This was calculated by reference to the date when the Commission failed to use its own medical service in making an assessment of loss but used the medical officer of the insurers. The interest of 8 per cent. per annum was the fixed rate applied.
LEONARDINI *v.* E.C. COMMISSION (No. 115/76) [1977] E.C.R. 735, European Ct.

1312. —— application for post—refusal to state reasons
An official of the Commission applied to the European Court to annul a decision of the Commission not to accept his application for a post of clerical officer. *Held,* there is no duty on the appointing authority to provide stated reasons for such a decision because such a statement might prejudice the candidate.
GANZINI *v.* E.C. COMMISSION (No. 101/77) [1978] E.C.R. 915, European Ct.

1313. —— contents of personal file—damages
The applicant, an official of the E.C. Commission, applied to the European Court for an annulment of an implied decision of the Commission rejecting his complaint that various damaging allegations were wrongly included in his per-sonal file. He also claimed damages. *Held,* the Commission proved to the satisfaction of the court that the allegations included on his personal file were justified by his behaviour. Thus the Commission had not infringed art. 24 of the Staff Regulations and his application for annulment and damages would be dismissed.
PIERRE GUILLOT *v.* E.C. COMMISSION (No. 43/74) [1977] E.C.R. 1309, European Ct.

1314. —— elections

Applicants, officials of the European Parliament, applied to the European Court for the annulment of elections to the Staff Committee of the European Parliament (held on March 18, 1975), because of various irregularities that had occurred in connection with the elections. *Held*, the rejection of the applicant's complaint seeking an acknowledgment of the irregular nature of the elections would be annulled and the Staff Committee disbanded (subject to any measures necessary in the interests of legal certainty).

RAPHAËL DE DAPPER *v.* EUROPEAN PARLIAMENT (No. 54/75) [1977] E.C.R. 471, European Ct.

[For interlocutory proceedings, see [1977] C.L.Y. 1294.]

1315. —— equality between officials—procedure

An official of the European Commission applied to the European Court for an annulment of the " Procedures to be implemented prior to decisions on the transfer from Category B to Category A of officials in the scientific and technical services," of decisions pursuant to these procedures and to art. 92 of the Staff Regulations. *Held*, as the provisions of this article are based on objective criteria, they cannot constitute a breach of the principle of equality between officials. Similarly, the " Procedures " have respected these criteria. The claim was therefore rejected.

JÄNSCH *v.* E.C. COMMISSION (No. 5/76) [1977] E.C.R. 1817, European Ct.

1316. —— expatriation allowance—origin and residence

An official of the E.C. Commission applied to the European Court for the annulment of the decision of the Commission, rejecting his complaints concerning his entitlement to expatriation allowance. *Held*, the period in which an application should be made may restart at any altered date. Art. 47 of the Staff Regulations of officials refers to those who continuously resided for more than six months in a place more than 25 kilometres from the seat of the Community, and art. 9 of these Regulations refers to the place where the person concerned lived permanently and was previously employed. " Place of origin " is a term of art used to determine the relevant place for annual or bi-annual travel expenses. Usually retrospective withdrawal of a wrong decision is strictly defined. Irregular payments of remuneration grants no vested rights in the recipient. There is no standard form of complaint for officials, and each complaint must be carefully considered by the Administration, who cannot be held liable for private legal costs in advising on a complaint. The latter claim may be vexatious.

HERPELS *v.* E.C. COMMISSION (No. 54/77) [1978] E.C.R. 585, European Ct.

1317. —— job competition—Commission's refusal to admit

Pending the hearing of his action for the annulment of a refusal by a Commission Selection Board to admit him to a competition, the applicant made an interlocutory application for the adoption of an interim measure under art. 83 *et seq.* of the Rules of Procedure to suspend proceedings in the competition. *Held*, dismissing the application, that the applicant had failed to make out either urgency or a prima facie case for taking such a measure, and the issues could not be prejudged by the Court; nor had he shown that the continuance of the competition proceedings would cause him irreparable damage, whereas a suspension would cause harm both to the candidates and the Commission.

AUTHIÉ *v.* E.C. COMMISSION (No. 19/78) [1978] E.C.R. 679, European Ct.

1318. The applicant, an official of the E.C. Commission, applied to the European Court for the annulment of a decision to refuse to admit him to a staff competition, of the competition itself and of the resulting appointment. *Held*, the provision that an appeal to the European Court can only be made if the person has previously made an official complaint under art. 91 (2) of the Staff Regulations does not cover decisions of a selection board. An official may prefer some duties to others, even if there is no improved financial benefit or status.

BERNHARD DIETHER RITTER VON WÜLLERSTORFF UND URBAIR *v.* E.C. COMMISSION (No. 7/77) [1978] E.C.R. 769, European Ct.

1319. —— **family allowances—remuneration**

An official of the E.C. Commission applied to the European Court for the annulment of a decision concerning certain family and dependant allowances. *Held*, art. 67 (2) of the Staff Regulations, which prohibits overlapping benefits, applies only to regular allowances which virtually comprise part of the official's remuneration. An ex gratia holiday allowance cannot be considered as an increase in the regular family allowance. Unless there are exceptional circumstances, errors and rectifications in the calculation of salaries are not grounds for claiming interest because of delay.

DEBOECK (NÉE GELDERS) *v.* E.C. COMMISSION (No. 106/76) [1977] E.C.R. 1623.

1320. A similar application to that made in Case No. 106/76 was made to the European Court by a further EC Commission official, with the same result (see § 1319).

EMER *v.* E.C. COMMISSION (No. 14/77) [1977] E.C.R. 1683.

1321. —— **interim order—staff competition**

The applicant, an official of the E.C. Commission, applied to the European Court to annul the decision of a Selection Board to refuse him admission to a certain competition. *Held*, if, in an interim order, the court allowed the tests in such a competition this would amount to a reversal of the Commission's decision and the main action would lose its purpose.

ENRICO SALERNO *v.* E.C. COMMISSION (No. 4/78R) [1978] E.C.R. 1, European Ct.

1322. —— **pensions—calculation of amount**

The applicant, a former official of the Commission, applied to the European Court of Justice for the annulment of the Commission decision of August 9, 1971, by which it refused to review the calculation of his rate of pension. He also requested the court to order the Commission, in calculating the proportional reduction of his pension for the period before the Staff Regulations came into force, to take into consideration the amount credited to his account under the previous temporary provident scheme. *Held*, application dismissed. In view of the principles governing the pension scheme established by the Staff Regulations, the Commission was justified in refusing to amend its calculation of the proportional reduction of the applicant's pension as desired by the applicant.

BRUNS *v.* E.C. COMMISSION (No. 95/76) [1977] E.C.R. 2401, European Ct.

1323. —— **periodic reports**

The applicant, a librarian at the European Parliament, applied to the European Court of Justice for the annulment of the applicant's periodic report for the period 1973/74 on the ground that the assessments made in relation to her constituted " serious acts of abuse of powers by a Director General in the performance of his administrative duties." *Held*, the application for annulment of a periodic report was admissible, as such a report is an important factor when an official is considered for promotion or takes part in competitions. Although these reports are made up of assessments which it is difficult for a court to review, that does not prevent their adoption from being vitiated for lack of authority, irregularity of form and procedure or patent error and misuse of discretionary power—defects capable of making them, unlawful. However, this application would be dismissed as the applicant had failed to establish a misuse of powers by the Director General.

MARGHERITA HEBRANT (NEE MACEVICIUS) *v.* EUROPEAN PARLIAMENT (No. 31/76) [1977] E.C.R. 883, European Ct.

1324. —— **physical unfitness—procedure**

The applicant, a probationer in the Netherlands typing pool of the European Commission, applied to the European Court for the annulment of an implied decision of the Commission involving another decision that she was physically unfit, and for compensation. *Held*, a statement of reasons rejecting in this case a complaint was deemed under art. 90 (2) of the Staff Regulations, sub-para. 4, to be the same as that for the decision which was the subject matter of an unanswered complaint, and they should be reviewed together. A decision to suspend recruitment because of physical unfitness adversely affects the employee within the meaning of art. 25 of the Staff Regulations and so reasons must be stated though with due regard to professional secrecy. In such a case, or wherever a person is gravely prejudiced by a decision, the administrative body is bound to give the person an opportunity to express his or her point of view.

MOLLET *v.* E.C. COMMISSION (No. 75/77) [1978] E.C.R. 897, European Ct.

1325. —— staff competition—effect of unauthorised disclosure—board's assessment of candidate's experience

The European Court, in rejecting an application for the annulment of a decision of the Selection Board for competition declining to accept the applicant as a candidate for an internal EEC staff competition, *held*, (1) the decision was not vitiated by an unauthorised disclosure of the decision, since it had already been taken at the time of the disclosure—even though it had not yet been committed to writing; (2) there could be no complaint about the board's assessment of whether the applicant had experience equivalent to a university degree, since it had been based on objective facts.

COSTACURTA *v.* E.C. COMMISSION (No. 73/76) [1977] E.C.R. 1163, European Ct.

1326. —— qualifications

An official of the E.C. Commission applied to the European Court for the annulment of a decision of the European Parliament refusing the applicant entry to a staff competition. *Held*, this decision, on the documents produced by the applicant, is one for the defendant to make. Where the competition is based on qualifications it is for the candidate to enclose them with the application form and it is not for the Selection Board to call for them.

ALLGAYER *v.* EUROPEAN PARLIAMENT (No. 74/77) [1978] E.C.R. 977, European Ct.

1327. —— termination of employment—temporary staff

An official of the European Parliament applied to the European Court for the annulment of a decision to terminate his contract of employment as a temporary staff member, alternatively against an implied decision contained in a letter to the same effect, or a decision that his complaint was inadmissible. *Held*, such termination of employment is expressly provided for by art. 47 of the Conditions of Employment of other servants and is contained in the contract of employment. No reasons for such termination need be given. The position of temporary staff is wholly different from permanent staff under the Staff Regulations.

SCHERTZER *v.* EUROPEAN PARLIAMENT (No. 25/68) [1977] E.C.R. 1729, European Ct.

1328. —— transfer—periodic reports

The applicant, an official in the scientific service of the European Atomic Energy Community, applied to the European Court for an annulment of certain administrative measures concerning his position and duties and for damages. *Held,* the court will consider whether a decision adversely affecting an official fully states the reasons upon which it is based. In the circumstances of the case the applicant's transfer was taken regularly in form and substance. Only the administration is responsible for the organisation of employment services and must have the power to alter the services of an employee or official. The administration also has the duty of ensuring that periodic reports are properly prepared on each official on dates set out in the Staff Regulations as such a report is an indispensable criterion of the official's assessment for administrative purposes. Damages were awarded for failure to draw up periodic reports.

JEAN-JACQUES GEIST *v.* E.C. COMMISSION (No. 61/76) [1977] E.C.R. 1419, European Ct.

[For interlocutory proceedings, see [1977] C.L.Y. 1297.]

1329. Patents—grant of licences—patentee's refusal—other licensees' disapproval

The Court of Appeal, 's-Hertogenbosch, Netherlands, on considering an appeal from a District Court of Breda, *held* that certain action by the appellant was maintaining or continuing action prohibited, under art. 85 (1) EEC, by the

E.C. Commission. The appellant, the owner of a Dutch patent, had refused to grant a licence in respect of that patent because of the disapproval of existing licensees. This had been prohibited as infringing this article by the Commission. A further refusal to grant a licence was claimed to be without regard to the disapproval of existing licensees, but the court decided that this further action imposed a heavy duty on the appellant to show it was not a continuation of the earlier action, and this onus had not been discharged.

N.V. HEIDEMAATSCHAPPIJ BEHEER *v.* ZUID NEDERLANDSCHE BRONBEMALING EN GRONDBORINGEN B.V. [1978] 1 C.M.L.R. 36, C.A. of 's-Hertogenbosch.

1330. Procedure—addition of defendant

The European Court considered a procedural point in an action for damages against the Commission. After the application was lodged, the applicant purported to extend the action against the E.C. Council. *Held,* the Rules of Procedure did not permit this change in the person of the defendant, and the Registrar of the court was ordered not to serve a reply upon the council.

HELLMUT STIMMUNG K.G. *v.* E.C. COMMISSION [1977] E.C.R. 2113, European Ct.

1331. —— interim measure—customs duties

The European Court considered an application for an interlocutory decision and the adoption of interim measures under Rule of Procedure 83 (1) of the Court, concerning art. 3 of Reg. 1778/77. *Held,* pending final judgment in the case upon a sum owed in customs duties by the applicant, the application of this article was suspended, costs also being reserved.

NACHI FUJIKOSHI CORP. *v.* E.C. COUNCIL [1977] E.C.R. 2107, European Ct.

1332. —— revision of judgment—new facts

An application was made to the European Court for revision of its judgment [1977] C.L.Y. 1303 on the grounds of discovery of a decisive fact unknown to the court and to the party claiming revision. *Held,* rejecting the application, that a subsequent judgment of another court may be considered as the discovery of a new fact but in the circumstances where this judgment merely confirmed earlier judgments and drew a foreseeable conclusion from them this did not amount to a new fact.

RAYMOND ELZ *v.* E.C. COMMISSION [1977] E.C.R. 1617, European Ct.

1333. —— withdrawal of applications

National Carbonising Co. requested the European Court of Justice for permission to withdraw its applications to the Court. This request was served on the Commission and the intervening parties who had no objection to the withdrawal. *Held,* pursuant to art. 78 of the Rules of Procedure of the Court, the applications (cases nos. 109 and 114/75) would be removed from the court Register.

NATIONAL CARBONISING CO. *v.* E.C. COMMISSION (Nos. 109 and 114/75 [1977] E.C.R. 381, European Ct.

1334. Quantitative restrictions—fixed minimum retail price—state aids

The Gerechthof, Amsterdam, referred several questions to the European Court under art. 177 EEC on the interpretation of arts. 30 to 37 and 92 to 94 EEC. *Held,* measures which are likely, inter alia, to hinder imports between Member States are within the meaning of the expression " measures having an equivalent effect to a quantitative restriction." Such a measure is a fixed minimum price although applicable without distinction to domestic and imported products as it is capable of having an effect on the marketing of imports. A short term and temporary measure of this kind infringes art. 30 despite its temporary nature. Art. 92 EEC should be interpreted to mean that a fixing of a minimum retail price by a public authority is not a state aid within the meaning of that article.

OPENBAAR MINISTERIE OF THE KINGDOM OF THE NETHERLANDS *v.* VAN TIGGELE (No. 82/77) [1978] E.C.R. 25, European Ct.

1335. —— origin of products—requirement to declare—preliminary rulings—relevance

The Tribunale of Saluzzo referred several questions to the European Court under art. 177 EEC for a preliminary ruling on the interpretation of art. 1

of Annex 1 to the Agreement between the EEC and Spain, Reg. No. 1524/70, and arts. 30 and 115 of the Treaty EEC, *Held*, the relevance of such questions referred is not for the European Court to assess. Between 1970 and 1971, the EEC/Spanish agreement was no obstacle to the application to table grapes of art. 155 EEC. Member States could continue to apply quantitative restrictions in existence prior to Reg. 2513/69 to Spanish table grapes between July 1 and December 31. Any administrative or penal measure which goes beyond what is strictly necessary for the purposes of enabling the importing Member State to obtain reasonable information of the movement of goods must be regarded as a measure having an effect equivalent to a quantitive restriction prohibited by the treaty. Asking for the country of origin on customs forms does not fall into this category but control of quality rules do not of themselves justify the requirement of documents of origin. Art. 8 of Reg. 158/66 penalises infringements without distinction as to origin of the goods. National measures which involve such distinction must be regarded as discriminatory and incompatible within art. 30 EEC.

LEONCE CAYROL *v.* GIOVANNI RIVOIRA & FIGLI [1977] E.C.R. 226, European Ct.

1336. Reference to European Court—annulment—Lomé Convention—discrimination

The European Court considered several questions referred to it under art. 177 EEC by the Cour d'Appel de Douai for a preliminary ruling concerning the interpretation of art. 62 of the Lomé Convention. A professional body, namely a Bar Council, had referred a question to the European Court but a national Court of Appeal had annulled this reference. *Held,* the European Court accepted such annulment and struck the case reference from its register. Art. 62 of the Lomé Convention has direct effect. However, nationals of signatory states are not bound to be treated as favourably as nationals of EEC Member States or as any other national of such signatory states.

Re RAZANATSIMBA (No. 65/77) [1978] 1 C.M.L.R. 246, European Ct.

1337. Regulations—interpretation—wine

The English Court of Appeal allowed an appeal by S Ltd., makers of Babycham Champagne Perry, from an order restraining them and HPB Ltd. from using in the course of trade certain expressions including " champagne," or the word " champagne " in any manner calculated to lead to confusion or deception. In the course of its judgment the court, at the invitation of counsel for the defendants, decided certain questions of Community law. *Held* (1) EEC regulations should be interpreted by reading and construing them as a whole, taking into account their objectives. If the operative language was doubtful, assistance could be gained from the recitals in the preamble, and if there was still a doubt it might be necessary to refer to the provisions of the Treaty under which the regulation was made; (2) art. 12 of reg. 817/70/EEC was concerned only with the organisation of the wine trade in the true sense and had no application to anything done by anyone not dealing in wines.

H. P. BULMER *v.* J. BOLLINGER S.A. [1977] 2 C.M.L.R. 625, C.A.

1338. Restrictive practices—cartel rules—requirement of premises

The E.C. Commission considered the rules of a Dutch trade association concerned with and controlling 80 per cent. of the distribution of bicycles in the Netherlands, involving retailers, wholesalers, assemblers and importers. *Held*, certain provisions of these rules infringed art. 85 (1) EEC and, in the circumstances, exemption under art. 85 (3) EEC would be exempted. These were, inter alia, a prohibition on firms recognised by this association from dealing with those not so recognised, certain restrictions on distribution levels and trading, and resale price maintenance. Similarly, the requirement for members to have premises in Holland was a competitive disadvantage to those not having premises.

P. DONCK *v.* CENTRAAL BUREAU VOOR DE RIJWIELHANDEL [1978] 2 C.M.L.R. 194, E.C. Commission.

133 ?. —— coal—concentration

The E.C. Commission considered submissions by the German Government concerning the authorisation of the applicant company for the acquisition of a 12·5 per cent. stake in a group of wholesale coal undertakings. *Decision:* this acquisition was authorised unconditionally despite the Federal German Government's opposition. However, this transaction between the newcomers and four existing undertakings was a concentration within the meaning of art. 66 (1) ECSC.

Re RUHRKOHLE HANDEL G.M.B.H. AND BAYERISCHER BRENNSTOFFHANDEL G.M.B.H. & Co. KG [1978] 3 C.M.L.R. 40, E.C. Commission.

1340. —— concealment of papers—search and specific delivery

The E.C. Commission considered the case of a steel undertaking that had withheld various documents when an anti-trust search was carried out on its premises by the Bundeskartellamt (the Federal German Cartel Office). Later the E.C. Commission investigators found that the documents in question were no longer on the premises. These documents concerned a suspected breach of art. 61 (1) E.C.S.C. *Held,* the Commission would make a further search at large of the premises of the undertaking and made an order for specific delivery of the documents.

Re DOCUMENTS OF STAHLWERKE RÖCHLING-BURBACH G.M.B.H. [1977] 2 C.M.L.R. D25, E.C. Commission Decision.

1341. —— concentrations—conditions

The E.C. Commission considered the acquisition by a Luxembourg steel company of 25 per cent. of the shares in a Belgian firm and all the shares in a German firm. In respect of the Belgian firm, the Luxembourg firm also commenced management financially and technically. *Decision*: the latter position brings to the Luxembourg firm control within the meaning of ECSC Decision 24/54 and the transaction was held to amount to a " concentration " within the meaning of art. 66 ECSC. In authorising such concentrations, the Commission may require a reduction of cross-shareholdings and abolition of interlocking directorships.

Re ARBED TAKEOVERS [1978] 2 C.M.L.R. 767, E.C. Commission.

1342. —— distributorship agreement

Brooke Bond Liebig Benelux N.V. concluded distribution agreements with the three main Belgian supermarket chains whereby, inter alia, each chain undertook to sell only Liebig spices, apart from its own brands, and to sell Liebig spices at the prices affixed at the time of production on condition that these prices were kept to by all other retailers. In return, Liebig undertook, inter alia, to give rebates to these chains and to guarantee them a profit. *Held*, the obligation in the agreements that the distributors sell only Liebig spices apart from spices under their own brands was reinforced by financial benefits, such as rebates, a profit guaranteed and system of resale price maintenance, and infringed art. 85 (1) EEC as it prevented the distributors from exercising their freedom of choice in respect of the purchase and resale of spices by tying them to a single supplier, except in respect of spices sold under their own brands. Further, the agreements restricted competition between spice producers by prohibiting the producers of other brands from selling their spices through these three distributors. Competition from other spice producers already established on the Belgian market would be seriously impeded by these agreements, and potential competition from producers wishing to penetrate the market would be frustrated further, particularly in view of Liebig's important position on the Belgian market. These restrictions on competition had a significant effect on trade between Member States. Thus, the Commission ordered the undertakings concerned to terminate the infringement of art. 85 (1) EEC.

THE COMMUNITY *v.* BROOKE BOND LIEBIG (No. 78/172) [1978] 2 C.M.L.R. D116, E.C. Commission Decision.

1343. —— dominant position

The E.C. Commission considered certain clauses in agreements between associations of growers and associations of dealers in vegetables and certain decisions by a dealers' association relating to access to vegetable auctions in Brittany. *Held,* a " cease and desist " order for rescission of these clauses would be issued. The following infringed art. 85 (1): first, agreements between producers and dealers requiring dealers to obtain all their supplies at certain auctions; secondly, a requirement for a dealer to have a packing station within a certain distance of the auction; thirdly, the requirement that to join such a dealers' association needed the consent of the majority of the Board of Directors of the association; fourthly, the requirement that dealers must purchase work and despatch goods on their own account only where the association or organisation has monopoly access to one of the auctions. The exemption from art. 85 (1) in art. 2 (1) of Reg. 26 does not apply to agreements between farmers' associations and dealers or to decisions made by dealers' associations alone.

GROUPEMENT D'EXPORTATION DU LEON *v.* SOCIÉTÉ D'INVESTISSEMENTS ET DE COOPERATION AGRICOLES [1978] 1 C.M.L.R. D66, E.C. Commission Decision.

1344. —— —— abuse—banana market

The European Court considered an application by United Brands Company to set aside a decision of the E.C. Commission for infringement of arts. 85 & 86 EEC, for moral damages, cancellation or reduction of the fine imposed by the Commission, and costs. This company is the largest group in the world banana market. *Held*, in determining the existence of a dominant position under art. 86 EEC, the court would have regard to the particular features of the product in question; the geographical area in which it is marketed; and the interchangeability of the product with other similar products, in this case bananas with other fruit. Having the ability to adjust supplies and prices indicates a limitation of competition. For this article's requirements, the undertaking must have a substantial part of the market though 40 to 45 per cent. share is not automatically enough and be in a position where effective competition can be prevented. Other undertakings will be included in this assessment of a dominant position if there is a close trading nexus between them such as, inter alia, the position that for 30 years the other undertaking had never attempted to act independently of the company under consideration. Where the latter sells twice as much as its competitor, and owns about 45 per cent. of the market and can impose considerable barriers to competition against new traders, it is effectively protected from competition. Its profit or loss is not computed in the assessment of a dominant position, but where customers continuously buy more from the company under consideration than to competitors, this is conclusive of this position. Various practices are an abuse of a dominant position; refusal without good cause to supply a long-standing customer; certain selective distribution actions, causing repercussions on competition between Member States; price calculation without including all the market factors; and prices without reasonable relation to the economic value of the product. The defendant must be given reasonable time in which to defend against a Commission's suit, but the particular company in this case must only have been unaware of art. 86 provisions through negligence. The fine was reduced, and each party ordered to pay their own costs.

UNITED BRANDS CO. AND UNITED BRANDS CONTINENTAL BV *v.* E.C. COMMISSION (No. 27/76) [1978] 1 C.M.L.R. 429.

[See also § 1280.]

1345. —— —— —— favouring regular customers

The European Court considered a decision of the E.C. Commission that the applicant oil companies had abused their dominant position during the O.P.E.C. oil crisis. The Commission had found that this abuse concerned a reduction of supply of petrol to the complainant that was greater than to their regular customers in the Netherlands. Held, the applicant was entitled to sue for annulment in the circumstances, particularly that the Commission decision concerned only past conduct, did not impose a fine and declared it was unlawful. The rules contained in art. 86 EEC prohibiting abuse of a dominant position continue in crisis situations, and the Commission must continue in these times to see they are observed. Favouring regular customers on such occasions is not an abuse of a dominant position.

BENZINE EN PETROLEUM HANDELSMAATSCHAPPIJ BV, BRITISH PETROLEUM RAFFINADERIJ NETHERLAND NV AND BRITISH PETROLEUM MAATSCHAPPIJ

NETHERLAND BV *v.* E.C. COMMISSION (No. 77/77) [1978] 3 C.M.L.R. 174, European Ct.

1346. —— —— —— oil industry—naphtha

The E.C. Commission reported its findings on the naphtha market for petrochemical use and the behaviour of the oil companies in the Seventh Report on Competition Policy of the E.C. Commission (1978). The purpose of the inquiry was to see if the conduct of the oil companies in the Community market was compatible with EEC competition rules. It concluded that between 1973 and 1975, following the oil crisis, there was no evidence of restrictive practices between these undertakings which infringed art. 85 EEC. Moreover, there was no evidence of abuse of any dominant position within the meaning of art. 86 EEC which called for action.

REPORT ON NAPHTHA [1978] 2 C.M.L.R. 722, E.C. Commission.

1347. —— —— —— spare parts

The E.C. Commission considered a Swedish company and subsidiaries that had a monopoly in the supply of spare parts for cash registers and refused to supply these except to its own subsidiaries and distributors. *Held,* together parent and subsidiaries should be considered an undertaking for art. 86 EEC. Such monopoly was sufficient to establish a dominant position within this article. Great Britain is a substantial part of the Common Market for the purposes of this article and such refusal without justification was an abuse of a dominant position. Similarly, it is an abuse to refuse to supply a main customer because it has the result in removing a major competitor in servicing the product. The supply of spare parts to distributors and subsidiaries only, restricts trade between Member States since a distributor in one Member State may not supply a non-distributor in another Member State. A fine was imposed.

LIPTON'S CASH REGISTERS AND BUSINESS EQUIPMENT *v.* HUGIN KASSA-REGISTER AB AND HUGIN CASH REGISTERS [1978] 1 C.M.L.R. D19, E.C. Commission Decision.

1348. —— electronic equipment—imposition of uniform technical standards and licensing provisions

The Commission considered agreements that Philips GmbH had made with undertakings in the consumer electronics industry whereby those undertakings agreed to adopt Philips' video cassette recorder (VCR) system and to observe uniform technical manufacturing standards for the VCR system. After receiving the Commission's statement of objections, the parties had informed the Commission that the agreements had been cancelled and requested a termination of proceedings. The Commission delivered a decision on these notified agreements despite the parties' request for them to desist, as in its opinion there was still a clear interest in establishing whether the restrictive practices in issue did fall within art. 85 (1) EEC. *Held,* the agreements fell within art. 85 (1) as they restricted competition within the EEC in that (1) the parties were required to observe the uniform technical standards for the manufacture of VCR equipment which meant that they were obliged to manufacture and distribute only cassettes and recorders conforming to the V.C.R. system licensed by Philips. They were prohibited from changing to manufacturing or distributing competing video cassette systems during the period of the agreements; (2) licensing provisions in the agreements provided that the parties granted each other royalty-free, non-exclusive and non-transferable licences under certain of their patents and patent licences, but that where a party terminated its agreement it forfeited the licences it had by virtue of being a party to the agreement while the remaining parties retained their licences under the patents of the terminating party.

Re AGREEMENTS ON VIDEO CASSETTE RECORDERS (No. 78/156) [1978] 2 C.M.L.R. 160, E.C. Commission Decision.

1349. —— ECSC—joint buying agency

The E.C. Commission considered a joint buying agreement between 14 Italian steel undertakings. These produced almost 40 per cent. of the electric-furnace steel and 16·5 per cent. of the crude steel in Italy. *Held,* this agreement infringed and was prohibited by art. 65 (1) ECSC. The offending parts of the agreement included the sharing of products and sources of supply by co-ordination of purchases of pre-reduced iron ore through a joint buying agency, and also the controlling of investment in, and production of, pre-reduced iron ore through the agency.

Re THE CONSORZIO ITALIANO DEI MINERALI PREVIDOTTI S.P.A. (COIMPRE) [1978] 1 C.M.L.R. D1.

1350. —— exchange of information

The E.C. Commission considered the situation of the exchange of commercial information concerning a whole industry where individual undertakings were not identified, and secondly, where there was such an exchange between named firms, usually confidentially. Further, it considered an agreement involving the spontaneous notification to all participants of all significant information on prices, in this case in the manufacturers of printing paper and stationery in the Netherlands and Belgium. *Held*, while the first situation prima facie did not distort and restrict competition, the second and third did, and therefore infringed art. 85 (1) EEC. Artificially created markets based on abnormally shared information and eliminating certain risks are incompatible with the EEC treaty. Exemption would not be granted under art. 85 (3) EEC in this case.

Re THE VEREENIGING VAN NEDERLANDSCHE PAPIERFABRIKANTEN (VNP) AND THE ASSOCIATION DES FABRICANTS DE PATES PAPIERS ET CARTONS DE BELGIQUE (COBELPA) [1977] 2 C.M.L.R. D28, E.C. Commission Decision.

1351. —— exclusive dealing agreement—export prohibition clause

M Co., a producer and supplier of sound recordings, brought an action under art. 173 EEC to annul a Commission Decision of December 1, 1976, which declared that certain restrictions on the export of records, tapes and cassettes, inserted by M Co. in an exclusive dealing agreement and in its terms and conditions of sale, infringed art. 85 (1) EEC and which fined M Co. 70,000 units of account. M Co. argued that the restrictions did not appreciably affect trade between Member States, and thus did not infringe art. 85 (1), in view of its insignificant position on the market in sound recordings, the nature of its products which are mainly intended for the German-speaking public and the nature of its customers. *Held*, application dismissed. The clauses prohibiting exports were such as to affect trade between Member States and infringed art. 85 (1) as, inter alia, (1) M Co.'s position on the market, if not strong, was of sufficient importance for its behaviour to be, in principle, capable of affecting intra-Community trade; (2) once it was established that M Co. had exported a minor part of its production to other Member States it was unnecessary to establish the extent to which M Co.'s production was aimed at German-speaking people. Such exports had led M Co. and certain of its customers to think them of sufficient importance to justify adopting the clauses. Furthermore the importance of M Co.'s German market led it to protect that market against the reimportation of products exported at low prices; (3) the fact that at present M Co.'s customers were not interested in effecting intra-Community trade did not mean that this state of affairs might not change from year to year; (4) it was sufficient that the export prohibition clauses were capable of appreciably affecting trade between Member States. The European Court stated that by its very nature a clause prohibiting exports constitutes a restriction on competition, whether it is drawn up on the initiative of the supplier or of the customer since the agreed purpose of the contracting parties is to isolate a part of the market. This is so even where in practice the supplier is not strict in enforcing the prohibition.

MILLER INTERNATIONAL SCHALLPLATTEN G.M.B.H. *v.* E.C. COMMISSION [1978] 2 C.M.L.R. 334, European Ct.

1352. —— exemption—specialisation

The E.C. Commission considered a specialisation agreement between a German and a French firm concerning the supply of clocks and watches. *Held*, the agreement, which had previous exemption under art. 85 (3) EEC, would be granted further exemption for 10 years in four of the agreement's aspects, namely certain mutual cessation of manufacture, supply of specialised articles at advantageous prices with the partners' trade mark in return for agreed deliveries, a restriction on third party purchases of certain specialised items, and agreed priority for marketing new articles.

Re THE AGREEMENT BETWEEN JAZ S.A. AND PETER-UHREN G.M.B.H. [1978] 2 C.M.L.R. 186, E.C. Commission.

1353. —— joint purchase—joint subsidiary

The E.C. Commission considered an agreement where the parties, various British steelmaking undertakings, agreed to allocate products and sources of supply through a joint subsidiary. Further, it was agreed to exchange price imporation for this aim. *Held*, these agreements fell within the prohibition in art. 65 (1) E.C.S.C.

Re STEELMAKING SUPPLIES [1977] 2 C.M.L.R. D58, E.C. Commission Decision.

1354. —— —— mutual transfer of orders

The E.C. Commission considered the case of certain coal wholesalers who agreed mutually to abandon voluntarily rights of direct access to various suppliers so that one or more retain the right. There was a risk that, following decline in demand, direct access to certain collieries might be lost. This scheme aimed to protect the participants' supplies of coal. In order to effect this there was a mutual transfer of orders and agreements not to sell to one another's customers. *Held*, this constituted a restriction and distortion on the normal play of competition within the meaning of art. 65 (1) E.C.S.C.

Re GERMAN COAL WHOLESALERS [1977] 2 C.M.L.R. D63, E.C. Commission Decision.

1355. —— joint venture

The Commission considered a joint venture agreement between SOPELEM and Vickers. The companies proposed to use a joint venture company as the basis for technical co-operation between them in the field of microscopy and for distributing certain of their products in the Common Market. The agreement was to last for three years and thereafter be determinable on six months' notice. *Held*, the agreement fell within art. 85 (1) EEC as it was made between competing manufacturers from two different Member States and affected trade between Member States. However, the agreement would be exempted under art. 85 (3) EEC, subject to a reporting obligation. The agreement was granted exemption as the parties would be able to develop a more comprehensive and technically advanced range of instruments more rapidly; the technology was to be shared; costs would be reduced by the standardisation of parts; each party would be able to expand on each other's distribution system and save costs and be more efficient. The reduction of costs would be of benefit to the consumer. Moreover, SOPELEM would have ceased to make microscopes, but for this agreement and a competitor on the market would have been lost. The two parties, in view of the other competitors in existence, could not eliminate competition in respect of a substantial part of the relevant products.

Re THE AGREEMENT BETWEEN SOPELEM, VICKERS & MICROSCOPES NACHET SA (No. 78/251) [1978] 2 C.M.L.R. 146, E.C. Commission Decision.

1356. The E.C. Commission considered an agreement between two British companies to develop sodium circulators for commercial fast nuclear reactors. *Held,* the agreement infringed art. 85 (1) EEC but would be granted exemption under art. 85 (2) subject to conditions. Joint ventures, provided there is unified joint control by the parties for all their activities relating to a certain product or products and despite there being no arrangements which depend for their validity or enforcement on joint ownership of a distinct company, may still constitute a joint venture proper. The Commission requested an amendment to the agreement so that the field of primary responsibility was attributed to each of the parties but without rigidly pre-determining exclusive areas of work for each party during the existence of the agreement. Where the parent companies are actual or potential competitors their participation in a joint venture is likely to impair free competition between them.

Re THE AGREEMENT BETWEEN THE GENERAL ELECTRIC CO. AND THE WEIR GROUP [1978] 1 C.M.L.R. D42, E.C Commission Decision.

1357. —— —— concentration—ECSC

The E.C. Commission considered the creation by two Italian steel producers of a joint subsidiary. To this subsidiary the original companies would transfer a proportion of their business, and the subsidiary would have 30 per cent. of its capital from one and 70 per cent. from the other. *Held,* the subsidiary was authorised under art. 66 (2) ECSC. In these circumstances the control exercised by the majority shareholder results in there being a concentration between it and the subsidiary within the meaning of art. 66 ECSC.

Re FRAMTEK [1978] 1 C.M.L.R. D17, E.C. Commission Decision.

1358. —— —— creation of business association

The E.C. Commission considered a joint venture between two undertakings in which a business association without legal personality was created. These two undertakings were competitors and had previously operated independently in various community and internal markets. However, they remained economically independent and were not holding companies. Each controlled 50 per cent. of the association created by the venture and both parties' consent was necessary for any major decision by it. *Held,* that this joint venture infringed art. 85 (1) EEC but exemption would be granted upon certain conditions under art. 85 (3) EEC. The association was found to be likely to alter the normal flow of trade having regard to the size of the undertakings involved. There was, however, no evidence of a merger. The lack of independence and the decision-making process of the association would have anti-competitive consequences because of the joint consultations which would take place.

Re DE LAVAL-STORK VOF [1977] 2 C.M.L.R. D69, E.C. Commission Decision.

1359. —— —— exclusive purchase—patent licences

The E.C. Commission considered an agreement between two undertakings dealing with the joint development of electronic control devices. *Held,* the part of the agreement which made it obligatory on one party to it to order all its supplies from the other party, infringed art. 85 (1) EEC. Similarly prohibited for the same reason was a stipulation which bound one of the parties to such an agreement so that its freedom was limited in its granting of licences to third parties under patents obtained through the joint development work.

Re THE AGREEMENT OF E.M.I. ELECRONICS AND H. JUNGHEINRICH & CO. [1978] 1 C.M.L.R. 398, E.C. Commission.

1360. —— national rules—fee for agreement notification

The Kammergericht considered an appeal against the fees charged by the Bundeskartellamt (Federal German Cartel Office) in respect of notifications by the applicant society of agreement concerning performing and broadcasting rights. Held, national and community rules in respect of restrictive practices co-exist and only when the EEC has reached a final decision must national rules avoid conflict.

GEMA *v.* BUNDESKARTELLAMT [1978] 2 C.M.L.R. 381, Kammergericht, Berlin.

1361. —— parallel exports—resale conditions

The E.C. Commission considered the pricing rules of a British undertaking which produced and marketed alcholic drink. *Held,* these rules were intended to restrict parallel exports into other EEC countries, and were prohibited as infringing art. 85 (1) ECC. No notification had been made of these rules to the Commission, thus no exemption would be granted under art. 85 (3) EEC. The objectionable restrictions were a prohibition on trade customers reselling spirits sold for delivery outside Great Britain, outside that state; also a prohibition on reselling under bond.

A. BULLOCH & CO. *v.* THE DISTILLERS CO. [1978] 1 C.M.L.R. 400, E.C. Commission.

1362. —— parallel imports—notification

The European Court considered a decision of the E.C. Commission to impose fines on a Dutch company for infringing community rules against restrictive practices. The case concerned an attempt at prohibiting parallel imports. This attempt was made by an exclusive distributor of an English supplier of goods under an exclusive trade mark. This company omitted full disclosure of relevant information when it notified the Commission of its agreement. *Held*, oral agreements which are mutually binding are agreements within art. 85 (1) EEC. Where only trade inside one Member State is affected, or between one Member State and the outside world, and inter-state trade in the Common Market is not appreciably affected, then the agreement does not infringe art. 85. An attempt by a trade mark holder to stop parallel imports and so enforce its monopoly will be regarded as an aggravating circumstance under art. 85 EEC. Full disclosure of ancillary concerted practices must be notified to the Commission under art. 15 (1) (*a*) of reg. 17 EEC.

TEPEA B.V. *v.* E.C. COMMISSION (No. 28/77) [1978] C.M.L.R. 392, European Ct.

1363. ——— ——— resale restrictions—exemption

The E.C. Commission considered various provisions in an exclusive licence agreement concerning the distribution of certain maize seed varieties in a Member State (Germany). The agreement aimed at protecting the territorial monopoly of the licensee. *Decision*, such an exclusive licence infringed art. 85 EEC Regulations in such licences which prohibit parallel imports restrict competition within the meaning of this article. The obligation upon the licensee for a national territory to fix resale prices with the licensor similarly restricts competition as does the requirement in such a licence for the purchase of two-thirds of the Member State's demand and not to produce more than one-third of that demand. Art. 2 of Reg. 26 does not apply to such licences as in the circumstances of the case a national market organisation was not involved. A restrictive agreement entered into by a state agency for agricultural research will not in the circumstances be covered by art. 90 (2) EEC. Conduct which might be harmful to the consumer cannot be a reason for the non-application of arts. 30, 34 or 85 EEC. Where exclusive propagation rights are granted by the holder of a right to breed and propagate which is given to a Community licensee this may be exempted under art. 85 (3) EEC. No exemption was however granted in this case.

Re THE AGREEMENT BETWEEN KURT EISELE AND THE INSTITUT NATIONAL DE RECHERCHE AGRONOMIQUE (INRA) [1978] 3 C.M.L.R. 434, E.C. Commission.

1364. ——— performing arts—investigation

The E.C. Commission considered the situation following the disruption by a German radio and television company of a planned world-wide broadcast by the Italian Radio and Television Organisation. The Germany company claimed that artists in the proposed Italian programme infringed exclusive contracts with it. *Decision*, artistes such as lead opera singers are undertakings within the meaning of art. 85 (1) EEC when they use commercially their performances. Where an undertaking is required to give information pursuant to a request under art. 11 of Reg. 17 it may not refuse because it is of the opinion that the agreement does not affect trade between Member States. The Germany company was required to produce certain information to the Commission.

Re UNITEL FILM- UND FERNSEH-PRODUKTIONSGESELLSCHAFT M.B.H. & CO. [1978] 3 C.M.L.R. 306, E.C. Commission.

1365. ——— price fixing—market sharing

The E.C. Commission considered a number of agreements between a British and a German-Swiss group which manufactured zip-fasteners. Together these groups dominated the Community market in zip-fasteners. Without formal decision, the parties voluntarily terminated alleged infringements. The latter had included provisions restricting licensees, freedom to fix sales prices, and agreements involving market sharing.

Re THE COMPLAINT BY YOSHIDA KOGYO KK [1978] 3 C.M.L.R. 44, E.C. Commission.

1366. ——— prohibition on export—signed circular constituting agreement

In 1975, by reason of price controls in Belgium, the prices of BMW cars were lower in Belgium than in other Member States. As a result, BMW cars were being re-exported from Belgium to other Member States which disturbed the BMW dealers in those other States because the latter's dealership agreement obliged them to provide guarantee service even on BMW cars that they had not sold themselves. On September 29, 1975, BMW Belgium sent a circular to all its Belgian dealers requesting them not to sell BMW cars outside Belgium, or to firms which proposed to sell them outside Belgium. The circular asked the dealers to agree to the proposals in the circular by signing and returning a copy of the circular. *Held*, the signed circular was an agreement within art. 85 (1) EEC, and by agreeing on the general export prohibition proposed in the circular BMW Belgium and the dealers involved were infringing art. 85 (1) and were fined. The Commission stated that where a motorvehicle manufacturer operates a distribution network based on sales by appointed dealers throughout the EEC and on concentration of sales promotion by each dealer primarily in his particular territory, and this network is reinforced by a general prohibition on exports by dealers even if the prohibition is directed at dealers in only one Member State, no particular proof is required of the extent to which appointed dealers have been dissuaded by the prohibition from selling to consumers outside their own allotted territory or would have been able to effect such sales if there had not been a prohibition.

Automobilimporte C. Heuer & MGH Motorgesellschaft mbH *v.* BMW Belgium NV (No. 78/155) [1978] 2 C.M.L.R. 126, E.C. Commission Decision.

1367. —— **resale conditions**

The E.C. Commission considered a ban on trade customers exporting Scotch whisky in bond out of the United Kingdom. This condition of resale was imposed by a Scotch whisky distilling company. *Decision*, this condition infringed art. 85 (1) EEC and no exemption would be granted. This condition effectively prevented unauthorised export. The mere fact that there was a sale by the manufacturer to European customers at a cheaper price than domestic wholesalers does not justify a formal prohibition on exports.

The Community *v.* Arthur Bell & Son [1978] 3 C.M.L.R. 298, E.C. Commission.

1368. The E.C. Commission considered various restrictions imposed by a Scotch whisky distiller on its trade customers. In particular it considered the conditions that purchasers of one brand could not resell it outside Great Britain and this condition must be included in subsales. Trade customers who buy this brand under bond may only resell or transfer it out of bond and after payment of excise duty upon removal of the product from bond. *Decision*, these conditions infringed art. 85 EEC and could not be given exemption under art. 85 (3) EEC.

Re The Notification by William Teacher and Sons [1978] 3 C.M.L.R. 290, E.C. Commission.

1369. —— **search of premises—delivery order**

The E.C. Commission considered agreements that were suspected of maintenance of local prices and of restricting interpenetration of markets. *Held*, a German association had refused to submit to investigation on its premises by E.C. representatives and the E.C. Commission would therefore issue a decision/warrant requiring not only access to the said premises but also, inter alia, delivery up of certain records of its relation with other associations.

Re The Business Records of the Vereinigung Deutscher Freiform-schmieden [1978] 1 C.M.L.R. D63, E.C. Commission Decision.

1370. —— **territorial limits—market sharing**

The E.C. Commission considered a territorial market-sharing clause in a notified contract between an English and a French company, concerned with the manufacture of precision devices for the armed forces and the off-shore oil industry. *Decision*: as the parties were actual and potential competitors, and each being of significant importance in its own country, the agreement which imposed territorial limitations involved mutual agreement not to engage in production or sale of products in each other's country of origin, namely France and Britain, infringed art. 85 (1) EEC. It could not be exempted under art. 85 (3) because this agreement was contrary to a principal objective of the EEC treaty.

Re The Notification by the Société Nationale des Poudres et Explosifs (SNPE) and Leafields Engineering [1978] 2 C.M.L.R. 758, E.C. Commission.

1371. —— **trade fair regulations—trade association**
    The E.C. Commission considered various provisions in the regulations of a motor trade association. These governed international exhibitions and included the stipulations, first, that vehicle manufacturers were prohibited from participating in such exhibitions not listed in the Association's Calendar, and secondly, that for any infringement of the rules a less favourable or a smaller stand may be allocated to the firm responsible in the country where the breach occurred. *Held*, these rules restricted competition within the meaning of art. 85 EEC.
    Re THE APPLICATION OF THE INTERNATIONAL PERMANENT BUREAU OF MOTOR MANUFACTURERS (B.P.I.C.A.) [1977] 2 C.M.L.R. D43, E.C. Commission Decision.

1372. —— **trade marks—licencees—exemption**
    The E.C. Commission considered certain conditions imposed on licensees of the trade mark and manufacture of the drink Campari. *Held*, these infringed art. 85 (1) EEC but would be exempted under art. 85 (3). The exclusivity of these licences and the obligation on licence holders not to sell competing products were restrictions on competition as was, inter alia, a ban on active sales outside certain territories. An export ban outside the EEC did not so infringe art. 85 (1). Similarly permissible was a requirement aimed at quality control that, inter alia, the licensee must follow the licensors instructions as to manufacture. Community law does not compel a licensor to reveal trade secrets to its licensee. A prohibition on assignment of the licence is permissible. In granting exemption, the Commission required to be notified of any relevant arbitral awards.
    Re THE AGREEMENTS OF DAVIDE CAMPARI-MILANO SpA [1978] 2 C.M.L.R. 397, E.C. Commission.

1373. —— —— **market sharing agreement**
    J. C. Penney Co. Inc. made an application to the Commission for negative clearance of an agreement settling litigation between it and Associated British Foods and others. Prior to the settlement, the parties had conflicting trade names and trade marks in a number of EEC Member States. The settlement was made on the basis, inter alia, that each side had exclusive right to one set of marks throughout the Common Market. *Held*, a settlement of litigation was an " agreement " within the meaning of art. 85 (1), but that in the circumstances of this case, it did not violate art. 85 (1).
    Re PENNEY'S TRADE MARK [1978] 2 C.M.L.R. D100, E.C. Commission Decision.

1374.   The E.C. Commission considered the position of two undertakings who exclusively used the same trade mark in different Member States. *Held*, that the two undertakings operated a geographical market-sharing agreement infringing art. 85 (1) EEC. However, an agreement between them permitting the circulation and marketing of these products, which had a common origin although the mark was in different colours in the respective countries, was outside art. 85 (1) even if it was concerted practice.
    Re PERSIL TRADE MARK [1978] 1 C.M.L.R. 395, E.C. Commission.

1375. Road traffic—duty to keep records
    The European Court considered several questions referred to it by the Tribunal Correctionnel de Charleroi under art. 177 EEC concerning the interpretation of art. 14 of Reg. 543/69. *Held*, in the context of the situation of a sub-contractor which hired out a driver to a transport undertaking, the latter was required as an " undertaking " within the meaning of this regulation to keep and store certain driving records. The former would only be under such a duty if national legislation imposed it.
    AUDITEUR DU TRAVAIL *v.* BERNARD DUFOUR, S.A. CREYF'S INTERIM AND S.A. CREYF'S INDUSTRIAL (No. 76/77) [1978] 1 C.M.L.R. 265, European Ct.

1376. Social security—attendance allowance—discrimination
    The U.K. National Insurance Commissioner considered the claim of an Irish national, born in Ireland and widow of an Irish worker, for an attendance allowance. *Held*, the Commissioner allowing the appeal, that the Irish

widow of an Irish worker was under art. 3 (1) of EEC Reg. 1408/71 to be placed, in relation to an attendance allowance, in the same position as if she were a British national born in the U.K. Art. 3 (1) of EEC Reg. 1408/71 read in the light of EEC rules prohibiting discrimination, in particular art. 7 EEC, had the effect of placing the claimant in the same position as if she had been born in Great Britain and thus she did not have to comply with a particular residency condition required of a British subject not born in the U.K. or of a British protected person by reg. 2 (1) (*d*) of the Social Security (Attendance Allowance) (No. 2) Regulations 1975.

Re RESIDENCE CONDITIONS [1978] 2 C.M.L.R. 287, National Insurance Commissioner, U.K.

1377. —— delay—inter-state arrangements

The British Ombudsman considered a complaint that the Department of Health and Social Security had been responsible for excessive delay in dealing with a man's claim to invalidity benefit due from the Italian Ministry of Labour and Social Security. The report of the Ombudsman criticised the British authorities but principally blamed the Italian Ministry. He spoke of the need to develop a quicker arrangement for dealing with claims.

Re ITALIAN SOCIAL INSURANCE PAYMENTS [1978] 3 C.M.L.R. 28, Parliamentary Commissioner for Administration.

1378. —— family allowance—overlapping

The European Court considered several questions referred to it by the Landessozialgericht, Nordrheinwestfalen, under art. 177 concerning the interpretation of art. 79 (3) of Regulation 1408/71 EEC. The case involved a claim for family allowance for two German children whose father died and whose mother remarried and who was living with them and their stepfather in Belgium. *Held*, this Regulation applies to protect these children as it applies to survivors of a worker where the survivors take up residence in another Member State. Family allowances under this Regulation become payable by virtue of actual occupation, even if the worker concerned is no longer working. Suspension of family or orphans' allowances is only justified where there is overlapping of benefit.

LAUMANN *v.* LANDESVERSICHERUNGSANSTALT RHEINPROVINZ (No. 115/77) [1978] 3 C.M.L.R. 201, European Ct.

1379. —— migrant workers

The Hoge Raad of the Netherlands referred two questions to the European Court of Justice under art. 177 EEC concerning the interpretation of art. 12 of Reg. No. 3 and of art. 13 of Reg. No. 1405/71 governing social security for migrant workers. *Held*, both arts. prohibited the State of residence from requiring payment, under its social security legislation, of contributions on the salary received by a worker in respect of work performed in another Member State and therefore subject to the social security legislation of that State.

H.O.A.G.M. PERENBOOM *v.* INSPECTEUR DER DIRECTE BELASTINGEN OF NIJMEGEN (No. 102/76) [1977] E.C.R. 815, European Ct.

1380. —— —— changes in national legislation

A German national worked in the Netherlands at a time when the social security legislation there was of type B (benefits dependent on duration of insurance periods). She subsequently worked in Germany. The Netherlands legislation was later changed to type A (benefits independent of insurance periods. The Raad van Beroep, Amsterdam, referred to the European Court a number of questions on the interpretation of arts. 40, 45 and 46 of reg. 1408/71/EEC, arising from the refusal of the Netherlands to grant an invalidity pension. *Held* (1) a worker was not to be deprived of the right to benefits merely because at the time when reg. 1408/71 (harmonisation of national systems of social security legislation) was adopted, the national legislation in force when the worker was insured had been replaced by different legislation; (2) "legislation" in art. 45 (3) of that regulation (whereby a worker at one time subject to type A legislation is deemed still so subject if he can establish a claim to benefits in another Member State) must be widely interpreted so as

to include measures in force at the time when the risk materialised as well as measures in force at the time when the worker was subject to the legislation.
BLOTTNER *v.* BESTUUR DER NIEUWE ALGEMENE BEDRIJFSVERENIGING (No. 109/76) [1977] E.C.R. 1141, European Ct.

1381. —— —— **claimant resident in Italy**
The Tribunal du Travail, Brussels, referred two questions to the European Court of Justice for a preliminary ruling under art. 177 EEC on the interpretation of arts. 2 (1) and 10 (1) of EEC Reg. No. 1408/71. *Held,* an Italian worker who qualified for Belgian social security benefits while working in the Belgian Congo and who would be entitled to those benefits if he were residing in Belgium or in a former Belgium colony, can take advantage of the "non-residence" clause in art. 10 (1) of Reg. No. 1408/71 while he is residing in Italy. Thus, he is entitled to payment of benefit from the Belgian social security authorities.
WALTER BOZZONE *v.* OFFICE DE SÉCURITÉ SOCIALE D'OUTRE-MER (No. 87/76) [1977] E.C.R. 687, European Ct.

1382. —— —— **contributions**
The French Cour de Cassation referred several questions to the European Court under art. 177 concerning the interpretation of Reg. 1408/71. *Held,* the payment of social security contributions in the United Kingdom identifies an employed person within the meaning of art. 1 (*a*) (ii) of the Regulation. Rights acquired by a person who can be so identified must be taken into account by any other Member States as if they were periods required for the acquisition of a right under its own legislation.
CAISSE PRIMAIRE D'ASSURANCE MALADIE D'EURE-ET-LOIRE *v.* ALICIA TESSIER, NÉE RECQ. (No. 84/77) [1978] E.C.R. 7, European Ct.

1383. —— —— **entitlement**
The Cour du Travail, Mons, referred several questions to the European Court under art. 177 EEC, concerning the interpretation of art. 12 of Reg. 1408/71. *Held,* while a worker is being paid a pension under national legislation alone, this Regulation does not prevent national rules being applied to him. Where national legislation proves less favourable than the application of the rules regarding aggregation and apportionment, the latter must be applied by virtue of art. 46 (1) of this Regulation.
FONDS NATIONAL DE RETRAITE DES OUVRIERS MINEURS *v.* GIOVANNI MURA (No. 22/77) [1977] E.C.R. 1699.

1384. The Tribunal du Travail, Charleroi referred a similar question to the European Court, with a similar result to Case 22/77 (see § 1383).
GRECO *v.* FONDS NATIONAL DE RETRAITE DES OUVRIERS MINEURS (No. 37/77) [1977] E.C.R. 1711.

1385. —— —— **family allowances**
The European Court considered several questions referred to it under art. 177 by the Tribunal du Travail at Brussels. The case concerned an Italian, employed in Belgium, whose wife and children resided in Italy where his wife was employed. He claimed to be entitled in Belgium to family allowance benefits. *Held,* work undertaken in a state where the family is not residing is not something which disentitles social security benefits under the overlapping of benefit rules in reg. 1408/71 (art. 73) and the suspension under art. 76 of entitlement to such benefits is not applicable in this type of case.
RAGAZZONI *v.* CAISSE DE COMPENSATION POUR ALLOCATIONS FAMILIALES "ASSUBEL" (No. 134/77) [1978] E.C.R. 963, European Ct.

1386 —— —— **invalidity and pension insurance**
The Bundessozialgericht, Bochum, requested the European Court of Justice to give a preliminary ruling under art. 177 EEC on the question whether an Italian national living in Italy who at no time had lived or worked in the Federal Republic of Germany or West Berlin is to be treated, by virtue of art. 8 of Reg. No. 3 of the Council of September 25, 1958, and of art. 3 (1) of Reg. No. 1408/71 of the Council of June 14, 1971, on the same footing as a German national when applying para. 108 (*c*) of the Reichsknappschafts-

gesetz (law of the Reich governing social security for mine workers), so far as concerns insurance periods which were completed before 1945 with the Reichsknappschaft under the law of the Reich outside the territory of the Federal Republic of Germany or West Berlin. The Italian in question had worked in a mine in Sudetenland from 1942 to 1943. *Held,* art. 8 of Reg. No. 3 and art. 3 (1) of Reg. No. 1408/71 do not apply to benefits such as those provided for in para. 108 (*c*) of the Reichsknappschaftsgesetz in respect of periods completed before 1945 outside the territory of the Federal Republic of Germany and of West Berlin. The payment of the benefits in question to nationals is discretionary where such nationals are residing abroad and are not to be regarded as social security.

CARLO FOSSI *v.* BUNDESKNAPPSCHAFT (No. 79/76) [1977] E.C.R. 667, European Ct.

1387. —— —— overlapping benefits
The Tribunal du Travail, Charleroi referred several questions to the European Court under art. 177 EEC concerning the interpretation of art. 51 EEC and art. 46 (3) of Reg. 1408/71. *Held,* if this article is applied in such a way that it diminishes the rights and limits the benefits that persons enjoy in Member States, this is incompatible with art. 51 EEC. The overlapping of benefit rules may only apply where it is necessary to aggregate insurance periods and apportion benefits.

RENATO MANZONI *v.* FONDS NATIONAL DE RETRAITE DES OUVRIERS MINEURS (No. 112/76) [1977] E.C.R. 1647.

1388. The Centrale Raad van Beroep referred a question to the European Court under art. 177 EEC for a preliminary ruling on the interpretation of arts. 12 (2) and 46 of Reg. 1408/71 EEC. The case concerned a widow, resident in the Netherlands, who was granted a Dutch pension for widows and who was also entitled to an old age pension in the Netherlands and Germany, because of her husband's employment there. The question was to what extent this Regulation limited national rules on overlapping benefits. *Held,* the Court's judgment was the same as the second part of its decision in case 98/77 (§ 1390).

BESTUUR VAN DE SOCIALE VERZEKERINGSBANK *v.* BOERBOOM-KERSJES (No. 105/77) [1978] E.C.R. 717, European Ct.

1389. The Tribunal du Travail at Brussels refered several questions to the European Court under art. 177 EEC concerning the interpretation of art. 11 (2), Reg. 3 and art. 9 (2) of Reg. 4/EEC. The case concerned an Italian who had worked in Belgium and Italy, and who was paid benefits in both countries. Belgium relied on the rules concerning overlapping of benefits and claimed the right to reduce them retrospectively and a refund of overpayment. *Held,* the restrictions in art. 11 (2) only apply to insured persons in so far as the benefits acquired by applying those regulations are concerned. However, Reg. 3 does not preclude the application to benefits acquired by virtue of only national legislation against the overlapping of benefits. Art. 9 (2) of Reg. 4 only applies after an award following " aggregation " and " apportionment."

NASSELLI *v.* CAISSE AUXILIAIRE D'ASSURANCE MALADIE-INVALIDITÉ (No. 83/77) [1978] E.C.R. 683, European Ct.

1390. The European Court considered several questions referred to it by the Centrale Raad van Beroep of the Netherlands under art. 177 EEC, concerning the interpretation of arts. 12 (2) and 46 of Reg. 1408/71. The case involved a man who had worked from 1929 to 1933 in Germany, and had voluntarily continued German social security contributions under a special scheme for Nazi victims until 1945. From 1933 to 1972, when he became disabled, he worked in the Netherlands. His Dutch disablement pension was reduced because he was paid a larger German pension. *Held,* (1) such contributions as these German contributions that had been bought, fell within art. 46 (2) of Reg. 574/72 of the Council; (2) provided a worker is receiving a pension under only national legislation, Reg. 1408/71 does not prohibit national rules against overlapping benefits from being applied to him. If national legislation is less favourable to the individual than the rules under art. 46 of Reg. 1408/71, the latter must be applied.

SCHAAP *v*. BESTUUR VAN DE BEDRIJFSVERENIGING VOOR BANKEN VERZEKERINGSWEZEN, GROOTHANDEL EN VRIJE BEROEPEN (No. 98/77) [1978] E.C.R. 707, European Ct.

1391. ——— treatment in several Member States

The Centrale Raad van Beroep referred several questions to the European Court under art. 177 EEC for a preliminary ruling on the interpretation of Reg. 1408/71, in particular art. 22 (1) & (2). The case concerned a resident of the Netherlands who was refused by the Dutch social security institution a refund of costs for hydrotherapy incurred in the Federal Republic of Germany, despite the fact that she was entitled to invalidity benefit under Dutch legislation. *Held*, the European Court under such a reference does not adjudicate upon the relevance of the questions asked. The phrase in art. 22 (1) " who satisfies the conditions of the legislation of the competent state for the entitlement to benefits " determines the persons who in principle are entitled to benefits under national law and the phrase " the treatment in question " in art. 22 (2) (second paragraph) refers to the person's disease or sickness for which treatment is given. The phrase " benefits in kind provided on behalf of the competent institution of the place of stay or residence " do not only refer to benefits due in the Member State of residence but includes any benefits which the competent institution has the power to give. " Authorisation " within art. 22 (2) may not be refused in cases where the treatment provided in the Member State in which the person resides is less effective than that in which the person concerned can receive in another Member State. The phrase " institution of the place of stay or residence " in art. 22 (1) (*c*) (i) refers to the institution empowered to provide benefits in the state of residence as set out in Annex 3, Reg. 574/72, amended by 878/73. The costs incurred in the payment of benefits by the institution of the state of residence are to be repaid.

BESTUUR VAN HET ALGEMEEN ZIEKENFONDS DRENTHE-PLATTELAND *v*. PIERIK (No. 117/77) [1978] E.C.R. 825, European Ct.

1392. ——— overlapping benefits—unemployment and widows benefit

The National Insurance Commissioner considered the case of an Irish widow claiming unemployment benefit payable in Britain while being paid a widow's pension in Ireland. *Held*, the unemployment benefit was not subject to any adjustment under the rules on the overlapping of benefits. Such EEC rules only apply in cases where the calculation of the benefit relies upon EEC legislation which it did not in this case. The decisions interpreting art. 11 (2) of Reg. 3 EEC apply where relevant to art. 12 (2) of Reg. 1408/71 which replaces it.

Re AN IRISH WIDOW [1978] 2 C.M.L.R. 178, National Insurance Commissioner.

1393. ——— procedure—contributions—Secretary of State

The National Insurance Commissioner considered a question whether the contribution conditions for unemployment benefit were satisfied in respect of a claimant who had been working in Germany throughout the relevant period paying only German contributions. *Held*, referring this question to the Secretary of State, that such questions under s. 93 (1) of the Social Security Act 1975 should be determined by the Secretary of State and relevant questions of EEC law should, after examination by the Commissioner, be similarly determined.

Re WORK IN GERMANY [1978] 2 C.M.L.R. 169, National Insurance Commissioner.

1394. ——— ——— place of claim

The National Insurance Commissioner considered the case of an Italian who made a claim for sickness benefit in Italy. He had paid some contributions in Britain and Italy. *Held*, the claim made in Italy would, in the circumstances, be treated as a claim made in Britain after it had been forwarded by the

Italian authorities. However, the claim was dismissed as inadequate contributions had been paid to qualify for benefit.

Re An Italian Claimant [1978] 2 C.M.L.R. 331, National Insurance Commissioner.

1395. —— reimbursement of social security contributions

The Landessozialgericht of Nordrhein-Westfalen referred several questions to the European Court of Justice under art. 177 concerning the interpretation of Reg. No. 3 and Reg. No. 1408/71 with a view to determining their effect, if any, on the reimbursement of social security contributions. *Held*, (1) the reimbursement of social security contributions comes within the scope of Reg. No. 3 and art. 4 of Reg. No. 1408/71; (2) provided the conditions laid down by the applicable national legislation are fulfilled, Reg. No. 3 does not prevent the reimbursement of social security contributions by reason of the fact that the individual involved falls within the ambit of another social security scheme after moving residence to another Member State; (3) under the system established by Reg. No. 3, the objectives pursued by the Treaty and by the Reg. itself did not justify the refusal of the reimbursement of social security contributions to a person who could claim the benefit of such reimbursement under a national legislation.

Gerda Jansen *v.* Landesversicherungsanstalt Rheinprovinz (No. 104/76) [1977] E.C.R. 829, European Ct.

1396. —— voluntary or optional continued insurance

The Tribunal du Travail, Charleroi asked the European Court of Justice for a preliminary ruling under art. 177 EEC on the interpretation of art. 9 (2) of Reg. No. 1408/71 of the Council of June 14, 1971. *Held*, the expression " voluntary or optional continued insurance " in art. 9 (2) of Reg. No. 1408/71 covers assimilation to periods of employment for the purposes of insurance for periods of study, whether or not there is any continuation of existing insurance.

Fernand Liègeois *v.* Office National des Pensions pour Travailleurs Salariés (No. 93/76) [1977] E.C.R. 543, European Ct.

1397. —— sickness benefit—contributions—Member States

The High Court, Queen's Bench Division referred several questions under art. 177 EEC to the European Court concerning the interpretation of art. 45 of reg. 1408/71. *Held*, this article requires that, where the right to invalidity benefit is dependent on sickness benefit only payable after completed insurance periods, such periods completed in one Member State must be treated as if completed in the Member State where a claim is made. Where such a claim must be made in a prescribed manner and time, a claim made properly in the State of residence will be sufficient. To this effect art. 36 of Reg. 574/72 will be read together with art. 51 E.E.C.

R. *v.* National Insurance Commissioner, *ex p.* Warry (No. 41/77) [1977] 2 C.M.L.R. 783, European Ct.

1398. —— —— disqualification

The National Insurance Commissioner referred several questions to the European Court under art. 177 (2) concerning an Irishman's claim for sickness benefit while he was in or near an Irish prison. Imprisonment disentitled claimants in English law. The questions posed were whether art. 7 EEC had direct effect and whether such a national rule infringed art. 19 (1) (*b*) or 22 (1) (*a*), Reg. 1408/71. *Held,* a national court need not have exhausted all possibility of deciding a case under national law before referring a case to the European Court.

Kenny *v.* Insurance Officer [1978] 1 C.M.L.R. 181, National Insurance Commissioner.

1399. —— unemployment—aggregation of insurance periods

The European Court considered the interpretation of art. 67 (1) of Regulation 1408/71 EEC, following a reference by the Belgian Cour de Cassation under art. 177 EEC. An Italian woman had worked 15 years in Italy and three months in Belgium. She became unemployed in Belgium and claimed benefit, despite a requirement there that she should have completed 22 months'

employment before being entitled to claim. *Held*, that the periods of employment in Italy should be included in the assessment in Belgium, provided the
employment in Italy was recognised by Italy as an insurance period(s). This
is so notwithstanding the proviso in art. 67 (1), Reg. 1408/71.

FRANGIAMORE *v.* OFFICE NATIONAL DE L'EMPLOI (No. 126/77) [1978] 3
C.M.L.R. 166, European Ct.

1400. —— —— failure to register

The National Insurance Commissioner considered a claim by an unemployed
Englishman who sought work in Germany for three months. He did not sign
on in Germany with the unemployment authority there, as required by Reg.
1408/71 (art. 69). *Decision*: this man was not entitled to unemployment benefit
during these three months, even though the fault was caused by bad advice
given by the English unemployment benefit office.

Re AN ABSENCE IN GERMANY [1978] 2 C.M.L.R. 603, National Insurance
Commissioner.

1401. —— —— search for work—reference to European Court

The National Insurance Commissioner considered a claim of an unemployed
person registered as such in Britain who went to look for work in Eire for
five days. *Held*, that this action did not disqualify him from benefit in Britain
for the period of absence by virtue of art. 69 of Reg. 1408/71. Because of
the small amount involved the Commissioner did not feel justified in making
a reference under art. 177 (2) despite the fact that he would have been
grateful for such assistance.

Re SEARCH FOR WORK IN IRELAND [1978] 2 C.M.L.R. 174, National Insurance
Commissioner.

1402. State aids—charges having an equivalent effect

The Verwaltungsgericht of Frankfurt-am-Main referred several questions to
the European Court of Justice for a preliminary ruling under art. 177 concerning the interpretation of arts. 9, 12, 13, 92, 93 and 95 of the EEC Treaty. The
questions arose out of proceedings whereby a German undertaking disputed
charges levied on it by the German Government (represented by the Bundesamt
für Ernährung und Forstwirtschaft) in respect of the processing of citrus
concentrates imported from Italy and third countries as being incompatible
with Community law. The charges being used to aid German agriculture,
food and forestry industries. *Held*, (1) art. 93 does not preclude a national
court from asking the European Court of Justice for a preliminary ruling
on the interpretation of art. 92. However, in the absence of implementing provisions within the meaning of art. 94, a national court does not have
jurisdiction to decide an action for a declaration that existing aid which has
not been the subject of a decision by the Commission requiring the Member
State to abolish or alter it, or a new aid which has been introduced in accordance with art. 93 (3), is incompatible with the Treaty; (2) except for the
reservation in art. 90 (2), art. 92 applies to all private and public undertakings
and to their entire production; (3) the prohibition in art. 92 (1) covers all
aid granted by a Member State or through State resources, no distinction
being made as to whether the aid is granted directly by the State or by
public or private bodies established or appointed by it to administer the
aid; (4) a measure adopted by the public authority and favouring certain
products or undertakings does not cease to be a gratuitous advantage by the
fact that it is wholly or partially financed by contributions exacted from the
undertakings concerned by the public authority; (5) where a Member State
infringes an obligation under the Treaty in connection with the prohibition in
art. 92, it is no justification that other Member States likewise fail to fulfil
that obligation; (6) where a charge satisfies the conditions characterising effects
equivalent to customs duties, the fact that it is applied at the stage of marketing or processing of the product after it has crossed the frontier is irrelevant
when the product is charged solely by reason of its crossing the frontier, which
factor excludes the domestic product from similar taxation; (7) there is,
generally, no discrimination such as is prohibited by art. 95 where internal
taxation applies to national products and to previously imported products on

their being processed into more elaborate products where there is no distinction between them as to rate, basis of assessment or conditions of payment by reason of their origin.

FIRMA STEINIKE UND WEINLIG v. FEDERAL REPUBLIC OF GERMANY (No. 78/76) [1977] E.C.R. 595, European Ct.

1403. —— **incompatibility with Community provisions**

The Pretore of Milan referred several questions to the European Court for a preliminary ruling under art. 177 concerning the interpretation of arts. 30, 92, 93 & 95 of the EEC Treaty. *Held*, (1) art. 30 has direct effect and creates individual rights, as from the end of the transitional period at the latest, which the national courts must protect; (2) the aids referred to in arts. 92 & 93 of the EEC Treaty do not as such fall within the scope of the prohibition of quantitative restrictions on imports and measures having equivalent effect laid down by art. 30, but the aspects of aid which are not necessary for the attainment of its object or for its proper functioning and which contravene this prohibition may for that reason be held to be incompatible with this provision; (3) the fact that an aspect of aid which is not necessary for the attainment of its object or for its proper functioning, is incompatible with a provision of the Treaty other than arts. 92 and 93 does not have the effect of making the aid as a whole void nor of rendering the system for financing that aid illegal; (4) since art. 95 refers to internal taxation of any kind, the fact that a tax or levy is collected by a body governed by public law other than the State, or is collected for its benefit, and is a tax charge which is special or appropriated for a specific purpose cannot prevent its falling within the scope of art. 95; (5) in applying art. 95, account should be taken not only of the rate of internal taxation imposed directly or indirectly on national and imported products but also the basis of assessment and the detailed rules for the imposition of tax. If differences in this respect result in the imported product being taxed at the same stage of production or marketing at a higher rate than the similar national product, the prohibition of art. 95 is infringed; (6) it is for the national court to decide whether the whole of any internal taxation which is discriminatory within the meaning of art. 95 or only that part of it which exceeds the tax assessed on the national product is not payable.

IANNELLI & VOLPI S.P.A. v. DITTA PAOLO MERONI (No. 74/76) [1977] E.C.R. 557, European Ct.

1404. Trade—imports—disguised prohibition

The Gerechtshof at Amsterdam considered an appeal from the Amsterdam District Court concerning the application by the Dutch of a prohibition against additives in cheese made to certain imported French cheeses. *Held*, there was no danger to health by these additives. Therefore to apply this prohibition, which mainly affected imported food from other Member States, constitutes a disguised prohibition on imported food and was unlawful under arts. 30 and 36 EEC.

GERDABEL NEDERLAND B.V. v. THE STATE [1978] 3 C.M.L.R. 336, Gerechtshof, Amsterdam.

1405. Trade marks—parallel imports—reference to European Court

The District Court in Rotterdam considered a dispute involving the repacking by an importer into Holland of British-made pills and the re-labelling of them with the British trade mark and with the importer's name. The situation concerned parallel imports and was similar to *Hoffmann-la Roche & Co. A.G. v. Centrafarm G.m.b.H.* [1977] C.L.Y. 1264 and [1978] C.L.Y. 1406. *Held*, the question of breach of the trade mark holders' rights depends upon the interpretation of art. 30 EEC. Where a question similar in substance to that before the court has been referred under art. 177 EEC to the European Court, proceedings would be stayed pending a decision in that case.

THE BOOTS CO. v. CENTRAFARM B.V. [1978] 3 C.M.L.R. 256, Rotterdam District Ct.

1406. —— **repacking—inter-state trade—dominant position**

The European Court considered several questions referred to it by the

Landgericht Freiburg under art. 177 EEC. The case concerned the import into Germany of pills manufactured in Britain which were repacked and relabelled in Germany with their British trade mark. *Held*, the court interpreted arts. 30 and 36 EEC so that, whereas the function of a trade mark is to ensure the identity of origin of the product to purchasers, the subject matter which includes this function is the guarantee to the owner of the trade mark of the exclusive right of marketing of the product for the first time and so protects him from competitors. Art. 36 (1) EEC permits a proprietor to stop the repacking and labelling with his trade mark by an importer without his authorisation. However, this article permits an importer to do so without permission if it is established that the use of the trade mark will, in the circumstances, contribute to the artificial partitioning of the markets between Member States, that repacking will not be detrimental to the product, that the trade mark owner is notified and that the new packing states that it has been repacked. Where the use of a trade mark is lawful under art. 36, it is not deemed contrary to art. 86 because the user has a dominant market position.

HOFFMANN LA ROCHE & CO. AG AND HOFFMANN-LA-ROCHE AG *v.* CENTRAFARM VERTRIEBSGESELLSCHAFT PHARMAZEUTISCHER ERZEUGNISSE MBH (No. 102/77) [1978] 3 C.M.L.R. 217, European Ct.

1407. Transport

COMMUNITY ROAD TRANSPORT RULES (EXEMPTIONS) REGULATIONS 1978 (No. 1158) [20p], made under the European Communities Act 1972 (c. 68), s. 2 (2); operative on August 17, 1978; give effect to exemptions, in respect of certain national transport operations, from provisions of Council Reg. 543/69 (relating to ages, and hours and conditions of work, of drivers) and of Council Reg. 1463/70 (recording equipment).

1408. Treaties, conventions and regulations

EUROPEAN COMMUNITIES (DEFINITION OF TREATIES) ORDER 1978 (No. 617) [10p], made under the European Communities Act 1972 (c. 68), s. 1; operative on dates to be published; declares specified treaties to be Community Treaties as defined in s. 1 (2) of the 1972 Act.

EUROPEAN COMMUNITIES (DEFINITION OF TREATIES) (No. 2) ORDER 1978 (No. 618) [10p], made under the European Communities Act 1972, s. 1; operative on a date to be published; declares specified treaties to be Community Treaties as defined in s. 1 (2) of the 1972 Act.

EUROPEAN COMMUNITIES (DEFINITION OF TREATIES) (No. 3) ORDER 1978 (No. 619) [19p], made under the European Communities Act 1972, s. 1; operative on a date to be published; declares specified treaties to be Community Treaties as defined in s. 1 (2) of the 1972 Act.

EUROPEAN COMMUNITIES (DEFINITION OF TREATIES) (No. 4) ORDER 1978 (No. 781) [10p], made under the European Communities Act 1972, s. 1; operative on a date to be published; declares the specified Treaty relating to elections by universal suffrage to the European Assembly to be a Community Treaty.

EUROPEAN COMMUNITIES (DEFINITION OF TREATIES) (No. 5) (JOINT EUROPEAN TORUS) ORDER 1978 (No. 1032) [10p], made under the European Communities Act 1972, s. 1; operative on July 26, 1978; declares the Exchange of Letters dated May 3, 1978 between the U.K. and the European Atomic Energy Community regarding privileges to be granted to the Joint European Torus to be a Community Treaty as defined by s. 1 (2) of the 1972 Act.

EUROPEAN COMMUNITIES (DEFINITION OF TREATIES) (No. 6) (INTERNATIONAL DEVELOPMENT ASSOCIATION) ORDER 1978 (No. 1103) [10p], made under the European Community Act 1972, s. 1; operative on a date to be notified in the *London Gazette*; declares the Agreement of May 2, 1978, between the EEC, its member states and the International Development Association to be a community treaty as defined in the 1972 Act.

EUROPEAN COMMUNITIES (DEFINITION OF TREATIES) (No. 7) (INTERNATIONAL WHEAT AGREEMENT) ORDER 1978 (No. 1104) [10p], made under the European Communities Act 1972, s. 1 (3); operative on a date to be notified in the *London Gazette*; declares the 1978 Protocols for the Fourth Extension of the Wheat Trade Convention and the Food Aid Convention constituting International Wheat Agreement 1971 (Cmnd. 4953), to be community treaties as defined in the 1972 Act.

1409. Treaty—import of obscene publications—evasion. See R. *v.* HENN; R. *v.* DARBY, § 562.

1410. Weights and measures—wine and grape must. See § 1500.

BOOKS AND ARTICLES. See *post,* pp. [4], [22].

EVIDENCE

1411. Admissibility—discretion of trial judge—affidavit relating to domicile

The debtor, served with a petition in bankruptcy, gave notice that he disputed the court's jurisdiction on the grounds of his domicile in Spain. He sought, however, to give evidence in the proceedings by way of affidavit. The petitioning creditor sought a direction that his affidavits should not be admitted if he failed to attend for cross-examination. The court refused to anticipate the exercise by the trial court of its discretion whether to admit the affidavit or not which should be exercised at the time of trial in the light of all the relevant circumstances: *Re* ROSS (A DEBTOR) (1978) 122 S.J. 680, C.A.

1412. —— welfare officer's report—hearsay material. See *Re* HOGUE AND HAINES (FORMERLY HOGUE), § 1989.

1413. —— " without prejudice "—communications before writ—infringement of trade mark and passing off actions. See CHOCOLADEFABRIKEN LINDT & SPRUNGLI A.G. *v.* NESTLÉ CO., § 2960.

1414. —— witness's statement—made some time after events—rule of practice only

[Fugitive Offenders Act 1967 (c. 68), s. 7.] In an application for extradition under s. 7 of the Fugitive Offenders Act 1967, the magistrate admitted depositions made by witnesses, notwithstanding that those witnesses had refreshed their memories by referring to statements made a month or more after the events recorded. *Held,* that the English rule that such statements must be made very shortly after the event if they were to be used for such a purpose was a rule of practice only, not of substance; accordingly the magistrate was not obliged to follow it and was entitled to admit the depositions: *Re* MILLER, *The Times,* October 25, 1978, D.C.

1415. Affidavit—admissibility—Beddoe proceedings—whether privileged—waiver

There is no general principle that privilege attaches to an affidavit filed in *Beddoe* proceedings so that it cannot be referred to in subsequent litigation.

In 1961 W granted G an option to purchase his farm at a fixed price; the option was not registered. In 1967 W conveyed the farm to E, his wife, for £500. When G soon thereafter gave notice exercising the option, neither W nor E complied. Two years after E's death, G commenced proceedings against her executors, W and D (G also being an executor) claiming, inter alia, specific performance of the option; by amendment G also claimed damages for conspiracy against W personally and E's estate on the grounds that the 1967 conveyance was a sham intended to defeat his option. By a *Beddoe* summons, W and D as executors sought directions on the litigation; for that purpose W filed an affidavit disclosing that the purpose of the conveyance had been to defeat G's option. W showed the affidavit to G. Later, on discovery, D disclosed W's affidavit in his list of documents with no claim of privilege. G's reply in his action relying on the admission in the affidavit was struck out on the grounds that the affidavit was privileged. By the time of trial W had died, his personal repersentatives being joined as defendants, as had G. G's personal representatives wished to introduce the affidavit in evidence. *Held,* that (1) the plaintiffs were not estopped *per rem judicatam* from producing the affidavit in evidence; (2) it offended against the right of a party to refer to any filed document for the affidavit to be treated as confidential; (3) in any event W, by showing the affidavit to G, and D, by including it in his list of documents, had waived any privilege; (4) W's estate was liable in damages for conspiracy in the light of the admission in W's affidavit); (5) G's claim in tort against E's estate was time-barred, having been commenced more than six months after the grant of representation; and (6) the claim for specific performance against E's estate failed as the conveyance had been for valuable, if inadequate consideration. (*Re Moritz* [1959] C.L.Y. 2591 considered.)

MIDLAND BANK TRUST CO. *v.* GREEN [1978] 3 All E.R. 555, Oliver J.

1416. —— contents—possession action by mortgagee
[R.S.C., Ord. 88, r. 6 (3) (4).]

The words " the amount of repayments " in R.S.C., Ord. 88, r. 6 (3) (*b*) mean the amount of repayments of principal made under the mortgage down to the date of the affidavit.

The building society sought possession of a house charged to them by way of legal mortgage. The branch manager swore an affidavit in support of the claim, giving the amount of the money advanced, the balance outstanding at that date, the monthly instalment of interest and the amount of arrears of interest at the date of the summons and at the date of the affidavit. A copy of the legal charge was exhibited thereto. The affidavit further stated: " I am informed and verily believe that the owner and his family were the only persons in occupation." The summons was adjourned to court for determination of whether R.S.C., Ord. 88, r. 6 (3) (*b*) required a statement in the affidavit of the total amount of repayments made under the legal charge and whether the statement of information and belief sufficiently complied with Ord. 88, r. 6 (4). *Held* that (1) the affidavit should have stated the amount of principal repaid under the mortgage; (2) since the order sought was a final order, the affidavit had to comply with Ord. 41, r. 5 (1) and therefore it had to contain only facts that the deponent could prove; accordingly the affidavit should contain an unqualified assertion of the building society's knowledge in accordance with R.S.C., Ord. 88, r. 6 (4).

NATIONWIDE BUILDING SOCIETY *v.* BATEMAN [1978] 1 W.L.R. 394, Goulding J.

1417. Blood tests
BLOOD TESTS (EVIDENCE OF PATERNITY) (AMENDMENT) REGULATIONS 1978 (No. 1266) [10p], made under the Family Law Reform Act 1969 (c. 46), s. 22; operative on September 25, 1978; increase the fees payable under S.I. 1971 No. 1861 in respect of blood tests carried out for the purpose of determining paternity in civil proceedings.

1418. Contract. See CONTRACT.

1419. Criminal cases. See CRIMINAL LAW; MAGISTERIAL LAW.

1420. Cross-examination—document used to refresh memory—matters beyond those upon which memory refreshed
[Aust.] In the course of giving evidence-in-chief, a medical witness for D refreshed his memory from his contemporaneously written medical report of an interview with and examination of D. Counsel for P cross-examined the witness about the document and asked some questions concerning matters contained in the document which were matters which the witness had not referred to in order to refresh his memory. After completion of cross-examination and re-examination and after the witness had left the witness box and the court, counsel for D made an application that counsel for P should be required to tender the medical report in evidence. *Held*, that counsel for P was not required to tender the report in evidence as the application had not been made in the course of cross-examination. (*Senat* v. *Senat* [1965] C.L.Y. 1586 referred to): HATZIPARADISSIS *v.* G.F.C. (MANUFACTURING) PTY. [1978] V.R. 181, Vict.Sup.Ct.

1421. Discovery. See also PRACTICE.

1422. —— proceedings in foreign court—letters rogatory—privilege against self-incrimination
[Civil Evidence Act 1968 (c. 64), s. 14; Evidence (Proceedings in Other Jurisdictions) Act 1975 (c. 34), ss. 1, 2, 3; Treaty of Rome, art. 85.]

At the request of a foreign tribunal, the High Court will order the production of specific documents in the possession of a person not party to the foreign proceedings, provided that those proceedings are not penal; but such person is entitled to claim privilege against self-incrimination if the evidence required is likely to render such person liable to financial sanctions under the Treaty of Rome.

W was the defendant in proceedings for breach of contract in the United States, W having failed to complete its contract to build power stations and supply them with uranium. W's defence to such proceedings was effectively that the contracts were frustrated due to the supervening circumstances that the cost of uranium had risen steeply in price. W discovered that there appeared to be in operation an international cartel amongst uranium producers regulating the supply and price of uranium; W wished to adduce evidence of the existence of the cartel in its defence. A United States court issued letters rogatory to the High Court seeking orders requiring representatives of an English company, R.T.Z., to attend for oral examination in London and for R.T.Z. to produce certain scheduled documents for use at the trial in the U.S. court. R.T.Z. claimed privilege against such orders on the ground that their evidence might expose them to penalties under arts. 85 and 86 of the Treaty of Rome. That claim was upheld by the High Court and the Court of Appeal. The judge of the U.S. court upheld a claim by witnesses to privilege under the Fifth Amendment. The U.S. Department of Justice then applied for an order in the U.S. court compelling testimony, which could not be used against the witnesses, on the grounds that it was required for a grand jury investigation into violations of the U.S. anti-trust laws and with a view to issuing criminal proceedings. *Held,* that (1) the master's order rightly gave effect to the letters rogatory in respect of the production of documents and the witnesses sought to be examined; (2) R.T.Z. was entitled to claim privilege; and (3) the intervention of the Department of Justice changed the character of the letters rogatory, as execution was now being sought for the purposes of exercising extraterritorial jurisdiction of the U.S. court in a penal matter. (*Triplex Safety Glass Co.* v. *Lancegaye Safety Glass (1934)* [1939] 2 K.B. 395, C.A. applied; *Radio Corp. of America* v. *Rauland Corp.* [1956] C.L.Y. 6731 considered.)

Re WESTINGHOUSE ELECTRIC CORP. URANIUM CONTRACT LITIGATION M.D.L. DOCKET NO. 235 (NO. 1) (NO. 2); RIO TINTO ZINC CORP. v. WESTINGHOUSE ELECTRIC CORP. [1978] 2 W.L.R. 81, H.L.

1423. Divorce cases. See DIVORCE AND MATRIMONIAL CAUSES.

1424. Documents—procedure for requiring production—licensing appeal—considerations of commercial confidentiality and complication of hearing. See WHITBREADS (WEST PENNINES) v. ENTWISTLE, § 1741.

1425. Estoppel. See ESTOPPEL.

1426. Expert's report—leave to adduce refused

The plaintiff served notice under R.S.C., Ord. 38, r. 40, of his intention to give evidence, at the trial of his running down action, in accordance with an engineer's report. It was plain on reading the report that it was arguing out the cause of the accident and was not really expert evidence. He was refused leave to adduce the evidence at the trial on an appeal on the summons for direction. He could not seek to get leave from the trial judge who could only act under r. 36 or Ord. 38: HINDS v. LONDON TRANSPORT EXECUTIVE, *The Times,* October 5, 1978, C.A.

1427. Foreign tribunals

EVIDENCE (PROCEEDINGS IN OTHER JURISDICTIONS) (CAYMAN ISLANDS) ORDER 1978 (No. 1890) [25p], made under the Evidence (Proceedings in Other Jurisdictions) Act 1975 (c. 34), s. 10 (3); operative on January 10, 1979; extends the provisions of the 1975 Act, which provides for the taking of evidence by courts on behalf of other courts, to the Cayman Islands.

EVIDENCE (PROCEEDINGS IN OTHER JURISDICTIONS) (FALKLAND ISLANDS AND DEPENDENCIES) ORDER 1978 (No. 1891) [25p], made under the Evidence (Proceedings in Other Jurisdictions) Act 1975, s. 10 (3); operative on January 10, 1979; extends the provisions of the 1975 Act which sets out a comprehensive code for the taking of evidence by courts on behalf of other courts to the Falkland Islands.

EVIDENCE (PROCEEDINGS IN OTHER JURISDICTIONS) (GIBRALTAR) ORDER 1978 (No. 1892) [10p], made under the Evidence (Proceedings in Other Jurisdictions)

Act 1975, s. 10 (3); operative on January 10, 1979; extends to Gibraltar the provisions of the 1975 Act that provide for the repeal of specified enactments.

EVIDENCE (PROCEEDINGS IN OTHER JURISDICTIONS) (SOVEREIGN BASE AREAS OF AKROTIRI AND DHEKELIA) ORDER 1978 (No. 1920) [25p], made under the Evidence (Proceedings in Other Jurisdictions) Act 1975, s. 10 (3); operative on January 10, 1979; extends the provisions of the 1975 Act to the Sovereign Base Areas of Akotiri and Dhekelia.

1428. Hearsay—exception to rule—statement of witness beyond the seas—whether court has discretion to exclude

[Civil Evidence Act 1968 (c. 64), ss. 2, 8 (1) (2); R.S.C., Ord. 38, rr. 21 (1), 22 (3), 25.]

Where a party seeks to give in evidence a statement of a person beyond the seas, the fact that that person is abroad is sufficient reason for admitting the statement and the court has no discretion to exclude it.

P Co. began an action against C to be indemnified against the total loss of a ship. C denied liability and gave notice under R.S.C., Ord. 38, r. 21 of his intention to give in evidence statements made by K, his solicitor, to show fraud on the part of P Co., stating that K might not be available as a witness at the trial because he was likely to be beyond the seas. P Co. contended at the hearing that under Ord. 38, r. 25, C was required to show that he had taken all reasonable steps to call the maker of the statements. Donaldson J. *held* that P Co. could only challenge whether one of the reasons set out in r. 25 applied. Thus C was entitled as of right to put the statements in evidence. On appeal *held,* dismissing the appeal, that on a true construction of the rules it was unnecessary, in such a case, to show that efforts had been made to secure the attendance of the maker of the statements. (*Rasool* v. *West Midlands Passenger Transport Executive* [1974] C.L.Y. 2948 approved.)

PIERMAY SHIPPING CO. S.A. v. CHESTER [1978] 1 W.L.R. 411, C.A.

1429. Negligence. See NEGLIGENCE.

1430. Oaths Act 1978 (c. 19)

This Act consolidates the Oaths Act 1838 and the Oaths Acts 1888 to 1977. Pt. I (ss. 1 and 2) relates to England, Wales and Northern Ireland: s. 1 sets out the manner in which an oath may be administered; s. 2 contains consequential amendments.

Pt. II (ss. 3–8) relates to the United Kingdom: s. 3 permits a person to swear with uplifted hand; s. 4 relates to the validity of oaths; s. 5 stipulates that a person may make a solemn affirmation instead of taking an oath; s. 6 sets out the form of affirmation; s. 7 contains repeals and savings; s. 8 gives the short title. The Act extends to Northern Ireland; Pt. I does not extend to Scotland.

The Act received the Royal Assent on June 30, 1978, and came into force on July 30, 1978.

1431. Privilege—lawyer and client correspondence—transmission to agents—trade mark dispute. See MCGREGOR CLOTHING CO.'S TRADE MARK, § 2970.

1432. —— self-incrimination—refusal to answer questions when called as a witness before Board of Inquiry

[Aust.] R was called upon to show cause under the Evidence Act 1958 why, when present before a Board of Inquiry, he had refused to answer questions within the Board's terms of inquiry. R gave as his ground for refusing to answer these questions his concern that his answers might tend to incriminate him. Before he was called to be examined before the Board, he had been charged with offences under the Public Service Act 1974. *Held*, inter alia, that the penalties and forfeitures which R was at risk of suffering under the Public Service Act were not of the nature (namely admonition, reprimand, fine, reduction in classification or salary, removal from office and appointment to another office, or dismissal) of those for which the privilege against self-incrimination and exposure to suffering penalty was conferred by the common law. A witness before a Board of Inquiry is required to answer a relevant question notwithstanding it might incriminate him unless the Board considers the answer might have a tendency to subject him to punishment for treason, felony or misdemeanour. (*Re Westinghouse Electrical Corp. Uranium Litigation* [1977] C.L.Y. 1366 distinguished): ATT.-GEN. (VICTORIA) *v.* RIACH [1978] V.R. 301, Vict. Sup.Ct.

1433. —— solicitor's correspondence—public policy

A solicitor, whilst acting for a client in a previous action in which the present plaintiffs had been parties, wrote letters to his client, the legal aid committee, and another firm of solicitors. On a hearing for taxation of the costs in this case, the plaintiffs discovered the letters and sued the solicitor for libel. The action was stayed, and an injunction granted to prevent the plaintiffs issuing further proceedings. In so far as the letters were covered by legal professional privilege, there was a complete defence to the action, and as the plaintiffs could not use letters disclosed in that action they could not use them in this case, on the grounds of public policy: HAYWARD *v.* WEGG-PROSSER (1978) 122 S.J. 792, Tudor-Evans J.

1434. Similar fact—admissibility—infringement of copyright—documents relating to earlier acts. See E. G. MUSIC *v.* S. F. (FILM) DISTRIBUTORS, § 345.

1435. —— when admissible

The plaintiff claimed damages for loss of a diamond which the defendant bank denied having ever received. The plaintiff sought to lead evidence of a similar incident where another customer of the same bank suffered such a loss; but it was ruled inadmissible. *Held,* the question whether or not the bank's method of keeping their customer's goods safe was put in issue. This evidence was therefore admissible to rebut the suggestion that the bank used all reasonable safeguards to protect the diamond. In this area of evidence, principles apply equally in both civil and criminal cases (*Makin* v. *Att.-Gen. for New South Wales* [1894] A.C. 57 considered): SATTIN *v.* NATIONAL UNION BANK (1978) 122 S.J. 367, C.A.

BOOKS AND ARTICLES. See *post,* pp. [4], [23].

EXECUTORS AND ADMINISTRATORS

1436. Fees—taxation of costs. See MALTBY *v.* D. J. FREEMAN & CO., § 2819.

1437. Grants of representation—stamp duty

The following Practice Direction was issued by the Principal Registry of the Family Division on February 28, 1978:

1. Where, for the purposes of applying for a grant of representation, it is necessary for the applicant to produce to the Principal or a District Probate Registry an original deed or other instrument, it is the practice of the Registry to examine the instrument to ensure that it has been properly executed and duly stamped under the Stamp Act 1891 before proceeding with the application. Where there is any doubt whether the instrument is duly stamped, the applicant will be asked to present the instrument to the Controller of Stamps (Inland Revenue) for adjudication before the issue of the grant.

2. To avoid delay in the issue of the grant in such cases, the Commissioners of Inland Revenue have agreed that the applicant may, if so desired, submit the original instrument to the Adjudication Section of the Office of the Controller of Stamps for preliminary noting, endorsement and return, provided that a written undertaking is at the same time given to the Controller by the solicitor applying for the grant of representation that he will, on or immediately after the issue of the grant, re-submit the original instrument to the Controller for formal adjudication and pay the stamp duty (if any) to which the instrument is adjudged liable.

3. In every case on the application for a grant, the original instrument (after inspection) will be returned as soon as practicable to the applicant, or his solicitor, by the probate registry. Practitioners are reminded, however, that where the application is for a grant to an assignee or assignees under Rule 22 of the Non-Contentious Probate Rules 1954, a copy of the original instrument of assignment must be lodged in the registry (see Rule 22 (3)).

[1978] 1 W.L.R. 430; [1978] 1 All E.R. 1046.

1438. Intestacy—surviving spouse—value of home greater than surviving spouse's interest—whether right to require appropriation of home

[Intestates' Estates Act 1952 (c. 64), Sched. 2, para. 1 (1).]

On intestacy, a surviving spouse only has power to require appropriation of the matrimonial home where the value of his or her interest exceeds the value of the house.

H died intestate. At the time of his death, H and his spouse occupied a house which was part of H's residuary estate. The value of the house was greater than the value of the wife's absolute interest in the estate. W required the appropriation of the home. *Held,* that the Act only allowed W to require appropriation if the value of her absolute interest in the estate of the intestate spouse exceeded the value of the house.

Re PHELPS (DECD.) [1978] 3 All E.R. 395, Foster J.

1439. Liability—plene administravit—defence after judgment—whether too late

The court has no jurisdiction to allow a personal representative to enter a defence pleading plene administravit, after judgment against a deceased's estate had been given. A defence based on an insufficiency of assets to satisfy the judgment was now precluded. Despite the sympathy felt by the court in the applicant's circumstances, even if the court had such jurisdiction, the relief sought was inappropriate where the personal representative's original defence had been struck out for failure to comply with an order for discovery: MIDLAND BANK TRUST CO. *v.* GREEN (NO. 2), *The Times,* July 5, 1978, Oliver J.

1440. Northern Ireland. See NORTHERN IRELAND.

1441. Probate—contentious matters—practice

Under s. 162 (1) (*b*) of the Supreme Court of Judicature (Consolidation) Act 1925, the former wife and son of the deceased applied to pass over the executors appointed in the will, who were willing and able to take a grant of probate, in favour of themselves as administrators. The procedure adopted was that contained in rr. 51 and 60 of the Non-Contentious Probate Rules, and involved 37 affidavits, upon which all deponents were cross-examined, taking up 11 working days. *Held,* dismissing the application, that much time and expense could have been saved if at an early stage it had been recognised that the case was to be hotly contentious; grounds of contention could then have been particularised by the pleadings, suitable directions could have been made, all oral evidence could have been put before the judge, and the matters could have been heard in open court: VAN HOORN *v.* VAN HOORN, *The Times,* November 30, 1978, Balcombe J.

1442. —— fees. See § 2370.

1443. —— grant—caveats entered—vexatious litigant

[Non-Contentious Probate Rules 1954 (S.I. 1954 No. 796), r. 44.] D nursed a grievance against the National Trust (the NT), owners of land adjoining D's cottages, the NT's local committee and the mortgagees of his cottages following an action in 1963 when it was held that there was access by foot only to the cottages. In January 1965 D issued a writ claiming damages against 31 defendants (including the NT, its local committee and the deceased) for defamation and conspiracy. In December 1965, D issued a further writ against seven defendants (including his former mortgagees, the purchasers of the cottages and the deceased) seeking to set aside the disposition of the cottages and obtain possession of them and the documents of title. Neither writ was served on the deceased prior to his death nor had a statement of claim been served on any defendant. On January 8, 1976, D entered a caveat in the deceased's estate. On February 3, P (the sole executrix and universal beneficiary of the deceased) issued a warning to that caveat which was served on February 12. On February 20, D took out a summons for directions under r. 44 (10) of the 1954 Rules, which he never served. On May 25, 1976, D issued a further writ (" the 1976 writ ") in the Chancery Division entitled in the matter of three estates (including that of the deceased and two other dead members of the local Committee) seeking an order against, inter alia, P that there be no grant in the deceased's estate (to P) but the appointment of a receiver, accounts and inquiries and other relief. The writ was indorsed by a Chancery Master with "leave to issue" under Ord. 76, r. 2 (2) (b), and a copy of the writ was transmitted to the Probate Registry. Neither the writ nor a statement of claim had ever been served on P. On June 10, 1977, D entered a new caveat (which was warned) and on January 12, 1978, D attempted to enter a further new caveat. On June 13, 1977, P applied by summons under both r. 44 (12) (c) and the inherent jurisdiction of the court for a grant notwithstanding the issue of the 1976 writ and notwithstanding the entry of the 1976 caveat and any further caveats. The Senior Registrar referred the summons to Payne J. *Held* (1) a grant of representation to the deceased's estate should be made to P (if entitled thereto) notwithstanding the issue of the 1976 writ and the entry of any past and present caveats because (a) the 1976 writ did not commence a "Probate action" within Ord. 76, r. 1 (2); (b) D had no beneficial interest in the deceased's estate; (c) the writ had not been served; and (d) the procedure adopted by D was vexatious and an abuse of the process of the court (*Heywood* v. *BDC Properties* (*No.* 2) [1963] C.L.Y. 1923 applied); (2) the grant could issue whether or not the time for the issue and service of a notice of appeal had expired and whether or not such a notice had been issued and served; (3) no further caveat should be entered in the estate of the deceased without the leave of a judge of the Family Division; and (4) a transcript of the judgment be sent to the Att.-Gen. for consideration by him whether an application should be made under s. 51 of the Judicature Act 1925: *Re* HANCOCK, DECD.; KILLEY v. PALLANT, January 16, 1978, Payne J. (*Ex rel. W. D. Ainger, Esq., Barrister.*)

1444. Proceedings against estates—no grant of probate made—official solicitor appointed only to accept service—judgment not enforceable
    [Proceedings Against Estates Act 1970 (c. 17), s. 2; R.S.C., Ord. 15, r. 6A.]
    Where the Official Solicitor is appointed only for the purpose of accepting service of proceedings against the estate of a deceased where no grant of probate has been made, judgment cannot be entered in default of appearance.
    The Official Solicitor consented under R.S.C., Ord. 15, r. 6A (5A), to being appointed to accept service of proceedings brought by the plaintiffs against the estate of the deceased, who had been domiciled outside the jurisdiction and in respect of whose estate no personal representatives had been appointed. The Official Solicitor declined to consent to being appointed for the purposes of taking any further step in the proceedings. He accepted service of the plaintiffs' writ but took no further action. The plaintiffs thereafter obtained judgment in default of appearance which judgment they sought to enforce in garnishee proceedings: they appealed against the Master's discharge of the garnishee order. *Held*, dismissing their appeal, that the judgment was a nullity, since there was no person against whom it could be enforced, the action being one brought in personam.
    Re AMIRTEYMOUR (DECD.) [1978] 3 All E.R. 637, C.A.

        BOOKS AND ARTICLES. See *post*, pp. [4], [24].

EXPLOSIONS AND EXPLOSIVES

1445. Licensing of stores
    EXPLOSIVES (LICENSING OF STORES) VARIATION OF FEES REGULATIONS 1978 (No. 270) [10p], made under the Health and Safety at Work etc. Act 1974 (c. 37), ss. 11 (2) (d), 15 (1) (3) (a), 50 (3) as amended by the Employment Protection Act 1975 (c. 71), s. 116, Sched. 15, para. 6; amends ss. 15 and 18 of the Explosives Act 1875 by increasing the maximum fees payable for a store licence and the renewal of a store licence.

1446. Northern Ireland. See NORTHERN IRELAND.

1447. Unlawful possession—pyrotechnic effect only—whether an issue for the jury
    [Explosive Substances Act 1883.] The defendant was charged with unlawful possession of an "explosive substance" in contravention of s. 4 (1) of the Explosive Substances Act 1883. Defence evidence was called that the substance would produce only a pyrotechnic effect, not an explosive one. The judge withdrew the issue from the jury, adopting the definition of "explosive" in

s. 3 of the Explosive Substances Act 1875, which included substances used to produce a pyrotechnic effect. The appeal against the judge's decision was dismissed: R. *v.* WHEATLEY (1978) 122 S.J. 791, C.A.

EXTRADITION

1448. **Australia to New Zealand—illegal arrest, detention and surrender—whether affects court's jurisdiction**

[N.Z.] 14 "Hell's Angels," including B, burst into a residence in New Zealand with weapons and several people were injured, one of whom died. B was arrested in Australia at the request of New Zealand police, without warrant or any authority and was put on the next plane to New Zealand. B said all the statutory safeguards under the Fugitive Offenders Act 1881 (U.K.), intended to protect individuals against arbitrary arrest or unwarrantable interference with their liberty and freedom of movement, had been disregarded. His arrest, detention and surrender were thus unlawful. *Held,* on B's appeal against conviction in New Zealand, that B was eventually lawfully arrested in New Zealand and the court therefore had jurisdiction, which should not be declined: R. *v.* BENNETT [1978] Crim.L.R. 44, C.A. New Zealand.

1449. **Discharge of order—fresh application on new grounds—habeas corpus**

[Fugitive Offenders Act 1967 (c. 68), s. 8 (3).] T has been granted leave to make a fresh application for habeas corpus under s. 8 (2) (*b*) of the 1967 Act, to be discharged from an order extraditing him to Singapore to face company law charges, even though a first application made on the grounds of s. 8 (3) (*a*) and (*c*) had been refused: *Ex p.* TARLING, *The Times*, June 24, 1978, D.C.

1450. **Fugitive offenders**

FRANCE (EXTRADITION) (AMENDMENT) ORDER 1978 (No. 455) [15p], made under the Extradition Act 1870 (c. 52), ss. 2, 17, 21; operative on April 16, 1978; extends the application of the Extradition Acts in the case of France to drug offences.

FEDERAL REPUBLIC OF GERMANY (EXTRADITION) (AMENDMENT) ORDER 1978 (No. 1403) [25p], made under the Extradition Act 1870, ss. 2 21; operative on October 3, 1978; applies the Extradition Acts 1970 to 1935 in the case of the Federal Republic of Germany and Land Berlin (West Berlin) in accordance with the Treaty between the U.K. and Germany for the Mutual Surrender of Fugitive Criminalsdated May 14, 1872, as reapplied by later agreements.

SPAIN (EXTRADITION) (REVOCATION) ORDER 1978 (No. 1523) [10p], made under the Extradition Act 1870, s. 21; operative on November 22, 1978; revokes the Orders in Council, S.R. & O. 1878 and S.R. & O. 1889 which applied the 1870 Act and the Extradition Act 1873 in the case of Spain following the termination on October 13, 1978, of the Treaty for the Mutual Surrender of Fugitive Criminals.

ISRAEL (EXTRADITION) (AMENDMENT) ORDER 1978 (No. 1623) [20p], made under the Extradition Act 1870, ss. 2 and 21; operative on December 14, 1978; amends the application of the Extradition Acts 1870–1895 in the case of Israel so as to reserve the right of the requested government not to extradite its nationals in accordance with the Agreement between the U.K. and the Government of Israel for the reciprocal extradition of criminals signed on April 4, 1960.

EXTRADITION (HIJACKING) (AMENDMENT) ORDER 1978 (No. 1887) [20p], made under the Extradition Act 1870, ss. 2, 17, 21 and the Hijacking Act 1971 (c. 70), ss. 3 (2), 6 (1) (3); operative on January 25, 1979; deletes the entry for Spain from Sched. 2 to S.I. 1971 No. 2102 and adds further specified countries to the Sched.

EXTRADITION (PROTECTION OF AIRCRAFT) (AMENDMENT) ORDER 1978 (No. 1888) [20p], made under the Extradition Act 1870, ss. 2, 17, 21 and the Protection of Aircraft Act 1973 (c. 47), ss. 5 (2), 27 (1) (3); operative on January 25, 1979; deletes Spain from Sched. 2 to S.I. 1973 No. 1756 and adds specified countries to the Sched.

EXTRADITION (TOKYO CONVENTION) (AMENDMENT) ORDER 1978 (No. 1889) [10p], made under the Extradition Act 1870, ss. 2, 17, 21 and the Tokyo Convention Act 1967 (c. 52), s. 2 (2); operative on January 25, 1979; applies the Extradition Acts 1870 to 1932 as amended to offences committed on board aircraft in flight registered in Peru and removes Spain from the list of states to which the Acts apply. It also removes Tuvalu from the list of territories to which the application of the Tokyo Convention has been extended.

FUGITIVE OFFENDERS (DESIGNATED COMMONWEALTH COUNTRIES) ORDER 1978 (No. 1905) [10p], made under the Fugitive Offenders Act 1967 (c. 68), s. 2 (1); operative on January 24, 1979; designates the Commonwealth of Dominica, the Solomon Islands and Tuvalu for the purposes of s. 1 of the 1967 Act.

1451. ------ **passage of time—unjust or oppressive**

[Fugitive Offenders Act 1967 (c. 68), s. 8 (3).]

By s. 8 (3) the High Court may order the release of a fugitive offender from custody if it appears that by reason of the passage of time it would be unjust or oppressive to return him.

In April 1973, P was shot dead in Cyprus by three terrorists one of whom was alleged to be K. K and his family left Cyprus for England in September 1974. In February 1976, the Attorney-General of Cyprus in a vastly changed government directed extradition proceedings against K, alleging participation in P's murder. In the magistrates' court, K denied participation and gave evidence of alibi. A witness B gave supporting evidence but stated he was unable to return to Cyprus to attend the trial for fear of ill-treatment or arrest. K was committed in custody and an appeal to the Divisional Court was dismissed. On appeal to the House of Lord, *held*, allowing the appeal, that by reason of the passage of time it would be unjust or oppressive to return K who would be deprived of the opportunity to call his alibi evidence, which would detract from the fairness of his trial. (*R. v. Governor of Pentonville Prison, ex p. Narang* [1977] C.L.Y. 1392 applied.)

KAKIS *v.* GOVERNOR OF THE REPUBLIC OF CYPRUS [1978] 1 W.L.R. 779, H.L.

1452. Genocide

EXTRADITION (GENOCIDE) (AMENDMENT) ORDER 1978 (No. 782) [10p], made under the Extradition Act 1870 (c. 52), s. 2; operative on June 29, 1978; applies the Extradition Acts as extended by the Genocide Act 1969 to the offence of genocide in the case of Austria being a state with which the U.K. has an extradition Treaty and which is also a party to the Convention on the Prevention and Punishment of the Crime of Genocide.

EXTRADITION (GENOCIDE) (AMENDMENT No. 2) ORDER 1978 (No. 1886) [10p], made under the Extradition Act 1870, s. 21; operative on January 25, 1979; amends S.I. 1970 No. 147 so as to omit the entries for those British possessions which have attained independence.

1453. Habeas corpus—evidence—Irish warrant executed in England

[Backing of Warrants (Republic of Ireland) Act 1965 (c. 45), s. 2 (2).]

Where evidence of the matters mentioned in s. 2 (2) of the Act is not before the justices, fresh or additional evidence of them is not admissible in a habeas corpus application.

N was arrested in England under a warrant issued in Ireland. The justices ordered his return. No evidence was called before them to show that the order should not be made. On the hearing for an application of habeas corpus, N sought to introduce evidence that he would be prosecuted for an offence of a political character on his return, and that he ought to be released pursuant to s. 2 (2) of the Act. *Held*, dismissing the application, that the matters mentioned in s. 2 (2) were matters which had to be shown to the satisfaction of the justices, and fresh or additional evidence on them was not admissible on a habeas corpus application.

Re NOBBS [1978] 3 All E.R. 390, D.C.

1454. Internationally Protected Persons Act 1978 (c. 17). See § 1730.

1455. Offences—defendant's acts under English law—whether prima facie case of fraud—powers of Divisional Court on application for writ of habeas corpus

The Divisional Court refused a writ of habeas corpus to secure T's release from committal on a charge of conspiracy to induce shareholders in a Singapore company, M & G, to accept an offer from HP, another Singapore company, for shares in HP in exchange for shares in M & G by dishonest concealment of facts. The Divisional Court discharged T from custody after his committal on charges of, in effect, conspiracy to steal and conspiracy to defraud connected with, inter alia, M & G and HP. The magistrate had declined to commit a co-defendant on such charges. *Held*, allowing T's appeal and dismissing the Singapore Republic Government's appeal, that the court had to fit the complex facts of the case into English legislation which was largely inappropriate to deal with them. The Divisional Court was not entitled to retry the case, but an extensive review of the facts and evidence and elaboration of the Divisional Court's judgment was necessitated by the complexity of the issues and lack of the detailed findings by the magistrate. T had always acted in accordance with professional advice. This tended to negative fraud. As no sufficient evidence of dishonesty was found by the Divisional Court on the charge concerning HP, the charge in respect of M & G ought also to be found to fail: TARLING *v.* SINGAPORE REPUBLIC GOVERNMENT [1978] Crim.L.R. 490, H.L.

1456. Suppression of terrorism

EXTRADITION (SUPPRESSION OF TERRORISM) ORDER 1978 (No. 1106) [25p], made under the Extradition Act 1870 (c. 52), s. 2; operative on October 25, 1978; applies the Extradition Acts to the European Convention on the Suppression of Terrorism.

1457. Supression of Terrorism Act 1978 (c. 26). See § 885.

FACTORIES

1458. Breach of statutory duty—obstruction on floor—whether reasonably practicable to prevent obstruction

[Factories Act 1961 (c. 34), s. 28 (1).]

The fact that employers were unaware of the existence of an obstruction on the factory floor does not mean that it was not reasonably practicable for them to keep such floor free of obstruction.

The employee was injured after tripping over a piece of wire in a badly lit part of the factory. The employers contended that since the wire had inadvertently got into that position and as they were unaware of it, they were not in breach of their duty under s. 28 of the Act to keep the floor free of obstruction as far as was reasonably practicable. *Held*, giving judgment for the employee, that the employers had failed to establish that it was not reasonably practicable for them to have prevented or removed the obstruction. (Dicta of Lord Reid in *Jenkins* v. *Allied Ironfounders* [1970] C.L.Y. 1076 applied.)

BENNETT *v.* RYLANDS WHITECROSS [1978] I.C.R. 1031, Kilner-Brown J.

1459. Building operations. See BUILDING AND ENGINEERING, ARCHITECTS AND SURVEYORS.

1460. Harbours and docks. See SHIPPING AND MARINE INSURANCE.

1461. Lighting

FACTORIES (STANDARDS OF LIGHTING) (REVOCATION) REGULATIONS 1978 (No. 1126) [10p], made under the Health and Safety at Work etc. Act 1974 (c. 37), ss. 11 (2) (*d*), 15 (1) (3) (*a*), 50 (3) as amended by the Employment Protection Act 1975 (c. 71), s. 116, Sched. 15, para. 6; operative on October 1, 1978; revokes S.R. & O. 1941 No. 94,

1462. Northern Ireland. See NORTHERN IRELAND.

1463. Shops. See SHOPS.

ARTICLES. See *post*, p. [24].

FAMILY ALLOWANCES

1464. Child benefit

CHILD BENEFIT (MISCELLANEOUS AMENDMENTS) REGULATIONS 1978 (No. 540) [15p], made under the Tribunals and Inquiries Act 1971 (c. 62), s. 10, and the Child Benefit Act 1975 (c. 61), ss. 6 (1), 7 (1), 24 (2) (4) (5), Sched. 1, para. 1; operative on May 5, 1978; amend S.I. 1976 No. 962 so as to correct an omission from the definition of "special questions." Also amend S.I. 1976 No. 964 so as to allow a claim to an increase of benefit to be treated, in certain circumstances, as a claim for the whole child benefit.

CHILD BENEFIT (GENERAL) AMENDMENT REGULATIONS 1978 (No. 1275) [10p], made under the Child Benefit Act 1975, s. 4 (1), Sched. 1, para. 2 (2); operative on August 31, 1978; amend S.I. 1976 No. 965 so as to provide that child benefit under the 1975 Act shall not be payable in respect of a child for any week after August 31, 1978, while that child is receiving financial support by virtue of arrangements made under s. 2 of the Employment and Training Act or during a period of interruption of full-time education immediately prior to receiving such financial support.

1465. Family income supplements

FAMILY INCOME SUPPLEMENTS (COMPUTATION) REGULATIONS 1978 (No. 1137) [10p], made under the Family Income Supplements Act 1970 (c. 55), ss. 2 (1), 3 (1), 3 (1A) and 10 (3), as amended by the Child Benefit Act 1975 (c. 61), Sched. 4, paras. 3 and 4; operative on November 14, 1978; specify the prescribed amount for any family and the weekly rate of benefit under the 1970 Act in accordance with the amendments made to the 1970 Act by the 1975 Act.

1466. National insurance. See NATIONAL INSURANCE.

FIRE SERVICE

1467. Appointments and promotion

FIRE SERVICES (APPOINTMENTS AND PROMOTION) REGULATIONS 1978 (No. 436) [25p], made under the Fire Services Act 1947 (c. 41), s. 18 (1) as amended by the Fire Services Act 1959 (c. 44); operative on June 1, 1978; consolidate with amendments S.I. 1965 No. 577 as amended by principally specifying the examinations which qualify for various ranks and transfers responsibility for examinations to the Fire Services Central Examinations Board.

1468. Pensions. See PENSIONS AND SUPERANNUATION.

BOOKS. See *post*, p. [4].

FIREARMS

1469. Certificate—whether Chief Officer of Police exercised discretion properly

[Firearms Act 1968 (c. 27), s. 7 (1).] The Crown Court quashed a Chief Officer of Police's refusal to renew a shotgun certificate in accordance with his policy of refusing renewals where the owner of the gun had a previous conviction involving arms. *Held*, refusing an application to quash the Crown Court's decision, that if such a policy were adopted it must admit of exceptions, and each case must be considered individually. The policy was not lawful if intended to be punitive. Punishment for poaching, and fitness to hold a shotgun certificate, were different questions: R. *v.* WAKEFIELD CROWN COURT, *ex p.* OLDFIELD [1978] Crim.L.R. 164, D.C.

1470. Fees

FIREARMS (VARIATION OF FEES) ORDER 1978 (No. 267) [10p], made under the Firearms Act 1968 (c. 27), s. 43; operative on April 1, 1978; increases the fees in respect of firearm certificates and shotgun certificates and in respect of the registration of firearms dealers and the new registration certificates issued to firearms dealers annually.

1471. Gun Barrel Proof Act 1978 (c. 9)

This Act makes provision for the United Kingdom to accede to the Convention for the Reciprocal Recognition of Proof Marks of Small Arms done at Brussels on July 1, 1969; it amends the Gun Barrel Proof Act 1868 and extends that Act and the Gun Barrel Proof Act 1950 to Scotland and Northern Ireland.

S. 1 amends certain section of the 1868 Act, and makes certain other provisions, with respect to convention proof marks; s. 2 provides for fines for certain offences under the 1868 Act, and declares that certain sections of that Act shall cease to have effect; s. 3 relates to the establishment of branch proof houses; s. 4 confers power upon the guardians to make certain rules and regulations; s. 5 permits the expression of measurements in rules and regulations made under s. 117 of the 1968 Act to be in metric or imperial units; s. 6 extends the Gun Barrel Proof Acts 1868 and 1950 to Scotland and Northern Ireland; s. 7 is the interpretation section; s. 8 makes certain minor consequential amendments and repeals; s. 9 deals with the citation of the Act.

The Act received the Royal Assent on May 5, 1978.

1472. —— commencement

GUN BARREL PROOF ACT 1978 (COMMENCEMENT No. 1) ORDER 1978 (No. 1587 (C. 46)) [10p], made under the Gun Barrel Proof Act 1978 (c. 9), s. 9 (3); operative on December 1, 1978; brings into force ss. 2–7, 8 (1) (part), (2), 9, Sched. 3 (part), Sched. 4.

1473. Northern Ireland. See NORTHERN IRELAND.

1474. Possession—" having with him " more than " possession "

[Firearms Act 1968 (c. 27), s. 18 (1).]

A jury should be directed that " having with him a firearm " means more than having " possession " of a firearm.

D had in his home a holdall containing, *inter alia,* a sawn-off shotgun. He was charged, *inter alia,* with " having with him a firearm with intent to commit an arrestable offence." The judge rejected a submission that there was no case to answer. He directed the jury that " having with him a firearm " was wider than carrying the firearm and extended to any " close physical link " with it. *Held*, that that ruling was correct, but that the judge should have gone on to direct the jury that something more than the legal concept of " possession " of the firearm was required. D's appeal was allowed.

R. *v.* KELT [1977] 1 W.L.R. 1365, C.A.

1475. —— rifle with rifling removed

[Firearms Act 1968 (c. 27), ss. 1, 57 (1).]

A rifle with the rifling removed can still discharge its original bullets so that it is still a firearm within the meaning of s. 57 of the Firearms Act 1968.

D removed the rifling from certain rifles which he possessed. When charged with possessing those rifles without a firearms certificate he contended that the removal of the rifling had turned them into smooth-bore guns covered by his shotgun certificate. *Held*, dismissing his appeal (Widgery C.J. dissenting), that as the guns could still be used as rifles, albeit with less accuracy, a firearms certificate was required.

CREASER *v.* TUNNICLIFFE [1977] 1 W.L.R. 1493, D.C.

1476. —— whether antique—burden of proof—evidence

B claimed that he kept a rifle and shotgun found in his flat because they were antiques. The trial judge directed the jury to convict B of possessing a firearm without a certificate, possessing a firearm having been sentenced to imprisonment for a term of three years or more, and possessing a shotgun without a certificate, since no expert evidence was to be called. *Held*, allowing B's appeal, that the burden was on the prosecution to prove that the firearms were not antiques and required a certificate, B having raised the issue. The issue was one of fact for the jury: R. *v.* BURKE [1978] Crim.L.R. 431, C.A.

FISH AND FISHERIES

1477. Diseases of fish

DISEASES OF FISH ORDER 1978 (No. 1022) [10p], made under the Diseases of Fish Act 1937 (c. 33), s. 13 and the Statutory Instruments Act 1946 (c. 36), s. 6 (2); operative on August 15, 1978; extends the provisions of the 1937 Act to bacterial kidney disease which affects fish of the salmon family.

1478. Fishery boards

ANGLIAN WATER AUTHORITY (SEA FISHERIES) REVOCATION ORDER 1978 (No. 74) [10p], made under the Sea Fisheries Regulation Act 1966 (c. 38), s. 18 (2); operative on April 1, 1978; revokes certain orders which conferred on the Board of Conservators of the Suffolk and Essex Fishery District (and on their successors the Anglian Water Authority) the powers of a local fisheries committee with respect to the area comprised in that district.

1479. Fishing boats

FISHING BOATS (FAROE ISLANDS) DESIGNATION ORDER 1978 (No. 191) [15p], made under the Fishery Limits Act 1976 (c. 86), s. 2 (1); operative on February 11, 1978; designates the Faroe Islands as a country whose registered fishing boats may fish in the areas specified in the Order for sea fish specified in relation to those areas.

FISHING BOATS (FAROE ISLANDS) DESIGNATION (No. 2) ORDER 1978 (No. 288) [15p], made under the Fishery Limits Act 1976, s. 2 (1); operative on March 3, 1978; designates the Faroe Islands as a country whose registered fishing boats may fish in the areas specified in the order for sea fish specified in relation to those areas.

FISHING BOATS (FAROE ISLANDS) DESIGNATION (No. 2) (VARIATION) ORDER 1978 (No. 490) [10p], made under the Fishery Limits Act 1976, ss. 2 (1), 6 (2); operative on March 31, 1978; extends the duration of S.I. 1978 No. 288 until June 1, 1978.

FISHING BOATS (FAROE ISLANDS) DESIGNATION (No. 2) (VARIATION) (No. 2) ORDER 1978 (No. 767), [10p], made under the Fishery Limits Act 1976, ss. 2 (1), 6 (2) and S.I. 1978 No. 272, art. 2 (3); operative on May 31, 1978; extends the duration of S.I. 1978 No. 288 until August 1, 1978.

FISHING BOATS (SPECIFIED COUNTRIES) DESIGNATION (No. 3) (VARIATION) ORDER 1978 (No. 772) [10p], made under the Fishery Limits Act 1976, ss. 2 (1), 6 (2) and S.I. 1978 No. 272, art. 2 (3); operative on June 1, 1978; varies S.I. 1977 No. 1084 by extending the designated areas in which fishing boats registered in Sweden may fish and amends the definitions of the sea fish they may fish for in those areas.

FISHING BOATS (FAROE ISLANDS) DESIGNATION (No. 3) ORDER 1978 (No. 1168) [20p], made under the Fishery Limits Act 1976, ss. 2 (1), 6 (2) and S.I. 1978 No. 272; operative on August 9, 1978; designates the Faroe Islands as a country whose registered boats may fish in areas specified in the order for sea fish specified in relation to those areas.

FISHING VESSELS (SAFETY PROVISIONS) (AMENDMENT) RULES 1978 (No. 1598) [10p], made under the Fishing Vessels (Safety Provisions) Act 1970 (c. 27), s. 2; operative on December 17, 1978; amend S.I. 1975 No. 330.

FISHING BOATS (FAROE ISLANDS) DESIGNATION (No. 3) (VARIATION) ORDER 1978 (No. 1650) [10p], made under the Fishery Limits Act 1976, ss. 2 (1), 6 (2), and S.I. 1978 (No. 272); operative on November 21, 1978; amend S.I. 1978 No. 1168 by permitting Faroese boats to fish for Norway pout and sprat in part of ICES area VIA.

FISHING BOATS (SPECIFIED COUNTRIES) DESIGNATION (No. 3) ORDER 1977 (VARIATION) (No. 2) ORDER 1978 (No. 1651) [20p], made under the Fishery Limits Act 1976, ss. 2 (1), 6 (2), and S.I. 1978 No. 272; operative on November 21, 1978; further varies S.I. 1977 No. 1084 by adjusting the designated areas where fishing boats registered in Spain and Sweden may fish, and amending the descriptions of sea fish for which they may fish in those areas.

SEA FISHING (SPECIFIED FOREIGN BOATS) LICENSING (No. 3) ORDER 1977 (VARIATION) ORDER 1978 (No. 1652) [20p], made under the Sea Fish (Conservation) Act 1967, ss. 4, 20 (1), as amended by the Fishery Limits Act 1976, s. 3, and S.I. 1978 No. 272; operative on November 21, 1978; further varies S.I. 1977 No. 942 by bringing fishing boats registered in Sweden and the Faroe Islands within its terms, and altering the arrangements in relation to Spanish vessels.

FISHING VESSELS (ACQUISITION AND IMPROVEMENT) (GRANTS) (VARIATION) SCHEME 1978 (No. 1820) [10p], made under the Sea Fish Industry Act 1970 (c. 11), ss. 44, 45, 57; operative on December 9, 1978; further varies S.I. 1976

No. 304 by substituting January 1, 1980 as the date by which relevant applications for a grant are to be approved.

FISHING VESSELS (SAFETY PROVISIONS) (AMENDMENT NO. 2) RULES 1978 (No. 1873) [25p], made under the Fishing Vessels (Safety Provisions) Act 1970, s. 7 (2), the Merchant Shipping Act 1894 (c. 60), s. 427 as substituted by the Merchant Shipping (Safety Convention) Act 1949 (c. 43), s. 2 and amended by the Merchant Shipping Act 1964 (c. 47), s. 9; operative on February 1, 1979; further amend S.I. 1975 No. 330 by making new safety provisions relating to distress flares and smoke signals.

FISHING BOATS (FAROE ISLANDS) DESIGNATION (No. 4) ORDER 1978 (No. 1950) [20p], made under the Fishery Limits Act 1976, ss. 2 (1) and 6 (2); operative on January 4, 1979; designates the Faroe Islands as a country whose registered boats may fish in certain specified areas for specified sea fish.

1480. Fishing rights

MORECAMBE BAY MUSSEL FISHERY ORDER 1978 (No. 1854) [20p], made under the Sea Fisheries (Shellfish) Act 1967 (c. 83), s. 1, as amended by the Sea Fisheries Act 1968 (c. 77), s. 15, and by the Fishery Limits Act 1976 (c. 86), s. 9 (1), Sched. 2, para. 15; operative on January 18, 1979; confers on Lancashire and Western Sea Fisheries Joint Committee the right of regulating a fishery for mussels over those parts of the seabed at the western end of Morecambe Bay.

1481. Import of Live Fish (Scotland) Act 1978 (c. 35)

This Act restricts in Scotland the import, keeping or release of live fish or shellfish.

S. 1 empowers the Secretary of State to limit the import, keeping or release of fish and fish eggs of species which are not native to Scotland; s. 2 deals with powers of Customs and Excise officials, police and authorised persons to enter and inspect land held by a person licensed under s. 1; s. 3 makes it an offence to import or keep fish specified in an order under s. 1, or to contravene terms of a licence under s. 1; s. 4 gives the short title. The Act extends to Scotland only.

The Act received the Royal Assent on July 20, 1978, and came into force on that date.

1482. Northern Ireland. See NORTHERN IRELAND.

1483. Oyster fisheries

UPPER COLLINS CREEK OYSTER AND CLAM FISHERY ORDER 1978 (No. 1596) [10p], made under the Sea Fisheries (Shellfish) Act 1967 (c. 83), s. 1, as amended by the Sea Fisheries Act 1968 (c. 77), s. 15 (1) (2); operative on December 1, 1978; confers on M. C. R. Emmett, Esq., and on B. R. J. Wright, Esq., a right of several or exclusive oyster and clam fishery on a portion of the bed of the River Blackwater in Essex known as Upper Collins Creek.

1484. Salmon fishing—taking fish during close time—whether mens rea necessary

[Salmon and Freshwater Fisheries Act 1975 (c. 51), s. 19.] D fished regularly with nets along the sea shore for various fish, not including salmon. He put a salmon, which he found dead in one of his nets, into his sack during the weekly close time for salmon. Another salmon was found alive in another net. Justices acquitted D of taking salmon during the weekly close time other than with a rod and line or putts and putchers, contrary to s. 19 of the 1975 Act, on the grounds that salmon was " taken " when caught and there was no evidence as to whether the salmon had entered the nets before the close time; furthermore, that D had no intention of catching salmon. *Held*, dismissing an appeal by the prosecutor, that under s. 19 there must be an intention to catch salmon to establish an offence : CAIN *v.* CAMPBELL [1978] Crim.L.R. 292, D.C.

1485. Sea Fish Industry Act 1970—relaxation

SEA FISH INDUSTRY ACT 1970 (RELAXATION OF TIME LIMITS) ORDER 1978 (No. 1822) [10p], made under the Sea Fish Industry Act 1970 (c. 3), s. 1 (2); operative on December 9, 1978; relaxes time limits contained in certain provisions of the 1970 Act by providing that those provisions shall have effect as if in each of them references to 1972 were references to 1979.

1486. Sea fishing

SEA FISH (CONSERVATION) (CHANNEL ISLANDS BOATS) ORDER 1978 (No. 280) [10p], made under the Sea Fish (Conservation) Act 1967 (c. 84), s. 24 (1) and the Fishery Limits Act 1976 (c. 86), s. 11 (3); operative on March 8, 1978; applies s. 4 of the 1967 Act (as substituted by s. 3 of the 1976 Act) to British fishing boats registered in any of the Channel Islands as it applies in relation to British fishing boats registered in the United Kingdom.

SEA FISH (CONSERVATION) (MANX BOATS) ORDER 1978 (No. 281) [10p], made under the Sea Fish (Conservation) Act 1967, s. 24 (1) and the Fishery Limits Act 1976, s. 11 (3); operative on March 8, 1978; applies s. 4 of the 1967 Act (as substituted by s. 3 of the 1976 Act) to British fishing boats registered in the Isle of Man as it applies in relation to British fishing boats registered in the United Kingdom.

EASTERN SEA FISHERIES DISTRICT (VARIATION) ORDER 1978 (No. 438) [25p], made under the Sea Fisheries Regulation Act 1966 (c. 38), s. 1; operative on April 1, 1978; enlarges the Eastern Sea Fisheries District and varies the constitution of the Eastern Local Fisheries Committee as a result of the Suffolk County Council being made a constituent council of the committee.

WEST COAST HERRING (PROHIBITION OF FISHING) ORDER 1978 (No. 930) [20p], made under the Sea Fish (Conservation) Act 1967, ss. 5 (1) (2), 15 as amended by the Sea Fisheries Act 1968 (c. 77), s. 22 (1), Sched. 1, para. 38 and the Fishery Limits Act 1976, s. 9 (1), Sched. 2, para. 16 (1); operative on July 6, 1978; prohibits the fishing for herring in the area of sea specified in the Order.

FISHING NETS (NORTH-EAST ATLANTIC) (VARIATION) ORDER 1978 (No. 946) [20p], made under the Sea Fish (Conservation) Act 1967, ss. 3, 15 as amended by the Sea Fisheries Act 1968, s. 22 (1), Sched. 1, para. 38 and the Fishery Limits Act 1976, s. 9 (1), Sched. 2, para. 16 (1); operative on July 11, 1978; amends S.I. 1977 No. 440 by reducing limits where a by-catch limit is fixed for fishing with small mesh nets to 10 per cent of the catch.

HADDOCK (NORTH SEA) LICENSING ORDER 1978 (No. 1285) [20p], made under the Sea Fish (Conservation) Act 1967, ss. 4, 15 as amended by the Sea Fisheries Act 1968 (c. 77), s. 22 (1), Sched. 1, Pt. II, para. 38 and the Fishery Limits Act 1976, ss. 3, 9 (1), Sched. 2, para. 16 (1); operative on September 18, 1978; prohibits fishing by British fishing boats registered in the U.K. for haddock in the North Sea except under licence, but exempts from this prohibition fishing by British boats of registered length less than 40 feet.

HADDOCK (RESTRICTIONS ON LANDING) (REVOCATION) ORDER 1978 (No. 1286) [10p], made under the Sea Fish (Conservation) Act 1967, ss. 6, 15, 20 (1) as amended by the Sea Fisheries Act 1968, s. 22 (1); Sched. 1, Pt. II, para. 38 and the Fishery Limits Act 1976, s. 9 (1), Sched. 2, para. 16 (1); operative on September 11, 1978; revokes S.I. 1977 No. 781.

WEST COAST HADDOCK (RESTRICTIONS ON LANDING) ORDER 1978 (No. 1287) [20p], made under the Sea Fish (Conservation) Act 1967, ss. 6, 15 as amended by the Sea Fisheries Act 1968, s. 22 (1), Sched. 1, para. 38 and the Fishery Limits Act 1976, s. 9 (1), Sched. 2, para. 16 (1); operative on September 11, 1978; prohibits the landing in the U.K. of haddock caught in waters off the West Coast of Scotland by a British fishing boat but excepts from this prohibition the landing of specified quantities of haddock.

IRISH SEA HERRING (PROHIBITION OF FISHING) ORDER 1978 (No. 1374) [20p], made under the Sea Fish (Conservation) Act 1967, ss. 5 (1) (2), 15 as amended by the Sea Fisheries Act 1968, s. 22 (1), Sched. 1, para. 38 and the Fishery Limits Act 1976, s. 9 (1), Sched. 2, para. 16 (1); operative on September 24, 1978; prohibits fishing for herring in a specified sea area until January 1, 1979.

NORWAY POUT (PROHIBITION OF FISHING) (NO. 3) (VARIATION) ORDER 1978 (No. 1379) [20p], made under the Sea Fish (Conservation) Act 1967, ss. 5 (1) (2), 15, 20 (1) as amended by the Sea Fisheries Act 1968, s. 22 (1), Sched. 1, para. 38 and the Fishery Limits Act 1967, s. 9 (1), Sched. 2, para. 16 (1); operative on October 1, 1978; varies S.I. 1977 No. 1756 by redefining the area within which the fishing for Norway Pout is prohibited.

ROCKALL HADDOCK (RESTRICTIONS ON LANDING) ORDER 1978 (No. 1413) [20p], made under the Sea Fish (Conservation) Act 1967, ss. 6, 15 as amended by the Sea Fisheries Act 1968, s. 22 (1), Sched. 1, para. 38 and by the Fishery Limits Act 1976, s. 9 (1), Sched. 2, para. 16 (1); operative on October 9, 1978; prohibits the landing in the U.K. of haddock caught in waters of Rockall by a British fishing boat. Also prohibits the landing of undersized haddock which may be lawfully landed.

MACKEREL LICENSING (MANX AND CHANNEL ISLANDS BOATS) ORDER 1978 (No. 1537) [20p], made under the Sea Fish (Conservation) Act 1967, s. 4; operative on November 5, 1978; prohibits fishing for mackerel by British fishing boats registered in the Isle of Man or any of the Channel Islands in ICES areas IV, VI, VII and VIII, unless that fishing is authorised by licence granted by a Fisheries Minister.

MACKEREL LICENSING (VARIATION) ORDER 1978 (No. 1538) [10p], made under the Sea Fish (Conservation) Act 1967, ss. 4 and 20 (1), as amended by the Fishery Limits Act 1976, s. 3, and S.I. 1978 No. 272; operative on November 5, 1978; varies S.I. 1977 No. 1497 which prohibits fishing without a licence by British fishing boats registered in the United Kingdom for mackerel in specified areas. The present order excepts from prohibition fishing by hand-line or fishing by British fishing boats whose registered length is less than 40 feet.

SOUTHERN SEA FISHERIES (VARIATION) ORDER 1978 (No. 1715) [20p], made under the Sea Fisheries Regulation Act 1966 (c. 38), ss. 1, 18 (1); operative on December 1, 1978; varies the description of the limits of the Southern Sea Fisheries District.

1487. —— conservation—EEC. See E.C. COMMISSION *v.* IRELAND, § 1246.

1488. Several fishery—extent—low water mark

A several fishery in private ownership is not necessarily confined to the area above the mean low water mark of ordinary tides; it may extend seaward as far as the low water mark at spring tides. (*Gann* v. *Free Fishers of Whitstable* (1865) 11 H.L.Cas. 193 applied): LOOSE *v.* CASTLETON, *The Times,* June 21, 1978, C.A.

1489. Shell fish

MENAI STRAIT (WEST) OYSTER, MUSSEL AND CLAM FISHERY ORDER 1978 (No. 243) [15p], made under the Sea Fisheries (Shellfish) Act 1967 (c. 83), s. 1, Sched. 1, as amended by the Sea Fisheries Act 1968 (c. 77), s. 15 (2), and S.I. 1969 No. 388; operative on March 23, 1978; confers upon the Local Fisheries Joint Committee for the Lancashire and Western Sea Fisheries District the right of several or exclusive fishery for specified shellfish over parts of the bed of the Menai Strait.

1489a. White fish industry

WHITE FISH AUTHORITY (RESEARCH AND DEVELOPMENT GRANTS) ORDER 1978 (No. 1821) [10p], made under the Sea Fish Industry Act 1970 (c. 11), s. 23 (2) and S.I. 1978 No. 272; operative on December 9, 1978; increases by £1 million to £6 million the aggregate amount of any grants payable to the White Fish Authority for the purpose of research or experiment or in providing plants for processing white fish or making ice.

FOOD AND DRUGS

1490. Additives and contaminants

The Government has published a report by the Food Additives and Contaminants Committee that recommends that changes should be made to the existing provisions of the Preservatives in Food Regulations 1975 (S.I. 1975 No. 1487), as amended, concerning the levels of nitrite and nitrate permitted in cured meats and certain cheeses. The report is available from H.M.S.O. [40p].

1491. Antioxidants

ANTIOXIDANTS IN FOOD REGULATIONS 1978 (No. 105) [35p], made under the Food and Drugs Act 1955 (c. 16), ss. 4, 7, 82, 123, as amended by the European Communities Act 1972 (c. 68), s. 4 (1), Sched. 4, para. 3 (1), as read with S.I. 1968 No. 1699; operative on February 28, 1978; re-enact S.I. 1974 No. 1120, as amended, which implemented Council Directive 70/357/EEC, on the approximation of the laws of the Member States concerning the antioxidants authorised for use in foodstuffs intended for human consumption.

1492. Bread

BREAD PRICES (NO. 2) ORDER 1976 (AMENDMENT) (NO. 5) ORDER 1978 (No. 516) [10p], made under the Prices Act 1974 (c. 24), s. 2 (1) (6) (8); operative on April 3, 1978; varies S.I. 1976 No. 2128 by increasing the maximum retail price of most bread loaves of 28 oz. or less.

BREAD PRICES (NO. 2) ORDER 1976 (AMENDMENT) (NO. 6) ORDER 1978 (No. 545) [10p], made under the Prices Act 1974, s. 2 (1) (6) (8); operative on May 2, 1978; provides that S.I. 1976 No. 2128 shall apply to bread sold in metric quantities.

BREAD (NO. 2) ORDER 1976 (AMENDMENT) (NO. 7) ORDER 1978 (No. 1790) [10p], made under the Prices Act 1974, s. 2 (1) (6) (8); operative December 11, 1978; varies S.I. 1976 No. 2128 by increasing the maximum retail price of most bread loaves of 800g or less.

1493. Butter

BUTTER PRICES ORDER 1978 (No. 97) [15p], made under the Prices Act 1974 (c. 24), s. 2 (1) (6) (8); operative on February 16, 1978; revokes S.I. 1977 No. 786 and reproduces with modifications the provisions of that Order which regulated the maximum price to be charged for butter subject to the EEC butter subsidy.

BUTTER PRICES (AMENDMENT) ORDER 1978 (No. 835) [10p], made under the Prices Act 1974, s. 2 (1) (6) (8); operative on July 1, 1978; varies S.I. 1978 No. 97 by increasing the maximum retail prices of butter.

CONCENTRATED BUTTER PRICES ORDER 1978 (No. 971) [10p], made under the Prices Act 1974, s. 2 (1) (4) (6); operative on August 14, 1978; regulates the maximum price which may be charged for the sale by retail of concentrated butter produced from butter sold from intervention stocks at a reduced price under the provisions of Commission Regulation (EEC) No. 649/78.

1494. Cheese

CHEESE PRICES ORDERS (REVOCATION) ORDER 1978 (No. 98) [10p], made under the Prices Act 1974 (c. 24), s. 2 (6); operative on February 16, 1978; revokes those provisions of S.I. 1976 No. 1929 remaining unrevoked, and S.I. 1977 No. 193.

PRICE MARKING (CHEESE) (AMENDMENT) ORDER 1978 (No. 133) [10p], made under the Prices Act 1974, s. 4 (3); operative on March 1, 1978; amends S.I. 1977 No. 1334, and makes provision for price marking of pre-packed natural cheeses.

1495. Coffee

COFFEE AND COFFEE PRODUCTS REGULATIONS 1978 (No. 1420) [40p], made under the Food and Drugs Act 1955 (c. 16), ss. 4, 7, 82, 123 as amended by the European Communities Act 1972 (c. 68), s. 4 (1), Sched. 4, para. 3 (1), as read with S.I. 1968 No. 1699 and S.I. 1978 No. 272; operative on July 12, 1980, save for Regs. 1, 2 and 16 which are operative on October 24, 1978; implement Council Directive No. 77/436/EEC on the approximation of the laws of the Member States relating to coffee extracts and chicory extracts.

1496. Colouring matters

COLOURING MATTER IN FOOD (AMENDMENT) REGULATIONS 1978 (No. 1787) [20p], made under the Food and Drugs Act 1955 (c. 16), ss. 4, 7, 123, as amended by the European Communities Act 1972 (c. 68), s. 4 (1), Sched. 4, para. 3 (1), as read with S.I. 1968 No. 1699 and S.I. 1978 No. 272; operative on January 1, 1979; amend S.I. 1973 No. 1340.

1497. Dangerous drugs. See CRIMINAL LAW; MEDICINE.

1498. Food subsidies

BUTTER SUBSIDY (PROTECTION OF COMMUNITY ARRANGEMENTS) REGULATIONS 1978 (No. 214) [15p], made under the European Communities Act 1972 (c. 68),

s. 2 (2); operative on March 20, 1978; enable the subsidy paid on butter under Council Reg. 880/77 to be recovered where the butter has been exported from the U.K. or has been used for manufacture.

BUTTER SUBSIDY (PROTECTION OF COMMUNITY ARRANGEMENTS) (AMENDMENT) REGULATIONS 1978 (No. 960) [10p], made under the European Communities Act 1972, s. 2 (2); operative on July 13, 1978; amend the definition of "subsidy payment" in S.I. 1978 No. 214 by adding a reference to Council Directive (EEC) No. 1040/78.

BUTTER SUBSIDY (PROTECTION OF COMMUNITY ARRANGEMENTS) (AMENDMENT No. 2) REGULATIONS 1978 (No. 1592) [10p], made under the European Communities Act 1972, s. 2 (2); operative on November, 9, 1978; further amend the definition of "subsidy payment" in S.I. 1978 No. 214 by adding a reference to Council Regulation (EEC) No. 2574/78 which has further amended Council Regulation (EEC) No. 880/77 on the granting of a consumer subsidy for butter.

1499. Import of food—official certificates

The Ministry of Agriculture, Fisheries and Food has issued the following circulars under the Imported Food Regulations 1968, as amended: 3/78 (South West Africa); 4/78 (Finland); 5/78 (Denmark); 6/78 (Hungary); 7/78 (France); 8/78 (France); 9/78 (Canada); 10/78 (Federal Republic of Germany); 11/78 (Switzerland); 12/78 (Belgium); 13/78 (Italy); 14/78 (Australia); 15/78 (Belgium); 16/78 (Sweden); 17/78 (Belgium); 18/78 (Federal Republic of Germany); 19/78 (Netherlands); 20/78 (Official Certificate Procedure—Poultry Meat); 21/78 (Austria); 22/78 (Denmark); 23/78 (France); 24/78 (Australia); 25/78 (Federal Republic of Germany); 26/78 (Argentina); 2778 (South Africa); 28/78 (Sweden); 29/78 (Finland); 30/78 (Norway); 31/78 (Republic of Ireland); 32/78 (Italy); 33/78 (Portugal); 34/78 (New Zealand); 35/78 (Netherlands); 25/78 (Federal Republic of Germany); 26/78 (Argentina); 27/78 (South Africa); 36/78 (Belguim); 37/78 (France); 38/78 (Sweden); 39/78 (Switzerland); 40/78 (Netherlands); 41/78 (Australia); 42/78 (Italy); 43/78 (Denmark); 44/78 (Federal Republic of Germany); 45/78 (Belgium); 46/78 (France); 47/78 (Hungary); 48/78 (Republic of Ireland); 49/78 (France); 50/78 (Australia); 51/78 (Belgium); 52/78 (Botswana); 53/78 (Netherlands); 54/78 (Denmark); 55/78 (France); 56/78 (Italy); 57/78 (Spain); 58/78 (Portugal); 59/78 (Argentina); 60/78 (Netherlands); 61/78 (Finland); 62/78 (Brazil); 63/78 (Denmark); 64/78 (Sweden); 65/78 (Belgium); 66/78 (Republic of Ireland); 67/68 (Switzerland); 68/78 (Ethiopia); 69/78 (Federal Republic of Germany); 70/78 (Austria).

1500. Labelling

PACKAGING AND LABELLING OF DANGEROUS SUBSTANCES REGULATIONS 1978 (No. 209) [£1], made under the European Communities Act 1972 (c. 68), s. 2, and the Health and Safety at Work, etc., Act 1974 (c. 37), ss. 11 (2) (*d*), 15 (1), (3) (*a*) (*c*), (4) (*b*), (6) (*b*) (*d*), 82 (3) (*a*), Sched. 3, para. 1 (1) (*b*), (4) as amended by the Employment Protection Act 1975 (c. 71), s. 116, Sched. 15, para. 6; operative for the purposes of Reg. 1 (*a*) on September 1, 1978, operative for all other purposes on March 1, 1979; implement as respects Great Britain the provisions of Directive 67/548/EEC as amended on the classification, packaging and labelling of dangerous substances.

PREPACKING AND LABELLING OF WINE AND GRAPE MUST (EEC REQUIREMENTS) REGULATIONS 1978 (No. 463) [35p], made under the European Communities Act 1972, s. 2 (2); operative on May 15, 1978; implement certain requirements relating to the prepackaging and labelling of wine and grape must imposed by Council Regulation (EEC) No. 2133/74.

LABELLING OF FOOD (AMENDMENT) REGULATIONS 1978 (No. 646) [10p], made under the Food and Drugs Act 1955 (c. 16), ss. 7, 82, 123 as read with S.I. 1968 No. 1699 and S.I. 1978 No. 272; Reg. 3 operative on April 1, 1980, the remainder operative on May 30, 1978; amend S.I. 1970 No. 400 and specify new appropriate designations for types of pilchard.

1501. Materials in contact with food

MATERIALS AND ARTICLES IN CONTACT WITH FOOD REGULATIONS 1978 (No. 1927) [30p], made under the European Communities Act 1972 (c. 68), s. 2 (2); operative on November 26, 1979; implement Council Directive No. 76/893/EEC on the approximation of the laws of Member States relating to materials and articles intended to come into contact with foodstuffs.

1502. Meat inspection

AUTHORISED OFFICERS (MEAT INSPECTION) REGULATIONS 1978 (No. 884) [10p], made under the Food and Drugs Act 1955 (c. 16), s. 86 (4) (*d*), as read with S.I. 1968 No. 1699 and S.I. 1978 No. 272; operative on July 7, 1978; prescribe the qualifications to be held by an officer of a council authorised to act in relation to the examination and seizure of meat.

1503. Milk

MILK (GREAT BRITAIN) (AMENDMENT) ORDER 1978 (No. 469) [10p], made under the Emergency Laws (Re-enactments and Repeals) Act 1964 (c. 60), ss. 6, 7 as extended by S.I. 1969 No. 1058 and S.I. 1974 No. 2139; operative on April 1, 1978; prescribes revised maximum prices for the sale in Great Britain of raw milk for heat treatment.

MILK (GREAT BRITAIN) (AMENDMENT) (No. 2) ORDER 1978 (No. 1382) [10p], made under the Emergency Laws (Re-enactments and Repeals) Act 1964, ss. 6, 7 as continued in force by S.I. 1969 No. 1058 and S.I. 1974 No. 2139; operative on October 1, 1978; provides that an additional charge for Channel Islands and South Devon milk may be made at a rate of 2·904p per litre between April and September, and at the rate of 3·124p between October and March.

MILK (GREAT BRITAIN) (AMENDMENT) (No. 3) ORDER 1978 (No. 1498) [20p], made under the Emergency Laws (Re-enactments and Repeals) Act 1964, ss. 6, 7, S.I. 1969 No. 1058 and S.I. 1974 No. 2139; operative on November 5, 1978; increases the maximum retail price of milk.

1504. Northern Ireland. See NORTHERN IRELAND.

1505. Poisons. See MEDICINE.

1506. Price marking

PRICE MARKING (FOOD) ORDER 1978 (No. 738) [20p], made under the Prices Act 1974 (c. 24), s. 4 (3); operative on July 1, 1978; requires the display of prices for the sale of food and drink for human consumption when an indication is given on any premises or at any place.

FOOD (PROHIBITION OF REPRICING) ORDER 1978 (No. 1014) [10p], made under the Prices Act 1974, s. 2 (1) (4) (6); operative on August 14, 1978; prohibits the repricing of food which has been displayed for retail sale marked with a price.

1507. Unfit for human consumption—sale—whether in " same state " after being deep frozen

[Food and Drugs Act 1955 (c. 16), ss. 8 (1) (*a*), 115 (1).]

Food may be described as being in the " same state " when thawed as when deep frozen.

D, who owned a food shop, bought some frozen pastry, which they put into their freezer. Eleven days later, when on a shelf where it had been placed to thaw, it was bought by a customer and found to be mouldy. D, when prosecuted for selling food intended for, but unfit for, human consumption, relied successfully on the defence that, notwithstanding the fact that the pastry was thawing, it was in the " same state " as when it was received from the supplier. *Held*, dismissing the prosecutor's appeal, that although the organic content of the pastry had changed by natural deterioration there was no evidence that the freezing and thawing had affected its state or that D had tampered with it, so that the justices could not be said to be wrong in concluding that the pastry was in the " same state," within the meaning of the Food and Drugs Act 1955, s. 115 (1), when sold as when supplied to D.

WALKER *v*. BAXTER'S BUTCHERS (1977) 76 L.G.R. 183, D.C.

1508. Welfare foods

WELFARE FOOD (AMENDMENT) ORDER 1978 (No. 269) [10p], made under the Emergency Laws (Re-enactments and Repeals) Act 1964 (c. 60), ss. 4, 7; operative on April 3, 1978; further amends S.I. 1977 No. 25 by adding an additional brand of modified dried milk to the list of those approved for the purposes of that Order.

WELFARE FOOD (AMENDMENT No. 2) ORDER 1978 (No. 1876) [10p], made under the Emergency Laws (Re-enactments and Repeals) Act 1964, ss. 4, 7; operative on January 15, 1979; further amends S.I. 1977 No. 25 by increasing the prices at which Children's Vitamin Drops and Vitamin Tablets for expectant and nursing mothers may be bought.

FORESTRY

1509. New Forest

NEW FOREST (CONFIRMATION OF BYELAWS OF THE VERDERERS OF THE NEW FOREST) ORDER 1978 (No. 1277) [25p], made under the New Forest Act 1877 (c. cxxi), s. 25 as extended by the New Forest Act 1949 (c. 69), s. 9 and amended by the New Forest Act 1964 (c. 83), s. 12; operative on October 4, 1978; confirms by-laws made by the Verderers amending and extending by-laws previously confirmed.

FRAUD, MISREPRESENTATION AND UNDUE INFLUENCE

1510. Fraud—damages—innocent breach of law—public policy

[Exchange Control Act 1947 (c. 14), s. 5.]

Where there is an innocent breach of the Exchange Control Act 1947, an action for damages may be allowed in order to recover damages for fraud in respect of money paid notwithstanding such breach.

P wanted a house in Spain. D had one. P paid money into D's bank account in England, although D lived in Spain. She was thus, innocently, in breach of s. 5 of the Exchange Control Act 1947. D was unable to give P the house, and disappeared. P sought to recover damages for D's fraud. *Held*, giving judgment for P, that as her claim was for damages for fraud, and not for the return of the money, and as her breach had been innocent, public policy did not prevent her from recovering damages.

SHELLEY *v.* PADDOCK [1978] 2 W.L.R. 877, Bristow J.

1511. Insurance fraud—appropriate sentence. See R. *v.* HALEWOOD, § 618.

1512. Misrepresentation—contract of employment—job offer—knowledge of employee's lack of experience

The defendants advertised in a newspaper for staff to work in an oil refinery in Libya and specified that applicants must have three years' experience of oil refinery work. The plaintiff, who was a chemical plant operator, applied but was initially rejected. His curriculum vitae made it clear he had no oil refinery experience. However, at a later date he was contacted by telephone and told that a post was available. He was interviewed by the second defendant who had his curriculum vitae and who told him that the work in Libya would be similar to his current work. He was also told that he would be allowed a period of familiarisation with the plant. He was not given any details of the work he would have to do. His contract, which he signed without reading, provided, inter alia, that (a) the plaintiff would undergo such tests as were required by the defendants and if he failed, then the contract would be void ab initio; and (b) if the defendants were required by their client to remove the plaintiff (for whatever reason), they could do so. The plaintiff left for Libya but his lack of experience made him unacceptable to the Libyan client and within two weeks his employment was terminated and he was repatriated. He was out of work for some months and it was almost a year before his earnings matched what he had earned before joining the defendants. By his action he claimed damages for misrepresentation and negligence on the part of the defendants; the misrepresentation being both by statement and by conduct in offering the job. *Held*, that (1) although in an ordinary case, when a man applies for a job he holds himself out as capable of fulfilling it, on these facts, where the defendants had details of the job offered and of the experience of the applicant, the plaintiff could and did rely on the representations of the defendants. There was a misrepresentation to which s. 2 of the Misrepresentation Act 1967 applied; (2) also, (applying *Hedley Byrne & Co.* v. *Heller & Partners* [1963] C.L.Y. 2416) there was a duty of care on the defendants and that duty had not been discharged; (3) accordingly, the plaintiff was entitled to damages, the correct basis of assessment being that laid down in *Doyle* v. *Olby (Ironmongers)* [1969] C.L.Y. 1528, namely all damage directly flowing from the tortious act (*i.e.* loss of earnings, travelling and other expenses involved in seeking new employment); (4) the plaintiff was awarded £400 general damages for worry and inconvenience: McNALLY v. WELLTRADE INTERNATIONAL, July 14, 1978, Sir Douglas Frank Q.C. (*Ex rel. Charles Douthwaite, Esq., Barrister.*)

1513. —— **insurance—agent using undue influence—whether contract concluded.**

P wished to invest the £90,000 standing in her bank account, and it was recommended that she put her money in the property bonds of D1, an insurance company. Accordingly, P met D2, D1's agent, who explained the nature and advantages of the property bond policy, and offered P D1's " liquidity facility." P then arranged a meeting between her accountant and D2, who explained the property bond and the liquidity facility, to which the accountant gave his approval. P and D2 then went to P's bank and P, after a discussion with the bank manager, handed over a cheque for £91,600 in D1's favour. Five or six months later, P requested that £50,000–£60,000 of her investment be returned to her. She was unwilling to accept a surrender value, and D2 were unwilling to return all the money P had paid to them. P claimed that she never intended to make this investment, but a short-term deposit with a similarly named building society; that D2 had misrepresented the nature of property bonds and had exercised undue influence to obtain P's application; and that no binding contract was ever concluded. *Held*, that (1) D2 owed a duty to give an adequate explanation of the nature of property bonds and the liquidity facility beyond the duty not to make misrepresentation without proper grounds; (2) such misrepresentations were never made by D2, and the question of negligence or lack of reasonable grounds did not arise; (3) this was supported by the fact that D2 was interviewed by P's accountant and bank manager; and within the limits of his duty, he was entitled to commend what he was offering; and, further, P knew that he was an insurance agent; (4) P and D2 were not ill-matched in terms of business capacity and influence; P had the benefit of independent advice, and the benefit which D1 took from her was in no way unconscionable; and there was accordingly no ground for equitable relief; (5) P's application form was an offer to invest the money accompanying it, and D2's allocation of units in their property bond fund to P an acceptance of that offer; the subsequent sending of the policy was merely a record of an antecedent agreement on the terms contained in it; (6) upon receipt of the policy, P was obliged to reject it expressly, if it or any part of it was not what she required or had been led to expect, within a reasonable time, and this she had not done. Accordingly, her claim failed on all the grounds advanced: RUST v. ABBEY LIFE ASSURANCE CO. [1978] 2 Lloyd's Rep. 386, C. M. Clothier, Q.C., Deputy Judge.

1514. —— **insurance broker—duration of policy.** See CHERRY v. ALLIED INSURANCE BROKERS, § 1695.

1515. —— **lease—failure to check information**

A description of premises wrongly representing the availability of unrestricted planning permission for their intended use amounts to a negligent misrepresentation in that this point could have been checked prior to the signing of the lease.

In 1971 the plaintiff property owners sought permission from the local planning authority to change its use from shop and living accommodation to offices, which permission was granted for part of the property only. Forgetting this, the plaintiffs offered to let the whole of the property to the defendants for use as offices for 15 years. Presuming planning permission existed, the defendants took possession immediately without making any of the usual searches and inquiries, leaving the details to their solicitors. They were then informed by their solicitors of the restrictions of the planning permission. The parties agreed the plaintiffs should apply for permission to use the whole property as offices. This was granted but for a limited period to expire on

October 31, 1977, for review in the light of a new road planning contemplated for the area. No alternative leasehold arrangement proved satisfactory and in April 1975 the defendants gave the plaintiffs a month's notice. The plaintiffs sought specific performance of the agreement for a lease. The defendants claimed they were absolved from carrying out the agreement on grounds of negligent misrepresentation, common mistake or illegality. *Held*, dismissing the plaintiffs' claim and rescinding the agreement, that (1) the plaintiffs were negligent in representing that the property had the requisite planning permission for a term of 15 years and in not checking that information. (*Re Davis and Carey* (1888) 40 Ch.D. 601 and *Charles Hunt* v. *Palmer* [1931] 2 Ch. 287 applied); (2) alternatively, belief in unrestricted planning permission was a fundamental mistake and the defendants were not at fault in failing to make the usual searches and inquiries as they owed no duty of care to the plaintiffs so to do. The defence of common mistake was therefore open to them; they did not cause the plaintiffs' forgetfulness (*Solle* v. *Butcher* (1949) C.L.C. 8914 and *Grist* v. *Bailey* [1966] C.L.Y. 1854 applied); (3) the fact they acceded to the negotiations and suggestions offered for other arrangements did not affect the defendants' claim. They were entitled to consider the possibilities then open to them during the period of uncertainty.

LAURENCE *v.* LEXCOURT HOLDINGS [1978] 2 All E.R. 810, Brian Dillon Q.C.

1516. Negligent misrepresentation—pre-contractual statement—absolute obligation
[Misrepresentation Act 1967 (c. 7), ss. 2 (1), 3.]

The liability of the representor under s. 2 (1) of the Act does not depend upon his being under a duty of care. In negotiations leading to a contract, the statute imposes an absolute obligation not to state facts which the representor cannot prove he had reasonable grounds to believe.

A Ltd., civil engineering contractors, entered negotiations with H Ltd. for the hire of two sea-going barges, owned by H Ltd., for carrying vast quantities of clay out to sea. At a meeting on July 11, 1974, the owners' marine manager orally represented to A Ltd. that the capacity of the barges was 1,600 tonnes deadweight. He based that figure on his recollection of an entry in Lloyd's Register which gave the capacities as 1,800 tonnes. The Register was erroneous, and the correct deadweight capacity was 1,055 tonnes, which could have been ascertained from the ship's document in possession of H Ltd. A Ltd. continued negotiations without obtaining any other figure for the vital matter of deadweight capacity, and took the barges into use under a charterparty. The charterparty included an exception clause that the charterers' acceptance at handing over the barges should be conclusive that they had examined them and found them fit for their purpose. After about six months' use, A Ltd. discovered the correct capacity and paid £20,000 for the hire, refusing to pay any more. H Ltd. withdrew the barges and issued proceedings claiming outstanding hire charges. A Ltd. denied liability, and counterclaimed for damages alleging, inter alia, (1) breaches of collateral warranties in the representations before contract; (2) negligence arising from a special relationship between the parties and (3) liability under s. 2 (1) of the Act. Bristow J. gave judgment for H Ltd. On appeal by A Ltd., and cross-notice by H Ltd., *held*, allowing the appeal in part, that (1) there was nothing in the pre-contract negotiations which could amount to a collateral warranty; (2) *per* Bridge and Shaw L.JJ., the misrepresentation at the meeting of July 11, 1974, as to the deadweight capacity, was a most material matter and H Ltd. had not proven that their marine manager had reasonable grounds for believing, and did believe, that the facts represented were true; (3) *per* Shaw and Bridge L.JJ., H Ltd. could not escape liability by reliance on the exception clause, since it was a provision which came within s. 3 of the Act and was therefore of no effect unless the court allowed reliance upon it as being " fair and reasonable in the circumstances of the case " and since it was not " fair and reasonable " to allow reliance upon it, the cross-appeal should be dismissed. *Per* Shaw L.J., A Ltd. also had a cause of action in negligence at common law.

HOWARD MARINE AND DREDGING CO. *v.* A. OGDEN & SONS (EXCAVATIONS) [1978] 2 W.L.R. 515, C.A.

1517. Undue influence—guarantee signed under business pressure—no wrongful act or abuse—whether enforceable

[Can.] A person signed, in the course of business, a guarantee of his company's debts in favour of a creditor. *Held*, he could not avoid the guarantee simply on the ground that he felt himself to be under pressure at the time. Where the creditor is unaware of the pressure, commits no wrongful act, and takes advantage of no personal relationship with the guarantor, there is no undue influence or unconscionability, and the guarantee is enforceable. (*Lloyds Bank* v. *Bundy* [1974] C.L.Y. 1691 distinguished): THERMO-FLO CORP. v. KURYLUK (1978) 84 D.L.R. (3d) 529, Nova Scotia Sup.Ct.

ARTICLES. See *post*, p. [24].

FRIENDLY SOCIETIES

1518. Dissolution—disposal of assets—objects of the society

[Friendly Societies Act 1896 (c. 25), s. 79 (4).]

A friendly society, upon dissolution, is not entitled to dispose of its assets other than in accordance with the declared objects of the society.

A police friendly society had as its objects the provision of relief to relatives of deceased members and the relief of members during sickness. Following reorganisation of police areas, the society was dissolved and it was resolved that the assets of the society should be applied, inter alia, by way of donation to other police benevolent funds. The trustee of the society sought directions as to whether he was entitled so to dispose of the funds. *Held*, that by virtue of s. 79 (4) of the 1896 Act, the trustee could dispose of such funds only amongst those entitled to them under the objects of the society or otherwise under the general law: the benevolent funds in question were not so entitled.

Re BUCKS. CONSTABULARY WIDOWS' AND ORPHANS' FUND FRIENDLY SOCIETY; THOMPSON v. HOLDSWORTH [1978] 1 W.L.R. 641, Megarry V.-C.

1519. ——— ——— surplus

[Friendly Societies Act 1896 (c. 25), s. 49 (1).] The object of the society was to provide by voluntary contributions from members for the relief of widows and orphans of deceased members. On dissolution of the society, the question was what was to happen to the surplus assets. By virtue of s. 49 on ceasing to be a member of the society, any interest in its funds also ceased. *Held*, the assets were held on trust for members in existence at the time of dissolution to the exclusion of any claim on behalf of the Crown as *bona vacantia* (*Re West Sussex Constabulary Widows, Children and Benevolent (1930) Fund* [1970] C.L.Y. 2632 distinguished): *Re* BUCKS CONSTABULARY WIDOWS AND ORPHANS FUND FRIENDLY SOCIETY (NO. 2), *The Times*, July 13, 1978, Walton J.

1520. Fees

FRIENDLY SOCIETIES (FEES) REGULATIONS 1978 (No. 1717) [20p], made under the Friendly Societies Act 1974 (c. 46), s. 104 (1) and S.I. 1971 No. 1900 art. 2; operative on January 1, 1979; increase the fees to be paid for matters to be transacted, and for the inspection of documents under the 1974 Act. They supersede S.I. 1977 No. 2001.

1521. Limits of benefit

FRIENDLY SOCIETIES (LIMITS OF BENEFITS) ORDER 1978 (No. 920) [10p], made under the Friendly Societies Act 1974 (c. 46), s. 64 (3); operative on July 31, 1978; raises the limit on the amounts which a member of a registered friendly society may be entitled to receive from one or more such societies under non-tax exempt business. The new limits are (i) £15,000 by way of gross sum under life or endowment business and, (ii) to £1,500 by way of annuity.

1522. Premium relief

FRIENDLY SOCIETIES (LIFE ASSURANCE PREMIUM RELIEF) (AMENDMENT) REGULATIONS 1978 (No. 1160) [10p], made under the Finance Act 1976 (c. 40), Sched. 4, para. 13; operative on September 4, 1978; amend S.I. 1977 No. 1143 so that when a friendly society adopts the prescribed scheme, the scheme will apply only to contributions due and payable after April 5, 1979.

GAME

1523. Northern Ireland. See NORTHERN IRELAND.

GAMING AND WAGERING

1524. Amusements with prizes

GAMING ACT (VARIATION OF MONETARY LIMITS) ORDER 1978 (No. 37) [10p], made under the Gaming Act 1968 (c. 65), ss. 34 (9) and 51 (4); operative on February 20, 1978; increases the maximum amounts which may be offered as prizes in amusements by means of machines provided at certain fairs, licensed club premises and other commercial entertainments under s. 34 of the 1968 Act.

1525. Betting duty—assessment—time limit

[Betting and Gaming Duties Act 1972, Sched. 1, para. 11.] G, an on-course bookmaker, pleaded guilty to offences of fraudulent evasion of betting duty between September and December 1974. The Commissioners made an estimate of unpaid duty between September 1971 and December 1974, and issued appropriate assessments. *Held*, that the assessments were good, para. 11 of Sched. 1 to the Betting and Gaming Duties Act 1972 giving the Commissioners powers of recovery unrestricted by time: CUSTOMS AND EXCISE COMMISSIONERS *v.* GUILE, *The Times*, November 17, 1978, Sheen J.

1526. Betting levy

HORSERACE BETTING LEVY SCHEMES (VARIATION OF SETTLEMENT PERIOD) ORDER 1978 (No. 496) [10p], made under the Horserace Betting Levy Act 1969 (c. 14), s. 1 (7); operative on May 1, 1978; provides that s. 1 (2) of the 1969 Act will come into force on August 1 in any year, instead of on October 1, in relation to the scheme for the year following.

1527. Betting shop—claim for money due—whether claim void

[Gaming Act 1845 (c. 109), s. 18.]
A firm of bookmakers cannot sue its employee on his contract of employment for breach of its instructions when entering a wagering transaction.

P Co., who owned betting shops, brought an action against D, who had been one of their managers, for damages for breach of his contract of employment in allowing customers to bet on credit contrary to their instructions. They argued that when the customers failed to pay, the money could not be recovered from them as the debt arose from wagering transactions, and that therefore the manager was liable for his own breach of contract. *Held*, the transaction was equally vitiated, vis-à-vis the manager under s. 18 of the Gaming Act 1845, and no suit could be maintained in any court to recover it. (*Hill* v. *William Hill (Park Lane)* (1949) C.L.C. 4254 applied; *Thomas Cheshire & Co.* v. *Vaughan Brothers & Co.* [1920] 3 K.B. 240 considered.)
A. R. DENNIS & CO. *v.* CAMPBELL [1978] 2 W.L.R. 429, C.A.

1528. Bingo

GAMING CLUBS (HOURS AND CHARGES) (AMENDMENT) REGULATIONS 1978 (No. 38) [10p], made under the Gaming Act 1968 (c. 65), ss. 14 (2) and 51; operative on February 20, 1978; increase the maximum charges which may be made for admission to gaming on bingo club premises in England and Wales from £1 to £1·50.

1529. Fees

GAMING ACT (VARIATION OF FEES) ORDER 1978 (No. 1847) [10p], made under the Gaming Act 1968 (c. 65), ss. 48 (5), 51 (4); operative on May 1, 1979; increases the fees payable under the 1968 Act for specified purposes.

1530. Gaming machines

GAMING MACHINE LICENCE DUTY (EXEMPTIONS) ORDER 1978 (No. 44) [10p], made under the Betting and Gaming Duties Act 1972 (c. 25), Sched. 4, para. 2A, as amended by the Finance (No. 2) Act 1975 (c. 45), s. 4; operative on February 20, 1978; extends the exemption from gaming machine licence duty in respect of machines provided at pleasure fairs.

1531. Licence—application—validity—technical defect

[Gaming Act 1968 (c. 65), s. 42 (1) (3) (7), Sched. 2, para. 6 (2) (4).]

The requirements as to notices and displays should not be so strictly construed against an applicant that he is defeated by a purely technical objection.

A company applied for a licence under the Gaming Act 1968, and drafted their application following an Atkins precedent. The application was properly drafted except that it commenced with words of authentication and terminated with the signature and address of the applicant, both matters not strictly required to be included in the notice. Objections to the application on the grounds that these extra words invalidated the notice, were upheld by the licensing authority. The Divisional Court refused mandamus. On appeal, *held*, allowing the appeal, that objection to the inclusion of the signature, name and address of the company secretary was purely technical and formalistic, and since the notice was otherwise valid an order for mandamus would issue. (Dicta of Denning M.R. in *R.* v. *Newcastle-upon-Tyne Gaming Licensing Committee, ex p. White Hart Enterprises* [1977] C.L.Y. 1467 applied; *R.* v. *Loughborough Gaming Licensing Committee, ex p. Hamblins Leisure Services* June 21, 1976, D.C. overruled).

R. *v.* BRIGHTON GAMING LICENSING COMMITTEE, *ex p.* COTEDALE [1978] 1 W.L.R. 1140, C.A.

1532. Pool betting duty

H.M. Customs and Excise have issued Notice No. 147 (November 1977): pool betting duty.

1533. Pools Competitions Act 1971—continuation

POOLS COMPETITIONS ACT 1971 (CONTINUANCE) ORDER 1978 (No. 778) [10p], made under the Pools Competitions Act 1971 (c. 57), s. 8 (2) (3); operative on July 26, 1978; continues in force the 1971 Act until July 26, 1979.

ARTICLES. See *post*, p. [24].

GAS AND GASWORKS

1534. Finance

GAS (CONSUMERS' DEPOSITS) (RATE OF INTEREST) ORDER 1978 (No. 1848) [10p], made under the Gas Act 1972 (c. 60), Sched. 4, para. 30 (2); operative on April 1, 1979; increases to 7 per cent. per annum the rate of interest payable by the British Gas Corporation on every sum of 50p deposited with them by way of security under the Gas Supply Code for every six months which it remains in their hands. S.I. 1950 No. 687 is accordingly revoked.

1535. Northern Ireland. See NORTHERN IRELAND.

1536. Pressure

GAS QUALITY (AMENDMENT) REGULATIONS 1978 (No. 230) [10p], made under the Gas Act 1972 (c. 60), s. 26 (1); operative on March 21, 1978; substitute a new Table in S.I. 1972 No. 1804 that specifies a minimum pressure of 12·5 millibars in relation to gas with a Wobbe number exceeding 1075 but not exceeding 1940.

1537. Rating. See RATING AND VALUATION.

GIFTS

1538. Validity—mental capacity—test to be applied—gift of donor's only valuable asset

Where a gift inter vivos is made of the donor's only valuable asset, a high degree of understanding on the part of the donor is required to validate such gift.

Shortly before her death, the deceased, then aged 64, transferred to her daughter ownership of her house, which represented her only valuable asset. At the time of so doing the deceased told a solicitor and an old friend who were present that she understood the effect of her actions. After her death

intestate, her two other daughters sought a declaration avoiding the gift and adduced evidence that at the time of making the gift the deceased was suffering from senile dementia to such an extent that she would not have understood that she was making an absolute gift. *Held,* granting the declaration, that since the effect of the gift was to disentitle the plaintiffs to any share in her estate, of which the house was the only valuable asset, which effect was not apparently explained to her and in view of the medical evidence, the transfer was void. (*Manches* v. *Trimborn* (1946) 115 L.J.K.B. 305 and *Gibbons* v. *Wright* [1956] C.L.Y. 5244 applied.)
Re BEANEY (DECD.) [1978] 1 W.L.R. 770, Martin Nourse, Q.C.

GUARANTEE AND INDEMNITY

1539. Guarantee—charterparty—proviso not fulfilled—no proceedings pending
O timechartered the Q to C, the charter providing that any dispute be referred to arbitration in London. G guaranteed to pay the obligations of C in regard to hire and any other sums due under the charter " provided always that G shall not be required to pay or discharge any liability of C to O so long as the legality thereof shall be contested in good faith by C in appropriate proceedings " (cl. 2). It was further provided by cl. 8 (*b*) that " the liability of G shall not in any way be affected, lessened or impaired by any omission neglect or forebearance on the part of O in enforcing the aforesaid payments by C." On redelivery of the Q, O claimed £40,000 against G, which they alleged was due under the charter. *Held*, on appeal, that (1) the proviso to cl. 2 did not operate here, since there were no proceedings in existence in which C were contesting anything, in good faith or otherwise; accordingly it could not be said that O's claim should be held up pending arbitration; (2) no term could be implied that O were not to claim against D until there had been an arbitration under the original charter, since this would conflict directly with cl. 8 (*b*); (3) accordingly, the terms of the proviso were not fulfilled, and the action against G had been properly brought and pursued: THE " QUEEN FREDERIKA " [1978] 2 Lloyd's Rep. 164, C.A.

1540. —— joint liability—release—effects
[Can.] D was a principal of CD Ltd. which had franchised outlets to CNR Ltd. CNR Ltd. was operated by one J. P loaned $15,000 by way of promissory notes signed by J to CNR Ltd. At the same time, a personal guarantee for the same amount was executed by D covering the liabilities of CD Ltd. " and/ or " CNR Ltd. Subsequently, D paid $10,600 to P. CD Ltd. was then sold to others. P sued and obtained judgment against J, CD Ltd., CNR Ltd. and D. The purchasers of CD Ltd. obtained a complete discharge without a reserve clause from P in return for the payment of a certain sum. Originally, D added CD Ltd. as a third party claiming an indemnity, but later abandoned that claim. *Held*, (1) P was entitled to judgment for $4,400. plus interest; (2) even though the release did not contain express reserving words, if there was knowledge and consent on behalf of the other judgment debtors, that was sufficient not to discharge them upon the release of one of them; (3) the creditor did not break any contract with any other surety by releasing one, and therefore that defence was not available to the debtor or remaining surety. It was incumbent upon the remaining surety, D, to show that the creditor, P, had so dealt with the other surety that his right of contribution from that other surety was affected. D, by abandoning his claim against the third party, determined his own right to contribution. (*Ward* v. *National Bank of New Zealand* (1883) 8 App.Cas. 755 applied): CANADIAN IMPERIAL BANK OF COMMERCE *v.* VOPNI [1978] 4 W.W.R. 76, Manitoba Queen's Bench.

1541. Return of deposit—letter of credit—injunction. See HOWE RICHARDSON SCALE CO. *v.* POLIMEX-CEKOP, § 141.

HAWKERS AND PEDLARS

1542. Northern Ireland. See NORTHERN IRELAND.

HIGHWAYS AND BRIDGES

1543. Bridges

COUNTY COUNCIL OF WEST SUSSEX (UPPER BEEDING: RIVER ADUR BRIDGE) SCHEME 1976 CONFIRMATION INSTRUMENT 1978 (No. 830) [25p], made under the Highways (Miscellaneous Provisions) Act 1961 (c. 63), s. 3; operative on a date to be published; confirms a scheme for the construction of a bridge over the River Adur.

COUNTY COUNCIL OF CAMBRIDGESHIRE (RIVER GREAT OUSE–ST. IVES BY-PASS BRIDGE) (No. 2) SCHEME 1977 CONFIRMATION INSTRUMENT 1978 (No. 1296) [25p], made under the Highways (Miscellaneous Provisions) Act 1961 s. 3; gives effect to a scheme for the bridging of the River Great Ouse near St. Ives.

1544. Construction of roads—grants—aids to industrial development. See § 973.

1545. Footpath—conflicting evidence of use—map conclusive

[National Parks and Access to the Countryside Act 1949 (c. 97), s. 32 (4) (*a*).]

Where a way is shown on a definitive map as a footpath, that is conclusive that the public has a right of way on foot only, whatever evidence there may be to the contrary.

The P council published in 1961 a definitive map showing a lane as a footpath. The lane gave access onto land which was later acquired by D. After later research showed the lane to have been used as a cartway, D sought to use it for vehicular access. The council sought a declaration that the lane could be used as a footpath. The judge held that although the definitive map was conclusive as to the lane being a footpath by virtue of s. 32 (4) of the National Parks and Access to the Countryside Act 1949, that did not preclude the existence of additional rights. On appeal by the council, *held,* dismissing the appeal, that objection could have been made when the map was being prepared, and the definitive map was conclusive in the absence of any special review that the lane was a footpath only. (Dicta of Browne L.J. in *R.* v. *Secretary of State for the Environment, ex p. Hood* [1975] C.L.Y. 2462 applied; *Att.-Gen.* v. *Honeywill* [1972] C.L.Y. 2540 disapproved.)

SUFFOLK COUNTY COUNCIL v. MASON [1978] 1 W.L.R. 716, C.A.

1546. —— diversion order—retroactive power

[Town and Country Planning Act 1971 (c. 78), ss. 209, 210.] Outline and detailed planning permission was granted subject to a condition requiring the retention of an adequate footpath until it was legally diverted. The builder laid out an alternative footpath and started work on a house over the existing footpath. At a public inquiry as to whether the Secretary of State should confirm the order to divert the footpath it was argued that he had no power to confirm having regard to the development already carried out. The order was confirmed. The applicants applied for the order to be quashed. *Held,* (1) an order under s. 210 made lawful what would otherwise be unlawful; (2) the Secretary of State had given proper reasons for his decision; (3) he had not acted outside his jurisdiction: ASHBY v. SECRETARY OF STATE FOR THE ENVIRONMENT [1978] J.P.L. 761, Sir Douglas Frank, Q.C.

1547. —— duty to maintain—footpath made slippery by ice and snow—liability to take protective measures

[Highways Act 1959 (c. 25), ss. 44 (1), 129, 295.]

Whilst a local authority is under a duty to take protective measures to render an ice-covered footpath safe for users, a plaintiff must establish that the authority acted unreasonably in not taking such measures.

The plaintiff's home adjoined a steep narrow footpath commonly used by local residents. During cold weather the plaintiff was injured after slipping on the impacted snow and ice upon the path's surface, which slippery surface had arisen as a result of wintry weather some few days previously. The defendants had been warned of the dangerous surface on the evening before the accident but although they gritted the path the next day, the plaintiff had already been injured. The plaintiff contended, inter alia, that the authority was in breach of its duty to maintain the highway under s. 44 of the 1959 Act and the trial judge accepted that a failure to salt or grit the footpath was a breach of such duty. *Held*, allowing the defendant's appeal, that (1) (*per* Geoff and Shaw L.JJ.) although the authority's duty to maintain extended to the taking of protective measures in case of snow and ice, the plaintiff had failed to establish that the authority had acted unreasonably in first treating the many major roads within its area or that it had delayed unreasonably in attending to the footpath; and (2) the common law claim for negligence failed since the authority had properly exercised its discretion in giving priority to major roads. (*Burnside* v. *Emerson* [1968] C.L.Y. 1762 and *Hereford and Worcester County Council* v. *Newman* [1975] C.L.Y. 1546 considered; *Anns* v. *Merton London Borough Council* [1977] C.L.Y. 2030 distinguished.)

HAYDON v. KENT COUNTY COUNCIL [1978] 2 W.L.R. 485, C.A.

1548. —— **evidence of use as bridleway—definitive map**

[National Parks and Access to the Countryside Act 1949 (c. 97), s. 33.] A definitive map made in 1953 showed a footpath. In 1972 parts of this path were reclassified as a bridlepath. Objections were made and the inspector excluded as irrelevant any evidence as to user prior to 1953. He recommended that the objections be allowed. The applicant sought an order of certiorari to quash the decision and mandamus directing the Secretary to hear the objections. *Held*, on a proper construction of the Act the evidence of user prior to 1953 should have been heard and had been wrongly excluded. Application allowed: R. v. SECRETARY OF STATE FOR THE ENVIRONMENT, *ex p.* STEWART [1978] J.P.L. 764, D.C.

1549. —— **highway authority—discretion to assert rights**

[Highways Act 1959 (c. 25), s. 116 (3), (5).]

The question of whether to institute proceedings under s. 116 of the Highways Act 1959, is one of discretion for the authority concerned. That section does impose upon them a primary duty to decide the status of a path.

Landowners erected barriers over land which local residents claimed to be a footpath, although its existence was not shown on definitive maps. One such resident sought an order of mandamus requiring the council to exercise a duty, imposed on it by s. 116 of the Highways Act 1959, to "assert and protect the rights of the public" in relation to the footpath. *Held*, refusing the application, that the council had a discretion whether to issue proceedings or not. The existence of the footpath was disputed and the council had no primary duty to determine its status.

R. v. LANCASHIRE COUNTY COUNCIL, *ex p.* GUYER (1977) 76 L.G.R. 290, D.C.

1550. Highways—road markings—removal—highway authority's duty of care

A highway authority owes to motorists a duty of care not to cause danger through the removal or obliteration of traffic signs.

At its junction with a major road, a minor road bore white line markings indicating the requirement to "give way." A bend in the minor road meant that a motorist would not see the junction until very close to it. During resurfacing work the white lines were obliterated and no other temporary warning signs were provided pending their restoration. The defendant driver drove out of the minor road colliding with a car on the major road. He claimed an indemnity from the highway authority against his liability to a passenger in the other car. *Held*, giving judgment for the defendant motorist, that the authority had failed in its duty to take reasonable steps to avoid causing or adding to danger, in particular by failing to provide temporary warning signs; that the defendant motorist by driving too fast was two-thirds responsible for the accident, but was entitled to an indemnity from the authority as to one-third. (*Anns* v. *Merton London Borough Council* [1977] C.L.Y. 2030 applied; *Sheppard* v. *Glossop Corporation* [1921] 3 K.B. 132 distinguished.)

BIRD v. PEARCE; SOMERSET COUNTY COUNCIL (THIRD PARTY) [1978] R.T.R. 290, Wood J.

1551. Motorways—inquiry—rules of evidence—post-inquiry proceedings

Strict rules of evidence do not apply to a motorway scheme inquiry: the inspector may allow statistics to be quoted from a book of which the witness is not the author, and refuse to permit cross-examination as to the reliability of the book.

At a motorway scheme inquiry, a witness gave evidence as to future traffic growth, relying upon the statistics and forecasts contained in the Department of Environment's standard reference book of which the witness was not the author. The inspector declined to allow cross-examination as to the reliability of the book. After the inspector recommended confirmation of the schemes, objectors sought the re-opening of the inquiry on the grounds of subsequent changes in circumstances. The Secretary of State declined to re-open the inquiry, indicating that he had taken account of, inter alia, changes in traffic forecasts since the inquiry. *Held,* refusing to quash that decision, that (1) no objection could be taken to the inspector's refusal to permit cross-examination upon the book's reliability; (2) the Secretary of State acting in an administrative capacity was entitled to consider fresh information. (*T. A. Miller* v. *Minister of Housing and Local Government* [1968] C.L.Y. 20 and dictum of Lord Reid in *Ridge* v. *Baldwin* [1963] C.L.Y. 2667, applied; *Nicholson* v. *Secretary of State for Energy* [1978] C.L.Y. 23, distinguished).

BUSHELL *v.* SECRETARY OF STATE FOR THE ENVIRONMENT (1978) 76 L.G.R. 460, Sir Douglas Frank Q.C.

1552. Negligence. See NEGLIGENCE.

1553. Northern Ireland. See NORTHERN IRELAND.

1554. Road traffic. See ROAD TRAFFIC.

1555. Special roads
S.I. 1978 Nos. 329 (M25–M11 to A12 Section) [10p]; 330 (M25–A10–M11 Section) [25p]; 623 (M42 Birmingham–Nottingham) [10p]; 755 (M25–River Wey Navigation Crossing) [20p]; 910 (A6127(M)–Newcastle upon Tyne Central Motorway East) [10p]; 1222 (M63–Stockport East/West By-Pass) [10p]; 1223 (M63–Stockport East/West By-Pass) [10p]; 1558 (M3–Compton-Bassett Section) [10p]; 1559 (M27–Chilworth–Windhover) [10p]; 1833 (M1 Motorway) [10p]; 1929 (A1 (M) Motorway–South Mimms Improvement) [10p]; 1977 (M25 Motorway) [10p]; 1978 (M25 Motorway).

1556. Street—disused road over a bridge—construction of statute. See STRATHCLYDE REGIONAL COUNCIL *v.* BRITISH RAILWAYS BOARD, § 2839.

1557. Street trading. See HAWKERS AND PEDLARS.

1558. Town and country planning. See TOWN AND COUNTRY PLANNING.

1559. Trunk roads
S.I. 1978 Nos. 22 (London–Fishguard) [10p]; 50 (Heathrow Airport Spur Road) [10p]; 128 (North of Oxford–South of Coventry) [15p]; 164 Doncaster–Kendal) [10p]; 165 (Snaith–Sunderland) [10p]; 219 (London–Inverness) [10p]; 226 (Penrith–Middlesbrough) [10p]; 227 (Penrith–Middlesbrough) [15p]; 248 (Levens Bridge–Carlisle) [15p]; 309 (Southampton–Bath) [10p]; 310 (Doncaster–Kendal) [10p]; 328 (London–King's Lynn) [10p]; 333 (Shrewsbury–Whitchurch–Warrington) [10p]; 334 (Winchester–Preston) [10p]; 335 (Winchester–Preston) [10p]; 336 Liverpool–Leeds–Hull) [10p]; 337 (Liverpool–Leeds–Hull) [10p]; 338 (Liverpool–Warrington–Stockport–Sheffield–Lincoln–Skegness) [10p]; 340 Swansea–Manchester [10p]; 341 (Manchester–Burnley) [10p]; 342 (Stoke-on-Trent–Lawton Gate) [10p]; 343 (Winchester–Preston) [10p]; 344 (London–Carlisle–Glasgow–Inverness) [10p] 345 (London–Carlisle–Glasgow–Inverness) [10p]; 346 (Preston–Blackpool) [10p]; 347 (Liverpool–Leeds–Hull) [10p]; 348 (London–Carlisle–Glasgow–Inverness) [10p]; 349 Swansea–Manchester) [10p]; 350 (Shotwick–Frodsham–Warrington) [10p]; 351 (Liverpool–Warrington–Stockport–Sheffield–Lincoln–Skegness) [10p]; 352 (Manchester–Burnley) [10p]; 353 (Winchester–Preston) [10p]; 354 (Liverpool–Warrington–Stockport–Sheffield–Lincoln–Skegness) [10p]; 355 (Liverpool–Warrington–Stockport–Sheffield–Lincoln–Skegness) [10p]; 356 (Winchester–Preston) [10p]; 361 (London–Norwich) [10p]; 376 (London–Fishguard) [25p]; 398 (London–Brighton) [10p]; 412 (Worcester–Wolverhampton–South of Stafford [10p]; 420 (East of Snaith–Sunderland) [15p]; 421 (East of Snaith–Sunderland) [10p]; 464 (Swansea–Manchester) [10p]; 476 (Liverpool–Leeds–Hull) [10p]; 477 (Widnes-

pool–Howden) [10p]; 478 (Widnespool–Howden) [10p]; 493 (Barnet Way, Barnet) [10p]; 497 (Newport–Worcester) [10p]; 501 (Ipswich–Norwich) [10p]; 525 (Greenodd–Barrow-in-Furness) [10p]; 537 (London–Edinburgh–Thurso) [10p]; 596 (Newport–Shrewsbury) [10p]; 614 (Exeter–Leeds) [10p]; 632 (Birmigham–Nottingham) [10p]; 711 (Bath–Lincoln) [10p]; 762 (Taunton–Fraddon) [10p]; 808 (London–Norwich) [10p]; 824 (London–Llandovery) [10p]; 839 (London–Norwich) [10p]; 845 (Southend Road, Walthamstow) [10p]; 848 (Newtown–Aberystwyth) [10p]; 875 (Exeter–Leeds) [10p]; 876 (Leeds–Scarborough) [10p]; 895 (London–Folkestone–Dover) [10p]; 897 (Newport–Shrewsbury) [10p]; 938 (Barnstaple, Rolle Street Bridge) [20p]; 939 (Preston–Leeds) [10p]; 968 (London–Cambridge–King's Lynn) [10p]; 983 (King's Lynn–Newark) [10p]; 1116 (North Circular Road, Brent) [10p]; 1183 (Birmingham–Great Yarmouth) [10p]; 1195 (Taunton–Fraddon) [10p]; 1206 (Norman Cross–Grimsby) [10p]; 1207 (London–Carlisle–Glasgow–Inverness) [10p]; 1209 (Dolgellau–South of Birkenhead) [19p]; 1269 (Penrith to Middlesbrough) [10p]; 1272 (York–Hull) [10p]; 1306 (Chester-Bangor and Dolgellau–South of Birkenhead) [25p]; 1444 (Glan–Usk Park to Llyswen) [10p]; 1492 (Shrewsbury–Dolgellau) [10p]; 1575 (Llandeilo–Carmarthen) [10p]; 1617 (Folkestone–Honiton) [10p]; 1655 (New Road, Rainham) [10p]; 1675 (Felixstowe–Weedon) [10p]; 1685 (Workington–Barons Cross) [10p]; 1705 (Maentwrog–East of Conway) [10p]; 1726 (North West of Doncaster–Kendal) [10p]; 1769 (London–Great Yarmouth) [10p]; 1770 (London–Great Yarmouth) [50p]; 1784 (Eastern Avenue, Redbridge) [10p]; 1807 (London–Folkestone–Dover) [10p]; 1922 (London–Folkestone–Dover) [10p]; 1923 (London–Folkestone–Dover) [10p]; 1924 (Widnes-pool–Howden) [10p]; 1925 (Widnespool–Howen) [10p]; 1935 (Birmingham–Great Yarmouth) [20p]; 1936 (A1 Trunk Road) [10p]; 1954 (London–Inverness) [10p]; 1969 (Bath–Lincoln) [10p]; 1970 (Birmingham–Great Yarmouth [10p]; 1974 (Liverpool–Leeds–Hull) [10p]; 1975 (Liverpool–Leeds–Hull [10p].

1560. —— **order—road mainly to be used by local traffic**
[Highways Act 1959 (c. 25), s. 7.]

The fact that a proposed trunk road will be mainly used by local traffic does not preclude the making of a trunk road order, provided that it was reasonable to conclude that such a road would improve the route for through traffic.

The applicant opposed a trunk road order providing for a direct route through Plymouth, and also improving facilities for local traffic; he sought to quash the order upon the grounds that the Secretary of State had no power to make such an order unless the new road was exclusively intended for use by through traffic. *Held,* dismissing the application, that the order was intra vires since the Secretary of State had bona fide and reasonably concluded that such a road would improve facilities for through traffic; the fact that it would also be used by the local traffic did not render the order ultra vires.

WATERS *v.* SECRETARY OF STATE FOR THE ENVIRONMENT (1977) 33 P. & C.R. 410, Slynn J.

ARTICLES. See *post,* p. [24].

HIRE PURCHASE

1561. Minimum deposit

HIRE-PURCHASE AND CREDIT SALE AGREEMENTS (CONTROL) (AMENDMENT) ORDER 1978 (No. 553) [10p], made under the Emergency Laws (Re-enactments and Repeals) Act 1964 (c. 60), ss. 1, 7; operative on May 2, 1978; varies the exemption from control under S.I. 1976 No. 1135 relating to credit sale agreements where the cash price is paid by way of an agreement for running-account credit. In place of the limitation of the exemption by reference to specified minimum payments, the exemption now applies where the cash price under the credit sale agreement does not exceed £1,000.

1562. Possession—owner's right—bona fide purchaser—whether presumptions apply
[Hire Purchase Act 1964 (c. 53), ss. 27, 28, 29.]

Presumptions that a purchaser of goods subject to a hire-purchase agreement acquires good title may not apply where all dispositions of the goods are known.

M entered a hire-purchase agreement with the defendants in respect of a car valued at £6,000. Soon thereafter M " sold " the car to S for £3,000, the car being sold thereafter to L and to D who let it on hire-purchase to the plaintiff company of which S was a director. The defendants then recovered possession of the car. The plaintiffs claimed, inter alia, the return of the car. The trial judge in dismissing the claim, ruled that the sale between M and S was not a genuine transaction. *Held*, dismissing the plaintiff's appeal, that the presumption under s. 28 of the 1964 Act was inapplicable since all dispositions of the car were known; further, that the lack of bona fides in the transaction between M and S prevented the passing of title.

SONECO *v.* BARCROSS FINANCE [1978] R.T.R. 444, C.A.

1563. Sale by hirer—breach of bailment agreement—right of finance company to immediate possession

The fact that a hire purchase agreement makes express provision for termination of the hire in the event of default by the hirer does not restrict the owner's common law right to terminate upon the hirer acting in a manner repugnant to the agreement.

The plaintiffs let a motor car to S upon hire purchase, S agreeing to pay therefor in instalments. The agreement expressly provided, inter alia, that S was not to remove any identification marks on the vehicle or to sell the vehicle without the owner's consent. Specific provision was made for the plaintiffs to terminate the hiring by written notice in the event of any breach by S of the agreement. Shortly after the hiring, S altered the car's registration number and entered the car in the defendant's car auction where it was sold and the proceeds paid to S. Thereafter, the plaintiffs served notice terminating the hiring. When the plaintiffs discovered the fact of the sale by the defendants, they claimed damages for conversion. The defendants contended, inter alia, that at the time of the sale the plaintiffs did not have the right to immediate possession. *Held*, giving judgment for the plaintiffs, that the plaintiffs became entitled to immediate possession of the car upon S changing the registration number and entering the car in the auction; the later notice of termination was superfluous. (*North General Wagon and Finance Co.* v. *Graham* (1950) C.L.C. 4454 applied.

UNION TRANSPORT FINANCE *v.* BRITISH CAR AUCTIONS [1978] 2 All E.R. 385, C.A.

1564. Value limit of agreements

HIRE-PURCHASE (INCREASE OF LIMIT OF VALUE) (GREAT BRITAIN) ORDER 1978 (No. 461) [10p], made under the Hire Purchase Act 1965 (c. 66), s. 3 and the Hire Purchase (Scotland) Act 1965 (c. 67), s. 3; operative on June 1 1978; amends s. 2 of both 1965 Acts by increasing the value limit of such agreements to £5,000.

ARTICLES. See *post*, p. [24].

HOUSING

1565. Clearance area—rehabilitation—no absolute duty upon council

[Housing Act 1957 (c. 56), as amended by the Housing Act 1974 (c. 44), ss. 49, 105 (4); Housing Act 1974 (c. 44), as amended by the Housing Rents and Subsidies Act 1975 (c. 6), s. 14.]

The fact that a local authority may have acquired a building for housing purposes does not prevent them from subsequently including the same in a clearance area and then demolishing it.

The council acquired houses in an area under its powers to acquire properties for housing. They fell into disrepair through neglect. This area was declared a clearance area and it was intended to demolish them. On an application by owners of other houses in the area for an injunction to restrain the demolition, *held,* refusing the application, that the council could include in a clearance area buildings acquired by them for the purpose of housing and then demolish them, even if the demolition requirement arose from their own neglect. It was within the council's discretion whether to rehabilitate an area or not, and one with which the courts would not interfere.

ATT.-GEN. *ex rel.* RIVERS-MOORE *v.* PORTSMOUTH CITY COUNCIL (1978) 76 L.G.R. 643, Walton J.

1566. —— —— whether practicable—inspector's decision at inquiry

At an inquiry following a compulsory purchase order under the Housing Act 1957, Pt. III, the central issue was whether the best way of dealing with the conditions in the clearance area was by way of demolition or rehabilitation. The inspector found rehabilitation not to be a reasonable proposition and that the cost would not be worthwhile. An objector appealed. *Held*, dismissing the appeal, the inspector had reached conclusions of fact based on the evidence and what he saw on inspection. He had properly not taken into account matters which the objectors had had no opportunity of dealing with: ALLEN *v.* SECRETARY OF STATE FOR THE ENVIRONMENT AND BOROUGH OF SUNDERLAND [1978] J.P.L. 621, Sir Douglas Frank, Q.C.

1567. Compulsory purchase. See COMPULSORY PURCHASE.

1568. Control order—house unlawfully sublet—whether occupiers for the purpose of control means " lawful occupiers "

[Housing Act 1964 (c. 56), s. 73.] The applicants owned premises which had been sub-let in breach of covenant. A possession order was obtained but suspended for 28 days. The council served a control order. The applicants applied for the order to be quashed. *Held*, (1) it was not necessary to decide whether " occupiers " meant lawful occupiers. The court inclined to the view that it meant all-in occupiers; (2) the landlord could appeal to the county court and argue that the council's real motive was to prevent them having to rehouse the occupants. Prerogative orders should be refused where there was an alternative remedy. Application dismissed: MILFORD PROPERTIES *v.* HAMMERSMITH LONDON BOROUGH [1978] J.P.L. 766, D.C.

1569. —— whether in multiple occupation—common lodging house

[Housing Act 1964 (C. 56), s. 73 (1) as amended by Housing Act 1969 (C. 33), s. 58.]

For the purposes of s. 73 (1) of the Housing Act 1964 " occupied " is to be widely construed as being synonymous with " lived in."

A control order was made by the local authority in respect of a house which had formerly been registered as a common lodging house and which, after the cessation of registration, had continued to be used for the purpose of accommodating up to 75 women, most of whom were mentally or otherwise deficient and some of whom stayed for one night only, others remaining for some years. The women were allowed in only between 4 p.m. and 10 a.m. and were provided with dormitory and washing facilities but no meals. On appeal by the owner against the control order, the County Court judge ruled that the women did not occupy the house within the meaning of s. 73 (1) of the 1964 Act. *Held*, allowing the local authority's appeal, that it was not necessary for the purposes of s. 73 (1) to show that the women had exclusive possession of some part of the house but only that they " lived in " in the house; and that on the facts, it could not be said that the transient population occupying the house did so as a single household. (*Simmons* v. *Pizzey* [1977] C.L.Y. 1520, considered; *Duffy* v. *Pilling* [1977] C.L.Y. 2917, distinguished.)

SILBERS *v.* SOUTHWARK LONDON BOROUGH COUNCIL (1978) 76 L.G.R. 421, C.A.

1570. Council house—possession—local authorities' powers

The mere fact that a local authority gives a " good tenant " notice to quit does not raise a prima facie case that they have abused or exceeded their statutory powers.

C Council served notice to quit on K, a council-house tenant, and commenced an action in the county court for possession. The only ground for possession was the termination of the tenancy by notice to quit. No breaches of regulations and conditions of the tenancy were alleged. K contended that the council were in breach of their duty in that they had failed to exercise their powers in good faith and to take into account all relevant considerations in deciding to evict her. At the hearing K gave evidence, C Council called no evidence. The judge found that K was a good tenant but held that that fact was insufficient to raise a prima facie case and made an order for possession. K appealed. *Held*, dismissing the appeal, that there was nothing on the facts proved to raise a prima facie case of abuse of powers by the council and that there was nothing in the defence which required the local authority to particularise their deliberations in the exercise of their statutory powers. (*Associated Provincial Picture Houses* v. *Wednesbury Corporation* (1948) C.L.C. 8107 applied; *Bristol District Council* v. *Clark* [1975] C.L.Y. 1581 considered.)

CANNOCK CHASE COUNCIL v. KELLY [1978] 1 W.L.R. 1, C.A.

1571. Duty of local authority—when arising
[Housing (Homeless Persons) Act 1977 (c. 48), ss. 4, 8.] The duty of a housing authority under s. 4 of the Housing (Homeless Persons) Act 1977 arises when the authority is satisfied that a person is homeless; it is not deferred until they notify their decision under s. 8: R. v. BEVERLEY BOROUGH COUNCIL, *The Times*, October 27, 1978, D.C.

1572. Fitness for habitation—repairs—reasonable expense—matters to be considered
[Housing Act 1957 (c. 56), ss. 9, 11, 39.] The respondent authority served notice under s. 9 stating that the house controlled by the appellants was unfit for human habitation and requiring them to execute specified works to render it fit. The appellants appealed to the county court pursuant to s. 11 contending that the house could not be rendered fit at reasonable expense. *Held*, allowing the appellants' appeal from the judge's confirmation of the s. 9 notice, the house could not have been made fit at reasonable expense. The judge had failed to consider (a) that the agreed cost of remedial works was subject to the possibility of further works being required when the house was opened up; (b) the high cost of borrowing money to carry out the works: ELLIS COPP & CO. v. RICHMOND-UPON-THAMES LONDON BOROUGH COUNCIL (1976) 245 E.G. 931, C.A.

1573. —— —— —— meaning of " value "
[Housing Act 1957 (c. 56), ss. 9 (1A) (inserted by Housing Act 1969 (c. 33), s. 72), 11 (1) (3), 39 (1).]

Where a landlord contends that it would be uneconomic to carry out works required by a local authority, the potential value of the house with vacant possession may be considered.

The local authority served notices on landlords requiring substantial repairs to be effected on them. The landlords contended that the cost of the repairs exceeded the value of their properties as occupied by their sitting tenants (but not otherwise). *Held*, allowing an appeal from the setting aside of those notices, that the local authority had properly had regard to the matters set out in s. 9 (1A) to the Housing Act 1957 and that the judge was wrong in failing to have regard to the fact that the landlords might have made a substantial profit by obtaining vacant possession of the houses.

HILLBANK PROPERTIES v. HACKNEY LONDON BOROUGH COUNCIL [1978] 3 W.L.R. 260, C.A.

1574. —— —— —— value of house when work complete
[Housing Act 1957 (c. 56), ss. 9 (1), 11 (1) (3), 39 (1).]
The " value " of a house to which regard must be had under s. 39 (1) of the Housing Act 1957 when considering whether it can be rendered fit for human habitation at reasonable expense, means its open market value.

The authority served a notice on P Co. under s. 9 (1) of the Housing Act 1957, stating that a house was unfit for human habitation and requiring them to carry out certain repairs. The present value of the house on the open market was £1,300. Its price after repair would be £1,900 and repairs would cost £1,800. P Co. appealed on the ground that the premises were not capable of being rendered fit for human habitation at reasonable expense. The authority argued that a gross rental from the premises of £9·25 per week for a prospective life of 15 or 20 years would produce a net value to the property of £4,000 or £6,000. The judge rejected that method of valuation and allowed P Co.'s appeal. On appeal by the authority, *held*, dismissing the appeal, that " value " meant open market value. (*Ellis Copp & Co.* v. *Richmond-upon-Thames London Borough Council* [1978] C.L.Y. 1572 and *Bacon* v. *Grimsby Corporation* (1950) C.L.C. 4473 considered.)

INWORTH PROPERTY CO. *v.* SOUTHWARK LONDON BOROUGH COUNCIL (1977) 34 P. & C.R. 186, C.A.

1575. Home purchase assistance

HOME PURCHASE ASSISTANCE (RECOGNISED SAVINGS INSTITUTIONS) ORDER 1978 (No. 1785) [10p], made under the Home Purchase Assistance and Housing Corporation Guarantee Act 1978 (c. 27), s. 2 (1) (7); operative on December 5, 1978; adds to the institutons specified in Pt. II of the Sched. as being recognised savings institutions.

1576. Home Purchase Assistance and Housing Corporation Guarantee Act 1978 (c. 27)

This Act authorises the use of public money to assist first-time purchasers of houses; it also increases the financial limit of the Housing Corporation's power to guarantee loans to housing associations.

S. 1 empowers the Secretary of State to make advances to recognised lending institutions enabling them to provide assistance to first-time purchasers of homes in Great Britain; and sets out the conditions on which such assistance shall be given; s. 2 deals with the administration of such advances and assistance; s. 3 amends building society law to take account of this Act; s. 4 relates to Northern Ireland; s. 5 increases to £300 million the Housing Corporation's power to guarantee loans; s. 6 contains the short title.

The Act received the Royal Assent on June 30, 1978, and ss. 4–6 came into force on that date. Ss. 1–3 came into force on such day as the Secretary of State shall order.

1577. —— appointed day

HOME PURCHASE ASSISTANCE AND HOUSING CORPORATION GUARANTEE ACT 1978 (APPOINTED DAY) ORDER 1978 (No. 1412 (C. 36)) [10p], made under the Home Purchase Assistance and Housing Corporation Guarantee Act 1978 (c. 27), s. 6 (2); operative on December 1, 1978; brings into force ss. 1 to 3 of the 1978 Act.

1578. Homes Insulation Act 1978 (c. 48)

This Act provides for local authority grants towards the thermal insulation of dwellings.

S. 1 directs local authorities to make grants towards the cost of works undertaken to improve the thermal insulation of dwellings in their areas, in accordance with schemes prepared by the Secretary of State and approved by Parliament, the first such scheme being defined by the section; s. 2 contains financial provisions for the making of grants; s. 3 contains certain provisions in relation to Northern Ireland, with the exception of which the Act does not apply there; s. 4 gives the short title.

The Act received the Royal Assent on July 31, 1978, and came into force on that date.

1579. Housing action area—notice to quit—landlord's failure to notify local authority of service

[Housing Act 1974 (c. 44), s. 47.]

Where a landlord purports to serve notice to quit within the provisions of s. 47 of the Act he commits an offence under that section if he fails to notify the local authority of such service even though the notice itself is invalid.

F, the landlord of a dwelling-house in a housing action area, served on the tenants a notice to quit which expired less than a month after the date of service and was therefore invalid. He failed to notify the local authority of the service of the notice and was convicted of an offence under s. 47 of the Act. The Crown Court allowed F's appeal on the ground that " notice to quit " in s. 47 of the Act meant valid notice to quit. The local authority appealed. *Held*, allowing the appeal, that F's purported service of the notice to quit was sufficient for the purpose of s. 47.

FAWCETT *v.* NEWCASTLE-UPON-TYNE CITY COUNCIL (1977) 75 L.G.R. 841, D.C.

1580. Housing (Financial Provisions) (Scotland) Act 1978, (c. 14)

This Act makes new provision for Scotland with respect to grants for housing authorities and grants and loans to voluntary organisations concerned with housing; it provides for grants and loans by local authorities to meet expenses of repairing houses in a state of disrepair; it makes further provisions for the improvement of houses below the tolerable standard, and makes certain adjustments to provisions affecting the rates and rents of housing owned by Scottish local authorities; the Act also makes minor amendments to various enactments relating to housing.

S. 1 directs that the Secretary of State shall make annual grants to Scottish local authorities for the purpose of assisting them in meeting housing needs in their areas, such grants to be known as " housing support grants " and having a fixed aggregate amount; s. 2 deals with the apportionment of the aggregate amount of the housing support grants between local authorities; s. 3 permits variations to housing support grant orders; s. 4 provides for grants to be payable to the Scottish Special Housing Association and to development corporations; s. 5 empowers the Secretary of State to give financial assistance to voluntary organisations concerned with housing; s. 6 confers a discretion upon the Secretary of State as to the time, manner and conditions of grants; s. 7 terminates certain exchequer payments to housing authorities; s. 8 inserts a section into the Housing (Scotland) Act 1974 to make provision for repairs grants by local authorities; s. 9 imposes a duty upon a local authority to offer loans to meet the expenses of repairs to houses; s. 10 confers a power upon local authorities to order the improvement of houses below tolerable standard outside housing action areas; s. 11 contains amendments relating to the housing revenue account; s. 12 makes alterations to the amount of rent rebate subsidy and rent allowance subsidy payable to a local authority; s. 13 relates to rent rebates and allowances paid to persons in receipt of supplementary benefit; s. 14 extends the powers of the Secretary of State in respect of limiting the rents of houses belonging to housing associations and to the Housing Corporation; s. 15 amends s. 2 of the Housing Rents and Subsidies (Scotland) Act 1975 (c. 28); s. 16 makes certain minor and consequential amendments and repeals; s. 17 makes financial provision for certain public expenses attributable to the Act; s. 18 is the interpretation section; s. 19 contains the short title. The Act extends to Scotland only.

The Act received the Royal Assent on May 25, and came into force on June 25, 1978, with the exception of s. 11, Sched. 2, paras. 31, 35 and 36, and Sched. 3 in part, which came into force on April 1, 1979.

1581. Housing (Homeless Persons) Act 1977—appropriate arrangements

HOUSING (HOMELESS PERSONS) (APPROPRIATE ARRANGEMENTS) ORDER 1978 (No. 69) [25p], made under the Housing (Homeless Persons) Act 1977 (c. 48), ss. 5 (8) (9) (a) (10); operative on January 21, 1978; directs that, for cases involving English or Welsh authorities, the " appropriate arrangements " under s. 5 (7) are to be the arrangements set out in the Schedule to this Order. The arrangements provide for any disputed question under s. 5 to be determined either by a person agreed upon by the two authorities concerned or in default by a person appointed by the chairman of the association representing the authorities.

HOUSING (HOMELESS PERSONS) (APPROPRIATE ARRANGEMENTS) (NO. 2) ORDER 1978 (No. 661) [20p], made under the Housing (Homeless Persons) Act 1977, s. 5 (8) (9) (a) and (10); operative on April 28, 1978; make appropriate arrangements in default of agreement between two Scottish housing authorities concerning the transfer of responsibility for a homeless person, for the determination of such disputes.

1582. Housing subsidies

ASSISTANCE FOR HOUSE PURCHASE AND IMPROVEMENT (QUALIFYING LENDERS) ORDER 1978 (No. 10) [10p], made under the Housing Subsidies Act 1967 (c. 29), ss. 27 and 32 (2); operative on February 1, 1978; by this Order the Secretary of State for the Environment prescribes a further body as a qualifying lender for the purposes of operating the option mortgage scheme under the 1967 Act.

ASSISTANCE FOR HOUSE PURCHASE AND IMPROVEMENT (VARIATION OF SUBSIDY) ORDER 1978 (No. 1699) [20p], made under the Housing Subsidies Act 1967, s. 28 (3)–(5); operative on December 4, 1978; provides new scales of percentages in relation to option mortgage subsidy payable under the 1967 Act.

1583. Northern Ireland. See NORTHERN IRELAND.

1584. Recovery of possession—housing authority—arrears of rent—order for possession not to be enforced without leave—tenant's failure to comply with informal agreement

Where an informal agreement as to payment of arrears of rent is made between a council and its tenant against whom a possession order has been made but ordered not to be enforced without leave, the court cannot refuse to allow the order to be enforced when the tenant has failed to comply with his agreement.

The plaintiff council obtained an order for possession of a council house upon the grounds of arrears of rent. The county court registrar was told that the council and the tenant had informally agreed that operation of the order would be deferred upon the tenant paying off the arrears at an agreed rate. Accordingly the possession order made in December 1975 was not to be enforced without leave of the court. The tenant failed to honour the agreement and ultimately in February 1977 the council sought leave to issue a warrant for possession. The registrar, upheld on appeal by the judge, refused leave and ordered that no warrant would issue so long as the tenant paid £4 per week off the arrears. *Held*, allowing the council's appeal, that although the court had a discretion to allow a short period—of four to six weeks—before the judgment was enforced, its discretion did not extend to refusing the council their undoubted right to possession. (*Jones* v. *Savery* (1951) C.L.C. 1938, *Air Ministry* v. *Harris* (1951) C.L.C. 1939 and *Bristol District Council* v. *Clark* [1975] C.L.Y. 1581, applied.)

BRISTOL CITY COUNCIL v. RAWLINS (1977) 34 P. & C.R. 12, C.A.

1585. Rent allowance subsidy

HOUSING FINANCE (RENT ALLOWANCE SUBSIDY) ORDER 1978 (No. 34) [10p], made under the Housing Finance Act 1972 (c. 47), s. 8 (4); operative on February 14, 1978; substitutes, for the year 1978–79, 100 per cent. as the amount of rent allowance subsidy payable to a local authority, *i.e.* 100 per cent. of the authority's standard amount of rent allowances for the year.

1586. Rent rebates

RENT REBATE AND RENT ALLOWANCE SCHEMES (ENGLAND AND WALES) REGULATIONS 1978 (No. 217) [10p], made under the Housing Finance Act 1972 (c. 47), s. 20 (2); operative on March 21, 1978; enable authorities to set the period for a rent rebate or allowance, in the case of non-pensioners, at up to nine months, where the grant of the rebate or allowance is notified during March or April in any year.

RENT REBATES AND RENT ALLOWANCES (STUDENTS) (ENGLAND AND WALES) REGULATIONS 1978 (No. 1078) [10p], made under the Housing Finance Act 1972, s. 25 (3) (c) (added by the Rent Act 1974 (c. 51), s. 11 (7) (b); operative on September 1, 1978; amend S.I. 1976 No. 1242 to increase to £7·70 the amount prescribed as the deduction to be made in calculating the rent which is eligible to be met by a rent rebate or a rent allowance under Part II of the 1972 Act, as amended, in the case of tenants who are students who have grants from public funds for the purpose of their full-time education.

RENT REBATE AND RENT ALLOWANCE SCHEMES (ENGLAND AND WALES) (No. 2) REGULATIONS 1978 (No. 1302) [25p], made under the Housing Finance Act 1972, s. 20 (2) (3); operative on September 30, 1978; vary Scheds, 3 and 4 to the 1972 Act.

1587. Town and country planning. See TOWN AND COUNTRY PLANNING.

BOOKS AND ARTICLES. See *post,* pp. [4], [24].

HUSBAND AND WIFE

1588. Abortion—husband's objection—whether any enforceable right

[Abortion Act 1967 (c. 87), s. 1.]

A husband has no enforceable right to prevent his wife having a legal abortion.

At a wife's behest two doctors certified in accordance with s. 1 of the 1967 Act that the continuance of her pregnancy would involve risk of injury to her physical or mental health. Her husband, who had not been consulted, objected and sought an injunction restraining her from having the abortion. *Held*, dismissing his application, that a husband has no enforceable legal or equitable right to prevent his wife having a legal abortion.

PATON *v.* BRITISH PREGNANCY ADVISORY SERVICE TRUSTEES [1978] 2 All E.R. 987, Sir George Baker P.

1589. Children. See MINORS.

1590. Couple living together as man and wife—order to vacate "matrimonial home"—effect of 1976 Act

[Domestic Violence and Matrimonial Proceedings Act 1976 (c. 50), ss. 1 (1) (2), 2 (1) (2).]

S. 1 of the Domestic Violence and Matrimonial Proceedings Act 1976 is not merely procedural; it gives the County Court power to grant an injunction excluding a violent person from the home, whether the parties are married or unmarried, and irrespective of any property rights vested in the person excluded. Such an injunction can be permanent, but will in most cases be temporary.

Per curiam: (1) the rule of stare decisis is still binding on the Court of Appeal; (2) a judge should not make use of proceedings in Parliament for the purposes of interpreting statutes.

M and W held a joint tenancy of a council flat. W left the home with their child due to M's violent behaviour. W obtained injunctions from a deputy county court judge under the Domestic Violence and Matrimonial Proceedings Act 1976 restraining M from molesting W or the child and excluding M from the home. Subsequently, after the decisions in *Cantliff* v. *Jenkins* and *B.* v. *B.*, the county court judge rescinded that part of the order which excluded M from the home. On appeal by W, a court of five judges of the Court of Appeal declined to follow their previous decisions, holding that it was not bound to do so where it was satisfied that they were clearly wrong and did not represent the will and intention of Parliament. They accordingly allowed the appeal and restored the deputy judge's order. On appeal by M to the House of Lords, *held*, dismissing the appeal, that s. 1 of the Domestic Violence and Matrimonial Proceedings Act 1976 gave jurisdiction to all county courts to grant an injunction and exclude a violent person from the home, whether married or not, irrespective of any property right vested in the person excluded. (*B.* v. *B.* (*Domestic Violence: Jurisdiction*) [1978] C.L.Y. 1591 and *Cantliff* v. *Jenkins* [1978] C.L.Y. 1592 overruled; *Practice Statement* (*Judicial Precedent*) [1966] C.L.Y. 9921 and *Young* v. *Bristol Aeroplane Co.* [1944] K.B. 718, C.A. considered.)

DAVIS *v.* JOHNSON [1978] 2 W.L.R. 553, H.L.

1591. [Domestic Violence and Matrimonial Proceedings Act 1976 (c. 50), s. 1.]

On its true construction, s. 1 of the Domestic Violence and Matrimonial Proceedings Act 1976 is a procedural provision which gives jurisdiction to the county court to grant specified injunctions independently of other relief; it does not alter the substantive law as to the rights of parties to occupy premises.

M and W lived together as man and wife since 1967 in a house of which M was sole tenant. They had two children who were born in 1967 and 1968. By 1977 their relationship had deteriorated, there was violence in the home and W left. The children stayed with M since W could find no accommodation for them. On W's application, a county court judge ordered that M vacate the house, that M be restrained from molesting W or the children, and he made provision for the care, custody and control of the children. On appeal by M, *held*, allowing the appeal, that (1) as M had an indefeasible right at common law to occupy the house as against W, the judge had no jurisdiction to order him to vacate it; (2) the children were well cared for by M and the court's inherent power to override property rights did not entitle it to make the order merely because it felt that the children would be better off with their mother; and (3) any contractual licence of W's to occupy the house would not have given the court power to evict M. Quaere, whether, as W had left, M and W were " living with each other in the same household." (*Montgomery* v. *Montgomery* [1964] C.L.Y. 1140 and *Stewart* v. *Stewart* [1972] C.L.Y. 1690 considered.)

B. *v.* B. (DOMESTIC VIOLENCE: JURISDICTION) [1978] 2 W.L.R. 160, C.A.

1592. [Domestic Violence and Matrimonial Proceedings Act 1976 (c. 50), s. 1.]
The Domestic Violence and Matrimonial Proceedings Act 1976 does not create any jurisdiction to exclude a joint tenant who is not a spouse from the enjoyment of premises.

M and W, who lived together as husband and wife, became joint tenants of a house. There was disharmony and violence and W left. She obtained injunctions in the county court under s. 1 of the Domestic Violence and Matrimonial Proceedings Act 1976 ordering M to vacate the premises and not to molest her or her child. On appeal by M, *held*, allowing the appeal, that s. 1 of the Act was a procedural provision which did not give the court power to override the common law property rights of the parties. (*B.* v. B. (*Domestic Violence: Jurisdiction*) [1978] C.L.Y. 1591 followed.)

CANTLIFF *v.* JENKINS [1978] 2 W.L.R. 177, C.A.

1593. Death of spouse—funeral expenses—liability of husband—limitation
[Can.] [Married Women's Property Act 1882 (c. 75).] The court *held* that since the enactment of the Married Women's Property Act 1882, a husband's common law liability for the funeral expenses of his deceased wife is limited to the difference between the amount of the expenses and her estate: PEARCE *v.* DIENSTHUBER (1978) 81 D.L.R. 286, Ontario C.A.

1594. Divorce. See DIVORCE AND MATRIMONIAL CAUSES.

1595. Domestic violence—injunction
The following Practice Direction was issued on July 21, 1978, by the Family Division:

To secure uniformity of practice, the President has issued the following note with the concurrence of the Lord Chancellor.

1. S. 1 (1) (*c*) of the Domestic Violence and Matrimonial Proceedings Act 1976 empowers a county court to include in an injunction provisions excluding a party from the matrimonial home or a part of the matrimonial home or from a specified area in which the matrimonial home is included. Where a power of arrest under s. 2 of the Act is attached to any injunction containing such provisions, the respondent is liable to be arrested if he enters the matrimonial home, or part thereof or specified area, at any time while the injunction remains in force.

2. It is within the discretion of the court to decide whether an injunction should be granted and, if so, for how long it should operate. But whenever an injunction is granted excluding one of the parties from the matrimonial home (or a part thereof or specified area), consideration should be given to imposing a time limit on the operation of the injunction. In most cases, a period of up to three months is likely to suffice, at least in the first instance. It will be open to the respondent in any event to apply for the discharge of the injunction before the expiry of the period fixed, for instance on the ground of reconciliation; and to the applicant to apply for an extension.

[1978] 1 W.L.R. 1123.

1596. —— —— duration
[Domestic Violence and Matrimonial Proceedings Act 1976 (c. 50), s. 1.]
An injunction granted under the Domestic Violence and Matrimonial Proceedings Act 1976 should either be expressly limited, or else it should be made clear to both parties that its protection is only for such reasonable time as will enable the woman to make other arrangements for her accommodation or, in the case of a wife, to enable the court to make property adjustment orders.

A and W were married and remained together for about a year. Subsequently, on W's application, a county court judge ordered H to vacate the matrimonial home under the Domestic Violence and Matrimonial Proceedings Act 1976. Both parties appealed. *Held*, dismissing both appeals on the question of the duration of the injunction, that if W did not either try to find somewhere else to live, or to get the marriage dissolved so that she or H could apply for a property adjustment order, then the injunction should be discharged. (*Davis* v. *Johnson* [1978] C.L.Y. 1590.

HOPPER v. HOPPER (NOTE) [1978] 1 W.L.R. 1342, C.A.

1597. —— **power of arrest—notice to be given to respondent**
[Domestic Violence and Matrimonial Proceedings Act 1976 (c. 50), s. 2.]
A court has power to attach a power of arrest to an injunction made in divorce proceedings or under s. 2 of the Domestic Violence and Matrimonial Proceedings Act 1976.

In divorce proceedings W applied for an order that H leave the matrimonial home, she also sought an order, although she did not notify H of this, that a power of arrest must be attached to the order. The trial judge doubted whether he had jurisdiction to attach such a power where proceedings were not brought under s. 2 of the Domestic Violence and Matrimonial Proceedings Act 1976. *Held,* allowing W's appeal, that there was such jurisdiction, but the power should be exercised only in exceptional circumstances and the husband should be given notice, if possible, of the nature of the relief sought.

LEWIS (A. H.) v. LEWIS (R. W. F.) [1978] 1 All E.R. 729, C.A.

1598. —— **power of High Court to grant injunctions**
[Domestic Violence and Matrimonial Proceedings Act 1976 (c. 50), s. 1.]
W issued an originating summons in the High Court for an injunction with a power of arrest to be attached; no other proceedings had been started. *Held,* granting the injunction without a power of arrest on W's undertaking to start proceedings, the words " without prejudice to the Jurisdiction of the High Court " in s. 1 of the 1976 Act meant that the existing jurisdiction of the High Court to grant injunctions remained unaffected by the section. A High Court judge could only attach a power of arrest to an injunction if proceedings for some substantive relief had been started: CRUTCHER v. CRUTCHER, *The Times* July 18, 1978, Payne J.

1599. Financial provision—appeal from registrar to county court judge—re-hearing
In matrimonial proceedings an appeal from a registrar to a county court judge is by way of re-hearing.

W appealed from an order of a county court registrar which awarded her financial relief ancillary to divorce proceedings. The county court judge declined to admit fresh evidence or to treat the case as a re-hearing. *Held,* allowing W's appeal, that the proceedings were governed by the Matrimonial Causes Rules 1977 and were in the nature of a re-hearing in which fresh evidence would be admitted and in which the judge's discretion would not be fettered by that previously exercised by the registrar.

G. (FORMERLY P.) v. P. (ANCILLARY RELIEF: APPEAL) [1977] 1 W.L.R. 1376, C.A.

1600. —— **lump sum—husband to receive future uncertain capital sum—wife's application stood over**
H was a warrant officer in the Army. When he retired, he would receive a gratuity based on his length of service. On divorce, W sought a lump sum payment. The trial judge ordered that H should pay W one quarter of this gratuity on its receipt. H appealed. *Held,* the amount received would depend on the length of H's service, and was presently unpredictable. The justice of a fixed percentage order could not be ascertained. H would be ordered to notify W of his receipt of the money and she could then apply for a lump sum payment, her present application being stood over till then: MORRIS v. MORRIS [1977] Fam. Law 244, C.A.

1601. Injunction—contempt of court—committal
[Domestic Violence and Matrimonial Proceedings Act 1976 (c. 50), s. 2 (3); R.S.C., Ord. 20, r. 11; C.C.R., Ord. 15, r. 22.] H1 was ordered by Swansea County Court not to molest his wife or remain in or enter the matrimonial

home; a power of arrest under s. 2 (3) of the 1976 Act was attached. He remained in the home and was arrested for breach of that order; he was committed to prison for contempt without limit of time being specified. W2 left the matrimonial home because of her husband's violence, and a month later the Court of Appeal ordered him to vacate the home to enable her to return. When she did so it was devoid of furniture and damaged. A county court judge committed H2 to prison " for a period of six months until further order." *Held*, allowing appeals by the Official Solicitor in respect of both husbands, both committal orders were bad. Neither of them properly specified the duration of committal (*Wellington* v. *Wellington* [1978] C.L.Y. 1606 applied) and they did not state the evidence, nor the particular contempts of which the husbands were guilty. No attempt should be made to remedy defects in a Court order without reference to a judge, and the slip rule could not be invoked in cases affecting the liberty of the subject: CINDERBY v. CINDERBY; PEKESIN v. PEKESIN, *The Times*, April 27, 1978, C.A.

1602. —— ex parte applications

The following Practice Note was issued by the Family Division on June 26, 1978:

The President is greatly concerned by the increasing number of applications being made *ex parte* in the Royal Courts of Justice for injunctions, which could and should have been made (if at all) on two clear days' notice to the other side, as required by the Rules.

An *ex parte* application should not be made, or granted, unless there is real immediate danger of serious injury or irreparable damage. A recent examination of *ex parte* applications shows that nearly 50 per cent. were unmeritorious, being made days, or even weeks, after the last incident of which complaint was made. This wastes time, causes needless expense, usually to the Legal Aid Fund, and is unjust to respondents.

Where notice of an application for an injunction is to be given and an early hearing date is sought, practitioners are reminded of the special arrangements which exist at the Royal Courts of Justice whereby the applicant's solicitor is able to select for the hearing any day on which the court is sitting. These arrangements are contained in President's Practice Direction dated July 10, 1972, [1972] C.L.Y. 1045.

[1978] 1 W.L.R. 925; [1978] 2 All E.R. 919.

1603. Injury to husband—wife's claim for loss of earnings—whether duty owed to spouse. See JACK v. ALEXANDER M'DOUGALL & CO. (ENGINEERS), § 714.

1604. Maintenance—magistrates' court—marriage of short duration

The parties married in 1942 and cohabited for two years thereafter. In 1945, W obtained maintenance of £2 per week (present value £12.66) which was reduced in 1948 to £1·50. In 1953 W obtained a divorce on grounds of desertion. W had worked after H left until 1970 when unable to continue because of osteoarthritis; at that time she was earning £34 per week. In 1977, when she was receiving £23·50 State benefits and the £1·50 maintenance, she applied to vary the 1948 order. *Held*, allowing her appeal from the justices' refusal to vary, the proper sum for H to pay was £12. The short duration of the marriage and the long period since its end should have a reducing but not nullifying effect on the order (*Krystman* v. *Krystman* [1973] C.L.Y. 926 and *Lombardi* v. *Lombardi* [1973] C.L.Y. 906 considered): McGRADY v. McGRADY [1978] Fam. Law 15, D.C.

1605. Matrimonial causes. See DIVORCE AND MATRIMONIAL CAUSES.

1606. Matrimonial home—breach of vacation order—failure to follow specified form for committal

W was committed to prison for seven days for breach of an order not to return to the matrimonial home. On release, he again returned and was arrested. He was brought before the judge on a Sunday; he was committed for contempt but the order for committal was left blank and none of the requisites had been completed. *Held*, W should be released immediately because of the defects: WELLINGTON v. WELLINGTON, *The Times*, March 22, 1978, C.A.

1607. —— exclusion—contempt—committal

[R.S.C., Ord. 52, r. 6.] H was ordered by Arnold J. on February 28, 1978, to vacate the former matrimonial home and not to return within 50 yards thereof, pursuant to an earlier order for sale on divorce proceedings. He failed to comply with the order and threatened prospective purchasers. On June 8, 1978, Lane J. heard evidence of H's breach of the earlier order in his absence and made a committal order. On June 28, 1978, the committal order was affirmed in H's presence. H appealed, contending insufficient particularity in the committal order. *Held,* dismissing the appeal, H knew he was in breach of the February order, and there was no need to specify in a High Court order that he had not vacated the house (*McIlraith* v. *Grady* [1967] C.L.Y. 3107 distinguished): KAVANAGH v. KAVANAGH, *The Times,* July 26, 1978, C.A.

1608. —— —— injunctions

The following Practice Note was issued by the Family Division on July 21, 1978:

1. S. 1 (1) (c) of the Domestic Violence and Matrimonial Proceedings Act 1976 empowers a county court to include in an injunction provisions excluding a party from the matrimonial home or a part of the matrimonial home or from a specified area in which the matrimonial home is included. Where a power of arrest under s. 2 of the Act is attached to any injunction containing such provisions, the respondent is liable to be arrested if he enters the matrimonial home or part thereof or specified area at any time while the injunction remains in force.

2. It is within the discretion of the court to decide whether an injunction should be granted and, if so, for how long it should operate. But whenever an injunction is granted excluding one of the parties from the matrimonial home (or a part thereof or specified area), consideration should be given to imposing a time limit on the operation of the injunction. In most cases a period of up to three months is likely to suffice, at least in the first instance. It will be open to the respondent in any event to apply for the discharge of the injunction before the expiry of the period fixed, for instance on the ground of reconciliation; and to the applicant to apply for an extension.

[1978] 2 All E.R. 1056.

1609. —— —— likelihood of violence

[Domestic Violence and Matrimonial Proceedings Act 1976 (c. 50), ss. 1 (1) (a) (b) (c), 2 (1).]

It is not an essential pre-requisite of an order that a party vacate the "matrimonial home" that there has been or will be physical violence.

The father and mother of two children were joint tenants of a council house. The mother left and took the two children to live with a neighbour in overcrowded conditions. Although there was no likelihood of violence from the father, the court made an order that he leave the house. *Held*, dismissing his appeal (but discharging a non-molestation order) that the primary consideration was the provision of a home for the children and that the fact that the father had not been violent did not prevent an order from being made.

SPINDLOW v. SPINDLOW [1978] 3 W.L.R. 777, C.A.

1610. —— —— order should not be applied for ex parte

A deputy judge ordered H to leave the matrimonial home at 6 p.m., notice being served on H at 3.30 p.m. after W's ex parte application. There was no allegation that H was violent. On appeal by H, *held*, the order ought not to have been made, as exclusion orders should only be made on notice, with both parties present. Solicitors making such future applications could be personally liable in costs: MASICH v. MASICH [1977] Fam. Law 245, C.A.

1611. —— —— parties sharing after divorce—test to be applied

In deciding whether to expel a spouse from the matrimonial home, the test the court should apply is: what is fair, just and reasonable, having regard to all the circumstances of the case.

Per curiam: The words "impossible" and "intolerable" in relation to such situations are subject to misuse and should be dropped.

Both before and after decree nisi of divorce, the parties lived at the matrimonial home with their three teenage children. There was considerable friction between H and W, and between H in particular and the children. W applied to exclude H from the matrimonial home which resulted in an order allowing H to remain but defining the use which he was permitted to make of the home. Further incidents occurred and W applied for a non-molestation injunction and an order that H vacate the matrimonial home. The judge granted the non-molestation injunction but, although he was satisfied that if H remained he would make life impossible for W and the children, he refused to exclude him from the home. W appealed. *Held*, allowing the appeal, that, applying the correct test, blame was irrelevant and that since W had to look after the children, H must be ordered to leave the matrimonial home. (*Bassett* v. *Bassett* [1975] C.L.Y. 1617 considered.)

WALKER v. WALKER [1978] 1 W.L.R. 533, C.A.

1612. —— —— **violent husband—children's interest paramount**
[Domestic Violence and Matrimonial Proceedings Act 1976 (c. 50), s. 1.]
Children's interests in the matrimonial home are paramount. A wife who is to look after them should not have to take her chance with a violent husband.

H, who admitted using violence to his wife on one occasion, lived in the matrimonial home. W had left with the five children and was living with her mother in crowded conditions. *Held*, allowing her appeal, that H should be ordered from the home to enable her to return. The children's interest was paramount and they should be back in the home with W looking after them.

RENNICK v. RENNICK [1977] 1 W.L.R. 1455, C.A.

1613. —— **gift—no direct financial contribution—wife's application for declaration of trust**
[Can.] In anticipation of his son, D, marrying P, D's father conveyed certain lands to D. A house was built on that land, and was paid for through a mortgage taken in D's name alone. P worked for the first five years of marriage and used her income for household purposes. P brought an action against her husband D, for a declaration that she was entitled to an interest in the property. *Held*, the action was dismissed. Since the land was a gift, and the house was paid for out of the mortgage proceeds, P made no direct financial contribution towards either the acquisition of the land nor to the building of the house. There was no common intention that P should have a share in the property. The mere sharing of household expenses between husband and wife creates no trust. (*Eves* v. *Eves* [1975] C.L.Y. 3110 referred to): COOK v. COOK [1978] 2 R.F.L. (2d) 204, Nfld.Sup.Ct.

1614. —— **tenancy—transfer—objection of landlord**
[Matrimonial Homes Act 1967 (c. 75), s. 7.] H was tenant of the matrimonial home, the landlord being his employer. H left his job, gave the landlord notice to terminate his tenancy, and moved out of the matrimonial home, leaving W with the children, aged 16 and 13. W was granted a decree nisi. It was accepted that W and the younger child would suffer severe hardship if forced to leave the matrimonial home. H consented to, but the landlord opposed, the transfer of the tenancy to W under s. 7 of the 1967 Act. *Held*, (1) the fact that the landlord opposed the transfer was not decisive; (2) the court should weigh the landlord's circumstances against the applicant's position; (3) if the order under s. 7 was granted, the landlords would still have their remedies under the Rent Acts, whereas if it were refused, the landlords would be better off and W worse off; (4) accordingly the order under s. 7 would be made. (*Hale* v. *Hale* [1975] C.L.Y. 1620 distinguished; *Thompson* v. *Thompson* [1975] C.L.Y. 1619, *Regan* v. *Regan* [1977] C.L.Y. 1547 and *Hutchings* v. *Hutchings* [1976] C.L.Y. 1392 considered): BUCKINGHAM v. BUCKINGHAM, May 12, 1978, Judge Kingham, Luton Cty.Ct. (*Ex rel N. E. Hickman, Esq., Solicitor.*)

1615. —— **transfer—executed without legal advice**
[Matrimonial Causes Act 1973 (c. 18), s. 25 (1).]
The court will not look with favour on assignments of proprietary interests in the matrimonial home made without the benefit of legal advice.

H and W married in 1954, and there were two children. In 1971 the matrimonial home was purchased in their joint names for £7,950. Then W formed an adulterous association with X, and she went off with him in 1973. In the same year, H's solicitors prepared a transfer of W's interest in the house to H, which W signed without having sought legal advice. H and W were divorced in 1974. In 1976 H remarried and lived on in the house with his new family. The house was now worth £20,250. W sought a lump sum and a property transfer order relating to the house under s. 23 of the Matrimonial Causes Act 1973. *Held,* even if the transfer by W to H had been valid, the court would ignore its effect. W had no doubt been under great emotional strain, and had not had legal advice. The transaction was something which should not be encouraged by the courts; however, it would be unjust to order H to sell the house where he lived with his family. Accordingly, he would be ordered to pay a lump sum of £3,500, which he could raise by way of second mortgage. (*Wachtel* v. *Wachtel* [1973] C.L.Y. 923 and *W.* v. *W.* (*Financial Provision: Lump Sum*) [1975] C.L.Y. 966 applied; dictum of Lord Denning M.R. in *Lloyd's Bank* v. *Bundy* [1974] C.L.Y. 1691, *H.* v. *H.* (*Family Provision: Remarriage*) [1975] C.L.Y. 1597 and *Cresswell* v. *Potter* (*Note*) [1978] C.L.Y. 1617 considered.)

BACKHOUSE *v.* BACKHOUSE [1978] 1 W.L.R. 243, Balcombe J.

1616. ——— ——— **preferable to a " Mesher " order**

[Matrimonial Causes Act 1973 (c. 18), s. 25 (1).]

In certain circumstances an outright transfer of a matrimonial home should be ordered in preference to a *Mesher* order.

H and W were married in 1957 and H bought the matrimonial home on a mortgage in 1963. They separated in 1971, H going to live in police quarters, W remaining in the house with the four children, two of whom were over 18. Rees J. made an order that the house should be sold when the younger child reached 17, both parties to have equal shares of the net proceeds of sale; he also ordered periodical payments for the two younger children. On appeal by W, *held,* allowing the appeal, that the case should be distinguished from *Mesher* v. *Mesher* [1973] C.L.Y. 1615, where both parties were about to marry. If this order were allowed to stand, in five years' time when the house was sold, each party would be left with no more than £2,500 after the Law Society's charge had been paid off. W would be homeless with inadequate capital for alternative accommodation. Yet she had made a considerable contribution to the family, especially since 1971, in comparison with H, who has been living a bachelor existence. It would therefore be ordered that H transfer his whole interest in the house to W and periodical payments for the children should be reduced to a nominal sum. (*Wachtel* v. *Wachtel* [1973] C.L.Y. 923 applied; *Mesher* v. *Mesher* [1973] C.L.Y. 1615 distinguished.)

HANLON *v.* HANLON [1978] 1 W.L.R. 592, C.A.

1617. ——— **wife's interest—deed of surrender—unconscionable bargain**

A requirement for independent advice on signing a document may be covered by an accompanying letter notifying the party of the effect of the document and suggesting that independent legal advice be obtained.

W, who was a van driver of moderate means, married H in 1955, and a house was purchased in H's name. In 1958, the house was sold and another one bought, with a mortgage, in the joint names of H and W. In June 1959, W went off with another man. In August H's solicitor sent an inquiry agent to W's home with a legal document which W signed. The effect of the document was that W surrendered her rights in the matrimonial home, and in return was released from her liability under the mortgage. The parties were divorced and the property sold. *Held,* that (1) within the requirements laid down in *Fry* v. *Lane* (1880) 40 Ch.D. 312, W was "poor and ignorant" in that she was a member of the lower income group and not highly educated. She was also "ignorant" in the context of property transactions; (2) the sale was at a "considerable undervalue" in that the release under the mortgage was worth far less than W's interest in the house; and (3) W was throughout without indepen-

dent advice. No explanation had been made to her as to the import of the document she had signed, and the transaction could not stand.
CRESSWELL *v.* POTTER [1978] 1 W.L.R. 255, Megarry J.

1618. —— —— equitable
[Land Registration Act 1925 (c. 21), s. 70 (1) (*g*).] When a mortgagor was in actual occupation of the matrimonial home, it could not be said his wife was also in actual occupation. Similarly if the wife were the mortgagor, the husband would not be in actual occupation. The rules relating to registered land were the same as for unregistered land. The one with legal title had actual occupation (*Caunce* v. *Caunce* [1969] C.L.Y. 2286 applied): BIRD *v.* SYME THOMPSON (1978) 122 S.J. 470, Templeman J.

1619. Matrimonial property—joint bank account used for husband's business—ownership
[Can.] W claimed a half share in a joint bank account. This was mostly used to hold moneys collected by H as a part-time salesman for which he was accountable to his employers. *Held,* the evidence showed that this account was in joint names purely as a matter of convenience. W was not entitled therefore to a half share in the balance left after deducting what was due to H's employers: BRUCE *v.* BRUCE (1976) 28 R.F.L. 190, New Brunswick Sup. Ct.

1620. —— Law Commission's Third Report. See § 1828.

1621. —— proceedings for causing damage—whether consent of D.P.P. required. See WOODLEY *v.* WOODLEY, § 445.

1622. Non-molestation order—rape of wife by husband—whether consent. See R. *v.* STEELE, § 589.

1623. Northern Ireland. See NORTHERN IRELAND.

1624. Transfer of property—wife's application—whether registrable as land charge. See WHITTINGHAM *v.* WHITTINGHAM; NATIONAL WESTMINSTER BANK (INTERVENER), § 1748.

1625. Widow's benefit. See NATIONAL INSURANCE.

ARTICLES. See *post,* p. [24].

INCOME TAX

1626. Appeal—case stated—validity—lack of evidence—Commissioner's assessment
[Taxes Managament Act 1970 (c. 9), s. 55 (3), as substituted by Finance (No. 2) Act 1975 (c. 45), s. 45 (1).] Estimated assessments were made on the taxpayer under Case II of Sched. D for the year 1975/76. No accounts were produced to the Commissioners, who, on application by the taxpayer, refused to order postponement of payment of tax. The taxpayer declared his dissatisfaction with the decision, and asked for a case to be stated. A case was duly stated, but it was signed by only one of the Commissioners who had heard the application. The taxpayer transmitted the case and set it down for appeal. On appeal, the taxpayer contended (i) that the case was defective, as it was signed by only one Commissioner, and (ii) that there was no evidence on which the Commissioners could reasonably have reached their conclusion that he was not overcharged to tax. *Held,* affirming the decision of Fox J., that (1) it was not open to the taxpayer to assert that the case was invalid and at the same time use it as the foundation of his appeal (*Norman* v. *Golder* (1944) 26 T.C. 293, followed), and (2) as there was no evidence before them relating to the taxpayer's income, the Commissioners could not have come to any other conclusion: PARIKH *v.* CURRIE [1978] S.T.C. 473, C.A.

1627. Assessment—appeal—final determination
The taxpayer company sought a declaration that their appeal against assessments to income and profits tax had not been " finally determined " by the Special Commissioners because the latter had not stated the amount of tax payable, merely an assessment of the income and profits assessable to tax, together with the necessary facts relating to the rate of tax. The Revenue had

agreed that, until final determination of the appeal, the taxpayer was not bound to pay the tax. *Held*, in favour of the Revenue, that (1) assessments ought to include a statement of the tax payable; but that (2) the Commissioners no longer had power to make or amend assessments, which were the functions of the tax inspector and the Board of the Inland Revenue. Accordingly, the appeal had already been determined, and the tax was payable: HALLAMSHIRE INDUSTRIAL FINANCE TRUST *v.* I.R.C., *The Times*, October 26, 1978, Browne-Wilkinson J.

1628. —— **back-duty—omission of profits from returns**
As a result of a protracted back-duty investigation, the inspector raised additional assessments for the years 1961/62 to 1966/67 inclusive in respect of business profits omitted from accounts, and assessments for 1968/69 to 1970/71 inclusive. When the assessments came before the Special Commissioners, they found that no business profits had been omitted during 1961/62 to 1964/65 inclusive, but that there was an unexplained increase in the taxpayer's assets and that profits of approximately £300 per year had been omitted. Therefore, they confirmed the assessments for 1965/66 to 1970/71 inclusive. *Held*, that the determination of the Commissioners was supported by the facts found: DRIVER *v.* I.R.C. [1977] T.R. 339, Ct. of Session.

1629. —— **trade—profits—pre-emption rights**
[Income Tax Act 1952 (c. 10), ss. 64, 514.]
The value of pre-emption rights is deductible in computing the profits of a trade of dealing in land.
The taxpayer company had a right of pre-emption in respect of certain land which had been requisitioned from it by the War Department in 1939. In 1962 the company exercised the right of pre-emption, re-acquiring the land for £42,000, and immediately re-sold it for £115,000. It was assessed to tax under Sched. D, Cases III to VIII. The company appealed against the assessment, and two days before the hearing notified the Revenue that it considered that the assessment should have been made under Case I. The Revenue accepted this contention. The Special Commissioners upheld the assessment, adjusting the figure in accordance with the Case I rules, and rejected the company's contention that in computing the Case I profits the value of its pre-emption should have been taken into account. *Held*, that (1) in the circumstances, the inspector having been seriously misled, the court should exercise its discretion under I.T.A. 1952, s. 514, to substitute an assessment under Case I for the assessment actually made (*Foulsham* v. *Pickles* [1925] A.C. 458, applied), and (2) the right of pre-emption was trading stock of the company, and in computing its trading profits should be brought in at valuation.
BATH AND WEST COUNTIES PROPERTY TRUST *v.* THOMAS [1977] 1 W.L.R. 1423, Walton J.

1630. Avoidance of tax—capital gains—disposal—sale into settlement—arm's length bargain
[Finance Act 1965 (c. 25), s. 22 (4) and (5), and Sched. 7, paras. 17 and 21.]
" Settlement " in the Finance Act 1965, Sched. 7, para. 21, does not extend to an arrangement without any element of bounty.
By way of a capital gains tax avoidance scheme, the taxpayer for full consideration paid to him by a Jersey company transferred shares to a Guernsey company on trust to pay the income thereof to the taxpayer during his life with remainder to the Jersey company. Two days later the taxpayer sold his life interest to a Bahamian company for full value. The taxpayer was assessed to tax on a sum of approximately £150,000 in respect of the transfer of the shares to the Guernsey company. *Held*, allowing the taxpayer's appeal from the decision of the Special Commissioners, that on the disposal of the shares to the Guernsey company, the Revenue could not rely on the Finance Act 1965, s. 22 (4), to substitute market value, the bargain being at arm's length, and the provisions of para. 21 of Sched. 7 to the Finance Act 1965 not operating to treat the taxpayer and the Guernsey company as " connected

persons "; in that provision, " settlement " does not extend to an arrangement having no element of bounty (*Bulmer* v. *I.R.C.* [1966] C.L.Y. 6173 and *I.R.C.* v. *Plummer* [1977] C.L.Y. 1619 applied).
BERRY *v.* WARNETT [1978] 1 W.L.R. 957, Goulding J.

1631. —— exchange of shares—value-shifting—exercise of control
Para. 15 (2), Sched. 7, to the Finance Act 1965 extends to the concerted exercise of collective control.
The vendors wished to sell their shares in company A to company B. They created company C, to which they sold the shares in company A in exchange for the issue of shares in company C. Immediately thereafter company C sold the shares in company A to company B. A fourth company registered in the Cayman Islands subsequently acquired shares in company C, and then took up preferred ordinary shares, commanding the greater part of the value of company C, on a rights issue, the controlling shareholders not taking up their entitlement to the shares. Goulding J. held that the arrangement was effective to avoid capital gains tax on the disposal of the shares in company A and that the value-shifting provisions of para. 15 (2) of Sched. 7 to the Finance Act 1965 did not apply to the acquisition of the preferred ordinary shares by the Cayman Islands company. *Held*, allowing the Crown's appeal, that the scheme failed at the second stage of value-shifting, as provisions of para. 15 (2) extended to control enjoyed by persons collectively, and there could be an exercise of such collective control without all the shareholders in question exercising their votes.
FLOOR *v.* DAVIS [1978] 3 W.L.R. 360, C.A.

1632. —— transfer of assets—associated operations
[Income Tax Act 1952 (c. 10), s. 412.] A discretionary settlement was made in 1942 under the law of Northern Ireland; the trustees were resident outside the United Kingdom. The trustees had power to accumulate income and to invest it, and to accumulate the resulting income thereof; they also had power to pay or apply capital for certain beneficiaries. Rental income arising to the trustees was accumulated and invested, and the resulting income was also accumulated. Between 1962 and 1966 capital appointments were made from the latter accumulations. The taxpayer received some of the funds appointed. He was assessed to income tax under I.T.A. 1952, s. 412, on the basis that he was chargeable in respect of the whole of the income of the settlement for the year in which the appointment was made and thereafter. Other beneficiaries were similarly assessed. However, the Revenue voluntarily restricted the aggregate of the assessments in respect of any year to the amount of the income actually received by the trustees in that year. The Special Commissioners upheld the assessments. *Held*, (1) that the trustees were persons resident outside the United Kingdom for the purposes of s. 412; (2) that the appointment of sub-accumulations was an " associated operation "; but (3) that the taxpayer's liability was limited to the amount actually appointed to him, and he fell to be assessed only in respect of the year in which the appointment was made (dictum of Earl Loreburn in *Drummond* v. *Collins* [1915] A.C. at p. 1017, applied): VESTEY *v.* I.R.C. [1977] S.T.C. 414, Walton J.

1633. Bonus—P.A.Y.E.
[Income and Corporation Taxes Act 1970 (c. 10), s. 204.] An annual bonus credited to a director's account with a company which he was free to draw on as he wished, was *held* to be a " payment " to which the P.A.Y.E. Regulations applied: GARFORTH *v.* NEWSMITH STAINLESS, *The Times,* November 22, 1978, Walton J.

1634. Capital allowances
CAPITAL ALLOWANCES (CORRESPONDING NORTHERN IRELAND GRANTS) ORDER 1978 (No. 53) [10p], made under the Capital Allowances Act 1968 (c. 3), ss. 84 (1) and 95 (6), as amended by the Finance Act 1972 (c. 41), s. 67 (3); operative on February 15, 1978; raises the limit of grants payable in Northern Ireland to 45 per cent., and applies to agreements entered into on or after August 1, 1977, but before April 1, 1980.

1635. —— boat converted into restaurant—whether " plant "
[Capital Allowances Act 1968 (c. 3), s. 18; Finance Act 1971 (c. 68), s. 41.]
A floating restaurant is not " plant " for the purposes of capital allowances.
The taxpayer company bought a vessel and converted it into a floating restaurant at a total cost of approximately £78,000. It claimed that the vessel was " plant," and that the money spent on the purchase and conversion qualified for capital allowance. *Held*, that the vessel was the place or setting where the business was carried on and did not constitute the apparatus or plant by means of which the business was carried on. Therefore, the expenditure did not qualify for capital allowances.
BENSON *v.* YARD ARM CLUB [1978] 2 All E.R. 958, Goulding J.

1636. Capital gains
CAPITAL GAINS TAX (EXEMPT GILT-EDGED SECURITIES) (NO. 1) ORDER 1978 (No. 141) [10p], made under the Finance Act 1969 (c. 32), s. 41 (2) (*i*); adds specified gilt-edged securities to the category of stocks and bonds which are exempt from tax on capital gains if held for more than 12 months.
CAPITAL GAINS TAX (EXEMPT GILT-EDGED SECURITIES) (NO. 2) ORDER 1978 (No. 1312) [10p], made under the Finance Act 1969, s. 41 (2); adds specified gilt-edged securities to the category of stocks and bonds exempt from capital gains tax if held for more than 12 months.
CAPITAL GAINS TAX (EXEMPT GILT-EDGED SECURITIES) (NO. 3) ORDER 1978 (No. 1838) [10p], made under the Finance Act 1969, s. 41 (2); adds specified gilt-edged securities to the category of stocks and bonds which are exempt from tax on capital gains if held for more than twelve months.

1637. —— assessment—damages for breaches of two contracts—prior agreement on apportionment not binding upon inspector
[Taxes Management Act 1970 (c. 9), s. 54 (1).]
An agreement in principle, leaving figures to be determined, does not bind the Inland Revenue under the Taxes Management Act 1970, s. 54.
The taxpayer brought claims against an investment trust in respect of breach of an agreement for the sale of shares, and breach of a service agreement. The claims were settled on payment of a global sum of £399,357, no apportionment being made. The inspector agreed that the amount fell to be apportioned as to damages for breach of the sale agreement and damages for breach of the service agreement, but he gave no indication of the amounts of the apportionments or as to the basis on which the apportionment was to be made. Subsequently, he assessed the whole amount to capital gains tax by attributing it to the share sale agreement. *Held*, affirming the decision of Foster J., that the agreement in principle which had been reached with the inspector did not preclude him from assessing the whole amount to capital gains tax.
DELBOURGO *v.* FIELD [1978] 2 All E.R. 193, C.A.

1638. —— assets—service contract
[Finance Act 1965 (c. 25), s. 22.]
Rights under a service contract are not " assets " for capital gains tax purposes.
The taxpayer company, a holding company, acquired the services of a director for a seven-year period on its acquisition of a subsidiary company. After two years the director paid the taxpayer company £50,000 for release from his obligations under the contract. *Held*, allowing the taxpayer company's appeal from the decision of Fox J., that non-assignable rights under a service contract for which no market value was ascertainable were not "assets " for capital gains tax purposes. (*Nokes* v. *Doncaster Amalgamated Collieries* [1940] A.C. 1014 applied.)
O'BRIEN *v.* BENSON'S HOSIERY (HOLDINGS) [1978] 3 W.L.R. 609, C.A.

1639. —— disposal—transfer of shares to trustee—absolutely entitled
[Finance Act 1965 (c. 25), s. 22 (5).]
Persons may be absolutely entitled against a trustee for the purposes of F.A. 1965, s. 22 (5), notwithstanding that their interests are interdependent by virtue of some contract or trust.

With a view to securing continued family control of a company, the taxpayer and 11 other shareholders in the company transferred their shareholdings to trustees to be held by them for 15 years on the terms of a shareholders' agreement. The Crown contended that the transfer of the shares to the trustees was a disposal for capital gains tax purposes. *Held*, applying *Stephenson* v. *Barclays Bank Trust Co.* [1975] C.L.Y. 1643, and *Kidson* v. *Macdonald* [1974] C.L.Y. 840, that the shareholders were "absolutely entitled" as against the trustees so that there had been no capital gains tax disposal on the transfer of the shares to the trustees.

BOOTH v. ELLARD [1978] 1 W.L.R. 927, Goulding J.

1640. —— **exemptions—annual payments due under covenant**
[Finance Act 1965 (c. 25), Sched. 7, para. 12 (*c*).]
Royalty payments may be annual payments within Finance Act 1965, Sched. 7, para. 12 (*c*).

The taxpayer company, which had a licence to exploit the xerographic process throughout the world in the U.S.A. and Canada, by agreements under seal surrendered its rights in respect of certain countries in consideration of a "royalty" of five per cent. on sales in those countries. It then resolved to pay a dividend to its shareholders to be satisfied by the distribution of its rights to royalty payments. It claimed that the royalty payments were "annual payments" within Finance Act 1965, Sched. 7, para. 12 (*c*), so that the disposal of those rights did not give rise to a liability for corporation tax on chargeable gains. *Held*, allowing the taxpayer company's appeal from the decision of Slade J., that the royalty payments were annual payments due under a covenant and were exempt from capital gains tax.

RANK XEROX v. LANE [1978] 2 All E.R. 1124, C.A.

1641. —— **land—development value**
[Finance Act 1965 (c. 25), Sched. 6, para. 23 (1) (*b*).]
Absence of planning permission does not exclude the application of the valuation provisions in para. 23 of Sched. 6 to the Finance Act 1965.

The taxpayer had inherited in 1962 22 acres of agricultural land which had a value for tax purposes of 11,581. He sold it in 1972 for 264,000, the price reflecting the hope or expectation that planning permission would be granted. He appealed against an assessment to capital gains tax in respect of the sale for the year 1971/72, contending that para. 23 of Sched. 6 to the Finance Act 1965 (which prescribes April 1965 value as the capital gains tax base cost) had no application where land was sold without planning consent, and that para. 24 (time-apportionment of gain) was the more appropriate method of computation. *Held*, affirming the decision of Fox J., that the land had to be valued as at April 6, 1965, since the application of the statutory hypothesis was not restricted to cases where planning permission existed at the date of sale.

WATKINS v. KIDSON [1978] 2 All E.R. 785, C.A.

1642. —— **sale of shares—deferred consideration**
[Finance Act 1965 (c. 25), s. 22.] The taxpayers sold shares partly for a fixed consideration to be paid immediately, and partly for a deferred consideration payable on certain contingencies. The Inland Revenue claimed that on the receipt of the deferred consideration there was a disposal of an asset (a chose in action) by the taxpayers for the purpose of capital gains tax, and made assessments to tax accordingly. *Held*, that there was no disposal of an asset within F.A. 1965, s. 22 (3), on the payment of the deferred consideration:

MARREN v. INGLES, *The Times*, July 13, 1978, Slade J.

1643. —— **settlement—disposal—absolute entitlement**
[Finance Act 1965, s. 25 (3).]
An "advance" of settled property by subjecting it to the trusts of a new settlement involves a disposal of the settled property for capital gains tax purposes.

Under a settlement created in 1955 the trustees had a discretionary power "to pay or apply" the whole or any part of the capital of the trust fund to or for the benefit of all, or any one or more, of the beneficiaries. They exercised this power by appointing that the settled property should be held on the trusts of a separate settlement (created in 1972 in favour of the beneficiaries) of which they were also the trustees. The Crown contended that the appointment effected by the trustees involved a deemed disposal by them of the settled property under F.A. 1965, s. 25 (3). *Held*, allowing the Crown's appeal from the decision of the Special Commissioners, that on the facts the 1955 settlement had come to an end in relation to the appointed assets, and that the trustees of the 1972 settlement had become " absolutely entitled " to those assets as against the trustees of the 1955 settlement, that expression not signifying beneficial entitlement.

HOARE TRUSTEES *v.* GARDNER; HART *v.* BRISCOE [1978] 1 All E.R. 791, Brightman J.

1644. Chargeable benefits

INCOME TAX (CASH EQUIVALENTS OF CAR BENEFITS) ORDER 1978 (No. 434) [10p], made under the Finance Act 1976 (c. 40), s. 64 (4); operative on April 6, 1978; prescribes the new level of cash equivalents on which directors and higher paid employees are chargeable to income tax in respect of the benefit of a car made available for private use by reasons of their employment. For this purpose, higher-paid employees are those earning at the rate of £7,500 or more a year.

1645. Child allowance—apportionment

[Income and Corporation Taxes Act 1970 (c. 10), ss. 10, 11.] A husband and wife, who had separated in March 1975, each claimed relief under ss. 10 and 11 of the I.C.T.A. 1970, in respect of their two children for the years 1973–74 and 1974–75. The General Commissioners apportioned relief, by reference to contributions to expenditure on the children, for the year 1973–74 as to 60 per cent. to the husband and 40 per cent. to the wife, and for 1974–75 as to 25 per cent. to the husband and 75 per cent. to the wife. For the latter year they had regard to the fact that contributions made by the husband under a court order were deductible in computing his total income for tax purposes. The husband appealed. *Held*, dismissing the appeal, that the findings of the Commissioners in the form of percentages by reference to the total expenditure on any child were sufficient for the purposes of s. 11 (3) and, faced with the conflicting evidence, represented a proper basis for the apportionment of the child relief: BUXTON *v.* BUXTON [1978] S.T.C. 122, Brightman J.

1646. —— entitlement—proof—Commissioner's decision

The taxpayer, having two wives under Mohammedan law, claimed child allowances in respect of four persons as his children by one or other of the wives. The General Commissioners came to the conclusion on the evidence before them, which consisted of certain affidavits obtained from the Yemen, that the taxpayer had not proved on the balance of probabilities that the children were his children, and they disallowed the claims for child allowances. *Held*, dismissing the appeal, that the Commissioners were entitled to reach their decision on the evidence before them, and their decision should not be disturbed: MOHSIN *v.* EDON [1978] S.T.C. 163, Brightman J.

1647. —— meaning of " custody "

[Income and Corporation Taxes Act 1970 (c. 10), s. 10 (1) (*b*).] Miss Ikpoh, a student of 23 years of age at Dublin University, was born the daughter of Chief Ikpoh, who subsequently renounced his rights over her in favour of Mr. Nwagbo, Mr. Nwagbo sent Miss Ikpoh money and paid her fees at Dublin University; Miss Ikpoh stayed with Mr. Nwagbo during vacations. *Held*, that Miss Ikpoh was not in the " custody " of Mr. Nwagbo for the purposes of I.C.T.A. 1970, s. 10 (1) (*b*), so that Mr. Nwagbo was not entitled to a child allowance in respect of her (*Kirby* v. *Leather* [1965] C.L.Y. 2285, followed): NWAGBO *v.* RISING [1978] S.T.C. 558, Fox J.

1648. Construction industry—deductions by contractors—exemption—powers of commissioners on appeal

[Finance (No. 2) Act 1975 (c. 45), ss. 69, 70.] G, a sub-contractor, applied for a certificate of exemption from s. 69 of the 1975 Act (which provides for contractors to deduct tax from payments made to sub-contractors). The certificate was refused because during the qualifying period G had failed to declare certain small amounts and had failed to make certain returns. He appealed and the commissioners held that the Board had been right to refuse the certificate, but that as K had rectified the faults they would issue one. On appeal, *held*, that the commissioners had no power to issue a certificate. The board had properly exercised their discretion and the commissioners could not exercise that discretion for them: KIRVELL *v.* GUY, *The Times,* November 29, 1978, Walton J.

1649. Distribution—date

The taxpayer company's balance sheet for the year ended March 31, 1967, showed a capital distribution of £67,564 on one side, the discharge of a loan account of £60,330 on the other side, and a balance of £7,234 under current liabilities as "unclaimed capital distribution." There was no record of any approval of the balance sheet or of the capital distribution until a meeting of August 5, 1968. The Crown claimed, and the Special Commissioners held, that the company had made the distribution on August 5, 1968, when the balance sheet was approved by the annual general meeting of the company. *Held*, that on the material before them the Special Commissioners were entitled to come to the conclusion that the distribution was made on August 5: JOHN PATERSON (MOTORS) *v.* I.R.C. [1978] S.T.C. 59, Ct. of Session

1650. Double taxation

DOUBLE TAXATION RELIEF (TAXES ON INCOME) (BOTSWANA) ORDER 1978 (No. 183) [35p], made under the Income and Corporation Taxes Act 1970 (c. 10), s. 497 (8); gives effect to the Agreement with Botswana scheduled to the Order so that shipping and air transport profits, certain trading profits not arising through a permanent establishment, pensions (other than government pensions) and the earnings of temporary business visitors are, subject to certain conditions, to be taxed only in the country of the taxpayer's residence.

DOUBLE TAXATION RELIEF (TAXES ON INCOME) (PHILIPPINES) ORDER 1978 (No. 184) [35p], made under the Income and Corporation Taxes Act 1970, s. 497 (8); gives effect to the Convention with the Philippines scheduled to the Order so that certain trading profits, pensions and the earnings of temporary business visitors are to be taxed only in the country of the taxpayer's residence.

DOUBLE TAXATION RELIEF (TAXES ON INCOME) (POLAND) ORDER 1978 (No. 282) [35p], made under the Income and Corporation Taxes Act 1970, s. 497, the Finance Act 1972 (c. 41), s. 98 (2) and the Finance Act 1965 (c. 25), s. 39; contains in the schedule a Convention with Poland, under which certain trading profits not arising through a permanent establishment, interest, pensions and the earnings of temporary business visitors are to be taxed only in the taxpayer's country of residence.

DOUBLE TAXATION RELIEF (TAXES ON INCOME) (GHANA) ORDER 1978 (No. 785) [40p], made under the Income and Corporation Taxes Act 1970, s. 497, the Finance Act 1972 (c. 41), s. 98 (2) and the Finance Act 1965 (c. 25), s. 39; gives effect to the Convention with Ghana that is set out in this Order relating to double taxation relief on income.

DOUBLE TAXATION RELIEF (TAXES ON INCOME) (REPUBLIC OF KOREA) ORDER 1978 (No. 786) [50p], made under the Income and Corporation Taxes Act 1970, s. 497, the Finance Act 1972, s. 98 (2) and the Finance Act 1965, s. 39; gives effect to the matters contained in the Convention with the Republic of Korea set out in this Order relating to double taxation relief on income.

DOUBLE TAXATION RELIEF (TAXES ON INCOME) (SINGAPORE) ORDER 1978 (No. 787) [25p], made under the Income and Corporation Taxes Act 1970, s. 497, the Finance Act 1972, s. 98 (2) and the Finance Act 1965, s. 39; gives effect to those agreements set out in a Protocol contained in this Order relating to double taxation relief in the United Kingdom and Singapore.

DOUBLE TAXATION RELIEF (TAXES ON INCOME) (HUNGARY) ORDER 1978 (No. 1056) [40p], made under the Income and Corporation Taxes Act 1970, s. 497, the Finance Act 1965, s. 39, and the Finance Act 1972, s. 98 (2); gives effect to a double taxation agreement with Hungary.

DOUBLE TAXATION RELIEF (TAXES ON INCOME) (SWITZERLAND) ORDER 1978 (No. 1408) [50p], made under the Income and Corporation Taxes Act

1970, s. 497 (8); in relation to Switzerland provides that certain trading profits not arising through a permanent establishment, interest, royalties, pensions and the earnings of temporary business visitors are (subject to certain conditions) to be taxed only in the country of the taxpayer's residence. Provision is made for students, capital gains, shipping and air transport.

1651. Finance Act 1978 (c. 42)

Part III (ss. 13, 14, 18–43) deals with income tax: s. 13 charges income tax for 1978–79; s. 14 provides for lower rate income tax; s. 18 deals with relief for interest on certain loans; s. 19 alters personal reliefs; s. 20 deals with child tax allowances and benefits in respect of children; s. 21 relates to maintenance payments; s. 22 deals with tax repayments to wives; s. 23 sets the threshold for benefits in kind for 1979–80; s. 24 increases the maximum tax-free payment for loss of employment; s. 25 deals with life policies; s. 26 relates to retirement annuities; s. 27 provides for relief for individuals carrying on a trade, profession or vocation partly abroad; s. 28 provides for relief for fluctuating profits for persons carrying on a trade of farming and market gardening; s. 29 states that persons employed as divers or diving supervisors are to be taxed under Sched. D. Case I; s. 30 relates to further relief for losses in early years of trade; s. 31 withdraws loss relief for dealing in commodity futures; s. 32 restricts relief on sales of land with the right to repurchase; s. 33 amends the deduction rate for sub-contractors in the construction industry; s. 34 contains exemptions for community land transactions; s. 35 alters the maximum and minimum amounts for calculating the relevant income for close companies; s. 36 relates to the acquisition of trades by close companies; s. 37 relates to capital allowances for long leases; s. 38 deals with capital allowances for hotels; s. 39 deals with capital allowances for agricultural and forestry works; s. 40 relates to capital allowances for sports grounds; s. 41 relates to the date for payment of tax for 1977–78; s. 42 deals with the deduction of tax from payments of interest in 1978–79; s. 43 relates to the repayment of tax paid under Police Regulations.

1652. —— capital gains

Pt. III (ss. 44–52) deals with capital gains tax: s. 44 provides for relief from capital gains tax for gains less than £9,500; s. 45 exempts from capital gains tax chattels sold for £2,000 or less; s. 46 provides for relief from capital gains tax for gifts of business assets; s. 47 relates to relief for replacement of business assets; s. 48 relates to the transfer of business on retirement; s. 49 provides for relief from capital gains tax in respect of loans to traders; s. 50 deals with relief for private residences; s. 51 relates to part disposals of land; s. 52 deals with the alteration of dispositions taking effect on death.

1653. —— profit sharing schemes

Pt. III (ss. 53–61) deals with profit sharing schemes: s. 53 relates to the appropriation of shares under approved profit sharing schemes; s. 54 sets out the period of retention, the release date and the appropriate percentage for approved profit sharing schemes; s. 55 relates to the disposal of scheme shares; s. 56 relates to capital receipts in respect of scheme-shares; s. 57 deals with company reconstructions and amalgamations in connection with profit sharing schemes; s. 58 relates to excess or unauthorised shares; s. 59 deals with P.A.Y.E. deduction of tax for approved profit sharing schemes; s. 60 relates to Sched. D deduction of payments to trustees; s. 61 contains definitions for this Part of the Act

1654. General Commissioners

The following orders have been made under the Taxes Management Act 1970 (c. 9), s. 2 (6):

Divisions of General Commissioners Orders 1978 Nos. 1, 2, 3, 18, 19 (amendment).

1655. Interest

INCOME TAX (OFFICIAL RATE OF INTEREST ON BENEFICIAL LOANS) ORDER 1978 (No. 28) [10p], made under the Finance Act 1976 (c. 40), s. 66 (9);

operative on April 6, 1978; prescribes the official rate of interest for the purposes of the charge to income tax under the 1976 Act in respect of certain cheap or interest-free loans, which directors and higher-paid employees obtain by reason of their employment.

1656. —— **account in bank's name—whether part of taxpayer's income**
[Income Tax Act 1952 (c. 10), s. 148.]
Interest on money deposited in the name of a bank as a security is taxable income of the depositor.

In 1965 the taxpayer gave a guarantee to a bank. In 1967 he opened a deposit account in the name of the bank by way of security for performance of his obligations under the guarantee. Two months later he opened a second deposit in the bank's name, again by way of security. In June 1967 interest was credited to the first deposit account, and a month later he transferred the balance on that account (including the interest) to the second deposit account. Until June 1969 interest was periodically credited to the second deposit account. The guarantee was then discharged, and the taxpayer withdrew the moneys standing to credit on the second deposit account. He was assessed to income tax under Sched. D, Case III, on the ground that for the years 1967–1970 he had received or been entitled to the interest on the deposit accounts within the Income Tax Act 1952, s. 148. *Held,* affirming the decision of Brightman J., that the interest paid enured immediately to the taxpayer's benefit and so was "received" by the taxpayer (*Whitworth Park Coal Co.* v. *I.R.C.* [1959] C.L.Y. 1534 distinguished).
DUNMORE v. McGOWAN [1978] 1 W.L.R. 617, C.A.

1657. Investment income—special charge—relevance of residence
[Finance Act 1968 (c. 44), s. 41.] The taxpayer appealed from an assessment to the special charge on investment income for the tax year 1967–68, on the ground that it was implicit in s. 41 (3) that the charge did not apply in respect of investment income arising during any part of the year of assessment after which the person in question had ceased to be resident in the U.K.; and that he was accordingly liable to the charge only in respect of income arising before his departure from the U.K. on January 29, 1968. *Held,* dismissing the appeal, that the charge was levied on an annual basis, and there was no provision for partial liability only: NEUBERGH v. I.R.C. [1978] S.T.C. 181, Brightman J.

1658. Life assurance premiums
INCOME TAX (LIFE ASSURANCE PREMIUM RELIEF) REGULATIONS 1978 (No. 1159) [25p], made under the Finance Act 1976 (c. 40), Sched. 4, para. 16, as amended by the Finance Act 1978 (c. 42), Sched. 3, para. 10; operative on April 6, 1979; provide that an individual who pays a premium on which relief is due will normally be entitled to deduct and retain an appropriate sum for relief, and the Inland Revenue will reimburse the life office for the consequent deficiency in its premium receipts.

1659. Northern Ireland. See NORTHERN IRELAND.

1660. P.A.Y.E.
INCOME TAX (EMPLOYMENTS) (No. 7) REGULATIONS 1978 (No. 326) [15p], made under the Income and Corporation Taxes Act 1970 (c. 10), s. 204; operative on April 6, 1978; modify the regulations relating to income tax under P.A.Y.E. They add the personal relief allowable under s. 14 of the 1970 Act (additional relief for widows and others having single-handed responsibility for children) to the reliefs for which no notice of coding need be given to the employee when there is an alteration in the rate of the relief.

1661. Penalties—notices—validity
[Taxes Management Act 1970 (c. 9), ss. 20, 98.] Notices were served on six companies under T.M.A. 1970, s. 20, requiring them to make all books, accounts and documents relating to their trading transactions available for inspection. Some of the notices extended to periods expired more than six years prior to the date of issue of the notices. In the case of two companies some notices related to periods for which no returns had been demanded. The companies failed to comply. Proceedings were commenced for penalties under T.M.A. 1970,

s. 98. *Held*, (1) that the six-year time limit did not apply to notices under s. 20; (2) that the penalty proceedings were effectually commenced by a minute signed by an Under-Secretary of State on behalf of the Revenue; but (3) that the notices relating to periods for which no returns had been demanded were invalid: B & S DISPLAYS *v.* I.R.C. [1978] S.T.C. 331, Goulding J.

1662. Post-war credits

POST-WAR CREDIT (INCOME TAX) ORDER 1978 (No. 662) [10p], made under the Finance Act 1972 (c. 41), s. 131 (3), as amended by the Finance Act 1976 (c. 40), s. 59; operative on July 1, 1978; provides that the right to repayment of post-war credit is extinguished where an applicant has not applied before December 31, 1978, and cannot produce a post-war credit certificate. It also provides that after December 31, 1978, no one shall be entitled to require that a post-war credit certificate be issued to him.

1663. Practice—appeal—case stated—effect

[Taxes Management Act 1970 (c. 9), s. 56.] The taxpayer unsuccessfully appealed against assessments to income tax made on him in respect of rent and bank deposit interest alleged to have been omitted from his tax returns. He required the Commissioners to state a case for the opinion of the High Court, and proceeded with the appeal by transmitting the case. At the hearing of the appeal he contended that the case stated was inaccurate and that the proceedings before the Commissioners had not been properly conducted. *Held*, dismissing the appeal, that the court had jurisdiction to consider only those facts found by the Commissioners and to determine the questions of law arising therefrom. The complaints raised by the taxpayer were appropriately made only by way of application to a Divisional Court of the Queen's Bench Division: YOANNOU *v.* HALL [1978] S.T.C. 600, Fox J.

1664. —— hearing—taxpayer not present—finding of fraud

Back duty assessments were made on the taxpayer for the years 1963–64 to 1975–76. The taxpayer appealed, but at the hearing of the appeal he was not present and was not represented. However, by letter he requested an adjournment, on the ground that he had consulted counsel. At the hearing the Crown made allegations of fraud or wilful default under Taxes Management Act 1970, s. 36, or alternatively neglect under s. 37 of that Act. The Commissioners refused the adjournment and found the taxpayer guilty of fraud for certain of the years. The taxpayer appealed, alleging breach of the rules of natural justice. *Held*, that while the question of adjournment was a question for the Commissioners, having regard to the nature of the charges refusal of the adjournment seriously prejudiced the taxpayer. The appeal was allowed and the case was remitted to be heard by different Commissioners (*Rose* v. *Humbles* [1972] C.L.Y. 1702 followed): OTTLEY *v.* MORRIS [1978] S.T.C. 594, Fox J.

1665. Profits—undisclosed bank deposit interest

[Taxes Management Act 1970 (c. 9), ss. 36, 37, 39, 50 and 118.] For the years 1958/59 to 1965/66 inclusive the taxpayer failed to include in his tax returns bank deposit interest of his wife. The General Commissioners accepted statements from the inspector showing amounts described as " profits not disclosed." They determined that the taxpayer had been guilty of neglect. The taxpayer challenged the determination on the ground that it was not supported by lawful evidence, and the case stated did not include any statement of the evidence relied upon by the Commissioners for their conclusion. *Held*, affirming the decision of Walton J., that the Commissioners were warranted in their conclusion that there had been neglect: JOHNSON *v.* SCOTT [1978] T.R. 121, C.A.

1666. Profits of trade—capital or revenue expenditure

Under a fifty-year lease the taxpayer company was liable to pay a variable rent computed by reference to its gross takings from petrol sales and catering and other services. The gross takings included the tobacco duty in the selling price of tobacco. The company paid to the landlord £122,000 to eliminate from the rental computation the tobacco duty contained in the sales of tobacco. It claimed to deduct this sum in computing its profits assessable to tax under Case I of Sched. D. *Held,* affirming the decision of Templeman J., that the payment procured an advantage which endured (see [1979] 1 W.L.R. 87) for the benefit of the trade; therefore, it was capital expenditure and not deductible in the computation of profits (*dictum* of Rowlatt J. in *Anglo-Persian Oil Co.* v. *Dale* (1932) 16 T.C. at p. 262, applied): TUCKER v. GRANADA MOTORWAY SERVICES [1978] S.T.C. 587, C.A.

1667. —— ex gratia payments

A voluntary payment made to acknowledge friendly relations with a trader and to maintain goodwill is not taxable as profits of his trade.

The taxpayer ran licensed catering establishments, many of which were held on tied tenancy agreements from another company, W. In 1968, W decided to call back 13 tenancies over a period of two years from January 1969. In this connection it made ex gratia payments to the taxpayer totalling approximately £80,000. The taxpayer was assessed to tax on the basis that the payments arising from the loss of tenancies were profits of its trade. The Special Commissioners found that the payments were made to acknowledge the long and friendly trading relationship between W and the taxpayer, and to maintain W's goodwill, and they held that the payments were not taxable. Walton J. affirmed the Commissioners' decision. *Held,* dismissing the appeal, that while every case had to be considered on its own facts, the payments were not receipts arising from the taxpayer's trade.

MURRAY v. GOODHEWS [1978] 1 W.L.R. 499, C.A.

1668. —— land—purpose of acquisition

The company was formed to develop and acquire properties. The Special Commissioners found as a fact that the properties were acquired for the purpose of retention as investments and not for the purpose of resale. In 1966 it was decided to liquidate the company and sell the properties. The reasons for this decision were changes in taxation and landlord and tenant legislation, and restrictions on credit and office building. The Special Commissioners held that the surplus on disposal of the properties attracted tax as a trading profit. *Held,* allowing the company's appeal from the decision of the Special Commissioners, that the Commissioners' finding that the properties were acquired with the definite intention of investment, and the fact that disposal arose from changed circumstances, led to the conclusion that the transactions were not in the course of trade, so that the surplus was not taxable as a trading receipt: SIMMONS (AS LIQUIDATOR OF LIONEL SIMMONS PROPERTIES) v. I.R.C. [1978] S.T.C. 344, Goulding J.

1669. —— objects of company—carry forward of loss. See AMERICAN LEAF BLENDING CO. SDN. BHD. v. DIRECTOR-GENERAL OF INLAND REVENUE, § 236.

1670. Returns—default—penalty

[Taxes Management Act 1970 (c. 9), s. 8.] The taxpayer failed to make a return as required by s. 8, T.M.A. 1970, and maintained that he did not have to do so as he was unemployed during the period in question. The General Commissioners awarded a penalty of £10. *Held,* that the penalty was properly imposed: GARNHAM v. I.R.C. [1977] T.R. 307, D.C.

1671. [Taxes Management Act 1970 (c. 9), ss. 8, 93, 118.] The taxpayer failed to make returns of income for the years 1972/73 to 1975/76 (inclusive), as required by T.M.A. 1970, s. 8. A penalty of £25 was imposed in respect of each of the three years to April 5, 1975. *Held,* that in the absence of satisfactory excuse, the penalties had been properly imposed: NAPIER v. I.R.C. [1977] T.R. 289, D.C.

1672. Schedule D—travelling expenses

[Income and Corporation Taxes Act 1970 (c. 10), s. 130 (*a*).]

Travelling expenses between house and work are not deductible in a Schedule D computation, even though the taxpayer calls in another place of work en route.

A dental surgeon called at his dental laboratory on his journeys between his home and his surgery, for the purpose of collecting dentures and discussing work with his technician. *Held,* the travelling expenses were not wholly and exclusively incurred for the purpose of his practice, and so were not deductible in computing profits for tax purposes.

SARGENT v. BARNES [1978] 1 W.L.R. 823, Oliver J.

1673. Schedule E

INCOME TAX (REPAYMENTS TO WIVES) REGULATIONS 1978 (No. 1117) [20p], made under the Finance Act 1978 (c. 42), s. 22 (6); operative on August 1, 1978; supplement the provisions of s. 22 of the 1978 Act for the repayment of Schedule E tax in certain circumstances to married women.

INCOME TAX (EMPLOYMENTS) (No. 8) REGULATIONS 1978 (No. 1196) [10p], made under the Income and Corporation Taxes Act 1970 (c. 10), s. 204; operative on September 8, 1978; modify the Regulations relating to Income Tax under P.A.Y.E. relating to the collection of tax.

1674. —— deductible expenses

[Income and Corporation Taxes Act 1970 (c. 10), s. 189.] A G.L.C. surveyor incurred expenditure on cleaning and repairing clothes which had become dirty and damaged during visits to construction sites. *Held,* the expenditure was not deductible in computing Sched. E income: WARD v. DUNN, *The Times,* November 21, 1978, Walton J.

1675. —— emoluments from office or employment—shares

[Finance Act 1965 (c. 25), Sched. 2, para. 1 (1).]

A preferential right, exercised by an employee to buy shares in his company before it went public, which turned out to be below the market price was not a taxable emolument of his employment.

A company sought a public quotation for its shares by offering shares for sale through a bank, but reserved 10 per cent. of the shares for certain of its employees at a fixed price. The taxpayer, being one of the employees in question, applied for and obtained 5,000 shares. On the first day of dealing the shares commanded a price in excess of the cost to the taxpayer. He was assessed to income tax under Sched. E in respect of the " profit." *Held,* dismissing the Crown's appeal, that the benefit was not an emolument of his employment, since it had been derived from the speculation which he made with his own money by acquiring the shares (*Hochstrasser* v. *Mayes* [1959] C.L.Y. 1543, applied).

TYRER v. SMART [1978] 1 W.L.R. 415, C.A.

1676. —— " office holder "

The taxpayer, a distinguished chartered civil engineer, was invited from time to time to act as an inspector to hold a local public inquiry under the Acquisition of Land (Authorisation Procedure) Act 1946. Until 1973, he had been assessed under Schedule D, Case II, on the fees he received in this capacity, but the Revenue then changed to making PAYE deductions from his fees on the basis that he was an " office " holder with s. 204 of the Income and Corporation Taxes Act 1970. *Held,* allowing the appeal of the Crown against the general commissioners' decision that he was taxable under Schedule D, that the taxpayer was the holder of an " office," and therefore such income was liable to Schedule E taxation: EDWARDS v. CLINCH, *The Times,* November 30, 1978, Walton J.

1677. Settlement—beneficial interest—whether vested

The question of whether or not an interest under a trust is or is not vested, is not affected by directions in the settlement as to the disposition of intermediate income.

One half of a trust fund was left on trust for S if he attained 30 years of age, but if he died under that age, on the trusts concerning D's half of the fund. There were corresponding provisions governing D's share. The trustees were directed to accumulate the income of the respective shares until the beneficiary attained the age of 22, and that s. 31 of the Trustee Act 1925 was to be applied with the substitution of the age 25 rather than 21 as regards the payment of income to the beneficiary. S and D were assessed to income tax in respect of the income of their shares arising between their respective 21st and 22nd birthdays, on the basis that they were entitled to such income since the direction to accumulate during those years was avoided by s. 164 of the Law of Property Act 1925. Foster J. allowed the appeals of S and D, holding that their interests were merely contingent and they were not entitled as of right to this income. *Held,* allowing the appeal of the Crown, that (1) the rule in *Phipps* v. *Ackers* (1842) 9 Cl. & Fin. 583 applied; (2) the interests of S and D were vested, liable to be divested; (3) they had therefore been correctly assessed to tax in respect of the income.

BROTHERTON v. I.R.C. [1978] 1 W.L.R. 610, C.A.

1678. —— beneficiaries' income

[Income and Corporation Taxes Act 1970 (c. 10), ss. 437, 444.] A and J had life interests under a settlement made by their father, the interests in remainder being in favour of their respective children, subject to their power to appoint income in favour of their respective surviving husbands. Subject to the foregoing, each of A and J had a general power of appointment by will. A married and had children, but J did not marry and had no children. By a deed of release and assignment in 1959, A released her contingent reversionary interest in J's share of the trust fund and revocably exercised her power of appointment in favour of her children. J died in 1963. In 1974 A revoked the appointment and re-appointed in favour of her children and grandchildren. *Held,* that the deed of release and assignment executed in 1959 was a " disposition " and a " settlement " within I.C.T.A. 1970, s. 444, with the consequence that liability for income tax arose under s. 437 in respect of income paid to, or applied for, the benefit of A's children after 1963, (*I.R.C.* v. *Buchanan* [1957] C.L.Y. 1706 applied): D'ABREU v. I.R.C. [1978] S.T.C. 538, Oliver J.

1679. Surtax—husband and wife—assessment—time limit

[Taxes Management Act 1970 (c. 9), s. 34; Income and Corporation Taxes Act 1970 (c. 10), s. 40 (2).]

A notice served under s. 359 of the Income Tax Act 1952 is subject to the six-year time limit prescribed by the Taxes Management Act 1970, s. 34.

The taxpayer's husband was assessed to surtax for the years 1961/62 and 1965/66. He died in 1973, leaving the surtax assessments unpaid. In 1974, the Commissioners of Inland Revenue issued a notice to the taxpayer under I.T.A. 1952, s. 359 (now I.C.T.A. 1970, s. 40) requiring her to pay that part of the tax attributable to her income. The taxpayer appealed, contending that the notice was ineffective in that it was outside the time limit prescribed by T.M.A. 1970, s. 34, for making assessments. *Held,* reversing the decision of Foster J., that a notice served under s. 359 was subject to the six-year time limit prescribed by T.M.A. 1970, s. 34.

JOHNSON v. I.R.C. [1978] 2 All E.R. 65, C.A.

1680. —— tax avoidance scheme—whether payments deductible

[Income and Corporation Taxes Act 1970 (c. 10), ss. 52, 53, 109, 434, 457 and 459.]

A transaction without any element of bounty is not a " settlement " for income tax purposes.

The taxpayer entered into an arm's length transaction with a charitable company whereby in consideration of the payment to him of a capital sum he covenanted to make payments to the company over a number of years. He claimed to deduct these payments in arriving at his total income for the purposes of surtax. The Crown disallowed the deduction, claiming that the payments were of a capital nature, or not made out of profits brought into charge to tax, or that the arrangement constituted a " settlement " for the purposes of I.C.T.A. 1970, s. 457, of which the taxpayer was the " settlor." *Held,* dismissing the Crown's appeal from the decision of Walton J., that the annuity payments were deductible. (*Bulmer* v. *I.R.C.* [1966] C.L.Y. 6173 applied.)

I.R.C. v. PLUMMER [1978] 3 W.L.R. 459, C.A.

1681. Tax advantage—counteraction—reasons—natural justice

[Income and Corporation Taxes Act 1970 (c. 10), ss. 460, 462.] The taxpayer sought declarations that a notification served on him by the Inland Revenue was void on the ground that it did not state the Inland Revenue's reasons for believing that s. 460 applied to him, and that the determination of the tribunal that there was a prima facie case for proceeding was void on the ground that, in arriving at their determination, the tribunal took into account a " counterstatement " of the Inland Revenue which contained a great deal of material which the taxpayer had had no opportunity of considering and answering. *Held*, dismissing the taxpayer's appeal from the decision of Oliver J., that the Inland Revenue and the tribunal had duly complied with the prescribed statutory procedure. In particular, the Inland Revenue was not required, by reason of natural justice or otherwise, to state its reasons for believing that the section might apply, and the tribunal was not precluded from taking into account material which the taxpayer had not seen. (*Wiseman* v. *Borneman* [1969] C.L.Y. 1748 followed): BALEN v. I.R.C. [1978] S.T.C. 420, C.A.

1682. —— **transaction in securities**

[Income and Corporation Taxes Act 1970 (c. 10), ss. 460–468.] K. Ltd., a property dealing company, engaged in a complicated series of transactions to avoid liability for tax and betterment levy in respect of the disposal of land. Subsequently, the shareholders in K. Ltd. exchanged their shares in that company for the issue to them of shares in P. Ltd., and K. Ltd. paid to P. Ltd. a group dividend approximately equal to the profits derived from the land transactions. Notices were issued under I.C.T.A. 1970, s. 460, and consequential assessments to income tax and surtax were made. *Held,* that the receipt of the shares in P. Ltd. constituted the receipt of a tax advantage, and that the assessments were in order and could be affirmed by the Commissioners: ANYSZ v. I.R.C.; MANOLESCUE v. I.R.C. [1978] S.T.C. 296, Browne-Wilkinson J.

1683. [Income and Corporation Taxes Act 1970 (c. 10), ss. 460–468.] K. Ltd., a property dealing company, carried out a number of complicated transactions designed to avoid liability for tax and betterment levy on the disposal of land. The shareholders in K. Ltd. then exchanged their shares in that company for shares in G. Ltd.; subsequently, K. Ltd. paid a group dividend to G. Ltd. These transactions having been completed, the cash in G. Ltd. was extracted (indirectly) by way of loans. *Held,* that the receipt of the shares in G Ltd. constituted a tax advantage which was properly counteracted under I.C.T.A. 1970, s. 460: WILLIAMS v. I.R.C. [1977] T.R. 331, Browne-Wilkinson J.

1684. [Income and Corporation Taxes Act 1970 (c. 10), ss. 460, 461, 466.] W Ltd. carried on the business of making and dealing in picture frames. In 1955 it bought a frame for 48 guineas. Seven years later it transpired that the frame held a very valuable painting. In 1967 the shareholders of W Ltd. caused the major part of its stock to be transferred to another of their companies. They then sold the shares in W Ltd., which still owned the valuable painting, to K Ltd. for £45,000. *Held*, that the transactions were caught by I.C.T.A. 1970, the shareholders having obtained a " tax advantage " from a " transaction in securities " in s. 461D circumstances: I.R.C. v. WIGGINS, *The Times*, November 21, 1978, Walton J.

1685. Tax avoidance—foreign earnings—partnership abroad

[Income and Corporation Taxes Act 1970 (c. 10), s. 122.]

Foreign income paid to a partnership abroad is not liable to U.K. income tax even though the partnership was set up to avoid tax.

With a view to avoiding liability for United Kingdom income tax on his substantial foreign earnings, the taxpayer formed a partnership with a Bahamian company to exploit his foreign activities. The taxpayer was entitled to 95 per cent of the partnership profits; but he did not remit them to the United Kingdom. *Held*, affirming the decision of Browne-Wilkinson J., that an effective partnership had been created and that there was no liability for United Kingdom income tax on the unremitted foreign income (*Colquhoun* v. *Brooks* (1889) 14 App.Cas. 493 applied).

NEWSTEAD v. FROST [1978] 1 W.L.R. 1441, C.A.

ARTICLES. See *post*, p. [25].

INDUSTRIAL SOCIETIES

1686. Industrial and provident societies

INDUSTRIAL AND PROVIDENT SOCIETIES (AMENDMENT OF FEES) REGULATIONS 1978 (No. 1729) [20p], made under the Industrial and Provident Societies

Act 1965 (c. 12), s. 70 (1) as applied by the Industrial and Provident Societies Act 1967 (c. 48), s. 7 (2); operative on January 1, 1979; increase the fees to be paid for matters to be transacted and for the inspection of documents under the 1965 and 1967 Acts. They supersede S.I. 1977 No. 2022 and amend S.I. 1967 No. 1310.

1687. Industrial and Provident Societies Act 1978 (c. 34)

This Act raises the amount of deposits which an industrial and provident society may take without carrying on the business of banking.

S. 1 raises the limit of deposits taken at any one time to £10, and the maximum amount which can be taken from any one depositor to £250; s. 2 empowers the chief registrar futher to alter limits; s. 3 gives the short title and extent. The Act applies to the Channel Islands but not to Northern Ireland.

The Act received the Royal Assent on July 20, 1978, and came into force on August 20, 1978.

INNKEEPERS

1688. Tenancy—surrender—manager appointed—whether continuity of employment for employees. See YOUNG v. DANIEL THWAITES & CO., § 1068.

INSURANCE

1689. Accident insurance—causation—whether accident direct and independent cause of death

[Can.] By the terms of an accident insurance policy, a certain sum was payable on death resulting from accidental bodily injuries " which are the direct and independent cause of the loss." By an exclusion, any loss caused or contributed to by disease was not to be considered as resulting from injury. The insured died from cardiac arrest induced by a motor vehicle accident. Evidence showed that his heart was previously diseased, but that the arrest was caused by the accident. In an action on the policy, *held*, the accident was the direct and independent cause of the insured's death; it could not be said that the disease was the cause, or contributing cause of death. (*Jason* v. *Batten* [1969] C.L.Y. 912 distinguished; *Caswell* v. *Powell Duffryn Associated Collieries* [1940] A.C. 152 referred to): ROBBINS v. TRAVELLERS INSURANCE CO. (1978) 84 D.L.R. (3d) 727, Ontario High Ct.

1690. Accounts and forms

INSURANCE COMPANIES (ACCOUNTS AND FORMS) (AMENDMENT) REGULATIONS 1978 (No. 721) [20p], made under the Insurance Companies Act 1974 (c. 49), ss. 13, 16, 17, 44, 85, 86; operative on July 31, 1978; amend S.I. 1968 No. 1408 to require insurance companies to reflect in accounts submitted thereunder, in respect of financial years ending on or after July 31, 1978, certain requirements of S.I. 1977 No. 1553 and S.I. 1978 No. 720.

1691. Agents—non disclosure

[Can.] In an action by the plaintiff arising out of her claim on a policy after the premises in question had burnt down, *held*, that where an agent is authorised to receive information from an assured, he is to be treated as the insurer's agent. Should he fail to pass on such information to the insurer, the policy is then enforceable by the insured against the insurer: GOLDSHLAGER v. ROYAL INSURANCE (1978) 84 D.L.R. (3d) 355, Ontario High Ct.

1692. Annuity contracts—winding up—inability to pay debts. See Re CAPITAL ANNUITIES, § 257.

1693. Brokers

INSURANCE BROKERS REGISTRATION COUNCIL (CONSTITUTION OF THE DISCIPLINARY COMMITTEE) RULES APPROVAL ORDER 1978 (No. 1457) [20p], made under the Insurance Brokers (Registration) Act 1977 (c. 46), ss. 27 (1), 28 (1); operative on October 31, 1978; approves rules made by the Council as to the constitution of the Disciplinary Committee and related matters.

INSURANCE BROKERS REGISTRATION COUNCIL (PROCEDURE OF THE DISCI-

PLINARY COMMITTEE) RULES APPROVAL ORDER 1978 (No. 1458) [30p], made under the Insurance Brokers (Registration) Act 1977, ss. 27 (1), 28 (1); operative on October 31, 1978; approves rules made by the Council as to the procedure to be followed before the Disciplinary Committee and related matters.

INSURANCE BROKERS REGISTRATION COUNCIL (DISCIPLINARY COMMITTEE) LEGAL ASSESSOR RULES 1978 (No. 1503) [10p], made under the Insurance Brokers (Registration) Act 1977, s. 20; operative on November 10, 1978; regulate the functions of the Legal Assessor appointed under s. 20 of the 1977 Act.

1693a. —— **agents for underwriters**

Insurance brokers have the authority of underwriters to effect interim motor insurance by the issue of cover notes, and members of the public dealing with brokers rightly regard them as the agents of the underwriters and not of the insured for these purposes. If such a broker informs the insured that he is covered, then the insurers are bound: STOCKTON v. MASON, *The Times*, June 27, 1978, C.A

1694. —— **duty of care—failure to give information to applicant for insurance**

An insurance broker effecting an insurance policy on behalf of an applicant owes him a duty of care to inform him of any exemptions under the policy which may affect the cover given.

The defendant insurance company offered motor insurance at low premium rates to certain categories of motorists; specifically excluded from such categories were, inter alios, " part-time musicians." The plaintiff approached the defendant brokers with a view to effecting a motor insurance and with their assistance completed a proposal form stating his occupation truthfully, as that of a property repairer. The plaintiff did not disclose, nor was he asked, that he was also a part-time musician. A policy was issued by the defendant insurers who subsequently denied liability in respect of damage suffered by the plaintiff in a motor accident on the grounds that the plaintiff as a part-time musician was excluded by the policy. At first instance the brokers were held liable to indemnify the plaintiff. *Held*, dismissing the brokers' appeal, that since they were aware of the exempted categories under the policy, they were in breach of their duty of care to the plaintiff in failing to inquire of him as to whether he fell within such exemptions.

MCNEALY v. PENNINE INSURANCE CO. [1978] R.T.R. 285, C.A.

1695. —— **misleading representations concerning policy—whether insured entitled to an indemnity**

P, manufacturers, were insured with G, insurers, against loss of profit and other consequential loss caused by destruction of or damage to P's business premises. P's insurance brokers, D, effected renewal of the annual policy. On June 8, 1974, P advised D that they had appointed K as their insurance brokers and told D to cease acting on their behalf as from June 19, 1974. D were also requested to cancel the policy as from that date, as P had taken out a similar insurance with other insurers. On August 13, 1974, P were advised that G would not cancel the policy or return the premium. On August 15, P cancelled the insurance policy with the new insurers but did not inform D. On August 21, G agreed to cancel the policy with effect from June 19, 1974, but D did not advise P of this fact. On August 29, 1974, there was a fire at P's premises which caused substantial consequential damage, in respect of which P had no cover. P claimed to be indemnified by D by way of damages for breach of contract or negligence. *Held*, (1) D, knowing and intending that what they said would be acted upon, had led P reasonably to believe that the policy with G was, and would remain, in force; P had relied on what they were told by D and cancelled the policy with the new insurers; (2) D had given information within their specialised knowledge and knew or ought to have known that it would be acted upon; (3) P were entitled to recover from D, as damages, such sum as they would have recovered under the policy with G if that policy had been in force on August 29, 1974. (*Hedley Byrne & Co.* v. *Heller & Partners* [1963] C.L.Y. 2416 applied): CHERRY v. ALLIED INSURANCE BROKERS [1978] 1 Lloyd's Rep. 274, Cantley J.

1696. Capital allowances—" war risk "—sunken dredger
[Capital Allowances Act 1968, s. 33 (7).] A dredger operating off Mauritius sucked up a number of shells which had been dumped by the British Armed Forces at the end of World War II. The dredger was sunk. The owners resisted a balancing charge on the insurance moneys, claiming that the loss of the dredger was due to a " war risk." *Held*, that the dumping of the shells was not a warlike operation and the exemption from the balancing charge given by Capital Allowances Act 1968, s. 33 (7), did not apply, and, in any event, the shells which caused the explosion were " fixed or floating objects " and so excluded from the exemption: COSTAIN-BLANKWOORT (U.K.) DREDGING Co. *v.* DAVENPORT, *The Times*, November 17, 1978, Walton J.

1697. Cover—motor accident—limitation of liability. See HARKER *v.* CALEDONIAN INSURANCE CO., § 2593.

1698. Exclusion clause—all-risks insurance—building contractor
[Can.] P, building contractors, were insured with D, insurers, under a contractor's all-risk insurance policy. The policy expressly excluded loss or damage caused, inter alia, by faulty or improper workmanship (cl. 7 (*a*) (ii)) or design (cl. 7 (*a*) (iii)). P contracted with M to build a sewage treatment plant, one of the components of which was a concrete tank. The specifications required steel struts to be laid across the top of the tank with each end welded to a plate let into the concrete wall of the tank. Before effecting the welding, P tested the tank by pouring water into it and one of the sides bulged. P repaired the tank at a cost in excess of Can.\$40,000 and claimed an indemnity from D. D denied liability on the ground that it was excluded by cl. 7. P contended that D were estopped by their conduct from denying liability, as P had repaired the tank on D's assurance that the loss was covered by the policy. *Held*, on appeal, (1) the words of cl. 7 were not ambiguous and the contra proferentem rule did not apply; (2) the lack of instructions as to the order in which the welding and testing was to be done could not constitute faulty or improper design, and D could not rely on cl. 7 (*a*) (iii); (3) testing before welding was improper workmanship and D could rely on cl. 7 (*a*) (ii); (4) on the evidence D were not estopped from denying liability. (*Cornish* v. *Accident Insurance Co.* (1889) 23 Q.B.D. 453 and *Combe* v. *Combe* (1951) C.L.C. 3014 applied): PENTAGON CONSTRUCTION (1969) Co. *v.* UNITED STATES FIDELITY AND GUARANTY CO. [1978] 1 Lloyd's Rep. 93, Brit.Col.C.A.

1699. —— passenger liability—whether passenger carried " by reason of " his contract of employment
A passenger whose contract of employment neither requires nor entitles him to be carried in a motor vehicle is not insured by a policy limited to persons carried by reason of or in pursuance of a contract of employment.
The driver of a lorry belonging to a timber company gave a lift to a forester whose duties included inspection of loads carried by the company's lorries, but who was not on duty at the time. The driver feared that to refuse the lift might subsequently cause difficulties when loads were inspected. The forester was killed as a result of the driver's negligence. The timber company sought an indemnity from their insurers under a provision of their policy providing cover for a passenger carried by reason or in pursuance of a contract of employment. Having failed in the local courts, the company appealed to the Privy Council. *Held*, dismissing the appeal, that since the forester's contract of employment did not entitle or require him to be carried in the lorry, he was not carried by reason of or in pursuance of such a contract. (*Izzard* v. *Universal Insurance Co.* [1937] A.C. 773 and *McSteen* v. *McCarthy* [1953] C.L.Y. 3225, applied.)
TAN KENG HONG *v.* NEW INDIA ASSURANCE CO. [1978] 1 W.L.R. 297, P.C.

1700. Fire insurance—premium—" cost of reinstatement " date of calculation
P let their premises to D for 21 years. D covenanted, inter alia, to pay to P a premium for keeping the premises insured " for the full cost of reinstatement against loss or damage by fire." D claimed that the " full cost of reinstatement " was the cost calculated on the date on which each annual premium was to be paid. *Held*, that (1) the parties must have intended

to contract on the basis that there would be delay between the casualty insured against and the completion of reinstatement, and to take into account the rise in building costs; (2) to cover themselves fully, P could expect a delay of at least 18 months from the date of the catastrophe, which could occur on the last day covered by the premium; (3) accordingly, reinstatement could be completed two and a half years from the date of payment of the premium; (4) P in assessing the cost of reinstatement in this way were acting bona fide within their power to insure the premises, and the premiums were fair and reasonable: GLENIFFER FINANCE CORP. *v.* BAMAR WOOD & PRODUCTS [1978] 2 Lloyd's Rep. 49, Forbes J.

1701. Friendly societies. See FRIENDLY SOCIETIES.

1702. Insurance Brokers (Registration) Act 1977—commencement

INSURANCE BROKERS (REGISTRATION) ACT 1977 (COMMENCEMENT No. 2) ORDER 1978 (No. 1393 (C. 35)) [10p], made under the Insurance Brokers (Registration) Act 1977 (c. 46), s. 30 (3); operative on October 20, 1978; brings into force the provisions of the 1977 Act that relate to the opening and maintenance of the register and list of its publications, erasure therefrom, restoration of names thereto, disciplinary cases and appeals, namely ss. 2–5, 9, 13–19 (3), 20.

1703. Insurance Brokers Registration Council

INSURANCE BROKERS REGISTRATION COUNCIL (CODE OF CONDUCT) APPROVAL ORDER 1978 (No. 1394) [20p], made under the Insurance Brokers (Registration) Act 1977 (c. 46), ss. 27 (1), 28 (1); operative on October 20, 1978; approves the Code of Conduct drawn up by the Insurance Brokers Registration Council for the purposes of the 1977 Act.

INSURANCE BROKERS REGISTRATION COUNCIL (REGISTRATION AND ENROLMENT) RULES APPROVAL ORDER 1978 (No. 1395) [25p], made under the Insurance Brokers (Registration) Act 1977, ss. 27 (1), 28 (1); operative on October 20, 1978; approves rules made by the council in relation to the register and list which are to be kept in pursuance of the 1977 Act.

INSURANCE BROKERS REGISTRATION COUNCIL (CONSTITUTION OF INVESTIGATING COMMITTEE) RULES APPROVAL ORDER 1978 (No. 1456) [20p], made under the Insurance Brokers (Registration) Act 1977, ss. 27 (1), 28 (1); operative on October 31, 1978; approves rules made by the Insurance Brokers Registration Council as to the constitution of the Investigating Committee.

1704. Insurance companies

INSURANCE COMPANIES (AUTHORISATION AND ACCOUNTS: GENERAL BUSINESS) REGULATIONS 1978 (No. 720) [30p], made under the European Communities Act 1972 (c. 68), s. 2 (2); operative on July 31, 1978; give effect to the provisions of Council Directive 73/239/EEC that require the taking up of the business of direct insurance other than life insurance to be subject to authorisation.

INSURANCE COMPANIES (CHANGES OF DIRECTOR, CONTROLLER OR MANAGER) REGULATIONS 1978 (No. 722) [20p], made under the Insurance Companies Act 1974 (c. 49), ss. 52–54, 85, 86; operative on July 31, 1978; supersede S.I. 1975 No. 959 and require certain additional information to be supplied in respect of directors, controllers and managers of insurance companies and, in conformity with S.I. 1975 No. 1023, draw attention to the requirement to disclose spent convictions when supplying particulars of previous convictions.

INSURANCE COMPANIES (DEPOSITS) REGULATIONS 1978 (No. 917) [20p], made under the Prevention of Fraud (Investments) Act 1958 (c. 45), s. 4 (2) (3) as amended by the Administration of Justice Act 1965 (c. 2), ss. 14 (3), 17 (1), Sched. 1; operative on July 31, 1978; contain provisions respecting deposits to be made by certain overseas companies carrying on insurance business or applying for authorisation to do so. These deposits are required by S.I. 1977 No. 1553 implementing Council Directive No. 73/239/EEC.

INSURANCE COMPANIES (NOTICE OF LONG-TERM POLICY) REGULATIONS 1978 (No. 1304) [25p], made under the Insurance Companies Act 1974, ss. 65, 85, 86; operative on January 1, 1980; prescribe the form and contents of the statutory notice which an insurer is required to send to the other party to an ordinary long-term insurance contract pursuant to s. 65 (1) of the 1974 Act.

1705. Life insurance—exclusion clause—whether deceased deliberately exposed himself to danger

Where a life insurance policy contains a clause exempting liability for death due to the insured's own criminal act, driving dangerously or whilst drunk will amount to a sufficient criminal act.

M was insured for £15,000 for accidental bodily injury resulting in his death. There was an exclusion clause in the case of death " directly or indirectly resulting from deliberate exposure to exceptional danger or the insured person's own criminal act." M drove dangerously whilst he had 261 mg. of alcohol in 100 ml. of blood, and was killed. The insurers repudiated liability under the policy. *Held*, (1) the death was caused by an accidental bodily injury; (2) M had not deliberately exposed himself to exceptional danger; but (3) " criminal act " covered all criminal offences which were not offences of inadvertence or negligence, including driving whilst under the influence of drink or dangerously, and the insurers were entitled to repudiate liability. (*Candler* v. *London & Lancashire Guarantee & Accident Co. of Canada* (1963) 40 D.L.R. (2d) 408 distinguished.)

MARCEL BELLER *v.* HAYDEN [1978] 2 W.L.R. 845, Judge Edgar Fay, Q.C.

1706. National Insurance. See NATIONAL INSURANCE; SOCIAL SECURITY.

1707. Non-disclosure—previous conviction—duty of brokers

In April 1974, T, brokers, insured P's house with D, insurers. In August 1974, the house was destroyed by fire. D denied liability because of P's non-disclosure of his criminal record, which P admitted but claimed that T knew about. *Held*, that (1) P ought to have disclosed his criminal past; (2) T in the ordinary course of business as brokers and D's agents had acquired some knowledge of P's past; (3) on these facts, P had no duty to disclose his past to T; (4) therefore D could not avoid the policy, but were entitled to be indemnified by T, who were plainly under a duty to disclose their knowledge to D. (*Bates* v. *Hewitt* (1867) 2 Q.B. 608 applied): WOOLCOTT *v.* EXCESS INSURANCE CO. [1978] 1 Lloyd's Rep. 633, Caulfield J.

1708. —— spent—whether insurers could amend pleadings

P1 and P2, whose premises had been partially destroyed by fire in November 1973, brought an action against the insurers, D, on the question of quantum under a policy issued in 1972. About 10 months before the trial in February 1978, D's solicitors learned that P1 had been convicted of an offence in 1961. This had become a spent conviction under the Rehabilitation of Offenders Act 1974 (c. 53), which was in force at the time of the trial, but not when the policy was issued. At the trial, D sought leave to amend the pleadings to raise the conviction as a material non-disclosure. *Held*, on appeal, that (1) an amendment should not be refused solely for the dilatoriness or negligence of the legal advisers, but should be granted whenever necessary to enable justice to be done between the parties, provided the delay did not prejudice the other party in the assertainment of the facts; (2) there was no such prejudice in this case; (3) by s. 7 (3) of the 1974 Act, the question of whether to admit evidence of the spent conviction was essentially for the " judicial authority ", that is, the judge trying the case, and it would be inappropriate to direct him on it (*Baker* (*G. L.*) v. *Medway Building and Supplies* [1959] C.L.Y. 2088 applied): REYNOLDS *v.* PHOENIX ASSURANCE CO. [1978] 2 Lloyd's Rep. 22, C.A.

1709. —— whether policy to be avoided

Non-disclosure of a conviction for a serious criminal offence by an insured entitles the insurer to avoid the policy of insurance.

The plaintiff was granted a mortgage advance by a building society whose application form, completed by the plaintiff, stated that the society would insure the property. No information was required to be supplied by the plaintiff for the purposes of such insurance which was arranged under a block policy held by the society with the defendants. The property was duly insured for £30,000, including the society's interest which was £12,000. Upon the property being destroyed by fire, the defendants indemnified the society, but claimed to be entitled to avoid the policy as against the plaintiff upon the grounds that he had failed to disclose a material fact, namely that he had previously been convicted of an offence of robbery and other offences. Evidence was accepted by the judge that the robbery conviction so increased the " moral hazard " that the insurance company would not have accepted the risk had it known of the same. *Held,* dismissing the plaintiff's claim, that the non-disclosure was a material non-disclosure of facts which a reasonable or prudent insurer might have treated as material and that accordingly the policy was avoided. (*Lambert* v. *Co-operative Insurance Society* [1976] C.L.Y. 1451, applied.) WOOLCOTT *v.* SUN ALLIANCE AND LONDON INSURANCE [1978] 1 W.L.R. 493, Caulfield J.

1710. Reinsurance—claim for money due under treaty—validity of arbitration clause —whether action should be stayed

In 1967 a treaty of reinsurance was made between P, insurers, and D, re-insurers, in respect of various all-risk policies. The broker's slip containing the terms of the agreement showed that P were to undertake all the primary insurances, that P were to retain 15 per cent. of the premiums for their own account and be liable for 15 per cent. of the losses, and that P were to cede the other 85 per cent. to various insurers, and of that 85 per cent., D were to receive $7\frac{1}{2}$ per cent. of the premiums and pay $7\frac{1}{2}$ per cent. of the losses. The slip also contained the words " Sub 100% R/1 and 1% our credit," indicating that D were to take 1 per cent. of the premiums and that this was a " fronting arrangement." The slip further showed that the reinsurance was based on an estimated premium income of £250,000. The treaty of reinsurance contained an arbitration clause which provided that all disputes arising out of the agreement should be referred to arbitration, and that the arbitrators should settle disputes according to an equitable, rather than a strictly legal, interpretation of the agreement. In July 1969, the treaty was renegotiated by P and D's agents. P's retention increased from 15 per cent. to $42\frac{1}{2}$ per cent., the shares of the reinsurers being reduced proportionately. In 1976, P claimed £70,000 from D as being due under the treaty. On December 3, 1976, P issued a specially indorsed writ. The indorsement was defective, and D applied to strike it out. P reissued the statement of claim, and took out a summons under R.S.C., Ord. 14, for summary judgment. D resisted the summons and applied to stay the proceedings on the ground that there was an arbitration clause. D alleged that they were not aware of the renegotiation. *Held,* (1) as regards the application under R.S.C., Ord. 14, it would not be right to enter judgment against D as their were several triable issues; (2) D's application to strike out the statement of claim was not a " step in the proceedings " within the meaning of s. 4 of the Arbitration Act 1950, such as to debar them from applying for a stay; (3) the arbitration clause was valid; (4) the action would be stayed: EAGLE STAR INSURANCE CO. *v.* YUVAL INSURANCE CO. [1978] 1 Lloyd's Rep. 357, C.A.

1711. Road traffic. See ROAD TRAFFIC.

1712. Settlement of claim—deed of release—executed by an insured of limited understanding—not binding

[Can.] An insurance adjuster, in entering into a settlement agreement with an accident victim obtained the latter's signature to a deed releasing all future claims arising out of the accident. On the insured purporting not to be bound by the deed, *held,* the adjuster owed the insured a duty to see that he understood the agreement was in final settlement of all claims. Where a victim is of limited education and agrees to settle the claim and executes a release without fully understanding its effect, the release is not binding. Where parties do not meet on equal terms, the stronger party cannot retain a benefit without showing that everything has been right and fair and reasonable on his part. (*Lloyd's Bank* v. *Bundy* [1974] C.L.Y. 1268 applied): BEACH *v.* EAMES (1978) 82 D.L.R. (3d) 736, County Ct. of Elgin, Ontario.

1713. Social security. See SOCIAL SECURITY.

1714. Unemployment benefit. See SOCIAL SECURITY.

1715. Value added tax. See VALUE ADDED TAX.

BOOKS AND ARTICLES. See *post,* pp. [5], [26].

INTERNATIONAL LAW

1716. African Development Bank

AFRICAN DEVELOPMENT BANK (PRIVILEGES) ORDER 1978 (No. 1884) [10p], made under the International Organisations Act 1968 (c. 48), s. 10 (1); operative on January 10, 1979; confers the legal capacities of a body corporate upon the African Development Bank and grants it to certain taxation exemptions.

1717. Aviation. See AVIATION.

1718. Common market. See EUROPEAN COMMUNITIES.

1719. Conflict of laws. See CONFLICT OF LAWS.

1720. Consular fees

CONSULAR FEES ORDER 1978 (No. 177) [25p], made under the Consular Salaries and Fees Act 1891 (c. 36), s. 2 (1), and the Fees (Increase) Act 1923 (c. 4), s. 8 (1); operative on March 6, 1978; revokes S.I. 1977 No. 46 and increases consular fees.

1721. Consular relations

CONSULAR RELATIONS (MERCHANT SHIPPING AND CIVIL AVIATION) (POLISH PEOPLE'S REPUBLIC) ORDER 1978 (No. 275) [15p], made under the Consular Relations Act 1968 (c. 18), ss. 4–6, 16 (2); operative on a date to be notified; provides, in relation to ships and aircraft (other than ships of war and military aircraft) of Poland, for limiting the jurisdiction of the courts of the U.K. to entertain proceedings relating to the remuneration or any contract of service of the master or commander or a member of the crew. It gives effect to the relevant provisions of the Consular Convention between the U.K. and Poland signed at London on February 23, 1967 (Cmnd. 4790), as amended by the Protocol signed at London on December 16, 1976 (Cmnd. 6740).

1722. Consuls

CONSULAR FEES REGULATIONS 1978 (No. 692) [20p], made under the Consular Salaries and Fees Act 1891 (c. 36), s. 2 (2), and the Fees (Increase) Act 1923 (c. 4), s. 8 (2); operative on May 25, 1978; prescribe the manner in which consular officers should deal with fees received by them.

ADMINISTRATION OF ESTATES BY CONSULAR OFFICERS (ESTONIA) (REVOCATION) ORDER 1978 (No. 779) [10p], made under the Consular Conventions Act 1949 (c. 29), s. 8; operative on June 21, 1978; revokes S.R. & O. 1939 No. 1451.

1723. Diplomatic privileges

COMMONWEALTH COUNTRIES AND REPUBLIC OF IRELAND (IMMUNITIES AND PRIVILEGES) (AMENDMENT) ORDER 1978 (No. 780) [10p], made under the Consular Relations Act 1968 (c. 18), ss. 12, 14, as amended by the Diplomatic and other Privileges Act 1971 (c. 64), s. 4; operative on June 29, 1978; corrects an error in S.I. 1977 No. 1627 which accorded partial relief from general rates to the Hong Kong Liaison Office.

1724. European Space Agency

EUROPEAN SPACE AGENCY (IMMUNITIES AND PRIVILEGES) ORDER 1978 (No. 1105) [25p], made under the International Organisations Act 1968 (c. 48), ss. 1 and 10 (3); operative on a date to be notified in the *London Gazette*; confers privileges and immunities upon the Agency, representatives of its Member States, its officers and experts.

1725. Extradition. See EXTRADITION.

1726. Fisheries. See FISH AND FISHERIES.

1727. Foreign compensation

FOREIGN COMPENSATION (FINANCIAL PROVISIONS) ORDER 1978 (No. 180) [10p], made under the Foreign Compensation Act 1950 (c. 12), s. 7 (2), and the Foreign Compensation Act 1962 (c. 4), s. 3 (3); operative on March 20, 1978; directs the Foreign Compensation Commission to pay into the Exchequer amounts in respect of the Commission's expenses in relation to the distribution of the Rumanian Compensation Fund.

1728. Immunities and privileges

INTERNATIONAL RUBBER STUDY GROUP (IMMUNITIES AND PRIVILEGES) ORDER 1978 (No. 181) [25p], made under the International Organisations Act 1968

(c. 48), s. 10 (1); operative on a date to be notified; confers privileges on the International Rubber Study Group and on its officers and representatives.

INTERNATIONAL LEAD AND ZINC STUDY GROUP (IMMUNITIES AND PRIVILEGES) ORDER 1978 (No. 1893) [25p], made under the International Organisations Act 1968, s. 10 (1); operative on a date to be notified in the London Gazette; confers privileges and immunities upon the Study Group, its officers, representatives of its members, and experts serving on committees on its behalf.

1729. International Development Association

INTERNATIONAL DEVELOPMENT ASSOCIATION (FIFTH REPLENISHMENT) ORDER 1978 (No. 472) [10p], made under the Overseas Aid Act 1968 (c. 57), s. 1 (5); operative on November 8, 1978; provides for the payment to the Association of a sum of £705,944·83 as an additional subscription carrying voting rights and a sum of £474,065,631·70 as an additional contribution not carrying voting rights.

1730. Internationally Protected Persons Act 1978 (c. 17)

This Act implements the convention on the prevention and punishment of crimes against Internationally Protected Persons (Cmnd. 6176).

S. 1 relates to attacks and threats of attacks on protected persons outside the U.K. and defines " protected person"; s. 2 contains provisions supplementary to s. 1; s. 3 states that an offence under s. 1 (3) (a) shall be included in the list of extradition crimes; s. 4 extends the application of the Act to the Channel Islands, the Isle of Man and other countries; s. 5 contains the short title.

The Act received the Royal Assent on June 30, 1978, and shall come into force on such day as Her Majesty may by Order in Council appoint.

1731. Overseas aid

ASIAN DEVELOPMENT BANK (FURTHER PAYMENTS TO CAPITAL STOCK) ORDER 1978 (No. 154) [15p], made under the Overseas Aid Act 1968 (c. 57), s. 2 (1), as amended by the International Finance, Trade and Aid Act 1977 (c. 6), s. 7 (2); operative on February 2, 1978; provides for the payment to the Asian Development Bank of sums not exceeding U.S.$101,250,000 of the value in effect on January 31, 1966, as further payments to the Bank by way of subscription to an issue of shares increasing the authorised stock of the Bank.

INTERNATIONAL FINANCE CORPORATION (FURTHER PAYMENT TO CAPITAL STOCK) ORDER 1978 (No. 1152) [10p], made under the Overseas Aid Act 1968, s. 2, as amended by the International Finance Trade and Aid Act 1977 (c. 6), s. 7 (2); operative on August 1, 1978; provides for a further payment to the Corporation of sums not exceeding U.S.$23,500,000 by way of subscription to an issue of shares increasing the Corporation's authorised stock.

1732. Poland

CONSULAR RELATIONS (PRIVILEGES AND IMMUNITIES) (POLISH PEOPLE'S REPUBLIC) ORDER 1978 (No. 1028) [20p], made under the Consular Relations Act 1968 (c. 18), ss. 3 (1), 14 (3); operative on a date to be notified in the *London Gazette*; provides with respect to consular posts in Poland for according privileges additional to those given by Sched. 1 to the 1968 Act, namely, relief from rates and taxes for certain residences, exemption from taxation for certain staff, similarly exemption from customs duties, diplomatic inviolability and immunity from jurisdiction for certain members of a consular post. The order gives effect to the Consular Convention between the U.K. and Poland, signed at London on February 23, 1967 (Cmnd. 4790).

1733. Rhodesia. See BRITISH COMMONWEALTH.

1734. Shipping

STATE IMMUNITY (MERCHANT SHIPPING) (UNION OF SOVIET SOCIALIST REPUBLICS) ORDER 1978 (No. 1524) [10p], made under the State Immunity Act 1978 (c. 33), s. 15 (1); operative on November 22, 1978; preserves the immunity from execution of ships and cargoes of the U.S.S.R. which would otherwise have been lost by virtue of s. 13 (4) of the 1978 Act and requires notice to be given to a Soviet consul before a warrant of arrest is issued in an action in rem against a ship of that State or cargo on it.

1735. South Africa

SOUTH AFRICA (UNITED NATIONS ARMS EMBARGO) (PROHIBITED TRANS-ACTIONS) ORDER 1978 (No. 277) [25p], made under the United Nations Act 1946 (c. 45), s. 1; operative on March 24, 1978; prohibits certain transactions relating to patents, registered designs and industrial information or techniques for the manufacture or maintenance of arms and certain associated goods in South Africa.

SOUTH AFRICA (UNITED NATIONS ARMS EMBARGO) (PROHIBITED TRANSAC-TIONS (AMENDMENT) ORDER 1978 (No. 1034) [10p], made under the United Nations Act 1946, s. 1; operative on August 24, 1978; replaces the reference in art. 3 (3) of S.I. 1978 No. 277 to the Export of Goods (Control) Order 1970, as amended, with a reference to the Export of Goods (Control) Order 1978.

SOUTH AFRICA (UNITED NATIONS ARMS EMBARGO) (PROHIBITED TRANSAC-TIONS) (GUERNSEY) ORDER 1978 (No. 1052) [25p], made under the United Nations Act 1946, s. 1; operative on September 1, 1978; extends to Guernsey and prohibits certain transactions relating to patents, registered designs and industrial information or techniques for the manufacture or maintenance of arms and certain associated goods in South Africa. It also confers powers to obtain evidence and information for the purposes of the Order.

SOUTH AFRICA (UNITED NATIONS ARMS EMBARGO) (PROHIBITED TRANSAC-TIONS) (ISLE OF MAN) ORDER 1978 (No. 1053) [20p], made under the United Nations Act 1946, s. 1; operative on September 1, 1978; prohibits in relation to the Isle of Man certain transactions relating to patents, registered designs and industrial information or techniques for manufacture or maintenance of arms in South Africa.

SOUTH AFRICA (UNITED NATIONS ARMS EMBARGO) (PROHIBITED TRANSAC-TIONS) (JERSEY) ORDER 1978 (No. 1054) [20p], made under the United Nations Act 1946, s. 1; operative on September 1, 1978; prohibits in Jersey certain transactions relating to patents, registered designs and industrial infor-mation or techniques for the manufacture or maintenance of arms and certain associated goods in South Africa.

SOUTH AFRICA (PROHIBITED EXPORTS AND TRANSACTIONS) (OVERSEAS TERRI-TORIES) ORDER 1978 (No. 1624) [40p], made under the United Nations Act 1946, s. 1; operative on December 14, 1978; applies to the Scheduled Territories and prohibits the export of certain goods intended for South Africa including transactions relating to patents, registered designs and industrial information or techniques relating to the manufacture or maintenance of arms and certain associated goods.

SOUTH AFRICA (PROHIBITED EXPORTS AND TRANSACTIONS (OVERSEAS TERRITO-RIES) (AMENDMENT) ORDER 1978 (No. 1894) [10p], made under the United Nations Act 1946, s. 1; operative on January 24, 1979; amends S.I. 1978 No. 1624.

SOUTH AFRICA (UNITED NATIONS ARMS EMBARGO) (PROHIBITED TRANSACTIONS) (AMENDMENT No. 2) ORDER 1978 (No. 1895) [10p], made under the United Nations Act 1946, s. 1; operative on January 24, 1979; amends S.I. 1978 No. 277.

SOUTH AFRICA (UNITED NATIONS ARMS EMBARGO) (PROHIBITED TRANSACTIONS) (GUERNSEY) (AMENDMENT) ORDER 1978 (No. 1896) [10p], made under the United Nations Act 1946, s. 1; operative on January 24, 1979; amends S.I. 1978 No. 1052.

SOUTH AFRICA (UNITED NATIONS ARMS EMBARGO) (PROHIBITED TRANSACTIONS) (ISLE OF MAN) (AMENDMENT) ORDER 1978 (No. 1897) [10p], made under the United Nations Act 1946, amends s. 1; operative on January 24, 1979; amends S.I. 1978 No. 1053.

SOUTH AFRICA (UNITED NATIONS ARMS EMBARGO) (PROHIBITED TRANSACTIONS) (JERSEY) (AMENDMENT) ORDER (No. 1898) [10p], made under the United Nations Act 1946, s. 1; operative on January 24, 1979; amends S.I. 1978 No. 1054 by including among the goods to which that order applies the specialised parts and components of apparatus, appliances and equipment in S.I. 1978 No. 796 as amended.

1736. Sovereign states—immunity from action—plaintiff suffering damages under contract with sovereign state

[Can.] One issue was considered: the degree of immunity which should be accorded to a sovereign state in litigation concerning a commercial contract. *Held,* the doctrine of restrictive immunity which holds that a sovereign state is not immune from being impleaded in the courts of another state where the cause of action concerns matters other than legislative or international transactions of the sovereign state is part of the law of Canada. (*Rahimtoola* v. *Nizam of Hyderabad* [1957] C.L.Y. 2864 applied): ZODIAK INTERNATIONAL PRODUCTS INC. *v.* POLISH PEOPLE'S REPUBLIC (1977) 81 D.L.R. 656, Quebec C.A.

1737. State Immunity Act 1978 (c. 33)

This Act provides for proceedings in the U.K. by or against other States, and for the effect of judgments given against the U.K. in the courts of States which are parties to the European Convention on State Immunity; it also makes new provision respecting the immunities and privileges of heads of States.

S. 1 gives a State general immunity from the jurisdiction of the U.K. courts; s. 2 states that a State is not immune as respects proceedings in which it has submitted to the jurisdiction of the U.K. courts; s. 3 states that a State is not immune as respects proceedings relating to commercial transactions and contracts to be performed in the U.K.; s. 4 stipulates that a State is not immune as respects proceedings relating to a contract of employment between the State and an individual where the contract was made or the work is to be performed in the U.K.; s. 5 exempts proceedings relating to personal injuries and damage to property caused by an act or omission in the U.K. from the immunity provisions; s. 6 states that a State is not immune as respects proceedings relating to ownership, possession and use of property in the U.K.; s. 7 provides for the exemption from immunity in proceedings relating to patents, trade marks, designs and plant breeders' rights; s. 8 stipulates that proceedings relating to a State's membership of a body corporate, unincorporated body or partnership are not immune; s. 9 relates to arbitration proceedings; s. 10 relates to the immunity of States regarding ships used for commercial purposes; s. 11 deals with proceedings relating to a State's liability for VAT, customs duties, agricultural levies and rates of commercial premises; s. 12 sets out the procedure for the service of process, and for obtaining judgment in default of appearance; s. 13 sets out certain reliefs and penalties which are not available against a State; s. 14 defines the States to which the immunities and privileges conferred by this Act apply; s. 15 empowers Her Majesty to restrict or extend any immunity or privilege by Order in Council; s. 16 deals with matters excluded from the provisions of this Act; s. 17 contains definitions in connection with ss. 1–16; s. 18 relates to the recognition of judgments given against the U.K. by a court in another convention State; s. 19 sets out exceptions to such recognition; s. 20 provides that the Diplomatic Privileges Act 1964 shall apply to heads of States, members of their family and their servants; s. 21 provides that a certificate given by the Secretary of State shall be conclusive evidence as to whether a country is a State for the purposes of this Act; s. 22 contains general definitions; s. 23 gives the short title and repeals. The Act extends to Northern Ireland.

The Act received the Royal Assent on June 30, 1978, and shall come into force on such date as the Lord Chancellor shall specify by statutory instrument.

1738. —— commencement

STATE IMMUNITY ACT 1978 (COMMENCEMENT) ORDER 1978 (No. 1572 (C. 44)) [10p], made under the State Immunity Act 1978 (c. 33), s. 23 (5); operative on November 22, 1978; brings into force the 1978 Act, which restricts the immunity which sovereign states can claim from the jurisdiction of civil court and tribunals in the U.K. and regulates the personal immunities of heads of state.

BOOKS AND ARTICLES. See *post,* pp. [5], [26].

INTOXICATING LIQUORS

1739. Beer

BEER REGULATIONS 1978 (No. 893) [70p], made under the Finance Act 1975 (c. 45), s. 16 (2), and the Customs and Excise Act 1952 (c. 44), ss. 127, 128, 131, 171, 250 and 263; operative on September 1, 1978; provide for the revenue control of the brewing of beer liable to excise duty; reproduce with modifications S.I. 1952 No. 2232.

1740. Licensing

DOVER HOVERPORT LICENSING (LIQUOR) ORDER 1978 (No. 225) [10p], made under the Licensing Act 1964 (c. 26), s. 87; operative on March 1, 1978; brings s. 87 of the 1964 Act into operation at Dover Hoverport.

LICENSING (FEES) ORDER 1978 (No. 1644) [20p], made under the Licensing Act 1964, ss. 29 (1), 198 (2); operative on January 1, 1979; revokes S.I. 1976 No. 1858 and substitutes new fees for the fees chargeable in respect of matters arising under the Licensing Act 1964.

1741. —— appeal—documentary evidence—commercial confidentiality

Licensing justices refused to make a provisional grant of an on-licence for a proposed public house. Brewers owned a public house situated near to the site of the proposed premises and were members of an association which opposed the application. The applicant having appealed to the Crown Court, applied to the Crown Court office for the issue of a witness summons requiring the brewers to produce at the hearing of the appeal documents relating to the trade of their nearby public house. The Court Office issued a document in a form prescribed for a witness order under the Criminal Procedure (Attendance of Witnesses) Act 1965. The brewers moved to set aside the witness order. Secondly, the witness order having been quashed, counsel for the appellant thereupon applied under s. 4 (8) of the Courts Act 1971, for the issue of a subpoena duces tecum requiring a named officer of the brewery to attend the hearing of the appeal and produce such documents as were in his possession on behalf of the brewery as related to (a) the brewery's sales during the three years prior to the justices' refusal to grant the appellant a licence; (b) the brewery's accounts during that period; (c) its wholesale and retail prices; and (d) prices paid by the brewery in respect of the purchase, up-keep and furnishing of its premises. *Held*, that (1) the appropriate procedure for securing the attendance of a witness at a Crown Court in civil proceedings is the issue of a writ of subpoena under Ord. 38, r. 14, R.S.C.; (2) a subpoena issued to secure the production at the hearing of an appeal against the refusal of a justices' on-licence of documents relating to the trade of rival brewers will be set aside on the ground that the value of the documentary evidence would be outweighed by considerations of commercial confidentiality and increased length and complexity of procedure: WHITBREADS (WEST PENNINES) *v.* ENTWISTLE, May 2, 1978, Judge David Q.C., Chester Crown Ct. (*Ex rel. Marilyn Mornington, Barrister.*)

1742. —— special occasion—no element of participation

[Licensing Act 1964 (c. 26).] A licensee sought a special order of exemption from licensing hours so that his customers could watch the World Cup matches. Orders of exemption granted by the magistrates were quashed by the Divisional Court since while the court could accept that it was a special occasion within the meaning of the Licensing Act 1964, it was also necessary for the licensee to show that the special occasion created a potential demand for liquor by those participating in the occasion. There was no element of participation here: R. *v.* LEICESTER JUSTICES, *ex p.* WATCHORN, *The Times*, June 9, 1978, D.C.

1743. —— —— Saturday prior to bank holiday

[Licensing Act 1964 (c. 26), s. 74.] A Saturday is not a " special occasion " for the purposes of s. 74 of the Licensing Act 1964 just because it falls before a Bank Holiday Monday: R. *v.* WENLOCK JUSTICES, *ex p.* FURBER, *The Times*, July 26, 1978, Tudor Evans J.

1744. Offences of drunkenness. See § 460.

BOOKS AND ARTICLES. See *post*, pp. [5], [27].

JURIES

1745. Allowances

JURORS' ALLOWANCES REGULATIONS 1978 (No. 1579) [10p], made under the Juries Act 1974 (c. 23), s. 19, as amended by the Administration of Justice Act 1977 (c. 38), Sched. 2, para. 4; operative on January 1, 1979; revoke and replace S.I. 1977 No. 4.

ARTICLES. See *post*, p. [27].

JURISPRUDENCE

BOOKS AND ARTICLES. See *post*, pp. [5], [27].

LAND CHARGES

1746. Estate contract—failure to register—extent of solicitor's duty. See MIDLAND BANK TRUST CO. *v.* HETT, STUBBS & KEMP (A FIRM), § 2822.

1747. Local land charges

LOCAL LAND CHARGES (AMENDMENT) RULES 1978 (No. 1638) [10p], made under the Local Land Charges Act 1975 (c. 76), s. 14; operative on November 17, 1978; provide for the temporary use of facsimiles of forms required in connection with local land charges.

1748. Registration—transfer of property—wife's claim registrable

[Land Charges Act 1972 (c. 61), ss. 5 (1) (*a*), 17; Matrimonial Causes Act 1973 (c. 18), s. 24.]

A wife's application in matrimonial proceedings for transfer of property to herself is registrable as a land charge, it being a lis pendens relating to specific land.

A wife applied in divorce proceedings for a transfer of residential property (not the matrimonial home) owned by her husband, subject to a mortgage. After the making of the application but prior to its determination the husband further charged the property in favour of a bank. Balcombe J. allowed the bank's appeal against the registrar's order setting aside such charge. *Held*, dismissing the wife's appeal, that the wife's application was a pending land action within the meaning of s. 17 (1) of the 1972 Act and registrable as such; and that accordingly failure to register rendered the application not binding upon the bank. (*Taylor* v. *Taylor* [1968] C.L.Y. 1826 and *Calgary and Edmonton Land Co.* v. *Dobinson* [1974] C.L.Y. 2045 considered.)

WHITTINGHAM *v.* WHITTINGHAM; NATIONAL WESTMINSTER BANK (INTERVENER) [1978] 2 W.L.R. 936, C.A.

LAND DRAINAGE

1749. Drainage authorities

SEVERN-TRENT WATER AUTHORITY (ALTERATION OF BOUNDARIES OF THE MELVERLEY INTERNAL DRAINAGE DISTRICT) ORDER 1977 (No. 79) [15p], made under the Land Drainage Act 1930 (c. 44), s. 4 (1) (*b*) as modified and applied by the Water Resources Act 1963 (c. 38), the Local Government Act 1972 (c. 20), s. 254 (3) as applied by the Water Act 1973 (c. 37) and the Land Drainage Act 1976 (c. 70), ss. 11 (1) (4), 109 (6), 117 (1), Sched. 6, para. 6; operative on January 9, 1978; modifies a Scheme for the alteration of the boundaries of the Melverley Internal Drainage District.

SEVERN-TRENT WATER AUTHORITY (ABOLITION OF THE BAGGYMOOR DRAINAGE DISTRICT) ORDER 1978 (No. 506) [15p], made under the Land Drainage Act 1930, s. 4 (1) (*b*) as amended and applied by the Water Act 1973 and under the Land Drainage Act 1976, ss. 11 (1), 117 (1), Sched. 6, para. 6; operative on March 28, 1978; abolishes on a day to be appointed the Baggymoor Drainage District and transfers all its rights, properties, liabilities and obligations to the Severn–Trent Water Authority.

NORTH WEST WATER AUTHORITY (ABOLITION OF THE NEWLAND MOSS AND THE RIVER DUDDON INTERNAL DRAINAGE DISTRICTS) ORDER 1978 (No. 843) [20p], made under the Land Drainage Act 1976, s. 11 (1); operative on June 5, 1978; gives effect to the abolition of the Newland Moss and the River Duddon

Internal Drainage Districts, transferring all their rights and property to the North West Water Authority.

ANGLIAN WATER AUTHORITY (ALTERATION OF BOUNDARIES OF THE WITHAM FOURTH DISTRICT INTERNAL DRAINAGE DISTRICT) ORDER 1978 (No. 1288) [20p], made under the Land Drainage Act 1976, s. 11 (1); operative on August 29, 1978; confirms a scheme for the alteration of the boundaries of the Witham Fourth District Internal Drainage District.

WELSH WATER AUTHORITY (ABOLITION OF THE VALLEY DRAINAGE DISTRICT) ORDER 1978 (No. 1371) [20p], made under the Land Drainage Act 1976, ss. 11 (1) (4), 109 (6), as read with S.I. 1978 No. 272; operative on September 18, 1978; confirms a scheme for the abolition of the Valley Drainage District and Board.

ANGLIAN DRAINAGE AUTHORITY (BEDFORDSHIRE AND RIVER IVEL INTERNAL DRAINAGE DISTRICT) ORDER 1978 (No. 1588) [25p], made under the Land Drainage Act 1976, s. 11 (1); operative on October 30, 1978; provides for the constitution of an internal drainage board for the new internal drainage district resulting from the amalgamation of the Bedford First and the River Ivel Internal Drainage Districts.

ANGLIAN WATER AUTHORITY (SOUTH HOLLAND INTERNAL DRAINAGE DISTRICT) (AMENDMENT) ORDER 1978 (No. 1589) [20p], made under the Land Drainage Act 1976, s. 11 (1); operative on October 30, 1978; confirms a scheme for the reconstitution of the South Holland Internal Drainage District.

NORTH-WEST WATER AUTHORITY (ABOLITION OF THE STALMINE, PREESALL AND HAMBLETON INTERNAL DRAINAGE DISTRICT) ORDER 1978 (No. 1590) [20p], made under the Land Drainage Act 1976, s. 11 (1); operative on October 30, 1978; confirms a scheme for the abolition of the Stalmine, Preesall and Hambleton Internal Drainage District.

1750. Drainage charges

GENERAL DRAINAGE CHARGE (ASCERTAINMENT) ORDER 1978 (No. 665) [10p], made under the Land Drainage Act 1976 (c. 70), s. 49 (1) (3); as amended by S.I. 1978 No. 319; operative on June 2, 1978; defines in relation to each local land drainage district of the Anglican Water Authority a factor in the formula prescribed by s. 49 (1) of the 1976 Act for ascertaining the amount of the general drainage charge raised by the Authority for each such district.

1750a. Drainage orders

Order made under the Land Drainage Act 1976 (c. 70), s. 11 (1):
S.I. 1978 No. 1819 (Black Sluice Internal Drainage District) [20p].

1751. Flood barriers

BARKING CREEKMOUTH (BARRIER) (VARIATION) ORDER 1978 (No. 558) [10p], made under the Thames Barrier and Flood Prevention Act 1972 (c. xlv), ss. 56, 59; operative on April 19, 1978; varies S.I. 1975 No. 1170 by altering the position of the proposed flood barrier at the mouth of Barking Creek.

DARTFORD CREEK (BARRIER) ORDER 1978 (No. 1125) [50p], made under the Thames Barrier and Flood Prevention Act 1972, s. 56; operative on August 4, 1978; empowers the Southern Water Authority to construct a flood barrier incorporating a movable gate across the mouth of Dartford Creek and to execute ancillary works.

1752. Land Drainage Act 1976—amendment

LAND DRAINAGE ACT 1976 (AMENDMENT) REGULATIONS 1978 (No. 319) [15p], made under the Agriculture (Miscellaneous Provisions) Act 1976 (c. 55), s. 7 (1), (2) (a) and (5); operative on April 1, 1978; amend the 1976 Act by substituting for references therein to areas expressed in imperial units references to areas expressed in metric units.

1753. Northern Ireland. See NORTHERN IRELAND.

1754. Sewerage. See PUBLIC HEALTH.

LAND REGISTRATION

1755. Credit accounts—office copies

The following Practice Direction was issued by the Chief Land Registrar on April 4, 1978:

CREDIT ACCOUNTS

Credit account facilities in the Registration of Title Department are currently available for the payment of office copies on an item basis. As from May 1, these facilities will be extended to include an application for a complete set of office copies for which a fee of £2·25 is payable under para. XII (1) in the Schedule to the Land Registration Fee Order 1976 (S.I. No. 1333).

A new print of form A44 will be issued in due course but in the meantime the existing form can be used despite the direction that a complete set of office copies can only be obtained when fees are prepaid. The practical effect of this change will be that, when a request is made for the fee to be paid through a credit account in respect of an application made either for a complete set of office copies or, on an itemised basis, for copies of the register, filed plan and " all " documents referred to on the register as being filed, a complete set of office copies will be issued. This will be charged on an item basis but with a maximum fee of £2·25 (subject to any excess due if there are plans to be copied which are not of normal size).

1756. District registries

LAND REGISTRATION (DISTRICT REGISTRIES) ORDER 1978 (No. 1162) [20p], made under the Land Registration Act 1925 (c. 21), ss. 132, 133; operative on October 30, 1978; replaces S.I. 1974 No. 1304 and constitutes a new district registry at Birkenhead.

1757. Documents—binding

The following Practice Direction was issued by the Chief Land Registrar on April 4, 1978 :

Binding of documents lodged for registration

Although it is appreciated that the appearance and durability of a document is important, nevertheless the use of plastic spines for binding can cause difficulties for the Land Registry. The department does not wish to insist unnecessarily on strict compliance with the Land Registration Rules with regard to the presentation of documents, but it is anxious to avoid the need to remove plastic binders where this becomes a matter of practical necessity. It must, therefore, be the general practice of the Land Registry not to accept documents bound with plastic spines if they will be required to be annexed to land or charge certificates or to be filed in the department. Principally, this concerns transfers and charges of registered land and certified copies thereof, and also copy documents required to accompany applications for first registration. If, however, there should be a problem in any particular case (*e.g.* as, where a large document affects numerous registered properties), the district land registrar of the appropriate district land registry should be consulted to see whether some special arrangement can be made.

1758. Official searches

LAND REGISTRATION (OFFICIAL SEARCHES) RULES 1978 (No. 1600), made under the Land Registration Act 1925 (c. 21), s. 144; operative on January 1, 1979; revoke and replace S.I. 1969 No. 1179 and extend from 15 to 20 days the period of priority conferred by an official search.

1759. Registration of title—companies

The following Practice Direction was issued by the Chief Land Registrar on April 4, 1978 :

Entry of company numbers on Register of Title

Although there is no requirement that a company's registered number should be supplied when application is made for the registration of a company as the proprietor of land or of a charge, nevertheless, at the request of The Law Society, the Chief Land Registrar has now made arrangements, in the case of a company incorporated in England and Wales, to enter the company's number on the register of title whenever this is so desired and the necessary information is furnished. Accordingly, if a company's number is provided with its name and address on the relevant form of application for registration (such as, *e.g.* forms 1E, 2E, 3E or A4 or A5), or if that number is stated in the transfer or other document lodged for registration, it will be entered in the register of title immediately following the company's name.

1760. Rules.
LAND REGISTRATION RULES 1978 (No. 1601) [20p], made under the Land Registration Act 1925 (c. 21), s. 144; operative on January 1, 1979; amend S.R. & O. 1925 No. 1093 and make fresh provision relating to the dates on which applications for registration are treated as having been delivered. They also clarify the provisions relating to competing priorities of applications and the cancellation of defective applications.

1761. Water. See WATER AND WATERWORKS.

ARTICLES. See *post*, p. [27].

LANDLORD AND TENANT

1762. Agricultural holdings. See AGRICULTURE.

1763. Assignment—consent of landlord—whether refusal reasonable—assignment resulting in existing tenant and proposed assignee being entitled to purchase freehold
A landlord may not be unreasonable in refusing his consent to an assignment of a lease where the assignment would result in the assignee being entitled to purchase the freehold under the Leasehold Reform Act 1967.

The plaintiff, long leaseholders, sought a declaration that the lessors were unreasonably withholding their consent to a proposed assignment of the lease to the plaintiff's sub-tenant (whose tenancy was protected under the Rent Acts). The lessors' stated reason for refusal was that such an assignment would enable the sub-tenant to purchase the freehold at low cost under the 1967 Act and that they were anxious to retain control of the large estate of which the subject premises formed part. The lessors offered to purchase the plaintiff's interest at a fair price. *Held*, allowing the lessor's appeal against the grant of the declaration, that in the circumstances, refusal of consent was reasonable. (*Re Gibbs and Houlder Brothers & Co.'s Lease* [1925] Ch. 575 and *Pimms v. Tallow Chandlers* [1964] C.L.Y. 2079 applied.)

BICKEL *v.* DUKE OF WESTMINSTER (1977) 34 P. & C.R. 22, C.A.

1764. Business tenancies—application for new lease—landlords to use premises for " business "—parish community centre
[Landlord and Tenant Act 1954 (c. 56), ss. 23 (2), 30.]
For the purposes of s. 30 (1) of the Landlord and Tenant Act 1954, the provision and running of a community centre is a " business."

The trustee company was empowered to execute trusts in connection with the Roman Catholic Church in England. As lessors of premises let for use as a country club, the trustees objected to the grant of a new lease under the 1954 Act upon the grounds (under s. 30 (1) (*g*)) that they intended to occupy the premises for the purposes of business carried on by themselves, the proposal being that the local parish priest should run the premises as a community centre and church meeting room for members of his congregation. *Held*, dismissing the tenant's appeal against refusal to order a new tenancy, that (1) the purpose contemplated by the trustees was a " business " within the meaning of s. 30 (1) (*g*) of the Act; and (2) it sufficed that the business was to be run by the parish priest as agent for the trustees.

PARKES *v.* WESTMINSTER ROMAN CATHOLIC DIOCESE TRUSTEE (1978) 36 P. & C.R. 22, C.A.

1765. —— —— leave to withdraw—no power to back-date order. See COVELL MATTHEWS & PARTNERS *v.* FRENCH WOOLS, § 2391.

1766. —— —— tenants' proposals in originating summons—whether capable of construction as offer
[Landlord and Tenant Act 1954 (c. 56), ss. 24A, 25, 34, 64.] T applied by originating summons in August 1975 for the grant of a new lease upon terms proposed in the summons or such other terms as the court might determine. L served a s. 25 notice and a summons pursuant to s. 24A for interim deter-

mination of rent. T served successive affidavits proposing decreases in rent
from the level originally proposed in their summons. In February 1977 L purported to accept T's proposals by letter. *Held,* on a preliminary point, (1) the
effect of s. 64 of the Act was to make the offer contained in the summons
an offer to take a tenancy from a date three months from the final disposition
of the summons. Accordingly, L's letter accepting a tenancy commencing in
October 1975 was not an acceptance of T's offer but a counter offer; (2) under
s. 34 of the Act, the rent falls to be determined at the date of the hearing, but
having regard to the likely date of the commencement of the tenancy in three
months' time: LOVELY & ORCHARD SERVICES *v.* DAEJAN INVESTMENTS (1977)
246 E.G. 651, Judge Finlay Q.C.

1767. —— **breach of restrictive covenant—meaning of " supermarket "**
    C Ltd. sought a declaration that T Ltd. were in breach of a covenant con-
tained in a lease between C Ltd. and T Ltd.'s predecessor in title, which
restricted the use of premises to the business of a supermarket for the sale of
a named range of articles, and other things ancillary thereto. C Ltd. claimed
that T Ltd. were in breach, as the premises comprised a freezer centre in
which sales of freezers made up 15 per cent. of the business. *Held,* dismissing
C Ltd.'s appeal from the judge's refusal to grant the declaration sought, the
premises were a supermarket even though not all the goods sold, namely the
freezers, were portable. " Supermarket " is a technical term of the distributive
trade, on which expert evidence is admissible: CALABAR (WOOLWICH) *v.* TESCO
STORES (1977) 245 E.G. 479, C.A.

1768. —— **notice to quit—bankrupt tenant—service on trustee**
    The defendant was a hairdresser and holder of a business tenancy. The
plaintiff landlords served notice to quit, under the Landlord and Tenant Act
1954, on July 11, 1977. No counter-notice was served, and on May 24,
1978, an order for possession was made. The defendant applied to set aside the
order on the ground that he had, with the plaintiffs' knowledge, been bankrupt
since 1973, and the notice should have been served on his trustee in bankruptcy.
Held, upholding this submission and setting aside the order, that (1) as the
tenancy by operation of law had vested in the trustee, the defendant could only
give effect to the order by disregarding his obligations to the trustee, and (2) the
defendant had no such right to give effect to the order: GATWICK INVESTMENTS
v. RADIVOJEVIC, September 8, 1978, Judge Pickering, Willesden County Ct.
(*Ex rel. John Harwood-Stevenson, Esq., Barrister.*)

1769. —— —— **validity**
    [Landlord and Tenant Act 1954 (c. 56), s. 24 (1) (5) (6); Landlord and Tenant
(Notices) Regulations 1957 (S.I. 1957 No. 1157), para. 4 (vii), App., Form 7 (as
amended by Landlord and Tenant (Notices) Regulations 1969 (S.I. 1969 No.
1771), para. 3, App.1, and Landlord and Tenant (Notices) Regulations 1973
(S.I. 1973 No. 792), para. 3).]
    A notice terminating a tenancy under s. 24 of the Landlord and Tenant Act
1954 will not be invalid merely because it fails to set out notes which are
irrelevant.
    L let a fish-and-chip shop to T. L wished to terminate the tenancy, but was
willing for T to have a new one. L gave notice under s. 24 of the Landlord
and Tenant Act 1954, stating that he would not oppose a new tenancy. The
notice was in the form prescribed by the 1957 Regulations, as amended by the
1969 and 1973 Regulations, but notes 4, 5 and 7 in Form 7 were omitted.
Notes 4 and 5 apply to a case where the landlord opposes a new tenancy.
Note 7 defines who a landlord is, and there was no uncertainty as to the
identity of L. The judge held that the notice was invalid. On appeal by L, *held,*
allowing the appeal, that the departure from the form was immaterial since the
omitted notes were irrelevant, and the notice was therefore valid. (*Bolton's
(House Furnishers)* v. *Oppenheim* [1959] C.L.Y. 1834, dictum of Barry J in
Barclays Bank v. *Ascott* [1961] C.L.Y. 4871 and *Lewis* v. *M.T.C. (Cars)* [1975]
C.L.Y. 1880 applied; *Sun Alliance and London Assurance Co.* v. *Hayman* [1975]
C.L.Y. 1881 considered.)
    TEGERDINE *v.* BROOKS (1978) 36 P. & C.R. 261, C.A.

1770. ——— " occupied for the purpose of business "—meaning—staff accommodation —must be necessary for staff duties
[Landlord and Tenant Act 1954 (c. 56), s. 23 (1).]
Premises are " occupied for the purposes of a business " within s. 23 (1) of the Landlord and Tenant Act 1954 if they are occupied for a purpose necessary to the furtherance of the business, not merely for the convenience of the business.
T used the premises to accommodate staff from a nearby hotel which he owned. L sought possession on the ground that T did not occupy the cottage as his residence. T claimed that the tenancy was one to which Pt. II of the Landlord and Tenant Act 1954 applied. The judge dismissed the proceedings. On appeal by L, *Held,* allowing the appeal, that the occupation of the cottage for the housing of the hotel's staff was not necessary for the furtherance of the business, but was merely for the convenience of the business, and therefore was not covered by Pt. II of this Act.
CHAPMAN v. FREEMAN [1978] 1 W.L.R. 1298, C.A.

1771. ——— ——— mixed purposes
[Landlord and Tenant Act 1954 (c. 56), s. 23 (1).]
Premises are " occupied for the purposes of a business or for those and other purposes " within s. 23 (1) of the Landlord and Tenant Act 1954, when business occupation constitutes a significant purpose of the occupation, as opposed to being merely incidental to residential occupation.
In the first case, T conducted an import business from the service flat which was his home. He used a local P.O. box number as his business address. L sought a declaration that T's tenancy was subject to Part II of the Landlord and Tenant Act 1954 because the premises were partly occupied for business purposes. The judge dismissed the claim on the ground that the business use was de minimis. In the second case, T, a doctor, obtained L's consent to carry on his profession in the maisonnette which was his home. He practised from consulting-rooms elsewhere, and only used his home once or twice in emergencies. L sought possession on the basis that the tenancy was covered by Pt. II of the 1954 Act. Both landlords appealed: *held,* allowing the appeal in the first case, that the business activity constituted a significant purpose of the occupation. In the second case, dismissing the appeal, that T's professional use of the premises was purely incidental to his residential occupation. *Per* Geoffrey Lane L.J.: the business occupation must exist both at the time the contractual tenancy comes to an end and at the date of service of the notice of determination.
CHERYL INVESTMENTS v. SALDANHA; ROYAL LIFE SAVING SOCIETY v. PAGE [1978] 1 W.L.R. 1329, C.A.

1772. ——— payment of landlord's costs—whether " penalty "
[Landlord and Tenant Act 1954 (c. 56), s. 38 (1).] A clause in a lease of business premises provided that the tenant should pay to the landlord all costs charges and expenses including legal costs which might be incurred by the landlord in proceedings under Pt. II of the Landlord and Tenant Act 1954. *Held,* that the clause was a " penalty " within s. 38 (1) of the Act, and so void: STEVENSON AND RUSH (HOLDINGS) v. LANGDON, *The Times,* November 23, 1978, C.A.

1773. ——— renewal—whether holding required by landlord for his business
[Landlord and Tenant Act 1954 (c. 56), s. 30 (1) (g).] A cricket club applied for a new tenancy of three and a half acres of the landlord's property, the remainder of which was used as a farm. The landlord opposed the grant on the ground that he intended to use the land for his business as a farmer. He gave an undertaking to that effect to the county court judge, who, on the other hand, heard evidence that the landlord's existing land was only farmed to 50 per cent. capacity. The judge granted the club a new tenancy, holding that the landlord did not have a present, fixed and genuine intention to farm the land. *Held,* dismissing the landlord's appeal, there were no grounds for disturbing the judge's decision; he had the right test in mind and the question was essentially one of fact. (*Betty's Cafés* v. *Phillips Furnishing Stores* [1958] C.L.Y. 1818 and

Espresso Coffee Machine v. *Guardian Assurance* [1959] C.L.Y. 1820 applied):
LIGHTCLIFFE AND DISTRICT CRICKET AND LAWN TENNIS CLUB v. WALTON (1977)
245 E.G. 393, C.A.

1774. —— **right of way**
[Landlord and Tenant Act 1954 (c. 56), s. 23 (1).]
Pt. II of the Landlord and Tenant Act 1954 has no application to the grant
of a right of way.

A local authority granted a waste disposal company a seven-year lease of the
right of way over the authority's land for the purposes of dumping waste. The
company served a request for a new tenancy of the right of way under Pt. II
of the Landlord and Tenant Act 1954, and the local authority served a
counter-notice opposing a new tenancy. *Held*, that Pt. II of the 1954 Act did not
apply to a mere right of way, since such an incorporated hereditament, though
capable of being " used," was not capable of being " occupied " for the purposes of a business within s. 23 (1). (Dictum of Sachs L.J. in *Lee-Verhulst*
(Investments) v. *Harwood Trust* [1972] C.L.Y. 1981 explained.)
LAND RECLAMATION CO. v. BASILDON DISTRICT COUNCIL [1978] 2 All E.R.
1162, Brightman J.

1775. —— **user—landlords' proposal to modify covenant restricting user**
[Landlord and Tenant Act 1954 (c. 56), s. 35.] The tenants' application for a
new tenancy of premises used for their business of retail cutlers was adjourned
into court for the judge to decide, pursuant to s. 35 of the Act, upon the
landlords' proposal that an existing covenant against user for purposes other
than the business of retail cutler without the landlords' written consent be
modified to include " such consent not to be unreasonably withheld." This proposal was likely to increase the rent by £1,750 p.a. and was opposed by the
tenants. *Held*, the covenant should not be so modified in the absence of any
special reason; if the tenants object they should not be forced to accept such
modification for higher rent: CHARLES CLEMENTS (LONDON) v. RANK CITY
WALL (1978) 246 E.G. 739, Goulding J.

1776. Conveyancing. See REAL PROPERTY AND CONVEYANCING.

**1777. Covenant—breach—whether frustrated—landlord unable to perform through
insolvency**
A landlord's obligation under a contract to maintain facilities in a lease is
not to be regarded as frustrated by reason only of the landlord's insolvency
rendering performance financially impossible.

Under a lease by virtue of which the plaintiff, as an elderly widow, occupied
a third floor flat, the landlords covenanted to supply and maintain a lift. Such
a lift operated until 1972, when repairs were required. The landlords bought a
new lift but because of their insolvency could not afford to install it. The plaintiff suffered hardship in that access to and from the flat was difficult without
the lift. In 1975, she issued proceedings seeking specific performance of the
covenant, and damages for breach thereof. The landlords contended that performance of the covenant had become frustrated. *Held*, making the decree,
that the landlord's obligation remained substantially the same as at the time
of making the lease, and that their insolvency did not frustrate the covenant;
nor did the hardship to them justify a refusal to order specific performance.
(*Davis Contractors* v. *Fareham Urban District Council* [1956] C.L.Y. 874 and
Jeune v. *Queen's Cross Properties* [1973] C.L.Y. 1899 applied.)
FRANCIS v. COWCLIFFE (1977) 33 P. & C.R. 368, D.C.

**1778. Covenant to insure—landlord's agency—implied obligations of landlord—
liability for breach**
The plaintiff was the assignee of a lease of a dwelling-house. The defendants
were the assignees of the reversion. The lease contained an express covenant
by the tenant to insure the house and keep it insured through the landlord's
agency under a specific type of policy in a named company. The plaintiff,
upon exchanging contracts for the assignment (which was completed on July
2, 1975) requested the defendants in a letter dated May 6, 1975, to effect an
insurance on her behalf with the named company and to furnish her with
details of previous insurances. The defendants replied on June 17, 1975, stating

only that they did not keep the details of the insurances affecting the premises but merely required that their interests be noted on the policies. No reference was made in the defendants' letter to the plaintiff's request to the defendants to effect an insurance of the demised premises. The matter rested there until a freak storm on August 14, 1975, caused damage amounting to £450 to the plaintiff's dwelling-house. *Held,* that there was an implied obligation on the defendants in the circumstances to effect an insurance of the premises upon request from the plaintiff notwithstanding the absence from the lease of any express covenant to that effect; but, because the plaintiff upon receipt of the defendants' letter was free to effect her own insurance and ought to have taken steps to effect such insurance of the property otherwise than through the defendants' agency in order to mitigate any loss which the plaintiff might suffer through the defendants' breach, the defendants were not liable in contract or otherwise for damages arising from non-insurance as long after June 17, 1975, as August 14, 1975: MITCHELL *v.* CO-OPERATIVE INSURANCE SOCIETY, May 10, 1978, Clerkenwell County Ct., Judge Dewar (*Ex. rel. Peter Cowell, Esq., Barrister.*)

1779. Covenant to repair—notice served under s. 146—whether costs incidental thereto recoverable as a debt or damages

[Law of Property Act 1925 (c. 60), s. 146; Leasehold Property (Repairs) Act 1938 (c. 34), ss. 1 and 2.]

Where a lease makes express provision for payment by the lessee of costs incidental to preparation and service of a notice to repair under s. 146 of the Law of Property Act 1925, such sum is recoverable as a debt without prior leave of the court if a counter-notice is served under the Leasehold Property (Repairs) Act 1938.

A lease provided that the lessee would pay on demand all costs incurred by the lessor incidental to the preparation and service of any statutory notice to repair. Notice under s. 146 of the 1925 Act was served by the lessors and the lessee duly carried out the repairs specified therein. The lessors thereupon successfully claimed some £150, being the legal and surveyor's costs incurred in connection with service of the notice. The lessee appealed, contending that since the lease had more than three years to run, the effect of the Leasehold Property (Repairs) Act 1938 was that the lessors could not recover such sum without the prior leave of the court, which leave had not been obtained. *Held,* dismissing the appeal, that the sum claimed was a contractual debt and therefore the claim was not subject to the 1938 Act. (*Bader Properties* v. *Linley Property Investments* [1968] C.L.Y. 2175 approved.)

MIDDLEGATE PROPERTIES *v.* GIDLOW-JACKSON (1977) 34 P. & C.R. 4, C.A.

1780. Forfeiture of lease—adjournment of hearing—whether justified

[County Court Act 1959 (c. 22), s. 191 (1).]

Although the judge in an action for possession upon forfeiture for non-payment of rent is entitled of his own motion to adjourn the hearing once for inquiry to be made as to the tenant's ability to pay arrears, a second adjournment without the plaintiff's consent is inappropriate where no new information has come to light.

The plaintiff lessors sought possession of the demised premises upon forfeiture of the lease for non-payment of rent. At the first hearing, the defendant sought to advance no defence, but the judge of his own motion adjourned the hearing upon learning that the defendant had some unspecified expectancy under a trust. Upon the adjourned hearing, it remained uncertain as to what amounts the defendant might receive thereunder and when he might receive the same; but the judge again adjourned the hearing for further inquiries, subject to the defendant undertaking to assign his interest in certain of such expected moneys to the plaintiffs. The plaintiffs sought an order of mandamus compelling the judge to hear the action. *Held,* that notwithstanding that s. 191 (1) (*b*) of the Act compelled a judge to order possession unless the outstanding rent is paid within a given period, a single adjournment lay within the judge's discretion; but that there had been no justification for a second adjournment; however, in the circumstances the making of an order of mandamus was not necessary, as the court was confident that the judge would now proceed with the hearing.

R. *v.* A CIRCUIT JUDGE (SITTING AS NORWICH COUNTY COURT), *ex p.* WATHEN (1977) 33 P. & C.R. 423, D.C.

1781. —— service of notice—right of tenant to apply for relief—whether lessor justified in refusing consent to assignment

[Law of Property Act 1925 (c. 20), s. 146.]

The fact that a lessor has commenced forfeiture proceedings may not justify the lessor in refusing licence to assign to a responsible assignee.

The defendant company was lessee of business premises under a lease containing a covenant against assignment except with the licence of the lessor, not to be unreasonably withheld in the case of a " responsible and respectable assignee." Under the lease, the lessor had a right of re-entry in the event of the liquidation of the lessee. On January 15, the lessee company passed a resolution to wind up; on February 5 the lessee's solicitors applied for licence to assign to another company. Discussions followed such application, until on February 24 the lessors, who had not previously known of the liqidation, wrote indicating their wish to exercise the right of re-entry and enclosing a s. 146 notice. Thereafter, the lessees offered guarantors for the proposed assignee, but the lessors contended that the question of assignment no longer arose. Foster J. granted the lessees relief against forfeiture and an order that consent to the assignment had been unreasonably withheld. *Held*, dismissing the lessor's appeal, that the lessees were entitled to seek relief after service of the s. 146 notice, and that the appellate court would not interfere with the trial judge's finding of fact as to whether the assignee was responsible and respectable. (*Quilter* v. *Mapleson* (1882) 9 Q.B.D. 672 applied; *Re Smith's Lease* (1951) C.L.C. 1839 approved).

PAKWOOD TRANSPORT *v.* 15 BEAUCHAMP PLACE (1978) 36 P. & C.R. 112, C.A.

1782. Furnished letting—resident landlord—second tenancy immediately following furnished letting—protection by virtue of transitional provisions

[Rent Act 1968 (c. 23), s. 5A (1) (*b*), as amended by Rent Act 1974 (c. 51), s. 2 (3), Sched. 2, para. (i); Rent Act 1974, s. 1 (1) (*a*); Sched. 3, para. 1 (1) (2).]

Where a tenancy is followed by a second fixed-term tenancy, the second tenancy will not necessarily be protected if the first tenancy lacked protection only because of the transitional provisions of the Rent Act 1974 and not by virtue of s. 5A of the Rent Act 1968.

P let D a fully furnished flat for two years from July 1, 1973. On July 1, 1975, P, who was a resident landlord, granted a further fixed-term tenancy for an 11 month period. On P's claim for possession at the end of that period D contended that the tenancy was protected because their previous tenancy had not been a protected tenancy by virtue of s. 5A of the Rent Act 1968. *Held*, dismissing the second defendant's appeal from the order for possession made by the judge, that the reason that the first tenancy had not been protected was the exemption contained in the transitional provisions of the Rent Act 1974 and not s. 5A of the Rent Act 1968.

STUBBS *v.* ASSOPARDI [1978] 1 W.L.R. 646, C.A.

1783. Holiday letting—evidential value of letting agreement

Whilst the labels used by the parties in describing their transaction are not conclusive, where a tenancy agreement expressly states the purpose for which it is made, that statement will stand as evidence of the purpose of the parties in making it.

B let a furnished house to M for a fixed three month period. The letting agreement, signed by M, described the letting as being for the purpose of a holiday. B sought possession at the end of the period. M denied that the letting had been for a holiday. The judge decided the issue in favour of M on the oral evidence of the parties, apparently without reference to the letting agreement. *Held*, allowing B's appeal, that the description used by the parties in the agreement was evidence of their purpose, and that it would be for M to show that the true purpose was different, which he could not be said to have done.

BUCHMANN *v.* MAY [1978] 2 All E.R. 993, C.A.

1784. Joint tenancy—agricultural holdings—validity of counter notice—authority of one joint tenant only

[Agricultural Holdings Act 1948 (c. 63), s. 24 (1).]

A counter-notice served in response to a landlord's notice to quit by one joint tenant without the consent or authority of the other is an invalid notice.

The plaintiffs were landlords of a freehold agricultural farm, the defendants joint tenants. A valid notice to quit was served on the joint tenants, whereupon one tenant, without the authority of the other, served a counter-notice under s. 24 (1) of the Act. On the plaintiffs' originating summons for a declaration that the counter-notice was of no effect, *held,* that one joint tenant is not " holder of the land under a contract of tenancy," merely one of the holders; that one joint tenant was not able to give a valid counter-notice without the authority of the other. (*Howson* v. *Buxton* (1928) 97 L.J.K.B. 749, C.A. distinguished : *Jacobs* v. *Chaudhuri* [1968] C.L.Y. 2191 and *T. M. Fairclough* v. *Berliner* (1931) 1 Ch. 60 applied.)

NEWMAN *v.* KEEDWELL (1978) 35 P. & C.R. 393, Fox J.

1785. —— deed of conveyance—construction—contributions towards purchase price —whether constructive trust to be implied

The doctrine of constructive trusts cannot apply to a transaction where there is an express declaration of trust.

A house was conveyed to the plaintiff and defendant as joint tenants in law and in equity. The plaintiff subsequently claimed that the defendant had only been joined on the transfer to satisfy mortgagees, he having contributed nothing towards the price and that, accordingly, the property was held on constructive trust for the benefit of the plaintiff alone. The plaintiff sought an order that the defendant transfer all his interest in the property. The defendant claimed an interest in the property on the grounds that he had paid £500 towards the price. The Master ruled that the defendant could not establish an interest unless he proved not only that he had paid £500, but that such sum was paid towards the purchase price. *Held,* allowing the defendants' appeal, that in the absence of recission by reason of fraud or mistake or of a claim to rectify the transfer, the express declaration of trust contained in the transfer precluded the implication of a constructive trust. (*Pettit* v. *Pettit* [1969] C.L.Y. 1639 and *Wilson* v. *Wilson* [1969] applied.)

PINK *v.* LAWRENCE (1978) 36 P. & C.R. 98, C.A.

1786. Lease—assignment—disclaimer by assignee on bankruptcy—liability of original tenant for rent

[Companies Act 1948 (c. 38), s. 323 (2).]

When the liquidators of a company or the trustee in bankruptcy of an individual disclaims a lease which has been assigned to the company or the individual, the original lessee will remain liable to the lessor for the rent throughout the term.

P Co. granted D a lease of business premises for a term of 20 years in 1971. The lease contained a covenant for payment of rent during the term from D. D assigned the lease to X Co. with P Co.'s consent. X Co. went into liquidation, and the liquidator disclaimed the lease. P Co. claimed the rent from D. *Held,* the disclaimer released the company only, and not the original lessee, therefore D was liable for the rent throughout the term. (*Hill* v. *East and West India Dock Co.* (1884) 9 App.Cas. 448 applied.)

WARNFORD INVESTMENTS *v.* DUCKWORTH [1978] 2 W.L.R. 741, Megarry V.-C.

1787. —— breach of condition—surety's bankruptcy—need for s. 146 notice

[Law of Property Act 1925 (c. 20), s. 146.]

Where there is a condition in a lease for re-entry in case of bankruptcy of a surety, there is a breach of condition within s. 146 of the Act if the surety goes bankrupt.

A lease contained a proviso for re-entry by the landlord in the event, inter alia, of the tenant or either of his sureties committing an act of bankruptcy. The tenant sublet part of the premises, contrary to a covenant in the lease, and the landlord gave notice under s. 146 of the Act specifying the breach and requiring the tenant to remedy the same. The landlord brought an action for possession on the ground of the unauthorised sub-letting and sought leave to amend the statement of claim to allege an act of bankruptcy by one of the sureties as a further ground. On the question of whether the landlord claiming re-entry on the latter ground should first serve a s. 146 notice, *held*, that breach of condition is not necessarily a voluntary or avoidable act on the part of the tenant, and ought reasonably to be interpreted as including the bankruptcy of a surety. The landlord, having failed to serve notice under s. 146, would not be given leave to amend the statement of claim.

HALLIARD PROPERTY CO. *v.* JACK SEGAL [1978] 1 W.L.R. 377, Goulding J.

1788. —— **covenant against sub-letting—occupiers as licensees**

Lambeth London Borough Council let a house to W at £400 rent p.a. W agreed not to assign, sub-let or part with possession. He divided his house between two applicants, each of whom had a partially furnished bedroom and the use of a common living room, kitchen and garden for £8 a week each. It was clear that the mere fact that a sub-tenancy was unlawful did not mean that the person concerned was not a householder. *Held*, the reasonable assumption, given W's limited rights, was that the applicants were living in the house as licensees, guests or friends. The court could not interfere unless there was a clear error of law (*R.* v. *Preston Supplementary Benefit Appeal Tribunal, ex p. Moore* [1975] C.L.Y. 3288 applied): HOLLAND *v.* SOUTH LONDON SUPPLEMENTARY BENEFITS APPEAL TRIBUNAL; SZCZELKUN *v.* SAME, *The Times*, June 2, 1978, C.A.

1789. —— **duty of landlord—adjoining vacant property—vandalism**

[Scot.] P rented property in a block owned by D. Other property in the block was left empty and unsecured. Vandals got into it and caused damage to P's flat. *Held*, knowing of the risks of vandalism in the area, D was under a duty to ensure the security of neighbouring vacant property to prevent damage being caused to P's property. (Dictum of Lord Macmillan in *Donoghue* v. *Stevenson*, 1932 S.L.T. at p. 339 applied): EVANS *v.* GLASGOW DISTRICT COUNCIL, 1978 S.L.T. 17, Outer House.

1790. —— **service of notices—implied general agency.**

Although no express agency is created, if a landlord and a tenant each allows another to deal with the demised premises upon his behalf, such other person has implied authority both to give and receive notices.

Each party to a fixed-term lease of business premises let by the plaintiff to the defendant received under the lease an option to determine the same by notice in writing. From an early stage the premises were in fact occupied by U, an associate of the defendants, to whom eventually all rent demands and correspondence were sent by the plaintiffs. From 1974 all such correspondence was sent to U by W, an associate of the plaintiffs. In August 1975, U served written notice upon W, purporting to exercise the option to determine the lease. The plaintiff sought a declaration that such notice was invalid as it should have been served by the defendants upon the plaintiffs. *Held*, refusing a declaration, that by standing by and allowing U and W to deal exclusively with the premises, both parties had allowed a general agency to arise, and that, accordingly, it was implicit that U had authority to give, and W to receive, such a notice. (*Jones* v. *Phipps* (1868) L.R. 3 Q.B. 567, considered.)

TOWNSEND CARRIERS *v.* PFIZER (1977) 33 P. & C.R. 361, Megarry V.-C.

1791. Leasehold reform—conveyance to lessee—meaning of " appurtenant "

[Leasehold Reform Act 1967 (c. 88).] The Leasehold Reform Act 1967 is exproprietary because it gives a tenant a compulsory right to have the freehold conveyed to him, and it should therefore not be construed too liberally. The word " appurtenant " in the Act referred to incorporeal rights appurtenant to the land, and not corporeal rights such as a piece of land outside the curtilage of the house that was let. The lessee in this case was not entitled to have a separate paddock conveyed to her together with the adjoining house: METHUEN-CAMPBELL *v.* WALTERS (1978) 122 S.J. 610, C.A.

1792. —— **Lands Tribunal decisions**

GRAINGER *v.* GUNTER ESTATE TRUSTEES (LR/8/1977) (1977) 246 E.G. 55 (determination under 1967 Act for price to be paid for freehold interest of mews house in South Kensington, the lease having 11 years unexpired. Landlord's expert's approach preferred on every point: (i) likely buyer a private investor not an institution applying a sophisticated form of valuation; (ii) sale prices of ground rent investments make unreliable comparisons; (iii) " adverse differential " approach to decapitalisation of site value to reach s. 15 rent and recapitalisation of s. 15 rent disapproved (*Official Custodian for Charities* v. *Goldridge* [1974] C.L.Y. 2101 applied.) The tribunal has little confidence in evidence from alleged comparables not inspected by expert witness.)

UGRINIC v. SHIPWAY (ESTATES) (1977) 244 E.G. 893 (in a reference for the determination under the 1967 Act of the price to be paid for the freehold interest of a typical semi-detached house in Telford New Town with an unexpired lease of 85 years, the Lands Tribunal *held* that (1) the anxiety-to-settle effect was not strong, as the difference in value between freehold and leasehold was relatively slight; (2) the investment market for long reversion ground rents was for many years not lively: sum determined at £220).

1793. —— price payable—clause in current lease purporting to affect value of freehold—whether void

[Leasehold Reform Act 1967 (c. 88), ss. 9 (1), 23 (1).]

The words " any agreement relating to a tenancy ' 'in s. 23 (1) of the Leasehold Reform Act 1967 are not restricted to agreements between the landlord and tenant.

T, a leaseholder, gave notice of her intention to acquire the freehold. The freeholders, before service of the notice, granted a longer concurrent lease to a property company containing a clause that, if that company granted a sublease to T, then the rent payable by it should be a market rent. With that clause, the valuation of freehold was agreed at £50 payable by T to the freeholders, and £250 to the reversioner; without it, £4,000 was agreed as payable to the freeholders alone. *Held*, allowing T's appeal from an order of the Lands Tribunal that the £4,000 was payable, that s. 23 (1) of the Leasehold Reform Act 1967 applied to the agreement between the freeholders and the company, so that the clause in that agreement was void in so far as it purported to affect the value of the freehold.

JONES v. WROTHAM PARK SETTLED ESTATES [1978] 3 W.L.R. 585, C.A.

1794. Licence—contractual and determinable—sale of house to cohabitee

A contractual licence to occupy for life cannot exist in the absence of express agreement between the parties.

K, and her husband bought a house in 1972, and K remained in the matrimonial home after breakdown of the marriage. K, was joined by C, the plaintiff, who became her lover. C bought the house, and shortly after brought an action for possession against K. The court declared a constructive trust enabling K to remain for life. On appeal, *held*, dismissing the appeal but varying the declaration, that K had a contractual licence terminable on reasonable notice, which in this case would be 12 months. (*Bannister* v. *Bannister* (1948) C.L.C. 9341 distinguished; *Errington* v. *Errington and Woods* [1952] C.L.Y. 1973 and *Tanner* v. *Tanner* [1976] C.L.Y. 2170 considered.)

CHANDLER v. KERLEY [1978] 1 W.L.R. 693, C.A.

1795. —— terms wider than usual—sham agreement

Where an agent orally tells lessees that a provision in the letting agreement which purports to prevent those lessees from having exclusive occupation, is only a legal formality and will not be put into effect, the letting agreement may be a sham, and the occupation a tenancy.

P wanted her house let. She showed D round a flat in it then referred him to her agent to negotiate an agreement. The agreement provided for non-exclusivity of occupation by D, but the agent told D that there would be no question of third parties occupying the flat. *Held*, that in view of what the agent told D, D effectively had exclusive possession of the flat; the agreement was a sham and D had a tenancy.

WALSH v. GRIFFITHS-JONES [1978] 2 All E.R. 1002, Lambeth County Ct.

1796. Licence or tenancy—informal family arrangement—court will impute a common intention to parties

Where a house is occupied under an informal family arrangement, the court must spell out the resulting legal relationship by imputing to the parties a common intention which they had never in fact formed.

In 1973 J's mother bought a house for J and his wife to live in under an informal arrangement whereby they would pay her £28·00 per month. The mother never pressed for the many payments that were not made. In possession proceedings, the mother alleged an oral agreement for a licence or alternatively a weekly tenancy terminated by notice to quit. J's wife contended that she was a protected tenant. The judge dismissed the action. On appeal, *held*, dismissing the appeal, that on the evidence, a joint contractual licence would be inferred, or a joint equitable licence (*per* Lord Denning M.R.) permitting the wife to remain in occupation on payment of £7 per week after J had left.

HARDWICK *v.* JOHNSON [1978] 1 W.L.R. 683, C.A.

1797. —— parties' intentions—separate licences granted to people living together
[Rent Act 1968 (c. 23), s. 105.]

Where the agreement between the parties truly is that a landlord should license two individuals each to occupy part of a room and each be responsible for a part of the consideration for the room, the letting may be a licence and not a tenancy.

Two people each entered into separate agreements with the owner of a dwelling house. Each was given a licence to occupy the dwelling, the owner reserving the right to use the room herself and to allow one other person to use it. Each covenanted to pay separate weekly instalments for their occupation. The judge held that a regulated furnished tenancy had been created. *Held*, allowing the the owner's appeal, that no agreement had been made which was contrary to public policy and that two separate licences had been created.

SOMMA *v.* HAZELHURST [1978] 1 W.L.R. 1014, C.A.

1797a. Mobile homes—term of leases—jurisdiction of court to extend
[Mobile Homes Act 1975 (c. 49).]

A judge has no jurisdiction under the Mobile Homes Act 1975 to grant terms of more than five years to residents on a site.

The owners of a caravan site offered terms of five years to residents on their site in accordance with their obligations under the Mobile Homes Act 1975. The residents were dissatisfied and sought longer terms. The agreements were amended in the county court by extending the five-year periods. *Held*, allowing the site owners' appeal, that the judge in the county court had no jurisdiction under the Act to grant terms longer than five years where the terms of the agreement complied with the requirements of the Act.

TAYLOR *v.* CALVERT [1978] 1 W.L.R. 899, C.A.

1798. Northern Ireland. See NORTHERN IRELAND.

1799. Possession—breach of covenant—provision tantamount to forfeiture—whether relief available.

A clause in a lease entitling the lessor to terminate a tenancy upon a given period of notice following breach of covenant is the same as a provision for forfeiture (though not expressed as such), and the tenant is entitled to claim relief.

A tenancy agreement provided, inter alia, that upon any breach of covenant by the tenant, the landlord might determine the tenancy upon three months' notice. The tenant being in arrears of rent, the landlord served such a notice and issued proceedings for possession. The outstanding rent was paid, but the tenants were denied relief, and possession was ordered. *Held*, allowing the tenant's appeal, that the provision for early termination by the landlord did not deprive the tenants of their right to claim relief. (*Chandless-Chandless* v. *Nicholson* [1942] 2 K.B. 321, applied.)

RICHARD CLARKE & CO. *v.* WIDNALL (1977) 33 P. & C.R. 339, C.A.

1800. —— council house—local authorities' powers. See CANNOCK CHASE COUNCIL *v.* KELLY, § 1570.

1801. —— County Court Rules, Ord. 26—evidence of tenancy—appropriateness of summary judgment. See PHSEROWSKY AND STANTON *v.* PHILLIPS, § 387.

1802. —— interim payment—bona fide counterclaim

Plaintiffs demised land to the second defendant for use as a garage and petrol station, who then purported to assign the lease to the first defendants without the plaintiffs' consent. The plaintiffs issued a writ of forfeiture. The first defendants claimed they had exercised an option to renew or alternatively it being a business tenancy and no notice having been served on them, the term continued under the Landlord and Tenant Act 1954. The plaintiffs sought an interim payment from the first defendants under R.S.C., Ord. 29, r. 18 for use and occupation of the land and for periodical payments thereafter pending the action. The first defendants in turn claimed damages for loss of sales due to harrassment. *Held*, r. 18 was concerned only with claims for possession of land where there was no bona fide counterclaim which might exceed the plaintiffs' claim. It would not be proper simply because the wording of the claim brought it within Ord. 29 instead of Ord. 14 to order an interim payment (*Moore* v. *Assignment Courier* [1977] C.L.Y. 2374 referred to): OLD GROVERY MANOR FARM *v.* W. SEYMOUR PLANT SALES (1978) 122 S.J. 457, Brightman J.

1803. —— " landlord by purchase " proviso—controlled tenancy converted to regulated tenancy—relevant date

[Rent Act 1977 (c. 42), Sched. 15, Pt. I, Case 9.] The plaintiff claimed possession under Case 9 of a flat that the defendant had lived in since 1939. The plaintiff purchased his interest in 1961, at which date the plaintiff's husband was the contractual tenant. At the date of the purchase the tenancy was a controlled tenancy. In 1962 the plaintiff's husband died, and the plaintiff became the statutory controlled tenant by transmission. On April 29, 1973, the tenancy was converted to a regulated tenancy by virtue of s. 35 of the Housing Finance Act 1972. On the question whether the plaintiff was a landlord by purchase and debarred from recovering possession under Case 9, *held*, that (1) the clog on the plaintiff's right to recover possession was not affected by the statutory transmission of the tenancy to the defendant (considering *Littlechild* v. *Holt* (1950) C.L.C. 8620 and *Wright* v. *Walford* [1955] C.L.Y. 2339), but (2) the words " in the case of a controlled tenancy " in the proviso " and the landlord did not become landlord by purchasing the dwelling-house or any interest therein after—(i) November 1, 1956, in the case of a controlled tenancy " meant " if the tenancy *is* a controlled tenancy," not " if the tenancy was at the date of the purchase a controlled tenancy." Accordingly, where a controlled tenancy had been converted to a regulated tenancy, the relevant date for the purpose of the proviso was March 23, 1965, and the plaintiff having purchased his interest in 1961 could recover possession: AGER *v.* BURNELL, October 26, 1978, Judge Corley, Ilford County Ct. (*Ex rel. David Lamming, Esq., Barrister.*)

1803a. —— power of court to suspend order

Ord. 26 of the County Court Rules gives no jurisdiction to the court to grant a stay of an order for possession of premises, other than by consent.

The County Court, having found that P had complied with the procedural requirements of Ord. 26 of the County Court Rules, made an order for possession of premises, but stayed the same for 14 days, without P's consent. *Held*, allowing P's appeal, that in the absence of consent he had no jurisdiction so to do.

SWORDHEATH PROPERTIES *v.* FLOYDD [1978] 1 All E.R. 721, C.A.

1804. —— recovery—claim by one of two owner-occupiers

[Rent Act 1968 (c. 23), s. 10, Sched. 3, Pt. II, Case 10.]

Where joint owners-occupiers let a house, they cannot reclaim possession under Case 10 if only one requires the house for his own residence.

The plaintiffs were joint owner-occupiers of a dwelling-house which they let furnished to the defendant, having served notice of their owner-occupation. After expiry of the term the defendant remained in occupation and the plaintiffs sought possession under Case 10 on the grounds that one of them required the premises as her residence. A county court judge dismissed the claim. *Held*, dismissing the plaintiff's appeal (Eveleigh L.J. dissenting) that only if the joint owner-occupiers together required the house as their joint residence could Case 10 be relied upon. (*McIntyre* v. *Hardcastle* (1948) C.L.C. 8614 applied.)

TILLING *v.* WHITEMAN [1978] 3 W.L.R. 137, C.A.

1805. —— trespass—damages

About 18 months after the expiry of a fixed term tenancy, landlords succeeded in obtaining an order for possession against the defendants, but were refused damages for trespass because they had failed to produce evidence that they would have been able to let the residential premises to suitable tenants after the expiry of the term. *Held,* allowing the landlords' appeal, that principle, common sense and authority indicated that if a landlord had established that an occupier of residential premises remained there as a trespasser, he was entitled, without bringing any evidence, to damages based, in the absence of special factors, on the amount of the annual letting value of the premises: SWORDHEATH PROPERTIES *v.* TABET (1978) 122 S.J. 862, C.A.

1806. Protected tenancies—joint tenants—whether remaining tenant entitled to benefit of statutory tenancy

[Rent Act 1968 (c. 23), s. 3 (1) (*a*).]

If a protected tenancy is granted to joint tenants and, before expiry of the contractual term one of them leaves, the remaining tenant is entitled to the benefit of the statutory tenancy when the term expires under s. 3 (1) (*a*) of the Rent Act 1968 (now s. 2 (1) of the Rent Act 1977).

L let a flat to A and B as joint tenants for a term expiring on December 25, 1976. The tenancy was protected under the Rent Act 1968. In October 1976 A left and never returned. B held over after December 25. L brought an action for possession, which the county court judge refused. On appeal by L, *held,* dismissing the appeal, that where there was a joint tenancy, " the tenant " in s. 3 (1) (*a*) of the Rent Act 1968 meant the joint tenants, or any one or more of them; accordingly B was entitled to the protection of the Act. (*Howson* v. *Buxton* (1928) 97 L.J.K.B. 749, C.A. applied.)

LLOYD *v.* SADLER [1978] 2 W.L.R. 721, C.A.

1807. —— possession—whether flat was tenant's home

T was the statutory tenant of a three-bedroomed flat. He occupied one bedroom when resident, his son and girl friend lived as man and wife in another bedroom, and his son's friend occupied the third. T paid the rent and rates and owned the furniture; the other occupants shared the expenses. T lived apart from his wife, for whom he had purchased a smaller flat, but visited her on average 1/2 nights per week; he also listed his wife's address as his " usual residential address " for certain business purposes. T kept his clothes in the subject flat and stayed there on average 2/3 nights a week, but travelled extensively on business trips abroad. L claimed possession on the following grounds: (1) T was not entitled to Rent Act protection as the subject flat was not his home; (2) if it was his home he had suitable alternative accommodation at his wife's flat; (3) T was in breach of covenants prohibiting (a) subletting, and (b) immoral user (his son and girl friend living together). *Held,* L's appeal from the judge's refusal to make a possession order, none of the enumerated grounds were well founded and the last " lacked substance or merit ": HEGLIBISTON ESTABLISHMENT *v.* HEYMAN (1977) 246 E.G. 567, C.A.

1808. —— " premium "—payments of rent in advance

[Rent Act 1968 (c. 23), ss. 85 (1), 91, 92 (1); Theft Act 1968 (c. 60), s. 16 (2).]

The payment of a returnable deposit is not a premium, or " any other pecuniary consideration in addition to rent " within s. 92 (1) of the Rent Act 1968, and is not unlawful under s. 85 (1). A conditional payment of rent in advance a day before a tenancy is due to begin is not a payment of rent in advance contrary to s. 91.

D called at an accommodation agency and signed a six months' tenancy agreement for a flat commencing the next day. The rent was £12 per week payable monthly in advance, and a returnable deposit of £48 was required against bills for services and depreciation. D made out a cheque for £96 in a false name against a bank account in which there was no money, and, having moved in, stopped the cheque. He was convicted of obtaining a pecuniary advantage, the evasion of the debt, by deception, contrary to s. 16 (2) of the Theft Act 1968. He appealed on the ground that the £48 deposit was an unlawful premium under ss. 85 and 92 (1) of the Rent Act 1968, and the £48 rent in advance was unlawfully required under s. 91, and that therefore neither were debts or charges under s. 16 (2) of the Theft Act. *Held,* dismissing the appeal, that both sums were lawfully payable, and were therefore debts or charges under s. 16 (1) and (2).

R. *v.* EWING (1977) 65 Cr.App.R. 4, C.A.

1808a. —— succession—male friend of female tenant—whether " member of family "
[Rent Act 1977 (c. 42), Sched. 1, para. 3.] On the death of a tenant, a man friend who had lived with her for five years claimed a tenancy by succession under para. 3 of Sched. 1 to the Rent Act 1977. *Held,* that their relationship lacked the element of permanence and the friend was not " a member of the original tenant's family " within the paragraph. (*Gammans* v. *Ekins* (1950) C.L.C. 8813 and *Dyson Holdings* v. *Fox* [1975] C.L.Y. 1909 considered): HELBY *v.* RAFFERTY, *The Times,* May 6, 1978, C.A. [*G. H.*]

1809. Rent—rent review—arbitration—extension of time. See S.I. PENSION TRUSTEES *v.* WILLIAM HUDSON, § 101.

1810. —— —— no strict compliance—whether provision directory or mandatory
[Law of Property Act 1925 (c. 20), s. 41.]
A rent revision clause in a lease specifies the machinery or guide-lines for ascertaining the open market rent, and its provisions are directory not mandatory.

A lease of shops for 21 years provided for a rent review at the end of 14 years, provided either party gave three months' notice and stated a suggested new rent with usual provisions as to arbitration in the event of non-agreement. The landlords served a notice in time but failed to suggest a new rent. The tenants took the point that the notice was invalid as the terms of the clause had not been strictly complied with. On originating summons before Graham J., it was held that, as a matter of construction, the words used in the clause were the essence of the contract. On the landlords' appeal, *held,* allowing the appeal, that the provisions requiring a statement of the suggested new rent were not of the essence of the contract, but merely part of the machinery for determining the new rent. They were directory, not mandatory, and their construction as such accorded with s. 41 of the 1925 Act. (*United Scientific Holdings* v. *Burnley Borough Council; Cheapside Land Developments* v. *Messels Service* [1977] C.L.Y. 1758 applied.)

DEAN AND CHAPTER OF CHICHESTER *v.* LENNARDS (1978) 35 P. & C.R. 309, C.A.

1811. —— —— period of statutory restriction—meaning of " fair rack-rent "
[Counter-Inflation (Business Rents) Order 1973 (S.I. No. 741), arts. 4, 14.]
A rent review clause contained in a lease made prior to the counter-inflation " rent freeze " may be enforced notwithstanding that at the date of the review rents are " frozen " pursuant to the counter-inflation policy.

A lease of business premises made in 1967 provided for an annual rental of £5,500 for the first seven years and that thereafter, at the lessor's option upon service of notice, the rent would be reviewed at a " fair rack rent " to be assessed by surveyors as if it was " payable " upon the premises being let on a seven-year term. By the review date in 1974, business rents had been " frozen " under the 1975 order. The lessee contended that by reason of the order " fair rack rent " was to be regarded as the " frozen " rent of £5,500. *Held,* allowing the lessor's appeal, that the review clause should be construed in the light of circumstances prevailing at the date of the lease; and that the surveyor or assessing the new rent could take into account the 1973 order, but was not prevented thereby from fixing a rent in excess of £5,500. (*Rawlance* v. *Croydon Corporation* [1952] C.L.Y. 1562 and *Newman* v. *Dorrington Developments* [1975] C.L.Y. 1903, distinguished.)

COMPTON GROUP *v.* ESTATES GAZETTE (1977) 36 P. & C.R. 148, C.A.

1812. —— —— " reasonable rent "—tenant's improvements

A " reasonable rent " for " demised premises " is a fine question of valuation. The provenance of any improvements to those premises can be disregarded.

A rent review clause provided that the rent should be " such sum as shall be assessed as a reasonable rent for the demised premises." The tenants contended that the valuation should take account of the fact that they themselves had improved the premises, *held*, finding for the landlords, that the question was a matter of valuation alone as to what rent was reasonable for those premises.

CUFF *v.* J. AND F. STONE PROPERTY CO. [1978] 3 W.L.R. (Note), Megarry V.-C.

1813. A " reasonable rent for the demised premises " means that rent which is reasonable for the premises as they are, taking into account improvements made by the tenant.

A rent review clause provided that the rent to be fixed was " a reasonable rent for the demised premises." The premises burnt down and were re-built, with many improvements, by the tenant. The landlord took out a summons to determine the basis on which rent should be assessed. *Held*, dismissing the tenant's appeal, Lords Wilberforce and Salmon dissenting, that " a reasonable rent for the demised premises " meant that which was reasonable for the premises (*i.e.* incorporating the improvements) and not that which it was reasonable for the tenant to pay.

PONSFORD *v.* H.M.S. AEROSOLS [1978] 3 W.L.R. 241, H.L.

1814. —— —— revision to represent " full yearly market rental "

Where a rent review clause provides for a full market rental, to be computed as the rent at which premises are worth to be let with vacant possession on the open market between a willing lessor and a willing lessee, such lessor and lessee are hypothetical parties, and any circumstances affecting the actual lessor and lessee are not to be taken into account unless they would also affect their hypothetical counterparts.

L Co. leased land and factory buildings to T Co. for 21 years. The lease contained a rent review clause enforceable after three years, the rent to be a full market rental. " Full market rental " was defined as the rent at which the premises were worth to be let with vacant possession on the open market between a willing lessor and a willing lessee for the remainder of the term on the conditions of the lease. *Held*, that the willing lessor and lessee were hypothetical persons not necessarily having any of the characteristics of their real counterparts; unaffected by personal ills such as cash-flow crises, mortgagees, the need to let or lease, or governmental pressures to maintain employment in the area. Circumstances affecting the real landlord and tenant were only relevant if they would also affect their hypothetical counterparts. (*I.R.C.* v. *Clay* [1914] 3 K.B. 466, C.A. and *Tomlinson* v. *Plymouth Argyle Football Co.* [1960] C.L.Y. 2701 applied.)

F. R. EVANS (LEEDS) *v.* ENGLISH ELECTRIC CO. (1978) 36 P. & C.R. 184, Donaldson J.

1815. —— whether new rent still inclusive

[Rent Act 1974 (c. 51), s. 5 (1).] Rent for a furnished flat registered inclusive of rates under Part VI of the 1968 Rent Act and subsequently by the 1974 Act " deemed " registered under Part IV of the 1968 Act, which provides for rent to be registered exclusive of rates, meant that the inclusive figure was not converted into an exclusive figure so as to entitle the landlord in effect to recover the rates from the tenant twice over: DOMINAL SECURITIES *v.* McLEOD, *The Times*, July 15, 1978, C.A.

1816. Rent restriction. See RENT RESTRICTION.

1817. Squatters—entitlement to let premises—obtaining by deception. See R. *v.* EDWARDS, § 564.

1818. Statutory tenancy—tenancy by succession—whether friend a member of the tenant's " family "

[Rent Act 1968 (c. 23), Sched. 1, para. 3.]

A platonic relationship between two adults living together for many years does not suffice to render them of the same "family" for the purposes of succession to a statutory tenancy.

In 1958 the defendant moved into a flat leased by an elderly widow and lived there with her until her death in 1976. Their relationship was platonic and became recognised by members of the widow's family as that of "aunt" and "nephew." After the widow's death, the defendant continued in occupation claiming to be the statutory tenant by succession, he being "a member of the original tenant's family" under Sched. 1, para. 3 to the Act. The plaintiff landlords appealed against the dismissal of their claim for possession. *Held,* allowing the appeal, that the defendant's relationship with the widow was not such as to make him a member of her family for the purposes of the Act. (*Gammans* v. *Ekins* [1950] 2 K.B. 328 and *Ross* v. *Collins* [1964] C.L.Y. 3153 applied.)

JORAM DEVELOPMENTS v. SHARRATT [1978] 2 All E.R. 948, C.A.

1819. Sub-lease—consent—reasonableness of landlords' refusal to grant

WL were tenants, by an assignment dated March 1974, of business premises with a self-contained furnished flat above, for a term of 14 years from June 1971. Under the lease the flat was only to be occupied on a furnished letting or a service tenancy basis. J had become the assignee of the reversion in November 1976. WL now wished to sub-let the flat to Mr. and Mrs. W but J refused his consent on the ground that Mr. and Mrs. W would become protected tenants which would thereby reduce the value of the premises. *Held,* J had unreasonably withheld his consent. This was not an "abnormal" sub-letting. The fact that the law had now changed was unfortunate to the landlord, but the clause had to be construed in the light of the Rent Act 1974 rather than with regard to the original intentions of the parties when the lease was granted. (*Swanson* v. *Forton* (1949) C.L.C. 5345, *Bookman* v. *Nathan* [1955] C.L.Y. 1492 approved; *Norfolk Capital* v. *Kitway* [1976] C.L.Y. 1519 and *Bickel* v. *Duke of Westminster* [1976] C.L.Y. 1518 considered): WEST LAYTON v. JOSEPH, January 26, 1978, Judge Wakley, Brentford County Ct. (*Ex rel. Richard Fernyhough, Esq., Barrister*).

1820. Tenancy—notice to quit—whether landlords exercising statutory powers

The plaintiffs, a registered housing association, were tenants of premises, part of which they sub-let to the defendants on the written understanding that such sub-tenancy was not protected and that the freeholders planned the clearance and demolition of the building by July 1978. Just before this date, the plaintiffs served a notice to quit upon the defendants, who resisted the plaintiffs' subsequent possession action on the grounds, inter alia, that the plaintiffs had, in 1975, been granted public funds from the Housing Corporation to carry out basic repairs to the flats, that plans for the demolition of the flats had since been abandoned, and that the plaintiffs, by acting in contravention of the purposes of the Housing Act 1974, were thus abusing statutory powers. *Held,* dismissing the appeal, that no such statutory powers existed, and the plaintiffs had served notice to quit merely in the course of their normal and essential activities: PEABODY HOUSING ASSOCIATION v. GREEN, 122 S.J. 862, C.A.

1821. —— whether protected—whether occupied for the purposes of a business

[Landlord and Tenant Act 1954 (c. 56), s. 23.]

Taking in lodgers and making virtually no profit out of it is not a "trade, profession or employment" within the meaning of s. 23 (2) of the Landlord and Tenant Act 1954.

Mrs. T, the tenant of a house, took lodgers, in three rooms, for which she received £14·50 rent in all. She paid for the gas and electricity and provided some food. It was agreed that the Rent Acts applied to the premises unless Pt. II of the Landlord and Tenant Act 1954 applied. *Held,* although taking in lodgers was Mrs. T's only gainful occupation, in view of the degree of the activity and its lack of commercial advantage it could not be regarded as a "trade, profession or employment." Accordingly, Mrs. T was a protected tenant under the Rent Acts. (*Abernethie* v. *A. M. and J. Kleiman* [1969] C.L.Y. 2035 applied; *Rolls* v. *Miller* (1884) 27 Ch.D. 71, C.A., *Thorn* v. *Madden* [1925] Ch. 847 and *Tendler* v. *Sproule* (1947) C.L.C. 8469 distinguished.)

LEWIS v. WELDCREST [1978] 1 W.L.R. 1107, C.A.

1822. Unlawful eviction—conduct—exemplary damages—not specifically claimed

Exemplary damages can be awarded for the unlawful eviction of a tenant.

L let a furnished maisonette to T in 1974. In October 1975, on T's application, the rent officer reduced the rent. Six days later, T returned home to find that L had got three men to invade the maisonette. They had bolted the door from the inside and thrown out all T's property, damaging some of it. A fortnight later, T obtained an injunction against L to restrain him from refusing T admission to the maisonette, L appealed to the Court of Appeal, and lost. In all, T had to sleep on the floor of a friend's house for 10 weeks. When he finally got back into the maisonette, it was dirty and disordered. T claimed damages limited to £1,000 for interference with his right to quiet enjoyment, and pleaded the circumstances. The county court judge described L's behaviour as "monstrous," and awarded £1,000 exemplary damages on the basis of trespass, although trespass was not pleaded as such. On appeal by L, *held*, dismissing the appeal, that the facts pleaded amounted to trespass, and exemplary damages could be awarded; the County Court rules did not require a claim for exemplary damages to be specifically pleaded and L's conduct justified the damages awarded. (Dicta of Lord Devlin in *Rookes* v. *Barnard* [1964] C.L.Y. 3703 and Lord Denning M.R. in *Re Vandervell's Trusts (No. 2)* [1974] C.L.Y. 3501 and *McCall* v. *Abelesz* [1976] C.L.Y. 1531 applied.)

DRANE v. EVANGELOU [1978] 1 W.L.R. 455, C.A.

BOOKS AND ARTICLES. See *post*, pp. [5], [27].

LAW REFORM

1823. Arbitration

The Commercial Court Committee, under the chairmanship of Donaldson J., have submitted a report to the Lord Chancellor recommending, inter alia, the amendment of s. 21 of the Arbitration Act 1950 and of the "case-stated" procedure. The Report is available from H.M.S.O. (Cmnd. No. 7284) [50p].

1824. Contract—interest on debts

The Law Commission has published a Report on Interest recommending that debtors should be made legally liable to pay interest on the amount they owe by imposing "statutory" interest, at the rate of 1 per cent. above the average minimum lending rate, which would start to run 28 days after the creditor has made formal demand for payment. The report is available from HMSO (Law Com. No. 88; Cmnd. 7229) [£2·10].

1825. Criminal law—mental element

The Law Commission has published its Report on the Mental Element in Crime, which examines the meaning and use of certain terms denoting mental states. The report is available from HMSO (Law Com. No. 89) [£1·60].

1826. —— sentence

The Home Secretary's Advisory Council on the Penal System has published its report entitled "Sentences of Imprisonment: A Review of Maximum Penalties." It is the first general review of the existing penalty structure for more than a century, and its main recommendation is a new approach to statutory maximum prison sentences. The report is available from HMSO [£3·75].

1827. Data protection

The Report of the Data Protection Committee, under the Chairmanship of Sir Norman Lindop, was published on December 5, 1978. The Committee recommends, that a Data Protection Authority be set up to, inter alia, prepare Codes of Practice for collecting or processing personal information, require registration of applications involving the handling of personal data, investigate complaints by data subjects against data users and hold hearings to resolve disputes. The Government will seek the news of computer users and others affected by these recommendations. The report is available from HMSO (Cmnd. 7341) [£6·00].

1828. Family law

The Law Commission have published their Third Report on Family Property: The Matrimonial Home (Co-ownership and Occupation Rights) and

Household Goods. Book One contains the Commission's detailed scheme for statutory co-ownership of the matrimonial home; Book Two is concerned with rights of occupation in the home; and Book Three recommends ways of protecting a wife or husband in the use and enjoyment of household goods. The report is available from HMSO (Law Com. No. 86) [£5·60].

1829. Gaming and wagering

The Royal Commission on Gambling has published its Final Report, which makes over 300 recommendations concerning all aspects of gambling activities. The Commission's proposals include the tightening of rules governing bingo clubs, fruit machines and casinos, the abolition of " spot-the-ball " competitions, the setting up of a new British horse-racing authority and a new national lottery for good causes. The report is available from H.M.S.O. (Cmnd. 7200) [£7·50].

1830. Law Commission's Annual Report

The Law Commission has published its 13th Annual Report for 1977–78, which outlines matters of general importance, reviews the year's progress on various law reform programmes, gives an account of work done outside such programmes and briefly draws attention to developments in the organisation and activities of the Commission. The report is available from HMSO (Law Com. No. 92) [£1·00].

1831. Statute law

The Law Commission and the Scottish Law Commission have published their Ninth Report on statute law revision, which proposes the repeal of 222 whole Acts and parts of another 136 Acts as being useless or outdated. Appendix 1 to the Report is a draft Statute Law (Repeals) Bill. The report is available from HMSO (Law Com. No. 87; Scot. Law Com. No. 48) [£1·65].

1832. —— interpretation

The Law Commission and the Scottish Law Commission have published their Report on the Interpretation Act 1889 and certain other enactments relating to the construction and operation of Acts of Parliament and other instruments. The appendix to the report contains various recommendations many of which have been given effect in the Interpretation Bill now going through Parliament. The report is available from HMSO (Law Com. No. 90; Scot. Law Com. No. 53) (Cmnd. 7235) [40p].

1833. Territorial limits

The Law Commission have published a report on the territorial and extra-territorial extent of the criminal law. This recommends a new method of measuring territorial limits, especially where territorial waters are to be covered, and makes proposals for including within the compass of the criminal law certain crimes committed at sea, such as hijacking a ship. The report is available from HMSO (Law Com. No. 91) [£1·85].

1834. Trustees and personal representatives

The Law Reform Committee have issued a Consultative Document asking for evidence on a number of points concerning the powers, rights and obligations of trustees and personal representatives. The Committee would be grateful for evidence from others besides those specifically consulted. Copies of the Consultative Document may be obtained on request from Mr. M. C. Blair, The Secretary of the Law Reform Committee, Lord Chancellor's Office, House of Lords, Westminster, S.W.1.

ARTICLES. See *post*, p. [28].

LEGAL HISTORY

ARTICLES. See *post*, p. [28].

LIBEL AND SLANDER

1835. Appeal—inability to pay costs—whether frivolous or vexatious

Three distinguished Africans were awarded libel damages totalling £66,000 against the defendant. On her appeal against the amount of damages, she admitted that she could not pay the costs if she lost. *Held*, that the appeal should not be struck out as frivolous and vexatious, and that security of £750 should be ordered for costs: OBOTE *v.* JUDITH COUNTESS OF LISTOWEL, *The Times*, May 9, 1978, C.A.

1836. Blasphemous libel—mens rea. See R. *v.* LEMON; R. *v.* GAY NEWS, § 420.

1837. Discovery of documents—privilege—extent. See LISZKAY *v.* BROUWER, § 2360.

1838. Inference—undertaking with damages—allegation of M.P.'s corruption in newspaper

The Observer newspaper and its political correspondent agreed to pay substantial damages for libel in an article which carried the headline: " Corruption: three M.P.s escape prosecution—exclusive." It was made clear in the article that Mr. Maudling was not one of the three M.P.s referred to in the headline, but the article carried a large photo of Mr. Maudling, and readers could have inferred that he was one of the M.P.s or was in a similar category: MAUDLING *v.* RAPHAEL, *The Times*, May 11, 1978, May J.

1839. Newspaper article—damages

A substantial sum was paid by way of damages to Lord Rothermere over an article in *The Sunday Times* suggesting that the management philosophy of Associated Newspapers, of which the plaintiff was chairman, had been one of waiting for the Beaverbrook Newspaper group to die, and that the failure of the plaintiff to acquire it was due to his inability to reach a firm decision: HARMSWORTH *v.* TIMES NEWSPAPERS, *The Times*, October 10, 1978, Tudor-Evans J.

1840. —— implication of hypocrisy

Mr. Michael Foot was awarded damages and costs against the *Daily Mail* who apologised for publishing an article in which it was alleged that he had received private treatment as a National Health Service patient, with the implication that he was hypocritical and insincere in his advocacy of egalitarianism: FOOT *v.* ASSOCIATED NEWSPAPERS GROUP, *The Times*, January 17, 1978, Bristow J.

1841. —— politicians

Mrs. Barbara Castle has been awarded damages for libel in articles in a newspaper which, by the heading "Parliament heads blacklist of Britain's nonattenders" next to a photograph of her, implied that she was shirking her duties: CASTLE *v.* ENGLISH, *The Times*, July 29, 1978, Milmo J.

1842. The *Daily Mail* had alleged that the eight plaintiffs were M.P.s who had absented themselves from their duties. The publishers, editor, and political correspondent now recognised that the allegations were untrue, and apologised to the plaintiffs, who had already been paid damages and costs: GRIEVE *v.* ASSOCIATED NEWSPAPERS GROUP, *The Times*, July 28, 1978, Milmo J.

1843. Right to sue—municipal corporations

[Can.] P, a municipal corporation incorporated under the provisions of the Municipal Act, commenced an action claiming the defendant television station had libelled the corporation and that the corporation's " trading and governing reputation and standing had been lowered." *Held*, on a point of law, that a municipal corporation enjoys a reputation delineated by those powers and obligations created by the Municipal Act and therefore it has the capacity to sue D for libel. (*South Hetton Coal Co.* v. *North-Eastern News Association* [1894] 1 Q.B. 133 applied; *Bognor Regis Urban District Council* v. *Campion* [1972] C.L.Y. 2032 followed): PRINCE GEORGE *v.* BRITISH COLUMBIA TELEVISION SYSTEM [1978] 3 W.W.R. 12, Brit.Col.Sup.Ct.

1844. Television programme—solicitors stated to be inefficient—damages

Miss Esther Rantzen and the B.B.C. apologised and agreed to pay substantial damages to three solicitors and a legal executive for libelling them in a programme, in stating that the firm with which they were connected was inefficient: NORTHAM *v.* BRITISH BROADCASTING CORP., *The Times*, July 14, 1978, Milmo J.

BOOKS AND ARTICLES. See *post,* pp. [6], [29].

LIMITATION OF ACTIONS

1845. Dismissal of action—relevance of previous action

[Limitation Act 1939 (c. 21), s. 2D (1) (3); Limitation Act 1975 (c. 54), s. 3.]

The fact that a first action might be struck out for delay does not mean that a second, time-barred action will not be allowed to proceed.

P issued a writ, on a personal injury claim, in 1971. Little further action took place, P believing that he had no good claim, until 1976 when, on the basis of a new report, he issued another writ for the same cause of action. On P's undertaking to discontinue the first action, Swanwick J. permitted the second one to continue. *Held,* dismissing D's appeal against that order, that P was entitled to have his right to continue tested, not against the criterion of whether the first action should be struck out for delay, but against the criteria set out in s. 2D of the Limitation Act 1939.

WALKLEY *v.* PRECISION FORGINGS [1978] 1 W.L.R. 1228, C.A.

1846. Carriage by road—C.M.R. Convention. See MULLER BATAVIER *v.* LAURENT TRANSPORT CO., § 203.

1847. Expiry of time—joinder of parties—effect of limitation. See GAWTHROP *v.* BOULTON, § 2381.

1848. Extension of time limit—personal injuries

[Limitation Act 1939 (c. 21), as amended by Limitation Act 1975 (c. 54).]

The court's discretion to extend the time limit for bringing an action for damages for personal injuries under s. 2D of the Limiation Act 1939 is unfettered; it is not confined to a residual class of exceptional cases.

Four plaintiffs in personal injury cases were granted applications by judges of the High Court to be allowed to proceed with claims that otherwise would have been statute-barred. In the first three cases, writs had been issued in time, but the solicitors had neglected to serve them in time or renew them. In each case the defendants were well aware of the claims. In the fourth case, a defendant driver had joined the tyre manufacturers as third parties. The plaintiff wished accordingly to join the tyre company as defendants, but the solicitors neglected to do so in time. All four defendants appealed. *Held,* dismissing the appeal, that the court had an unfettered discretion to extend time, and in each case there was an overwhelming case for exercising that discretion in favour of the plaintiffs; the plaintiffs would be greatly prejudiced by being statute-barred due to their solicitors' mistakes, whereas the defendants had known the nature of the claims throughout, and would not be prejudiced at all. (*Heaven* v. *Road and Rail Wagons* [1965] C.L.Y. 3252 considered; dicta in *Birkett* v. *James* [1977] C.L.Y. 2410 distinguished.)

FIRMAN *v.* ELLIS [1978] 3 W.L.R. 1, C.A.

1849. Unreasonable delay—interrogatory re previous legal advice—whether required to answer—whether relevant

[Limitation Act 1939 (c. 21), s. 2D, as inserted by Limitation Act 1975 (c. 54), s. 1.]

Where a plaintiff seeks leave to proceed under s. 2D of the 1939 Act, the court is entitled to know in general terms the nature of the legal advice given to the plaintiff in so far as it is relevant to the question of unreasonable delay.

J brought an action for negligence in respect of damage suffered seven years previously. The defence raised limitation, and the plaintiff replied that it was only a recent opinion from leading counsel that had enabled her to get legal aid to commence proceedings. The defence served interrogatories asking whether previous legal advice had been favourable or unfavourable. The plaintiff refused to answer and an appeal to the judge requiring her to answer was dismissed. On appeal, *held,* allowing the appeal, that in this case whether counsel's advice was favourable or unfavourable was relevant to the question of unreasonable delay.

JONES *v.* G. D. SEARLE & CO. [1978] 3 All E.R. 654, C.A.

ARTICLES. See *post,* pp. [29].

LOANS

1850. Moneylenders. See MONEYLENDERS.

LOCAL GOVERNMENT

1851. Alteration to areas

LOCAL GOVERNMENT AREA CHANGES (AMENDMENT) REGULATIONS 1978 (No. 247) [25p], made under the Local Government Act 1972 (c. 70), s. 67 (1) (2), Sched. 10, para. 9; operative on March 30, 1978; extends the general provisions of S.I. 1976 No. 246, in relation to alterations to local government areas, in accordance with s. 67 (1) (2) of the 1972 Act.

1852. Attendance allowance

LOCAL GOVERNMENT (ALLOWANCES) (AMENDMENT) REGULATIONS 1978 (No. 1795) [10p], made under the Local Government Act 1972 (c. 70), ss. 173, 178; operative on December 29, 1978; increase the maximum rate of attendance allowance payable to members of a local authority for the performance of an approved duty.

LOCAL GOVERNMENT (ALLOWANCES) (AMENDMENT) (No. 2) REGULATIONS 1978 (No. 1917) [10p], made under the Local Government Act 1972, ss. 173, 178; operative on January 23, 1979; increases the maximum rates of financial loss allowance payable to any member of a body to which s. 173 of the 1972 Act applies, and who is not entitled to attendance allowances for the performance of approved duties.

1853. —— meaning of " councillor "

[Local Government Act 1972 (c. 70), s. 173 (1).]

The words " any member of a local authority who is a councillor " refer to members of a local authority who are councillors of that particular authority.

H was an elected councillor of a district council. D Council appointed her as a member of a national park committee and she was by virtue of s. 177 (3) of the Act deemed to be a member of the D Council for the purposes of ss. 173 to 176 of the Act. H was not entitled to financial loss allowances in respect of her attendance at the committee meetings but claimed that being a " member of a local authority who is a councillor " she was entitled, under s. 173 (1) of the Act, to be paid an attendance allowance in respect of such meetings. *Held*, dismissing the claim, that s. 173 (1) did not include persons deemed to be members of a local authority who were only councillors of another authority.

HOPSON *v.* DEVON COUNTY COUNCIL [1978] 1 All E.R. 1205, Megarry V.-C.

1854. Boundaries

NEW FOREST AND SOUTHAMPTON (AREAS) ORDER 1978 (No. 129) [15p], made under the Local Government Act 1972 (c. 70), ss. 47, 51 (1) (2), 67 (4); operative for the purposes of art. 2 on March 6, 1978, for all other purposes operative on April 1, 1978; establishes a length of the centre for the time being of the River Trent as the boundary between the District of New Forest and the City of Southampton.

1855. —— new proposals—objective of electoral equality—ratio of electors to councillors

[Local Government Act 1972 (c. 70), Sched. 11, para. 3 (2) (3).]

The object of para. 3 (2) of Sched. 11 to the Local Government Act 1972 is to get as near as possible to " one voter one vote of equal weight "; it requires the Boundary Commission to adopt an arrangement which is as close to electoral equality " as nearly as may be," and not just " approximately " or " within reasonable range of it."

In 1975 the Boundary Commission was revising the electoral arrangements of the London Borough of Enfield, under the Local Government Act 1972. Under para. 3 (2) of Sched. 11 to the Act, having regard to any change in the number or distribution of the local government electors of the borough likely to take place within the period of five years immediately following the consideration, the ratio of the number of electors to the number of councillors to be elected was to be " as nearly as may be " the same in every ward of the borough. An assistant commissioner was appointed to carry out an investigation and report to the commission. The local authority submitted an arrangement which provided for 70 councillors; the maximum divergence from the mesne figure which produced equality in the ratio of electors to councillors was 0.15 in 1976 and 0.2 in 1981. The assistant commissioner rejected the scheme because of his decision about the size of the council, and not on the grounds of electoral equality. He went on to say that on the electoral ratio basis, the local authority's scheme was almost perfect. He chose instead a scheme providing for 66 councillors. The scheme eventually adopted was one with 66 councillors which produced a maximum divergence in the ratio of electors to councillors of 0.25 in 1976 and over 0.2 in 1981. *Held*, para. 3 (2) of Sched. 11 to the 1972 Act required the commission to adopt an arrangement whereby the ratio was "as nearly as may be" the same in every ward, not just "approximately" or "within reasonable range of it." The 66 councillor scheme was significantly inferior to the 70 councillor scheme, the mandatory requirement of para. 3 (2) (*a*) had been disregarded, and the local authority was entitled to a declaration to that effect.

ENFIELD LONDON BOROUGH COUNCIL *v*. LOCAL GOVERNMENT BOUNDARY COMMISSION FOR ENGLAND [1978] 2 All E.R. 1073, Bristow J.

1856. City of Sheffield

CITY OF SHEFFIELD (LOCAL ACT REPEAL) ORDER 1978 (No. 316) [10p], made under the Local Government (Miscellaneous Provisions) Act 1976 (c. 57), s. 81; operative on April 1, 1978; the city council have resolved that as from April 1, 1978 the provisions of Part II of the 1976 Act (hackney carriages and private hire vehicles) are to apply to Sheffield, and this order accordingly repeals the Sheffield City Council Act 1975 (c. xv).

1857. Compulsory purchase. See COMPULSORY PURCHASE.

1858. Diseases of animals. See ANIMALS.

1859. Education. See EDUCATION.

1860. Electoral divisions

Orders made under the Local Government Act 1972 (c. 70), s. 51 (1):

S.I. 1978 Nos. 43 (District of South Kesteven [15p]; 45 District of Selby [15p]; 46 (District of Mid Suffolk) [15p]; 47 (District of Teignbridge) [15p]; 48 (City of Westminster) [15p]; 49 (District of Wychavon) [15p]; 63 (Borough of Tower Hamlets) [15p]; 87 (District of Basildon) [15p]; 88 (City of Chester) [15p]; 89 (London Borough of Harrow) [15p]; 90 (District of Vale of White Horse) [15p]; 231 (District of Derwentside) [15p]; 437 (Borough of Hastings) [15p]; 482 (District of South Holland) [15p]; 610 (Borough of Sandwell) [15p]; 753 (Borough of Hove) [10p]; 990 (District of West Lindsey) [25p]; 1246 (District of Allerdale) [20p]; 1247 (Borough of Edmundsbury) [20p] 1299 (Borough of Erewash) [20p]; 1300 (Borough of Warrington) [20p]; 1356 (District of Kerries) [20p]; 1370 (District of Carrick [10p]; 1434 (District of Adur) [20p]; 1435 (District of Cotswold) [20p]; 1436 (Borough of Ipswich) [20p]; 1437 (Borough of Macclesfield) [25p]; 1438 (District of North Norfolk) [20p]; 1439 (District of Thanet) [20p]; 1465 (Borough of Copeland) [20p]; 1473 (District of Cherwell) [25p]; 1494 (District of Bolsover) [20p]; 1495 (District of Wyre Forest) [20p]; 1505 (District of Penwith) [20p]; 1552 (Borough of Chesterfield) [20p]; 1553 (Borough of Gosport) [20p]; 1591 (District of the Wrekin) [20p]; 1604 (Borough of Grimsby) [20p]; 1605 (Borough of Oldham) [25p]; 1606 (Borough of Solihull) [20p]; 1611 (District of Amber Valley) [20p]; 1612 (District of Breckland) [25p]; 1613 (City of Derby) [25p]; 1639 (Borough of Barnsley) [20p]; 1640 (District of Wokingham) [25p]; 1664 (Borough of Northampton) [20p]; 1665 (District of South Lakeland) [25p]; 1690 (City of Durham) [20p]; 1694 (Borough of Weymouth and Portland) [20p]; 1722 (Borough of Bury) [20p]; 1749 (District of Dover) [20p]; 1750 (City of Lincoln) [20p]; 1751 (District of Torridge) [20p]; 1768 (District of North East Derbyshire) [20p]; 1783 (City of St. Albans) [20p]; 1792 (Borough of Newcastle-under-Lyme) [25p]; 1793 (City of Plymouth) [20p]; 1806 (District of North Cornwall) [20p]; 1813 (Borough of Bournemouth) [20p]; 1814 (District of Hambleton) [20p]; 1841 (Borough of Christchurch) [10p]; 1842 (District of East Devon) [25p]; 1843 (District of Leominster) [30p]; 1859 (District of Easington) [20p]; 1860 (District of Forest Heath) [10p]; 1861 (District of Horsham) [20p]; 1862 (Borough of Rugby) [20p]; 1863 (Borough of Sefton) [20p]; 1864 (District of Shepway) [20p].

1861. Highways. See HIGHWAYS AND BRIDGES.

1862. Housing. See HOUSING.

1863. Lancashire County Council (General Powers) Act 1968—extension
    LANCASHIRE COUNTY COUNCIL (GENERAL POWERS) ACT 1968 (EXTENSION OF TIME) ORDER 1978 (No. 1453) [10p], made under the Lancashire County Council (General Powers) Act 1968 (c. xxix), s. 5 (3); operative on December 1, 1978; extends the powers contained in section 5 of the 1968 Act until December 31, 1988.

1864. Land drainage. See LAND DRAINAGE.

1865. Licence fees
    BERKSHIRE COUNTY COUNCIL ACT 1953 (VARIATION OF LICENCE FEES) ORDER 1978 (No. 473) [10p], made under the Local Government Act 1966 (c. 42), ss. 35 (2), 40; operative on May 1, 1978; provides for the Berkshire County Council increasing the maximum fees which may be fixed by them under s. 74 of the Berkshire County Council Act 1953 on application for the grant or renewal of licences for various purposes.
    CITY OF MANCHESTER (VARIATION OF LICENSING AND REGISTRATION FEES) ORDER 1978 (No. 844) [10p], made under the Manchester Corporation Act 1967 (c. xl), s. 43 and Sched. 1, as amended by the Manchester Corporation (General Powers) Act 1971 (c. lxvii), s. 23 (3); operative on September 1, 1978; amends the provisions of three local Acts in force in Manchester so as to increase the fees or maximum fees which the Manchester City Council may charge under those provisions in respect of the licensing of brokers, and dealers in secondhand goods, the registration of entertainment clubs and the licensing of street trading.

1866. Local authorities
    LOCAL AUTHORITIES (ARMORIAL BEARINGS) ORDER 1978 (No. 1025) [10p], made under the Local Government Act 1972 (c. 70), s. 247; operative on August 21, 1978; confers on the local authorities specified in the Schedule the right to bear and use the armorial bearings formerly borne and used by the local authorities specified in the Schedule.

1867. Local commissioner—complaint—jurisdiction
    The mother of children taken into care complained of various injustices suffered by her. The council sought an order to restrain the investigation by the local Ombudsman. *Held,* no specific complaint of maladministration was necessary. The Commissioner could investigate all complaints. The only limit on the Commissioner was that he must not arrive at a conclusion hostile to the local authority based upon a finding that there was a faulty or wrong decision unless it was linked to some other act of maladministration: R. *v.* LOCAL COMMISSIONER FOR ADMINISTRATION FOR NORTH AND NORTH-EAST AREA OF ENGLAND, *ex p.* BRADFORD CITY METROPOLITAN COUNCIL [1978] J.P.L. 767, C.A.

1868. Local Government Act 1972—miscellaneous provisions
    LOCAL AUTHORITIES ETC. (MISCELLANEOUS PROVISION) ORDER 1978 (No. 440) [25p], made under the Local Government Act 1972 (c. 70), s. 254 (1) (*a*), 2 (*a*), (*c*), and the London Government Act 1963 (c. 33), s. 84 (1) (*a*), (2) (*a*); operative on May 8, 1978; makes further provision incidental, consequential, transitional and supplementary to the 1972 Act.

1869. Local Government Act 1974—commencement
    LOCAL GOVERNMENT ACT 1974 (COMMENCEMENT No. 3) ORDER 1978 (No. 1583 (C. 45)) [10p], made under the Local Government Act 1974 (c. 7), s. 43 (2), (3); operative on April 1, 1979; brings into force part of Sched. 8.

1870. Local Government Act 1978 (c. 39)
    This Act amends the Local Government Act 1974 with respect to Local Commissioners' investigations.
    S. 1 amends the Local Government Act 1974, s. 31, and the Local Govern-

ment (Scotland) Act 1975, s. 29, so as to empower authorities to incur expenditure to remedy injustices caused by maladministration; s. 2 gives the short title.

The Act received the Royal Assent on July 20, 1978, and came into force on that date.

1871. Local Government (Scotland) Act 1978 (c. 4)

This Act amends the law relating to the valuation and rating of land and heritages in Scotland occupied by certain utilities and bodies; makes further provision with respect to payments to the Commissioner for Local Administration in Scotland and his officers: postpones the repeal of the Burgh Police (Scotland) Acts 1892 to 1911 and of certain local statutory provisions; and makes minor amendments to the Countryside (Scotland) Act 1967 and the Local Government (Scotland) Act 1973.

S. 1 amends s. 6 of the Local Government (Scotland) Act 1975; s. 2 particularises the lands and heritages to which s. 6 of the Local Government Act 1975 applies; s. 3 contains transitional provisions; s. 4 provides for payments to the Commissioner for Local Administration and his officers; s. 5 postpones the repeal of the Burgh Police (Scotland) Acts 1892 to 1911 and certain local statutory provisions; s. 6 allows for extra expenses resulting from the provisions of the Act to be defrayed out of funds provided by Parliament; s. 7 contains the short title, and extends the Act to Scotland only.

The Act received the Royal Assent on March 23, and came into force on that date except for para. 2 of the Schedule which came into force on January 1, 1979.

1872. Local enactments

CITY OF EXETER (LOCAL ACT REPEALS) ORDER 1978 (No. 651) [10p], made under the Local Government (Miscellaneous Provisions) Act 1976 (c. 57), s. 81; operative on June 1, 1978; provides for the application of Pt. II of the 1976 Act to the district of Exeter.

CITY OF MANCHESTER (LOCAL ACTS REPEALS) ORDER 1978 (No. 739) [20p], made under the Local Government (Miscellaneous Provisions) Act 1976, s. 81; operative on June 25, 1978; repeals the provisions of four local Acts that are specified because the Manchester City Council have adopted the provisions of Pt. II of the 1976 Act.

1873. Locus standi—tree preservation order—breach. See KENT COUNTY COUNCIL *v.* BATCHELOR (No. 2), § 2910.

1874. London. See LONDON.

1875. National health service. See NATIONAL HEALTH.

1876. Northern Ireland. See NORTHERN IRELAND.

1877. Pensions. See PENSIONS AND SUPERANNUATION.

1878. Powers—housing—possession. See CANNOCK CHASE COUNCIL *v.* KELLY, § 1570.

1879. Public health. See PUBLIC HEALTH.

1880. Rating. See RATING AND VALUATION.

1881. Refuse Disposal (Amenity) Act 1978 (c. 3)

This Act consolidates certain enactments relating to abandoned vehicles and other refuse.

S. 1 places a duty upon local authorities to provide places where refuse may be deposited, at all reasonable times, free of charge, by any person; s. 2 makes unauthorised dumping a summary offence, and attaches penalties thereto; s. 3 places a duty on local authorities to remove any vehicle abandoned on their land in the open air, or on a highway; s. 4 empowers a local authority to dispose of any vehicle coming into its custody by operation of s. 3, and makes provision for owners' claims; s. 5 directs that expenses incurred by an authority under these provisions may be recovered as a debt from any persons responsible; s. 6 covers the removal and disposal of other abandoned refuse; s. 7 concerns the authorisation for compulsory acquisition by an authority of any land needed for the purposes of the Act; s. 8 confers certain powers of entry, extends provisions for the service of notices and the furnishing of information, upon authorities in carrying out the purposes of this Act; s. 9 deals with the Secretary of State's power to extend this Act to the Scilly Isles; s. 10 covers the method by which the Act will be implemented; s. 11 is the interpretation section; s. 12 makes certain consequential amendments, repeals and savings; s. 13 contains the short title, and provides that the Act shall not extend to Northern Ireland.

The Act received the Royal Assent on March 23, 1978, and came into force on April 23, 1978, with the exceptions of ss. 1 (8), 4 (2) and 6 (8), which will come into force on days to be appointed by the Secretary of State.

1882. Rent. See RENT RESTRICTION.

1883. Reorganisation—compensation—alternative employment—whether reasonably comparable

[Local Government (Compensation) Regulations 1974 (S.I. 1974 No. 463), regs. 2 (2), 7 (i) (a) (f) (i) (4), 11 (i) (a) (e) (ii) (2), 39.]

Part-time employments must be considered together in determining whether alternative employment offered is " comparable."

H held two part-time posts with a water authority. As a result of a reorganisation, those employments ceased. Alternative offers of employment made to him did not compensate him for the loss of one of the part-time posts. The Industrial Tribunal disregarded that fact in dismissing his appeal against the refusal of the authority to pay compensation for loss of employment to him. *Held*, allowing his appeal, that (i) the two part-time posts should have been considered together in determining what was the lost employment so that the loss of one of the part-time employments ought not to have been disregarded; (ii) the loss of employment was attributable to the Water Act 1973 since it arose from a reorganisation made necessary by it, so that compensation was payable.

HARPER *v.* NORTH WEST WATER AUTHORITY (1978) 76 L.G.R. 631, Forbes J.

1884. —— —— loss of employment—whether " attributable " to 1972 Act

[Local Government Act 1972 (c. 70), s. 259 (1); Local Government (Compensation) Regulations 1974 (S.I. 1974 No. 463), regs. 7 (1), 11 (1).]

Compensation for loss of employment is only payable under s. 259 (1) of the Local Government Act 1972 where the operation of the Act, or a subordinate instrument, itself contributes to the loss of employment.

M was employed as manager of an airport. In the 1974 reorganisation of local government areas, a new authority became responsible for the airport and, for financial reasons, agreed to various changes in the running of the airport. M became redundant and applied for compensation. The tribunal dismissed the claim; Griffiths J. allowed the applicant's appeal. *Held*, on appeal by the new council that compensation under s. 259 (1) of the Act was only payable where the operation of the Act or instrument contributed to loss, not where, as here, the loss of employment was due to a voluntary change in administrative policy.

MALLETT *v.* RESTORMEL BOROUGH COUNCIL [1978] I.C.R. 725, C.A.

1885. [Local Government Act 1972 (c. 70), s. 259 (1); Local Government (Compensation) Regulations 1974 (S.I. No. 463), reg. 4 (1).]

Loss of employment is " attributable to " the provisions of the Local Government Act 1972 only if there is some causal connection between those provisions and the loss of employment.

A was the town clerk of a local borough council. When local government was reorganised pursuant to the provisions of the Local Government Act 1972, he was made chief executive of the new district council. After he had occupied that post for a year, the new council reviewed its operations and, in the interests of economy, dispensed with his post. A applied for compensation on the ground that his loss of employment was " attributable to " the provisions of the Local Government Act 1972, under reg. 4 (1) of the Local Government (Compensation) Regulations 1974. The district council refused his claim. An industrial tribunal and the High Court dismissed his application on the ground that his loss of employment was due solely to this council's change of policy in its management structure. On appeal by A to the Court of Appeal, *held*, that although A would not have held the post of chief executive but for the 1972 Act which created the council which employed him, his loss of employment was not due to the Act but to the council's change of policy. (*Mallett* v. *Restormel Borough Council* [1978] C.L.Y. 1884 considered.)

WALSH v. ROTHER DISTRICT COUNCIL [1978] 3 All E.R. 881, C.A.

1886. Scilly Isles
ISLES OF SCILLY ORDER 1978 (No. 1844) [40p], made under the Local Government Act 1972 (c. 70), ss. 256, 266 (2); operative on February 1, 1979; contains provisions applying the 1972 Act to the Scilly Isles and for the constitution of the Council of the Isles of Scilly.

1887. Sewerage. See PUBLIC HEALTH.

1888. Shops. See SHOPS.

1889. Town and country planning. See TOWN AND COUNTRY PLANNING.

1890. Water. See WATER AND WATERWORKS.

ARTICLES. See *post*, p. [29].

LONDON
1891. Housing
LONDON BOROUGH OF HARROW (TRANSFER OF HOUSING ACCOMMODATION ETC.) ORDER 1978 (No. 240) [25p], made under the London Government Act 1963 (c. 33), s. 23 (3); operative on April 1, 1978; gives effect to the terms agreed between Harrow Council and the Borough of Hertsmere for the transfer of housing accommodation to the latter council.

LONDON BOROUGH OF HAVERING (TRANSFER OF HOUSING ACCOMMODATION ETC.) ORDER 1978 (No. 763) [20p], made under the London Government Act 1963, s. 23 (3); operative on July 1, 1978; provides for the transfer of housing accommodation from the Borough of Havering to the District Council of Basildon.

1892. Police—pay. See § 2306.

1893. Town and country planning
TOWN AND COUNTRY PLANNING (LOCAL PLANNING AUTHORITIES IN GREATER LONDON) REGULATIONS 1978 (No. 602) [25p], made under the Town and Country Planning Act 1971 (c. 78), s. 287, Sched. 3, paras. 3, 7; operative on May 19, 1978; re-enact with amendments S.I. 1965 No. 679, S.I. 1967 No. 430 and S.I. 1974 No. 450; prescribe the classes of development in respect of which the Greater London Council are the local planning authority for the purposes of the 1971 Act.

MAGISTERIAL LAW
1894. Adoption. See MINORS.

1895. Appeal—election of court—leave to appeal out of time
[Magistrates' Courts Act 1952 (c. 55), s. 87 (4).] The defendant was convicted in his absence by a magistrates' court of an offence under the Air Navigation Order. Two days within the time limit for appeal, the defendant gave notice of appeal to the Crown Court and simultaneously required the justices to state a case for the Divisional Court. After the expiry of time for appeal, the requirement to state a case was withdrawn, and the defendant sought to continue with his appeal to the Crown Court. On an application to the Crown Court for leave to appeal out of time, *held*, s. 87 (4) of the Magistrates' Courts Act 1952 was designed to prevent a dissatisfied defendant from seeking to appeal to the Divisional Court, and then changing his mind and appealing instead to the Crown Court. The defendant must make a clear election of the court to which he will appeal. To seek simultaneously to appeal to both courts was no election. Accordingly, s. 87 (4) did not operate to debar the defendant from appealing to the Crown Court. The court would therefore exercise its discretion and give the

defendant leave to appeal out of time: KIRK v. CIVIL AVIATION AUTHORITY, May 16, 1978, Judge Clarke, Exeter Crown Ct. (*Ex rel. J. P. Maurice, Esq., Barrister.*)

1896. Binding over—magistrates' powers

Magistrates bound X over for 12 months in the sum of £100, and ordered him to keep away from a certain nightclub for a year. He had not been convicted of any offence. *Held*, quashing the orders, that (1) on the evidence before the Crown Court, there was no real apprehension that a breach of the peace was likely to be committed by X; (2) justices' ancient power to bind over to keep the peace was general, and did not permit particular prohibitions more suitably dealt with by injunction or other process: LISTER v. MORGAN [1978] Crim.L.R. 292, Birmingham Crown Ct.

1897. Certiorari—burden of establishing case

C applied for certiorari to quash convictions of exceeding speed limits. C said that the chairman of the bench had said " we believe both witnesses " (*i.e.* the prosecution witness and C), and " It is most difficult to decide cases where the evidence is directly opposite. In the previous case we gave the benefit of the doubt to the defence; this case we give it the other way." The chairman stated in her affidavit that although she could not recall her exact words, the Bench had been satisfied that the charge was proved. *Held*, dismissing the application, that it was an almost inflexible rule of the Divisional Court that it would not attempt to dispose of cases by certiorari when a conflict of evidence on fact was involved: R. v. ABINGDON (COUNTY) MAGISTRATES' COURT, ex p. CLIFFORD [1978] Crim.L.R. 165, D.C.

1898. Children and young persons

MAGISTRATES' COURTS (CHILDREN AND YOUNG PERSONS) (AMENDMENT) RULES 1978 (No. 869) (L. 23)) [50p], made under the Justices of the Peace Act 1949 (c. 101), s. 15, as extended by the Magistrates' Courts Act 1952 (c. 55), s. 122 and the Children and Young Persons Act 1969 (c. 54), ss. 18 (2) (*b*), 32B; operative on July 17, 1978; amends the 1970 Rules to take account of the coming into force of ss. 34, 36 and 37 of the Criminal Law Act 1977, and to take account of the Bail Act 1976.

1899. Committal proceedings—criminal libel—evidence of prosecutor's bad character —whether admissible

At committal proceedings for criminal libel evidence of the general bad character of the prosecutor is not admissible.

The defendants were alleged in a private prosecution to have committed criminal libel. At the committal proceedings the magistrate ruled that evidence as to the general bad reputation of the prosecutor was inadmissible during such proceedings. The defendants applied to set aside the committal orders made. *Held*, refusing the application, that such evidence, like the statutory defence of justification, became relevant only at trial and was not admissible in committal proceedings (*R.* v. *Carden* (1879) 5 Q.B.D. 1, applied).

R. v. WELLS STREET STIPENDIARY MAGISTRATE, ex p. DEAKIN [1978] 1 W.L.R. 1008, D.C.

1900. —— joinder of defendants—whether valid

Magistrates may hold a joint committal of two or more defendants upon different charges which could properly be tried together on indictment, notwithstanding the defendant's objections to such procedure.

A magistrates' court decided to hold joint committal proceedings in respect of a charge against the applicant of wilfully illtreating a child, and a charge against the child's father of its murder. The applicant sought to restrain the magistrate from so acting. *Held*, refusing the application, that the proposed course accorded with established practice and that there was no statutory prohibition relating thereto. (*R.* v. *Assim* [1966] C.L.Y. 2499 applied; *Aldus* v. *Watson* [1973] C.L.Y. 2085 considered.)

R. v. CAMBERWELL GREEN STIPENDIARY MAGISTRATE, ex p. CHRISTIE [1978] 2 W.L.R. 794, D.C.

1901. —— mandamus—whether available during proceedings

The High Court has no jurisdiction to issue mandamus in respect of the conduct of committal proceedings until such proceedings are concluded.

During the course of committal proceedings the examining magistrate refused to allow cross-examination by the defence upon a certain subject. The proceedings were adjourned and the defendant applied for an order of mandamus directing the magistrate to admit such cross-examination. *Held*, refusing the application, that the court had no jurisdiction until determination of the committal proceedings (*R.* v. *Carden* (1879) 5 Q.B.D. 1, followed).

R. *v.* WELLS STREET STIPENDIARY MAGISTRATE, *ex p.* SEILLON [1978] 1 W.L.R. 1002, D.C.

1902. Criminal Law Act 1977—commencement. See § 450.

1903. Domestic Proceedings and Magistrates' Courts Act 1978 (c. 22)

This Act provides anew for matrimonial proceedings in magistrates' courts, and amends enactments relating to other proceedings so as to eliminate certain differences between the law relating to those proceedings and the law relating to matrimonial proceedings in magistrates' courts.

Pt. I deals with matrimonial proceedings in magistrates' courts: s. 1 sets out the grounds of application for financial provision; s. 2 confers powers upon the court to make orders for financial provision; s. 3 stipulates matters to which the court is to have regard in exercising its powers under s. 2; s. 4 limits the duration of orders for financial provision for a party to a marriage; s. 5 states the age limit for making orders for financial provision for children and the duration of such orders; s. 6 relates to orders for payments agreed upon by the parties; s. 7 concerns the powers of the court where parties are living apart by agreement; s. 8 deals with orders for the custody of children; s. 9 states the powers of the court in providing supervision of children; s. 10 defines the court's powers to commit children to the care of a local authority; s. 11 makes provision for maintenance for children where orders under ss. 8–10 are made; s. 12 contains supplementary provisions in respect of the court's powers under ss. 8–10; s. 13 governs disputes between persons holding parental rights and duties jointly; s. 14 relates to access to children by grandparents; s. 15 sets out the principle on which questions relating to the custody and upbringing of children are to be decided; s. 16 confers powers on the court to make orders for the protection of a party to a marriage or a child of the family; s. 17 contains supplementary provisions with respect to s. 16; s. 18 confers powers of arrest where s. 16 orders are breached; s. 19 deals with interim orders; s. 20 provides for the variation, revival and revocation of orders for periodical payments; s. 21 provides for the variation and revocation of orders relating to the custody of children; s. 22 permits the variation of instalments of lump sums; s. 23 contains supplementary provisions in respect of variations and revocations of orders; s. 24 governs proceedings by or against a person outside England and Wales for variation or revocation of orders; s. 25 deals with the effect on certain orders of parties living together; s. 26 relates to reconciliation; s. 27 provides for orders to be refused where cases are more suitable for the High Court; s. 28 stipulates the powers of the High Court and county courts in relation to certain orders made under Pt. I; s. 29 deals with appeals; s. 30 makes provisions as to jurisdiction and procedure; s. 31 directs the constitution of courts; s. 32 concerns the enforcement of orders for payment of money; s. 33 relates to the enforcement of orders for custody; s. 34 restricts the removal of a child from England and Wales; s. 35 provides for the making of orders for repayment, in certain cases, of sums paid after the cessation of an order by reason of remarriage.

Pt. II amends the Guardianship of Minors Acts 1971 and 1973: s. 36 clarifies the meaning of custody in the Guardianship of Minors Acts 1971 and 1973; s. 37 makes further provisions with regard to custody orders; s. 38 amends the provisions relating to age-limits on orders for custody; s. 39 restricts the removal of minors from England and Wales; s. 40 permits access to minors by grandparents; s. 41 extends the powers of the court to make orders for maintenance; s. 42 relates to the duration of maintenance orders; s. 43 makes further provision as to orders for maintenance; s. 44 deals with maintenance for children in the case of local authorities; s. 45 concerns interim orders: s. 46 states the effect on certain orders of parents living together; s. 47 defines the jurisdiction and powers of magistrates' courts; s. 48 specifies the orders made on appeal from a magistrates' court.

Pt. III amends other enactments relating to domestic proceedings; s. 49 affects the jurisdiction of magistrates' courts; s. 50 relates to the contents of affiliation orders; s. 51 specifies the persons entitled to payments under affiliation orders; s. 52 stipulates an age limit for affiliation orders, and their duration; s. 53 provides for the revocation and variation of affiliation orders; s. 54 affects the date of operation of orders under Pt. I of the Maintenance Orders (Reciprocal Enforcement) Act 1972 (" the 1972 Act "); s. 55 interprets Pt. I of the 1972 Act as respects Scotland; s. 56 concerns magistrates' courts having jurisdiction to hear applications for affiliation orders under s. 27 of the 1972 Act; s. 57 deals with complaints by spouses in convention countries for recovery in England and Wales of maintenance from their other spouse; s. 58 relates to complaints by former spouses in convention countries for recovery in England and Wales of maintenance from another spouse; s. 59 covers complaints by former wives in convention countries for recovery in Northern Ireland of maintenance from former husbands; s. 60 further amends the maintenance Orders (Reciprocal Enforcement) Act 1972 as respects Scotland; s. 61 covers the eligibility for Legal Aid in Scotland for proceedings under the aforesaid Act; s. 62 amends s. 4 of the Matrimonial Causes Act 1973; s. 63 amends s. 27 of the same Act; s. 64 extends the court's powers to make orders for maintenance and access under s. 34 of the Children Act 1975; s. 65 further provides for the maintenance of a child subject to a custodianship order; s. 66 affects the variation and revocation of orders for periodical payments; s. 67 makes provisions relating to lump sums; s. 68 amends s. 36 of the Children Act 1975; s. 69 relates to custodianship orders made on application under Pt. I of this Act or under the Guardianship of Minors Act 1971; s. 70 restricts the removal of a child from England and Wales; s. 71 deals with orders made on appeal from a magistrates' court; s. 72 alters the age limits for certain orders made on refusal of adoption order; s. 73 directs hearing in private of adoption proceedings; s. 74 makes provisions affecting Convention adoption orders.

Pt. IV amends Pt. II of the Magistrates' Court Act 1952: s. 75 confers jurisdiction to deal with complaints; s. 76 extends the power to vary orders for periodical payments; s. 77 makes provision as to payments required to be made to a child, etc.; s. 78 sets out penalties for disobeying orders other than for the payment of money; s. 79 re-defines " domestic proceedings "; s. 80 defines " domestic courts "; s. 81 stipulates people who may be present during the hearing of domestic proceedings; s. 82 restricts reporting by newspapers of domestic proceedings; s. 83 affects probation officer's reports on the means of parties.

Pt. V contains supplementary provisions: s. 84 relates to giving reasons for decisions in domestic proceedings; s. 85 gives directions where periodical payments are payable by one person under more than one order; s. 86 amends the Administration of Justice Act 1964; s. 87 relates to expenses; s. 88 is the interpretation section; s. 89 contains transitional provisions, amendments, repeals and provides for commencement; s. 90 gives the short title, and directs that, except for certain provisions, the Act does not extend to Scotland and Northern Ireland.

The Act received the Royal Assent on June 30, 1978, and will come into force on a date or dates to be appointed. Ss. 86, 88 (5), 89 (except subs. (2) (a)), 90, Scheds. 1, 3 (part) came into force on July 18, 1978.

1904. —— commencement

DOMESTIC PROCEEDINGS AND MAGISTRATES' COURTS ACT 1978 (COMMENCEMENT NO. 1) ORDER 1978 (No. 997 (C. 25)) [10p], made under the Domestic Proceedings and Magistrates' Courts Act 1978 (c. 22), s. 89 (3); operative forthwith; brings into force ss. 86, 88 (5), 89 save for subs. 2 (a), 90, Scheds. 1 and 3 in so far as they relate to s. 2.

DOMESTIC PROCEEDINGS AND MAGISTRATES' COURTS ACT 1978 (COMMENCEMENT NO. 2) ORDER 1978 (No. 1489 (C. 42)) [20p], made under the Domestic

Proceedings and Magistrates' Courts Act 1978, s. 89 (3); operative on November 20, 1978; brings into force ss. 73, 74, 87, 89 (2) (*a*), Sched. 2, paras. 17, 18, 19 (*b*) (*c*), 45 (*b*), 49–53, Sched. 3 in part.

1905. Evidence—fingerprints—discretion to order taking

[Magistrates' Courts Act 1952 (c. 52), s. 40.] D, who had been arrested for unlawful damage, objected to an order under s. 40 of the 1952 Act that his fingerprints should be taken, on the ground that such evidence was equivalent to an oral or written confession. The justices stated a case for the High Court's opinion without concluding the case. *Held*, that (1) justices had a discretion to order fingerprints of persons over 14, under s. 40, whenever they saw fit and the discretion had been exercised properly; (2) cases should be concluded by justices before being sent to the High Court on appeal: GEORGE *v.* COOMBE [1978] Crim.L.R. 47, D.C.

1906. Fines

The Home Office have published Research Study No. 46, " Fines in Magistrates' Courts." This is the result of a survey done on the general level of fines imposed for indictable offences, and suggests possible economic, rather than statutory, reasons for their apparent low level. It also gives information about the proportion of fines remaining unpaid, and contains detailed analyses of fines imposed for specific indictable offences. The study will be available from HMSO.

1907. Food and drugs. See FOOD AND DRUGS.

1908. Forms

MAGISTRATES' COURTS (FORMS) (AMENDMENT) RULES 1978 (No. 146 (L.1)) [75p], made under the Justices of the Peace Act 1949 (c. 101), s. 15, as extended by the Magistrates' Courts Act 1952 (c. 55), s. 122 and the Bail Act 1976 (c. 63), s. 5 (1); operative on April 17, 1978; amend S.I. 1968 No. 1919 in consequence of the Bail Act 1976 coming into force.

MAGISTRATES' COURTS (FORMS) (AMENDMENT) (No. 2) RULES 1978 (No. 757 (L. 18)) [30p], made under the Justices of the Peace Act 1949, s. 15 as extended by the Magistrates' Courts Act 1952, s. 122; operative on July 17, 1978; amend S.I. 1968 No. 1919 in consequence of the coming into force of certain provisions of Pt. III of the Criminal Law Act 1977.

1909. Gaming. See GAMING AND WAGERING.

1910. Highways. See HIGHWAYS AND BRIDGES.

1911. Indictable offences. See CRIMINAL LAW.

1912. Information—amendment—immaterial surplusage in summons

[Magistrates' Courts Act 1952 (c. 55), s. 100; Road Traffic Act 1972 (c. 20), s. 9 (3).]

Words in an information which are mere surplusage and do not mislead the defendant may be disregarded.

The defendant was arrested for driving while unfit through drink and at the police station he failed to provide a duly requested laboratory specimen. He was summoned for failing to provide such specimen " being a person who had been in charge of a motor vehicle." The justices found all the constituent elements of the offence under s. 9 (3) to be proved but dismissed the information on the grounds that the wording of the summons, inasmuch as it referred to the defendant being " in charge," was incorrect, the prosecutor having declined their invitation to amend the summons by deletion. *Held*, allowing the prosecutor's appeal, that the words were mere surplusage and therefore irrelevant; that since all the ingredients of the offence were found to be proved, the justices would be directed to convict (*Commissioner of Police for the Metropolis* v. *Curran* [1975] C.L.Y. 2943 applied).

ROBERTS *v.* GRIFFITHS [1978] R.T.R. 362, D.C.

1913. —— continuing period—whether bad for duplicity

[Town and Country Planning Act 1971 (c. 78), s. 89 (5).]

An information alleging breach of an enforcement notice since a certain date, alleges a separate offence each day since that date, and is therefore void for duplicity.

In 1975 the Council preferred an information against D that he had, since January 8, 1972, used land in contravention of an enforcement notice, and D was convicted. On appeal by D, *held*, allowing the appeal, that as the information charged more than one offence, it was void for duplicity, and the conviction must be quashed. (*Ex p. Burnby* [1901] 2 K.B. 458, D.C. not followed.)

PARRY v. FOREST OF DEAN DISTRICT COUNCIL (1976) 34 P. & C.R. 209, D.C.

1914. —— whether defective—offences misdescribed

D was charged with offences under the Town and Country Planning Act 1971, s. 89 (5). One information alleged contravention of an enforcement notice requiring discontinuance of use for sale and supply of motor vehicles, the contravention being use as a store for cars. The other information alleged contravention of a notice prohibiting use as a store, the contravention being use for sale of vehicles. *Held*, allowing D's appeal against convictions, that both informations were defective, one not complying with the enforcement notices and the other not disclosing any offence: DRAKES v. COLEY [1978] Crim.L.R. 493, D.C.

1915. Judicial review—justices' ruling on admissibility of evidence—adjournment—High Court without jurisdiction—correct procedure

At B's trial justices refused to admit evidence relating to other charges as similar fact evidence. The case was adjourned and the prosecution applied to the Divisional Court for a judicial review of the ruling. *Held*, that the trial should have continued and the prosecution should then have appealed by way of case stated in the event of acquittal. The court had no jurisdiction in the matter as the case was still pending (*R. v. Carden* (1879) 5 Q.B.D. 1 applied): R. v. ROCHFORD JUSTICES, *ex p.* BUCK [1978] Crim.L.R. 492, D.C.

1916. Jurisdiction—licensing application—not " an extension of an industrial tribunal "

[Licensing Act 1964 (c. 26), s. 8.] A licensee was dismissed, and the managing director of the company owning the premises applied under s. 8 of the Licensing Act 1964 for a protection order. The justices refused the application since they did not wish to prejudice the licensee's application for reinstatement, to be made on the ground of unfair dismissal. *Held*, that the justices had misdirected themselves, and should have confined themselves to their duties under the Licensing Act; they should not have acted as " an extension of the industrial tribunal ": R. v. MELKSHAM JUSTICES, *ex p.* COLLINS, *The Times*, April 10, 1978, D.C.

1917. Justices

JUSTICES OF THE PEACE (SIZE AND CHAIRMANSHIP OF BENCH) (AMENDMENT) RULES 1978 (No. 1163 (L. 27)) [20p], made under the Justices of the Peace Act 1949 (c. 101), s. 13 as modified by the Administration of Justice Act 1964 (c. 42), s. 33 and as amended by the Justices of the Peace Act 1968 (c. 69), s. 3 and the Administration of Justice Act 1977 (c. 38), s. 21; operative on October 1, 1978; amends S.I. 1964 No. 1107 with regard to the method of election of chairmen and one or more deputy chairmen of the justices for a petty sessions area.

1918. Justices' clerks

JUSTICES' CLERKS (AMENDMENT) RULES 1978 (No. 754 (L. 17)) [10p], made under the Justices of the Peace Act 1949 (c. 101), s. 15 as extended by the Justices of the Peace Act 1968 (c. 69), s. 5; operative on July 17, 1978; amend S.I. 1970 No. 231 so as to provide that a justices' clerk may do those things which a single justice of the peace may do under ss. 24 (4A), 44A (3) of the Criminal Justice Act 1967.

1919. Justices of the Peace Acts—compensation

JUSTICES OF THE PEACE ACT 1949 (COMPENSATION) REGULATIONS 1978 (No. 1682) [£1·00], made under the Justices of the Peace Act 1949 (c. 101), s. 42, as extended by the Administration of Justice Act 1964 (c. 42), s. 32, and as amended by the Local Government Act 1972 (c. 70), Sched. 27, para. 12, and by the Superannuation Act 1972 (c. 11), s. 24; operative on December 20, 1978; provide for the payment of compensation to or in respect of justices' clerks and their assistants who suffer loss of office or loss or diminution of emoluments which is attributable to reorganisation.

1920. Licensing—fees. See § 1740.

1921. —— renewal application—grant of new licence—jurisdiction of justices
W was the holder of a music and dancing licence granted under s. 51 of the Public Health Acts Amendment Act 1890. He applied to the licensing justices for the renewal of the licence. The justices instead granted a new licence subject to a condition as to the hours of user which was materially different to, and more limited than, the condition concerning hours of user contained in the current licence. W appealed against the imposition of that condition. *Held,* an applicant for the renewal of an existing licence was seeking no more than a precise repetition of what he had had before. Since W was merely seeking the renewal of his licence, the justices had no jurisdiction on that application to grant him something substantially different from what he had had before by imposing a new condition. That result could only be achieved by instructing the applicant to make an application for a new licence. Further, the justices had no jurisdiction on an application for a renewal of a licence to grant a new licence. The appeal would therefore be allowed. (*Marsden* v. *Birmingham Licensing Justices* [1975] C.L.Y. 2057 followed; dictum of Lord Cockburn C.J. in *Marwick* v. *Codlin* (1874) L.R. 9 Q.B. at 514 applied): WOOD v. ST. HELENS LICENSING JUSTICES, August 15, 1978, Judge Temple, Liverpool Crown Ct. (*Ex rel. Marilyn Mornington, Barrister*).

1922. Magistrates' Courts rules
MAGISTRATES' COURTS (AMENDMENT) (NO. 2) RULES 1978 (No. 758 (L.19)) [20p], made under the Justices of the Peace Act 1949 (c. 101), s. 15 as extended by the Magistrates' Courts Act 1952 (c. 55), s. 122; operative on July 17, 1978; amend S.I. 1968 No. 1920 in consequence of the coming into force of certain provisions of Pt. III of the Criminal Law Act 1977.

1923. Matrimonial causes. See DIVORCE AND MATRIMONIAL CAUSES.

1924. Northern Ireland. See NORTHERN IRELAND.

1925. Petty sessional divisions
PETTY SESSIONAL DIVISIONS (NOTTINGHAMSHIRE) ORDER 1978 (No. 644) [20p], made under the Justices of the Peace Act 1949 (c. 101), s. 18 (1); as amended by the Local Government Act 1972 (c. 70), Sched. 27, para. 6; operative immediately for the purposes of para. 2 to the Sched., otherwise operative on June 1, 1978; provides for the combination of the divisions of Mansfield (Borough) and Mansfield (County) to form the new division of Mansfield and the combination of the divisions of Newark and Southwell to form the new division of Newark and Southwell.
PETTY SESSIONAL DIVISIONS (DERBYSHIRE) ORDER 1978 (No. 671) [25p], made under the Justices of the Peace Act 1949, s. 18 (1) as amended by the Local Government Act 1972, Sched. 27, para. 6; operative on July 1, 1978 save for Sched. 3, para. 2 which is operative immediately; provides for the reorganisation of the petty sessional divisions of Alfreton, Ashbourne, Bakewell, Belper, Derby, Derby County, Appletree, Matlock and South Derbyshire.
PETTY SESSIONAL DIVISIONS (GWYNEDD) ORDER 1978 (No. 777) [20p], made under the Justices of the Peace Act 1949, s. 18 (1) as amended by the Local Government Act 1972, Sched. 27, para. 6; operative on July 1, 1978 save for Sched. 1, para. 2 to the Order which is operative immediately; provides for the petty sessional divisions of Caernarvon and Gwyrfai to be combined to form a new petty sessional division of Caernarvon and Gwyrfai.
PETTY SESSIONAL DIVISIONS (CAMBRIDGESHIRE) ORDER 1978 (No. 1124) [25p], made under the Justices of the Peace Act 1949, s. 18, as amended by the Local Government Act 1972, Sched. 27, para. 6; operative on September 1, 1978, save for reg. 2 which is operative forthwith; provides for the abolition of the petty sessional divisions of Huntingdon and Norman Cross, Hurstingstone, Ramsey, Soke of Peterborough and Whittlesey and the formation from the areas comprised therein of two new petty sessional divisions known as the Huntingdon division and the Peterborough division.

PETTY SESSIONAL DIVISIONS (BUCKINGHAMSHIRE) ORDER 1978 (No. 1365) [20p], made under the Justices of the Peace Act 1949, s. 18 (1) as amended by the Local Government Act 1972, Sched. 27, para. 6; operative December 1, 1978, save for para. 2 of the Schedule which is operative forthwith; provides for the petty sessional divisions of Fenny Stratford, Newport Pagnell and Stony Stratford to be combined to form a new petty sessional division of Milton Keynes.

PETTY SESSIONAL DIVISIONS (CHESHIRE) ORDER 1978 (No. 1952) [10p], made under the Justices of the Peace Act 1949, s. 18 (1) as amended by the Local Government Act 1972, Sched. 27, para. 6; operative on February 1, 1979, provides for the renaming of the petty sessional division of Ellesmere Port as Ellesmere Port and Neston.

1926. Plea—change of plea—justices' discretion

Justices retain a discretion to consider a change of plea although the defendant who pleaded guilty is legally represented at the time of pleading.

Per curiam. It will be very rare for it to be incumbent upon justices to permit a change of plea where the defendant is legally represented and makes no application to change his plea.

By their solicitor, the defendant company pleaded guilty to offences of permitting their drivers to work excessive hours, the solicitor being, wrongly, of the opinion that the offences were absolute. He mitigated upon the basis that the offences were committed without the defendants' knowledge since they relied wholly upon their transport manager; the latter gave evidence and was examined by the justices who subsequently fined the defendants. The defendants appealed unsuccessfully to the Crown Court contending that on hearing the mitigation the justices should have ordered a change of plea. The Crown Court ruled, inter alia, that the justices had no discretion to direct a change of plea by a represented defendant unless an application was made. *Held*, dismissing the defendants' appeal, that the pleas were clearly unequivocal; the justices did retain a discretion notwithstanding the absence of application but on the facts there was no reason to suppose such discretion had been exercised wrongly. (*S.* (*An Infant*) v. *Recorder of Manchester* [1969] C.L.Y. 2189 applied; *R.* v. *Durham Quarter Sessions, ex p. Virgo* [1952] C.L.Y. 2103, considered.)

P. FOSTER (HAULAGE) v. ROBERTS [1978] R.T.R. 302, D.C.

1927. Practice—discovery of documents—care proceedings—whether local authority obliged to disclose relevant documents. See R. v. GREENWICH JUVENILE COURT, *ex p.* GREENWICH LONDON BOROUGH COUNCIL, § 1977.

1928. —— refusal to state a case—requirement of affidavit

[Review of Justices' Decisions Act 1872 (c. 26).] The Lord Chief Justice observed that the failure of justices to make an affidavit under the provisions of the Review of Justices Decisions Act 1872 had doubled the length of the hearing, and commented that it would have been courteous of the justices to make such an affidavit, after refusing to state a case: R. v. DAEJAN PROPERTIES, *ex p.* MERTON LONDON BOROUGH COUNCIL, *The Times*, April 25, 1978, D.C.

1929. Probation

PROBATION ORDERS (VARIATION OF STATUTORY LIMITS) ORDER 1978 (No. 474) [10p], made under the Powers of Criminal Courts Act 1973 (c. 62), s. 2 (9) and the Criminal Law Act 1977 (c. 45), s. 57 (1); operative on May 15, 1978; amends s. 2 (1) of the 1973 Act to reduce from one year to six months the minimum period of supervision a court may specify in making a probation order.

COMBINED PROBATION AND AFTER-CARE AREAS (NOTTINGHAMSHIRE) ORDER 1978 (No. 652) [10p], made under the Powers of Criminal Courts Act 1973, s. 54 (4), Sched. 3, para. 1 as extended by S.I. 1974 No. 529; operative on June 1, 1978; amends S.I. 1974 No. 529 to take account of the combination of the petty sessional divisions of Mansfield (Borough) and Mansfield (County) in the new division of Mansfield and the petty sessional divisions of Newark and Southwell in the new division of Newark and Southwell.

COMBINED PROBATION AND AFTER-CARE AREAS (DERBYSHIRE) ORDER 1978 (No. 813) [10p], made under the Powers of Criminal Courts Act 1973,

s. 54 (4), Sched. 3, para. 1 as extended by S.I. 1974 No. 529; operative on July 1, 1978, save for art. 3 which is operative immediately; amends S.I. 1974 No. 529 to take account of the reorganisation of the petty sessional divisions in Derbyshire effected by S.I. 1978 No. 671.

COMBINED PROBATION AND AFTER-CARE AREAS (NORTH WALES) ORDER 1978 (No. 814) [10p], made under the Powers of Criminal Courts 1973, s. 54 (4), Sched. 3, para. 1 as extended by S.I. 1974 No. 529; operative on July 1, 1978; amends S.I. 1974 No. 529 to take account of the combination of the petty sessional divisions of Caernarvon and Gwyrfai effected by S.I. 1978 No. 777.

COMBINED PROBATION AND AFTER-CARE AREAS (CAMBRIDGESHIRE) ORDER 1978 (No. 1192) [10p], made under the Powers of Criminal Courts Act 1973, s. 54 (4) and Sched. 3, para. 1, as extended by S.I. 1974 No. 529, art. 3; operative on September 1, 1978, save for art. 3 which is operative forthwith; amends S.I. 1974 No. 529 to take account of the combination of the petty sessional divisions of Huntingdon and Norman Cross, Hurstingstone, Ramsey, Soke of Peterborough and Whittlesey in the new petty sessional divisions of Huntingdon and Peterborough effected in S.I. 1978 No. 1124.

COMBINED PROBATION AND AFTER-CARE AREAS (BUCKINGHAMSHIRE) ORDER 1978 (No. 1400) [10p], made under the Powers of Criminal Courts Act 1973, s. 54 (4), Sched. 3, para. 1 extended by S.I. 1974 No. 529, art. 3; operative on December 1, 1978; amends S.I. 1974 No. 529 to take account of the combination of certain petty sessional divisions into the new division of Milton Keynes effected by S.I. 1978 No. 1365.

1930. —— statistics

The annual volume of probation and after-care statistics is published for the first time by the Home Office. In previous years the report has only been available in limited numbers. The report, which is in five volumes, is entitled " Probation and After-care Statistics: England and Wales 1977 " and brings together these statistics for 1977, giving comparable figures for previous years. The report is available from the Home Office [£1·95].

1931. Procedure

MAGISTRATES' COURTS (AMENDMENT) RULES 1978 (No. 147 (L.2)) [25p], made under the Justices of the Peace Act 1949 (c. 101), s. 15, as extended by the Magistrates' Courts Act 1952 (c. 55), s. 122 and the Bail Act 1976 (c. 63), ss. 5 (1), 8 (4); operative on April 17, 1978; amends S.I. 1968 No. 1920, in consequence of the Bail Act 1976 coming into force, principally to prescribe the manner in which bail decisions are to be recorded.

1932. Sentence—refusal to hear mitigation—Court of Appeal's powers

Justices sentenced R to three months' imprisonment without allowing R's counsel to mitigate. *Held*, that (1) an order of certiorari quashing the decision should be granted; (2) however, an order of mandamus directing the justices to hear the mitigation would be refused and the case would not be remitted, as the court had power to substitute any sentence the justices could have imposed, by virtue of the Administration of Justice Act 1960, s. 16 (1). Having considered the mitigation, the court decided that the original sentence should stand: R. *v.* BILLERICAY JUSTICES, *ex p.* RUMSEY [1978] Crim.L.R. 305, D.C.

1933. Weights and measures. See WEIGHTS AND MEASURES.

BOOKS AND ARTICLES. See *post*, pp. [6], [29].

MARKETS AND FAIRS

1934. Rival market—extent of local authority's franchise—injunction

The defendant company proposed to establish on one floor of their shopping centre a series of booths, from which trading would take place on Thursdays, Fridays and Saturdays. The local authority of the market town three and a half miles away sought an interlocutory injunction three months before trading was due to commence. *Held*, the defendants' activities would constitute a market, the plaintiff would suffer damage and was entitled to prevent the levying of a rival market within six and two-thirds of a mile. Interlocutory injunction granted: NORTHAMPTON BOROUGH COUNCIL *v.* MIDLANDS DEVELOPMENT GROUP OF COMPANIES [1978] J.P.L. 543, Walton J.

1935. —— whether nuisance

A rival market was set up to be held on the same day, within the common law distance of 6⅔ miles of a franchise market. *Held*, there was an irrebuttable presumption actionable without proof of damage that this amounted to a nuisance, unless it was held under licence from the franchise owner or was itself the subject of a concurrent market franchise. The injunction would therefore be granted against the new market: TAMWORTH BOROUGH COUNCIL *v.* FAZELEY TOWN COUNCIL (1978) S.J. 699, Vivian Price Q.C.

MEDICINE

1936. Advertising

MEDICINES (ADVERTISING TO MEDICAL AND DENTAL PRACTITIONERS) REGULATIONS 1978 (No. 1020) [30p], made under the Medicines Act 1968 (c. 67), ss. 95, 129 (5); operative on December 1, 1978; regulate advertisements directed to medical and dental practitioners for medicinal products administered to human beings.

1937. Committee on Radiation from Radioactive Medicinal Products

MEDICINES (COMMITTEE ON RADIATION FROM RADIOACTIVE MEDICINAL PRODUCTS) ORDER 1978 (No. 1005) [10p], made under the Medicines Act 1968 (c. 67), s. 4 (1); operative on January 1, 1978; establishes the Committee on Radiation from Radioactive Medicinal Products for the purpose of giving advice with respect to the safety, quality and efficacy, in relation to radiation, of any substance or article for human use to which any provision of the 1968 Act is applicable.

1938. Dentists

ANCILLARY DENTAL WORKERS (AMENDMENT) REGULATIONS 1978 (No. 1128) [10p], made under the Dentists Act 1957 (c. 28), s. 41 (9); operative on December 1, 1978; further amend S.I. 1968 No. 357 by increasing the fee for first enrolment to £4 and the fee for the retention of a name in a Roll to £3.

1939. Fees

MEDICINES (FEES) REGULATIONS 1978 (No. 1121) [60p], made under the Medicines Act 1971 (c. 69), s. 1 (1) and (2); operative on September 1, 1978; consolidate the regulations prescribing fees payable in connection with certificates and licences granted under the 1968 Act.

1940. Food and drugs. See FOOD AND DRUGS.

1941. General Medical Council

GENERAL MEDICAL COUNCIL (REGISTRATION (FEES) REGULATIONS) ORDER OF COUNCIL 1978 (No. 1772) [25p], made under the Medical Act 1969 (c. 40), s. 5; operative on February 15, 1979; prescribe the fees payable to the G.M.C. under the Medical Acts 1956 to 1978 in respect of making entries in the register of medical practitioners and increase the annual retention fee to £10.

GENERAL MEDICAL COUNCIL DISCIPLINARY COMMITTEE (PROCEDURE) (AMENDMENT) RULES ORDER OF COUNCIL 1978 (No. 1796) [20p], made under the Medical Act 1956 (c. 76), s. 37 (1) as amended by the Medical Act 1969, s. 13; operative on January 1, 1979; makes new provision for the hearing of disciplinary proceedings in private and increasing the number of elected members of the Penal Cases Committee of the Council.

1942. Licences

MEDICINES (INTRA-UTERINE CONTRACEPTIVE DEVICES) (APPOINTED DAY) ORDER 1978 (No. 1138) [20p], made under the Medicines Act 1968 (c. 67), s. 16 (1); appoints October 1, 1978, as the day from which the licensing restrictions on marketing, manufacture and wholesale dealing imposed by ss. 7 and 8 of the 1968 Act and the restrictions on clinical trials imposed by s. 31 of that Act shall subject to certain transitional provisions, apply to intra-uterine contraceptive devices.

MEDICINES (INTRA-UTERINE CONTRACEPTIVE DEVICES) (AMENDMENT TO EXEMPTION FROM LICENCES) ORDER 1978 (No. 1139) [20p], made under the Medicines Act 1968, ss. 13 (2), 15 (1), 23 (4), 35 (8), 129 (4); operative on October 1, 1978; amends certain earlier orders containing various exemptions from the provisions of the 1968 Act as to licensing and clinical trials so as to make those orders apply to intra-uterine contraceptive devices.

MEDICINES (LICENSING OF INTRA-UTERINE CONTRACEPTIVE DEVICES) (MIS-CELLANEOUS AMENDMENTS) REGULATIONS 1978 (No. 1140) [20p], made under the Medicines Act 1968, ss. 18, 85 (1) (4), 86 (1), 91 (2) (3), 129 (1); operative on October 1, 1978; amend S.I. 1971 No. 974 and S.I. 1976 No. 1726 so as to make them apply to intra-uterine contraceptive devices as they apply to medicinal products.

1943. Medical Act 1978 (c. 12)

This Act provides for the constitution and functions of the General Medical Council and certain of its committees; it also amends the Medical Acts regarding medical education, the registration of medical practitioners and their professional conduct and fitness to practice.

S. 1 sets out the constitution of the General Medical Council; s. 2 makes supplementary provisions regarding the constitution; s. 3 provides for branch councils to be set up in England, Wales, Scotland and Northern Ireland; s. 4 empowers Her Majesty in Council to amend the Medical Acts 1956–1969 in the event of the termination of the 1927 Agreement regarding the registration and control of medical practitioners made with the Republic of Ireland; s. 5 gives the General Council power to advise on professional conduct or medical ethics; s. 6 establishes the Professional Conduct Committee, the Health Committee and the Preliminary Proceedings Committee and provides for rules to be made regarding the constitution of these committees; s. 7 sets out the powers of the Professional Conduct Committee where a fully registered person is judged guilty of serious professional misconduct or has been convicted of a criminal offence; s. 8 sets out the powers of the Health Committee where the fitness to practise of a fully registered person has been judged to be seriously impaired by reason of his physical or mental condition; s. 9 empowers the Professional Conduct Committee or the Health Committee to order immediate suspension after a finding of professional misconduct or unfitness to practise, if satisfied that such an order is necessary for the protection of the public or is in the best interests of the person; s. 10 enables the General Council to erase an entry from the register if satisfied that such an entry has been fraudulently procured or incorrectly made; s. 11 sets out the procedure for appeals from decisions made under ss. 7, 8 or 10; s. 12 relates to the restoration of names to the register following an erasure under s. 7; s. 13 sets out the functions of the Preliminary Proceedings Committee regarding proceedings as to professional misconduct and unfitness to practise; s. 14 and Sched. 4 set out provisions supplementary to ss. 7–13; s. 15 establishes the Education Committee with the general function of promoting high standards of medical education; s. 16 amends the Medical Act 1956, s. 15, regarding the experience required for full registration.

S. 17 and Sched. 5 provide for the replacement of ss. 18–26 of the Medical Act 1956 relating to the registration of overseas qualified practitioners by ss. 18–28 of the 1978 Act; s. 18 sets out the criteria which must be satisfied before a person with overseas qualifications may be fully registered; s. 19 relates to the registration of further overseas qualifications obtained by a person registered under s. 18; s. 20 states the requirements as to experience in connection with the full registration of a person with recognised overseas qualifications; s. 21 relates to the provisional registration of practitioners having recognised overseas qualifications; s. 22 deals with the limited registration of practitioners having overseas qualifications; s. 23 sets out the procedure for the erasure from the register of a person having limited registration; s. 24 provides for a register of practitioners with limited registration to be kept by the Registrar; s. 25 relates to the full registration of persons with limited registration; s. 26 provides for the temporary full registration of visiting overseas doctors; s. 27 establishes the Review Board for Overseas Qualified Practitioners; s. 28 sets out the functions of the Review Board; s. 29 states until the repeal of ss. 18 and 23 of the Medical Act 1956 is operative, an applicant for registration under those sections must show he has the necessary knowledge of English.

S. 30 contains definitions; s. 31 makes minor amendments, repeals and savings; s. 32 gives the short title. The Act extends to Northern Ireland.

The Act received the Royal Assent on May 5, 1978, and ss. 4, 17 and 32 came into force on that date. Ss. 1 (part) 2, 30 and 31 (part) came into force on August 28, 1978; s. 29 came into force on December 1, 1978; ss. 22–28 and 31 (part) came into force on February 15, 1979.

1944. —— commencement

MEDICAL ACT 1978 (COMMENCEMENT NO. 1) ORDER 1978 (No. 1035 (C. 29)) [20p], made under the Medical Act 1978 (c. 12), s. 32 (2); brings into force ss. 1 (part), 2, 30 and 31 (part) on August 23, 1978; s. 29 on December 1, 1978; ss. 22–28 and 31 (part) on February 15, 1979.

1945. Medical practitioners

MEDICAL PRACTITIONERS (NEWFOUNDLAND, CANADA) (REVOCATION) ORDER 1978 (No. 283) [10p], made under the Medical Act 1956 (c. 76), s. 19 (2); revokes S.R. & O. 1913 No. 1364 without prejudicing the rights of persons already registered in accordance with that order.

1946. Medicinal products

MEDICINES (FLUTED BOTTLES) REGULATIONS 1978 (No. 40) [25p], made under the Medicines Act 1968 (c. 67), ss. 87 (1), 91 (2), (3) and 129 (5); operative on February 1, 1978; impose a prohibition upon the sale or supply of certain medicinal products for external use except in bottles which are recognisable by touch.

MEDICINES (LABELLING AND ADVERTISING TO THE PUBLIC) REGULATIONS 1978 (No. 41) [35p], made under the Medicines Act 1968, ss. 85 (1), 86 (1), 91 (2), 95 (1)–(3), (5), (6) and 129 (5); operative on February 1, 1978; impose requirements relating to the prohibition, restrictions and requirements for advertisements directed to the public relating to medicinal products.

MEDICINES (PRESCRIPTION ONLY) AMENDMENT ORDER 1978 (No. 189) [15p], made under the Medicines Act 1968, ss. 58 (1), (4) (a) and 129 (4); operative on February 11, 1978; provides a temporary exemption for six months for certain medicinal products for human and animal use from the restrictions applicable to prescription only medicines by virtue of s. 58 (2) of the 1968 Act.

MEDICINES (LABELLING) (SPECIAL TRANSITIONAL) REGULATIONS 1978 (No. 190) [15p], made under the Medicines Act 1968, ss. 85 (1), 129 (5); operative on February 11, 1978; provide a transitional period of six months for the labelling of those products which, but for the exemption introduced by S.I. 1978 No. 189, would have satisfied the requirements of S.I. 1976 No. 1726.

MEDICINES (EXEMPTION FROM LICENCES) (IMPORTATION) ORDER 1978 (No. 1461) [20p], made under the Medicines Act 1968, ss. 13 (2) (3), 15 (1) (2); operative on November 3, 1978; exempts from the restrictions imposed by s. 7 of the 1968 Act the importation and sale or supply of certain medicinal products for human use.

1947. National health. See NATIONAL HEALTH.

1948. Northern Ireland. See NORTHERN IRELAND.

1949. Nurses

NURSES AGENCIES AMENDMENT REGULATIONS 1978 (No. 1443) [10p], made under the Nurses Agencies Act 1957 (c. 16), ss. 1 (1) (*d*), 2 (2), 7; operative on November 1, 1978; amends S.I. 1961 No. 1214 so as to provide that nurses registered or enrolled in Scotland or Northern Ireland are among the classes of persons a nurses' agency in England or Wales is authorised to supply.

1950. Opticians

GENERAL OPTICAL COUNCIL (MEMBERSHIP) ORDER OF COUNCIL 1978 (No. 1410) [10p], made under the Opticians Act 1958 (c. 32), Sched., para. 13 (1); operative on October 31, 1978; increases to three the number of elected members of the General Optical Council representing registered dispensing opticians.

1951. Pharmacists

PHARMACEUTICAL SOCIETY (STATUTORY COMMITTEE) ORDER OF COUNCIL 1978 (No. 20) [25p], made under the Pharmacy Act 1954 (c. 61), Sched. 1, para. 5 (1), and the Medicines Act 1968 (c. 67); operative on February 1, 1978; supersede S.I. 1957 No. 754.

1952. Poisons

POISONS RULES 1978 (No. 1) [60p], made under the Poisons Act 1972 (c. 66), s. 7; operative immediately after the coming into operation of the 1972 Act; replace S.I. 1972 No. 1939, and have effect only in relation to non-medicinal poisons.

POISONS LIST ORDER 1978 (No. 2) [15p], made under the Poisons Act 1972, s. 2; operative immediately after the coming into force of the 1972 Act; amends the poisons list—the amended list is set out in the Schedule to the Order.

POISONS (AMENDMENT) RULES 1978 (No. 672) [10p], made under the Poisons Act 1972, s. 7; operative on June 26, 1978; amend S.I. 1978 No. 1 so as to relieve from specified obligations of those Rules poisons that fall within the scope of S.I. 1970 No. 209.

1953. Prescriptions

MEDICINES (PRESCRIPTION ONLY) AMENDMENT (NO. 2) ORDER 1978 (No. 987) [50p], made under the Medicines Act 1968 (c. 67), ss. 58 (1), (4), 129 (4); operative on August 11, 1978; amends S.I. 1977 No. 2127 by making changes to the descriptions and classes of medicinal products that are prescription-only medicines.

1954. Radioactive substances

MEDICINES (RADIOACTIVE SUBSTANCES) ORDER 1978 (No. 1004) [20p], made under the Medicines Act 1968 (c. 67), s. 104 (1); operative on January 1, 1979; extends the application of specified provisions of the 1968 Act to certain articles and substances that are, contain or generate radioactive substances.

MEDICINES (ADMINISTRATION OF RADIOACTIVE SUBSTANCES) REGULATIONS 1978 (No. 1006) [25p], made under the Medicines Act 1968, s. 60; operative on July 1, 1980, except as to arts. 1 and 3, which shall come into operation on January 1, 1979; prohibit the administration of radioactive medicinal products except by doctors or dentists holding a certificate issued by the Health Ministers in respect of radioactive medicinal products or persons acting under the directions of such a doctor or dentist. The regulations also include provision as to the grant, duration, renewal, suspension, variation and revocation of certificates, provide for the appointment of a committee to advise the Health Ministers, and provide a procedure enabling applicants for or holders of a certificate to make representations in writing or to be heard by an appointed person before a certificate is refused, suspended or revoked.

1955. Sale

MEDICINES (PHARMACY AND GENERAL SALE EXEMPTION) AMENDMENT ORDER 1978 (No. 988) [30p], made under the Medicines Act 1968 (c. 67), ss. 57 (1), 129 (4); operative on August 11, 1978; amends S.I. 1977 No. 2133 by modifying the range of medicinal products which may be sold or supplied in certain circumstances by registered ophthalmic opticians free from the restrictions imposed by s. 52 of the 1968 Act.

MEDICINES (SALE OR SUPPLY) (MISCELLANEOUS PROVISIONS) AMENDMENT REGULATIONS 1978 (No. 989) [20p], made under the Medicines Act 1968, ss. 61, 66 (1); operative on August 11, 1978; modify the range of prescription-only medicines that may be sold by way of wholesale dealing by certain persons to registered ophthalmic opticians and permit sale by way of wholesale dealing by those persons of certain prescription-only medicines to persons who are allowed to administer them under the temporary exemption granted by art. 11B of S.I. 1977 No. 2132, as amended.

1956. Supply of medicines

MEDICINES (COLLECTION AND DELIVERY ARRANGEMENTS—EXEMPTION) ORDER 1978 (No. 1421) [10p], made under the Medicines Act 1968 (c. 67), s. 57 (1); operative on October 30, 1978; provides exemption for the restrictions imposed by ss. 52 and 53 of the Medicines Act 1968 where medicines for human use are supplied at premises which are not a registered pharmacy and such medicines have been dispensed in accordance with a prescription as part of certain collection and delivery arrangements.

1957. Veterinary drugs

MEDICINES (EXEMPTIONS FROM RESTRICTIONS ON THE RETAIL SALE OR SUPPLY OF VETERINARY DRUGS) (AMENDMENT) ORDER 1978 (No. 1001) [70p], made under the Medicines Act 1968 (c. 67), ss. 57 (1), (2) and 129 (4); operative on August 11, 1978; amends S.I. 1977 No. 2167.

1958. Veterinary surgery

VETERINARY SURGEONS AND VETERINARY PRACTITIONERS (REGISTRATION) (AMENDMENT) REGULATIONS ORDER IN COUNCIL 1978 (No. 1809) [10p], made under the Veterinary Surgeons Act 1966 (c. 36), ss. 11, 25 (1); further amend S.I. 1967 No. 395 by increasing various fees payable in respect of registration and retention of names in the registers.

BOOKS AND ARTICLES. See *post,* pp. [6], [29].

MEETINGS

BOOKS. See *post,* p. [6].

MENTAL HEALTH

1959. Insanity. See CRIMINAL LAW; DIVORCE AND MATRIMONIAL CAUSES.

BOOKS AND ARTICLES. See *post,* pp. [3], [29].

MINING LAW

1960. Coal industry

REDUNDANT MINEWORKERS AND CONCESSIONARY COAL (PAYMENTS SCHEMES) ORDER 1978 (No. 415) [45p], made under the Coal Industry Act 1977 (c. 39), s. 7 (1); operative on March 25, 1978; establishes schemes for the payment of benefits to mineworkers and other coal industry employees made redundant between March 25, 1978, and March 29, 1981, and for the re-imbursement of the N.C.B. for the cost of providing concessionary coal to redundant men.

MINEWORKERS' PENSION SCHEME (LIMIT ON CONTRIBUTIONS) ORDER 1978 (No. 416) [10p], made under the Coal Board (Finance) Act 1976 (c. 1), s. 2 (4); operative on March 20, 1978; substitutes a maximum sum of £34 million for that stipulated in s. 2 (3) (*b*) of the 1976 Act for the financial year 1977–78 and subsequent years.

COAL MINES (RESPIRABLE DUST) (AMENDMENT) REGULATIONS 1978 (No. 807) [10p], made under the Health and Safety at Work etc. Act 1974 (c. 37), ss. 11 (2) (*d*), 15 (1), 50 (3) as amended by the Employment Protection Act 1975 (c. 71), s. 116, Sched. 15, para. 6; operative on July 4, 1978; amends S.I. 1975 No. 1433 by lowering the levels of respirable dust in Scheds. 1 and 2.

1961. Ironstone mining

IRONSTONE RESTORATION FUND (RATES OF CONTRIBUTION) ORDER 1978 (No. 195) [15p], made under the Mineral Workings Act 1971 (c. 71), ss. 1 (2), (3), 2 and 5; operative on April 1, 1978; prescribes the full and reduced rates of contribution to be paid by ironstone operators towards the Fund under s. 1 of the 1971 Act in respect of ironstone extracted on or after April 1, 1971.

IRONSTONE RESTORATION FUND (STANDARD RATE) ORDER 1978 (No. 196) [10p], made under the Mineral Workings Act 1971, ss. 3 and 5; operative on April 1, 1978; raises the standard rate of payment to ironstone operators to £708 per acre in respect of all work completed after March 31, 1978.

1962. Metrication of measurements

COAL AND OTHER MINES (METRICATION) REGULATIONS 1978 (No. 1648) [80p], made under the Health and Safety at Work etc. Act 1974 (c. 37), ss. 15 (1) (3) (*a*), 49 (1) (2) (4), 82 (3) (*a*), as amended by the Employment Protection Act 1975 (c. 71), s. 116, Sched. 15, paras. 6 and 15; operative on

December 12, 1978; amend the scheduled regulations by substituting for the measurements expressed in imperial units, measurements expressed in metric units so as to preserve the effect of the various provisions except to the extent necessary to obtain amounts expressed in convenient and suitable terms.

1963. Minerals—title—effect of Crown reservation—not applying to mineral tailings dumped on land

[Can.] The village of Princeton leased to K certain lands, subject to the reservations expressed in the Crown grant which read in part " to raise and get thereout any minerals, precious or base." The village covenanted in the lease that it held title " to the tailings materials presently situate " on the said land. SM Ltd. entered into an agreement with K and advanced to him $22,000. K then refused to make further payments, asserting that title to the minerals in the tailings was the property of the Crown, provincial, and not that of K. SM Ltd. claimed rescission. *Held,* there was a valid lease as the village was the owner of the tailings materials, including the minerals therein. The intention of the parties to the Crown grant cannot have been to reserve title in the Crown to minerals in tailings which were then regarded as of no practical value, placed on the land by men, and which later may have become practicably recoverable as a result of technological advances. (*Borys* v. *Canadian Pacific Ry.* [1953] C.L.Y. 2662 and *Barnard-Argue-Roth-Stearns Oil & Gas. Co.* v. *Farquharson* [1912] A.C. 864 considered; *Boileau* v. *Heath* [1898] 2 Ch. 301 and *Rogers* v. *Longsdon* [1966] C.L.Y. 6112 applied): SEYMOUR MANAGEMENT v. KENDRICK [1978] 3 W.W.R. 202, Brit.Col.Sup.Ct.

1964. Mines and Quarries

MINES AND QUARRIES ACT 1954 (MODIFICATION) REGULATIONS 1978 (No. 1951) [10p], made under the Health and Safety at Work etc. Act 1974 (c. 37), s. 15 (1), (3) (*a*), as amended by the Employment Protection Act 1975 (c. 71), s. 116, Sched. 15, para. 6; operative on January 23, 1979; amend the 1954 Act, s. 148; to require the Mining Qualifications Board to ascertain the fitness of candidates for such certificates as by virtue of health and safety regulations are to be operated on their recommendation.

1965. Opencast coal mining

OPENCAST COAL (RATE OF INTEREST ON COMPENSATION) ORDER 1978 (No. 255) [10p], made under the Opencast Coal Act 1958 (c. 69), ss. 35 (8), 49 (4); operative on March 27, 1978; decrease the rate of interest, payable in addition to compensation in certain circumstances, to 7¼ per cent. per annum.

OPENCAST COAL (RATE OF INTEREST ON COMPENSATION) (No. 2) ORDER 1978 (No. 735) [10p], made under the Opencast Coal Act 1958, ss. 35 (8), 49 (4); operative on June 21, 1978; increases the rate of interest to 9½ per cent. per annum payable on compensation in certain circumstances and revokes S.I. No. 255.

OPENCAST COAL (RATE OF INTEREST ON COMPENSATION) (No. 3) ORDER 1978 (No. 1419) [10p], made under the Opencast Coal Act 1958, ss. 35 (8), 49 (4); operative on October 26, 1978; increases the rate of interest to 10½ per cent. per annum payable in certain circumstances and revokes S.I. 1978 No. 735.

OPENCAST COAL (RATE OF INTEREST ON COMPENSATION) (No. 4) ORDER 1978 (No. 1802) [10p], made under the Opencast Coal Act 1958, ss. 35 (8), 49 (4); operative on January 3, 1979; increases to 13 per cent. per annum the interest payable on compensation in certain circumstances.

1966. —— authorisation—natural justice. See NICHOLSON v. SECRETARY OF STATE FOR ENERGY, § 23.

ARTICLES. See *post,* p. [29].

MINORS

1967. Access—child born by artificial insemination—father's rôle

The father lived with a woman who was unable to have further children, and her two children. He decided to pay a woman £3,000 to have a child by artificial insemination which would be brought up by the father and his cohabitee after birth. At birth the mother refused to yield up the child and no money was paid to her. The father sought care and control, or alternatively access, in wardship proceedings. *Held,* the mother would be given care and control under a supervision order, and the wardship would continue until majority. The father should have controlled access and also discharge his financial responsibilities towards the child: A. *v.* C. (1978) 8 Fam. Law 170, Comyn J.

1968. —— **putative father**

The parties met in 1973 when the mother was aged 19 and the father 39. The child was born in April 1975, and in December 1976 cohabitation ceased. The putative father was divorced and had no contact with his children of the marriage. He now lived on licensed premises, had a drink problem, had threatened to abduct the child and had attempted suicide. He appealed against the justices' refusal to allow him access. *Held,* dismissing the appeal, the welfare of the child was the paramount consideration but the justices had properly exercised their discretion and were entitled to take note of the mother's genuine fear of access and its effect on the child's welfare: M *v.* J [1978] Fam. Law 12, D.C.

1969. The child was born to an unmarried mother in January 1976. At the time of the justices' hearing, the child was being cared for by the mother and the putative father was paying £7 maintenance. The justices granted the putative father reasonable access. The mother appealed, contending that access would involve the child in the strain between its parents and that she wanted to start a new life. *Held,* dismissing the appeal, the justices had correctly exercised their discretion by considering the child's welfare (*M.* v. *M.* [1973] C.L.Y. 2160 applied): S *v.* O [1978] Fam. Law 11, D.C.

1970. Adoption

CONVENTION ADOPTION RULES 1978 (No. 417 (L. 7)) [25p], made under the Adoption Act 1958 (c. 5), s. 9 (3) and the Adoption Act 1968 (c. 53), s. 12 (1); operative on the date on which s. 24 of the Children Act 1975 comes into force; make provision in England and Wales for proceedings under s. 24 of the 1975 Act and s. 6 of the Adoption Act 1968, and apply the Adoption (High Court) Rules 1976 (S.I. 1976 No. 1645) with the modifications necessitated by the specific provisions relating to proceedings under the Hague Convention on Jurisdiction, Applicable Law and Recognition of Decrees Relating to Adoptions.

CONVENTION ADOPTION (AUSTRIA AND SWITZERLAND) ORDER 1978 (No. 1431) [20p], made under the Adoption Act 1968, ss. 7 (4), 11 (1) and the Children Act 1975 (c. 72), ss. 24 (8), 107 (1); operative on October 23, 1978; designates Austria and Switzerland as Convention countries for the purposes of the 1968 and 1975 Acts and specifies the provisions of those countries which prohibit adoption have been notified to the U.K. pursuant to the Convention relating to Adoptions concluded at The Hague on November 15, 1965.

CONVENTION ADOPTION (MISCELLANEOUS PROVISIONS) ORDER 1978 (No. 1432) [20p], made under the Adoption Act 1968, ss. 4 (3), 7 (4), 11 (1) and the Children Act 1975, s. 107 (1); operative on October 23, 1978; contains the definitions of " convention adoption," " British territory," " specified country " and " United Kingdom national " for the purposes of the 1968 Act and the 1975 Act in respect of the Convention on Jurisdiction, Applicable Law and Recognition of Decrees relating to Adoption concluded at The Hague on November 15, 1965.

ADOPTION (COUNTY COURT) (AMENDMENT) RULES 1978 (No. 1518 (L.34)) [10p], made under the Adoption Act 1958, s. 9 (3), as amended by the Children Act 1975, Sched. 3, para. 22; operative on November 20, 1978; amend S.I. 1976 No. 1644 by revoking the provisions requiring certain types of adoption proceedings to be heard in chambers. These provisions have now been superseded by s. 73 of the Domestic Proceedings and Magistrates' Courts Act 1978.

ADOPTION (HIGH COURT) (AMENDMENT) RULES 1978 (No. 1519) (L.35)) [10p], made under the Adoption Act 1958, s. 9 (3), and the Adoption Act 1968, s. 12 (1), as amended by the Children Act 1975, Scheds. 3, para. 22, 4, Pt. III;

operative on November 20, 1978; amend S.I. 1976 No. 1645 and the Convention Adoption Rules 1978 by revoking the provisions permitting certain types of adoption proceedings to be heard in chambers. These provisions have been superseded by s. 73 of the Domestic Proceedings and Magistrates' Courts Act 1978.

1971. —— **guardianship—proceedings transferred from County Court to High Court**

The following Practice Direction was issued by the Principal Registry of the Family Division on October 27, 1978:

R.S.C., Ord. 90, r. 10 provides that an application for an order under s. 16 (1) of the Guardianship of Minors Act 1971 or s. 101 (1) of the Children Act 1975 for the removal of guardianship or adoption proceedings from a County Court into the High Court shall be made by originating summons issued out of the Principal Registry. Unless the court otherwise directs, the summons need not be served on any person, and the application for the removal of the proceedings may be heard by a registrar.

The following procedure shall apply on any such application:—

(1) The originating summons shall be in Form No. 11 of Appendix A to the R.S.C. (*Ex parte* originating summons), suitably amended, and shall be supported by affidavit or other evidence, including, where appropriate, the written consent of the other party or parties to the application; the fee in respect of an application is £2 (Supreme Court Fees Order 1975 (S.I. No. 1343 (L. 15), Fee No. 2);

(2) Both copies of the summons will be retained in the Registry and will be referred, together with the supporting evidence, to the Registrar of the day for consideration;

(3) If the Registrar requires personal attendance on the summons, the Registry will fix a date and will send the sealed copy summons to the applicant's solicitor with a date and time of hearing noted thereon: notice of the hearing must then be given to the other party or parties by the applicant's solicitor;

(4) When the Registrar makes an order for the removal of the proceedings to the High Court, the Registry will serve a copy on the applicant, but it is the responsibility of the applicant to serve the other party or parties and to send a copy of the order to the Registrar of the county court from which the proceedings are to be removed so that he may arrange for the physical removal of the documents referred to in Ord. 16, r. 19 of the County Court Rules 1936 to the " proper officer " of the High Court; for the purposes of R.S.C., Ord. 90, r. 10 (4), the " proper officer " shall be the Senior Registrar of the Principal Registry of the Family Division;

(5) On receipt of the documents referred to in para. (4) above, the Registry will give notice to all parties of the removal of the proceedings to the High Court, together with the High Court file reference number.

[1978] 1 W.L.R. 1456; [1978] 3 All E.R. 960.

1972. —— **order failed to consider child's welfare**

The boy's father, his mother's first husband, had died when the boy was two. The mother had remarried a divorced man who had two girls by the former marriage, and she then had a child by her new husband. The mother and stepfather applied to adopt the boy, now aged nine; the paternal grandparents who wished to retain contact with him, and had set up a trust for him, opposed the application. *Held*, allowing the grandparents' appeal from the justices' adoption order, the boy was already integrated in his new family, and the justices had failed to consider his welfare in severing him from his grandparents: *Re* L. A. (A MINOR), *The Times*, April 27, 1978, D.C.

1973. Adoption Act 1968—commencement

ADOPTION ACT 1968 (COMMENCEMENT No. 2) ORDER 1978 (No. 1430 (C.37)) [10p], made under the Adoption Act 1968 (c. 53), s. 14 (2); operative on October 23, 1978; brings into force ss. 5–7, 8 (1), 9 of the 1968 Act.

1974. Adoption (Scotland) Act 1978 (c. 28)

This Act consolidates the enactments relating to adoption in Scotland.

Pt. I (ss. 1–11) relates to the Adoption Service: s. 1 establishes the Adoption Service; s. 2 sets out the functions of a local authority's social work committee;

s. 3 relates to the application to the Secretary of State for approval of acting as an adoption society; s. 4 deals with the withdrawal of such approval; s. 5 sets out the procedure on refusal to approve, or withdrawal of approval from adoption societies; s. 6 states that in reaching any decision relating to the adoption, a court's or adoption agency's first consideration should be the welfare of the child; s. 7 states that an adoption agency should have regard to the wishes of the child's parents or guardians as to the religious upbringing of the child; s. 8 relates to inactive or defunct adoption societies; s. 9 deals with the regulation of adoption agencies; s. 10 relates to the inspection of books of approved adoption societies; s. 11 places restrictions on the arranging of adoptions and the placing of children.

Pt. II (ss. 12–26) relates to adoption orders: s. 12 defines " adoption order "; s. 13 requires a child to live with the adopters for 13 weeks before an adoption order is made; s. 14 relates to adoption by married couples; s. 15 relates to adoption by one person; s. 16 states that an adoption order shall not be made unless each parent or guardian of the child has freely agreed to the adoption; s. 17 relates to Convention adoption orders; s. 18 sets out the procedure for freeing a child for adoption; s. 19 deals with progress reports to former parents; s. 20 relates to the revocation of a s. 18 order; s. 21 deals with the transfer of parental rights and duties from one adoption agency to another; s. 22 requires an applicant for an adoption order to notify his local authority, at least three months before the date of the order, of his intention to make such application; s. 23 deals with reports to be submitted to the court by an adoption agency; s. 24 sets out restrictions on the making of an adoption order; s. 25 deals with interim orders; s. 26 relates to the care of a child on the refusal of an adoption order.

Pt. III (ss. 27–37) relates to the care and protection of children awaiting adoption: s. 27 places restrictions on the removal of a child where an adoption has been agreed or an application has been made under s. 18; s. 28 places restrictions on the removal of a child where the applicant has provided a home for the child for five years; s. 29 deals with the return of a child removed in breach of ss. 27 or 28; s. 30 relates to the return of children placed for adoption by adoption agencies; s. 31 sets out the application of s. 30 where a child has not been placed for adoption; s. 32 defines " protected child "; s. 33 sets out the duty of local authorities to secure the well-being of protected children; s. 34 relates to the removal of protected children from unsuitable surroundings; s. 35 states that a person who has a protected child in his care must notify the local authority of any change in his permanent address; s. 36 sets out offences relating to protected children; s. 37 contains miscellaneous provisions relating to protected children.

Pt. IV (ss. 38–44) relates to the status of adopted children: s. 38 gives the meaning of " adoption order " in this Part of the Act; s. 39 sets out the status of an adopted child; s. 40 relates to the citizenship of an adopted child; s. 41 relates to miscellaneous enactments; s. 42 deals with pensions payable to children; s. 43 relates to insurance; s. 44 states the effect of s. 39 on succession and inter vivos deeds.

Pt. V (ss. 45–48) relates to the registration and revocation of adoption orders and Convention adoptions: s. 45 deals with the Adopted Children Register to be maintained by the Registrar-General for Scotland; s. 46 relates to the revocation of the adoption of an illegitimate child on the marriage of its natural parents; s. 47 relates to the annulment of overseas adoptions; s. 48 contains supplementary provisions.

Pt. VI (ss. 49–67) contains miscellaneous and supplementary provisions: s. 49 relates to the adoption of children abroad; s. 50 places a restriction on the removal of children for adoption outside Great Britain; s. 51 places prohibitions on payments for adoption or for the giving of consent to an adoption; s. 52 places restrictions on advertisements relating to adoptions; s. 53 sets out the effect of determinations and orders made in England and Wales and overseas in adoption proceedings: s. 54 relates to evidence of adoption in England and Wales and Northern Ireland; s. 55 relates to evidence of agreement and consent; s. 56 deals with courts; s. 57 states that all proceedings under

Pt. II, s. 29 or 49 shall be heard and determined in private; s. 58 relates to curators ad litem and reporting officers; s. 59 provides for procedural rules to be made; s. 60 relates to orders, rules and regulations; s. 61 refers to offences by corporate bodies; s. 62 deals with service of notices; s. 63 relates to nationality; s. 64 defines " internal law "; s. 65 contains other definitions; s. 66 contains transitional provisions, amendments and repeals; s. 67 gives the short title. The Act extends to Scotland only.

The Act received the Royal Assent on July 20, 1978, and shall come into force on such day as the Secretary of State shall appoint.

1975. Blood tests—paternity. See § 1417.

1976. Borstal detention—sentence. See CRIMINAL LAW.

1977. Care proceedings—production of documents—mother's witness summons— whether case records protected

[Magistrates' Courts Act 1952 (c. 55), s. 77.]

S. 77 of the Act is restricted to getting the witness on documents into the precincts of the court and does not require the court to decide whether or not particular documents are privileged.

In proceedings under s. 4 of the Children Act 1948 the mother of the two children concerned served on the local authority a witness summons under s. 77 of the 1952 Act requiring them to produce at the hearing all documents in their possession relating to the children. The local authority opposed the application on the ground that the summons would oblige them to produce a case file which was privileged from production and was not relevant to the complaint before the court. The juvenile court concluded that apart from certain notes the documents were not protected against publication and made an order requiring production of the file. The local authority applied for an order of certiorari to quash the order. *Held*, quashing the order, that (1) there was no general power of discovery in the magistrates' court and even if the documents were brought to the court none of them could be put before the court unless a representative of the local authority gave evidence and referred to the file and the documents concerned were shown to be relevant; (2) the court should have considered the availability to production of the documents, document by document or class by class.

R. *v.* GREENWICH JUVENILE COURT, *ex p.* GREENWICH LONDON BOROUGH COUNCIL (1977) 76 L.G.R. 99, D.C.

1978. —— wishes of children aged 12 and 9

The two children of the marriage, who since 1974 when their parents' marriage broke down had been in their father's custody, wished to be with their mother. The judge gave custody to the mother, saying that he thought that the children were old enough to decide what they wish to do. The father appealed. *Held*, dismissing the appeal, the judge's decision was right although it involved no criticism of the father or the woman with whom he was now living: MARSH *v.* MARSH (1978) 8 Fam. Law 103, C.A.

1979. Change of surname—divorce of parents

The mother of children aged three and four applied to change their surname from that of their father, from whom she was divorced, to that of their step-father. The natural father would not agree to this. *Held*, that there were two irreconcilable judicial approaches to this question: namely, the two recent decisions of the Court of Appeal in *R.* v. *R.* (*Child*: *Surname*) [1977] C.L.Y. 1937, and in *D.* v. *B.* (*Surname*: *Birth Registration*) [1978] C.L.Y. 2026, on the one hand; and the series of decisions of the Court of Appeal and the High Court, culminating in *Re W.G.* [1976] C.L.Y. 1766, the Practice Direction of August 6, 1969 [1969] C.L.Y. 2296, and the Matrimonial Causes Rules 1977, r. 92 (8), on the other hand. In this case, the court took the view that a change of name was a judicial consideration of some importance as affecting the best interests and the psychological welfare of the children. The natural father was someone with whom it would be beneficial for the children to maintain a close connection. A marriage could be dissolved, but not parenthood. Mother's application refused: L. *v.* F., *The Times*, August 1, 1978, Latey J.

1980. Children Act 1975—commencement

CHILDREN ACT 1975 (COMMENCEMENT No. 3) ORDER 1978 (No. 1433 (C.38)) [10p], made under the Children Act 1975 (c. 72), s. 108 (2) (8); operative on October 23, 1978; brings into force s. 24 of the 1975 Act.

1981. Custody—appeal—mother's ability to cope—need for welfare report

The mother left the matrimonial home in Cornwall and took the two daughters aged six and two with her to Kettering where she obtained a job as a nurse. The judge granted interim custody to the father on the understanding that the paternal grandparents would look after the children with access, including staying access, to the mother. The mother appealed. *Held,* dismissing the appeal, the judge saw both parents and had doubts about the mother's ability to cope with the children. A welfare report would be ordered as a matter of great urgency and the issue as to final custody decided by a different judge: R. *v.* R. (1978) 8 Fam. Law 169, C.A.

1982. —— baby girl to father

The parties married in 1974 and the baby girl, aged six months at the time of the magistrates' court hearing, was conceived in August 1976. The parties then joined an organisation called " The Sealed Knot " and met H, a spiritual consultant, with whom the mother committed adultery beginning in October 1976. The baby was born in May 1977 and on Christmas Day 1977 the mother left to live with H, described by the court as a " mountebank and philanderer." The father took the baby to the maternal grandmother. The justices awarded custody to the father and care and control to the maternal grandmother. *Held,* dismissing the mother's appeal, that her insistence on living with H, whose attitude to women was obnoxious, prevented her having custody of the girl in an environment in which H was present: HUTCHINSON *v.* HUTCHINSON [1978] Fam.Law 140, D.C.

1983. —— change of child's name informally by mother

M, who was awarded custody, care and control of the three children, after the divorce, registered them at school as Dell, being unaware of the prohibition against changing their name in the order. The children knew their name was Crick, but they used Dell and were unconcerned. *Held,* no order would be made as to the use of the name Dell, but the divorce judge's order should be amended to provide that M was not obliged to change their name back to Crick: (R. v. R. *(Child: Surname)* [1977] C.L.Y. 1937 considered): CRICK *v.* CRICK [1977] Fam. Law. 239, C.A.

1984. —— informal hearing—necessity for proper trial

In a custody hearing at Ilford County Court, counsel for the father briefly outlined the facts, the judge read all the affidavits and had an informal discussion with the father and mother. *Held,* the case involved a number of real issues, and should have been tried in the ordinary way. Although some informality was permissible, this case went far beyond the bounds of permissive informality. Custody cases should be conducted with great care. A re-trial would be ordered: JENKINS *v.* JENKINS, *The Times,* June 30, 1978, C.A.

1985. —— jurisdiction—residence

[Guardianship of Minors Act 1971 (c. 3), s. 15.] The parties lived in Scotland with their three children. The mother left the father, and took the children over the border into Cumbria. Four days later, she applied by means of a summons under the 1971 Act for custody and maintenance in the Carlisle Magistrates' Court. Ten days after that application the older boy went back to live with his father. At the hearing before the justices, the mother expressed her intention to acquire accommodation in Scotland, and return her children to school there as quickly as possible. The justices gave custody of the three children to the father. *Held,* allowing the mother's appeal, s. 15 of the 1971 Act gave jurisdiction only if the mother resided in England. On the facts, the justices were wrong to accept jurisdiction, as the mother's visit was insufficiently permanent. (*Fox* v. *Stirk* [1970] C.L.Y. 858 applied): *Re* IRVING (MINORS), *The Times,* April 25, 1978, D.C.

1986. —— to mother—no change necessary

After divorce in 1973, both parties remarried and the mother, who had taken the children (a boy and girl now aged 12 and 10 respectively) with her on separation, was granted custody. The father appealed contending (i) the judge had given too much weight to preserving the status quo; (ii) the step-father ill-treated the children; (iii) the children had previously expressed a wish to be with their father. *Held,* dismissing the appeal, no real reason had been given which justified a change. The " ill-treatment " was no more than lawful correction. The girl was clearly attached to her mother and it would be wrong to split the children after so long with her: *Re* C. (MINORS) (1978) 8 Fam. Law 202, C.A.

1987. —— whether sufficient attention to children's wishes

The mother was given custody of the parties' three children, two daughters aged 14 and 13 and a son aged 10, with a condition she should reside in the matrimonial home until the youngest child became 18. The father appealed, contending that the judge had given insufficient attention to the daughters' wish to stay with him. He sought an order that he remain in the matrimonial home with the daughters until the youngest became 18. *Held,* dismissing the appeal, the daughters' wishes had been very much influenced by the father. If his proposals succeeded the children would be split and the mother and son would have to vacate the matrimonial home with nowhere to live: DONCHEFF *v.* DONCHEFF (1978) 8 Fam. Law 205, C.A.

1988. —— wardship—application to take child out of jurisdiction

The mother had custody of the parties' son under a magistrates' court order of September 1977 against which the father was appealing. In May 1978 she sought to take the boy to India for six weeks' holiday during term-time. The father, having failed to get an undertaking that she would bring him back to England, issued a wardship summons. The mother obtained leave in the wardship proceedings to take the child out of the jurisdiction, her counsel giving the desired undertaking. The father appealed. *Held,* allowing the appeal, it was wrong to take a 12-year-old away from school for six weeks and take him to India at the hottest time of the year if both could be avoided: *Re* A. (A MINOR) (1978) 8 Fam. Law 201, C.A.

1989. —— welfare officer's report—nature and extent of matters to be canvassed by report—whether hearsay material admissible

[Aust.] In the course of hearing competing applications for custody of a nine-year-old child, it was *held,* that (1) once a welfare report has been ordered and prepared, the discretion imposed in the court to admit the report into evidence is without limitation and such a report can be admitted even though it contains hearsay material; (2) the admission of a welfare report into evidence does not supplement the duty of the trial judge to listen to and weigh up the evidence and form his own conclusions; (3) it is undesirable for a welfare officer to annex to a report copies of reports and statements of other persons. (*Official Solicitor* v. *K.* [1963] C.L.Y. 1807 followed): *Re* HOGUE AND HAINES (FORMERLY HOGUE) [1977] 29 F.L.R. 186, Fam.Ct. of Aust.

1990. Habeas corpus—wrong procedure in Family Division

A 15-year-old girl failed to return home from school and her father was informed that she was in the care of the local authority as she did not wish to live with her parents. He applied for leave to issue a writ of habeas corpus against the local authority. *Held,* dismissing the application, although the local authority had given the father little information, it was clear that the girl did not wish to live with her parents. Habeas corpus was the wrong procedure in the Family Division; wardship would be preferable: *Re* K (A MINOR) (1978) 122 S.J. 626, Bush J.

1991. Juvenile courts. See MAGISTERIAL LAW.

1992. Local authorities—child in care—access arrangements—whether wardship proceedings appropriate—evidence

[Children Act 1948 (c. 43), s. 2 (1).]
Where a child is in the care of the local authority pursuant to s. 2 of the

Act the court will only make the child a ward or continue the wardship where there is a positive advantage in the child remaining a ward.

Per curiam: Although in wardship proceedings the interests of the child may require a modification of the normal rules of procedure in the discretion of the judge, evidence should in general be treated in the normal way as in proceedings between adversaries and the court should not receive affidavits from one party which have not been delivered to the other.

In 1974 D was received into care by the local authority at the request of his mother. Both parents were receiving treatment at a mental hospital. In 1975 the local authority passed resolutions pursuant to s. 2 of the Act assuming parental rights. The mother objected but justices hearing her complaint ordered that the resolution assuming her rights should not lapse. Access was arranged but the mother became dissatisfied with proposed limitations and issued an originating summons asking that D be made a ward of court; that he should remain in the care of the local authority but that the court should issue directions relating to his education, welfare and to the mother's access. The judge confirmed the wardship and ordered the local authority to file their evidence within one month. The local authority applied for directions as to the manner in which they should present their evidence since they were concerned about certain sources of confidential information being revealed to the mother. The registrar referred the matter to the judge in chambers. At the hearing the local authority asked that the case be dealt with summarily contending that D should be de-warded. *Held*, dismissing the summons, that there was no ground for the court to override the views of the local authority about access and this was a case where the future of the child during his minority could be safely left to be regulated by the local authority; accordingly the child would cease to be a ward of court. (*Re M. (An Infant)* [1961] C.L.Y. 4336 and dictum of Ormrod L.J. in *Re Y. (A Minor) (Child in Care: Access)* [1975] C.L.Y. 2201 applied.)

Re D. F. (A MINOR) (1971) 76 L.G.R. 133, Dunn J.

1993. —— —— **assumption of parental rights**
[Children Act 1948 (c. 43) s. 2 (1) (*b*) (v), s. 2 (4); Children Act 1975 (c. 72), s. 57.] The child was in local authority care under s. 1 of the 1948 Act and the authority passed a resolution under s. 2 (1) (*b*) (v) vesting parental rights in itself. The parent, on receipt of notice of the resolution, served a counter-notice under s. 2 (4), and the authority complained to the juvenile court, which held that it had no jurisdiction because of the Court of Appeal decision in *Johns* v. *Jones* [1978] C.L.Y. 1994. The authority applied for judicial review to the Divisional Court and appealed to the Court of Appeal from that court's refusal. *Held*, refusing the applications, but granting the authority leave to appeal to the House of Lords, the appeal should be expedited: LEWISHAM LONDON BOROUGH COUNCIL v. LEWISHAM JUVENILE COURT JUSTICES, *The Times*, November 1, 1978, C.A.

1994. —— —— **return to mother—power of authority to assume parental rights**
[Children Act 1948 (c. 43), ss. 1 (3), 2 (1), as amended and substituted by Children Act 1975 (c. 72), s. 57.]
The power of a local authority to assume parental rights over a child exists only where that child is in its care.
A child was placed in voluntary care by her mother. When the mother asked for her back, the local authority passed a resolution under s. 2 of the Children Act 1948 (as amended) assuming parental rights over the child. The juvenile court confirmed that resolution. *Held*, allowing the mother's appeal from the refusal by the Divisional Court to quash the resolution, that the power to make such a resolution existed only when the child was in its care under s. 1 of the Children Act and that the child had ceased to be in its care under that section the moment the mother withdrew her authority by requesting the return of the child to her.

JOHNS v. JONES [1978] 3 W.L.R. 792, C.A.

1995. Maintenance. See DIVORCE AND MATRIMONIAL CAUSES.

1996. —— **arrears—suspended committal order**
On the mother's complaint of arrears of maintenance, the justices ordered the arrears to be paid at £10 per week and enforced that order by a suspended committal order. The father appealed on motion to the Divisional Court. *Held,* dismissing the appeal on its merits, the only procedure for appealing from an order enforcing payment of arrears due under the Guardianship of Minors Act 1971 made in the magistrates' court, is by way of case stated on a point of law (*Griffiths* v. *Griffiths* (1909) 25 T.L.R. 454 and *Re Stern (an Infant)* (1950) C.L.C. 3057 applied): *Re* K. (MINORS), *The Times,* November 8, 1978, D.C.

1997. Northern Ireland. See NORTHERN IRELAND.

1998. Protection of Children Act 1978 (c. 37). See § 583.

1999. Referral to children's hearing—appeal against refusal—whether hearing had reached a decision
[Scot.] [Social Works (Scotland) Act 1968 (c. 49), ss. 42, 49.] A child accused of an assault was referred to a children's hearing, which would not accept the referral. The child and his parents sought to appeal to the Sheriff, under s. 49, against the refusal of the children's hearing to accept the referral under s. 42. *Held,* they could only appeal against a decision of the hearing, and its declining to hear the case further, pending the outcome of an application to the sheriff, did not constitute a decision. H. AND H. *v.* M'GREGOR, 1973 S.C. 95, Second Division.

2000. Social security. See SOCIAL SECURITY.

2001. Wardship—application—Registrar's jurisdiction
[R.S.C., Ord. 90, r. 12.]
Although R.S.C., Ord. 90, r. 12, purports to give a registrar jurisdiction to make an order for care and control in wardship proceedings, such cases should be heard by the appropriate judge.
The paternal grandmother issued an originating summons making L a ward of court and applied for care and control. The application was heard by a deputy registrar who made an order for care and control in her favour. L's mother appealed. *Held,* allowing the appeal, that even if the deputy registrar had jurisdiction, the proper practice was for him to give directions for the hearing to proceed before the appropriate judge dealing with such business in that district registry.
Re L. (A MINOR) (WARDSHIP: PRACTICE) (PRACTICE NOTE) [1978] 1 W.L.R. 181, C.A.

2002. —— **child already in care—parents leaving the country—exercise of jurisdiction**
[Children and Young Persons Act 1969 (c. 54), s. 1.]
The High Court may exercise its wardship jurisdiction notwithstanding an existing care order to a local authority, where the parents of the ward intend to leave the jurisdiction and return to their homeland
The three-year-old child of Pakistani parents was committed to the care of a local authority by a juvenile court by reason of her suffering serious non-accidental injuries probably caused by one of her parents. The parents subsequently wished to return permanently to Pakistan and successfully sought an order making the child a ward of court, together with leave to take the child out of the jurisdiction (and out of the local authorities care and control). *Held,* dismissing the local authority's appeal, that the circumstances were sufficiently special to justify the exercise of the wardship jurisdiction notwithstanding the existing order under the 1969 Act and that the judge had correctly exercised his discretion in considering the best interests of the child's future welfare. (*Re M (An Infant)* [1961] C.L.Y. 4336 and *Re T (A.J.J.) (An Infant)* [1970] C.L.Y. 1360, distinguished.)
Re H (A MINOR) (WARDSHIP: JURISDICTION) [1978] 2 W.L.R. 608, C.A.

2003. —— **court's duty to investigate—conflicting views of parties**
[Children Act 1948 (c. 43), s. 2 (i).]
Where the Official Solicitor as guardian ad litem takes a different view from the council in whose care a child is as to the welfare of that child, the court will, in the exercise of its wardship jurisdiction, investigate the different views.

A child was in care. Paternal relatives wished to look after him. The authority did not agree. The relatives took out a wardship summons, and the authority did not object to the appointment of the Official Solicitor as guardian ad litem. He upheld the views of the relatives. *Held,* that the court would investigate which view should prevail and would not decline jurisdiction simply because the child had been placed in the care of the local authority.

Re D (A MINOR) (1978) 76 L.G.R. 653, Balcombe J.

2004. —— **divorce—declaration of satisfaction—child maintained by social security.** See COOK *v.* COOK, § 799.

2005. —— **kidnapping—jurisdiction of English court**
F and M were divorced. M had remarried and lived in California with the three children of the marriage. M died. Contrary to the order of the Californian court, F kidnapped them and brought them to England. Here, the step-father made them wards of court and applied to take them back to California. *Held,* on a consideration of the Californian court's likely decision, that F should have the children so that they would return to England, the English court could assume jurisdiction. No such order as the step-father sought would be made: *Re* N. C., J. C. AND A. C. (MINORS) [1977] Fam. Law 240, C.A.

2006. —— **not to be used as form of appeal from county court**
The child in question had been the subject of adoption proceedings in the county court. The proposed adoptor, rather than appealing, applied to the High Court to decide the child's care and control under the wardship jurisdiction. *Held,* that the High Court, in potential conflicts between itself and a lower court, would not permit the wardship procedure to be used to reverse the judge's order by the back door. The High Court would not accept jurisdiction without special reasons. The child should cease to be a ward of court and should be returned to the mother: *Re* S. (A MINOR), *The Times,* October 31, 1978, Dunn J.

2007. —— **proceedings—inappropriate where ward involved in future criminal proceedings**
The ward, aged 17, was the complainant in a forthcoming rape trial. The defence sought an order that her medical records be available to them, and that she be examined by a psychiatrist: both orders were refused by the trial judge. The mother instituted wardship proceedings, and the Official Solicitor issued a summons for directions as to whether the defence were entitled to the orders sought. *Held,* dismissing the summons, there was no reason for the court to overrule the mother's objections to the defence applications, but in the circumstances, the use of the wardship jurisdiction was inappropriate and improper: *Re* D (A MINOR) (1978) 122 S.J. 643, Dunn J.

BOOKS AND ARTICLES. See *post,* pp. [6], [30].

MONEY

2008. Banking. See BANKING.

2009. Counterfeit coins—meaning of " utter." See R. *v.* WALMSLEY, DEREYA AND JACKSON, § 442.

2010. Currency—fluctuating rate of exchange—sale of goods. See PARSONS & Co. *v.* ELECTRICITY TRUST, § 2644.

2011. Exchange control. See REVENUE AND FINANCE.

2012. Loans. See MONEYLENDERS.

2013. Mortgages. See MORTGAGES.

ARTICLES. See *post,* p. [30].

MONEYLENDERS

2014. Temporary loans—through solicitor—whether moneylending
[Moneylenders Act 1900 (c. 51), s. 6.] While looking for a long term investment, a retired estate agent who provided temporary loans on dilapidated

properties through a solicitor was *held*, not to be carrying on the business of a moneylender: OFFEN *v.* SMITH, *The Times*, November 15, 1978, C.A.

ARTICLES. See *post*, p. [30].

MORTGAGES

2015. Building societies. See BUILDING SOCIETIES.

2016. Home Purchase Assistance and Housing Corporation Guarantee Act 1978. See § 1576.

2017. Mortgage brokers—commission—whether payable—no binding commitment. See GREENBRIER MORTGAGE INVESTMENTS *v.* J. E. ONGMAN & SONS, § 33.

2018. Possession—action not bona fide—brought by wife as mortgagee
  A houseowner charged his house to the bank and then let it in breach of the conditions of the charge. The bank declined to bring possession proceedings, but assigned the charge to the owner's wife. On her action for possession, *held*, that it was brought for the benefit of the owner and not bona fide to protect the security and, accordingly, was not within the provisions of the Rent Acts entitling a mortgagee to recover possession of a dwelling house: QUENNELL *v.* MALTBY, *The Times*, November 17, 1978, C.A.

2019. —— mortgagee's wife claiming overriding interest
  The plaintiff bank applied for summary possession of mortgaged premises, the charging deed having contained a covenant by the mortgagor to guarantee debts and liabilities up to £40,000 of a company, now in liquidation, in which he had an interest. One ground, inter alia, for opposing the bank's claim to enforce its security, was that the mortgagor's wife had an overriding interest by virtue of having contributed to the purchase price and having been in "actual occupation" at the dates of the mortgage and the registration. *Held*, granting summary judgment for possession to the plaintiffs, that the mortgagor's wife was unable to make out more than a "minor interest" within s. 3 of the Land Registration Act 1925; and s. 70 (1) (*g*) of the Law of Property Act 1925 could not include occupation by the spouse of a legal owner without introducing an element of absurdity into the law: WILLIAM & GLYN'S BANK *v.* BOLAND, *The Times*, April 28, 1978, Templeman J.

2020. —— mortgagor's refusal to comply with order—writ of restitution. See ABBEY NATIONAL BUILDING SOCIETY *v.* MORRIS, § 383.

2021. —— recovery—evidence—contents of affidavit. See NATIONWIDE BUILDING SOCIETY *v.* BATEMAN, § 1416.

2022. —— —— rateable value of property—High Court jurisdiction. See P. B. FROST *v.* GREEN, § 2463.

2023. Repayment—foreign currency—whether clog on equity
  A collateral stipulation in a mortgage which does not clog the equity is only objectionable if it is unfair and unconscionable, *i.e.* imposed in a morally reprehensible manner, not merely if it is unreasonable.
  M lent P £36,000 secured by a mortgage in 1966. Cl. 6 of the mortgage linked repayment to the Swiss franc which at the date of the loan was worth less than 9p. When P wished to redeem the mortgage in 1976, the Swiss franc was worth 25p, thus trebling the amount of sterling required for redemption. P contended that the clause was void either on the grounds that it was contrary to public policy, or that it was unconscionable and a clog on the equity. *Held*, that the clause was not contrary to public policy; it was not a clog on the equity of redemption, and both parties had been of equal bargaining power, so, whilst possibly unreasonable, such a term was not unconscionable. The court could not rewrite an improvident contract, and the term would have to stand. (*Kreglinger* v. *New Patagonia Meat and Cold Storage Co.* [1914] A.C. 25; *Knightsbridge Estates Trust* v. *Byrne* [1939] Ch. 441, and dicta of Lord Hodson in *White and Carter (Councils)* v. *McGregor* [1962] A.C. 413, applied; *Cityland and Property (Holdings)* v. *Dabrah* [1967] C.L.Y. 2533 distinguished;

dicta of Denning L.J. in *Treseden-Griffin* v. *Co-operative Insurance Society* [1956] C.L.Y. 4946 not followed.)

MULTISERVICE BOOKBINDING *v.* MARDEN [1978] 2 W.L.R. 535, Browne-Wilkinson J.

2024. Sale—duty of mortgagee

A bank loan, secured on leasehold property, was guaranteed by the defendants. *Held*, that the bank owed the defendants no duty to obtain the best price when the security was realised. (*Cuckmere Brick Co.* v. *Mutual Finance* [1971] C.L.Y. 7479 distinguished): BARCLAYS BANK *v.* THIENEL, *The Times*, June 16, 1978, Thesiger J.

2025. Title deeds—loss by mortgagee—duty of care—whether mortgagor entitled to indemnity

A mortgagee in possession of title deeds cannot be sued for negligence resulting in their loss, nor can compensation in equity be awarded before redemption.

B acquired the freehold interest of certain property and charged the leasehold interest to a third party, who admitted receiving the relevant deeds. B later contracted to sell property comprising part of the charged property but could not produce satisfactory documents of title, entitling the purchaser to damages. B sought an indemnity from the third party who had failed to produce the documents. *Held*, that the third party as mortgagee was owner of the documents and therefore owed no one a duty of care in respect of them; that the equitable relief of compensation in respect of their loss was only available on redemption. (*Gilligan and Nugent* v. *National Bank* [1901] 2 I.R. 513 applied.)

BROWNING *v.* HANDILAND GROUP (1978) 35 P. & C.R. 345, Rubin J.

ARTICLES. See *post*, p. [30].

NAME

2026. Change of surname—effects of deed poll

At common law a surname is the name by which a person is generally known and the effect of changing it by deed poll is merely evidential.

H and W married in 1970, but separated in 1975 when W was pregnant. W went to live with another man, and changed her surname to his by deed poll. The child was registered at birth in the mother's name without H's consent. H was granted an order by Lane J. that, inter alia, the Register and deed poll be altered to show the child's name as being that of H. On appeal by W, *held*, allowing the appeal, that (1) the effect of changing a name by deed poll was merely evidential, and the order to execute a fresh deed poll would be set aside; (2) the surname to be entered in the register was the surname by which it was intended the child should be known, which was the child's new name in this case.

D. *v.* B. (SURNAME: BIRTH REGISTRATION) [1978] 3 W.L.R. 573, C.A.

2027. Nom-de-plume—journalist—proof of use and reputation. See SYKES *v.* FAIRFAX AND SONS, § 2986.

2028. Surname—change of child's name. See CRICK *v.* CRICK, § 1983.

2029. Trade name. See TRADE MARKS AND TRADE NAMES.

BOOKS AND ARTICLES. See *post*, pp. [7], [30].

NATIONAL HEALTH

203 Annual report

The Department of Health and Social Security have published their annual report for 1977. It gives estimated yearly spending on health and personal social services in the country, and also contains sections on such considerations as the record number of patients, fewer nurses in training, and the state of industrial relations within the National Health Service. This report is available as a Command Paper from H.M.S.O.

2031. Central Health Services Council

CENTRAL HEALTH SERVICES COUNCIL (VARIATION OF CONSTITUTION) AMENDMENT ORDER 1978 (No. 339) [10p], made under the National Health Service Act 1977 (c. 49), s. 6 (2); operative on April 10, 1978; amends S.I. 1974 No. 186 by increasing the minimum and maximum numbers of nominated members of the Council.

CENTRAL HEALTH SERVICES COUNCIL (VARIATION OF CONSTITUTION) AMENDMENT (NO. 2) ORDER 1978 (No. 489) [10p], made under the National Health Service Act 1977, s. 6 (2); operative on May 1, 1978; revokes S.I. 1978 No. 339 and increases the maximum and minimum numbers of the Council.

2032. Charges

NATIONAL HEALTH SERVICE (DENTAL AND OPTICAL CHARGES) REGULATIONS 1978 (No. 950) [25p], made under the National Health Service Act 1977 (c. 49), ss. 77, 78 (1), 79, Sched. 12, paras. 1 (1), 2 (1) (2), 3; operative on August 7, 1978; put into a consolidated form provisions relating to charges for dental treatment and dental and optical appliances formerly contained in S.I. 1971 No. 340 and other regulations, including amending regulations which are superseded and revoked.

2033. Community health councils

NATIONAL HEALTH SERVICE (COMMUNITY HEALTH COUNCILS) AMENDMENT REGULATIONS 1978 (No. 21) [10p], made under the National Health Service Act 1977 (c. 49), s. 20 (3), Sched. 7, para. 2 (a); operative on February 8, 1978; alter the date of termination of office of members of Community Health Councils from June 30 to August 31.

2034. Contributions. See NATIONAL INSURANCE.

2035. Finance

GENERAL PRACTICE FINANCE CORPORATION (INCREASE OF BORROWING POWERS) ORDER 1978 (No. 921) [10p], made under the National Health Service Act 1966 (c. 8), s. 6 (3); operative on July 12, 1978; raises the maximum aggregate amount which may be borrowed by the General Practice Finance Corporation to £25 million.

2036. Health authorities

NATIONAL HEALTH SERVICE (HEALTH AUTHORITIES: MEMBERSHIP) AMENDMENT REGULATIONS 1978 (No. 228) [10p], made under the National Health Service Act 1977 (c. 49), Sched. 5, para. 12 (a); operative on March 21, 1978; amend S.I. 1977 No. 1103 by altering the provisions governing the tenure of office of Area Health Authorities in Wales.

2037. Local health authorities

WHITSTABLE PORT HEALTH AUTHORITY ORDER 1978 (No. 685) [20p], made under the Public Health Act 1936 (c. 49), ss. 2, 3 as extended by the Control of Pollution Act 1974 (c. 40), s. 108, Sched. 3, para. 6; operative on June 12, 1978; constitutes the Port of Whitstable as a port health district and constitutes the Canterbury City Council as port health authority for that district.

2038. Medical practitioners—wages paid to ancillary staff—whether exclusion of wives and dependants unjust

[Health Services and Public Health Act 1968 (c. 46), s. 29 (1); National Health Service (General Medical and Pharmaceutical Services) Regulations 1974 (S.I. 1974 No. 160), reg. 24 (1).] The 1974 Regulations provided for the reimbursement by the National Health Service to doctors of 70 per cent. of the salary paid to their ancillary staff, but excluded wives or dependants of doctors from this provision. *Held*, this exclusion was unjust and oppressive, and was not based on a consideration of all the essential facts. It was not, however, contrary to the Sex Discrimination Act 1975, ss. 1 and 3: GLANVILL *v.* SECRETARY OF STATE FOR HEALTH AND SOCIAL SERVICES, *The Times*, July 29, 1978, Talbot J.

2039. National Health Service (Scotland) Act 1978 (c. 29)

This Act consolidates enactments relating to the National Health Service in Scotland.

Pt. I (ss. 1–17) deals with organisation: s. 1 sets out the general duty of the Secretary of State with regard to the health service; s. 2 establishes the

Health Boards; s. 3 establishes the Scottish Medical Practices Committee; s. 4 establishes the Scottish Dental Estimates Board; s. 5 sets up the Scottish Health Service Planning Council; s. 6 deals with national consultative committees; s. 7 relates to the establishing of local health councils; s. 8 relates to University Liaison Committees; s. 9 deals with the recognition of local consultative committees; s. 10 sets up the Common Services Agency; s. 11 establishes the Scottish Hospital Trust; s. 12 establishes the Scottish Hospital Endowments Research Trust; s. 13 relates to co-operation between Health Boards and other authorities; s. 14 authorises Health Boards to designate medical officers to exercise functions assigned to them; s. 15 deals with the supply of goods and services to local authorities; s. 16 authorises the Secretary of State to assist certain voluntary organisations; s. 17 relates to the furnishing of overseas aid by Health Boards and the Common Services Agency.

Pt. II (ss. 18–35) deals with the provision of services: s. 18 sets out the duty of the Secretary of State to provide medical and other services; s. 19 relates to arrangements and regulations for general medical services; s. 20 deals with applications by medical practitioners to provide general medical services; s. 21 sets out a requirement that a medical practitioner applying under s. 20 must have suitable experience; s. 22 provides for regulations to be made as to s. 21; s. 23 relates to the distribution of general medical services; s. 24 provides for regulations to be made concerning additional functions of the Medical Practices Committee; s. 25 relates to arrangements for the provision of general dental services; s. 26 relates to arrangements for the provision of general ophthalmic services; s. 27 relates to arrangements for the provision of pharmaceutical services; s. 28 deals with persons authorised to provide pharmaceutical services; s. 29 sets up a tribunal for inquiring about the disqualification of persons providing services; s. 30 relates to the removal of a disqualification; s. 31 relates to disqualification provisions in England and Wales or Northern Ireland; s. 32 provides for regulations to be made as to ss. 29–31; s. 33 sets out the powers of the Secretary of State where he considers services to be inadequate; s. 34 provides for regulations to be made regarding the choice of medical practitioners in certain cases; s. 35 places a prohibition on the sale of medical practices.

Pt. III (ss. 36–48) relates to other services and facilities: s. 36 sets out the duty of the Secretary of State regarding accommodation and services; s. 37 empowers the Secretary of State to make arrangements for the prevention of illness, care and after-care; s. 38 relates to the care of mothers and young children; s. 39 sets out the duty of the Secretary of State to provide for the medical and dental inspection, supervision and treatment of pupils and young persons; s. 40 deals with vaccination and immunisation; s. 41 sets out the duty of the Secretary of State relating to family planning; s. 42 relates to health education; s. 43 concerns the control of the spread of infectious disease; s. 44 relates to supplies of blood and other substances; s. 45 sets out the duty of the Secretary of State regarding ambulances; s. 46 provides for vehicles for persons suffering from physical defect or disability; s. 47 relates to the availability of facilities for teaching and research; s. 48 relates to residential and practice accommodation.

Pt. IV (ss. 49–78) relates to the Secretary of State's powers: s. 49 empowers the Secretary of State to provide for the control of the maximum prices of medical supplies; s. 50 sets out additional powers relating to accommodation and services; s. 51 deals with the exercise of the power under s. 50 in relation to private patients; s. 52 makes additional provisions as to charges under s. 50; s. 53 sets out additional powers as to the disposal and production of goods; s. 54 places a restriction on the Secretary of State's powers under ss. 44, 50 and 53; s. 55 authorises the Secretary of State to make hospital accommodation available on part payment of charges; s. 56 relates to expenses payable by resident patients who are remuneratively employed; s. 57 relates to the provision of accommodation and services for private resident patients; s. 58 relates to the provision of accommodation and services for private non-resident patients; s. 59 concerns the withdrawal of facilities available for private patients; s. 60 relates to the revocation of authorisations under ss. 57 or 58; s. 61 makes further provision regarding the revocation of s. 58 authorisations;

s. 62 sets out the principles to be considered when making revocations under ss. 60 or 61; s. 63 places restrictions on authorisations under ss. 57 or 58; s. 64 relates to applications for permission to use health service facilities for private patients; s. 65 sets out the duty of the Secretary of State to provide information to the Health Services Board; s. 66 relates to the publication of matters under ss. 60 and 63; s. 67 imposes a duty on the Secretary of State to publish an annual report on the extent in Scotland of facilities for private patients; s. 68 defines " common waiting lists "; s. 69 provides for regulations to be made for charges for drugs, medicines or appliances or pharmaceutical services; s. 70 provides for regulations to be made for charges for dental or optical appliances; s. 71 relates to charges for dental treatment; s. 72 provides for regulations to be made for charges in respect of services provided under ss. 37, 38 and 41; s. 73 relates to charges for more expensive supplies; s. 74 provides for charges to be made for certain repairs and replacements; s. 75 relates to sums otherwise payable to those providing services; s. 76 deals with inquiries; s. 77 sets out the powers of the Secretary of State in relation to the default of certain bodies; s. 78 sets out the emergency powers of the Secretary of State.

Pt. V (ss. 79–89) deals with property and finance: s. 79 empowers the Secretary of State to purchase land and movable property; s. 80 states that property vested in the Secretary of State is free of trusts; s. 81 gives voluntary organisations a power to transfer property to the Secretary of State; s. 82 relates to the use and administration of certain endowments and other property held by Health Boards; s. 83 gives Health Boards and local health councils a power to hold property on trust; s. 84 relates to the power of trustees to make payments to Health Boards; s. 85 authorises the expenses of certain bodies, and travelling expenses and receipts, to be paid by the Secretary of State; s. 86 states that each Health Board and the Common Services Agency must keep accounts; s. 87 provides for regulations to be made regarding financial arrangements of certain Boards; s. 88 relates to the payment by the Secretary of State of allowances and remuneration to members of certain bodies connected with the health service; s. 89 deals with superannuation for officers of certain hospitals.

Pt. VI (ss. 90–97) relates to the Health Service Commissioner for Scotland: s. 90 establishes the Health Service Commissioner for Scotland and sets out the tenure of his office; s. 91 deals with the salary and pension of the Commissioner; s. 92 authorises the Commissioner to appoint officers to assist him; s. 93 deals with bodies and action subject to the Commissioner's investigation; s. 94 sets out the procedure relating to complaints; s. 95 states that certain provisions of the Parliamentary Commissioner Act 1967 are applicable to the Commissioner; s. 96 relates to reports by the Commissioner; s. 97 contains definitions.

Pt. VII (ss. 98–110) contains miscellaneous and supplementary provisions: s. 98 provides for regulations to be made for the making and recovery of charges in respect of persons not ordinarily resident in Great Britain; s. 99 relates to the evasion of charges; s. 100 provides for accommodation for persons displaced in the course of development; s. 101 applies s. 166 of the Public Health (Scotland) Act 1897 to Health Boards and the Common Services Agency; s. 102 relates to the management of state hospitals; s. 103 relates to arbitration of questions; s. 104 exempts certain conveyances, agreements and assignations from stamp duty; s. 105 relates to the exercise of the power to make orders, regulations and directions; s. 106 relates to supplementary regulatory powers; s. 107 relates to local enactments; s. 108 contains definitions; s. 109 contains transitional provisions and savings, and amendments and repeals; s. 110 gives the short title. The Act extends to Scotland only.

The Act received the Royal Assent on July 20, 1978, and came into force on January 1, 1979.

2040. National insurance. See NATIONAL INSURANCE.

2041. Northern Ireland. See NORTHERN IRELAND.

2042. Pensions. See PENSIONS AND SUPERANNUATION.

2043. Prescription charges

PRESCRIPTION PRICING AUTHORITY CONSTITUTION ORDER 1978 (No. 331) [15p], made under the National Health Services Act 1977 (c. 49), s. 11; operative on April 1, 1978; provides for the Authority a new Constitution.

PRESCRIPTION PRICING AUTHORITY REGULATIONS 1978 (No. 332) [15p], made under the National Health Service Act 1977, Sched. 5, paras. 10, 12; operative on April 1, 1978; provide for the consultations to be carried out by the Secretary of State before making appointments to the Prescription Pricing Authority.

2044. Professions supplementary to medicine

NATIONAL HEALTH SERVICE (PROFESSIONS SUPPLEMENTARY TO MEDICINE) AMENDMENT REGULATIONS 1978 (No. 1090) [10p], made under the National Health Service Act 1977 (c. 49), Sched. 5, paras. 10 (1), 11 (1); operative on October 1, 1978; amend S.I. 1974 No. 494 by substituting certain classifications of specified professions and by providing that a person not registered under the Professions Supplementary to Medicine Act 1960 may not be employed by a local authority unless similarly employed on June 29, 1964, or immediately before April 1, 1974.

2045. Transfer of property

NATIONAL HEALTH SERVICE (TRANSFER OF TRUST PROPERTY—TOOTING BEC HOSPITAL) ORDER 1978 (No. 1072) [10p], made under the National Health Service Act 1977 (c. 49), s. 92 (1); operative on August 25, 1978; provides for the transfer between health authorities of property by reason of a change in arrangements for the administration of Tooting Bec Hospital.

NATIONAL INSURANCE

2046. Family allowances. See FAMILY ALLOWANCES.

2047. National health service. See NATIONAL HEALTH.

2048. Northern Ireland. See NORTHERN IRELAND.

2049. Pensions. See § 2270.

2050. Social security. See SOCIAL SECURITY.

2051. Supplementary benefit. See SOCIAL SECURITY.

ARTICLES. See *post,* p. [30].

NEGLIGENCE

2051a. Architects—planning permission—validity—failure to advise client

An architect was instructed to design an office of under 10,000 sq. ft. so that an office development permit was not required. The building designed included a car park and caretaker's flat which did take the building over 10,000 sq. ft., but the planning officer of the council said that these were not designated as office space. The council granted planning permission. In fact the statement was wrong, and the council had no power in law to grant permission. The architect was liable in negligence for acting on the statement and for failing to advise his client that the planning permission might be wrong in law and of no effect: B. L. HOLDINGS *v.* ROBERT J. WOOD AND PARTNERS, *The Times,* July 21, 1978, Gibson J.

2052. Breach of statutory duty—local authority—statutory remedy

A statute such as the Chronically Sick and Disabled Persons Act 1970, does not give a right of action at law to a disappointed sick person. When the claim is that a local authority have failed to discharge any of their functions under the Act, the remedy lies with the default powers of the Minister under s. 36 of the National Assistance Act 1948 on representation to him. Since the remedy was provided by statute, no other remedy was available. (*Southwark London Borough Council* v. *Williams* [1971] C.L.Y. 9950 followed): WYATT v. HILLINGDON LONDON BOROUGH COUNCIL, *The Times,* May 11, 1978, C.A.

2053. —— **road excavation**

In October 1973, the defendants temporarily reinstated an excavation which they had made in the road in Churchill Road, Walthamstow, London E.17, and gave notice to the local authority under the provisions of the Public Utilities Street Works Act 1950, to permanently reinstate. On February 4, 1974, before the excavation had been permanently reinstated and thus while the defendants were still responsible for that section of the highway, the plaintiff alleged that he tripped over the temporary reinstatement and his momentum caused him to stagger some 25 feet before falling, hitting his head and shoulder against the kerb. *Held*, that the excavation was some 3 feet 3 inches × 5 feet 5 inches. It had sunk, causing a depression of about one inch. Inevitably in the roadway one finds undulations and the surface is not to be judged by the standards of a bowling green. In the circumstances of this case, a depression of one inch was not dangerous. Further, in view of the place of the fall, the plaintiff did not trip over the reinstated excavation. Plaintiff's claim dismissed. (*Littler* v. *Liverpool Corporation* [1968] C.L.Y. 1747, and *Meggs* v. *Liverpool Corporation* [1967] C.L.Y. 1808 considered): COHEN v. BRITISH GAS CORP., January 11, 1978, Judge Lynbery, Q.C. (*Ex rel. B. C. Brooks, Esq., Solicitor.*)

2054. —— **unlit metal plate projecting one-eighth of an inch—public pavement**

A metal plate projecting, unlit, one-eighth of an inch from the pavement may constitute a negligent danger to users of the highway.

Per curiam: Where either or both parties are dissatisfied with the county court judge's note of the evidence, then, as with the judge's note of his summing up, any addition or emendation they agreed on should be submitted to the judge as early as possible so that he may consider the matter and correct his own note.

The electricity board's employees dug a hole in the pavement for a junction box. They covered it with a specially made metal plate which projected one-eighth of an inch. An old lady fell over it and broke her wrist. The county court judge awarded her damages for negligence, in that the plate had not been lit. On appeal, *held*, dismissing the appeal, that the plate was a new and unexpected addition to the roadway, and the judge's finding had been correct. (*Griffiths* v. *Liverpool Corporation* [1966] C.L.Y. 5600, *Meggs* v. *Liverpool Corporation* [1967] C.L.Y. 1808 and *Littler* v. *Liverpool Corporation* [1968] C.L.Y. 1747 distinguished.)

PITMAN v. SOUTHERN ELECTRICITY BOARD (1978) 76 L.G.R. 579, C.A.

2055. Collision—error of judgment—" agony of the moment "—competitor's risk

On February 20, 1977, during the course of a dinghy race at Hillingdon Sailing Base, P's sailing dinghy was caught by a gust of wind and capsized. D was in his sailing dinghy, competing in the race, and was about 25 yards astern of P and a little downwind. As P capsized, D bore away a little in order to pass between P and the bank but as he did so P righted his dinghy, which began to drift rapidly astern. D tried to bear away further but the bow of his dinghy collided with P's dinghy on its starboard side by the transom at an angle of 30° leading aft and causing damage. P claimed the cost of repairs from D. *Held*, on the facts, that (1) when P capsized, D could have stopped (by falling right off or turning into the wind) or he could have turned upwind to pass P or he could have turned downwind to pass P. D chose to turn downwind, but did not do so enough to allow himself sufficient room; (2) although this did amount to an error of judgment, the decision had to be made quickly; it was made in the " agony of the moment," and thus did not amount to negligence; (3) even if D's conduct did amount to negligence it was not reckless nor was it wilful, but was the kind of mistake which competitors voluntarily accept. P's claim dismissed. (*Wooldridge* v. *Sumner* [1962] C.L.Y. 2033, *Sims* v. *Leigh Rugby Club* [1969] C.L.Y. 2400 and *White* v. *Blackmore* [1972] C.L.Y. 2375 considered; *The Volute* [1922] 1 A.C. 129 applied): BETON v. TOONE, July 11, 1978, Judge Leonard, Mayor's and City of London Ct. (*Ex rel. Jervis Kay, Esq., Barrister.*)

2056. Contributory negligence—no specific pleading

Where no plea of contributory negligence is made by a defendant, the court should not, of its own volition, make such a finding.

Following a road accident, the plaintiff sued the driver of an articulated lorry for negligence. The driver did not serve a defence nor appear. The judge held P one-third to blame for the accident. *Held*, allowing P's appeal, that no such finding should have been made in the absence of a plea of contributory negligence by the defendant.

FOOKES v. SLAYTOR [1978] 1 W.L.R. 1293, C.A.

2057. —— **road accident—failure to wear seat belt—burden of proof—phobia.** See CONDON v. CONDON, § 2611.

2058. —— —— —— **drunken driver.** See TRAYNOR v. DONOVAN, § 2612.

2059. —— —— —— **principles for apportioning blame.** See GREGORY v. KELLY, § 2610.

2060. Damages. See also DAMAGES.

2061. —— **measure—house rendered uninhabitable—whether re-instatement cost recoverable**

[Can.] Crude oil escaped from D's pipeline and saturated P's home and land. D admitted liability, but contended that P was not entitled to anything for the replacement of the house, soil and trees because the part of the property on which they were situated was zoned " commercial," and if sold for commercial purposes, it would exceed its residential value, with or without the buildings. Alternatively, D argued that its liability extended only to replacement cost, less depreciation. P claimed for the replacement value, as they had already received zoning approval to rebuild a residential house, and as the house was situated next to a vintage car museum which they operated. *Held*, P was entitled to replacement cost, as they would not be able to find another location as convenient to them. As there was no evidence that a new home would be worth any more to P than the old one, there was no deduction made for depreciation. (*C. R. Taylor* (*Wholesale*) v. *Hepworths* [1977] C.L.Y. 2020 applied): JENS v. MANNIX Co. [1978] 5 W.W.R. 486, Brit.Col.Sup.Ct.

2062. Defective premises—vendors—duty of care

A husband and wife, the defendants, built a restaurant on land which they owned, and themselves, and/or a plumber working for them, installed in it a hot water system. The defendants operated the restaurant for some months, and then sold and conveyed the land with the restaurant, its fixtures and fittings and goodwill, to the plaintiffs. The plaintiffs alleged in their pleadings (i) that the defendants knew at the time of building the restaurant that they might soon sell it; (ii) that the hot water system was negligently designed and/or installed; and (iii) that, after conveyance, the hot water system malfunctioned, causing physical damage and financial loss to the plaintiffs. On the trial of preliminary issues of law based upon the allegations made in the plaintiffs' pleadings, *held*: (1) the defendants owed to the plaintiffs a duty of care in the tort of negligence, whereby, if the facts pleaded by the plaintiffs were proved, the plaintiffs were entitled to recover damages from the defendants in respect of their damage and loss, notwithstanding the defendants' earlier disposal of all interest in the property and that the defendants were not professional builders; and (2) condition 12 (3) of the Law Society's Conditions of Sale (1970 edition), which was incorporated in the contract for sale of the land and restaurant, and which provided that the plaintiffs should " be deemed to buy with full notice in all respects of the actual state and condition of the property and . . . shall take the property as it is," did not exempt the defendants from liability for negligence and could not afford them a defence. (*Dicta* in *Anns* v. *Merton London Borough Council* [1977] C.L.Y. 2030, followed): HONE v. BENSON, February 17, 1978, Judge Fay, Q.C. (*Ex rel. Roy McAuley, Esq., Barrister.*)

2063. Duty of care—breach—driving whilst disqualified—passenger's knowledge

[Aust.] P was a passenger in a motor car who was injured in an accident caused by the driver's negligence. P was aware the driver did not hold a driving licence and had been disqualified from holding one. The driver pleaded that at the time of the accident, P and he were jointly participating in the commission of a crime, and therefore he did not owe P a duty of care. *Held*, P's participation in the driver's offence did not deprive P of the right of action which would otherwise have existed for breach of the driver's duty of care: HARRISON v. JACKSON (1977) 16 S.A.S.R. 182, Sth.Aust.Sup.Ct.

2064. —— **children buying ice-cream from van—liability of owner and driver**

[Can.] The infant plaintiff, having bought ice-cream from an ice-cream van parked at the curb, dashed into the street and was struck by a passing car. The driver of the ice-cream van was an untrained 19-year-old student. After serving the infant plaintiff, he served her brother. At that time, the car was some distance behind the van. Had the driver of the van looked through the large glass windows at the rear of the van, he could not have failed to see that the two children would be in imminent danger of being struck. *Held*, his failure to warn them before they started to cross the road of the danger from cars was negligence, as was his failure to take the precaution of looking through his windows. With regard to the liability of the mother, she had given the children clear instructions how to cross the road, and specifically reminded them on this occasion to " watch out for cars." The standard of care put on her is that of mothers in the area where an ice-cream van stopped in order to attract young children: she was not contributorily negligent. Mothers are entitled to rely on drivers of ice-cream vans to exercise care towards the children attracted by the vehicle. (*Robins v. National Trust Co.* [1927] A.C. 515 applied): ARNOLD v. TENO (1978) 83 D.L.R. (3d) 609, Canada Sup.Ct.

2065. —— **defective goods—proper supervision of work no defence**

A manufacturer can be vicariously liable for the negligence of his workmen notwithstanding the fact that he has a good system of work and adequate supervision.

P was standing on a wooden case which caved in, so that he fell. It caved in because it had been badly nailed together. He sued the manufacturer, who denied liability since he had an adequate system of manufacture and provided adequate supervision. *Held*, that the plaintiff could succeed. The manufacturer was vicariously liable for the negligence of his workmen.

HILL v. JAMES CROWE (CASES) [1978] 1 All E.R. 812, Mackenna J.

2066. —— **garage owner—car left in street—stolen**

No greater standard of care is required of a garage owner than is expected of a prudent owner who takes steps to immobilise his vehicle in some way.

The plaintiff was owner of a motor caravan with a defective gearbox. He drove the vehicle to the defendant's premises, and was instructed to leave it in a side street, from which it was stolen two days later. Evidence at the trial indicated that the vehicle could only be moved with great difficulty. The plaintiff succeeded at first instance. On appeal, *held*, allowing the appeal, that no higher standard of care was required of a garage owner than that exhibited by an owner who immobolised his vehicle in some way. Since the vehicle was as immobile as could be expected, the defendants were not negligent.

COWAN v. BLACKWILL MOTOR CARAVAN CONVERSIONS [1978] R.T.R. 421, C.A.

2067. —— **house builders—land subject to natural landslides—action in contract and tort**

Builders and developers may be liable in negligence to purchasers of a house built upon land which, although surveyed by the contractors, was not appreciated to be subject to landslides.

A, a builder, purchased laid and sold the same to B, a developer, B thereafter financing the building of dwelling-houses thereon by A. A and B had inspected the land prior to its purchase but had failed to inspect and/or appreciate the significance of the sub-soil of adjoining land which to an expert would have indicated that the land to be developed, which was on a hillside, was liable to be affected by landslides. In 1971 the plaintiffs purchased from B one of the houses which had been properly constructed by A. In 1974 a landslide removed part of the garden thereof and the house was doomed since within 10 years at most further landslips were expected to destroy the house, which therefore became valueless. The plaintiffs claimed damages from A and B for negligence and also against B for a breach of a contractual warranty that the house was built in " an efficient and workmanlike manner and of proper materials and so as to be fit for habitation." Crichton J. held that both A and B were negligent but declined to enter judgment against B for breach of warranty although he found that they were in breach. On appeal and cross-appeal, *held*, (1) that B were in breach of the warranty since the words " and so as to be fit for habitation " were not to be limited in their meaning by the preceding words and that clearly the house was not fit for habitation; (2) the plaintiffs were entitled to judgment against B in both contract and tort; (3) A, the builders, were liable in negligence since their duty to act as careful and competent builders upon the facts of this case extended beyond a duty to build the house properly and with adequate foundations. (*Esso Petroleum Co.* v. *Mardon* [1976] C.L.Y. 341 and *Anns* v. *Merton London Borough Council* [1977] C.L.Y. 2030 applied; *Dutton* v. *Bognor Regis Urban District Council* [1972] C.L.Y. 2352 considered.)

BATTY *v.* METROPOLITAN PROPERTY REALISATIONS [1978] 2 W.L.R. 500, C.A.

2068. —— **foreseeability—whether act of vandalism amounts to novus actus interveniens**

[Scot.] A man sustained severe injuries when knocked down and trampled upon by a crowd at a football ground. The crowd made a deliberate attack on a gate, which eventually gave way, and then surged through, carrying P in with them. There was no suggestion of contributory fault by P. It was established that (1) no one had inspected the part of the gate that gave way prior to the accident; (2) no one had applied his mind to problems of crowd safety resulting from the gate being broken down; (3) the gate was corroded in part; (4) there was no safety device to keep the gate in position and that such devices were common-place and effective; and (5) the occupiers knew of other similar incidents at their and other football grounds. *Held*, (1) it was reasonably foreseeable by the occupiers that there might be an attempt by an unruly crowd to force the gate; (2) the behaviour of the crowd did not amount to a novus actus interveniens breaking the causal link; (3) accordingly, the occupiers were liable. (*Home Office* v. *Dorset Yacht Co.* [1970] C.L.Y. 1849 applied): HOSIE *v.* ARBROATH FOOTBALL CLUB, 1978 S.L.T. 122, Outer House.

2069. —— **owed by Home Office—sexual offender in prison—attack**

E, a prisoner serving a sentence for sexual offences on young girls, was attacked and seriously injured by fellow prisoners in a lavatory a few days after being taken off r. 43 restrictions, under which he had been segregated from other prisoners. *Held*, that the defendants had a duty to exercise reasonable care for prisoners and greater care and supervision over prisoners potentially more at risk than other prisoners. The prison officers in the canvas shop where E worked should have been told that he had just been taken off r. 43 and should have taken reasonable steps to guard him against attack to which they knew he might be subject. However, E's claim failed, as a spontaneous attack in the lavatory like this would not have been anticipated, and thus no breach of duty leading to the injury was shown: EGERTON *v.* HOME OFFICE [1978] Crim.L.R. 494, May J.

2070. —— **owner of chartered vessel—loading of cargo.** See THE RED JACKET, § 2728.

2071. —— **surveyor's report—measure of damages**

[Scot.] In reliance on a surveyor's report, a purchaser bought a house which had dry-rot not mentioned by the report. *Held*, the measure of damages was the amount required to put the purchaser in the position he would have been in had the surveyor fulfilled the duty of care incumbent on him; that is, the difference between the value of the house in its assumed condition and the value of its actual state. (*Philips* v. *Ward* [1956] C.L.Y. 936 followed): UPSTONE *v.* G. D. W. CARNEGIE & CO., 1978 S.L.T. 4, Sheriff Principal R., Reid Q.C.

2072. —— **users of highway—misleading signals—failure to keep a proper look-out —apportionment of liability.** See WADSWORTH *v.* GILLESPIE, § 2534.

2073. —— **whether owed by mortgagee towards mortgagor—loss of title deeds.** See BROWNING *v.* HANDILAND GROUP, § 2025.

2074. Economic loss—remoteness—duty of care—multiple test to be used

[Can.] P1 and P2 purchased some charter flight tickets from a travel agency, of which D was vice-president. The tickets were to be used by P1 and P2 and their close relatives. D promised to drive some of the family to the airport. As a result of his gross negligence in so doing, the father of D1 was killed in a road accident. As a result of the death, none of the other members of the family boarded the flight. Because the tickets were for a charter flight, neither P1 nor P2 was able to recover the cost of the tickets from either the airline nor the travel agency. In an action for damages for economic loss suffered as a result of D's negligence, *held*, there should be judgment for P1 and P2. While some of the cases consider the question as one of duty and others as one of remoteness, all are dealing with the same issue. There is a multiple test: (1) there must be a duty owed by D to P; (2) there must have been a breach of that duty; and (3) the damages suffered by P as a result of that breach must not be too remote or, put another way, it must have been reasonably foreseeable. D knew that if P1 and P2 did not board the charter flight, they would be unable to recover the cost of their tickets. He also knew—or is presumed to know—that if he negligently prevented the father from making the trip, P1 and P2 would not go; that is, D had the knowledge, or means of knowledge, that P1 and P2 individually would be likely to suffer economic loss as a consequence of his negligence, and he owed them a duty of care not to cause them such loss by his negligent act. (*Spartan Steel and Alloys* v. *Martin & Co. (Contractors)* [1972] C.L.Y. 2341; *Overseas Tankship (U.K.)* v. *Morts Dock and Engineering Co.* [1961] C.L.Y. 2343; *Anns* v. *Merton London Borough Council* [1977] C.L.Y. 2030 referred to): YUMEROVSKI v. DANI (1978) 83 D.L.R. (3d) 558, Middlesex County Ct., Ont.

2075. Exclusion of liability—by-law—common law duty

[Singapore Harbour Board By-Laws (Straits Settlements Gazette, December 5, 1913), by-law 26.]

By-law 26 does not exclude or transfer the liability at common law of the port authority for the negligence of their employees in the course of their employment.

The deceased was a member of a gang of stevedores, all of whom were employed by the Singapore port authority. Whilst engaged in loading a ship the deceased was injured in an accident caused by the negligence of a fellow workman. He subsequently died and the administrator of his estate claimed damages for personal injuries against the port authority. The trial judge dismissed the action on the ground that by-law 26 exempted the port authority from liability. The Court of Appeal dismissed the administrator's appeal. On appeal to the Judicial Committee, *held*, allowing the appeal, that by-law 26 did not exempt the port authority and they were liable in respect of the injuries. (*Alishakkar* v. *Port of Singapore Authority* (unreported), August 16, 1973, overruled, in part. Decision of the Court of Appeal in Singapore reversed.)

KARUPPAN BHOOMIDAS v. PORT OF SINGAPORE AUTHORITY [1978] 1 W.L.R. 189, P.C.

2076. Failure to repair—loss of profits—damages

[Can.] The roof of the plaintiff's building constructed in 1973 collapsed early in 1974 as a result of the negligent manufacture and preparation of plans by the defendants. Because of lack of funds, the plaintiff was unable to make repairs promptly. As a result, because of inflation and continued loss of profits, the plaintiff's losses were much greater than they would have been if repairs could have been made promptly. *Held*, there should be judgment for the plaintiff based on what would have been the costs of repairs and loss of profits if the building had been repaired promptly. (*Dredger " Liesbosch "* v. *S.S. Edison* [1933] A.C. 449 applied): ALBERTA CARRIERS v. R. VOLLAN (ALTA.) (1977) 81 D.L.R. 672, Alberta Sup.Ct.

2077. Liability—accident—two defendants—only first defendant culpable—indemnity from second defendant

[Can.] The plaintiffs were injured in a motor accident caused by the first defendant's negligence. Immediately after the collision, another car, driven by the second defendant, collided with the plaintiff. *Held,* they were able to recover all their damages from the first defendant. Such damages as were caused by the second defendant occurred by virtue of the situation into which the first defendant had placed them. As between the first and second defendants, for the first defendant to claim any indemnity he had to show what proportion of blame the second defendant bore. As he could not show this, he was unable to succeed in such a claim: WARD *v.* PALAMARCHUK AND PELECH [1977] 6 W.W.R. 193, Alberta Sup.Ct.

2078. —— **barristers—immunity narrowed.** See SAIF ALI *v.* SYDNEY MITCHELL AND CO. (A FIRM), § 2323.

2079. —— **exclusion—independent contractors—lost cargo.** See THE FEDERAL SCHELDE, § 2695.

2080. ——**harbour authority—damage to cargo—exclusion of liability**
[Kenya] A crude oil tower belonging to P was shipped on the A for carriage from Liverpool to Mombasa under a bill of lading which stated, by cl. 29, that no independent contractor employed by the carrier should be under any liability whatsoever to the shipper, consignee or owner of the goods for any loss or damage arising from any act, neglect or default on his part while acting in the course of his employment. At Kilindi Harbour, Mombasa, the tower was damaged when it was being lowered by a floating crane operated by D, the harbour authority. P claimed damages in negligence. D contended that they were exempt from liability by reason of reg. 61 (1) (*g*) of the East African Harbours Regulations and cl. 29 of the bill of lading. Reg. 61 (1) stated, inter alia, that lifting by cranes provided by the harbour authority was performed upon the condition that no liability whatsoever should attach to the authority for any damage, howsoever caused, to the goods. P maintained that the regulation was ultra vires the East African Harbours Act, s. 76 (1), under which it was made. The Act stated, inter alia, that the authority could make regulations with respect to the services provided for the maintenance of order in any harbour. *Held,* by the High Ct. of Kenya (1) on the facts D had been negligent; they were in breach of reg. 184 (1) as the wire ropes had not been examined and tested by a competent person; and also in breach of reg. 187, as there were no markings on the ropes denoting their safe working loads; (2) reg. 61 (1) was ultra vires; (3) D could not rely on cl. 29. (*The Eurymedon* [1973] C.L.Y. 3095, not followed): LUMMUS CO. *v.* EAST AFRICAN HARBOURS CORP. [1978] 1 Lloyd's Rep. 317, High Ct. of Kenya.

2081. —— **of manufacturer, retailer, owner and his agent respectively—sale of defective towing coupling**
The coupling between a vehicle and trailer driven by D2, D1's servant, broke, and the trailer came into collision with a car, as a result of which P, a mother and daughter, were injured and the father and son killed. The coupling had been sold to D1 by D4, who had purchased it from D3, the manufacturers. On P's claim in negligence, *held,* that (1) the defects in the coupling were readily foreseeable by an appropriately skilled engineer, and accordingly D3 were liable in tort to P; (2) D1 and D2 were liable in tort to P for continuing to use the coupling in a state which had been manifestly damaged for months; (3) D4 were not liable to P in tort since they had no reason to doubt the suitability or design of the coupling, and were under no duty to inspect the ancillary equipment of the vehicle; (3) D1's claim against D4 under s. 14 of the Sale of Goods Act 1893 succeeded in so far as the coupling was not suitable for the purpose for which it was provided, but D1 was not entitled to damages to the extent of his liability to P because the continued use of the coupling when it was manifestly broken was not in the contemplation of the parties, and accordingly the damage was not caused by the breach of contract. Claim dismissed: LAMBERT *v.* LEWIS [1978] 1 Lloyd's Rep. 610, Stocker J.

2082. —— **personal injury of employee—course of employment—insurer's indemnity**
P, an employee of D, who were building contractors constructing a gas refinery at Bid Boland, Iran, was injured whilst a passenger in a vehicle owned by D due to negligent driving by D's driver. The vehicle was on its way from

D's office at Abadan to the construction site 170 km. away where P was told he was required. There was no public transport between Abadan and Bid Boland where P had a house, and D provided transport for all employees travelling to and from the construction site. D were insured with A, underwriters, against legal liability in respect of accidental bodily injury to persons carried, inter alia, in a licensed motor vehicle belonging to D. The policy expressly excluded liability in respect of any accident, injury or liability to any person arising out of, and in the course of, employment by D. D were also insured with B, under an employer's liability insurance policy covering them in respect of bodily injury to an employee caused, and arising out of, and in the course of, employment by D. P claimed damages from D who settled the claim. D claimed an indemnity from A and B. *Held,* (1) for a man to be in the course of his employment he must be doing something which it is his duty to his employer to do; on the facts, it was part of P's employment to travel on D's vehicle from the office at Abadan to the construction site; (2) the accident arose in the course of P's employment, and B were liable to indemnify D. (*St. Helen's Colliery Co.* v. *Hewitson* [1924] A.C. 58, applied): PATERSON v. COSTAIN & PRESS (OVERSEAS) [1978] 1 Lloyd's Rep. 86, Talbot J.

2083. —— **rescuer principle—car negligently driven into train**
    [Can.] The conductor of a train was a rescuer. D's negligence in driving his car created the need for his own rescue. If the conductor had not come to his rescue, D could have aggravated his existing injuries. *Held,* the conductor did not act in a wanton manner but in an unselfish, responsible way. It should be reasonably foreseeable to the driver of a car who carelessly runs into a train that someone will come to his aid. (*Videan* v. *British Transport Commission* [1963] C.L.Y. 233 applied): CANADIAN NATIONAL RAILWAY CO. v. BAKTY (1978) 82 D.L.R. (3d) 731, Haldimand County Ct., Ontario.

2084. —— **unborn child**
    A boy, now 6, suffered from injuries sustained while he was still en ventre sa mère when his mother sustained a car collision with the defendant. The defendant admitted that the boy had a cause of action at common law, and the court entered judgment for him. This was the first action in an English court where such an admission had been made: WILLIAMS v. LUFF, *The Times,* February 14, 1978, O'Connor J.

2085. **Master and servant—employee robbed**
    Plaintiff was robbed when he collected the weekly wages (about £1,500) for his firm. *Held,* that on the facts the employers were guilty of negligence in failing to employ a security firm to collect the wages: CHARLTON v. FORREST PRINTING INK CO., *The Times,* October 19, 1978, Forbes J.

2086. **Manufacturer's negligence—no contractual relationship—no damage to persons or property—damages for economic loss**
    [Can.] P sued D1, the manufacturer of heating units which P had purchased from D2, in negligence as the heaters did not work and had to be replaced. D1 made a motion to dispose of a point of law prior to trial, namely that P could not claim for recovery of damages for economic loss in a negligence action without there being damage to person or property. *Held,* there was no cause of action against D1 as there was no contractual relationship, express or implied, between the plaintiff and the manufacturer. (*Anns* v. *Merton London Borough Council* [1977] C.L.Y. 2030 considered): ITAL-CANADIAN INVESTMENTS v. NORTH SHORE PLUMBING AND HEATING CO. [1978] 4 W.W.R. 289, Brit.Col.Sup.Ct.

2087. **Northern Ireland.** See NORTHERN IRELAND.

2088. **Product liability—burden of proof—plaintiff must prove existence of defect before product left manufacturer's hands**
    [Can.] In an action against a manufacturer by a person complaining of injury by a defective product, it was *held* that P must show, on the balance of probabilities, that the product was defective when it left the manufacturer's hands; and he can show this by proving that, on the balance of probabilities, the defect complained of was not added after the product left

the manufacturer's hands. (*Donoghue* v. *Stevenson* [1932] A.C. 562; *Evans* v. *Triplex Safety Glass Co.* [1936] 1 All E.R. 283, and *Mason* v. *Williams* [1955] C.L.Y. 1857 referred to): SMITH v. INGLIS (1978) 83 D.L.R. (3d) 215, Nova Scotia Sup.Ct.

2089. —— **herbicide—inadequate warning as to use—liability for reduced crop yield**
 [Can.] P, a farmer of 25 years' experience, used Treflan, a herbicide manufactured by D, on fields to be used for flax. The instructions warned of dangers if certain crops were to be grown, but did not mention flax. *Held*, failure to inform P of the risks attendant on using Treflan when planting flax was negligent on D's part. D was liable in respect of the reduction in yield: LABRECQUE v. SASKATCHEWAN WHEAT POOL AND ELI LILLEY & CO. (CANADA) (1977) 6 W.W.R. 122, Saskatchewan Q.B.

2090. —— **neurosurgery—patient not informed of risks.** See REIBL v. HUGHES, § 2852.

2091. Shareholders—right of minority shareholders to sue. See DANIELS v. DANIELS, § 241.

2092. Solicitor—failure to register land charge—extent of duty. See MIDLAND BANK TRUST CO. v. HETT, STUBBS & KEMP (A FIRM), § 2822.

2093. —— **will witnessed by beneficiary's wife—test of damages.** See WHITTINGHAM v. CREASE, § 2825.

2094. Special precautions—country lane—large bus
 Where a large bus is using a small lane there are no special precautions, over and above the existence of reasonable care, which its owners should necessarily take.
 P's car was five feet five inches wide. A bus coming in the opposite direction was eight feet two inches wide. The road was 17 feet six inches wide. There was a collision between them. The deputy county court judge, allowing an amendment to plead (and refusing a request for an adjournment to consider the allegation) that the owners of the bus should have taken some special precautions in view of the width of their vehicle, made a finding of negligence against the defendants. *Held*, allowing their appeal, that those precautions were impracticable and perhaps unlawful. There had been enough room for the two vehicles to pass, and the defendants had not been negligent.
 THROWER v. THAMES VALLEY AND ALDERSHOT BUS CO. [1978] R.T.R. 271, C.A.

2095. Standard of care—doctor—wrong diagnosis—correct diagnosis not practicable —whether doctor liable
 [Can.] D, a doctor on a house call, diagnosed 'flu in his patient, although the symptoms were not those of 'flu. In fact, the patient subsequently died of meningitis. *Held,* the doctor was not, by failing to diagnose meningitis, falling short of the standard of care expected of a normal, prudent practitioner, he was nevertheless liable, because he should have known the patient was not suffering from influenza and should have arranged for hospital tests to determine the correct diagnosis: DALE v. MUNTHALI (1978) 78 D.L.R. 588, Ontario High Ct.

2096. Vandalism—duty of landlord—property adjoining vacant property. See EVANS v. GLASGOW DISTRICT COUNCIL, § 1789.

BOOKS AND ARTICLES. See *post*, pp. [7], [30].

NORTHERN IRELAND

2097. Administrative Law
 SALARIES (COMPTROLLER AND AUDITOR-GENERAL AND OTHERS) ORDER (NORTHERN IRELAND) 1978 (No. 303) [10p], made under S.I. 1973 No. 1086 (N.I. 14), art. 4 operative on December 1, 1978; increases the salaries of the comptroller and auditor-general, the parliamentary commissioner and the commissioner for complaints, revokes the 1977 (No. 188) Order.
 PARLIAMENTARY COMMISSIONER FOR ADMINISTRATION AND COMMISSIONER FOR COMPLAINTS (PENSION) ORDER (NORTHERN IRELAND) 1978 (No. 304) [10p],

made under the Parliamentary Commissioner Act (Northern Ireland) 1969 (c. 10), s. 2 (3) and the Commissioner for Complaints Act (Northern Ireland) 1969 (c. 25), s. 13 (1); operative on December 1, 1978; amends the definition of " last annual salary " in the 1973 (No. 455) Order.

LANDS TRIBUNAL (SALARIES) ORDER (NORTHERN IRELAND) 1978 (No. 305) [10p], made under the Lands Tribunal and Compensation Act (Northern Ireland) 1964 (c. 29), s. 2 (5); operative on December 1, 1978; increases the salaries of members of the lands tribunal; revokes the 1977 (No. 189) Order.

2098. Adoption (Hague Convention) Act (Northern Ireland) 1969 (c. 22)—commencement

ADOPTION (1969 HAGUE CONVENTION ACT) (COMMENCEMENT) ORDER (NORTHERN IRELAND) 1978 (No. 271 (C. 12)) [10p], made under the Adoption (Hague Convention) Act (Northern Ireland) 1969, s. 13 (2) and the Northern Ireland Act 1974 (c. 28), Sched. 1, para. 2 (1) (2); brings the remaining provisions of the Adoption (Hague Convention) Act (Northern Ireland) 1969 into operation on October 23, 1978.

2099. Agriculture

AGRICULTURE (TRACTOR CABS) REGULATIONS (NORTHERN IRELAND) 1978 (No. 33) [25p], made under the Agriculture (Safety, Health and Welfare Provisions) Act (Northern Ireland) 1959 (c. 24), s. 1; operative on April 1, 1978; require certain tractors used in agriculture to be fitted with safety cabs; revoke the 1970 (No. 52) Regulations.

PIGS (FEED PRICE ALLOWANCE) (AMENDMENT) SCHEME (NORTHERN IRELAND) 1978 (No. 47) [10p], made under the Agriculture (Temporary Assistance) Act (Northern Ireland) 1954 (c. 31), s. 1, as amended by the Agriculture (Temporary Assistance) Act (Northern Ireland) 1957 (c. 3); operative on April 1, 1978; increases the maximum amount payable under certain feed price allowance schemes and extends the period within which the amount may be spent.

EGGS (FEED PRICE ALLOWANCE) (AMENDMENT) SCHEME (NORTHERN IRELAND) 1978 (No. 48) [10p], made under the Agriculture (Temporary Assistance) Act (Northern Ireland) 1954, s. 1, as amended by the Agriculture (Temporary Assistance) (Amendment) Act (Northern Ireland) 1957, operative on April 1, 1978; increases the maximum amount payable under various feed price allowance schemes.

POULTRY (FEED PRICE ALLOWANCE) (AMENDMENT) SCHEME (NORTHERN IRELAND) 1978 (No. 49) [10p], made under the Agriculture (Temporary Assistance) Act (Northern Ireland) 1954, s. 1, as amended by the Agriculture (Temporary Assistance) (Amendment) Act (Northern Ireland) 1957; operative on April 1, 1978; increases the maximum amount payable under various feed price allowance schemes.

BACON CURERS' (LICENCES AND RETURNS) (AMENDMENT) REGULATIONS (NORTHERN IRELAND) 1978 (No. 52) [40p], made under the Agricultural Produce (Meat Regulation and Pig Industry) Act (Northern Ireland) 1962 (c. 13), ss. 15, 20; operative on April 3, 1978; amend certain forms in the 1966 (No. 27) Regulations

RECORDING AND PERFORMANCE TESTING (BEEF CATTLE) SCHEME (NORTHERN IRELAND) 1978 (No. 66) [15p], made under the Agriculture Act (Northern Ireland) 1949 (c. 2), s. 9, as amended by S.I. 1977 No. 1245 (N.I. 12), art. 5; operative on April 10, 1978; requires records to be kept for certain beef breeding herds and selected beef bulls; authorises the payment of premiums to the owners of certain bulls.

BEEF HERD IMPROVEMENT SCHEME (NORTHERN IRELAND) 1978 (No. 67) [10p], made under the Agriculture Act (Northern Ireland) 1949, s. 9, as amended by S.I. 1977 No. 1245, art. 5; operative on April 10, 1978; allows payments to be made to owners of certain cows in respect of their artificial insemination.

SHEEP HEADAGE PAYMENTS SCHEME (NORTHERN IRELAND) 1978 (No. 68) [11p], made under the Agriculture (Temporary Assistance) Act (Northern Ireland) 1954, s. 1, as amended by the Agriculture (Temporary Assistance)

(Amendment) Act (Northern Ireland) 1957; operative on March 27, 1978; authorises headage payments for certain home-bred sheep.

SEED POTATO (IMPROVEMENT) SCHEME (NORTHERN IRELAND) 1978 (NO. 111) [15p], made under the Agriculture (Temporary Assistance) Act (Northern Ireland) 1954, s. 1, as amended by the Agriculture (Temporary Assistance) (Amendment) Act (Northern Ireland) 1957, operative on May 26, 1978; authorises the payment of grants in respect of measures to increase the efficiency of the seed potato industry; revokes the 1977 (No. 226) scheme.

AGRICULTURE ACT 1949 (AMENDMENT) REGULATIONS (NORTHERN IRELAND) 1978 (No. 133) [10p], made under S.I. 1977 No. 1245 (N.I. 12), art. 20 (1) (a) (2) (a); operative on July 1, 1978; substitute a metric unit in s. 43 (1) of the Agriculture Act (Northern Ireland) 1949.

EMPLOYMENT IN AGRICULTURE (AMENDMENT) SCHEME (NORTHERN IRELAND) 1978 (No. 155) [10p], made under the Agriculture (Temporary Assistance) Act (Northern Ireland) 1954, s. 1, as amended by the Agriculture (Temporary Assistance) (Amendment) Act (Northern Ireland) 1957; operative on July 24, 1978; increases the amount payable under, and extends the duration of, the 1972 (No. 230) Scheme.

MILK RECORDING SCHEME (NORTHERN IRELAND) 1978 (No. 189) [20p], made under the Agriculture Act (Northern Ireland) 1949, s. 9, as amended by S.I. 1977 No. 1245 (N.I. 12), art. 5; operative on September 4, 1978; provides a means for assessing the breeding value of dairy cattle; revokes the 1971 (No. 340) scheme.

SOLID PACK APPLES (QUALITY) (AMENDMENT) REGULATIONS (NORTHERN IRELAND) 1978 (No. 207) [10p], made under the Horticulture Act (Northern Ireland) 1966 (c. 15), ss. 13, 17, 18, 33; operative on September 15, 1978; amend the 1977 (No. 67) Regulations by deleting references to heat treatment of certain apples and amending a definition.

SHEEP IMPROVEMENT SCHEME (NORTHERN IRELAND) 1978 (No. 211) [25p], made under the Agriculture Act (Northern Ireland) 1949, as amended by S.I. 1977 No. 1245 (N.I. 12), art. 5; operative on August 30, 1978; increases manhire payments to certain flock owners of sheep; revokes the 1972 (No. 163) and 1975 (No. 329) Schemes.

BLACK FACE RAMS SCHEME (NORTHERN IRELAND) 1978 (No. 212) [20p], made under the Agriculture Act (Northern Ireland) 1949, s. 9, as amended by S.I. 1977 No. 1245, art. 5; operative on August 30, 1978; increases grants to purchasers of approved black face rams; revokes the 1971 (No. 256) and 1973 (No. 205) Schemes.

SEEDS (FEES) REGULATIONS (NORTHERN IRELAND) 1978 (No. 226) [30p], made under the Seeds Act (Northern Ireland) 1965 (c. 22), ss. 1 (2), 2 (2) (4), as amended by the 1972 (No. 351) order; operative on September 11, 1978; increase fees under certain Regulations on seeds; revoke the 1977 (No. 187) Regulations.

MARKETING OF POTATOES (AMENDMENT) REGULATIONS (NORTHERN IRELAND) 1978 (No. 237) [10p], made under the Marketing of Potatoes Act (Northern Ireland) 1964 (c. 8), ss. 3 (3), 7 (2), 11; operative on October 1, 1978; increase the fee for inspecting potatoes to 70p per tonne.

FERTILIZERS (SAMPLING AND ANALYSIS) REGULATIONS (NORTHERN IRELAND) 1978 (No. 240) [£2], made under the Agriculture Act (Northern Ireland) 1970 (c. 40), ss. 66 (1), 74A, 75 (1), 77, 78 (2) (4) (6), 79 (1) (2) (9), 84, 86; operative on October 1, 1978; deal with the sampling and analysis of fertilisers.

PIG PRODUCTION DEVELOPMENT (CONTRIBUTION) ORDER (NORTHERN IRELAND) 1978 (No. 255) [10p], made under the Pig Production Development Act (Northern Ireland) 1964 (c. 25), s. 4 (1), as amended by S.I. 1977 No. 1245 (N.I. 12), art. 12; operative on October 2, 1978; reduces the amount payable by pig producers to the pig production development fund; revokes the 1977 (No. 245) Order.

EUROPEAN COMMUNITIES EGGS (MARKETING STANDARDS) (AMENDMENT) REGULATIONS (NORTHERN IRELAND) 1978 (No. 300) [20p], made under the European Communities Act 1972 (c. 68), s. 2 (2); operative on November 16, 1978; make detailed amendments of the 1973 (No. 23) Regulations.

2100. Animals

DISEASES OF ANIMALS (SCHEDULED SUBSTANCES EXEMPTION) ORDER (NORTHERN IRELAND) 1977 (No. 358) [10p], made under the Diseases of Animals Act (Northern Ireland) 1958 (c. 13), s. 32A (1); operative on February 1, 1978; permits commercial animal feeding stuffs manufacturers to have in their possession two arsenical feed additives for certain purposes.

ANIMALS AND POULTRY QUARANTINE FEES ORDER (NORTHERN IRELAND) 1978 (No. 58) [15p], made under the Diseases of Animals Act (Northern Ireland) 1958, s. 43A, as inserted by the Agriculture (Miscellaneous Provisions) Act (Northern Ireland) 1965 (c. 3), s. 13 and amended by S.I. 1977 No. 1245, art. 12; operative on April 1, 1978; prescribes fees payable to the Department of Agriculture for the care and housing of quarantined animals and poultry.

TUBERCULOSIS CONTROL (AMENDMENT) ORDER (NORTHERN IRELAND) 1978 (No. 164) [10p], made under the Diseases of Animals Act (Northern Ireland) 1958, ss. 10, 53, Sched. 2; operative on July 17, 1978; increases limits of compensation under the 1964 (No. 31) Order.

BRUCELLOSIS CONTROL (AMENDMENT) ORDER (NORTHERN IRELAND) 1978 (No. 165) [10p], made under the Diseases of Animals Act (Northern Ireland) 1958, ss. 3, 5, 10, 13, 18, 53, Sched. 2, operative on July 17, 1978; increases limits of compensation under the 1972 (No. 94) Order and makes detailed amendments in that Order.

JOHNE'S DISEASE (COMPENSATION) ORDER (NORTHERN IRELAND) 1978 (No. 205) [10p], made under the Diseases of Animals Act (Northern Ireland) 1958, ss. 10, 53; operative on September 1, 1978; specifies the compensation for animals slaughtered on account of Johne's disease.

WARBLE FLY (TREATMENT) SCHEME (AMENDMENT) ORDER (NORTHERN IRELAND) 1978 (No. 228) [20p], made under the Diseases of Animals Act (Northern Ireland) 1958, s. 3B; operative on September 15, 1978; makes detailed amendments of the 1976 (No. 245) Order.

IMPORTATION OF BEES REGULATIONS (NORTHERN IRELAND) 1978 (No. 239) [20p], made under the Bee Pest Prevention Act (Northern Ireland) 1945 (c. 1), s. 4A; operative on October 2, 1978; prohibit the importation into Northern Ireland of bees in fixed-comb hives and bees which have not been certified free of disease; revoke the 1955 (No. 83) Regulations.

SHEEP SCAB (AMENDMENT) ORDER (NORTHERN IRELAND) 1978 (No. 247) [20p], made under the Diseases of Animals Act (Northern Ireland) 1958, ss. 5, 7, 8, 13, 14, 23, 25, 53; operative on September 30, 1978; amends the 1970 (No. 240) Order by adding provisions for the control and prevention of sheep scab.

ARTIFICIAL INSEMINATION (PIGS) REGULATIONS (NORTHERN IRELAND) 1978 (No. 321) [20p], made under S.I. 1975 No. 1834 (N.I. 17), art. 5; operative on December 1, 1978; provide for the licensing of private centres for the artificial insemination of pigs and for certain controls of boar semen.

2101. Building, engineering, architects and surveyors

CONTROL OF NOISE (CODE OF PRACTICE FOR CONSTRUCTION SITES) ORDER (NORTHERN IRELAND) 1978 (No. 349) [10p], made under S.I. 1978 No. 1049 (N.I. 19), arts. 51, 86; operative on December 18, 1978; approves a B.S.I. code of practice for noise control on construction and demolition sites.

BUILDING REGULATIONS (NORTHERN IRELAND) ORDER 1978 (No. 1038) (N.I. 8) [40p], made under the Northern Ireland Act 1974 (c. 28), Sched. 1, para. 1; operative on days to be appointed; widens the purposes for which building regulations may be made; makes procedures for the approval of building plans more flexible; introduces new provisions as to continuing requirements, enables building regulations to be applied to work by the Crown and provides for civil liability for damage caused by breach of duty under the regulations.

2102. Building societies

BUILDING SOCIETIES (FEES) (AMENDMENT) REGULATIONS (NORTHERN IRELAND) 1978 (No. 28) [15p], made under the Building Societies Act (Northern Ireland) 1967 (c. 31), s. 123 (1); operative on April 1, 1978; increase certain fees payable under the Act; revoke the 1976 (No. 192) Regulations.

BUILDING SOCIETIES (AUTHORISED INVESTMENTS) ORDER (NORTHERN IRELAND) 1978 (No. 59) [25p], made under the Building Societies Act (Northern Ireland) 1967, s. 58 (1); operative on May 1, 1978; specifies the manner in which building societies incorporated under the Act may invest their surplus funds.

2103. Charities—condition that burial plot be maintained—whether valid charitable gift

[Glebe Lands, Representative Church Body, Ireland, Act 1875 (c. 42), s. 4; Charities Act (Northern Ireland) 1964 (c. 33), s. 22.] T devised a house and about 42 acres of land to the property-holding body of the Church of Ireland (" the R.C.B.") in trust to use the income for the maintenance of a church. The following conditions were imposed—(a) to keep a burial plot in repair; (b) not to sell the land or plough it, but only to let it yearly for grazing in conacre; (c) not to let the house. T's executor took out a summons for the construction of the will. *Held,* that (1) the trust for the church was a valid charitable trust which was not invalidated by the condition for the repair of the burial plot; as there was no gift over in the event of a breach of the condition, the condition was precatory only; (2) T had a general charitable intention and since conditions (b) and (c) had ceased to provide a suitable and effective method of using the property they would be removed under s. 22 (1) (*e*) (iii) of the Charities Act (Northern Ireland) 1964; (3) condition (c) could not take away the Department of Finance's jurisdiction to authorise a sale under s. 18 of the Charities Act (Northern Ireland) 1964 or the court's power to authorise a sale; (4) s. 4 of the Glebe Lands, Representative Church Body, Ireland Act 1875 does not operate to defeat an otherwise valid charitable trust and since the R.C.B. had elected not to accept the trust another trustee would be appointed in its place: *Re* STEELE; NORTHERN BANK EXECUTOR & TRUSTEE CO. *v.* LINTON [1976] N.I. 66, Murray J.

2104. Chronically Sick and Disabled Persons (Northern Ireland) Act 1978 (c. 53)

This Act makes further provision for the welfare of chronically sick and disabled persons in Northern Ireland.

S. 1 relates to information as to the need for, and existence of social welfare services; s. 2 enumerates various kinds of social welfare provision available: s. 3 directs the Northern Ireland Housing Executive to have regard to the special needs of the chronically sick and disabled; s. 4 concerns access to, and facilities at, premises open to the public; ss. 5 and 6 relate to the provision of public sanitary conveniences; s. 7 directs the display of signs at buildings complying with ss. 4–6; s. 8 concerns access to, and facilities at, university and school buildings; s. 9 relates to the appointment of advisory committees; s. 10 deals with the co-option of chronically sick or disabled persons by committees of Health and Social Services Boards; s. 11 similarly relates to committees of district councils; s. 12 deals with the separation of younger from older patients; s. 13 concerns the dissemination of information as to accommodation of younger and older persons; s. 14 directs the issue of badges for display on motor vehicles used by disabled persons; s. 15 relates to information about special educational treatment for the deaf-blind; s. 16 does likewise for autistic and certain other children; s. 17 similarly relates to the provision of special educational treatment for dyslexic children; s. 18 empowers the Department of Health and Social Services for Northern Ireland to define certain expressions used in this Act: s. 19 provides for the enacting of secondary legislation; s. 20 is the interpretation section: s. 21 gives the short title, and states that the Act extends to Northern Ireland only.

The Act received the Royal Assent on July 31, 1978, and shall come into force on such day or days as the Secretary of State may by order appoint.

2105. Company law

COMPANIES (NORTHERN IRELAND) ORDER 1978 (No. 1042) (N.I. 12) [£2·50], made under the Northern Ireland Act 1974 (c. 28), Sched. 1, para. 1; operative on days to be appointed; arts. 3–9 relate to the duty to prepare, lay and deliver accounts by reference to accounting reference periods, art. 10 concerns group accounts, arts. 11–13 deal with accounts for companies incorporated outside, but carrying on business within, Northern Ireland; arts. 14–24 relate to accounts, including statements in holding companies' and subsidiaries of information about their subsidiaries and holding company, respectively, particulars as to directors, salaries, pensions and emoluments and of salaries of employees; art. 25 concerns accounting records; arts. 26–33 deal with auditors and auditors' reports; art. 34 contains miscellaneous amendments about accounts and audit; arts. 35–43 penalise dealings by directors, their spouses or children in certain options and contain provisions for securing disclosure of certain material facts; arts. 44–52 relate to directors' reports; arts. 53–56 to disqualification orders prohibiting persons from participating in the management of companies, arts. 57, 58, to returns about directors and other officers; arts. 59–64 effect miscellaneous amendments concerning directors; arts. 65–67 relate to the official assignee for company liquidations; art. 68 concerns applications for winding up; arts. 69–78 deal with liquidators, arts. 79, 80, with committees of inspection and arts. 81–84 with the general powers of the court in winding up; arts. 85–99 set out provisions about every mode of winding up, including provisions about preferential payments; arts. 100–113 relate to the inspection of companies and their books and papers; arts. 114–117 contain provisions for securing the disclosure of substantial individual interests in share capital carrying unrestricted voting rights; arts. 118–120 relate to the re-registration of companies and arts. 121, 122 to names used by Part X companies; arts. 123–128 concern documents, forms and business letters, arts. 129, 130, company transactions, art. 131, registered offices, art. 132, official seals and arts. 133–135 certain partnerships; arts. 136–148 effect miscellaneous amendments of the Companies Act (Northern Ireland) 1960; arts. 149–153 are supplementary.

2106. —— **winding up—sale by liquidator—powers of court**
[Companies Act (Northern Ireland) 1960 (c. 22), s. 227.] A hotel in Newcastle was advertised for sale on the instructions of an official liquidator, who was appointed by the court to wind up a private company. No advertisement was published in local newspapers and no sale board erected at the hotel. One week after the advertisement, the liquidator instructed his estate agent to accept the best offer, over a specified figure, received that day. An oral agreement was made with a prospective purchaser. The draft conditions of sale prepared for the liquidator provided that the sale was subject to the consent of the chief clerk of the High Court. Three days after the oral agreement for sale M, a shareholder, offered a higher price; the liquidator informed him that the property had been sold, although no contract had been signed. The liquidator sought the chief clerk's approval of the sale, erroneously stating that a contract had been signed and failing to mention M's offer. The chief clerk approved the sale and later confirmed it. M applied under s. 227 of the Companies Act (Northern Ireland) 1960 to set aside the sale. *Held*, that (1) the chief clerk has no function in relation to a liquidator's power of sale under s. 227 (2) of the 1960 Act; (2) under s. 227 (3) of the 1960 Act all the activities of the liquidator are under the court's control and that an application under it may be made by a contributory, including the holder of fully-paid shares in a solvent company; (3) the liquidator would be restrained from completing the contract, as he was in breach of his statutory fiduciary duty to obtain the best possible price for the hotel; (4) as the liquidator was in breach of that duty and guilty of gross carelessness he was not entitled to include his own costs in the costs of the winding up; (5) the liquidator should pay M's costs but, as he had relied on professional advice, he could include half of those costs in the costs of the winding up: *Re* BROOK COTTAGE [1976] N.I. 78, Murray J.

2107. Compulsory purchase
COMPULSORY ACQUISITION (INTEREST) ORDER (NORTHERN IRELAND) 1978 (No. 248) [10p], made under the Administrative and Financial Provisions Act (Northern Ireland) 1956 (c. 17), s. 14 and the Local Government Act (Northern Ireland) 1972 (c. 9), Sched. 6, para. 18; operative on October 4, 1978; increases to 11½ per cent. p.a. the rate of interest on compensation payable under specified Acts for compulsorily acquired land.

2108. —— **Lands Tribunal decisions**
FENNING *v.* NORTHERN IRELAND HOUSING EXECUTIVE, R/10/1977 (compensation for dwelling-house in Lisburn, Co. Down).

GRAY *v.* DEPARTMENT OF THE ENVIRONMENT FOR NORTHERN IRELAND, R/6/1978 (compensation for land in Fivemiletown, Co. Tyrone).

ULSTER FARMERS MART CO. *v.* NORTHERN IRELAND HOUSING EXECUTIVE, R/15/1977 (compensation for land at Enniskillen, Co. Fermanagh).

2109. Constitutional law—Act of Northern Ireland Parliament regulating sea fisheries —whether ultra vires

[Government of Ireland Act 1920 (c. 67), s. 10; Ireland (Confirmation of Agreement) Act 1925 (c. 77), s. 1 (2); Fisheries Act (Northern Ireland) 1966 (c. 17), s. 99.] M was charged with illegal fishing off the Northern Ireland coast contrary to s. 99 of the Fisheries Act (Northern Ireland) 1966. The complaint was dismissed. On appeal, *held,* (1) Northern Ireland, as constituted by the Government of Ireland Act 1920, includes the former rights of the United Kingdom in and over the territorial waters adjoining Northern Ireland; (2) the powers of the Northern Ireland Parliament included power to make laws in relation to those territorial waters; (3) the powers relating to fisheries under s. 10 of the 1920 Act included sea fisheries and were transferred to the Government and Parliament of Northern Ireland by s. 1 (2) of the Ireland (Confirmation of Agreement) Act 1925; (4) the validity of an Act of the United Kingdom Parliament cannot be challenged in a Northern Ireland court: D.P.P. *v.* MCNEILL [1975] N.I. 177, C.A.

2110. Coroners

CORONERS (SALARIES, FEES AND EXPENSES) (AMENDMENT) RULES (NORTHERN IRELAND) 1978 (No. 177) [10p], made under the Coroners Act (Northern Ireland) 1959 (c. 15), s. 36 (1) (*a*); operative on August 14, 1978; increase the maximum fee payable to persons assisting at post-mortem examinations.

CORONERS (SALARIES, FEES AND EXPENSES) (AMENDMENT No. 2) RULES (NORTHERN IRELAND) 1978 (No. 190) [20p], made under the Coroners Act (Northern Ireland) 1959, s. 36 (1) (*a*); operative on September 1, 1978; increase amounts payable for jury service at inquests.

CORONERS (SALARIES) (AMENDMENT) RULES (NORTHERN IRELAND) 1978 (No. 227) [10p], made under the Coroners Act (Northern Ireland) 1959, s. 36 (1) (a); operative on December 1, 1978; increases the Belfast coroner's salary

2111. County court practice

COUNTY COURTS (COSTS IN AFFILIATION AND SEPARATION AND MAINTENANCE APPEALS) (AMENDMENT) RULES (NORTHERN IRELAND) 1978 (No. 39) [10p], made under the County Courts Act (Northern Ireland) 1959 (c. 25), s. 146; operative on April 1, 1978; amend the 1966 (No. 276) Rules by including appeals under the Maintenance Orders (Reciprocal Enforcement) Act 1972 and increasing the maximum sum for certain costs.

COUNTY COURT (COSTS) (AMENDMENT) RULES (NORTHERN IRELAND) 1978 (No. 56) [10p], made under the County Courts Act (Northern Ireland) 1959, s. 146; operative on April 1, 1978; amend the scale for the plaintiff's costs on default and summary civil bills, and in undefended actions in the county court.

COUNTY COURT (CRIMINAL DAMAGE COMPENSATION) RULES (NORTHERN IRE-LAND) 1978 (No. 135) [70p], made under the County Courts Act (Northern Ireland) 1959, s. 146 and S.I. 1977 No. 1247 (N.I. 14), arts. 12, 14, 15; operative on July 1, 1978; prescribe county court procedure for the purposes of that S.I.

COUNTY COURT (FAIR EMPLOYMENT ACT) RULES (NORTHERN IRELAND) 1978 (No. 151) [30p], made under the County Courts Act (Northern Ireland) 1959, s. 146 and the Fair Employment (Northern Ireland) Act 1976, s. 45; operative on July 10, 1978; prescribe county court procedure in relation to certain matters under the Fair Employment (Northern Ireland) Act 1976.

COUNTY COURT (CRIMINAL INJURIES TO THE PERSON) (COMPENSATION) (AMENDMENT) RULES (NORTHERN IRELAND) 1978 (No. 195) [10p], made under the County Courts Act (Northern Ireland) 1959, s. 146 and S.I. 1977 No. 1248 (N.I. 15), art. 14; operative on September 1, 1978; amend two periods in the 1977 (No. 313) Rules.

COUNTY COURT (CRIMINAL INJURIES TO PROPERTY) (COMPENSATION) (AMEND-

MENT) RULES (NORTHERN IRELAND) 1978 (No. 196) [10p], made under the County Courts Act (Northern Ireland) 1959, s. 146 and the Criminal Injuries to Property (Compensation) Act (Northern Ireland) 1971 (c. 38), s. 8 (1) (2); operative on September 1, 1978; amend the 1973 (No. 166) Rules in relation to appeals to the county court and payments into that court.

2112. Criminal law

PROTECTION OF CHILDREN (NORTHERN IRELAND) ORDER 1978 (No. 1047) (N.I. 17) [25p], made under the Northern Ireland Act 1974 (c. 28), Sched. 1, para. 1; operative on August 26, 1978; creates certain offences relating to taking, distributing and showing indecent films and photographs of children under 16.

THEFT (NORTHERN IRELAND) ORDER 1978 (No. 1407) (N.I. 23) [20p], made under the Northern Ireland Act 1974 (c. 28), Sched. 1, para. 1; operative on November 1, 1978; replaces s. 16 (2) (*a*) of the Theft Act (Northern Ireland) 1969 (c. 16) with other provisions against fraudulent conduct.

REHABILITATION OF OFFENDERS (NORTHERN IRELAND) ORDER 1978 (No. 1908 (N.I. 27)) [40p], made under the Northern Ireland Act 1974, Sched. 1, para. 1, operative on a day to be appointed; provides for the rehabilitation, after specified periods, of offenders who have not been convicted of a serious offence; it also penalises the unauathorised disclosure of spent convictions and amends the law of defamation.

2113. —— attempt—impossibility

A's car was impossible to drive at the time of an accident. A, unaware of the extent of the damage, tried unsuccessfully to drive the car. A was convicted of attempting to drive the car while under the influence of drink. On appeal, *held* that A should not have been convicted since it had been physically impossible to commit the substantive offence (*Haughton* v. *Smith* [1974] C.L.Y. 637 applied): CLEMENTS v. DOHERTY [1975] N.I. 152, C.A.

2114. —— attempted murder—escaping prisoner—use of reasonable force

M, a soldier, was in charge of an army patrol in a hostile area shortly after an explosion occurred; the patrol arrested W. M shot W when W tried to escape, after calling on W to stop. M was charged with attempted murder and with causing grievous bodily harm. *Held*, that M was not guilty, since he was entitled to use reasonable force to prevent an escape from lawful custody: R. *v.* MACNAUGHTON [1975] N.I. 203, Lowry L.C.J.

2115. —— criminal damage—compensation

CRIMINAL DAMAGE (COMPENSATION) (NORTHERN IRELAND) REGULATIONS 1978 (No. 72) [25p], made under S.I. 1977 No. 1247 (N.I. 14), arts. 7, 21 (2) (3); operative on April 1, 1978; prescribe certain matters for the purposes of that S.I.

2116. —— —— —— mortgaged premises—whether compensation held on trust for mortgagee or subject to lien

C mortgaged premises to a bank by the deposit of the title deeds. In 1971 the premises were destroyed. C claimed compensation under the Criminal Injuries Acts (Northern Ireland) 1957 to 1971. At C's request the bank sent the title deeds to C's solicitors on their receipt, which stated that they held the deeds as agents of the bank and, subject to the bank's lien on the deeds. The chief enforcement officer was appointed receiver of any compensation payable. £900 compensation was paid to him. The bank's claim that it was entitled to the compensation in priority to the receiver was rejected. On appeal, *held* (1) that the bank was not entitled to the compensation, the receiver did not hold the compensation as trustee for the banker, since if it had been paid to C he would not have held it on a constructive trust; (2) that the bank's lien on the title deeds did not attach to the compensation which was never in the hands of C's solicitors: *Re* JUDGMENTS (ENFORCEMENT) ACT (NORTHERN IRELAND) 1969 [1975] N.I. 147, Gibson J.

2117. —— —— —— public house destroyed—loss of profits

G owned a public house which was totally destroyed by a bomb in March, 1973. He could not rebuild it because of planning restrictions and did not restart his business until August 1, 1975, after he had acquired other premises. On an application for compensation under the Criminal Injuries Acts (Northern

Ireland) 1956 to 1970, he was awarded an agreed sum representing the market value of the public house, plus £15,000 for loss of profits. On appeal, *held,* that G was entitled only to the market value of the property; since that value included an element for future profits, by receiving compensation for that value, G had the full measure of what he had had before the destruction of the premises: GILMURRAY *v.* SECRETARY OF STATE [1976] N.I. 28, C.A.

2118. —— —— —— **raid by armed men—whether persons tumultuously assembled**
[Criminal Injuries to Property (Compensation) Act (Northern Ireland) 1971 (c. 38), s. 3 (2).] F's premises were raided by a gang of eight to 10 men, some armed, who stole a considerable number of TV sets. F claimed compensation under s. 3 (2) of the Criminal Injuries to Property (Compensation) Act (Northern Ireland) 1971 for the unlawful removal of the sets. On appeal, *held,* that as the men were not tumultuously assembled, no compensation was payable: FOSTERS OF CASTLEREAGH *v.* SECRETARY OF STATE [1978] N.I. 25, Gibson L.J.

2119. —— —— —— **whether power to include interest on award**
[Law Reform (Miscellaneous Provisions) Act (Northern Ireland) 1937 (c. 9), s. 17.] M's premises were damaged by an explosion. M was awarded compensation under the Criminal Injuries Act (Northern Ireland) 1957, together with interest on the compensation. On appeal, *held,* that " damages " in s. 17 (1) of the Law Reform (Miscellaneous Provisions) Act (Northern Ireland) 1937 did not include compensation under an Act. Accordingly there was no power under that section to order the payment of interest between the date of the criminal damage and the date of the award: McCAUGHEY *v.* SECRETARY OF STATE FOR NORTHERN IRELAND [1975] N.I. 133, C.A.

2120. —— **criminal injuries compensation—augmented police pension—whether deductible in full**
[Criminal Injuries to Persons (Compensation) Act (Northern Ireland) 1968 (c. 9), s. 4 (6) (*c*).] A policeman was murdered and R, his widow, became entitled to an augmented pension. R claimed compensation for the murder of her husband, from which only the " augmented " part of her pension was deducted. On appeal, *held,* that in a claim under s. 4 (6 (*c*) of the Criminal Injuries to Persons (Compensation) Act (Northern Ireland) 1968 arising out of a death, all pensions payable as a result of that death must be wholly taken into account: ROLSTON *v.* SECRETARY OF STATE FOR NORTHERN IRELAND [1975] N.I. 195, C.A.

2121. —— —— **death of applicant—whether right of action survived death**
[Criminal Injury to Persons (Compensation) Act (Northern Ireland) 1968 (c. 9), s. 3 (2).] B's husband claimed compensation under the Criminal Injuries to Persons (Compensation) Act (Northern Ireland) 1968, but died before the claim was determined. B was administratrix of his estate, the county court judge allowed the claim. On appeal, *held,* that where a right to compensation is based on a statute, the right survives the death of the person claiming the compensation and passes to his personal representative: BENSON *v.* SECRETARY OF STATE [1976] N.I. 36, C.A.

2122. —— **disorderly behaviour offence described in summons as committed " together " with other named persons—whether essential ingredient**
C and three others were charged separately with disorderly behaviour. The summonses described the offence as committed together with the other named persons. The summonses were dismissed. On appeal, *held,* that acting together was not an essential ingredient of disorderly behaviour: McMORRIS *v.* CONLON [1975] N.I. 145, C.A.

2123. —— **evidence—statement by accused—whether accused subjected to torture or inhuman or degrading treatment**
[Northern Ireland (Emergency Provisions) Act 1973 (c. 53), s. 6.] The accused were charged with murder. The only evidence of their complicity consisted of their statements. Prima facie evidence was given that they had been subjected to torture or inhuman or degrading treatment. *Held,* that the onus on the prosecution, under s. 6 of the Northern Ireland (Emergency Provisions) Act 1973, to show that statements have not been obtained by such

treatment must be discharged beyond reasonable doubt: R. *v.* HETHERINGTON [1975] N.I. 164, Lowry L.C.J.

2124. —— trial—submission of no case to answer

W was charged with two offences. He was tried on indictment by a judge without a jury, and convicted. On appeal, *held,* that there is no rule that a judge must accede to a submission of no case at the close of the prosecution case if at that stage he has not been satisfied beyond a reasonable doubt of the accused's guilt: R. *v.* WILSON [1975] N.I. 210, C.C.A.

2125. Damages—fatal accident

P's husband was killed in an accident. At his death he was an electrician aged 26. In an action under the Fatal Accidents Acts (Northern Ireland) 1846 to 1959, P was awarded damages of £30,500. On appeal, *held,* that the damages awarded were not excessive or unreasonable: SCOTT *v.* POLLOCK [1976] N.I. 1, C.A.

2126. Deeds and bonds

REGISTRATION OF DEEDS (FEES) ORDER (NORTHERN IRELAND) 1978 (No. 40) [15p], made under the Registration of Deeds Act (Northern Ireland) 1970 (c. 25), s. 16; operative on April 1, 1978; specifies fees payable under the Act, revokes the 1976 (No. 145) Order.

2127. Divorce and matrimonial causes

MATRIMONIAL CAUSES (1978 ORDER) (COMMENCEMENT No. 1) ORDER (NORTHERN IRELAND) 1978 (No. 276 (C. 13)) [10p], made under S.I. 1978 No. 1045 (N.I. 15), art. 1 (2); brings art. 56 of that S.I. into operation on October 16, 1978.

MATRIMONIAL CAUSES (NORTHERN IRELAND) ORDER 1978 (No. 1045) (N.I. 15)) [£1·00], made under the Northern Ireland Act 1974 (c. 28), Sched. 1, para. 1; operative on days to be appointed; art. 3 allows divorce on the breakdown of marriage to be determined by reference to specified facts, arts. 4–12 relate to divorce; arts. 13, 14 specify the grounds on which marriages are void and voidable; arts. 15, 16 set out the court's jurisdiction in nullity proceedings and bars to relief where marriages are voidable; art. 17 relates to marriages governed by foreign law; art. 18 deals with the effect of decrees of nullity on voidable marriages; arts. 19–21 concern other matrimonial suits; art. 22 relates to relief for respondents; arts. 23–42 deal with financial relief for the parties to a marriage and the children of the family; in particular the court may order either spouse to make financial provision for the other spouse or a child of the family and vary settlements; arts. 43–47 concern the protection and custody of children; arts. 48–49 relate to the court; art. 50 allows the court to grant matrimonial relief in respect of polygamous marriages; art. 51 deals with collusion, art. 52 with evidence, art. 53 with parties to proceedings and art. 54 with matrimonial causes rules; art. 55 extends s. 17 of the Married Women's Property Act 1882; art. 56 amends the Summary Jurisdiction (Separation and Maintenance) Act (Northern Ireland) 1945; art. 57 abolishes the right to claim damages for adultery, art. 58 abolishes actions for enticement and harbouring of a spouse; art. 59 abolishes the right to claim restitution of conjugal rights; art. 60 abolishes the wife's agency of necessity; art. 61 sets out the effect of divorce on certain subsequent marriages.

2128. Education

EDUCATION AND LIBRARY BOARDS (CONFERENCES) (AMENDMENT) REGULATIONS (NORTHERN IRELAND) 1978 (No. 53) [10p], made under S.I. 1972 No. 1263 (N.I. 12), arts. 81 (2), 125; operative on March 20, 1978; increase allowances payable to persons authorised by education and library boards to attend conferences.

TEACHERS' SALARIES REGULATIONS (NORTHERN IRELAND) 1978 (No. 129) [80p], made under S.I. 1972 No. 1263 (N.I. 12), arts. 57, 125; operative on May 30, 1978; revise salaries for teachers in primary schools, secondary schools (except technical intermediate schools) and special schools and for peripatetic and supply teachers; revoke the 1976 (No. 128) and 1977 (Nos. 29, 140) Regulations.

TEACHERS' SUPERANNUATION (AMENDMENT) REGULATIONS (NORTHERN IRE-

LAND) 1978 (No. 147) [20p], made under S.I. 1972 No. 1073 (N.I. 10), art. 11, Sched. 3; operative on July 14, 1978; provide for the payment of superannuation allowances to teachers aged 50 or over whose service is terminated for certain reasons; make detailed amendments of the 1977 (No. 260) Regulations.

INSTITUTIONS OF FURTHER EDUCATION SALARIES (AMENDMENT) REGULATIONS (NORTHERN IRELAND) 1978 (No. 153) [20p], made under S.I. 1972 No. 1263 (N.I. 12), arts. 57, 125, and the Administrative and Financial Provisions Act (Northern Ireland) 1962 (c. 7), s. 18; operative on June 29, 1978; revise salaries for teachers in recognised further education institutions.

SECONDARY SCHOOLS (GRANT CONDITIONS) (AMENDMENT) REGULATIONS (NORTHERN IRELAND) 1978 (No. 175) [10p], made under S.I. 1972 No. 1263 (N.I. 12), arts. 57, 58, 105, 125; operative on August 1, 1978; increase the rate above which salary grant is payable in respect of teachers on the authorised staff of voluntary grammar schools.

MILK AND MEALS (AMENDMENT) REGULATIONS (NORTHERN IRELAND) 1978 (No. 182) [10p], made under S.I. 1972 No. 1263, arts 46, 47, 125; operative on September 1, 1978; require education and library boards and other school authorities to provide milk for pupils attending primary schools or parts of secondary schools which are used for primary education.

MAINTENANCE ALLOWANCES (PUPILS OVER COMPULSORY SCHOOL AGE) (AMENDMENT) REGULATIONS (NORTHERN IRELAND) 1978 (No. 214) [20p], made under S.I. 1972 No. 1263 (N.I. 12), arts. 39, 125; operative on September 1, 1978; increase maintenance allowances for pupils over compulsory school age following full-time courses at grant-aided schools or further education institutions.

COLLEGE OF EDUCATION SALARIES (AMENDMENT) REGULATIONS (NORTHERN IRELAND) 1978 (No. 216) [20p], made under the Administrative and Financial Provisions Act (Northern Ireland) 1962, s. 18 and S.I. 1972 No. 1263, arts. 57, 125; operative on July 31, 1978; raise salaries for teachers in education colleges; revoke the 1977 (No. 169) Regulations.

GRAMMAR SCHOOL PUPILS' (ADMISSION, GRANTS AND ALLOWANCES) REGULA-TIONS (NORTHERN IRELAND) 1978 (No. 217) [20p], made under S.I. 1972 No. 1263, arts. 21, 39, 105, 125; operative on September 1, 1978; abolish grammar school scholarships and introduce grants to grammar schools for certain pupils; revoke the 1973 (No. 427) Regulations.

ULSTER POLYTECHNIC REGULATIONS (NORTHERN IRELAND) 1978 (No. 279) [30p], made under the Ulster College Act (Northern Ireland) 1968 (c. 14), ss. 1, 9; operative on October 24, 1978; retitle the Governors of the Ulster College as the Governors of the Ulster Polytechnic; change the membership and structure of the Governors; revoke the 1975 (No. 181) Regulations.

TEACHERS' COMPULSORY ABSENCE AND MATERNITY LEAVE (AMENDMENT) REGULATIONS (NORTHERN IRELAND) 1978 (No. 294) [10p], made under S.I. 1972 No. 1263 (N.I. 12), arts. 57, 58, 125; operative on November 1, 1978; amend the 1976 (No. 323) Regulations as respects maternity leave.

EDUCATION (NORTHERN IRELAND) ORDER 1978 (No. 1040) (N.I. 10) [40p], made under the Northern Ireland Act 1974 (c. 28), Sched. 1, para. 1; operative on August 8, 1978; art. 3 deals with committees of boards and art. 4 with grants to certain voluntary schools; art. 5 relates to proposals as to primary and secondary education, art. 6 to awards, art. 7 to the selection of students for teacher training and art. 8 to teachers; art. 9 concerns loans to officers of boards for certain purposes, art. 10 the compulsory acquisition of land for the purposes of certain schools and art. 11 building grants for voluntary schools; art. 12 relates to accounts and audit, art. 13 to the vacation of office by mem-bers of boards, art. 14 to the appointment of an assessor to an examinations board and art. 15 to arrangements regarding certain examinations; art. 16 deals with the Ulster college and art. 17 with the sports council's accounts.

2129. Education (Northern Ireland) Act 1978 (c. 13)

This Act facilitates the establishment in Northern Ireland of schools likely to be attended by pupils of different religious affiliations or cultural traditions.

S. 1 facilitates the establishment of "controlled integrated schools," as de-fined, the management committees of which are to be nominated in accordance with Sched. 4A to the Education and Libraries (Northern Ireland) Order 1972 (S.I. 1972 No. 1263 (N.I. 12)), and the schemes for which may be submitted, after statutory consultation with parents, by the education and libraries board to the Department of Education for Northern Ireland for approval; s. 2 deals with the management of controlled integrated schools; s. 3 makes certain supplementary provisions; s. 4 contains the short title and provides for interpretation. The Act extends to Northern Ireland only.

The Act received the Royal Assent on May 25, 1978, and came into force on that date.

2130. Election law

REPRESENTATION OF THE PEOPLE (NORTHERN IRELAND) (AMENDMENT) REGULATIONS 1978 (No. 198) [10p], made under the Representation of the People Act 1949 (c. 68), ss. 42 and 171 (5); operative on February 15, 1978; increase the fee payable for copies of the register of electors prepared in accordance with S.I. 1969 No. 905.

ELECTORAL LAW (DISTRICT COUNCIL REGISTRATION EXPENSES) REGULATIONS (NORTHERN IRELAND) 1978 (No. 213) [10p], made under S.I. 1972 No. 1264 (N.I. 13), art. 7 (7); operative on December 1, 1978; prescribes a proportion for art. 7 (7) of that S.I.

2131. Electricity

Order made under S.I. 1972 No. 1072 (N.I. 9), art. 31: S.R. 1978 No. 311 (Castlederg) [10p].

2132. Emergency laws

PAYMENTS FOR DEBT (COSTS OF COLLECTION) ORDER (NORTHERN IRELAND) 1978 (No. 231) [10p], made under the Payments for Debt (Emergency Provisions) Act (Northern Ireland) 1971 (c. 30), s. 2; operative on September 25, 1978; requires payment of the cost of collecting, from certain public funds, of debts due for electricity or gas and specifies the basis for calculating that cost.

2133. Employment

EMPLOYMENT AND TRAINING (CONTINUANCE) ORDER (NORTHERN IRELAND) 1978 (No. 54) [10p]; made under S.I. No. 1043 (N.I. 16), art. 65 (3); operative on March 31, 1978; postpones to March 31, 1979, the cesser of powers of the Department of Manpower Services under s. 5A of the Employment and Training Act (Northern Ireland) 1950.

INDUSTRIAL RELATIONS (VARIATION OF LIMITS) ORDER (NORTHERN IRELAND) 1977 (No. 381) [15p], made under S.I. 1976 No. 1043 (N.I. 16), arts. 70, 80 (3) and S.I. 1976 No. 2147 (N.I. 28), arts. 5 (5), 63 (4); operative on February 1, 1978; increases certain financial limits in those S.I.s and the Contracts of Employment and Redundancy Payments Act (Northern Ireland) 1965.

INDUSTRIAL RELATIONS (1976 No. 2 ORDER) (COMMENCEMENT No. 3) ORDER (NORTHERN IRELAND) 1978 (No. 232 (C. 9)) [10p], made under S.I. 1976 No. 2147, art. 1 and the Northern Ireland Act 1974 (c. 28), Sched. 1, para. 2 (1) (2); brings arts. 50 to 54 of that S.I. into operation on October 9, 1978.

CODE OF PRACTICE (DISCLOSURE OF INFORMATION) (COMMENCEMENT) ORDER (NORTHERN IRELAND) 1978 (No. 233 (C. 10)) [10p], made under S.I. 1976 No. 1043, art. 14A (5); specifies October 9, 1978, as the date on which the code of practice on disclosure of information to trade unions for collective bargaining purposes takes effect.

CODE OF PRACTICE (DISCIPLINARY PRACTICE AND PROCEDURES) (COMMENCEMENT) ORDER (NORTHERN IRELAND) 1978 (No. 296) [10p], made under S.I. 1976 No. 1043 art. 14A (7); brings the code of practice in disciplinary practice and procedures issued by the labour relations agency into operation on November 6, 1978.

HEALTH AND SAFETY AT WORK (NORTHERN IRELAND) ORDER 1978 (No. 1039 (N.I. 9) [90p], made under the Northern Ireland Act 1974 (c. 28), Sched. 1, para. 1; operative on days to be appointed; arts. 1–3 are introductory; arts. 4–8 set out general duties of employers, self-employed, persons concerned with premises, manufacturers and employees; art. 9 imposes a duty not to interfere with or misuse things provided under certain provisions; art. 10 prevents employers from charging for things done or provided under specified provisions; art. 11 sets out duties of departments; arts. 12–15 relate to the health and safety agency; art. 16 concerns investigations and inquiries; arts. 17–19 authorise the making of health and safety regulations and the approval of codes of practice; arts. 20–28 deal with enforcement; arts. 29, 30 with obtaining and disclosing information, arts. 31–39 with offences and art. 40 with finance; arts. 41–47 are miscellaneous and supplementary; arts. 48–51 concern the employment medical advisory service; arts. 52–56 are miscellaneous and general.

2134. —— **industrial training**

INDUSTRIAL TRAINING (GRANTS AND LOANS) ORDER (NORTHERN IRELAND) 1978 (No. 27) [10p], made under the Industrial Training Act (Northern Ireland) 1964 (c. 18), s. 5 (3); operative on April 1, 1978; increases the aggregate of the grants and loans that may be made to industrial training boards.

Orders made under the Industrial Training Act (Northern Ireland) 1964, s. 4:

S.R. 1978 Nos. 159 (engineering industry) [20p]; 160 (food and drink industry) [20p]; 161 (textiles industry) [20p]; 162 (distributive industry) [20p]; 163 (construction industry) [20p]; 170 (catering industry) [20p]; 183 (clothing and footwear industry) [25p]; 184 (road transport industry) [25p].

2135. —— **wages councils**

AERATED WATERS WAGES COUNCIL (NORTHERN IRELAND) (ABOLITION) ORDER (NORTHERN IRELAND) 1978 (No. 166) [10p], made under the Wages Councils Act (Northern Ireland) 1945 (c. 21), s. 6; operative on May 5, 1978; abolishes the aerated waters wages council; revokes the 1950 (No. 62) Order.

BRUSH AND BROOM WAGES COUNCIL (NORTHERN IRELAND) (ABOLITION) ORDER (NORTHERN IRELAND) 1978 (No. 167) [10p], made under the Wages Councils Act (Northern Ireland) 1945, s. 6; operative on May 5, 1978; abolishes the brush and broom wages council; revokes the 1950 (No. 15) Order.

Orders made under the Wages Councils Act (Northern Ireland) 1945, s. 10:

S.R. 1977 Nos. 364 (road haulage) [15p]; 365 (readymade and wholesale bespoke tailoring) [15p]; 366 (laundry) [10p]; 367 (dressmaking and women's light clothing) [15p]; 368 (dressmaking and women's light clothing—No. 2) [10p]; 369 (shirtmaking) [10p]; 370 (retail bespoke tailoring) [15p]; 371 (boot and shoe repairing) [10p]; 372 (retail bespoke tailoring) [10p]; 373 (paper box) [15p].

S.R. 1978 Nos. 69 (linen and cotton handkerchief and household goods and linen piece goods) [15p]; 79 (sugar confectionery and food preserving) [25p]; 88 (catering) [10p]; 89 (baking) [25p]; 94 (baking—holidays) [25p]; 138 (laundry) [10p]; 154 (ready made and wholesale bespoke tailoring) [20p]; 241 (dressmaking and women's light clothing) [20p]; 242 (dressmaking and women's light clothing—No. 2) ([20p], 243 (road haulage) [20p], 250 (paper box) [20p], 254 (shirtmaking) [20p], 263 (boot and shoe) [20p], 264 (shirtmaking—holidays) [10p], 274 (readymade and wholesale bespoke tailoring) [20p].

2136. Factories

FACTORIES (STANDARDS OF LIGHTING) (REVOCATION) REGULATIONS (NORTHERN IRELAND) 1978 (No. 306) [10p], made under the Factories Act (Northern Ireland) 1965 (c. 20), s. 5 (2); operative on December 19, 1978; revoke the 1941 (No. 94) Regulations.

2137. Family allowances

CHILD BENEFIT (MISCELLANEOUS AMENDMENTS) REGULATIONS (NORTHERN IRELAND) 1978 (No. 106) [15p], made under S.I. 1975 No. 1504 (N.I. 16), arts. 2 (3) (5) (6), 8 (1), 9 (1), Sched. 1, para. 1 and the Social Security (Northern Ireland) Act 1975 (c. 15), s. 119 (3); operative on May 5, 1978; make detailed amendments of the 1976 (Nos. 225, 226) Regulations.

CHILD BENEFIT AND SOCIAL SECURITY (FIXING AND ADJUSTMENT OF RATES) (AMENDMENT) REGULATIONS (NORTHERN IRELAND) 1978 (No. 203) [20p], made under S.I. 1975 No. 1504 (N.I. 16), arts 7, 19 (1); operative, as to part, on November 13, 1978, and as to the remainder, on April 2, 1979; increase child benefit.

FAMILY INCOME SUPPLEMENTS (COMPUTATION) REGULATIONS (NORTHERN IRE-
LAND) 1978 (No. 238) [10p], made under the Family Income Supplements
Act (Northern Ireland) 1971 (c. 8), ss. 2 (1), 3 (14); operative on November 14,
1978; specify the prescribed amount for families and weekly rates of benefit
under the Act; revoke the 1977 (No. 257) Regulations.

CHILD BENEFIT (GENERAL) (AMENDMENT) REGULATIONS (NORTHERN IRE-
LAND) 1978 (No. 251) [10p], made under S.I. 1975 No. 1504, art. 6,
Sched. 1, para. 2 (2); operative on August 31, 1978; amend the 1976 (No. 226)
Regulations by providing that child benefit is not payable for a child while he
receiving financial support by virtue of payments made under certain Acts.

FAMILY INCOME SUPPLEMENTS (GENERAL) (AMENDMENT) REGULATIONS
(NORTHERN IRELAND) 1978 (No. 293) [10p], made under the Family Income
Supplements Act (Northern Ireland) 1971, s. 4 (2) (*b*); operative on
November 1, 1978; amend the 1971 (No. 122) Regulations by providing that
certain rent allowances may be disregarded when calculating income for the
purpose of determining entitlement to benefit.

2138. Fire service

FIREMEN'S PENSION SCHEMES (AMENDMENT) ORDER (NORTHERN IRELAND)
1978 (No. 24) [25p], made under the Fire Services Act (Northern Ireland)
1969 (c. 13), s. 17; operative on March 14, 1978; amends the 1973 (No. 393)
Order and increases certain provisions and awards.

FIREMEN'S PENSION SCHEME (AMENDMENT NO. 2) ORDER (NORTHERN IRELAND)
1978 (No. 100) [35p], made under the Fire Services Act (Northern Ireland)
1969, s. 17; operative on April 1, 1978; increases the amounts so certain
awards for firemen and the widows of firemen.

2139. Firearms—possession—suspicious circumstances—onus of proof

[Northern Ireland (Emergency Provisions) Act 1973 (c. 53), s. 7.] A car
containing the accused—three men and one woman—was stopped. The woman
was found to be concealing two loaded pistols under her clothes. The accused
were charged with possession of the pistols and ammunition in suspicious
circumstances. *Held,* that s. 7 of the Northern Ireland (Emergency Provisions)
Act 1973 is intended to be invoked where there almost certainly exists in one
of a number of persons a guilty possession but without using s. 7 it is not
possible to lay it at the door of any one of them. Accordingly, since the woman
was clearly guilty, s. 7 could not be employed against the other accused: R. *v.*
LAVERY [1976] N.I. 148, Murray J.

2140. Fish and fisheries

FISHERIES (LICENCE DUTIES) BYELAWS (NORTHERN IRELAND) 1977 (No. 355)
[15p], made under the Fisheries Act (Northern Ireland) 1966 (c. 17), s. 26;
operative on January 1, 1978; increase certain licence duties for fishing and
dealers; revoke the 1976 (No. 356) Byelaws.

RAINBOW TROUT WATERS BYELAWS (NORTHERN IRELAND) 1977 (No. 356)
[10p], made under the Fisheries Act (Northern Ireland) 1966, s. 26; operative
on January 1, 1978; designate certain waters as rainbow trout waters without a
close season; revoke the 1976 (No. 355) Byelaws.

FOYLE AREA (CLOSE SEASONS FOR ANGLING) REGULATIONS 1978 (No. 50)
[10p], made under the Foyle Fisheries Act 1952 (Eire No. 5), s. 13 and the
Foyle Fisheries Act (Northern Ireland) 1952 (c. 5), s. 13; operative on March
10, 1978; permit the angling season on the River Foyle, Lough Foyle and the
River Finn and its lakes and tributaries to open on March 1 in each year;
revoke the 1974 (No. 13) Regulations.

FOYLE AREA (LICENSING OF FISHING ENGINES) (AMENDMENT) REGULATIONS
1978 (No. 98) [10p], made under the Foyle Fisheries Act 1952, s. 13 and
the Foyle Fisheries Act (Northern Ireland) 1952, s. 13; operative on May 1,
1978; increase licence fees for nets in the Foyle area.

FOYLE AREA (LICENSING OF FISHING ENGINES) (AMENDMENT NO. 2) REGU-
LATIONS 1978 (No. 115) [20p], made under the Foyle Fisheries Act 1952,
s. 13 and the Foyle Fisheries Act (Northern Ireland) 1952, s. 13; operative on
May 1, 1978; specify licence fees for nets in the Foyle area; revoke the 1978
(No. 98) Regulations.

RISK OF INFECTION (FISH) ORDER (NORTHERN IRELAND) 1978 (No. 185) [10p], made under the Diseases of Fish Act (Northern Ireland) 1967 (c. 7), s. 3; operative on September 1, 1978; prohibits the bringing into Northern Ireland of salmonidae fish unless they are brought from the Republic of Ireland or an authorisation is obtained from the Department of Agriculture; revokes the 1976 (No. 109) Order.

ESCALLOP (FISHING METHODS) REVOCATION REGULATIONS (NORTHERN IRELAND) 1978 (No. 218) [10p], made under the Fisheries Act (Northern Ireland) 1966, ss. 19, 124; operative on October 1, 1978; revoke the 1977 (No. 108) Regulations.

HERRING (RESTRICTION OF FISHING) REGULATIONS (NORTHERN IRELAND) 1978 (No. 277) [20p], made under the Fisheries Act (Northern Ireland) 1966, ss. 19, 124; operative on September 20, 1978; prohibit the use of fishing boats of 35 feet or longer for catching herring between September 20 and December 31, 1978, within a specified area; also prohibit, subject to an exception between September 20 and October 27, 1978, the use of fishing boats under 35 feet during that period in the same area.

HERRING (RESTRICTION OF FISHING) (AMENDMENT) REGULATIONS (NORTHERN IRELAND) 1978 (No. 286) [10p], made under the Fisheries Act (Northern Ireland) 1966, ss. 19, 124; operative on September 26, 1978, at 6 p.m.; revoke the 1978 (No. 227) Regulations in so far as they confer a limited exemption for fishing boats under 35 feet.

FISHERIES (LICENCE DUTIES) BYELAWS (NORTHERN IRELAND) 1978 (No. 339) [20p], made under the Fisheries Act (Northern Ireland) 1966, s. 26; operative on January 1, 1979; increase certain licence fees.

2141. Food and drugs

ANTIOXIDANTS IN FOOD REGULATIONS (NORTHERN IRELAND) 1978 (No. 112) [35p], made under the Food and Drugs Act (Northern Ireland) 1958 (c. 27), ss. 4, 7, 68, 68A; operative on June 8, 1978; replace, with detailed amendments, and revoke, the 1974 (No. 197) Regulations.

LABELLING OF FOOD (AMENDMENT) REGULATIONS (NORTHERN IRELAND) 1978 (No. 206) [20p], made under the Food and Drugs Act (Northern Ireland) 1958, ss. 6, 68; operative, as to part on September 4, 1978 and, as to the remainder, on April 1, 1980; specify designations for certain pilchards.

MILK (NORTHERN IRELAND) (AMENDMENT) ORDER 1978 (No. 470) [10p]; made under the Emergency Laws (Re-enactments and Repeals) Act 1964 (c. 60), ss. 7, 22 (3) and S.I. 1969 No. 1058 as amended; operative on April 1, 1978; prescribes revised maximum prices for the sale in Northern Ireland of raw milk for heat treatment.

MILK (NORTHERN IRELAND) (AMENDMENT) (NO. 2) ORDER 1978 (No. 1491) [20], made under the Emergency Laws (Re-enactments and Repeals) Act 1964, ss. 6, 7, 22 (3), S.I. 1969 No. 1058 and S.I. 1974 No. 2139; operative on November 1, 1978; increases the maximum retail price of milk.

2142. Forestry

FORESTRY ACT (NORTHERN IRELAND) 1953 (AMENDMENT) REGULATIONS (NORTHERN IRELAND) 1978 (No. 130) [10p], made under S.I. 1977 No. 1245 (N.I. 12), art. 20 (1) (a) (b) (2) (a); operative on July 1, 1978; substitute metric units in the Forestry Act (Northern Ireland) 1953.

2143. Friendly societies

FRIENDLY SOCIETIES (FEES) (AMENDMENT) REGULATIONS (NORTHERN IRELAND) 1978 (No. 30) [15p], made under the Friendly Societies Act (Northern Ireland) 1970 (c. 31), ss. 98, 100; operative on April 1, 1978; increase fees payable under the Act; revoke the 1976 (No. 193) Regulations.

FRIENDLY SOCIETIES (LIMITS OF BENEFITS) ORDER (NORTHERN IRELAND) 1978 (No. 261) [10p], made under the Friendly Societies Act (Northern Ireland) 1970, s. 55 (4); operative on November 30, 1978; increases amounts which members of friendly societies may receive from one or more societies under non-tax exempt business.

FRIENDLY SOCIETIES (LIFE ASSURANCE PREMIUM RELIEF) REGULATIONS (NORTHERN IRELAND) 1978 (No. 285) [30p], made under the Finance Act 1976 (c. 40), Sched. 4, para. 13; operative on November 1, 1978; authorise certain friendly societies and their branches to adopt schemes under which tax relief on contributions on friendly society contracts may be effected by the payer retaining or having refunded 17½ per cent. of the contribution.

2144. Game

GAME PRESERVATION (GROUSE, PARTRIDGE AND HEN PHEASANTS) ORDER (NORTHERN IRELAND) 1978 (No. 199) [10p], made under the Game Preservation Act (Northern Ireland) 1928 (c. 25), ss. 7C (1), 7F and the Northern Ireland Act 1974 (c. 28), Sched. 1, para. 2 (1) (2); operative on August 11, 1978; prohibits, subject to exemptions, the killing of hen pheasants during the normal open season; restricts dealings in hen pheasants and grouse and prohibits the shooting or taking of partridge.

2145. Gaming and wagering—gaming machines on bookmaker's premises—whether offence

[Betting and Lotteries Act (Northern Ireland) 1957 (c. 19), s. 13 (1) (*a*).] E, licensed bookmaker and L, his manager, were charged with offences arising out of the installation of two gaming machines on the bookmaker's premises. A fixed percentage of the money inserted in the machines was yielded as profit to the owner of the machine. E and L were convicted of carrying on a business other than bookmaking on licensed premises contrary to s. 13 (1) (*a*) of the Betting and Lotteries Act (Northern Ireland) 1957. On appeal, *held*, that in operating the machines the essential element of a bet was missing since the player played against the machine and not its owner. Accordingly, the appellants were rightly convicted: SEAY *v.* EASTWOOD [1976] N.I. 8, C.A.

2146. Gas and gasworks

COMPENSATION FOR LIMITATION OF PRICES (GAS) ORDER (NORTHERN IRELAND) 1978 (No. 104) [10p], made under S.I. 1977 No. 427 (N.I. 3), art. 2 (1); operative on June 1, 1978; specifies the amount of compensation payable to certain gas undertakings for loss incurred because of price limitations.

2147. Highways and bridges

Orders made under S.I. 1975 No. 1040 (N.I. 10), art. 3 (1):
S.R. 1977 No. 375 (Madam's Bank bridge, Co. Londonderry) [25p]; 1978 No. 75 (New West Bridge, Enniskillen) [15p].
Order made under the Special Roads Act (Northern Ireland) 1963 (c. 12), ss. 1, 2, 5, 7, 16, 26:
S.R. No. 1978 No. 310 (M2—Whitla St. extension) [20p].

2148. Hire-purchase

HIRE-PURCHASE (INCREASE OF LIMIT OF VALUE) ORDER (NORTHERN IRELAND) 1978 (No. 97) [10p], made under the Hire-Purchase Act (Northern Ireland) 1966 (c. 42), s. 3 (1) and the Northern Ireland Constitution Act 1973 (c. 36), Sched. 5, para. 4 (2); operative on June 1, 1978; increases a limit specified in s. 2 of the 1966 Act to £5,000.

2149. Housing

HOUSING (DETERMINATION OF UNFITNESS) ORDER (NORTHERN IRELAND) 1978 (No. 22) [10p], made under the Housing (Ireland) Act 1919 (c. 45), s. 6 (6) and the Planning and Housing Act (Northern Ireland) 1931 (c. 12), s. 29 (7); operative on April 1, 1978; specifies 15 as the multiplier for the purposes of s. 6 (6) of the 1919 Act and s. 29 (7) of the 1931 Act.

SMALL DWELLINGS ACQUISITION (MARKET VALUE) ORDER (NORTHERN IRELAND) 1978 (No. 178) [10p], made under the Small Dwellings Acquisition Act (Northern Ireland) 1947 (c. 8), s. 1; operative on August 1, 1978; raises to £15,000 the limit on the market value of houses in respect of which advances may be made under the Small Dwellings Acquisition Acts (Northern Ireland) 1899 to 1948; revokes the 1954 (No. 145) Order.

HOUSING (IMPROVEMENT, INTERMEDIATE AND REPAIRS GRANTS) ORDER (NORTHERN IRELAND) 1978 (No. 267) [10p], made under S.I. 1976 No. 1780 (N.I. 25), arts. 44, 46; operative on October 1, 1978; increases certain percentages and limits in arts. 44 and 46 of that S.I.

HOME PURCHASE ASSISTANCE (1978 ORDER) (COMMENCEMENT) ORDER (NORTHERN IRELAND) 1978 (No. 309) (C. 15) [10p], made under S.I. 1978

No. 1043 (N.I. 13), art. 1 and the Northern Ireland Act 1974 (c. 28), Sched. 1, para. 2 (1) (2); brings that S.I. into operation on December 1, 1978.

HOME PURCHASE ASSISTANCE (NORTHERN IRELAND) ORDER 1978 (No. 1043) (N.I. 13) [10p], made under the Northern Ireland Act 1974, Sched. 1, para. 1; operative on an appointed day; enables the Department of the Environment to make advances to recognised lending institutions to enable them to provide assistance to first-time home purchasers.

HOMES INSULATION SCHEME ORDER (NORTHERN IRELAND) 1978 (No. 335) [20p], made under S.I. 1978 No. 1406 (N.I. 22), art. 3 (1)–(3) (8); operative on December 1, 1978; specifies for the purposes of that S.I. works of roof space insulation, descriptions of dwellings and categories of persons who may apply for grant.

HOMES INSULATION (NORTHERN IRELAND) ORDER 1978 (No. 1406 (N.I. 22)) [10p], made under the Northern Ireland Act 1974, Sched. 1, para. 1, operative on October 6, 1978; authorises the housing executive to provide financial assistance for private householders towards the cost of measures to improve thermal insulation of buildings.

2150. Husband and wife—matrimonial home—extent of wife's interest
[Married Women's Property Act 1882 (c. 75), s. 17.] Land was let to H and W in 1956. The purchase of the land, and of the house later built on it, was financed by a mortgage, for which W supplied the deposit. H first paid the mortgage instalments out of his earnings, but they were later met out of their joint earnings until H and W separated in June 1969. After June 1969, the instalments were paid by W out of her earnings, except for a seven-month period. W brought an originating summons to determine the extent of her interest in the matrimonial home. *Held,* that (1) H and W had taken the property jointly and until 1969 neither had, by their payments, expected or intended to extend the beneficial interest each had originally acquired; (2) although W had full use of the house after 1969, she was entitled to recover one-half of her payments (except for the seven-month period when H contributed to the household expenses) as H was at fault; (3) the sums awarded to W, including costs, should be charged on H's interest in the property: McKEOWN *v.* McKEOWN [1975] N.I. 139, Lord MacDermott.

2151. Industrial societies
INDUSTRIAL AND PROVIDENT SOCIETIES (FEES) (AMENDMENT) REGULATIONS (NORTHERN IRELAND) 1978 (No. 29) [15p], made under the Industrial and Provident Societies Act (Northern Ireland) 1969 (c. 24), s. 97; operative on April 1, 1978; increase fees payable under the Act; revoke the 1976 (No. 194) Regulations.

INDUSTRIAL AND PROVIDENT SOCIETIES (CREDIT UNION FEES) (AMENDMENT) REGULATIONS (NORTHERN IRELAND) 1978 (No. 31) [15p], made under the Industrial and Provident Societies Act (Northern Ireland) 1969, s. 97; operative on April 1, 1978; increase fees payable under the Act in relation to credit unions; revoke the 1976 (No. 195) Regulations.

INDUSTRIAL ASSURANCE (LIFE ASSURANCE PREMIUM RELIEF) REGULATIONS (NORTHERN IRELAND) 1978 (No. 131) [10p], made under the Industrial Assurance Act (Northern Ireland) 1924 (c. 21), s. 43 (1) and the Finance Act 1976 (c. 40), Sched. 4, para. 13; operative on July 3, 1978; authorise industrial assurance companies and collecting societies to adopt schemes under which tax relief on certain policies may be effected by the premium payer retaining or having refunded $17\frac{1}{2}$ per cent. of the premiums.

INDUSTRIAL ASSURANCE (PREMIUM RECEIPT BOOKS) (AMENDMENT) REGULATIONS (NORTHERN IRELAND) 1978 (No. 132) [10p], made under the Industrial Assurance Act (Northern Ireland) 1924, s. 43 (1) and the Industrial Assurance and Friendly Societies Act (Northern Ireland) 1948 (c. 22), s. 8 (2); operative on July 3, 1978; amend the 1949 (No. 3) Regulations as respects entries in receipt books.

2151a. Intoxicating liquors
LICENSING (NORTHERN IRELAND) ORDER 1978 (No. 1044) (N.I. 14) [20p], made under the Northern Ireland Act 1974 (c. 28), Sched. 1, para 1; operative

on August 8, 1978; authorises the renewal of certain licences to sell intoxicating liquor notwithstanding that the premises in question have ceased to exist or that the business has been discontinued.

2152. Intoxicating liquors—licensing—whether premises in vicinity of other premises
[Licensing Act (Northern Ireland) 1971 (c. 13), Sched. 1, Part I, para. 4.] H was granted a provisional off-licence for premises on the outskirts of Newtownards. T, who had premises in the centre of Newtownards, objected to the grant of the licence. *Held*, that under para. 4 of Pt. I of Sched. 1 to the Licensing Act (Northern Ireland) 1971 T was not entitled to be heard as an objector as his premises were not in the vicinity of H's premises: HUNT *v.* TOHILL [1976] N.I. 73, McGonigal J.

2153. Judicature (Northern Ireland) Act 1978 (c. 23)
This Act provides for the constitution, jurisdiction and proceedings of the Supreme Court of Judicature of Northern Ireland; it establishes, as part of that Court, a Crown Court to try indictments and exercise other jurisdiction in criminal cases on the abolition of courts of assize. It also provides for the administration of the courts of Northern Ireland, for certain rules of law in judicial matters, and amends the law relating to magistrates' courts, county courts and justices of the peace in Northern Ireland.

Pt. I (ss. 1–15) deals with the constitution of the Supreme Court of Judicature of Northern Ireland: s. 1 sets out the three courts of which this shall consist; s. 2 regulates the composition of the High Court; s. 3 regulates the composition of the Court of Appeal; s. 4 regulates the composition of the Crown Court; s. 5 sets out the three divisions of the High Court; s. 6 empowers the judges of one court to assist in another court; s. 7 provides for further assistance in the transaction of judicial business; s. 8 contains further provisions as to persons rendering judicial assistance; s. 9 stipulates the necessary qualifications for judges in each court; s. 10 allocates precedence among the judges; s. 11 provides for the exercise of the functions of the Lord Chief Justice; s. 12 relates to the appointment of judges; s. 13 defines the conditions of tenure by judges; s. 14 enables their vacation of office; s. 15 empowers judges to act in cases relating to rates and taxes.

Pt. II (ss. 16–33) deals with the High Court: s. 16 defines the general jurisdiction of the High Court and its judges; s. 17 governs the assignment of business to the judges; s. 18 relates to the hearing of applications for judicial review by the High Court; s. 19 empowers the court to grant a stay of proceedings or appropriate interim relief on an application under s. 18; s. 20 provides for an award of damages in addition to, or in lieu of, such relief; s. 21 confers a power to remit the matter, or to reverse or vary the decision; s. 22 extends the supervisory powers of the High Court; s. 23 governs declaratory judgments; s. 24 provides for injunctions to issue where public offices have been abused; s. 25 deals with the power of the High Court to vary a sentence on certiorari; s. 26 sets out the High Court's jurisdiction in relation to wards of court; s. 27 provides for their maintenance; s. 28 confers jurisdiction with respect to the property and affairs of psychiatric patients; s. 29 co-ordinates different jurisdictions in relation to persons under a disability; s. 30 directs that the High Court is to have exclusive original jurisdiction in admiralty matters; s. 31 permits the remittal and removal of various civil matters to a county court; s. 32 permits the imposition of a restriction on the institution of vexatious actions; s. 33 empowers the court to order the execution of instruments.

Pt. III (ss. 34–45) deals with the Court of Appeal and the House of Lords: s. 34 sets out the general jurisdiction of the Court of Appeal; s. 35 regulates its appellate functions; s. 36 relates to its composition; s. 37 defines the powers of a single judge in the Court of Appeal; s. 38 confers further powers upon the court for purposes of appeals; s. 39 deals with certain appeals under the Criminal Appeal Act 1968; s. 40 deals with appeals to the House of Lords under the same Act; s. 41 relates to appeals to the House of Lords in other criminal matters; s. 42 has reference to appeals in civil cases; s. 43 re-iterates the provision for appeals directly to the House of Lords from the High Court in certain circumstances; s. 44 provides for appeals in cases of contempt of court; s. 45 governs the right of appeal in habeas corpus proceedings.

Pt. IV (ss. 46–53) is concerned with the Crown Court: s. 46 confers upon the Crown Court exclusive jurisdiction in trials on indictment; s. 47 relates to the exercise of its jurisdiction; s. 48 regulates proceedings on committal for trial; s. 49 deals with the effects of sentences, or other orders, imposed by the Crown Court; s. 50 states who may have a right of audience in the Crown Court; s. 51 sets out the process to compel appearance before the Crown Court; s. 52 provides for rules of practice and procedure in the Crown Court to be made by the Crown Court Rules Committee; s. 53 governs the composition and appointment of this committee.

Pt. V (ss. 54–67) relates to practice, procedure and trials: s. 54 provides for the establishment of a Supreme Court Rules Committee; s. 55 sets out the Committee's rule-making duties; s. 56 concerns the control and publication of such rules; s. 57 provides for the making of rules to regulate the sittings of the High Court and Court of Appeal; s. 58 relates to the composition and location of these two courts; s. 59 governs the award of costs of proceedings; s. 60 pertains to the taxation of costs; s. 61 permits the calling in of specially qualified assessors; s. 62 indicates the conditions on which a trial shall or may be had with a jury; s. 63 regulates the trial of a challenge for cause in civil proceedings; s. 64 relates to the composition of juries in civil actions; s. 65 provides for the making of rules of court, governing juries in civil actions; s. 66 renders certain judicially signed or sealed affidavits taken abroad admissable in evidence without the usual formalities; s. 67 relates to subpoenas in other parts of the U.K.

Pt. VI (ss. 68–76) is concerned with departments and officers: s. 68 provides for the establishment of certain departments of the Supreme Court; s. 69 sets up a unified and distinct civil service, to be called the Northern Ireland Court Service; s. 70 deals with the appointment and qualification of statutory officers within this Service; s. 71 governs their tenure of office; s. 72 relates to their superannuation; s. 73 contains restrictions on practice; s. 74 permits the appointment of deputies or temporary officers; s. 75 permits the appointment of an Official Solicitor to the Supreme Court; s. 76 arranges for the automatic vesting of property, held in their official capacity by certain officers, in their successors.

Pt. VII (ss. 77–85) relates to funds in court: s. 77 concerns the role of the Accountant General; s. 78 states his duty to keep proper accounts of funds in court; s. 79 makes it incumbent upon him also to keep a bank account in respect of court funds; s. 80 arranges for payments or transfers of funds to be by way of this account; s. 81 relates to the investment of funds in court; s. 82 empowers the Lord Chancellor to make rules for all transactions concerning funds in court; s. 83 renders certain investment provisions of the Administration of Justice Act 1965 (c. 2), applicable to funds in court; s. 84 concerns statutory deposits; s. 85 provides for any default by a Court Service official in respect of money, securities or statutory deposits, to be made good by the Lord Chancellor.

Pt. VIII (ss. 86–94) sets out rules of law in judicial matters generally: s. 86 provides for the concurrent administration of law and equity to continue; s. 87 modifies the law on the assignment of debts and choses in action; s. 88 states that certain stipulations are not to be of the essence of contracts; s. 89 relates to mergers of interests in estates; s. 90 relates to equitable waste; s. 91 empowers the High Court and county court to make orders for sale, grant mandatory and other injunctions and appoint receivers in certain circumstances; s. 92 permits the award of damages in addition to, or in lieu of, injunctions and decrees of specific performance; s. 93 relates to suits for possession of land by mortgagors; s. 94 deals with relief from ejection.

Pt. IX (ss. 95–102) governs inferior courts: s. 95 amends ss. 1 and 2 of the County Courts Act (Northern Ireland) 1959 (c. 25); s. 96 amends provisions of the same Act that relate to times of sittings of county courts; s. 97 enables circuit registrars to exercise civil jurisdiction in certain matters; s. 98 amends existing legislation with respect to the appointment and assignment of county court judges; s. 99 states the qualifications necessary for county court judges and deputy judges; s. 100 alters the law on the appointment and assignment of resident magistrates; s. 101 provides for the designation of petty sessions districts and their administration; s. 102 is supplementary.

Pt. X (ss. 103–117) contains miscellaneous matters: s. 103 deals with the appointment of magistrates; s. 104 makes certain provisions regarding under-sheriffs; s. 105 states that solicitors shall be officers of the Supreme Court; s. 106 confers a right of audience upon solicitors for certain causes in the High Court and Court of Appeal; s. 107 sets out the qualifications for holding office of solicitors who have been barristers, and vice versa; s. 108 provides for election courts; s. 109 relates to the evolvement, etc. of instruments; s. 110 deals with court bonds; s. 111 governs the loss of negotiable instruments; s. 112 provides for the appointment of commissioners of oaths, notaries public and for the taking of affidavits; s. 113 permits the appointment of conveyancing counsel; s. 114 states other law in Northern Ireland courts; s. 115 governs the use of official seals; s. 116 relates to fees; s. 117 directs the transfer of certain functions relating to the courts to the Lord Chancellor.

Pt. XI (ss. 118–123) concerns interpretation and general matters: s. 118 deals with the application of this Act to the Crown; s. 119 provides for the making and control of subordinate legislation; s. 120 is the interpretation section; s. 121 contains financial provisions; s. 122 consists of minor and consequential amendments, transitional provisions and repeals; s. 123 is the short title.

The Act received the Royal Assent on June 30, 1978, and shall come into force on such day or days as the Lord Chancellor may by order appoint. Ss. 52, 53, 54 (2)–(4) (6), 55 (3), 46 (1)–(3), 99, 107, 116, 118, 121, 122 (1) (part), 122 (2) (part), and 123, and Sched. 5 (part), and 6, paras. 7, 10, came into force on August 21, 1978.

2154. —— commencement

JUDICATURE (NORTHERN IRELAND) ACT 1978 (COMMENCEMENT NO.1) ORDER 1978 (No. 1101 (C. 31)) [20p], made under the Judicature (Northern Ireland) Act 1978 (c. 23), s. 123 (2) (3); operative on August 21, 1978; brings into force ss. 52, 53, 54 (2) (3) (4) (6), 55 (3), 56 (1) (2) (3), 99, 107, 116, 118, 121, 122 (1) in part, 122 (2) in part, 123, Scheds. 5 so far as it relates to other specified statutes, 6, paras. 7, 10 so far as it relates to para. 7, so far as it relates to the repeal of specified statutory provisions.

2155. Juries

JURORS (PAYMENTS) ORDER (NORTHERN IRELAND) 1978 (No. 192) [15p], made under the Juries Act (Northern Ireland) 1953 (c. 19), s. 1; operative on September 1, 1978; increases travelling and attendance allowances for jurors; revokes the 1977 (No. 216) Order.

2156. Land registration—rectification

[Local Registration of Title (Ireland) Act 1891 (c. 66), s. 34.] S applied for the rectification of an official error in a land registry map. *Held*, that (1) the court's jurisdiction under s. 34 of the Local Registration of Title (Ireland) Act 1891 to rectify an error (a) is exercisable only against a party to the instrument or transaction as respects which the application is made, or who is a voluntary transferee from such a party; (b) is exercisable if the proposed rectification will cause loss or damage to such a party or transferee; (c) is not affected by the fact that the proposed rectification will result in property being taken away from such a party if, apart from the error, he was never entitled in law to it; and (2) that, since the respondents were neither parties to the instrument or transactions in question nor volunteers taking under a transfer from such parties, the application would be refused: *Re* SKELTON [1976] N.I. 132, Murray J.

2157. Landlord and tenant

RENT (1978 ORDER) (COMMENCEMENT) ORDER (NORTHERN IRELAND) 1978 (No. 245 (C. 11)) [10p], made under S.I. 1978 No. 1050 (N.I. 20), art. 1 and the Northern Ireland Act 1974 (c. 28), Sched. 1, para. 2 (1) (2); brings that S.I. into operation on October 1, 1978.

RENT BOOK REGULATIONS (NORTHERN IRELAND) 1978 (No. 253) [20p], made under S.I. 1978 No. 1050, arts. 38 (2), 74; operative on October 1, 1978; set out particulars and information to be included in rent books supplied by landlords of certain houses.

RENT ASSESSMENT COMMITTEES REGULATIONS (NORTHERN IRELAND) 1978 (No. 259) [20p], made under S.I. 1978 No. 1050, art. 74 (1) (c); operative on October 1, 1978; specify the procedures of rent assessment committees.

RENT (FORMS) REGULATIONS (NORTHERN IRELAND) 1978 (No. 260) [40p], made under S.I. 1978 No. 1050, art. 74 (1); operative on October 1, 1978; prescribe forms for that S.I. and the information to be contained in the register of rents.

RENT ALLOWANCE SCHEME (STATUTORY PARTICULARS) REGULATIONS (NORTHERN IRELAND) 1978 (No. 265) [10p], made under S.I. 1978 No. 1050, arts. 60 (5), 74 (1); operative on October 1, 1978; specify particulars to be furnished of rent allowance schemes.

RENT (NORTHERN IRELAND) ORDER 1978 (No. 1050) (N.I. 20) [£1·00], made under the Northern Ireland Act 1974, Sched. 1, para. 1; operative on days to be appointed; replaces, and repeals, the Rent Restrictions Acts (Northern Ireland) 1920 to 1967. Where those Acts applied to a dwelling-house immediately before the Order's commencement, a tenancy in the house is classified as a regulated or a restricted tenancy, tenants under both classes of tenancy enjoy security of tenure, subject to Sched. 4. Rents under restricted tenancies are limited to the rents payable before the Order's commencement. Rent under regulated tenancies are two and a half times the net annual value unless a rent assessment committee determines otherwise. However, until it does so the maximum weekly rent under a regulated tenancy is £8 and maximum monthly rent £35. Rent assessment committees must have regard to the rents payable for comparable houses let by the housing executive (art. 27 (2) (3)). Rents may be registered and the level of registered rents varied by the Department of the Environment. Arts. 41–45 specify the terms to be implied in regulated tenancies; arts. 46–48 set out procedures for the enforcement, by landlord or tenant, of repairing obligations under regulated tenancies; Pt. VIII prohibits premiums or loans being required for the grant or assignment of certain tenancies; Pt. IX affords protection to tenants against unlawful eviction and harassment; art. 59 relates to rent allowances for certain tenants; art. 62 requires 4 weeks' notice for valid notices to quit under tenancies of dwelling-houses.

2158. —— **business tenancies—Lands Tribunal decisions**

LAVERY v. BAYLIS, BT/16/1977 (grant of new tenancy of premises in Lurgan for a term of five years at a rent of £180 p.a., the former tenancy being weekly at a rent of £2·50 per week).

MCCONVILLE v. QUINN, BT/21/1978 (objection to grant of new tenancy upheld on ground that the landlord intended to occupy the premises for the purposes of a business to be carried on by him).

WILLIAM KELLY (SUPERMARKETS) v. NORTHERN BANK EXECUTOR & TRUSTEE CO. AND HEWITT (WRIGHT (DECD.)) BT/48/49/1977 (grant of new tenancies of premises in Strabane, Co. Tyrone, for six years at £5,600 and £1,000 p.a., the former tenancies being for seven years at £1,406 p.a. and two years, seven months at £850 p.a.).

2159. —— **leasehold enfranchisement—Lands Tribunal decision**

STANFIELD v. FLYNN, R/11/1977 (compensation for acquisition by tenant of fee simple in premises let to him subject to rent of £25 p.a., *held*, to be £300).

2160. Local government

BELFAST CORPORATION SUPERANNUATION REVOCATION (AMENDMENT) REGULATIONS (NORTHERN IRELAND) 1978 (No. 2) [10p], made under S.I. 1972 No. 1073 (N.I. 10), art. 10; operative on February 17, 1978; revoke a provision relating to a valuation of a superannuation fund in the 1973 (No. 89) Regulations.

LOCAL GOVERNMENT (GENERAL GRANT) ORDER (NORTHERN IRELAND) 1978 (No. 9) [10p], made under S.I. 1972 No. 1999 (N.I. 22), Sched. 1, Part I, para. 3 (1); operative on January 10, 1978; specifies districts to be taken into account in calculating the standard penny rate products for the year ending March 31, 1979.

COUNCILLORS (TRAVELLING AND SUBSISTENCE ALLOWANCES) REGULATIONS (NORTHERN IRELAND) 1978 (No. 57) [15p], made under the Local Government Act (Northern Ireland) 1972 (c. 9), s. 36; operative on April 14, 1978; increase certain travelling and subsistence allowances payable to councillors and committee members of district councils; revoke the 1976 (No. 293) Regulations.

2161. Magisterial law

MAGISTRATES' COURTS (COSTS IN AFFILIATION AND SEPARATION AND MAINTENANCE PROCEEDINGS) (AMENDMENT) RULES (NORTHERN IRELAND) 1978 (No. 193) [15p], made under the Magistrates' Courts Act (Northern Ireland) 1964 (c. 21), s. 23; operative on September 1, 1978; amend the 1966 (No. 277) Rules by including proceedings under the Maintenance Orders (Reciprocal Enforcement) Act 1972 and increasing to £60 the maximum costs recoverable for a solicitor's remuneration and outlay or for counsel's fees.

MAGISTRATES' COURTS (COSTS IN CRIMINAL CASES) RULES (NORTHERN IRELAND) 1978 (No. 194) [10p], made under the Magistrates' Courts Act (Northern Ireland) 1964, s. 23 and the Costs in Criminal Cases Act (Northern Ireland) 1968 (c. 10), s. 7 (3); operative on September 1, 1978; increase certain amounts allowable in connection with the attendance of witnesses in prosecutions in magistrates' courts.

REMAND (TEMPORARY PROVISIONS) (NORTHERN IRELAND) ORDER 1978 (No. 1585 (N.I. 24)) [10p], made under the Northern Ireland Act 1974 (c. 28), Sched. 1, para. 1; operative on November 6, 1978; for a three-month period, makes it unnecessary for an accused to be brought before a magistrates' court at the end of any period in remand.

REMAND (TEMPORARY PROVISIONS) (NORTHERN IRELAND) ORDER 1978 (CESSATION) ORDER 1978 (No. 340) [10p], made under S.I. 1978 No. 1585 (N.I. 24), art. 4 (2) (*b*); operative on November 13, 1978; provides that art. 3 of that S.I. ceases to be in force.

Order made under the Magistrates' Courts Act (Northern Ireland) 1964 (c. 21), s. 21 (3) (*a*):

S.R. 1978 No. 299 (all petty sessions) [30p].

2162. —— appeal—case stated—requirement to transmit within specified time—mandatory

[Magistrates' Courts Act (Northern Ireland) 1964 (c. 21), s. 146 (8).] Following his summary conviction, O applied for a case stated which was sent to him by the petty sessions clerk on May 16, 1974. O's solicitors did not send it to the Court of Appeal until December 17, 1974. *Held*, that the requirement in s. 146 (8) of the Magistrates' Courts Act (Northern Ireland) 1964 to transmit a case stated to the Court of Appeal within 14 days from its despatch by the clerk is mandatory and not directory. Accordingly the appeal could not be heard: DOLAN *v.* O'HARA [1975] N.I. 129, C.A.

2163. Medicine

MEDICINES (PROHIBITION OF IMPORTATION AND POSSESSION OF VETERINARY DRUGS) ORDER (NORTHERN IRELAND) 1977 (No. 359) [15p], made under the Medicines Act 1968 (c. 67), ss. 62 (1) (*a*), 134, Sched. 4, para. 6, 7; operative on February 1, 1978; prohibits the importation, landing and possession of certain veterinary drugs except by authorised or listed persons.

MISUSE OF DRUGS (LICENCE FEES) (AMENDMENT) REGULATIONS (NORTHERN IRELAND) 1978 (No. 6) [10p], made under the Misuse of Drugs Act 1971 (c. 38), ss. 30, 31, 38; operative on April 1, 1978; increase fees for licences under the Act.

PHARMACY (1976 ORDER) (COMMENCEMENT) ORDER (NORTHERN IRELAND) 1978 (No. 11) (C. 1) [10p], made under the Northern Ireland Act 1974 (c. 28), Sched. 1, para. 2 (1) (2) and S.I. 1976 No. 1213 (N.I. 22), art. 1; brings that S.I. into operation on February 1, 1978.

POISONS (1976 ORDER) (COMMENCEMENT) ORDER (NORTHERN IRELAND) 1978 (No. 12) (C. 2) [10p], made under the Northern Ireland Act 1974, Sched. 1, para. 2 (1) (2) and S.I. 1976 No. 1214 (N.I. 23), art. 1 (2); brings that S.I. into operation on February 1, 1978.

PHARMACEUTICAL SOCIETY OF NORTHERN IRELAND (GENERAL) REGULATIONS 1978 (No. 168) [20p], made under S.I. 1976 No. 1213 (N.I. 22), art. 5; operative on July 31, 1978; prescribe conditions under which candidates for membership of the pharmaceutical society may be registered as students, the qualifications and conditions for registration as pharmaceutical chemists and the annual fees payable by members of the society; revoke the 1974 (No. 69) and 1976 (No. 171) Regulations.

PHARMACEUTICAL SOCIETY OF NORTHERN IRELAND (GENERAL) (AMENDMENT) REGULATIONS 1978 (No. 219) [20p], made under S.I. 1976 No. 1213 art. 5; operative on August 1, 1978; prescribe conditions under which candidates for membership of the pharmaceutical society may be registered as students, the qualifications for registration as pharmaceutical chemists and the annual fee for membership of the society.

2164. Mining law

MINERAL DEVELOPMENT (FEES) (AMENDMENT) REGULATIONS (NORTHERN IRELAND) 1978 (No. 137) [10p], made under the Mineral Development Act (Northern Ireland) 1969 (c. 35), s. 49; operative on July 1, 1978; increase fees for certain licences, leases, permissions and permits under the Act.

2165. Mortgages

OPTION MORTGAGE (RATES OF INTEREST) ORDER (NORTHERN IRELAND) 1978 (No. 83) [15p], made under S.I. 1978 No. 457 (N.I. 2), art. 11; operative on April 1, 1978; specifies rates of interest for calculating option mortgage subsidy.

OPTION MORTGAGE (GUARANTEE OF ADVANCES) ORDER (NORTHERN IRELAND) 1978 (No. 84) [10p], made under S.I. 1978 No. 457 (N.I. 2), art. 14 (2); operative on April 1, 1978; specifies April 1, 1978, as the appointed day for the purposes of art. 14 (1) of that S.I.

OPTION MORTGAGE (QUALIFYING LENDERS) ORDER (NORTHERN IRELAND) 1978 (No. 85) [10p], made under S.I. 1978 No. 457, art. 10; operative on April 1, 1978; specifies certain bodies as qualifying lenders for the purposes of that S.I.

OPTION MORTGAGE (QUALIFYING LENDERS) (No. 2) ORDER (NORTHERN IRELAND) 1978 (No. 113) [10p], made under S.I. 1978 No. 457, art. 2; operative on June 1, 1978; specifies two bodies as qualifying lenders for the purpose of the option mortgage scheme.

OPTION MORTGAGE (QUALIFYING LENDERS) (No. 3) ORDER (NORTHERN IRELAND) 1978 (No. 252) [10p], made under S.I. 1978 No. 457, art. 10; operative on October 1, 1978; specifies the Londonderry Provident Building Society as a qualifying lender for the purposes of that S.I.

2166. National health

HEALTH AND PERSONAL SOCIAL SERVICES (GENERAL OPHTHALMIC SERVICES) (AMENDMENT) REGULATIONS (NORTHERN IRELAND) 1978 (No. 21) [10p], made under the Northern Ireland Act 1974 (c. 28), Sched. 1, para. 2 (1) (2) and S.I. 1972 No. 1265 (N.I. 14), arts. 62, 98, 106, 107, Sched. 15; operative on March 1, 1978; amend the 1975 (No. 372) Regulations in relation to exceptions from charges for the replacement or repair of optical appliances and several minor matters.

WELFARE FOODS (AMENDMENT) REGULATIONS (NORTHERN IRELAND) 1978 (No. 64) [10p], made under the Welfare Foods Act (Northern Ireland) 1968 (c. 26), s. 1 (3) (a); operative on April 3, 1978; enable certain young children to receive free welfare milk and approve a brand of dried milk.

NATIONAL INSURANCE (HEALTH SERVICES SUPERANNUATION SCHEME—MODIFICATION AND NON-PARTICIPATION) REGULATIONS (NORTHERN IRELAND) 1978 (No. 292) [30p], made under the National Insurance Act (Northern Ireland) 1966 (c. 6), s. 103 and S.I. 1972 No. 1073 (N.I. 10), arts. 12, 14; operative on December 1, 1978; modify benefits under the health service superannuation scheme in connection with graduated benefit; revoke the 1966 (No. 280) and 1969 (No. 282) Regulations.

HEALTH SERVICES (SUPERANNUATION) (AMENDMENT) REGULATIONS (NORTHERN IRELAND) 1978 (No. 301) [60p], made under S.I. 1972 No. 1073 (N.I. 10), arts. 12, 14; operative on October 6, 1978; amend the 1962 (No. 237) Regulations as respects the superannuation of certain persons in the health services.

HEALTH SERVICES (SUPERANNUATION) (WAR SERVICE, ETC.) REGULATIONS

(NORTHERN IRELAND) 1978 (No. 324) [30p], made under S.I. 1972 No. 1073 (N.I. 10), arts. 12, 14; operative on December 15, 1978; provide for the reckoning of war service of certain members of the health services superannuation scheme.

HEALTH AND PERSONAL SOCIAL SERVICES (NORTHERN IRELAND) ORDER 1978 (No. 1907 (N.I. 26)) [30p], made under the Northern Ireland Act 1974, Sched. 1, para. 7; operative on January 21, 1979; arts. 3–7 prohibit the sale of cigarettes and tobacco products to persons apparently under 16; art. 8 relates to vocational experience which medical practitioners must have before being included in certain lists; arts. 9–19 contain detailed amendments to legislation dealing with health matters.

2167. Negligence—hire of machine operator—whether independent contractor

P, an employee of D, was injured by a mechanical digger driven by W. W was the owner of the hire firm from which D had hired the digger. W was told to dig certain trenches, but was not given directions as to the operation of the digger. On P's claim for damages, the jury found that W was negligent and that D was his employer. On appeal, *held*, allowing the appeal (O'Donnell J. dissenting) that the evidence pointed only to a hiring arrangement and not to W's employment by D: MAGUIRE *v.* P. J. LAGAN (CONTRACTORS) [1976] N.I. 49, C.A.

2168. Northern Ireland Act 1974—extension

NORTHERN IRELAND ACT 1974 (INTERIM PERIOD EXTENSION) ORDER 1978 (No. 957) [10p], made under the Northern Ireland Act 1974 (c. 28), s. 1 (4); operative on July 10, 1978; extends until July 16, 1979, the period specified in s. 1 (4) of the 1974 Act.

2169. Northern Ireland (Emergency Provisions) Act 1978 (c. 5)

This Act consolidates, with certain exceptions, the Northern Ireland (Emergency Provisions) Act 1973, the Northern Ireland (Young Persons) Act 1974 and the Northern Ireland (Emergency Provisions) (Amendment) Act 1975.

S. 1 makes provision in respect of preliminary inquiries into scheduled offences; s. 2 delimits the power to grant bail in a case involving a scheduled offence; s. 3 concerns the grant of Legal Aid for bail applications in cases where a scheduled offence is charged; s. 4 governs the power to hold young persons charged with scheduled offences in custody; s. 5 relates to directions given by the Secretary of State in respect of s. 4; s. 6 lays down the court for trial on indictment of a scheduled offence; s. 7 stipulates the mode of trial; s. 8 covers admissions made by persons charged with one or more scheduled offences; s. 9 indicates the burden and standard of proof in relation to offences of possessing a proscribed article; s. 10 directs the treatment of young persons convicted of scheduled offences; s. 11 relates to powers of arrest of suspected terrorists; s. 12 covers their detention; s. 13 confers a general power of arrest and seizure upon constables; s. 14 confers powers of arrest and detention, without warrant, upon constables and members of H.M. forces on duty; s. 15 extends these powers to searches for munitions and radio transmitters; s. 17 deals with the powers of explosives inspectors; s. 18 grants powers to stop and question persons; s. 19 relates to general powers of entry, and authorised interferences with property rights, and restrictions on highways; s. 20 contains supplementary provisions; s. 21 lists certain proscribed organisations, and creates certain offences in connection with these organisations; s. 22 prohibits the collection, publication, etc., of information likely to be useful to terrorists; s. 23 makes it an offence to give or receive training or instruction in the making or use of firearms, explosives or explosive substances; s. 24 makes it an offence to comply with an order that an assembly of three or more people should disperse; s. 25 prohibits dressing or behaving in a public place like a member of a proscribed organisation; s. 26 concerns the summary offence of wearing a hood or mask to conceal identity; s. 27 contains supplementary regulations for preserving the peace; s. 28 provides for compensation to be paid by the Secretary of State for any taking, occupation, destruction or damage, of any real or personal property under this Act; s. 29 restricts certain prosecutions; s. 30 relates to the definition of a " scheduled offence "; s. 31 is the interpretation section; s. 32 gives directions for orders and regulations to be made under the Act; s. 33 deals with commencement, duration, expiry and revival of the Act's provisions; s. 34 contains certain consequential amendments; s. 35 contains transitional provisions, savings and repeals; s. 36 contains the short title; the Act applies to Northern Ireland only.

The Act received the Royal Assent of March 23, 1978, and came into operation on June 1, 1978, except for the secondary legislation made under s. 32, and s. 33 itself.

2170. —— continuation

NORTHERN IRELAND (EMERGENCY PROVISIONS) ACT 1978 (CONTINUANCE) ORDER 1978 (No. 958) [10p], made under the Northern Ireland (Emergency Provisions) Act 1978 (c. 5), s. 33 (3) (_a_); operative on July 25, 1978; continues in force the temporary provisions of the 1978 Act for six months from July 25, 1978.

NORTHERN IRELAND (EMERGENCY PROVISIONS) ACT 1978 (CONTINUANCE) (No. 2) ORDER 1978 (No. 1865) [10p], made under the Northern Ireland (Emergency Provisions) Act 1978, s. 33 (3) (_a_); operative on January 25, 1979; continues in force the temporary provisions of the 1978 Act for a further six months.

2171. Pensions and superannuation

JUDICIAL PENSIONS (WIDOWS' AND CHILDREN'S BENEFITS) REGULATIONS (NORTHERN IRELAND) 1978 (No. 15) [25p], made under the Administration of Justice Act 1973 (c. 15), s. 10 (8), Sched. 3; operative on February 1, 1978; provide for the contributions to be made by holders of certain judicial and other offices towards increased superannuation benefits for widows and children.

TEACHERS' SUPERANNUATION (CONTRACTED-OUT EMPLOYMENT) REGULATIONS (NORTHERN IRELAND) 1978 (No. 16) [15p], made under S.I. 1975 No. 1503 (N.I. 15), art. 53, Sched. 2, para. 8, as amended by S.I. 1977 No. 610 (N.I. 11), art. 18 (18); operative on February 20, 1978; deal with the operation of Part IV of S.I. 1975 No. 1503 in relation to certain teachers.

PENSIONS (CLERKS OF THE CROWN AND PEACE—REQUISITE BENEFITS) ORDER (NORTHERN IRELAND) 1978 (No. 103) [25p], made under S.I. 1975 No. 1503 (N.I. 15), art. 61; operative on April 21, 1978; modifies the pension scheme for clerks of the Crown and Peace.

PENSIONS APPEAL TRIBUNALS (NORTHERN IRELAND) (AMENDMENT) RULES 1978 (No. 117) [10p], made under the Pension Appeal Tribunals Act 1943 (c. 39), Sched., para. 5; operative on June 5, 1978; increase the maximum fee payable to a medical specialist or other expert for giving his opinion to the pensions appeal tribunal.

OCCUPATIONAL PENSION SCHEMES (CERTIFICATION OF EMPLOYMENTS—HEALTH SERVICES) REGULATIONS (NORTHERN IRELAND) 1978 (No. 121) [20p], made under S.I. 1975 No. 1503 (N.I. 15), art. 53, Sched. 2, para. 8, as amended by S.I. 1977 No. 610 (N.I. 11), art. 18 (18); operative on June 12, 1978; treat the Department of Health and Social Services as the employer of employees in the health services for certain occupational pension purposes and deem employment in those services to be employment under a single employer for the purpose of specified provisions of the 1975 Order.

PENSIONS APPEAL TRIBUNALS (NORTHERN IRELAND) RULES 1978 (No. 169) [20p], made under the Pensions Appeal Tribunals Act 1943, Sched., para. 5, as amended by the Administration of Justice Act 1977 (c. 38); operative on July 31, 1978; amend the 1972 (No. 267) Rules as respects expenses and allowances

PENSIONS INCREASE (ANNUAL REVIEW) ORDER (NORTHERN IRELAND) 1978 (No. 269) [20p], made under the Pensions (Increase) Act (Northern Ireland) 1971 (c. 35), ss. 2, 9 (4), as amended by S.I. 1972 No. 1073) (N.I. 10) art. 20 and S.I. 1974 No. 1267 (N.I. 2), arts, 3, 5; operative on December 1, 1969; increases certain public service pensions.

PENSIONS INCREASE (MODIFICATION) REGULATIONS (NORTHERN IRELAND) 1978 (No. 270) [10p], made under the Pensions (Increase) Act (Northern Ireland) 1971, s. 5 (3); apply the Act and the 1978 (No. 269) Order to pensions payable under the Belfast Corporation Act (Northern Ireland) 1943, whenever they began.

PENSIONS (REQUISITE BENEFITS) ORDER (NORTHERN IRELAND) 1978 (No. 307) [20p], made under S.I. 1975 No. 1503 (N.I. 15), art. 61 (1); operative on November 9, 1978; modify occupational pension schemes for the holders of certain public offices.

2172. Petroleum

PETROLEUM PRODUCTION (FEES) (AMENDMENT) REGULATIONS (NORTHERN IRELAND) 1978 (No. 136) [10p], made under the Petroleum (Production) Act (Northern Ireland) 1964 (c. 28), s. 13; increase fees for petroleum licences under the Act.

2173. Police

ROYAL ULSTER CONSTABULARY PENSIONS (AMENDMENT) REGULATIONS 1978 (No. 73) [35p], made under the Police Act (Northern Ireland) 1970 (c. 9), s. 25; operative on April 6, 1978; amend the 1973 (No. 317) Regulations as respects the transfer of superannuation rights from other employments, the superannuation of officers who rejoin the R.U.C. and certain other matters.

ROYAL ULSTER CONSTABULARY (AMENDMENT) REGULATIONS 1978 (No. 92) [25p], made under the Police Act (Northern Ireland) 1970, s. 25; operative on May 1, 1978; increase the pay and certain allowances of specified members of the R.U.C.

POLICE CADETS (AMENDMENT) REGULATIONS (NORTHERN IRELAND) 1978 (No. 93) [10p], made under the Police Act (Northern Ireland) 1970, s. 10; operative on May 1, 1978; increase the pay of, and board and lodging charges for, police cadets.

ROYAL ULSTER CONSTABULARY (AMENDMENT No. 2) REGULATIONS 1978 (No. 280) [25p], made under the Police Act (Northern Ireland) 1970, s. 25; operative on October 9, 1978; increase the pay of members of the R.U.C. with ranks not higher than that of chief superintendent.

POLICE CADETS (AMENDMENT No. 2) REGULATIONS (NORTHERN IRELAND) 1978 (No. 281) [10p], made under the Police Act (Northern Ireland) 1970, s. 10; operative on October 9, 1978; increase the pay of police cadets and the charge for certain board and lodging.

ROYAL ULSTER CONSTABULARY PENSIONS (AMENDMENT No. 3) REGULATIONS 1978 (No. 346) [20p], made under the Police Act (Northern Ireland) 1970, s. 25; operative on December 1, 1978; increase certain widow's pensions and children's allowances for members of the R.U.C.

ULSTER SPECIAL CONSTABULARY PENSIONS (AMENDMENT) REGULATIONS 1978 (No. 347) [10p], made under the Police Act (Northern Ireland) 1970, s. 33 (2); operative on December 1, 1978; increase widows' pensions and childrens' allowances for members of the U.S.C.

2174. Practice

RULES OF THE SUPREME COURT (NORTHERN IRELAND) (CONVENTION ADOPTIONS ETC.) 1978 (No. 128) [40p], made under the Northern Ireland Act 1962 (c. 30), s. 7; operative on the commencement of s. 1 of the Adoption (Hague Convention) Act (Northern Ireland) 1969; amend R.S.C. as respects matters relating to adoptions.

RULES OF THE SUPREME COURT (NORTHERN IRELAND) (CAPITAL TRANSFER TAX APPEALS) 1978 (No. 180) [20p], made under the Northern Ireland Act 1962, s. 7; operative on September 4, 1978; permit service out of the jurisdiction in proceedings to recover estate duty or capital transfer tax; specify the procedure for appeals in certain capital tax proceedings.

RULES OF THE SUPREME COURT (NORTHERN IRELAND) (MISCELLANEOUS) 1978 (No. 181) [10p], made under the Northern Ireland Act 1962, s. 7; operative on September 4, 1978; apply Ord. 59A to appeals, references and applications to the High Court under the Land Registration Act (Northern Ireland) 1970; amend Ord. 60A by delegating certain matters to registrars; amend Ord. 88 by requiring the official assignee to take part in the examination of bankrupts.

RULES OF THE SUPREME COURT (NORTHERN IRELAND) (SITTINGS AND VACATIONS) 1978 (No. 287) [10p], made under the Northern Ireland Act 1962, s. 7; operative on October 25, 1978; amend R.S.C., Ord. 63 by extending the recess in the Michaelmas sittings and shortening the Christmas vacation.

2175. —— debt collection

PAYMENTS FOR DEBT (AMENDMENT) (NORTHERN IRELAND) ORDER 1978 (No. 1046) (N.I. 16) [10p], made under the Northern Ireland Act 1974 (c. 28), Sched. 1, para. 1; operative on August 8, 1978; authorises the making of an order requiring the payment of interest or costs of collection on sums recoverable under the Payments for Debt (Emergency Provisions) Act (Northern Ireland) 1971 in respect of debts and charges for electricity or gas.

2176. —— legal aid

LEGAL ADVICE AND ASSISTANCE (FINANCIAL CONDITIONS) REGULATIONS (NORTHERN IRELAND) 1978 (No. 186) [10p], made under the Legal Aid and Advice Act (Northern Ireland) 1965 (c. 8), ss. 7C, 14; operative on September 1, 1978; increase to £23 a week the disposable income above which a person receiving legal advice and assistance is required to pay a contribution.

LEGAL ADVICE AND ASSISTANCE (FINANCIAL CONDITIONS) (NO. 2) REGULATIONS (NORTHERN IRELAND) 1978 (No. 187) [10p], made under the Legal Aid and Advice Act (Northern Ireland) 1965, ss. 7 (2), 14; operative on September 1, 1978; increase disposable income and capital limits for the availability of legal advice and assistance.

LEGAL AID (GENERAL) (AMENDMENT) REGULATIONS (NORTHERN IRELAND) 1978 (No. 188) [10p], made under the Legal Aid and Advice Act (Northern Ireland) 1965, ss. 3, 14; operative on September 1, 1978; increase certain amounts in the 1965 (No. 217) Regulations and add supplementary benefit and family income supplements to the prescribed exemptions from the charge imposed by s. 3 (6) of the Act.

LEGAL AID (ASSESSMENT OF RESOURCES) (AMENDMENT) REGULATIONS (NORTHERN IRELAND) 1978 (No. 191) [10p], made under the Legal Aid and Advice Act (Northern Ireland) 1965, s. 4; operative on September 1, 1978; amend the 1965 (No. 218) Regulations by increasing certain amounts and excluding certain allowances and interests from the assessment of disposable income or capital.

LEGAL AID IN CRIMINAL CASES (STATEMENT OF MEANS) RULES (NORTHERN IRELAND) 1978 (No. 200) [20p], made under the Legal Aid and Advice Act (Northern Ireland) 1965, ss. 24 (1), 27 (3); operative on September 1, 1978; provide a new form of statement of means which, in criminal proceedings, applicants for legal aid under certain provisions may be required to furnish under s. 24 of the Act; revoke the 1966 (No. 55) Rules.

LEGAL AID AND ASSISTANCE REGULATIONS (NORTHERN IRELAND) 1978 (No. 201) (C. 8) [20p], made under the Legal Aid and Advice Act (Northern Ireland) 1965, ss. 1, 4, 7A to E, 14; operative on September 1, 1978; provide for legal advice and assistance to be given under the Act by solicitors to those found by them to be financially eligible for it.

LEGAL AID, ADVICE AND ASSISTANCE (1977 ORDER) (COMMENCEMENT NO. 2) ORDER (NORTHERN IRELAND) 1978 (No. 215) [10p], made under S.I. 1977 No. 1252 (N.I.) 19), art. 1 (2); brings art. 3 (3) (pt.) (6)–(8) (9) of, and the Sched. to, that S.I. into operation on September 1, 1978.

LEGAL ADVICE AND ASSISTANCE (FINANCIAL CONDITIONS) (NO. 3) REGULATIONS (NORTHERN IRELAND) 1978 (No. 337) [10p], made under the Legal Aid and Advice Act (Northern Ireland) 1965, ss. 7 (2), 14; operative on December 15, 1978; increase disposable income and capital limits to £52 a week and £365.

LEGAL ADVICE AND ASSISTANCE (FINANCIAL CONDITIONS) (NO. 4) REGULATIONS (NORTHERN IRELAND) 1978 (No. 338) [10p], made under the Legal Aid and Advice Act (Northern Ireland) 1965, ss. 7C, 14; operative on December 15, 1978; increase to £25 a week the disposable income above which a person receiving legal aid and advice is required to make a contribution.

LEGAL ADVICE AND ASSISTANCE (AMENDMENT) REGULATIONS (NORTHERN IRELAND) 1978 (No. 341) [10p], made under the Legal Aid and Advice Act (Northern Ireland) 1965, ss. 4, 14; increase allowances for dependants in assessing disposable capital.

2177. —— writ—county court jurisdiction increased—whether action could be remitted

[Northern Ireland (Remittal and Removal of Proceedings) Order 1971 (S.I. 1971 No. 875), art. 3 (1).] P issued in the High Court a writ for damages in respect of a claim in tort when the limit on the county court's jurisdiction was £300. That jurisdiction was later increased to £1,000. D issued a summons for the remittal of the action to the county court. An order for that purpose was made. On appeal, *held,* that art. 3 (1) of S.I. 1971 No. 875 fell to be applied as the legislation stood at the date of the hearing of the application and that the order for remittal was therefore properly made: WARNOCK *v.* HARLAND & WOLFF [1976] N.I. 156, C.A.

2178. —— —— extension of time for service

After a car accident in which two drivers were killed, P served two writs claiming negligence as administratix of the driver of one of the cars and as committee of his passenger. No grant of administration had been taken out to the estate of the other driver and the writs named his personal representative (using that description) as defendant. After twelve months from the issue of the writs P applied for an order extending the time for their service. *Held,* that the time for serving the writs would be extended, as there were exceptional circumstances arising out of the refusal of L's widow to take out a grant: McCLELLAN *v.* PERSONAL REPRESENTATIVE OF LOVE (DECD.) [1976] N.I. 126, MacDermott J.

2179. **Prisons**

PRISON RULES (NORTHERN IRELAND) 1978 (No. 336) [10p], made under the Prison Act (Northern Ireland) 1953 (c. 18), s. 13; operative on November 3, 1978; amend the 1954 (No. 7) Rules in relation to emergencies.

2180. **Public health**

INTEREST ON RECOVERABLE SANITATION EXPENSES ORDER (NORTHERN IRELAND) 1978 (No. 249) [10p], made under the Public Health and Local Government (Miscellaneous Provisions) Act (Northern Ireland) 1962 (c. 12), s. 5; operative on October 4, 1978; increases to 11½ per cent. p.a. the rate of interest on certain expenses recoverable by district councils under the Public Health (Ireland) Act 1878; revokes the 1977 (No. 362) Order.

POLLUTION CONTROL AND LOCAL GOVERNMENT (NORTHERN IRELAND) ORDER 1978 (No. 1049) (N.I. 19) [£1·50], made under the Northern Ireland Act 1974 (c. 28), Sched. 1, para. 1; operative on days to be appointed; arts. 3, 4 relate to waste disposal arrangements and plans; arts. 5–13 concern the licensing of the disposal of controlled waste; arts. 14–20 deal with the collection and removal of waste; arts. 21–24 relate to the disposal and reclamation of waste; arts. 25–28 concern street cleaning and litter and arts. 29–32 motor vehicles; arts. 33–36 are supplemental; art. 37 requires district councils to make periodical noise inspections; arts. 38, 39 relate to summary proceedings to deal with noise, arts. 40, 41, noise on construction sites, art. 42, noise in streets, art. 43–47, noise abatement zones and art. 48, noise from plant or machinery; arts. 49–54 are supplemental; arts. 55–63 deal with the pollution of the atmosphere; art. 64 amends provisions relating to water; arts. 65–87 are miscellaneous and general.

2181. **Rating and valuation**

RATES (REGIONAL RATE AND REDUCTION OF REGIONAL RATE ON DWELLINGS) ORDER (NORTHERN IRELAND) 1978 (No. 23) [10p], made under S.I. 1977 No. 2157 (N.I. 28), arts. 7, 27; operative on April 1, 1978; fixes the regional rate for the year ending March 31, 1979, and the amount by which it is reduced for dwelling-houses.

RATE REBATE (AMENDMENT) ORDER (NORTHERN IRELAND) 1978 (No. 32) [10p], made under S.I. 1977 No. 2157, art. 28; operative on April 1, 1978; increases to £3·20 the maximum weekly rate rebate.

RATE REBATE (AMENDMENT NO. 2) ORDER (NORTHERN IRELAND) 1978 (No. 297) [20p], made under S.I. 1977 No. 2157 (N.I. 28), art. 28; operative on November 13, 1978; amends the 1974 (No. 65) Order as respects needs allowances, deductions for non-dependants and rebates; revokes the 1976 (No. 302) and 1977 (No. 281) Orders.

2182. —— Lands Tribunal decisions

BURNS v. COMMISSIONER OF VALUATION, VR/21/1977 (unsuccessful appeal against the valuation of a dwelling-house in Sion Mills, Co. Tyrone).

BYFORD v. COMMISSIONER OF VALUATION, VR/38/1977 (unsuccessful appeal against the valuation of a shopping centre at Newtownards, Co. Down).

DONNELLY v. COMMISSIONER OF VALUATION, VR/48/1978 (unsuccessful appeal against the valuation of a dwelling-house in St. James Parade, Belfast).

DUGGAN v. COMMISSIONER OF VALUATION, VR/71/1977 (appeal against the valuation of a public-house at Ormeau Road, Belfast, the tribunal holding that it was less attractive to hypothetical tenants than comparable licensed premises because of past bomb and other attacks and that it was expensive to staff and run and keep fit for trade).

FAGAN v. COMMISSIONER OF VALUATION, VR/53/1978 (appeal against the valuation of a bungalow in Lurgan, Co. Armagh, the tribunal holding that the valuation should be reduced on account of unpleasant conditions arising from building operations nearby).

GRANT v. COMMISSIONER OF VALUATION, VR/98/1977 (appeal against the valuation of a shop in Crumlin, Co. Antrim).

HUME v. COMMISSIONER OF VALUATION, VR/97/1977 (unsuccessful appeal against the valuation of a dwelling-house in Cultra, Holywood, Co. Antrim).

JUNIOR v. COMMISSIONER OF VALUATION, VR/5/1977 (buildings on farm which were occasionally used to service machinery and equipment for work which was not on agricultural land occupied by the ratepayer *held* to be used solely in connection with agricultural operations as the time they were used for other purposes was not substantial).

KANE v. COMMISSIONER OF VALUATION, VR/3/1978 (valuation of bungalow in Lurgan, Co. Armagh, the tribunal reducing the valuation by about 10 per cent. on account of defective woodwork in window frames and elsewhere).

McCONNELL v. COMMISSIONER OF VALUATION, VR/15/1977 (appeal against the valuation of a dwelling-house in Castlereagh district, the tribunal reducing the valuation by £10).

McKEE v. COMMISSIONER OF VALUATION, VR/6/1978 (valuation of dwelling-house in Newtownabbey, Co. Antrim).

WELSHMAN v. COMMISSIONER OF VALUATION, VR/39/1978 (unsuccessful appeal against the valuation of a dwelling-house at Newforge Lane, Belfast).

WHITE v. COMMISSIONER OF VALUATION, VR/68/1977 (unsuccessful appeal against valuation of bungalow in Cookstown, Co. Tyrone).

WILLEY v. COMMISSIONER OF VALUATION, VR/99/1977 (unsuccessful appeal against the valuation of a bungalow in Bangor, Co. Down).

2183. Real property and conveyancing

PROPERTY (1978 ORDER) (COMMENCEMENT) ORDER (NORTHERN IRELAND) 1978 (No. 134 (C. 7)) [10p], made under S.I. 1978 No. 459 (N.I. 4), art. 1 (2); brings that S.I. into operation on June 1, 1978.

2184. Revenue and finance

CONTROL OF BORROWING (AMENDMENT) ORDER (NORTHERN IRELAND) 1978 (No. 4) [10p], made under the Loans Guarantee and Borrowing Regulation Act (Northern Ireland) 1946 (c. 18), s. 2; operative on February 13, 1978; amends the 1962 (No. 187) Order in relation to transactions involving borrowing or raising money in Northern Ireland by or on behalf of persons resident outside the United Kingdom or by or on behalf of certain investment trust companies and a definition; revokes the 1970 (No. 253) Order.

GOVERNMENT LOANS FUND (FEES) REGULATIONS (NORTHERN IRELAND) 1978 (No. 71) [10p], made under the Government Loans Act (Northern Ireland) 1957 (c. 10), ss. 3 (2), 27; operative on April 1, 1978; specify fees payable by certain borrowers from the government loans fund; revoke the 1967 (No. 39) and 1974 (No. 174) Regulations.

CONTROL OF BORROWING (AMENDMENT) (NO. 2) ORDER (NORTHERN IRELAND) 1978 (No. 99) [10p], made under the Loans Guarantee and Borrowing Regulation Act (Northern Ireland) 1946, s. 2; operative on May 15, 1978: substitute references to district councils in the 1962 (No. 187) and 1978 (No. 4) Orders.

ULSTER SAVINGS CERTIFICATES (AMENDMENT) REGULATIONS 1978 (No. 142) [20p], made under the Exchequer and Financial Provisions Act (Northern Ireland) 1950 (c. 3), ss. 15 (1), 16 (1), as amended by the Administrative and Financial Provisions Act (Northern Ireland) 1962 (c. 7), s. 2; operative on June 17, 1978; extend the currency of 14th issue Ulster savings certificates for two years and increase the maximum holding to 3,000 units.

9½% ULSTER DEVELOPMENT BONDS (SECOND ISSUE) ORDER (NORTHERN IRELAND) 1978 (No. 256) [20p], made under the Exchequer and Financial Provisions Act (Northern Ireland) 1950, s. 11 (1); operative on November 20, 1978; governs the issue, purchase and other matters relating to 9½ per cent. Ulster development bonds (second issue).

9½% ULSTER DEVELOPMENT BONDS (SECOND CONVERSION ISSUE) ORDER (NORTHERN IRELAND) 1978 (No. 257) [20p], made under the Exchequer and Financial Provisions Act (Northern Ireland) 1950, s. 11 (1); operative on November 20, 1978; provides for the creation of a new conversion issue of Ulster development bonds and for the exchange of matured issues of existing bonds for the new bonds.

ULSTER SAVINGS CERTIFICATES (INDEX LINKED RETIREMENT ISSUE) (AMENDMENT) REGULATIONS 1978 (No. 266) [10p], made under the Exchequer and Financial Provisions Act (Northern Ireland) 1950, s. 15 (1); operative on October 2, 1978; increase to 70 units the maximum permitted holding of Ulster savings certificates of the index linked issue.

PREVENTION OF FRAUD (INVESTMENTS) ACT LICENSING (AMENDMENT) REGULATIONS (NORTHERN IRELAND) 1978 (No. 298) [10p], made under the Prevention of Fraud (Investments) Act (Northern Ireland) 1940 (c. 9), ss. 3, 19; operative on December 1, 1978; increase fees for principals' and representatives' licences under the 1945 (No. 130) Regulations.

APPROPRIATION (NO. 2) (NORTHERN IRELAND) ORDER 1978 (No. 1036) (N.I. 6) [25p], made under the Northern Ireland Act 1974 (c. 28), Sched. 1, para. 1; operative on July 25, 1978; authorises the issue of sums out of the consolidated fund and appropriates those sums for specified services.

APPROPRIATION (NO. 3) (NORTHERN IRELAND) ORDER 1978 (No. 1037) (N.I. 7) [10p], made under the Northern Ireland Act 1974, Sched. 1, para. 1; operative on July 25, 1978; authorises the issue of a sum out of the consolidated fund and appropriates that sum for a specified service.

FINANCIAL PROVISIONS (NORTHERN IRELAND) 1978 (No. 1041) (N.I. 11) [30p.], made under the Northern Ireland Act 1974, Sched. 1, para. 1; operative on August 8, 1978, except for arts. 5, 12, 13 and Sched. 3, Part II, which are operative on April 1, 1979; increases limits on sums which may be issued out of the consolidated fund for certain purposes and limits on grants for capital works relating to harbours, allows the maxima of certain payments to district councillors and members of education and library boards to be determined by the relevant departments; abolishes the Ulster land fund and the housing commutation fund.

APPROPRIATION (NO. 4) (NORTHERN IRELAND) ORDER 1978 (No. 1906) (N.I. 25) [25p], made under the Northern Ireland Act 1974, Sched. 1, para. 1; operative on December 20, 1978; authorises the issue of a further sum out of the consolidated fund for the year ending March 31, 1979, and appropriates that sum for specified services.

2185. Road traffic

HEAVY GOODS VEHICLES (DRIVERS' LICENCES) (AMENDMENT) REGULATIONS (NORTHERN IRELAND) 1977 (No. 382) [10p], made under the Road Traffic Act (Northern Ireland) 1970 (c. 2), ss. 66 (3) (c), 71; operative on December 29, 1977; exclude fire fighting salvage vehicles when being driven by members of the armed forces from the provisions of the Act about heavy goods vehicle drivers' licences.

ROAD TRAFFIC (DRIVERS' AGES AND HOURS OF WORK) (1976 ORDER) (COMMENCEMENT NO. 2) ORDER (NORTHERN IRELAND) 1978 (No. 17) (C. 3) [10p], made under the Northern Ireland Act 1974 (c. 28), Sched. 1, para. 2 (1) (2) and S.I. 1976 No. 581 (N.I. 11), art. 1 (3); brings arts. 4 and 6 (part) of, and Sched. 3 (part) to, that S.I. into operation on February 6, 1978.

COMMUNITY DRIVERS' HOURS RULES (TEMPORARY MODIFICATIONS) REGULA-
TIONS (NORTHERN IRELAND) 1978 (No. 18) [25p], made under the European
Communities Act 1972 (c. 68), s. 2 (2); operative on February 6, 1978;
implement an EEC decision allowing a phased introduction of an EEC Regulation relating to the hours of drivers of passenger and goods vehicles.

MOTOR CARS (DRIVING INSTRUCTION) (AMENDMENT) REGULATIONS (NOR-
THERN IRELAND) 1978 (No. 76) [10p], made under the Road Traffic Act
(Northern Ireland) 1970, ss. 117, 117C, 189; operative on April 28, 1978;
amend the 1974 (No. 109) Regulations in relation to the period for which
certain applicants must have held specified licences.

PUBLIC SERVICE VEHICLES (AMENDMENT) REGULATIONS (NORTHERN IRELAND)
1978 (No. 80) [10p], made under the Road Traffic Act (Northern Ireland)
1970, ss. 61, 189; operative on April 3, 1978; amend the 1965 (No. 161)
Regulations in relation to payments for journeys in one-man operated buses.

ROAD TRAFFIC (FIXED PENALTY) (PROCEDURE) (AMENDMENT) REGULATIONS
(NORTHERN IRELAND) 1978 (No. 139) [10p], made under the Road Traffic Act
(Northern Ireland) 1970, ss. 172 (4), 175 (4), 189; operative on July 1,
1978; amend the 1966 (No. 116) Regulations so that references to the clerk of
petty sessions include the payments officer at the fixed penalty notice office,
Belfast.

ROAD TRAFFIC (PAYMENT OF FIXED PENALTY) ORDER (NORTHERN IRELAND)
1978 (No. 140) [10p], made under the Road Traffic Act (Northern Ireland)
1970, s. 175 (1); operative on July 1, 1978; require fixed penalties for certain
offences in the petty sessions districts of Bangor, Belfast, Carrickfergus, Lisburn
and Newtownards to be paid at the fixed penalty notice office, Belfast.

MOTOR CYCLES (WEARING OF PROTECTIVE HEADGEAR) REGULATIONS (NOR-
THERN IRELAND) 1978 (No. 152) [20p], made under the Road Traffic Act
(Northern Ireland) 1970, ss. 114, 189; operative on August 1, 1978; replace
and revoke the 1973 (No. 115) Regulations.

MOTOR VEHICLES (CONSTRUCTION AND USE) (AMENDMENT) REGULATIONS
(NORTHERN IRELAND) 1978 (No. 208) [30p], made under the Road Traffic Act
(Northern Ireland) 1970, ss. 26, 27 189; operative on September 1, 1978;
amend the 1976 (No. 320) Regulations.

MOTOR VEHICLES (DRIVING LICENCES) (AMENDMENT) REGULATIONS (NOR-
THERN IRELAND) 1978 (No. 209) [20p], made under the Road Traffic Act
(Northern Ireland) 1970, ss. 2, 15, 189 and S.I. 1976 No. 581 (N.I. 11), art. 3,
Sched. 1, para. 6, Sched. 2, para. 1; operative on September 1, 1978; amend
the 1965 (No. 42) Regulations as respects mopeds; revoke the 1971 (No. 384)
Regulations.

MOTOR VEHICLES (INVALID CARRIAGES) (AMENDMENT) REGULATIONS (NOR-
THERN IRELAND) 1978 (No. 210) [10p], made under the Road Traffic Act
(Northern Ireland) 1970, ss. 30 (2), 189; operative on September 1, 1978;
increase the maximum unladen weight of invalid carriages to 10 cwt.

MOTOR VEHICLES (MAXIMUM SPEED) (AMENDMENT) REGULATIONS (NORTHERN
IRELAND) 1978 (No. 268) [10p], made under the Road Traffic Act (Northern
Ireland) 1970, ss. 26, 189; operative on October 18, 1978; amend the 1973
(No. 504) Regulations as respects the maximum speed at which certain trailers
may be drawn.

ROAD VEHICLES (REGISTRATION AND LICENSING) (AMENDMENT) REGULATIONS
(NORTHERN IRELAND) 1978 (No. 1541) [10p], made under the Vehicles (Excise)
Act (Northern Ireland) 1972 (c. 10) (N.I.), ss. 23, 34, as modified by s. 37 (1)
and Sched. 9, Part I, para. 20; operative on November 17, 1978; further amend
S.R. & O. 1973 No. 490 as a result of the exemption from vehicle excise duty
for persons in receipt of a mobility allowance.

ROADS AND ROAD TRAFFIC (NORTHERN IRELAND) ORDER 1978 (No. 1051)
(N.I. 21) [70p], made under the Northern Ireland Act 1974, Sched. 1, para.
1; operative, as to arts. 6, 10 (2), on August 25, 1978, and, as to the remainder,
on days to be appointed; arts. 3–5 contain provisions as to the control of
builders' skips on, and their removal from, roads; art. 6 amends the law relating
to the licensing of drivers of vehicles; art. 7 prohibits the fitting and sale of
defective or unsuitable vehicle parts; art. 8 amends the law relating to heavy

goods vehicle drivers' licences; art. 9 allows the prohibition of the driving of foreign vehicles in specified circumstances; art. 10 relates to deposits and securities in lieu of third party insurance; art. 11 concerns reckless driving and art. 12, traffic surveys; art. 13 increases penalties; the remaining provisions are supplemental.

Orders made under the Road Traffic Act (Northern Ireland) 1970:

S. 19: 1978 Nos. 288 (Newcastle) [10p]; 312 (Coleraine) [40p]; 343 (Lisnaskea) [10p].

S. 20: S.R. 1978 Nos. 55 (Ballysillan Park, Belfast) [10p]; 70 (Portadown, Warrenpoint and Armagh) [10p]; 150 (Killead Road, Co. Antrim) [10p]; 295 (Rawbrae Rd., Whitehead) [10p]; 318 (Hollow Rd., Islandmagee) [10p].

S. 25: S.R. 1978 Nos. 61 (Londonderry) [10p]; 156 Belfast—prohibition of right or left-hand turn) [30p].

S. 43 (4): S.R. 1978 N. 45 (Lisburn, Co. Antrim) [10p]; 290 (Belfast, Cos. Antrim, Armagh, Down, Londonderry) [40p]; 291 (Cos. Antrim, Down) [10p].

S. 44 (1): S.R. 1977 No. 379 (Belfast–Newtonwnards) [10p].

S. 44 (4): S.R. 1978 Nos. 65 (Belfast—Newtownards) [10p]; 258 (Belfast—Newtownards) [10p].

S. 60: S.R. 1978 No. 319 (taxi stands–Newry) [10p].

S. 89: S.R. 1978 Nos. 123 (Antrim, Toome and Randalstown) [20p]; 273 (Belfast—off-street parking) [20p]; 316 (Ballymena, Larne) [30p].

Order made under the Special Roads Act (Northern Ireland) 1963 (c. 12), s. 16 (3):

S.R. 1978 No. 289 (classes of traffic) [20p].

Order made under the Special Roads Act (Northern Ireland) 1963 (c. 12), s. 20 and the Road Traffic Act (Northern Ireland) 1970 (c. 2), s. 22:

S.R. 1978 No. 234 (M1) [10p].

Order made under the Special Roads Act (Northern Ireland) 1963 (c. 12), s. 20 and the Road Traffic Act (Northern Ireland) 1970 (c. 2), s. 44 (1):

S.R. 1978 No. 235 (M1) [10p].

2186. —— permitting use of motor vehicle without proper insurance—whether absolute offence

[Road Traffic Act (Northern Ireland) 1970 (c. 2), s. 75 (1).] The respondent was charged under s. 75 (1) of the Road Traffic Act (Northern Ireland) 1970 with permitting B to use a motor vehicle without third party insurance being in force for its use by B. The case was dismissed because mens rea was not proved. On appeal, *held,* that s. 75 (1) created an absolute offence in which mens rea was not involved: REID *v.* HALL [1975] N.I. 171, C.A.

2187. Shipping and marine insurance

STRANGFORD LOUGH FERRY (REVISION OF CHARGES) ORDER (NORTHERN IRELAND) 1978 (No. 14) [10p], made under the Down County Council (Strangford Lough Ferry) Act (Northern Ireland) 1967 (c. ii), s. 6; operative on March 6, 1978; increases tolls on the Strangford Lough Ferry.

LOUGH ERNE (NAVIGATION) BY-LAWS (NORTHERN IRELAND) 1978 (No. 43) [35p], made under S.I. 1973 No. 69 (N.I. 1), art. 41, Sched. 7; operative on April 1, 1978; require certain vessels using Lough Erne to be licensed and to carry safety equipment; regulate the use of Lough Erne by boats.

SHIPBUILDING (REDUNDANCY PAYMENTS SCHEME) (NORTHERN IRELAND) ORDER 1978 (No. 1127) [30p], made under the Shipbuilding (Redundancy Payments) Act 1978 (c. 11), ss. 1, 2; operative on August 2, 1978; establishes under the 1978 Act a scheme for Northern Ireland for the payment of benefits to employees of any company engaged in shipbuilding who is made redundant or transferred to less well-paid employment during the period of two years beginning on July 1, 1977.

Order made under the Harbours Act (Northern Ireland) 1970 (c. 1), s. 1: S.R. 1978 No. 51 (Portrush) [15p].

2187a. Shops

SHOPS (NORTHERN IRELAND) ORDER 1978 (No. 1909 (N.I. 28)) [10p], made under the Northern Ireland Act 1974 (c. 28), Sched. 1, para. 1; operative on January 3, 1979; enables shops to stay open 6 days a week if district councils make orders allowing them to do so.

2188. Social security

SOCIAL SECURITY (ISLE OF MAN) ORDER (NORTHERN IRELAND) 1977 (No. 378) [25p], made under the Social Security (Northern Ireland) Act 1975 (c. 15), s. 134, as amended and extended by the Social Security (Miscellaneous Provisions) Act 1977 (c. 5), s. 20 (3) (4); operative on January 1, 1978; modifies the 1975 Act to give effect to an agreement on social security with the Isle of Man.

SOCIAL SECURITY PENSIONS (1975 ORDER) (COMMENCEMENT No. 11) ORDER (NORTHERN IRELAND) 1977 (No. 380) (C. 23) [25p], made under S.I. 1975 No. 1503 (N.I. 15), art. 1 (3) (4); provides that for the purpose of causing employments to be contracted-out employments for the purposes of Art. 29 of that Order, Art. 32 (1) (*b*) and (*c*) come into force on October 6, 1978.

SOCIAL SECURITY (CONTRIBUTIONS) (CONSEQUENTIAL AMENDMENTS) (AMENDMENT No. 2) REGULATIONS (NORTHERN IRELAND) 1977 (No. 383) [10p], made under S.I. 1975 No. 1503 (N.I. 15), art. 3; operative on April 6, 1978; substitute lower and upper earnings limits in the 1976 (No. 35) Regulations.

SOCIAL SECURITY (CONTRIBUTIONS, RE-RATING) ORDER (NORTHERN IRELAND) 1978 (No. 10) [10p], made under the Social Security (Northern Ireland) Act 1975, s. 120 and S.I. 1977 No. 610 (N.I. 11), art. 3 (7); operative on April 6, 1978; alters contributions, and certain limits and amounts relating to contributions, under the 1975 Act.

STATE SCHEME PREMIUMS (ACTUARIAL TABLES) REGULATIONS (NORTHERN IRELAND) 1978 (No. 35) [50p], made under S.I. 1975 No. 1503 (N.I. 15), arts. 46 (7), 47 (4); operative on April 6, 1978; prescribe actuarial tables for the purposes of certain provisions of that S.I.; revoke the 1976 (No. 292) Regulations.

SOCIAL SECURITY (CONTRIBUTIONS, RE-RATING) CONSEQUENTIAL AMENDMENT REGULATIONS (NORTHERN IRELAND) 1978 (No. 41) [10p], made under the Social Security (Northern Ireland) Act 1975, s. 124 (1); operative on April 6, 1978; increase the percentage rate of secondary Class 1 contributions in respect of certain mariners; reduce Class 2 contributions payable by share fishermen.

SUPPLEMENTARY BENEFITS (1977 ORDER) (COMMENCEMENT) ORDER (NORTHERN IRELAND) 1978 (No. 42) (C. 5) [10p], made under the Northern Ireland Act 1974 (c. 28), Sched. 1, para. 2 (1) (2) and S.I. 1977 No. 2156 (N.I. 27), art. 1 (2); brings that S.I., except arts. 1, 2 (1), into operation on March 20, 1978.

CONTRACTED-OUT EMPLOYMENT (MISCELLANEOUS PROVISIONS) REGULATIONS (NORTHERN IRELAND) 1978 (No. 74) [25p], made under S.I. 1975 No. 1503 (N.I. 15), arts. 42 (3), 45 (4), 46 (3), 47 (1) (2); operative on April 6, 1978; provide that, for certain purposes and in particular cases, contracted-out employment is to be treated as not having terminated; make detailed amendments of various Regulations.

SOCIAL SECURITY (CREDITS) AMENDMENT AND (EARNINGS FACTOR) TRANSITIONAL REGULATIONS (NORTHERN IRELAND) 1978 (No. 77) [10p], made under the Social Security (Northern Ireland) Act 1975, s. 13 (4) and S.I. 1975 No. 1503 (N.I. 15), art. 72 (1); operative on April 6, 1978; make detailed amendments of the 1975 (No. 113) Regulations.

SOCIAL SECURITY (GRADUATED RETIREMENT BENEFIT) REGULATIONS (NORTHERN IRELAND) 1978 (No. 78) [15p], made under the National Insurance Act (Northern Ireland) 1966 (c. 6), ss. 35 (5), 36 (4); operative on April 5, 1978; provide for certain persons who, on April 5, 1975, had rights or prospective rights to, or expectations of, graduated retirement benefit under ss. 35 and 36 of the 1966 Act and who have deferred their retirement beyond pensionable age.

SOCIAL SECURITY PENSIONS (1975 ORDER) (COMMENCEMENT No. 12) ORDER (NORTHERN IRELAND) 1978 (No. 81) (C. 6) [10p], made under S.I. 1975 No. 1503, art. 1 (3); brings arts. 24, 74 (1) (part) of, and Sched. 5, paras. 29 to 31, 33 of, that S.I. into operation on June 7, 1978, and September 20, 1978, for certain purposes and September 6, 1978, and December 20, 1978, for other purposes.

SOCIAL SECURITY (CONTRIBUTIONS) (SPECIAL ANNUAL MAXIMUM) REGULA-
TIONS (NORTHERN IRELAND) 1978 (No. 86) [10p], made under the Social
Security (Northern Ireland) Act 1975, s. 11 (1) (2); operative on April 6, 1978;
prescribe the maximum amount of class 1 contributions for certain earners.

SOCIAL SECURITY (UNEMPLOYMENT, SICKNESS AND INVALIDITY BENEFIT)
(AMENDMENT) REGULATIONS (NORTHERN IRELAND) 1978 (No. 87) [10p], made
under the Social Security (Northern Ireland) Act 1975, s. 17 (1) (a) (ii); operative on May 5, 1978; amend the 1975 (No. 86) Regulations as respects medical
certificates.

SOCIAL SECURITY (MISCELLANEOUS AMENDMENTS) REGULATIONS (NORTHERN
IRELAND) 1978 (No. 90) [15p], made under the Social Security (Northern
Ireland) Act 1975, ss. 3 (2), 35 (1), 37A, 49, 79 (1), 80 (2) (b), 84, 85, 126,
Sched. 17; operative on April 3, 1978; make miscellaneous amendments of
Regulations made or having effect under the Act.

SOCIAL SECURITY (CONTRIBUTIONS) (CONSEQUENTIAL AMENDMENT) REGULA-
TIONS) (NORTHERN IRELAND) 1978 (No. 91) [10p], made under the Social
Security (Northern Ireland) Act 1975, s. 124 (1); operative on April 6, 1978;
amend the 1975 (No. 319) Regulations in relation to contributions on mariners'
earnings.

SOCIAL SECURITY (CONTRIBUTIONS) (AMENDMENT) REGULATIONS (NORTHERN
IRELAND) 1978 (No. 95) [25p], made under the Social Security (Northern
Ireland) Act 1975, Sched. 1, paras. 5 (1), 6 (1) (h) (m); operative on April 6,
1978; amend the 1975 (No. 319) Regulations in relation to class 1 contributions
and earnings-related contributions.

SOCIAL SECURITY (MOBILITY ALLOWANCE) UP-RATING ORDER (NORTHERN
IRELAND) 1978 (No. 96) [10p], made under the Social Security (Northern
Ireland) Act 1975, s. 120; operative on July 5, 1978; increases to £10 the
weekly rate of mobility allowance.

SOCIAL SECURITY (WIDOW'S BENEFIT AND RETIREMENT PENSIONS) (AMEND-
MENT) REGULATIONS (NORTHERN IRELAND) 1978 (No. 101) [25p], made under
the Social Security (Northern Ireland) Act 1975, ss. 30 (3), 33 (2) (3) and S.I.
1975 No. 1503, art. 22, Sched. 1, paras. 2 (2) (a), 3, as amended by S.I. 1977
No. 610 (N.I. 11), art. 4; operative on April 6, 1979; amend the 1975 (No. 12)
Regulations in relation to elections, increments to certain pensions, benefit at
reduced rate for certain persons and substitution of the contribution record
of a former spouse.

SOCIAL SECURITY PENSIONS (HOME RESPONSIBILITIES AND MISCELLANEOUS
AMENDMENTS) REGULATIONS (NORTHERN IRELAND) 1978 (No. 102) [15p], made
under the Social Security (Northern Ireland) Act 1975, ss. 33 (2), 125 (1),
Sched. 3, para. 5 (6) (7); operative on April 6, 1979; define an expression in
that para.; make detailed amendments of the 1975 (No. 19) Regulations.

SOCIAL SECURITY (GRADUATED RETIREMENT BENEFIT) (NO. 2) REGULATIONS
(NORTHERN IRELAND) 1978 (No. 105) [25p], made under the Social Security
(Consequential Provisons) Act 1975 (c. 18), Sched. 3, paras. 3, 7, 9 and S.I.
1975 No. 1503 (N.I. 15), art. 26 (1); operative, as to part on December 6,
1978, and as to the remainder, on April 6, 1979; revoke the 1975 (No. 96) Regulations and contain provisions for the continuance, with modifications, of
ss. 35 and 36 of the National Insurance Act (Northern Ireland) 1966.

SOCIAL SECURITY (OVERLAPPING BENEFITS) (AMENDMENT) REGULATIONS
(NORTHERN IRELAND) 1978 (No. 107) [25p], made under the Social Security
(Northern Ireland) Act 1975, s. 85; operative on April 6, 1979; amend
the 1975 (No. 94) Regulations so as to make provision in respect of benefits
payable under S.I. 1975 No. 1503.

SOCIAL SECURITY (WIDOW'S AND WIDOWER'S INVALIDITY PENSIONS) REGULA-
TIONS (NORTHERN IRELAND) 1978 (No. 108) [10p], made under S.I. 1975 No.
1503 (N.I. 15), arts. 17 (5) (b), 18 (1) (b) (2) (a) (5) (b) and S.I. 1977 No. 610
(N.I. 11), art. 13 (6); operative on April 6, 1979; deal with the calculation of
invalidity benefit and category A retirement pension for certain classes of
widows and widowers and prescribe periods for the purposes of art. 18 of
S.I. 1975 No. 610.

SOCIAL SECURITY BENEFIT (PERSONS ABROAD) REGULATIONS (NORTHERN

IRELAND) 1978 (No. 114) [35p], made under the Social Security (Northern Ireland) Act 1975, ss. 21 (3), 30 (3), 32 (5), 82 (5), 114 (1), 126 and the Social Security (Consequential Provisions) Act 1975, s. 2, Sched. 3, para. 3; operative on June 12, 1978; consolidate and revoke the 1975 (No. 103) and related Regulations.

SOCIAL SECURITY (UNEMPLOYMENT, SICKNESS AND INVALIDITY BENEFIT) (AMENDMENT No. 2) REGULATIONS (NORTHERN IRELAND) 1978 (No. 120) [10p], made under the Social Security (Northern Ireland) Act 1975, s. 17 (2) (a); amend the 1975 (No. 86) in relation to days which are not to be treated as days of unemployment.

SOCIAL SECURITY (MOBILITY ALLOWANCE) (VEHICLE SCHEME BENEFICIARIES) (AMENDMENT) REGULATIONS (NORTHERN IRELAND) 1978 (No. 149) [10p], made under S.I. 1977 No. 610 (N.I. 11), art. 10 (1); operative on June 2, 1978; amend the definition of " vehicle scheme beneficiary " in the 1977 (No. 242) Regulations.

SOCIAL SECURITY BENEFITS UP-RATING ORDER (NORTHERN IRELAND) 1978 (No. 202) [30p], made under the Social Security (Northern Ireland) Act 1975, s. 120, as extended by S.I. 1975 No. 1503 (N.I. 15), art. 25; operative on November 13, 1978; increases certain benefits and increases of benefit; revokes the 1977 (No. 246) Order.

SUPPLEMENTARY BENEFIT (DETERMINATION OF REQUIREMENTS) REGULATIONS (NORTHERN IRELAND) 1978 (No. 204) [20p], made under S.I. 1977 No. 2156 (N.I. 27), art. 4 (2) (3); operative on November 13, 1978; increase weekly sums allowed in calculating requirements for the purpose of supplementary pension or allowance; revoke the 1971 (No. 188), 1972 (No. 181), 1973 (No. 64) and 1977 (No. 231) Regulations.

SOCIAL SECURITY (MAXIMUM ADDITIONAL COMPONENT) REGULATIONS (NORTHERN IRELAND) 1978 (No. 220) [10p], made under S.I. 1975 No. 1503, art. 11 (3); operative on April 6, 1979; prescribe a maximum additional component up to which additional components in category A pensions of surviving spouses may be increased.

SOCIAL SECURITY (MOBILITY ALLOWANCE) (MOTABILITY PAYMENT ARRANGEMENTS) REGULATIONS (NORTHERN IRELAND) 1978 (No. 222) [10p], made under the Social Security (Northern Ireland) Act 1975, s. 81 (4) (d); operative on August 31, 1978; prescribe circumstances in which mobility allowance may be paid to someone other than the beneficiary in connection with arrangements made by the charity " Motability."

CONTRACTING-OUT AND PRESERVATION (FURTHER PROVISIONS) REGULATIONS (NORTHERN IRELAND) 1978 (No. 230) [20p], made under S.I. 1975 No. 1503, art. 40 (1), Sched. 2, para. 9, Sched. 3, para. 9 (3); operative on August 28, 1978; amend the 1976 (Nos. 29 and 153) Regulations as respects the transfer of accrued rights between schemes without members' consent.

SUPPLEMENTARY BENEFIT (GENERAL) (AMENDMENT) REGULATIONS (NORTHERN IRELAND) 1978 (No. 236) [10p], made under S.I. 1977 No. 2156 (N.I. 27), art. 19 (1) (2), Sched. 1, para. 13; operative on November 13, 1978; increase to £3·90 per week the weekly sum taken to be the personal requirements of applicants for supplementary benefit who are in residential accommodation; revoke the 1977 (No. 262) Regulations.

SOCIAL SECURITY BENEFITS UP-RATING REGULATIONS (NORTHERN IRELAND) 1978 (No. 262) [20p], made under the Social Security (Northern Ireland) Act 1975, ss. 17 (2) (a), 36 (9) (b), 58 (3), 126, Sched. 14, para. 2 (1) and the Social Security (Consequential Provisions) Act 1975 (c.18), s. 2 (1), Sched. 3, para. 7; operative as to part, on November 13, 1978, and, as to the remainder, on April 6, 1979; specify circumstances in which certain awards of benefit are not automatically altered by virtue of para. 2 of Sched. 14 to the Social Security (Northern Ireland) Act 1975 and increase earnings limits for certain benefits.

SOCIAL SECURITY (NON-CONTRIBUTORY INVALIDITY PENSION) (AMENDMENT) REGULATIONS 1978 (No. 275) [10p], made under the Social Security (Northern Ireland) Act 1975, s. 36 (7); operative on September 13, 1978; amend the 1975 (No. 202) Regulations as respects circumstances in which women are to be treated as incapable or not incapable of performing normal household duties.

SOCIAL SECURITY (CATEGORISATION OF EARNERS) (AMENDMENT) REGULATIONS (NORTHERN IRELAND) 1978 (No. 308) [10p], made under the Social Security (Northern Ireland) Act 1975, s. 2 (2) (a); operative on November 20, 1978; disregard for contribution purposes employments of certain persons in connection with elections or referendums.

SOCIAL SECURITY (OVERLAPPING BENEFITS) (AMENDMENT NO. 2) REGULATIONS (NORTHERN IRELAND) 1978 (No. 326) [20p], made under the Social Security (Northern Ireland) Act 1975, s. 85; operative on November 16, 1978; amend the 1975 (No. 94) Regulations as respects priority of entitlement where more than one person is entitled to an increase of benefit in respect of the same child.

2189. Town and country planning

PLANNING (AMENDMENT) (NORTHERN IRELAND) ORDER 1978 (No. 1048) (N.I. 18) [30p], made under the Northern Ireland Act 1974 (c. 28), Sched. 1, para. 1, operative on August 25, 1978 except for art. 4 which is operative on an appointed day; art. 3 excludes compensation in certain cases where planning permission is revoked; art. 4 relates to the control of demolition in conservation areas, art. 5 to grants relating to conservation areas and art. 6 to traffic signs following orders under art. 77 of the Planning (Northern Ireland) Order 1972; art. 7 deals with the period for serving enforcement notices, art. 8 with the powers of the planning appeals commission and art. 9 with the definition of " road " in the Planning Order; art. 10 relates to references to development plans in that Order; arts. 11 and 12 concern stop notices; art. 13 confers rights of entry on the planning appeals commission; art. 14 extends a power to require information; arts. 15 and 16 relate to " blight "; art. 17 authorises the acquisition of other estates in land following purchases under certain notices; arts. 18 to 20 are miscellaneous.

2190. —— blight notice—inability to sell house at reasonable price—whether material detriment

[Planning and Land Compensation Act (Northern Ireland) 1971 (c. 23), s. 6 (4).] H had attempted to sell his house, but had been unable to obtain any reasonable offers due to road proposals involving the acquisition of part of his garden. He served a blight notice which the Lands Tribunal declared valid. On a case stated, held, that the notice was valid since " material detriment " in s. 6 (4) of the Planning and Land Compensation Act (Northern Ireland) 1971 includes detriment reflected in market value caused by the proposed physical operations: HILL v. DEPARTMENT OF THE ENVIRONMENT [1976] N.I. 43, C.A.

2191. —— —— Lands Tribunal decisions

JEFFERS v. DEPARTMENT OF THE ENVIRONMENT FOR NORTHERN IRELAND, R/7/1977 (blight notice held to be valid, the tribunal finding that the applicant genuinely wished to sell and made reasonable efforts to sell the property, which was in a comprehensive development area in Belfast).

MITCHELL v. DEPARTMENT OF THE ENVIRONMENT FOR NORTHERN IRELAND, R/18/1977 (counter-notice to blight notice held to be valid on the ground that the Department had shown that it did not propose to acquire any part of the relevant land within 15 years from the date of the counter-notice).

2192. —— planning application inaccurately advertised—whether planning permission valid

[Planning (Northern Ireland) Order 1972 (S.I. 1972 No. 1634), art. 15 (a).] M applied to D for permission to make structural alterations to premises and to change their use. Owing to D's error, the statutory advertisement did not refer to the change of use. D granted planning permission to M. M sought a declaration that the permission was valid. Held, that (1) art. 15 (a) of S.I. 1972 No. 1634 requires an advertisement whose terms bring home to the mind of a reasonably intelligent and careful reader any material change of use for which permission is sought; (2) the requirement in art. 15 (a) of proper notice is mandatory; (3) since the advertisement was not a valid notice the grant of planning permission was invalid: MORELLI v. DEPARTMENT OF THE ENVIRONMENT [1976] N.I. 159, Murray J.

2193. Trade and industry

PRICE MARKING (MEAT) ORDER (NORTHERN IRELAND) 1978 (No. 60) [15p], made under the Prices Act 1974 (c. 24), s. 4; operative on April 1, 1978; requires, subject to exceptions, the price of meat offered or exposed for retail sale in display areas of premises to be indicated.

CATERING ESTABLISHMENTS (SELF-CATERING) REGULATIONS (NORTHERN IRELAND) 1978 (No. 179) [15p], made under the Development of Tourist Traffic Act (Northern Ireland) 1948 (c. 4), ss. 11, 13, 34 and S.I. 1977 No. 2153 (N.I. 24), art. 3; operative on September 1, 1978; prescribe qualifications for the registration of self-catering establishments.

STATISTICS OF TRADE (AMENDMENT) ORDER (NORTHERN IRELAND) 1978 (No. 272) [10p], made under the Statistics of Trade Act (Northern Ireland) 1949 (c. 7), s. 9 (1) (a); operative on December 1, 1978; prescribes additional information about which persons carrying on certain undertakings may be required to furnish returns.

PERAMBULATORS AND PUSHCHAIRS (SAFETY) REGULATIONS (NORTHERN IRELAND 1978 (No. 329) [20p], made under the Consumer Protection Act (Northern Ireland) 1965 (c. 14), s. 1; operative as to certain goods on January 1, 1979, and, in any other case, on July 1, 1979; specify, by reference to B.S.I. standards, safety requirements for prams and pushchairs.

COSMETIC PRODUCTS REGULATIONS (NORTHERN IRELAND) 1978 (No. 342) [£1·75], made under the Consumer Protection Act (Northern Ireland) 1965, s. 1; operative on various dates between December 11, 1978, and July 29, 1981; specify standards for cosmetic products.

2194. Transport

PUBLIC SERVICE VEHICLES (DEFINITION OF BUS SERVICE) REGULATIONS (NORTHERN IRELAND) 1977 (No. 357) [10p], made under the Finance Act (Northern Ireland) 1966 (c. 21) s. 14 (7); operative on January 30, 1978; increase to 21p the minimum fare for the purposes of s. 14 of the Act; revoke the 1973 (No. 53) Regulations.

ROAD FREIGHT TRANSPORT LICENSING (AMENDMENT) REGULATIONS (NORTHERN IRELAND) 1978 (No. 46) [10p], made under the Transport Act (Northern Ireland) 1967 (c. 37), s. 45 (d) (e); operative on April 1, 1978; provide for the review of suspensions or revocations of road freight vehicle licences.

2195. Weights and measures

WEIGHTS AND MEASURES (1976 ACT) (SCHEDULE 5) (COMMENCEMENT) ORDER (NORTHERN IRELAND) 1978 (No. 20) (C. 4) [10p], made under the Weights and Measures Act 1976 (c. 77), Sched. 5, para. 4 (1); brings Sched. 5 to the Act into operation on April 1, 1978.

WEIGHTS AND MEASURES (SUGAR) (AMENDMENT) ORDER (NORTHERN IRELAND) 1978 (No. 116) [10p], made under the Weights and Measures Act (Northern Ireland) 1967 (c. 6), s. 15 (2) (3) (5); operative on June 30, 1978; requires prepacked sugar and sugar in containers to be sold only in a range of metric weights after July 31, 1978.

WEIGHTS AND MEASURES (CHEESE) ORDER (NORTHERN IRELAND) 1978 (No. 122) [10p], made under the Weights and Measures Act (Northern Ireland) 1967, s. 15 (2) (3) (5); operative on June 30, 1978; requires cheese which is not pre-packed to be sold by retail, by net weight or, in certain circumstances, by gross weight.

WEIGHTS AND MEASURES (MARKING AND ABBREVIATIONS) (AMENDMENT) REGULATIONS (NORTHERN IRELAND) 1978 (No. 126) [20p], made under the Weights and Measures Act (Northern Ireland) 1967, ss. 8 (1) (f), 15 (4) (a) (d); operative on July 1, 1978; amend the 1976 (No. 126) Regulations as respects the marking and making up of certain containers of goods in metric units.

2196. Wills—construction—conditional gift—whether condition void for uncertainty

By his will, T left his interest in a business to his brother, subject to the payment of £4,000 to the executors within six months from his death, or satisfactory arrangements being made for payment. A later provision stated that if the sum was not paid, or satisfactory arrangements for payment were not made, the gift was to be revoked and to fall into residue. The £4,000 was never paid. *Held,* that the condition about payment was a condition subsequent, which was void for uncertainty since there was no indication what arrangements would be satisfactory. T's brother therefore took the gift free from the condition imposing a forfeiture, but subject to the obligation to pay £4,000 to the trustee: *Re* PORTER; LOGAN *v.* NORTHERN BANK [1975] N.I. 157, Lowry L.C.J.

2197. —— —— gift of shares subsequently disposed of—whether general or specific
T's will, made in 1971, contained five legacies of £1,000 stock in the Canadian Pacific Railway Co. T had held sterling stock in that company, but in 1967 she had exercised an option to convert it into dollar stock. After making her will, T sold the dollar stock and held no stock in the company at her death. On a summons to determine whether the legacies were general or specific, *held,* that the legacies were general and payable out of residue since, if T had retained the stock, the legacies would have been specific: *Re* HARRISON [1976] N.I. 120, Gibson L.J.

2198. Workmen's compensation
WORKMEN'S COMPENSATION (SUPPLEMENTATION) (AMENDMENT) REGULATIONS (NORTHERN IRELAND) 1978 (No. 315) [20p], made under the Industrial Injuries and Diseases (Northern Ireland Old Cases) Act 1975 (c. 17), ss. 2, 4 (1); operative on November 15, 1975; adjust intermediate rates of lesser incapacity allowance.

ARTICLES. See *post,* p. [31].

NUISANCE

2199. Abnormal user—whether plaintiff's interest is one that the law will protect—proper measure of damages
[Can.] D, a public utility, located an electric power installation very close to P's cable television operation. This resulted in interference with the reception and transmission of television signals. P was forced to stop supplying one television channel to its subscribers. *Held* (1) there should be judgment for P because although the harm suffered was not of a physical nature or personal discomfort, P's interest in the use and enjoyment of its land had been interfered with by D; (2) P's complaint was also in negligence: that D knew or should have known that its activity would adversely affect the cable system. As to damages, P lost no subscribers and maintained the same level of income. It would cost at least $200,000 to restore the lost channel. That cost was wholly out of proportion to the value of the channel to P, and was not a reasonable basis for measuring damages. (*Bridlington Relay* v. *Yorkshire Electricity Board* [1965] C.L.Y. 3159 disapproved; *Hole* v. *Harrisons* [1972] C.L.Y. 825; *Harbutt's Plasticine* v. *Wayne Tank and Pump Co.* [1970] C.L.Y. 362 referred to): NOR-VIDEO SERVICES *v.* ONTARIO HYDRO (1978) 84 D.L.R. (3d) 221, Ont.H.C.J.

2200. Damages—appropriate plaintiff—nuisance continuing when plaintiff acquired interest
The victim of a continuing nuisance causing damage to his property is entitled to recover the cost of remedying such damage, including that which occurred prior to his acquiring an interest in the property.
The roots of a tree for which the defendants were responsible encroached onto a house, the lease of which was owned by the plaintiff's father, causing damage to the same. The father transferred the lease to the plaintiff so that the latter could obtain finance for the necessary remedial work. Upon the plaintiff claiming damages for the cost of such work, the defendants contended that the plaintiff could not recover in respect of damage occurring prior to his acquisition of the leasehold interest. *Held,* rejecting such contention, that the nuisance was continuing at the time of such acquisition and that the total cost of remedying the damage caused was therefore recoverable. (*Thompson* v. *Gibson* (1841) 7 M. & W. 456 applied; *Malone* v. *Laskey* [1907] 2 K.B. 141, and dictum of Lord Denning M.R. in *Sparham-Souter* v. *Town and Country Development* (*Essex*) [1976] C.L.Y. 1873 considered.)
MASTERS *v.* BRENT LONDON BOROUGH COUNCIL [1978] 2 W.L.R. 768, Talbot J.

2201. Natural causes—earth-fall—duty of defendants

Owners of land who are aware of the danger of damage being caused to adjoining property by natural land-slips owe a duty to take reasonable steps to prevent such damage occurring.

A geological mound on the defendant's land had for years been subject to natural erosion and slips, and small amounts of soil and rubble had fallen onto the plaintiffs' adjoining properties. Complaint was periodically made to the defendants. In 1976, the defendants' attention was drawn to a large crack in the mound near the plaintiffs' properties but the defendants took no action, contending that they were not responsible for natural land movement. A substantial fall of land followed damaging the plaintiffs' property, and thereafter the plaintiffs claimed damages and sought abatement of the nuisance by way of mandatory injunction. *Held*, for the plaintiffs, that the defendants knew of the danger but failed to take steps to prevent a substantial fall such as had occurred and were accordingly liable for the damage suffered; but that, in view of remedial work since satisfactorily carried out by the defendants, a mandatory injunction was inappropriate. (*Margate Pier and Harbour Proprietors* v. *Margate Town Council* (1869) 20 L.T. 564, *Davey* v. *Harrow Corporation* [1957] C.L.Y. 241 and *Goldman* v. *Hargrave* [1966] C.L.Y. 8145 applied; *Sedleigh-Denfield* v. *O'Callaghan* [1940] A.C. 880 and *Neath Rural District Council* v. *Williams* (1951) C.L.C. 6972 considered.)

LEAKEY v. NATIONAL TRUST FOR PLACES OF HISTORIC INTEREST OR NATURAL BEAUTY [1978] 2 W.L.R. 774, O'Connor J.

2202. Noise—Control of Pollution Act 1974—injunction

[Control of Pollution Act 1974 (c. 40), s. 58 (8).]

A local authority may bring proceedings for an injunction to restrain a noise which is a nuisance under s. 58 (8) of the Control of Pollution Act 1974 rather than bringing a prosecution under s. 58 (4).

Residents complained to the local authority about a 24-hour " taxi care centre " because of the noise it made. The local authority served a notice requiring the company to cease operations between 11 p.m. and 7 a.m. under s. 58 (1) of the Control of Pollution Act 1974. The company lodged an appeal to the magistrates' court, and, as they were not entitled to do, continued their operations unabated. Instead of prosecuting the company under s. 58 (4) the local authority applied to the High Court for an injunction under s. 58 (8). The magistrates then adjourned the appeal. The High Court judge refused the injunction on the ground that the statutory procedures had not been exhausted, and the issue should be decided by the magistrates. On appeal by the local authority, *held*, allowing the appeal, that the local authority was entitled to seek an injunction instead of prosecuting, and was entitled to the relief sought.

HAMMERSMITH BOROUGH COUNCIL v. MAGNUM AUTOMATED FORECOURTS [1978] 1 W.L.R. 50, C.A.

2203. —— playground—damages

Noise emanating from the unrestricted use of a children's playground can amount to a nuisance.

D and his wife owned a small hotel which had a pleasant garden with grazing land beyond. The local council built a housing estate on the grazing land with a playground sited adjacent to the hotel garden. When the playground opened, children of all ages played in it from dawn to dusk. The noise emanating therefrom became so intolerable to D's wife that she left the hotel. D complained to the council but as no agreement was reached he commenced proceedings against them alleging nuisance. He applied for an interim injunction. The council gave an undertaking to shut the playground. The playground was reopened on terms that it should be used between 12.30 p.m. and 6.30 p.m. by children under 12 years. D still found the noise a nuisance. On trial of the action, *held*, giving judgment for D, that (1) for the short period of unrestricted use the noise emanating from the playground amounted to a nuisance in law and the court would award £200 damages; (2) after the opening hours were restricted the noise caused grave aggravation but did not amount to a nuisance and the injunction should be varied to allow opening between 10 a.m. and 6.30 p.m.

DUNTON *v.* DOVER DISTRICT COUNCIL (1977) 76 L.G.R. 87, Griffiths J.

2204. Northern Ireland. See NORTHERN IRELAND.

2205. Obstruction of light to greenhouse—prescriptive right

[Prescription Act 1832, s. 3.] The defendant neighbours had obstructed the light to the plaintiff's greenhouse by parking a caravan and erecting a fence between the two gardens, the plaintiff's garden being at a lower level. *Held*, it was a building within s. 3 (*Clifford* v. *Holt* [1899] 1 Ch. 698 applied) and its use over a 20-year period, at all material times as a normal greenhouse in a private garden gave the plaintiffs a prescriptive right to such light required for its continuing use (*Colls* v. *Home & Colonial Stores* [1904] A.C. 179 applied). In this instance, the right to light meant all the benefits of light including warmth from the sun, but in certain cases, *e.g.* solar heating, such benefits may be separated and a different result could be reached: ALLEN *v.* GREENWOOD, *The Times*, October 17, 1978, C.A.

ARTICLES. See *post*, p. [31]

OPEN SPACES AND RECREATION GROUNDS

2206. Parks regulations—no dogs allowed—whether by-law oppressive

A by-law of Burnley Borough Council prohibiting any person from causing any dog belonging to him or in his charge to enter or remain in specified pleasure grounds, other than a guide dog accompanied by a blind person, was not manifestly unjust or an oppressive or gratuitous interference with the rights of others which a reasonable council would not countenance (*Kruse* v. *Johnson* [1898] 2 Q.B. 91 followed). The council was therefore entitled to appropriate relief to ensure observation of the by-law: BURNLEY BOROUGH COUNCIL *v.* ENGLAND, *The Times*, July 15, 1978, Hugh Francis Q.C.

[See also § 2.]

ARTICLES. See *post*, p. [31]

PARLIAMENT

2207. Elections. See ELECTION LAW.

2208. House of Commons (Administration) Act 1978 (c. 36)

This Act makes further provision for the administration of the House of Commons.

S. 1 sets up the House of Commons Commission, and states who is to be a member of the Commission; s. 2 sets out the functions of the Commission; s. 3 deals with financial provisions; s. 4 relates to the House Departments; s. 5 contains the short title and definitions.

The Act received the Royal Assent on July 20, 1978, and ss. 1, 3–5 and Scheds. 1 and 2, paras. 1, 2, came into force on that date. S. 2 and Scheds. 2, paras. 3–5, and 3 came into force on January 1, 1979.

2208a. House of Commons Members' Fund

Resolution of the House of Commons dated November 30, 1978, passed in pursuance of the House of Commons Members' Fund Act 1948 (c. 36):

S. 3: S.I. 1978 No. 1771 (periodical payments—past members and widows) [10p].

2209. Ministers. See CONSTITUTIONAL LAW.

2210. Ministerial salaries

MINISTERIAL AND OTHER SALARIES ORDER 1978 (No. 1102) [20p], made under the Ministerial and other Salaries Act 1975 (c. 27), s. 1 (4), operative on July 31, 1978; increases by 10 per cent. the annual salaries payable under the 1975 Act to certain Ministers, certain Members of the Opposition and to the Speaker.

2211. Northern Ireland. See NORTHERN IRELAND.

2212. Parliamentary Commissioner
    PARLIAMENTARY COMMISSIONER ORDER 1978 (No. 616) [10p], made under the Parliamentary Commissioner Act 1967 (c. 13), s. 4 (2); operative on May 25, 1978; adds the Forestry Commission to the list of departments and authorities which are subject to investigation by the Parliamentary Commissioner for Administration.

2213. Pensions. See § 2263.

2214. Statutes. See STATUTES AND ORDERS.
                                  ARTICLES. See *post*, p. [31]

PARTNERSHIP

PATENTS AND DESIGNS

2215. Amendment—covetousness—ambiguity
    [Patents Act 1949 (c. 87), ss. 29, 31.] The applicants' main claim related to an organic polymeric material containing a certain grey dye. The material was suitable for films resistant to halation and light piping effects. A possible opponent with a subsequently published specification had not objected although aware of the applicants' suit. The applicants applied to amend the main claim to grey film " suitable for use as a photographic film base " produced from the polymeric, and to introduce subsidiary claims. The hearing officer found, inter alia, the main claim of unjustified width and refused to allow the amendments proposed. The applicants appealed. *Held* (1) the original claims were not covetous being limited to dye mixed from two components from a possible four chemicals; (2) the proposed amendment did not introduce ambiguity; (3) the subsidiary claims should be allowed since they derived from the description in the body of the specification, although incorporating some features not originally claimed. (*Howlett's Patent* [1941] 38 R.P.C. 238 distinguished; *Davidson's Patent* [1936] 53 R.P.C. 453 followed): IMPERIAL CHEMICAL INDUSTRIES (WHYTE'S) PATENT [1978] R.P.C. 11, Patents Appeal Tribunal.

2216. —— post-dating—fair basis
    The application related to a claim to an encapsulation process in which dissolved calcium or aluminium drops were coated with alginate and then treated with dissolved calcium or aluminium ions. Simulated fruit berries were produced with a firm skin. The applicants sought to amend the specification, alleging that the process had two separate aspects. The examiner refused. The applicants appealed. *Held*, the original specification did not suggest that a satisfactory product could be obtained by the latter process only. The amendment should not be allowed without post-dating: UNILEVER (SNEATH'S) APPLICATION [1978] R.P.C. 617, Patents Appeal Tribunal.

2217. Appeals—appointment of Registrar of Patent Appeals
    The following Practice Direction was issued by the Chancery Division on May 18, 1978 :
    1. Under R.S.C., Ord. 104, r. 14 (17), the Chief Master has nominated Mr. D. F. James, at present the Registrar of the Patents Appeal Tribunal, to be the " proper officer " of the Patents Court for the purposes of appeals from the Comptroller-General of Patents, Designs and Trade Marks. He will be known as the Registrar of Patent Appeals. The Registrars of the Chancery Division will continue to perform their present duties in infringement actions and other patent business.
    2. (*a*) Appeals from the Comptroller must be brought by originating motion (Ord. 104, r. 14 (1)). The originating motion (in the rule called " notice of appeal ") is issued by lodging copies with the Registrar of Patent Appeals (Room 152). If the Registrar of Patent Appeals and his deputy are not available, the copies may be lodged in the Chief Master's Secretariat (Room 169).
    (*b*) Two copies of the originating motion (notice of appeal) will be required, one of which must be stamped with a £10 fee (Fee 8), and the other of which will be sealed and returned to the appellant. (*c*) A respondent's notice under

Ord. 104, r. 14 (9), asking that the decision of the Comptroller be varied, must be stamped £5 (Fee 36).

[1978] 1 W.L.R. 855; [1978] 2 All E.R. 464.

2218. —— number of judges

The following Practice Direction was issued by the Patents Court on May 23, 1978:

S. 97 (2) of the Patents Act 1977, which comes into operation on June 1, 1978, provides that for the hearing of appeals from the comptroller the Patents Court may consist of one or more judges in accordance with directions given by or on behalf of the Lord Chancellor.

For the hearing of such appeals the Patents Court will consist of a single judge unless, in any particular case, the Senior Judge of the Court or, in his absence, another nominated judge, directs that is shall consist of two judges.

[1978] 2 All E.R. 464.

2219. Application—manner of manufacture

[N.Z.] [New Zealand Patents Act 1953, ss. 2, 51; Statute of Monopolies, s. 6.] Certain known chemical compounds were found by the applicant to treat leukaemia. Claims 1–12 related to a method of treatment, claims 13–28 to a package consisting of a container and indications of the suitability of the drug for such treatment. *Held*, rejecting all claims (1) claims 1–12 did not relate to an invention, as they were a method of treatment not resulting in a vendible product; (2) claims 13–28 did not relate to a manner of new manufacture; (3) claims 29 to 34 related to a new use of a known substance for the purpose of medical treatment of a human being, and did not relate to a manner of new manufacture (*Maeder* v. *Ronda* [1943] N.Z.L.R. 122 and *Re Ciba-Geigy A.B. (Durr's) Applications* [1977] C.L.Y. 2203 applied): WELLCOME FOUNDATION (HITCHINGS') APPLICATION [1978] F.S.R. 51, N.Z. Patent Office.

2220. —— medical and cosmetic treatment—method of cleaning teeth

Applications for a patent referred to methods of removing dental plaque, preventing calculus, and removing carios material from teeth. The hearing officer rejected the claims since they were for medical treatment, for the treatment or cure of disease. A claim to a method of cleaning teeth was allowed. The applicants appealed. *Held,* (1) all the claims should be rejected because they included medical treatment; (2) the claim to a method of cleaning teeth could be amended so as to limit it to cosmetic effects, in which case it would be allowed: ORAL HEALTH PRODUCTS INC. (HALSTEAD'S) APPLICATION [1977] R.P.C. 612, Graham J.

2221. —— post-dating

[Patents and Designs Act 1907 (c. 29); Patents and Designs Act 1949 (c. 87); Patents Rules 1978 (S.I. 1978 No. 216).] The applicants filed a complete specification on December 6, 1973. On September 6, 1976, the applicants applied for post-dating of one month. They had given no notice extending the period for putting their application in order until September 19. The notice would have been in time if the post-dating application had been complied with. *Held*, directing the application to proceed so long as the possibility existed that the applicant could comply with the requirements of s. 12, the application retained its full vitality and effect; (2) the application for post-dating in this case should therefore have been processed: ASSOCIATED BRITISH COMBUSTION'S APPLICATION [1978] R.P.C. 582, C.A.

2222. —— preventive dental treatment

[Patents Act 1949 (c. 87), ss. 41, 101.] On application to patent, the claims were to (1) a method of repairing defects in the surface of the tooth; (2) a method of sealing the tooth surface; (3) a method of drying hard tooth surfaces. *Held*, rejecting all the claims as being methods of medical treatment, (1) the filling of cavities was an integral part of the treatment of dental cavities, and any treatment of the tooth cavity prior to filling was part of the treatment; (2) sealing the pits and fissures was preventive medical treatment: LEE PHARMACEUTICALS' APPLICATIONS [1978] R.P.C. 51, Patents Office.

2223. —— priority—first foreign filing

[Patents Act 1949 (c. 87), s. 1.] Applicants claimed a priority based on a United States application. An inventor had made a yet earlier U.S. application. The examiner objected. The applicants appealed. *Held*, (1) the earlier U.S. application was to protect a process the subject of the present application; (2) the present application described the effect of performing the process described in the earlier application: ENGEL AND ANDERSON'S APPLICATION [1978] R.P.C. 608, Whitford J.

2224. —— whether new manner of manufacture

A patent application related to a method and means of speech instruction. Instructions and marks indicating accent and rhythm were used. The hearing officer refused the application. On appeal, *held,* there was no novel presentation of words and no new manner of manufacture. There was no invention to be protected by the Act: DIXON'S APPLICATION [1978] R.P.C. 687, Whitford J.

2225. Convention application—fair basis—construction

[Patents Act 1949 (c. 87), s. 14.] The applicants claimed priority from two applications in Japan in 1969, for registration of utility models of automatic cloth-cutting machines. The opponents alleged that claimed features of the machine were not disclosed in the utility models. The superintending examiner found that one application was not fairly based on the Japanese applications, but allowed the second claim, which could be seen to be derived from disclosure in the priority documents. The superintending examiner referred to knowledge " before 1970." The opponents appealed. *Held*, (1) the superintending examiner had assessed the facts and the law correctly; (2) the examiner's decision was justifiable on the evidence, although it is necessary to construe an application solely in the light of knowledge at the date of the application: MUTO INDUSTRIAL CO.'S APPLICATION [1978] R.P.C. 70, Graham J.

2226. Conversion—patent of addition—discretion of Comptroller

[Patents Act 1949 (c. 87), ss. 26, 29.] Applicants for conversion sought to convert one patent into a patent of addition for the other. The application was refused because the conversion might validate a patent which was the subject of High Court proceedings. The applicants appealed. They undertook not to seek any remedy in respect of the patent for which conversion sought. *Held*, (1) the word " may " should be construed as " must " at times in the Patents Act; (2) if the Comptroller was satisfied that the provisions of the statute were complied with, he must permit conversion: AKTIEBOLAGET CELLOPLAST'S APPLICATION [1978] R.P.C. 239, Whitford J.

2227. Designs

DESIGNS (AMENDMENT) RULES 1978 (No. 907) [25p], made under the Registered Designs Act 1949 (c. 88), ss. 36, 40 as amended by the Patents and Designs (Renewals, Extensions and Fees) Act 1961 (c. 25); operative on July 3, 1978 save for Rule 3 which is operative on October 2, 1978; amend S.I. 1949 No. 2368 to increase certain fees payable under them.

DESIGNS (AMENDMENT No. 2) RULES 1978 (No. 1151) [25p], made under the Registered Designs Act 1949, ss. 36 and 40, as amended by the Patents and Designs (Renewals, Extensions and Fees) Act 1961; operative on August 10, 1978, except rule 3, which is operative on October 2, 1978; increase fees payable under S.I. 1949 No. 2368.

2228. —— infringement—injunction—balance of convenience

The plaintiffs alleged that the defendants had copied one of their dress designs, and were selling it at a lower price. The plaintiffs were granted an ex parte injunction, restraining the defendants from " selling, distributing or disposing of ladies' dresses which are substantially copied from the plaintiffs' designs." *Held*, at the inter partes hearing, the matter could be dealt with in damages, and, in view of the dispute on the facts, the injunction should be discharged. The injunction was framed so widely that it would be embarrassing for the defendants to comply with it: ALJOSE FASHIONS *v.* ALFRED YOUNG & Co. [1978] F.S.R. 365, C.A.

2229. The plaintiffs alleged that the second defendants had copied and manufactured, and the third defendants retailed, a dress designed by the plaintiffs. An ex parte injunction was granted against the second defendants. At the hearing inter partes, *held*, (1) damages would not be an adequate remedy to the plaintiffs; (2) an injunction against the defendants would do unquantifiable damage; (3) the balance of convenience lay with the plaintiffs because the alleged infringer had produced goods for the market when the plaintiffs' goods had been on the market for some time. The judge was, however, bound by *Aljose Fashions* v. *Alfred Young & Co.* [1978] C.L.Y. 2228. Injunction refused: MONET OF LONDON v. SYBIL RICHARDS [1978] F.S.R. 368, Browne-Wilkinson J.

2230. —— **registration—novel feature invisible at time of purchase**
[Registered Designs Act 1949 (c. 88), s. 1 (2) (3).] The applicants designed a chocolate egg, the inner and outer layers of which contrasted in colour. Registration was refused because the novel features could be seen only when the egg was broken. The applicants appealed. *Held*, that (1) provided that the features claimed were features of the finished article, the features need not be judged at the time when an article was bought. (*AMP Inc.* v. *Utilux Pty.* [1972] C.L.Y. 2593 considered and explained): P. FERRERO AND C.S.PA'S APPLICATION [1978] R.P.C. 473, Whitford J.

2231. European Patent Organisation
EUROPEAN PATENT ORGANISATION (IMMUNITIES AND PRIVILEGES) ORDER 1978 (No. 179) [25p], made under the International Organisations Act 1968 (c. 48), s. 10 (1); operative on February 10, 1978; confers privileges and immunities on the European Patent Organisation, representatives of its members, officers of the European Patent Office and experts.

2232. Fees
The European Patent Organisation has issued the following rules relating to fees:

Article 1

General

The following shall be levied in accordance with the provisions contained in these Rules:
(a) Fees due to be paid to the European Patent Office (hereinafter referred to as the Office) as provided for in the Convention and in the Implementing Regulations and the fees and costs which the President of the Office lays down pursuant to art. 3, para. 1;
(b) fees and costs pursuant to the Patent Cooperation Treaty (hereinafter referred to as the PCT), the amounts of which may be fixed by the Office.

Article 2

Fees provided for in the Convention and in the Implementing Regulations

The fees due to be paid to the Office under Article 1 shall be as follows:

	DM
1. Filing fee (art. 78, para. 2, of the Convention)	450
2. Search fee in respect of	
— a European or supplementary European search (art. 78, para. 2; r. 46, para. 1; r. 104b, para. 3; and art. 157, para. 2 (*b*) of the Convention)	1,450
— an international search (r. 16.1, PCT and r. 104a, para. 1, of the Convention)	1,700
3. Designation fee for each Contracting State designated (art. 79, para. 2, of the Convention)	225
4. Renewal fees for European Patent applications (art. 86, para. 1, of the Convention)	
— for the 3rd year, calculated from the date of filing of the application	330

4. Renewal fees for European Patent applications—*cont.*   DM
   — for the 4th year, calculated from the date of filing
      of the application   440
   — for the 5th year, calculated from the date of filing
      of the application   550
   — for the 6th year, calculated from the date of filing
      of the application   675
   — for the 7th year, calculated from the date of filing
      of the application   800
   — for the 8th year, calculated from the date of filing
      of the application   975
   — for the 9th year, calculated from the date of filing
      of the application   1,150
   — for the 10th and each subsequent year, calculated
      from the date of filing of the application   1,400
5. Additional fee for belated payment of a renewal fee for   10 per cent.
   the European patent application (art. 86, para. 2, of the   of the belated
   Convention)   renewal fee
6. Examination fee (art 94, para. 2, of the Convention)   1,725
7. Fee for grant (art. 97, para. 2 (*b*), of the Convention)   330
8. Fee for printing the European patent specification (art.
   97, para. 2 (*b*), of the Convention) for each page of the
   application in the form in which it is to be printed   —
9. Fee for printing a new specification of the European
   patent (art. 102, para. 3 (*b*), of the Convention)—flat-
   rate fee   —
10. Opposition fee (art. 99, para. 1, and art. 105, para. 2,
    of the Convention)   450
11. Fee for appeal (art. 108 of the Convention)   550
12. Fee for further processing (art. 121, para. 2, of the
    Convention   100
13. Fee for re-establishment of rights (art. 122, para. 3, of
    the Convention)   100
14. Conversion fee (art. 136, para. 1, and art. 140 of the
    Convention)   50
15. Claims fee for the 11th and each subsequent fee (r. 31,
    para. 1 and 2)   50
16. Fee for the awarding of costs (r. 63, para. 3)   50
17. Fee for the conservation of evidence (r. 75, para. 3)   50
18. Transmittal fee for an international application (art.
    152, para. 3, of the Convention)   150
19. National fee for an international application (art. 158,
    para. 2, and r. 104b, para. 1, of the Convention)   450
20. Fee for the preliminary examination of an international
    application (r. 58, PCT)   1,000

Article 3
Fees, costs and prices laid down by the President of the Office

1. The President of the Office shall lay down the amount of the administrative fees provided for in the Implementing Regulations and, where appropriate, the amount of the fees and costs for any services rendered by the Office other than those specified in art. 2.

2. He shall also lay down the prices of the publications referred to in arts. 93, 98, 103 and 129 of the Convention.

3. The amount of the fees, costs and prices referred to in paras. 1 and 2 shall be published in the *Official Journal* of the European Patent Office.

Article 4
Due date for fees

1. Fees in respect of which the due date is not specified in the provisions of the Convention or of the PCT or of the Implementing Regulations thereto

shall be due on the date of receipt of the request for the service incurring the fee concerned.

2. The President of the Office may decide not to make services within the meaning of para. 1 dependent upon the advance payment of the corresponding fee.

Article 5
Payment of fees

1. Subect to the provisions of art. 6, the fees due to the Office shall be paid in Deutsche Mark or in a currency freely convertible into Deutsche Mark:

    (a) by payment or transfer to a bank account held by the Office;

    (b) by payment or transfer to a Giro account held by the Office;

    (c) by money order;

    (d) by delivery or remittance of cheques which are drawn on a banking establishment in the Federal Republic of Germany or the Netherlands and which are made payable to the Office;

    (e) by cash payment.

2. The President of the Office may allow other methods of paying fees than those set out in para. 1, in particular by means of fees, vouchers or deposit accounts held with the European Patent Office.

Article 6
Currencies

1. Payments or transfers to a bank account or a Giro account in accordance with art. 5, para. 1 (*a*) and (*b*), shall be made in the currency of the State in which that account is held.

2. Payments in accordance with art. 5, para. 1 (*d*), shall be made in Deutsche Mark or Dutch guilders.

3. Payments in accordance with art. 5, para. 1 (*c*) and (*e*), shall be made in Deutsche Mark, or, where they are made to the branch at The Hague or any sub-office set up pursuant to art. 7 of the Convention which is empowered to receive payments, in the currency of the State in which such branch or sub-office is located.

4. For payments to the Office made in currencies other than Deutsche Mark, the President of the Office shall, after consulting the Budget and Finance Committee if appropriate, lay down the equivalents in such other currencies of the fees in Deutsche Mark payable pursuant to these Rules. In doing so, he shall ensure that fluctuations in monetary rates of exchange are not prejudicial to the Office. The amounts determined in this way shall be published in the *Official Journal* of the European Patent Office. Revised amounts shall be binding on all payments for fees which are due 10 days or more after such publication; the President of the Office may, however, shorten this period.

Article 7
Particulars concerning payments

1. Every payment must indicate the name of the person making the payment and must contain the necessary particulars to enable the Office to establish immediately the purpose of the payment.

2. If the purpose of the payment cannot immediately be established, the Office shall require the person making the payment to notify it in writing of this purpose within such period as it may specify. If he does not comply with this request in due time the payment shall be considered not to have been made.

Article 8
Date to be considered as the date on which payment is made

1. The date on which any payment shall be considered to have been made to the Office shall be as follows:

    (a) in the cases referred to in art. 5, para. 1 (*a*) and (*b*): the date on which the amount of the payment or of the transfer is entered in a bank account or a Giro account held by the Office;

(b) in the cases referred to in art. 5, para. 1 (c) and (e): the date of receipt of the amount of the money order or of the cash payment or the date on which the amount of the money order is entered in a Giro account held by the Office;

(c) in the case referred to in art. 5, para. 1 (d): the date of receipt of the cheque at the Office, provided that the cheque is met.

2. Where the President of the Office allows, in accordance with the provisions of art. 5, para. 2, other methods of paying fees than those set out in art. 5, para. 1, he shall also lay down the date on which such payment shall be considered to have been made.

3. Where, under the provisions of paras. 1 and 2, payment of a fee is not considered to have been made until after the expiry of the period in which it should have been made, it shall be considered that this period has been observed if evidence is provided to the Office that the person who made the payment fulfilled one of the following conditions in a Contracting State not later than 10 days before the expiry of such period:

(a) he effected the payment through a banking establishment or a post office;

(b) he duly gave an order to a banking establishment or a post office to transfer the amount of the payment;

(c) he dispatched at a post office a letter bearing the address of the Office and containing a cheque within the meaning of art. 5, para. 1 (d), provided that the cheque is met.

The Office may request the person who made the payment to produce such evidence within such period as it may specify. If he fails to comply with this request or if the evidence is insufficient, the period for payment shall be considered not to have been observed.

Article 9

Insufficiency of the amount paid

1. A time limit for payment shall in principle be deemed to have been observed only if the full amount of the fee has been paid in due time. If the fee is not paid in full, the amount which has been paid shall be refunded after the period for payment has expired. The Office may, however, insofar as this is possible within the time remaining before the end of the period, give the person making the payment the opportunity to pay the amount lacking. It may also, where this is considered justified, overlook any small amounts lacking without prejudice to the rights of the person making the payment.

2. Where the request for grant of a European patent designates more than one Contracting State in accordance with art. 79, para. 1, of the Convention, and the amount paid is insufficient to cover all the designation fees, the amount paid shall be applied according to the specifications made by the applicant at the time of payment. If the applicant makes no such specifications at the time of payment, these fees shall be deemed to be paid only for as many designations as are covered by the amount paid and in the order in which the Contracting States are designated in the request.

Article 10

Refund of the fee for the European search report

1. The search fee shall be refunded fully or in part if the European search report is based on an earlier search report already prepared by the Office on an application whose priority is claimed for the European patent application or which is the earlier application within the meaning of art. 76 of the Convention or the original application within the meaning of r. 15 of the Implementing Regulations thereto.

2. The search fee may be refunded fully or in part if the European search report is based on an international search report prepared under the provisions of the PCT by the European Patent Office or by any other International Searching Authority.

3. The amount of any refund allowed under paras. 1 or 2 shall be 25, 50, 75 or 100 per cent. of the search fee, depending upon the extent to which the Office benefits from the earlier search report or the international search report.

4. The search fee shall be fully refunded if the European search report relates to a European divisional application and is based entirely on an earlier search report on the earlier application.

5. The search fee shall be fully refunded if the European patent application is withdrawn or refused or deemed to be withdrawn at a time when the Office has not yet begun to draw up the European search report.

Article 11
Decisions fixing costs which are subject to appeal

In accordance with art. 106, para. 5, of the Convention, decisions fixing the amount of costs of opposition proceedings may be appealed if the amount is in excess of the fee for appeal.

Article 12
Reduction of fees

1. The reduction laid down in r. 6, para. 3, of the Convention shall be 20 per cent. of the filing fee, opposition fee and fee for appeal.

2. The reduction laid down in r. 104b, para. 5, of the Convention shall be 50 per cent. of the examination fee.

Article 13
Transitional provision

The provisions of art. 10, paras. 1 and 3, shall also apply if the Office is able to base itself on a search report prepared by the International Patent Institute at The Hague on an application whose priority is claimed for the European patent application.

Article 14
Entry into force

These Rules shall enter into force on *

* This date will have to be fixed by the Administrative Council and must in any event be *later* than the date of publication of the Rules in the *Official Journal* of the European Patent Office.
[1973] 3 F.S.R. 608.

2233. Infringement—experiments—interlocutory injunction—discovery, research and experiments leading to invention

[Patents Act 1949 (c. 87), s. 32 (1).] On two motions for directions in a patent action, the patent in suit related to a synthetic absorbable suture of polymeric material. The plaintiff sued for an infringement and the defendants counterclaimed for revocation of the patents. The pleadings were closed, and in 1973 an interlocutory injunction restrained the defendants from marketing an article allegedly infringing the patent. The defendant sought repetition of two experiments of the plaintiffs on the first motion, and further discovery on the second. *Held,* (1) that experiments which could be repeated within a reasonable time should be carried out; (2) postponement of the trial should be avoided since the plaintiffs might suffer a substantial increase in liability for damages in view of the injunction; (3) the defendants were entitled to documents relating to (a) processes used in manufacture of the suture, but not those relating to experimental work leading to adoption of these processes, (b) research and development leading to the invention to date of publication of the patent, and (c) use of certain examples in the specification prior to the plaintiffs' experiments in chief; (4) discovery of all research and experiments would be oppressive and occasion delay; nevertheless full discovery of the experimental research was necessary to determine sufficiency because there was no comparable prior art: AMERICAN CYANAMID CO. *v.* ETHICON [1977] F.S.R. 593, C.A.

2234. —— **imminent expiry of patent—balance of convenience**
The plaintiffs incurred heavy capital expenditure in launching their product and at the time of action the market was improving. One patent had 14 months to run. The defendants brought an allegedly infringing product from Austria to the U.K. The trial judge declined to grant an interlocutory injunction. The plaintiffs appealed. *Held* allowing the appeal, that (1) damage would be impossible to assess after expiry of the patent; (2) the defendants' business would not suffer greatly by a delay in launching. They should not have the opportunity to establish their business before the expiry of the patent; (3) the balance of convenience favoured the plaintiffs: CORRUPLAST *v.* GEORGE HARRISON (AGENCIES) [1978] R.P.C. 761 C.A.

2235. —— **importation—" pith and marrow " doctrine**
[Patents Act 1949 (c. 87), s. 4 (3).] B was the patentee of Ampicillin and other antibiotics. The second defendants were their licensees. The first defendants were a wholly-owned subsidiary of the second defendants, and imported and sold in the U.K. Hetacillin, an acetone derivative of Ampicillin. B alleged that the doctrine applied whereby the importation of a product manufactured abroad infringed a U.K. patent if, had the product been manufactured in the U.K., it would have infringed the U.K. patent. B alleged that this doctrine should be extended to cover new products. The defendants alleged that the doctrine was inapplicable on account of the need for precise claiming, and that if B's claims were sufficiently broad to embrace Hetacillin they lacked fair basis. The defendants alleged that the " pith and marrow " doctrine was inapplicable for the same reasons. *Held*, (1) the " pith and marrow " doctrine should be applied in this case because the new product Hetacillin was a temporary reproduction of Ampicillin; (2) the importation of Hetacillin infringed two patents which covered the whole process of manufacture of Ampicillin; (3) the Patents Act 1949, s. 4 (3), did not affect the doctrine of infringing importation, but for the doctrine to be applied, the process must have played more than a trifling or unimportant part in the manufacture abroad of the product: BEECHAM GROUP *v.* BRISTOL LABORATORIES [1978] R.P.C. 153, H.L.

2236. —— **no loss to patentee**
D imported a chemical in bulk form which they intended to export in tablet form. The patentees obtained an injunction to restrain infringement. At the trial, the defendants' contention that no infringement occurred if the patentee suffered no loss was rejected. The defendants appealed. *Held*, the patentees were entitled to a remedy for infringement even if they could not show that economic loss would occur: SMITHKLINE CORP. *v.* D.D.S.A. PHARMACEUTICALS [1978] F.S.R. 109, C.A.

2237. —— **procedure—want of prosecution—discretion of trial judge**
An action was commenced in 1971 for a continuing infringement of a patent. The parties communicated until the end of 1973. In December 1977, the plaintiffs gave notice of intention to proceed. The defendants brought a motion to strike out the action for want of prosecution. The trial judge found that the delay was faintly excusable and that the defendants had shown no real prejudice. The defendants appealed. *Held*, (1) the dalay had been inexcusable; (2) the judge had exercised his discretion reasonably on the issue of prejudice and the Court of Appeal should not interfere with it. (*Birkett* v. *James* [1977] C.L.Y. 2410 applied): COMPAGNIE FRANÇAISE DE TÉLÉVISION *v.* THORN CONSUMER ELECTRONICS [1978] R.P.C. 735, C.A.

2238. —— **reasonable trial—prior user—confidential information**
[Patents Act 1949 (c. 87), s. 32 (2) (*a*).] The plaintiff designed a prototype lift in his house, and applied for a patent. The plaintiff discussed with the defendants the possibility of manufacture on a commercial scale. The plaintiff gave details and drawings to the defendants who constructed one lift in accordance with those instructions. The defendants later put on the market a lift incorporating a feature of the plaintiff's design. This feature was removed

after the sale of 378 such lifts. The defendants admitted that the plaintiff's lift had contributed to their design, but alleged that its features and principles of operation were all drawn from common knowledge. On application for an injunction, *held*, (1) the information was given to the defendants in circumstances of confidence; (2) use by the plaintiff, and sight of it by visitors before the defendants were involved, did not amount to prior user; (3) the plaintiff was entitled to damages for those lifts manufactured with his essential feature incorporated; (4) when the defendants modified their lift, the information was no longer confidential: HARRISON *v.* PROJECT AND DESIGN CO. (REDCAR) [1978] F.S.R. 81, Graham J.

2239. International convention

PATENTS ETC. (REPUBLIC OF KOREA) (CONVENTION) ORDER 1978 (No. 187) [10p], made under the Patents Act 1949 (c. 87), s. 68 (1), and the Registered Designs Act 1949 (c. 88), s. 13; made with a view to the fulfilment of an arrangement with the Republic of Korea, and declares that Republic to be a Convention country for all the purposes of the Acts relating to patents and designs.

2240. Opposition—obviousness and anticipation—inadequate classification of cited specification

[Patents Act 1949 (c. 87), s. 14.] In opposition proceedings, anticipation and obviousness were alleged in the light of P's specification. The specification of P had been classified in the Patent Office library only under " Alloys " and should have been classified for cross-referencing purposes under " process for obtaining coherent bodies from powdered metals." The applicants argued that P's specification would not have come to the attention of the notional skilled addressee and should not be considered on the issue of obviousness. *Held*, (1) P's specification was relevant, despite the inadequate classification; (2) modification of the applicants' claim avoided anticipation and obviousness had not been clearly established (*I.C.I.* (*Pointer's*) *Application* [1977] C.L.Y. 2192 distinguished): ASEA AKTIEBOLAG'S APPLICATION [1978] F.S.R. 115, Whitford J.

2241. —— prior publication

[Patents Act 1949 (c. 87), ss. 50 (2), 51 (2) (*d*).] Prior publication and obviousness were alleged in opposition proceedings. The inventor had read a paper at a meeting of a learned society, and the subject was published in four periodicals. *Held*, (1) the inventor had implicitly given consent to worldwide publication; (2) publication in this country was not occasioned by the reading of the paper to the society in Canada; (3) neither the paper nor the publications were transactions of the society, and they were not published under the society's auspices: RALPH M. PARSONS CO. (BEAVON'S) APPLICATION [1978] F.S.R. 226, Patents Office.

2242. —— specification—insufficiency—amendment

[Patents Act 1949 (c. 87), ss. 4, 14 (1) (9).] Application related to a class of compounds for use as solvents in the making of colour-former solutions. The specification was amended to read " dissolved in a solvent comprising " certain named compounds. The hearing officer found that the description of how the invention was to be put into effect was sufficient, but that the invention was not sufficiently described since it appeared from the specification that some compounds were solids at working temperatures whereas, prior to amendment, it appeared that some compounds were low viscosity liquids. The applicants appealed. *Held*, dismissing the appeal, that (1) the specification related only to compounds in which the solvent was a liquid at working temperatures; (2) the invention must be sufficiently and fairly described before the tribunal could consider whether the specification in fact adequately described the method by which the invention should be performed: FUJI PHOTO FILM CO. (KIRITANI'S) APPLICATION [1978] R.P.C. 413, Whitford J.

2243. Patent—grant of licence—disapproval of other licensees. See N.V. HEIDEMAATSCHAPPIJ BEHEER *v.* ZUID NEDERLANDSCHE BRONBEMALING EN GRONDBOBINGEN B.V., § 1329.

2244. Patent agents

REGISTER OF PATENT AGENTS RULES 1978 (No. 1093) [25p], made under the Patents Act 1977 (c. 37), s. 123, operative on September 1, 1978; regulate the registration of patent agents and the suspension of the right to act as such an agent.

2245. Patents Act 1977—commencement

PATENTS ACT 1977 (COMMENCEMENT NO. 2) ORDER 1978 (No. 586 (C. 14)) [10p], made under the Patents Act 1977 (c. 37), s. 132 (5); operative on June 1, 1978; brings into force ss. 1–52, 53 (part), 54–59, 60 (part), 61–76, 77 (part), 78 (part), 79–83, 89–113, 115–129, 131 and 132 (part) of, and Scheds. 1–5 and 6 (part) to the 1977 Act.

2246. —— modification

PATENTS ACT 1977 (ISLE OF MAN) ORDER 1978 (No. 621) [10p], made under the Patents Act 1977 (c. 37), s. 132 (2); operative on June 1, 1978; modifies the 1977 Act in its application to the Isle of Man.

2247. Practice—convention application—service by post

[Patents Rules 1968 (S.I. 1968 No. 1389), rr. 6, 152.] A patent agent gave a convention application form to an employee to deliver to the Patent Office on the last day on which the application should be received. The form was not delivered until next day. *Held,* on appeal, that (1) delivery by an employee was not service by post within r. 6 of the Patents Rules 1968; (2) the mistake was not a procedural error which could be rectified: FUJISAWA PHARMACEUTI-CAL CO.'s APPLICATION [1978] F.S.R. 187, C.A.

2248. —— costs—discretion of judge. See SCHERER *v.* COUNTING INSTRUMENTS § 2341.

2249. —— priority of application—post-dating

[Registered Designs Act 1949 (c. 62), ss. 14, 21; Patent and Designs Act 1907 (c. 29), s. 70; Designs Rules 1949 (S.I. 1949 No. 2368), rr. 27, 51.] Priority was claimed from an application filed in France. The Convention documents were filed one day outside the required three-month period. The applicants applied to post-date the filing of their application by one day, in order to uphold their claim to priority. *Held,* on appeal, the Registrar was correct in his decision, that in view of the Registered Design Rules 1949, rr. 27 (2) and 51, he could not permit post-dating: ALLIBERT'S EXPLOITATION APPLICATION [1978] R.P.C. 261, Whitford J.

2250. —— stay of execution—invalid patents—public interest

[R.S.C., Ord. 59, r. 13.] The plaintiff companies were proprietors of four patents. In four actions for infringement, the trial judge found that one patent was valid and had been infringed, but that the other three were invalid. A stay of execution was ordered, pending appeal, on the account of profits and on the injunction. The plaintiffs appealed against the stay. *Held,* (1) the judge had not erred in principle; (2) there was a public interest in avoiding abortive expenditure which in this case would be great if the defendants succeeded on appeal: J. LUCAS (BATTERIES) *v.* GAEDOR [1978] F.S.R. 159, C.A.

2251. Pre-acceptance proceedings—anticipation

[Patents Act 1949 (c. 87), s. 7.] The examiner objected that a prior publi-cation existed in respect of the applicants' invention. The prior publication was of two claims for a chemical process involving the treatment of cells. The applicants did not assert that any question of a selection invention arose. Applying *Merck and Co. (Macek's) Patent* [1967] C.L.Y. 2989, the hearing officer identified three distinct claims to each isomer, and found anticipation. *Held,* allowing the appeal, that a large number of possible isomers and processes could be delivered from a reading of the prior specification, and anticipation was not sufficiently clearly established: KOCH-LIGHT LABORATORIES' APPLICA-TION [1978] R.P.C. 291, Whitford J.

2252. —— whether claim might cover unrelated inventions—clarity and fair basis

In pre-acceptance proceedings, the claim was for a new cephalosporin, its salts, and " pharmaceutically acceptable bioprecursors therefor." Bioprecursors derive from the cephalosporin and revert thereto in the body. It was accepted that these could include compounds fundamentally different from the cephalosporin. The hearing officer rejected the claim for lack of clarity, and because inventive ingenuity might be required for production of the bioprecursors. *Held*, on appeal, the application should proceed, since the claims were not so broad that they might cover an invention unrelated to that described. Here the inventor had claimed anything which, when absorbed into the body, was reconverted into cephalosporin. (*Beecham Group* v. *Bristol Laboratories* [1967] C.L.Y. 2938 applied): BEECHAM GROUP'S APPLICATION [1977] F.S.R. 565, Graham J.

2253. Prohibited transactions—South Africa. See § 1735.

2254. Registration—literary or artistic character—article not judged solely by eye
[Registered Designs Act 1949 (c. 88), s. 1; Patents and Designs Act 1907 (c. 29), s. 93; Designs Rules 1949 (S.I. 1949 No. 2368), r. 26.] The applicants designed a pre-printed computer print-out stock form or web. It consisted of folded paper with perforations at the side and alternating bands of colour on the white background. These made the print-out easier to read, so that the rows of print could be closer together and overall economy was effected. Registration was refused and the applicants appealed. *Held*, (1) the article was not printed matter of a primarily literary or artistic character; (2) the form was not a design within the meaning of the Registered Designs Act 1949, s. 1 (3), because although the bands appealed to the eye, they were not to be judged solely by the eye. The customer would choose the forms because the bands of colour made the article more useful to him (*Re Littlewoods Pool's Application* (1949) C.L.C. 7043 distinguished; *AMP Inc.* v. *Utilux Proprietary* [1972] C.L.Y. 2593 applied: LAMSON INDUSTRIES' APPLICATION [1978] R.P.C. 1, Whitford J.

2255. Revocation—insufficiency—obviousness
[Patents Act 1949 (c. 87), s. 33.] The patent related to maltitol which was a known substance which could be used as an artificial sweetener. The patentees had discovered that a certain quality was non-calorific. The claim stated " without an increase in the calorific value of the food materials." The superintending examiner found these words surplusage, and revoked the patent as being bad for anticipation and obviousness. The Patents Appeal Tribunal dismissed the patentees' appeal. The patentees appealed further. *Held*, (1) the words were not surplusage; (2) the heavy onus, in revocation proceedings, of establishing insufficiency and anticipation, had not been discharged; (3) the patentees had made an inventive step. The appeal should be allowed: HAYASHIBARA CO.'S PATENT [1977] F.S.R. 582, C.A.

2256. —— patent of addition—anticipation—by main patent
[Patents Act 1949 (c. 87), s. 14 (1) (*g*), 31.] The patent of addition claimed a process for increasing plant resistance to diseases by application of one or more phosphoric acid derivatives similar to those in the main patent. The applicants for revocation alleged prior claiming, anticipation and insufficiency. *Held*, (1) the invention was too broadly described; (2) effecting the treatment in the main patent amounted to the process claimed in the patent of addition, and therefore anticipation was established: AMCHEM PRODUCTS INC.'s PATENT [1978] R.P.C. 271, Whitford J.

2257. Rules
PATENTS RULES 1978 (No. 216) [£1·60], made under the Patents Act 1977 (c. 37), ss. 14 (4) (6) and (8), 25 (5), 32 (2), 72 (3), 78 (4), 92 (3) (4), 97 (1) (*d*); 115 (1), (3), 120 (1), 123 and 127; operative on June 1, 1978; revoke and replace previous Rules so that, inter alia, provision is made for applications to the comptroller by employees for compensation for certain inventions, and provision is made in relation to international applications for patents.

BOOKS AND ARTICLES. See *post*, pp. [7], [31].

PENSIONS AND SUPERANNUATION

2258. British Railways
BRITISH RAILWAYS BOARD (FUNDING OF PENSION SCHEMES) (No. 5) ORDER 1978 (No. 1295) [20p], made under the Railways Act 1974 (c. 48), ss. 5, 6;

operative on October 1, 1978; prescribes the sum of £37,680,737 as the sum to be provided by the Board, and to be paid by the Board in instalments between April 1, 1979, and April 1, 1986, for the purpose of effecting a partial funding of the Board's obligations in connection with certain of their pension schemes.

BRITISH RAILWAYS BOARD (WINDING UP OF CLOSED PENSION FUNDS) ORDER 1978 (No. 1358) [25p], made under the Transport Act 1962 (c. 46), s. 74; operative on October 11, 1978; amends the terms of specified funds so as to permit the employment of any member of the funds to be contracted-out of the earnings-related component of the state pension scheme provided for in the Social Security Pensions Act 1975.

BRITISH RAILWAYS BOARD (FUNDING OF PENSION SCHEMES) (NO. 6) ORDER 1978 (No. 1763) [25p], made under the Railways Act 1974, ss. 5 and 6; operative on January 1, 1979; increases the sum to be provided by the BRB.

2259. Commutation

PENSIONS COMMUTATION (AMENDMENT) REGULATIONS 1978 (No. 1257) [25p], made under the Pensions Commutation Act 1871 (c. 36), ss. 4, 7 and the Pensions Commutation Act 1882 (c. 44), s. 3; operative on September 1, 1978; provides for officers of the Armed Forces to apply for commutation of their pensions during the period of 28 days ending on their last day of service and substitute the tables giving the commutation rates.

2260. Contracting-out

CONTRACTED-OUT EMPLOYMENT (MISCELLANEOUS PROVISIONS) REGULATIONS 1978 (No. 250) [25p], made under the Social Security Pensions Act 1975 (c. 60), ss. 40 (3), 43 (4), 44 (3), 45 (1) (2), Sched. 2, para. 1, 6; operative on April 6, 1978; make miscellaneous provisions in connection with the contracting-out of occupational pension schemes.

CONTRACTED-OUT EMPLOYMENT (MISCELLANEOUS PROVISIONS) (NO. 2) REGULATIONS 1978 (No. 1827) [20p], made under the Social Security Act 1973 (c. 38), s. 66 (7), and the Social Security Pensions Act 1975, s. 31 (5), Sched. 2, paras. 1 and 9; operative on January 9, 1979; provide that where an election with a view to the issue, variation or surrender of a contracting-out certificate meets the conditions prescribed the requirements for the giving of notices and consultation may be dispensed with.

2261. —— local government

LOCAL GOVERNMENT SUPERANNUATION (SOCIAL SECURITY—REQUIREMENTS FOR CONTRACTING-OUT) REGULATIONS 1978 (No. 1738) [40p], made under the Superannuation Act 1972 (c. 11), ss. 7 and 12 operative on December 30, 1978; after the local government superannuation scheme in the principal regulations to meet the requirements of the Social Security Pensions Act 1975.

2262. —— miscellaneous offices

PENSIONS (MISCELLANEOUS OFFICES) (REQUISITE BENEFITS) ORDER 1978 (No. 552) [25p], made under the Social Security Act 1973 (c. 38), s. 65; operative on April 21, 1978; modifies the pension schemes for the holders of specified offices so as to meet contracting-out requirements.

2263. —— Parliament

PARLIAMENTARY AND OTHER PENSIONS (CONTRACTED-OUT PROVISIONS) ORDER 1978 (No. 891) [20p], made under the Social Security Act 1973 (c. 38), s. 65; operative on June 28, 1978; modifies the Parliamentary and other Pensions Act 1972 to enable the provisions of that Act to become a contracted-out pension scheme.

2264. Coroners

SOCIAL SECURITY (MODIFICATION OF CORONERS (AMENDMENT) ACT 1926) ORDER 1978 (No. 374) [10p], made under the Social Security Act 1973 (c. 38), ss. 65 and 96; operative on April 6, 1978; modifies the 1926 Act relating to the payment of pensions to coroners.

2265. Earnings rule

The Department of Health and Social Security have published a report entitled "The Earnings Rule for Retirement Pensioners and the Wives of

Retirement and Invalidity Pensioners." This concludes that, although the Government remains committed to ending the earnings rule which affects certain retirement pensioners who work, this cannot be done immediately because of the cost. The report is available from HMSO (House of Commons Paper 697).

2266. Fire service

FIREMEN'S PENSION SCHEME (AMENDMENT) ORDER 1978 (No. 1228) [40p], made under the Fire Services Act 1947 (c. 41), s. 26 as extended by the Reserve and Auxiliary Forces (Protection of Civil Interests) Act 1951 (c. 65), s. 42 and the Superannuation Act 1972 (c. 11), ss. 12, 16; operative on October 1, 1978; amends S.I. 1973 No. 966 to provide a new method for transferring superannuation rights where a person enters a fire brigade from certain other forms of pensionable employment or enters such employment after leaving a fire brigade.

FIREMEN'S PENSION SCHEME (AMENDMENT) (No. 2) ORDER 1978 (No. 1349) [40p], made under the Fire Services Act 1947, s. 26 as amended and extended by the Reserve and Auxiliary Forces (Protection of Civil Interests) Act 1951, s. 42, and the Superannuation Act 1972 (c. 11), ss. 12, 16; operative on October 6, 1978; amend S.I. 1973 No. 966 to enable that scheme to satisfy the requirements for the issue of a contracting-out certificate under the Social Security Pensions Act 1975, s. 31.

FIREMEN'S PENSION SCHEME (AMENDMENT) (No. 3) ORDER 1978 (No. 1577) [25p], made under the Fire Services Act 1947, s. 26, as amended by the Reserve and Auxiliary Forces (Protection of Civil Interests) Act 1951, s. 42, and the Superannuation Act 1972, ss. 12, 16; operative on December 1, 1978; amend S.I. 1973 No. 966 and increases the flat rates to which reference is made when determining the amounts of certain awards.

2266a. Judicial officers

PENSIONS INCREASE (JUDICIAL PENSIONS) (AMENDMENT) REGULATIONS 1978 (No. 1808) [20p], made under the Pensions (Increase) Act 1971 (c. 56), s. 5 (3) (4); operative on January 5, 1979; amend S.I. 1972 No. 71 by removing the multiplier which was formerly used for calculating increases to pensions of former Lord Chancellors which is now replaced by a new provision which expressly restricts the pension so that it cannot exceed that of the present Lord Chancellor should he resign his office.

2267. Local government

LOCAL GOVERNMENT SUPERANNUATION (AMENDMENT) REGULATIONS 1978 (No. 266) [35p], made under the National Insurance Act 1965 (c. 51), s. 110 (1) (*a*) and the Superannuation Act 1972 (c. 11), ss. 7, 12; operative on March 30, 1978; amend S.I. 1974 No. 520 with regard to qualifications to participate in a superannuation scheme.

LOCAL GOVERNMENT SUPERANNUATION (AMENDMENT) (No. 2) REGULATIONS 1978 (No. 822) [20p], made under the Superannuation Act 1972, ss. 7, 12, operative on July 6, 1978; provide for coroners who are not subject to S.I. 1974 No. 520 to become superannuated under those Regulations.

LOCAL GOVERNMENT SUPERANNUATION (AMENDMENT) (No. 3) REGULATIONS 1978 (No. 1739) [50p], made under the Superannuation Act 1972, ss. 7, 12; operative on December 30, 1978; further amend S.I. 1974 No. 520.

2268. National Health Service

NATIONAL HEALTH SERVICE (SUPERANNUATION) (AMENDMENT) REGULATIONS 1978 (No. 1353) [40p], made under the Superannuation Act 1972 (c. 11), ss. 10, 11; operative on October 6, 1978; further amend S.I. 1961 No. 1441, which provide for the superannuation of persons engaged in the National Health Service.

2269. National Insurance. See NATIONAL INSURANCE.

2270. National Insurance Commissioners

NATIONAL INSURANCE COMMISSIONERS' PENSIONS (PRESERVATION OF BENEFITS) ORDER 1978 (No. 407) [15p], made under the Social Security Act 1973 (c. 38), ss. 64, 65; operative on April 6, 1978; modifies the pension scheme for the Chief and other National Insurance Commissioners.

NATIONAL INSURANCE COMMISSIONERS' PENSIONS (REQUISITE BENEFITS) ORDER 1978 (No. 408) [25p], made under the Social Security Act 1973, s. 65, operative on April 6, 1978; modifies the pensions scheme for the Chief and other National Insurance Commissioners.

NATIONAL INSURANCE COMMISSIONERS' PENSIONS (REQUISITE BENEFITS) AMENDMENT ORDER 1978 (No. 1368) [10p], made under the Social Security Act 1973, ss. 64, 65; operative on October 13, 1978; amends S.I. 1978 No. 408 so as to provide that where a Commissioner dies after ceasing to hold office, having completed less than five years of qualifying service, his widow shall be entitled to a pension of not less than her guaranteed minimum.

2271. Northern Ireland. See NORTHERN IRELAND.

2272. Occupational schemes

OCCUPATIONAL PENSION SCHEMES (PUBLIC SERVICE PENSION SCHEMES) REGULATIONS 1978 (No. 289) [10p], made under the Social Security Act 1973 (c. 38), s. 51 (3) (b) and the Social Security Pensions Act 1975 (c. 60), s. 66 (1); operative on March 30, 1978; provides that specified occupational pension schemes are to be treated for the purposes of Part II of the 1973 Act and Parts III and IV of the 1975 Act as public social pension schemes.

OCCUPATIONAL PENSION SCHEMES (PUBLIC SERVICE PENSION SCHEMES) (AMENDMENT) REGULATIONS 1978 (No. 1355) [10p], made under the Social Security Act 1973, s. 51 (3) (b), and the Social Security Pensions Act 1975 (c. 60), s. 66 (1); operative on October 11, 1978; amend S.I. 1978 No. 289, so as to add three further occupational pension schemes to the Schedule to those regulations.

2273. Parliamentary pensions

PARLIAMENTARY PENSIONS (PURCHASE OF ADDED YEARS) ORDER 1978 (No. 1837) [30p], made under the Parliamentary Pensions Act 1978 (c. 56), s. 11; operative on January 5, 1979; provides for the purchase of added years of reckonable pensionable service either by periodical contributions or by lump sum payment by Members of the House of Commons serving on or after August 2, 1978.

2274. Parliamentary Pensions Act 1978 (c. 56)

This Act further provides for contributory pension schemes for Members of the House of Commons and for holders of certain ministerial and other offices.

S. 1 directs the payment of pensions to Members on early retirement; s. 2 relates to ill-health pensions based on service as a Member; s. 3 deals with ill-health pensions based on service as an office-holder; s. 4 is concerned with ill-health pensions for those no longer Members or office-holders; s. 5 deals with medical evidence for purposes of ss. 2–4; s. 6 relates to widowers' pensions; s. 7 makes further provision with respect to widows', widowers' and children's pensions; s. 8 provides for short-term pensions for widows, widowers and children; s. 9 has to do with children's pensions; s. 10 directs the method of payment of gratuities on the death of a Member or office-holder; s. 11 arranges for the purchase of added years; s. 12 amends the provisions for calculating reckonable service; s. 13 relates to participation by holders of qualifying offices; s. 14 directs an increase of contributions from Parliamentary remuneration; s. 15 sets out future changes in the basis of contributions to, and payments out of, the Fund; s. 16 reduces the reckonable service needed for a pension under s. 9 of the Parliamentary and other Pensions Act 1972 (c. 48); s. 17 relates to the duration of pensions, and makes provision for partial abatement; s. 18 deals with transfers to and from overseas pensions schemes; s. 19 amends s. 30 (3) of the Parliamentary and other Pensions Act 1972; s. 20 stipulates the rate of interest for the purposes of the 1972 Act; s. 21 makes certain financial provisions; s. 22 deals with the citation and construction of this Act, and makes minor and consequential repeals and amendments.

The Act received the Royal Assent on August 2, 1978, and came into force on that date.

2275. Pensioners Payments Act 1978 (c. 58)

This Act makes provision for lump sum payments to pensioners.

S. 1 makes provisions corresponding to those made in the Pensioners Payments Act 1977, mutatis mutandis; s. 2 gives the short title.

The Act received the Royal Assent on November 23, 1978, and came into force on that date.

2276. Pensions appeal tribunals

PENSIONS APPEAL TRIBUNALS (ENGLAND AND WALES) (AMENDMENT) RULES 1978 (No. 607) [15p], made under the Pensions Appeal Tribunals Act 1943 (c. 39), Sched., para. 5, as amended by the Administration of Justice Act 1977 (c. 38) and after consultation under the Tribunals and Inquiries Act 1971 (c. 62), s. 10; operative on May 23, 1978; amends S.I. 1971 No. 769 in relation to allowances.

PENSIONS APPEAL TRIBUNALS (ENGLAND AND WALES) (AMENDMENT No. 2) RULES 1978 (No. 1780) [10p], made under the Pensions Appeal Tribunals Act 1943, Sched. 1, para. 5 as amended by the Administration of Justice Act 1977, and under the Tribunals and Inquiries Act 1971, s. 10; operative on January 15, 1979; further amends S.I. 1971 No. 769.

2277. Pensions increase

PENSIONS INCREASE (COMPENSATION TO STAFF OF GRANT-AIDED COLLEGES) (SCOTLAND) REGULATIONS 1978 (No. 210) [10p], made under the Pensions (Increase) Act 1971 (c. 56), s. 5 (2); operative on March 17, 1978; apply the 1971 Act to pensions payable under Pt. IV or V of S.I. 1977 No. 1777.

PENSIONS INCREASE (WELSH DEVELOPMENT AGENCY) REGULATIONS 1978 (No. 211) [10p], made under the Pensions (Increase) Act 1971, s. 5 (2) and (4); operative on March 17, 1978; replace S.I. 1977 No. 136.

2278. Police

POLICE PENSIONS (AMENDMENT) REGULATIONS 1978 (No. 375) [15p], made under the Police Pensions Act 1976 (c. 35), ss. 1, 3 and 4; operative on April 6, 1978; amend S.I. 1973 No. 428 and S.I. 1977 No. 2173 relating to the new method of transferring superannuation rights where a person enters a police force from certain other forms of pensionable employment or enters such employment after leaving a police force.

POLICE PENSIONS (AMENDMENT) (No. 2) REGULATIONS 1978 (No. 1348) [40p], made under the Police Pensions Act 1976, ss. 1, 3, 4; operative on October 6, 1978; amend S.I. 1973 No. 428 so as to enable those regulations to satisfy the requirements for the issue of a contracting-out certificate under the Social Security Pensions Act 1975, s. 31.

POLICE PENSIONS (AMENDMENT) (No. 3) REGULATIONS 1978 (No. 1578) [20p], made under the Police Pensions Act 1976, ss. 1, 3, 5; operative on December 1, 1978; amend S.I. 1973 No. 428 and S.I. 1971 No. 232 by increasing the flat rates to which reference is made for the purpose of determining the amounts of certain widows' pensions and children's allowances.

POLICE PENSIONS (LUMP SUM PAYMENTS TO WIDOWS) REGULATIONS 1978 (No. 1691) [10p], made under the Police Pensions Act 1976, ss. 1, 3, 5, the Pensioners' Payments Act 1977 (c. 51), s. 1 and the Pensioners' Payments Act 1978 (c. 58), s. 1 (1); operative on December 4, 1978; provide for the payment of a gratuity of £10 in the case of a policeman's widow in receipt of a discretionary increase in her pension under S.I. 1971 No. 232 in the week beginning December 4, 1978.

2279. Retirement age

The Department of Health and Social Security have published a discussion document on the elderly, which, inter alia, discusses the possibility of changes in the state retirement pension ages for men and women. The report is available from HMSO [95p].

2280. Retirement pensions

SOCIAL SECURITY (GRADUATED RETIREMENT BENEFIT) REGULATIONS 1978 (No. 391) [10p], made under the National Insurance Act 1965 (c. 51), ss. 36 (5), 37 (4); operative on April 5, 1978; provide for certain persons who had rights or prospective rights to, or expectations of, graduated retirement benefit under ss. 36 and 37 the 1965 Act and who have deferred their retirement beyond retirement age.

SOCIAL SECURITY (WIDOW'S BENEFIT AND RETIREMENT PENSIONS) AMENDMENT REGULATIONS 1978 (No. 392) [25p], made under the Social Security Act 1975 (c. 14), ss. 30 (3), 33 (2) (3), 139 (1), the Social Security Pensions Act 1975 (c. 60), ss. 20, 61 (1) (e), Sched. 1, paras. 2 (2) (a), 3 as amended by the Social Security (Miscellaneous Provisions) Act 1977 (c. 5), s. 3; operative on April 6, 1979; amends S.I. 1974 No. 2059 consequential on the passing of the Social Security Pensions Act 1975.

SOCIAL SECURITY (GRADUATED RETIREMENT BENEFIT) (No. 2) REGULATIONS 1978 (No. 393) [25p], made under the Social Security (Consequential Provisions) Act 1975 (c. 18), s. 2 (1), Sched. 3, paras. 3, 7, 9, the Social Security Pensions Act 1975, ss. 24 (1), 61 (1) (e) and the Social Security Act 1975 s. 139 (1); regs. 1 and 2 operative on April 6, 1978, remainder for the purposes of reg. 1 (3) operative on December 6, 1978 and the remainder for all other purposes operative on April 6, 1979; revoke S.I. 1975 No. 557 and provide for the continuing in force of ss. 36 and 37 of the National Insurance Act 1965.

2281. Royal Irish Constabulary

ROYAL IRISH CONSTABULARY (LUMP SUM PAYMENTS TO WIDOWS) REGULATIONS 1978 (No. 1692) [10p], made under the Royal Irish Constabulary (Widows' Pensions) Act 1954 (c. 17), s. 1; operative on December 4, 1978; provide for the payment of an additional £10 in the case of a widow in receipt of an allowance or pension under S.I. 1971 No. 1469 during the week beginning December 4, 1978 if she is not entitled to a payment by virtue of s. 1 (1) of the Pensioners' Payments Act 1978.

2282. State scheme premiums

STATE SCHEME PREMIUMS (ACTUARIAL TABLES) REGULATIONS 1978 (No. 134) [35p], made under the Social Security Pensions Act 1975 (c. 60), ss. 44 (7), 45 (4), 46 (2); operative on April 6, 1978; prescribe tables in accordance with which the Secretary of State is required to calculate the cost of providing guaranteed minimum pensions.

2283. Surviving spouses

SOCIAL SECURITY (MAXIMUM ADDITIONAL COMPONENT) REGULATIONS 1978 (No. 949) [10p], made under the Social Security Pensions Act 1975 (c. 60), s. 9 (3); operative on April 6, 1979; prescribe a maximum additional component for the purposes of s. 9 (3) of the 1975 Act which makes provision for circumstances in which the additional components in the Category A retirement pensions of surviving spouses should be increased up to that maximum.

2284. Teachers

TEACHERS' SUPERANNUATION (AMENDMENT) REGULATIONS 1978 (No. 422) [25p], made under the Superannuation Act 1972 (c. 11), ss. 9, 12, Sched. 3; operative on April 17, 1978; amend S.I. 1976 No. 1987 by providing that if a teacher who is over 50 but has not yet attained the age of 60 and is made redundant, the allowances under the 1976 Regulations shall be paid to him.

TEACHERS' SUPERANNUATION (AMENDMENT) (No. 2) REGULATIONS 1978 (No. 1422) [30p], made under the Superannuation Act 1972, ss. 9, 12, Sched. 3; operative on October 6, 1978; amend S.I. 1976 No. 1987 to take account of the requirements to be satisfied by an occupational pension scheme if it is to be a contracted-out scheme for the purposes of the Social Security Pensions Act 1975.

TEACHERS' SUPERANNUATION (AMENDMENT) (No. 3) REGULATIONS 1978 (No. 1512) [20p], made under the Superannuation Act 1972, ss. 9, 12, Sched. 3; operative on December 1, 1978; amend S.I. 1976 No. 1987 by restating Reg. 6 of the principal Regulations.

2285. Transfer of rights

CONTRACTING-OUT AND PRESERVATION (FURTHER PROVISIONS) REGULATIONS 1978 (No. 1089) [20p], made under the Social Security Act 1973 (c. 38), Sched. 16, para. 9 (3) and the Social Security Pensions Act 1975 (c. 60), s. 38 (1), Sched. 2, para. 9; operative on August 28, 1978; amend S.I. 1975 No. 2101 so as to provide that on a transfer of accrued rights between schemes without the member's consent the trustees or administrators of the transferring scheme must be of the opinion that the rights allowed in the other scheme are at least equal in value to the rights transferred. They also amend S.I. 1973 No. 1469.

2286. Transport

NATIONAL FREIGHT CORPORATION (FUNDING OF PENSION SCHEMES) (NO. 2) ORDER 1978 (No. 1764) [10p], made under the Transport Act 1978 (c. 55), ss. 19, 20; operative on January 1, 1979; provides for the variation of the sum which the Corporation is to provide for funding certain obligations owed in respect of the pension schemes that are specified.

2287. War pensions

WAR PENSIONS (AMENDMENT OF PREVIOUS INSTRUMENTS) ORDER 1978 (No. 278) [25p], made under the Social Security (Miscellaneous Provisions) Act 1977 (c. 5), s. 12 (1); operative on April 3, 1978; amends commencing dates of awards, rates of pensions and allowances in respect of children of members of the naval, military or air forces.

PERSONAL INJURIES (CIVILIANS) (AMENDMENT) SCHEME 1978 (No. 384) [15p], made under the Personal Injuries (Emergency Provisions) Act 1939 (c. 82), s. 2; operative on April 3, 1978; amends S.I. 1976 No. 585 by amending commencing dates of awards in general. It also amends rates of pensions and allowances in respect of children of civilians injured or killed in the 1939–45 War and makes transitional provisions in respect of persons who, before the coming into operation of the scheme, were qualified to receive payment of pensions or allowances but were not entitled to benefit under the Child Benefit Act 1975.

WAR PENSIONS (AMENDMENT OF PREVIOUS INSTRUMENTS) (NO. 2) ORDER 1978 (No. 1404) [80p], made under the Social Security (Miscellaneous Provisions) Act 1977, s. 12 (1); operative on November 13, 1978; further amends the Order in Council of September 25, 1964, and increases the rates of retired pay, pensions, gratuities and allowances in respect of disablement and death due to service in the 1914–18 War and after September 3, 1939.

WAR PENSIONS (PRE-CONSOLIDATION AMENDMENT) ORDER 1978 (No. 1405) [30p], made under the Social Security (Miscellaneous Provisions) Act 1977 s. 12 (1); operative on January 1, 1978; revokes certain specified instruments that provided for war pensions for servicemen and makes a new provision for the date at which the amount of a gratuity is to be calculated.

PERSONAL INJURIES (CIVILIANS) AMENDMENT (NO. 2) SCHEME 1978 (No. 1426) [25p], made under the Personal Injuries (Emergency Provisions) Act 1939, s. 2; operative on November 13, 1978; further amends S.I. 1976 No. 585 by increasing the rates of retired pay, pensions, gratuities and allowances in respect of disablement and death in the 1939–45 War.

NAVAL, MILITARY AND AIR FORCES, ETC. (DISABLEMENT AND DEATH) SERVICE PENSIONS ORDER 1978 (No. 1525) [£2], made under the Social Security (Miscellaneous Provisions) Act 1977, s. 12 (1); operative on January 1, 1979; consolidates into a single instrument the Order in Council of September 25, 1964, the Royal Warrant of December 19, 1964, and the Order of Her Majesty of September 24, 1964, which provided for pensions and other awards in respect of disablement or death due to service in the naval, military or air forces during the 1914 World War and after September 2, 1939.

NAVAL, MILITARY AND AIR FORCE ETC. (MODIFICATION OF ENACTMENTS AND OTHER INSTRUMENTS) ORDER 1978 (No. 1526) [25p], made under the Social Security (Miscellaneous Provisions) Act 1977, s. 12 (1), S.I. 1978 Nos. 1405, 1525; operative on January 1, 1979, is made in consequence of S.I. 1978 Nos. 1405 and 1525. It makes provision for references in Acts and instruments to those war pensions instruments and to pensions and other benefits provided by them to be construed as including references to the Consolidation.

INJURIES IN WAR (SHORE EMPLOYMENTS) COMPENSATION (AMENDMENT) SCHEME 1978 (No. 1629) [10p], made under the Injuries in War Compensation Act 1914 (Session 2) (c. 18), s. 1, as amended by the Defence (Transfer of Functions) (No. 1) Order 1964 (S.I. 1964 No. 488), and the Defence (Transfer of Functions) Act 1964 (c. 15), s. 1 (1) (3); operative on November 13, 1978;

provides that the maximum weekly allowance, payable under the Injuries in War (Shore Employments) Compensation Schemes 1914–1977, shall be increased from £28·60 to £31·90 and other allowances be increased proportionately.

NAVAL, MILITARY AND AIR FORCES ETC. (DISABLEMENT AND DEATH) SERVICE PENSIONS AMENDMENT ORDER 1978 (No. 1902) [20p], made under the Social Security (Miscellaneous Provisions) Act 1977, s. 12 (1); operative on January 24, 1979; amends S.I. 1978 No. 1525. It substitutes a new Table 1A in Sched. 2 and up-rates the rate of part-time treatment allowance. It restores the condition, formerly in art. 12 (6) of the 1964 war pensions instruments, that a woman member of the forces shall not be eligible for an increase of her basic disablement pension in respect of a child of whom her husband is the father or adoptive father unless he is dependent on her and is incapable of self-support and in need.

2288. The Minister of the Disabled has announced increases in the rates of car maintenance allowance paid to disabled war pensioners. As from July 15, 1978, allowances, paid on the scale relating to the age of the car in question, will rise from £35 to £50 a year (for the first two years), £55 to £90 per year (for the third and fourth years), and £65 to £150 per year (for the fifth and subsequent years). The private car maintenance allowance will also be increased, as from July 5, 1978, to £250 per year, tax free and exempt from vehicle excise duty.

2289. The Minister for the Disabled has announced that, as from November 1978, a pension will be awarded to war widows whose husbands were receiving a constant attendance allowance at the part-day rate at the time of their deaths.

2290. The Department of Health and Social Security have published a report on the administration of the War Pensions Scheme. This is available from HMSO (H.C. No. 546) [£1·50].

BOOKS AND ARTICLES. See *post,* pp. [7], [31].

PERSONAL PROPERTY

ARTICLES. See *post,* p. [31].

PETROLEUM

2291. Continental shelf

PETROLEUM (PRODUCTION) (AMENDMENT) REGULATIONS 1978 (No. 929) [20p], made under the Petroleum (Production) Act 1934 (c. 36), s. 6 as applied by the Continental Shelf Act 1964 (c. 29), s. 1 (3); operative on July 26, 1978; amend S.I. 1976 No. 1129 by providing for an increase in the fee payable by applicants for petroleum production licences.

2292. Licence fees

PETROLEUM (REGULATION) ACTS 1928 AND 1936 (VARIATION OF FEES) REGULATIONS 1978 (No. 635) [10p], made under the Health and Safety at Work, etc. Act 1974 (c. 37), ss. 11 (2) (d), 15 (1) (3) (a), 50 (3) as amended by the Employment Protection Act 1975 (c. 71), s. 116, Sched. 15, para. 6; operative on July 1, 1978; modifies the Petroleum (Consolidation) Act 1928 by substituting a new Sched. for the First Sched. of that Act and s. 1 (4) of the Petroleum (Transfer of Licences) Act 1936 by increasing the fee payable for the transfer of a petroleum-spirit licence.

2293. Prices

PETROL PRICES (DISPLAY) ORDER 1978 (No. 1389) [25p], made under the Prices Act 1974 (c. 24), s. 4, as amended by the Price Commission Act 1977 (c. 33), s. 16; arts. 1 and 5 operative on October 18, 1978, arts. 2 to 4 operative on December 20, 1978; supersedes S.I. 1977 No. 1057 and makes provision for the display of petrol prices.

ARTICLES. See *post,* p. [31].

POLICE

2294. Chief Inspector of Constabulary

Her Majesty's Chief Inspector of Constabulary, Sir Colin Woods, has published his annual report for 1977, which discusses, inter alia, the problems facing the police in dealing with political demonstrations. The report is available from HMSO (H.C. 545) [£2·25].

2295. Judges' Rules. See § 531.

2296. Metropolitan police

The Commissioner of Police of the Metropolis, Sir David McNee, published his annual report for 1977. It surveys such issues as the Force's declining manpower in the face of a sharply rising rate of reported crimes, and its massive public order commitments in the face of severe financial cutbacks. It also contains detailed comments of the setting up of the Royal Commission on Criminal Procedure, on police pay, bail abuse, community relations, women in the Force, and the law on obscene publications. The Report is available from HMSO (Cmnd. 7238) [£2·10].

2297. Police cadets

POLICE CADETS (AMENDMENT) REGULATIONS 1978 (No. 1239) [10p], made under the Police Act 1964 (c. 48), s. 35 and the Police Act 1969 (c. 63), s. 4 (4); operative on September 1, 1978; amend S.I. 1968 No. 25 by increasing the pay of police cadets and the charges payable by them for board and lodgings provided by police authorities.

2298. Police Complaints Board

The Police Complaints Board, set up under the Police Act 1976, have published their first annual report, covering the period June 1–December 31, 1977; it is available from H.M.S.O. [50p].

2299. Powers—retention of property—for use in evidence—not for payment of compensation. See MALONE v. METROPOLITAN POLICE COMMISSIONER, § 458.

2300. Powers of arrest—arrest before inquiries made

The Court of Appeal stated that, except under the Prevention of Terrorism (Temporary Provisions) Act 1976, the police had no power to arrest anyone so that they could make inquiries about him. When they had enough evidence to prefer a charge they should do so without delay and bring the accused person before a magistrate as soon as practicable in accordance with s. 38 (4) of the Magistrates Courts Act 1952. Parliament might have to decide whether the police should have such powers: R. v. HOUGHTON; R. v. FRANCIOSY, *The Times*, June 23, 1978, C.A.

2301. —— arrestable offences with or without warrant—unnecessary fetter

A police constable who wishes to make an arrest on warrant in a civil matter must have the warrant in his possession or very near. The reason is that it is essential for the person arrested to be able to " buy " his freedom from arrest by payment of the sum stated in the warrant. A constable making an arrest otherwise is not acting in the execution of his duty, within the meaning of s. 51 of the Police Act 1964. The Lord Chief Justice said that the existing law produced an unnecessary fetter on the powers of the police: DE COSTA SMALL v. KIRKPATRICK, *The Times*, October 24, 1978, D.C.

2302. —— entry to effect—constables not acting in course of duty. See R. v. MCKENZIE AND DAVIS, § 413.

2303. —— obstruction in course of duty

W, a solicitor, refused to allow two police officers to take away from X a ring which they thought to be stolen unless they gave a receipt. One officer then arrested W for obstructing him in the execution of his duty. W was acquitted of this offence by magistrates. *Held*, that a police officer has power to arrest without a warrant a person who wilfully obstructs him in the execution of his duty only if the nature of the obstruction was such as to cause, or be likely to cause, a breach of the peace or was calculated to prevent the lawful arrest of another. Accordingly, W's claim for damages succeeded: WERSHOF v. METROPOLITAN POLICE COMMISSIONER [1978] Crim.L.R. 424, May J.

2304. Procedure—corruption in public life. See § 435.

2305. Search warrant—clients' forged documents on solicitor's premises—solicitor's right to be heard

[Forgery Act 1913 (c. 27), s. 16 (1).]

A search warrant may be granted to search for forged documents held in a solicitor's office on behalf of his client. Solicitors acting for a number of defendants had in their possession a power of attorney, allegedly forged, granting a power of attorney to one of the defendants. A search warrant was issued empowering the police to enter the solicitors' office to search for that document. *Held*, refusing the solicitor's application for certiorari to quash the warrant, that s. 16 of the Forgery Act 1913 gave no right to a person to be heard before a search warrant was issued against him. The sections included " any forged document " which included a power of attorney. No question of there being any " lawful authority or excuse " arose since any privilege which the solicitors had in respect of the documents was the privilege of their clients who had no " lawful authority or excuse " within the meaning of the Act of 1913.

R. *v.* PETERBOROUGH JUSTICES, *ex p.* HICKS [1977] 1 W.L.R. 1371, D.C.

2306. Terms of employment

POLICE (AMENDMENT) REGULATIONS 1978 (No. 1169) [25p], made under the Police Act 1964 (c. 48), s. 33; operative on September 1, 1978; increase rates of pay, confer a London allowance on members of the City of London and Metropolitan police forces, and end the undermanning allowance payable to members of certain police forces.

BOOKS AND ARTICLES. See *post*, pp. [7], [31].

POST OFFICE

2307. Northern Ireland. See NORTHERN IRELAND.

2308. Telecommunications. See TELECOMMUNICATIONS.

2309. Trade unions. See TRADE UNIONS.

PRACTICE

2310. Admiralty. See SHIPPING AND MARINE INSURANCE.

2311. Adoption. See MINORS.

2312. Appeal—bankruptcy. See Practice Direction, § 143.

2313. —— contempt of criminal proceedings—Civil Division

Appeal against a finding that a defendant in criminal proceedings has been guilty of a contempt of the court of trial lies, if at all, to the civil division of the Court of Appeal: R. *v.* TIBBITS (1978) 122 S.J. 761, C.A.

2314. —— financial provision—appeals to Divisional Court—single judge. See PRACTICE DIRECTION, § 795.

2315. —— from magistrates' court—election of court in which appeal is to be heard —simultaneous applications. See KIRK *v.* CIVIL AVIATION AUTHORITY, § 1895.

2316. —— judge's dismissal of appeal against Order 14 judgment

The defendant appealed to the judge in chambers after a master had entered judgment in the plaintiffs' favour under R.S.C., Ord. 14. At the appeal, which had already been adjourned on the defendant's request, the defendant was unable to attend, and the judge dismissed the appeal. *Held*, that although the defendant had a right to challenge the judge's order in the Court of Appeal, and although in this particular case the Court of Appeal would entertain his appeal direct, as a general rule the correct course for such a party to take would be to apply to the judge to set aside his order and hear the appeal, otherwise the Court of Appeal would be flooded with such business: ROYAL BANK OF CANADA *v.* GHOSH, *The Times*, November 30, 1978, C.A.

2317. —— minors—application by solicitors to obtain documents

It is open to solicitors having difficulty in obtaining documents or justices' reasons in any appeal concerning a child to apply to a single judge of the Family Division for an order for production so that further delay can be prevented: *Re* B (A MINOR), *The Times,* October 26, 1978, D.C.

2318. —— **numerous previous appeals—whether " adverse influence "**
The Church of Scientology of California, which has appeared on eight occasions in the last decade before the Master of the Rolls, has successfully applied for another appeal to be heard in a division of the court not presided over by him, stating that they believe that there is " an unconscious adverse influence." *Per* Shaw L.J.: it is almost impossible to resist the application even though the grounds are not merely slight but non-existent: *Ex p.* CHURCH OF SCIENTOLOGY OF CALIFORNIA, *The Times,* February 21, 1978, C.A.

2319. —— **patents—Registrar of Patents Appeals.** See PRACTICE DIRECTION, § 2217.

2320. Appearance—substitution of conditional for unconditional—court's discretion
[R.S.C., Ord. 21, r. 1.]
R.S.C., Ord. 21, r. 1, gives the court a complete discretion to give leave to withdraw an appearance, the exercise of which depends on the facts of each case.
The plaintiff in an action obtained leave to join X Co. as defendants by an order which was outside the limitation period. X Co. gave their solicitors authority to enter an appearance to the action, and a solicitors' clerk entered an unconditional appearance. The judge, on appeal from the master, gave X Co. leave to withdraw the unconditional appearance and to enter instead a conditional appearance. The plaintiff contended that the judge could grant leave only where the appearance had been entered by mistake due to absence of authority. *Held,* dismissing the appeal, that the judge had a discretion to make the order, which he had exercised properly. (*Somportex* v. *Philadelphia Chewing Gum Corp.* [1968] C.L.Y. 3049 explained.)
FIRTH v. JOHN MOWLEM & CO. [1978] 3 All E.R. 331, C.A.

2321. Application for judicial review—simultaneous proceedings in Chancery Division
Where an application for judicial review can be made in the Queen's Bench Divisional Court, it is wrong for the applicant to pursue the alternative of seeking a declaration in the Chancery Division: UPPAL v. HOME OFFICE, *The Times,* November 11, 1978, C.A.

2322. Attachment of earnings—pension—whether " in respect of disablement "
[Attachment of Earnings Act 1971 (c. 32), s. 24.], M, a fireman, retired in 1972 as he was permanently disabled by osteo-arthritis. He thereafter received a pension from the council. His wife applied for an attachment of earnings order to secure maintenance payments. *Held,* M's position was calculated solely on the length of his service not by reference to his disablement. It was therefore like an ordinary fireman's pension and was not exempt from attachment. MILES v. MILES, *The Times,* November 29, 1978, C.A.

2323. Barristers—negligence—immunity—narrowed to include only trial and immediate pre-trial work
A barrister's immunity from actions in negligence is based on public policy and extends only to work performed in court or to work intimately connected with such a performance.
P, a passenger in a car, sued the husband of the driver of another car for negligence in the manner of his wife's driving, alleging that she drove as his agent. That husband denied his wife's agency and alleged contributory negligence by P's driver. Counsel, who was consulted about these allegations, did not advise joinder of either the wife or P's driver. The claim became time barred and had to be discontinued against the driver. P sued his solicitors who joined the barrister as third party. *Held,* allowing P's appeal, that the barrister had an immunity extending to barristers (and to solicitors) which covered work performed in court and work intimately connected with the conduct of the cause in court but each piece of the pre-trial work had to be considered separately in the light of this test. This was not such a case and the action could proceed.
SAIF ALI v. SYDNEY MITCHELL AND CO. (A FIRM) [1978] 3 W.L.R. 849, H.L.

2324. Certiorari—county court—" final and conclusive " determination—whether certiorari lies

[County Courts Act 1959 (c. 22), s. 107; Housing Act 1974 (c. 44), Sched. 8, para. 2 (2).]

Certiorari will lie in respect of misconstruction of statutory words amounting to an error in law by a county court judge vested with jurisdiction to make a " final and conclusive " determination.

A tenant under a long lease claimed that the installation by him of a central heating system amounted to a structural alteration entitling him to a reduction in rateable value for the purposes of the Leasehold Reform Act 1967. The matter came before a county court judge, whose determination was by virtue of Sched. 8, para. 2 (2), of the 1974 Act " final and conclusive," who held that the work was not a structural alteration. The Divisional Court refused to issue certiorari. *Held*, allowing the tenant's appeal (Geoffrey Lane L.J. dissenting), that the wording of para. 2 (2) did not exclude the remedy of certiorari where the judge had erred in law in construing " structural alteration . . . or addition " within the definition of which the work here fell as it involved substantial alteration to the fabric of the house. (*R.* v. *Hurst, ex p. Smith* [1960] C.L.Y. 1107 and *Anisminic* v. *Foreign Compensation Commission* [1968] C.L.Y. 1866 applied.)

PEARLMAN *v.* KEEPERS AND GOVERNORS OF HARROW SCHOOL [1978] 3 W.L.R. 736, C.A.

2325. —— disciplinary body—whether available. See R. *v.* BOARD OF VISITORS OF HULL PRISON, *ex p.* ST. GERMAIN, § 2429.

2326. Chancery Division—business outside London—long vacation

The following Practice Direction was issued by the Chancery Division on July 14, 1978:

During the Long Vacation Vice Chancellor Blackett-Ord or his deputy will sit at the crown court, Courts of Justice, Crown Square, Manchester at 11 a.m. on Wednesdays August 2, 9, 16, 23, 30; September 6, 13, 20, 27 and on such other days as may be necessary for the purpose of hearing such applications which may require to be immediately or promptly heard as are within his jurisdiction and according to the practice in the Chancery Division are usually heard in court or by the judge in chambers personally.

Papers for use in court. The following papers must reach the cause clerk (Chancery Division) in the Manchester District Registry, Quay Street, Manchester M60 9DJ before 1 p.m. two days previous to the day on which the application is to be made:

(*a*) a certificate of counsel that the case requires to be immediately or promptly heard and stating concisely the reasons,

(*b*) a copy of the notice of motion bearing the district registry seal,

(*c*) a copy of the writ and of the pleadings (if any),

(*d*) unless the case is proceeding in the Manchester District Registry an extra copy of (*b*) and (*c*) above and office copy affidavits in support and in answer (if any).

If the case is proceeding in a district registry other than the Manchester District Registry, the papers should be lodged at that registry one day prior to the day on which they are to reach the cause clerk at Manchester for transmission to him. In emergencies papers in such cases may be sent to him direct by post.

Solicitors should apply at once to the clerk in court for the return of their papers as soon as the application has been disposed of.

When the vacation judge is not sitting, applications may be made, but only in cases of extreme urgency, to him personally. His address must first be obtained from the officer in charge of his list at the Manchester District Registry and telephonic communication to the vacation judge is not to be made except after reference to that officer, unless the registry is closed when the need first appears.

Application may also be made by prepaid letter, accompanied by counsel's brief, office copy affidavits in support and a minute on a separate sheet of papers signed by counsel, of the order to which he may consider the applicant entitled and also an envelope sufficiently stamped, capable of receiving the papers and addressed to The District Registrar, Manchester District Registry, Quay Street, Manchester M60 9DJ, to whom the papers will be returned by the Vice-Chancellor.

(1978) 122 S.J. 512.

2327. —— **setting down for trial—obligation on solicitors for case to be ready**

Brightman J. has warned solicitors that it is their duty to be ready for trial within 28 days of setting down unless an application is made for a date to be fixed. As in this case the delay was not the fault of the litigants, the hearing would be deferred and the action would not be put at the end of the list: RAMAGE-GIBSON v. RADCLIFF, *The Times,* March 9, 1978, Brightman J.

2328. —— **trial—listing of cases**

The following Practice Direction was issued by the Chancery Division on May 23, 1978:

In order to assist solicitors in foreseeing when their cases in the Chancery Division are likely to be heard, two improvements in the system of listing will be made as from the beginning of the next sittings on June 6, 1978. These will not affect cases for which a date has been fixed, or cases in Part 1 of the Witness List which, by agreement, are " floating " on and after some agreed date.

First, the notice of setting down, which the Clerk of the Lists sends to the solicitors for all parties as soon as a case in Part 2 of the Witness List or in the Non-Witness List is set down for hearing, will in future state a date on and after which the solicitors should watch the weekly Warned List, published each Friday, for further information. This date will be fixed according to the state of the list when the notice is sent out, and it will give warning that there is a strong probability that the case will be in the Warned List on or soon after that date.

Second, the weekly Warned List for cases in Part 2 of the Witness List, published each Friday, will in future, in addition to the present list of cases warned for hearing on or after the following Monday, contain a further list of cases warned for hearing on or after the following Monday week. This will ensure that at least a week's notice will be given before the case is in the list for hearing.

[1978] 1 W.L.R. 757; [1978] 2 All E.R. 645.

2329. The following Practice Direction was issued by Sir Robert Megarry V.-C. on November 27, 1978:

It may assist solicitors who have cases in Part 2 of the Witness List in the Chancery Division if I say something about the progress of that list. In recent weeks many cases have been disposed of, and so cases now waiting for hearing have the prospect of being heard sooner than was previously expected. One result is that solicitors who, under the procedure set out in the Practice Direction of May 23 last [1978] C.L.Y. 2328, have been advised to watch the Warned List as from the beginning of December or January are finding that their cases are beginning to come into the list now.

It must be emphasised that the date from which solicitors are advised to watch the Warned List does not, and cannot, give any guarantee that the case will not appear in the list earlier. It is necessarily no more than an estimate based on the information available at the time, given in an attempt to assist the profession. It is hoped that in normal circumstances the estimate will be reasonably accurate; but from time to time there are liable to be occasions, such as the present, when the progress of the list will outrun the estimate. All reasonable efforts will be made to assist those who are put in any difficulty by this acceleration; and it is hoped that solicitors will do their best to co-operate. In any case, those who have been advised to watch the Warned List as from the beginning of December or January next should watch it from now onwards.

The Times, November 28, 1978.

2330. Commercial Court—working party

The following Practice Note was issued by the Queen's Bench Division on February 15, 1978:

Since the Commercial Court was established in 1895, all concerned have sought to improve its procedures with the object of providing a speedy, efficient and therefore economical service. With a view to furthering this process, the Commercial Court Committee has established a Working Party to study the Court's procedures. The Working Party would welcome suggestions for improvements from those with experience of the work of the Court. They should be sent to Mr. J. L. Powell, the Secretary of the Commercial Court Committee, at Lord Chancellor's Office, Romney House, Marsham Street, London, SW1. [1978] 1 Lloyd's Rep. 423.

2331. Companies. See COMPANY LAW.

2332. Companies Court—long vacation—schemes and reductions

The following Practice Direction was issued by the Chancery Division on February 23, 1978:

1. Practice Direction No. 3 of 1977 [1977] C.L.Y. 280 set out arrangements for hearing in the long vacation, 1977, certain applications concerning schemes of arrangement and reductions of capital, capital redemption reserve funds and share premium accounts.

2. It has been decided to extend the arrangements set out in that Practice Direction to future long vacations, until further notice.

3. The days on which a judge of the Companies Court will be available for sitting will be an early Wednesday in August (this year August 9) and each Wednesday in September.

4. It is emphasised that any party wishing to make an application to the registrar or to have a petition heard by the judge during the long vacation under this Practice Direction should give the earliest possible warning of this fact to the office of the Companies Court Registrar before the long vacation begins. It will not be necessary at that stage to disclose the name of any party.

[1978] 1 W.L.R. 429; [1978] 1 All E.R. 820.

2333. Consent order —effect—enforceability

On the granting of a decree nisi in an undefended suit the parties resolved all matters in contention in an agreement, signed by them and the registrar, which was made a rule of court. Subsequently, W sought to commit H for breach of the agreement and H submitted the agreement was not an order of the court so there was no power to make a committal order. *Held*, dismissing H's preliminary point, the agreement had the same effect as an order or judgment of the court (*Green* v. *Rozen* [1955] C.L.Y. 2136 and *Pasley* v. *Pasley* [1964] C.L.Y. 1139 considered): HERBERT v. HERBERT (1978) 122 S.J. 826, A. S. Myerson, Q.C.

2334. —— family provision. See PRACTICE DIRECTION, § 3093.

2335. Contempt

A Green Paper has been published, inviting public discussion of the law on contempt of court. The paper raises four main questions for discussion: (1) the stage in legal proceedings at which the media should become strictly liable for contempt; (2) proposed defences against strict liability; (3) liability for conduct deliberately intended to prejudice legal proceedings; and (4) bringing pressure or influence to bear upon a party to legal proceedings. The paper is available from H.M.S.O. Cmnd. 7145. [45p.]

2336. —— committal—motion by litigant in person—Chancery Division

[R.S.C., Ord. 52, rr. 2, 4.]

In future, litigants in person in proceedings in the Chancery Division will be entitled to make applications to commit for contempt of court.

The practice of the Queen's Bench Division is to allow litigants in person to make applications for committal for contempt. It is undesirable for there to be material differences in practice between the divisions of the High Court and henceforth a similar liberty will be extended to litigants in person in the Chancery Division.

BEVAN v. HASTINGS JONES [1978] 1 W.L.R. 294, Goulding J.

2337. —— deliberate flouting of justices' ruling—identity of witness disclosed
[Official Secrets Act 1920 (c. 75), s. 8 (4).]
To publish deliberately the name of a witness whom a court had directed be identified only by an initial is a contempt of court.

At committal proceedings for offences under the Official Secrets Act 1920 the prosecution called as a witness a " Colonel B," whose name was disclosed in writing to the court and to counsel but not otherwise, the court acceding to the prosecution's application for his identity not to be disclosed in the interests of national safety. The respondent thereafter deliberately published Colonel B's real name. *Held*, that by deliberately flouting a valid ruling of the court, the respondents were in contempt (*Re Att.-Gen.'s Application; Att.-Gen.* v. *Butterworth* [1962] C.L.Y. 2384 applied).

ATT.-GEN. v. LEVELLER MAGAZINE [1978] 3 W.L.R. 395, D.C.

2338. —— inferior court—local valuation court
[General Rate Act 1967 (c. 9), s. 76; R.S.C., Ord. 52, r. 1 (2).]
A local valuation court acting pursuant to s. 76 of the General Rate Act 1967 is an " inferior court " within R.S.C., Ord. 52, r. 1, and is therefore entitled to protection from contempt.

The B.B.C. planned to re-broadcast a television programme about the efforts of a sect called " the Exclusive Brethren " to get rating relief for their places of worship in Andover. The programme dealt with issues about to be considered by a local valuation court. *Held*, that such a court was clearly entitled to protection from such a contempt. (Dicta of Fry L.J. in *Royal Aquarium and Summer and Winter Garden Society* v. *Parkinson* [1892] 1 Q.B. 431, at 446, applied; *Mersey Docks and Harbour Board* v. *West Derby Assessment Committee* [1932] 1 K.B. 40, distinguished.)

ATT.-GEN. v. BRITISH BROADCASTING CORP.; DIBLE v. BRITISH BROADCASTING CORP. [1978] 1 W.L.R. 477, D.C.

2339. —— injunction—restraint of publication—findings of Ministerial inquiry while action pending
[Aust.] An action arose from a contract for the construction of bridges on a railway line. While that action was pending, the Minister of Transport ordered an inquiry into the safety of bridges in general, including those which were the subject of the above action. E, party to that action, sought an injunction to restrain publication of the findings of the inquiry on the ground that publication would prejudice the fair trial of the action. *Held*, upon the Minister undertaking not to publish the findings unless he considered he was under a public duty to do so, the application should be refused. There is no body of law to suggest that a judge may restrain a Minister from performing one of his functions in good faith and intra vires. The court must protect (a) the public interest of the general community in ensuring that the judicial system remains unimpaired, and (b) the private interest of the litigants in ensuring that the particular trial in which they are involved is fairly conducted to a conclusion. (*Att.-Gen.* v. *Times Newspapers* [1973] C.L.Y. 2618 applied): EGAN v. COMMONWEALTH MINISTER FOR TRANSPORT (No. 2) (1976) 15 S.A.S.R. 408, S.Aust.Sup.Ct.

2340. —— redress for deprivation of liberty—jurisdiction
[Trinidad and Tobago (Constitution) Order 1962 (S.I. 1962 No. 1875), Sched. 2, ss. 1 (*a*), 2, 3, 6.]
S. 6 of the Constitution of Trinidad and Tobago gives to the High Court of those places jurisdiction to determine allegations of contraventions of human rights and fundamental freedoms.

M, a barrister, was imprisoned for seven days for contempt of court. He applied to the High Court claiming redress for his right (under s. 1 of the Constitution) not to be deprived of his liberty save by due process of law. The application failed. The committal order was subsequently quashed after he had served his sentence. His appeal against the failure of his application was later dismissed on the grounds that there had been no contravention of the Constitution. *Held*, allowing his appeal to the Judicial Committee of the Privy Council from the dismissal of that appeal, that there had been such a contravention and that (1) the High Court had jurisdiction to enquire whether there had been a contravention of the freedoms and rights given by the Constitution; (2) there had been such a contravention, the applicant not having been told the reason for his committal, and (3) the redress sought could and should include monetary compensation.

MAHARAJ *v.* ATT.-GEN. OF TRINIDAD AND TOBAGO (No. 2) [1978] 2 W.L.R. 902, P.C.

2341. Costs—discretion of judge—refusal of application to strike out proceedings

[Supreme Court of Judicature (Consolidation) Act 1925 (c. 49), ss. 50, 31 (1) (*h*); Patents Act 1949 (c. 87), s. 65.] The plaintiffs instituted proceedings in 1972 and 1974 alleging infringement of patents and misuse of confidential information. In 1976 the plaintiffs issued notice of intention to proceed, and the defendants applied to strike out both actions for want of prosecution. Whitford J. refused both applications, since no prejudice had occurred. He ordered the plaintiffs to pay the defendants' costs. The plaintiffs appealed. *Held*, (1) there was no ground on which the judge could exercise his discretion to order the plaintiffs to pay the defendants' costs; (2) an order that costs be in the cause should be substituted: SCHERER *v.* COUNTING INSTRUMENTS [1977] F.S.R. 569, Whitford J.

2342. —— examination of judgment debtor

The following Practice Direction was issued by the Queen's Bench Division on January 9, 1978:

In order to enable the more effective and more convenient exercise of the power to deal with the costs of an application orally to examine the judgment debtor and of the examination thereunder under R.S.C., Ord. 48, especially in cases where such an examination is ordered by the High Court to take place in the County Court, the Practice Form No. PF. 102, which provides the form of such an order and that such costs shall be "in the discretion of the master making the order," shall be amended by deleting the words set out above in quotes and substituting therefor the words "in the discretion of the master or registrar in whose court the examination has taken place."

2343. —— partner in court—difficult case

On the taxation of costs of a difficult case in the Court of Appeal, the registrar reduced from £75 to £25 a day a solicitor's claim for attendance allowance at court. On appeal, *held*, the scale allowed £3–£15 a day which was insufficient to cover the costs of an experienced solicitor. Here there was no need to disturb the registrar's assessment: MARTIN *v.* MARTIN, *The Times*, May 17, 1978, Payne J.

2344. —— taxation

The following Practice Direction was issued by the Chief Taxing Master on April 4, 1978:

A rearrangement of the procedure for expediting the work of the post-taxation section of the Supreme Court Taxing Office will take effect on June 6, and for this purpose:

1. The masters and their clerks will be divided into two groups A and B as under:

Group A	
Masters	Chambers room
Chief Master Graham-Green	
Master Matthews	
Master Horne	293
Master Berkeley	

Group B

Masters		*Chambers room*
Master Razzall		
Master Clews		315
Master Wright		
Master Martyn		

2. The post taxation section, at present located on the third floor room 252, will be divided between the two groups of chambers and located on the second floor in rooms 293 and 315.

3. The rota clerk will remain in room 294.

4. From the above mentioned date therefore, all work relating to vouching and lodging of completed bills for certificate and all other queries will be dealt with according to the group to which it relates, namely: Group A, room 293; Group B, room 315.

122 S.J. 304.

2345. —— —— **basis—liquidation.** See Re NATION LIFE INSURANCE CO. (IN LIQUIDATION), § 248.

2346. —— —— **solicitor's professional misconduct.** See SHARP v. SHARP, § 2829.

2347. —— —— **computerised time sheets**

Practising solicitors who make use of computing systems to record costs should retain their files, including attendance notes and time sheets, until the conclusion of taxation and the review of taxation, probably even until the payment of costs: *Re* KINGSLEY (DECD.), *The Times,* June 17, 1978, Payne J.

2348. —— —— **power to allow objection to taxation out of time**

[R.S.C., Ords. 3, 62.] After divorce and ancillary proceedings, W's solicitors claimed £10,000 costs and the registrar agreed that sum on taxation on July 14, 1978. H's solicitors did not attempt to lodge objections until August 15, after the 14 days allowed by Ord. 62 had expired, as the member of the firm dealing with the case had left. *Held*, allowing H's appeal from the registrar's refusal to grant him leave to extend the time available for filing objections, the discretionary power given by Ord. 3 extended to such applications despite the wording of Ord. 62. (*Re Furber* (1898) S.J. 613; *Brown* v. *Youde* [1967] C.L.Y. 3123 and *Maltby* v. *Freeman* [1976] C.L.Y. 2128 applied): THORNE *v.* THORNE, *The Times,* November 10, 1978, Comyn J.

2349. —— **whether order should be made against Legal Aid Fund**

Following the practice direction in *Maynard* v. *Osmond* [1978] C.L.Y. 2395, the Court of Appeal made an order for £100 costs against a legally aided appellant whose appeal had been withdrawn and said that it was minded to make an order for the balance of the costs against the Legal Aid Fund, but the order was not to be drawn up for 10 weeks to enable the fund to make representations: SCARTH *v.* JACOBS-PATON, *The Times,* November 2, 1978, C.A.

2350. Court of Appeal—transcripts

The following Practice Note was issued by Lord Denning M.R. on February 24, 1978:

Before we start this morning, I would like to say a word about the transcripts which have been kept of the Court of Appeal judgments. For many years Mr. Fisher of the Bar Library has instigated and carried on a system of indexing and calendaring all the transcripts of the Civil Divisions of the Court of Appeal. This has proved to be of the greatest value. The transcripts have been kept in the Bar Library from which people have been readily able to find transcripts on the subjects they have been dealing with and have been able to refer to them whenever they wished. This, if I may say so, has been almost entirely due to the excellent work of Mr. Fisher who has been in the Bar Library for so many years. Anybody who wanted to has been able to go to the Bar Library for these transcripts, and their references are also in the reports.

Now there has been a change. In future the transcripts are going to be kept in the Supreme Court Library. The work is going to be continued, as it has been so valuable, but the transcripts are going to be reported in a slightly different way. For example, if there is a case like *Smith* v. *Fraser* on July 19, 1977, it will now appear as " *Smith* v. *Fraser*, July 19, 1977, Court of Appeal (Civil Division) Transcript No. 178 of 1977, C.A." So in future people will know where they are. In fact the transcripts have already been transferred from the Library to the Supreme Court Library.

I would like to take this opportunity of thanking Mr. Fisher and all those concerned for the great and valuable work which they have done.

NOTE

On April 19, 1951, Viscount Jowitt L.C. issued a direction for the taking of an official note of all judgments in the Court of Appeal (Civil Division), and the indexing an filing of a copy of each in the Bar Library. From the beginning of January 1978, these copies have been held in the Supreme Court Library. Parties requiring copies of them can obtain them from the shorthand writers on payment of the usual charges.

These arrangements do not apply to transcripts of the judgments of the Court of Appeal (Criminal Division). These are filed in the Criminal Appeal Office which may be asked for assistance in appropriate circumstances, *e.g.* where counsel is aware of an unreported case or where clarification of an existing report is required. Counsel who propose to refer to such transcripts should satisfy themselves that arrangements are being made for copies to be available to the court and to other counsel concerned: see statement from Lord Chancellor's office of February 1978.

[1978] 1 W.L.R. 600.

2351. Crown Court—business—Practice Direction. See § 453.

2352. Damages—assessment—copy of judgment

The following Practice Direction was issued by the Queen's Bench Division on January 9, 1978:

In order to reduce the expense and delay in bespeaking an office copy of the judgment for the purpose of obtaining an appointment before a master for the assessment of damages or interest under R.S.C., Ord. 37, the practice of requiring an office copy of the judgment has been discontinued.

For this purpose, a plain copy of the judgment certified by the solicitor of a party to be a true copy thereof, or alternatively a photo-copy of the judgment bearing the seal of the court will suffice, and this should be used for the recording of the appropriate fee, the stamp for the assignment of a master, the date and time specified by him for the appointment, and for the recording of the Master's finding.

2353. Discovery—affidavits used in matrimonial proceedings—use in other proceedings—public interest

Where there two conflict, the public interest of encouraging the fullest disclosure of means in matrimonial proceedings by protecting its confidentiality outweighs the public interest of a full disclosure of information in an application for security costs.

X was involved in two cases in different divisions of the High Court. In the Family Division, he was defendant in his former wife's application to vary a maintenance agreement. In those proceedings he had filed two affidavits of means. In the Queen's Bench Division, X's company had applied as plaintiff for summary judgment in an action against D Co. D Co. applied for security for costs, exhibiting copies of X's two affidavits of means in the Family Division case. X sought an injunction in the Chancery Division restraining D Co. from disclosing or using the affidavits, and an order to deliver them up. *Held*, granting the injunction and the order, that matrimonial proceedings involved the status and future provision for the parties, often for their whole lives, whereas security for costs was a relatively minor matter of litigation, and the fullest disclosure of means in matrimonial proceedings should be encouraged by protecting its confidentiality. (Dicta of Lord Diplock in *D.* v. *National Society for the Prevention of Cruelty to Children* [1977] C.L.Y. 2324, of Talbot J. in *Distillers Co.* (*Bio-chemicals*) v. *Times Newspapers* [1975] C.L.Y. 2616, and of

Lord Denning M.R. in *Riddick* v. *Thames Board Mills* [1977] C.L.Y. 1368 applied.)

MEDWAY v. DOUBLELOCK [1978] 1 All E.R. 1261, Goulding J.

2354. —— Anton Piller order—jurisdiction

The plaintiffs sought *ex parte* an *Anton Piller* order, and further sought an order that (1) the defendants should permit the plaintiffs' representatives to enter and inspect any other premises under the control of the defendants; and that (2) two addresses in Scotland be included in the order. *Held,* (1) only in special circumstances would the court make an *Anton Piller* order describing the premises to be searched in general terms; (2) the court exercised its discretion not to make the order in respect of premises in Scotland: PROTECTOR ALARMS v. MAXIM ALARMS [1978] F.S.R. 442, Goulding J.

2355. —— confidential documents disclosed in English patent proceedings—whether use in Dutch proceedings permissible

Two simultaneous actions were taking place, one in England, the other in Holland. A file of selected documents, disclosed on discovery and released from confidentiality, was agreed in the English action. The appellants wished to use the file in the Dutch proceedings and so appealed against the refusal of an order releasing them from their undertaking that the files were not to be disclosed to anyone else. *Held,* in dismissing the appeal, there was a real possibility that as a result of the contents of the file being made available as evidence, the respondents would be faced with the problem of not putting forward all the confidential documents (of which the agreed file was but a part) which might be material to explain or amplify the file, that would otherwise be made available to all the world. The file could therefore not be used in the Dutch proceedings: HALCON INTERNATIONAL INC. v. SHELL TRANSPORT AND TRADING CO. (1978) 122 S.J. 645, C.A.

2356. —— hospital records—no power to limit production to medical advisers

[Administration of Justice Act 1970 (c. 31), s. 32 (1).]

Where a party to proceedings is entitled to production by a third party of hospital records, the court has no power to limit production to persons other than the party concerned.

The defendants in a personal injuries action sought an order under s. 32 of the 1970 Act directing the appellant board to produce hospital records relating to the treatment of the plaintiff in the action. The appellants contended that such order should be limited to production to medical advisers nominated by the parties, but the order made required production to the defendant's legal advisers. *Held,* dismissing the appeal, that s. 32 (1) specified that production was to be " to the applicant," which would include his legal advisers, and did not empower the court to order or limit production to some other person. (*Dunning* v. *United Liverpool Hospital's Board of Governors* [1973] C.L.Y. 2645, *Davidson* v. *Lloyd Aircraft Services* [1974] C.L.Y. 2987 and *Deistung* v. *South West Metropolitan Regional Hospital Board* [1975] C.L.Y. 2611 overruled.)

McIVOR v. SOUTHERN HEALTH AND SOCIAL SERVICES BOARD [1978] 1 W.L.R. 757, H.L.

2357. —— industrial tribunal—complaint of racial discrimination

On a complaint of racial discrimination to an industrial tribunal, the applicant obtained an order for discovery of certain documents relating to fellow-employees. The employers appealed on the ground that disclosure would be a breach of confidentiality. *Held,* allowing the appeal, and applying *Science Research Council* v. *Nassé* [1978] C.L.Y. 1034, that the chairman of the tribunal should look at such documents at the hearing of the complaint and see if there was any prima facie prospect of the confidential material being relevant to issues in the litigation, and if, therefore, it was a case in which the interests of justice required that discovery should be ordered: BRITISH RAILWAYS BOARD v. NATARAJAN (1978) 122 S.J. 861, E.A.T.

2358. —— matrimonial proceedings—company documents. See B. v. B., § 809.

2359. —— pre-trial—identification of potential parties

There is no reason in principle why a court should not order a party to give information as to other potential parties during the course of an action on an ex parte application.

P, on an ex parte application, sought an injunction pending trial restraining D from taking mussels from his fishery. He also sought an order that D identify persons on board his boat and on other boats who had also been seen fishing on P's fishery. *Held,* making that order and granting the injunction that it was proper to do so where circumstances required it, in this case, if D was innocent, he would suffer no harm by disclosing the information and P's fishery appeared, on his case, to be in imminent danger from poachers.

LOOSE *v.* WILLIAMSON [1978] 1 W.L.R. 639, Goulding J.

2360. —— privilege—extent—libel action

[Can.] D, insurance adjusters, were hired by an insurance company to investigate a claim made by P; they wrote reports which P alleged to be libellous. P then commenced action for libel and applied for an order directing D to produce documents which D claimed were privileged. *Held,* the documents were privileged only in P's action on the policy of insurance, and not in the action for libel, as the privilege did not extend to parties outside the first action. (*Schneider* v. *Leigh* [1955] C.L.Y. 2119 applied): LISZKAY *v.* BROUWER [1978] 3 W.W.R. 566, Brit.Col.Sup.Ct.

2361. —— —— whether accident inquiry report privileged

W, the widow of a train driver brought a claim against British Rail Board under the Fatal Accidents Acts. On discovery of documents, the Board did not disclose their notes of the inquiry held concerning the accident, stating that the purpose of the inquiry was to assess the legal liability and the notes were therefore privileged. W challenged the claim of privilege. *Held,* Lord Denning M.R. dissenting, the documents were obtained for the purpose of helping the Board's solicitors in preparing its case in anticipated litigation, and were therefore privileged. (*Birmingham & Midland Water Omnibus Co.* v. *London and North Western Railway Co.* [1913] 3 K.B. 850 and *Ogden* v. *London Electric Railway Co.* (1933) 49 T.L.R. 542 followed): WAUGH *v.* BRITISH RAILWAYS BOARD, *The Times,* July 29, 1978, C.A.

2362. —— statement to police—defamation proceedings

[N.Z.] A made a statement to police when he was charged. The prosecutor referred to the statement in detail, which included allegations of criminal conduct on T's part. In defamation proceedings against A, T claimed an order for production of the statement and inspection. *Held,* that it was not realistic to say that the maker of the statement would be influenced in his willingness to give the police information by the prospect of disclosure. Accordingly disclosure could not be refused on the ground of public policy: APPERLEY *v.* TIPPENE [1978] Crim.L.R. 632, N.Z.C.A.

2363. —— whether production injurious to public interest

In an action brought against the Bank of England by B Co., concerning the purchase by the Bank of shares held by B Co. as an attempt to help B Co.'s financial difficulties, the Bank refused to produce certain documents relating to communications between the Bank and the Government regarding the transaction. *Held,* these documents were high-level policy documents which should be withheld from production in the public interest. They did not materially assist B Co.'s case: BURMAH OIL CO. *v.* BANK OF ENGLAND; ATT.-GEN. INTERVENING, *The Times,* July 29, 1978, Foster J.

2364. Documents—photostatic copies—legibility

The following statement was made by Megarry V.-C. on February 3, 1978: Megarry V.-C. said that in recent weeks a number of cases came before him in which photostatic copies of documents provided for the use of the court, particularly as exhibits, had been far from legible. In some cases the copies had been so pallid and indistinct that the documents had had to be deciphered word by word, and guesses made about words or phrases which disclosed only an odd letter or two of their content. Sometimes the paper had been improperly centred in the copying process, so that one or two lines had been omitted from the bottom of the page, or the first half dozen letters of each line been omitted at the left hand margin. Some copies managed to combine those faults, and in one recent case most of the clause on which the whole case turned was put before his lordship in a deplorably indistinct copy which had been heavily underlined, and the solicitors concerned had failed to bring the original to court. His lordship wished to make it plain that he regarded solicitors as being personally responsible for the legibility and completeness of any copies of documents that they put before the court. It was not enough for them to assume that any photostatic copies would be legible and complete: they or some responsible member of their staff must see that in fact they were in that state. If in future illegible or incomplete copies of relevant documents were put before the court, the solicitor concerned should expect to be required to provide an explanation, either in person or by affidavit, and he should also expect there to be consequences in costs. In this connection his lordship drew attention once again to the requirements of para. 5 of the *Practice Direction* [1970] C.L.Y. 2245, to be found at p. 632 of the current Supreme Court Practice.

(1978) 122 S.J. 147.

2365. Domestic violence—injunction. See PRACTICE DIRECTION, § 1595.

2366. Evidence. See EVIDENCE.

2367. Extension of time—summonses

The following Practice Direction was issued by the Queen's Bench Division on January 13, 1978:

1. As from February 1, 1978, a summons for hearing by a master of the Queen's Bench Division asking only for the extension of any period of time will be issued for hearing before the Practice Master of the day at 10.30 a.m. and will be made returnable two days from the date of its issue, excluding Saturdays, Sundays, any Bank Holidays or other day on which the Central Office is closed.

2. Such a summons must be served at least one day before the day specified therein for its hearing (see R.S.C., Ord. 32, Rule 3).

3. It should also be emphasised that the mere issue or service of such a summons will not by itself operate to extend any relevant period of time or to stay proceedings.

4. This Practice Direction will not extend to District Registries.

[1978] 1 W.L.R. 131; [1978] 1 All E.R. 723.

2368. Family Division—directions for trial—defended cases—pre-trial review

The following Practice Direction was issued by the Family Division on December 19, 1978.

1. The proviso to r. 33 (4) of the Matrimonial Causes Rules 1977 enables a registrar to treat a request for directions for trial in a defended cause as a summons for directions under R.S.C. Ord. 25. In that event, the registrar is required to give the parties notice of a date, time and place at which the request will be considered (a " pre-trial review "). The provisions of R.S.C. Ord. 34, r. 5 (3) (which provide for the parties to furnish the Court with any information it may require as to the state of readiness of the case for trial) are applied to defended matrimonial causes by r. 46 (4) of the Matrimonial Causes Rules 1977.

2. As from the beginning of the Hilary Term 1979, every request for directions for trial relating to a defended matrimonial cause proceeding in the Principal Registry will be referred to a registrar for a pre-trial review appointment to be fixed. Appointments are likely to be fixed for hearing from February onwards.

3. The prime objective behind the pre-trial review procedure is to enable the registrar to ascertain the true state of the case and to give such directions as are necessary for its " just, expeditious and economic disposal." In practice, in those District Registries where the system of pre-trial review has been applied to matrimonial causes, it has been found that under the registrar's guidance the parties are often able to compose their differences, or to drop unsubstantial charges and defences, and to concentrate on the main issues in dispute. Experience in the District Registries has shown that, following pre-trial review, many cases proceed undefended under the special procedure, with

consent orders as to financial provision or in respect of the custody of, or access
to, the children. Where contested issues remain, the registrar is able to give
directions to facilitate their expeditious determination at the subsequent hearing
before the Judge.

4. To avoid possible adjournments and delay, it is especially important
that the parties are represented on a pre-trial review hearing by their legal
advisers who are fully conversant with the facts of the case, including Counsel
if he has been so instructed. The personal attendance of the parties on the
review hearing is normally desirable.

This Practice Direction is issued with the approval of the President of the
Family Division.

[1979] 1 W.L.R. 2.

2369. —— injunctions—ex parte applications. See PRACTICE NOTE, § 1602.

2370. Fees

SUPREME COURT FEES (AMENDMENT) ORDER 1978 (No. 1244 (L.30)), made
under the Supreme Court of Judicature (Consolidation) Act 1925 (c. 49), s. 213,
operative on October 2, 1978; increases to £25 the fee payable on the issue of
a writ or other originating process in the High Court except in the case of a
writ for a liquidated sum not exceeding £2,000, and replaces all existing fees
payable in the Court Funds Office with a new fee payable on a search of the
records of unclaimed balances.

SUPREME COURT (NON-CONTENTIOUS PROBATE) FEES (AMENDMENT) ORDER
1978 (No. 1298 (L.32)), made under the Supreme Court of Judicature (Consolidation) Act 1925, s. 213, and the Public Offices Fees Act 1879 (c. 58), ss. 2,
3; operative on October 2, 1978; amends S.I. 1975 No. 1344, as amended by
substituting for the scale of charges an ad valorem fee of £2·50 per £1,000 of
the value estate where it does not exceed £100,000 while raising the figure at
which no fee is payable to £2,000.

2371. Foreign judgment. See CONFLICT OF LAWS.

2372. Funds

FUNDS IN COURT (INVESTMENT) (AMENDMENT) REGULATIONS 1978 (No. 468)
[10p], made under the Administration of Justice Act 1965 (c. 2), s. 12 (1);
operative on April 25, 1978; amend S.I. 1970 No. 1400 by adding to the list of
prescribed securities.

SUPREME COURT FUNDS (AMENDMENT) RULES 1978 (No. 751 (L. 16)) [20p],
made under the Administration of Justice Act 1965, s. 7 (1); operative
on July 3, 1978; amend S.I. 1975 No. 1803 to enable funds ordered by the
E.A.T. to be lodged in court to be dealt with by the Accountant General
and to enable the court to order the final disposal of effects which have
remained deposited in court unclaimed for more than 25 years.

**2373. High Court—transfer of proceedings to different division—judicial discretion—
convenience**

[Supreme Court of Judicature (Consolidation) Act 1925 (c. 49), s. 58; R.S.C.,
Ord. 72, r. 1, Ord. 88, r. 2.]

A judge may of his own motion transfer a case from one division of the
High Court to another, if the action could properly be brought in the other
division and if it would be more convenient for the case to be transferred.

The plaintiff bank sought summary judgment upon an action brought by it
in the Queen's Bench Division for the recovery of moneys owed by the defendant. Judgment was entered by the Master, and the defendant's application for
the action to be transferred to the Chancery Division (since the moneys were
secured by a mortgage, although no action had been taken to foreclose) was
dismissed. *Held*, dismissing the defendant's appeal, that although the court had
power to order such transfer, it was not appropriate here, but that since the
case involved banking it would be assigned to the Commercial Court.

MIDLAND BANK *v.* STAMPS [1978] 1 W.L.R. 635, Donaldson J.

**2374. House of Lords—costs—petition for leave to appeal—petitions referred and not
referred for oral hearing.**

The following Practice Direction was issued by the House of Lords on
November 10, 1977:

The Appeal Committee have determined:

1. Where a petition for leave to appeal is *not* referred for an oral hearing, costs may be awarded as follows: (*a*) To a legally aided petitioner, reasonable costs incurred in preparing papers for the Appeal Committee. (*b*) To a legally aided respondent, only those costs necessarily incurred in attending client, petitioners' agents, perusing petition and entering appearance. (*c*) To an unassisted respondent where the petitioner is legally aided, payment out of the legal aid fund of costs incurred by him at (*b*) above. (*d*) Where neither party is legally aided, respondents will be allowed only the costs at (*b*) above. Applications for such party and party costs must be made in writing to the Judicial Office.

2. Where a petition *is* referred for an oral hearing, application for costs must be made at the conclusion of the hearing.

3. Direction No. 9 in the Directions as to Procedure and Standing Orders is amended accordingly and should be read subject to the terms of this direction.

4. This direction also applies to petitions for leave to appeal in criminal matters.

[1978] 1 W.L.R. 132.

2375. Industrial court. See EMPLOYMENT; TRADE AND INDUSTRY; TRADE UNIONS.

2376. Injunction—Mareva injunction—foreign debenture having priority

A *Mareva* injunction gives a right *in personam* and does not prevail against a pre-existing debenture, even if the debenture consists of a floating charge which does not crystallise until after the granting of the injunction.

The claimants were in dispute with respondents, an Irish company with no place of business in the United Kingdom, concerning a charterparty. Pending determination of arbitration the claimants obtained a *Mareva* injunction restraining the respondents from removing from the jurisdiction assets up to the value of U.S. $700,000. Thereafter the arbitration was compromised but the respondents failed to pay the agreed amount and the claimants obtained judgment for $282,000. The respondents' only asset in England was some £70,000 on bank deposit. A receiver appointed under a debenture registered in Ireland prior to the dispute arising, whereunder a floating charge upon all the respondents' assets had been created, applied to discharge the injunction. The floating charge had crystallised after the making of the injunction but prior to the claimants obtaining the money judgment. Donaldson J. discharged the injunction. *Held,* dismissing the claimants' appeal, that the application to discharge would be treated as if made by the debenture-holder, since he and not the receiver was the proper applicant; that the debenture-holder had priority over the claimants since the relevant date was that of the creation of the floating charge and not its crystallisation; and that the respondents had no rights of disposition over the deposit account, so that a *Mareva* injunction directed to them was of no effect in respect of the debenture-holders' rights. (*Rasu Maritime S.A.* v. *Perusahaan Pertambangan Minyak Dan Gas Bumi Negara (Pertamina)* [1977] C.L.Y. 2346, *The Siskina; Siskina (Cargo Owners)* v. *Distos Compania Naviera S.A.* [1977] C.L.Y. 2344 and *Galbraith* v. *Grimshaw* [1910] A.C. 508, considered.)

CRETANOR MARITIME CO. *v.* IRISH MARINE MANAGEMENT [1978] 1 W.L.R. 966, C.A.

2377. —— to restrain criminal offence—unauthorised recordings

[Dramatic and Musical Performers' Protection Acts 1925–1972.]

When a private or corporate person can show a private right which is being interfered with by a criminal act, causing or threatening to cause him special damage over and above the damage to the public in general, the court has jurisdiction in equity to grant an injunction ex parte restraining the defendant from damaging that interest.

The Dramatic and Musical Performers' Protection Acts 1925–1972 make it a criminal offence to record dramatic or musical performers or to distribute records without permission. Thirty performers and authorised recording companies applied for an injunction against a " bootlegger " who was damaging their interest by making unauthorised recordings of their performances. The nature of the injunction sought was that of an " Anton Piller " order, which was the order commonly made against " pirates " who infringed copyright by copying and distributing records without authorisation. No such civil wrong was committed by " bootleggers," merely the crime prohibited by the Acts. The application was refused at first instance. On appeal, *held,* allowing the appeal (Shaw L.J. dissenting), that since the recording companies were clearly losing sales, and the performers royalties, there was an interference with a private right causing damage over and above damage to the public in general, and the court would exercise its jurisdiction to grant injunctions restraining the defendant from committing any acts in contravention of s. 1 of the Act of 1958 or interfering with contractual relations and ordering him to deliver up all recordings in his possession. (*Anton Piller K.G.* v. *Manufacturing Processes* [1976] C.L.Y. 2136 and dicta in *Gouriet* v. *Union of Post Office Workers* [1977] C.L.Y. 690 applied; *Institute of Patent Agents* v. *Lockwood* [1894] A.C. 347; *Musical Performers' Protection Association* v. *British International Pictures* (1930) 46 T.L.R. 485 and *Apple Corps.* v. *Lingasong* [1977] C.L.Y. 408 distinguished.)

Ex p. ISLAND RECORDS [1978] 3 W.L.R. 23, C.A.

2378. —— to restrain payment of moneys—whether " just or convenient "

[Aust.] A contract between a contractor and the Melbourne and Met. Board of Works for the laying of pipes, reserved to the Board a discretion to pay money directly to an approved sub-contractor if it was established to the satisfaction of the engineer in chief of the Board that the contractor had defaulted in payment of moneys due and payable to the approved sub-contractor. Money was owed by the Board to the contractor under the contract. P, a sub-contractor, claimed to be entitled to payment for work done under the sub-contract and damages from the contractor and sought injunctions to restrain payment by the Board to the contractor of the money owing under the contract. The contractor disputed that it was liable to P under the sub-contract and in addition complained that P had breached the sub-contract and it advanced a cross-claim for damages. *Held,* that (1) P had not established a prima facie case that the contractor would, after taking into account the cross-claim, be shown to be liable to P; (2) in the circumstances, it had not been demonstrated that it was " just and convenient " that an interlocutory injunction be granted. (*Nippon Yusen Kaisha* v. *Karageorgis* [1975] C.L.Y. 3167. and *Marera Compania Naviera S.A.* v. *International Bulk Carriers* [1975] C.L.Y. 3169 considered): J. D. BARRY PTY. *v.* M. & E. CONSTRUCTIONS PTY. [1978] V.R. 185, Vict.Sup.Ct.

2379. Interlocutory injunction—restraining defendant from dealing with personalty in dispute—plaintiff creditor—fraudulent conveyance

[Can.] P, the holder of two promissory notes made by D, sued D on the notes and also for the price of goods sold and delivered by P to D. Further, P claimed to set aside a conveyance between D and a third party of a quantity of personal property, and claimed an interim and permanent injunction restraining D from selling or dealing with the goods in question. *Held,* where an action is brought to set aside a conveyance of personal property, an interlocutory injunction may be granted restraining D from dealing with the property pending the outcome of the action if the applicant can demonstrate that he is a creditor, and if it can be shown that fraud has been committed. It is sufficient if the court is satisfied that there is a strong indication that the conveyance may have been fraudulent: ROBERT REISER INC. *v.* NADORE FOOD PROCESSING EQUIPMENT (1978) 81 D.L.R. 278, Ontario High Ct.

2380. Interlocutory proceedings—appeal out of time

On October 4, 1977, an order was made that (a) the defence be struck out unless further and better particulars were served within 21 days; (b) unless the plaintiff served further and better particulars of the Reply and Re-Amended Statement of Claim, the claim should be struck out. On December 7, the plaintiff issued a summons. *Held,* despite the plaintiff's failure to serve the further and better particulars the court would exercise its discretion to extend time until December 8. Leave to appeal out of time against the October 4 order was granted. The defendant's particulars complied with the order and

the defence and counterclaim should not be struck out: R. LAWS PLAN-BUILD
v. GLOBE PICTURE THEATRES (BRISTOL) (1978) 8 Build.L.R. 29, Judge Fay Q.C.

2381. Joinder of parties—effects of limitation—adjournment to a judge

[R.S.C., Ord. 32, r. 14.]

A party added to proceedings as a defendant after expiry of the limitation
period is not debarred from raising the defence of limitation by reason of the
writ having been issued within the limitation period.

B, a solicitor, was trustee of a testatrix's estate, of which the plaintiff was
the residuary beneficiary. B was in partnership with K until 1971, each retaining
an interest in the other's practice until B's death in 1973, whereupon B's
wife discovered (and notified the plaintiff accordingly) that B had fraudulently
converted part of the testatrix's estate. The plaintiff in 1975 issued proceedings
against B's wife as his personal representative. In 1977 the plaintiff sought by
summons to add K as a defendant on the grounds that as B's partner he was
liable for B's fraudulent acts. K opposed the application on the grounds,
inter alia, that if he was so added he would be deprived of the limitation
defence. After making the order adding K as a defendant, the Master declined
K's application to adjourn the summons to the judge because K was not at that
stage a " party " within the meaning of R.S.C. Ord. 32, r. 14. *Held,* allowing
K's motion for the summons to be adjourned to the judge, that Ord. 32, r. 14
conferred the right to require an adjournment to the judge upon any party
to the summons and not solely to existing parties to the proceedings; but that
K could properly be joined as a defendant since he would not thereby be
debarred from raising the defence of limitation (although in any event since the
plaintiff could not have discovered the fraud until 1973, she could still commence
proceedings against K). (*Lucy* v. *W. T. Henley's Telegraph Works* [1969]
C.L.Y. 2103 distinguished.)

GAWTHROP v. BOULTON [1978] 3 All E.R. 615, Walton J.

2382. Judges

MINIMUM NUMBER OF JUDGES ORDER 1978 (No. 1057) [10p], made under
the Administration of Justice Act 1968 (c. 5), s. 1 (2); operative on July 25,
1978; increases the maximum number of ordinary judges of the Court of
Appeal to 18.

2383. The Home Secretary has published the Report of the Working Party on
Judicial Studies and Information (chairman: Bridge L.J.). The report recommends that judicial study programmes for newly appointed judges should be
set up, to prepare judges for their role as sentencers. The report is available
from H.M.S.O. [£1].

2384. Judgment—entry—consent order—whether can be set aside

[Aust.] Following terms of settlement arrived at between the parties to an
action in the court, judgment by consent was entered for P. Subsequently D
gave notice of motion to set the judgment aside which was consented to by P,
new terms of settlement having been arrived at between the parties. *Held,* while,
as a general rule, a perfected judgment cannot be set aside, the court possesses
inherent jurisdiction to set aside a judgment by consent of the parties, providing
that to do so would cause no particular injury to a third party. Accordingly,
as there was a suggestion that third parties might be so affected, the court
should decline to make an order unless satisfied that third party rights were
either unaffected by or not material to the setting aside of the judgment.
(Dicta of Romer J. in *Ainsworth* v. *Wilding* [1896] 1 Ch. 673 at p. 677
applied; *Hammond* v. *Schofield* [1891] 1 Q.B. 453 referred to): PERMANENT
TRUSTEE CO. (CANBERRA) v. STOCKS & HOLDINGS (CANBERRA) PTY. (1976) 28
F.L.R. 195, Sup.Ct. of Aust.Cap.Terr.

2385. —— stay of execution—interests of all creditors

[Rules of the Supreme Court, Ord. 47, s. 1.] The plaintiffs had obtained
judgment for £7,561, the price of programmes ordered by the defendant football club; but a stay of execution, upon terms that the club should pay 20 per
cent. of the debt within 28 days, was ordered by the Divisional Court. The
club had recently acquired bad debts, but its other unsecured creditors had
agreed to an informal moratorium, and the club was now in a position to

begin paying off its debts. *Held*, dismissing the plaintiffs' appeal against the staying order, the court must consider the other creditors in exercising its discretion over staying a judgment. (Dicta of Megaw L.J. in *Burston Finance* v. *Godfrey* [1976] C.L.Y. 143, and of Buckley L.J. in *Rainbow* v. *Moorgate Properties* [1975] C.L.Y. 2596, applied): PRESTIGE PUBLICATIONS v. CHELSEA FOOTBALL AND ATHLETIC CO., *The Times*, April 29, 1978, C.A.

2386. Judicial statistics

The annual report of judicial statistics for 1977 has been published. It contains, inter alia, statistics relating to the House of Lords, Court of Appeal, the High Court, and the Judicial Committee of the Privy Council. The report is available from H.M.S.O. (Cmnd. 7254) [£3·25].

2387. Juries. See JURIES.

2388. Jurisdiction—leave to serve outside jurisdiction

[R.S.C., Ord. 11, r. 1 (1) (*h*).] If a plaintiff avers that false or negligent misrepresentations have been made in telephone conversations or telex to him in this country by someone outside the jurisdiction, then his action is founded on a tort committed within the jurisdiction within Ord. 11, r. 1 (1) (*h*), and he may apply for leave to serve out of the jurisdiction. (*Cordova Land Co.* v. *Victor Bros Inc.* [1966] C.L.Y. 9912 and *Monro* v. *American Cyanamid & Chemical Corp.* [1944] 1 K.B. 42 distinguished): DIAMOND v. BANK OF LONDON AND MONTREAL, *The Times*, November 10, 1978, C.A.

2389. —— mortgage action—property not liable to be rated. See P. B. FROST v. GREEN, § 2463.

2390. —— natural forum for action—stay of proceedings

An action begun in England may be stayed where (a) the defendant is able to satisfy the court that there is another forum to whose jurisdiction he is amenable in which justice can be done between the parties at substantially less inconvenience or expense, and (b) the stay does not deprive the plaintiff of a legitimate personal or juridical advantage which would be available to him if he invoked the jurisdiction of the English court.

Four Scotsmen living and working in Scotland sustained injuries in industrial accidents in Scotland. All the defendants were English companies having their registered offices in England. The plaintiffs, on the advice of experienced solicitors, issued proceedings in England. The defendant companies applied to stay the actions in England, leaving the plaintiffs to bring their claims in Scotland, the natural forum. They contended that the disadvantage to them of contesting the claims in England was oppressive and that the plaintiffs had shown no reasonable justification for choosing to litigate in England. They further alleged that there had recently been a deliberate policy of bringing, in English courts, proceedings arising out of Scottish industrial accidents where the only connection with England was that the defendants were English companies registered in England. They claimed that their cases should be considered in the light of the cumulative effect of that policy. The plaintiffs relied upon the affidavits of their solicitors which contended that damages might be higher, and the legal process shorter and cheaper, in England. In the first two cases, Goff J. refused to stay the actions, and his decision was upheld on appeal. In the other two cases, Griffiths J. considered himself bound by the decision of the Court of Appeal. The defendants appealed. *Held*, allowing the appeals, that the defendants had shown that the natural forum was Scotland, where they could be tried at substantially less inconvenience and expense, and the plaintiffs had failed to discharge the consequent onus upon them of showing that they would be deprived of some real personal or juridical advantage. The actions should be stayed. *Per* Lord Diplock: in so deciding, it was relevant to consider substantial waste of time and effort if it became a common practice to bring in England actions arising out of industrial injuries in Scotland when the matters were referred by trade unions to English solicitors acting for them. (Test in *St. Pierre* v. *South American Stores* [1936] 1 K.B. 382, 393, C.A., modified; *The Atlantic Star* [1973] C.L.Y. 2702, H.L., explained; decision of Court of Appeal [1977] C.L.Y. 2359 reversed.)

MACSHANNON v. ROCKWARE GLASS [1978] 2 W.L.R. 362, H.L.

2391. Leave to discontinue or withdraw—no power to back-date order

[Landlord and Tenant Act 1954 (c. 56), s. 64 (2); R.S.C., Ord. 21, r. 3.]

The "date of withdrawal" of an application before the High Court for a new business tenancy is the date upon which leave to discontinue is granted; the court has no power to back-date the order.

Per curiam: It is anomalous that in the county court leave is not required in order to withdraw proceedings.

In March 1973, tenants applied to the High Court for a new business tenancy under the 1954 Act. In December 1975 they vacated the premises and in January 1976 applied under Ord. 21, r. 3, for leave to discontinue the proceedings. At the landlord's request the application was adjourned to the judge and was set down for hearing in July 1976 but was not in fact decided until October 1976. The parties agreed that any order of discontinuance should be treated as having been made in July. Graham J. gave leave to discontinue taking effect from July. The tenants appealed, contending that the court had power to order discontinuance operating retrospectively to take effect from an earlier date. *Held*, dismissing the appeal, that the court had no such power.

COVELL MATTHEWS & PARTNERS *v.* FRENCH WOOLS (1977) 35 P. & C.R. 107; [1978] 2 All E.R. 800, C.A.

2392. Legal aid

The 27th Legal Aid Annual Reports [1976–77] have been published by H.M.S.O. The reports contain the Report of The Law Society on their administration of the legal aid scheme and the Report of the Lord Chancellor's Legal Aid Advisory Committee on legal aid in civil causes and legal services generally. H.C. Paper No. 172. [£2·65.]

2393. LEGAL ADVICE AND ASSISTANCE (FINANCIAL CONDITIONS) REGULATIONS 1978 (No. 1567) [10p], made under the Legal Aid Act 1974 (c. 4), ss. 4, 20; operative on November 27, 1978; increase to £25 a week the disposable income above which a person receiving legal advice and assistance under the 1974 Act is required to pay a contribution, and make consequential amendments to the scale of contributions.

LEGAL AID AND ASSISTANCE (FINANCIAL CONDITIONS) (NO. 2) REGULATIONS 1978 (No. 1568) [10p], made under the Legal Aid Act 1974, ss. 1, 20; operative on November 27, 1978; increase the disposable income limit for the availability of legal advice and assistance to £52 a week and increase the disposable capital limit to £365.

LEGAL ADVICE AND ASSISTANCE (AMENDMENT) REGULATIONS 1978 (No. 1569) [10p], made under the Legal Aid Act 1974, ss. 11, 20; operative on November 27, 1978; increase allowances for dependants in the assessment of disposable capital. The allowance for the first dependant is increased to £200, for the second to £120 and for every other dependant £60.

LEGAL AID (ASSESSMENT OF RESOURCES) (AMENDMENT) REGULATIONS 1978 (No. 1570) [10p] made under the Legal Aid Act 1974, ss. 11, 20; operative on November 27, 1978; increase the allowances for dependants in the assessment of disposable capital. The allowance for the first dependant is increased to £200, for the second to £120 and for every other dependant to £60.

LEGAL AID (FINANCIAL CONDITIONS) REGULATIONS 1978 (No. 1571) [10p], made under the Legal Aid Act 1974, ss. 6, 9, 20; operative on November 27, 1978; increases the financial limits of eligibility for legal aid laid down in the 1974 Act. It makes legal aid available to those with disposable incomes of not more than £2,600 a year and available without the payment of a contribution to those with disposable incomes of not less than £815 a year. The capital limits are increased respectively to £1,700 and £365.

2394. —— assessment—change of circumstances

[Legal Aid (Assessment of Resources) Regulations) 1960 (S.I. 1960 No. 1471), as amended.] The interpretation of the 1960 Regulations by an Area Committee has been criticised by Payne J. In 1968 P was granted a civil aid certificate to defend his wife's petition for divorce; at that time his disposable income was £693 per annum. Since then his position had changed so that by 1978 he had a net income of £8,000. The Supplementary Benefits Commission was asked to consider reassessment but stated that the computation period had expired and the change in P's circumstances would be ignored. The judge queried whether *Moss* v. *Moss* [1956] C.L.Y. 6871 had been followed, as he felt it was still applicable today: PATEL v. PATEL, *The Times,* November 29, 1978, Payne J.

2395. —— **costs of successful unassisted public authority—constitutionally important point**

[Legal Aid Act 1974 (c. 4), s. 13 (2).] It may be " just and equitable " for the legal aid fund to be ordered to pay the costs of a successful unassisted party under s. 13 (2) of the Legal Aid Act 1974 even if the unassisted party is a public authority such as a police authority; this may particularly be the case if a point of constitutional importance has to be elucidated, and legal aid is accordingly granted for an appeal: MAYNARD v. OSMOND, *The Times,* October 5, 1978, C.A.

2396. —— **grant on eve of trial—costs attributable**

[Legal Aid Act 1974 (c. 4), ss. 13 (1), 14 (5).]

The words " attributable to that part " in s. 14 (5) of the Act mean that part of the proceedings in connection with which the assisted party received legal aid.

W was granted a legal aid certificate on the eve of a hearing concerning custody of the three children of the marriage. Custody was granted to M, who was an unassisted person. The judge granted H a proportion of his costs against the legal aid fund indicating that they should include the costs of preparation and delivery of briefs to counsel and preparation for trial. The taxing registrar referred the matter back to the judge on the question whether costs incurred prior to the date of W's legal aid certificate were recoverable having regard to s. 14 (5) of the Act. The judge held that the costs of preparation for trial were " attributable " to the hearing for which W received legal aid and were recoverable. The Law Society appealed. *Held,* allowing the appeal, that W received legal aid for " that part " of the proceedings after the issue of her legal aid certificate and the costs incurred by H prior to that date could not be " attributable to that part " within s. 14 (5) of the Act. (Decision of Latey J. reversed.) S. *v.* S. (UNASSISTED PARTY'S COSTS) [1978] 1 W.L.R. 11, C.A.

2397. —— **mother in care proceedings—legislation not yet brought into force**

A mother applied for judicial review of a refusal by magistrates to grant her legal aid to be separately represented in proceedings to have her 12-year-old son taken into care by the local authority under s. 1 of the Children and Young Persons Act 1969. All parties agreed that she should be separately represented; and her counsel agrued that she came within the phrase " a person brought before a juvenile court " in s. 28 (3) of the Legal Aid Act 1974. *Held,* by a majority dismissing the application, that, regrettably, the only provisions permitting the grant of legal aid to a party other than the relevant minor, had not yet been brought into force: namely ss. 64 and 65 of the Children Act 1975, enacted on November 12, 1975: R. v. WELWYN JUSTICES, *ex p.* S., *The Times,* November 30, 1978, C.A.

2398. —— **transmission of applications between Member States of the Council of Europe**

The agreement of the Council of Europe relating to the transmission of applications for legal aid between Member States has now been ratified by the United Kingdom and came into operation on February 17, 1978. Its purpose is to facilitate the steps which must be taken by any person of limited means in order to obtain legal aid in any civil, commercial or administrative matters in a contracting state of the Council of Europe other than that of his residence. The agreement designates a transmitting authority in each Member State, to which a resident of that State may make his application. The transmitting authority refers the application to the receiving authority of the foreign state, and will deal with all resulting problems without any necessity for the applicant to communicate with the foreign authority personally.

The transmitting and receiving authority for England and Wales is the Law Society; for Scotland the Scottish Legal Aid Central Committee, and for Northern Ireland the Incorporated Law Society of Northern Ireland.

2399. Litigant in person—duty of judge to make decision clear

The C.A. has emphasised the duty of a judge before whom a litigant appears in person to give clear reasons for his decision, and to deal with special care with the case of the party against whom he decides: BOWMAN *v.* McKEOWN, *The Times*, November 23, 1978, C.A.

2400. Masters' Practice Direction No. 19—amendment

The following Practice Direction was issued by the Queen's Bench Division on November 2, 1978:

In order to assist the county court to exercise its powers of control and investment over the funds of persons under disability required by an order of the High Court to be transmitted or to be paid into the county court, it is desirable that such orders should be indorsed with the age and date of birth of the plaintiff and the number of the legal aid certificate if any. Accordingly, the second sentence of para. 4 of this direction should be deleted and the following substituted: " In both cases, there shall be indorsed on the order the name and address of the next friend of any infant or patient who is the party for whose benefit the money is being transmitted or paid into the county court, the age and date of birth of the infant or patient as the case may be, the number of the legal aid certificate, if any, and the name and address of the plaintiff's solicitors and their office reference number."

(1978) 122 S.J. 780.

2401. Oaths Act 1978 (c. 19). See § 1430.

2402. Order 14—interest—discretion of court

[Law Reform (Miscellaneous Provisions) Act 1934 (c. 41), s. 3 (1).] In fully contested Order 14 proceedings the court had jurisdiction to award interest under the very wide discretion given by s. 3 (1) of the 1934 Act, which applies to any proceedings " tried " in any court of record where, inter alia, judgment was given in debt. (Dictum of Lord Denning M.R. in *Wallersteiner* v. *Moir* [1975] C.L.Y. 2602 agreed with): TOMKINS *v.* TOMKINS, *The Times*, May 24, 1978, Megarry V.-C.

2403. —— judgment—whether proceedings " tried "—power to award interest

[Law Reform (Miscellaneous Provisions) Act 1934 (c. 41), s. 3; R.S.C., Ord. 14.]

A case in which summary judgment is awarded under Ord. 14 has been " tried " in court and accordingly the court has power to award interest.

The plaintiffs obtained judgment under Ord. 14 for some £50,000, but the judge declined to award interest thereon up to the date of judgment. *Held*, allowing their appeal, that the court had jurisdiction to award interest under s. 3 of the 1934 Act and in its discretion would award interest at the rate of 9 per cent. per annum for six months preceding the judgment.

GARDENER STEEL *v.* SHEFFIELD BROTHERS (PROFILES) [1978] 1 W.L.R. 916, C.A.

2404. Originating summons—striking out—affidavit in support

[R.S.C., Ord. 18, r. 19 (1) (*a*) (2) (3.]

On an application under Ord. 18, r. 19 (1) (*a*), to strike out an originating summons, the prohibition under r. 19 (2) does not apply to an affidavit which had already been put in as supporting the originating summons.

Per curiam: The operation of Ord. 18, r. 19, in the case of originating summonses is something that the Rules Committee might with advantage consider.

K issued an originating summons, with supporting affidavit, against S and H, the executors of a will, claiming as a beneficiary under the will an order for the administration of the estate of the testator and ancillary relief. The executors issued a summons under R.S.C., Ord. 18, r. 19 (1) (*a*), seeking an order that the proceedings be dismissed on the grounds that K had no locus standi to bring them, and that they disclosed no cause of action. The argument before the Master was on the footing that the affidavit in support was before the court. When the executors' summons was adjourned to the judge, K objected to the admissibility of his own affidavit. He contended that it fell within the prohibition in Ord. 18, r. 19 (2), and so had to be excluded from consideration.

Held, dismissing the executors' summons, that (1) Ord. 18, r. 19 (3), could be read as requiring a degree of flexibility to avoid leaving most originating summonses outside the practical operation of r. 19 and that, since the supporting affidavit had already been used before the Master without objection, the unity of proceedings in the Chancery Division prevented it from being excluded at the hearing before the judge; (2) it was impossible to say that K had no locus standi and had no cause of action.

KNAPMAN *v.* SERVIAN; *Re* CAINES (DECD.) [1978] 1 W.L.R. 540, Megarry V.-C.

2405. Payments into court—postal facilities

The following direction was issued by the Finance Office of the Lord Chancellor's Department during September 1978 :

1. *Introduction*
   1.1 With a view to offering improved facilities to litigants and solicitors, it has been decided that payments into the High Court in London may in future be effected by post.
   1.2 Normally, the most expeditious method of lodgment into Court is by personal attendance at the Court Funds Office, in London. These facilities will continue as before.
   1.3 From October 2, 1978, it will be possible to effect lodgments in certain categories of cases by post, thus avoiding personal attendances at the Court Office.
   1.4 The various categories of lodgments which may or may not be carried out by the new method are set out in para. 6. The detailed requirements of acceptable postal lodgments are set out in the schedule to this notice [not printed here].

2. *Responsibility of correct lodgment*
   2.1 It is the responsibility of the solicitor concerned (or party, if acting in person) to ensure that all procedures outlined in this notice are fully complied with.
   2.2 Where, for any reason, time is of the essence, particularly having regard to any period of limitation which may be involved, solicitors and parties must be particularly careful in making use of the post for lodgments into court. Wherever the use may create difficulties as regards any time-factor to be observed, the solicitor or party concerned should carefully consider whether it would not be better and safer to effect lodgment by personal attendance at the Court Funds Office.
   2.3 It will not be possible for the Court Funds Office to enter into correspondence or telephonic communication in respect of any lodgment for which a party has chosen to use postal facilities; nor can the Court Funds office accept any responsibility for any defect, error or omission in any document sent to it through the post. Any application which, by such defect etc., cannot be accepted for lodgment will be returned to the sender with the reason for rejection stated. Any queries on such matters may require personal attendance at the Court Funds Office.

3. *Date of payment into court*
   3.1 On receipt, postal lodgments will be dealt with in all respects in the same manner as personal lodgments made on the same date.
   3.2 All relevant documents received will have, affixed, an official Court Funds Office stamp showing the date and time of receipt. Date of lodgment will be the date of notification of clearance of the cheque (see para. 4.3).

4. *Procedure for lodgments*
   4.1 All applications for lodgment by post must include :
      (a) A request for direction for lodgment in respect of each separate payment into Court. (See Schedule.) Delay will often be avoided if care is taken to see that this form is properly completed and signed.
      (b) Any other supporting documents required—as set out in schedule.

(c) A remittance for the sum(s) to be lodged (see para. 4.3).

(d) An envelope of adequate size, properly addressed to the sender, for the return of any relevant documents and/or receipts.
N.B. NO FEE IS PAYABLE.

4.2 *Address for lodgment*

In actions proceeding in the Royal Courts of Justice: all postal lodgments together with the requisite documents must be posted in a prepaid envelope properly addressed to:

> The Principal,
> Court Funds Office,
> Royal Courts of Justice,
> Strand,
> London WC2A 2LL.

4.3 *Remittances*

Payments into court should be made by banker's draft, cheque, postal orders or other accepted form of negotiable instrument. All remittances should be made payable to " THE ACCOUNTANT GENERAL OF THE SUPREME COURT " and crossed. Bank notes and bankers' drafts should be forwarded by registered post.

Payments by cheque may be subject to a clearance period which is normally between six and 14 working days.

5. *Application to District Registries*

Postal facilities will also be available in District Registries of the High Court, with such variations as the circumstances may require. Intending users of this facility should contact their nearest District Registry to enquire as to exact requirements in a particular type of case.

6. *Categories of lodgments which may or may not be lodged by post*

6.1 The following general types of lodgment may be effected by post, subject to the exceptions outlined in para. 6.2:

(a) Lodgments directed by court order—all divisions.

(b) Lodgments on request pursuant to Ord. 22, R.S.C.

(c) Lodgments under the provisions of Exchange Control Acts.

(d) Lodgments made under various statutes (e.g. Compulsory Purchase of Land Acts, Road Traffic Act 1972 etc.).

6.2 The following categories of lodgments CANNOT be accepted by post:

(a) All lodgments made in foreign currency.

(b) All lodgments of boxes and sealed packets.

(c) Lodgments in Chancery, Q.B., Family and Admiralty Divisions where the consent of a Master or Registrar is required before a lodgment can be authorised.

(d) Lodgments under the Trustee Act 1925 where an affidavit is required to be sworn and filed before the lodgment may be made.

(e) All lodgments of securities. It should be noted that such lodgments are made in accordance with individual instructions provided by the C.F.O. as and when they are required to be made, and not in accordance with this notice.

[1978] 122 S.J. 684.

2406. Pleadings—amendment—introduction of insured's undisclosed criminal offence. See REYNOLDS *v.* PHOENIX ASSURANCE CO., § 1708.

2407. —— **negligence—necessity for specific pleading.** See FOOKES *v.* SLAYTOR, § 2056.

2408. —— **particulars—alleged racial discrimination by local authority against schoolchildren**

[Race Relations Act 1968 (c. 71), s. 19; Race Relations Act 1976 (c. 74), s. 79, Sched. 2, para. 3.]

On an allegation that a local authority is discriminating against an ethnic group of schoolchildren by dispersing them into different areas, particulars need not be given of the identities of the children until after discovery.

The Race Relations Board brought proceedings under s. 19 of the Race Relations Act 1968 against a local authority, alleging that the local authority was discriminating against its Asian children in one area by dispersing them to schools outside the area. The particulars of claim did not particularise the children discriminated against and the local authority sought those particulars prior to delivering their defence. The registrar ordered the defence to be delivered within 21 days and the authority appealed. The authority also applied to strike out the particulars of claim as disclosing no cause of action; alternatively, they applied for an order that they should not be required to deliver a defence until they had received the particulars they sought. The judge refused the orders sought. On appeal by the local authority, *held*, dismissing the appeal, that the pleadings disclosed a reasonably arguable cause of action, and that particulars need not be given until after discovery.

COMMISSION FOR RACIAL EQUALITY *v.* EALING LONDON BOROUGH COUNCIL [1978] 1 W.L.R. 112, C.A.

2409. Privy Council. See PRIVY COUNCIL PRACTICE.

2410. Probate. See EXECUTORS AND ADMINISTRATORS.

2411. Rules of the Supreme Court

RULES OF THE SUPREME COURT (AMENDMENT No. 2) 1978 (No. 359 (L.5)) [10p], made under the Supreme Court of Judicature (Consolidation) Act 1925 (c. 49), s. 99 (4); operative on April 24, 1978; amends the Rules of the Supreme Court so as to revoke the provision that, on an appeal by case stated from the Crown Court, the relevant facts and questions of law may be stated by reference to an annexed copy of the judgment, order or decision; to provide for an appeal from the decision of a Master or a Registrar of the Family Division in interpleader or garnishee proceedings or on an application for a charging order or in proceedings under s. 17 of the Married Woman's Property Act 1882 to lie to a judge in chambers instead of the Court of Appeal; to substitute new fixed costs for the basic costs allowable under Appendix 3 to Order 62 where not less than £1,200 is recovered.

RULES OF THE SUPREME COURT (AMENDMENT No. 3) 1978 (No. 579 (L.11)) [35p], made under the Supreme Court of Judicature (Consolidation) Act 1925, s. 99 (4); operative on June 1, 1978; amends the Rules of the Supreme Court to take into account the Torts (Interference with Goods) Act 1977 and the Patents Act 1977; enables appeals to the High Court under the Matrimonial Proceedings (Magistrates' Courts) Act 1960 to be heard and determined by a single judge where only the amount of any weekly payments is in issue.

RULES OF THE SUPREME COURT (AMENDMENT No. 4) 1978 (No. 1066 (L. 26)) [20p], made under the Supreme Court of Judicature (Consolidation) Act 1925, s. 99 (4); operative on September 1, 1978; amends the Rules of the Supreme Court to enable the court to allow service of a writ in a Member State of the EEC where the claim is for an agricultural levy or other sum to which Directive No. 76/308/EEC applies, to give the court power to order that damages be assessed by a master, to provide that an application for leave to enforce an arbitration award may be made ex parte by affidavit instead of by originating summons.

2412. —— amendment—applications for judicial review

[R.S.C., Ord. 53, r. 5 (2).] The divisional court, on granting leave to make an application for judicial review and an order for certiorari, directed for the first time that the application should be made by motion to a single judge sitting in open court, in accordance with the new Ord. 53, r. 5 (2). The Lord Chief Justice commented that the divisional court would look with interest on the operation of this change in practice: R. *v.* SECRETARY OF STATE FOR THE ENVIRONMENT, *ex p.* STEWART, April 21, 1978, D.C. (*Ex rel. M. Farmer, Esq,. Barrister.*)

2413. —— —— bail. See § 416.

2414. Sentence. See CRIMINAL LAW; MAGISTERIAL LAW.

2415. Service of process—foreign company—address for service—whether place of business

A writ was served on the defendants, a company registered under the laws of

Panama, at an address in London. The service was set aside since the plaintiffs had not discharged the onus on them of showing that at the relevant date of service the London address was a place of business established by the defendants in London: BETHLEHEM STEEL CORP. *v.* UNIVERSAL GAS AND OIL CO. INC., *The Times*, August 3, 1978, H.L.

2416. —— summons—Sundays

On a summons for committal to prison (in breach of injunction) of the husband respondent, the question arose as to whether the service of the summons for committal was effective, having been served on the previous Sunday. The learned judge applied R.S.C. Ord. 37, r. 4 (1): " Non-compliance with Rules " in relaxation of Ord. 8, r. 3: " No service on a Sunday ": MOOGAN *v.* MOOGAN, September 28, 1978, Judge Wickham, Liverpool County Ct. (*Ex rel. Richard Murray, Esq., Barrister.*)

2417. Transfer of proceedings—minors—adoption or guardianship. See PRACTICE DIRECTION, § 1971.

2418. Trial—transcripts—alleged inaccuracies—guidelines

The following Practice Note was given by Lawton L.J. in the Court of Appeal on May 3, 1978:

For the guidance of counsel and solicitors, I would like to point out that the practice which should be followed by those suggesting that the transcript is inaccurate, is to tell the registrar what is alleged. He will then take the matter up with the shorthand writers and, if necessary, with the trial judge. It is unfair to the trial judge for the court to proceed on an assumption of fact which is not in accordance with the transcript of evidence. The transcript may be wrong; but so may also be those who think they have recorded accurately what the judge has said. It is in everybody's interest that matters of this kind should be cleared up.

(1978) 67 Cr.App.R. 50.

2419. Want of prosecution—abuse of process—second action similar to first

Where a defendant applies to strike out an action after the expiry of a period of limitation, it is for the plaintiff to establish that, by reason of the existence of a second action, it is futile to strike out the first one.

P claimed an order for specific purpose for the sale of shares. Some six years later, he brought a second action for a declaration that he owned the shares. D sought to strike out the first action for want of prosecution and the second as an abuse of process of the court. *Held*, that (i) there had been such delay in prosecuting the first action as to justify its striking out, and that this would be done since P had failed to show that the existence of a second action made such striking out futile as the second action might itself fall victim to the doctrine of laches; and (ii) the second action, although similar to the first, and facing greater difficulties, did not, by reason of those facts alone constitute an abuse of process of the court. It would not be struck out.

JOYCE *v.* JOYCE [1978] 1 W.L.R. 117, Megarry V.-C.

2420. —— acquiescence in delay

The Court of Appeal allowed an appeal by a plaintiff from an order striking out for want of prosecution his claim for injuries sustained by the defendant's negligent driving. The injury was sustained in January 1969 and the delay was deplorable, but the defendant's insurers' solicitors had acquiesced in the position and had struck too soon. It was a strong thing to dismiss a claim by a plaintiff who was otherwise entitled to a substantial award of damages: GREEN *v.* HARDISTY, *The Times*, March 14, 1978, C.A.

2421. —— delay—awaiting the outcome of proceedings before the E.C. Commission

The defendants brought motions to dismiss the plaintiffs' actions on the ground of inexcusable delay. The plaintiffs' actions commenced in 1969 and 1970 and alleged infringements of their patent rights. By their amended defence, the defendants stated, inter alia, that the plaintiffs were not entitled to the relief claimed by virtue of arts. 85 and 86 EEC. An associated company of the defendants then filed a complaint with the Commission relating to the plaintiffs' activities. The plaintiffs took the view that, before proceeding further with the action, it would be desirable to await the outcome of the action taken before the E.C. Commission. *Held*, the motions would be dismissed as, although delay had occurred, it was not inexcusable; both parties had thought that the outcome of the proceedings before the E.C. Commission might well be of great importance to the resolution of the EEC issue in the litigation before the English High Court. Thus, it could not be said that the plaintiffs had not a valid excuse for not proceeding.

AERO ZIPP FASTENERS *v.* YKK FASTENERS (U.K.) [1977] 2 C.M.L.R. 88, Whitford J.

2422. ⸺ ⸺ whether equitable to proceed

[Limitation Act 1939 (c. 21), s. 2D.] H was injured in a work accident in 1953. In 1973, while seeking advice on another matter, his solicitor told him he might still have a claim against the Coal Board. A writ was issued in 1976 and was served nearly a year later. The Coal Board applied for the action to be dismissed. *Held*, the determination as to whether it is equitable to allow the action to proceed need not be deferred until trial but could be dealt with on a summons. Here it was plain that it was no longer equitable for this action to proceed: HATTAM *v.* NATIONAL COAL BOARD, *The Times*, October 28, 1978, C.A.

2423. ⸺ infant plaintiff—right to issue fresh writ when 18—no help to defendant

[Limitation Act 1939 (c. 21), s. 22.] P was injured by D's car in 1967, when she was two years old. A writ was issued by P's father in 1967 and was served in 1968, but there was no further action until 1977. *Held*, although there had been inordinate and inexcusable delay, the action would not be dismissed for want of prosecution. Under s. 22 of the 1939 Act, P had an absolute right to issue a fresh writ when she attained 18, and it would be of no help to D to dismiss the present action. Although the extended limitation period in s. 22 had been granted to protect infants from their, and their parents', ignorance of the law, the protection should not be whittled away by depriving P, whose parents had known the law, of her right to sue. (*Birkett v. James* [1977] C.L.Y. 2410 followed; dicta of Lord Denning M.R. in *Biss v. Lambeth, Southwark and Lewisham Area Health Authority (Teaching)* [1978] C.L.Y. 2425 not followed): TOLLEY *v.* MORRIS, *The Times*, May 17 1978, C.A.

2424. ⸺ more than one defendant

If one of two defendants applies for an action to be dismissed for want of prosecution and it appears that the other defendant has acquiesced in or contributed to the delay, then the court may allow the action to continue against the latter defendant only; but that is exceptional, and it will often be held that the action should, on broad grounds of justice, continue against both. The note to R.S.C., Ord. 25, r. 1, is, however, wrong in suggesting that that course will always be followed: KELLY *v.* MARLEY TILE CO. (1977) 122 S.J. 17, C.A.

2425. ⸺ prejudice to defendant

[Limitation Act 1939 (c. 21), ss. 2A (4) (*b*), 2D (1) (3), as added by Limitation Act 1975 (c. 54), s. 1.]

In determining whether an action should be dismissed for want of prosecution because of delay after the writ has been issued, the court has to consider the resulting prejudice to both a fair trial and to the defendants.

From April 1965 to January 1966, B was an in-patient at a hospital run by the authority, suffering from multiple sclerosis. She contracted severe bed sores. In 1966, after being moved to a specialist hospital, she was granted legal aid to pursue a claim in negligence against the nursing staff. After correspondence between the parties, counsel advised against continuing the action and no further steps were taken. In 1973, the Multiple Sclerosis Society encouraged her to renew her claim and, armed with an opinion from the director of the specialist hospital, she was granted leave by the Court of Appeal under s. 1 of the Limitation Act 1963 to bring her action. After pleadings were closed, there was a period of nine months when no further steps were taken on B's behalf. Subsequently, she changed her solicitors, but the health authority applied for the action to be dismissed for want of prosecution. The master granted the application, but the decision was reversed by the judge. On appeal by the health authority, *held*, allowing the appeal, that in considering the prejudice to the defendant, the recent delay had to be considered against the background of substantial delay before the writ was issued. Under the Limitation Acts of 1939 to 1975, and especially s. 2D (3) of the 1939 Act, the judge had to exercise his discretion whether to allow the action to proceed in all the circumstances; as the health authority had been substantially prejudiced by the further nine months' delay, the action would be dismissed for want of prosecution. *Per* Lord Denning M.R.: prejudice to a defendant is not limited to the death or disappearance of witnesses or their fading memories, or in the loss or destruction of records. There is much prejudice in having an action hanging over one's head indefinitely. (*Birkett* v. *James* [1977] C.L.Y. 2410 distinguished.)

BISS *v.* LAMBETH, SOUTHWARK AND LEWISHAM AREA HEALTH AUTHORITY (TEACHING) [1978] 1 W.L.R. 382, C.A.

2426. ⸺ third party proceedings

In an action for damages for personal injuries by P against D, TP were joined as third parties. There were substantial delays. After the expiration of the limitation period for P's action, TP applied for the dismissal of the action and of the third party proceedings, for want of prosecution. *Held*, that (1) the principles to be applied to the third party proceedings were the same as those which would be applied on an application to strike out an action made by the defendant; (2) although there had been inordinate and inexcusable delay, there was no such prejudice as would justify the striking out of the third party proceedings; and (3) the third party had no right to make an application to strike out the action. (*Birkett* v. *James* [1977] C.L.Y. 2410 applied): ENOCH *v.* NATIONAL COAL BOARD, *The Times*, March 17, 1978, Milmo J.

2427. Wards of court. See MINORS.

2428. Witnesses. See EVIDENCE.

BOOKS AND ARTICLES. See *post*, pp. [9], [32].

PRESS

BOOKS AND ARTICLES. See *post*, pp. [7], [32].

PRISONS

2429. Board of visitors' decisions—subject to judicial review

[Prison Act 1952 (c. 52).] Disciplinary decisions of the prison visitors under the Prison Act 1952 are judicial in character and subject to review by the High Court. (*Ex p. Fry* [1954] C.L.Y. 818 not followed; *Ridge* v. *Baldwin* [1963] C.L.Y. 2667 applied; decision of D.C. [1977] C.L.Y. 2285 reversed): R. *v.* BOARD OF VISITORS OF HULL PRISON, *ex p.* ST. GERMAIN, *The Times*, October 4, 1978, C.A.

2430. Northern Ireland. See NORTHERN IRELAND.

2431. Prisoners—sexual offenders liable to attack—duty of care owed by Home Office. See EGERTON *v.* HOME OFFICE, § 2069.

BOOKS AND ARTICLES. See *post*, pp. [7], [32].

PRIVY COUNCIL PRACTICE

2432. Appeals

MALAYSIA (APPEALS TO PRIVY COUNCIL) ORDER 1978 (No. 182) [25p], made under the Malaya Independence Act 1957 (c. 60), s. 3, and the Malaysia Act 1963 (c. 35), s. 5; operative on March 2, 1978; amends and consolidates Orders conferring jurisdiction on the Judicial Committee of the Privy Council in respect of appeals from Malaysia.

2433. ⸺ reference from Governor-General of New Zealand—jurisdiction

[N.Z.] [Crimes Act 1961 (New Zealand), s. 406 (*b*).] The Governor-General referred T's application to quash two convictions in the exercise of the

Crown's prerogative of mercy to the Court of Appeal for its opinion under s. 406 (*b*) of the Crimes Act 1961. The Court of Appeal gave an opinion against T. *Held*, dismissing T's petition, that the opinion was not binding on the Governor-General and no appeal against the Court of Appeal's opinion lies to the Privy Council: THOMAS *v.* THE QUEEN [1978] Crim.L.R. 753, P.C.

2434. Barbados

JUDICIAL COMMITTEE (BARBADOS) ORDER 1978 (No. 620) [10p], made under the Judicial Committee Amendment Act 1895 (c. 44), s. 1 (1); operative on May 17, 1978; names the Supreme Court of Barbados as a superior court for the purposes of s. 1 (1) of the 1895 Act.

2435. Jurisdiction—Malaysian appeals

Dismissing a petition, the Judicial Committee *held,* that it had no jurisdiction to hear appeals from Malaysia in criminal and constitutional matters except where the petition was lodged before January 1, 1978; even though, in this case, notice of intended application for leave to appeal had been lodged in Malaysia before January 1, pursuant to the Malaysian Courts of Judicature (Amendment) Act 1976: LEE KOK ENG *v.* PUBLIC PROSECUTOR, *The Times,* October 31, 1978, P.C.

ARTICLES. See *post,* p. [32].

PUBLIC AUTHORITIES AND PUBLIC OFFICERS

ARTICLES. See *post,* p. [32].

PUBLIC ENTERTAINMENTS

2436. Blackburn

BOROUGH OF BLACKBURN (PUBLIC ENTERTAINMENT) ORDER 1978 (No. 1595) [10p], made under the Local Government Act 1972 (c. 70), s. 262 (8) (11); operative on May 5, 1979; repeals the Blackburn Improvement Act 1882, s. 197, and the Darwen Corporation Act 1887, s. 110, which provide for the regulation of places for dancing, music and other entertainment in Blackburn and Darwen.

2437. Cinema

CINEMATOGRAPH FILMS (COLLECTION OF LEVY) (AMENDMENT No. 6) REGULATIONS 1978 (No. 1092) [10p], made under the Cinematograph Films Act 1957 (c. 21), s. 2 (7); operative on September 24, 1978; amend S.I. 1968 No. 1077 by increasing to 17½p the portion of the payment for admission which is not liable to levy and by increasing to £1,100 the amount by reference to which total or partial exemption from payment of levy is allowed in respect of cinemas at which takings are small.

FEES FOR CINEMATOGRAPH LICENCES (VARIATION) ORDER 1978 (No. 1387) [10p], made under the Local Government Act 1966 (c. 42), ss. 35 (2), 40 (2), Sched. 3, Pt. II; operative on November 1, 1978; raises the maximum fees payable for the grant, renewal and transfer of licences issued under the Cinematograph Act 1909, s. 2, for the use of premises in England and Wales.

2438. Films

FILMS (REGISTRATION) (AMENDMENT) REGULATIONS 1978 (No. 1632) [30p], made under the Films Act 1960 (c. 57), s. 44, as amended by the Films Act 1970 (c. 26), s. 20, as further amended by the European Communities Act 1972 (c. 68), s. 8; operative on January 1, 1979; further amend S.I. 1970 No. 1858 by prescribing a new form of application for the registration of films.

2439. Safety of sports grounds

SAFETY OF SPORTS GROUNDS (DESIGNATION) ORDER 1978 (No. 1091) [10p], made under the Safety of Sports Grounds Act 1975 (c. 52), ss. 1 (1), 18 (4); operative on January 1, 1979; designates certain sports stadia as stadia requiring safety certificates under the 1975 Act.

2440. Television. See TELECOMMUNICATIONS.

2441. Theatres

THEATRES (LICENCE APPLICATION FEES) (AMENDMENT) ORDER 1978 (No. 1388) [10p], made under the Theatres Act 1968 (c. 54), Sched. 1, para. 3 (1)

(2); operative on November 1, 1978; amends S.I. 1968 No. 1315 by raising the fees for the grant, renewal or transfer of licences for the use of premises for the public performance of a play in England and Wales under the 1968 Act.

2442. Theatres Trust (Scotland) Act 1978 (c. 24)

This Act extends the Theatres Trust Act 1976 to Scotland.

S. 1 amends the 1976 Act so that it extends to Scotland; s. 2 gives the short title.

The Act received the Royal Assent on June 30, 1978, and came into force on that date.

PUBLIC HEALTH

2443. Aviation

PUBLIC HEALTH (AIRCRAFT) (AMENDMENT) REGULATIONS 1978 (No. 286) [25p], made under the Public Health Act 1936 (c. 49), s. 143 as modified by the Civil Aviation Act 1949 (c. 67), s. 69, Sched. 11, the Civil Aviation Act 1971 (c. 75), s. 32 and the Airports Authority Act 1975 (c. 78), s. 15; operative on April 1, 1978; amend S.I. 1970 No. 1880 which provide for public health control over aircraft arriving in or leaving England and Wales.

2444. Building. See BUILDING AND ENGINEERING; ARCHITECTS AND SURVEYORS.

2445. Control of Pollution Act 1974—commencement

CONTROL OF POLLUTION ACT 1974 (COMMENCEMENT No. 13) ORDER 1978 (No. 954 (C. 23)) [10p], made under the Control of Pollution Act 1974 (c. 40), s. 109 (2); operative on August 1, 1978; brings into force s. 13 (3) (5) (8) of the 1974 Act.

2446. Detergents

DETERGENTS (COMPOSITION) REGULATIONS 1978 (No. 564) [25p], made under the European Communities Act 1972 (c. 68), s. 2 (2), and S.I. 1972 No. 1811; operative on January 1, 1979; give effect to Council Directives 73/404/EEC and 73/405/EEC which relate to the biodegradability of surface active agents in detergents, particularly those that are anionic.

DETERGENTS (COMPOSITION) (AMENDMENT) REGULATIONS 1978 (No. 1546) [10p), made under the European Communities Act 1972, s. 2 (2), and S.I. 1972 No. 1811; operative on January 1, 1979; amend S.I. 1978 No. 564 by amending the definition of "detergent" in those Regulations.

2447. Food and drugs. See FOOD AND DRUGS.

2448. Hazardous substances

HAZARDOUS SUBSTANCES (LABELLING OF ROAD TANKERS) REGULATIONS 1978 (No. 1702) [70p], made under the Health and Safety at Work etc. Act 1974 (c. 37), ss. 11 (2) (d), 15 (1)–(6), 50 (2) (3), Sched. 3, paras. 1 (4), 3, as amended by the Employment Protection Act 1975 (c. 71), s. 116, Sched. 15, para. 6; operative on March 28, 1979; impose requirements for notices to be displayed on road tankers which are being used for the conveyance by road of prescribed hazardous substances.

2449. Health inspector—right to prosecute—proof of appointment. See CAMPBELL *v.* WALLSEND SLIPWAY AND ENGINEERING CO., § 580.

2450. Medicine. See MEDICINE.

2451. National Health. See NATIONAL HEALTH.

2452. Northern Ireland. See NORTHERN IRELAND.

2453. Port health authorities

DOVER PORT HEALTH AUTHORITY ORDER 1978 (No. 819) [20p], made under the Public Health Act 1936 (c. 49), ss. 2, 3 as amended by the Control of Pollution Act 1974 (c. 40), s. 108, Sched. 3, para. 6; operative on August 1, 1978; constitutes the Port of Dover as a port health district and constitutes the District Council of Dover as port health authority for that district.

RAMSGATE PORT HEALTH AUTHORITY ORDER 1978 (No. 1695) [20p], made under the Public Health Act 1936, ss. 2, 3 as extended by the Control of Pollution Act 1974, s. 108, Sched. 3, para. 6; operative on December 30, 1978; constitutes the Port of Ramsgate as a port health district and constitutes the District Council of Thanet as port health authority for that district.

2454. Sewage—sewer laid under public highway—whether " acquired " by local authority

[Public Health Act 1936 (c. 49), ss. 15, 20.]

A sewer privately laid under a public highway may become public property by application of the maxim " quicquid plantatur solo, solo cedit."

The plaintiffs purchased land and built houses thereon in reliance upon the local authority having indicated the presence of a public sewer running beneath the nearby public highway. Such sewer had been constructed 15 years previously by the defendants to serve houses built by them and adjoined a public sewer. The authority had approved the construction of the sewer and, although intending to adopt it, had never formally done so. After the plaintiffs had built the houses and connected their drainage to the sewer, the defendants sealed off the plaintiffs' connection. The plaintiffs sought, inter alia, a declaration that the sewer was a public sewer. *Held*, making the declaration, that although no formal resolution had been passed, the sewer had been "acquired" by the local authority within the meaning of s. 20 (1) (6) of the 1936 Act, since the sewer had ceased to be a chattel and had become part of the land. (*Simmons* v. *Midford* [1969] C.L.Y. 3038 distinguished.)

ROYCO HOMES v. EATONWILL CONSTRUCTION; THREE RIVERS DISTRICT COUNCIL, THIRD PARTY [1978] 2 W.L.R. 957, Hugh Francis, Q.C.

2455. Ships

PUBLIC HEALTH (SHIPS) (AMENDMENT) REGULATIONS 1978 (No. 287) [25p], made under the Public Health Act 1936 (c. 49), s. 143; operative on April 1, 1978; further amend S.I. 1970 No. 1881, which provide for public health control over ships arriving in or leaving England and Wales.

2456. Smoke abatement

SMOKE CONTROL AREAS (AUTHORISED FUELS) REGULATIONS 1978 (No. 99) [10p], made under the Clean Air Act 1956 (c. 52), s. 34 (1); operative on February 24, 1978; declare "Palmalite" ovoid briquettes to be an authorised fuel.

SMOKE CONTROL AREAS (EXEMPTED FIREPLACES) ORDER 1978 (No. 1609) [10p], made under the Clean Air Act 1956, s. 11 (4); operative on December 11, 1978; exempts a class of fireplace comprising certain types of the Spänex Wood Fired Air Heater from the provisions of s. 11 of the 1956 Act.

2457. Water. See WATER AND WATERWORKS.

ARTICLES. See *post*, p. [32].

RAILWAYS

2458. Fares—intent to avoid payment

[Regulation of Railways Act 1889 (c. 57), s. 5 (3) (*a*), amended by Transport Act 1962 (c. 46), s. 84 (2).]

There is no reason to import into s. 5 (3) (*a*) of the 1889 Act the word " permanently."

Per curiam: If a person buys a ticket for a destination but, when he travels, intends to travel beyond that destination without previously paying for the additional distance, he travels that additional distance with intent to avoid the required payment. If he fails to tender the outstanding balance of the fare, at latest, when passing the ticket collector at his final destination, the requisite intent to avoid payment is proved.

C repeatedly purchased a 10p ticket for a journey on the London Underground longer than that covered by the fare. On leaving the station at his intended destination he handed to the ticket collector the 10p ticket and a form indicating his intention to pay the additional fare only on request at some future date. He was charged with an offence contrary to s. 5 (3) (*a*) of the 1889 Act. At the hearing, he contended that it was not proved that he intended permanently to avoid payment of the correct fare, and that the information should be dismissed. The magistrate found that intent to avoid payment was proved, and C was convicted. On appeal, *held,* dismissing the appeal, that an intention not to pay unless later requested was an intention to avoid payment within s. 5 (3) (*a*) of the Act.

CORBYN *v.* SAUNDERS [1978] 1 W.L.R. 400, D.C.

2459. Light railways

LOUGHBOROUGH AND BIRSTALL LIGHT RAILWAY ORDER 1978 (No. 471) [25p], made under the Light Railways Act 1896 (c. 48), ss. 3, 7, 9, 10, 11 as amended by the Light Railways Act 1912 (c. 19) and the Railways Act 1921 (c. 55), Pt. V; operative on April 3, 1978; makes provisions relating to the operation of the Loughborough and Birstall Light Railway by the Great Central Railway Company (1976) Ltd.

STRATHSPEY LIGHT RAILWAY ORDER 1978 (No. 871) [25p], made under the Light Railways Act 1896, s. 10 as amended by the Railways Act 1921 operative on June 26, 1978; makes provisions for the operation of the Strathspey Light Railway.

WHITBY AND PICKERING LIGHT RAILWAY (AMENDMENT) ORDER 1978 (No. 952) [20p], made under the Light Railways Act 1896, s. 24, as amended by the Light Railways Act 1912 and the Railways Act 1921, Pt. V; operative on July 16, 1978; makes provision concerning railway services provided by the company.

ISLE OF WIGHT (HAVENSTREET AND WOOTTON) LIGHT RAILWAY ORDER 1978 (No. 1119) [25p], made under the Light Railways Act 1896, ss. 3, 7, 9–12, as amended by the Light Railways Act 1912 and the Railways Act 1921, Pt. V; operative on August 11, 1978; makes provisions for the operation of the Isle of Wight Railway Co. Ltd.

CRANMORE LIGHT RAILWAY ORDER 1978 (No. 1937) [20p], made under the Light Railways Act 1896, ss. 7, 9, 10–12, 18, as amended by the Light Railways Act 1912, and by the Railways Act 1921, Part V; operative on December 21, 1978; transfers from the British Railways Board to the East Somerset Railway Co. the railway described in the Schedule.

ARTICLES. See *post,* p. [32].

RATING AND VALUATION

2460. Agricultural land

RATING ENACTMENTS (AGRICULTURAL LAND AND AGRICULTURAL BUILDING) (AMENDMENT) REGULATIONS 1978 (No. 318) [10p], made under Agriculture (Miscellaneous Provisions) Act 1976 (c. 55), s. 7 (1) (2) (*a*); operative on April 1, 1978; amend the definition of " agricultural land " in s. 26 (3) of the General Rate Act 1967 and the definition of " agricultural building " in s. 2 of the Rating Act 1967 by substituting references therein to areas expressed in imperial units references to areas expressed in metric units.

2460a. Appeal—jurisdiction—distress warrant

[Supreme Court of Judicature (Consolidation) Act 1925 (c. 49), s. 31 (1) (*a*).]

An application to a magistrates' court for the issue of a distress warrant for non-payment of rates is not a " criminal cause or matter " within s. 31 (1) (*a*) of the Supreme Court of Judicature (Consolidation) Act 1925.

A group of buildings comprising a three-storey house and two small factories were listed as a single hereditament and described as a " workshop and store." The defendant occupied one of the two factories and a first floor office in the house. After the defendant refused to pay rates in respect of the whole hereditament, the rating authority sought the issue of a distress warrant from a magistrates' court which refused to authorise such issue. The Divisional Court then allowed the appeal by the rating authority. *Held,* allowing the defendant's appeal, that (1) an application to a magistrates' court for the issue of a distress warrant was not a " criminal cause or matter " within s. 31 (1) (*a*) and accordingly an appeal lay to the Court of Appeal from a decision of the Divisional Court; (2) the Divisional Court was wrong in holding that the part occupied

by the defendant fulfilled the description in the valuation list and the defendant was therefore not liable for any part of the rates claimed.
CAMDEN LONDON BOROUGH COUNCIL *v.* HERWALD [1978] 3 W.L.R. 47, C.A.

2461. Charities
RATING (CHARITABLE INSTITUTIONS) ORDER 1978 (No. 218) [10p], made under the General Rate Act 1967 (c. 9), s. 40 (3); operative on March 21, 1978; amends Sched. 8 to the 1967 Act by omitting from the said Sched. the permanent private halls in the University of Oxford.

2462. Docks and harbours—" authority conferred by or under a statute "
[General Rate Act 1967 (c. 9), s. 35 (2) (*c*); Docks and Harbours (Valuation) Order 1971 (S.I. 1971 No. 561), art. 2 (i).]
The words " under authority conferred by or under any enactment " *in* relation to the carrying on of a dock or harbour undertaking in the General Rate Act 1967, s. 35, are not wide enough to cover a statutory approval of the place where the undertaking is carried out.
H carried on a dock undertaking at Harwich harbour. The hereditament which they occupied was an approved wharf under the Customs and Excise Act 1952. Special rating provisions apply to dock or harbour undertakings carried on " under authority conferred by or under any enactment." *Held,* dismissing H's appeal, that that referred to the undertaking itself, not the place where it was carried on, and that the approvals given to the premises under the Customs and Excise Act 1952 did not entitle H to the benefit of the rating provisions applicable to such undertakings.
HARWICH DOCK CO. *v.* I.R.C. (1978) 76 L.G.R. 238, H.L.

2463. Hereditament—not liable to be rated—net annual value—whether within county court jurisdiction
[Administration of Justice Act 1970 (c. 31), s. 37 (1); County Courts Act 1959 (c. 22), ss. 48, 200 (2) (*b*).]
Property which is not liable to be rated is to be taken to have net annual value for rating equal to its value by the year. Where this is greater than £1,000, the High Court has jurisdiction.
In 1977, the defendant G charged by way of legal mortgage two separate parcels of land. Upon G's failure to comply with a notice to repay an instalment, the plaintiffs F took out a High Court summons. The rateable value of one parcel was £742, but the other parcel was not liable to be rated, though its annual value exceeded £258. It was contended that the High Court had no jurisdiction to hear the summons. *Held,* that for jurisdictional purposes, where one property had no annual value for rating, its rateable value was to be assessed by reference to s. 200 (2) (*b*) of the 1959 Act; accordingly it would be taken to have a value for rating equal to its value by the year. Since this exceeded £258, the mortgaged property had a rateable value of over £1,000 and was therefore within High Court jurisdiction. (*Trustees of Manchester Unity Life Insurance Collecting Society* v. *Sadler* [1974] C.L.Y. 2432 considered.)
P. B. FROST *v.* GREEN [1978] 2 All E.R. 206, Slade J.

2464. Lands Tribunal decisions
CENTRAL HOTELS (CRANSTON) *v.* RIDGEON (LVC/671/1975) (1977) 245 E.G. 577 (the appellant ratepayers occupied an hotel on the perimeter of Heathrow Airport and claimed 50 per cent. end-allowances for location, standard of accommodation and general disabilities on comparison with assessments of nine other hotels in the vicinity of the airport. *Held,* such end-allowances are not to be rejected merely because of their size or the disparity suggested between the appeal property and comparables, but they should be reduced to 37½ per cent.).
ECCLES *v.* HANFORD (Ref. No. LVC/371/1975) (successful appeal against a rating assessment on a four-bedroom house on the northern bank of the River Kennet. There were seven sluice gates within the appeal, hereditaments which needed to be reset every time the flow of water in the river altered. In winter, the gates might need to be reset three times a day. The tribunal made a deduction of £150 from the assessment, to take into account the disability

caused by the need to operate the sluice gates, which could only be discharged by the tenant, as the hypothetical landlord's obligation could only cover their repair and maintenance).

FAIRHURST *v.* GREIG (LVC/260/1976) [1978] J.P.L. 256 (the valuation officer added £10 for car space to the rateable value of a house. The ratepayer objected to this and also claimed a temporary reduction in assessment because the estate was not finished and there was a nuisance caused by contractors vehicles. *Held,* the assessment of £290 gross value should be confirmed since (1) in the General Rate Act 1967, s. 20 (1), the value which " would have been ascribed " means the " value which would properly have been ascribed," although the onus was on the valuation officer who sought to increase an assessment which he found under-assessed. Here it was permissible to take £3 per square metre for similar houses on the other estates with a £10 increase for car space; (2) the nuisance was not such as to persuade a hypothetical landlord to reduce his rent for the first year of his tenancy and should not be taken into account.)

HARDY & CO. (FURNISHERS) *v.* BARTLETT (LVC/836/1975) (1977) 245 E.G. 759 (ratepayers, occupiers of a shop at extreme end of High Street in Birmingham suburb, appealed against LVC's decision. *Held,* dismissing the appeal, the accepted assessments of the valuation officers' comparables was preferable to the ratepayers' adjusted actual rents basis. A 10 per cent. allowance was made for the disability of a small area masked by a boutique at the front of the appeal hereditament, but no allowance for quantity was allowed).

HART *v.* SMITH (LVC/2/1977) (1977) 246 E.G. 143. (Appeal against V.O.'s proposal for individual caravan situated on quiet holiday retreat within easy reach of Lake District. *Held,* allowing the appeal, (1) no valid comparison lies between a caravan and a permanent house; (2) It is unrealistic to derive rental value of separately let caravan from fraction of rental value of whole caravan site.)

HAUPTFUHRER *v.* THOMPSON (LVC/623/1977) (1977) 246 E.G. 407 (appellant acquired lease of Grade I listed palladian villa in Richmond, Surrey, for a premium of £8,500 in consideration of his expending £35,000 on its restoration and improvement. A grant from the Historic Buildings Council was subject to the condition that ground and first floors should be open to public view at reasonable times by appointment. The LVC reduced gross valuation to £14,000. The appellant appealed contending that the local authority publicised the house but contributed nothing to it and that no tenant on the open market would rent it for £1,400 p.a. *Held,* dismissing the appeal, the basic gross value was not excessive against comparables, distinguishing *Castle Howard Estate* v. *Phillipson* [1960] C.L.Y. 2669).

JONES *v.* DAVIES (Ref. No. LVC/863/1976) (1977) 244 E.G. 897 (in an appeal, the issue was whether buildings used for a mink farm were agricultural buildings and so exempt from rates under s. 2 of the Rating Act 1971. *Held,* the buildings were not used for breeding of livestock kept for the production of food or wool as required by the Act. Although mink carcases were fed to ducks and trout the production of food was not the main purpose of keeping the mink, and the ordinary use of the word " wool " does not cover the soft under-hair of mink).

LIVERPOOL CITY COUNCIL *v.* BRITISH TRANSPORT HOTELS AND GIBBONS (LVC/876/1976) (1977) 246 E.G. 491 (BTH owned hereditaments which it used as hotel until 1971, thereafter for storage. In 1975 BTH made a proposal for an alteration in the valuation list, namely deletion of the hereditament from the list. Before LVC hearing, BTH and G agreed on reduction in valuation instead of deletion; accordingly, LVC directed an alteration in valuation on the hearing of application for deletion. *Held,* it had no power to do so under s. 69 of the 1967 Act; it could only strike out the entry in the valuation list or reject the proposal).

MIDLAND BANK *v.* LANHAM, LVC/28, 29/1975 (the question at issue in this case was whether part of an office block used by a bank as a training school for its employees should be valued for rating purposes on the basis of its use as a training school or as offices. The tribunal *held* that the hereditament must be valued rebus sic stantibus; that its value as thus restricted must be related to the hereditament in its existing physical state; that the use of the hereditament must be taken to be within the same mode or category as the existing use but that all alternative uses to which the hereditament in its existing state could be put in the real world must be taken as being within the same mode or category where the existence of competing bidders could be established by evidence; but that the evidence of the valuation officer that a rent for a comparable training school in a commercial building was lower than office rents, even though rents for training schools had formerly been the same as those for offices and even though it might be inferred here that office tenants would be in competition, must on the facts of the case lead to the assumption that there would be no competing bid from prospective office tenants such as would influence the rent a tenant of this hereditament would be prepared to pay for the floors used as a training school. The tribunal did not consider that it was part of its role to determine issues of planning, but that in so far as the existence of planning restrictions and the necessity to obtain planning permission for change of use were factors which would affect the minds of tenants in the real world, they must have an influence on value).

PRICE v. SMITH (LVC/197/1977) (1977) 246 E.G. 145. (Appeal against V.O's proposal for 7-year-old caravan on Lake District Site, on ground that brand-new caravans carried similar rating values. 7-year-old caravan having much lower capital value than new caravans; evidence shows older caravans have lower letting values also. *Held*, age of caravan an indicator of internal layout and amenities, and therefore a proper factor affecting rental values. Appeal allowed.)

SHEPPARD'S APPEAL (LVC/192–193/1977) (1977) 245 E.G. 665 (valuation officer appealed against LVC's determination of ratepayers' claim for rate reduction because of six month nuisance resulting from sewer-laying outside their premises. *Held*, allowing the appeal, (1) LVC's specification of dates usurped prerogative of rating authority; (2) LVC wrong to make two reductions on one proposal; (3) LVC wrong to make reduction followed by increase; (4) LVC right to reduce rateable value in some measure as six months nuisance not too transient. Court of Appeal's observations on transience in *Dick Hampton (Earth Moving)* v. *Lewis* (1975) C.L.Y. 2776, although relating to rateable occupation, were applicable to effect of nuisance on rental value).

STRAND HOTELS v. HAMPSHER (LVC/615/1975) (1977) 244 E.G. 977 (the appellants appealed against the respondent's assessments on Tower Hotel, St. Katharine's Dock made in February 1974 and February 1975 when the hotel was open to the public but partly still in contractors' hands. Additional bedrooms were available by 1975. The appellants' valuations on profits basis were rejected and no justification was found for end-allowances deductions, but the valuation officer's valuations on unit-prices-per-room basis were adjusted after comparison with other Central London Hotels and the appeal accordingly allowed).

WALLS v. NATIONAL CAR PARKS, LVC/229–230/1976 (reference was to determine rating assessments of two multi-storey car parks. The valuation officer adopted a direct approach valuation, founded on an analysis of lease rents. He added 5 per cent. for repairs and insurance and 13·67 per cent. for inflation. No adjustment was to be made for security of tenure. *Held*, this valuation was to be preferred to the ratepayer's, based on estimated gross takings for 1973–74 related to comparables from other disparate cities).

2465. Liability for rates—obligation of husband—agreement by wife to pay rates

A husband's obligation to pay rates in respect of the former matrimonial home, which continues to be occupied by his wife and child, is not discharged by an agreement by the wife to pay the rates out of a weekly allowance paid to her by the husband. (*Cardiff Corporation* v. *Robinson* [1956] C.L.Y. 7289 applied): CHARNWOOD BOROUGH COUNCIL v. GARNER, *The Times*, November 21, 1978, D.C.

2465a. ——— ——— separated husband having no interest in home

Where a wife who is judicially separated from her husband is and always has been the sole owner of the matrimonial home, and the husband has never been responsible for maintaining the home for his wife and children and owns no interest in the home, he cannot be deemed to be its occupier for rating purposes: BROWN v. OXFORD CITY COUNCIL, *The Times*, June 24, 1978,

2466. Northern Ireland. See NORTHERN IRELAND.

2467. Rate rebates

RATE REBATE (AMENDMENT) REGULATIONS 1978 (No. 387) [15p], made under the Local Government Act 1974 (c. 7), s. 11 (1); operative on April 1, 1978; amend the statutory rate rebate scheme provided in S.I. 1974 No. 411. The maximum rebate is increased from £3·00 to £4·50 in the G.L.C. area, and from £2·50 to £3·20 elsewhere.

RATE REBATE REGULATIONS 1978 (No. 1504) [40p], made under the Local Government Act 1974, s. 11 (1); operative on November 13, 1978; consolidate with amendments certain specified instruments which are revoked. They set out the statutory rate rebate scheme for the grant by rating authorities to residential occupiers of rebates from rates. They increase the minimum rebate to 10p.

2468. Rate support grant

RATE SUPPORT GRANT (SPECIFIED BODIES) REGULATIONS 1978 (No. 171) [10p], made under the Local Government Act 1974 (c. 7), s. 2 (7) (a); operative on April 1, 1978; specify bodies (in addition to those bodies specified in S.I. 1974 No. 788, S.I. 1975 No. 5 and S.I. 1976 No. 214, in relation to whose services the power to defray expenditure applies.

RATE SUPPORT GRANT REGULATIONS 1978 (No. 1701) [40p], made under the Local Government Act 1974, ss. 2 (4), 10 (3), Sched. 2, paras. 2, 6, 9, 11 and the General Rate Act 1967 (c. 9), s. 48 (4); operative on April 1, 1979; provide for carrying into effect the provisions of the 1974 Act with respect to the payment of rate support grants to local authorities for the year 1979–80.

RATE SUPPORT GRANT ORDER 1978 (No. 1867) [40p], made under the Local Government Act 1974, s. 3 (1); operative on December 16, 1978; fixes and prescribes the rate support grant for the financial year 1979–80.

RATE SUPPORT GRANT (INCREASE) ORDER 1978 (No. 1868) [10p], made under the Local Government Act 1974, s. 4; operative on December 16, 1978; further increases the aggregate amount of supplementary grant for transport purposes for the financial year 1977–78.

RATE SUPPORT GRANT (INCREASE) (No. 2) ORDER 1978 (No. 1869) [40p], made under the Local Government Act 1974, s. 4; operative on December 16, 1978; increases the rate support grants for the financial year 1978–79.

2469. Rateable value—proposal to alter not served—valuation list conclusive

[General Rate Act 1967 (c. 9), ss. 67 (6) (7), 87.]

Where the valuation list is altered to match a proposal for alteration which was never served, magistrates cannot go behind the list in determining whether to issue a distress warrant for non-payment.

A proposal to alter the valuation of premises never came to the attention of the occupier, who consequently did not object to it. The valuation list was altered accordingly. When a demand was made for the increased amount, the occupier refused to pay and a distress warrant was issued by the magistrates. *Held*, dismissing the occupier's appeal against the issue of that warrant, that the magistrates were correct in accepting the valuation list as conclusive evidence of the rateable value.

COUNTY AND NIMBUS ESTATES v. EALING LONDON BOROUGH COUNCIL (1978) 76 L.G.R. 624, D.C.

2470. Rating—derating—change of use—" dock purposes "

[Scot.] [Rating and Valuation (Apportionment) Act 1928 (c. 44), ss. 5, 6.] Land used as part of a dock undertaking may be derated under s. 5, and if s. 5 applies, s. 6 excludes any part of the land used for transport purposes from the provisions normally applying to it. Application was made to derate a fish market, used for sorting and processing fish once it vested in the Harbour Board, which was a dock authority who used it in connection with their dock undertaking. *Held*, this transfer was a material change in circumstances justifying derating, as the land thereby became used for the dock undertaking and did not remain occupied and used for warehousing merchandise not being transported: ABERDEEN HARBOUR BOARD v. ASSESSOR FOR THE CITY OF ABERDEEN, 1973 S.C. 76, L.V.A.C.

2470a. Rating (Disabled Persons) Act 1978 (c. 40)

This Act amends the law relating to relief from rates in respect of premises used by disabled persons and invalids.

S. 1 provides for rebates for hereditaments with special facilities for disabled persons; s. 2 relates to rebates for institutions for the disabled; s. 3 deals with administration and appeals; s. 4 provides for rebates for land and heritages in Scotland with special facilities for disabled persons; s. 5 relates to rebates for institutions in Scotland for the disabled; s. 6 deals with administration and appeals in Scotland; s. 7 provides for the alteration of the valuation roll in Scotland; s. 8 contains definitions; s. 9 gives the short title. The Act does not extend to Northern Ireland.

The Act received the Royal Assent on July 20, 1978, and came into force on April 1, 1979.

2471. Rating surcharge—unoccupied premises—whether a "dwelling-house" or a "commercial building"

[General Rate Act 1967 (c. 9), ss. 17A (1), 17B (2) (as amended by Local Government Act 1974 (c. 7), s. 16), 115, Sched. 13 para. 2 (1).]

A "dwelling-house" within the meaning of the Act need not necessarily be a building actually in use as a dwelling-house in order to be excluded from the category of commercial building.

V Ltd. purchased the lease of a building which had been used in the past both as a dwelling-house and for letting rooms, and remained capable of being used for either purpose. The building remained unoccupied for six months while V Ltd. arranged for its conversion into separate units. The rating authority complained against V Ltd. that it had failed to pay a rating surcharge demanded under s. 17A of the 1967 Act, contending that the building was a "commercial building." The justices dismissed the complaint on the ground that the building was a "dwelling-house" within the meaning of s. 115 of the Act and was therefore not a commercial building. The rating authority appealed. *Held*, dismissing the appeal, that a dwelling-house within the meaning of the Act was a building which existed for the use of, or was of a kind that was used for, a dwelling-house and the justices were right. ROYAL BOROUGH OF KENSINGTON AND CHELSEA v. VICTORIA WINE CO. [1977] 75 L.G.R. 835, D.C.

2472. Unoccupied premises—electricity board—showroom—whether "occupied and used"

[General Rate Act 1967 (c. 9), ss. 17 (1) (a), 34 (1) (2) (b), Sched. 1, para. 1 (1).]

S. 34 (2) (b) of the Act operates only if the electricity board premises are used as well as occupied as a showroom.

Premises of the electricity board were occupied and used as a showroom until November 1974. Thereafter they remained unoccupied and unused until August 1975. The rating authority passed a resolution under s. 17 of the Act bringing into effect Sched. 1 to the Act and rated the electricity board during the relevant period. The rate was not paid and the rating authority applied for a distress warrant. The magistrate held that the premises were not liable to be rated by virtue of s. 34 (1) and (2) (b) of the Act since they were not occupied or used by the electricity board but that they could be rated by virtue of Sched. 1 and accordingly issued a warrant. On appeal by the electricity board, *held*, allowing the appeal, that Sched. 1, para. 1 (1) did not deem user to continue as well as occupation therefore since the premises were not "occupied and used" as a showroom during the relevant period they were exempt from rating by virtue of s. 34 (1) of the Act. TOWER HAMLETS LONDON BOROUGH COUNCIL v. LONDON ELECTRICITY BOARD [1977] 75 L.G.R. 810, D.C.

2473. Valuation

VALUATION LISTS (POSTPONEMENT) ORDER 1978 (No. 993) [10p], made under the General Rate Act 1975 (c. 5), s. 1 (2); operative on July 18, 1978; postpones the coming into force of new valuation lists until April 1, 1981.

2474. —— factors reducing value—harassment by neighbour—nil valuation
[General Rate Act 1967 (c. 9), s. 19; Housing Act 1961 (c. 65), s. 19 (as amended by Housing Act 1969 (c. 33), ss. 61, 62.]
Harassment of a ratepayer by neighbours is a factor to be considered in assessing the rateable value of premises; a nil or nominal valuation is possible notwithstanding that the ratepayer is in beneficial occupation.
The ratepayer had for some 25 years occupied a first floor flat which had fallen into extreme dilapidation and had become unfit for habitation. In anticipation of a closing order the ratepayer remained in occupation so as to protect her position and qualify for rehousing. Although an order had been made limiting the number of households in the whole house to one, from 1973 to 1975 the ground floor flat was occupied by two families comprising 13 persons with whom the ratepayer had to share a bathroom and through whose flat was access to such bathroom. In 1974 the ratepayer applied for the flat to be reassessed at a nil value, the 1973 values being £260, gross, and £190, rateable. The tribunal reduced such values to £70 and £39 respectively but refused to take account of harassment by neighbouring occupants or to make a nil assessment in view of the ratepayer's beneficial occupation. *Held*, allowing the ratepayer's appeal, that (1) harassment was a factor to be considered; (2) the ratepayer was not to be equated with a hypothetical tenant under s. 19 (6) of the 1967 Act, since it may be that no one else would willingly pay anything for such premises, and that a nil or nominal valuation could be made notwithstanding beneficial occupation by the ratepayer. (*British Transport Commission* v. *Hingley* [1961] C.L.Y. 7486 applied.)
BLACK v. OLIVER [1978] 2 W.L.R. 923, C.A.

2475. —— new hereditament—powers under s. 6 of 1967 Act
[General Rate Act 1967 (c. 9), ss. 2 (4), 6.] The valuation officer made a proposal for inclusion of the respondent's newly erected hereditament into the valuation list. The rating authority took action to obtain rates more quickly by exercising powers under s. 6 of the 1967 Act to make amendments in the rate. The respondents failed to pay their rates contending that the authority had sought to include in the rate a sum which had not appeared in the valuation list at all contrary to its powers under s. 2 (4) of the Act. *Held*, allowing the authority's appeal by case stated, provided that a proposal by the valuation officer had been made, the rating authority may use its powers under s. 6 to bring a new hereditament into charge—despite the apparent conflict between s. 2 (4) and s. 6 of the Act: NEWCASTLE-UNDER-LYME BOROUGH COUNCIL v. KETTLE (1977) 245 E.G. 1027, D.C.

2476. —— profits basis of valuation—relevance of exceptional profit
[Scot.] A valuation of a harbour was made on the basis of its profit in the preceeding five years. It was contended that an excessive, unprecedented profit in one year should be disregarded for rating purposes. *Held*, it was correct to have regard to such a profit as the basis for the assessment was the fact of the previous five years' profit, not speculation as to future profits: ASSESSOR FOR FIFE v. ANSTRUTHER UNION HARBOUR BOARD COMMISSIONERS, 1973 S.C. 88, L.V.A.C.

2477. —— rates—relationship to interest rates
[Scot.] [Valuation and Rating (Scotland) Act 1956 (c. 60), s. 6 (8).] In assessing the net annual value of two distilleries, the assessor arrived at a decapitalisation rate of 6 per cent. on land and buildings, and 7 per cent. on plant, using the interest rate on money lent. *Held*, this was a proper basis for an assessment, but the valuation committee erred in holding that s. 6 (8) imposed no burden on a landlord of replacing worn out buildings, and so its reduction of the rate to 6 per cent. overall would be reversed: SCOTTISH MALT DISTILLERIES v. ASSESSOR FOR COUNTY OF BANFF, 1973 S.C. 63, L.V.A.C.

ARTICLES. See *post*, p. [32].

REAL PROPERTY AND CONVEYANCING

2478. Covenants—restrictive covenant—enclosure of swimming pool—no breach of covenant to build private dwelling-houses

P sought an injunction to restrain D from constructing a building to enclose an existing swimming-pool claiming that (1) a building scheme was in force and, accordingly, (2) D would breach a covenant that "no building other than private dwelling-houses shall be erected." *Held*, refusing the injunction, (1) there was no evidence of a building scheme (*Elliston* v. *Reacher* [1908] 2 Ch. 374 applied); (2) the enclosure of the swimming pool was for use ancillary to D's house and so did not breach the covenant: HARLOW v. HARTOG (1977) 245 E.G. 140, Sir Douglas Frank, Q.C.

2479. —— —— Lands Tribunal decisions

Re ACLAND'S APPLICATION, LP/25/1976 (in an application for discharge or modification of a restriction imposed in a conveyance in 1960, forbidding alteration to the external plan of a dwelling-house without the consent of the vendor, the applicant contended that changes in the character of the neighbourhood rendered the restriction obsolete, that reasonable user was impeded without benefit to the covenantee's successors, and that in signing an undated document acquiescing in the development they had agreed to the discharge of the restriction. *Held*, (1) the restriction was not obsolete; (2) on the evidence, the objectors had not consented to the proposed development; (3) the planning permission granted to the applicants proved only that the specified development was not contrary to public interest; (4) the objectors would be injured by the proposed development, and money would not be adequate compensation).

Re L.H.M. DEVELOPMENTS' AND ROBERT BARNES' APPLICATION LP/22/1977 (an application to erect four houses in contravention of a restrictive covenant was rejected on the grounds that the covenant secured practical benefits of substantial value or advantage to the objector in that it enabled her to control the form of development possible upon the subject land, which was important to her, as any house built upon that land would be visible from her house and would result in her moving from there; that control by a restrictive covenant could be more severe than that possible by a planning authority; that the public interest was not so important or immediate here as to warrant interference with private rights).

Re PEARSON'S APPLICATION LP/14/1977 (application to use outbuildings of a house in Cubbington, Warwickshire, as a home for retired ladies in contravention of a restrictive covenant imposed in 1970. The original covenantee and a company producing dumpers, of which the former was controlling shareholder, objected on the grounds that such a use of the applicant's land would prevent the objectors from obtaining planning permission to exploit their industrial use of adjoining land. The tribunal permitted the proposed modification as they did not believe that planning permission would be forthcoming for the uses of the adjoining land which the objectors had in mind, except upon a very temporary basis, and he did not believe that the objectors would be injured by the modification).

2480. —— —— owner of benefited land purchasing burdened land—unity of seisin

Where the fees simple of land benefited, and of land burdened by restrictive covenants become vested in the same person, the restrictive covenants are extinguished unless the common owner recreates them.

P purchased agricultural land which was part of the estate of a mansion house. To protect the view of the house P covenanted with V, the vendor, to use the land for agricultural purposes only and not to erect any building. X bought the mansion and its grounds, and subsequently also about half of P's land. X sold some of the land to the defendants, and some burdened land to the plaintiff. The plaintiff sought a declaration that X's purchase of the burdened land had created unity of seisin and that the land was no longer subject to the covenants. *Held*, that since the common owner had not re-imposed the covenants when dividing up and selling the land, the plaintiff was entitled to a declaration that the covenants were extinguished. (Dictum of Lord Cross of Chelsea in *Texaco Antilles* v. *Kernochan* [1973] C.L.Y. 2793 applied.)

Re TILTWOOD, SUSSEX; BARRETT v. BOND [1978] 3 W.L.R. 474, Foster J.

2481. Exchange of contracts—by telephone

There was no binding contract where solicitors purported to dispense with exchange of contracts and bind their clients immediately to the sale of a house. The issue concerned the validity of the practice of solicitors exchanging contracts by telephone, where there had to be a simultaneous sale and purchase in a chain of vendors and purchasers, and thereby agreeing that a binding contract existed before the formalities of exchange had been completed. The fundamental rule was that in the absence of specific authority solicitors are not the agents of their clients to conclude a contract for them (*Lockett* v. *Norman-Wright* [1925] Ch. 56, 62 applied). All the arrangements had been made through estate agents " subject to contract," a well understood phrase which imports actual exchange. Exchange by telephone was a bad practice which did not achieve its object: DOMB v. ISOZ, *The Times*, August 8, 1978, Brian Dillon Q.C.

2482. Fees—solicitors—fair and reasonable sum. See TREASURY SOLICITOR v. REGESTER, § 2817.

2483. Joint tenancy—whether property held in resulting trust—quit claim deed—no intention to end joint tenancy

[Can.] P sued, in her personal capacity, her deceased mother's estate of which she was the administratrix, claiming that land registered in the name of her mother was in part held on a resulting trust for herself and her mother in joint tenancy. The land was first registered solely in the mother's name in 1958, and was later conveyed into joint tenancy in 1962. In 1964 the mother convinced P to sign a quit claim deed because she mistrusted P's current boy friend. P contributed to the mortgage payments continuously from 1958 to 1967. The mother continued to live in the house until her death in 1975. *Held,* the house was held by the deceased on a resulting trust. The parties intended originally that there be a joint tenancy and there was no evidence that, in signing the quit claim deed, P intended a gift to the mother of any of her interest in the property. Further, the quit claim deed did not sever the joint tenancy, as neither party intended it to change the right of survivorship. (Dicta of Lord Denning M.R. in *Burgess* v. *Rawnsley* [1975] C.L.Y. 3115 applied): GROVES v. CHRISTIANSEN [1978] 4 W.W.R. 64, Brit.Col.Sup.Ct.

2484. Land charges. See LAND CHARGES.

2485. Land obligation—variation—impractibility of variation—whether obligation unduly burdensome

[Scot.] [Conveyancing and Feudal Reform (Scotland) Act 1970 (c. 35), s. 1 (3) (*b*) (*c*).] A burdened proprietor may apply to have varied a land obligation if it is unduly burdensome compared with the benefits it confers, or if it impedes the reasonable use of the land. The obligation in question restricted the use of the land which it was desired to use as a supermarket. *Held,* the proprietors' application for variation failed because, even if the obligation were varied, access problems and planning permission would still prevent use as a supermarket. The obligation was not unduly burdensome, and did not impede any reasonable use of land: MURRAYFIELD ICE RINK v. SCOTTISH RUGBY UNION TRUSTEES, 1973 S.C. 21, Second Division.

2486. Land registration. See LAND REGISTRATION.

2487. Licence—misconduct of licensee—whether licence revocable

Once an equitable licence to occupy premises is established, it cannot be determined by misconduct.

In 1972 S was held by a county court to have an equitable licence to occupy a cottage for life pursuant to a prior family arrangement. The cottage together with the adjoining cottage and a paddock were sold to W. S created difficulties for W in relation to his use of the paddock and occupation of the adjoining cottage. W brought an action for possession of the cottage occupied by S. The judge held that the misconduct had been such as to determine the equitable licence and granted possession to W. S. appealed. *Held,* allowing the appeal, that the misconduct did not determine the licence. *Per* Lord Denning M.R.: in an extreme case an equitable licence might be revoked. *Per* Goff and Cumming-Bruce L.JJ.: when a party raises an equity of the present character and it is alleged against him that his own behaviour has been wrong, the court has to decide on the facts at the date of the hearing whether he is entitled to equitable relief.

WILLIAMS *v.* STAITE [1978] 2 W.L.R. 825, C.A.

2488. Mortgages. See MORTGAGES.

2489. Northern Ireland. See NORTHERN IRELAND.

2490. Option to purchase—Beddoe application—failure to register option. See MIDLAND BANK TRUST CO. *v.* GREEN, § 1415.

2491. Party wall—extension to outside wall by one party—whether " lawful "
[Bristol Corporation Act 1926 (c. xcix), s. 93 (1).]
The words " it shall be lawful " in the Bristol Corporation Act 1962, s. 93 (1), do not confer title to do that which involves encroachment on the proprietary right of another.

D built up part of his garden wall, which was a party wall. P brought an action for damages and for an injunction requiring the removal of that part of the built-up party wall which was built on his part of the wall. D contended that by virtue of s. 93 (1) of the Bristol Corporation Act 1926 he was entitled to build up the wall as he had. *Held,* allowing P's appeal, that this was not so. S. 93 (1) provides that " it shall be lawful for the owner or part owner of any party wall to raise the same provided that the wall when raised will be of the substance required by any by-law." This section did not confer any title to encroach on the proprietary rights of another.

MOSS *v.* SMITH (1977) 76 L.G.R. 284, C.A.

2492. Purchaser acting as vendor's agent—duty to disclose—fiduciary relationship. See ENGLISH *v.* DEDHAM VALE PROPERTIES, § 3060.

2493. Registered land. See LAND REGISTRATION.

2494. Rentcharges
RENTCHARGES REGULATIONS 1978 (No. 16) [25p], made under the Rentcharges Act 1977 (c. 30), ss. 4 (5), 8 (2), 9 (3), 12, 15 (2) (3); operative on February 1, 1978, prescribe various forms.

2495. Rentcharges Act 1977—commencement
RENTCHARGES ACT 1977 (COMMENCEMENT) ORDER 1978 (No. 15 (C. 2)) [10p], made under the Rentcharges Act 1977 (c. 30), s. 18 (2); operative on February 1, 1978; brings into force those provisions not already in operation, which deal principally with the procedures for the apportionment and redemptions and implied covenants affecting rentcharges.

2496. Restrictive burden—whether binding
[Scot.] [Conveyancing (Scotland) Act 1874 (c. 94), s. 32.] In 1913, the feuar of land agreed that it should remain unbuilt on, and this was expressed as a real burden binding on the land, which was subsequently divided up and sold, subject to the agreement. Application was made to the Dean of Guild Court for warrant to allow a plot to be built on. The superiors objected on the basis of the agreement. *Held,* the Dean of Guild Court could hear the application although the applicants, only being conditional purchasers, were not infeft. The agreement bound the land under s. 32 of the Act as a real burden affecting it: GORRIE AND BANKS *v.* BURGH OF MUSSELBURGH, 1973 S.C. 33, First Division.

2497. Right of pre-emption—whether creating interest in land
Properly constructed rights of pre-emption create interests in land.
In 1944, L and his wife conveyed to R part of a parcel of land and retained the remainder for their own occupation. The conveyance contained in cl. (B) a covenant by the vendors and their successors in title for the benefit of R and his successors in title that whilst R and the vendors were alive neither the vendors nor the survivor of them would sell or concur in selling all or

any part of the retained lands without giving R the option of purchasing the retained lands. That covenant was duly registered under the Land Charges Act 1925. By 1965 the land purchased by R had been conveyed with the benefit of the covenant to B and his wife. The retained land was occupied by P under a 21-year lease which gave P an option to purchase the retained land after the death of the survivor of L and his wife. In 1969 L's wife died. By 1971 L's health had deteriorated and his nephew was appointed as his receiver under the Mental Health Act 1959. Funds were urgently needed for his support and, with the authority of the Court of Protection, agreement was reached to sell the retained lands to B and his wife pursuant to cl. (B) of the 1944 conveyance. Completion took place after L's death in 1973 and soon afterwards P served a notice purporting to exercise his option to purchase the retained lands. P claimed, *inter alia,* specific performance of the contract of sale allegedly arising therefrom and an order that the conveyance of the retained lands to B and his wife be set aside on the basis that they had conspired with L's nephew to interfere with his contractual rights. *Held,* dismissing the claims, that (1) the right of pre-emption of the retained lands contained in the cl. (B) covenant created an interest in land and since it was registered it took precedence over the option to purchase conferred on P; (2) the sale to B and his wife was valid and effective; (3) it was impossible to imply into the lease of the land to P any term that L and his wife would not during their lives sell or concur in selling the retained lands since the possibility of a sale under cl. (B) of the 1944 conveyance was accepted by P when the lease was negotiated; (4) the defendants lacked the necessary knowledge to render them guilty of conspiracy. (*Murray* v. *Two Strokes* [1973] C.L.Y. 1881 and *Imperial Chemical Industries* v. *Sussman* (unreported), May 28, 1976, not followed; *Manchester Ship Canal Co.* v. *Manchester Racecourse Co.* [1901] 2 Ch. 37 distinguished; *London and South Western Railway Co.* v. *Gomm* [1881] 20 Ch.D. 562, and *First National Securities* v. *Chiltern District Council* [1975] C.L.Y. 1823 considered.)
PRITCHARD *v.* BRIGGS [1978] 2 W.L.R. 317, Walton J.

2498. Sale of land. See VENDOR AND PURCHASER.

2499. ——— option in lease—validity—amendment by notary
    [Can.] A lease of land which included an option to purchase was drawn up by a notary acting for both parties. He deleted part of the lease as he felt he thereby expressed the parties' true intentions, then notified them of his action. The lessor sought to resist the lessee's exercise of the option, claiming that the deed had been rendered a nullity by the alteration. *Held,* the notary's deletion did not better express the parties' true intentions. However, rectification would be made and the option enforced, because, if the notary had acted as a stranger, his alteration was a nullity, and if he acted as both parties' agent then they, having been notified and done nothing, had acquiesced in his deletion. (*Suffell* v. *Bank of England* (1882) 9 Q.B.D. 555 considered): JOHNSON *v.* TROBAK [1977] 6 W.W.R. 289, Brit. Col. C.A.

2500. ——— plan for identification only—boundaries unclear—whether reference to plan permissible
    Where the identity of property to be conveyed is not made explicit in the description of the parcels, an annexed plan described as " for identification only " can be used to elucidate the identity of the property.
    In 1920 in an auction by X of certain lots of land, M Ltd. bought lot 795, which was described as "coloured yellow on the sales plan." The sale particulars referred to a 1915 ordinance survey map, in which the parcel of land was larger than the description of it in the sales plan. The conveyance plan corresponded with the sales plan. In 1972, after a series of conveyances and other transactions, the plaintiffs bought from X the fee simple in some land included in the 1915 O.S. map but not in the yellow portion on the sales plan. The defendants, thinking the land was theirs, had already built on it. The plaintiffs contended the land was theirs by virtue of the 1972 conveyance, the defendants that it had been conveyed in 1921 and they were entitled to possession. The trial judge found for the defendants. On appeal, *held,* allowing the appeal, that although a plan annexed to a conveyance and marked

"for identification only" could not contradict anything explicit in the description of the parcels, it could be used to elucidate the identity of the property where this was not explicit. Here reference could be made to the plans to determine the extent of the land conveyed.

WIGGINTON AND MILNER v. WINSTER ENGINEERING [1978] 3 All E.R. 436, C.A.

2500a. —— time of the essence—rescission of contract

After serving on the purchasers a notice to complete, expiring on December 1, the vendors introduced the purchasers to M, who agreed with the purchasers to take an assignment of the contract, and arranged with the vendors a completion date of December 6, later extended to January 28. But M failed to complete also, and on February 7 the vendors sent the purchasers a letter rescinding the contract, and referring, inter alia, to interest payable under the contract. The vendors then brought proceedings against the purchasers and obtained damages. The purchasers brought the present action against their solicitors, claiming that the latter had negligently given them wrong advice. *Held,* (1) time had not ceased to be of the essence of the contract on February 7, since the extensions given to M had been indulgences granted to him personally. There had been no act vis-à-vis the purchasers constituting a waiver by the vendors of the requirement to complete; (2) the contract had been rescinded in the sense that the vendors had accepted the purchasers' repudiation and retained their rights under the contract, and not in the sense that they had treated the contract as annulled *ab initio*. If annulment had been intended, the vendors would not have referred to interest in their letter. Consequently, damages had been rightly recoverable, and the solicitors had not been negligent. *Per* Goff L.J., the vendors had been entitled to accept the purchasers' repudiation and recover damages, whether or not they could rescind *ab initio*: BUCKLAND v. FARMAR AND MOODY (A FIRM), *The Times,* February 17, 1978, C.A.

2501. —— whether contract existed—requirement of writing—enforceability

[Law of Property Act 1925 (c. 20), s. 40.]

A contract to do something which has the effect of disposing of an interest in land is a contract to dispose of an interest in land within s. 40 of the Act.

D Ltd. negotiated with F Ltd. for the sale of certain properties. D Ltd. alleged that there was an oral agreement that F Ltd. would exchange contracts for the sale of the properties if D Ltd. attended at their offices with a draft contract in terms already agreed and a banker's draft for the deposit. D Ltd. complied with those conditions, but F Ltd. refused to exchange contracts. D Ltd. claimed damages for breach of the oral agreement. The judge struck out the statement of claim as disclosing no cause of action in that there was no note or memorandum of the agreement sufficient to satisfy s. 40 (1) of the Act. D Ltd. appealed. *Held,* dismissing the appeal, that (1) D Ltd., having satisfied the conditions specified, there was a valid unilateral contract of which F Ltd. were in breach; although the unilateral contract was not for the sale of land or an interest in land, s. 40 of the Act applied to it and, in the absence of a memorandum in writing, there had to be an act of part performance before it could be enforced; (2) D Ltd.'s acts did not point to there being some contract so there was no act of part performance to exclude the provisions of s. 40 (1) of the Act. (*Warlow* v. *Harrison* (1858) 1 El. & El. 295 and *Johnson* v. *Boyes* [1899] 2 Ch. 73 distinguished; *Steadman* v. *Steadman* [1974] C.L.Y. 3968 applied.)

DAULIA v. FOUR MILLBANK NOMINEES [1978] 2 W.L.R. 621, C.A.

2502. Stamp duties. See STAMP DUTIES.

2503. Tenancy in common—right to revenue—obligation to account—benefits of occupation

[Can.] On their father's death, the parties each inherited a one-third interest in two quarter sections of land. On their mother's death, P inherited her one-third share in the NW. quarter, and D her one-third share in the SW. quarter. D remained on the land throughout, farming both quarters. P asked for judgment in an amount equal to his share of the revenue since the mother's death, and an order either directing the sale of the land, or transferring the interest of P in the SW. quarter to D, and the interest of D in the NW. quarter to P. *Held*, P was not entitled to a share in the revenue. Under common law, there was no obligation to account between tenants in common, and s. 27 of the Statute of Queen Anne, 1705, applied only where revenue came from an outside source, not where one tenant has enjoyed more of the benefit of the subject or made more of his occupation. An order transferring P's interest in the SW. quarter to D, and D's interest in the NW. quarter to P was made: REID v. REID [1978] 4 W.W.R. 460, Sask.Q.B.

2504. Town and country planning. See TOWN AND COUNTRY PLANNING.

2505. Trusts. See SETTLEMENTS AND TRUSTS.

BOOKS AND ARTICLES. See *post*, pp. [7], [33].

REGISTRATION OF BIRTHS, DEATHS AND MARRIAGES

2506. Northern Ireland. See NORTHERN IRELAND.

RENT RESTRICTION

2507. Fair rent—rent officer's jurisdiction—no withdrawal because tenant has vacated premises
[Rent Act 1968 (c. 23), s. 44 (1) (6).]
In the absence of an express withdrawal of an application to fix a fair rent, a rent officer should not automatically treat an application which has not been pursued as withdrawn since the public interest may require that a fair rent is determined.

In March 1976, the applicant applied for the registration of a fair rent in respect of premises occupied by him as a statutory tenant. The rent officer inspected the premises and in July 1976 wrote to the applicant and the landlord inviting both to a consultation. Unbeknown to the rent officer the applicant had vacated the premises by the date of the letter. After no one attended the proposed consultation; thereafter the rent officer indicated that since the applicant was no longer the tenant and in view of his failure to attend the consultation, he, the rent officer, would treat the application as withdrawn. Upon the applicant's application for mandamus requiring the officer to determine a fair rent, *held*, granting the application, (1) that the rent officer retained jurisdiction to determine the applicant notwithstanding the applicant's vacation of the premises since the relevant date for the purposes of conferring jurisdiction was that upon which the application was made; (2) that although it was right to consider that the applicant had been at fault, the fact that little money was involved and that the applicant had no continuing interest in the premises, the public interest outweighed such considerations since, inter alia, the fixing of a rent for these premises might influence rents on other properties in the area. (*R.* v. *West London Rent Tribunal, ex p. Napier* [1965] C.L.Y. 3383 and *Hanson* v. *Church Commissioners for England* [1977] C.L.Y. 2520 applied.) R. v. LAMBETH RENT OFFICER, *ex p.* FOX (1978) 35 P. & C.R. 65, D.C.

2508. Forms
RENT REGULATIONS (FORMS, ETC.) REGULATIONS 1978 (No. 495) [60p], made under the Rent Act 1977 (c. 42), ss. 60 (1), 74 (1), 117 (1); operative on June 19, 1978; prescribe the forms to be used for the purposes of Parts III and IV of, and Scheds. 11 and 12 to, the Rent Act 1977.

2509. Procedure—recovery of possession
RENT (COUNTY COURT PROCEEDINGS) (CASE 11) RULES 1978 (No. 1961 (L. 40)) [20p], made under the Rent Act 1977 (c. 42), s. 142; operative on March 12, 1979; provide a summary procedure for the recovery of possession by owner-occupiers as an alternative to the ordinary proceedings in the County Court where the claim falls within Case 11 of Sched. 15 to the 1977 Act.

2510. Rent assessment committee—no need to follow particular valuation method
[Rent Act 1968 (c. 23), s. 46; Rent Assessment Committees (England and

Wales) Regulations 1971 (S.I. 1971 No. 1065), reg. 5.] L appealed against decisions of a rent assessment committee. *Held*, dismissing the appeal, (1) failure to consider capital values of properties was not an error of law by the committee as there was no obligation to follow any particular valuation method; (2) the committee was not obliged to give its reasons when fixing a fair rent; (3) in the absence of a tenancy agreement the committee could not say that improvements were within the terms of any agreement; (4) the duty to supply all relevant documents to the parties before the hearing does not extend to those documents which come to light thereafter (principles in *Guppys (Bridport)* v. *Sandoe* (1975) C.L.Y. 1862 applied): GUPPYS PROPER-TIES v. KNOTT; GUPPYS PROPERTIES v. STRUTT (1977) 245 E.G. 1023, D.C.

2511. Rent tribunal—jurisdiction—applicant neither tenant nor contractual licensee
[Rent Act 1968 (c. 23), Part VI.] L let a furnished room to A on a holiday tenancy. A was married to the applicant but left her before the tenancy expired and she continued to pay the rent. After the expiry of the tenancy when she had stopped paying the rent, the applicant applied to a rent tribunal for consideration of rent and security of tenure. The tribunal granted her application. L applied for a writ of certiorari to quash the tribunal's decision. *Held*, quashing the decision, neither rent paid by the applicant before the expiry of the holiday tenancy nor events after the application could enable the tribunal to find that the applicant was a tenant or contractual licensee: R. v. KENSINGTON AND CHELSEA RENT TRIBUNAL, *ex p.* BARRETT (1977) 245 E.G. 397, D.C.

2512. Statutory tenancy—agriculture
RENT (AGRICULTURE) (RENT REGISTRATION) REGULATIONS 1978 (No. 494) [15p], made under the Rent Act 1977 (c. 42), s. 74 (1) as applied by the Rent (Agriculture) Act 1976 (c. 80), s. 13; operative on June 19, 1978; prescribe the application form for the registration of a fair rent for a statutory tenancy arising under the 1976 Act and the particulars to be given in that form.

ARTICLES. See *post*, p. [33].

REVENUE AND FINANCE

2513. Appropriation Act 1978 (c. 57)
This Act applies a sum out of the Consolidated Fund to the service of the year ending on March 31, 1979; it also appropriates the supplies granted in this Session of Parliament, and repeals certain Consolidated Fund and Appropriation Acts.
S. 1 provides for the issue out of the Consolidated Fund for the year ending March 31, 1979; s. 2 deals with the appropriation of sums voted for supply services; s. 3 repeals certain enactments; s. 4 contains the short title.
The Act received the Royal Assent on August 2, 1978, and came into force on that date.

2514. Capital transfer tax. See CAPITAL TAXATION.

2515. Coinage
TRIAL OF THE PYX (AMENDMENT) ORDER 1978 (No. 185) [10p], made under the Coinage Act 1971 (c. 24), s. 8 (2), (3); operative on February 10, 1978; amends S.I. 1975 No. 2192 by giving to the Queen's Remembrancer the right to decide whether the whole or part only of the verdict of the jury shall be read out in his presence.

2516. Consolidated Fund Act 1978 (c. 7)
This Act provides for the issue of certain monies out of the Consolidated Fund.
The Act received the Royal Assent on March 23, 1978, and came into force on that date.

2517. Consolidated Fund (No. 2) Act 1978 (c. 59)
This Act provides for the issue of certain moneys out of the Consolidated Fund.

The Act received the Royal Assent on December 14, 1978, and came into force on that date.

2518. Counter-inflation

COUNTER-INFLATION (PRICE CODE) ORDER 1978 (No. 1082) [10p], made under the Counter-Inflation Act 1973 (c. 9), s. 2, as amended by the Prices Act 1974 (c. 24) and the Price Commission Act 1977 (c. 33); operative on August 1, 1978; revokes S.I. 1977 No. 1272 and substitutes a new Price Code, differing from its predecessor in that it is addressed solely to the Price Commission in relation to their remaining functions under the 1973 Act, and it does not now make provision for controls on prices and profit margins since, after July 31, 1978, the Commission will have no power to enforce such provisions contained in a Code.

PRICES AND CHARGES (NOTIFICATION OF INCREASES) ORDER 1978 (No. 1083) [40p], made under the Counter-Inflation Act 1973, ss. 5, 15, Sched. 3, paras. 1 (1) (2) (4) (6), 2 (2), as amended under the Prices Act 1974 and the Price Commission Act 1977, ss. 14, 15 (4); operative on August 1, 1978; replaces S.I. 1977 No. 1281 and makes provision for notification to the Price Commission of proposed increases in prices and charges.

COUNTER-INFLATION (DIVIDENDS) (AMENDMENT) ORDER 1978 (No. 1454) [10p], made under the the Counter-Inflation Act 1973, s. 10, Sched. 3, para. 1 (1) (4) (6); operative on October 11, 1978; amends S.I. 1973 No. 659 by providing for the reduction, in certain circumstances, of the maximum amount of ordinary dividends which a company is permitted to declare for a financial year without Treasury consent.

2519. Customs and Excise. See CUSTOMS AND EXCISE.

2520. Death duties. See DEATH DUTIES.

2521. Dividends Act 1978 (c. 54)

This Act extends the duration of s. 10 of the Counter-Inflation Act 1973 (c. 9).

S. 1 provides that s. 10 of the Counter-Inflation Act 1973, which enables the Treasury to restrict the declaration and payment of ordinary dividends by companies at any time when that section is in force, shall be extended in duration until July 31, 1979, and shall then expire; s. 2 contains the short title, and extends the Act to Northern Ireland.

The Act received the Royal Assent on July 31, 1978, and came into force on that date.

2522. Double taxation. See INCOME TAX.

2523. Exchange control

EXCHANGE CONTROL (AUTHORISED DEALERS AND DEPOSITARIES) (AMENDMENT) ORDER 1978 (No. 581) [15p], made under the Exchange Control Act 1947 (c. 14), ss. 36 (5), 42 (1); operative on May 8, 1978; amends the lists of the banks and other persons who may deal in gold and foreign currencies and those who are entitled to act as authorised depositaries.

EXCHANGE CONTROL (PURCHASE OF FOREIGN CURRENCY) (AMENDMENT) ORDER 1978 (No. 756) [10p], made under the Exchange Control Act 1947, ss. 31, 36 (5); operative on June 19, 1978; adds Bank Leumi (U.K.) Ltd. and the National Giro to the Sched. of S.I. 1970 No. 789.

EXCHANGE CONTROL (AUTHORISED DEALERS AND DEPOSITARIES) ORDER 1978 (No. 1599) [40p], made under the Exchange Control Act 1947, ss. 36 (5), 42 (1); operative on November 28, 1978; supersedes S.I. 1977 No. 501 and lists those persons authorised under the 1947 Act to deal in gold, and gold and foreign currencies, and act as authorised depositaries for the purposes of Pt. III of the Act.

EXCHANGE CONTROL (PURCHASE OF FOREIGN CURRENCY) (AMENDMENT) (No. 2) ORDER 1978 (No. 1683) [10p], made under the Exchange Control Act 1947, ss. 31, 36 (5); operative on December 18, 1978; adds the Standard Chartered Bank (C.I.) Ltd. to the Sched. to S.I. 1970 No. 789.

EXCHANGE CONTROL (AUTHORISED DEALERS AND DEPOSITARIES) (AMENDMENT) (No. 2) ORDER 1978 (No. 1942) [10p], made under the Exchange

Control Act 1947, ss. 36 (5), 42 (1); operative on January 2, 1979; amends S.I. 1978 No. 1599 in particular the lists of those entitled to act as authorised depositaries.

2524. Fiduciary note issue

FIDUCIARY NOTE ISSUE (EXTENSION OF PERIOD) ORDER 1978 (No. 224) [10p], made under the Currency and Bank Notes Act 1954 (c. 12), s. 2 (7); operative on March 14, 1978; extends for a further two years the period during which the fiduciary note issue may stand at amounts continuously exceeding £1,575 million.

2525. Finance Act 1978 (c. 42)

The several matters with which the Act deals are noted under their appropriate titles. Thus for Part I (customs and excise), see § 688; for Part II (value added tax), see § 3032; for Part III (income tax, capital gains tax and corporation tax), see §§ 362, 1651–1653; for Part IV (capital transfer tax), see § 202.

Pt. V (ss. 75–80) contains miscellaneous and supplementary provisions: s. 75 relates to national insurance surcharge; s. 76 states that the effective date of s. 13 of the Development Land Tax Act 1976 shall be March 13, 1980; s. 77 relates to disclosure of information to tax authorities in other Member States; s. 78 relates to local loans; s. 79 deals with pre-consolidation amendments; s. 80 gives the short title.

The Act received the Royal Assent on July 31, 1978, and came into force on that date.

2526. Local government finance. See LOCAL GOVERNMENT.

2527. Northern Ireland. See NORTHERN IRELAND.

2528. Premium savings bonds

PREMIUM SAVINGS BONDS (AMENDMENT) REGULATIONS 1978 (No. 1297) [10p], made under the National Debt Act 1972 (c. 65), s. 11; operative on September 11, 1978; amend S.I. 1972 No. 765 so as to increase the maximum permitted holding of premium savings bonds from 2,000 bond units to 3,000 bond units.

2529. Price Commission

EVER READY COMPANY (GREAT BRITAIN) LTD. (PRICES) ORDER 1978 (No. 445) [10p], made under the Price Commission Act 1977 (c. 33), s. 7 (5) (a); operative on March 20, 1978; restricts increases in the prices of zinc carbon dry (primary) batteries which had been proposed by the Ever Ready Company.

2530. Purchase tax. See PURCHASE TAX.

2531. Savings certificates

SAVINGS CERTIFICATES (AMENDMENT) REGULATIONS 1978 (No. 788) [10p], made under the National Debt Act 1972 (c. 65), s. 11; operative on July 1, 1978; amend S.I. 1972 No. 641 and increase the maximum permitted holding of the 14th Issue of National Savings Certificates to 3,000 unit certificates.

SAVINGS CERTIFICATES (AMENDMENT) (No. 2) REGULATIONS 1978 (No. 1334) [10p], made under the National Debt Act 1972, s. 11; operative on October 2, 1978; amend S.I. 1972 No. 641 to increase the maximum permitted holding of the 15th Issue of National Savings Certificates from 50 (purchase price £500) to 70 (purchase price £700).

SAVINGS CERTIFICATES (AMENDMENT) (No. 3) REGULATIONS 1978 (No. 1855) [10p], made under the National Debt Act 1972, s. 11; operative on January 29, 1979; amend S.I. 1972 No. 641 to provide that the maximum permitted holding of the 18th Issue of National Savings Certificates shall be 150 at a purchase price of £10.

2532. Stamp duties. See STAMP DUTIES.

BOOKS AND ARTICLES. See *post,* pp. [8], [33].

ROAD TRAFFIC

2533. Accident—failing to stop and/or report accident—two offences—relevance of statement of facts

[Road Traffic Act 1972 (c. 20), s. 25.]

S. 25 of the Road Traffic Act 1972 creates two separate offences: a motorist may be convicted of both failing to stop and to report an accident.

The defendant was convicted of failing to stop and failing to report an accident. He appealed, contending that he should not have been convicted of both, s. 25 creating only one offence. He further complained that he was prevented from cross-examining a prosecution witness upon the contents of a statement of facts served with the summonses. *Held*, dismissing the appeal, that (1) s. 25 creates two separate offences; (2) the statement of facts was not relevant upon the case being contested, and in any event was not a statement made by the witness.

ROPER *v.* SULLIVAN [1978] R.T.R. 181, D.C.

2534. —— misleading signals—apportionment of liability

The defendant drove a motorcar along a minor road to a major road, the exit to which was governed by a statutory " Give way " sign. The plaintiff was driving his motorcycle along the major road. The defendant looked towards him on two occasions before he reached the junction, and saw his left indicator was signalling to turn left. In reliance on the signal, the defendant commenced to enter the major road and the plaintiff who drove straight on collided with the defendant's motorcar. The judge found that the plaintiff had knocked the lever of his indicator accidentally and was unaware that it was flashing. *Held*, the defendant failed in her duty of care in not taking a further look to satisfy herself that the plaintiff was indeed turning to the left. The plaintiff had failed in his duty of care in driving along the major road giving a misleading signal. On the particular facts of this case, liability would be apportioned two thirds against the defendant motorist and one third against the plaintiff motorcyclist. (*Another* v. *Probert* [1968] C.L.Y. 3422a and *Grange Motors* v. *Spencer* [1969] C.L.Y. 2430 considered): WADSWORTH *v.* GILLESPIE, November 9, 1978, Sir Basil Neild sitting as a judge in the High Court, Leeds. (*Ex rel. Messrs. Lee and Priestley, Solicitors.*)

[For quantum, see § 764.]

2535. Competitions and trials

MOTOR VEHICLES (COMPETITION AND TRIALS) (AMENDMENT) REGULATIONS 1978 (No. 481) [10p], made under the Road Traffic Act 1972 (c. 20), ss. 15, 199 (2); operative on April 26, 1978; increases the fees payable to the R.A.C. for the authorisation of events in so far as they take place, in whole or in part, in England or Wales.

2536. Construction and use

MOTOR VEHICLES (CONSTRUCTION AND USE) REGULATIONS 1978 (No. 1017) [£2·50], made under the Road Traffic Act 1972 (c. 20), ss. 34 (5), 40 (1)–(3), 65 (1) (2), 199 (2); operative on August 30, 1978; consolidate S.I. 1973 No. 24 with specified amending regulations with minor drafting amendments.

WEIGHING OF MOTOR VEHICLES (USE OF DYNAMIC AXLE WEIGHING MACHINES) REGULATIONS 1978 (No. 1180) [20p], made under the Road Traffic Act 1972, ss. 160 (1) (1A) (5), 199 (2), as amended by the Road Traffic Act 1974 (c. 50), s. 14; operative on September 15, 1978; make provision for facilitating the use of dynamic axle weighing machines in order to ascertain the weights transmitted to the road surface by the wheels of each axle of a motor vehicle or trailer, and, in consequence, the gross weight of the motor vehicle or trailer.

MOTOR VEHICLES (CONSTRUCTION AND USE) (AMENDMENT) REGULATIONS 1978 (No. 1233) [25p], made under the Road Traffic Act 1972, s. 40 (1) (3); operative on September 29, 1978; amend S.I. 1978 No. 1017 by introducing new provisions as to seat belt anchorage points and seat belts.

MOTOR VEHICLES (CONSTRUCTION AND USE) (AMENDMENT) (NO. 2) REGULATIONS 1978 (No. 1234) [10p], made under the Road Traffic Act 1972, s. 40 (1) (3); operative on October 1, 1978; amend S.I. 1978 No. 1017.

MOTOR VEHICLES (CONSTRUCTION AND USE) (AMENDMENT) (NO. 3) REGU-

LATIONS 1978 (No. 1235) [20p], made under the Road Traffic Act 1972, s. 40 (1) (3); operative on October 1, 1978; amend S.I. 1978 No. 1017.

MOTOR VEHICLES (CONSTRUCTION AND USE) (AMENDMENT (No. 4) REGULATIONS 1978 (No. 1263) [10p], made under the Road Traffic Act 1972, s. 40 (1) and (3); operative on October 1, 1978; amend S.I. 1978 No. 1017, and the markings with which certain vehicles manufactured on or after October 1, 1976, and first used on or after April 1, 1977, are required to be marked in relation to the emission of gaseous pollutants by the engine are varied to include a marking designated as an approval mark by S.I. 1978 No. 1111.

MOTOR VEHICLES (CONSTRUCTION AND USE) (AMENDMENT) (No. 5) REGULATIONS 1978 (No. 1317) [10p], made under the Road Traffic Act 1972, s. 40 (1) (3), 199 (2); operative on October 1, 1978; further amend S.I. 1978 No. 1017 by introducing a requirement that on and after March 6, 1979, in all motor vehicles in a certain class there shall be carried a notice indicating any overall height which exceeds 12 feet.

2537. —— **moped—use without excise licence or test certificate—whether " mechanically propelled vehicle "**

[Vehicles (Excise) Act 1971 (c. 10), s. 8 (1); Road Traffic Act 1972 (c. 20), ss. 44 (1), 190 (1).]

A moped which is not in mechanical working order remains a " mechanically propelled vehicle " provided that there is a reasonable prospect of it being made mechanically mobile again.

The defendant was charged with using a moped without an excise licence or M.O.T. certificate. The moped was not in mechanically working order and the defendant was pedalling it along the road, taking it for mechanical repairs. Justices dismissed the charges concluding that the moped was being used as a pedal cycle and was not a " mechanically propelled vehicle." Held, allowing the prosecutor's appeal, that since the moped had been constructed as a mechanically propelled vehicle and was clearly intended by the defendant to be restored to such condition, it remained such a vehicle notwithstanding its mechanical breakdown. (R. v. Tahsin [1970] C.L.Y. 2567 and Binks v. Department of the Environment [1975] C.L.Y. 3038 applied.)

MCEACHRAN v. HURST [1978] R.T.R. 462, D.C.

2538. —— **odometer—false reading—disclaimer notice.** See WALTHAM FOREST LONDON BOROUGH COUNCIL v. T. G. WHEATLEY (CENTRAL GARAGE) (No. 2.), § 2653.

2539. —— **tread pattern**

[Road Traffic Act 1972 (c. 20), s. 40 (1) (5); Motor Vehicles (Construction and Use) Regulations 1973 (S.I. 1973 No. 24), reg. 99 (1) (f).]

The tread of a tyre is that part in contact with the road in normal driving conditions.

The pattern on D's tyres was five ridges (" lands ") and four grooves. In many places the tyres were smooth and the outer groove worn away. D contended that the measurement of the tread pattern should be taken from the centre of the land between the third and fourth grooves. Held, dismissing their appeal, that the expression " tread pattern " did not include an area of flat rubber so that the tread pattern stopped where there was no more pattern to probe or measure.

SANDFORD v. BUTCHER [1978] R.T.R. 132, D.C.

2540. —— **" using " by partner in firm—vehicle driven by employee**

D, a partner in a firm, was charged with using a vehicle with tyres of insufficient tread, on the road contrary to reg. 99 (1) (f) of the 1973 Regulations and s. 40 (5) of the 1972 Act. The vehicle had been driven by an employee of the firm during the course of his employment. D took no part in the day-to-day management of the firm nor in the maintenance of the vehicle. Held, allowing the prosecutor's appeal against a finding of no case to answer, that " use " included use by the driver or his employer: PASSMOOR v. GIBBONS [1978] Crim.L.R. 498, D.C.

2541. Crown roads

CROWN ROADS (INDUSTRIAL ESTATES) (APPLICATION OF ROAD TRAFFIC ENACTMENTS) ORDER 1978 (No. 749) [10], made under the Transport Act

1968 (c. 73), ss. 149, 157; operative on June 23, 1978; applies certain road traffic enactments to the roads in certain industrial estates in the north east of England.

CROWN ROADS (QUEENS AVENUE AND ALISON'S ROAD, ALDERSHOT) (APPLICATION OF ROAD TRAFFIC ENACTMENTS) ORDER 1978 (No. 802) [10p], made under the Transport Act 1968, ss. 149, 157; operative on June 30, 1978; applies certain road traffic enactments to the above-named roads, which are Crown roads.

2542. Cycle racing

CYCLE RACING ON HIGHWAYS (SPECIAL AUTHORISATION) (ENGLAND AND WALES) REGULATIONS 1978 (No. 254) [25p], made under the Road Traffic Act 1972 (c. 20), s. 20 (2) and (3); operative on March 17, 1978; vary S.I. 1960 No. 250 (bicycle races) by increasing the maximum number of competitors who may take part to 84 in the case of the " Tour of Britain (Milk Race) " and to 60 in other cases.

2543. Dangerous driving—charge preferred of careless driving—whether valid procedure more than six months after offence

[Road Traffic Act 1972 (c. 20), Sched. 4, Pt. V, para. 4; Magistrates' Courts Act 1952 (c. 55), s. 104.] S was charged with dangerous driving. More than six months after the incident giving rise to the charge, justices dismissed the charge, caused a charge of driving without due care and attention to be preferred by virtue of their power under Sched. 4, Pt. V, para. 4 to the 1972 Act, and convicted. *Held,* dismissing B's application for an order quashing the conviction, that the preferring of the charge of driving without due care and attention was not invalid by virtue of s. 104 of the 1952 Act which prohibited trial by magistrates of informations laid more than six months from commission of the offence. It was not appropriate to describe proceedings under para. 4 as the trial of an information: R. *v.* COVENTRY JUSTICES, *ex p.* SAYERS [1978] Crim.L.R. 364, D.C.

2544. —— disqualification—sentence—momentary inattention

[Road Traffic Act 1972 (c. 20), s. 93 (1).]

Where dangerous driving arises out of momentary inattention rather than recklessness, a period of three years' disqualification may be too severe.

M, a bus driver of 27 years' experience, drove into a woman on a pedestrian crossing and killed her. He was ordered to be disqualified for three years, on the basis that he " could not see that what he had done was dangerous." *Held,* that the period would be reduced to 12 months as M was guilty of momentary inattention rather than recklessness.

R. *v.* MILLER [1978] R.T.R. 98, C.A.

2545. —— —— seriousness of separate incidents—whether affecting seriousness of offence

[Road Traffic Act 1972 (c. 20), s. 93 (2), Sched. 4, Part I.]

Where a dangerous driving charge relates to a period of driving in which separate incidents occur, the judge is in a position to form a view as to the nature of the driving which the jury found " dangerous."

In K's trial for dangerous driving which related to three separate incidents on the same night, emphasis was placed by the prosecution on one of the three incidents. The jury convicted and K was disqualified for 12 months. K appealed on the basis that if the one incident was analysed it was not of itself sufficiently serious to justify disqualification. *Held,* dismissing the appeal, that the judge, having heard the evidence, was in a position to form a view as to the nature of the driving which the jury found " dangerous."

R. *v.* KENNEDY [1978] R.T.R. 418, C.A.

2546. —— insurance policy—whether " criminal act." See MARCEL BELLER *v.* HAYDEN, § 1705.

2547. —— mens rea—automatism

" Hysterical fugue," rendering a driver's mind shut to moral inhibitions, is no defence to dangerous driving.

After involvement in an accident, the defendant drove off in a manner which was manifestly dangerous avoiding pursuing police officers and a road block and finally escaping. When seen later, the defendant claimed to remember nothing of the incident. At his trial, the defendant adduced medical evidence to support his defence that the accident had left him in a state of hysterical fugue and that although he knew he had been trying to get away from the scene of the accident, he did not know why and he had driven without conscious thought. He was convicted after a ruling that such evidence did not provide a defence. *Held*, dismissing his appeal, that although insanity and automatism provided a defence to a charge of dangerous driving, the defendant's state of mind was not such that he had no idea of what he was doing: at the time, he was clearly driving purposefully although his mind may have been closed to moral inhibitions.

R. *v.* Isitt [1978] R.T.R. 211, C.A.

2548. —— identity of driver—vehicle number essential

In a case where the identity of a driver is in issue there must be some evidence to show that the defendant was the driver of the vehicle involved.

Witnesses saw a white Vauxhall car being driven dangerously. One witness recorded its number, which she did not give in evidence. The prosecution relied on a police form which gave the date and place of the alleged offence and requested details of the driver of car no. MPO 494J. C admitted he drove a vehicle of that number. He was convicted, the justices being of the opinion that the police could only have got that number from the witness concerned. *Held*, allowing C's appeal, that the police form was insufficient on its own and that the witness should have been able to link the car, whose actions were described in the form, with the registration number written on it. (*Jones* v. *Metcalfe* [1967] C.L.Y. 751 applied.)

Cattermole *v.* Millar [1978] R.T.R. 258, D.C.

2549. Death by dangerous driving—accused giving evidence against co-accused—whether charged with same offence. R. *v.* Hills, § 529.

2550. —— sentence—effect of change in legislation. See R. *v.* Eadie, § 594.

2551. —— —— inadvertence. See R. *v.* Heslop, § 608.

2552. —— —— repeated offences. See R. *v.* McLaughlin, § 610.

2553. Drink or drugs—arrest—validity of

[Road Traffic Act 1972 (c. 20), ss. 6, 8.]

A motorist already under arrest for a non-motoring offence may be validly re-arrested after failing a properly-requested breath test.

The appellant decamped after crashing his car and assaulted a police officer who chased and caught him; he was arrested for the assault. At the police station he provided a positive breath test and was re-arrested under s. 8 (2) of the 1972 Act. A blood specimen subsequently provided proved to contain alcohol in excess of the prescribed limit. He appealed against his conviction for driving with excess alcohol on the grounds that he had not been validly arrested. *Held*, dismissing the appeal, that there is no reason why a person already under restraint cannot validly be re-arrested for a different offence.

R. *v.* Hatton (Francis) [1978] R.T.R. 357, C.A.

2554. —— —— —— failure to give reasons

S was seen driving unusually, was stopped and told by a police officer that his breath smelt of alcohol and his speech was incomprehensible. S suddenly drove off, was stopped and was arrested. A struggle ensued, and at the police station his violence prevented an examination of him by a doctor. The only issue was whether S had been told of the reason for his arrest when arrested. The Recorder failed to direct the jury that an officer must give reasons for an arrest unless to do so was impracticable, and failed to refer to the evidence on this point. *Held*, allowing S's appeal against conviction of failing to provide a specimen for a laboratory test, that the summing up was defective: R. *v.* Sullivan [1977] Crim.L.R. 751, C.A.

2555. —— blood or urine specimen—consent—refusal to sign form

[Road Traffic Act 1972 (c. 20), s. 9 (1) (3) (5).]

A defendant is entitled, before he signs a form consenting to give blood, to read it.

D, an arrested motorist, agreed to provide a specimen of blood provided that he could read the consent form which he was being asked to sign. On appeal against his conviction for failing to provide a specimen of blood, *held*, allowing his appeal, that this was not a case of a conditional acceptance amounting to a refusal, because there had been an agreement to provide a sample of blood.

HIER *v.* READ [1978] R.T.R. 114, D.C.

2556. ────── ──── **election for blood test as second specimen—no requirement to wait an hour**

[Scot.] [Road Traffic Act 1972 (c. 20), ss. 6 and 9.] A, having provided the first of two urine specimens under the procedure of s. 9 then elected to provide a specimen of blood rather than a second urine sample. *Held*, it was not necessary therefore to wait an hour after the urine specimen to take the blood specimen : POWELL *v.* MACNEILL, 1976 J.C. 30, High Ct. of Justiciary.

2557. ────── ──── **failure to provide—doctor's permission**

[Road Traffic Act 1972 (c. 20), s. 9 (2) (3) (7).]

There is no requirement that the notification to a medical practitioner by a constable of an intention to take a blood test must be made out of earshot of a patient.

L was an injured motorist in hospital as a patient. He heard a constable notify the doctor of his intention to require provision of a blood or urine sample. Justices found that that prevented the doctor from making any effective decision as to his patient's welfare, so that the purpose of s. 9 (2) of the Road Traffic Act 1972 would be negated. *Held*, allowing P's appeal, that there was nothing in that Act requiring such a request to be made out of earshot of the patient.

OXFORD *v.* LOWTON [1978] R.T.R. 237, D.C.

2558. ────── ──── ──── **drink taken after accident—whether " special reasons "**

[Road Traffic Act 1972 (c. 20), s. 93 (1).]

The fact that a motorist, who has been convicted of failing to provide a laboratory specimen, would have had a defence to any charge based upon the specimen's analysis is not a special reason for not disqualifying.

The defendant was convicted of failing to provide a laboratory specimen following an accident in which he had been involved. The justices accepted that after the accident but before the request for the specimen he had consumed alcohol and would therefore have had a defence to a charge of driving with excess alcohol had he provided a specimen; they found that special reasons were thereby made out and declined to disqualify. *Held*, allowing the prosecutor's appeal, that such facts did not amount to " special reasons." (*Glendinning* v. *Bell* [1973] C.L.Y. 2907 overruled.)

COURTMAN *v.* MASTERSON [1978] R.T.R. 457, D.C.

2559. ────── ──── ──── **" reasonable excuse "**

[Scot.] [Road Traffic Act 1972 (c. 20), s. 9 (3.] Following a positive breath test M was required to provide blood or urine specimen. He agreed to supply blood but refused to allow the doctor to take capillary blood from his thumb after five attempts to take blood from the veins of his arms had failed. He refused to provide urine. *Held*, dismissing M's appeal against conviction and disqualification, that the onus was on M to establish reasonable excuse both for failing to supply blood and for failing to supply urine. His reason was insufficient and could not be a special reason for not disqualifying : MACDONALD *v.* MACKENZIE [1978] Crim.L.R. 694, High Ct. of Justiciary.

2560. ────── ──── ──── **significance of refusal for jury**

[Road Traffic Act 1972 (c. 20), ss. 5 (1) (5), 7 (1), 9 (3).]

Where a reason is given for a refusal to provide a specimen of blood or urine, then it is doubtful if that refusal is of any weight in considering whether or not an appellant is too drunk to drive his car.

A was arrested. An hour later he was asked to take a breath test or supply a specimen. He refused. He said that he was not a driver an hour after he had been stopped. The jury were directed that his refusal could be taken as supporting prosecution evidence or rebutting defence evidence about A's

condition. *Held*, that A's appeal would be allowed. Some direction should have been given to the jury about the reason given by A for his refusal.
R. *v.* HILLMAN [1978] R.T.R. 124, C.A.

2561. —— —— —— **stipulation that to be taken by particular doctor**
[Road Traffic Act 1972 (c. 20), ss. 9, 12 (2).]
A person is not to be regarded as refusing to provide a blood specimen if he stipulates that it should be taken by his own doctor who is present at the time of the stipulation being made.
The appellant was arrested after failing to take a breath test and at the police station agreed to provide a specimen of blood. The police doctor and the appellant's own doctor attended at the station, whereupon the appellant stated that he was willing to provide the specimen but only if taken by his own doctor. He was charged with and convicted of failing without reasonable excuse to provide a specimen. The Crown Court upheld the conviction. *Held*, allowing this appeal, that the appellant was willing to comply with the requirements of ss. 9 and 12 of the Act inasmuch as s. 12 (2) required only that the specimen be taken by " a medical practitioner "; accordingly the imposition of a condition by him did not amount to a refusal.
BAYLISS *v.* THAMES VALLEY POLICE CHIEF CONSTABLE [1978] R.T.R. 328, D.C.

2562. —— —— —— **whether refusal to be inferred**
[Road Traffic Act 1972 (c. 20), s. 9 (3).] W was requested at a police station to give a specimen of blood or urine. He replied " You can have blood, but you can't have urine." When asked to give a urine specimen, he said : " What's the quickest way out of this place? " He was told that failure to supply a specimen would be treated as refusal to do so, but when the request was repeated W made the same reply. *Held*, dismissing W's appeal against conviction of failing to provide a specimen under s. 9 (3) of the 1972 Act, that the justices were entitled to draw the inference that W had refused to provide a specimen :
WILKINSON *v.* BUTTON [1978] Crim.L.R. 436, D.C.

2563. —— —— **first discarded, second lost, third after time limit—whether analysis evidence admissible**
[Road Traffic Act 1972 (c. 20), ss. 5 (1), 6 (1), 7 (1) (2) (3), 8 (5), 9 (1) (3) (6).]
Evidence of analysis of a urine sample provided outside the one-hour limit is admissible on a s. 5 (1) charge but not on a s. 6 (1) charge.
M elected to provide a urine sample at the station. The first sample was disregarded, the second was knocked over and the contents lost, the third was provided 20 minutes over the hour. M was tried on s. 5 (1) and s. 6 (1) charges. The trial judge held that the analysis evidence was admissible only on the s. 5 (1) " unfit " charge, not on the excess alcohol s. 6 (1) charge. M was convicted under s. 5 (1). On appeal on the basis that evidence was wrongly admitted, *held*, dismissing the appeal, that (1) the code under s. 7 was distinguishable from that under s. 9, in that the latter charge was of a technical nature involving automatic penal consequences, where under ss. 5 and 7 the analysis could only go to support the case against a defendant; (2) since M provided a specimen at a material time, the first being disregarded, and the third within an hour of the second, the provisions of s. 7 (2) and 7 (3) were complied with (*R.* v. *Hyams* [1972] C.L.Y. 3012 distinguished.)
R. *v.* MOORE [1978] R.T.R. 384, C.A.

2564. —— —— **hospital procedure—failure to tell doctor all information**
[Scot.] M was taken to hospital following an accident involving a van he was driving. The police told the doctor in charge of their intention to require a breath specimen and, if it was positive, a blood or urine sample and the doctor raised no objection. *Held*, dismissing M's appeal, that it was not necessary for the police to mention to the doctor the warning as to penalties for refusal which had to be given to M : McGUINESS *v.* THAW [1978] Crim.L.R. 696, High Ct. of Justiciary.

2565. —— —— **relevant time to assess blood alcohol level for purposes of conviction**
[Scot.] [Road Traffic Act 1972 (c. 20), s. 6 (1).] A provided a specimen of blood which, on analysis, had 82 milligrammes of alcohol per 100 millilitres

of blood. Evidence showed a likelihood that, although at the time the specimen was taken he exceeded the limit, whilst he was driving his blood was still absorbing alcohol and so he would have been under the limit. He was therefore acquitted. The prosecutor appealed by way of case stated. *Held*, the time when an accused's blood's alcohol content was relevant was when the specimen was taken. Accordingly, A should be convicted: TUDHOPE v. WILLIAMSON, 1976 J.C. 17, High Ct. of Justiciary.

2566. —— **breath test—bag inflated in two breaths—whether test valid**
[Road Traffic Act 1972 (c. 20), s. 8 (1) (3) (4); Alcotest Instructions Book, paras. 3, 4.]
A breath test in which a motorist disobeys police instructions to inflate the bag in one breath, and, to the knowledge of the officer, inflates it in two, is nevertheless a valid test.
A constable, aware of the Alcotest instructions, told a driver to inflate the bag in one continuous breath. The driver, in the constable's presence, inflated it in two. The test was positive. The Attorney-General referred the matter to the court for an answer as to whether the test was valid. *Held*, that since there was no reason to suppose that breach of the manufacturer's instructions in this way would render the test favourable to the crown, or potentially prejudicial to the defendant, the test was valid. (Dicta in *Webber* v. *Carey* [1970] C.L.Y. 2528 and *Walker* v. *Lovell* [1975] C.L.Y. 2561 applied.)
ATT.-GEN.'S REFERENCE (No. 1 OF 1978) [1978] R.T.R. 377, C.A.

2567. —— —— **burst bag—no effect on validity of test**
[Road Traffic Act 1972 (c. 20), ss. 8 (1) (4), 12 (1).]
A breath test will not be invalidated if the Alcotest bag bursts as the driver finishes blowing into it.
A took a breath test. The crystals in the Alcotest tube changed green, indicating a positive test. The bag then burst. *Held*, dismissing A's appeal, that that did not invalidate the test. The crystals had changed green before the bag was fully inflated; the extra breath would not have changed them back again.
R. v. KAPLAN [1978] R.T.R. 119, C.A.

2568. —— —— **court's discretion to exclude**
Some time after an accident, police walked into S's house through a door which was ajar, opened another door, walked through S's living room and kitchen to his bedroom where he was in bed, and required him to provide a specimen of breath. He did so after initial objections, and it was positive. *Held*, that (1) the evidence of the positive breath test was admissible although illegally obtained; (2) the court would exercise its discretion to exclude the evidence since the conduct of the police, in entering S's bedroom without invitation and in later intentionally omitting from the depositions reference to a second police officer who had been present, was " in other respects reprehensible." (*Scott* v. *Baker* [1968] C.L.Y. 3428 considered; *Jeffrey* v. *Black* [1977] C.L.Y. 2263 applied): R. v. SMITH (BENJAMIN WALTER) [1978] Crim.L.R. 296, Preston Crown Ct.

2569. —— —— **failure to inflate bag—no inspection of crystals—whether arrest valid**
[Road Traffic Act 1972 (c. 20), ss. 8 (1) (3) (5), 9 (1), 12 (3); Alcotest Instructions Book, paras. 3, 4.]
A constable may infer from his observations that there has been a failure to provide a breath sample, and provided the jury are satisfied that the arrest is for the right reason, the arrest is valid.
R was required to blow into the Alcotest device for the proper period, but blew for such a short time that the bag did not start to inflate. R was arrested for failing to provide a sample of breath. An issue arose as to the validity of arrest on the question of whether the constable examined the crystals before arresting under s. 8 (5). The jury were directed that there was no absolute principle of law requiring a constable to examine the crystals before arrest. R was convicted. On appeal, *held*, dismissing the appeal, that the issue had to be properly left to the jury as to the correctness of the reason for arrest, but the constable having inferred, from the minimal air blown into the bag, without

examining the crystals, that R had failed to provide a breath specimen, the arrest was valid. (*Walker* v. *Lovell* [1975] C.L.Y. 2961 distinguished.)
R. v. REY [1978] R.T.R. 413, C.A.

2570. —— —— **green stain must pass line**
[Road Traffic Act 1972 (c. 20), ss. 8 (1) (4), 12 (1).]
A breath test is positive only if the green reaction stain passes the ring on the Alcotest.
P took a breath test. The constable who took it saw the crystals in the Alcotest turn green up to the line. A sergeant, returning to the scene after the test, described it as positive. In cross-examination he wrongly gave the test for a positive result as being if the crystals turned green " up to or beyond the line " (they must pass it). The justices, satisfied of the sergeant's bona fides, convicted P. *Held*, allowing his appeal, that the bona fides of the sergeant were irrelevant. The green stain should have passed the line, as set out in the instructions for use of the Alcotest, and it had not done so.
PARSLEY v. BEARD [1978] R.T.R. 263, D.C.

2571. —— —— **partial inflation of bag—crystals not examined**
[Road Traffic Act 1972 (c. 20), s. 9 (1) (*b*).]
Where a defendant inflates an Alcotest bag only partially, the true evaluation of the test must either be that it is positive or that there has been a failure to provide such a test.
K partially inflated an Alcotest bag. The constable did not examine the result. D was required to submit a specimen of blood, which he did. It showed that he had excess alcohol in his blood. The justices were of the view that the constable should have considered, in the first instance, whether or not the test was positive. *Held*, allowing P's appeal, that this was not so. The requirement for the specimen of blood had been validly made in any event, since there must have been either a positive result or a failure to take the test.
SHEPHERD v. KAVULOK [1978] R.T.R. 85, D.C.

2572. —— —— **refusal—driving or attempting to drive**
[Scot.] [Road Traffic Act 1972 (c. 20), s. 8 (1).] Police followed a car driven by M, whom they suspected to have consumed alcohol. The car stopped and drove off again. When it was finally stopped, a woman who had been M's passenger was driving. M refused to give a breath specimen. *Held*, dismissing M's appeal against conviction for refusing to provide a specimen, that the requirement was proper as it was part of a single chain of events: MORRISON v. PIRIE [1978] Crim.L.R. 695, High Ct. of Justiciary.

2573. —— —— **requirement to evaluate whether test positive or negative**
[Road Traffic Act (c. 20), ss. 8 (1) (*b*) (3) (4) (5), 9 (1).]
Where an Alcotest bag is partially inflated, a constable should not arrest for a failure to provide a specimen without deciding whether or not the test is positive.
S, in three blows, only partially inflated an Alcotest bag. The police constable arrested him without checking the result of the test. *Held*, allowing S's appeal, that as some air had entered the bag, the constable should have inspected it to decide whether to make an arrest on a positive result or on a failure to supply a specimen of breath.
SENEVIRATNE v. BISHOP [1978] R.T.R. 92, D.C.

2574. —— —— **suspicion of involvement in accident—alternative ground**
[Road Traffic Act 1972 (c. 20), s. 8.]
A request for a breath test made by reason of a suspicion that a driver had been in an accident may be justified on the alternative ground of suspicion of his having alcohol in the body provided that such alternative suspicion existed and is proved.
The defendant was stopped while driving along a road by a constable who, erroneously, suspected the defendant to have been in an accident; upon stopping him, the constable noticed signs of alcohol having been taken. The defendant failed to take a breath test, was arrested, and subsequently provided a blood specimen. He was charged with failing to provide a breath test and with driving

with excess alcohol. Justices dismissed both charges on the ground that the constable did not suspect the presence of alcohol in the defendant's body when he required the breath specimen. *Held*, dismissing the prosecutor's appeal, that although a specimen could be requested and/or the request justified on alternative grounds, there was here no evidence that the constable had addressed his mind to the question of whether the defendant had consumed alcohol. (*Atkinson* v. *Walker* [1975] C.L.Y. 2957 explained.)

CLEMENTS *v*. DAMS [1978] R.T.R. 206, D.C.

2575. —— —— —— **direction to jury**
[Road Traffic Act 1972 (c. 20), s. 8 (2).]
Where the validity of a breath test requirement depends upon the occurrence of an accident, the jury must be clearly directed that it must be established that the motorist's vehicle had been involved in an accident, and not merely that a police officer had a reasonable suspicion that it had.

The appellant was convicted of driving with excess alcohol, he having been arrested for refusing to provide a specimen of breath after, according to the prosecution, being involved in an accident. The appellant denied being so involved. The trial judge's direction did not make it clear that it was essential that it be proved that an accident had in fact occurred. *Held*, allowing the appeal, that such omission amounted to a material misdirection.

R. *v*. VARDY [1978] R.T.R. 202, C.A.

2576. —— —— **whether driving at time—moving traffic offence**
[Road Traffic Act 1972 (c. 20), s. 8 (1).]
A breath test required by a constable suspecting a driver to have consumed alcohol when he was no longer driving may nonetheless be valid where the driver has been stopped for committing a moving traffic offence.

A driver was stopped by police for driving with a defective rear light. After some five minutes, the officer noticed symptoms of alcohol having been consumed, and required provision of a specimen of breath which proved positive. The driver was arrested and subsequently charged with driving with excess alcohol. Justices dismissed the information on the grounds that the driver was no longer driving at the time of the request. *Held*, allowing the prosecutor's appeal, that the requirement for a breath specimen was alternatively justified under s. 8 (1) (*b*) of the Act; that the justices had been referred to the moving traffic offence so that it would not be oppressive to decide the appeal on that ground; and that the justices were wrong in thinking that a request under s. 8 (1) (*b*) had to be made while the defendant was still driving. (*Atkinson* v. *Walker* [1975] C.L.Y. 2957 followed.)

RICKWOOD *v*. COCHRANE [1978] R.T.R. 218, D.C.

2577. —— **driving or attempting to drive—car incapable of being driven**
[Road Traffic Act 1972 (c. 20), s. 6 (1).]
A motorist may be "attempting to drive" a motor vehicle notwithstanding that a mechanical failure has rendered the car immobile.

Whilst the defendant was driving his car up a hill, the car stopped and would not proceed further. The defendant was found by police officers in the driving seat "revving" the car engine in an apparent effort to make the car go. In fact, the clutch had burnt out and the car was undrivable. The defendant was later convicted of attempting to drive the car having consumed alcohol in excess of the prescribed limit. *Held*, dismissing his appeal, that the fact that the car was not propellable under its own resources did not affect the fact that the defendant was attempting to drive it. (*R*. v. *Smith* (*Roger*) [1974] C.L.Y. 637 and *R*. v. *Bates* [1973] C.L.Y. 2931, considered.)

R. *v*. FARRANCE [1978] R.T.R. 225, C.A.

2578. [Road Traffic Act 1972 (c. 20), s. 6 (1).]
Where a motorist's defence to a drink-driving charge is that he was not driving at the time of suspicion arising because of mechanical breakdown, the jury have only to decide whether the car was capable of being driven.

The appellant was seen by police to stop his car in the roadway, two of its tyres being completely deflated. The car later proved incapable of being driven and had to be towed away. Some two minutes after the car had stopped, the officer spoke to the appellant and noticed that his breath smelt of alcohol. He was breathalysed and in due course found to have an excess of alcohol in his body. He was convicted of driving with excess alcohol after the judge had directed the jury that the only relevant consideration for them in determining whether he was driving was the time lapse between his stopping and the officer's suspicion forming. *Held,* allowing his appeal, that the jury were misdirected, since they should have been required to consider whether the car was being driven and whether the defendant was prevented from driving it by reason of the breakdown at the time of the officer's suspicion forming. (*Edkins* v. *Knowles* [1973] C.L.Y. 2925 applied.)

R. *v.* NEILSON [1978] R.T.R. 232, C.A.

2579. —— **driving whilst unfit—statutory definition of " road "—hotel driveway— available to part of the public**

[Scot.] [Road Traffic Act 1972 (c. 20), s. 196 (1).] D was charged with driving a vehicle on a road with his ability to drive impaired by his having consumed alcohol. The " road " in question was the drive way of an hotel, used only by hotel patrons. *Held,* the road was open to all customers of the hotel. It was not necessary that the road be accessible to the general public so long as it was accessible to some part of the public, *i.e.* those availing themselves of the manager's invitation or permission to use the road. D was therefore within the section and so guilty of an offence (*Harrison* v. *Hill,* 1932 J.C. 13 distinguished): DUNNE v. KEANE, 1976 J.C. 39, High Ct. of Justiciary.

2580. —— **sentence—first offence**

[Road Traffic Act 1972 (c. 20), s. 6 (1).]

The court does not recognise any principle of sentencing that a custodial offence is not to be imposed for a first breathalyser offence.

M was convicted of driving with excess alcohol in the blood. He had several previous convictions, many connected with motoring. He had previously been sent to prison for driving while disqualified. *Held,* dismissing his appeal against an immediate custodial sentence of six months, that there was no reason why imprisonment should not be imposed for a first breathalyser offence; regard should be had to the motorist's record and the circumstances of the offence.

R. *v.* NOKES [1978] R.T.R. 101, C.A.

2581. Drivers' hours

COMMUNITY DRIVERS' HOURS RULES (TEMPORARY MODIFICATIONS) REGULATIONS 1978 (No. 7) [15p], made under the European Communities Act 1972 (c. 68), s. 2 (2); operative on January 26, 1978; implement the decision of the EEC authorising the United Kingdom Government to take measures derogating from arts. 7, 11 and 12 of Reg. 543/69 (EEC), relating to hours and conditions of work of drivers in the road transport industry.

DRIVERS' HOURS (HARMONISATION WITH COMMUNITY RULES) REGULATIONS 1978 (No. 1157) [30p], made under the Transport Act 1968 (c. 73), s. 95 (1) and (1A), as amended by the Road Traffic (Drivers' Ages and Hours of Work) Act 1976 (c. 3), s. 2; operative on August 17, 1978; provide for adjusting the terms of s. 96 of the 1968 Act so as to take into account the relevant community rules.

DRIVERS' HOURS (GOODS VEHICLES) (EXEMPTIONS) REGULATIONS 1978 (No. 1364) [40p], made under the Transport Act 1968, ss. 96 (10), 101 (6); operative on October 17, 1978; revoke and replace S.I. 1972 No. 574 to provide exemptions from s. 96 (1) of the 1968 Act to enable drivers of goods vehicles to deal with cases of emergency and to meet certain special needs.

DRIVERS' HOURS (KEEPING OF RECORDS) (AMENDMENT) REGULATIONS 1978 (No. 1878) [25p], made under the Transport Act 1968, ss. 98, 101 (2) as amended by the European Communities Act 1972, s. 4 (1), Sched. 4, para. 9 (2) (c) and the Road Traffic (Drivers' Ages and Hours of Work) Act 1976, s. 2 (1); operative on February 1, 1979; amend S.I. 1976 No. 1447 principally to provide for a simplified form of drivers' record book to be used by short distance freight drivers who do not spend more than four hours in driving in the course of a working day. The application of European Community rules to national transport operations is also clarified.

DRIVERS' HOURS (KEEPING OF RECORDS) (AMENDMENT) (No. 2) REGULA-
TIONS 1978 (No. 1938) [10p], made under the European Communities Act
1972, ss. 2, 4 (1), Sched. 4, para. 9 (2) (c); the Transport Act 1968, s. 101 (1)
(6) and the Road Traffic (Drivers' Ages and Hours of Work) Act 1976, s. 2 (1);
operative on February 1, 1979; amend S.I. 1976 No. 1447 so as to render it
unnecessary for the drivers of British passenger vehicles on national transport
operations to enter in the weekly reports in their drivers' record books particulars of the time spent in the course of their employment on activities other
than driving.

2582. Driving instruction

MOTOR CARS (DRIVING INSTRUCTION) (AMENDMENT) REGULATIONS 1978 (No.
1316) [10p], made under the Road Traffic Act 1972 (c. 20), ss. 128, 129, 133,
142; operative on October 1, 1978; amend S.I. 1977 No. 1043 so as to increase
specified fees relating to driving instruction.

2583. Driving licences

HEAVY GOODS VEHICLES (DRIVERS' LICENCES) (AMENDMENT) REGULATIONS
1978 (No. 669) [10p], made under the Road Traffic Act 1972 (c. 20), ss. 119,
120 (1), 124, 199 (2); operative on June 1, 1978; amend S.I. 1977 No. 1309 so
as to increase the fee payable by a person who applies for a heavy goods
vehicle driving licence from £24 to £30.

MOTOR VEHICLES (DRIVING LICENCES) (AMENDMENT) REGULATIONS 1978
(No. 697) [20p], made under the Road Traffic Act 1972, ss. 85 (2), 88 (2),
107, 199 (2); operative on June 1, 1978; amend S.I. 1976 No. 1076 in relation
to the conditions attached to a provisional licence and increases the driving test
fee to £7·30.

MOTOR VEHICLES (DRIVING LICENCES) (AMENDMENT) (No. 2) REGULATIONS
1978 (No. 1109) [20p], made under the Road Traffic Act 1972, ss. 88 (1)
(2), 107, 199 (2); operative on August 31, 1978; amend S.I. 1976 No. 1076 so as
to remove from May 1, 1979, the concessionary fee of £1 for a driving licence
payable by persons over 65, and to add Barra to the category of islands
excluded from the exemption from Reg. 8 (1) (a) of the 1976 Regulations.

2584. Driving whilst disqualified—passenger's knowledge—injury—duty of care owed.

See HARRISON v. JACKSON, § 2063.

2585. Driving without reasonable consideration—notice of intended prosecution— where defendant has no knowledge of accident

[Road Traffic Act 1972 (c. 20), s. 179.] S's car was involved in an accident
when S was driving it but S did not realise that this was so. He was not given
any warning of intended prosecution in accordance with s. 179 of the 1972
Act but was prosecuted and convicted of driving without reasonable consideration. *Held*, that as S did not know of the accident and had not shut
his eyes to the obvious, s. 179 (3A) did not apply to exclude the need for
notice of intended prosecution (*Harding* v. *Price* (1948) C.L.C. 8998 and
Hampson v. *Powell* [1970] C.L.Y. 2508 considered): METROPOLITAN POLICE
v. SCARLETT [1978] Crim.L.R. 234, Inner London Crown Ct.

2586. Driving without due care and attention—whether defendant "driving"— hypoglycaemia

[Scot.] [Road Traffic Act 1972 (c. 20), s. 3.] S drove a car for miles,
colliding three times with other vehicles. Evidence was given that he was
diabetic and had been in a state of hypoglycaemia. *Held*, that the test of
whether S was driving was whether he was in conscious control and his movements were voluntary. He was convicted and given an absolute discharge:
FARRELL v. STIRLING [1978] Crim.L.R. 696, Sheriff Ct.

2587. Driving without licence or insurance—burden of proof

[Scot.] [Road Traffic Act 1972 (c. 20), ss. 84 (1), 143 (1).] W failed to provide his licence and insurance when required to do so. In evidence he admitted
having neither. *Held*, allowing the prosecutor's appeal against W's acquittal
of driving without a licence and without insurance, that the burden of proof
was on W to displace the inference raised by the prosecution case: MILNE v.
WHALEY [1978] Crim.L.R. 695, High Ct. of Justiciary.

2588. Goods vehicles

GOODS VEHICLES (PLATING AND TESTING) (AMENDMENT) REGULATIONS 1978 (No. 867) [10p], made under the Road Traffic Act 1972 (c. 20), ss. 45 (1) (6), 199 (2); operative on July 1, 1978; further amend S.I. 1971 No. 352 by increasing certain specified fees.

GOODS VEHICLES (PLATING AND TESTING) (AMENDMENT) (NO. 2) REGULATIONS 1978 (No. 1018) [10p], made under the Road Traffic Act 1972, ss. 45 (1), 199 (2); operative on August 30, 1978; amend S.I. 1971 No. 352 by defining " converter dolly " and providing that these regulations shall cover converter dollies which do not exceed 1,020 kilograms.

GOODS VEHICLES (OPERATORS' LICENCES) (TEMPORARY USE IN GREAT BRITAIN) (AMENDMENT) REGULATIONS 1978 (No. 1110) [20p], made under the Transport Act 1968 (c. 73), s. 91 (1) (4) (5) (8); operative on August 31, 1978; amend S.I. 1975 No. 1046 and exempts foreign vehicles being temporarily used in Britain, in certain instances, from the requirement to have an operator's licence.

2589. —— dangerous load—whether knowledge of circumstances necessary

[Road Traffic Act 1972 (c. 20), s. 40 (5) (*b*); Motor Vehicles (Construction and Use) Regulations 1973 (S.I. 1973 No. 24), reg. 90 (2) (as substituted by reg. 12 (*b*) of the Motor Vehicles (Construction and Use) (Amendment) Regulations 1976 (S.I. 1976 No. 317).]

In deciding whether danger was, or was likely to be, caused within reg. 90 (2) of the 1973 Regulations it must be determined according to the factual circumstances regardless of the knowledge of the defendant.

An articulated lorry was loaded with three prepacked coils of steel, each attached to a pallet by three steel straps. The lorry driver checked the straps as the load was secured and the sides of the vehicle were chained in position. The lorry was driven on a road, one coil fell off and the other two shifted because, unknown to the driver, the straps had come loose. Both the driver and the lorry owner were charged with use of the vehicle contrary to reg. 90 (2) of the 1973 Regulations and s. 40 (5) of the Act. The justices dismissed the informations on the ground that the load had been secured so that danger was not likely to be caused by reason of the load falling from the vehicle. The prosecutor appealed. *Held*, allowing the appeal, that this was an absolute offence and the facts spoke for themselves. The case would be remitted to the justices with a direction to convict. (*Cornish* v. *Ferry Masters* [1975] C.L.Y. 2908 applied; *Friend* v. *Western British Road Services* [1976] C.L.Y. 2375 explained.)

DENT v. COLEMAN [1978] R.T.R. 1, D.C.

2590. Highways. See HIGHWAYS AND BRIDGES.

2591. Insurance—condition of policy—driving licence—heavy goods vehicle

[Road Traffic Act 1972 (c. 20), s. 143.] H appealed against conviction in his absence by justices for driving a heavy goods vehicle without insurance. There was a policy in force permitting driving by any person who " holds a licence to drive the vehicle or has held and is not disqualified for [*sic*] holding or obtaining such a licence." At the time of the offence H had held and was not disqualified from holding or obtaining an ordinary driving licence for the class of vehicle in question, but he did not hold and had never held a heavy goods vehicle licence. The court rejected a submission of no case to answer, and held that H did not comply with the policy condition: POLICE v. HEPPER, May 23, 1978, Deputy Judge Raw, Knightsbridge Crown Ct. (*Ex rel. Robin Spon-Smith, Esq., Barrister.*)

2592. —— third party—cover for " social, domestic and pleasure purposes "—primary purpose of journey

In deciding whether a car is used for " social, domestic and pleasure purposes " or for business purposes, regard must be had to the primary purpose of the user.

A father assisting his son in his business agreed to drive, in his son's car, the son's employee who was suffering from toothache to a dentist and/or home on his own way home for lunch. En route the car was involved in an accident in which one person died and another was injured. Judgment was awarded against both father and son for some £45,000 and the father in third party proceedings unsuccessfully claimed an indemnity from his own insurers who insured him to drive any car " for social, domestic and pleasure purposes." *Held*, dismissing the father's appeal, that the primary purpose of the journey was a business purpose of the son and was therefore not covered by the policy; alternatively that the fact that one of the purposes for which the car was being driven was a business purpose sufficed to defeat the claim. (*Passmore* v. *Vulcan Boiler and General Insurance Co.* [1936] 154 L.T. 258, considered.]

SEDDON *v.* BINIONS, ZURICH INSURANCE & CO. (THIRD PARTY); STORK *v.* BINIONS, ZURICH INSURANCE (THIRD PARTY) [1978] R.T.R. 163, C.A.

2593. —— —— **insurer's liability limited—recovery of excess**

[Motor Vehicles Insurance (Third Party Risks) Ordinance 1958, British Honduras, ss. 3, 4 (1) (*b*), 20 (1).]

There are no grounds for interfering with the plain meaning of the British Honduras Ordinance limiting an insurer's liability for third party risks.

S. 4 (1) (*b*) of the British Honduras Ordinance required that to be valid third party motor insurance need not be required to cover liability in excess of 4,000 dollars (£1,000). An action was brought in England by the father of the victim of a road accident who was awarded some £44,000 damages against the responsible driver who was unable to pay any sum. The driver was insured with the defendants under a policy limiting liability for third party risks to £1,000. The action was brought under s. 20 of the Ordinance which enabled recovery from the insurers of any amount payable under the relevant insurance policy. The insurers paid £1,000 but declined further payment in reliance upon the limitation of liability. *Held*, giving judgment for the insurers, that the wording of s. 4 (1) was plain and unambiguous and that the insurer's liability was limited accordingly.

HARKER *v.* CALEDONIAN INSURANCE CO. [1978] R.T.R. 143, Donaldson J.

2593a. —— **uninsured driver—knowledge or belief of plaintiff**

The plaintiff told the defendant that she (plaintiff) was not insured to drive her car and that she needed an insured driver to drive it; the defendant, who was insured to drive another car, volunteered to drive the plaintiff's car. In the course of the journey she was injured by his negligence; it emerged that defendant's insurance did not cover his driving of the car. *Held*, that the plaintiff did not " know or have reason to believe " that there was no contract of insurance within cl. 6 (1) (*c*) (ii) of the M.I.B. agreement and, accordingly, the M.I.B. were bound to indemnify her under the agreement: PORTER *v.* ADDO; PORTER *v.* MOTOR INSURERS' BUREAU, *The Times*, May 18, 1978, Forbes J.

2594. —— **validity—motorist failing to disclose disqualification**

[Road Traffic Act 1972 (c. 20), s. 143 (1).]

An insurance policy obtained by a disqualified driver without disclosure of disqualification is voidable, as opposed to void ab initio, and the cover given remains in force until the insurers avoid the policy.

The defendant, a disqualified driver, obtained motor insurance by not disclosing this disqualification to the insurers. During the currency of the policy, the defendant was observed driving and was charged, inter alia, with using a vehicle without insurance. Justices dismissed the information on the grounds that the defendant was in possession of a cover note which had not been cancelled. *Held*, dismissing the prosecutor's appeal, that the policy was voidable at the instance of the insurers and remained valid for the purposes of s. 143 of the Act until avoided. (*Durrant* v. *Maclaren* [1956] C.L.Y. 7846.)

ADAMS *v.* DUNNE [1978] R.T.R. 281, D.C.

2595. Lighting

ROAD VEHICLES LIGHTING (AMENDMENT) REGULATIONS 1978 (No. 1261) [10p], made under the Road Traffic Act 1972 (c. 20), ss. 40 (1), 68 (1)–(3), 73 (1)–(3), 78 (2), 199 (2); operative on September 23, 1978; amend S.I. 1971 No. 694 so as to avoid references in those Regulations to fog lamps applying to rear fog lamps by replacing references to fog lamps by references to front fog lamps.

ROAD VEHICLES (USE OF LIGHTS DURING DAYTIME) (AMENDMENT) REGULATIONS 1978 (No. 1262) [10p], made under the Road Traffic Act 1972, ss. 40 (1) (2A) (3), 199 (2) as amended by the Road Traffic Act 1974 (c. 50), s. 9 (1); operative on September 23, 1978; amend S.I. 1975 No. 245 by substituting for the reference to one fog lamp a reference to one front fog lamp so as to avoid this reference including a rear fog lamp.

2596. London traffic. See LONDON.

2597. Motor vehicles

MOTOR VEHICLES (TYPE APPROVAL) (GREAT BRITAIN) (AMENDMENT) REGULATIONS 1978 (No. 293) [10p], made under the Road Traffic Act 1972 (c. 20), ss. 47 (1), 50 (1) and 51 (1), as amended by the Road Traffic Act 1974 (c. 50), s. 10; operative on March 31, 1978; postpone by four months the coming into operation of the scheme for the compulsory type approval of certain motor vehicles and their parts.

MOTOR VEHICLES (DESIGNATION OF APPROVAL MARKS) (AMENDMENT) REGULATIONS 1978 (No. 1111) [25p], made under the Road Traffic Act 1972, ss. 63 (1), 199 (2), as amended by S.I. 1973 No. 1193; operative on August 30, 1978; further amend S.I. 1976 No. 2226 by adding to the markings designated as approval markings.

MOTOR VEHICLES (TYPE APPROVAL) (AMENDMENT) REGULATIONS 1978 (No. 1112) [10p], made under the European Communities Act 1972 (c. 68), s. 2 (2); operative on August 30, 1978; amend S.I. 1973 No. 1199.

MOTOR VEHICLES (TYPE APPROVAL) (AMENDMENT) (NO. 2) REGULATIONS 1978 (No. 1236) [10p], made under the European Communities Act 1972, s. 2 (2); operative on October 1, 1978; further amend S.I. 1973 No. 1199.

MOTOR VEHICLES (TYPE APPROVAL) (GREAT BRITAIN) (AMENDMENT) (NO. 2) REGULATIONS 1978 (No. 1237) [10p], made under the Road Traffic Act 1972, ss. 47 (1), 50 (1), 199 (2) as amended by the Road Traffic Act 1974 (c. 50), s. 10, Sched. 2; operative on October 1, 1978; further amend S.I. 1976 No. 937 by providing that windscreens manufactured in France and which have French approval marking are exempt from the requirement that the glass shall comply with certain British Standards Specifications.

ROAD VEHICLES (REAR FOG LAMPS) REGULATIONS 1978 (No. 1260) [25p], made under the Road Traffic Act 1972, ss. 40 (1) (2A) and (3), 41 (3), as amended by the Road Traffic Act 1974, s. 91 (1) (2); operative on September 23, 1978; provide that all motor vehicles made on or after October 1, 1979, shall be equipped with either one rear fog lamp marked with an approval mark, or two lamps, fitted so as to form a pair, and all such vehicles shall be equipped with a tell-tale.

MOTOR VEHICLES (TYPE APPROVAL) (GREAT BRITAIN) (AMENDMENT) (NO. 3) REGULATIONS 1978 (No. 1318) [10p], made under the Road Traffic Act 1972 ss. 47 (1), 50 (1), 199 (2), as amended and extended by the Road Traffic Act 1974 (c. 50), s. 10; operative on October 1, 1978; further amend S.I. 1976 No. 937 by postponing for one further year the application of the type approval scheme to motor vehicles constructed or assembled by persons not ordinarily engaged in the trade or business of manufacturing motor vehicles.

MOTOR VEHICLES (TYPE APPROVAL) (GREAT BRITAIN) (AMENDMENT) (NO. 4) REGULATIONS 1978 (No. 1319) [40p], made under the Road Traffic Act 1972, ss. 47 (1), 50 (1), as amended and extended by the Road Traffic Act 1974, s. 10, Sched. 2; operative on October 1, 1978; further amend S.I. 1976 No. 937 and make provision for seat belts and seat belt anchorage points.

MOTOR VEHICLES (TYPE APPROVAL) (GREAT BRITAIN) (FEES) (AMENDMENT) REGULATIONS 1978 (No. 1320) [30p], made under the Road Traffic Act 1972, s. 50 (1), as amended by the Road Traffic Act 1974, s. 10, Sched. 2; operative on October 1, 1978; amend S.I. 1976 No. 1439 so as to provide a new scale of fees for an approval certificate.

MOTOR VEHICLES (TYPE APPROVAL AND APPROVAL MARKS) (FEES) (AMENDMENT) REGULATIONS 1978 (No. 1321)) [40p], made under the Finance Act 1973

(c. 51), s. 56 (1) (2); operative on October 1, 1978; amend S.I. 1976 No. 1465 by increasing certain fees by replacing Sched. 1 of those regulations.

MOTOR VEHICLES (TYPE APPROVAL) (GREAT BRITAIN) (FEES) (AMENDMENT) (No. 2) REGULATIONS 1978 (No. 1810) [10p], made under the Road Traffic Act 1972, ss. 50 (1), 199 (2) as amended by the Road Traffic Act 1974, s. 10, Sched. 2; operative on January 10, 1979; further amend S.I. 1976 No. 1466 by adding fees for the examination of seat belts to a new standard and for the examination of rear fog lamps.

MOTOR VEHICLES (TYPE APPROVAL) (GREAT BRITAIN) (AMENDMENT) (No. 5) REGULATIONS 1978 (No. 1811) [40p], made under the Road Traffic Act 1972, ss. 47 (1), 50 (1), as amended by the Road Traffic Act 1974, s. 10 and Sched. 2; operative on January 10, 1979; amend further S.I. 1976 No. 937.

MOTOR VEHICLES (TYPE APPROVAL AND APPROVAL MARKS) (FEES) (AMENDMENT) (No. 2) REGULATIONS 1978 (No. 1831) [10p], made under the Finance Act 1973, s. 56 (1) (2); operative on January 1, 1979; amend S.I. 1976 No. 1465 so as to prescribe the fees payable for the testing of vehicle parts being the heating systems for the passenger compartment of motor vehicles and the wheel guards of motor vehicles.

MOTOR VEHICLES (TYPE APPROVAL) (AMENDMENT) (No. 3) REGULATIONS 1978 (No. 1832) [25p], made under the European Communities Act 1972, s. 2 (2); operative on January 12, 1979; amend S.I. 1973 No. 1199.

MOTOR VEHICLES (DESIGNATION OF APPROVAL MARKS) (AMENDMENT) (No. 2) REGULATIONS 1978 (No. 1870) [10p], made under the Road Traffic Act 1972, ss. 63 (1), 199 (2) as amended by S.I. 1973 No. 1193; operative on January 19, 1979; further amend S.I. 1976 No. 2226 by designating further approval marks in relation to vehicles approved in respect of radio interference suppression, rear fog lamps and speedometers.

2598. —— **definition—mechanical condition—" use "**

[Scot.] [Road Traffic Act 1972 (c. 20), ss. 44 (1), 143 (13), 190.] E's motor car, which he had decided not to have repaired, was left parked on a road outside his house. It was found to have a flat battery and locked rear wheels. E was charged with using a motor vehicle with no insurance and no M.O.T. *Held*, s. 190 (1) defines a motor vehicle as " a mechanically propelled vehicle intended or adapted for use on roads." Only when a vehicle's mechanical condition was such as to offend against common sense in calling it a " mechanically propelled vehicle " did it cease to be a motor vehicle. E's car had by no means reached such a stage. The meaning of " use " in ss. 44 and 143 was determined according to the mischief each section aimed at; E was " using " his car with respect to the insurance offence but not to the M.O.T. offence (*Smart* v. *Allan* [1962] C.L.Y. 2723 applied; *Hewer* v. *Cutler* [1974] C.L.Y. 3397 considered): TUDHOPE v. EVERY, 1976 J.C. 42, High Ct. of Justiciary.

2599. Northern Ireland. See NORTHERN IRELAND.

2599a. Offence—notice of intended prosecution—" at the time the offence was committed "

[Road Traffic Act 1972 (c. 20), s. 179 (2) (*a*).] A warning of intended prosecution given orally two and a half hours after allegedly dangerous driving may be given " at the time the offence was committed " within s. 179 (2) (*a*) of the Road Traffic Act 1972; it is a question of fact and degree. (*Jollye* v. *Dale* [1960] C.L.Y. 2806 and *Sinclair* v. *Clark* [1962] C.L.Y. 2653 applied): R. v. OKIKE, *The Times*, October 5, 1978, C.A.

2600. Offences

The annual volume " Offences Relating to Motor Vehicles 1977 " has been published by the Home Office. The report shows, inter alia, that the number of motor vehicle offences dealt with by written warning, fixed penalty notice or prosecution in court in England and Wales in 1977 fell by about 4 per cent. compared with 1976. For the first time, the volume contains a commentary on the statistics over the past 10 years. The report is available from HMSO. (Cmnd. 7349) [£1·75].

2601. Parking

CONTROL OF PARKING IN GOODS VEHICLE LOADING AREAS ORDERS (PROCEDURE) REGULATIONS 1978 (No. 1347) [25p], made under the Road Traffic Regulation Act 1967 (c. 76), ss. 84C (2)–(4) (6), 107 (2), as applied by the Local Government (Miscellaneous Provisions) Act 1976 (c. 57), s. 37 (4); operative on October 12, 1978; lays down the procedure to be followed by the G.L.C. and by county councils in England and Wales in connection with the making by them of orders under s. 37 of the 1976 Act for controlling the parking of vehicles in areas used for loading or unloading goods vehicles.

CONTROL OF OFF-STREET PARKING (ENGLAND AND WALES) ORDER (No. 1535) [40p], made under the Transport Act 1978 (c. 55), s. 11; operative on December 1, 1978; applies, with appropriate modifications, the provisions of s. 36 and Sched. 5 to the Transport (London) Act 1969 (c. 35) to England (outside Greater London) and to Wales.

2602. —— fines—power of authority to allow discount

[Road Traffic Regulation Act 1967 (c. 76), s. 31.] The defendant authority made an order under s. 31 of the Road Traffic Regulation Act 1967 providing for payment of a £10 charge in respect of vehicles left too long in parking places. The authority intended to allow a discount, being prepared to accept £1·50 paid within seven days, in full satisfaction. *Held,* that although the authority was probably not entitled to give the discount, the order itself was not ultra vires. (*Yabbicom* v. *King* [1899] 1 Q.B. 444 considered; *Kruse* v. *Johnson* [1898] 2 Q.B. 91 applied): STARTIN v. SOLIHULL METROPOLITAN BOROUGH COUNCIL, *The Times,* October 7, 1978, O'Connor J.

2603. Public service vehicles

PUBLIC SERVICE VEHICLES (LOST PROPERTY) REGULATIONS 1978 (No. 1684) [25p], made under the Road Traffic Act 1960 (c. 16), ss. 160, 260 (2); operative on January 1, 1979; make provision as respects property accidently left in or on public service vehicles.

2604. Records—duty to keep—EEC. See AUDITEUR DU TRAVAIL v. BERNARD DUFOUR, S.A. CREYF'S INTERIM AND S.A. CREYF'S INDUSTRIAL, § 1375.

2605. Refuse Disposal (Amenity) Act 1978 (c. 3). See § 1881.

2606. Registration and licensing

ROAD VEHICLES (REGISTRATION AND LICENSING) (AMENDMENT) REGULATIONS 1978 (No. 1536) [10p], made under the Vehicles (Excise) Act 1971 (c. 10), ss. 23, 37, 39 (1), Sched. 7, Pt. I, para. 20; operative on November 17, 1978; amend S.I. 1971 No. 450 as a consequence of the coming into force of s. 8 of the Finance Act 1978 which extends the exemptions from vehicle excise duty to persons in receipt of a mobility allowance.

2607. Removal of vehicles

REMOVAL AND DISPOSAL OF VEHICLES (LOADING AREAS) (MODIFICATIONS OF ENACTMENTS) REGULATIONS 1978 (No. 889) [25p], made under the Local Government (Miscellaneous Provisions) Act 1976 (c. 57), s. 37 (7); operative on July 19, 1978; adapt the provisions of the Road Traffic Regulation Act 1967 relating to the removal, storage and disposal of vehicles left on roads so that they relate also to vehicles standing in a prohibited goods vehicle parking area.

REMOVAL AND DISPOSAL OF VEHICLES (LOADING AREAS) REGULATIONS 1978 (No. 1345) [20p], made under the Road Traffic Regulation Act 1967 (c. 76), ss. 20, 52, 53, as altered by S.I. 1967 No. 1900, as amended by the Local Government Act 1972 (c. 70), Sched. 19, and the Road Traffic Act 1974 (c. 50), s. 19, and as continued in effect (as altered) by the Statute Law (Repeals) Act 1976 (c. 16), s. 2 (3), and as modified by S.I. 1978 No. 889; operative on October 12, 1978; make provision for the removal and disposal of vehicles under the 1967 Act as those sections have been applied in relation to vehicles in any part of a loading area while the parking of such vehicles on that part is prohibited.

REMOVAL AND DISPOSAL OF VEHICLES (AMENDMENT) REGULATIONS 1978 (No. 1346) [10p], made under the Refuse Disposal (Amenity) Act 1978 (c. 3), ss.

4 (5), 5 (1), and the Road Traffic Regulation Act 1967, ss. 52 (1), 53 (3), as altered by S.I. 1967 No. 1900 and continued in effect by the Statute Law (Repeals) Act 1976 (c. 16), s. 2 (3); operative on October 12, 1978; increases the charges payable under S.I. 1968 No. 43.

2608. Road Traffic (Drivers' Ages and Hours of Work) Act 1976—commencement

ROAD TRAFFIC (DRIVERS' AGES AND HOURS OF WORK) ACT 1976 (COMMENCEMENT NO. 2) ORDER 1978 (No. 6 (C. 1) [10p], made under the Road Traffic (Drivers' Ages and Hours of Work) Act 1976 (c. 3), s. 4 (2) (3) (4); operative on January 26, 1978; brings into force s. 2 of the 1976 Act.

2609. Sale of vehicle. See SALE OF GOODS.

2610. Seat belts—failure to wear—contributory negligence—principles of apportionment of blame

[Road Traffic Act 1972 (c. 20), s. 148 (3).]

In road accident cases, where the passenger is plaintiff, respective faults are not to be assessed by attempted mathematical computation, but by looking at the matter generally and doing justice in sharing out the blame.

G was a passenger in a car, driven by K, which was involved in a road accident in which G suffered injuries. The car, to G's knowledge, had a defective foot brake; G was not wearing a seat belt, and the injuries he suffered were attributable to that failure. *Held,* giving judgment for the plaintiff, that (1) in view of s. 148 (3) of the Act, volenti non fit injuria was not available; (2) contributory negligence was established; (3) the respective faults of the parties was not to be measured by taking percentages attributable to different aspects of negligence in a mathematical computation, but by looking at the matter generally and doing justice in sharing out the blame.

GREGORY *v.* KELLY [1978] R.T.R. 426, Kenneth Jones J.

2611. —— —— —— proof

A defendant wishing to prove contributory negligence by reason of a car passenger's failure to wear a seat belt must elicit evidence that the plaintiff failed to take reasonable care and that any failure contributed to the injuries.

The plaintiff was injured in a motor accident, she being the passenger in a car driven by the defendant; her main injury resulted from a piece of glass striking her eye. The plaintiff denied the defendant's allegation of contributory negligence due to her failure to wear a seat belt. An agreed medical report stated that the injury " probably " would have been less severe had she worn a belt. She gave evidence that she refrained from so doing due to claustrophobia. The defendant called no evidence. *Held,* giving judgment for the plaintiff, that in the absence of an admission, it was incumbent upon the defendant to adduce evidence in support of his allegation of contributory negligence; the plaintiff's phobia was, on the evidence, genuine and excused her failure to wear the belt; the medical evidence did not state any basis for the conclusion as to the probable effect of wearing the belt; and accordingly no contributory negligence was established. (*Froom* v. *Butcher* [1975] C.L.Y. 2295 considered.)

CONDON *v.* CONDON [1978] R.T.R. 483, Bristow J.

[For quantum of damages, see § 738.]

2612. —— —— drunken driver—whether plaintiff contributorily negligent

The plaintiff was a front seat passenger in a car driven by the defendant. She was not wearing a seat belt as she shared the seat with a second passenger. The judge accepted medical evidence to the effect that she would have suffered different but equally severe injuries had she worn a seat belt. The defendant was convicted of driving with 168 milligrammes of alcohol in his blood. The judge also accepted the plaintiff's evidence that she did not observe any indication prior to accepting the lift from the defendant, whom she had first met half an hour previously in a public-house, that his driving ability might be impaired. She called police evidence to confirm that symptoms of such excessive consumption of alcohol were not necessarily apparent to a lay person. *Held,* that there should be no deduction from a 100 per cent. award of damages: TRAYNOR *v.* DONOVAN, October 20, 1978, Sheldon J. (*Ex rel. J. Sofer, Esq., Barrister.*)

2613. Speed limit

70 MILES PER HOUR, 60 MILES PER HOUR AND 50 MILES PER HOUR (TEMPORARY SPEED LIMIT) (CONTINUATION) ORDER 1978 (No. 1548) [10p], made under the Road Traffic Regulation Act 1967 (c. 76), s. 77 (3); operative on November 30, 1978; continues indefinitely the provisions of the 70 miles per hour, 60 miles per hour and 50 miles per hour (Temporary Speed Limit) Order 1977, as varied, which provided for a 70 m.p.h. general speed limit on dual carriageway roads (not being motorways) and 60 m.p.h. general speed limit on single carriageway roads (not being motorways), with certain exceptions.

2614. Statutory statement of ownership—notice—no evidence of recipient being owner of car with fixed penalty notice affixed

[Road Traffic Act 1974 s. 1 (2) (6) (7).]

The Act does not require the police to have reasonable grounds for suspecting that the recipient of a notice under s. 1 (6) is the owner of the vehicle to which the fixed penalty notice had been affixed.

W was served with a notice under s. 1 (6) of the Act giving particulars of a fixed penalty for an alleged parking offence. He did not pay the fixed penalty and did not furnish a statutory statement of ownership or facts in compliance with the notice. He was charged with an offence contrary to s. 1 (7) of the Act. At the hearing he did not appear and no evidence was adduced to establish that he was the owner of the car at the time of the alleged parking offence. The justices dismissed the information on the ground that there was no evidence to connect W with the car to which the fixed penalty notice had been affixed. The prosecutor appealed. On the question of whether the Act required the police to have reasonable grounds for suspecting that W, as the recipient of the notice under s. 1 (6), was the car owner, *held*, allowing the appeal, that the justices had taken a view of s. 1 (7) not open to them and the case would be remitted for the hearing to proceed.

HEDGES *v.* WRAY [1977] R.T.R. 433, Goff J.

2615. Testing of vehicles

MOTOR VEHICLES (TESTS) (AMENDMENT) REGULATIONS 1978 (No. 1574) [10p], made under the Road Traffic Act 1972 (c. 20), ss. 43 (6), 199 (2); operative on December 1, 1978; amend S.I. 1976 No. 1977 by increasing the fee for the examination of a motor bicycle to £2·70 and the fee for examining any other vehicle to which the 1976 Regulations apply to £4·50.

2616. Traffic regulation

LONDON AUTHORITIES' TRAFFIC ORDERS (PROCEDURE) (AMENDMENT) REGULATIONS 1978 (No. 707) [20p], made under the Road Traffic Regulation Act 1967 (c. 76), ss. 84c (2) (3) (4), 107 (2) as amended by the Transport Act 1968 (c. 73), Pt. IX; operative on June 15, 1978; amend S.I. 1972 No. 729 which prescribe the procedure to be followed in connection with the making of traffic regulations, parking place and speed limit orders under the 1967 Act.

CONTROL OF ROAD-SIDE SALES ORDERS (PROCEDURE) REGULATIONS 1978 (No. 932) [30p], made under the Road Traffic Regulation Act 1967, ss. 84C (2)–(6), 107 (2), as applied by the Local Government (Miscellaneous Provisions) Act 1976 (c. 57), s. 7 (3); operative on August 2, 1978; lays down the procedure to be followed by highway authorities in connection with the making by them of orders under s. 7 of the 1976 Act for controlling road-side sales.

2617. Transport tribunal decisions. See TRANSPORT.

2618. Value added tax. See VALUE ADDED TAX.

BOOKS AND ARTICLES. See *post,* pp. [8], [34].

SALE OF GOODS

2619. C.i.f. contract—prohibition of export—force majeure. See BREMER HANDELSGESELLSCHAFT M.B.H. *v.* MACKPRANG JR, § 2646.

2620. Conditions and warranties—implied condition of fitness—seller not informed of purpose

[Can.] P assembled hair-dryers for sale to a retailer. D manufactured the motors for the hair-dryers. The motors were not inherently defective. However, P requested certain modifications to D's original design, which resulted in greater stress. Consequently many of the dryers failed. On appeal, *held*, that P had not made known to D the particular purpose for which the goods were required so as to show reliance on D's skill and judgment. The final product was designed by P, and the stress was caused by the modification requested by P. P had only relied in part on D's skill and judgment, and in part on its own. There was no breach of condition (*Ashington Piggeries* v. *Christopher Hill* [1971] C.L.Y. 10517 referred to): VENUS ELECTRIC v. BREVEZ PRODUCTS [1978] 85 D.L.R. (3d) 282, Ontario C.A.

2621. —— **merchantability—exclusion of liability—whether contract subject to exclusion clause**

[Sale of Goods Act 1897 (c. 71), s. 14, as amended by Supply of Goods (Implied Terms) Act 1973 (c. 13).]

A seller wishing to rely upon an exclusion clause must make clear to the buyer that the same is incorporated into the contract.

A vehicle was offered for sale at an auction; the auction conditions, advertised by posters in the auction room, included an exclusion of all rights by a buyer to " return " vehicles and/or claim damages. The vehicle failed to reach its reserve price and soon thereafter the defendant negotiated through the auctioneer to buy it by private treaty. The vehicle broke down almost immediately and the defendant returned it to the auctioneer and stopped his cheque for the price. The plaintiffs claimed the price, relying upon the auction conditions. *Held*, giving judgment for the defendant, that the vehicle was not of merchantable quality; that the defendant had bought it in a transaction separate to the auction and the auctioneer had not made it clear to the defendant that the auction conditions applied (and that had they done so it was not certain that the condition was apt to exclude the buyer's statutory rights).

D. & M. TRAILERS (HALIFAX) v. STIRLING [1978] R.T.R. 468, C.A.

2622. —— —— **measure of damages.** See JACKSON v. CHRYSLER ACCEPTANCES; MINORIES GARAGE (THIRD PARTY), § 786.

2623. —— —— **suitability for purpose—defective towing coupling—retailer's liability.** See LAMBERT v. LEWIS, § 2081.

2624. Consumer credit

CONSUMER CREDIT (EXEMPT AGREEMENTS) (AMENDMENT) ORDER 1978 (No. 126) [10p], made under the Consumer Credit Act 1974 (c. 39), s. 16 (3), (9); operative on March 1, 1978, specifies further bodies to be included in the Schedule to S.I. 1977 No. 326.

CONSUMER CREDIT (EXEMPT AGREEMENTS) (AMENDMENT No. 2) ORDER 1978 (No. 1616) [10p], made under the Consumer Credit Act 1974, ss. 16 (1) (3) (4) (9), 182 (2) (4); operative on December 8, 1978; further varies S.I. 1977 No. 326 by specifying further bodies to be included in the schedule to that Order.

2625. Consumer protection

NIGHTWEAR (SAFETY) ORDER 1978 (No. 1728) [10p], made under the Consumer Safety Act 1978 (c. 38), s. 3 (1) (*a*) (2), Sched. 1, para. 5; operative on December 1, 1978; prohibits the supply of children's nightwear which has been treated with or contains Tris (2, 3-dibromopropyl) phosphate.

2626. Consumer Safety Act 1978 (c. 38). See § 2917.

2627. Contract—breach—nomination of vessel—whether buyers entitled to extension of time for loading

V sold soya beans to P by a contract dated July 1, 1974, incorporating the terms of the standard Anec f.o.b. contract 1974. This provided, by cl. 7, that P give V at least 15 days' notice of the earliest time of arrival of the vessel; by cl. 10 that P pay carrying charges in the event of any or all the goods not being on board by the last day of the period of delivery; and by cl. 14 that all terms and conditions not in contradiction with the Anec form to be as per G.A.F.T.A. 64. This provided, by cl. 7, that P could claim an extension of time for tendering suitable tonnage by notifying V not later than the last day of the specified period for the delivery. On July 19, P nominated two vessels, stating their respective e.t.a. to be July 27 and August 3. On July 22, V rejected both nominations as not in accordance with cl. 7 of the Anec form and considered the contract null and void. P rejected this, and called for an extension of loading time under cl. 7 of G.A.F.T.A. 64. On July 23, P nominated a third vessel, due to arrive on August 7. V again rejected nomination, and advised P that the contract was null and void. P again invoked cl. 7 of G.A.F.T.A. 64, but on July 29 accepted the repudiation as an anticipatory breach of the contract. On a special case stated, *held*, that (1) failure to comply with cl. 7 of the Anec form was a breach of a condition rather than of a mere warranty; (2) taking cl. 10 of the Anec form by itself against the common law background, P had the option of treating the contract as terminated through breach of a condition in the event of the goods not being on board by the last day of the period of delivery; (3) the provisions of cl. 7 of the Anec form rendered inapplicable the provisions of cl. 7 of G.A.F.T.A. 64; (4) cl. 10 of the Anec form contradicted with the extension provisons of cl. 7 of G.A.F.T.A. 64, and in accordance with cl. 14 of the Anec form, cl. 10 prevailed; (5) therefore V succeeded, as P was not entitled to any extension under cl. 7 of G.A.F.T.A. 64 (*Finnish Government* (*Ministry of Food*) v. *H. Ford & Co.* (1921) 6 Ll.L.Rep. 188; *Tradax Export S.A.* v. *André & Cie S.A.* [1976] C.L.Y. 2464 applied): BREMER HANDELSGESELLSCHAFT M.B.H. v. J. H. RAYNER & Co. [1978] 2 Lloyd's Rep. 73, Mocatta J.

2628. Delivery—delay—force majeure—extension of shipment period

By a contract in the F.O.S.F.A. 54 form, V sold oil to P for shipment December 1974/January 1975. Cl. 15, the force Majeure clause, provided, inter alia, that "should shipment of goods be prevented at any time during the last 30 days of the contract shipment period by reason of strikes or any other cause comprehended by the term force majeure at port/s of loading or elsewhere preventing transport of the goods to such port/s, the time allowed for shipment shall be extended to 30 days beyond the termination of such cause." V intended to ship on the C on January 4 but were unable to do so in time because of strikes. The oil was in fact shipped on board the K on February 1 and 2, but bills of lading were issued on January 31, both V and P being unaware of the deception. Upon discovery of the deception, P sought damages for breach of contract. On a special case stated, *held*, that (1) to come within cl. 15, V merely had to show that shipment was prevented by one of the specified causes at the time at which shipment was intended; (2) V had proved that the strikes had made shipment more difficult on January 4, but not that they had prevented shipment, and so could not rely on cl. 15. Judgment for P: THE KASTELLON [1978] 2 Lloyd's Rep. 203, Donaldson J.

2629. —— goods not in conformity with contract—whether buyers lost right of rejection

V contracted to sell to P three consignments of South African crude maize oil, specifying, inter alia, a 2 to 3 per cent. ffa content. The first two consignments were resold to G, who rejected them on the basis that they contained semi-refined, not crude, oil, and P claimed damages from V. The third consignment was not resold, but 17 days after delivery, P purported to reject it. On a special case stated, *held* that (1) in respect of the first two consignments, P had failed to show that the crude South African oil of 2 to 3 ffa content that they had contracted to buy was worth more than the semi-refined South African oil of the same ffa content that they had received; (2) in respect of the third consignment, it could not be held, in the absence of a finding of fact other than that 17 days had elapsed before an analysis of the oil was put in hand, that P had no reasonable opportunity for examination and s. 34 of the Sale of Goods Act 1893 applied. Judgment for V: ALGEMENE OLIEHANDEL INTERNATIONAL B.V. v. BUNGE S.A. [1978] 2 Lloyd's Rep. 207, Donaldson J.

2630. —— whether delivery order complied with contract

In October 1973, S bought 700 tons of groundnut extraction from R, delivery 350 tons in each of November and December 1973, partly in order to meet an obligation to deliver 100 tons to P in November 1973. On November 5, 1973,

P sold 10 tons to Y for " prompt " delivery, and Y immediately sold on to R for
" prompt " delivery. All the contracts were on GAFTA 109 form, and stipulated delivery ex store/silo at Avonmouth GAFTA 109 provided, *inter alia,*
that if sold prompt, the delivery period was to be 14 consecutive days from the
contract date; that sellers were to have the contracted goods available for
delivery in good condition from the first day of the delivery period; and that
delivery/transfer orders should be for the contract quantity. At Avonmouth,
goods were stored by the port authority (PBA), who maintained a register of
those to whose order the goods were held. Deliveries under such contracts could
be actual or constructive. Constructive delivery took place by means of delivery
orders (to be handed by the seller to the buyer against payment), and advice
notes sent to, and registered by, PBA (to inform them of the transfer). On
November 5 PBA received and registered an advice note and delivery order
showing a transfer from R to S. On November 6, PBA received a telex advice
from P of the respective transfers of 100 tons from S to P, and of 10 tons
from P to Y. On November 7, the delivery order by Y in favour of R was
received by PBA. On November 8, PBA received the documents confirming the
transfers notified in the telex of November 6. On November 8, actual delivery
of 10 tons was made by PBA to R. P claimed that S's tender of the delivery
order for 100 tons was a bad tender, and claimed repayment of the purchase
price with interest. *Held,* (1) S's tender of delivery was good, and S were under
no liability to P; (2) " available for delivery " meant that the contracted goods
had to be in such a state of availability for delivery from and including the first
day of the delivery period that they could be delivered as soon, in a commercial
sense, as buyers required sellers to deliver; (3) " contracted goods " meant that
the goods had to be identified, even if only as part of an identified bulk, and had
to be in a deliverable state; (4) S could have procured immediate delivery, and
there was no evidence to suggest that the goods were not in an immediately
deliverable state: EUROPEAN GRAIN AND SHIPPING *v.* DAVID GEDDES (PROTEINS)
[1977] 2 Lloyd's Rep. 591, Donaldson J.

2631. Duty of seller—whether performance impossible—executive action. See
EXPORTELISA S.A. *v.* GUISEPPE ROCCO & FIGLI SOC. COLL., § 324.

2632. F.o.b. contract—non-delivery—prohibition on export—appeal procedure. See
PROVIMI HELLAS A.E. *v.* WARINCO A.G., § 89.

2633. Hire purchase. See HIRE PURCHASE.

**2634. Implied terms—unroadworthy condition of motorvehicle—damages for incon-
venience.** See GASCOIGNE *v.* BRITISH CREDIT TRUST, § 711.

2635. Manufacturer's negligence—no contractual relationship—economic loss. See
    ITAL-CANADIAN INVESTMENTS *v.* NORTH SHORE PLUMBING AND HEATING CO.,
    § 2086.

**2636. Non-acceptance—goods sold on " as is " basis—whether seller could claim
balance of price.**
    By a contract on LCTA form 64 dated November 30, 1967, S sold to P 8,000
m.t. 5 per cent. more or less of barley at $57 per m.t. f.o.b., stowed/trimmed
Lattakia, shipment 4,000 m.t. in December 1967 and 4,000 m.t. in January 1968.
The contract provided, inter alia, " Weight and quality: final at loading as per
Superintendence Company Certificate. Payment: cash against documents on
presentation." P tendered the vessel A for loading of 2,000 m.t. of barley, and
loading was completed on February 17. Of this 913 m.t. were appropriated
to the December shipment and 1,086 m.t. to the January shipment. A certificate of quality was issued which stated, inter alia, that impurities and foreign
substances amounted to 4·10 per cent. On February 24, the A reached Ravenna
before the documents and the cargo was discharged into silo space. On March
1, P learned of the contents of the quality certificate and complained to S
about the excessive quantity of foreign matter. S rejected this protest on the
grounds that the contract provided: " Quality: final at loading as per Superintendence Certificate." On March 8, S presented the shipping documents to P
who refused to pay for them. The parties agreed without prejudice that the
goods be sold " as is " for a net price of £89,242. S claimed that they had

suffered $26,728.24 loss being the net price, including penalties (due *to* the late tender of the A), and the proceeds of resale. *Held,* (1) in the absence of any agreement that the provision as to impurities was a condition, the court should construe the provision as an intermediate term; only a serious and substantial breach of which entitled rejection; (2) if there had been no provision as to quality final certificate, the breach of provision as to impurities would not have entitled rejection of the goods but would have entitled P to an allowance; the fact that the certificate showed a minor breach did not make any difference; (3) this was not a case where there can be no acceptance or waiver unless there were an unequivocal representation acted upon by the seller; (4) S were entitled to treat the resale price as the market price of goods and were entitled to recover $26,728.24 as damages for non-acceptance from P. (*Cehave N.V.* v. *Bremer Handelgesellschaft* [1975] C.L.Y. 3041, and *Hong Kong Fir Shipping Co.* v. *Kawasaki Kisen Kaisha* [1961] C.L.Y. 8255, applied): TRADAX INTERNACIONAL S.A. *v.* GOLDSCHMIDT S.A. [1977] 2 Lloyd's Rep. 604, Slynn, J.

2637. Non-delivery—force majeure—invalid notice

By a contract dated December 19, 1972. V sold to P 1,000 tonnes of soya bean meal c.i.f. Rotterdam for shipment 500 tonnes each April and May 1973. The contract incorporated the terms of G.A.F.T.A. 100, which provided, inter alia, that provided the shipper gave proper notice, the shipment period could be extended by eight days, under cl. 9, and by cl. 22, for two months in case of force majeure. On April 25, 1973, V telexed P invoking cl. 22 owing to flooding conditions on the Mississippi River. On May 3, 1973, V telexed P declaring extensions under both cl. 9 and cl. 22. On July 13, P telexed V to the effect that despite the force majeure extension, the first shipment had taken place under a bill of lading dated May 31, which indicated normalisation of the river, and calling for the April shipment with a bill of lading dated not later than June 30. V never tendered the April shipment. On a special case stated, *held*, that (1) the cl. 9 notice was invalid as not being in terms a notice by a shipper as required in cl. 9, and P was not precluded from relying on such invalidity; (2) it was not established that the second cl. 22 notice was invalid as being out of time; (3) both parties were precluded from treating either cl. 22 notice as invalid, having treated them as valid; but the cl. 9 notice was never accepted by P, no matter what V's beliefs, and V were liable to P in damages. (*Panchaud Freres S.A.* v. *Etablissements General Grain Co.* [1970] C.L.Y. 2604 and *Toepfer* v. *Cremer* [1975] C.L.Y. 3059 followed): BUNGE G.M.B.H. *v.* ALFRED C. TOEPFER [1978] 1 Lloyd's Rep. 506, Brandon J.

2638. ——— waiver

By a contract dated April 25, 1973, to which G.A.F.T.A. 100 and 125 applied, V sold to P 500 tonnes of soya bean meal in instalments. Owing to the U.S. Government's embargo on soya bean meal, V were unable to ship the June instalment, part of which was shipped in August. On September 3, V sent to P a notice of appropriation in respect of the 60 tonnes balance, shipped on the C under a bill of lading dated August 16, 1973. On September 7, P accepted V's "notifications" "subject to reserves." On September 21, P rejected the notice of appropriation as uncontractual. The C completed discharge on September 12. V contended that P's conduct relieved them from any obligation to tender shipping documents. By telex, on September 27, 1973, P held V in default for failure to present documents and nominated their arbitrator. V contended that P's claim was time barred under the G.A.F.T.A Arbitration Rules 125, which provided, inter alia, that the arbitrator was to be nominated and the claim made within three months of the contract time of shipment. On a special case stated, *held* that (1) on September 21, P took the clear stand that a bill of lading dated August 16, 1973, was not contractual; and P's earlier acceptance of V's "notifications" "without reserves" was not a waiver of their contractual right to a June bill of lading; (2) V was not in default for failure to present documents on September 27, since P never fully accepted the notice of appropriation, and rejected it as "not contractual" after the discharge of the C; (3) the contract time of shipment ended on June 30, and P's telex of September 27 was within the three months laid down by the G.A.F.T.A. Rules; (4) although V were not in default for not presenting documents, they were for not having given a valid notice of appropriation, and so the telex of September 27 satisfied the very general provisions of the G.A.F.T.A. Rules; (5) these were two different causes of action, and since P had rejected any tender by the C because of the date of the bill of lading, V cannot have been prejudiced when the default was put on its proper footing; (6) V was liable to P in damages for breach of contract. (*Finagrain S.A.* v. *Kruse S.A.* [1977] C.L.Y. 2669 applied): BUNGE S.A. v. SCHLESWIG-HOLSTEINISCHE LANDWIRTSCHAFTLICHE HAUPTGENOSSEN-SCHAFT EINGETR G.M.B.H. [1978] 1 Lloyd's Rep. 480, Mocatta J.

2639. Passing of property—title to manufactured goods—manufacturer as supplier's bailee

Under a contractual term, a supplier retained title to the goods until the buyer had paid him in full. The effect of this was that there was a fiduciary relationship between the manufacturer, who acted as bailee, and the supplier, and in those circumstances the equitable remedy of tracing could be used. (*Aluminium Industrie BV* v. *Romalpa* [1976] C.L.Y. 2474 and *Re Hallett's Estate* (1880) 13 Ch.D. 696 applied): BORDEN v. SCOTTISH TIMBER PRODUCTS, *The Times*, November 16, 1978, Judge Rubin.

2640. Payment—delivery of documents—delay

By a contract dated December 19, 1972, under GAFTA form 100, S agreed to sell to P, inter alia, 300 m.t. of U.S. soya bean meal, for June shipment at U.S. $158 per m.t., c.i.f. Rotterdam; Cl. 10 (*a*) provided, inter alia, that a shipper was to give notice of appropriation to his buyer within 10 days of the date of the bill of lading. Cl. 10 (*b*) provided that each subsequent seller was to give notice of appropriation to his buyer within the above period, but if notice of appropriation were received by a subsequent seller on or after that period, his notice of appropriation was to be deemed to be in time if despatched either on the same calendar day, if received after 1600 on any business day, or not later than the next business day, if received after 1600 hours or on a non-business day. S were not shippers. In June 1973, the U.S. Government imposed export controls on soya bean meal, and S did not deliver any goods. On July 11, 1973, P gave S seven days in which to make a contracted appropriation. On July 12, S claimed prohibition in respect of approximately 60 per cent. of 100 m.t., and gave notice of appropriation in respect of 39.2 m.t. (40 per cent.), the date of the bill of lading being June 18. S replied that they would accept this tender as part fulfilment, if full proof were furnished that this appropriation was contractual. S did not give any notice of appropriation with regard to 200 m.t., and on July 16 P declared S in default in respect of this quantity and claimed arbitration. On a special case stated, held, (1) S's obligation under cl. 10 (*b*) was to give notice of appropriation on or before July 10, and if they did not do so, P were entitled to claim default at once; P were entitled to succeed in relation to the 200 m.t.; (2) as to the 39.2 m.t., prima facie, the giving of a notice of appropriation on July 12 was not in compliance with the contract; S were unable to cure this defect because they could not prove that they and all intermediate sellers had complied with the contractual timetables, and S were in default in respect of the 39.2 m.t.; (3) S were liable to P in damages for non-fulfilment; damages were to be calculated by reference to the market value of July 10, 1973. (*Toepfer* v. *Cremer* [1975] C.L.Y. 3059, applied): BUNGE G.M.B.H. v. C.C.V. LANDBOUW BELANG G.A. [1978] 1 Lloyd's Rep. 217, Donaldson J.

2641. On a c.i.f. sale, the payment clause provided for payment against documents not later than 20 days after date of bill of lading; the ship grounded and the documents were not presented until two months after the date of the bills of lading. *Held*, that the sellers were in breach of the obligation, and the buyers were entitled to reject the documents: ALFRED C. TOEPFER (HAMBURG) v. VERHEIJDENS VEERVOEDER COMMISSIEHANDEL (ROTTERDAM), *The Times*, April 26, 1978, Donaldson J.

2642. Performance—default—quantum of damages

By three contracts on GAFTA form 79A, dated January 1975, S agreed to sell to P 1,250 tons, 1,500 tons and 5,000 tons respectively, of English Horse and/or Tic beans, 10 per cent. more or less at P's option, f.o.b. Lowestoft, at £68 for the first two contracts and £68·50 for the third, shipment to be made between February 1 and April 15, 1975. Cl. 17 (a) of GAFTA 79A stipulated that, in the case of non-fulfilment of the contract by one party, the other party should give the defaulter notice of his intention either to sell elsewhere, and demand that the defaulter should make good the loss incurred in such sale; or to claim such losses at arbitration. On February 15, 1975, P took delivery of 919 tons under the second contract. No other delivery was taken under any of the contracts. The market prices of the beans fell, and at the end of each shipment period they were £63, £65 and £62·50, respectively. On April 15, S sent P a telex informing them that they were in default and that they intended to sell out against them. A dispute arose as to the quantum of damages. *Held,* (1) S were entitled to damages based on the difference between the contract prices and the market price; cl. 17 (a) contained no option in the sense of an irrevocable election, but merely a choice of remedies; (2) P were in breach before the end of each shipment period, but were not entitled to have damages assessed by reference to such earlier dates. S were entitled to have damages assessed by reference to the end of the respective shipment periods; (3) the effect of P's contractual option on the quantum of damages had not been raised before the Board of Appeal and could only be decided before the court if no additional facts which might have been found could affect it. Question of buyer's option remitted to Board of Appeal. (*Yamashita Shinnihon Steamship Co.* v. *Elios S.p.A.* [1977] C.L.Y. 2736 applied): KYPRIANOU PHOEBUS D. COY. *v.* WM. H. PIM JNR. & CO. [1977] 2 Lloyd's Rep. 570, Kerr J.

2643. Price

DISTRIBUTION OF FOOTWEAR (PRICES) ORDER (No. 1307) [20p], made under the Price Commission Act 1977 (c. 33), ss. 11 (1), 12 (3) (6); operative on October 1, 1978; requires certain distributors specialising in the retail distribution of footwear to restrict their retail prices so that their gross margins do not exceed a level determined by reference to margins achieved in specified earlier periods.

2644. —— currency—fluctuating rates of exchange—provisions in tender

[Aust.] D called for tenders for the supply and delivery of plant. The specification for tenderers required the price of individual items to be stated in the currency of the country of manufacture, but the total price to be stated in Australian currency, with the rate of exchange specified. P, an English firm, submitted an appropriate tender which was accepted. By the time payment was due there had been a variation in the rate of exchange. The question arose whether the price was to be paid in Australian currency to the value, at the date of payment, of the amounts specified in the tender in English currency, or in Australian currency based on the rate of exchange between the currencies specified in the tender. *Held,* under the contract D was required to pay the price in Australian currency specified in the tender without regard to any subsequent fluctuation in the rate of exchange: PARSONS & CO. *v.* ELECTRICITY TRUST (1976) 16 S.A.S.R. 93, South Aust.Sup.Ct.

2645. Product liability—infected seed—whether buyers' loss of profit recoverable from sellers

V, potato seed merchants, had for some time done business with P, farmers, subject to the standard conditions of the National Association of Seed Potato Merchants. These provided, inter alia, that notice of rejection be made within three days of delivery, and that under no circumstances should damages for any claim arising out of the contract exceed the contract price (cl. 5); and that V should not be responsible for any disease which might develop after delivery other than provided by cl. 5 (cl. 3 (a)). In February 1974, P bought 20 tons of seed, which after planting proved infected by virus Y, which was discernible upon examination, not of the seed, but of the previous season's crop. V claimed £2,273 for seed sold to P in 1974, and P counterclaimed £6,000 loss of profits in respect of the infected seed. *Held,* that (1) there was no oral warranty that the infected seeds would produce the same results as, or that they were sold by sample related to, previous consignment; (2) since P could not have known of the infection within three day of delivery, that part of cl. 5 was unenforceable and provided no defence to V; (3) cl. 5 was not restricted to patent defects; but even if it was, the restriction only applied to the first part, and not the very wide wording of the final part; (4) cl. 3 (*a*) had the effect of limiting P's claim to the contract price under cl. 5; (5) cl. 5 placed the risk of damage exceeding the contract price on P. It had been approved for many years by merchants and farmers, and could not be said to be unfair or unreasonable under s. 55 of the Sale of Goods Act 1893; (6) the limitation of liability in cl. 5 was clearly intended to cover the innocent sale of infected seed, and V was not disentitled from relying on it by their breach of s. 14 of the Sale of Goods Act 1893 in that the goods were not reasonably fit for their purpose. P's counterclaim limited to the contract price, *i.e.* £634: R. W. GREEN *v.* CADE BROS. FARMS [1978] 1 Lloyd's Rep. 602, Griffiths J.

2646. Prohibition of export—force majeure

The Court of Appeal considered the GAFTA form 100 in a claim over the non-shipment of soya bean meal. The sellers claimed exemption from liability because of an embargo imposed by the U.S. Government, but they were held not to have proved that they were prevented by the embargo from fulfilling the contract. The buyer had however waived defects in the notices and their timing since they led the sellers to believe that they would not rely on the defects, and it would be unjust and unfair to allow them to do so: the sellers' appeal was allowed in part: BREMER HANDELSGESELLSCHAFT M.B.H. *v.* MACKPRANG JR, *The Times*, November 17, 1978, C.A.

2647. Repudiation—date from which damages to be assessed—Hong Kong

[H.K.] [Sale of Goods Ordinance (Laws of Hong Kong, 1964 rev., c. 26), s. 53 (3); Sale of Goods Act 1893 (c. 71), s. 51 (3).]

Where one party repudiates a contract, damages fall to be assessed under s. 53 (3) of the Sale of Goods Ordinance by reference to the date at which the other party accepts that repudiation.

There was a contract for sale and delivery of cotton yarn in instalments as demanded by the buyer on reasonable notice. The sellers then failed to make supplies and on July 31, 1978 wrote to the buyers saying that they were treating the contract as cancelled. The buyers continued to press them for deliveries, but on November 28 accepted the repudiation and issued proceedings. The selling had been HK$1,335 per bale. The buyers claimed the difference between that and the market price on July 31, 1973, which was HK$3,325 per bale. By November 28 the market price had dropped substantially, and the measure of damage that much the less. *Held*, the measure of damages was the difference between the selling price and the market price at the time of acceptance of the repudiation in November. (*Millett* v. *Van Heek & Co.* [1921] 2 K.B. 369, C.A. applied.)

TAI HING COTTON MILL *v.* KAMSING KNITTING FACTORY (A FIRM) [1978] 2 W.L.R. 62, P.C.

2648. —— non-acceptance of one instalment—whether whole contract repudiated

By a contract dated May 22, 1973, S agreed to sell to P 2000 m.t. of rapeseed oil of good wholesome merchantable quality, f.o.b. Genoa, 1000 tons to be shipped in each of the months September and October, 1973. On October 5, P rejected the first shipment on the ground that the colour was too dark, and that it was thus not in accordance with specification. P asked S to replace the oil, and requested arbitration. On October 9, the parties agreed loading dates for the October shipment and P nominated a vessel. Meanwhile, the vessel carrying the September oil returned to Genoa. On October 19, P confirmed their refusal to take up the documents for the September oil and claimed arbitration. S informed P that they could only provide oil for the October shipment which was similar in quality to that of the September shipment, and advised P that if the October shipment were refused S would consider P in breach of contract. On October 22, P replied by telex " we call your attention to the fact that the parcel must be wholesome and merchantable. Any other oil will be refused and we shall take you to arbitration." On October 23, S accepted P's refusal to take up the documents and to pay for the September oil as a repudiation of the whole contract, and claimed arbitration. With regard to the September shipment, the arbitrator found that S took possession of the goods, thereby releasing P from their contractual obligations, and with regard to the October shipment found S in default. S appealed against the October oil award. On a special case stated from the Committee of Appeal of FOSFA, *held*, (1) it was not the law that any refusal to accept delivery of the first shipment automatically amounted to a repudiation of the whole contract; (2) if S had waited until the time came for delivery of the October oil and P had then indicated that they would reject it, P's conduct would then have been renunciatory and S would have been entitled to treat the contract as at an end; (3) S were liable to P for the non-fulfilment of the October portion of the contract. (*James Shaffer* v. *Findlay Durham and Brodie* [1953] C.L.Y. 674 referred to): WARINCO A.G. v. SAMOR S.P.A. [1977] 2 Lloyd's Rep. 582, Donaldson J.

2649. Street trading. See HAWKERS AND PEDLARS.

2650. Terms—buyer's right to sample and supervise weighing—effect of arbitration clause

V sold to P soya bean meal f.o.b. one Gulf port. The contract provided, inter alia, "Quality and condition final at loading port as *per* official certificate," "Weight: Final at loading as *per* weight certificate." Sampling was not dealt with as such; but provision was made for other conditions and arbitration to be governed by G.A.F.T.A. 119, which provided, inter alia, for sampling "if required by buyers, at time and place of shipment. . . ." During loading, P arrived to supervise weighting and to take samples, but the shippers, S, refused to grant the facilities unless asked to do so by V. P delivered a formal letter of protest to the elevator operators, E (who were acting on the instructions of S), but not to S or V, and as charterers of the vessel, refused to allow E to resume loading. P refused to take up and pay for the shipping documents. The dispute was referred to arbitration, and V sought to obtain security for their claim in the Italian courts, thus causing financial loss to P. On a special case stated, *held*, that (1) there was no right to supervise weighing, since the parties had made their own special bargain in this respect, and this excluded the right to supervise weighing under G.A.F.T.A. 119; (2) since an official certificate was to be final as regards quality and condition, there was no commercial purpose in taking samples for use in arbitration, and so no right to take samples; but if there were, it was only "if required by buyers," and such request must be made by P to V a reasonable time before shipment and not, as here, during shipment to E, who had no connection with V; (3) if, contrary to this view, there were a contractual obligation to allow the taking of samples and the supervision of weighing, P had failed to show that breach of it was of such a nature as to determine the contract, or that V did not intend to comply with the terms of the contract; (4) even if a weight certificate is a shipping document, failure to tender it does not constitute a fundamental breach, unless the failure amounts to a refusal. P alone were in breach of contract as far as loading and payment was concerned; (5) the Italian proceedings were legal proceedings in respect of the dispute before a final award had been made, even if not designed to determine the dispute, and accordingly were prohibited by the G.A.F.T.A. arbitration rules; (6) P's counterclaim for loss caused by the Italian proceedings was a "dispute arising out of the contract" and the arbitration had jurisdiction to entertain it: MANTOVANI v. CARAPELLI S.p.A. [1978] 2 Lloyd's Rep. 63, Donaldson J.

2651. —— notice of appropriation—need for strict compliance—seller's duty

By a contract dated June 1, 1972, on GAFTA form 100, S sold to P a quantity of U.S. soya bean meal c.i.f. Rotterdam shipment April, 1973. Cl. 10 of GAFTA 100 provided, inter alia, for the dispatch of a notice of appropriation by each seller in a string of sales to his buyer within ten days (or within a time deemed to be within this period) from the date of the bill(s) of lading where shipment was from U.S. Gulf, Atlantic or Lake Ports. On May 16, S, who were intermediate buyers in a string of sales, received a notice of appropriation from their sellers, G, stating that 209 tons of U.S. soya bean meal were being shipped on the I under a bill of lading dated April 5, 1973. S passed this appropriation to P who received it on May 17 and on the same day rejected the notice on the ground that the notice of appropriation was out of time. On May 18, S replied maintaining their tender and asking P to confirm acceptance, otherwise the contract would be declared void. On the same day, P sent a telex requiring S to prove a string of sales and the times of transmission of notices of appropriation. No proof of a string was given to P and on July 13 P declared S in default. On a special case stated, *held,* (1) the provisions of cl. 10 had to be strictly complied with. Strict compliance involved the shipper and all subsequent sellers sending notices of appropriation on a date which either was, or was deemed to be, within the ten day period; (2) it was for S to prove on the balance of probabilities that every seller had dispatched his notice of appropriation in time and that the notice was good; (3) S's obligation was to appropriate a parcel shipped under a bill of lading dated not later than April 30 and to dispatch a notice of appropriation of that parcel to P not later than May 10; it was only on May 10 that S were in default. (*Bremer Handelsgesellschaft m.b.H.* v. *Mackprang Jr.* [1978] C.L.Y. 2646 referred to): TRADAX EXPORT S.A. *v.* ANDRE & CIE. S.A. [1977] 2 Lloyd's Rep. 484, Donaldson J.

2652. Trade descriptions

TRADE DESCRIPTIONS (INDICATION OF ORIGIN) (EXEMPTIONS No. 11) DIRECTIONS 1978 (No. 1153) [10p], made under the Trade Descriptions Act 1972 (c. 34), s. 1 (5); operative on September 1, 1978; exclude s. 1 (2) of the 1972 Act in relation to gramophone records.

2653. —— false odometer reading—disclaimer notice—effect—evidence of " due diligence " required

[Trade Descriptions Act 1968 (c. 29), ss. 1, 34.]

For a disclaimer notice to be effective in negativing a false trade description, it must be sufficiently proximate to the description in order to " neutralise " the falsity thereof.

The defendant car dealers offered for sale a car bearing a false mileage on the odometer. A notice on the wall of the office inside their premises stated that " mileage . . . cannot be guaranteed accurate." They were summonsed for offering to supply the car with a false trade description. The defendants notified the prosecutor that they were selling the car on behalf of a third party who unbeknown to them had, as he now admitted, replaced the original odometer. At the hearing the defendants did not call such third party. The justices dismissed the information. *Held,* allowing the prosecutor's appeal, that (1) the disclaimer notice was not sufficiently proximate to the car to be effective; (2) there was no evidence before the justices to support the defendants' contentions that a third party had changed the odometer and that they had shown due diligence.

WALTHAM FOREST LONDON BOROUGH COUNCIL *v.* T. G. WHEATLEY (CENTRAL GARAGE) (No. 2) [1978] R.T.R. 333, D.C.

2654. —— false price indication

[Trade Descriptions Act 1968 (c. 29), s. 11 (2).]

Where there is no indication in an advertisement of the limits of an offer to sell at a reduced price, the fact that the purchase price is part discharged by a trade-in, does not affect the situation existing at the time when the advertisement appeared.

The defendants unconditionally offered to sell a motorcycle listed at £580 for £540. The defendants agreed to accept £90 as part-exchange on a vehicle trade-in, but only on the full price of £580. The defendants were found guilty of an offence under s. 11 (2) of the 1968 Act by the magistrate, but were successful in their appeal to the Crown Court. On appeal by the prosecutor, *held,* allowing the appeal and remitting the case to the Crown Court, that s. 11 (2) was concerned with the offer which induced a sale, rather than with legal analysis of the contract; that the fact that the purchase price was part discharged by a trade-in did not affect the situation existing at the time of the advertisement. (*Doble* v. *David Greig* [1972] C.L.Y. 3125 applied; *Barnes* v. *Watts Tyre & Rubber Co.* [1978] C.L.Y. 2655 distinguished.)

READ BROS. CYCLES v. WALTHAM FOREST BOROUGH COUNCIL [1978] R.T.R. 397, D.C.

2655. —— —— **offer not applying to credit cheque payment—whether offer at price less than factually offered**

[Trade Descriptions Act 1968 (c. 29), s. 11 (2).]

An offer of goods at a price, subject to a condition, which perhaps is not disclosed to the purchaser, that payment must not be by a certain method which the trader holds himself out as normally willing to accept, falls short of what is required by the language of s. 11 (2) of the Act.

M went to the defendants' premises where he was offered four tyres at a price of £6·50 each, the recommended price being £10. M proposed to pay for the tyres by means of a form of credit card. The defendants' name appeared in a booklet as being willing to accept this form of credit card. When M proffered the credit card he was told that the offer only applied to cash sales, and agreed to pay the full price, by credit card and the balance in cash. The stipendiary magistrate acquitted; the prosecutor appealed by way of case stated. *Held*, dismissing the appeal, that the tyres were offered at £6·50, albeit subject to a condition that ought to have been disclosed. There was no offer, or indication likely to be taken as such, to sell these goods at a lesser price. Once the condition was disclosed the parties entered an entirely new bargain.

BARNES v. WATTS TYRE AND RUBBER CO. [1978] R.T.R. 405 (NOTE), D.C.

BOOKS AND ARTICLES. See *post*, pp. [8], [34].

SAVINGS BANKS

2656. Fees

SAVINGS BANKS (REGISTRAR'S FEES) (AMENDMENT) WARRANT 1978 (No. 615) [10p], made under the Trustee Savings Bank Act 1969 (c. 50), s. 88 and the National Savings Bank Act 1971 (c. 29), s. 11 as applied by S.I. 1972 No. 641, Reg. 29 (4), S.I. 1972 No. 765, Reg. 22 (4) and S.I. 1969 No. 1342, Reg. 18 (4); operative on April 25, 1978; amends S.I. 1976 No. 738 by widening the definition of " the Registrar " to include a deputy appointed by the Chief Registrar of Friendly Societies. It replaces S.I. 1977 No. 482.

2657. National Savings Bank

NATIONAL SAVINGS BANK (AMENDMENT) REGULATIONS 1978 (No. 888) [10p], made under the National Savings Banks Act 1971 (c. 29), s. 2 (1); operative on July 14, 1978; increase from £3,000 to £5,000 the limit on the amount which may be repaid on death without proof that no death duties or capital transfer tax are payable.

NATIONAL SAVINGS BANK (AMENDMENT) (No. 2) REGULATIONS 1978 (No. 1594) [10p], made under the National Savings Bank Act 1971, s. 2 (1); operative on December 6, 1978; amend S.I. 1972 No. 764 so as to allow deposits of less than 25p in the case of ordinary accounts and £1 in the case of investment accounts if they are presented directly to the principal office of the N.S.B.

NATIONAL SAVINGS BANK (INVESTMENT DEPOSITS) (INVESTMENT) ORDER 1978 (No. 1839) [10p], made under the National Savings Bank Act 1971, s. 22; operative on December 14, 1978; revokes S.I. 1966 No. 735 and specifies the investments in which the National Debt Commissioners may invest any balance in the National Savings Bank Investment Account Fund. These investments are drawn from the Trusteee Investment Act 1961, Sched. 1, Pt. II.

2658. Trustee savings banks

TRUSTEE SAVINGS BANKS (INTEREST-BEARING RECEIPTS) ORDER 1978 (No. 605) [10p], made under Trustee Savings Banks Act 1969 (c. 50), s. 34 (2) (4) as amended by the Finance Act 1970 (c. 24), s. 34 (3); operative on May 21, 1978; reduces the rate of interest allowed to trustee savings banks on sums standing to their credit in the fund for the Banks for Saving to £7·25 per cent. per annum.

TRUSTEE SAVINGS BANKS (TRANSFER OF STOCKS) ORDER 1978 (No. 1718) [10p], made under the Trustees Savings Banks Act 1976 (c. 4), s. 33 (2) (4); operative on December 24, 1978; makes provision for stocks registered in such parts of the National Savings Stock Register as are kept by trustee savings banks to be transferred to that part of the Register which is kept by the Director of Savings.

2659. Trustee Savings Banks Act 1976—commencement

TRUSTEE SAVINGS BANKS ACT 1976 (COMMENCEMENT No. 5) ORDER 1978 (No. 533 (C. 12)) [10p], made under the Trustee Savings Banks Act 1976 (c. 4), s. 38 (3); operative on April 28, 1978; brings into force ss. 10 (1), 10 (3), 36 (2) (part) of, and Sched. 6 to the 1976 Act.

TRUSTEE SAVINGS BANKS ACT 1976 (COMMENCEMENT No. 6) ORDER 1978 (No. 1079 (C. 30)) [10p], made under the Trustee Savings Banks Act 1976, s. 38 (3); operative on August 18, 1978; brings into force ss. 12 (3), 36 (1) (2), Sched. 5, para. 15 (*a*) in part and Sched. 6 in part.

2660. Trustee Savings Banks Act 1978 (c. 16)

This Act clarifies and amends the law relating to the investment and borrowing by trustee savings banks.

S. 1 sets out the investment powers of trustee savings banks; s. 2 states that the duty to invest with National Debt Commissioners is confined to certain deposits in savings accounts; s. 3 sets out the power of trustee savings banks to borrow money; s. 4 deals with the application of the Act to the Isle of Man and the Channel Islands; s. 5 contains the short title and definitions. The Act extends to Northern Ireland.

The Act received the Royal Assent on June 30, 1978, and came into force on that date.

SEA AND SEASHORE

2661. Continental shelf

CONTINENTAL SHELF (DESIGNATION OF ADDITIONAL AREAS) ORDER 1978 (No. 178) [10p], made under S.I. 1964 No. 697, S.I. 1965 No. 1531, S.I. 1968 No. 891, S.I. 1971 No. 594, S.I. 1974 No. 1489, S.I. 1976 No. 1153 and S.I. 1977 No. 1871; designates an area of the Continental Shelf to the north-west of the Shetland Islands as an area in which the rights of the U.K. with respect to the sea bed and subsoil and their natural resources may be exercised.

CONTINENTAL SHELF (PROTECTION OF INSTALLATIONS) ORDER 1978 (No. 260) [15p], made under the Continental Shelf Act 1964 (c. 29), s. 2 (1); operative on March 31, 1978; specifies as safety zones certain areas surrounding designated offshore installations and prohibits ships from entering such zones without permission, also replaces all previous Orders in force before the making of this Order.

CONTINENTAL SHELF (JURISDICTION) (AMENDMENT) ORDER 1978 (No. 454) [10p], made under the Continental Shelf Act 1964, ss. 3 (2) (4), 6, 7; operative on April 24, 1978; includes in the areas of the United Kingdom Continental Shelf treated respectively as English and Scottish areas for the purposes of the civil law of the two countries, the new areas designated as part of the shelf by S.I. 1977 No. 1871 and S.I. 1978 No. 178.

CONTINENTAL SHELF (PROTECTION OF INSTALLATIONS) (No. 2) ORDER 1978 (No. 673) [10p], made under the Continental Shelf Act 1964, s. 2 (1); operative on May 6, 1978; specifies as a safety zone a sea area, being an area within a radius of 500 metres of a specified offshore installation and prohibits ships from entering the zone.

CONTINENTAL SHELF (PROTECTION OF INSTALLATIONS) (No. 3) ORDER 1978 (No. 733) [10p], made under the Continental Shelf Act 1964, s. 2 (1); operative on May 19, 1978; specifies as a safety zone a sea area in which there is an offshore installation and prohibits ships from entering that zone without permission.

CONTINENTAL SHELF (PROTECTION OF INSTALLATIONS) (No. 4) ORDER 1978 (No. 890) [10p], made under the Continental Shelf Act 1964, s. 2 (1); operative on June 22, 1978; specifies as a safety zone a certain sea area and prohibits ships from entering the zone without permission.

CONTINENTAL SHELF (PROTECTION OF INSTALLATIONS) (NO. 5) ORDER 1978 (No. 935) [10p], made under the Continental Shelf Act 1964, s. 2 (1); operative on July 6, 1978; specifies as a safety zone a sea area around certain offshore installations and prohibits ships from entering the zone except with permission.

CONTINENTAL SHELF (JURISDICTION) (AMENDMENT) (NO. 2) ORDER 1978 (No. 1024) [10p] made under the Continental Shelf Act 1964, ss. 3 (2), (4), 6 and 7; operative on August 23, 1978; includes in the areas of the United Kingdom Continental Shelf treated as English areas for the purposes of the civil law of England and Wales and related matters, the new areas designated as part of the Shelf by S.I. 1978 No. 1029.

CONTINENTAL SHELF (DESIGNATION OF ADDITIONAL AREAS) (NO. 2) ORDER 1978 (No. 1029) [10p], made under the Continental Shelf Act 1964, s. 1 (7); designates an area of the Continental Shelf in the South-Western approaches to the English Channel as an area in which the rights of the U.K. with respect to the sea bed and subsoil and their natural resources may be exercised.

CONTINENTAL SHELF (PROTECTION OF INSTALLATIONS) (VARIATION) ORDER 1978 (No. 1411) [10p], made under the Continental Shelf Act 1964, s. 2 (1) (3); operative on October 3, 1978; varies S.I. 1978 No. 260 by deleting one zone from the list of specified safety zones.

2662. Fisheries. See FISH AND FISHERIES.

2663. Offshore installations

OFFSHORE INSTALLATIONS (FIRE-FIGHTING EQUIPMENT) REGULATIONS 1978 (No. 611) [25p], made under the Mineral Workings (Offshore Installations) Act 1971 (c. 61), ss. 6, 7, Sched. 1, paras. 1 (1), 3, 4 (1), 7, 9, 11, 12, 14 as extended and amended by the Petroleum and Submarine Pipe-lines Act 1975 (c. 74), s. 44; operative on April 1, 1979; require the provision of fire-fighting equipment on fixed and mobil offshore installations maintained for the under-water exploitation and exploration of mineral resources in waters to which the 1971 Act applies.

OFFSHORE INSTALLATIONS (LIFE-SAVING APPLIANCES) (AMENDMENT) REGULA-TIONS 1978 (No. 931) [10p], made under the Mineral Workings (Offshore Installations) Act 1971, s. 6, as extended and amended by the Petroleum and Submarine Pipe-lines Act 1975 (c. 74), s. 44; operative on August 2, 1978; substitute a new table for calculating the fees chargeable for life-safety examiners of appliances on offshore installations.

2663a. Pollution—safety at sea—proposed new legislation. See § 2749.

2664. Shipping. See SHIPPING AND MARINE INSURANCE.

ARTICLES. See *post*, p. [35].

SETTLEMENTS AND TRUSTS

2665. Accumulations—power of trustees—whether void—corporate settlor

[Law of Property Act 1925 (c. 20), s. 164 (1).]

A corporate settlor is not a person within s. 164 of the 1925 Act, and a settlement made by a corporation is not therefore subject to the rule against accumulation of income.

A company entered into a trust deed for the benefit of its employees, and a clause in the trust deed gave the trustees in effect the power of accumulation. The trustees sought a declaration as to whether this power contravened the rule against accumulations. *Held*, that the original Accumulations Act 1800 was intended to be confined to natural persons, and that on a true construction of s. 164 (1) a corporate settlor was not a person and not therefore subject to the rule against accumulations.

Re DODWELL & CO.'S TRUST DEED [1978] 3 All E.R. 738, Walton J.

2666. Construction—uncertainty—beneficiary's wife to be " of Jewish blood and Jewish faith "

A settlement providing for payment of an income to a beneficiary so long as he is of the Jewish faith and married and living with an " approved wife " of Jewish blood from at least one parent brought up in and not having departed from the Jewish faith, any doubt to be resolved by one of two designated rabbis, is not void for uncertainty.

T set up trusts in 1912 providing that an income should be paid to the successors to his baronetcy providing that each was of the Jewish faith and married and living with an " approved wife " or, if separated, certified by one of two designated chief rabbis as being so through no fault of his. " An approved wife " was defined as a wife " of the Jewish blood by one or both of her parents and who has been brought up in and has never departed from and at the date of her marriage continues to worship according to the Jewish faith as to which facts in case of dispute or doubt the decision of " one of the two designated chief rabbis shall be conclusive." If the beneficiary should marry a non-approved wife, he would lose the income except for £400. The third baronet married an approved wife and had two sons by her. Then she divorced him and he married a woman who was not an approved wife. On the question of certainty, Whitford J. held that if there had been uncertainty, it was cured by the provision as to the chief rabbi being able to resolve disputes. On appeal, *held,* dismissing the appeal, that " Jewish blood " meant " some " Jewish blood and there was no uncertainty in the bequest, though, *per* Lord Denning, there was no reason why, if there was, the settlor should not delegate to a chief rabbi the decision as to facts in case of dispute or doubt. (*Clayton* v. *Ramsden* [1943] A.C. 320, distinguished; *Dundee General Hospitals Board of Management* v. *Walker* [1952] C.L.Y. 3649 considered.)

Re TUCK'S SETTLEMENT TRUSTS; PUBLIC TRUSTEE v. TUCK [1978] 2 W.L.R. 411, C.A.

2667. Constructive trust—deed of covenance—whether tenancy held by one tenant on trust for co-tenant. See PINK v. LAWRENCE, § 1785.

2668. Conveyancing. See REAL PROPERTY AND CONVEYANCING.

2669. Northern Ireland. See NORTHERN IRELAND.

2670. Powers of appointment. See POWERS.

2671. Public trustee

PUBLIC TRUSTEE (FEES) (AMENDMENT) ORDER 1978 (No. 373) [10p], made under the Public Trustee Act 1906 (c. 55), s. 9, as amended by the Public Trustee (Fees) Act 1957 (c. 12), s. 1, and the Administration of Justice Act 1965 (c. 2), s. 2 (1); operative on April 1, 1978; increases the standard rate of the administration fee from 1 per cent. to 1 1/10 per cent. while retaining the rate of 1 per cent. for trusts accepted on or after April 1, 1977.

2672. Settlement—vesting of contingent interests—liability to income tax. See BROTHERTON v. I.R.C., § 1677.

2673. Trust—division of trust fund—beneficiary entitled to half income of undivided fund

[Universities and Colleges (Trusts) Act 1943 (c. 9), s. 2 (1).]

An interest in half the income of an undivided trust fund is different from the whole income from a divided half of that fund.

A college and a school were beneficiaries under a trust. In 1950 a scheme put forward by the college was approved by Order in Council whereby the college divided each holding relating to the fund in half. Half was retained in a general trust scheme devised by the college and half excluded. The school was not consulted. The trust fund income received by the college became greater than that received by the school. The school sought, and obtained, a declaration that it was entitled to one-half the net income from the whole fund. *Held*, dismissing an appeal by the college, that an interest in half the income of an undivided trust fund was not the same as an interest in the whole income of a divided half of that fund; s. 2 (1) of the Universities and Colleges (Trusts) Act 1943 gave no power for any alteration of the beneficial interest in the trust (it dealt only with capital) so that, in the absence of acquiescence by the school, there could have been no such alteration.

Re FREESTON'S CHARITY [1978] 1 W.L.R. 741, C.A.

2674. Trustees—power to compromise litigation

[Trustee Act 1925 (c. 19), s. 15.]

Trustees have power to accept a compromise of court proceedings if they think it desirable and fair to all the beneficiaries.

Trustees of a settlement, the property of which included several valuable chattels, were directed on a summons for directions issued by them to issue proceedings. Thereupon the other parties to those proceedings offered a compromise. A beneficiary under the settlement took the point that the trustees had no power to accept the compromise. *Held,* that the trustees did have such power if they thought it desirable and fair to all the beneficiaries, and that it was not necessary for all the beneficiaries to consent before they accepted the compromise.

Re EARL OF STAFFORD (DECD.); ROYAL BANK OF SCOTLAND *v.* BYNG [1978] 3 W.L.R. 223, Megarry V.-C.

2675. —— remuneration—jurisdiction of court to increase

The inherent jurisdiction of the court to award remuneration to a trustee is exceptional and will only be exercised sparingly.

In 1966 and 1969, when parts of the Strand Estate became added to a trust, the trustees became involved in an exceptional and unforeseeable amount of development work, made even more complex by the introduction of capital transfer tax. The trustees applied to the court for authority to charge for their services beyond the charges envisaged by the trust instrument. *Held,* that (1) the court would exercise its inherent power to award remuneration sparingly, and would not order the general level of remuneration fixed by the trust instrument once the trust had been unconditionally accepted, unless the remuneration contemplated was derisory; (2) the trustees were implicitly authorised to be remunerated for the extra work involved in the development work, but not for the extra fiscal work; (3) the rates fixed by the trust instrument would not be altered; but (4) the buildings on which the rates were based could be revalued.

Re DUKE OF NORFOLK'S SETTLEMENT; EARL PERTH *v.* FITZALAN-HOWARD [1978] 3 W.L.R. 655, Walton J.

ARTICLES. See *post,* p. [35].

SHERIFFS

2676. Sheriff's fees—VAT

The following Practice Direction was issued by the Queen's Bench Division on December 28, 1977:

1. As from January 3, 1978, by virtue of the Sheriffs' Fees (Amendment No. 2) Order 1977 (S.I. 1977 No. 2111), the amount of the appropriate Value Added Tax must be paid in addition to the amount of any prescribed sheriff's fee where that tax is chargeable in respect of the service to which the fee relates.

2. Accordingly, as from January 3, 1978, any party delivering a writ of execution to a High Sheriff to be executed by him or serving a request for the endorsement of the manner in which such writ has been executed under R.S.C., Ord. 47, r. 9 must at the time of such delivery or service pay the Value Added Tax at the appropriate rate *in addition* to the prescribed sheriffs' fee.

[1978] 1 W.L.R. 144.

ARTICLES. See *post,* p. [35].

SHIPPING AND MARINE INSURANCE

2677. Admiralty—practice—action in personam—service of writ on foreign company

L, the owners of the T, chartered the vessel to C. C contracted to carry a cargo of bagged resin belonging to O from Finland to Hong Kong and Thailand. The cargo was damaged en route and on December 23, 1975, O issued a writ in personam against L and C claiming damages. On November 26, 1976, the writ was served personally on G, named as the president and director of L (a Panamanian company) in the register of companies in Panama. L entered a conditional appearance and on January 19, 1977, applied to the Admiralty Registrar to set aside the service of the writ on the ground that service on G was not good service on them. *Held,* on appeal, (1) unless a foreign company was carrying on business within the jurisdiction it could not be served with process within the jurisdiction; (2) there was no evidence that L was carrying on business in England in November 1976, when service of the writ on G took place; (3) R.S.C., Ord. 65, r. 3 was not applicable. THE THEODOHOS [1977] 2 Lloyd's Rep. 428, Brandon J.

2678. —— —— action in rem—jurisdiction

In 1976, a cargo of newsprint was carried on the A (owned by O) from Hanko, Finland, to Tokyo under bills of lading incorporating the Hague Rules which provided, inter alia, that the vessel was to be discharged from all liability in respect of loss or damage unless suit were brought within one year after delivery of the goods. On arrival at Tokyo, the cargo was found to be damaged, and on May 5, 1977, the consignees of the cargo (P) issued a writ against O, claiming damages. On August 11, 1977, the A was arrested under s. 3 (4) of the Administration of Justice Act 1956, which provided, inter alia, that the Admiralty jurisdiction of the High Court could be invoked by an action in rem, if the owner of the vessel at the time the cause of action arose was the beneficial owner of all the shares in the vessel at the time the proceedings were commenced. The affidavit evidence indicated that when the cause of action arose, the vessel belonged to A, a Panamanian company owned in part by a company, S, and in part by a Swiss company, K. In August 1976, the A was transferred to L Ltd., which was also owned by S. In December 1976, L Ltd. was purchased by AN, a company owned by eight individuals and in February 1977, the vessel was transferred to Y Ltd., a company created by AN. D applied for (1) the writ, and all subsequent proceedings, to be set aside on the ground that the court had no jurisdiction over the A or its owners; and (2) the claim indorsed on the writ to be struck out on the ground that the action was time barred. P contended that in February 1977, when the A was transferred from L Ltd. to Y Ltd., the beneficial owner of the companies, and therefore the beneficial owner of the A, was the same person, *i.e.* AN. *Held,* (1) the court could look behind the registered owner to determine the beneficial ownership; (2) s. 3 (4) did not limit the court to a consideration of who was the registered owner, or who was the legal owner, of the shares in the vessel; (3) the persons who beneficially owned the shares in the A were not the owners at the time the cause of action arose; (4) it was for P to prove on the balance of probabilities that, at the time the action was brought, the A was beneficially owned by the same person who was the owner at the time the cause of action arose; (5) on the facts, this was not a case in which the jurisdiction of the court to strike out ought to be exercised. (*Saloman* v. *Saloman and Co.* [1897] A.C. 22, referred to): THE AVENTICUM [1978] 1 Lloyd's Rep. 184, Slynn J.

2679. —— —— practice of naming sister ships in writ considered

[Administration of Justice Act 1956 (c. 46), s. 3 (4); R.S.C., Ord. 6, r. 8.]

Cargo owners may invoke the Admiralty jurisdiction by an action in rem either against the ship or against a sister-ship; they may issue, but not serve, both writs, then elect to serve one of the writs either upon the ship, or upon the sister-ship conveniently at a place within the jurisdiction.

In May 1973, P, cargo-owners, contracted with D for the carriage of sugar on D's vessel, the B, from Dunkirk to Dar-es-Salaam. P claimed that there was short delivery of 325 bags valued at £3,409. The time limit of P's claim expired on June 17, 1974, as the cargo was carried on Hague Rules terms, but this was extended by consent to December 17, 1975. On December 13, 1974, P issued writs in two actions in respect of their claim, the first action being in rem against sister-ships of the B and the second being in rem against the B, and in personam against D. On December 10, 1975, P renewed the writs in both actions. On May 17, P discovered that the V, a sister-ship of the B, was within the jurisdiction, and requested M, the London agents of the mutual insurance association, K, with whom the B was entered at the time of the carriage, to provide an undertaking so as to avoid the arrest of the V. M provided a letter of undertaking stating that in consideration of P consenting to the release from arrest, they undertook to instruct solicitors to accept service on behalf of D of proceedings brought by P within 14 days of a request to do so, and to enter an appearance thereto. On September 27 P requested M to nominate solicitors to accept service of proceedings against D. On October 4, the writ in the second action was served, and on November 10, 1976, D entered a conditional appearance. On November 23, D applied for (1) an order that that action be stayed or dismissed, as P had already invoked the court's jurisdiction in rem in respect of the claim in bringing the sister-ship action, and (2) an order that the renewal of the writ and subsequent service be set aside on the ground that the renewal was wrongly allowed. On December 10, 1976, P renewed the writ in the sister-ship action for a second time, and on April 18, 1977, P filed a cross-notice of motion, asking for an order that D perform their undertaking by instructing solicitors to accept service of the writ on their behalf and enter an appearance thereto. *Held,* (1) P were entitled to institute proceedings in rem against more than one of D's ships, provided that they only served proceedings on, and arrested, one of such ships. P were also entitled to issue one writ against the B, and another against the sister-ships; (2) alternatively, s. 3 (4) of the Administration of Justice Act 1956 gave P the option to invoke the admiralty jurisdiction of the court in rem either against the B, or any one of her sister-ships. The court could compel P so to elect, but could not compel P to continue against a sister-ship rather than the B because the sister-ship writ was issued first; on the facts P had elected against the B; (3) although P had not shown that the writs could not have been served during their currency, they had acted reasonably in relying on the established practice. D had not been prejudiced by service being accepted some 10 months after renewal and the court would exercise its discretion by upholding the renewal; (4) the instructing of solicitors to enter a conditional appearance was not a breach of the undertaking. (Dicta of Pearson J. in *Societé Generale de Paris* v. *Dreyfus Brothers* (1885) 29 Ch.D. 239, 242–243, of Farwell L.J. in *The Hagen* [1908] P. 189, 201, and of Lord Denning M.R. and Megaw L.J. in *The Banco* [1971] C.L.Y. 10748 applied.)

THE BERNY [1978] 2 W.L.R. 387, Brandon J.

2680. —— —— addition of defendant

On August 30, 1975, 25,300 tonnes of Argentine sorghum owned by M was loaded on D's bulk carrier, the P, for carriage to Kobe, Japan. On arrival in Kobe in October, 1975, the cargo was found to be damaged by sea water due to gaps in the hatch-covers. The damage amounted to £40,000 and in February, 1976, the P was arrested in Rotterdam. The P was released on an undertaking being given by D's P and I Club to honour any claim against "the owners" in respect of the cargo. In September and November, 1976, M issued a writ and statement of claim against D and applied for summary judgment under R.S.C., Ord. 14. On March 29, 1977, D served a defence denying liability and alleging that the P had been time-chartered to U. M applied to join U as additional defendants but U contended that they could not be joined as they would be deprived of their defence under the Hague Rules, art. III, r. 6, which provided that the carrier and the ship should be discharged from all liability in respect of loss or damage to cargo unless the suit were brought within one year after delivery of the goods. M had honestly and reasonably believed that D were responsible and were accepting liability. *Held,* on appeal, (1) this was a case where leave ought to be given to M to join U even though the one year had expired; (2) R.S.C., Ord. 15, r. 6, gave a wide discretion to add a defendant, and that discretion extended to a case where the one-year limitation under the Hague Rules had expired. (*Lucy* v. *Henleys* (*W. T.*) *Telegraph Works Co.* [1969] C.L.Y. 2103, applied): THE PUERTO ACEVEDO [1978] 1 Lloyd's Rep. 38, C.A.

2681. —— —— **arrest of ship—separate causes of action**

[Sing.] By a charterparty dated September 1, 1970, O, the owners of the I, time chartered the vessel to C, hire to be paid by instalments. On July 22, 1976, O alleged that C owed them hire amounting to U.S. $7,230,711. On July 24, 1976, O arrested C's vessel the PS. O had already arrested a sister-ship, the P for non-payment of hire due under the same charterparty. C applied to set aside the writ in rem and warrant of arrest directed against the PS. *Held*, on appeal, (1) a fresh cause of action arose each time there was a failure to pay an instalment on the due date; there was no doctrine of merger; (2) the words " claim " and " cause of action " in s. 4 (4) of the High Court (Admiralty Jurisdiction) Act had the same meaning; the arrests of the P and the PS were in respect of two claims, each of which were founded on a different cause of action; (3) O were entitled to arrest the PS. (*The Banco* [1971] C.L.Y. 10748 distinguished): THE PERMINA SAMUDRA XIV [1978] 1 Lloyd's Rep. 315, Sing.C.A.

2682. —— —— —— **whether violation of due process**

[U.S.] On December 17, 1975, E, as disponent owners, voyage chartered the A to W for the carriage of a cargo of about 4,000 long tons of sugar from Corinto, Nicaragua to one of several U.S. ports. On December 18, 1975, W sold 4,000 long tons of the cargo to P. The A arrived in Baltimore on January 31, 1976, and P's representative there suspected that the cargo was wet. A marine surveyor and a lawyer, W, instructed by E, went on board the A and investigated the cargo damage. A marine surveyor engaged by P arrived on the A to begin his survey but, at the request of W, left the vessel, P's representative remained on board. On February 2, 1976, P filed a complaint *in rem* against the A, and *in personam* against D, the owners of the A. The vessel was arrested the same day. D's counsel received notice that the suit had been filed and that the arrest had been made. On February 3, D filed a motion to dismiss the complaint on the ground, inter alia, that the arrest procedure violated the due process clause of the Fifth Amendment. *Held*, (1) at the time of the filing of the suit, D knew the nature of the claim and were in possession of more facts on which it was based than P; (2) D were entitled to an immediate, post-seizure consideration by a judicial officer of the validity of the action taken, but, on the facts, the failure of the judicial officer to review the pleadings before the arrest of the vessel did not amount to a constitutional violation; (3) P had sought in good faith to determine the amount of loss before the arrest and seizure, and D had disentitled themselves to equitable relief. (*Techem Chemicals Co.* v. *H/T Choyo Maru* (1976) 4/6 P.Supp. 960, distinguished): THE ALEXANDROS T. [1978] 1 Lloyd's Rep. 109, Maryland District Ct.

2683. —— —— **arrest of sister-ship—non-payment of hire—action in rem**

[Sing.] By a charterparty dated September 1, 1970, O, the owners of the I, time-chartered the vessel to C. On July 22, 1976, O alleged that C owed them hire amounting to U.S. $7,230,711. O arrested C's vessel, the P (the I's sister-ship), in respect of their claim. C contended that by the true construction of s. 4 (4) of the High Court (Admiralty Jurisdiction) Act, a sister-ship could only be arrested if at the time the action was brought, it was beneficially owned by the person who was the beneficial owner of the ship in connection with which the claim made in the action arose; and that O were thus not entitled to bring proceedings against the P. S. 3 of the Act provided, inter alia, that the Admiralty court had jurisdiction to hear any claim arising out of any agreement relating to the use or hire of a ship. S. 4 (4) provided, inter alia, that in the case of any claim arising out of such an agreement " where the person who would have been liable in an action in personam was, when the cause of action arose, the owner or charterer or person in possession or control of the ship, the Admiralty jurisdiction of the court may . . . be invoked by an action in rem against (a) that ship, if at the time when the action is brought it is beneficially owned as respects all the shares therein by that person; or (b) any other ship which at the time when the action is brought, is beneficially owned as aforesaid." *Held*, (1) the terms of s. 4 (4) were unambiguous and it was unnecessary to look at the International Convention Relating to the Arrest of Seagoing Ships, 1952, to arrive at the proper construction; further, Singapore was not a party to, nor had it acceded to, that Convention; (2) O were entitled to invoke the Admiralty jurisdiction of the High Court against the P; (3) the word " charterer " in s. 4 (4) did not mean charterer by demise. (*Salomon* v. *Customs and Excise Commissioners* [1966] C.L.Y. 3080 applied): THE PERMINA 108 [1978] 1 Lloyd's Rep. 311, Sing.C.A.

2684. ——— ——— **interpleader—court's wide jurisdiction—payment of hire charges**

E, bankers, made loans to various companies owned by C to facilitate the purchase of a fleet of ships. The loans were guaranteed by C and secured by mortgages by the companies. Further security in the form of bearer stock in the companies was handed to the bank by way of pledge. E then called in the loan and began to realise their securities. E sold some of the ships, but three of them were on time-charter to P and for a time the charter hire was paid to E who used the proceeds to pay out current expenses on the ships and in reduction of part of the outstanding indebtedness. C contended that the loans and all dealings with E were void on the ground that E were unregistered moneylenders and that C were entitled to the charter hire. P paid the hire on the three ships into a joint account and claimed interpleader relief. E contended that disbursements and expenses incurred in operating and maintaining the vessels should be paid to them out of the joint account. *Held,* on appeal, (1) the jurisdiction of the court under R.S.C., Ord. 17, r. 8 was very wide; (2) under the court's inherent jurisdiction, when an interpleader was taken out, the court could make such order as it thought fit even though it interfered with the rights of the parties; (3) it was fair and just that the disbursements and expenses should come out of the moneys paid into the joint account: B.P. BENZIN UND PETROLEUM A.G. *v.* EUROPEAN AMERICAN BANKING CORP. [1978] 1 Lloyd's Rep. 364, C.A.

2685. ——— ——— **intervention by charterers—charge on insurance monies**

In September, 1972, O, the owners of the PF, time-chartered the vessel to C for five years. The charter provided, by cl. 14, that C were to have a lien on the vessel for all moneys paid in advance and not earned and for the value of fuel in bunkers and for all claims for damages arising from any breach of the charter by O. In 1974, P made a loan of U.S. $7½ million to O's parent company. The loan was guaranteed by O and by a mortgage on the PF. Further, an insurance policy which had been taken out by O in respect of the hull and machinery and in respect of disbursements on the PF was assigned to the bank. The vessel sank in February 1975 and O claimed on the policy of insurance. C claimed that O owned them various sums of money under the charter and obtained a Mareva injunction restraining O by themselves, their servants or agents from disposing of the insurance proceeds. The underwriters paid a sum in respect of the insurance claim to D, brokers. In October 1977, P brought an action against D and O claiming that the insurance moneys should be paid over to them. C applied to intervene under R.S.C., Ord. 15, r. 6 (2) (b) (ii) on the ground that they had a lien under cl. 14 and this gave them an equitable charge on the insurance moneys. *Held,* on appeal, C's application to intervene was plainly within the words of R.S.C., Ord. 15, r. 6 (2) (*b*) (ii), and C would be allowed to intervene: PANGLOBAL FRIENDSHIP [1978] 1 Lloyd's Rep. 368, C.A.

2686. ——— ——— **jurisdiction—arbitration clause—action in rem**

[Hong Kong.] [Administration of Justice Act 1956 (c. 46), s. 3 (4).] P voyage-chartered the A to D, it being a term of the charterparty that disputes arising under it be referred to arbitration in London. A dispute having arisen in respect of payment of freight, P commenced proceedings in rem in Hong Kong and arrested the L, a vessel belonging to D. Upon D's application for the release of the L, for want of jurisdiction under the Administration of Justice Act 1956, s. 3 (4), and for a stay of proceedings and the unconditional release of the L because of the reference to arbitration, *held* that (1) the court could not hear the action in rem, since the word " charterer " in s. 3 (4) applies to a demised charterer only, and accordingly the L was not a sister ship of the A; (2) even if the court could hear the action in rem it would require P to elect whether to proceed in Hong Kong or to continue the arbitration in London; (3) if P elected to continue the arbitration, the court could not retain the vessel in Hong Kong pending awards to be made in London. (*The Moschanthy* [1971] C.L.Y. 10766; *The Golden Trader* [1974] C.L.Y. 3552 applied): THE LEDESCO UNO [1978] 2 Lloyd's Rep. 99, Li J.

2687. —— —— —— whether master signed bill of lading as agent of shipowners

[Can.] P's goods were shipped for a voyage from Finland to Canada on D1, the E, which had been timechartered to D3 by D2, whose master had signed the bills of lading. The goods were not delivered. P appealed against the finding of the Federal Court (Trial Division) that P's contract of carriage was not with D2, and D2 contended that the Trial Division had no jurisdiction to hear the case. *Held*, on appeal, that (1) the claim was clearly one which arose " out of any agreement relating to the carriage of goods in . . . a ship " within the meaning of s. 22 (2) (i) of the Federal Court Act; (2) this section conferred jurisdiction on the Trial Division, since in the light of *Quebec North Shore Paper Co.* v. *Canadian Pacific* (1977) 71 D.L.R. (3d) 111, read with *McNamara Construction (Western)* v. *The Queen* (1977) 75 D.L.R. (3d) 273, s. 101 of the British North America Act 1867 was to be read as authorising Parliament to confer jurisdiction on the Federal Court to administer *existing* federal law, whether statute or regulation or common law; (3) the trial judge erred in not holding that P's contract of carriage was with D2: THE EVIE W [1978] 2 Lloyd's Rep. 216, Federal C.A.

2688. —— —— maritime lien—salvage—determination of priorities between salvors and wage claimants

In June 1977 the salved vessel L was sold under an order for sale pendente lite for a net sum after deduction of the Admiralty Marshal's expenses of £24,863·26. In October 1977 the salvors applied by notice of motion for judgment in default of appearance in their action for remuneration and were awarded £22,000 with interest and costs. At the same time, the master and crew of the L applied for judgment in default of appearance in their action for wages and repatriation expenses amounting to £17,000. On the salvors' application to determine the priorities between them and the master and crew, *held*, that (1) the long-established rule that a maritime lien for salvage has priority over all liens attaching before the services, should not be departed from unless it would produce a plainly unjust result on the special facts of a case; (2) the salvor had managed to preserve property out of which the claims of the master and crew could have been satisfied, but this benefit was lost by the delay in selling the L; (3) accordingly, the principle that a salvor's lien took priority over all earlier liens including those of wage claimants applied; (4) the salvors' claims ranked before the claim for wages and for master's disbursements, whether they were earned or made before or after the salvage services. (*The Gustaf* (1862) Lush. 506; *The Elin* (1883) 8 P.D. 39; *The Inna* (1938) 60 Ll.L.Rep. 414 applied): THE LYRMA (No. 2) [1978] 2 Lloyd's Rep. 30, Brandon J.

2689. —— —— mortgage of ship—costs of appraisement and sale of ship

By a written agreement dated April 26, 1974, R agreed to lend U.S. $1,650,000 to F to assist F in purchasing the M which was to be registered in Liberia. The debt was to be secured by a first preferred mortgage on the M. The M was purchased and registered in Liberia, and on June 19, 1974, F executed the mortgage in favour of K. On July 1, 1974, the mortgage was duly recorded on the Liberian register. In September, 1974, the parties agreed to transfer the M to the Greek registry and on November 7 the Greek authorities issued a certificate of provisional registration. In December 1974, a further agreement was made between F and K for an additional loan of U.S. $300,000 which was to be secured by a second mortgage on the M. On December 10, F duly executed the second mortgage. On January 31, 1976, a certificate of permanent registration of the M in Greece was issued. On March 2, 1976, the first and second mortgages were registered in Greece. On September 22, 1976, F voyage chartered the M to N. F did not pay the sums due under the mortgages. On January 6, 1977, K began an action in rem, and arrested the M. On February 7, 1977, K issued a notice of motion asking for, inter alia, an order for the appraisement and sale of the ship pendente lite on the ground that she was a wasting asset. F resisted the application on the ground that the mortgages were invalid and unenforceable. N, as inter-veners in the action, applied for the release of the vessel on the ground that the arrest was unlawful interference with their rights. At first instance it was held that (1) F had, on the facts, so dealt with the M as to impair K's security; (2) an order for the release of a ship made in interlocutory proceed-ings should only be made in a clear case, and this was not such a case; (3) it was unreasonable to keep the M under arrest at great expense until the action came on, with the result that, if K succeeded in their claim, the amount recovered would be reduced by the costs incurred; (4) the interests of third parties might be less affected by a sale pendente lite than a prolonged arrest. It was ordered, inter alia, that expenses of discharging and storing the cargo incurred by the Admiralty Marshal should form part of his expenses in executing the commission for appraisement and sale. K appealed against the order, and contended that the cargo-owners should pay these expenses, each in proportion to his own parcel. The cargo-owners contended that the cargo, ought to be released to them free of these expenses. *Held*, on appeal, (1) an intermediate course would be adopted; (2) K were entitled to the protection of the court, and thus when the cargo was claimed, the cargo-owners should only be entitled to take away their cargo on terms: either they could pay the discharging costs, or they had to give appropriate security for the amount ultimately held to be due when the rights of the parties had been ascertained: THE MYRTO [1978] 1 Lloyd's Rep. 11, C.A.

2690. Arbitration—charterparty—stay of action—wrongful repudiation

[Arbitration Act 1975 (c. 3), s. 1 (1); R.S.C., Ord. 14, rr. 1 (1), 3 (1).]
Where there is an arbitration agreement, the defendants are entitled to a stay of proceedings in a court, and the plaintiffs cannot gain summary judg-ment where there is a complete dispute as to the quantum of damages even though liability generally is admitted.

P Co. let a ship to D Co. on a charterparty for five years, which contained an arbitration clause. D Co. repudiated the charterparty two years early. P Co. brought an action against D Co. for wrongful repudiation for $4,000,000, and applied for summary judgment under R.S.C., Ord. 14. D Co. admitted liability for wrongful repudiation but denied the amount of the damages claimed, and they applied for an order under s. 1 (1) of the Arbitration Act 1975 that the proceedings be stayed and the matter referred to arbitration under the arbitration clause. The order was granted, and P Co. appealed on the ground that they were entitled to summary judgment for that part of the damages that was indisputably due to them, and that the court need not refer the matter to arbitration where liability was not disputed. *Held*, dismiss-ing the appeal, that (1) there was a dispute between the parties with regard to the matter agreed to be referred, and therefore a stay of proceedings must be granted; (2) P Co. were not entitled to summary judgment, as in this particular case it was impossible to quantify any particular part of their claim which was indisputably due. (*Moore* v. *Assignment Courier* [1977] C.L.Y. 2734 applied; *Lazarus* v. *Smith* [1908] 2 K.B. 266 distinguished.)

ASSOCIATED BULK CARRIERS v. KOCH SHIPPING INC.; THE FUOHSAN MARU [1978] 2 All E.R. 254, C.A.

2691. —— construction of clause—demurrage

By a charterparty dated August 12, 1974, O voyage chartered the I to C for the carriage of a cargo from Taft, Louisiana to Tanjung Priok, Indonesia. The charter provided, by cl. 13, that general average and arbitration were to be settled according to the York-Antwerp Rules 1950 in London. The I arrived at Tanjung Priok and O brought a claim for demurrage. O applied under the Arbitration Act 1950, s. 10, for the appointment of a sole arbitrator since C refused to concur in such appointment. *Held*, on appeal, (1) cl. 13 provided for disputes arising out of a general average adjustment to be arbi-trated in London; adjustment was also to be made in London; (2) cl. 13 did not cover a dispute as to demurrage or any other dispute other than a dispute as to general average. (*Union of India* v. *E.B. Aabys Rederi A/S* [1974] C.L.Y. 3550, applied): THE IOANNA [1978] 1 Lloyd's Rep. 238, C.A.

2692. —— **jurisdiction—bill of lading.** See THE AGELOS RAPHAEL, § 104.

2693. Carriage by sea
    CARRIAGE OF GOODS BY SEA (PARTIES TO CONVENTION) ORDER 1978 (No. 1885) [10p], made under the Carriage of Goods by Sea Act 1971 (c. 19), s. 2; revokes S.I. 1977 No. 1236 and certifies the contracting parties to the 1924 Brussels Convention as amended.

2694. —— **bill of lading—freight—whether calculable on intaken quantity.** See THE METULA, § 2730.

2695. —— —— **negligence of independent contractors with carrier—exclusion of liability**
    [Can.] C, general agents, contracted with P to receive a containerised cargo of copper and to see to its shipment at Montreal for delivery to Antwerp. P were given an engagement note which provided that all the terms and conditions of C's bill of lading were incorporated into it. The bill of lading stated, in cl. 5, that the carrier or his agent should not be liable for loss or damage to the goods during the period before loading and (by cl. 18) that no servant or agent of the carrier or independent contractor employed by the carrier should be under any liability whatsoever to the owner of the goods for any loss or damage arising from any act, neglect or default on his part while acting in the course of his employment. S, stevedores, contracted with C to receive the goods at Montreal, to keep them in their possession until the vessel's arrival, and then to load them on the F which was owned by B. The cargo arrived at Montreal where the containers were sealed and left in an outdoor storage area. After discharge of the F at Antwerp, some of the cargo was found to be missing. P claimed damages from C, S and B. *Held,* (1) on the facts, the loss occurred at Montreal; (2) C and S had been negligent; (3) since the negligence was not " gross negligence," C could rely on cl. 5 of the bill of lading; (4) S could rely on cl. 18 as that constituted a valid stipulation *pour autrui* (*The Eurymedon* [1973] C.L.Y. 3095 considered): THE FEDERAL SCHELDE [1978] 1 Lloyd's Rep. 285, Sup.Ct. of Quebec.

2696. —— —— **negligence of wharfinger—carrier's liability**
    In April 1970, a cargo of frozen meat was shipped in good order and condition on the A, a passenger and refrigerated vessel owned by D, for carriage from New Zealand to London under bills of lading which expressly incorporated the Hague Rules as enacted in New Zealand's Sea Carriage of Goods Act 1940. The material clauses of the bills were cll. 2, 3 (*c*) and 9. Cl. 2 exempted the carrier (D) his agents or servants from liability for damage to goods, howsoever and wheresoever caused, even if caused by negligence, prior to loading on or subsequent to their discharge from the vessel. The clause stated that the goods subsequent to discharge were at owner's sole risk. Cl. 3 (*c*) authorised the carrier to carry the cargo to or from the vessel in, inter alia, any craft and contained a general exemption from liability for damage or delay to the cargo whilst in the craft, even if caused by negligence. Cl. 9 provided, inter alia, for delivery of the goods from the vessel to be taken immediately the vessel was ready to discharge. The A was due to arrive in London on Saturday, May 23, 1970, but as Monday, May 25 was a bank holiday, discharge could not begin until Tuesday, May 26. As the A had a schedule to keep, D contracted with C to effect lighterage and cold storage of the cargo, and advised cargo-owners, P, of the arrangements by letter dated May 19, 1970. They were further advised that storage would be at D's expense for 28 days. P made no objection to the arrangements. A number of insulated and refrigerated barges were used in the operations, but owing to industrial action there were delays in landing the goods and a proportion of the goods spoiled. P brought an action against D claiming £16,731·80 for damage to cargo. The question for the court's decision was whether D was liable for C's negligence. *Held,* (1) in taking industrial action in the form of a go-slow and an overtime ban, the dock-workers had acted negligently towards P; (2) on the facts, the lightening done by D was not autho-

rised by cl. 3 (c) of the bill of lading and P were prevented by the arrangement for cold storage from performing their obligations under cl. 9 (a) with regard to taking delivery; (3) P had by their conduct accepted the arrangement; such acceptance gave rise to fresh arrangements, implied by conduct, between P and D that the arrangement should be adopted; (4) cl. 2 (a) did not extend to fresh agreements going outside the original bill of lading contracts; D dealt with the goods under the arrangement, as common law bailees for reward; and D were liable for the negligence of C's employees; (5) on the evidence, about 25 per cent. of the damage would probably have occurred in any case and P were therefore entitled to recover 75 per cent. of the damages claimed, *i.e.* £12,548·85. (*British Road Services* v. *Arthur Crutchley & Co.* [1968] C.L.Y. 172, applied): THE ARAWA [1977] 2 Lloyd's Rep. 416, Brandon J.

2697. —— —— when " clean "

Sellers were entitled to be paid the price under the rules of the Refined Sugar Association upon tender of " clean bills of lading." The time to consider whether or not the bill was " clean " was the time of shipment. The bill was " clean " if it cast no doubt on the condition of the goods at that time and did not assert that the shipowner has any claim against the goods. The seller was not concerned with events happening after that time, and the fact that the bill had a notation added recording the fate of the goods after shipment did not render it "unclean": GOLODETZ & CO. INC. *v.* CZARNIKOW-RIONDA CO. INC., *The Times*, November 22, 1978, Donaldson J.

2698. —— carrying charges—late nomination of vessel—whether carrying charges a penalty

V sold to P 13,000 tonnes of maize under a contract incorporating G.A.F.T.A. 64, the shipment period being October 14 to October 23, 1974. By cl. 6, P was to notify V ten days before the earlier date of the name of the vessel and the expected date of readiness to load. By cl. 13 (1), V could at their discretion grant an extension of this time, provided P pay a sum at a rate calculated on tonnes per day late. On October 4 V nominated the shipment period, thus requiring P to nominate the vessel on the same day. P nominated the vessel on October 23. V claimed the carrying charges incurred due to late nomination and interest. On a special case stated, *held*, that (1) cl. 13 (1) was not a penalty clause in respect of late nomination, but a clause giving P the option to apply for an extension and V the option to grant it on specific terms; (2) even if they were not a genuine pre-estimate of the damages, the charges were not an agreed specified sum to be paid in the event of a breach of the contract and thus not a penalty; (3) the calculation should be made from the earliest date on which P could have nominated the vessel, *i.e.* October 5; (4) carrying charges did not include interest, since they were not defined in the contract but were words in common commercial use to which normal commercial meaning was to be given; (5) in a commercial arbitration, interest should ordinarily be included in an award for damages, where sufficient information was available: THOS. P. GONZALEZ CORP. *v.* F. R. WARING (INTERNATIONAL) (PTY.) [1978] 1 Lloyd's Rep. 494, Ackner J.

2699. —— charterparty—agency—whether defendants party to charter—whether defendants bound by arbitration clause

P, a Greek company, chartered their ship, the S, in the Gencon form, the charter referring to C, a Cypriot company, " as charterers." By para. 9 of the pre-charter negotiations, P had required that " if in C/P charterers are a foreign company then same to be countersigned by the authorised original charterers registered in Greece "; and cl. 29 of the charter provided that " Freight and demurrage will be guaranteed by actual charterer D [a Greek company]." The charter was signed by P and C, and the reverse side of the Gencon form and p. 4 by D. Further, of the four addenda, the second was signed by C and D, and the others by C only. The S suffered damage, the cost of repair exceeding $200,000, and P wished to pursue their claim in arbitration against D. D denied that they were liable under the charter, or, alternatively, that P were barred from proceeding against them having previously elected to start arbitration proceedings against C. *Held,* (1) it was difficult to take the view that D were liable only as guarantors, since they had signed the charter in two places, were described in it as actual charterers, and had signed one of the addenda; (2) since D as f.o.b. purchaser had to provide the carrying vessel, it was natural to expect them to be liable as charterers, and the words "actual charterers" in cl. 29 were apt to describe the commercial realities; (3) P's requirement under para. 9 explained D's signatures on the charter and showed that D were accepting liability as charterers; and D were also liable under the three addenda not signed by them, in view of what had gone before; (4) accordingly D were a party to the charter and were bound by the arbitration clause; (5) D had in no way been prejudiced by P's first proceeding against C; (6) since D did not know until a late stage that D were possessed of far more substantial means than C, it was not possible to say that what they had done was done with full knowledge of the facts; (7) accordingly there had been no conduct on P's part amounting to an election barring their claim in arbitration against D. Judgment for P. (*Clarkson Booker* v. *Andjel* [1964] C.L.Y. 23 applied): PYXIS SPECIAL SHIPPING CO. v. DRITSAS & KAGLIS BROS.; THE SCAPLAKE [1978] 2 Lloyd's Rep. 380, Mocatta J.

2700. —— —— **breach of terms—change of management—summary judgment**

On November 26, 1971, G, as time-chartered owners of the H, time-chartered the vessel to D for five years from the date of delivery, which, by cl. 2, was not to be before May 25, 1974. The charter provided, by cl. 48, that the time charter was made on the understanding that the H was owned and managed by L, and that L had the option of selling the H during the currency of the charter. On February 7, 1975, the terms of the charter were varied by an addendum to which L, G, D and buyers of the H, M, were parties, providing that, in consequence of the transfer of the ownership of the H to M, the rights and obligations of G under the time-charter were to be transferred to M. C were expressly stated to be managing agents of the H. By an assignment made on February 26, 1973, M assigned all moneys received and receivable under the charter to P, and notice of assignment was given to D. M then informed D that M would transfer the management from C to T. D objected to the appointment of new managers without their consent and repudiated the charter. On December 31, 1976, P issued a writ claiming U.S.$128,034, being the amount of charter hire due, and applied for summary judgment under R.S.C., Ord. 14. *Held*, on appeal, that neither on the question of whether M were entitled to change managers without D's consent, nor on the question of whether, if M were in breach of contract, their breach amounted to a repudiation, could it be said that D's case was unarguable: THE KATINGO COLOCOTRONIS [1978] 1 Lloyd's Rep. 20, C.A.

2701. —— —— **consecutive voyages—freight—applicable rate**

By a consecutive voyage charter dated May 21, 1973, O, the owners of the B, let the vessel to C for as many consecutive voyages as she could perform within 24 months. Cl. 1 of the charter provided, inter alia, that the B should deliver the cargo "on being paid freight in accordance with the rate provided by Worldscale as amended at 92·5 per cent." The charter further provided that freight was payable upon completion of discharge of the cargo on presentation of O's freight invoice (cl. 2), and that all terms and conditions of Worldscale Tanker nominal freight scale applied to the charter (cl. 33). The B performed her first voyage towards the end of the 1973 and C paid the freight calculated in accordance with Worldscale 1973. In 1974, the B performed four voyages and C paid freight in respect of each voyage calculated in accordance with Worldscale 1974. In 1975, the last four voyages were performed. O presented their invoice claiming payment on the basis of Worldscale 1975. C contended that they should be paying on the basis of Worldscale 1973 and paid for the last four voyages on this basis. O claimed the balance of freight in respect of the 1975 voyages. On a special case stated, *held*, the applicable Worldscale in respect of each voyage was the Worldscale published at the time of the accrual of the obligation to pay freight for that particular voyage, and O were entitled to the outstanding balance of freight: THE BUNGAMAWAR [1978] 1 Lloyd's Rep. 263, Goff J.

2702. —— —— **damage to jetty—master signed conditions of berth—indemnity of terminal—owners' liability**

D, the owners of the P, chartered the vessel to C. C ordered her to the plaintiffs' oil terminal at Freeport in the Bahamas to load a cargo of fuel. Before the P was allowed to berth alongside a jetty at the terminal, the master was required to, and did, sign a form headed " conditions of use of the jetties and berths." The form provided, inter alia, that every vessel brought along-side the plaintiffs' berths and facilities remained at the sole risk of the owners (cl. 2 (*a*)); and that if " during, or by reason of, the use " by the vessel of, inter alia, the berths and facilities, the berths or facilities were damaged from " whatsoever cause arising," the vessel and her owners should indemnify the plaintiffs against all loss and damage, notwithstanding that such loss or damage was contributed to or caused by the negligence of the plaintiffs or their servants (cl. 2 (*d*)). Cl. 6 provided that the conditions should be con-strued according to English law. On March 26, 1971, the P was lying along-side the jetty when the wind freshened and the sea got up. The jetty was damaged and the plaintiffs alleged that the P had ranged against it. They claimed $800,000 compensation under cl. 2 (*d*). D contended that the document had no contractual effect at all and, alternatively, even if it did, the master had no authority express, implied or ostensible, to conclude a contract con-taining cl. 2 (*d*). *Held,* that (1) the evidence on D's shipowner's insurance cover indicated that, in the tanker trade there was a general practice of master's being required to sign, and signing, documents of the same class, and, thus, had implied and ostensible authority to do so; these documents were generally regarded as liable to have contractual effect; (2) on the facts, the document had contractual effect; (3) on the evidence, the master had acted within the scope of his express authority; he must also have had implied authority since his orders were to berth at the terminal and he could not have done so without signing the document : THE POLYDUKE [1978] 1 Lloyd's Rep. 211, Kerr J.

2703. —— —— **delay—failure of ship to achieve warranted speed—" accident "**

An unexpected encrustation of the hull of a ship with molluscs rendering the ship incapable of achieving a speed warranted in the charterparty amounts to an " accident " entitling the charterers to withhold extra hire occasioned by the delay thus caused.

A charterparty included a warranty that the ship was capable of steaming at " about 14½ knots in good weather." After the date thereof, but prior to delivery of the ship, the hull of the ship unbeknown to the owners became encrusted with molluscs while berthed at a location where such molluscs were uncommon. Such encrustation reduced the average fair-weather speed of the ship to some 10½ knots. Upon redelivery of the ship, the charterers withheld some 5 days hire, relying, inter alia, upon a clause of the charterparty excluding liability to pay hire for time lost due to " damage to hull or other accident . . . hindering or preventing the efficient working of the vessel." *Held,* that the charterers were entitled to withhold such hire, since the encrustation of the hull was unexpected and out of the ordinary course of things, and therefore was an " accident." (Dicta of Willes J. in *Fenwick* v. *Schmalz* (1868) L.R. 3 C.P. at p. 316, and of Lord Halsbury L.C. in *Hamilton, Fraser & Co.* v. *Pandorf & Co.* (1887) 12 App.Cas. 518 applied.)

COSMOS BULK TRANSPORT INC. *v.* CHINA NATIONAL FOREIGN TRADE TRANS-PORTATION CORP.; THE APOLLONIUS [1978] 1 All E.R. 322, Mocatta J.

2704. —— —— —— **no right of set-off against damages claimed**

O voyage-chartered the A to C in the Gencon form. The charterparty was for a lump-sum freight, free in and out fully stowed, the freight to be fully prepaid on signing bills of lading. The loading ports were Dar es Salaam and Basrah, and the discharging port was Jeddah. Delays occurred during the voyage and C withheld $12,500, the balance of the freight, claiming to off-set a larger amount as damages for failure to prosecute the voyage with reasonable dispatch. On June 11, 1976, O issued a writ claiming the balance of freight and C applied for a stay of the proceedings pursuant to the Arbitration Act 1975, s. 1. *Held,* on appeal, the well-established principle that there was no right of set-off for claims for damages for breach of charter against a claim for freight, had to be applied. (*The Brede* [1973] C.L.Y. 3103 and *The Aries* [1977] C.L.Y. 2741, applied): THE ALFA NORD [1977] 2 Lloyd's Rep. 434, C.A.

2705. —— —— demurrage—free pratique—off-hire clause—liability of charterers

On October 3, 1970, O, the owners of the A, time-chartered the vessel to C on the New York Produce Exchange form, for a period of three years. Cl. 15 of the charter (the off-hire clause) provided, inter alia, that " in the event of loss of time from any other cause whatsoever preventing the full working of the vessel the payment of hire shall cease for the time thereby lost." In March 1972, the A discharged her cargo at Naples. Two members of the crew were disembarked as they had typhus. The A was ordered to Lower Buchanan, Liberia, to load a cargo. On March 27, 1972, at 22.24 hours, the A anchored off the port of Lower Buchanan. At that time, and until 05.00 hours on March 28, the only available berth was occupied. At 23.00 on March 27, the A was inspected by health officers. Free pratique was granted at 10.30 on March 29. At 11.18 hours the A began loading. C claimed that the A was off-hire from 03.30 hours on March 28 to 10.30 hours on March 29 and deducted from hire $11,721.50. O contended that C were not entitled to rely on cl. 15, as the delay was due to outside interference by the port health authorities. On a special case stated, *held*, (1) the word " whatsoever " in cl. 15 excluded the application of the ejusdem generis rule so as to limit the " other causes " to those of the same genus as previously enumerated; however, the words " preventing the full working of the vessel " and the general content of the charter limited the meaning; (2) the action taken by the port health authorities did prevent the full working of the vessel and did bring the off-hire clause into play; (3) since the earliest the A could have entered the berth was 05.00 hours on March 28, C were liable for hire, bunkers and stamps for four and a half hours between 00.30 and 05.00 hours on March 28 since that time would have been lost anyhow. (*Mareva Navigation Co.* v. *Canaria Amadora S.A.* [1977] C.L.Y. 2757 referred to): THE APOLLO [1978] 1 Lloyd's Rep. 200, Mocatta J.

2706. —— —— —— frustration

On October 12, 1973, O, the owners of the Z, voyage-chartered the vessel to C for the carriage of 155,000 tons 5 per cent. more or less in O's option of crude oil/dirty petroleum products from Ras Tanura in Saudi Arabia, to one or two safe European ports, at C's option. The charter provided for laytime of 72 running hours (including Sundays and holidays), weather permitting, and, by cl. 10, for freight to be payable as if the vessel were loaded with a full and complete cargo. By cl. 13, the charter was to be governed by English law. On October 16, 1973, C exercised their option to discharge at Porto Torres, Italy, and on October 28, O exercised their option for a quantity of 155,000 tons. Due to a decision of the Saudi Arabian Government to cut oil production on October 17, C's oil suppliers in Ras Tanura imposed a rationing scheme upon its customers, and C were only able to load 144,086 tons. The Z incurred demurrage at the loading and unloading ports. O claimed dead freight and demurrage. C contended that the charter had been frustrated, and that it would have been impossible or illegal to load the full cargo. On a special case stated, *held*, (1) C were under a duty, in the absence of an exceptions clause, to provide a cargo of the contractual description and quantity at the agreed loading port or to pay dead freight and also to load in the laytime or to pay demurrage; (2) difficulties or delays in the country of shipment were not capable of bringing the doctrine of frustration into operation; (3) the shortage did not result from illegality but from the rationing system: THE ZUIHO MARU [1977] 2 Lloyd's Rep. 552, Kerr J.

2707. —— —— —— laytime

Once laytime has expired, provisions as to time not counting towards laytime have no further application, and will not go to reduce damages payable by charterers for failure to complete the discharging operation in the stipulated time.

O Co. chartered the D to C Co. to carry wheat from Philadelphia to Hsingkang. By cl. 15 of the Baltimore berth grain form, at discharging charterers had the option at any time to treat at their expense ship's holds/compartments and/or cargo, and time so used not to count. The D arrived in the roads in Hsingkang on October 3. Permitted laytime started on October 4 and expired on October 26. From November 9 to 12, while the D was still in the roads, the charterers had the cargo fumigated, the ship berthed on December 6. O Co. claimed demurrage for the whole period after the expiration of laytime. C Co. contended that by cl. 15 the period spent on fumigation was excluded from the calculation. *Held*, the words in cl. 15 were not apt to exclude that period; they had no further application once laytime had expired. (Decision of C.A. [1977] C.L.Y. 2745 reversed.)

Dias Compania Naviera S.A. *v.* Louis Dreyfus Corp. [1978] 1 W.L.R. 261, H.L.

2708.   In 1973, O, as disponent owners, voyage chartered the F on the Centrocon form of charter to C for the carriage of a cargo of grain from Buenos Aires to Korea. The charter provided, inter alia, that the time for discharging was to commence from 1 p.m. if notice of readiness were delivered before noon, and from 8 a.m. the following working day if delivered during office hours in the afternoon, but that time lost in waiting for a berth was to count as discharging time. The cargo was to be discharged at the average rate of 1,000 long tons per weather working day of 24 consecutive hours, Sundays and Holidays excepted, even if used. The F anchored in the roads at the port of Nampo, Korea at 17.10 hours on June 7, 1973. At 18.30 hours on Saturday, June 9, notice of readiness was tendered. From June 11 until July 5, 1973 the F lay in the river when she began shifting to a quay berth. A dispute arose as to the period between 18.30 hours on June 9, and 23.00 hours on July 5, 1973. C contended that laytime began to run at 13.00 hours on June 11, 1973, Sundays and non-weather working days excepted, and would have expired on or about July 5, and that about £22,000 would have been payable in demurrage. O contended that the "time lost" provision operated continuously from the arrival of the vessel at the roads, without regard to Sundays or non-weather working days, that laytime was exhausted on June 25, 1973, and that C's liability for demurrage was about £37,000. On a special case stated, *held*, on appeal, (1) as a result of the decision in *The Darrah* [1976] C.L.Y. 2551, the owners were only entitled to £22,982·40 which C had paid in May, 1975; (2) the umpire had awarded O the sum of £37,142·74, together with interest from November 27, 1973, until the date of the award, *i.e.* February 4, 1975, and although the principal sum was now erroneous, there was no reason why it should not be corrected so that the award would be £22,982·40, together with interest at 9 per cent. from November 27, 1973, until the date of the award. Award remitted to umpire: The Finix [1978] 1 Lloyd's Rep. 16, C.A.

2709. —— —— **payable in foreign currency**

Under a charterparty, freight was calculated in U.S. dollars but was payable in sterling in London. The owners claimed that the relevant rates of exchange were those at the dates of payment and not at the date when demurrage was incurred. On appeal, *held*, affirming the decision of Donaldson J., that demurrage was different from freight; the rate of exchange should be taken at the day of payment and not at the day of calculation. (*Miliangos* v. *George Frank (Textiles)* [1975] C.L.Y. 2657 followed): George Veflings Rederi A/S *v.* President of India; Monrovia Tramp Shipping Co. *v.* Same (1978) 122 S.J. 843, C.A.

2710. —— —— **forum for arbitration.** See The Rena K, § 91.

2711. —— —— **freight—whether advance payment could be recovered**

P sold 3,750 tons of copra f.o.b. Quelimane in Mozambique to X and Y, who asked P to act as their agents in making arrangements with the carriers, M. M arranged to time-charter D's vessel, the G, but were required to pay in advance sums representing 30 days' hire and and the costs of bunkers on board amounting to U.S.$110,760. D knew nothing of the identity of P or of the nature of the cargo. M asked P to make an advance payment of freight, and P agreed to pay U.S.$60,000, and sent an advice note to D's bank which stated, inter alia, " payment by order of P. Freight on copra for shipment per m.v. G from Quelimane to Karachi." D were told of the receipt of the money, but not of the terms of the advice note or the identity of P, and assumed that M had paid the money on account of hire. D pressed M for further payment, and when this was not forthcoming, withdrew the G. The U.S.$60,000 was not refunded, D contending that it had been received on account of hire payable by M, and that they had no knowledge of P and no contract for the carriage of copra. *Held*, that (1) P's sole interest was in the carriage of the copra and they never intended to do other than make an advance payment of freight; (2) accordingly, on the terms of the advice note D were entitled to retain the money until freight became due (upon production of shipped bills of lading) and then apply it to satisfy any claim against M; but when a situation arose in which the money could never become due, D became obliged to repay it to P: AFRO PRODUCE (SUPPLIES) *v.* METALFA SHIPPING CO.; THE GEORGIOS [1978] 2 Lloyd's Rep. 197, Donaldson J.

2712. —— —— —— **hire—assignment—whether charterers entitled to treat charter as repudiated**

M timechartered the O to C for 10 years, it being a term of the charter that where the hire fixed by the London Tanker Brokers Panel was less than $3.49775 per dwt. per month, " C will pay no less than $3.49775 per dwt. per month. Any amount which C so pay in excess of the amount payable shall be deemed advance hire which shall be repayable with interest [and] may be deducted by C from hire during any subsequent period during which the relevant Panel rate exceeds $3.49775 and to the extent only of such excess." A side letter from M to C contained the funding arrangements, and included an unconditional and irrevocable guarantee to pay within three days of demand the difference between the Panel rate of hire and the minimum payable under the charter. The O was delivered in May 1973, and in August 1973 M secured a loan from P on the security, inter alia, of moneys due under the charter, at the same time instructing C to pay such moneys to P as assignees. P had been sent the charterparty, but not the side letter. In April 1975 the L.T.B.P. fixed hire at $1.50, and M paid to C the funding payments until September 1975, when they ceased to do so on the grounds that they were entitled to a set-off against hire due under other charters. From January 1976, C refused to continue to pay hire, treating the charter as at an end due to O's wrongful repudiation of it, and P learned of the side letter for the first time. In July 1976 the O was laid up with the consent and at the expense of P, and in September 1976 the O was transferred from M to P, who then recognised that the charter was at an end and claimed full hire from January to September 1976. *Held*, that (1) C were not entitled to repudiate the charter if M repudiated their obligations under the side letter, since the letter and the charter were carefully designed to operate independently of each other; (2) P and M were not estopped from denying that the charter and the side letter constituted a single transaction since there was no representation or collateral warranty to this effect; (3) M were not obliged to accept C's repudiation and treat the charter as at an end; (4) since the risk that M would act as they did regarding the funding arrangements was obvious and foreseen by C, C's conduct was the proximate cause of P's loss and not the causa sine qua non; (5) on the evidence, P had shown that they had suffered substantial loss and their loan to M had not been satisfied; (6) the charter came to an end in July 1976, since M and P could not lay up the O and in the same breath say that the charter was still in existence; and C were liable to pay hire until that date: GATOR SHIPPING CORP. *v.* TRANS-ASIATIC OIL S.A. AND OCCIDENTAL SHIPPING ESTABLISHMENT; THE ODENFELD [1978] 2 Lloyd's Rep. 357, Kerr J.

2713. —— —— —— **nomination of vessel—breach of contract.** See BREMER *v.* HANDELSGESELLSCHAFT M.B.H. *v.* J. H. RAYNER & CO., § 2627.

2714. —— —— —— **repudiation by owners.** See THE LORFRI, THE NANFRI, THE BENFRI, § 2731.

2715. —— —— **jurisdiction—balance of convenience.** See THE AGELOS RAPHAEL, § 104.

2716. —— —— laytime—commencement

By a charterparty dated August 19, 1976, on the Centrocon form, O chartered the P to C for the carriage of a cargo of grain from the Plate to one safe berth Seaforth, Liverpool. The charter provided, inter alia, that time was to count at the discharge port from the first working period on the next business day following the P's customs clearance and receipt of written notice of readiness during ordinary office hours by charterers' agents whether in berth or not (cl. 47). Cl. 49 provided that C were to have the liberty of ordering the P to discharge at a second safe wharf or berth if required, cost of shifting including bunkers used for C's account and time occupied in shifting to count. Cl. 50 provided, that in the event that the P was unable to berth immediately upon arrival on account of congestion, the P was to present notice of readiness in accordance with cl. 47 from arrival at the Mersey Bar, time to count accordingly, but time from berth becoming available within the port until the P's arrival in the berth not to count. The P arrived at the Mersey Bar anchorage at 16.45 on November 4 and at 16.50 gave notice of readiness. C rejected the notice on the ground that the P had not been cleared by customs. O ordered the P to proceed to a lay-by berth, obtained customs clearance and served a notice of readiness on November 8 at 12.00. C accepted the notice. A dispute arose between the parties as to whether the first notice was valid. On a special case stated, *held*, that (1) cl. 50 had to be read in relation to the charter which provided that the P was to discharge at " one safe berth Seaforth "; the words " to berth," " from berth " and " arrival in berth " meant discharging berth; (2) as this was a berth charter and the discharging berth was unavailable owing to congestion when the P reached Mersey Bar, cl. 50 came into operation and the notice of readiness given on November 4 was valid; (3) laytime commenced at 08.00 on November 5; (4) cl. 49 was not of any assistance to C. (*Schuler* v. *Wickman Machine Tool Sales* [1973] C.L.Y. 396 referred to): THE PUERTO ROCCA [1978] 1 Lloyd's Rep. 252, Mocatta J.

2717. —— —— —— —— port congested

O voyage-chartered the F to C to carry granite blocks from Lourenço Marques to Yorkshire. The charter provided, inter alia, by cl. 6, that time for loading was to count from 8 a.m. after the ship had reported as ready and in free pratique whether in berth or not; and by cl. 26 that " if through congestion at the port of discharge, and loading steamer is kept waiting off the port, lay days are to commence to count as per cl. 6, but not until 36 hours from arrival (Sundays and holidays excepted)." The F anchored at the Lourenço Marques pilot station at 14.30 on July 12, 1974, and gave notice of readiness, but owing to the congestion at the port, was not able to move to the inner harbour and be granted free pratique until 09.15 on August 1. *Held*, on appeal, that (1) reporting and being ready and obtaining free pratique was not a condition precedent to the operation of cl. 26; (2) the burden of waiting time through congestion was cast by cl. 6 upon C; (3) the parties had chosen to advance the commencement of laytime, which therefore commenced notwithstanding that the ship had neither reported, nor was ready, nor had received free pratique under cl. 6. Accordingly, laytime commenced at 02.30 on Monday, July 15, *i.e.* 36 hours after arrival at the pilot station, Sundays excepted: LOGS AND TIMBER PRODUCTS (SINGAPORE) PTE. v. KEELEY GRANITE (PTY.); THE FREIJO [1978] 2 Lloyd's Rep. 1, C.A.

2718. —— —— —— effect of words " weather permitting working days "

O chartered two vessels to C by a charterparty which provided, inter alia, that cargo was to be discharged free of risk to the vessels " at the average rate of 750 metric tons per day of 24 consecutive hours per weather permitting working day "; and, by cl. 6, that time lost in waiting for a berth should count as laytime. While the vessels were waiting for berths after notice of readiness had been tendered, there were periods when rain would have prevented discharge had the vessels been in berth. On a special case stated, *held*, that (1) " weather permitting working day " meant a day on which work would have been done but for the weather preventing it; (2) the object of cl. 6 was to put both parties in the same position when a berth was not available as they would have been in if it had been available; and that accordingly, if the periods of rain would have prevented discharge which would otherwise have taken place had the vessels been in berth, they must be deducted from laytime before the vessels reached their berths. (*The Darrah* [1976] C.L.Y. 2551 applied): THE CAMELIA AND THE MAGNOLIA [1978] 2 Lloyd's Rep. 182, Brandon J.

2719. —— —— owners' withdrawal of vessel—hire paid in advance

Where owners know that there has been an underpayment of hire, they must elect between withdrawing the vessel and refunding the hire or allowing the charterparty to continue.

A charterparty provided for a gross payment of the hire charge " except for the last months' hire " when deductions could be made from it. The charterers, believing a particular month to be the last month's hire, paid the charge after making deductions, and the owners accepted that payment before withdrawing the vessel on the grounds that the charterers were " in default of payment " as provided by the charterparty. *Held*, allowing the charterer's appeal, that because they had acted honestly and reasonably in making a net payment they were not " in default of payment " and further that, by accepting the hire paid (and requesting particulars of the deductions) the owners had chosen to treat the charterparty as continuing, so that their withdrawal of the vessel was wrongful.

CHINA NATIONAL FOREIGN TRADE TRANSPORTATION CORP. *v.* EVLOGIA SHIPPING CO. S.A. OF PANAMA; THE MIHALIOS XILAS [1978] 1 W.L.R. 1257, C.A.

2720. —— —— premature delivery and acceptance of notice of readiness—estoppel

Charterers who accept and affirm a premature delivery of notice of readiness will be estopped from denying it.

By a charterparty on a Baltimore Form C grain charter, owners chartered a vessel to charterers for the carriage of grain. By cl. 13 of the charterparty, notification of the vessel's readiness at port of discharge had to be delivered at the office of the receivers, or their agents, at or before 4 p.m. on official working days, vessel also having been entered at the custom house, and the laydays would then commence at 8.00 a.m. on the next business day, whether in berth or not, whether in port or not, whether in free pratique or not. The vessel arrived in the roads of the port of discharge at 8.26 a.m. on October 15, 1976, and the master immediately gave notice of readiness which the receivers, who were the agents of the charterers, accepted. Although it was at the immediate and effective disposition of the charterers, the vessel was unable to proceed to a discharging berth. The receivers then confirmed the acceptance in subsequent cables. The vessel proceeded to berth on November 26, and at 18.20 hours, free pratique and customs clearance were obtained, and customs entry effected. The owners contended that laytime commenced at 08.00 hours on October 16, 1976. The charterers contended that it commenced 08.00 hours on November 27. The difference amounted to some U.S. $160,000. *Held*, the receivers had acted within their authority as agents for the charterers when they accepted the notice of readiness, they had subsequently confirmed the acceptance, and the charterers were estopped from denying it. Laytime therefore ran from October 16. (Dicta of Buckley and Roskill L.JJ. in *E. L. Oldendorff & Co. G.m.b.H.* v. *Tradax Export S.A.* [1973] C.L.Y. 3100 applied.)

THE SHACKLEFORD; SURREY SHIPPING CO. *v.* COMPAGNIE CONTINENTALE (FRANCE) S.A. [1978] 1 W.L.R. 1080, C.A.

2721. —— —— redelivery—whether owners bound to pay for excess bunkers

In March, 1974, O, the owners of the CD, time-chartered the vessel to C, in the New York Produce Exchange form, for a minimum of three to a maximum of four consecutive months at C's option. The charter provided, by cl. 2, that C, whilst on hire, should provide and pay for all fuel except as otherwise agreed and, by cl. 3, that O were to take over and pay for all fuel remaining on board the CD at the port of redelivery at $85 per long ton for fuel oil and $120 per long ton for diesel oil, and that the CD was to be redelivered with sufficient bunkers to reach the nearest main bunkering port. On April 24, 1974, the CD was delivered and redelivery was between July 24 and August 24, 1974. On July 23, C gave notice of redelivery on or about August 3, 1974, at Kakagawa, Japan. On August 1, 1974, the CD was at Kobe, about 30 miles from Kakagawa and she had then enough bunkers on board to take her to Kakagawa. At that time the price of fuel oil and diesel oil at Kobe was $56 and $103 per long ton, respectively. C then notified O that the CD would be redelivered with full bunkers on board and O would be required to purchase all fuel remaining on board pursuant to cl. 3. On August 2, O instructed the master not to accept further bunkers. C claimed damages for breach of contract. *Held,* on appeal, that (1) on the facts, C's intention was to take on additional bunkers solely to make a trading profit; (2) since they were not needed for the chartered service, the master was entitled to refuse C's request; (3) there was no breach of contract; THE CAPTAIN DIAMANTIS [1978] 1 Lloyd's Rep. 346, C.A.

2722. —— —— **unseaworthiness—owner's liability—contribution from charterer**

On January 14, 1966, O, the owners of the E, voyage-chartered the vessel, in the Baltime Berth Grain form C, to C for the carriage of a cargo of wheat from Portland, U.S.A., to Bombay. The charter included the Jason clause which provided, inter alia, that if O exercised due diligence to make the E seaworthy in all respects and to have her properly supplied, C should contribute with O in general average where danger, damage or disaster resulted from any latent defect in the E, her machinery, or from unseaworthiness (even if existing at the time of shipment or at the beginning of the voyage). The E ran out of fuel oil while en route to Yokahama, a bunkering port, and the E had to be towed to Yokahama. O claimed a general average contribution. C contended that the Jason clause prevented recovery of such contribution, since O had failed to use due diligence to make the E seaworthy at the beginning of the voyage. *Held*, on appeal, that (1) the E was unseaworthy at the beginning of the voyage because she had insufficient bunkers and/or because they were of the wrong quality; (2) the unseaworthiness was the cause of the casualty; (3) contribution in general average was irrecoverable from C: THE EVJE (NO. 2) [1978] 1 Lloyd's Rep. 351, C.A.

2723. —— —— **vessel suffered ranging damage—unsafe berth—whether charterers liable**

I, the owners of the K, time-chartered the vessel to C on the New York Produce Exchange form for a round voyage via safe ports including Valparaiso. In May 1973, the K was ordered to Baron Wharf in Valparaiso, which was outside the shelter of the breakwater. In the event of bad weather, vessels sometimes had to leave the berth to avoid hull damage and to do so required a pilot, a tug, and unencumbered water in the immediate vicinity for manoeuvring. During the night May 18/19, 1973, the weather deteriorated, and at 1400 hours the bad weather warning light was displayed. The master prepared to move the vessel out of the berth and by 0500 hrs. the pilot was on board. By 0545 hrs. the tug was alongside. The K was prevented from leaving as two other vessels were anchored close by and remained so until 0850. The K suffered ranging damage by contact with the pier. I claimed damages from C. On a special case stated, *held,* (1) there was no evidence of any system to ensure that vessels using the berth would have adequate searoom if they had to leave in a hurry; the berth was thus an unsafe berth; (2) there was no finding that it was not foreseeable or was an abnormal occurrence for a master of an anchored vessel to be unable or unwilling to move his vessel at very short notice; the lack of safety of the berth lay in the risk that the vessel might be trapped by lack of searoom. (*Leeds Shipping Co.* v. *Société Française Bunge* [1958] C.L.Y. 3144 referred to): THE KHIAN SEA [1977] 2 Lloyd's Rep. 439, Donaldson J.

2724. —— —— **warranty as to safe port—whether delay amounted to frustration**

Where a vessel had been delayed in a port, partly as a result of the situation of the river in which the port was situated, and there was an express warranty in the charterparty that the port was safe, the question whether the charterers were in breach of this warranty depended on whether the delay was such as to frustrate the commercial adventure: it was not enough that the delay was commercially unacceptable: UNITRAMP *v.* GARNAC GRAIN CO. INC., *The Times,* November 13, 1978, C.A.

2725. —— —— **whether contract concluded—subject to trial voyage**

P, who were starch manufacturers at Woolwich, wished to import starch in slurry form from another factory at Koog a/d Zaan, Holland which had a loading quay. The quay was three miles from a lock. The depth of water over the sill of the lock varied greatly and restricted the size of vessels which could pass through. On August 11, 1975, D, the owners of the J offered her by telex to P to carry starch in slurry form and proposed a time-charter for one year from September 1, 1975, at £350 per day. On August 13, P sent a telex to D stating that they accepted the offer " subject to satisfactory completion of two trial voyages " by the J from Koog to Woolwich, the duration to be for a minimum of six months with option to cancel on both sides, and at a maximum rate of £325 per day. Telephone conversations took place between the parties and a voyage charterparty for two voyages was entered into. P paid for equipment to keep the starch in slurry form to be installed in the J. On the first voyage the equipment failed to keep the starch in slurry form and on the second voyage it was found that the K had scraped her keel on the sill and that a quantity of the starch had precipitated. On September 23, P informed D that they no longer wished to time charter the K for economic reasons. D claimed arbitration under the time charter. P applied for (i) a declaration that no time charterparty had been concluded and (ii) the arbitrator had no jurisdiction to determine any claim under it and (iii) an order restraining the arbitrator from hearing any claim made by D. *Held,* (1) there was no concluded contract between the parties; (2) the words " subject to satisfactory completion of two trial voyages " had to be construed subject to bona fides, and the subject-matter of the completion had to be limited to, inter alia, loading, unloading, agitation of cargo, and the navigation of the vessel; (3) the failure of the first voyage meant that there had been no satisfactory performance of two trial voyages; (4) although P gave a bad reason for repudiating the charterparty, they were entitled to rely upon any good reason available to justify their refusal to perform it; (5) a declaration that there was no concluded contract would be granted. (*Astra Trust* v. *Adams and Williams* [1969] C.L.Y. 507, and *British and Benington* v. *North West Cachar Tea* [1923] A.C. 48, applied): THE JOHN S. DARBYSHIRE [1977] 2 Lloyd's Rep. 457, Mocatta J.

2726. —— **consecutive voyages—redelivery date**

D, disponent owners, chartered the O to C " for consecutive voyages commencing October 1970, through November/December 1971." After eight voyages, the O made her last discharge at Tilbury on November 5, 1971. D required C to employ the O on a further voyage, since under the head charter they could not redeliver her before November 17. C refused, and D claimed that in so doing they were in breach of the sub-charter. *Held,* on appeal, that " commencing October 1970 through November/December 1971 " meant that the O was to be redelivered to D during the month of November and December 1971, and not that the last voyage was to commence in those months: THE OAKWOOD [1978] 2 Lloyd's Rep. 10, C.A.

2727. —— **contract—prohibition of export—notice**

V contracted to sell to P soya beans c.i.f. Rotterdam to be shipped from the U.S.A. at 280 tons per month in each of the months May to December 1973. The contract was in the GAFTA 100 form, which provided, by cl. 21, that any unfulfilled part of the contract might be cancelled, inter alia, in case of any executive act done by the government of the territory where the ports of shipment were situate preventing fulfilment; and by cl. 22, for an extension of the shipment period in the case of force majeure, strikes, etc., and that notice should be given stating the port or ports of loading from which the goods were intended to be shipped. In June 1973 the U.S. Government placed an embargo on the export of soya beans which was to be subject to quota restrictions. V claimed damages for non-delivery of the June shipment. *Held,* on appeal, that (1) under the terms of the GAFTA contract, the time of giving a cl. 22 notice was the time of its dispatch, and accordingly V's notice was in time; (2) the requirement that V must state the port or ports of loading from which the goods were intended to be shipped must be interpreted as meaning intended to be shipped as a consequence of the event constituting force majeure; but " the usual ports on the Lakes/East Coast/Gulf " could not properly be regarded as a nomination, and accordingly V's notice was bad; (3) the embargo made it impossible for V to make the June shipment legally unless the period were extended, which V were under no obligation to do; (4) the subsequent conduct of P showed that they had waived their right to challenge the validity of V's cl. 22 notice; (5) the validity of V's cl. 21 notice was not dependent on V's showing that they would have shipped but for the embargo; it was for P to show that it was not the embargo that prevented shipment. Judgment for V. (*Tradax Export S.A.* v. *André & Cie S.A.* [1976] C.L.Y. 2464 applied): BREMER HANDELSGESELLSCHAFT M.B.H. v. VANDEN AVENNE IZEGEM P.V.B.A. [1978] 2 Lloyd's Rep. 109, H.L.

2728. —— damage to goods—negligence of owner—unseaworthiness

[U.S.A.] P were the shippers and consignees of containerised deck cargo carried on the R (owned by A) from New York to Yokahama. En route to Yokahama, the R encountered heavy weather, and one of the containers containing tin ingots, which had been loaded by Y under a contract with M, broke loose. 43 of the containers were swept overboard and seven were damaged. *Held*, by the District Court of New York that (1) although Y and M had caused the tin ingots to be stowed in a negligent manner, this was not the proximate cause of the loss and damage; (2) the container for the ingots was structurally unsound and its condition was the proximate cause of the loss and damage; (3) A had not exercised due diligence to make the R seaworthy, as required by the United States Carriage of Goods by Sea Act 1936, s. 4 (1); they should not have permitted the container, which was part of her equipment, to be loaded on board, and A were solely responsible for the loss and damage: THE RED JACKET [1978] 1 Lloyd's Rep. 300, U.S.Dist.Ct.

2729. —— delay—force majeure. See THE KASTELLON, § 2628.

2730. —— freight—computation—loss of part of cargo

O voyage-chartered the M to C in the Exxonvoy 1969 form. Cl. 2 provided, inter alia: " Freight . . . shall be computed on intake quantity . . . payment of freight shall be made by C without discount upon delivery of cargo at destination. . . ." The M loaded with 190,415 tons of oil in the Persian Gulf for carriage to Chile, but stranded en route and lost part of the cargo. C paid freight on the 138,195·3 tons actually delivered, and O claimed the balance between this and the value of the intake quantity. *Held*, on appeal, that (1) the purpose of having the computation made on the intake quantity was that freight should be ascertained then, though payable at the destination; (2) although cl. 2 did not refer to lump sum freight properly so-called, it had the same characteristics in that freight was to be paid on the intake quantity even if there was a shortage: THE METULA [1978] 2 Lloyd's Rep. 5, C.A.

2731. —— hire—repudiation by owner

Shipowners, who threatened action which would have ruined charterers' trade, were *held* to have repudiated the contract so that the charterers were entitled to terminate the charters. The question of equitable set-off was not settled as there had been no definite findings of fact: THE LORFRI, THE NANFRI, THE BENFRI, *The Times*, November 29, 1978, H.L.

2732. C.i.f. contract—inter-office trading—whether notice of appropriation valid

V's H office had sold to P 1,000 tonnes of meal, shipment in June 1974 c.i.f. Rotterdam. In May 1974, V's H office sold to their M office, and in June 1974 the M office sold to the H office, 1,000 tonnes of meal, both shipments June 1974 c.i.f. Rotterdam. Notices of appropriation were passed down the line, and, P having protested that they were out of time, the H office revealed that the notices had gone H office—M office—H office—P. P then protested that the M office did not count as a " subsequent seller," and that accordingly the notices were too late; also that the notice gave the wrong bill of lading number. On a special case stated, *held,* that (1) there could be a string of contracts including " contracts " between the M office and the H office, provided they were genuine arm's length trading transactions, and accordingly, the notice was given in time; (2) if the notice contained inaccurate information not required by the contract, P could not complain if it was immaterial; and since, at the time the notice was given, the bill of lading number was immaterial, P. could not reject the documents: BREMER HANDELSGESELLSCHAFT M.B.H. *v.* TOEPFER [1978] 1 Lloyd's Rep. 643, Donaldson J.

2733. Collision

COLLISION REGULATIONS AND DISTRESS SIGNALS (AMENDMENT) ORDER 1978 (No. 462) [10p], made under the Merchant Shipping Act 1894 (c. 60), ss. 418, 424, 738; operative on May 1, 1978; further amends S.I. 1977 No. 982 by adding further countries to the list of countries to whose vessels the Collision Regulations and Distress Signals Rules applies.

COLLISION REGULATIONS AND DISTRESS SIGNALS (AMENDMENT No. 2) ORDER 1978 (No. 1059) [10p], made under the Merchant Shipping Act 1894, ss. 418, 424, 738; operative on September 1, 1978; further amend S.I. 1977 No. 982.

MERSEY CHANNEL (COLLISION RULES) ORDER 1978 (No. 1914) [25p], made under the Merchant Shipping Act 1894, s. 421 (2) as extended by the Mersey Channels Act 1897 (c. 21), s. 2; operative on March 11, 1979; revokes S.I. 1960 No. 977 and S.I. 1970 No. 160 and makes new rules concerning the lights and signals to be exhibited and the steps for avoiding collision to be taken by vessels navigating in the River Mersey.

2734. —— crossing vessels—apportionment of blame

[U.S.A.] On September 24, 1974, a collision occurred on the River M between the tug L, owned by P, which was towing a barge, the B, and a tanker, the A, owned by D. The A, her cargo (owned by H and E), and the B were damaged. The A was proceeding up river at full speed, about 400 ft. from the east bank. The L and her tow were proceeding down river. P claimed that the L was in the centre or just to the east of the centre. Visibility was good. The pilot on the A first sighted the L when she was about five miles distant. The pilot, thinking that there was no room to pass port to port, ordered the A to change course from 330 degrees to 325 degrees, so that the vessels would pass starboard to starboard. The A cut across the course of the L which rammed her broadside on. P claimed that the L had sounded a single whistle blast (requesting a port to port passage) when the vessels were about threequarters of a mile apart and a three blast danger signal when the A swung to port, followed by four blasts to signify that her engines were in reverse and that she continued to sound a series of three-whistle blasts until the collision. D claimed that they only heard the last danger signal. Art. 18, r. I, of the Inland Rules of the Road (33 U.S.C., para. 203) provided, inter alia, that when steam vessels were on reciprocal or nearly reciprocal courses they should pass port to port and either vessel should sound one short whistle blast which the other should answer by one short blast. Art. 18, r. III, provided that when a vessel failed to understand the course or intention of an approaching vessel, it should sound a danger signal and that the vessel should reduce its speed or reverse its engines. *Held,* (1) there had been sufficient room to pass port to port; one whistle blast was sounded by the L at about threequarters of a mile and the danger signal when the vessels were within half a mile of each other; (2) the A was in breach of art. 18, r. I, by failing to pass port to port, and by failing to signal her intention to pass starboard to starboard; (3) the A was negligent in failing to contact the L by radio, contrary to the Vessel Bridge-to-Bridge Communication Act, 33 U.S.C., para. 1201; (4) the L was in breach of art. 18, r. III, by failing to signal its failure to understand the A's intentions and to take action in time to avoid the collision; (5) the A was 85 per cent. to blame, the L 15 per cent. to blame; (6) H and E could claim in full from P, and P could then recover 85 per cent. of moneys paid to H and E from the A: THE ANCO PRINCESS [1978] 1 Lloyd's Rep. 293, U.S.Dist.Ct.

2735. At about noon on March 19, 1969, the G and the Z collided in the North Sea, in fog. G was on a southerly course making 10½–11 knots and Z was on a northerly course making 12½–13 knots through the northward traffic route of the separation scheme through the Dover Strait, the angle between the two courses being about 21°. On first sighting each other about two minutes before the collision, Z had crossed ahead of G and was bearing about 5° on G's starboard bow. G was bearing about 26° on Z's starboard bow, about $\frac{2}{3}-\frac{3}{4}$ mile distant. At this time G put her wheel 15° to port and stopped her engines, and Z put her wheel hard to starboard and her engines to full astern. Shortly after, Z's stern struck G's starboard side forward, penetrating deeply at about 80° leading forward. About three hours later, G sank. *Held*, that (1) both ships were seriously to blame for bad radar lookout, excessive speed in fog, and failure to reduce speed before a close-quarters situation developed; Z was further at fault in turning to starboard on sighting; (2) G should have steered a more westerly course to line up with the southbound traffic route and avoid unnecessary encounters with northbound traffic; (3) Z's speed was more excessive than that of G; (4) accordingly Z was substantially more to blame than G. Z was 60 per cent. to blame; G 40 per cent. to blame: THE ZAGLEBIE DABROWSKIE (No. 1) [1978] 1 Lloyd's Rep. 564, Brandon J.

2736. —— —— **meaning of " overtaking "**
    [Collision Regulations (Ships and Seaplanes on the Water) and Signals of Distress (Ships) Order 1965 (S.I. 1965 No. 1525), reg. 24.]
    A vessel is an " overtaking vessel " when it is " coming up with " another vessel and not merely when a risk of collision exists.
    P's vessel was approaching D's vessel. An hour before the collision the vessels were three miles apart. Half an hour later, P's vessel changed from an over-taking to a crossing course. The vessels were then about a mile apart and it was then that the collision risk arose. *Held*, allowing D's appeal, that P's vessel was the " overtaking vessel " within reg. 24 of the 1965 regulations and thus was the give-way ship. Notwithstanding P's vessel's change of course before the collision it had become the " overtaking vessel " at a time when it could properly be said to be " coming up with " D's vessel.
    THE NOWY SACZ [1977] 3 W.L.R. 979, C.A.

2737. —— —— **total loss of ship and cargo—whether caused by master's negligence**
    At about noon on March 19, 1969, the G and the Z collided in the North Sea, in fog. Z's stern striking G's starboard side forward, penetrating deeply at about 80° leading forward. After Z had drawn clear, G went down by the head and listed substantially to starboard as a result of her nos. 2 and 3 holds flooding. Her master decided that no. 1 hold would soon also flood and that therefore G was bound to sink shortly, and 20 minutes after the collision abandoned ship. Three hours after the collision, the G sank in deep water and was totally lost with all her cargo. The question arose whether the loss was caused by the collision or by the negligence of the master in abandoning ship instead of beaching her on the Fairy Bank, about four miles to the S.E. *Held*, (1) this depended primarily on the requirements of good seamanship in the very special and difficult circumstances of the case; (2) while the master was pre-cipitate in abandoning ship, he was not negligent in not trying to beach her; (3) the issue whether G could have been saved by tugs had not been pleaded, and there was insufficient evidence on which to decide it; (4) the master was not guilty of any causative negligence after the collision, which was the sole cause of the sinking: THE ZAGLEBIE DABROWSKIE (No. 2) [1978] 1 Lloyd's Rep. 573, Brandon J.

2738. —— **loss of cargo—liability of ship-owners—whether limited**
    [Merchant Shipping (Liability of Shipowners and Others) Act 1958 (c. 62), s. 5.] On an application for release of a security under s. 5 of the Merchant Shipping (Liability of Shipowners and Others) Act 1958, the shipowners must show that the collision occurred without their actual fault or privity. It is not enough for them to show that they have a prima facie case on that issue; they must go further and show that there is no serious question to be tried: THE WLADYSLAW LOKOTIEK, *The Times*, June 16, 1978, Brandon J.

2739. —— **narrow channel—apportionment of liability**
    At about dawn on August 24, 1974, a collision occurred between P's ship, the A, and D's ship, the C, in the Eastham Channel in the port of Liverpool, which, it was agreed, was a narrow channel to which r. 25 (*a*) of the Collision Regulations applied. Whilst waiting for the A to come out of the Queen Elizabeth II lock, the C had been pushed by the wind to her port side of the

channel, and was slowly proceeding up the edge of the channel on that side. At about 0459 hours the A was seen to be coming out of the lock by the C, which at 0505 hours decided to return to her starboard side of the channel, in order to pass the A port to port, and accordingly put her wheel to starboard, her engines to half ahead, and sounded one short blast. At about 0506 hours the A, upon realising that the C's intention was not, as expected, to wait at the side of the channel until the A was past, stopped her engines, put her wheel hard to port and sounded two short blasts. As each fully realised the intention of the other, both ships put their engines full astern and sounded three short blasts. However, the stern of the C struck the starboard shoulder of the A at an angle of about 50° leading aft on the A, the total damage caused being £150,000. *Held*, that (1) the C was not at fault in allowing herself to be pushed to her port side of the channel, but was at grave fault and in the plainest breach of r. 25 (*a*) in not crossing back in the proper time; (2) the A was at fault in not appreciating the possibility that the C might intend to cross back, and accordingly failing to keep well to her own starboard side of the channel at reduced speed; and in not porting a lookout outside the wheelhouse, and accordingly not hearing the one short blast sounded by the C; (3) the fault of the C was more culpable or causative than the faults of the A and a fair division of liability was C, 70 per cent. and A, 30 per cent.: THE CITY OF LEEDS [1978] 2 Lloyd's Rep. 346, Brandon J.

2740. Crew accommodation

MERCHANT SHIPPING (CREW ACCOMMODATION) REGULATIONS 1978 (No. 795) [£1·50], made under the Merchant Shipping Act 1970 (c. 36), ss. 20, 68, 92, 99 (2); operative on July 1, 1978; revoke S.I. 1953 No. 1036, as amended, and reproduce them with amendments, implementing the International Labour Organisation Convention.

2741. Fees

MERCHANT SHIPPING (FEES) REGULATIONS 1978 (No. 600) [60p], made under the Merchant Shipping Act 1948 (c. 44), s. 1, 3, 5 (3), the Merchant Shipping (Safety Convention) Act 1949 (c. 43), s. 33, as extended by the Merchant Shipping Act 1964 (c. 47), s. 2 (4), the Merchant Shipping (Load Lines) Act 1967 (c. 27), s. 26, the Fishing Vessels (Safety Provisions) Act 1970 (c. 27), s. 84, the Merchant Shipping Act 1974 (c. 43), s. 17, Sched. 5; operative on July 1, 1978, save for reg. 3 (2) and Part XI to the Sched. which is operative on May 22, 1978; revokes S.I. 1977 No. 2049 and S.I. 1975 No. 1692 and re-enact the fees laid down in those regs. except where fees are prescribed in respect of specified matters.

2742. Fishing. See FISH AND FISHERIES.

2743. Harbours and docks

POOLE HARBOUR PORT HEALTH AUTHORITY ORDER 1978 (No. 383) [15p], made under the Public Health Act 1936 (c. 49), ss. 2, 3, 9 (1), as extended by the Control of Pollution Act 1974 (c. 40), s. 108 and Sched. 3, para. 6; operative on April 10, 1978; constitutes the Port of Poole as a port health district and constitutes the Council of the Borough of Poole as port health authority for that district.

NEWLYN PIER AND HARBOUR REVISION ORDER 1978 (No. 427) [35p], made under the Harbours Act 1964, s. 14, Sched. 3; operative on March 16, 1978; provides the Newlyn Pier and Harbour Commissions with certain specified powers.

SHOREHAM PORT AUTHORITY REVISION ORDER 1978 (No. 647) [40p], made under the Harbours Act 1964, s. 14; operative on April 25, 1978; amends the constitution of the Shoreham Port Authority by giving persons representative of bodies engaged in the oil industry a right to consult the Secretary of State in the appointment of one member of the Authority.

MONTROSE HARBOUR (CONSTITUTION) REVISION ORDER 1978 (No. 919) [25p], made under the Harbours Act 1964, s. 14; operative on June 29, 1978; reconstitutes the Board of the Montrose Harbour Trustees.

TEES AND HARTLEPOOL PORT AUTHORITY (CONSTITUTION) REVISION ORDER 1978 (No. 941) [25p], made under the Harbours Act 1964, s. 15; operative on July 4, 1978; reconstitutes the Tees and Hartlepool Port Authority.

DOVER HARBOUR REVISION ORDER 1978 (No. 1069) [20p], made under the Harbours Act 1964, s. 14; operative on July 18, 1978; increases to one international nautical mile from the harbour the area within which the harbour master may exercise his powers, reduces to six months the period which must elapse before the authority may sell goods on which charges have not been paid, and makes provisions regulating the entry of dangerous goods into the harbour.

DOCKYARD PORT OF CHATHAM ORDER 1978 (No. 1880) [25p], made under the Dockyard Ports Regulation Act 1865 (c. 125), ss. 3, 5 and 6, as amended by the Criminal Justice Act 1967 (c. 80), s. 92 (2), Sched. 3, Pt. II; operative on January 24, 1979; provides for, inter alia, the display of signals at night warning vessels to keep clear of the entrance to the Chatham Dockyard locks, and for minor adjustment of the limit of the Dockyard Port across the Swale.

DOCKYARD PORT OF PORTSMOUTH ORDER 1978 (No. 1881) [30p], made under the Dockyard Ports Regulation Act 1865, ss. 3, 5, 7 as amended by the Criminal Justice Act 1967, s. 92 (2), Sched. 3, Pt. II; operative on January 24, 1979; provides for defining the limits of the dockyard port, the appointment of a Queen's Harbour Master for the port, the making of rules concerning the lights or signals to be carried or used and the steps to be taken to avoid collision of vessels using the port.

2744. Marine insurance—mutual insurance association—method of making calls on members to contribute to losses

On January 1, 1971, C, shipowners, were admitted to membership of the mutual insurance association, R. C were insured in respect of strikes of persons working on shore only and not crew strike risks, whereas some of the other members were insured against both types of risk. R. 5 of the association provided that the association and the owner of a vessel applying for membership had to agree on the daily sum to be insured and the contributing value of the vessel; r. 14 provided that the directors had to decide on the amount of "advance calls" and "supplementary calls" to be made on members; and r. 20 provided for the continuation of the insurance of a vessel after the end of the current period. C's membership continued during the policy year 1971, and ceased on September 30, 1972, but they remained liable for supplementary calls in respect of that policy year. Supplementary calls were made by R but C refused to pay them. *Held*, on appeal from a special case stated, (1) the association were not bound to administer as a separate fund the calls and claims of those members insuring against shore risks only, to the exclusion of calls and claims of members insuring against other or additional risks; (2) the association were bound to levy " advance " and " supplementary " calls on all members at the same basic percentage or rate per unit of currency of the contributing values of their entered vessels; as regards " supplementary " calls, there was an alternative basis of a percentage of the " advance " call: VOLKSWAGENWERK AG v. INTERNATIONAL MUTUAL STRIKES ASSURANCE CO. (BERMUDA) [1977] 2 Lloyd's Rep. 503, C.A.

2745. —— non-disclosure—indemnity—effect of " held covered " clause

P, who were insurance brokers, placed cargo insurance with D, underwriters, in respect of a cargo of enamelware to be carried from Hong Kong to Monrovia. The policy incorporated the Institute Cargo Clauses (All Risks) which, by cl. 4, stated: "Held covered at premium to be arranged in case of any omission or error in the description of the interest." The clause stipulated that prompt notice should be given to underwriters when the assured became aware of an event which was " held covered." The goods, which were an end of stock purchase, were described as " enamelware (cups and plates) in wooden cases." In fact, large quantities were neither cups nor plates and part of the cargo was packed in cartons. A proportion of the enamelware had been touched up by overpainting. On arrival in Monrovia some of the goods were found to be damaged. The cargo-owner, C, claimed damages from P in the Liberian courts. P contended that they were not D's agents, and did not put forward any defence on the merits. C obtained judgment against them and when judgment was not satisfied P's assistant was arrested. To obtain his release, P had to pay the sum claimed. P sought an indemnity from D on the ground that D were liable to them in quasi-contract. D denied liability on the grounds of non-disclosure, or misrepresentation of material facts. P contended that D had waived disclosure as to the cartons being included as well as wooden cases and that they were entitled to rely on the " held covered " clause. *Held,* (1) as to the claim in quasi-contract, P had been compelled to pay by Liberian legal process, and compulsion by a foreign system of law was sufficient; (2) D would not have been liable on the policy if sued by C, as there had been material non-disclosure; (3) disclosure as to the presence of the cartons had not been waived; (4) P could not rely on the " held covered " clause, as the clause applied only if the premium to be arranged could be described as a reasonable commercial rate; on the facts, no underwriter would have quoted such a rate on " all risk terms " unless protected by an f.p.a. warranty: LIBERIAN INSURANCE AGENCY INC. *v.* MOSSE [1977] 2 Lloyd's Rep. 560, Donaldson J.

2746. —— rectification of policy—coverage on a " per vessel " or " per occurrence " basis

[U.S.] M owned a number of barges and a tug which were insured under a protection and indemnity (" P and I ") policy which was due to expire on April 30, 1971. M requested their brokers to obtain coverage with other insurers and additional coverage of U.S. $10,000,000. The brokers obtained umbrella coverage in respect of $5,000,000 from P as from February 1, 1971, and $5,000,000 from F. In February 1971, M discovered that each vessel was insured separately under the existing primary cover and the total coverage of U.S. $654,400 would only exist if all the vessels were involved in a single accident. M instructed the brokers to obtain an excess protection and indemnity policy. D agreed to provide such cover as from February 24, 1971. The policy was on a " per vessel " basis. A new " P and I " policy was issued by N, replacing the original policy as from May 1, 1971. On January 7, 1972, two of M's barges were being towed by M's tug when they exploded. The barges were destroyed and a bridge and other property were damaged. P paid U.S. $2,650,103 and D U.S. $554,400. P claimed U.S. $1,008,800 from D on the ground that this was the additional amount for which D were liable under their policy. D denied liability on the ground that the coverage under their policy was " per occurrence " and not " per vessel " and although the policy stated that it was on a " per vessel " basis, a mistake had been made, and the policy should be reformed (*i.e.* rectified) so as to give effect to the true intention of the parties which was that the coverage was to be on a " per occurrence," basis. *Held,* that (1) under the law of Illinois where all the contracts took place, the equitable relief of reformation of a written instrument was available where the instrument failed to express the real agreement between the parties due to a mutual mistake of fact; (2) on the evidence, D had not shown that there was such a mistake: AMERICAN EMPLOYERS INSURANCE CO. *v.* ST. PAUL FIRE AND MARINE INSURANCE CO. [1978] 1 Lloyd's Rep. 417, U.S. Dist. Ct.

2747. Merchant shipping

MERCHANT SHIPPING (PROVISIONS AND WATER) (AMENDMENT) REGULATIONS 1978 (No. 36) [15p], made under the Merchant Shipping Act 1970 (c. 36), s. 21; operative on March 1, 1978; amend S.I. 1972 No. 1871.

MERCHANT SHIPPING (STERLING EQUIVALENTS) (VARIOUS ENACTMENTS) ORDER 1978 (No. 54) [15p], made under the Merchant Shipping (Liability of Shipowners and Others) Act 1958 (c. 62), s. 1 (3), the Carriage of Goods by Sea Act 1971 (c. 19), s. 1 (5), the Merchant Shipping (Oil Pollution) Act 1971 (c. 59), s. 4 (4), the Merchant Shipping Act 1974 (c. 43), s. 9, and the Unfair Contract Terms Act 1977 (c. 50), s. 28 (4); operative on February 1, 1978; specifies the sterling amounts which are to be taken as equivalent to the amounts expressed in gold francs in the 1958 and 1971 Acts.

MERCHANT SHIPPING (SMOOTH AND PARTIALLY SMOOTH WATERS) (AMENDMENT) RULES 1978 (No. 801) [10p], made under the Merchant Shipping Act 1894 (c. 60), s. 427 as substituted by the Merchant Shipping (Safety Convention) Act 1949 (c. 43), s. 2 as amended by the Merchant Shipping Act 1964 (c. 47), s. 9 and by the Fishing Vessels (Safety Provisions) Act 1970 (c. 27), s. 2 (1); operative on June 30, 1978; amend S.I. 1977 No. 252 by specifying two more areas of smooth and partially smooth waters in respect of Sullom Voe and Newport.

MERCHANT SHIPPING (INDEMNIFICATION OF SHIPOWNERS) ORDER 1978 (No. 1467) [10p], made under the Merchant Shipping Act 1974, s. 5 (4) (*a*); operative on October 16, 1978; prescribes the requirements when considering the liability of shipowners by reference to s. 5 (4) (*a*) of the 1974 Act.

MERCHANT SHIPPING (STERLING EQUIVALENTS) (VARIOUS ENACTMENTS) (No. 2) ORDER 1978 (No. 1468) [10p], made under the Merchant Shipping (Liability of Shipowners and Others) Act 1958, s. 1 (3), the Carriage of Goods by Sea Act 1971, s. 1 (5), the Merchant Shipping (Oil Pollution) Act 1971, s. 4 (4), the Merchant Shipping Act 1974, ss. 1 (7), (9) and the Unfair Contract Terms Act 1977, s. 28 (4); operative on October 16, 1978; specifies the sterling amounts which are to be taken as equivalent to the amounts expressed in gold francs in specified enactments, namely those set out above.

MERCHANT SHIPPING (REGISTRAR OF BRITISH SHIPS IN BERMUDA) ORDER 1978 (No. 1522) [10p], made under the Merchant Shipping Act 1948, s. 4; operative on November 22, 1978; provides that the Registrar of British Ships in Bermuda shall be the Registrar of Shipping, Bermuda.

MERCHANT SHIPPING (REGISTRATION OF GOVERNMENT SHIPS) ORDER 1978 (No. 1533)) [10p], made under the Merchant Shipping Act 1906, s. 50; operative on November 22, 1978; applies the provisions of s. 3 of the Merchant Shipping (Mercantile Marine Fund) Act 1898 to Government ships.

MERCHANT SHIPPING (DANGEROUS GOODS) RULES 1978 (No. 1543) [25p], made under the Merchant Shipping (Safety Convention) Act 1949 (c. 43), s. 23; operative on December 29, 1978; supersede S.I. 1965 No. 1067 as amended and provide for dangerous goods.

MERCHANT SHIPPING (REGISTRATION OF COLONIAL GOVERNMENT SHIPS) (AMENDMENT) ORDER 1978 (No. 1628) [10p], made under the Merchant Shipping Act 1906, s. 80; operative on December 14, 1978; extends the provisions of S.I. 1963 No. 1631 to ships belonging to or operated by the government of Saint Vincent.

MERCHANT SHIPPING (DISCIPLINARY OFFENCES) (AMENDMENT) REGULATIONS 1978 (No. 1754) [10p], made under the Merchant Shipping Act 1979, s. 34; operative on January 1, 1979; further amend S.I. 1972 No. 1294.

MERCHANT SHIPPING (OFFICIAL LOG BOOKS) (AMENDMENT) REGULATIONS 1978 (No. 1755) [20p], made under the Merchant Shipping Act 1970, s. 68; operative on January 1, 1979; prescribe additional particulars to be entered in official log books by masters when a seaman is charged with certain acts of misconduct.

MERCHANT SHIPPING (CREW AGREEMENTS, LISTS OF CREW AND DISCHARGE OF SEAMEN) (AMENDMENT) REGULATIONS 1978 (No. 1756) [10p], made under the Merchant Shipping Act 1970, s. 3; operative on January 1, 1979; provide that a seaman, employed under a crew agreement requiring him to comply with a code of conduct, can be discharged outside the U.K. without the consent of a proper officer if the master is satisfied that the seaman has committed a certain act of misconduct.

MERCHANT SHIPPING (LIFE-SAVING APPLIANCES) (AMENDMENT) RULES 1978 (No. 1874) [25p], made under the Merchant Shipping Act 1894, s. 427 as substituted by the Merchant Shipping (Safety Convention) Act 1949, s. 2 and amended by the Merchant Shipping Act 1964, s. 9; operative on February 1, 1979; further amend S.I. 1965 No. 1105 in relation to smoke signals and distress flares.

2748. —— code of practice

The Department of Trade (Marine Division) have published a code of safe working practices for merchant seamen, which aims to give merchant seamen in their place of work protection similar to that enjoyed by workers on shore under health and safety at work legislation. The code is based on the recommendations of the Steering Committee set up in 1974, and covers such subjects as working and protective clothing and equipment, emergency procedures, access to and movement on board the ship, cargo handling, work in galleys and overhaul of machinery. The code is available from HMSO [£3·50].

2749. —— safety and pollution at sea

The Department of Trade published on May 15, 1978, a White Paper (Cmnd. 7217) entitled: Action on Safety and Pollution at Sea: New Merchant Shipping Bill. The paper deals with four main areas, namely pollution, pilotage, discipline, and health and safety; and appends the proposed new legislation in draft form. The White Paper is available from HMSO [£1·35].

2750. Merchant Shipping Act 1970—commencement

MERCHANT SHIPPING ACT 1970 (COMMENCEMENT NO. 5) ORDER 1978 (No. 797 (C. 19)) [10p], made under the Merchant Shipping Act 1970 (c. 36), s. 101 (4); operative on July 1, 1978; brings into force s. 100 (3) and Sched. 5 so far as they relate to specified repeals.

2751. Merchant Shipping Act 1974—commencement

MERCHANT SHIPPING ACT 1974 (COMMENCEMENT NO. 3) ORDER 1978 (No. 1466 (C. 41)) [10p], made under the Merchant Shipping Act 1974 (c. 43), s. 24 (2) (3); operative on October 16, 1978; brings into force ss. 1, 2 4–8 of the 1974 Act in respect of the Fund set up by the International Convention on the Establishment of an International Fund for Compensation for Oil Pollution Damage 1971.

2752. Navigation

RIVER HULL (NAVIGATION) RULES (AMENDMENT) ORDER 1978 (No. 1062) [10p], made under the Merchant Shipping Act 1894 (c. 60), s. 421 (2); operative on August 16, 1978; amends S.I. 1957 No. 2051 by designating on a plan deposited at the Guildhall, Kingston upon Hull, and at the offices of the Department of Trade at Sunley House, Holborn, London, a part of the river within which vessels must now moor; and by amending the cross-reference to the current Collision Regulations and Distress Signals Order, made in 1977.

2753. —— negligence—near collision—liability

On the evening of December 22, 1972, P's vessel, the P, was proceeding down the River Tagus within the port of Lisbon at a speed of about 12½ knots. D's ship, the S, was proceeding up the river at about 9 knots. Visibility was good. The local regulations which governed navigation in the port and its approaches provided, inter alia, that the north and south channels were " narrow channels " (art. 522) and that ships entering the north channel had to give priority of passage, steering to port, to ships leaving by the south channel and for that purpose never pass to the south of the " transit line of the Mama-Caxias beacons " (art. 5241). The regulations further provided that a ship leaving by the south channel did not have to give way to a vessel to starboard entering by the north channel and should not pass to the north of the " transit line " of the Mama-Caxias beacons (art. 5242). Those on board the P first observed the S by radar about three miles distant, and having decided that the S was coming up in the middle of the north channel, assumed that the vessels would pass port to port in accordance with the usual rule governing navigation of ships in narrow channels, *i.e.* r. 25 (*a*) of the Collision Regulations 1960. The pilot on the S, which had entered the north channel, heard on the VHF radio that the P was on her way outward through the port. The S altered course to port. Those on board the S first observed the P when she was some distance away on the starboard bow. The pilot on board the S expected the P to make the usual alteration of course of about 40 deg. to port at the bend in the river and that the ships would pass starboard to starboard. The two ships approached each other and got in a situation where there was a danger of collision. Both ships took avoiding action and P ran aground on the north side of the river sustaining damage. P brought down an action against D claiming damages on the ground that the near collision and the resultant grounding were solely caused by the negligent navigation of the S. *Held*, (1) under art. 5241 the S was bound to give the P priority of passage by steering to port and keeping to the north of the Mama-Caxias line; (2) the S was not at fault in steering to port after entering the river by the north channel and remaining to the north of the Mama-Caxias line; r. 25 (*a*) of the Collision Regulations was, by virtue of r. 30, subject to the effect of local regulations; (3) as long as the S was com-

plying with art. 5241 she was right to navigate so as to pass the P starboard
to starboard; (4) the cause of the casualty was the failure of those on board
the P to appreciate correctly where in the river the S was coming up; the
master of the P did not have fully in his mind arts. 5241 and 5242: THE
STELLA ANTARES [1978] 1 Lloyd's Rep. 41, Brandon J.

2754. Noise levels in ships

The Department of Trade have published " The Code of Practice for Noise
Levels in Ships," which aims to limit maximum noise levels and reduce
exposure to noise on all United Kingdom registered ships with the exception
of private pleasure craft. It makes recommendations which would provide a
basis for those responsible for designing, building and owning or managing
ships. The Code is available from H.M.S.O. [£2·00].

2755. Northern Ireland. See NORTHERN IRELAND.

2756. Offshore installations. See SEA AND SEASHORE.

2757. Oil pollution

PREVENTION OF OIL POLLUTION (CONVENTION COUNTRIES) (ADDITIONAL
COUNTRIES) ORDER 1978 (No. 188) [10p], made under the Prevention of Oil
Pollution Act 1971 (c. 60), s. 21 (3); operative on March 10, 1978; declares
that the governments of specified countries have accepted the International
Convention for the Prevention of Pollution of the Sea by Oil 1954.

2758. Pilotage

PILOTAGE AUTHORITIES (RETURNS) ORDER 1978 (No. 852) [25p], made under
the Pilotage Act 1913 (c. 31), s. 22; operative on August 1, 1978; revokes S.I.
1965 No. 170 and prescribes revised forms of returns to be furnished by
pilotage authorities.

LONDON PILOTAGE (AMENDMENT) ORDER 1978 (No. 1540) [25p], made
under the Pilotage Act 1913, s. 7; operative on December 8, 1978; amends
the Pilotage Order (London) Confirmation Act 1913 by providing for the
reconstitution of the Pilotage Committee of the Trinity House for the London
Pilotage District and by amending the powers and duties delegated to the
Committee.

2759. Protection of wrecks

PROTECTION OF WRECKS (DESIGNATION No. 1) ORDER 1978 (No. 199) [10p],
made under the Protection of Wrecks Act 1973 (c. 33), s. 1 (4); operative on
March 8, 1978; designates as restricted areas for the purposes of the 1973
Act two areas round the sites of wrecked vessels, or what may prove to be
wrecked vessels, of historical and archaeological importance.

PROTECTION OF WRECKS (DESIGNATION No. 2) ORDER 1978 (No. 321) [10p],
made under the Protection of Wrecks Act 1973, s. 1 (1), (2) and (4);
operative on March 31, 1978; designates as a restricted area for the purposes
of the 1973 Act an area off Rome Head, Plymouth, round the site of a wrecked
vessel which may prove to be H.M.S. " Coronation " which is of historical
and archeological importance.

PROTECTION OF WRECKS (DESIGNATION No. 3) ORDER 1978 (No. 664) [10p],
made under the Protection of Wrecks Act 1973, s. 1 (1) (2) (4); operative on June 1, 1978; designates a restricted area for the purposes of the 1973
Act an area in the South Mouth of the Out Skerries, Scotland, which is the
site of a wreck.

PROTECTION OF WRECKS (DESIGNATION No. 4) ORDER 1978 (No. 764) [10p],
made under the Protection of Wrecks Act 1973, s. 1 (1) (2) (4); operative
on May 26, 1978; designates as a restricted area for the purposes of the 1973
Act an area of Langdon Bay, Dover.

2760. Sale of ship—delivery—whether survey " up to date "—whether buyers entitled to refuse

In November 1971, negotiation for the sale of the B by V to P began in
accordance with the Norwegian Memorandum of Agreement, which provided,
inter alia, by cl. 17, " the vessel is to be delivered with continuous machinery
survey cycle up to date at time of delivery." The survey cycle had begun in
November 1968 in accordance with r. 808 of Lloyd's Rules, which provided

that " the various items of machinery should be open for survey in rotation to ensure that the interval between consecutive examinations of each item will not exceed five years. In general approximately one-fifth of the machinery should be examined each year." On January 15, 1972, P telexed to V, " sale confirmed Dollars 680,000 cash. But view survey cycle to be up to date time delivery P anticipate this will be about 75 per cent." When the B was tendered on April 7, 1972, P refused to accept delivery, contending, inter alia, that V had not complied with cl. 17 since only 25 per cent. of the items had been surveyed in the three and a half years of the current cycle, and that V were in breach of an implied obligation to notify Lloyd's that the B, before the date of delivery, had suffered wear and tear affecting the maintenance of her class. On a special case stated, held, allowing V's appeal, that (1) the words " about 75 per cent." in P's telex were not part of the contract; (2) the requirement in r. 808 that one-fifth of the machinery should be examined each year was not part of the contractual stipulation; the rule meant that every item must have been done within the five-year cycle, and not that there had to be an even spread over the five years; (3) there was no implied term that V would notify Lloyd's of any items of wear and tear which might affect class: COMPANIA DE NAVEGACION POHING S.A. *v.* SEA TANKER SHIPPING (PTE); THE BUENA TRADER [1978] 2 Lloyd's Rep. 325, C.A.

2761. —— interest on refund—interest rates and currency applicable

P, German shipowners, contracted through S for the construction of two ships by M for M£522,500 each. By a " side letter " there was also an agreed sum paid by P of M£52,500 per ship (a " plus-up " of 10 per cent.) for extra equipment which P could take at their option and if they did not do so, P were entitled to a refund. P did not take any extra equipment and claimed the return of the M£105,000 from M who denied that they had knowledge of the " side letter " and its terms, and contended that S had no authority to enter into such an agreement. The substance of the action was settled and M conceded that they were liable to return M£105,000, subject to a counterclaim of M£3,443·15 on account of disbursements made by them on P's behalf. The vessels were delivered on March 7 and May 7, 1972, respectively, and P contended that they were entitled to the return of M£52,500 for each ship on those dates. M contended that P and M had agreed that P were not entitled to a refund until four years from the delivery dates, *i.e.* not until March 7 and May 7, 1976, and thus P were only entitled to interest from those dates until September 6, 1976, when the sum of M£105,500 less M£3,443·15 was repaid. M also contended that Maltese rates of interest should be applied since the Maltese pound was the currency of account. P argued that English commercial rates, which were substantially higher, should apply. *Held,* (1) on the evidence, the 10 per cent. " plus-up " was returnable at the time of the delivery of the ships in March and May, 1972; (2) as regards P's claim for interest, interest should run from April 10, 1972, and as regards M's claim for interest on the disbursements, from March 25, 1972; (3) the prima facie loss to P due to M's failure to make the refund in 1972 was that they had to find an equivalent sum from other sources in Germany; thus, interest based on German commercial borrowing rates between 1972 and 1976 should apply; (4) P were entitled to interest payable in Maltese currency; (5) M should be awarded interest on that disbursements at the commercial rate in Malta between 1972 and 1976. (*Miliangos* v. *George Frank* (*Textiles*) [1976] C.L.Y. 2178 considered): HELMSING SCHIFFAHRTS G.M.B.H. *v.* MALTA DRYDOCKS CORP. [1977] 2 Lloyd's Rep. 444, Kerr J.

2762. Salvage—award for services—percentage of salvage value

On December 5, 1976, D's vessel, the L, was off the Devonshire coast in a Southerly wind force 9–10, when her cargo shifted and she developed a list to starboard, and experienced trouble with her radar and steering. On December 6, P's tug, the A, in answer to the L's Mayday signal, found the L abandoned, and with great difficulty towed her to anchor in Torbay, where pumping and diving services were carried out. P brought an action for remuneration for the services, and arrested the L, which in June 1977 was sold for £32,500 under an order for sale pendente lite. On P's application by notice for judgment in default of appearance, *held,* that (1) the true salved value of the L was about £55,000; (2) considering the serious risk involved, the high status of P and the lack of alternative tug assistance, P would be awarded £22,000, i.e. 40 per cent. of the salved value: THE LYRMA (No. 1) [1978] 2 Lloyd's Rep. 27, Brandon J.

2763. —— **contract—whether master had authority to sign agreement**

On February 6, 1977, P's vessel the U, grounded 13 miles south-west of Singapore. After unsuccessfully attempting to refloat her, at 1412 on February 8 the master cabled for assistance to the ship's managers, T, who at 1503 replied that a suitable tug would be dispatched from Singapore. At 1640, the captain of D's tug, the S, offered to salve the U, and the master, mistakenly believing the S to be the tug sent from Singapore, signed Lloyd's Standard Form. At 1805, the master received a cable from T that the tug A would reach him by noon on February 9, whereupon he told the captain that he was to do no more with regard to the salvage of the U. On February 9 the A arrived and successfully refloated the U on February 10. P contended that the Lloyd's form was not a valid contract on the grounds of (a) mispresentation; (b) want of authority; (c) mistake; and (d) non-disclosure. *Held*, that (1) the allegation that the captain had misrepresented himself as " from the agents " failed on the evidence; (2) the implied actual authority of the master was not limited to the ordinary maritime law of salvage, but extended to acceptance of any reasonable contract for services; (3) T's instructions limited the master's authority to acceptance of the services of the A; (4) though the master had no actual authority to accept Lloyd's form, he had ostensible authority to do so, and D and the captain should not be taken to have been aware of any restriction in his authority; (5) the master's mistake could not affect the validity of the contract, since the captain ought not to be taken to have known of it; (6) there was no good reason why Lloyd's Standard Form should be regarded as a contract uberrimae fidei; (7) the ordinary law relating to rescission for fraudulent and innocent misrepresentation should apply to salvage contracts in the same way as to all other contracts; (8) the equitable jurisdiction of the Admiralty Court to refuse to enforce an inequitable salvage contract was sufficient protection against nondisclosure of material facts; (9) even if such contracts were uberrimae fidei, the captain was under no duty to disclose that he had arrived by chance, and not by arrangement between P and D; and P were not entitled to succeed on any of these grounds: THE UNIQUE MARINER [1978] 1 Lloyd's Rep. 438, Brandon J.

2764. Seamen

MERCHANT SHIPPING (SEAMEN'S DOCUMENTS) (AMENDMENT) REGULATIONS 1978 (No. 107) [10p], made under the Merchant Shipping Act 1970, ss. 71 and 99 (2); operative on March 1, 1978; amend S.I. 1972 No. 1295 by amending the requirement for a seaman to furnish to the superintendent, on application for a British Seaman's Card or discharge book, a black and white photograph of himself. The photograph can now be coloured or black and white and three copies of it will be necessary where a seaman applies for both card and discharge book.

MERCHANT SHIPPING (CERTIFICATION OF DECK OFFICERS) (AMENDMENT) REGULATIONS 1978 (No. 430) [15p], made under the Merchant Shipping Act 1970 (c. 36), ss. 43, 99 (2); operative on September 1, 1978; amends S.I. 1977 No. 1152 by providing for certain specified types of certificates of competency.

MERCHANT SHIPPING (SEAMEN'S DOCUMENTS) (AMENDMENT No. 5) REGULATIONS 1978 (No. 979) [10p], made under the Merchant Shipping Act 1970 ss. 71, 99 (2); operative on September 1, 1978; amend S.I. 1972 No. 1295 by providing that details of any pension fund of which a British seaman may be a member may be recorded in discharge books by an official of the Merchant Navy Establishment Administration.

MERCHANT SHIPPING (CONFIRMATION OF LEGISLATION) (HONG KONG) ORDER 1978 (No. 1061) [10p], made under the Merchant Shipping Act 1894 (c. 60), s. 735 (1); operative on September 1, 1978; confirms the Merchant Shipping (Amendment) Ordinance of the Colony of Hong Kong which repeals s. 126 of the 1894 Act and s. 58 of the Merchant Shipping Act 1906 and substituted corresponding provisions of the Merchant Shipping Act 1948 in respect of the qualifications for the engagement of able-bodied seamen in British ships registered in Hong Kong and the recognition of Commonwealth certificates of competency as A.B.

MERCHANT SHIPPING (CERTIFICATES OF COMPETENCY AS A.B.) (HONG KONG) ORDER 1978 (No. 1532) [10p], made under the Merchant Shipping Act 1948 (c. 44), s. 5; operative on December 1, 1978; provides for the recognition in the U.K. of certificates of competency as A.B. granted in Hong Kong.

MERCHANT SHIPPING (SEAMEN'S WAGES AND ACCOUNTS) (AMENDMENT) REGULATIONS 1978 (No. 1757) [10p], made under the Merchant Shipping Act 1970, ss. 9, 99 (2); operative on January 1, 1979; amend S.I. 1972 No. 1700 by authorising a deduction from the wages of a seaman who has committed one of a number of specified acts of misconduct.

MERCHANT SHIPPING (SEAMEN'S DOCUMENTS) (No. 1758) [10p], made under the Merchant Shipping Act 1970, ss. 71, 99 (2) operative on January 1, 1979; amend S.I. 1972 No. 1295 by requiring a seaman to surrender his discharge book upon the recommendation of a shore-based disciplinary committee for certain misconduct.

2765. Ship-broker. See AGENCY.

2766. Shipbuilding

SHIPBUILDING INDUSTRY (PENSION SCHEMES) REGULATIONS 1978 (No. 232) [15p], made under the Aircraft and Shipbuilding Industries Act 1977 (c. 3), s. 49 (4) and (11); operative on March 20, 1978; make provision with respect to the pension rights of employees of companies which have become wholly owned subsidiaries of British shipbuilders, and to those of employees and members of that Corporation.

SHIPBUILDING (REDUNDANCY PAYMENTS SCHEME) (GREAT BRITAIN) ORDER 1978 (No. 1191) [30p], made under the Shipbuilding (Redundancy Payments) Act 1978 (c. 11), ss. 1 (1); operative on August 4, 1978; establishes under the 1978 Act a scheme for the payment of benefits to employees of British Shipbuilders who are made redundant or transferred to less well-paid employment.

2767. ——— inadequately ventilated vessel—employee failing to observe employers' instructions—whether a defence for employers

[Shipbuilding and Ship-repairing Regulations 1960 (S.I. 1960 No. 1932), reg. 50 (a).] X, an acting chargehand employed by V Co., entered an inadequately ventilated vessel without observing V Co.'s procedure, known to X, for testing spaces and certifying them safe for entry. Justices held that a chargehand was a responsible person acting on V Co.'s behalf and V Co.'s procedure complied with reg. 50 (a) of the 1960 Regulations. *Held,* allowing an appeal against V Co.'s acquittal of an offence under reg. 50 (a), that as the vessel had not actually been tested or certified safe for entry by a responsible person, V Co. were not entitled to the exemption under reg. 50 (a): LINDSAY v. VICKERS [1978] Crim.L.R. 55, D.C.

2768. Shipbuilding (Redundancy Payments) Act 1978 (c. 11)

This Act provides for the making of supplementary payments to or in respect of employees of shipbuilding companies in respect of redundancy or transfer to less well-paid employment.

S. 1 enables the Secretary of State to make schemes for Great Britain and Northern Ireland providing for payments to be made to redundant workers in the shipbuilding industry; s. 2 sets out supplementary provisions relating to such schemes, s. 3 sets out financial provisions relating to the schemes; s. 4 gives the short title. The Act extends to Northern Ireland.

The Act received the Royal Assent on May 5, 1978, and came into force on that date.

2769. Soviet Union—immunity of ships and cargoes. See § 1734.

2770. Unseaworthiness—damage to cargo—whether shipowners exercised due diligence to make vessel seaworthy

On June 13, 1973, D's vessel, the H, left Piraeus for Mombasa via intermediate ports, arriving at Mombasa, the turn-around port, on August 21. On August 30, she left Mombasa on the homeward journey and called at Lourenço

Marques to load 5,252 bags of asbestos, belonging to P, for carriage to Venice. On arrival at Venice, 3,182 bags of asbestos were found to be damaged by seawater. It was agreed that they were in good order and condition when shipped and that the seawater had entered through a leaking seam. On P's action for damages, *held,* that (1) D could rely on the incursion of seawater through an undetected defect in the plating as a classic case of damage by perils of the sea unless P could show that the H was unseaworthy when she loaded the asbestos; (2) on the evidence, the defect must have been caused by a severe blow; but in the absence of any incident recorded in the logbooks, it was impossible to say whether the damage was sustained before or after loading the asbestos; (3) it was just as likely that the incident occurred after loading as before loading, and P had failed to prove that the H was unseaworthy before the commencement of the voyage; (4) D had complied with their obligation to exercise due diligence in that the H was fully classed and had undergone her annual dry docking in December 1972; intermediate examinations were carried out by a superintending engineer in Piraeus at the end of each round trip; and the master and chief officer carried out routine inspections in the course of the voyage; (5) failure to carry out a detailed examination at the turn-around port did not amount to a want of due diligence; (6) if the defect existed before loading the asbestos it was a true latent defect, and D had not only discharged the burden imposed on them by art. IV, r. 1 of the Hague Rules, but could also rely on the exception and latent defects contained in art. IV, r. 2 (*p*); (7) P had failed to show that either the scuppers or the sounding pipes were blocked at the commencement of the voyage, and so had failed to show that the H was unseaworthy in either respect. Judgment for D: THE HELLENIC DOLPHIN [1978] 2 Lloyds Rep. 336, Lloyd J.

BOOKS AND ARTICLES. See *post,* pp. [9], [35].

SHOPS

2771. Premises—Sunday market—field

[Shops Act 1950 (c. 28), ss. 53, 58; Town and Country Planning General Development Order 1977 (S.I. 1977 No. 289), art. 4 (3) (*b*).]

The word " premises " in the Shops Act 1950 contains the concept of a building. A local authority is entitled to prohibit a field from being used as a market.

N Ltd., a Jewish controlled company applied to register a piece of land which they intended to use as a Sunday market under the Shops Act 1950. The local authority refused so to register it and prohibited, under art. 4 of the Town and Country Planning General Development Order 1977, use of the land as such a market. On an application by the local authority for an interlocutory injunction, pending an application for mandamus being made to the Divisional Court by N Ltd., *held,* granting the injunction, that (1) as there was no building in the field, the field was not a shop within the meaning of the Shops Act 1950; (2) the local authority were entitled to prohibit the use of the land as they had done.

THANET DISTRICT COUNCIL *v.* NINEDRIVE [1978] 1 All E.R. 703, Walton J.

2772. Sale of goods. See SALE OF GOODS.

2773. Sunday trading—market stalls—whether land for market is " shop "

[Shops Act 1950 (c. 28), ss. 53, 58, 74.] F Ltd. occupied land which it started using as an open-air market on Sundays, for sales of a kind not permitted by Sched. 5 to the 1950 Act. There were about 270 stalls, only one of which was operated by F Ltd. itself. F Ltd. applied to the plaintiff local authority for registration of the whole land as a shop under s. 53, stating that the majority of its directors were of the Jewish faith. The authority refused the application and sought an injunction restraining the use of the land as a market in contravention of the 1950 Act. *Held,* granting the injunction, that the whole was not a " shop " in the meaning of s. 53. S. 58 extended the meaning of shop to " any place where any trade is carried on," but that applied only to the individual stalls. Each stallholder could apply for registration, but there could be no overall registration: CHICHESTER DISTRICT COUNCIL v. FLOCKGLEN (1977) 122 S.J. 61, Fox J.

SOCIAL SECURITY

2774. Attendance allowance—discrimination—EEC. See *Re* RESIDENCE CONDITIONS, § 1376.

2775. Benefits

SOCIAL SECURITY (UNEMPLOYMENT, SICKNESS AND INVALIDITY BENEFIT) AMENDMENT REGULATIONS 1978 (No. 394) [10p], made under the Social Security Act 1975 (c. 14), s. 17 (1) (*a*); operative on March 17, 1978; amend S.I. 1975 No. 564 so as to provide the requisite medical certificates for the purpose of deeming persons incapable of work should indicate that abstention from work consequential on a specific disease or disablement is for precautionary or convalescent reasons.

SOCIAL SECURITY (MISCELLANEOUS AMENDMENTS) REGULATIONS 1978 (No. 433) [15p], made under the Social Security Act 1975, ss. 3 (2), 49, 79 (1), 80 (2), 84, 85, 131, Sched. 20, as amended by the Social Security (Miscellaneous Provisions) Act 1977 (c. 5), s. 17 (2) and the Child Benefit Act 1975 (c. 61), s. 21 (1), Sched. 4; operative on April 3, 1978; amend certain specified statutory instruments in their application to various types of benefit.

SOCIAL SECURITY PENSIONS (HOME RESPONSIBILITIES AND MISCELLANEOUS AMENDMENTS) REGULATIONS 1978 (No. 508) [15p], made under the Social Security Act 1975, ss. 33 (2), 130 (1), 139 (1), Sched. 3, para. 5 (6) (7), as amended by the Social Security Pensions Act 1975 (c. 60), s. 19; operative on April 6, 1978; define the expression " precluded from regular employment by responsibilities at home " in Sched. 3, para. 5 (6) (7) of the Social Security Act 1975.

SOCIAL SECURITY (OVERLAPPING BENEFITS) AMENDMENT REGULATIONS 1978 (No. 524) [25p], made under the Social Security Act 1975, ss. 85, 139 (1) and the Social Security Pensions Act 1975; operative on April 6, 1978; amend S.I. 1975 No. 554 so as to make provision in respect of benefits payable under the Social Security Pensions Act 1975.

SOCIAL SECURITY (WIDOW'S AND WIDOWER'S INVALIDITY PENSIONS) REGULATIONS 1978 (No. 529) [10p], made under the Social Security Pensions Act 1975, ss. 15 (5) (*b*), 16 (1) (*b*) (2) (*a*) (5) (*b*), 61 (1) (*e*) as amended by the Social Security (Miscellaneous Provisions) Act 1977, ss. 4 (4), 17 (6), and the Social Security Act 1975, s. 139 (1); operative on April 6, 1978; provide for rates of invalidity pension and Category A retirement pension for certain class of widows and widowers.

SOCIAL SECURITY (UNEMPLOYMENT, SICKNESS AND INVALIDITY BENEFIT) AMENDMENT (No. 2) REGULATIONS 1978 (No. 608) [10p], made under the Social Security Act 1975, s. 17 (2) (a); operative on May 15, 1978; amend S.I. 1975 No. 564 so as to provide that a day in respect of which a person, whose employment as such has not been terminated, receives a payment by virtue of a scheme set up under s. 1 of the Employment Subsidies Act 1978 is not to be treated as a day of unemployment.

SOCIAL SECURITY BENEFITS UP-RATING ORDER 1978 (No. 912) [30p], made under the Social Security Act 1975, s. 124, and the Child Benefit Act 1975 (c. 61), s. 17 (4); operative on November 13, 1978; alters the rates and amounts of benefits specified in Pts. I, III, IV and V of Sched. 4 to the 1975 Act, and the rate of graduated retirement benefit under the National Insurance Act 1965.

CHILD BENEFIT AND SOCIAL SECURITY (FIXING AND ADJUSTMENT OF RATES) AMENDMENT REGULATIONS 1978 (No. 914) [20p], made under the Child Benefit Act 1975, ss. 5, 17 (1); operative on November 13, 1978, save for Reg. 2 (4) which is operative on April 2, 1979, amend S.I. 1976 No. 1267 by providing for higher rates of child benefit under the 1975 Act.

SOCIAL SECURITY BENEFITS UP-RATING REGULATIONS 1978 (No. 1123) [20p], made under the Social Security Act 1975, ss. 17 (2) (*a*), 36 (9) (*b*), 58 (3), 131, 139 (1) (2), Sched. 14, para. 2 (1), Sched. 15, para. 17; the Social Security (Consequential Provisions) Act 1975 (c. 18), s. 2 (1), Sched. 3, para. 7, and S.I. 1978 No. 912; operative on November 13, 1978, save for Reg. 8 which is operative on April 6, 1979; these Regulations which were made in consequence of S.I. 1978 No. 912, specify the circumstances in which altered rates of benefit payable are not automatically altered. They apply the provisions of S.I. 1975 No. 563 to the increases of benefit provided by virtue of the Up-rating Order. They amend S.I. 1975 Nos. 559, 564 and 1058 so as to raise to £572 per annum, or £11 per week, the earnings limits in respect of work which a person in receipt of benefit may do in certain circumstances.

SOCIAL SECURITY (UNEMPLOYMENT, SICKNESS AND INVALIDITY BENEFIT) AMENDMENT (No. 3) REGULATIONS 1978 (No. 1213) [10p], made under the Social Security Act 1975, s. 17 (2) (a); operative on September 11, 1978; further amend S.I. 1975 No. 564 so as to include an officer of the Manpower Services Commission as one of the officers to whom a person claiming unemployment benefit may be required to report by the Secretary of State.

SOCIAL SECURITY (NON-CONTRIBUTORY INVALIDITY PENSION) AMENDMENT REGULATIONS 1978 (No. 1340) [10p], made under the Social Security Act 1975, s. 36 (7); operative on September 13, 1978; amend Reg. 13A of S.I. 1975 No. 1058 and specifies not only the circumstances in which a woman is to be treated as incapable of performing normal household duties but also the circumstances in which she is to be treated as not incapable of performing such duties.

SOCIAL SECURITY (OVERLAPPING BENEFITS) AMENDMENT (No. 2) REGULATIONS 1978 (No. 1511) [20p], made under the Social Security Act 1975, s. 85; operative on November 16, 1978; provide that where more than one person is entitled to receive an increase of benefit in respect of the same child, priority of entitlement among those persons claiming such an increase shall be given first to a person to whom Child Benefit had been awarded in respect of the child for the period for which the increase is claimed.

2776. —— **overlapping—EEC.** See *Re* AN IRISH WIDOW, § 1392.

2777. —— **rates**
[Social Security Act 1975 (c. 14), s. 125 (1) (2).]
The Secretary of State on a review of weekly sums payable as pensions under s. 125 of the Social Security Act 1975, may compensate for any underestimation in a previous up-rating order if he wishes, but he is not under any duty to do so.
The Secretary of State reviewed the weekly rate of category A retirement pensions in May 1975, pursuant to s. 125 of the Social Security Act 1975. He concluded that the weekly rate had not retained its value in relation to the general level of earnings and prices, and made an up-rating order which came into effect in November 1975. After a further review, he made a further up-rating order in November 1976 in view of changes since the order of 1975. The plaintiffs, who were beneficiaries of category A retirement pensions, sought declarations that the 1976 order was not made pursuant to a review carried out in accordance with s. 125 (1). On a preliminary issue, Megarry V.-C. held that the period of review was from the date when the 1975 order came into effect, as opposed to the date of the preceding review, and dismissed the action. The plaintiffs appealed, contending that the Secretary of State was under a duty on a review to ascertain whether the sums in the previous order had been properly estimated, and if there was an under-estimation to make such an increase as would make good the under-estimation as well as any subsequent loss in value. *Held*, dismissing the appeal, that although there was nothing to preclude the Secretary of State from considering whether the sum in the 1975 order was under-estimated and compensating for it in the order of 1976, he was under no duty to do so. The Secretary of State had properly considered only whether the weekly rate in the order of 1975 had retained its value, and the order of 1976 was valid.
METZGER *v*. DEPARTMENT OF HEALTH AND SOCIAL SECURITY [1978] 1 W.L.R. 1046, C.A.

2778. Capacity for work—insurance officer's discretion
[Social Security (Unemployment, Sickness and Invalidity Benefit) Regulations 1975 (No. 564), reg. 3 (1).] On the true construction of reg. 3 (1) of

the Social Security (Unemployment, Sickness and Invalidity Benefit) Regulations 1975, the insurance officer has a discretion to determine whether a claimant is to be deemed to be incapable of work; he is not obliged so to determine simply because the claimant's doctor certifies that work is inadvisable: R. v. NATIONAL INSURANCE COMMISSIONER, ex p. DEPARTMENT OF HEALTH AND SOCIAL SECURITY, *The Times*, November 11, 1978, D.C.

2779. Categorisation of earners

SOCIAL SECURITY (CATEGORISATION OF EARNERS) AMENDMENT REGULATIONS 1978 (No. 1462) [10p], made under the Social Security Act 1975 (c. 14), s. 2 (2) (*a*); operative on November 3, 1978; further amend S.I. 1975 No. 528.

SOCIAL SECURITY (CATEGORISATION OF EARNERS) REGULATIONS 1978 (No. 1689) [30p], made under the Social Security Act 1975, ss. 2 (2), 4 (4) and (5), Sched. 1, para. 6 (1) (*k*); operative on December 27, 1978; consolidate S.I. 1975 No. 528, S.I. 1976 No. 404, S.I. 1977 Nos. 1015 and 1987 (*i.e.* regs. 1 (2) (*a*) and 2–7 inclusive), and S.I. 1978 No. 1462.

2780. Charges for accommodation

NATIONAL ASSISTANCE (CHARGES FOR ACCOMMODATION) REGULATIONS 1978 (No. 1073) [20p], made under the National Assistance Act 1948 (c. 29), s. 22; operative on November 13, 1978; supersede S.I. 1977 No. 1069. The minimum weekly amount which a person is required to pay for accommodation managed by a local authority under Pt. II of the 1948 Act is increased from £14 to £15·60. Weekly amounts for children are similarly increased.

2781. Child benefit. See FAMILY ALLOWANCES.

2782. Claims

SOCIAL SECURITY (CLAIMS AND PAYMENTS) (UNEMPLOYMENT BENEFIT TRANSITORY PROVISIONS) AMENDMENT REGULATIONS 1978 (No. 1000) [10p], made under the Social Security Act 1975 (c. 14), s. 79 (1) (3); operative on September 1, 1978; amend S.I. 1977 No. 1289 by increasing to two years the period specified in those regulations during which certain claims for unemployment benefit, made at certain specified unemployment benefit offices, may be made for a period falling partly after the date on which the claim is made.

2783. Computation of earnings

SOCIAL SECURITY BENEFIT (COMPUTATION OF EARNINGS) REGULATIONS 1978 (No. 1698) [25p], made under the Social Security Act 1975 (c. 14), ss. 3 (2), 66 (3), 82 (4), 119 (3) and 131; operative on January 1, 1979; provide for the way in which the earnings of a person to whom benefit is payable or of such a person's dependant are to be calculated or estimated for the purposes of the 1975 Act.

2784. Contributions

SOCIAL SECURITY (CONTRIBUTIONS, RE-RATING) CONSEQUENTIAL AMENDMENT REGULATIONS 1978 (No. 70) [10p], made under the Social Security Act 1975 (c. 14), ss. 128 (2) (*a*) and 129 (1), and the Social Security (Northern Ireland) Act 1975 (c. 15), s. 123; operative on April 6, 1978; amend S.I. 1975 No. 492.

SOCIAL SECURITY (CREDITS) AMENDMENT AND (EARNINGS FACTOR) TRANSITIONAL REGULATIONS 1978 (No. 409) [10p], made under the Social Security Act 1975, ss. 13 (4), 139 (1) and the Social Security Pensions Act 1975 (c. 60), s. 63 (1); operative on April 6, 1978; make minor amendments to S.I. 1975 No. 556 resulting from amendments made to the Social Security Act 1975 by the Social Security Pensions Act 1975 relating to the satisfaction of contribution conditions and rates of contributions.

SOCIAL SECURITY (CONTRIBUTIONS) (SPECIAL ANNUAL MAXIMUM) REGULATIONS 1978 (No. 410) [10p], made under the Social Security Act 1975, s. 11 (1) (2); operative on April 6, 1978; make provision for a special annual maximum of primary Class 1 contributions payable at the rate of 6.5 per cent. in the year ending April 5, 1979 in respect of employment which is not contracted-out employment by earners who reach pensionable age in that year.

SOCIAL SECURITY (CONTRIBUTIONS) AMENDMENT REGULATIONS 1978 (No. 423) [15p], made under the Social Security Act 1975, s. 139, Sched. 1, paras. 5 (1), 6 (1) (*h*) (*m*); operative on April 6, 1978; make provision relating to Class I contributions wrongly paid at the non-contracted-out rate in respect of an employment which is contracted-out to be returned after deduction of contributions at the contracted-out rate.

SOCIAL SECURITY (CONTRIBUTIONS) CONSEQUENTIAL AMENDMENT REGULATIONS 1978 (No. 507) [10p], made under the Social Security Act 1975, ss. 1, 129 (1) and S.I. 1977 No. 2180; operative on April 6, 1978; amend S.I. 1975 No. 492 and make provision for contributions payable in respect of mariner's earnings.

SOCIAL SECURITY (CONTRIBUTIONS) AMENDMENT (NO. 2) REGULATIONS 1978 (No. 821) [10p], made under the Social Security Act 1975, ss. 134 (6), 139; operative on July 1, 1978; amend S.I. 1975 No. 492 by modifying the provisions of s. 134 (4) of the 1975 Act by providing for no allocation to the Maternity Pay Fund from secondary Class 1 contributions paid in respect of members of the forces.

SOCIAL SECURITY (CONTRIBUTIONS) (EARNINGS LIMITS) AMENDMENT REGULATIONS 1978 (No. 1669) [10p], made under the Social Security Pensions Act 1975, ss. 1, 61 (1) (a) and the Social Security Act 1975, s. 139; operative on April 6, 1979; further amend S.I. 1975 No. 492 by substituting a new lower and upper earnings limit for Class 1 contributions for the tax year beginning April 6, 1979.

SOCIAL SECURITY (CONTRIBUTIONS) AMENDMENT (NO. 3) REGULATIONS 1978 No. 1703) [10p], made under the Social Security Act 1975, ss. 3, 9 (7), Sched. 1, para. 6 (1) (m); operative on January 4, 1979, except Reg. 2, which is operative on April 6, 1979; provide that a payment to defray or a contribution towards travelling expenses paid to a disabled person under s. 15 of the Disabled Persons (Employment) Act 1944 and earnings derived from a profit-sharing scheme to which the Finance Act 1978 applies shall be disregarded for the purposes of earnings-related contributions.

SOCIAL SECURITY (CONTRIBUTIONS, RE-RATING) ORDER 1978 (No. 1840) [10p], made under the Social Security Act 1975, s. 120; operative on April 6, 1979; raises the rates of class 2 and 3 contributions payable under the 1975 Act.

SOCIAL SECURITY (CONTRIBUTIONS) (MARINERS) AMENDMENT REGULATIONS 1978 (No. 1877) [20p], made under the Social Security Act 1975, ss. 3 (2), 129 (1), 139, Sched. 1, para. 6 (1) (d) and the Social Security (Consequential Provisions) Act 1975 (c. 18), Sched. 3, para. 9; operative on April 6, 1979; further amend S.I. 1975 No. 492 by providing for mariners employed on British ships.

2785. Family income supplements. See FAMILY ALLOWANCES.

2786. Industrial disablement benefit—prescribed disease—occupational deafness

C was employed as a boiler engineer with the same firm from 1938–1960 and again from 1965 to the date of his claim. His work required him to use pneumatic percussive tools on cast material fittings for boilers. After 1961 the type of boiler and fittings changed but C did some maintenance and repair work on old boilers. *Held*, that (1) as no degree of frequency of use of prescribed tools was specified, any such use, provided it was not so infrequent as to be negligible, would satisfy the provisions; (2) since 1965, C's use of pneumatic percussive tools was not so infrequent as to be negligible; (3) occupational deafness was prescribed in relation to C as he had been employed for not less than 20 years in an occupation involving the use of pneumatic percussive tools in the finishing or dressing of cast metal and he had not ceased to be so employed when he made his claim: DECISION No. R (I) 1/78.

2787. Industrial injuries benefit

The Industrial Injuries Advisory Council have published a report on the operation of the provisions for occupational deafness. The report recommends, inter alia, that industrial injuries benefits for occupational deafness should be extended to workers in certain noisy occupations. The report is available from HMSO (Cmnd. 7266) [70p.]

2788. The Industrial Injuries Advisory Council has been asked by the Secretary of State for Social Services to consider, in the light of the Royal Commission on Civil Liability and Compensation for Personal Injury, whether (a) any changes should be made in the terms of the list of prescribed industrial diseases under the Social Security industrial injuries scheme; and (b) whether industrial injuries benefits should be made available to any individual who can show that his disease is occupational in origin and a particular risk of his occupation.

2789. Invalidity pension—period of incapacity—regulations

The claimant, who had had polio, had never been able to work. He applied for a long term non-contributory invalidity pension, for which he had to be incapable for a total of 196 days before the day of his claim. A regulation provided that a day absent from Great Britain did not rank as a day of incapacity, and the claimant had gone to the West Indies for the sake of his health. He claimed that the regulation was ultra vires the Secretary of State; but it was *held* that the Social Security Act 1975 intended to provide a broad scheme which the Secretary of State could adapt by regulations, and so the regulation was intra vires: R. *v.* NATIONAL INSURANCE COMMISSIONER, *ex p.* FLEETWOOD (1978) 122 S.J. 146, D.C.

2790. Migrant workers—EEC—changes in national legislation. See BLOTTNER *v.* BESTUUR DER NIEUWE ALGEMENE BEDRIJFSVERENIGING, § 1380.

2791. Mobility allowance

MOBILITY ALLOWANCE UP-RATING ORDER 1978 (No. 475) [10p], made under the Social Security Act 1975 (c. 14), s. 124; operative on July 5, 1978; increases the weekly rate of mobility allowance.

MOBILITY ALLOWANCE (VEHICLE SCHEME BENEFICIARIES) AMENDMENT REGU-LATIONS 1978 (No. 743) [10p], made under the Social Security (Miscellaneous Provisions) Act 1977 (c. 5), s. 13 (1); operative on May 26, 1978; amend S.I. 1977 No. 1229 prescribing categories of persons to whom s. 13 of the 1977 Act applies so as to require that where persons have either been provided with, or applied for, a vehicle, it is a power driven vehicle controlled by the occupant.

MOBILITY ALLOWANCE (MOTABILITY PAYMENT ARRANGEMENTS) REGULATIONS 1978 (No. 1131) [10p], made under the Social Security Act 1975, s. 81 (1) (4) (*d*); operative on August 31, 1978; prescribe the circumstances in which mobility allowance payable under s. 37A of the 1975 Act may be paid to someone other than the beneficiary where that beneficiary is provided with a vehicle under arrangements made by the charity motability.

2792. Reciprocal agreements

SOCIAL SECURITY (JERSEY AND GUERNSEY) ORDER 1978 (No. 1527) [50p], made under the Social Security Act 1975 (c. 14), s. 143 (1); operative on November 6, 1978; makes provision for the modification of the 1975 Act in relation to Jersey and Guernsey.

2793. Sickness benefit—contributions—EEC—Member States. See R. *v.* NATIONAL INSURANCE COMMISSIONER, *ex p.* WARRY, § 1397.

2794. —— EEC—disqualification. See KENNY *v.* INSURANCE OFFICER, § 1398.

2795. —— incapacity for work—" alternative work " test

[Social Security Act 1975 (c. 14), s. 17 (1) (*a*) (ii).] A former furniture salesman aged 48, suffering from osteo-arthritis of spine and hypertension, was in receipt of sickness or invalidity benefit continuously from August 23, 1976. It was the opinion of separate officers of the Scottish Home and Health Department's regional medical service who examined him on January 13 and February 8, 1977, respectively, that he was incapable of work of the kind in which he had been previously employed, but that other work within specific limits would be possible for him. *Held*, that (1) the claimant had failed to show that he was incapable of work " which the person could reasonably be expected to do," in the words of the section, from February 25 till March 29; (2) it is inappropriate to lay down any specific period which must elapse before the " alternative work " test can properly be applied; (3) in order to determine at what stage it is reasonable to expect a claimant to change his occupation, factors such as the nature of the claimant's usual occupation, how long he has been thus employed, whether his incapacity is long or short term, and his adaptability to a new form of employment, must all be considered, as well as his age, education, experience and state of health: DECISION No. R(S) 2/78.

2796. —— place of claim. See *Re* AN ITALIAN CLAIMANT, § 1394.

2797. Social Security Pensions Act 1975—commencement

SOCIAL SECURITY PENSIONS ACT 1975 (COMMENCEMENT NO. 12) ORDER 1978 (No. 367 (C. 8)) [10p], made under the Social Security Pensions Act 1975 (c. 60), s. 67 (1) (2); operative on April 5, 1978; brings into force provisions of the 1975 Act relating to mobility allowance on appointed days in relation to specified age groups.

2798. Special hardship allowance—pneumoconiosis in coalmines—whether capable of employment of equivalent standard

[Social Security Act 1975 (c. 14), s. 60 (1).]

A miner, who by reason of pneumoconiosis is able only to work in approved dust conditions but who is prevented from doing so by some other (non-industrial) illness, is not entitled to a special hardship allowance.

The applicant developed pneumoconiosis whilst working as a coal miner in 1959. He was advised to continue in such employment provided that he worked in approved dust conditions: he was periodically medically examined and his disability was assessed at not more than 10 per cent. In 1975, he ceased employment in the mines due to breathlessness which was attributable to hypertension. His application for a special hardship allowance under s. 60 of the 1975 Act was refused. *Held*, refusing to issue certiorari, that although the applicant satisfied s. 60 (1) (*a*) of the Act in that he could only work in approved dust conditions, his application was defeated by s. 60 (1) (*b*) in that he could, but for the onset of hypertension, have continued " employment of an equivalent standard."

R. *v.* NATIONAL INSURANCE COMMISSIONERS, *ex p.* STEEL [1978] 3 All E.R. 78, D.C.

2799. Supplementary benefits

SUPPLEMENTARY BENEFITS (DETERMINATION OF REQUIREMENTS) REGULATIONS 1978 (No. 913) [20p], made under the Supplementary Benefits Act 1976 (c. 71), s. 2 (2) (3); operative on November 13, 1978; vary the provisions of Sched. 1, Pt. II, to the 1976 Act by increasing certain weekly amounts.

SUPPLEMENTARY BENEFITS (GENERAL) AMENDMENT REGULATIONS 1978 (No. 1459) [10p], made under the Supplementary Benefits Act 1976, ss. 2 (2), 5 as amended by the Social Security (Miscellaneous Provisions) Act 1977 (c. 5), s. 14 (4); operative on November 13, 1978; further amend S.I. 1977 No. 1141 by including the Manpower Services Commission among those bodies with which a person may register for employment and provides in respect of the day when changes in the amount of, or terminations of entitlement to, benefit take effect.

2800. The Department of Health and Social Security have published a report by a team of D.H.S.S. officials, entitled " Social Assistance: A Review of the Supplementary Benefits Scheme in Great Britain," which sets out a number of possibilities for improving and simplifying the supplementary benefits scheme. The report is available free from the D.H.S.S. Information Division, Leaflets Unit, Block 4, Government Buildings, Honeypot Lane, Stanmore, Middlesex, HA7 1AY.

2801. The Supplementary Benefits Commission have published their Annual Report for 1977. This deals in particular with two new proposals, namely, a single housing benefit scheme for all low-income householders, and a new scheme to help poorer people pay their fuel bills. The report is published as a Command Paper by HMSO.

2802. —— medical requirements—exceptional circumstances

[Supplementary Benefits Act 1976 (c. 71), s. 1 (3), Sched. 1, para. 4 (1) (*a*).]

Para. 4 (1) (*a*) of Sched. 1 to the Supplementary Benefits Act 1976, which gives the Supplementary Benefits Commission a discretion to award exceptional payments if they consider it appropriate, overrides s. 1 (3) of the Act, which excludes medical requirements.

Mrs. W was crippled with multiple sclerosis and was provided by various authorities with electrical aids, including a wheelchair, hoists and a ripple mattress. Mr. W applied to the Supplementary Benefits Commission for payments towards the extra electricity. The Appeal Tribunal held that no payment could be made since s. 1 (3) of the Supplementary Benefits Act 1976 excluded medical requirements. Mr. W applied for an order of certiorari to quash the decision. *Held,* granting the order, that (1) the tribunal had erred in law in not considering each item separately; (2) by para. 4 (1) (*a*) of Sched. 1, the tribunal had a discretion to make exceptional payments, in the exercise of which they were not restricted by s. 1 (3).

R. *v.* WEST LONDON SUPPLEMENTARY BENEFITS APPEAL TRIBUNAL, *ex p.* WYATT [1978] 1 W.L.R. 240, D.C.

2803. —— osteopathic treatment—whether commission has overriding discretion
[Supplementary Benefits Act 1976 (c. 71), ss. 6, 7.]
Osteopathic treatment is a medical or surgical requirement within s. 6 of the Supplementary Benefits Act 1976, and is therefore not a matter in respect of which supplementary benefit can be paid; further, the commission has no discretion under s. 7 to override the provisions of s. 6.

C, the claimant, applied for supplementary benefit in respect of osteopathic treatment. The Supplementary Benefits Commission rejected the application on the ground that it was a medical or surgical requirement, and therefore not a matter in respect of which benefit was payable, by reason of s. 6 of the Supplementary Benefits Act 1976. The Supplementary Benefits Appeal Tribunal overturned that finding, and awarded C £200. The commission applied for an order of certiorari to quash the tribunal's order. C contended that, in any event, s. 7 gave the commission an overriding discretion, subject to the test of unreasonableness, to make a single payment " to meet an exceptional need " if it thought fit. *Held,* (1) the treatment was a medical or surgical requirement within s. 6; (2) the commission had no discretion to override the terms of s. 6 by virtue of the provisions of s. 7. (*R. v. Preston Supplementary Benefits Appeal Tribunal, ex p. Moore* [1975] C.L.Y. 3288 considered.)

R. *v.* PETERBOROUGH SUPPLEMENTARY BENEFITS APPEAL TRIBUNAL, *ex p.* SUPPLEMENTARY BENEFITS COMMISSION [1978] 3 All E.R. 887, D.C.

2804. —— resources—money received while on strike
[Supplementary Benefits Act 1976 (c. 71), ss. 8 (1), 17 (1).] F, a fireman, was on strike from November 14, 1977, to January 16, 1978. On November 15 he received his salary for the month ending November 31, 1977, but at a later date he repaid half of this salary because of the strike. In November 1977 he applied for supplementary benefits for his wife and children; the tribunal held he was not entitled to an allowance before December 15, 1977, as he had received his salary up to November 30 and that money was his " resources " for the period ending December 14, 1977. *Held,* the money in question had not been earned and had had to be repaid; it should therefore have been disregarded when calculating F's resources for supplementary benefit: R. *v.* BOLTON SUPPLE-MENTARY BENEFITS APPEAL TRIBUNAL, *ex p.* FORDHAM, *The Times,* November 28, 1978, Sheen J.

2805. —— termination of employment—final wages in arrears
[Supplementary Benefits Act 1976 (c. 71).] A person paid wages in arrears, whose employment is terminated, is not entitled to immediate payment of supplementary benefit under the Supplementary Benefits Act 1976; his final wages are " resources " for the following period notwithstanding that they are referable to the period before termination. (Dictum of Lord Denning M.R. in *R. v. Preston Supplementary Benefits Appeal Tribunal, ex p. Moore* [1975] C.L.Y. 3288 followed): SUPPLEMENTARY BENEFITS COMMISSION *v.* RILEY, *The Times,* November 15, 1978, Sheen J.

2806. Unemployment benefit—absence—EEC. See *Re* SEARCH FOR WORK IN IRELAND, § 1401.

2807. —— entitlement—special capital payment—redundant member of armed forces
[Social Security (Unemployment, Sickness and Invalidity Benefit) Regulations 1975 (S.I. 1975 No. 564), reg. 7 (1) (*d*).]
The special capital payment received under a government scheme by a member of the armed forces on redundancy is not a payment in lieu of remuneration, disqualifying him from receiving unemployment benefit.

S was a squadron leader. He was made redundant, and received a special capital sum under a government scheme in lieu of a redundancy payment. Loss of remuneration was one, but only one, of the factors in its calculation. The Chief National Insurance Commissioner held that he was thereby disqualified from receiving unemployment benefit. *Held*, granting an order of certiorari and quashing the decision, that that payment was not one in lieu of remuneration, so that it did not disqualify him from receiving unemployment benefit.

R. *v.* NATIONAL INSURANCE COMMISSIONER, *ex p.* STRATTON [1978] 1 W.L.R. 1041, D.C.

2808. —— **migrant workers—EEC.** See CAISSE PRIMAIRE D'ASSURANCE MALADIE D'EURE-ET-LOIRE *v.* ALICIA TESSIER, NÉE RECQ, § 1382, KUYKEN *v.* RIJKS-DIENST VOOR ARBEIDSVOORZIENING, § 1254, and MARIS *v.* RIJKSDIENST VOOR WERKNEMERSPENSIONEN, § 1251.

2809. —— **trade dispute—dispute over protective clothing**
[Social Security Act 1975 (c. 14), s. 19 (2) (*b*).] The claimants were employed by a contractor responsible for the erection of boilers at a new power station. Their trade union claimed the provision of free protective clothing; the employer offered to supply the clothing on payment by the employees. On the breakdown of negotiations, the claimants stopped work. They contended that the dispute was not a trade dispute within the meaning of s. 19 (2) (*b*) of the 1975 Act. *Held*, that a dispute concerned with obligations or rights under the Health and Safety at Work etc. Act 1974 must necessarily be " connected with the conditions of employment " and therefore by definition a trade dispute: DECISION NO. R(U) 5/77.

2810. —— **whether engaged in employment—attending council meetings—whether attendance allowance " earnings "**
[Social Security (Unemployment, Sickness and Invalidity Benefit) Regulations 1975 (S.I. 1975 No. 564).] The claimant made a late claim for unemployment benefit. The insurance officer accepted good cause for the delay, but held that benefit was not payable for the 64 days on which the claimant had attended local authority meetings and for which he received £5 or £10 depending on the duration. *Held*, that the claimant was engaged in employment on those days and the attendance allowance constituted " earnings derived from that employment " which exceeded 75 pence per day, within reg. 7 (1) (*h*) of the 1975 Regulations: DECISION NO. R(U) 6/77.

2811. —— —— **calculation of income**
[Social Security (Unemployment, Sickness and Invalidity Benefit) Regulations 1975 (S.I. 1975 No. 564).] The claimant, while fully employed, also owned, in equal partnership with his wife, a fruit farm, on which the claimant worked in the evenings and at weekends. Three cottages on the farm were let to ordinary tenants unconnected with the farm. The claimant lost his full-time employment and claimed unemployment benefit; he continued to work on the farm as before. The profits of the farm for that accounting year came to £715, which included £925 in respect of rent from the cottages. *Held*, that (1) " employment " in reg. 7 (1) (*h*) of the 1975 Regulations included any business, and the claimant was thus at the material time engaged in employment; (2) that employment was consistent with full-time employment; but (3) the rents of the cottages should be disregarded in calculating the profits as the cottages were not used in the business, and therefore his earnings from the business did not exceed 75 pence per day: DECISION NO. R(U) 3/77.

2812. —— —— **consistency test**
[Social Security (Unemployment, Sickness and Invalidity Benefit) Regulations 1975 (S.I. 1975 No. 564).] The claimant became unemployed in April 1975. In August 1975 he and his wife, in equal partnership, opened a gift shop and coffee house in which the claimant worked full-time. In the first 14 weeks of trading, the estimated profits totalled £159; losses were incurred in five weeks and profits in nine weeks. *Held*, that (1) in order to calculate whether or not the claimant's earnings exceeded 75 pence per day, as set out in reg. 7 (1) (*h*) of the 1975 Regulations, his daily earnings rate should

be calculated separately for each week; thus his earnings only exceeded that amount in six of the 14 weeks; (2) satisfaction of the consistency test in reg. 7 (1) (*h*) requires that the occupation must be capable of being followed by the claimant concurrently with full-time employment; (3) the claimant's self-employment was consistent with full-time employment: DECISION No. R(U) 4/77.

2813. —— —— **forward disallowance**
[Social Security (Unemployment, Sickness and Invalidity Benefit) Regulations 1975 (S.I. 1975 No. 564), reg. 7 (1) (*h*).] Because of short-time working in C's normal full-time employment, for three months C did not work on alternate Mondays and Fridays. On Monday evenings during term time he worked for two hours for the County Council as a part-time table tennis coach at a Youth Centre, earning £3·23 per hour. *Held,* unemployment benefit was not payable for the Monday he worked at the Youth Centre whilst on short-time, as he was engaged in an employment from which he earned more than 75p, under reg. 7 (1) (*h*). There was however, no continuing feature in the disallowance for that day which would justify the imposition of a forward allowance for other days: DECISION No. R(U) 1/78.

2814. Welfare foods. See FOOD AND DRUGS.

BOOKS AND ARTICLES. See *post,* pp. [9], [36].

SOLICITORS

2815. Authority—to appeal—no express instructions. See R. *v.* McCREADY; R. *v.* HURD, § 528.

2816. Disciplinary proceedings—Singapore—appeal to Privy Council. See HILBORNE *v.* LAW SOCIETY OF SINGAPORE, § 175.

2817. Fees—conveyancing—fair and reasonable sum
[Solicitors Remuneration Order 1972 (S.I. 1972 No. 1139).]
An hourly cost rate applied to recorded time only, and other such arithmetical calculations, likewise final taxation figures in reported cases, are not primary sources for assessing a fair and reasonable sum for work done, and are to be used as cross-checks only.
The Department of the Environment sought a review of solicitors' professional charges of £9,000, excluding disbursements, in connection with the preparation, settlement and completion of a lease of offices. The total value of the land was about £2m. The lease was for 40 years at a rental of £190,035 per annum. The taxing master ordered that the costs be reduced to £6,900. The solicitors appealed from that order. *Held,* allowing the appeal, that (1) hourly cost rate applied to recorded time was only one of a number of cross-checks, since the determination of a fair and reasonable sum was a matter of judgment, and not of arithmetical calculation; (2) remuneration should not be disproportionate to the value of the property; ½ per cent. on the first £250,000 in a major transaction, and thereafter regressing, provided a reasonable method of assessment, but this figure should not be added to the remuneration for other elements; it is merely a check that the provisional figure bears a reasonable relationship to the value of the property; (3) the nature of the client's interest in the property was irrelevant; what mattered was the nature of the transaction, the skill and responsibility required of the solicitors, and the value of the property. In the circumstances, a reasonable and fair remuneration was £8,000. (Dictum of Walton J. in *Maltby* v. *D. J. Freeman & Co.* [1978] C.L.Y. 2819 applied; *Property and Reversionary Investment Corp.* v. *Secretary of State for the Environment* [1975] C.L.Y. 3292 explained.)
TREASURY SOLICITOR *v.* REGESTER [1978] 1 W.L.R. 446, Donaldson J.

2818. —— **taxation—basis—telephone calls**
A firm of solicitors appealed against the taxing master's assessment that £13 per hour was adequate for work done in proceedings for a matrimonial injunction and leave to petition within three years of marriage. *Held,* allowing the appeal, the rate of £13 plus 50 per cent. for care and attention was adequate

remuneration. Per curiam, it was logical to charge for time spent on telephone calls which saved interviews at the same rate as the interviews, but such calls should be recorded, aggregated and allowed on taxation at an hourly rate. Routine calls should be charged as in the past as substitutes for letters: BWANAOGA v. BWANAOGA, *The Times*, October 4, 1978, Payne J.

2819. —— —— remuneration for administration of estate

[Supreme Court (Non-Contentious Probate Costs) Rules 1956 (S.I. No. 552), r. 1.]

The logical starting point in assessing costs is the time expended by the solicitor, although it must be borne in mind that the problems of the office may be considered extensively in the solicitor's spare time. Where a large estate is involved, the most important consideration will be the nature and value of the property involved.

D. J. Freeman & Co., solicitors, charged A and B, executors, £11,175 for administering an estate worth £1,616,615. A, who was a surveyor, had assisted them by carrying out valuations, and their instructions were terminated before all the work was carried out. A and B applied to the Law Society for a certificate as to the fairness of the bill, and the Law Society certified that £8,500 would have been a more appropriate charge. A and B then had the bill taxed, and the taxation came to £10,500. On a review of the taxation, *held*, that (1) in assessing costs, care must be taken not to duplicate charges under the seven heads provided by r. 1 of the Supreme Court (Non-Contentions Probate) Rules 1956; (2) the logical place to start was head 5, the time expended, bearing in mind that a professional man seldom stopped thinking of the day's problems when he left the office; (3) where a large estate was involved, the most important head was head 6, the nature and value of the property involved, based on reducing percentages of successive bands; for an estate of the size and variety of the present one, the appropriate percentages were: on the first £$\frac{1}{4}$m., 1$\frac{1}{2}$ per cent.; on the next $\frac{3}{4}$m., $\frac{1}{2}$ per cent.; on the next £1$\frac{1}{2}$m., $\frac{1}{8}$ per cent. Therefore, bearing in mind the work done by A, and the early termination of the solicitors' instructions, the proper figure was £8,500. (*Property and Reversionary Investment Corp.* v. *Secretary of State for the Environment* [1975] C.L.Y. 3292 applied.)

MALTBY v. D. J. FREEMAN & Co. [1978] 1 W.L.R. 431, Walton J.

2820. Lay Observer

The Lay Observer has published, pursuant to s. 45 of the Solicitors Act 1974 (c. 47), his Third Annual Report for the year ending February 16, 1978. The report examines allegations made by or on behalf of members of the public concerning The Law Society's treatment of complaints about solicitors' conduct. The report is available from H.M.S.O. [35p].

2821. Negligence—assessment of damages

R instructed O Ltd., his solicitors, to draw up a contract of sale of three shops for £120,000 payable in four instalments. The contract in April 1973 provided for vacant possession to be given on completion but the tenants in the shops were protected by Part II of the Landlord and Tenant Act 1954 so this condition could not be fulfilled. In an attempt to mitigate the loss, a second agreement was made in January 1974 in which title was conveyed to the purchasers without vacant possession, but if the purchasers had not obtained vacant possession in six months R must repurchase the property for the £90,000 already paid. The purchasers could not get vacant possession and R could not repay the £90,000 as O Ltd. well knew. At the end of six months the premises were worth less than £90,000. The purchasers sued R for breach of the January 1974 agreement; only quantum was in issue. O Ltd. appealed against quantum in R's negligence action against them, contending that the January 1974 agreement broke the causation from their admitted negligence in April 1973. *Held*, R was entitled to damages which could reasonably be in contemplation at the time of the breach as being not unlikely to flow as a consequence of the breach (*Koufos* v. *C. Czarnikow* [1967] C.L.Y. 3623 applied). The January 1974 agreement was a reasonable remedial measure which unfortunately proved costly and R was not precluded from recovering against O Ltd. such damages as were awarded against him in the action by the purchasers (dicta of Lord Macmillan in *Banco de Portugal* v. *Waterlow* [1932] A.C. 452 at p. 506 applied): RUMSEY v. OWEN, WHITE AND CATLIN (1977) 245 E.G. 225, C.A.

2822. —— **failure to register land charge—extent of duty—limitation**

A solicitor who fails to register an estate contract may continue to be under a duty to so register until such time as a third party's transaction renders registration ineffectual.

In 1961 W granted to G an option to purchase W's farm, the option being drawn up by the defendant solicitors who failed to register it as an estate contract; thereafter on a number of occasions G consulted the defendants concerning the option. In 1967 W conveyed the farm to his wife, intending to defeat the option. An action brought later by G against W and W's wife's executors was largely unsuccessful. In 1972 G commenced an action against the defendants alleging negligence and/or breach of professional duty. On the question whether the claim was statute-barred, *held,* that the defendants were liable in tort for negligence in failing to register and the cause of action did not accrue until damage was suffered by the conveyance in 1967, which was within the limitation period; the defendant's contractual duty also continued up to the date of the conveyance which effectively defeated the option. (*Hedley Byrne & Co.* v. *Heller & Partners* [1963] C.L.Y. 2416 and *Esso Petroleum* v. *Mardon* [1976] C.L.Y. 341, applied; *Bean* v. *Wade* (1885) 2 T.L.R. 157, distinguished; *Cook* v. *Swinfen* [1967] C.L.Y. 3114 and *Heywood* v. *Wellers* [1975] C.L.Y. 2350, not followed.)

MIDLAND BANK TRUST CO. v. HETT, STUBBS & KEMP (A FIRM) [1978] 3 W.L.R. 167, Oliver J.

2823. —— **failure to search commons register**

A solicitor acting in the purchase of previously undeveloped land may be negligent in failing to search the commons register, in particular when he is aware of the importance to the purchaser of the land being unencumbered.

The plaintiffs engaged the defendant solicitors to act for them in the purchase of land which they intended to use for industrial development. The vendor's solicitors, in answer to the inquiries before contract, stated that no rights of common existed over the land " to the vendor's knowledge." Notwithstanding that the vacant land was disclosed upon the previous conveyances to have once belonged to the lord of the manor, no search of the commons register was made. After completion of the sale, the plaintiffs immediately agreed to resell the land but the resale was delayed because the defendants searched the commons register and found therein that rights of common had—erroneously—been registered. The delay was occasioned whilst the register was rectified. *Held,* giving judgment for the plaintiffs in their action for negligence, that since the defendants knew of the importance to the plaintiffs of the land being entirely unencumbered, they were negligent in not searching the commons register.

G. & K. LADENBAU (U.K.) v. CRAWLEY & DE REYA [1978] 1 W.L.R. 226, Mocatta J.

2824. —— **inexcusable delay by counsel—action dismissed for want of prosecution**

A pending action was dismissed for want of prosecution. The solicitors were guilty of inexcusable delay in their conduct of the action. The papers had been sent to counsel for his opinion and he was also dilatory. The solicitors were also liable for this delay since where counsel was dilatory, the solicitors should withdraw their instructions and pass them to another counsel; the solicitors were therefore in breach of duty to the plaintiff whose action had been dismissed: MAINZ v. JAMES AND CHARLES DODD, *The Times,* July 21, 1978, Watkins J.

2825. —— **test of damages—will witnessed by beneficiary's spouse**

[Can.] C, a solicitor with the defendant firm, drew up a will for a testator in January 1968. Under the will, P, who was one of the testator's five children, was the residual beneficiary. C requested P's wife to witness the will when it was executed. The testator died in 1973; in 1974 the testator's other four children filed a petition for relief and in January 1976 the gift of residue to P was declared void. P sued the defendant firm in negligence. *Held*, D was liable as C was negligent in that he did not exercise a reasonable degree of skill in the circumstances. Despite the fact that there was no contractual relationship between C and P, but only between C and the testator, C was liable for damages suffered by P as he had undertaken the responsibility of the proper execution of the will and there was an implied duty owed by C to P. The measure of damages was not the difference between what P would have received under the will and what he received by intestate succession, but rather the difference between what he would have received had the petition for relief been heard, and what he received by intestate succession: WHITTINGHAM v. CREASE [1978] 5 W.W.R. 45, Brit.Col.Sup.Ct.

2826. Practice. See PRACTICE.

2827. Practising certificate—failure to renew—whether "unqualified person" bars firm from recovering costs

[Solicitors Act 1957 (c. 27), ss. 18 (1) (2) (*b*), 23; Partnership Act 1890, (c. 39), ss. 5, 34.]

The rule that no unqualified person shall act as a solicitor in s. 18 of the Solicitors Act 1957, applies to an individual, not to a firm; the lapse of one partner's practising certificate brings about the automatic dissolution of the partnership under s. 34 of the Partnership Act.

P Co., a firm of solicitors, acted for D in a High Court action from January to December 1973. Throughout that period, S. a partner, had inadvertently allowed his practising certificate to lapse. S had not had anything to do with the conduct of D's case. D refused to pay P Co.'s costs, contending that by s. 18 of the Solicitors Act 1957, P Co. were debarred from recovering them. *Held*, that only the individual was debarred. When one partner's practising certificate lapsed, the partnership has dissolved by s. 34 of the Partnership Act 1890, and thereafter there came into an existence by conduct a new partnership of the remaining partners. There was no claim for work done by S, and therefore D was liable for P Co.'s costs. (Dictum of Gorell Barnes P. in *Hill* v. *Clifford* [1907] 2 Ch. 236, 255, *R.* v. *Kupfer* [1915] 2 K.B. 321, *Hugh Stevenson & Sons* v. *Aktiengesellschaft für Cartonnagen Industrie* [1918] A.C. 239, *Freeman* v. *Cooke* (1848) 2 Ex. 654 and *Scarf* v. *Jardine* (1882) 7 App.Cas. 345 applied; *Martin* v. *Sherry* [1905] 2 I.R. 62 considered.)

HUDGELL YEATES & CO. v. WATSON [1978] 2 W.L.R. 661, C.A.

2828. Privilege—client's forged document—search warrant—right to be heard. See *R.* v. PETERBOROUGH JUSTICES, *ex p.* HICKS, § 2305.

2829. Professional misconduct—personal liability for costs—basis of taxation

In protracted matrimonial proceedings, the wife's solicitor was guilty of grave professional misconduct in acting against her own client's interest and contrary to her instructions. As a result both parties suffered protracted delay and distress and were put to unnecessary expense. The judge in chambers made an indemnity order, and directed taxation on a solicitor and own client basis. *Held*, dismissing the wife's solicitor's appeal, under R.S.C., Ord. 62, r. 8, the court may direct a solicitor personally to indemnify any party against costs which have been incurred improperly, or by any misconduct or default. When such an order is appropriate the costs should be taxed on a solicitor and own client basis. Thus, in this case, the order should provide for the solicitor to indemnify the husband against the costs in question, the costs to be taxed, if not agreed, on a solicitor and own client basis. Taxation on a party and party basis would not amount to a full indemnity. (Decision of Latey J., *sub nom. S.* v. *S.* affirmed; *Jakeman* v. *Jakeman and Turner* [1964] C.L.Y. 1055 considered; dictum of Sachs J. in *Edwards* v. *Edwards* [1958] C.L.Y. 957 not followed): SHARP v. SHARP, October 31, 1978, C.A. (*Ex rel.* Malcolm Knott, Esq., Barrister.)

2830. —— powers of inquiry committee to initiate investigation

An advocate and solicitor of Singapore was struck off the roll for professional misconduct. On appeal, the Privy Council *held* that the inquiry committee could begin an inquiry or investigation on a written complaint

not supported by any affidavit or statutory declaration: CHAN CHOW WANG
v. LAW SOCIETY OF SINGAPORE (1978) 122 S.J. 626, P.C.

2831. —— trial—intimidation of witnesses
During the trial of X and others, X's solicitor, Y, introduced into the well
of the court near the witness-box a Soho rent collector, Z, known to
prosecution witnesses as being involved in activities in the twilight world. Z
gave the impression he was connected with the trial. Counsel being concerned
that Z's presence might intimidate witnesses, the judge ordered Z to sit in
the public gallery. Y had told the court that Z was involved in the case, and
on the third day of trial told the police that he wanted Z to return to the
court. The main prosecution witness told a disciplinary tribunal, investigating
Y's conduct, that he would have been too afraid to give evidence had he seen
Z. *Held,* dismissing Y's appeal from an order that his name be struck off the
roll, that there was sufficient evidence to support the finding that Y had
introduced Z to the well of the court to exercise an improper kind of control
over witnesses: *Re* A SOLICITOR [1978] Crim.L.R. 309, D.C.

2832. Restraint of trade—balance of convenience—former practice sending work. See
CRAMPTON AND BROWN *v.* ROBERTSON, § 330.

**2833. Settlement of claim—settlement contrary to instructions—whether client bound
by settlement**
[Can.] P sought to enforce a settlement of proceedings which had been
agreed between the parties' solicitors. D claimed the settlement was substantially different from the one they had instructed their solicitor to make.
Held, as their solicitor had acted outside his authority in making such a
settlement, D was not bound by it: BANK OF MONTREAL *v.* ARVEE CEDAR
MILLS [1977] 6 W.W.R. 447 Brit.Col.Sup.Ct.

BOOKS AND ARTICLES. See *post,* pp. [9], [36].

STAMP DUTIES

2834. Loan capital—issue
[Finance Act 1899 (c. 9), s. 8 (1) (5).]
The mere acceptance of money on loan does not constitute the " issue " of
loan capital.
The taxpayer company was incorporated to lend money on first mortgages
of agricultural or farming estates. It was empowered to raise money on deben-
tures or debenture stock. To facilitate the raising of moneys it entered into
arrangements with the Ministry of Agriculture and Fisheries, whereby the
Ministry made advances to establish and maintain a guarantee fund for the
company. The Inland Revenue contended, and Walton J. held, that the acceptance of such advances constituted the " issue " of loan capital within s. 8 (1)
of the Finance Act 1899, and that the capital, having the character of borrowed
money, attracted liability to stamp duty. *Held,* allowing the appeal, (1) that the
mere acceptance of money on loan does not constitute an " issue " within F.A.
1899, s. 8 (1), but there must be some overt act on the part of the debtor
recognising the creditor's rights and perfecting his title; (2) in any event,
" issue " signifies a business transaction on market or commercial terms between
parties at arm's length.
AGRICULTURAL MORTGAGE CORP. *v.* I.R.C. [1978] 1 All E.R. 248, C.A.

2835. Practice direction—grant of representation—adjudication. See § 1437.

**2836. Relief—reconstruction or reorganisation of company—" particular existing
company "—unlimited company**
[Finance Act 1927 (c. 10), s. 55 (1).]
The expression " particular existing company " in the Finance Act 1927,
s. 55 (1), extends to an unlimited company.
C Ltd. purchased the whole of the issued share capital of Cadogan, an
unlimited company, by increasing its share capital and allotting the increase
to the Cadogan shareholders. Relief from stamp duty was available on the
statement of increase of capital and the instruments of transfer of shares only if
Cadogan were a " particular existing company " within the Finance Act 1927,

s. 55 (1). *Held*, that the relief was available, since " particular existing company " did not signify a limited liability company only. (*Nestlé Co.* v. *I.R.C.* [1953] C.L.Y. 3484 distinguished).

CHELSEA LAND & INVESTMENT CO. *v.* I.R.C. [1978] 2 All E.R. 113, C.A.

2837. Rent—contingent rent—whether " reserved "
[Stamp Act 1891 (c. 39), Sched. 1.]
A contingent rent is a rent " reserved " by a lease under para. 3 of the head of charge " Lease or Tack " in Sched. 1 to the Stamp Act 1891.
The Council granted a head lease of a site to the Norwich Union for a term of 125 years at an annual rent of £17,500. Norwich Union granted an underlease of the site to the Council for 125 years less one day, the Council undertaking to construct a building, and Norwich Union undertaking to reimburse the cost up to £1,300,000. The rent payable under the underlease was (a) a yearly rent, equivalent to 8.142 per cent. of the total expenditure of Norwich Union, up to £1,300,000, on specified items which included (i) legal costs quantified at £2,500, and (ii) building costs; and (b) a yearly rent of £17,500. The Crown assessed the underlease to ad valorem duty under para. 3 of the head of charge " Lease or Tack " in Sched. 1 to the Stamp Act 1891, on a rent of (1) £105,846 (*i.e.* 8.142 per cent. of £1,300,000); and (2) £17,500. *Held*, that the rent of £105,846 was properly described as a rent payable on a contingency, and was correctly assessed to ad valorem duty. (Dicta of Collins M.R. in *Underground Electric Railways Co. of London* v. *I.R.C.* [1905] 1 K.B. at 182, and of Lord Radcliffe in *Independent Television Authority* v. *I.R.C.* [1960] C.L.Y. 3039, applied).

COVENTRY CITY COUNCIL *v.* I.R.C. [1978] 1 All E.R. 1107, Brightman J.

STATUTES AND ORDERS

2838. Construction—guidelines laid down by court—unambiguous statutes
Guidelines laid down by courts or industrial tribunals in applying statutes to particular facts are not binding legal rules. Where a legal right is created by statute, the statute alone is law and judges cannot add to or subtract from the law as expressed in the statute.
W was dismissed for not taking the agreed time for lunch on the day the factory closed for the Christmas period. She was not given an opportunity to explain her conduct. The industrial tribunal held that the employers had acted reasonably in treating her misconduct as a sufficient reason for dismissing her. On appeal, it was submitted that the tribunal had failed to follow guidelines laid down in previous decisions of courts and tribunals, and that such failure was an error of law which entitled the appeal tribunal to interfere. *Held*, the statute was clear and unambiguous and the guidelines created no legal precedent. However, the tribunal had misdirected in applying the law to the facts, and the appeal would be allowed.

WELLS *v.* DERWENT PLASTICS [1978] I.C.R. 424, E.A.T.

2839. —— " street "—whether disused road over a bridge is a street
[Scot.] [Public Utilities Street Works Act 1950 (c. 39), s. 1 (3).] " Any length of a highway (other than a waterway), roadway, lane, footway, alley or passage, any square or court, and any length of land laid out as a way, whether it is for the time being formed as a way or not, irrespective of whether the highway, road or other thing in question is a thoroughfare or not " is the statutory definition of a street. The case revolved around whether a disused road running across a bridge was therefore a street. *Held*, the words of the statute are wide enough to constitute it as a length of land laid out as a way, and consequently a street: STRATHCLYDE REGIONAL COUNCIL *v.* BRITISH RAILWAYS BOARD, 1978 S.L.T. 8, Sheriff Principal R., Reid Q.C.

2840. Interpretation—Law Commissions' report. See § 1832.

2841. Interpretation Act 1978 (c. 30)
This Act consolidates the Interpretation Act 1889 and other enactments.
S. 1 relates to words of enactment; s. 2 deals with amendments or repeals in the same session; s. 3 deals with judicial notice; s. 4 relates to the time of

commencement of an Act; s. 5 and Sched. 1 relate to definitions; s. 6 deals with gender and number; s. 7 refers to references to service by post; s. 8 relates to references to distance; s. 9 deals with references to time of day. s. 10 deals with references to the sovereign; s. 11 refers to the construction of subordinate legislation; s. 12 relates to the continuity of powers and duties; s. 13 refers to the anticipatory exercise of powers; s. 14 deals with the implied power to amend; s. 15 relates to the repeal of a repealing enactment; s. 16 relates to general savings provisions; s. 17 refers to repeals and re-enactments. s. 18 relates to duplicated offences; s. 19 deals with citation of other Acts; s. 20 relates to references to other enactments; s. 21 contains definitions; s. 22 deals with the application of this Act to Acts and Measures; s. 23 deals with the application of this Act to other instruments; s. 24 relates to the application of this Act to Northern Ireland; s. 25 contains repeals and savings; s. 26 gives the commencement date; s. 27 gives the short title.

The Act received the Royal Assent on July 20, 1978, and came into force on January 1, 1979.

2842. Parliament See PARLIAMENT.

2843. Revision of statutes—Law Commissions' report. See § 1831.

2844. Royal Assent

The following Acts received the Royal Assent during 1978:

Adoption (Scotland) Act 1978 (c. 28), July 20 [£1], §§ 1974, 3144.

Appropriation Act 1978 (c. 57), August 2 [£1·25], § 2513.

Chronically Sick and Disabled Persons (Northern Ireland) Act 1978 (c. 53), July 31 [30p], § 2104.

Civil Aviation Act 1978 (c. 8), March 23 [45p], § 129.

Civil Liability (Contribution) Act 1978 (c. 47), July 31 [30p], § 2853.

Commonwealth Development Corporation Act 1978 (c. 2), March 23 [35p], § 161.

Community Service by Offenders (Scotland) Act 1978 (c. 49), July 31 [40p], §§ 425, 3196.

Consolidated Fund Act 1978 (c. 7), March 23 [10p], § 2516.

Consolidated Fund (No. 2) Act 1978 (c. 59), December 14 [10p], § 2517.

Consumer Safety Act 1978 (c. 38), July 20 [60p], § 2917.

Co-operative Development Agency Act 1978 (c. 21), June 30 [30p], § 2919.

Dividends Act 1978 (c. 54), July 31 [10p], § 2521.

Domestic Proceedings and Magistrates' Courts Act 1978 (c. 22), June 30 [£1·85], § 1903.

Education (Northern Ireland) Act 1978 (c. 13), May 25 [20p], § 2129.

Employment (Continental Shelf) Act 1978 (c. 46), July 31, [10p], § 925.

Employment Protection (Consolidation) Act 1978 (c. 44), July 31 [£3], § 928.

Employment Subsidies Act 1978 (c. 6), March 23 [15p], § 929.

European Assembly Elections Act 1978 (c. 10), May 5 [40p], § 1275.

Export Guarantees and Overseas Investment Act 1978 (c. 18), June 30 [40p], § 2924.

Finance Act 1978 (c. 42), July 31 [£2], §§ 202, 362, 688, 1651, 1652, 1653, 2525, 3032.

Gun Barrel Proof Act 1978 (c. 9), May 5 [40p], § 1471.

Home Purchase Assistance and Housing Corporation Guarantees Act 1978 (c. 27), June 30 [25p], § 1576.

Homes Insulation Act 1978 (c. 48), July 31 [20p], § 1578.

House of Commons (Administration) Act 1978 (c. 36), July 20 [30p], § 2208.

Housing (Financial Provisions) (Scotland) Act 1978 (c. 14), May 25 [70p], §§ 1580, 3149.

Import of Live Fish (Scotland) Act 1978 (c. 35), July 20 [20p], §§ 1481, 3357.

Independent Broadcasting Authority Act 1978 (c. 43), July 31 [10p], § 2847.

Industrial and Provident Societies Act 1978 (c. 34), July 20 [20p], § 1687.

Inner Urban Areas Act 1978 (c. 50), July 31 [40p], § 2881.

Internationally Protected Persons Act 1978 (c. 17), June 30 [20p], § 1730.

Interpretation Act 1978 (c. 30), July 20 [40p], § 2841.
Iron and Steel (Amendment) Act 1978 (c. 41), July 20 [10p], § 2935a.
Judicature (Northern Ireland) Act 1978 (c. 23), June 30 [25p], § 2153.
Local Government Act 1978 (c. 39), July 20 [10p], § 1870.
Local Government (Scotland) Act 1978 (c. 4), March 23 [25p], §§ 1871, 3493.
Medical Act 1978 (c. 12), May 5 [£1·25], § 1943.
National Health Service (Scotland) Act 1978 (c. 29), July 20 [£2], §§ 2039, 3524.
Northern Ireland (Emergency Provisions) Act 1978 (c. 5), March 23 [60p], § 2169.
Nuclear Safeguards and Electricity (Finance) Act 1978 (c. 25), June 30 [25p], § 116.
Oaths Act 1978 (c. 19), June 30 [20p], § 1430.
Parliamentary Pensions Act (c. 56), August 2 [50p], § 2274.
Participation Agreements Act 1978 (c. 1), February 23 [10p], § 2939.
Pensioners Payments Act 1978 (c. 58), November 23 [10p], § 2275.
Protection of Children Act 1978 (c. 37), July 20 [25p], § 583.
Rating (Disabled Persons) Act 1978 (c. 40), July 20 [40p], § 2470a.
Refuse Disposal (Amenity) Act 1978 (c. 3), March 23 [35p], § 1881.
Representation of the People Act 1978 (c. 32), July 20 [10p], § 877a.
Scotland Act 1978 (c. 51), July 31 [£1·75], §§ 295, 3179.
Shipbuilding (Redundancy Payments) Act 1978 (c. 11), May 5 [20p], § 2768.
Solomon Islands Act 1978 (c. 15), May 25 [30p], § 179.
State Immunity Act 1978 (c. 33), July 20 [40p], § 1737.
Statute Law (Repeals) Act 1978 (c. 45), July 31 [90p], § 2845.
Suppression of Terrorism Act 1978 (c. 26), June 30 [40p], § 885.
Theatres Trust (Scotland) Act 1978 (c. 24), June 30 [10p], §§ 2442, 3608.
Theft Act 1978 (c. 31), July 20 [25p], § 642.
Transport Act 1978 (c. 55), August 2 [60p], § 3022.
Trustee Savings Banks Act 1978 (c. 16), June 30 [25p], § 2660.
Tuvalu Act 1978 (c. 20), June 30 [25p], § 181.
Wales Act 1978 (c. 52), July 31 [£1·75], § 297.

The following Measures received the Royal Assent during 1978:
Church of England (Miscellaneous Provisions) Measure (No. 3), June 30 [50p], § 845.
Dioceses Measure 1978 (No. 1), February 2 [50p], § 847.
Parochial Registers and Records Measure (No. 2), February 2 [50p], § 851.

2845. Statute Law (Repeals) Act 1978 (c. 45)

This Act promotes the reform of the statute law by the repeal, in accordance with recommendations of the Law Commission and the Scottish Law Commission, of certain enactments, or parts of enactments, which are no longer of practical utility. The Act also facilitates the citation of statutes.

S. 1 provides for the repeal of certain enactments set out in Sched. 1 to the Act, and also for the consequential amendments contained in Sched. 2; s. 2 gives effect to Sched. 3 to the Act, which facilitates the citation of certain enactments; s. 3 extends the Act to Northern Ireland, and also, upon Orders in Council being made, to the Channel Islands or the Isle of Man; s. 4 contains the short title.

The Act received the Royal Assent on July 31, 1978, and came into force on that date.

ARTICLES. See *post*, p. [36].

STOCK EXCHANGE

ARTICLES. See *post*, p. [36].

TELECOMMUNICATIONS

2846. Fees

WIRELESS TELEGRAPHY (GENERAL LICENCE CHARGES) (AMENDMENT) REGULA-TIONS 1978 (No. 12) [15p], made under the Wireless Telegraphy Act 1949 (c.

54), s. 2 (1) as extended by S.I. 1952 Nos. 1899, 1900; operative on February 1, 1978; increase the fees payable on the issue, renewal and variation of certain wireless telegraphy licences.

2847. Independent Broadcasting Authority Act 1978 (c. 43)

This Act extends the period during which television and local sound broadcasting services are to be provided by the Independent Broadcasting Authority, and makes certain provisions as regards the broadcasting of proceedings in Parliament and by local authorities.

S. 1 extends the duration of the Independent Broadcasting Authority's function until December 31, 1981; s. 2 excludes s. 4 (2) and (5) of the Independent Broadcasting Authority Act 1973, as respects proceedings in Parliament and the proceedings of local authorities; s. 3 contains the short title, and states that the Act shall extend to Northern Ireland, and also, if Orders in Council so direct, to the Isle of Man and the Channel Islands.

The Act received the Royal Assent on July 31, 1978, and came into force on that date.

2848. Post Office See POST OFFICE.

2849. Telegraph

WIRELESS TELEGRAPHY (ISLE OF MAN) ORDER 1978 (No. 1055) [10p], made under the Wireless Telegraphy Act 1967 (c. 72), s. 15 (6); operative on August 1, 1978; extends to the Isle of Man the 1967 Act, s. 11, as amended by the Criminal Law Act 1977, with exceptions and modifications.

WIRELESS TELEGRAPHY (CONTROL OF INTERFERENCE FROM HOUSEHOLD APPLIANCES, PORTABLE TOOLS ETC.) REGULATIONS 1978 (No. 1267) [20p], made under the Wireless Telegraphy Act 1949 (c. 54), ss. 9, 10 and S.I. 1952 Nos. 1899, 1900; operative on April 1, 1979, save for those Regs. applying to lighting dimmers which are operative on November 1, 1979; implement Council Directive No. 76/889/EEC relating to the control of radio interference caused by household appliances, portable tools and other equipment. Also provides that a person who fails to comply with these regs. may be served with a notice under ss. 11, 12 of the 1949 Act and that any person who contravenes the provisions of a such a notice shall be guilty of an offence.

WIRELESS TELEGRAPHY (CONTROL OF INTERFERENCE FROM FLUORESCENT LIGHTING APPARATUS) REGULATIONS 1978 (No. 1268) [20p], made under the Wireless Telegraphy Act 1949, ss. 9, 10, as extended by S.I. 1952 Nos. 1899, 1900; operative on January 1, 1979; implement Council Directive No. 76/890/EEC relating to the suppression of radio interference with regard to fluorescent lighting apparatus and apply to any luminaire which is fitted with a starter and which forms, or is designed to form, part of such apparatus. Also provides that a person who fails to comply with these regs. may be served with a notice under ss. 11, 12 of the 1949 Act and any person who contravenes the provisions of such a notice shall be guilty of an offence.

2850. Television licences

WIRELESS TELEGRAPHY (BROADCAST LICENCE CHARGES & EXEMPTION) (AMENDMENT) REGULATIONS 1978 (No. 1680) [10p], made under the Wireless Telegraphy Act 1949 (c. 54), s. 2 (1) as extended by S.I. 1952 Nos. 1899, 1900; operative on November 25, 1978; raises the amount of the basic fee for television licences to £10 in the case of monochrome and to £25 in the case of colour.

TIME

2851. Limitations of actions. See LIMITATION OF ACTIONS.

TORT

2852. Battery—neurosurgery—consent—patient not informed of true risks—whether true consent

[Can.] On examining R, H, a neurosurgeon, reached the conclusion that R needed surgery to clear a blocked artery and prevent a stroke in later life.

He did not tell R that 4 per cent. of such operations were fatal, and another 10 per cent. disabling. R consented. During surgery, R suffered a stroke which left him paralysed. He sued in both negligence and battery. *Held*, although the surgery itself was not negligently performed, he could recover in both. Battery requires absence of consent; R's consent, given in ignorance of the high risks involved in such surgery, was no consent at all, and the operation therefore constituted battery. In respect of the negligence claim, it is a concomitant of the physician's duty of care to ensure informed consent to treatment. As this had not been obtained, H had been negligent in treating R. (*Kelly* v. *Hazlett* (1976) 75 D.L.R. 536 followed): REIBL v. HUGHES (1977) 78 D.L.R. 35, Haines J.

2853. Civil Liability (Contribution) Act 1978 (c. 47)

This Act makes new provision for contribution between two or more persons who are jointly and/or severally liable for the same damage and may be required to pay compensation for the same damage, and for persons jointly liable for the same debt or damage.

S. 1 defines the circumstances in which a person liable in respect of damage may recover contribution from another similarly liable for the same damage; s. 2 provides for the assessment of such contribution; s. 3 deals with proceedings against persons jointly liable for the same debt or damage; s. 4 relates to successive actions against persons liable (jointly or otherwise) for the same damage; s. 5 states the application of the Act to the Crown; s. 6 is the interpretation section; s. 7 contains savings provisions; s. 8 deals with the application of the Act to Northern Ireland; s. 9 sets out consequential amendments and repeals; s. 10 gives the short title, and states that, with the exception of para. 1 of Sched. 1, the Act does not extend to Scotland.

The Act received the Royal Assent on July 31, 1978, and came into force on January 1, 1979.

2854. Crown proceedings. See PRACTICE.

2855. Damages. See DAMAGES.

2856. —— quantum—defective manufacture—delayed repairs. See ALBERTA CARRIERS v. R. VOLLAN (ALTA.), § 2076.

2857. Defamation. See LIBEL AND SLANDER.

2858. Negligence. See NEGLIGENCE.

2859. Nuisance. See NUISANCE.

2860. Passing off. See TRADE MARKS AND TRADE NAMES.

2861. Pearson Report. See § 717.

2862. Torts (Interference with Goods) Act 1977—commencement

TORTS (INTERFERENCE WITH GOODS) ACT 1977 (COMMENCEMENT NO. 2) ORDER 1978 (No. 627 (C. 15)) [10p], made under the Torts (Interference with Goods) Act 1977 (c. 32), s. 17 (2); brings into force the remaining provisions of the 1977 Act on June 1, 1978.

2863. Volenti non fit injuria. See NEGLIGENCE.

BOOKS AND ARTICLES. See *post,* pp. [9], [36].

TOWN AND COUNTRY PLANNING

2864. Acquisition of land

ACQUISITION OF LAND (RATE OF INTEREST AFTER ENTRY) (No. 3) REGULATIONS 1978 (No. 1741) [10p], made under the Land Compensation Act 1961 (c. 33), s. 32 (1); operative on January 4, 1979; increase from $12\frac{1}{2}$ per cent. to 14 per cent. per annum the rate of interest payable where entry is made, before payment of compensation, on land which is being purchased compulsorily.

ACQUISITION OF LAND (RATE OF INTEREST AFTER ENTRY) (SCOTLAND) (No. 3) REGULATIONS 1978 (No. 1742) [10p], made under the Land Compensation (Scotland) Act 1963 (c. 51), s. 40 (1); operative on January 4, 1979; increase from 12½ to 14 per cent. per annum the rate of interest payable where entry is made on land in Scotland which is being compulsorily purchased, before payment of compensation.

2865. Blight notice—Lands Tribunal decision

COMLEY *v.* KENT COUNTY COUNCIL (Ref. No. 52/1977) (1977) 34 P. & C.R. 218 (on the council's area town centre map, part of the road in which C's house was situated was shown to be " pedestrianised " together with the High Street into which it ran. The remainder of the road was shown as an access road, and the land on which C's house stood was shown as a new turning area for access. C served a blight notice. The council objected, on the ground that the map was part of an informal plan, and did not form part of the development plan. *Held,* the town map was only advisory and a guide to developers as it was not part of a development plan and could not be submitted to the Secretary of State. The authority's objection was well-founded).

2866. Caravan sites—site licence—electricity cut off—whether " protected site "

[Caravan Sites Act 1968 (c. 52), ss. 1 (2) 3 (1).]

Where a defendant fails through his own fault to obtain a site licence, his site may for the purpose of prosecuting him be a " protected site " within the meaning of the Caravan Sites Act 1968, s. 1 (2).

D owned land which he let as a caravan site. A site licence was refused because of his failure to obtain planning permission. He was subsequently charged with " persistently withdrawing a service [electricity] reasonably required on a protected site " contrary to s. 3 (1) of the Caravan Sites Act 1968. *Held,* allowing P's appeal from the dismissal by justices of the information, that the site was within the meaning of the term " protected site " so that D could not rely on his own failure to obtain a licence to absolve him from the requirements of the Caravan Sites Act 1968.

HOOPER *v.* EAGLESTONE (1977) 76 L.G.R. 308, D.C.

2867. Change of use—conversion to flats—detrimental to character of house

The owner of a large house obtained planning permission to build additional residential accommodation and three garages. This was carried out. A subsequent intending purchaser sought to turn the property into two units and sell off one. The application was refused. An inquiry was held and the inspector concluded that the material change of use would be out of character, detrimental to the amenity and unsatisfactory. The applicant sought for the decision to be quashed. *Held,* the inspector had properly arrived at his decision: WAKELIN *v.* SECRETARY OF STATE FOR THE ENVIRONMENT AND ST. ALBANS DISTRICT COUNCIL [1978] J.P.L. 769, C.A.

2868. —— permission to convert to showroom—sale of different goods

Planning permission was given for the modernisation of a large garage and petrol station, including the conversion of an existing workshop to a retail showroom. Later, a supermarket company acquired the showroom and used it as a retail supermarket. *Held,* that the mere sale of the showroom had not created a new planning unit; there was an implicit restriction in the permission that only automobile goods would be sold in the showroom; and accordingly the authority were entitled to serve an enforcement notice to end the unauthorised change of use: KWIK SAVE DISCOUNT GROUP *v.* SECRETARY OF STATE FOR WALES, *The Times,* June 29, 1978, D.C.

2869. Compulsory purchase. See COMPULSORY PURCHASE.

2870. Discontinuance order—meaning of " use of land "—scrap metal storage

[Town and Country Planning Act 1971 (c. 78), ss. 22 (1), 51 (1), 290 (1).]

" Use " of land comprises activities which are done in, alongside, or on the land but do not interfere with the actual physical characteristics of the land; " operations " comprise activities which result in some physical alteration to the land, which has some degree of permanence.

P stored and sorted scrap on the land in the Peak National Park, a well-known beauty spot, thereby creating an eyesore. The planning authority served a discontinuance order under s. 51 of the Town and Country Planning Act 1971. Ultimately, the Secretary of State confirmed the order. The judge, however, quashed it on the ground that the sorting of the scrap was an " operation " on the land under s. 290 (1) and therefore excluded from s. 51. On appeal, *held,* allowing the appeal, that the storing and sorting of scrap caused no physical alteration to the land, and was therefore a " use " within s. 51, rather than an " operation " within s. 290 (1).

PARKES v. SECRETARY OF STATE FOR THE ENVIRONMENT [1978] 1 W.L.R. 1308, C.A.

2871. Enforcement notice—builder's merchant's warehouse—meaning of " warehouse "

A " warehouse " means a place at which goods are stored; premises used primarily for the sale by retail of goods are not being used as a warehouse.

The appellants carried on the business of a " do-it-yourself supermarket " selling building supplies mainly by retail in premises for which planning permission had been granted for use as a " builders merchants' warehouse." An enforcement notice required them to cease user of the premises for the retailing of goods. The Secretary of State upheld the notice. *Held,* dismissing the appeal, that the use to which the premises was being put was clearly not that of a " warehouse " within the ordinary meaning of that word. (*LTSS Print and Supply Services* v. *Hackney London Borough Council* [1976] C.L.Y. 2691, applied.)

MONOMART (WAREHOUSES) v. SECRETARY OF STATE FOR THE ENVIRONMENT (1977) 34 P. & C.R. 305, D.C.

2872. —— material change of use—correct planning unit

A commenced repairs of cars and machinery in 1960. There were three buildings on the land he used. He moved from one to another, eventually using all three. An enforcement notice was served alleging material change of use. At the inquiry the council contended that there had been no significant industrial use of the land before December 31, 1963, and that there had been a change of use because the industrial use moved from one building to the other. The Secretary of State found that the correct planning unit was the whole site and that the use had been established in 1960. He quashed the enforcement notice and the council appealed. *Held,* the Secretary of State had reached the right decision on the evidence before him. No evidence of concurrent farming use had been adduced before the inspector and there had been no evidence of intensification of user by the industrial use taking over the whole site. (*Wipperman* v. *Barking London Borough Council* [1966] C.L.Y. 11832 applied): BROMSGROVE BOROUGH COUNCIL v. SECRETARY OF STATE FOR THE ENVIRONMENT [1977] J.P.L. 797, D.C.

2873. —— —— whether sufficient evidence for Secretary of State's decision

An enforcement notice alleged that a material change of use had taken place by selling in a farm shop agricultural produce not grown on the land. Evidence showed that since 1962, 20 per cent. of the produce was purchased for resale. The Secretary of State quashed the notice on the ground that the change took place before January 1, 1964. The Council applied for the decision to be quashed. *Held,* although the contribution from outside was small, it was sufficient to justify the Secretary of State in reaching his decision. (*Williams* v. *Minister of Housing and Local Government* [1967] C.L.Y. 3817 applied): BROMLEY LONDON BOROUGH v. GEORGE HAELTSCHI AND SON AND THE SECRETARY OF STATE FOR THE ENVIRONMENT [1978] J.P.L. 45, D.C.

2874. —— —— whether terms of notice overriding existing use rights

A single building which is part of a planning unit may be restricted even though there is no material change of use of the planning unit as a whole.

P acquired in 1969 a farm with a shop where produce from the holding, and from other sources, was sold. Planning permission was granted to erect a building for storage purposes, subject to the condition that it was to be used only for the storage of implements and produce of the farm. P then used the building for the wholesale distribution of fruit and vegetables not produced on the farm. An enforcement notice was served alleging material change of use, and requiring it to be discontinued. On appeal, the Secretary of State upheld the notice. On P's application for the notice to be quashed, he contended that so long as the activities on the planning unit as a whole did not amount to a material change of use, he could move those activities around the planning unit as he pleased. *Held*, dismissing the appeal, that the building had no use rights other than those conferred by the planning permission, and the enforcement notice was valid. (*Petticoat Lane Rentals* v. *Secretary of State for the Environment* [1971] C.L.Y. 11485; *Mansi* v. *Elstree Rural District Council* [1964] C.L.Y. 3580 distinguished.)

HILLIARD *v.* SECRETARY OF STATE FOR THE ENVIRONMENT (1977) 34 P. & C.R. 193, D.C.

:2875. —— non-compliance—whether continuing offence
[Town and Country Planning Act 1971 (c. 78), s. 89 (1) (6).]
Failing to take steps specified in an enforcement notice, contrary to the Town and Country Planning Act 1971, is not a continuing offence.

An enforcement notice was served on N, who did not comply with it, nor seek an extension of time for compliance. The local authority's prosecution of N for failing to comply with the directions contained in the notice was dismissed. *Held*, dismissing their appeal, that the offence alleged under s. 89 of the Town and Country Planning Act 1971 was not a continuing offence; time for complying with the notice could not be unilaterally extended by the authority without application by the land owner and that the local authority, having issued their summons out of time from the original offence, could not now succeed.

ST. ALBANS DISTRICT COUNCIL *v.* NORMAN HARPER AUTOSALES (1977) 76 L.G.R. 300, D.C.

:2876. —— storage of caravans not within " warehouse " use
[Town and Country Planning (Use Classes) Order 1972 (S.I. 1972 No. 1385).]
The respondent was charged with failing to comply with an enforcement notice requiring him to remove two caravans for which no planning consent had been given. The justices accepted his submission that the planning consent he had obtained—to use the land for warehousing and as a storage depot—covered the present storage of caravans. *Held*, allowing the appeal by case stated, the justices were wrong to accept that submission. The presence of caravans contravened the permitted use: HOOPER *v.* SLATER (1977) 245 E.G. 573, D.C.

:2877. —— to stop market use—validity—permanent use
[Town and Country Planning General Development Order 1973 (S.I. 1973 No. 31), art. 3 (1), Sched. 1, Class IV.2.]
For the purposes of the 14-day exemption in favour of markets under Class IV.2 of Sched. 1 to and art. 3 (1) of the Town and Country Planning General Development Order 1973, a distinction must be drawn between a general and temporary casual use which is permitted by the Order and the beginning of a permanent use, which is not.

P operated a Sunday market on a football ground. After he had done so on a total of nine Sundays, the local authority served an enforcement notice on him requiring discontinuance of such use. P appealed and the Secretary of State dismissed his appeal. P appealed, contending that the notice was premature, since he had not used the land for market purposes for a total of 14 days under Class IV.2 of Sched. 1 to the 1973 Order. *Held*, dismissing the appeal, that there had been ample evidence to show that the use was permanent, and not temporary, which was not covered by the General Development Order. (*Miller-Mead* v. *Minister of Housing and Local Government* [1963] C.L.Y. 3406 applied.)

TIDSWELL *v.* SECRETARY OF STATE FOR THE ENVIRONMENT (1976) 34 P. & C.R. 152, C.A.

:2878. Gypsy encampments
GIPSY ENCAMPMENTS (DESIGNATION OF THE COUNTY OF DORSET) ORDER 1978 (No. 1221) [10p], made under the Caravan Sites Act 1968 (c. 52), s. 12 (1); operative on September 21, 1978; designates the County of Dorset for the purposes of s. 10 of the 1968 Act, which prohibits the siting of caravans in certain areas for the purpose of residing for any period.

:2879. Industrial development certificates
TOWN AND COUNTRY PLANNING (SCOTLAND) (INDUSTRIAL DEVELOPMENT CERTIFICATES: EXEMPTION) ORDER 1978 (No. 327) [10p], made under the Town

and Country Planning (Scotland) Act 1972 (c. 52), ss. 67, 273; operative on April 1, 1978; amends s. 66 (1) of the 1972 Act by providing for an industrial development certificate if the floor space exceeds 15,000 square feet.

2880. Inner urban areas

INNER URBAN AREAS (DESIGNATED DISTRICTS) (ENGLAND AND WALES) ORDER 1978 (No. 1314) [10p], made under the Inner Urban Areas Act 1978 (c. 50), ss. 1 (1) and 15; operative on September 29, 1978; specifies designated district authorities for the purposes of the Act.

INNER URBAN AREAS (DESIGNATED DISTRICTS) (ENGLAND AND WALES) (No. 2) ORDER 1978 (No. 1486) [10p], made under the Inner Urban Areas Act 1978, ss. 1 (1), 15; operative on November 13, 1978; specifies the district of Wolverhampton as a designated district for the purposes of the 1978 Act.

2881. Inner Urban Areas Act 1978 (c. 50)

This Act makes provision as respects inner urban areas in Great Britain in which there exists special social need, and amends s. 8 of the Local Employment Act 1972.

S. 1 empowers the Secretary of State to designate districts for the purposes of the Act; s. 2 permits the making of loans by designated district authorities, to persons acquiring, or carrying out works on, land within the designated district; s. 3 deals with loans and grants for establishing common ownership and co-operative enterprises; s. 4 relates to the procedure for declaring areas to be, and for making changes in, industrial improvement areas; s. 5 specifies certain works for which designated district authorities may make grants or loans; s. 6 likewise permits the making of grants for converting or improving industrial or commercial buildings within an industrial improvement area; s. 7 enables the Secretary of State or Ministers to enter into arrangements with district councils that contain parts of inner urban areas, for the purpose of alleviating special social need; s. 8 defines " special areas " with designated districts; s. 9 empowers designated district authorities to make loans for site preparation work in special areas; s. 10 also permits the making of grants towards rents under leases of industrial or commercial buildings within special areas; s. 11 similarly permits grants towards loan interest; s. 12 makes certain provisions regarding the adoption of local plans; s. 13 confers power on designated district authorities to incur expenditure for certain purposes not otherwise authorised; s. 14 allows grants towards the acquisition of, or works on, derelict and other land in Greater London; s. 15 makes provision for secondary legislation under the Act; s. 16 deals with grants to national voluntary bodies; s. 17 is concerned with financial arrangements; s. 18 is the interpretation section; s. 19 gives the short title, and states that the Act does not extend to Northern Ireland.

The Act received the Royal Assent on July 31, 1978, and came into force on that date.

2882. Land compensation—depreciation of interest—conduct of hearing

[Land Compensation Act 1973 (c. 26), ss. 1, 16 (1).]

A member of the Lands Tribunal hearing a disputed claim for compensation exceeds his jurisdiction if he conducts his own experiments, in effect giving evidence to himself.

The appellant contended that alterations to a bend in the road opposite his house had caused increased noise and vibration from traffic and he claimed compensation under s. 1 of the 1973 Act. The member of the Lands Tribunal hearing the claim received evidence from both sides and in addition visited the site and conducted an experiment by himself driving along the road and round the bend. He concluded that the alterations had not increased noise and vibration. *Held,* dismissing his appeal, that although the member of the tribunal had exceeded his jurisdiction by conducting his own experiments (as opposed to simply visiting the site which was permissible) no miscarriage of justice had occurred, his conclusion being inevitable in view of the other, admissible, evidence before him.

HICKMOTT *v.* DORSET COUNTY COUNCIL (1977) 35 P. & C.R. 195, C.A.

2883. Listed building—application for demolition—Secretary of State rejecting findings of fact

[Town and Country Planning (Inquiries Procedure) Rules 1974 (S.I. 1974 No. 419), r. 12.] The college applied for consent to demolish a listed building. An inquiry was held and the inspector found that the defects were mostly superficial and easily remediable. The Secretary of State stated that the building if restored would be unlikely to be disposed of and he granted consent to demolition. The council applied to quash the decision, *Held*, the Secretary of State had wrongly not accepted the inspector's findings of fact. The Secretary's reason was unintelligible since there was no evidence as to whether the building could be disposed of if repaired. There had been a breach of the Inquiries Procedure Rules and the decision should be quashed: THANET DISTRICT COUNCIL *v.* SECRETARY OF STATE FOR THE ENVIRONMENT AND CORPUS CHRISTI COLLEGE, OXFORD [1978] J.P.L. 250, Sir Douglas Frank Q.C.

2884. —— church—whether permission needed for partial demolition. See *Re* ST. LUKE'S, CHEETHAM, § 844.

2885. London—local plans. See § 1893.

2886. Northern Ireland. See NORTHERN IRELAND.

2887. Planning permission—condition—personal permission to lapse after five years

The applicants started to use premises as an accountancy training school. An enforcement notice was served and an appeal against the notice and against refusal of planning permission was heard. The inspector recommended that a permission be granted, personal to the applicants for use of the premises as an accountancy training school. The Secretary of State added a condition that the permission was to lapse after five years. *Held*, the minister's reasons for imposing the time condition were not proper and adequate, and the condition must be quashed. (*Givandan* v. *Minister of Housing and Local Government* [1966] C.L.Y. 11724 applied): THE ACCOUNTANCY TUITION CENTRE *v.* SECRETARY OF STATE FOR THE ENVIRONMENT AND LONDON BOROUGH OF HACKNEY [1977] J.P.L. 792, Sir Douglas Frank Q.C.

2888. —— —— required for " temporary use "—whether valid

[Town and Country Planning Act 1971 (c. 78), ss. 29, 30.]

Planning permission, an application for which may properly be construed as relating to temporary use, may validly be subjected to a condition requiring removal of the buildings by a specified date.

Two large hangars were all that remained of a wartime airfield set in rural surroundings. In 1959 planning permission was given for their use for storing fertilisers and farm products on condition the hangars were removed by 1970. In 1962 the respondent company obtained permission to use the hangars for storing rubber products on condition that the buildings were removed by the end of 1972. Prior thereto, the respondent's application for a 30-year extension was rejected on the grounds that such uses conflicted with the development plan, enforcement notices were served after the respondents continued the use after 1972 but after an inquiry the Secretary of State (later upheld by the Divisional Court) held that the condition for removal was invalid as it was extraneous to the proposed user. *Held*, allowing the local authority's appeal, that inasmuch as the respondents were aware of the development plan and the policy of removing wartime buildings at the time of their application for planning permission, such application was to be regarded as for permission for temporary user and the condition for removal fairly and reasonably related thereto. (*Fawcett Properties* v. *Buckingham County Council* [1960] C.L.Y. 3110 and *Mixnam's Properties* v. *Chertsey Urban District Council* [1964] C.L.Y. 3556 considered.)

NEWBURY DISTRICT COUNCIL *v.* SECRETARY OF STATE FOR THE ENVIRONMENT [1978] 1 W.L.R. 1241, C.A.

2889. —— —— whether ultra vires

[Town and Country Planning Act 1971 (c. 78), s. 30 (1) (*a*).]

Where planning permission is sought for an extension to existing premises, conditions affecting operations in such existing premises may validly be imposed if the extension will materially affect the nature of operations therein.

Planning permission was sought for an extension to a factory which had been built pursuant to unconditional planning permission. The planning authority granted permission but subject to conditions, *inter alia*, regulating the hours during which machinery could be used in the existing factory and the levels of noise emanating therefrom. After an inquiry the Secretary of State concluded that such conditions were ultra vires inasmuch as they related to the existing premises. *Held*, quashing the Secretary of State's decision, that the conditions were valid since the purpose of the extension was to enable the existing factory to be used for longer hours, any increase in noise levels being at least partly due to the factory being used in conjunction with the extension. (Dicta of Lord Denning M.R. in *Pyx Granite Co.* v. *Ministry of Housing and Local Government* [1959] C.L.Y. 3260 and *Kingston-upon-Thames Royal London Borough Council* v. *Secretary of State for the Environment* [1974] C.L.Y. 3762 applied.)

PENWITH DISTRICT COUNCIL v. SECRETARY OF STATE FOR THE ENVIRONMENT (1977) 34 P. & C.R. 269, Sir Douglas Franks, Q.C.

2890. —— —— whether unreasonable—estoppel

Applicants for planning permission to extract sand and gravel offered to provide visibility splays for access on to the highway. This involved purchasing extra land. They also offered to make road improvements. No s. 52 agreement was concluded. The Secretary of State granted permission subject to a condition that ". . . splays be provided in accordance with a scheme to be agreed. . . ." Objectors applied for the decision to be quashed. *Held*, (1) the decision was not unreasonable; (2) the developer would be estopped from denying that the permission was conditional on their compliance with the undertaking: HILDENBOROUGH VILLAGE PRESERVATION ASSOCIATION v. SECRETARY OF STATE FOR THE ENVIRONMENT AND HALL AGGREGATES (SOUTH EAST) [1978] J.P.L. 708, Sir Douglas Frank, Q.C.

2891. —— development—demolition of existing building

The applicants demolished an existing building in a yard, intending to erect a new one. Planning permission was refused. An inquiry was held. The applicants applied to the High Court to quash the decision. *Held*, (1) the inspector had set out his reasons adequately and with sufficient clarity. He was entitled to look at the state of affairs after the development had been carried out. Demolition of an existing building gave no ground for granting planning permission for rebuilding: MAGOA SERVICES v. SECRETARY OF STATE FOR THE ENVIRONMENT AND BROMLEY LONDON BOROUGH [1978] J.P.L. 383, Sir Douglas Frank, Q.C.

2892. —— economic considerations

It is not a ground for refusing planning permission that the proposed development can be carried out only at a loss; it is for the developer, not the authority, to make the economic decision whether to carry out the development. (*Murphy (J.) & Sons* v. *Secretary of State for the Environment* [1973] C.L.Y. 3256 applied): WALTERS v. SECRETARY OF STATE FOR WALES, *The Times*, November 8, 1978, Sir Douglas Frank Q.C.

2893. —— further application—whether valid

A further application for approval of modified proposals is within the ambit of the original outline planning permission. There is nothing in the relevant planning legislation which prohibits the holder of outline permission from applying for more than one approval of reserved matters covering the same ground.

On September 5, 1973, outline planning permission was granted to the plaintiff developers by the local planning authority for a large scale comprehensive development of an eight acre site in the city centre. This provided for demolition of all existing buildings including one house in particular brought in to accommodate the planning authority's own proposed road construction plans. The permission related to the whole development in principle only, and detailed plans of each particular phase were to be approved by the authority. Further, the gross floor space of the development for all users was not to exceed 1,000,000 sq. ft. Plans of the particularised first phase were submitted in

December 1973 and approved in February 1974 conditional in that this approval was part only of an agreed overall phasing construction programme for the whole site. In April and June 1974, the particular house was listed under s. 54 of the Town and Country Planning Act 1971, of special architectural or historic interest. Its demolition therefore became an offence and so modified plans were submitted which while preserving the house meant an unavoidable increase in the overall floor space of the development. Permission was refused by the planning authority, but the High Court declared it a valid application. *Held*, dismissing the planning authority's appeal, that (1) the modified plans constituted a valid application of matters reserved for approval by the original outline planning permission. The application need not cover all the reserved matters outstanding; approval may be sought in stages; (2) it would be wholly unreasonable if the listing of a building could frustrate the original scheme of the development. The increase in floor space was a direct result of the retention of the listed building and was not outside the ambit of the original permission.

HERON CORP. *v.* MANCHESTER CITY COUNCIL [1978] 1 W.L.R. 937, C.A.

2894. —— Green Belt policy—two houses on site of one existing

On premises where there was an existing house, the applicant applied for planning permission to build a pair of semi-detached houses. The authority granted permission for one house, and the inspector refused the applicant's appeal. Application was made to the High Court to quash the decision. *Held*, the decision was valid. The inspector had applied the Green Belt policy. The authority was not obliged to grant any permission at all: GRAINGER *v.* SECRETARY OF STATE FOR THE ENVIRONMENT [1978] J.P.L. 631, Sir Douglas Frank, Q.C.

2895. —— gypsies—formal consultations

[Caravan Sites Act 1968 (c. 52), s. 6 (1).] In accordance with their statutory duty to provide adequate accommodation for gypsies residing in their area, the council in 1976 granted itself planning permission to develop a site. The applicant sought an order for certiorari on the ground that the council had failed to have regard to the wishes of the gypsy community. *Held*, no formal consultation took place but there had been sufficient interchange of views over a long period. There was no obligation to have organised consultations: R. *v.* SHEFFIELD CITY COUNCIL, *ex p.* MANSFIELD [1978] J.P.L. 465, D.C.

2896. —— inquiry—natural justice—inquiry procedure

On application for planning permission to build a house in the curtilage of an existing house, the inspector took into account the architectural quality of the existing house, but declined to hear expert evidence on the matter. Planning permission was granted and the council applied to the High Court for the decision to be set aside. *Held*, refusing the order, that the inspector was entitled to take into account what he saw on his own view, without reconvening the inquiry, if, as here, what he saw served simply to underline some point which was varied at the inquiry. The refusal to allow expert evidence as to architectural merit did not amount to a breach of the rules of natural justice because the inspector was entitled to decide that he could judge for himself: WINCHESTER CITY COUNCIL *v.* SECRETARY OF STATE FOR THE ENVIRONMENT AND ECCLES [1978] J.P.L. 467, Forbes J.

2897. —— reference of application to Secretary of State—failure to notify applicant

[Town and Country Planning Act 1971 (c. 78), s. 245; Town and Country Planning General Development Order 1973 (S.I. 1973 No. 31), art. 15; Town and Country Planning (Inquiries Procedure) Rules 1969 (S.I. 1969 No. 1092), r. 6 (1).]

Failure to serve in due time an applicant for planning permission with notice of the Secretary of State's direction referring the application to him for decision, is not a ground for quashing a subsequent refusal of permission where the applicant does eventually receive notice of the inquiry to be held, and is not substantially prejudiced in being prevented from fully putting his case.

The applicant sought planning permission to extend his existing caravan site. Negotiations with officials of the local planning authority resulted in the applicant being led to believe that permission would not be refused. In March 1973, the Secretary of State directed that the application be called-in for decision by him, but the local authority failed to serve such direction upon the applicant, in breach of art. 15 of the 1973 Order; nor did it serve a statement under r. 6 (1) of the 1969 Rules. In July 1973 a committee of the planning authority purported to give permission for the development. The applicant incurred considerable expense in improving and preparing the new site, while remaining ignorant of the direction until service of notice of the date of an inquiry in February 1974. At the inquiry in October 1974, the applicant gave evidence in support of his application. Upon permission ultimately being refused, the applicant applied to quash the decision under s. 245 of the Act, by reason of the failure of the planning authority to serve the requisite notices. *Held*, dismissing the application, that (1) failure to comply with art. 15 was not a ground for an application under s. 245; (2) in any event, the applicant was not substantially prejudiced since he did finally receive adequate notice of the hearing and was able to present his case thereat.

DAVIES *v.* SECRETARY OF STATE FOR WALES (1977) 33 P. & C.R. 330, Sir Douglas Franks, Q.C.

2898. —— refusal—propriety of minister's decision

The applicants sought planning permission to build a supermarket. An inquiry was held and the inspector recommended that outline planning permission be granted. The Secretary of State refused to grant the permission. The applicant applied for the decision to be quashed. *Held*, the Secretary had made his decision in the light of the inspector's findings of facts and only disagreed with his conclusion; (2) the Secretary had not taken improper matters into consideration; (3) he had made it clear why he had differed from the inspector; (4) no break of natural justice had occurred: J. SAINSBURY *v.* SECRETARY OF STATE FOR THE ENVIRONMENT AND COLCHESTER BOROUGH COUNCIL [1978] J.P.L. 379, Graham Eyre, Q.C.

2899. —— —— structure plan—natural justice—policy

The Secretary of State allowed an appeal in respect of an application to build 14 houses, subject to the condition that an access road to a larger adjacent site be provided if necessary. An appeal in respect of a larger site was rejected on account of prematurity and inadequacy of services. Two years later, two applications were rejected. DFP applied for an order to quash the decisions on the grounds that the decision was obscurely expressed, that the Secretary of State had not considered the relevant matter, and that a breach of natural justice had occurred. *Held*, the structure plan provided that future growth was to be discouraged except on a limited scale in certain circumstances. There was no definable local need for housing. The problems leading to the refusal of planning permission in 1973 had been resolved, but there were now decisive policy objections. There was no reason for the Minister to explain his change of policy. The structure plan was properly formulated. The inspector's decision was amply clear. The decision must stand: D.F.P. (MIDLANDS) *v.* SECRETARY OF STATE FOR THE ENVIRONMENT [1978] J.P.L. 319, Bristow J.

2900. —— refusal to supply documents—documents supplied at hearing—adjournment refused—breach of natural justice

[Town & Country Planning Act 1971 (c. 78), s. 245; Town and Country Planning (Inquiries Procedure) Rules 1974 (S.I. 1974 No. 419), rr. 6 (4) and 10 (5).]

When a planning authority refuses, prior to a planning inquiry to supply documents requested by the applicant and no adequate opportunity is given to the applicant to consider the same, a decision based upon the inspector's report may be quashed for breach of the rules of natural justice.

The applicant company appealed against a planning authority's refusal of planning permission. Prior to the inquiry the company requested to be supplied with copies of documents relating, inter alia, to the authority having canvassed opposition to its proposals from local residents. Such copies were not supplied until the day of the inquiry, whereupon the inspector refused an application for an adjournment to allow the documents to be studied, permitting the applicant's director and representatives only an extended luncheon break in which to peruse them. The Secretary of State dismissed the applicant's appeal in reliance upon the inspector's report. The applicant sought unsuccessfully to have such decision quashed. *Held,* allowing the applicants' appeal, that the authority's failure to supply the documents breached r. 6 (4) of the 1974 Rules and that the inspector had failed to allow the applicant an adequate opportunity to consider the documents as required by r. 10 (5) thereof; and that accordingly, although the outcome may not have been different had full opportunity been given to study the documents, natural justice demanded the quashing of the decision. (*Hibernian Property Co.* v. *Secretary of State for the Environment* [1974] C.L.Y. 379, approved.)

PERFORMANCE CARS v. SECRETARY OF STATE FOR THE ENVIRONMENT (1977) 34 P. & C.R. 92, C.A.

2901. —— representations by council—existing use rights—estoppel

[Town and Country Planning Act 1971 (c. 78), ss. 53, 94.] The plaintiffs bought a site and buildings of a disused factory intending to demolish and build for a fish meal and fish oil factory. They informed the council. The council later refused planning permission. Enforcement notices were served. The company sought a declaration that the council was estopped from denying that planning permission was unnecessary. *Held,* (1) on the facts, there was no relevant representation as to existing use rights, and if there were it was not acted upon; (2) the defendant council could not be estopped from performing their duty; (3) estoppel in development control can only apply to a s. 53 application, and not to applications for planning permission: WESTERN FISH PRODUCTS v. PENWITH DISTRICT COUNCIL AND THE SECRETARY OF STATE FOR THE ENVIRONMENT [1978] J.P.L. 627, C.A.

2902. —— residential area—adaptation of office premises—economic considerations

The cost of conversion is a material consideration in determining whether office premises can reasonably be adapted for residential use.

The local planning authority for Mayfair, pursuant to their declared policy of refusing business user permission where premises could " reasonably be . . . adapted for use for residential occupation," refused to extend temporary planning permission for business user of premises occupied as offices by the applicants. At an inquiry, the inspector found that it was not currently economically viable to convert the premises into flats and recommended an extension of business user permission. The Secretary of State refused to accept the recommendation on the grounds that the cost of conversion did not warrant an exception to the declared policy. *Held,* quashing the decision, that the economic viability was a material consideration in deciding whether conversion could reasonably be made, and that if he had considered the same, the Secretary of State could only reasonably have concluded that conversion could not reasonably be achieved. (*Sovmots Investments* v. *Secretary of State for the Environment* [1977] C.L.Y. 333; *Hambledon and Chiddingfold Parish Councils* v. *Secretary of State for the Environment* [1976] C.L.Y. 2676 considered.)

NIARCHOS (LONDON) v. SECRETARY OF STATE FOR THE ENVIRONMENT (1978) 76 L.G.R. 480, Sir Douglas Frank Q.C.

2903. —— Secretary of State's decision—power to amend ambiguity—failure to give reasons

[Town and Country Planning Act 1971 (c. 78), s. 245.] The Secretary of State decided to allow an appeal against an enforcement notice, and to grant planning permission. In his decision letter, it was stated that " planning permission with conditions will therefore be granted for the retail trading. . . ." In another part of the decision, there was no reference to conditions. The Secretary of State affirmed that the inclusion of the words was an error. The council applied to quash the decision. *Held,* the decision letter did not deal with the essential question of why retail trading should be allowed in unlimited terms. This constituted a failure to give reasons relating to an important matter. Decision quashed: PRESTON BOROUGH COUNCIL v. SECRETARY OF STATE FOR THE ENVIRONMENT AND E.L.S. WHOLESALE (WOLVERHAMPTON) [1978] J.P.L. 548, Slynn J.

2904. —— **statutory undertaker—existing rights**
[Town and Country Planning Act 1971 (c. 78), ss. 222, 245; Town and Country Planning General Development Order 1973 (S.I. 1973 No. 31), art. 3 (1), Sched. 1, Class XVIII.C.]
On an application for planning permission by a statutory undertaker, existing planning rights are capable of being a material consideration and should not be ignored by the Secretary of State.
The North Surrey Water Board applied for planning permission to build storage buildings, garages and offices. The application was refused, as being in conflict with the green belt policy. The Water Board appealed to the Secretary of State. An inquiry was held. The Water Board claimed that they enjoyed wide permitted development rights as statutory undertakers under Class XVIII.C of Sched. 1 to the Town and Country Planning General Development Order 1973. The inspector concluded that if the site was not operational land, the appeal would undoubtedly be dismissed on its planning merits; but if it was operational land of a statutory undertaker, then the appeal should be allowed. The Secretary of State took the view that the decision should rest merely on the merits, and not on the question of present planning rights, and the appeal was dismissed. The Water Board appealed against that decision, arguing also that the inspector had failed to record certain arguments and authorities in his report. *Held*, (1) the inspector was not bound to record legal submissions except where necessary to make the case presented intelligible to the Secretary of State; but (2) existing planning rights were capable of being a material consideration. The Secretary of State had therefore misdirected himself, and his decision must be quashed. (*A.B. Motor Co. of Hull* v. *Minister of Housing and Local Government* [1969] C.L.Y. 442 and *Wells* v. *Minister of Housing and Local Government* [1967] C.L.Y. 3843 referred to.)
NORTH SURREY WATER CO. *v.* SECRETARY OF STATE FOR THE ENVIRONMENT (1976) 34 P. & C.R. 140, Slynn J.

2905. —— **" within curtilage of a dwelling-house "—stone-cladding on walls**
[Town and Country Planning General Development Order 1977 (S.I. No. 289, Sched. 1, art. 3.]
Planning permission is not required where it is sought to add stone-cladding to the walls of a dwelling-house, provided that such cladding will not project beyond the front building-line of the house, such building-line being ascertained by reference to the window-sills and any moulding surrounds which may be attached to the brickwork.
Two householders wished to face their houses with stone-cladding but planning permission was refused. Ultimately, the Secretary of State ruled that permission was not required since the cladding would not project beyond the sills and window surrounds which projected three inches from the brickwork, such sills being part of the " wall " of the house within the meaning of class 1 (*c*) set out in Sched. 1 to the order. *Held*, dismissing the council's appeal, that it was permissible for the Secretary of State so to construe the wording of class 1 (*c*); that nothing in classes 1 and 2 in the Schedule required that planning permission be obtained for the present proposals. (*LTSS Print and Supply Services* v. *Hackney London Borough Council* [1976] C.L.Y. 2691 applied.)
BRADFORD METROPOLITAN DISTRICT COUNCIL *v.* SECRETARY OF STATE FOR THE ENVIRONMENT (1978) 76 L.G.R. 454, Griffiths J.

2906. Public inquiry—inspector's report deficient—admissibility of further evidence before court
[Town and Country Planning (Inquiries Procedure) Rules (S.I. 1974 No. 419).] A applied for planning permission which was refused on the ground, inter alia, that the development would be contrary to the provisions of the council planning policy, and that there was enough land released for housing. An inquiry was held, and the Secretary of State accepted the inspector's recommendation and granted planning permission. The inspector had wrongly reported that an increase of 12,000 in the population necessitated further development land, but did not report that the increase was anticipated because of the taking up of already existing planning permissions and commitments.

The local authority applied for the decision to be quashed on the ground that the Inquiries Procedure Rules 1974 had not been complied with. *Held,* affidavit evidence of what took place at the inquiry was admissible (1) to show that a particular matter of real importance had been left out of the inspector's report, so that the Secretary of State was unaware of it; or (2) to show that a matter of importance had been completely misunderstood. In this case, the Inquiries Procedure Rules 1974, r. 12, had not been complied with, and the decision should be quashed: EAST HAMPSHIRE DISTRICT COUNCIL *v.* SECRETARY OF STATE FOR THE ENVIRONMENT [1978] J.P.L. 182, Slynn J.

2907. Structure and local plans

TOWN AND COUNTRY PLANNING (REPEAL OF PROVISIONS NO. 13) (WEST MIDLANDS (PART)) ORDER 1978 (No. 724) [20p], made under the Town and Country Planning Act 1971 (c. 78), ss. 21 (2), 287; operative on June 28, 1978; repeals for the area covered by a structure plan approved for specified parts of the West Midlands the provisions of the 1971 Act relating to development plans which are contained in Scheds. 5, Pt. 1, 5 to that Act.

TOWN AND COUNTRY PLANNING (REPEAL OF PROVISIONS NO. 12) (EAST SUSSEX) ORDER 1978 (No. 726) [10p], made under the Town and Country Planning Act 1971, ss. 21 (2), 287; operative on June 28, 1978; repeals for the area covered by a structure plan that has been approved for the County of East Sussex the provisions of the Town and Country Planning Act 1971 relating to development plans which are contained in Scheds. 5, Pt. I, and 6 to that Act.

2908. Town and Country Planning Act 1971—commencement

TOWN AND COUNTRY PLANNING ACT 1971 (COMMENCEMENT NO. 39) (STAFFORD-SHIRE) ORDER 1978 (No. 557 (C. 13)) [15p], made under the Town and Country Planning Act 1971 (c. 78), ss. 21, 287; brings into operation on May 23, 1978, for the specified parts of Staffordshire, s. 20 of, and Sched. 23, Pt. I to the 1971 Act.

TOWN AND COUNTRY PLANNING ACT 1971 (COMMENCEMENT NO. 41) (WEST MIDLANDS (PART)) ORDER 1978 (No. 725 (C. 17)) [20p], made under the Town and Country Planning Act 1971, ss. 21, 287; operative on June 28, 1978; brings into force for specified parts of the County of West Midlands s. 20 and Sched. 23, Pt. I of the 1971 Act.

TOWN AND COUNTRY PLANNING ACT 1971 (COMMENCEMENT NO. 40) (EAST SUSSEX) ORDER 1978 (No. 727 (C. 18)) [10p], made under the Town and Country Planning Act 1971, ss. 21, 287; operative on June 29, 1978; brings into force s. 20 and Sched. 23, Pt. I in relation to East Sussex.

2909. —— repeals

TOWN AND COUNTRY PLANNING (REPEAL OF PROVISIONS NO. 11) (STAFFORD-SHIRE) ORDER 1978 (No. 556) [15p], made under the Town and Country Planning Act 1971 (c. 78), ss. 21 (2), 287; operative on May 23, 1978; repeals for scheduled areas the 1971 Act provisions relating to development plans which are contained in Sched. 5 and 6 to that Act.

2910. Tree preservation—breach—locus standi of local authority

[Local Government Act 1972 (c. 70), s. 222.]

A local authority may bring proceedings under s. 222 of the Local Government Act in its own name if seeking to promote or protect the interests of local inhabitants.

The local authority obtained an injunction restraining the defendant from damaging trees on his land, such trees being subject to preservation orders. Subsequent committal proceedings for alleged breach of the injunction were dismissed by the Court of Appeal for want of evidence of the breach. The local authority subsequently commenced further committal proceedings for further alleged breaches. The defendant applied to discharge the injunction and for adjournment of the committal proceedings on the grounds, inter alia, that the authority was not entitled to sue in its own name. *Held,* refusing the application, that (1) in view of the Court of Appeal having previously accepted jurisdiction, the court was bound to accept jurisdiction; (2) under s. 222 of the Act the local authority could bring such proceedings in its own name since its purpose was to protect the interests of local inhabitants. (*Solihull Metropolitan Borough Council* v. *Maxfern* [1976] C.L.Y. 1646 and *Stafford Borough Council* v. *Elkenford* [1977] C.L.Y. 2874 applied.)

KENT COUNTY COUNCIL v. BATCHELOR (No. 2) (1978) 76 L.G.R. 714, Talbot J.

2911. **Vendor and purchaser.** See VENDOR AND PURCHASER.

2912. **Windscale and Calder Works**

TOWN AND COUNTRY PLANNING (WINDSCALE AND CALDER WORKS) SPECIAL DEVELOPMENT ORDER 1978 (No. 523) [15p], made under the Town and Country Planning Act 1971 (c. 78), ss. 24, 287; operative on May 15, 1978; grants planning permission, subject to conditions, for the erection of a plant for the reprocessing of spent uranium oxide nuclear fuels at Windscale.

BOOKS AND ARTICLES. See *post*, pp. [7], [37].

TRADE AND INDUSTRY

2913. **Building industry.** See BUILDING AND ENGINEERING.

2914. **Coal industry.** See MINING LAW.

2915. **Consumer protection**

CONSUMER TRANSACTIONS (RESTRICTIONS ON STATEMENTS) (AMENDMENT) ORDER 1978 (No. 127) [10p], made under the Fair Trading Act 1973 (c. 41), ss. 22, 134 (2); operative on February 1, 1978; amends S.I. 1976 No. 1813 consequentially on the repeal by the Unfair Contract Terms Act 1977 (c. 50) and the re-enactment, in ss. 6 and 20 of that Act, of certain provisions of the Sale of Goods Act 1893 and the Supply of Goods (Implied Terms) Act 1973.

BABIES' DUMMIES (SAFETY) REGULATIONS 1978 (No. 836) [20p], made under the Consumer Protection Act 1961 (c. 40), ss. 1 (5), 2 (4), Sched., para. 3; operative on October 1, 1978, save for Reg. 4 (3) which is operative on January 1, 1980; impose requirements in relation to the safety of babies' dummies.

COSMETIC PRODUCTS REGULATIONS 1978 (No. 1354) [£1·00], made under the Consumer Protection Act 1961, s. 1 (5); operative on October 15, 1978, save for Regs. 4, 5 which are operative in specific circumstances on either January 1, 1979, or July 29, 1979; implement Council Directive No. 76/768/EEC relating to cosmetic products.

PERAMBULATORS AND PUSHCHAIRS (SAFETY) REGULATIONS 1978 (No. 1372) [20p], made under the Consumer Protection Act 1961, ss. 1 (5), 2 (4), Sched., para. 3; operative in part on January 1, 1979, and otherwise operative on July 1, 1979; impose requirements relating to the safety of perambulators and pushchairs.

2916. —— **safety of goods—liability of manufacturer—all reasonable precautions taken**

L.F. Co. bought toys from French manufacturers and supplied them to a shop who sold them on. The toys contravened the Toys (Safety) Regulations 1974 as the lead content of the paint thereon was too high. L.F. Co.'s practice was to place all orders subject to a condition that the goods complied with current regulations and the local trading standards department was invited to take samples for analysis at any time. Written undertakings from foreign manufacturers were obtained. *Held*, allowing an appeal against an acquittal on the ground that L.F. Co. had taken all reasonable precautions to avoid commission of an offence under the Consumer Protection Act 1961, that there were very few cases where a certificate alone sufficed when a company could have had a sample analysed: TAYLOR v. LAWRENCE FRASER (BRISTOL) [1978] Crim.L.R. 43, D.C.

2917. **Consumer Safety Act 1978 (c. 38)**

This Act makes further provision with respect to the safety of consumers.

S. 1 empowers the Secretary of State to make safety regulations in respect of goods; s. 2 deals with offences against the safety regulations; s. 3 authorises the Secretary of State to make orders or serve notices prohibiting the supply of goods or giving warning of danger from goods; s. 4 empowers the Secretary of State to obtain information, and makes it an offence to fail to comply with a notice requesting information; s. 5 relates to the enforcement of safety regulations; s. 6 sets out the civil liability of a person on whom obligations are imposed by safety regulations; s. 7 contains supplementary provisions; s. 8 provides for the payment of expenses, and stipulates that the Secretary of State shall lay a report before Parliament at least once every five years, on the exercise of his functions under this Act; s. 9 contains definitions; deals with repeals and transitional provisions; s. 10 sets out the application of this Act to Northern Ireland; s. 11 gives the short title.

The Act received the Royal Assent on July 20, 1978, and shall come into force on such day or days as the Secretary of State shall appoint. Ss. 1–9, 10 (part), and Scheds. 1 and 2 came into force on November 1, 1978.

2918. —— commencement

CONSUMER SAFETY ACT 1978 (COMMENCEMENT No. 1) ORDER 1978 (No. 1445 (C. 40)) [10p], made under the Consumer Safety Act 1978 (c. 38), s. 12 (2); operative on November 1, 1978; brings into force all the provisions of the 1978 Act save for s. 10 (1) and Sched. 3.

2919. Co-operative Development Agency Act 1978 (c. 21)

This Act gives effect to the report of the Working Group on a Co-operative Development Agency (Cmnd. 6972).

S. 1 establishes a body corporate to be known as the Co-operative Development Agency, and provides for the appointment of a chairman and members; s. 2 sets out the functions of the Agency, namely to promote the principles and represent the interests of the co-operative movement; s. 3 sets out the powers of the Agency; s. 4 provides that the Secretary of State may make grants to the Agency not exceeding £900,000; s. 5 relates to the keeping of accounts and the auditing of such accounts; s. 6 stipulates that the Agency must make an annual report of its operations to the Secretary of State; s. 7 contains financial provisions; s. 8 gives the short title. The Act extends to Northern Ireland.

The Act received the Royal Assent on June 30, 1978, and came into force on that date.

2920. Counter-inflation. See REVENUE AND FINANCE.

2921. Development of inventions

DEVELOPMENT OF INVENTIONS (INCREASE OF LIMITS) ORDER 1978 (No. 382) [10p], made under the Development of Inventions Act 1967 (c. 32), s. 4 (2); operative on April 24, 1978; raises from £20,000 to £250,000 the aggregate amount of assistance which the National Research Development Corporation may, without the approval of the Secretary of State, give to any person in any year, under s. 4 (2) of the 1967 Act.

2922. Employment. See EMPLOYMENT.

2923. Export guarantees

EXPORT GUARANTEES (EXTENSION OF PERIOD) (No. 2) ORDER 1978 (No. 322) [10p]; made under the Export Guarantees Act 1975 (c. 38), s. 5 (4); operative on March 4, 1978; extends the export guarantee period by a further year from March 26, 1978.

2924. Export Guarantees and Overseas Investment Act 1978 (c. 18)

This Act consolidates the Export Guarantees Act 1975, and ss. 1 and 2 of the Overseas Investment and Export Guarantees Act 1972.

S. 1 empowers the Secretary of State to give guarantees in connection with the export, manufacture, treatment or distribution of goods to persons carrying on business in the U.K.; s. 2 enables the Secretary of State to give such guarantees as are expedient in the national interest; s. 3 relates to loans and interest grants which the Secretary of State may make; s. 4 empowers the Secretary of State to acquire any securities which he has guaranteed under this Act; s. 5 deals with payments to exporters in respect of cost increases; s. 6 sets limits on the commitments of the Secretary of State under this Act; s. 7 deals with the application of the limits on commitments to foreign currency transactions; s. 8 sets out the circumstances in which the limit in s. 6 (2) may be exceeded; s. 9 obliges the Secretary of State to publish quarterly returns relating to guarantees under this Act; s. 10 relates to contracts entered into under this Act with a controlled company; s. 11 empowers the Secretary of State to make arrangements for meeting non-commercial risks; s. 12 relates to the functions of the Export Credits Guarantee Department and the Export Guarantees Advisory Council; s. 13 states that an order made under this Act must first be laid in draft before the House of Commons and approved by a resolution; s. 14 deals with expenses and receipts; s. 15 contains definitions; s. 16 gives the short title, and contains repeals and revocations. The Act extends to Northern Ireland.

The Act received the Royal Assent on June 30, 1978, and came into force on July 30, 1978.

2925. Fair trading—Director General—investigation

[Fair Trading Act 1973 (c. 41).] The Director General of Fair Trading applied for an order directing the defendants to restrain from continuing the course of conduct which led to their being convicted, under the Food and Drugs Act 1955, of 46 offences between 1973 and 1976 of having alien matters in their bread. The court accepted undertakings from the director of the defendant company that they would take all reasonable precautions and exercise all diligence in the future : DIRECTOR GENERAL OF FAIR TRADING *v.* SMITHS BAKERIES (WESTFIELD), *The Times,* May 12, 1978, Restrictive Practices Court.

2926. False trade description. See SALE OF GOODS.

2927. Financial assistance

FINANCIAL ASSISTANCE FOR INDUSTRY (INCREASE OF LIMIT) ORDER 1978 (No. 812) [10p], made under the Industry Act 1972 (c. 63), s. 8 (7) as amended by the Industry (Amendment) Act 1976 (c. 73), s. 1; operative on June 3, 1978; increases the aggregate limit of guarantees and loans to £1,100 million.

2928. Hallmarks

SHEFFIELD ASSAY OFFICE ORDER 1978 (No. 639) [40p], made under the Hallmarking Act 1973 (c. 43), s. 16 (1) (*c*) (3), Sched. 6, para. 6; operative on April 20, 1978; confers powers upon and varies existing statutory provisions relating to the Guardians of the Standard of Wrought Plate within the Town of Sheffield.

2929. Industrial assurance

INDUSTRIAL ASSURANCE (LIFE ASSURANCE PREMIUM RELIEF) (AMENDMENT) REGULATIONS 1978 (No. 1161) [10p], made under the Finance Act 1976 (c. 40), Sched. 4, para. 13; operative on September 4, 1978; amend S.I. 1977 No. 1144 so that where an industrial assurance company adopts the prescribed scheme, the scheme will only apply to premium payments due and payable after April 5, 1979.

2930. Industrial democracy

The Government has issued a White Paper on industrial democracy, which discusses, inter alia, company strategy and board level representation. The paper is available from HMSO. Cmnd. 7231. [50p.]

2931. Industrial development

SPECIAL DEVELOPMENT AREAS ORDER 1978 (No. 1141) [20p], made under the Industry Act 1972 (c. 63), s. 1 (4); operative on August 24, 1978; designates the specified areas as special development areas for the purposes of s. 1 of the 1972 Act.

2932. —— road scheme—grants. See § 973.

2933. Industrial relations. See EMPLOYMENT; TRADE UNIONS.

2934. Industrial training

INDUSTRIAL TRAINING (TRANSFER OF THE ACTIVITIES OF ESTABLISHMENTS) ORDER 1978 (No. 448) [25p], made under the Industrial Training Act 1964 (c. 16), s. 9A (2) as inserted by the Employment and Training Act 1973 (c. 50), s. 6, Sched. 2, Pt. I, para. 13; operative on April 24, 1978; transfers the activities of specified industrial training boards to other industrial training boards.

INDUSTRIAL TRAINING (TRANSFER OF THE ACTIVITIES OF ESTABLISHMENTS) (No. 2) ORDER 1978 (No. 1225) [25p], made under the Industrial Training Act 1964, s. 9A (2), as inserted by the Employment and Training Act 1973 (c. 50), s. 6, Sched. 2, Pt. I, para. 13; operative on October 1, 1978; except for art. 3 which is operative on September 25; transfers the activities of specified industrial training boards.

INDUSTRIAL TRAINING (TRANSFER OF THE ACTIVITIES OF ESTABLISHMENTS) (No. 3) ORDER 1978 (No. 1643) [20p], made under the Industrial Training Act 1964, s. 9A (2), as inserted by the Employment and Training Act 1973, s. 6, Sched. 2, para. 13, Pt. I; operative on December 12, 1978; transfers the activities of the establishments specified in the Schedule from the industry of the industrial training board established by the industrial training order as specified to the industry of the board established by the order as further specified.

S.I. 1978 Nos. 57 (levy—petroleum) [25p]; 233 (levy—iron and steel) [25p]; 242 (levy—knitting, lace and net) [25p]; 362 (levy—air transport and travel) [25p]; 363 (levy—distributive industry) [25p]; 432 (levy—clothing and allied products) [25p]; 546 (levy—footwear, leather and fur skin) [25p]; 547 (levy—hotel and catering) [25p]; 612 (levy—engineering) [25p]; 613 (levy—paper and paper products) [25p]; 675 (levy—food, drink and tobacco) [20p]; 688 (levy—shipbuilding) [20p]; 759 (levy—printing and publishing) [20p]; 773 (levy—chemical and allied products) [25p]; 841 (levy—furniture and timber) [25p]; 940 (levy—road transport) [25p]; 1021 (levy—cotton and allied textiles [25p]; 1132 (levy—ceramic, glass and mineral products [30p]; 1305 (levy—wool, jute and flax) [25p]; 1471 (levy—construction board) [30p]; 1547 (levy—rubber and plastic processing) [25p]; 1830 (levy—carpet) [25p].

2935. Investment

INVESTMENT GRANTS TERMINATION (No. 8) ORDER 1978 (No. 73) [10p], made under the Investment and Building Grants Act 1971 (c. 51), s. 1 (6); operative on February 20, 1978; specifies certain dates by which applications for investment grant in respect of expenditure incurred before a related date or period must be made; also makes provision for the form of application.

2935a. Iron and Steel (Amendment) Act 1978 (c. 41)

This Act increases the limit on the sums borrowed by, or paid by the Secretary of State to, the British Steel Corporation.

S. 1 amends s. 19 of the Iron and Steel Act 1975 so as to increase the borrowing powers of the British Steel Corporation; s. 2 gives the short title.

The Act received the Royal Assent on July 20, 1978, and came into force on that date.

2936. National Enterprise Board

NATIONAL ENTERPRISE BOARD (FINANCIAL LIMIT) ORDER 1978 (No. 580) [10p], made under the Industry Act 1975 (c. 68), ss. 8 (2) (3), 38 (1); operative on April 15, 1978; specifies the maximum limit under s. 8 (2) of the 1975 Act as £1,000 million.

2937. —— breach of statutory duty—whether actionable at suit of private individuals

[Industry Act 1975 (c. 68), s. 7; National Enterprise Board (Guideline) Directions 1976 (Cmnd. 5710).]

Since no specific remedy for breach of statutory duty by the National Enterprise Board is provided by statute, private individuals may sue in respect thereof, provided that they can show that the alleged breach occasioned them some peculiar injury additional to that suffered by the public.

The plaintiff tanners sought a declaration that the National Enterprise Board was acting in breach of its statutory duties in providing financial assistance to a minority tanning company, it being contended that the Board was in breach of its obligations as to investments as laid down in the 1976 Directions and further that by its actions it was showing undue preference to the minority interest to the prejudice of the plaintiffs' business. The Board sought to strike out the action on the grounds, inter alia, that the plaintiffs had no locus standi under the 1975 Act to prosecute the same. *Held*, dismissing the application, that the plaintiffs had an arguable case that the Board had acted in breach of statutory duties and that by virtue thereof the plaintiffs had suffered some peculiar injury to their business and that no great commercial inconvenience would be occasioned by the action proceeding. (Dicta of Cozens-Hardy M.R. in *Dyson* v. *Att.-Gen.* [1911] 1 K.B. 410 applied; *Phillips* v. *Britannia Hygienic Laundry* [1923] 2 K.B. 832 and *Cutler* v. *Wandsworth Stadium* (1949) C.L.C. 4241 considered.)

BOOTH & CO. (INTERNATIONAL) v. NATIONAL ENTERPRISE BOARD [1978] 3 All E.R. 624, Forbes J.

2938. Northern Ireland. See NORTHERN IRELAND.

2939. Participation Agreements Act 1978 (c. 1)
This Act excludes the application of the Restrictive Trade Practices Act 1976 in relation to certain agreements.

S. 1 retrospectively exempts from registration under the Restrictive Trade Practices Acts 1976 and 1956, agreements which are certified by the Secretary of State to be participation agreements, as defined, and which provide for majority state participation in United Kingdom offshore petroleum; s. 2 contains the short title.

The Act received the Royal Assent on February 23, 1978, and came into force on that date.

2939a. Prices
INDICATION OF PRICES (BEDS) ORDER 1978 (No. 1716) [20p], made under the Price Commission Act 1977 (c. 33), s. 11 (1); operative on March 1, 1979; prohibits in respect of beds any indication by a person that beds for sale by him may be sold by a person buying them at a particular price and further provides that dual price marking of beds shall be prohibited.

2940. Redundancy. See EMPLOYMENT.

2941. Restrictive covenant—injunction restraining use of confidential information
An injunction will be granted to restrain the breach of a reasonable covenant not to disclose confidential information.

P had a large mail order business. D worked for them. He had details of their bi-annual catalogue which formed the basis of their trade. He was subject to a covenant that he would not work for P's principal rivals for a year following any cessation of his employment with P. He left P's employment and refused to undertake not to breach that covenant. *Held*, granting an injunction restraining him from so doing, that P was entitled to have his trade secrets protected and that the covenant was a reasonable one which should be enforced.

LITTLEWOODS ORGANISATION v. HARRIS [1977] 1 W.L.R. 1472, C.A.

2942. Restrictive trade practices—failure to register agreement—injunction to restrain from enforcing other agreements.
[Restrictive Trade Practices Act 1976 (c. 34), s. 35.]
Although a respondent may have been party only to one unregistered agreement in restraint of trade, where there has been a clear breach of the law, the court is justified in granting an injunction restraining the enforcement of other agreements.

The respondent companies were parties to an agreement containing restriction or information provisions registrable under the 1976 Act but which they failed to register. Upon application by the Director-General of Fair Trading for injunctions restraining enforcement of such agreement, appropriate undertakings were given. Thereafter injunctions were sought restraining the respondents from enforcing other agreements contravening the Act, whereupon certain respondents contended that since they were parties only to one unregistered agreement, such an injunction was not justified. *Held*, rejecting such contention, that the law as to registration was sufficiently clear and established so that even one breach justified the seeking of a wider injunction. (*Re Flushing Cistern Makers' Agreement* [1973] C.L.Y. 3302 applied.)

Re AGREEMENTS RELATING TO THE SUPPLY OF BREAD [1977] I.C.R. 946, R.P.Ct.

2943. **Shipbuilding (Redundancy Payments) Act 1978 (c. 11).** See § 2768.

2944. **Shipping.** See SHIPPING AND MARINE INSURANCE.

2945. **Smell.** See NUISANCE.

2946. **Statistics**
CENSUS OF PRODUCTION (1979) (RETURNS AND EXEMPTED PERSONS) ORDER 1978 (No. 1573) [10p], made under the Statistics of Trade Act 1947 (c. 39), ss. 2, 11; operative on December 31, 1978; prescribes the matters about which a person carrying on an undertaking may be required to furnish returns for the purposes of the Census of Production being taken in 1979 and exempts from that obligation any person carrying on an undertaking in the exploration for and extraction of petroleum on land and offshore.

2947. **Trade Unions.** See TRADE UNIONS.

2948. **Transport.** See TRANSPORT.

BOOKS AND ARTICLES. See *post,* pp. [9], [37].

TRADE MARKS AND TRADE NAMES

2949. **Application—opposition—inherent distinctiveness**
[Trade Marks Act 1938 (c. 22), ss. 9, 10, 11, 17.] The applicant sought to register MULTILIGHT with a border for light fittings in Part A. The mark had been used since 1939. *Held,* (1) the mark bore a direct reference to the character and quality of the goods; (2) although the word was distinctive in practice, the word lacked inherent distinctiveness; (3) registration refused: MULTILIGHT TRADE MARK [1978] R.P.C. 601, Board of Trade.

2950. —— —— **likelihood of confusion**
[Trade Marks Act 1938 (c. 22), s. 11; Treaty of Rome, art. 30.] Application was made to register the mark ADVOKAAT in association with DE BEUKE-LAER for liqueur made in Belgium. The opponents contended that the mark was confined to Dutch drinks. The applicants contended that in Western Europe the word did not denote Dutch alcoholic beverages and that the Labelling of Food Regulations was restrictive, contrary to the Treaty of Rome. *Held,* (1) evidence as to the position in Western Europe was irrelevant; (2) Dutch Advocaat enjoyed a reputation in England and was associated with Dutch origin, and the applicant's mark would confuse. Registration must be refused: ADVOKAAT TRADE MARK [1978] R.P.C. 252, Trade Marks Registry.

2951. [Trade Marks Act 1938 (c. 22), ss. 9, 10, 11, 17, 22.] The application of B.A. was to register a facsimile of his signature in respect of clothes. The opponents alleged confusion on account of their use of the mark BARRY ARTIST, that the mark was incapable of distinguishing, and that B.A. was not the proprietor of the mark. *Held,* (1) the applicant had not assigned the mark to the opponent and the mark was his normal signature; (2) at the date of application B.A. had not used the mark in the course of merchanting. Evidence was necessary to determine whether his designing was sufficient connection in the course of trade: (3) the opponents' use was legitimate and the applicant had failed to establish that confusion was unlikely to occur: BARRY ARTIST TRADE MARK [1978] R.P.C. 703, Trade Marks Registry.

2952. [Trade Marks Act 1938 (C. 22), ss. 11, 12.] The applicants applied to register the mark MARGARET ROSE which they had used since 1967 for furniture and fittings. The opponents were proprietors of the mark ENGLISH ROSE for bedroom and bathroom fittings. They adduced evidence that confusion was likely. *Held,* refusing the application, that (1) the registrar must decide whether the marks were too close; (2) the opponents' mark was well known and there was danger of confusion: MARGARET ROSE TRADE MARK [1978] R.P.C. 55, Trade Marks Registry.

2953. [Trade Marks Act 1938 (c. 22), ss. 11, 12.]
Application to register POL-RAMA as a trade mark for sunglasses with polarising lenses was opposed by the proprietors of the mark POLAROID. *Held,* the words were not visually or phonetically similar and in the circum-

stances no confusion was likely to arise. (*Aristoc* v. *Rysta* [1945] 62 R.P.C. 65 followed): POL-RAMA Trade Mark [1977] R.P.C. 581, Trade Marks Registry.

2954.   [Trade Marks Act 1938 (c. 22), ss. 9, 10, 12.] On application to register RHEUMATON for diagnostic laboratory reagents, objection was taken that the word would be confused with RHEUMANOSTICON. The applicants showed that " Rheuma " was a known prefix and that laboratory staff are careful when ordering. *Held*, (1) RHEUMATON was not an ordinary word " with some trifling addition "; (2) there was no likelihood of confusion in this particular case: RHEUMATON Trade Mark [1978] R.P.C. 406, Trade Marks Registry.

2955.   [Trade Marks Act 1938 (c. 22), s. 11, 12 (1).] The mark TURBOTORCH was used in connection with gas blow-torches. The applicants sought to register the mark TURBOGAZ for similar goods. The applicants contended that the prefix Turbo was descriptive and that in the suffix Gaz they had a reputation by reason of a series of marks which they owned. *Held*, refusing registration, (1) " Turbo " was not descriptive; (2) " Gaz " was not sufficiently distinctive to prevent confusion and the applicants' reputation in the mark was not in the profession in which blow-torches were used: TURBOGAZ Trade Mark [1978] R.P.C. 206, Trade Marks Registry.

2956. —— —— —— **opponents' prior mark removed**
    [Trade Marks Act 1938 (c. 22), ss. 7, 11, 12, 29.]
    Application was made on December 10, 1971, to register the mark KERAION. The opponents' mark KERATON was applied for on May 19, 1971, and registration ceased to have effect on October 11, 1973, since no proprietor was registered within the prescribed period. The opponents had used their mark in Italy but not in the U.K. *Held*, (1) the relevant date for assessing whether KERATON prevented registration of the applicants' mark was the date of registration of the mark being applied for; (2) use of the opponents' mark in the U.K. was not grounds for prevention of registration in the U.K.; (3) it had not been established that the opponents' mark was known to a substantial number of people in the U.K.; (4) there was a likelihood of confusion between the two marks, particularly in view of their visual similarity. (" *Polymat* " *Trade Mark* [1968] C.L.Y. 3935 followed): KERAION Trade Mark [1977] R.P.C. 588, Trade Marks Registry.

2957. —— —— —— **user of mark by opponent's company**
    [Trade Marks Act 1938 (c. 22), ss. 11, 12.] The applicants applied to register the mark ZING, for, inter alia, golf clubs. The opponents owned the mark PING for golf clubs which were sold through a company of which the opponent was majority shareholder. *Held*, (1) the company controlled by the opponent was in the position of a registered user, and reputation in the mark was for the benefit of the opponent; (2) the marks were similar both visually and aurally and confusion was likely to arise. (*Bostitch Trade Mark* [1963] C.L.Y. 3520 and *Smith Hayden's Application* [1946] 63 R.P.C. 97 followed): ZING Trade Mark [1978] R.P.C. 47, Trade Marks Registry.

2958. —— —— **whether invented word—whether sufficiently distinctive**
    [Trade Marks Act 1938 (c. 22), ss. 9, 10, 11, 17.] Objection was made on application to register the mark SAFEMIX for thermostatic valves for mixing hot and cold water. *Held*, refusing the application that, (1) the mark consisted of two dictionary words joined. The mark was not invented; (2) the mark bore a direct reference to the character and quality of the goods; (3) the word SAFEMIX was not sufficiently distinctive: SAFEMIX Trade Mark [1978] R.P.C. 397, Trade Marks Registry.

2959. European Communities. See European Communities.

2960. Infringement—evidence—" without prejudice "—dealings prior to writ
    [Civil Evidence Act 1968 (c. 64), s. 18 (5).] In a telephone call and two telexes to the defendants, the parties discussed the possibility of settlement of the matter in issue. The words " without prejudice " were not used. In proceedings for interlocutory relief for passing-off, and for infringement of a registered trade mark, it was *held* that the communications were inadmissible and without prejudice, and that the court probably had no discretion to admit

such evidence: CHOCOLADEFABRIKEN LINDT & SPRUNGLI A.G. *v.* NESTLÉ CO. [1978] R.P.C. 287, Megarry V.-C.

2961. Passing-off—aerosol container with domed closing device—likelihood of deception

[S.A.] The plaintiff marketed a body spray in an aerosol container with a domed cap. B intended to market a body spray in an identical aerosol container but with different name and decoration. The plaintiff alleged it had a reputation in the unique shape or configuration of its closed container and that B's product would deceive or confuse the purchase. *Held,* (1) the plaintiff must show that the defendant's use of the feature was calculated to deceive and thereby injure the plaintiff's goodwill; (2) there was no evidence that the device indicated to a purchaser that the product was the plaintiff's; (3) no likelihood of confusion had been proved. Interdict refused: ADCOCK-INGRAM PRODUCTS *v.* BEECHAM S.A. (PTY.) [1978] R.P.C. 232, Sup.Ct. of South Africa.

2962 —— beverage—whether goods distinctive—unfair trading

The plaintiffs sold Advocaat and had a substantial goodwill and reputation in the name. In 1974, the defendants manufactured " Old English Advocaat." The plaintiffs did not prove that any purchaser of the defendants' product supposed it to be that of the plaintiff. An injunction was granted. The defendants appealed. *Held,* allowing the appeal, that (1) in passing-off proceedings, the plaintiff must show that he has a right of property in a business or goodwill likely to be injured by misrepresentation; (2) the name Advocaat was not sufficiently distinctive to be the basis of a proprietory right. As a trade name it was publici juris; (3) the tort of unfair trading is not committed when A uses a name accurately and B does so inaccurately, although B misleads the public in a way injurious to A; (4) the trade name of a product can only be protected in passing-off proceedings if it is distinctive of the goods of one particular producer or group if the products have a character and reputation peculiar to their products: ERVEN WARNINK B.V. *v.* T. TOWNEND AND SONS (HULL) [1978] F.S.R. 473, C.A.

2963. —— gas cylinders—no interlocutory injunction

The defendant filled, at the request of customers, Calor Gas cylinders with other gases. The plaintiff sought an interlocutory injunction, alleging passing off of other gases as the plaintiffs', and inducing customers to break contracts with the plaintiff. *Held,* dismissing the plaintiffs' appeal, that (1) the evidence did not suggest that the customer's breach of contract had been induced by the defendants; (2) the judge was entitled to find that the balance of convenience favoured the defendants: CALOR GAS *v.* CARGOES CARGAS [1978] F.S.R. 182, C.A.

2964. —— interim injunction—when granted—names of newspapers

The differences were so great between a proposed newspaper and an established one, with a similarity in name, that putting the two side by side only " a moron in a hurry " could be confused. Interlocutory relief would be granted only where there seemed some likelihood that the plaintiffs would be entitled to an injunction at the trial of the action. However, even if, on the evidence, the plaintiffs had shown an arguable case, entitlement to interlocutory relief would not automatically follow where there was a certainty of unquantifiable damage to the defendants which it was clear a plaintiff was unlikely to be able to pay. Here the promotion, advance advertising costs and the consequent free publicity of the venture could not be quantified: MORNING STAR CO-OPERATIVE SOCIETY *v.* EXPRESS NEWSPAPERS, *The Times,* October 19, 1978, Foster J.

2965. —— numerals for machinery—whether distinctive

The plaintiffs manufactured mechanical excavators known as the " 580 " series. The excavation bucket was five-eighths of a cubic yard. The defendants marketed an excavator called " 580." In a passing-off action, the defendants contended that they were merely using a number which had a descriptive connotation, and was available for anyone to use. *Held,* (1) " 580 " was not obviously a descriptive term; (2) no satisfactory reason for the defendants' use of the designation had been shown; (3) the balance of convenience favoured the plaintiffs. Injunction granted: HYMAC *v.* PRIESTMAN BROTHERS [1978] R.P.C. 495, Walton J.

2966. —— restaurant—deception and confusion

[Aust.] The plaintiffs registered the name " Giovanni's " as a trade mark. They owned a number of restaurants and the name was used on licence in connection with prepared foods. The defendants owned and ran " Papa Giovanni's Pizza House and Restaurant " and had done so since before the plaintiffs' registration. The plaintiffs sought an injunction. *Held*, there had been no deliberate passing off, and no misrepresentation by the defendant and the passing off action failed; (2) the defendants' mark was deceptively similar to the plaintiffs'. The defendants had established the statutory defence in that the actual use of the name by the defendants was not likely to deceive or confuse or to be taken as indicating a connection with the plaintiffs: MARC A. HAMMOND PTY. *v.* PAPA CARMINE PTY. [1978] R.P.C. 697, Sup.Ct. of New South Wales.

2967. —— scent—interlocutory injunction

The plaintiffs, manufacturers of perfume and soap, sought an injunction to restrain the defendants from selling their foam bath together with a bottle of low quality scent bearing a mark resembling that of the plaintiffs. *Held*, (1) there was an arguable case that the get-up represented that the plaintiffs had authorised the scent to be sold in conjunction with their own foam bath; (2) there was a likelihood of damage to the plaintiffs' goodwill; (3) the interlocutory injunction would preserve the status quo: MORNY *v.* BALL AND ROGERS (1975) [1978] F.S.R. 91, Goulding J.

2968. —— toothpaste—deception and confusion

The plaintiffs alleged infringement of their trademark " Colgate " and passing off of their toothpaste. The facts were agreed. The trial judge of the Supreme Court of Trinidad found no evidence of deception or confusion. The defendant called no evidence and offered no explanation. The judge refused to allow evidence that the prefix TRIN used by the defendant in their product named TRINGATE meant " made in Trinidad." The plaintiffs appealed. *Held*, (1) the rejected evidence was relevant and admissible; (2) the Court of Appeal was in a position to determine whether confusion or deception had occurred, and it was clear that the ordinary purchaser would be misled by the name and get-up of the defendant's product; (3) both trade marks had been infringed and the defendant was liable for passing off: COLGATE PALMOLIVE *v.* K. F. PATTRON [1978] R.P.C. 635, P.C.

2969. —— whisky—injunction—balance of convenience

The plaintiffs had a reputation in " Red Label " whisky. The defendants intended to produce " Red Label " cigarettes. The plaintiffs alleged passing-off, and sought an interlocutory injunction. *Held*, there was a certainty of unquantifiable damage to the defendants if the injunction were granted, and only a risk of unquantifiable damage to the plaintiff if it were refused. There was a serious issue to be tried. Injunction refused: JOHN WALKER & SONS *v.* ROTHMANS INTERNATIONAL [1978] F.S.R. 357, Brightman J.

2970. Procedure—privilege—lawyer and client correspondence—transmission to agents

S, an American attorney advising intervenors, wrote to the trade mark agents acting for the intervenors in the U.K. The letter contained legal advice. *Held*, the letter between S and the American intervenors was privileged, and such privilege was not lost by transmission for action to their agents in this country: MCGREGOR CLOTHING CO.'S TRADE MARK [1978] F.S.R. 354, Whitford J.

2971. Rectification—partial assignment—disassociation

[Trade Marks Act 1938 (c. 22), ss. 12, 22, 23.] C applied to register the mark COLT PHANTOM. CA applied to register the mark PHANTOM. C took an assignment of one of RR's old PHANTOM registrations in so far as it related to ventilating machines. RR was the proprietor of two other PHANTOM marks and no disassociation was carried out. CA applied for rectification on the ground that partial rectification was forbidden and the assignment by RR to C was void. *Held*, the Trade Marks Act 1938, s. 23, applied only to an assignment of a mark in respect of all goods. An assignment contravening s. 22 (4) was prima facie void. S. 22 (7) applied to postpone the effect of assignment only where it was in gross: PHANTOM TRADE MARK [1978] R.P.C. 245, C.A.

2972. —— person aggrieved—registered user no longer in existence
    [Trade Marks Act 1938 (c. 22), ss. 11, 13 (1), 28, 32 (1), 68; Trade Marks Rules 1938 (S.I. 1938 No. 661), r. 84.] Registered proprietors of the mark had delegated full function of quality control of MOLYSLIP products to D. The registered users had been wound up in 1968. The mark had been used by the interveners L and S, the holding company of the proprietors and the registered users. The applicants for rectification were responsible for MOLYSLIP product guarantees in South Africa. Marketing was carried out by another member of the applicants' group of companies, and they wished to trade under the mark in the U.K. The applicants alleged that the proprietors had permitted the mark to be used so as to render it no longer distinctive of the goods. The proprietors contended that the applicants were not persons aggrieved. *Held*, (1) the applicants were persons aggrieved as they were close to, and controlled by, a company in the applicants' group; (2) the absence of an existing registered user was immaterial; (3) the proprietors had committed no appropriate blameworthy act so as to justify rectification. The delegation to D of quality control had not severed the connection between the proprietors and the goods: MOLY-SLIP TRADE MARK [1978] R.P.C. 211, Trade Marks Registry.

2973. Registration—descriptive word—whether inherently capable of distinguishing goods
    On application to register " CHUNKY " in respect of dog food, the opponents alleged that the word was a well-known adjective used in promotion of animal foodstuffs. The word was present in the dictionary, but little used. The Registrar allowed the application to proceed. The opponents appealed. *Held*, the word was not of such a nature as to be inherently incapable of being distinguished. Appeal dismissed: CHUNKY TRADE MARK [1978] F.S.R. 322, Whitford J.

2974. —— direct reference to character—foreign word
    [Eire] [Trade Marks Act 1963 (Eire), ss. 17, 57.] Application was to register " KIKU " as a trade mark for perfumes. The word meant chrysanthemum in Japanese. The Controller refused registration. Kenny J. held the mark registrable. The Controller appealed. *Held*, there was no direct reference to goods, since the person who heard it would have to perform the additional act of translation in order to appreciate the reference: KIKU TRADE MARK [1978] F.S.R. 246, Sup.Ct. of Ireland.

2975. —— registered user—requirements
    [Aust.] [Trade Marks Act 1955 (Com), s. 103.] The first appellant was the Japanese proprietor of a device mark and word mark "Pioneer." The second appellant was a Victoria company. In 1974 the second appellant was appointed exclusive licensee. He had since 1973 promoted and imported the goods. The appellants applied for registration of the second appellants as registered users. The registrar required endorsement of the register to the effect that the appellants would not invoke s. 103 (1), to complain if goods of the registered owner were imported into Australia. The second appellant refused. The application was refused and the appellants appealed. *Held*, (1) where use of a trade mark was licensed, the trade mark was valid if the connection in the course of trade with the registered proprietor was maintained; (2) the Registrar was not authorised to insist upon the acceptance of an endorsement on the register; (3) for user to be registrable, the mark must be attached to the goods somewhere; (4) it was not necessary that the use of the mark by the proposed user should indicate a connection with the user to the exclusion of the proprietor; (5) registration of user could relate to a class of goods; (6) " public interest " in s. 74 (3) referred to the likelihood of deceiving the public; (7) the Registrar should pay costs. He had conceded that the original reason for requiring the application was invalid: PIONEER

ELECTRONIC CORP. *v.* REGISTRAR OF TRADE MARKS [1978] R.P.C. 716, High Ct. of Australia.

2976. —— surname—distinctive for Part B

[Eire] [Trade Marks Act 1963 (Eire), ss. 16, 17, 18.] The Controller refused to register the mark " KREUZER " since it was a surname and no evidence of distinctiveness was adduced. *Held,* on appeal, that (1) the word could not be registered in Part A, since it was a surname; (2) the word was so unusual in Ireland as to be capable of distinguishing the applicant's goods, and could be registered in Part B: KREUZER TRADE MARK [1978] F.S.R. 239, High Ct. of Ireland.

2977. —— or geographical name—sufficiently distinctive in Ireland

[Eire] [Trade Marks Act 1963 (Eire), ss. 16, 17.] The Controller refused to register the word " FARAH " as a trade name as it was a surname and a geographical name. *Held,* on appeal, (1) the word FARAH did not convey a surname to the Irish, and was therefore not a name within the meaning of the Act; (2) the word did not convey a geographical name to the Irish, and therefore FARAH was not a geographical name within the meaning of the Act; (3) the word was sufficiently unusual to be adapted to distinguish the applicant's goods and was not precluded from registration: FARAH TRADE MARK [1978] F.S.R. 234, High Ct. of Ireland.

2978. —— suspension of application—likelihood of confusion—effect of removal of similar mark

[Trade Marks Act 1938 (c. 22), ss. 12, 17, 20.] On application to register RUNNER for smoking products, there was official objection because the mark RUMMER was registered for rum-flavoured tobacco products. Renewal fees for the mark RUMMER were overdue. The applicants requested that the application be suspended for nine months. *Held,* refusing the application, (1) RUMMER should be deemed " already on the register " for one year from the date of removal; (2) RUNNER was likely to be confused with RUMMER; (3) suspension of the application was not reasonable: RUNNER TRADE MARK [1978] R.P.C. 402, Trade Marks Registry.

2979. —— whether additional evidence can be admitted on appeal from the Registrar

[Trade Marks Act 1938 (c. 22), ss. 9, 10, 17, 18.] The registrar refused an application to register the mark DISCO-VISION for video-discs on the grounds that the mark directly referred to the character and quality of the goods. On appeal the applicants applied to adduce further evidence that the mark was capable of distinguishing the goods. *Held,* (1) the court could not admit evidence not before the registrar; (2) the registrar had considered all relevant matters and had correctly decided that the words were descriptive of the goods in respect of which application was made. (" *Weldmesh* " *Trade Mark* [1966] C.L.Y. 121 77 referred to): DISCO-VISION TRADE MARK [1977] R.P.C. 594, Whitford J.

2980. Trade mark—alteration—to appearance rather than meaning

[Trade Marks Act 1938 (c. 22), s. 35; Trade Marks Rules 1938 (S.R. & O. 1938 No. 661), r. 89.]

The applicants proposed to alter the mark PELICAN from italic to capital form. Alternatively they sought to substitute the letter K for the letter C. The hearing officer refused both alterations. The applicants appealed in respect of the second alteration. *Held,* allowing the appeal, that (1) the alteration would slightly alter the appearance, but would not change the meaning of the trade mark, since it would be recognised either as a German word, or a mere mis-spelling of " Pelican ": PELICAN TRADE MARK [1978] R.P.C. 424, Board of Trade.

2981. —— licence—exemptions—EEC. See *Re* THE AGREEMENTS OF DAVIDE CAMPARI-MILANO SPA, § 1372.

2982. —— market sharing arrangement—different nations—whether concerted practice. See PERSIL TRADE MARK, § 1374.

2983. —— **removal from register—honest concurrent user—court's discretion**
[Trade Marks Act 1938 (c. 22), ss. 12 (2), 52.]
The mark " BALI " was expunged from the register in 1969, on account of similarity to the mark " BERLEI." In May 1969, BALI applied to re-register the mark, relying on honest concurrent user from 1962 to 1969. *Held*, on appeal by BERLEI, (1) the use by BALI was honest concurrent user; (2) the court should exercise its discretion to refuse registration. (*Alex Pirie and Son's Application* (1933) 50 R.P.C. 147 applied): BALI TRADE MARK (No. 2) [1978] F.S.R. 193, Fox J.

2984. Trade marks
TRADE MARKS (AMENDMENT) RULES 1978 (No. 1120) [30p], made under the Trade Marks Act 1938 (c. 22), ss. 40, 41; operative on August 8, 1978, save for Rule 3 which is operative on November 1, 1978; further amend S.R. & O. 1938 No. 661 so as to increase certain fees payable under them.

2985. Trade name—infringement—EEC. See TERRAPIN (OVERSEAS) *v.* TERRANOVA INDUSTRIE C.A. KAPFERER & CO., § 1309.

2986. —— **nom-de-plume of newspaper columnist—proof of user and reputation**
[Aust.] The plaintiff, a journalist, invented a fictitious character called " Pierpoint " and wrote a column in that name, in the defendants' newspaper. The plaintiff wished to write a " Pierpoint " column in another journal and sought an injunction to restrain the defendants from publishing articles under that name written by other journalists. *Held*, (1) the inventor and user of a nom-de-plume must show user of the name and a reputation in the name. The plaintiff had shown that he had become identified in the minds of readers with the name; (2) no term by which the pseudonym was to belong to the defendant was to be implied into the plaintiff's contract of employment. Injunction granted: SYKES *v.* FAIRFAX AND SONS [1978] F.S.R. 313, Sup.Ct. of New South Wales.

2987. —— **use of word " champagne "—EEC regulations.** See H. P. BULMER *v.* J. BOLLINGER S.A., § 1337.

ARTICLES. See *post*, p. [38].

TRADE UNIONS

2988. Activities—" appropriate time "—dismissal of employee. See ZUCKER *v.* ASTRID JEWELS, § 1170.

2989. Amalgamation
TRADE UNIONS AND EMPLOYERS' ASSOCIATIONS (AMALGAMATIONS, ETC.) (AMENDMENT) REGULATIONS 1978 (No. 1344) [10p], made under the Trade Union (Amalgamations, etc.) Act 1964 (c. 24), s. 7, and the Trade Union and Labour Relations Act 1974 (c. 52), s. 8 (4); operative on November 1, 1978; increase the fees payable to the Certification Officer in connection with amalgamations and transfers of engagements between trade unions or un-incorporated employers' associations, for the approval of changes of name by listed trade unions and employers' associations and for the inspection of documents.

2989a. Bargaining rights—duty of ACAS to encourage collective bargaining
[Employment Protection Act 1975 (c. 71), s. 1.] The duty imposed on the Advisory Conciliation and Arbitration Service (ACAS) by s. 1 of the Employ-ment Protection Act 1975, to encourage the extension of collective bargaining, although an important aspect of promoting the improvement of industrial relations, is not subject to the latter duty; a report by ACAS founded on the view that the improvement of industrial relations was its " over-riding duty " has been declared to be a nullity: U.K. ASSOCIATION OF PROFESSIONAL ENGINEERS *v.* ADVISORY CONCILIATION AND ARBITRATION SERVICE, *The Times*, July 1, 1978, May J.

2990. Certification of independence
CERTIFICATION OFFICER (AMENDMENT OF FEES) REGULATIONS 1978 (No. 1329) [10p], made under the Employment Protection Act 1975 (c. 71), s. 8 (2);

operative on November 1, 1978; increase from £21 to £50 the fee payable to the Certification Officer by a trade union on application for a certificate of independence.

2991. —— factors to be considered by certification officer

In deciding whether or not an association of employees is entitled to a certificate of independence from their employers, the certification officer should issue a certificate if the association satisfies the test of independence at the time; he should not pay too much attention to future possibilities.

Eight hundred employees formed a staff association to resist nationalisation, with the co-operation of the employers. They applied for certification as an independent trade union under s. 8 (1) of the Employment Protection Act 1975. The certification officer refused a certificate of independence on the ground that, although the association was not at the time under the control of the employers within s. 30 (1) (*a*) of the Labour Relations Act 1974, it was not free from liability to interference by the employers under s. 30 (1) (*b*). The company was then nationalised. On appeal by the association on the ground that they were not liable to interference by their new employers, *held*, allowing the appeal, that the certification officer in considering general criteria as opposed to factors peculiar to the case, had considered factors that were not germane to the issue, and the association, which had in fact become independent, should be granted a certificate of independence.

ASSOCIATION OF H.S.D. (HATFIELD) EMPLOYEES *v.* CERTIFICATION OFFICER [1978] I.C.R. 21, E.A.T.

2992. —— meaning of " independent trade union "—risk of interference by employers —certification officer's decision

[Trade Union and Labour Relations Act 1974 (c. 52), s. 30.] The proper test to be applied in the definition of " independent trade union " in s. 30 (1) is: was the staff association exposed to the risk of interference by the employers tending towards control? If that is so then clearly there is no independence. The degree of likelihood of the risk of interference is irrelevant provided it is not insignificant or de minimis. It is undesirable that the certification officer, who makes the initial decision as to the independence of a trade union, should undergo cross-examination about his decision not to grant a certificate of independence: SQUIBB UNITED KINGDOM STAFF ASSOCIATION *v.* CERTIFICATION OFFICER, *The Times*, October 10, 1978, C.A.

2993. Consultation with unions—redundancy—whether each building site a separate establishment. See BARRATT DEVELOPMENTS (BRADFORD) *v.* UNION OF CONSTRUCTION, ALLIED TRADES AND TECHNICIANS, § 1006.

2994. Contribution—arrears—meaning of " not a member of a specified union "— union membership agreement—unfair dismissal. See SCOTT *v.* E. AND E. KAYE, § 1134.

2995. Membership—closed shop agreement—local authority employer—whether ultra vires

[Local Government Act 1972 (c. 70), s. 111 (1); Trade Union and Labour Relations Act 1974 (c. 52), Sched. 1, para. 6 (5).]

A closed shop agreement entered into by a local authority employer is not ultra vires the authority.

The council entered into an agreement with several trade unions whereby all council employees were required to join a trade union, failing which they would be dismissed; an exception was made for employees objecting on religious grounds. The applicant sought an order of mandamus prohibiting enforcements of the agreement. *Held*, dismissing the application, that (1) the agreement was not ultra vires; (2) the provision for freedom of conscience in the Convention for the Protection of Human Rights and Fundamental Freedoms was subject to the 1974 Act.

R. *v.* GREATER LONDON COUNCIL, *ex p.* BURGESS [1978] I.C.R. 991, D.C.

2996. —— employer's threat against member employees—whether " action " within s. 53—calculation of compensation

[Employment Protection Act 1975 (c. 71), ss. 53 (1), 56.]

S. 53 of the Employment Protection Act 1978 exists to compensate employees, rather than to fine employers, and therefore what should be considered in assessing compensation is the employee's pecuniary and non-pecuniary injury.

Quaere: whether a threat by an employer can constitute "action" within the section.

A tribunal held that threats by the company's chairman that he would rather close the company down than recognise the union constituted action short of dismissal for the purpose of deterring employees from becoming or remaining members of an independent trade union, contrary to s. 53 of the Employment Protection Act 1975. In assessing compensation, the tribunal ordered the company to pay the employees' out-of-pocket expenses of attending the hearing and one day's pay. The tribunal stated that apart from that they did not propose to impose any pecuniary penalty on the company. On appeal by the employees, *held*, allowing the appeal, that the tribunal should have based its award on the employees' pecuniary and non-pecuniary injury. The case would therefore be remitted to a differently constituted tribunal for re-hearing.

BRASSINGTON *v.* CAULDON WHOLESALE [1978] I.C.R. 405, E.A.T.

2997. Natural justice—disciplinary proceedings—bias of chairman—lack of jurisdiction

Any union member facing disciplinary proceedings is entitled to a proper tribunal and a tribunal is not properly constituted if the chairman is personally involved and likely to be biased.

The plaintiffs, members of a miners' union, gave evidence on behalf of a newspaper successfully sued for libel by S, president of the union, on behalf of the union. Subsequently, the plaintiffs were charged with detrimental conduct and the charges were found proved by a committee chaired by S and affirmed by an area council also chaired by S. Their applications for interlocutory injunctions and declarations on grounds of breach of natural justice were granted by Judge Rubin, who also found that the proceedings were a contempt of court. On the plaintiffs' motions for judgment to be entered against the union, *held*, giving judgment for the plaintiffs, that S as plaintiff in the libel proceedings and then as chairman of the various committees that heard the charges must inevitably have appeared biased, so that the tribunal was not properly constituted; that a domestic tribunal had no power to punish a witness in legal proceedings. The proceedings were vitiated not because there was a contempt of court, but on grounds of lack of jurisdiction. (*Australian Workers Union* v. *Bowen No. 2* (1948) C.L.C. 10395 and *Hannam* v. *Bradford Corporation* [1970] C.L.Y. 852 considered.)

ROEBUCK *v.* NATIONAL UNION OF MINEWORKERS (YORKSHIRE AREA) No. 2 [1978] I.C.R. 676, Templeman J.

2998. Recognition—consultation—redundancy

[Employment Protection Act 1975 (c. 71), s. 99; Trade Union and Labour Relations Act 1974 (c. 52), s. 29 (1).] A.B. Co. made four employees redundant on May 28, 1976, without consulting N.U.G.S.A.T. A.B. Co. were members of a trade section of the British Jewellers' Association which had negotiated a succession of agreements concerning terms and conditions of employment with N.U.G.S.A.T. Eight A.B. Co. employees joined N.U.G.S.A.T. on May 5, 1976, and on May 20, 1976, a meeting was held between A.B. Co. and N.U.G.S.A.T.'s district secretary to discuss the wages of one employee, although no agreement was reached. *Held*, dismissing the union' appeal, that A.B. Co. had not "recognised" N.U.G.S.A.T. within the 1975 Act, s. 99. An act of recognition is only established by evidence of an actual agreement or clear and distinct conduct showing implied agreement. Discussion between management and a union about matters referred to in the 1974 Act, s. 29 (1) is not in itself sufficient. Nor was the Association the agent of A.B. Co. in any way; thus its actions could not impose recognition on A.B. Co.: NATIONAL UNION OF GOLD, SILVER AND ALLIED TRADES *v.* ALBURY BROTHERS [1978] I.R.L.R. 504, C.A.

2999. —— reference to Acas—Acas deferring inquiries—whether bound to proceed forthwith

[Employment Protection Act (c. 71), s. 12.]

Where a recognition issue is referred to Acas it has a discretion to defer taking various inquiries in fulfilment of its statutory duty, subject to an over-riding requirement of reasonableness.

A recognition dispute had arisen in a company involving three unions. The T.U.C. disputes committee ordered one of the unions to cease recruitment and not seek recognition. This same union then referred the dispute to Acas, while issuing a writ against the T.U.C. claiming a declaration that its award was invalid. Directions were given for a speedy trial of this action and Acas decided to defer its inquiries pending the outcome. The union commenced proceedings against Acas claiming that it was in breach of the statutory duty and should proceed forthwith. *Held*, that the word " when " in s. 12 (1) of the 1975 Act means no more than " after," so that Acas had a discretion to defer its inquiries, if reasonable, and if the circumstances rendered it desirable. (*Grunwick Processing Laboratories* v. *Acas* [1978] C.L.Y. 3000 referred to.)

ENGINEERS AND MANAGERS' ASSOCIATION v. ADVISORY, CONCILIATION AND ARBITRATION SERVICE [1978] I.C.R. 875, Oliver J.

3000. —— —— **duty to canvass workers' opinions**
[Employment Protection Act 1975 (c. 71), ss. 11, 12, 14.]
Prior to recommending that a trade union is recognised by an employer, ACAS has an unqualified duty to ascertain the opinions of the workers who are affected, and cannot make such recommendation unless the view of the majority of workers is ascertained.

After a strike at the plaintiffs' factory, the strikers were dismissed (being about one-third of the work force). A number of the strikers joined a trade union which unsuccessfully sought recognition by the plaintiffs. The union made application to ACAS under the 1975 Act. ACAS circulated the union members to ascertain their views but did not contact the remaining workers still employed at the factory since they were unable to obtain the names and addresses from the plaintiffs. Upon receipt of the views of the minority canvassed, ACAS recommended that the union be recognised. The Court of Appeal allowed the plaintiffs' appeal from refusal of a declaration that the recommendation was void. *Held*, dismissing the appeal by ACAS, that the recommendation was void, since ACAS could not properly make such a recommendation having failed to consult the majority of the work force affected.

GRUNWICK PROCESSING LABORATORIES v. ADVISORY CONCILIATION AND ARBITRATION SERVICE [1978] 2 W.L.R. 277, H.L.

3001. —— —— **questionnaire—breach of natural justice**
[Employment Protection Act 1975 (c. 71), ss. 12, 14 (1) (3).]
S. 14 (1) of the Act imposes upon A.C.A.S. a duty to seek to discover all facts relevant to enable them to make their report and, if necessary, recommendation on the recognition issue referred to it.

Both A.S.T.M.S., an independent trade union, and a staff association, had a substantial membership among the employees of an insurance company. Neither had a majority of employees as members. On the day the 1975 Act came into force, A.S.T.M.S., under s. 11 of the Act, referred the question of its recognition by the insurance company to A.C.A.S. No settlement by conciliation was reached. After consultation with the staff association, A.C.A.S. proposed to issue a questionnaire to the company's employees. P, on behalf of the staff association criticised the questionnaire as being unfairly biased against the staff association. A.C.A.S. decided to proceed with its issue. P sought an injunction to prevent them doing so and a declaration that the issue of the questionnaire was an unlawful exercise by A.C.A.S. of its discretion under s. 14 (1) of the Act. A.S.T.M.S. issued a summons asking to be joined as a defendant. At the hearing, P submitted unchallenged evidence that the questionnaire lacked symmetry in that it named A.S.T.M.S. but not the staff association, and was unlikely to provide A.C.A.S. with the relevant facts as to the wishes of the employees about representation. *Held*, granting the declaration sought adjoining A.S.T.M.S. as a defendant, that (1) A.C.A.S. had misdirected itself in considering that the correct basis for inquiries was to ascertain only the support for A.S.T.M.S. rather than seeking to discover the degree of support amongst employees for unions other than the referring union; (2) since the result of the recognition issue might result in a recommendation for or against recognition of A.S.T.M.S.,

it would be in breach of natural justice for the court to reach a decision without giving them an opportunity to be heard. (*Associated Provincial Picture Houses* v. *Wednesbury Corporation* (1948) C.L.C. 8107 applied.)
POWLEY *v.* A.C.A.S. [1978] I.C.R. 123, Browne-Wilkinson J.

3002. Rules—construction—miscount in election
By a clerical error a candidate in a branch election of the National Graphical Association was given 1,000 too many votes and declared elected. The plaintiff should have been elected. On the construction of the rules of the Association, it was *held* that they had power, rather than order a re-count, to declare the result of the ballot null and void and to hold a new ballot: SALTS *v.* NATIONAL GRAPHICAL ASSOCIATION, *The Times*, May 16, 1978, Judge Lewis Hawser Q.C.

3003. —— —— presumed intentions
The same canons of construction are to be applied to the rules of an association as to any written document and the court must reasonably interpret them to accord with what must have been intended.
The plaintiff association was a trade union managed by an annually elected council. One of the association rules, r. 43, provided for alteration of the rules at the annual general meeting; another, r. 34, for the holding of a referendum on any question the result of which was binding on the council. There was a divergence of views as to the construction of these rules in relation to alteration of the rules. In originating summons proceedings, the judge held that the procedure under both rules could be invoked in order to change them. The Court of Appeal allowed the appeal in part. On appeal, *held*, allowing the appeal again in part, that the same canons of construction were to be applied to rules of association, interpreting them so as to accord with presumed intentions, which in this case meant that a referendum decision under r. 34 could rescind or annul a general meeting in accordance with r. 43. Further, that where a proposed alteration at a general meeting failed to get the required majority, a subsequent referendum could operate to override that procedure, but only if the resolution was initiated through the general meeting procedure.
BRITISH ACTORS' EQUITY ASSOCIATION *v.* GORING [1978] I.C.R. 791, H.L.

3004. Trade dispute—whether in contemplation or furtherance of—interlocutory injunction
[Trade Union and Labour Relations Act 1974 (c. 52), ss. 13 (1), 17 (2), (as amended by Trade Union and Labour Relations (Amendment) Act 1976 (c. 7), s. 3 (2) and Employment Protection Act 1973 (c. 71), Sched. 6, Pt. III).]
When considering the balance of convenience in determining whether or not to grant an interlocutory injunction, wider considerations apply than merely the question of damages.
The circulation of P's newspaper increased when another newspaper stopped production. D sought to persuade P's employees against distributing the extra circulation. P sought an interlocutory injunction against D. D who claimed to be acting " in furtherance of " a trade dispute. *Held,* allowing P's appeal and granting the injunction, that the only dispute being between the other newspaper and its employees, it was doubtful if D would, at trial, have been said to have been acting " in furtherance of " a trade dispute; other questions, such as the requirements of the public, was relevant, as well as the question of eventual damages, and that, on balance, an injunction should be granted against D.
BEAVERBROOK NEWSPAPERS *v.* KEYS [1978] I.C.R. 582, C.A.

3005. [Trade Union and Labour Relations Act 1974 (c. 52), s. 13.] X recruited a crew of Indian seamen for their bulk carrier under articles to expire in October 1978 at rates of pay agreed between the crew's union and the Indian National Maritime Board. Such rates were well below those paid to seamen from other countries. X's bulk carrier flew the Liberian flag as a flag of convenience. On September 14, 1978, the ship was blacked by the I.T.F., the world-wide federation of seamen's unions, and not allowed to leave Glasgow docks. X were willing to agree to the I.T.F.'s demands that the crew be employed on I.T.F. terms with back pay accordingly but the crew refused to sign the I.T.F.

articles. The crew were therefore repatriated and a Greek crew was engaged which agreed a Greek collective agreement giving them benefits equivalent to the I.T.F. agreement. The new crew would not sign the I.T.F. articles. *Held*, that the High Court had erred in refusing an interlocutory injunction restraining officials of the I.T.F. from continuing the "blacking" of the carrier. Although a trade dispute existed between X and the I.T.F., it was an open question whether the I.T.F.'s actions were "in contemplation or furtherance" of that dispute within the 1974 Act, s. 13. The balance of convenience favoured the grant of an interlocutory injunction. In deciding whether an act is in contemplation or furtherance of a trade dispute, motives for the act will be considered. The I.T.F.'s demand was so unreasonable that it stamped the I.T.F. as intermeddlers and the suggestion that there was an ulterior motive related to flags of inconvenience was sufficiently strong to merit full consideration. (*Conway* v. *Wade* (1909) A.C. 506 applied): STAR SEA TRANSPORT CORP. OF MONROVIA v. SLATER, LAUGHTON AND COLLARBONE [1978] I.R.L.R. 507, C.A.

3006. Union funds—payment of members' fines—whether lawful

A resolution by a union to pay its members' fines is not contrary to public policy if it is passed after the offences were committed; the situation might be different if repeated resolutions led members to expect indemnification against the consequences of future offences.

The union was authorised by its rules to assist members "in such legal matters or proceedings as it deems necessary to protect the interests of the union." Union members were fined for offences arising from picketing. The union passed a resolution to indemnify its members for offences not involving violence. A member of the union sought an injunction to restrain the union from appropriating its funds to that purpose. *Held*, refusing the application, that the resolution was within the rules of the union, and was not against public policy. The situation might have been different after repeated resolutions to the same effect.

DRAKE v. MORGAN [1978] I.C.R. 56, Forbes J.

3007. Union membership agreement—unfair dismissal—members of different union. See HIMPFEN v. ALLIED RECORDS, § 1175.

3008. —— —— onus on employer to prove employee is not union member. See BLUE STAR SHIP MANAGEMENT v. WILLIAMS, § 1173.

ARTICLES. See *post*, p. [38].

TRANSPORT

3009. Buses

COMMUNITY BUS REGULATIONS 1978 (No. 1313) [40p], made under the Road Traffic Act 1972 (c. 20), ss. 40 (1) (3), 199 (2), the Transport Act 1978 (c. 55), ss. 5 (6) (9), 8 (1), Sched. 2, para. 5, and the Road Traffic Act 1960 (c. 16), ss. 160 (1), 260 (2); operative on November 1, 1978; make provision for vehicles being used to provide a community bus service in accordance with s. 5 of the 1978 Act or as a contract carriage in accordance with s. 6 of that Act.

3010. Compensation—Lands Tribunal decision

BRECON'S EXECUTORS v. BRITISH WATERWAYS BOARD (Ref /48/1975) (1977) 245 E.G. 57. (The claimants sought compensation under s. 105 (7) of the Transport Act 1968 for the extinguishment of rights to use boats on the Monmouthshire and Brecon Canal, such rights being granted to them by a Local Act of 1793. *Held*, (1) the rights were for pleasure boats however propelled; (2) compensation should not be payable only for financial loss; (3) claimants' valuation based on estimated increases in licence charges following inflation rejected (*Young* v. *Percival* [1974] C.L.Y. 832 applied); (4) claimants awarded £400 per boat on basis of sale of dwellings to occupiers wishing to use boats).

3011. Hovercraft

HOVERCRAFT (FEES) REGULATIONS 1978 (No. 483) [35p], made under S.I.

1972 No. 674, operative on April 20, 1978; revokes S.I. 1972 No. 852 as amended, and provides for fees in respect of the maintenance of hovercraft.

HOVERCRAFT (APPLICATION OF ENACTMENTS) (AMENDMENT) ORDER 1978 (No. 1913) [10p], made under the Hovercraft Act 1968 (c. 59), s. 1 (4); operative on December 29, 1978; amends S.I. 1972 No. 971.

3012. Industrial training levy—liability—company providing labour for oil companies—whether an employer

G.M.S. Co. principally provided a "payroll service" for oil companies, supplying labour for them, in particular for manning petrol stations. *Held*, that G.M.S. Co. were employers within the road transport industry, liable to pay the Road Transport Industry Training Board's levy: GARAGE MANAGEMENT SERVICES *v.* ROAD TRANSPORT INDUSTRY TRAINING BOARD (1978) 13 I.T.R. 117, Industrial Tribunal.

3013. London Transport

LONDON TRANSPORT (LOST PROPERTY) (AMENDMENT) REGULATIONS 1978 (No. 1791) [20p], made under the London Passenger Transport Act 1933 (c. 14), s. 106 as amended by the Transport Act 1962 (c. 46), s. 68 (1) and the Transport (London) Act 1969 (c. 35), s. 17, Sched. 3, para. 6 (1); operative on January 1, 1979; amend S.I. 1971 No. 2125 so as to introduce a new scale of charges payable on the return of property left in vehicles of London Transport.

3014. Minibuses

MINIBUS (DESIGNATED BODIES) (AMENDMENT) ORDER 1978 (No. 1930) [20p], made under the Minibus Act 1977 (c. 25), s. 1 (3); operative on January 26, 1979; amends S.I. 1977 No. 1709 by designating further bodies who may grant permits under the 1977 Act.

MINIBUS (PERMITS) (AMENDMENT) REGULATIONS 1978 (No. 1931) [10p], made under the Minibus Act 1977, s. 3 (1); operative on January 26, 1979; amend S.I. 1977 No. 1708 by prescribing new conditions which must be fulfilled by the driver of a minibus.

3015. National Freight Corporation

NATIONAL FREIGHT CORPORATION (CENTRAL TRUST) ORDER 1978 (No. 1290) [20p], made under the Transport Act 1962 (c. 46), s. 74; operative on October 1, 1978; provides for the transfer of the assets and liabilities of certain pension schemes of the National Freight Corporation to the trustees of a central trust established by the Corporation in connection with the funding of pension scheme obligations under s. 19 of the Transport Act 1978.

NATIONAL FREIGHT CORPORATION (FUNDING OF PENSION SCHEMES) (NO. 1) ORDER 1978 (No. 1294) [20p], made under the Transport Act 1978 (c. 55), ss. 19, 20; operative on October 1, 1978; prescribes the sum of £73,149,364 as the sum to be provided by the Corporation for the partial funding of the obligations of the Corporation and certain subsidiaries in connection with the Corporation's pension schemes.

3016. Northern Ireland. See NORTHERN IRELAND.

3017. Public service vehicles

PUBLIC SERVICE VEHICLES (LICENCES AND CERTIFICATES) (AMENDMENT) REGULATIONS 1978 (No. 1315) [10p], made under the Road Traffic Act 1960 (c. 16), ss. 139A, 158–160, as amended by the Transport Act 1978 (c. 55), s. 8 (1), Sched. 2, paras. 3, 5; operative on November 1, 1978; amend S.I. 1952 No. 900 by replacing the regulation relating to application for a licence for services.

3018. Railways. See RAILWAYS.

3019. Road Traffic. See ROAD TRAFFIC.

3020. Salaries—compulsory transfer—compensation—whether loss attributable to transfer

[Transport Act 1968 (c. 73), s. 135 (1); British Transport (Compensation to Employees) Regulations 1970 (S.I. 1970 No. 187), regs. 12, 13.] On January 1, 1969, T and other employees of British Rail were transferred to employment with NF Co. Initially his remuneration remained the same as if he had not been transferred, but between 1972 and 1974 a divergence developed between T's rate of pay and that of comparable employees of British Rail. T sought compensation under the 1970 Regulations, which provided for compensation for any worsening of position "properly attributable to the transfer." At first instance, it was held that T was entitled to compensation, and the Court of Appeal upheld this decision. On appeal, *held,* allowing the appeal (Lord Wilberforce and Viscount Dilhorne dissenting), that on the proper construction of s. 135 (1) and the regulations, T had not shown that the worsening of his position was attributable to his transfer: TUCK v. NATIONAL FREIGHT CORP., *The Times,* November 28, 1978, H.L.

3021. Shipping. See SHIPPING AND MARINE INSURANCE.

3022. Transport Act 1978 (c. 55)

This Act provides for the planning and development of public passenger transport services in England and Wales; for public service vehicle licensing, the regulation of goods vehicles and parking; and for amendments concerning British Rail, Freightliners Limited, the finances of the National Freight Corporation and other public sector transport bodies.

S. 1 sets out new passenger transport policies to be implemented in county areas; s. 2 requires the publication of a five-year plan for each non-metropolitan county council's public transport system; s. 3 relates to agreements with transport operators; s. 4 requires details of concessionary fare schemes to be included in such plans; s. 5 is concerned with the authorisation of community bus services; s. 6 governs car-sharing for social and other purposes; s. 7 amends the law relating to road service licences and permits; s. 8 amends the law governing lorries; s. 9 modifies drivers' hours as a result of EEC rules; s. 10 affects bicycles; s. 11 states the duty of the British Railways Board; s. 12 has to do with British Rail's public service obligations; s. 13 arranges for the transfer of the controlling interest in Freightliners Limited from the National Freight Corporation to the British Railways Board; s. 14 amends the Railways Act 1974 (c. 48), s. 8; s. 15 directs the reduction of the capital debt of the National Freight Corporation; s. 16 permits the making of capital grants to the corporation; s. 17 provides for the funding of pension obligations; s. 18 makes supplementary provisions to s. 17; s. 19 directs travel concessions for transferred employees; s. 20 contains amendments to transport supplementary grants; s. 21 makes general financial provisions; s. 22 concerns commencement, interpretation and repeals; s. 23 gives the short title, and states that the Act does not extend to Northern Ireland except for ss. 13, 15–19, and 21–23, but does extend to Scotland with the exception of ss. 1–4, and 20.

The Act received the Royal Assent on August 2, 1978.

3023. —— commencement

TRANSPORT ACT 1978 (COMMENCEMENT NO. 1) ORDER 1978 (No. 1150 (C. 32)) [10p]; made under the Transport Act 1978 (c. 55), s. 24 (1); operative on August 4, 1978; brings into force ss. 15, 17, 18, 21, 23, 24 (part) of and Sched. 4 (part) to the 1978 Act.

TRANSPORT ACT 1978 (COMMENCEMENT NO. 2) ORDER 1978 (No. 1187 (C. 33)) [20p], made under the Transport Act 1978, s. 24 (1); brings into force on September 1, 1978, ss. 1–4, 7, 8 (part), 10–14, 16, 22 and 24 (4) (part) of and Scheds. 1, 2 (part) and 4 (part) to the 1978 Act; brings into force on November 1, 1978, ss. 5, 6, 8 (part), 9 and 24 (4) (part) of and Scheds. 2 (part), 3, and 4 (part) to the 1978 Act.

TRANSPORT ACT 1978 (COMMENCEMENT NO. 3) ORDER 1978 (No. 1289 (C. 34)), made under the Transport Act 1978, ss. 20 (1) and 24 (1); operative on October 1, 1978; brings into force the provisions of ss. 19 and 20 of the Transport Act 1978 which relate to the funding of certain pension obligations of the National Freight Corporation.

ARTICLES. See *post,* p. [38].

TRESPASS

ARTICLES. See *post,* p. [38].

TROVER AND DETINUE

3024. Detinue—property in police custody—common law action independent of statutory procedure

The plaintiff brought a claim against the defendant in detinue in respect of a motor car which was in the defendant's possession by virtue of an order under s. 43 of the Powers of Criminal Courts Act 1973. The plaintiff, who claimed to be the owner of the car, was then entitled to claim its return under s. 1 of the Police Act 1897. To succeed, she had to prove ownership, as well as satisfy the conditions contained in s. 43 (3) of the 1973 Act, which apply wherever property is in police possession subject to a court order under s. 43 (1). Under s. 43 (4) (*b*), the claimant had to satisfy the court that she did not consent to the article being used for crime, nor suspect that it would be so used. The plaintiff applied to the magistrates' court under s. 1 of the 1973 Act, but they refused to entertain her application, apparently relying on *Raymond Lyons & Co.* v. *Metropolitan Police Commissioner* [1975] C.L.Y. 2574. In the present case, the plaintiff was found to be the owner of the car, but the question was whether she was entitled to bring an action in detinue independently of the aforesaid statutory procedure. *Held,* that a claimant to property the subject of a s. 43 order need not be confined to a remedy under the statutory law and procedure laid down under the Police Property Act 1897, s. 1, and the Powers of the Criminal Courts Act 1973, s. 43 (4). If a claim is brought under that procedure, the conditions contained in s. 43 (4) will apply. A claimant is equally free to pursue a remedy at common law which exists independently of statute, in which event the requirements of s. 43 (4) have no application: DAVIS *v.* HAMPSHIRE POLICE AUTHORITY, November 30, 1978, Judge McCreery Q.C., Winchester Crown Ct. (*Ex rel. M. J. Nicholls, Esq., Barrister*).

UNIVERSITIES

3025. Education. See EDUCATION.

3026. Membership—visitor—jurisdiction of court

The jurisdiction of the visitor to a university is sole and exclusive; the court has no jurisdiction over such matters save for the issue of orders of prohibition and mandamus.

P was a member of Bradford University reading computer science. He failed his first year examinations, and the university required him to withdraw. P applied to re-enter. The university refused his application without improved " A " levels. P brought an action against the university, seeking a declaration that he had unlawfully been refused re-admission, and an injunction and exemplary damages. The university contended that its visitor had exclusive jurisdiction. It was the Crown's right under the university's charter to appoint a visitor, and no appointment had been made. *Held,* refusing the relief claimed, that (1) in the absence of an appointment, the Crown was the visitor to the university, and its power was to be exercised by the Lord Chancellor; (2) the visitor's duty was exclusive, and included questions as to the lawful entry and removal of members. The court had no jurisdiction save for prohibition and mandamus, and the action must be dismissed. (*R.* v. *Hertford College* (1878) 3 Q.B.D. 693 followed.)

PATEL *v.* UNIVERSITY OF BRADFORD SENATE [1978] 3 All E.R. 841, Megarry V.-C.

3027. Universities and College Estates Act 1925—amendment

UNIVERSITIES AND COLLEGE ESTATES ACT 1925 (AMENDMENT) REGULATIONS 1978 (No. 443) [10p], made under the Agriculture (Miscellaneous Provisions) Act 1976 (c. 55), s. 7 (1) (2) (*a*); operative on April 19, 1978; amend the 1925 Act substituting the word " hectare " for the word " acre."

VALUE ADDED TAX

3027a. Assessment—appeal—jurisdiction

[Finance Act 1972 (c. 41), s. 31 (6).]

The proper remedy where an assessment of VAT is made is to appeal to the

VAT tribunal; the taxpayer cannot defend the Commissioners' summons for final judgment on the assessments by querying the amount assessed.

Per curiam: the provisions of the 1941 Act can cause hardship and injustice, and should be applied with an understanding of the difficulties faced by the taxable person, in particular the small trader.

H failed to make returns of VAT for certain periods and he was assessed to tax; he did not appeal. The Commissioners sought summary judgment and H asked for leave to defend. *Held,* leave should not be given. The proper remedy was to have appealed against the assessments to the VAT tribunal. CUSTOMS AND EXCISE COMMISSIONERS *v.* HOLVEY [1978] 2 W.L.R. 155 Pain J.

3028. —— **period covered—limitation**

[Finance Act 1972 (c. 41), s. 31.] G Ltd.'s VAT returns having been found to be incorrect, the Commissioners made an assessment for a 21-month period and not for several successive three-month accounting periods. *Held,* that the assessment for the longer period was valid, but that the limitation period for making assessments prescribed by F.A. 1972, s. 31, must be taken to run from the end of the first accounting period included in the assessment: S. J. GRANGE *v.* CUSTOMS AND EXCISE COMMISSIONERS, *The Times,* November 22, 1978, C.A.

3029. —— **whether correct basis—boats**

[Value Added Tax (Boats and Outboard Motors) Order 1975 (S.I. 1977 No. 745).] The taxpayer company, which bought boat hulls and fitted them out for re-sale, was assessed to VAT on the difference between the consideration given for the purchase of the hulls and the re-sale price, with no allowance for the fitting out costs. *Held,* that the basis of assessment was correct: WYVERN SHIPPING CO. *v.* CUSTOMS AND EXCISE, *The Times,* June 16, 1978, Neill J.

3030. Customs and excise guide

H.M. Customs and Excise have issued Notice No. 700 (September 1978): VAT: supplement to general guide.

3031. Deductions of input tax—meaning of " business " activities

The National Water Council's functions were varied. It contended that everything it did came under the rubric of " business " in the Finance Act 1972 (c. 41), and hence that it could reclaim input tax on VAT. The court *held* that "business" comprehended activities not limited to profit-making ones, and could include training and education facilities; but governmental functions, including advisory functions to ministers and their superannuation scheme, were disqualified. The input tax deductions would therefore be apportioned: NATIONAL WATER COUNCIL *v.* CUSTOMS AND EXCISE COMMISSIONERS (1978) 122 S.J. 627, Q.B.D., Neill J.

3032. Finance Act 1978 (c. 42)

Part II (ss. 11 and 12) relates to value added tax: s. 11 increases the figures relating to liability for registration: s. 12 provides for relief for bad debts.

3033. General regulations

VALUE ADDED TAX (GENERAL) (AMENDMENT) REGULATIONS 1978 (No. 532) [25p], made under the Finance Act 1972 (c. 41), ss. 3 (8), 4 (3), 18, 33, 35 (1); Regs. 1, 2 and 8 operative on April 29, 1978, the remainder operative on May 4, 1978; amend various provisions of, and add a new Part to, S.I. 1977 No. 1759.

VALUE ADDED TAX (GENERAL) (AMENDMENT) (NO. 2) REGULATIONS 1978 (No. 972) [25p], made under the Finance Act 1972, ss. 3 (1), 12 (7), 30; operative on October 1, 1978; amends S.I. 1977 No. 1759 by substituting new Regs. 49 and 50.

3034. Gifts to employees—course of business

[Finance Act 1972 (c. 41), s. 2.] R.H.M. Bakeries (Northern) made gifts of clocks and other articles to employees who had completed 25 years' service. *Held,* that the articles were supplied in the course of the company's business and that it was accountable for VAT in respect of the supplies: R.H.M. BAKERIES (NORTHERN) *v.* CUSTOMS AND EXCISE COMMISSIONERS, *The Times,* July 5, 1978, Neill J.

3035. Group supplies—retrospective treatment

[Finance Act 1972 (c. 41), s. 21.] Following a re-organisation within the Save And Prosper Group, a particular subsidiary company was not registered or included in the Group registration. Consequently, inter-company supplies became chargeable to tax. Save And Prosper applied for retrospective group treatment. *Held*, that the Commissioners of Customs and Excise had power to entertain an application for retrospective group treatment, and that they should proceed to consider the application: CUSTOMS AND EXCISE COMMISSIONERS *v*. SAVE AND PROSPER GROUP, *The Times*, July 13, 1978, Neill J.

3036. Higher rate—goods " suitable " for use

[Finance (No. 2) Act 1975 (c. 45), s. 17, Sched. 7, Group 3.]

" Suitable " in Sched. 7, Group 3, of the 1975 Act does not mean " designed " or " adapted for."

The taxpayer company, which supplied sailing and other recreational equipment, sold couplings and winches which were standard fittings for linking a trailer to a towing vehicle. The question was whether the couplings and winches attracted value added tax at the higher rate as being " goods of a kind suitable for use as parts of " trailers or trolleys when used as accessories to boats. *Held*, that " suitable " meant only " well fitted for " or " suited for " and not " designed " or " adapted for," so that the winches and couplings supplied were chargeable with value added tax at the higher rate.

CUSTOMS AND EXCISE COMMISSIONERS *v*. MECHANICAL SERVICES (TRAILER ENGINEERS) [1978] 1 W.L.R. 56, D.C.

3037. Isle of Man

VALUE ADDED TAX (UNITED KINGDOM AND ISLE OF MAN) (CONSOLIDATION) ORDER 1978 (No. 273) [25p], made under the Finance Act 1972 (c. 41), s. 50; operative on March 1, 1978; makes provision for the consolidation of VAT in the United Kingdom in relation to the Isle of Man.

VALUE ADDED TAX (UNITED KINGDOM AND ISLE OF MAN) ORDER 1978 (No. 1621) [20p], made under the Finance Act 1972, s. 50; operative on November 15, 1978; provides that VAT be charged under either the 1972 Act or the Value Added Tax and other Taxes Act 1973 as if references therein to the United Kingdom or the Isle of Man included both places but that the tax is not charged under both Acts in respect of the same transaction.

3038. Margin scheme—adequacy of records—review of commissioners' discretion

[Finance Act 1972 (c. 41), s. 40 (1); Value Added Tax (Works of Art, Antiques and Scientific Collections) Order 1972 (S.I. 1972 No. 1971), arts. 3 (5), 4.] The taxpayer company accounted for value added tax on antique coins in accordance with the Value Added Tax (Works of Art, Antiques and Scientific Collections) Order 1972. The Order requires certain records and accounts to be kept, as specified by the Commissioners by notice. The taxpayer failed to keep appropriate records, and was assessed to tax by the Commissioners. The taxpayer appealed. In their statement of case the Commissioners stated that they did not recognise the records which the taxpayer had kept and that their refusal to do so was within their discretion and not subject to review by the tribunal. *Held*, allowing the Commissioners' appeal from the decision of the tribunal, that the sufficiency of the records was within the Commissioners' discretion and not subject to review: CUSTOMS AND EXCISE COMMISSIONERS *v*. J. H. CORBITT (NUMISMATISTS) [1978] S.T.C. 531, Neill J.

3039. Registration/deregistration threshold

H.M. Customs and Excise have issued Notice No. 731A (April 1978): increased turnover value limits for registration.

3040. Relief

VALUE ADDED TAX (BAD DEBT RELIEF) REGULATIONS 1978 (No. 1129) [25p], made under the Finance Act 1978 (c. 42), s. 12 (3) and (4); operative on October 2, 1978; regulate the administration of relief for VAT included in bad debts incurred on supplies where the debtor becomes formally insolvent after October 1, 1978.

3041. Retailers

H.M. Customs and Excise have issued Notice No. 727 (October 1977): Special schemes for retailers.

3042. Returns—cessation of trading

[Finance Act 1972 (c. 41), s. 38 (7); Value Added Tax (General) Regulations 1975 (S.I. 1975 No. 2204), reg. 51 (1).]

A person registered for value added tax remains liable to make returns even if he has ceased to trade.

The defendant, a haulage contractor, was registered for value added tax purposes. He ceased trading, but took no steps to have his registration cancelled. Thereafter he failed to make value added tax returns. The justices dismissed the information on the ground that any return furnished would have been a nil return. *Held,* allowing the prosecutor's appeal, that so long as the defendant remained registered, he was liable to comply with the regulations requiring the making of returns.

KEOGH v. GORDON [1978] 1 W.L.R. 1383, D.C.

3043. Review

H.M. Customs and Excise have issued Notice No. 734 (April 1978): review of value added tax.

3044. Service contract—single or separate supplies of feedstuff

[Finance Act 1972, ss. 10 (4), 12 (2), Sched. 4, Group 1, general item 2.] The taxpayer, a farmer, kept stallions for the service of mares. Under a contract with the owner of a mare he assumed a number of obligations (*e.g.* to accommodate the mare, to feed it, etc.). A fee of £100 was charged, together with a weekly accommodation charge. A VAT Tribunal held that each contract constituted a number of separate supplies, and, in particular, that the supply of feeding stuffs fell to be zero-rated. *Held,* allowing the Crown's appeal, that the obligation under the contract constituted the supply of a single service, namely, the service of keeping the mare (dictum of Lord Denning M.R. in *British Railways Board* v. *Customs and Excise Commissioners* [1977] C.L.Y. 3133 applied): CUSTOMS AND EXCISE COMMISSIONERS v. SCOTT [1978] S.T.C. 191, D.C.

3045. Sheriffs' fees. See § 2676.

3046. Tribunal decisions

Antiques—numismatist—records—discretion

J. H. CORBITT (NUMISMATISTS) v. THE COMMISSIONERS (1977) V.A.T.T.R. 194 (the appellant—a numismatist—accounted for VAT on antique coins in accordance with Value Added Tax (Works of Art, Antiques and Scientific Collections) Order 1972 (S.I. 1972 No. 1971). The Order requires certain records and accounts to be kept, as specified by the Commissioners by notice. The appellant failed to keep appropriate records, and was assessed to tax by the Commissioners. The appellant appealed; but in their statement of case, the Commissioners stated that they did not recognise the records which he had kept, and that their refusal to do so was within their discretion and not subject to review by the tribunal. *Held,* that the tribunal had jurisdiction to review the exercise by the Commissioners of their discretionary powers).

—— *records—estoppel*

MILLER v. THE COMMISSIONERS (1977) V.A.T.T.R. 241 (the appellant, who carried on an antique business at Rickmansworth, decided to account for VAT under the "margin" scheme, but failed to keep sufficient records for this purpose, as required by Notice No. 712. He also carried on business in partnership with his son at Chorley Wood. The Commissioners disallowed certain input tax claimed in connection with this business because of failure to produce the relevant tax invoices. An officer of the Customs and Excise had visited the appellant's business on a routine visit and inspected his account book, but had made no comment thereon. The Commissioners had assessed the appellant on the basis that no partnership had existed in respect of the Chorley Wood business, but conceded that if such partnership existed the assessment fell to be adjusted. *Held,* that (1) the records kept in relation to the

Rickmansworth business were inadequate; (2) because of failure to produce the relevant tax invoices the input tax claimed was properly disallowed; (3) the Chorley Wood business was carried on in partnership, and the assessment fell to be reduced in accordance with the Commissioners' agreement).

Assessment—erroneous basis of computation

FRIEL *v.* THE COMMISSIONERS [1977] V.A.T.T.R. 147 (an officer of H.M. Customs and Excise examined the records and books of the appellant, a publican, and from such examination concluded that the appellant's VAT returns were incomplete or incorrect. An assessment to VAT was then made on the appellant in an amount computed by the officer, who in making the computation had erroneously used tax-inclusive figures for the purchases of stock and tax-exclusive figures for sales, and had made no allowance for off-licence sales. *Held*, that the assessment had not been made by the Commissioners " to the best of their judgment " as required by Finance Act 1972, s. 31 (1), and so should be withdrawn).

Boats—letting on hire—holiday accommodation—estoppel

D. A. W. OSBORNE OF DARBY BROS. *v.* THE COMMISSIONERS (1977) V.A.T.T.R. 257 (the appellant hired out cabin cruisers as holiday accommodation, and allowed hirers to hire a dinghy at an additional charge. Tax was charged at the standard rate. Officers of the Customs and Excise visited boat owners, and were made aware that tax was charged at the standard rate on the hire of dinghies, but they made no comment thereon. Subsequently, assessments were raised on the basis that tax should have been charged at the higher rate. *Held*, that (1) the dinghy was an optional extra and not part of the supply of holiday accommodation, and so was taxable at the higher rate; (2) there had been no sufficient representation by the Commissioners to found estoppel).

Building—demolition—reconstruction—repair

THOMAS BRIGGS (LONDON) *v.* THE COMMISSIONERS (1977) V.A.T.T.R. 213 (a three-storey wing of a factory was badly damaged by fire. It being too expensive to restore the wing as before, the owner had the damaged third floor demolished, and a flat roof built on the top of the second floor. The Commissioners decided that the works were by way of repair, and taxable at the standard rate. *Held*, applying *Lurcott* v. *Wakely & Wheeler* [1911] 1 K.B. 905, that the works were a renewal and replacement of a subordinate part of a building, and accordingly were works of repair).

Course for foreign students—" used "—zero-rating

G. & B. PRACTICAL MANAGEMENT DEVELOPMENT *v.* THE COMMISSIONERS [1977] V.A.T.T.R. 128 (the appellant company ran a six-week management course for students from Nigeria, all of whom returned to employment in Nigeria on completion of the course. *Held,* that the services supplied by the company in providing the course were " not used by a person present in the United Kingdom," and so were zero-rated under Finance Act 1972, Sched. 4, Group 9, item 6).

Education—business—scientology

CHURCH OF SCIENTOLOGY OF CALIFORNIA *v.* THE COMMISSIONERS [1977] V.A.T.T.R. 278 (the appellant, a religious membership corporation, established in California, provided scientology courses, and sold books, E-meters (a device designed to measure physical responses to mental stimuli) and scientology emblems. *Held*, that it was carrying on a business for tax purposes (not being education of a kind provided by a university), and was assessable to value added tax).

Food—mobile van—premises

JAMES *v.* THE COMMISSIONERS [1977] V.A.T.T.R. 155 (the sale of hot dogs and hamburgers to the public from mobile vans *held* to be the making of zero-rated supplies, and, if the vans were " premises " for the purposes of the supplies, the supplies were not consumed on those premises).

SPRAGGE v. THE COMMISSIONERS [1977] V.A.T.T.R. 162 (the appellant sold hot dogs and hamburgers from a mobile van which he parked on a site adjacent to the public highway. The Commissioners assessed him to VAT in respect of supplies made in the course of catering. *Held*, allowing the appeal, that for supplies to be made in the course of catering there must be premises available on which the food may be consumed. As the public highway does not constitute premises for the consumption of food, the supplies were not made in the course of catering).

Group of companies—services—disbursements—cancellation of charges
BRITISH UNITED SHOE MACHINERY CO. v. THE COMMISSIONERS (1977) V.A.T.T.R. 187 (B.U.S.M. paid for goods and services supplied to other group companies, but for VAT purposes was separately registered from certain of its subsidiaries. It accounted to the Commissioners for tax charged on invoices to the subsidiaries. One subsidiary, although a partially exempt trader, deducted the whole amount of the tax charged as input tax. The Commissioners sought to recover the tax from the subsidiary. B.U.S.M. then issued to the subsidiary a series of credit notes purporting to cancel the charges. *Held*, that the credit notes were ineffective as being contrary to public policy; that certain of the payments made by B.U.S.M. (*e.g.* travel tickets) were disbursements as agent for the subsidiary and not taxable supplies; but certain other charges (for rent, etc.) were for taxable supplies).

Hearing—computational errors—costs
BROWN v. THE COMMISSIONERS (1977) V.A.T.T.R. 253 (an assessment was made against the appellants in respect of undeclared tax. A hearing fixed for January 26, 1977, had to be adjourned because the Commissioners failed to give the appellants sufficient access to certain documents. At the adjourned hearing the assessment was upheld, but subsequently arithmetical errors were found in the tribunal's calculation. The amount of tax was eventually agreed. The appellants applied for an award of costs. *Held*, that they should be awarded the costs of the abortive hearing of January 26, 1977, but not of the subsequent hearing (*Shaikh Khalique Ahmad* v. *Customs and Excise Commissioners* [1977] C.L.Y. 3131 distinguished).

Input tax—builder—heating appliances
F. BOOKER BUILDERS & CONTRACTORS v. THE COMMISSIONERS (1977) V.A.T.T.R. 203 (the appellant built a number of new houses, installing in the lounge of each a radiant convector gas fire. The Commissioners ruled that the gas fires were not " articles of a kind ordinarily installed by builders as fixtures " for the purposes of art. 3 of the Input Tax (Exceptions) (No. 1) Order 1972, and accordingly disallowed the appellant's claim for input tax. *Held*, that the articles qualified as articles of a kind ordinarily installed by builders as fixtures (*F. Austin (Leyton)* v. *Customs and Excise Commissioners* [1968] C.L.Y. 3281 applied).

—— *goods acquired in another's name*
BOOTH v. THE COMMISSIONERS [1977] V.A.T.T.R. 133 (the appellant, a wholesaler of hairdressing requisites, was able to obtain certain products only by the device of arranging for the order to be placed with the manufacturer in the name of another wholesaler. The invoice for the goods was made out to such other wholesaler, but the appellant paid the whole amount invoiced. He claimed to deduct the VAT paid as input tax. *Held*, that the property in the goods supplied passed to the appellant, and that he was entitled to deduct as input tax the VAT charged on the supply of those goods).

—— *incorrect amounts charged*
PODIUM INVESTMENTS v. THE COMMISSIONERS [1977] V.A.T.T.R. 121 (the appellant company entered into two contracts with a firm of builders (which subsequently went bankrupt) for building works which involved both alterations and repairs and maintenance. The builders charged the appellant value added tax in incorrect amounts. The appellant sought to deduct as input tax the amount

actually charged, although it was incorrect. *Held*, that input tax deductible under Finance Act 1972, s. 3, is the tax " chargeable " and not the tax " charged," where that is a different amount).

Input tax—invoices issued in fictitious names—fraud—onus of proof
F. G. CONSTRUCTION CO. *v.* THE COMMISSIONERS [1977] V.A.T.T.R. 178 (the appellant company engaged sub-contractors for the purposes of its business of building and civil engineering contractors. It claimed to have made payments to certain sub-contractors on the basis of invoices purporting to have been issued by them. It transpired that the invoices had been issued in fictitious names and that the persons in question had never rendered any VAT returns. The Commissioners made an assessment to recover the amount previously deducted by the appellant as input tax. *Held*, that the burden of displacing the assessment rested upon the appellant, and that in the circumstances they were unable to do this, as they had neglected to keep proper records of the work and they had no documents to show that the sub-contractors in question had in fact been engaged by them).

—— *selling agents—petrol*
BERBROOKE FASHIONS *v.* THE COMMISSIONERS [1977] V.A.T.T.R. 168 (the appellants, retailers of women's clothing, engaged selling agents who arranged home parties to be held at which goods were displayed and sold. The agents were paid a commission based upon the takings at the parties. The work involved the agents in travel, and the costs were covered by the agents purchasing petrol out of moneys in their possession but belonging to the appellants. They obtained invoices for the petrol in the names of the appellants. The appellants sought to deduct the VAT on the petrol as input tax. *Held*, dismissing the appeal, that the agents were independent contractors and not employees, and the petrol was supplied to them, and not to the appellants for the purposes of their business).

Leases—garages—storage
WILSON *v.* THE COMMISSIONERS (1977) V.A.T.T.R. 225 (the appellant took leases of three garages on terms restricting their use as garages for motor vehicles or general storage purposes. He used two for general storage purposes, and parked his car in the third. *Held*, that in each lease there was a grant of facilities for parking a motor vehicle, and tax was chargeable at the standard rate).

—— *holiday accommodation*
SHEPPARD *v.* THE COMMISSIONERS [1977] V.A.T.T.R. 272 (mainly in an attempt to avoid the application of the Rent Acts, the taxpayer advertised furnished flats as holiday accommodation. However, more than half of the flats were occupied by persons not on holiday. *Held*, that as the flats were held out as holiday accommodation, the lettings were taxable supplies).

Practice—adjournment—discretion
BUTTERFIELD *v.* THE COMMISSIONERS [1977] V.A.T.T.R. 152 (the appellant, who had twice unsuccessfully requested deferment of the hearing to allow proper preparation of his case, telephoned the tribunal on the morning fixed for the hearing, and explained that he was unable to attend and that his accountant had not been able to prepare the case in time for the hearing. *Held*, treating the telephone call by the appellant as an application for an adjournment, that, having regard to the circumstances, the application should be refused, and, there being no evidence to displace the assessment, the appeal against the assessment should be dismissed).

Records—assessments—basis of computation
NOLAN *v.* THE COMMISSIONERS (1977) V.A.T.T.R. 219 (the Commissioners were dissatisfied with the returns put in by the appellant, who ran a wool shop. They made an assessment based upon estimated purchases of stock during a period, allowing a mark-up of 47.5 per cent. The appellant appealed,

criticising the computation on the ground that it took no account of opening and closing stock figures, and made no allowance for inflation. The Commissioners revised their computation to allow for inflation by calculating the output for each period by reference to purchases of stock for the corresponding period in the previous year. *Held,* that the assessment should be reduced to the amount of the revised computation).

Refund of tax—do-it-yourself builder
KENNELL *v.* THE COMMISSIONERS [1977] V.A.T.T.R. 265 (the taxpayer planned and supervised the construction of a house for himself, engaging contractors to carry out part of the works, but himself digging the foundations, putting in some of the plumbing, installing fixtures and doing the decoration. He claimed a refund of tax on materials purchased. *Held,* that he was a " person constructing a dwelling " and entitled to a refund of tax).

Tennis and squash club—floodlighting fees
ST. ANNES-ON-SEA LAWN TENNIS CLUB *v.* THE COMMISSIONERS (1977) V.A.T.T.R. 229 (the club provided facilities for its members to play tennis and squash. They paid fees on admission and annual subscriptions. During winter, in the case of tennis, and at all times for squash, it was necessary to have artificial lighting; this was provided by the club on payment of special charges which exceeded the cost of the electricity. *Held,* that in consideration of the light fees facilities for tennis and squash were supplied, and that the supplies were taxable at the standard rate).

3047. Zero-rating and exemptions
VALUE ADDED TAX (CONSOLIDATION) ORDER 1978 (No. 1064) [60p], made under the Finance Act 1972 (c. 41), ss. 12 (4), 13 (2), 43 (1), as amended by the Finance Act 1977 (c. 36) and the Finance (No. 2) Act 1975 (c. 45), s. 17 (2); operative on September 4, 1978; replaces S.I. 1977 No. 2092 and remedies an error in that Order and consolidates the description of goods or services that are zero-rated or exempt from VAT.

ARTICLES. See *post,* p. [38].

VENDOR AND PURCHASER

3048. Contract for sale—illegality—intention to defraud mortgagee—effect of locus poenitentiae rule
[Can.] P and V effected two documents, one purporting to show the purchase price as $135,000, the other as $117,000. The true price was $117,000; the higher price was designed to enable P to obtain a larger mortgage. V refused to complete and pleaded this illegality. *Held,* specific performance would be denied; as P was seeking to defraud the mortgagee, he was relying on an illegal contract. If he sought to rely on the locus poenitentiae rule, he could only recover such payment as he had made before his repentance of the illegality. As his deposit had already been returned to him he had no cause of action (*Alexander* v. *Rayson* [1936] 1 K.B. 169, applied): ZIMMERMAN *v.* LETKEMAN [1977] 6 W.W.R. 741, Sup.Ct. of Canada.

3049. —— offer to third party—honest but mistaken belief in non-existence of contract—third party's entitlement to damages—quantum
[Can.] D agreed to sell land to T and subsequently, but mistakenly, thinking the contract with T had fallen through, agreed to sell it to P. T then sued successfully for specific performance, D complied with the decree and P sued for damages. D argued that damages were limited by the rule in *Bain* v. *Fothergill* as this was an innocent failure to make good title. P argued that D's inability to convey was caused by their own fault and was not a defect in title, to which alone the rule applied. The trial judge held that the rule applied, and P's damages were limited to the return of their deposit with interest, the cost of investigating title, and solicitor's fees. On appeal, *held,* D were entitled to the benefit of the rule in *Bain* v. *Fothergill,* even if they were reckless, so long as they were not fraudulent. (*Bain* v. *Fothergill* (1874) L.R. 7 H.L. 158;

Day v. *Singleton* [1899] 2 Ch. 320 applied.): A.V.G. MANAGEMENT SCIENCE v. BARWELL DEVELOPMENTS [1978] 83 D.L.R. (3d) 702, Brit.Col. C.A.

3050. —— oral agreement—entry into possession—whether sufficient act of part performance

[Aus.] The respondents went into possession of the appellants' house under an oral agreement whereby the respondents should pay off the mortgage and effect repairs on it and then the appellants would convey it to them. Subsequently the respondents sought specific performance of the agreement and relied upon their taking possession as an act of part performance. *Held,* they were entitled to do so. It is enough that the acts done are unequivocally, and in their own nature, referable to some contract of the general nature of that alleged. Here, the giving and taking of possession were sufficient acts of part performance in themselves. (*Maddison* v. *Alderson* (1888) 8 App.Cas. 467, applied): REGENT v. MILLETT (1976) 133 C.L.R. 679, High Ct. of Aus.

3051. —— vacant possession—unoccupiable

Purchaser found notice on door of his house limiting the occupiers of the house to one household, by virtue of a local authority direction under the Housing Act 1961, s. 19. Since there was a tenant on the first floor, the ground floor was unoccupiable. *Held,* a house sold with vacant possession of the ground floor meant the vendors were under a contractual obligation to deliver the property in a state to be occupied. The vendors could not contract to give vacant possession in a negative sense, that the property was in fact empty, but could not be occupied: TOPFELL v. GALLEY PROPERTIES, *The Times,* October 27, 1978, Templeman J.

3052. Conveyancing. See REAL PROPERTY AND CONVEYANCING.

3053. Covenants. See REAL PROPERTY AND CONVEYANCING.

3054. Negligence—duty of care—conditions of sale. See HONE v. BENSON, § 2062.

3055. Northern Ireland. See NORTHERN IRELAND.

3055a. Notice to complete—ineffective—return of deposit

By a contract dated December 4, 1972, the defendants agreed to sell a leasehold house to the plaintiff for £33,000. The plaintiff paid a deposit of £3,300. After exchange of contracts and delivery of an abstract of title, the defendants served notice to complete, but the plaintiff was unable to pay the purchase price within the 28-day completion period, and the defendants then purported to rescind the contract and forfeit the deposit. The plaintiff issued his writ when the defendants refused to return the deposit. At the time of the contract, there were three charges upon the property; known to the defendants' solicitors, who accompanied their notice to complete with a letter undertaking to satisfy these charges out of the proceeds of sale, thus conveying a free title to the plaintiff. *Held,* ordering a return of the deposit to the plaintiff, that the defendants were not in fact ready to complete on service of their notice, since they needed to be sure that the only charges on the register were the ones they were undertaking to discharge. Their notice to complete was therefore ineffectual. In all the circumstances, it could not be said that the plaintiff's delay in completing was so unreasonable as to entitle the defendants to treat the contract as at an end. It was therefore unnecessary to consider the plaintiff's claim under s. 49 (2) of the Law of Property Act 1925; where an order for return of the deposit would only have been made on proof of exceptional circumstances: COLE v. ROSE (1978) 122 S.J. 193, D.C.

3056. —— validity—whether can supersede a decree of specific performance

The carrying out of an order for specific performance is primarily a matter for the court, so that other contractual conditions inconsistent with the order may become inapplicable.

The purchaser of property obtained an order for specific performance requiring the vendor to complete. When the purchaser subsequently delayed completion the vendor gave a 28 day completion notice in accordance with cl. 19 of the Law Society's Contract for Sale 1970 edition, which governed the contract, and on the purchaser's failure to comply with that notice sought an order forfeiting the deposit and giving him leave to re-sell the property.

Held, dismissing his motion, that the enforcement of the order for specific performance was a matter for the court, so that cl. 19 did not apply after the order for specific performance had been made, so that the completion notice was accordingly bad.

SINGH (SUDAGAR) *v.* NAZEER [1978] 3 W.L.R. 785, Megarry V.-C.

3057. Option to purchase land—declaration procedure

[N.Z.] [Land Settlement Promotion and Land Acquisition Act 1952 (No. 34 of 1952), ss. 23 (1), 24 (1).]

On a true construction of ss. 23 (1) and 24 (1) of the Act, a contract or agreement for an option to purchase land is a transaction to which s. 24 applies.

Per curiam. The Illegal Contracts Act 1970 is available in relation to an illegality arising from a declaration which does not sufficiently comply with the requirements of the 1952 Act.

In 1971 R leased a dairy farm to H for five years. The lease contained an option to purchase the farm at any time during the term upon notice, and upon filing a declaration to comply with the requirements of the 1952 Act. H filed a declaration pursuant to s. 24 of the Act referring to himself as the lessee and making no mention of the option. R gave notice that he would not proceed with the option on the grounds that s. 23 of the Act had not been complied with, in that the statutory declaration related solely to the lease and not to the option, and further that the declaration procedure under s. 24 was not available to an option holder. Alternatively, if it was available, that in relation to the option, the declaration filed did not comply with s. 24 (1) (*d*). H applied for a declaration that the option was valid and enforceable; alternatively, if the option was unlawful, that it should be validated by an order under the Illegal Contracts Act 1970. The Supreme Court granted the declaration. The Court of Appeal held that the declaration procedure under s. 24 of the 1952 Act was available to an option holder, and that the declaration filed complied with s. 24 (1) (*d*) in relation to the option. R appealed to the Judicial Committee. *Held,* dismissing the appeal, that the declaration procedure under s. 24 was available to a landless man who acquired land by grant of an option to purchase, as well as to one acquiring by lease or by simple purchase; and since no form was prescribed for the declaration, that made by H complied strictly with the requirements of s. 24 (1) (*d*), thus the option was valid. (*Harding* v. *Coburn* [1976] 2 N.Z.L.R. 577 approved; decision of the Court of Appeal of New Zealand [1976] 2 N.Z.L.R. 589 affirmed.)

ROSS *v.* HENDERSON [1978] 2 W.L.R. 354, P.C.

3058. —— refusal to convey—damages

[Chancery Amendment Act 1858 (Lord Cairn's Act) (c. 27), s. 2.]

The rule in *Bain* v. *Fothergill* may be excluded where a defendant fails to show that he has used his best endeavours to fulfil his part of the contract.

P agreed with D that, if their partnership should be dissolved, P would have an option to buy a house owned jointly by D and his wife. On dissolution the wife refused to sell the house. On P's claim for damages, *held,* that (1) to restrict P's damages to his costs under the rule in *Bain* v. *Fothergill,* D had to show, and had failed to show in this case, that he had used his best endeavours to perform his part of the contract; and (2) the damages should be assessed on the basis of the value of the realty as at the judgment date, with a year's back-dating to take account of P's delay. (*Bain* v. *Fothergill* (1874) L.R. 7 H.L. 158 considered.)

MALHOTRA *v.* CHOUDHURY [1978] 3 W.L.R. 825, C.A.

3059. Possession—improvements by prospective purchaser—no contract of sale—entitlement to compensation

[Can.] A prospective purchaser of land entered into possession and improved the land with the knowledge and acquiescence of the owner, but no agreement for sale was ever concluded. *Held,* the improver is entitled to compensation on the basis of restitution, in order to avoid unjust enrichment. (*Fibrosa Spolka Akcyjna* v. *Fairbairn Lawson Combe Barbour* [1943] A.C. 32 applied): PREEPER *v.* PREEPER (1978) 84 D.L.R. (3d) 74, Nova Scotia Sup.Ct.

3060. Purchaser acting as vendor's agent—duty to disclose

When in the course of negotiations for the sale of land the purchaser, purporting to be the agent of the vendor and using the vendor's name without the vendor's knowledge, takes some action regarding the property such as making a planning application or entering a contract of sale, which might if disclosed affect the vendor's decision whether or not to conclude the contract, a fiduciary relationship arises; then the purchaser must disclose the facts prior to concluding the contract and if he fails, he is liable to account for his profit.

D Co. were negotiating for the sale of P's house and land for £7,750. D Co. made a planning application in P's name without P's consent seven days before contracts were exchanged. Outline planning permission to build was granted but P was not informed and completion took place. P, having learnt of the successful application sought rescission of the contract. *Held*, granting the application that D Co. was under a duty to account to P for the profits received as a result of the successful planning application. (Dictum of Lord Denning M.R. in *Phipps* v. *Boardman* [1965] C.L.Y. 3575, C.A. applied; *With* v. *O'Flanagan* [1936] Ch. 575, C.A. distinguished.)

ENGLISH *v*. DEDHAM VALE PROPERTIES [1978] 1 W.L.R. 93, Slade J.

3061. Sale of land—evidence of earlier contract for sale—presumption of abandonment

[Land Registration Act 1925 (c. 21), s. 13 (c).]

The court will presume facts on which the title to land depends in circumstances where a jury would formerly have been directed so to presume.

The vendors sold land as trustees at auction. Subsequent examination of the title showed a pre-existing contract for sale made in 1912, the details of which were not available and which was described as " suspended " on terms which were not known. Goulding J. held, on a vendor and purchaser summons, that the trustees had failed to provide good title. *Held,* allowing the trustee's appeal, that the facts as to title would be presumed in circumstances where a jury would formerly have been directed so to presume them and that here there was overwhelming evidence to support the presumption that performance of the contract of 1912 had been abandoned. The trustees were not, however, entitled to a declaration as to registration under the Land Registration Act 1925, s. 13 (which was unnecessary in the circumstances), since that section did not give the court an original jurisdiction over land.

M.E.P.C. *v*. CHRISTIAN-EDWARDS [1978] 3 W.L.R. 230, C.A.

3062. Specific performance—contract to sell council house—whether enforceable—correspondence and conduct of parties

In deciding whether the parties have reached a binding agreement, the court should look at the correspondence between the parties as a whole and at the conduct of the parties to see if they have agreed on all material terms.

G was the tenant and occupier of a council house owned by M Corp., by whom he had been employed for 16 years. In November 1970, M Corp. sent G a form and a brochure giving details of how he could buy the house. G completed the form and returned it, requesting information as to its price. In February 1971, M Corp. wrote informing G of the price, and saying that if he wished to purchase the house, he should return the enclosed application. G completed the form, leaving the price blank, and returned it with a covering letter asking for consideration to be given to defects in the path to the house. M Corp. replied that the price had been fixed according to the condition of the property. G wrote back asking the corporation to " carry on with the purchase as per my application." M Corp. took the house off the list of tenant-occupied houses and G did some work on the house. The political control of M Corp. changed and they resolved not to sell council houses except where legally binding contracts had been previously concluded. G was notified that the sale would not proceed. On G's claim, the county court judge found that the contract for sale was complete and ordered specific performance. On appeal by M Corp., *held,* dismissing the appeal (Geoffrey Lane L.J. dissenting), that in the light of the correspondence as a whole, and the conduct of the parties, there was a concluded agreement for the sale of the house. (*Brogden* v. *Metropolitan Railway Co.* (1877) 2 App.Cas. 666 and *Storer* v. *Manchester City Council* [1974] C.L.Y. 3932 considered.)

GIBSON *v*. MANCHESTER CITY COUNCIL [1978] 1 W.L.R. 520, C.A.

3063. —— **jurisdiction to award damages—damages in lieu**
[Chancery Amendment Act 1858 (c. 27), s. 2.]
A person who sues for specific performance may not subsequently treat the contract as discharged and sue for its breach, but damages may be awarded where an order for specific performance proves abortive.
P agreed to sell properties to D. D failed to complete and an order for specific performance was made. Mortgagees of the properties then enforced their securities by selling the properties. P's contract price with D would have been enough to redeem the properties; the mortgagees' sale price was not. P moved for an order that D should pay the balance of the purchase price to him. *Held,* allowing P's appeal, that (1) as P could no longer perform his part of the contract it would be wrong to compel D to pay the balance of the purchase price under the order for specific performance; (2) as P had sued for specific performance he could not elect to have the contract treated as discharged by breach and sue for damages; but (3) where an order for specific performance is no longer capable of being worked out an order for damages could be made by reason of the jurisdiction given by the Chancery Amendment Act 1858, s. 2, and would be made in this case.
JOHNSON *v.* AGNEW [1978] 2 W.L.R. 806, C.A.

3064. Title—registration of vendor as owner
[Aus.] V contracted to sell land to P. V was not at the time registered as owner himself but was purchasing the land from a third party. The land became subject to planning restrictions. P refused to complete. *Held,* as V was able to effect a transfer to P by the third party he was able to give a good title which P must accept. Specific performance would be granted to V:
MERITON APARTMENTS PTY. *v.* McLAURIN AND TAIT (DEVELOPMENTS (1976) 133 C.L.R. 671, High Ct. of Aus.

ARTICLES. See *post,* p. [38].

WATER AND WATERWORKS

3064a. Charges
WATER CHARGES EQUALISATION ORDER 1978 (No. 1921) [25p], made under the Water Charges Equalisation Act 1977 (c. 41), ss. 1 (1) (2) (7) (8), 2, 3 (1) (5); operative on December 21, 1978; provides for the payment of an Equalisation levy for the year 1979 by specified statutory water undertakers and/or payment to be made out of those levies to other specified water undertakers.

3065. Drainage. See LAND DRAINAGE.

3066. Northern Ireland. See NORTHERN IRELAND.

3067. Sewerage. See PUBLIC HEALTH.

3068. Water authority—provision of new main—whether " necessary "—deposit
[Water Act 1945 (c. 42).] The plaintiffs were property developers and wanted the defendant water authority to provide water to their site. Since the existing mains were fully used, the authority proposed to lay a new main and asked the plaintiffs for a deposit. The plaintiffs claimed a declaration that no deposit was appropriate since the main was not a " necessary main " within the Act. It was *held* that the main was necessary since it would start from the nearest point where there was an adequate supply of water and not necessarily the nearest geographical point. If this was the purpose of the main, it did not matter that other customers could be supplied en route: ROYCO HOMES *v.* SOUTHERN WATER AUTHORITY (1978) 122 S.J. 627, Forbes J.

3069. Water authorities
WATER AUTHORITIES (COLLECTION OF CHARGES) ORDER 1978 (No. 285) [35p], made under the Local Government Act 1972 (c. 70), s. 254 (1) (*a*), (2) (*c*), as applied by the Water Act 1973 (c. 37), s. 34 (1), Sched. 6; operative on March 31, 1978; provides for the collection and recovery on behalf of water authorities, by local authorities who are rating authorities, of charges for the supply of water and for sewerage services during the year beginning on April 1, 1978.

WELSH NATIONAL WATER DEVELOPMENT AUTHORITY (LLYN CWELLYN DIS-
CHARGE) ORDER 1978 (No. 325) [10p], made under the Water Resources Act
1971 (c. 34), s. 1; operative on March 31, 1978; authorises the discharge of
water into the Afon Gwynfai from Llyn Cwellyn after the construction of
certain works authorised by S.I. 1977 No. 2179.

WELSH NATIONAL WATER DEVELOPMENT AUTHORITY (CHANGE OF NAME)
ORDER 1978 (No. 520) [10p], made under the Water Act 1973, s. 2 (5);
operative on April 2, 1978; changes the name of the Welsh National Water
Development Authority to the Welsh Water Authority.

NORTH WEST WATER AUTHORITY (ABOLITION OF THE WINDERMOOR INTERNAL
DRAINAGE DISTRICT) ORDER 1978 (No. 595) [15p], made under the Land
Drainage Act 1976 (c. 70), s. 11 (1); operative on April 17, 1978; abolishes
the Windermoor Internal Drainage District and transfers all its rights and
property to the North West Water Authority.

WATER AUTHORITIES (CONTROL OF DISCHARGES) ORDER 1978 (No. 1210)
[25p], made under the Local Government Act 1972, s. 254 (1) (*a*), (2) (*c*) and
the Water Act 1973, s. 34 (1); operative on September 15, 1978; lays down
procedures for the discharge of trade or sewage effluent by water authorities.

YORKSHIRE WATER AUTHORITY (ARKENGARTHDALE: LANGTHWAITE INTAKE)
ORDER 1978 (No. 1645) [25p], made under the Water Act 1945, s. 23,
as extended by the Water Act 1948 (c. 22), s. 3, and the Compulsory Purchase
Act 1965 (c. 56), s. 33 (2); operative on November 13, 1978; authorises the
Yorkshire Water Authority to construct a reservoir and to carry out minor works
on Arkengarthdale Moor, and to acquire land for the purpose.

SOUTH WEST WATER AUTHORITY (COLLIFORD RESERVOIR) ORDER 1978 (No.
1945) [25p], made under the Water Resources Act 1963, s. 67 and the Compulsory Purchase Act 1965, s. 36; operative on January 11, 1979; makes provision for the construction of the Cilliford Reservoir by the South West
Water Authority.

3070. Water orders

Orders made under the Water Act 1945 (c. 42):

S. 19 (6) proviso: S.I. 1978 Nos. 3 (Southern) [10p]; 4 (Thames) [10p]; 5
(Yorkshire); 19 (South Derbyshire) [10p]; 27 (South Cumberland, Stockport
and District and Calder); 39 (Rickmansworth and Uxbridge Valley) [10p];
51 (Kesteven and North East Lincolnshire) [10p]; 52 (South Lincolnshire)
[10p]; 60 (Tees Valley and Cleveland) [10p]; 61 (Wessex) [10p]; 86
(Newcastle and Gateshead) [10p]; 166 (Radnorshire and North Breconshire)
[10p]; 213 (Middle Thames) [10p]; 261 (Yorkshire) [10p]; 262 (Eastbourne) [10p]; 263 (Lee Valley) [10p]; 264 (Anglian) [10p]; 265 (Thames)
[10p]; 403 (North West) [10p]; 404 (North Surrey) [10p]; 406 (Severn–
Trent) [10p]; 509 (Folkestone and District) [10p]; 511 (Portsmouth) [10p];
572 (York Waterworks) [10p]; 636 (South Staffordshire) [10p]; 666
(Welsh Water) [10p]; 667 (Welsh Water) [10p]; 668 (Welsh Water) [10p];
853 (Yorkshire) [10p]; 902 (Wessex) [10p]; 903 (North West) [10p]; 904
(Mid Kent) [10p]; 905 (Severn–Trent) [10p]; 906 (Yorkshire) [10p]; 1084
(Yorkshire) [10p]; 1184 (Severn–Trent) [10p]; 1193 (Yorkshire) [10p]; 1229
(Northumbrian Water Authority) [10p]; 1230 (Hartlepools Water Company)
[10p]; 1231 (Thames Water Authority) [10p]; 1232 (Thames Water Authority)
[10p]; 1369 (North West Water) [10p]; 1380 (Yorkshire Water) [10p]; 1381
(North West Water) [10p]; 1414 (East Worcestershire) [10p]; 1415 (Bourne-
mouth and District Water) [10p]; 1416 (Sunderland and South Shields Water)
[10p]; 1447 (East Surrey) [10p]; 1448 (Yorkshire Water) [10p]; 1506 (West
Hampshire) [10p]; 1561 (Southern Water) [10p]; 1620 (Mid-Sussex) [10p];
1666 (Chester Water) [10p]; 1667 (Northumbrian Water) [10p]; 1672 (Anglian
Water) [10p]; 1673 (Severn–Trent) [10p]; 1674 (West Trent) [10p]; 1740
(Anglian Water) [10p]; 1849 (Southern Water) [10p]; 1940 (Cambridge Water)
[10p]; 1955 (Severn–Trent) [10p].

S. 23: S.I. 1978 Nos. 142 (South West) [10p]; 143 (Wessex Water) [15p];
268 (West Kent) [25p]; 510 (South West) [10p]; 628 (South West) [10p];
653 (Severn–Trent) [15p]; 827 (Severn–Trent) [10p]; 829 (Wessex) [20p];
899 (Welsh) [20p]; 1194 (Bournemouth and District) [10p]; 1198 (Severn–
Trent) [20p]; 1200 (Severn–Trent) [20p]; 1276 (Anglian Water) [10p]; 1482

(East Surrey) [25p]; 1586 (Anglian Water) [10p]; 1782 (Wessex) [20p]; 1932 (Portsmouth Water) [20p].

S. 28: S.I. 1978 No. 986 (Cambridge) [25p].

S. 32: S.I. 1978 Nos. 405 (East Worcestershire) [10p]; 881 (Cambridge) [10p]; 1240 (West Hampshire) [10p].

S. 33: S.I. 1978 Nos. 1240 (West Hampshire) [10p]; 1249 (Bristol Waterworks) [10p]; 1823 (Hartlepools Water) [10p].

S. 50: S.I. 1978 Nos. 405 (East Worcestershire) [10p]; 881 (Cambridge) [10p]; 1240 (West Hampshire) [10p]; 1482 (East Surrey) [25p]; 1932 (Portsmouth Water) [20p].

Orders made under the Water Resources Act 1963 (c. 38), s. 67, and the Water Resources Act 1971 (c. 34), s. 1:

S.I. 1978 No. 898 (Welsh Water Authority) [20p]; 1199 (Severn–Trent) [10p].

WEIGHTS AND MEASURES

3071. Coffee and chicory extracts

Weights and Measures Act 1963 (Coffee Extracts and Chicory Extracts) Order 1978 (No. 1081) [20p], made under the Weights and Measures Act 1963 (c. 31), ss. 21 (2) (3) (5), 54 (2) (3); operative on July 1, 1979; implements Council Directive No. 77/436/EEC as to the prescribed range of metric quantities, and quantity marking, relating to extracts of coffee and chicory, and supersedes Pts. VIII and XI of Sched. 4 to the 1963 Act.

3072. Cubic measures

Cubic Measures (Ballast and Agricultural Materials) Regulations 1978 (No. 1962) [25p], made under the Weights and Measures Act 1963 (c. 31), ss. 11 (1) (3), 14 (1) and 58; operative on February 1, 1979; replace S.I. 1970 No. 1712.

3073. Measuring instruments

Measuring Instruments (EEC Requirements) (Amendment) Regulations 1978 (No. 25) [10p], made under the European Communities Act 1972 (c. 68), s. 2 (2); operative on February 20, 1978; amend S.I. 1975 No. 1173.

Measuring Instruments (EEC Requirements) (Fees) Regulations 1978 (No. 26) [15p], made under the Finance Act 1973 (c. 4), s. 56 (1) and (2); operative on February 20, 1978; prescribe the fees payable in connection with services provided by the Department of Prices and Consumer Protection in respect of EEC pattern approval of the following measuring instruments— meters for liquids other than water, ancillary equipment for such meters, material measures of length and continuous totalising weighing machines.

3074. Pre-packed goods

Weights and Measures Act 1963 (Various Goods) (Termination of Imperial Quantities) Order 1978 (No. 1080) [20p], made under the Weights and Measures Act 1963 (c. 31), ss. 21 (2) (3) (5), 54 (1) (2) (4); operative on July 28, 1978; amend S.I. 1973 No. 1967, S.I. 1975 Nos. 1178 and 1179 and S.I. 1976 No. 431 so as to provide for the withdrawal of the ranges of imperial weights respectively prescribed in each Order as those in which the various goods concerned may be pre-packed.

3075. ——— wine and grape must. See § 1500.

3076. Solid fuel

Weights and Measures (Solid Fuel) Regulations 1978 (No. 238) [10p], made under the Weights and Measures Act 1963 (c. 31), s. 21 (4), Sched. 6, para. 3C (3), as amended by the Weights and Measures Etc. Act 1976 (c. 77), Sched. 4; operative on April 1, 1978; prescribe the manner in which information required to be displayed on a vehicle shall be displayed where solid fuel is carried on the highway for sale in open containers made up in metric quantities.

3077. Units of measurement

Units of Measurement Regulations 1978 (No. 484), [25p], made under the European Communities Act 1972 (c. 68), s. 2 (2); operative on April 27, 1978; implement the requirement of Council Directive No. 71/354/EEC.

3078. Weights and Measures Act 1963

Weights and Measures Act 1963 (Potatoes) Order 1978 (No. 741) [10p], made under the Weights and Measures Act 1963 (c. 31), ss. 21 (2) (3)

(5), 54 (1)–(4); operative on June 1, 1978; provides that Sched. 4, Pt. VII (save for para. 7) shall cease to apply to potatoes.

WILLS

3079. Construction—certainty—admissibility of written memorandum—gift to "worthy causes"
  A gift in a will to "worthy causes" is void for uncertainty.
  T bequeathed her residuary estate to "such worthy causes as have been communicated by me to my trustees in my lifetime." T never communicated any such causes to her trustees before her death. The solicitor who prepared the will had prepared a memorandum of the circumstances surrounding the preparation of the will, referring to discussions between himself and T as to what institutions should benefit. The solicitor later died. *Held*, (1) documents showing that the expression "worthy causes" was used in a special sense were inadmissible; (2) "worthy causes" could not be confined to charitable causes, and the gift was void for uncertainty. The property would therefore pass as on intestacy. (*Shore* v. *Wilson* (1842) 9 Cl. & F. 355 and *Re Gillingham Bus Disaster Fund* [1958] C.L.Y. 385 considered.)
  Re ATKINSON'S WILL TRUSTS; ATKINSON v. HALL [1978] 1 W.L.R. 586, Megarry V.-C.

3080. —— contemplation of marriage—gift to "my fiancée"
  [N.Z.]. [Wills Act 1837 (c. 26), ss. 13, 18.] The deceased's will was made before he married. It contained a gift to "my fiancée G. F." *Held*, such an expression did not indicate that the will was made in contemplation of marriage; it was therefore revoked by the deceased's subsequent marriage and he died intestate (*Re Langston* [1953] P. 100 not followed): *Re* WHALE [1977] 2 N.Z.L.R. 1, Wild C.J.

3081. —— residuary gift—whether partial intestacy—property abroad and at home
  [Administration of Estates Act 1925 (c. 23), s. 49 (1) (*a*) (*aa*).]
  Expressions of intent relating to hotchpot and partial intestacy are capable of embracing beneficial interests in property abroad as well as at home.
  T lived in England from 1943 to 1948; he married and had three children. He returned to Nigeria, his first marriage having been dissolved, where he remarried and had a daughter A. T died in 1965. Cl. 3 of the will left his second wife all rents from his leasehold property in Nigeria for the maintenance and training of his daughter A, and for the maintenance of his aged mother. Cl. 5 left the second wife the residue upon trust for the same purposes. His mother, however, had predeceased him; his second wife died in 1970 and A's education was completed in 1975. T was domiciled in Nigeria but owned property in London as well as Lagos. On a summons by P, a son of the first marriage, to determine whether the residue was held on trust for the purposes and persons set out in cl. 3 or was held on a partial intestacy, *held*, the court would construe such expressions of purpose as indicating the motive for making an absolute gift. This was equality of gifts without equality of motive. A and the personal representatives of the widow were beneficially entitled to the residue in equal shares absolutely. (*Re St. Andrews Trust* [1905] 2 Ch. 48 and dictum of Page Wood V.-C. in *Re Sanderson's Trust* (1857) 3 K. & J. 497 applied; *Re Trusts of Abbott Fund* [1900] 2 Ch. 326 distinguished.)
  Re OSOBA (DECD.); OSOBA v. OSOBA [1978] 1 W.L.R. 791, Megarry V.-C.

3082. —— voidable marriage
  [Wills Act 1837 (c. 26), s. 18; Matrimonial Causes Act 1973 (c. 18), s. 12.]
  A will made before marriage will be revoked by that marriage even if the marriage is voidable under s. 12 of the Matrimonial Causes Act 1973.
  The deceased made a will under which D was a beneficiary. He then married P. On his death P sought letters of administration. D counterclaimed for a pronouncement in favour of the will on the grounds that at the time of the marriage the deceased's state of mind was such that he could not understand the nature of the ceremony or consent to the marriage, so that the marriage was voidable. *Held*, dismissing D's appeal against an order striking out his defence and counterclaim, that even though the marriage might have been

voidable, such a marriage, whether subsequently annulled or not, always operated under s. 18 of the Wills Act 1837 to revoke an earlier will of the party to a marriage.

Re ROBERTS (DECD.) [1978] 1 W.L.R. 653, C.A.

3083. —— words of explanation—division of residue—" small amounts "
In deciding whether words in a will are words of qualification or explanation, regard may be had to the testator's probable wishes.

The testator by his will bequeathed sums varying between £25 and £250 to some 25 legatees and directed that the residue be " divided between those beneficiaries who have only received small amounts." The residue amounted to some £14,000. The executor sought directions as to disposal of the residue. *Held*, that (1) the court should have regard to any punctuation in the original handwritten will notwithstanding that Probate had been granted to a typed copy; (2) such punctuation marginally indicated that the words " small amounts " were intended as words of explanation which construction was consonant with the testator's probable intentions; and (3) accordingly the residue should be divided between all the legatees, equal division having the attraction of simplicity which would probably have appealed to the testator. (Dictum of Astbury J. in *Re Battie-Wrightson* [1920] 2 Ch. 330 applied; *Re Bower's Settlement Trusts* [1942] Ch. 197 considered.)

Re STEEL (DECD.); PUBLIC TRUSTEE *v.* CHRISTIAN AID SOCIETY [1978] 2 W.L.R. 950, Megarry V.-C.

3084. Death duties. See DEATH DUTIES.

3085. Deposit of documents
WILLS (DEPOSIT FOR SAFE CUSTODY) REGULATIONS 1978 (No. 1724) [20p], made under the Supreme Court of Judicature (Consolidation) Act 1925 (c. 49), s. 172; operative on February 1, 1979; provide that the Principal Registry of the Family Division shall be the depository for the safe custody of testamentary documents of living persons which are under the control of the High Court, and regulate the procedure for the lodgment and withdrawal of such documents.

3086. Family provision—county court jurisdiction. See § 381.

3087. —— intestacy—whether son a dependant
[Inheritance (Provision for Family and Dependants) Act 1975 (c. 63), s. 2.]
The plaintiff adult son of the deceased could not claim under his father's intestacy. He could not, at 46, in good health and employment, be said to be dependent upon his father despite the joint occupation of their home. The deceased during his life was under no obligation to maintain or contribute to the plaintiff's maintenance: *Re* COVENTRY, DECEASED, *The Times*, November 14, 1978, Oliver J.

3088. —— legitimate son
[Inheritance (Provision for Family and Dependants) Act 1975 (c. 63), s. 1 (1) (*e*).] By his will, made in 1971, the deceased bequeathed all his property to his legitimate son contingent upon his attaining the age of 25. The deceased had divorced in 1971 and been granted the custody of his son. In June 1972, the applicant, then aged 18 with an illegitimate daughter, became his common law wife; her daughter was adopted on the deceased's insistence. A son was born of that union in 1974, and the deceased died in 1976. *Held*, the applicant came within the provisions of s. 1 (1) (*e*) of the 1975 Act and was entitled to a lump sum of £5,000; the remainder of the estate (valued at £25,000–35,000) would be divided equally between the boys: C. A. *v.* C. C., *The Times*, November 17, 1978, Sir George Baker.

3089. —— " maintenance "—no implication of destitution
[Inheritance (Provision for Family and Dependants) Act 1975 (c. 63), ss. 1, 3.]
The deceased owned a house in Essex and a half-share in a house in London owned jointly with her son-in-law. Her 1963 will devised the Essex house to her son, her half-share in the London house to her daughter, and divided the residue equally between them. Shortly before her death she sold her Essex house and bought another, expressing her intention to alter her will to devise the new house to her son. She did not do so and the new house fell into residue.

The son issued a summons under the 1975 Act and the daughter contended that, as the son was not in need of " maintenance," the summons did not come within the Act. *Held*, ordering the transfer of the new house to the son, the deceased had always intended the son to have one house and the daughter the other. " Maintenance " in the 1975 Act did not mean that an applicant had to be destitute before applying: *Re* CHRISTIE (DECD.); CHRISTIE *v.* KEBLE (1978) 122 S.J. 663, Vivian Price, Q.C.

3090. —— **master's decision—dissatisfied party**
The following Practice Direction was issued by the Chancery Division on April 5, 1978:
1. Applications under the Inheritance (Provision for Family and Dependants) Act 1975 are now frequently heard and disposed of by masters. The question arises how the case is to proceed if a party is dissatisfied with the master's decision.
2. It is open to the master, with the consent of the parties, to try the case in court under Ord. 36, r. 9, and if he does so an appeal lies to the Court of Appeal under Ord. 58, r. 3.
3. If, however, the case is heard in chambers, a dissatisfied party must apply for an adjournment to the judge, in which case there must be a rehearing, normally in court.
4. Though the judge or the parties may require any cross-examination on affidavits or other oral evidence to be heard again in full, in most cases this should not be necessary if a full note or a transcript of the evidence before the master has been made.
5. A master hearing a case in chambers should therefore ensure, if possible, that the proceedings before him are recorded by a shorthand writer or a recording instrument. If he is unable to arrange this he should take as full a note as practicable of the oral evidence given before him. On the adjournment to the judge there should be sent to the judge, with the affidavits, a transcript or copy of the master's note of the oral evidence and a transcript or copy of the master's judgment.
6. No provision should be made for the attendance of witnesses at the rehearing before the judge unless a judge so directs. A party requiring such a direction should apply to the master to adjourn that question to a judge in chambers as a preliminary point.
[1978] 1 W.L.R. 585; [1978] 2 All E.R. 167.

3091. —— **persons entitled to apply—testator had maintained plaintiff unwillingly**
[Inheritance (Provision for Family and Dependants) Act 1975 (c. 63), s. 1 (1) (*e*).] A female plaintiff aged 71 claimed to be entitled to apply for reasonable financial provision from her deceased brother's estate. The plaintiff had been widowed one year before brother's death and was left in hard financial circumstances. An unmarried sister of the testator, who for some time during his life had received £10 per week, persuaded him partly to maintain the plaintiff. The testator reluctantly agreed to divide the £10 per week between his sisters and paid the plaintiff £5 per week for the six months prior to his death in April 1976. By his will dated March 7, 1975, executed three months before the plaintiff was widowed, the testator gave the unmarried sister an annuity of £520 but left the plaintiff nothing. The residuary legatee was the second defendant who had been first an employee and later a director of the testator's private company. She had worked for and then with the testator for 23 years and was in comfortable financial circumstances. The net estate before payment of C.T.T. was £44,210·02. *Held*, that (1) the plaintiff had proved that she was a qualified applicant within the meaning of s. 1 (1) (*e*) of the 1975 Act (*Re Wilkinson* (*decd.*) [1977] C.L.Y. 3175 followed); (2) the testator had not made reasonable financial provision for the plaintiff by his will; (3) provision which the court would make must take into account the fact that the maintenance paid to the plaintiff by the testator during his lifetime had been made grudgingly and accordingly reasonable financial provision would be restricted to that made by the testator. Because a weekly sum of £5 p.w. would adversely affect the plaintiff's rent and rate rebates, a capital sum of £2,000 would be awarded:

Re VINER (DECD.); KREEGER *v.* COOPER, January 25, 1978, Master Chamberlain. (*Ex rel. J. L. Davies, Esq., Barrister.*)

3092. —— **polygamous marriage—whether first wife entitled to claim provision**
[Inheritance (Provision for Family and Dependants) Act 1975 (c. 63), s. 1 (1) (*a*).]

A wife is entitled to make a claim for provision from her husband's estate, despite the fact that the marriage was polygamous.

W married H in India in 1937, the marriage being polygamous under Indian law. H later remarried, and both he and his two wives acquired an English domicile of choice. H died leaving all his estate to his second wife. The plaintiff applied for reasonable provision from his estate. *Held*, the plaintiff was the " wife of the deceased " and therefore entitled to make a claim despite the fact that the marriage was polygamous. (*Hyde* v. *Hyde and Woodmansee* (1866) L.R. 1 P.D. 130 distinguished.)
Re SEHOTA, DECD. [1978] 3 All E.R. 385, Foster J.

3093. Grants of representation—indorsement of orders
The following Practice Direction was issued by the Chancery Division on November 8, 1978:

1. In June 1953, Vaisey J. directed that a consent order made in proceedings under the Inheritance (Family Provision) Act 1938, all parties being sui juris, was not an order under that Act and accordingly that no memorandum of the order should be indorsed on the probate or letters of administration, but that it was otherwise if a compromise was approved by the court on behalf of a party not sui juris (see note to Ord. 104, r. 13, at p. 1999/137 of the *Annual Practice* 1966). This ruling is equally applicable to consent orders in proceedings in the Chancery Division under the Inheritance (Provision for Family and Dependants) Act 1975 (" the 1975 Act ").

2. In the Family Division, memoranda of all consent orders in proceedings under the 1975 Act are indorsed on the probate or letters of administration whether or not the parties are all sui juris.

3. To avoid any divergence of practice between two Divisions having concurrent jurisdiction, the direction of Vaisey J. is now withdrawn. In future, every final order embodying terms of compromise made in proceedings in the Chancery Division under the 1975 Act shall contain a direction that a memorandum thereof shall be indorsed on, or permanently annexed to, the probate of letters of administration, and a copy thereof shall be sent to the Principal Registry of the Family Division with the relevant grant of probate or letters of administration for indorsement, notwithstanding that any particular order may not, strictly speaking, be an order under the 1975 Act.

(1978) 122 S.J. 780.

3094. Probate. See EXECUTORS AND ADMINISTRATORS.

3095. Revocation—typed copy—error in letters of administration
[Administration of Justice Act 1970 (c. 31), s. 17.] The deceased drew up her will duly executed and witnessed. All trace of it, however, had been lost although typewritten copies, one marked " signed 26/11/69," were found after her death in a locked attaché case deposited at her bank. Dispute arose, for in order to obtain a grant of probate P required the consent of J as the deceased's next-of-kin. J contended that the will had been revoked or lost, and successfully applied for letters of administration. However, owing to an error the warning required an entry of appearance within 80 days, as opposed to the usual eight. *Held*, the will was carefully and lucidly made and had never been revoked. The court therefore found for the lost will on the basis of the supposed copy and ordered that the letters of administration be revoked under s. 17 since there had been an irregularity in their issue. (*Welch* v. *Phillips* (1836) 1 Moore P.C. 302 referred to): *Re* DAVIES (DECD.); PANTON v. JONES, *The Times*, May 23, 1978, Judge Mervyn Davies.

3096. —— **will witnessed by beneficiary's husband**
[Wills Act 1837 (c. 26), ss. 14, 15.] The testatrix by her will left her entire estate to her sister with a codicil that if her sister should predecease her,

the estate would go to her niece, the plaintiff. On her sister's death, the testatrix in a second will appointed the plaintiff executrix leaving her the estate. Although duly executed, this will was witnessed by the plaintiff's husband. *Held*, ss. 14 and 15 of the Wills Act precluded the plaintiff taking any benefit under the later will and further, if the revocation clause took effect the earlier gift to the plaintiff would also fail. In the special circumstances, given the clear intention that the plaintiff was to benefit, the later will would stand without the revocation clause and the three testamentary documents taken together should be treated as the deceased's will: IN THE ESTATE OF CRANNIS (DECD.); MANSELL *v.* CRANNIS (1978) 122 S.J. 489, Browne-Wilkinson J.

3097. Trusts. See SETTLEMENTS AND TRUSTS.

3098. Validity—gift to family and friends
A direction by a testatrix that those of her family and friends who wished to might purchase any picture, not specifically bequeathed by her will, at an advantageous price, was upheld as valid since it was possible to say of one or more persons that they qualified (*Re Allen* [1954] C.L.Y. 3479 followed as applied in *Re Tuck's Settlement Trusts* [1978] C.L.Y. 2666.) " Family " means all blood relations of the testatrix: *Re* BARLOW'S WILL TRUSTS; ROYAL EXCHANGE ASSURANCE *v.* NATIONAL COUNCIL OF SOCIAL SERVICE (1978) 122 S.J. 646, Browne-Wilkinson J

3099. —— holograph—purported execution in Switzerland
[Wills Act 1963 (c. 44), s. 1.] The deceased, a British subject domiciled in England, purported to execute a holograph will in Switzerland during a short visit there. He died, as a result of a road accident in England, on February 18, 1977. The purported will was written on a sheet of hotel paper in his own hand, except for the printed address at the top of the sheet. It was signed and dated but not witnessed. The plaintiff, the deceased's mother, sought an order against the will, under which the defendants were the principal beneficiaries. *Held*, s. 1 of the Wills Act provided that a will was to be treated as properly executed if, inter alia, its execution conforms to the internal law in force in the territory where it was executed, *i.e.* Switzerland. Expert evidence showed that, under Swiss law, the fact that the place of execution was printed proved fatal to the will's validity. An English court was therefore entitled to find the will invalid by reason of its non-compliance with the Swiss provision: *Re* KANANI (DECD.) (1978) 122 S.J. 611, Judge Mervyn Davies.

3100. —— witnessed by beneficiary's wife—solicitor's negligence. See WHITTINGHAM *v.* CREASE, § 2825.

BOOKS AND ARTICLES. See *post*, pp. [10], [38].

WORDS AND PHRASES

3101. Cumulative table

Appropriate time, 1053; 1170.
Arrangements, 1039.
Attributable to that part, 2396.
Cannabis, 545.
Employee, 1116.
Immovable property, 1297.
Independent trade union, 2992.
Knowingly, 524.
Learning, 563.
Liable to interference, 2992.
Material particular, 507.
Objection, 222.
Occupied for the purposes of a business, 1770.
Ordinary appeal, 1296.
Overtaking vessel, 2736.
Person aggrieved, 224.

Premises, 2771.
Protected site, 2866.
Records of a business, 493.
Road, 2579.
Same offence, 529.
Set-off, 261.
Settlement, 1630.
Special circumstances, 1000.
Street, 2839.
Suitable, 3036.
Trade, profession or employment, 1821.
Use of land, 2870.
Utter, 442.
Value, 1573, 1574.
Warehouse, 2871.
Whole family, 16.
With leave, 868.

WORKMEN'S COMPENSATION

3102. Supplementation

WORKMEN'S COMPENSATION (SUPPLEMENTATION) (AMENDMENT) SCHEME 1978 (No. 1460) [20p], made under the Industrial Injuries and Diseases (Old Cases) Act 1975 (c. 16), ss. 2, 4 (2), and in consequence of S.I. 1978 No. 912; operative on November 15, 1978; amends S.I. 1966 No. 165 by making adjustments to the intermediate rates of lesser incapacity allowance.

BOOKS AND ARTICLES

BOOKS

*[The books published in 1978 are grouped under their appropriate " Current Law "
headings. Books relating to countries outside the jurisdiction are placed under the headings
BRITISH COMMONWEALTH and INTERNATIONAL LAW, except that books relating to Scotland
will be found under the heading SCOTLAND and tax books have been grouped under the
collective heading REVENUE LAW.]*

ACCOUNTANCY
Card, Richard and James Jennifer—Law for Accountancy Students. [Cased, £8·95.
Paperback, £5·95.]
Willott, Robert—Current Accounting Law and Practice 1978. [Paperback, £10·50.]
Fulbrook, Julian—Administrative Justice and the Unemployed (Cambridge Studies in
Labour and Social Law, Vol. 1). [Cased, £11.]
Wade, H. W. R.—Administrative Law, Fourth Edition. [Cased,£15. Paperback, £8·50.]

ADVERTISING
Lawson R. G.—Advertising Law. [Cased, £8·75.]

AGRICULTURE
Muir Watt Agricultural Holdings. Second supplement to the 12th ed. by J. Muir Watt.
[Paperback, £9.]

ANIMALS
Sandys-Winch, Godfrey—Animal Law. [Paperback, £4·50.]

BANKING
Gheerbrant, P. A.—Cases in Banking Law. 2nd ed. M. & E. Handbooks. [Paperback,
95p.]
Hudson, Halmer—Tolley's Exchange Control. [Paperback, £1·50.]
Pennington, R. R. and Hudson, A. H.—Commercial Banking Law (Legal Topics Series).
[Paperback, £6.]

BANKRUPTCY
Collins, Hugh C. (Ed.)—Wearing's Notes on Bankruptcy in County Courts. 7th ed.
(Oyez Practice Notes). [Paperback, £4·25.]
Cruchley's Handbook on Bankruptcy Law and Practice. 3rd ed. by Michael Crystal and
Brinsley Nicholson. [Cased, £15.]
Eales, P. G. and De Vos, P. A.—A Guide to Bankruptcy. [Paperback, £3·80.]
Fletcher, I. F.—Law of Bankruptcy (Legal Topics Series). [Paperback, £6·50.]

BRITISH COMMONWEALTH
Australia
Finn, P. D.—Fiduciary Obligations. [Bound.]
Lewis's Australian Bankruptcy Law. 7th ed. by D. J. Rose. [Cased and Paperback.]
McDonald, Henry and Meek's Australian Bankruptcy Law and Practice. 5th ed. by C.
Darvall and N. T. F. Fernon. [Loose-leaf.]
Macken, J. J., Moloney, C. and McCarry, G. J.—The Common Law of Employment.
[Cased and Paperback.]
Sykes, E. I.—The Law of Securities. [Cased and Limp.]
Tomasic, Roman (Ed.)—Lawyers and the Community (Law in Society). [Paperback,
£5·95.]
Tomasic, Roman (Ed.)—Understanding Lawyers (Law in Society). [Paperback, £5·95.]
Canada
Choate, Claire, E.—Discovery in Canada (Carswell's Practice Series). [Cased.]
Hogg, Peter Wardell—Constitutional Law of Canada. [Cased.]
Kavanagh, John A.—A Guide to Judicial Review (Carswell's Practice Series). [Cased.]
McCaughan, Margaret Morrison—The Legal Status of Married Women in Canada
(Family Law Series). [Cased.]

BOOKS AND ARTICLES

BRITISH COMMONWEALTH—*continued*

Canada—continued

Reasons, Charles E. and Rich, Robert M.—The Sociology of Law—A Conflict Perspective. [Paperback, £6.]

Sarna, Lazas—The Law of Declaratory Judgements. [Cased.]

Tetley, William—Marine Cargo Claims. 2nd ed. [Cased, £25.]

Wakeling, Audrey A.—Corroboration in Canadian Law (Carswell's Criminal Law Series). [Cased.]

Watt, David—Criminal Law Precedents. In two loose-leaf volumes. [Loose-leaf.]

New Zealand

Arthur, C. M.—Estate Planning in New Zealand. [Cased.]

Doyle, M. W.—Criminal Procedure. [Paperback.]

Hinde, G. W., McMorland, D. W. and Sim, P. B. A.—Land Law. In two volumes. Volume 1 [Cased, £39·50. Limp, £31]. Volume 2 [Details to be announced].

Nigeria

The Nigerian Law Journal Vol. 10, 1976. Ed. by Professor A. B. Kasunmu. [Cased, £10. Paperback, £6·50.]

Papua New Guinea

Chalmers, D. R. C. and Paliwala, A. H.—An Introduction to the Law of Papua New Guinea. [Cased.]

Goldring, J.—The Constitution of Papua New Guinea—A study in legal nationalism. [Cased and Limp.]

BUILDING AND ENGINEERING. ARCHITECTS AND SURVEYORS

AJ Legal Handbook. 2nd ed. Ed. by Evelyn Freeth and Peter Davey [Cased, £12·50. Paperback, £7·95.]

Keating, Donald—Building Contracts. 4th ed. [Cased, £19.]

Parry's Valuation and Conversion Tables. 10th ed. by A. W. Davidson. [Cased, £7.]

Shaw's Commentary on the Building Regulations 1976, by William H. Cutmore. [Loose-leaf, £16.]

Turner, Dennis F.—Building Contracts. 3rd ed. [Cased, £8·50.]

Uff, John—Construction Law. 2nd ed. (Concise College Texts). [Cased, £5·70, Paperback, £3·40.]

Whyte, W. S. and Powell-Smith, Vincent—The Building Regulations—Explained and Illustrated. 5th ed. [Cased, £8·95. Paperback, £4·95.]

Wood R. D.—Building and Civil Engineering Claims. 2nd ed. [Cased, £8·50.]

CARRIERS

Ridley, Jasper—The Law of the Carriage of Goods by Land, Sea and Air. 5th ed. by Geoffrey Whitehead. [Paperback, £5·65.]

CHANNEL ISLANDS

Deloitte, Haskins and Sells—The Channel Islands—Basic Business Information. [Paperback, £2·50.]

Tolley's Taxation in the Channel Islands and Isle of Man 1977, by David G. Young. [Paperback, £3.]

COMPANY LAW

Butterworths Company Law Handbook. Ed. by Keith Walmsley. [Limp, £7.]

Chilvers, David and Shewell, Paul—Receivership Manual. [Limp, £7·50.]

Franks, John A.—The Company Director and the Law. 2nd ed. (It's your law series). [Paperback, £3·95.]

Gough, W. J.—Company Charges. [Cased, £25.]

Kerr on Receivers. 15th ed. by R. Walton. [Cased, £17.]

Magnus, S. W. and Estrin, M.—Companies Law and Practice. 5th ed. [Cased, £47·50.]

Nelson's Tables: Company Procedure. 6th revised ed. by C. N. Gorman. [Paperback, £2·95.]

Oliver, M. C.—Company Law. 6th ed. (M & E Handbooks). [Paperback, £1·75.]

Page, G. Terry—An Employer's Guide to Disclosure of Information. [Cased, £8.]

Pitfield, Ronald R.—Company Law Made Simple (Made Simple). [Paperback, £1·95.]

Sealy, L. S.—Cases and Materials on Company Law. 2nd ed. [Cased, £13·50. Paperback, £9.]

Topham and Ivamy's Company Law. 16th ed. by E. R. Hardy Ivamy. [Cased, £10. Paperback, £6·50.]

Topham and Ivamy's Company Law. Scottish Supplement to the 15th ed. by David M. Walker. [Paperback, £1·60.]

Tricker, R. I.—The Independent Director. [Paperback, £4·50.]

COMPULSORY PURCHASE

Corfield, S., Frederick and Carnwath, R. J. A.—Compulsory Acquisition and Compensation. [Cased, £27.]

Davies, Keith—Law of Compulsory Purchase and Compensation. 3rd ed. [Paperback, £7·50.]

COMPUTERS

Tapper, Colin—Computer Law (Business Data Processing). [Cased, £6·95.]

CONSTITUTIONAL LAW

Grant, Lawrence et al.—Civil Liberty: The NCCL Guide to Your Rights. 3rd ed. [Paperback, £1·75.]

Leeds, C. A.—Guide to British Government. 3rd ed. [Paperback, £1·80.]

O. Hood Phillips' Constitutional and Administrative Law. 6th ed. by O. Hood Phillips and Paul Jackson. [Cased, £8·50. Paperback, £6.]

Walker, D. J. and Redman, Michael J.—Racial Discrimination. [Paperback, £5·50.]

Yardley, D. C. M.—Introduction to British Constitutional Law. 5th ed. [Cased, £8·95. Paperback, £4·95.]

CONTRACT

Bowden, Gerald F. and Morris, Alan S.—An Introduction to the Law of Contract and Tort. [Paperback, £5.]

Lawson, Richard—Exclusion Clauses after the Unfair Contract Terms Act. [Limp, £5.]

Major W. T.—The Law of Contract. 5th ed. (M & E Handbooks). [Paperback, £2.]

Rogers, W. V. H. and Clarke, M. G.—The Unfair Contract Terms Act 1977. [Paperback, 75 pence.]

Thompson, Peter K.—Unfair Contract Terms Act 1977. [Cased, £6·50.]

Yates, David—Exclusion Clauses in Contracts (Modern Legal Studies). [Cased, £4·85. Paperback, £2·85.]

COUNTY COURT PRACTICE

The County Court Practice 1978 by Judge H. S. Ruttle, R. C. L. Gregory, Michael Birks and Mr. Registrar A. M. Myers. [Cased, £30.]

COURT OF PROTECTION PRACTICE

Heywood and Massey: Court of Protection Practice. 10th ed. by Eric R. Taylor. [Cased, £26·75.]

CRIMINAL LAW

Aldridge, Trevor M.—Criminal Law Act 1977. [Cased, £13·50.]

Baldwin, John and Bottomley, A. Keith—Criminal Justice—Selected Readings. [Cased. Paperback, £4·85.]

Cracknell's Law Students' Companion: Criminal Law. 3rd ed. by T. Gore and C. L. Maundy. [Paperback, £4·95.]

Dhavan, Rajeer and Davies, Christie (Eds.)—Censorship and Obscenity (Law in Society Series). [Cased, £7·95.]

Fallon, Peter—Crown Court Practice: Trial. [Cased, £30.]

Glazebrook, P. R. (Ed.)—Reshaping the Criminal Law. [Cased, £12·50.]

Graham-Green et al.—Criminal Costs and Legal Aid. First supplement to 3rd ed. [Paperback, £5·50.]

Griew, Edward—The Criminal Law Act 1977. [Paperback, £2·40.]

Griew, Edward—The Theft Acts 1968 and 1978. 3rd ed. [Cased, £9·25. Paperback, £6·25.]

Grygier, Tadensz—Social Protection Code: A New Model of Criminal Justice (The American Series of Foreign Penal Codes). [Cased, £10.]

Hall, Stuart, Critcher, Chas. et al.—Policing the Crisis (Critical Social Studies). [Cased, £12·50. Paperback, £4·95.]

Hallett, Heather—Criminal Law Act 1977 Part III. [Limp, £2·80.]

Harris, Brian—The New Law of Bail. [Limp, £3.]

Morrish, Peter and McLean, Ian—The Crown Court. 9th ed. [Cased, £8.]

Smith, J. C. and Hogan, Brian—Criminal Law. 4th ed. [Cased, £14·75. Paperback, £9·75.]

Williams, Glanville—Textbook of Criminal Law. [Cased, £16. Paperback, £10.]

CRIMINOLOGY

West, D. V., Roy, C., Nichols, F. L.—Understanding Sexual Attacks (Cambridge Studies in Criminology). [Cased, £7·95. Paperback, £2·80.]

Wootton, Barbara—Crime and Penal Policy. [Cased, £5·95.]

BOOKS AND ARTICLES

DIVORCE AND MATRIMONIAL CAUSES
>Freeman, M. D. A.—The Domestic Proceedings and Magistrates' Courts Act 1978 (Current Law Statute Reports). [Paperback, £2·20.]
>Friedman, Gil—How to Conduct Your Own Divorce. Revised ed. [Cased, £5·95.]
>Rayden's Law and Practice in Divorce and Family Matters. 3rd Cumulative Supplement to 12th ed. Ed. in Chief: Joseph Jackson. [Cased, £15.]

EASEMENTS AND PRESCRIPTIONS
>Jackson, Paul—The Law of Easements and Profits. [Cased, £18.]

EMPLOYMENT
>Anderman, Steven D.—The Law of Unfair Dismissal. [Cased, £12·50. Paperback, £8·50.]
>Bercusson, Brian—Fair Wages Resolutions (Studies in Labour and Social Law, Vol. 2). [Cased, £14·50.]
>Golzen, Godfrey et al.—Working for Yourself—The Daily Telegraph guide to Self Employment. 2nd revised ed. [Paperback, £2·50.]
>Schofield, P. G. and Burke, C.—Cases and Statutes on Labour Law (Concise College Casenotes). [Paperback, £3·85.]
>Selwyn's Law of Employment. 2nd ed. by Norman M. Selwyn. [Paperback, £5·95.]
>Tolley's Employment Handbook by Elizabeth Slade. [Paperback, £6·50.]

EQUITY
>Goff, S., Robert and Jones Gareth—The Law of Restitution. 2nd ed. [Cased, £27·50.]
>Oakley, A. J.—Constructive Trusts (Modern Legal Studies). [Cased, £4·35. Paperback, £2·65.]

EUROPEAN COMMUNITIES
>Bellamy, C. W. and Child, Graham D.—Common Market Law of Competition. 2nd ed. [Cased, £19·75.]
>Brinkhorst, L. J. and Schermers, H. G.—Judicial Remedies in the European Communities. 2nd revised ed. [Limp, £17·50.]
>E.E.C. Competition Law. Ed. by Barlo Beckerleg. [Paperback, £6·50.]

EVIDENCE
>Curzon, L. B.—Law of Evidence (M & E Handbooks). [Paperback, £2·25.]
>Eggleston, Richard—Evidence, Proof and Probability (Law in Context). [Cased, £8. Paperback, £4·50.]
>Phipson on Evidence by J. H. Buzzard, R. May and M. N. Howard (Common Law Library No. 10). 1st Supplement. [Paperback, £2.]

EXECUTORS AND ADMINISTRATORS
>Bailey, R. C.—Nelson's Tables: Administration of Estates. Revised 6th ed. [Paperback, £1·25.]
>Maudsley, R. H. and Burn, E. H.—Trusts and Trustees: Cases and Materials. 2nd ed. [Cased, £16·50. Paperback £12.]

FAMILY LAW
>Eekelaar, John—Family Law and Social Policy (Law in Context). [Cased, £11. Paperback, £7·50.]
>Martyn, John G. Ross—The Modern Law of Family Provision. [Paperback, £3.]

FIRE SERVICE
>Taylor, Jane and Cooke, Gordon (Eds.)—The Fire Precautions Act in Practice. [Cased, £6·95. Paperback, £4·95.]

HEALTH AND SAFETY
>Dewis, M.—The Law on Health and Safety at Work. [Cased, £7·50.]
>Smith, Peter—Industrial Injuries Benefits. [Cased, £8·50.]

HOTELS
>Field, David—Hotel and Catering Law. 3rd ed. (Concise College Texts). [Cased, £5. Paperback, £3.]

HOUSING
>Hoath, David—Council Housing (Modern Legal Studies). [Cased, £4. Paperback, £2·50.]
>Macey, John P. and Baker, Charles Vivian—Housing Management. 3rd ed. [Cased, £15. Paperback, £8.]
>Partington, Martin—The Housing (Homeless Persons) Act 1977 and Code of Guidance. [Paperback, £1·50.]

BOOKS

INSURANCE

Houseman's Law of Life Assurance. 9th ed. by B. P. A. Davies. [Cased, £15. Paperback, £9.]

Ivamy, E. R. Hardy—Fire and Motor Insurance. 3rd ed. (Butterworth's Insurance Library). [Cased, £18.]

INTERNATIONAL LAW

Goodwin-Gill, Guy S.—International Law and the Movement of Persons between States. [Cased, £14.]

International Commission of Jurists—Human Rights in a One-Party State. [Paperback, £1·80.]

Lauterpacht, Hersch—International Law. Vol. 4: The Law of Peace, Parts VII–VIII. Ed. by E. Lauterpacht. [Cased £35.]

Belgium

The Unity of Strict Law. Ed. by Ralph A. Newman (Vol. II of the Unity of Law). [Paperback.]

Italy

The Italian Penal Code. Ed. by John Delaney (American Series of Foreign Penal Codes No. 23). [Cased, £15.]

Middle East

Corporate Development in the Middle East. Ed. by Robert Nelson. [Paperback, £15.]

The Netherlands

Audretsch, H. A. H.—Supervision in European Community Law. [Cased.]

The International Law of the Ocean Development. Two loose-leaf binders. [Loose-leaf.]

Vermes, M.—The Fundamental Questions of Criminology. Translated by Dr. I. Decsény. [Cased.]

Republic of Ireland

Tolley's Taxation in the Republic of Ireland 1977–78 by Eric L. Harvey and Nigel A. D. Lambert. [Paperback, £4·50.]

South Africa

Gibson, J. T. R. and Cowrie, R. G.—South African Mercantile and Company Law. 4th ed. [Bound and Paperback.]

Jacobs, Marcus—The Law of Arbitration in South Africa. [Cased.]

Shrand, David—The Law and Practice of Insolvency, Winding-up of Companies and Judicial Management. 3rd ed.

UAE

Nafa, M. A.—United Arab Emirates Company and Business Law. [Cased, £35.]

INTOXICATING LIQUOR

Paterson's Licensing Acts, 1978. 86th ed. by J. N. Martin. [Cased, £20.]

JURISPRUDENCE

Anderson S. Norman—Liberty, Law and Justice (Hamlyn Lectures). [Cased, £5. Paperback, £2·25.]

Atiyah, P. S.—From Principles to Pragmatism. [Paperback, 95p.]

Cross, Rupert—Precedent in English Law. 3rd ed. (Clarendon Law Series). [Cased, £5·95.]

David, Renee and Brierley, John—Major Legal Systems in the World Today. 2nd ed. [Cased, £14. Paperback, £9.]

Friedman, Lawrence M.—Law and Society—An Introduction (Prentice-Hall Foundations of Modern Sociology Series). [Paperback, £3·60.]

Frost, Anne and Howard, Coral—Representation and Administrative Tribunals (Routledge Direct Editions). [Paperback, £2·95.]

Harvey, Brian W. (Ed.)—The Lawyer and Justice. [Cased, £6.]

Hooker, M. B.—A Concise Legal History of South-East Asia. [Cased, £12.]

Hunt, Alan—The Sociological Movement in Law. [Paperback, £3·95.]

Kahn-Freund, Otto—Selected Writings. [Cased, £10.]

Kiralfy, A. K. R.—The English Legal System. 6th ed. [Cased, £6·85. Paperback, £4·25.]

Smith, K. and Keenan, D. J.—English Law. 6th ed. [Limp, £5·50.]

Stacey, Frank—Ombudsmen Compared. [Cased, £10.]

Unger, Roberto Maugabeira—Law in Modern Society—Towards a Criticism of Social Theory. [Paperback, £3.]

Watson, Alan—The Nature of Law. [Cased, £3·75.]

LANDLORD AND TENANT

Aldridge, Trevor M.—Letting Business Premises. 3rd ed. (Oyez Practitioner Series). [Paperback, £7·50.]

BOOKS AND ARTICLES

LANDLORD AND TENANT—*continued*

Aldridge, Trevor M. with Johnson, Tony A.—Managing Business Property. [Cased, £12·50.]

Arden, Andrew—Housing: Security and Rent Control (Social Work and Law). [Paperback, £3·35.]

Farrand, J. T.—The Rent Act 1977 and The Protection from Eviction Act 1977. [Paperback, £5.]

Lewis and Holland: Landlord and Tenant. 2nd ed. by C. Burke. [Cased, £8·95. Paperback, £5·95.]

Magnus, S. W.—The Rent Act 1977. [Cased, £34.]

Pettit, Philip H.—Landlord and Tenant under the Rent Act 1977. [Cased, £16.]

Woodfall Landlord and Tenant. 28th ed. by V. G. Wellings assisted by G. N. Huskinson. [Three loose-leaf volumes, £95.]

LIBEL AND SLANDER

Duncan, Colin and Neill, Brian—Defamation. [Cased, £13·50.]

MAGISTERIAL LAW

Anthony and Berryman's Magistrates' Court Guide, 1978. Ed. by C. J. Acred. [Limp, £5·20.]

Gerlis, Stephen—Summary Matrimonial and Guardianship Orders. 5th ed. (Oyez Practice Notes). [Paperback, £6.]

Henham, John A.—Magistrates' Summary Jurisdiction—Guide to Sentencing Powers. 5th ed. [Paperback, £1·50.]

McLean, Ian and Morrish, Peter—The Magistrates' Court. 4th ed. [Cased, £5·75.]

Stone's Justices Manual, 1978. 110th ed. Ed. by John Richman and A. T. Draycott. Three Volumes. [Cased in plastic carrier, £35.]

MEDICINE

Mason, J. K.—Forensic Medicine for Lawyers. [Cased, £12·50.]

MEETINGS

Hall, L.—Meetings 2nd ed. (M & E Handbooks). [Paperback, £1·50.]

MINORS

Anderson, Richard—Representation in the Juvenile Court (Routledge Direct Editions). [Paperback, £2·95.]

Austin, Patricia M.—Notes on Juvenile Court Law. 10th ed. [Limp, £1·80.]

Baxter, Ian and Eberts, Mary (Eds.)—The Child and the Courts (Carswell's Family Law Series). [Cased, £14.]

Bevan, Hugh K. and Parry, Martin L.—Children Act 1975. [Cased, £13·50.]

Feldman, Linda—Care Proceedings (Oyez Practitioner Series). [Paperback, £6.]

Hall, Jean Graham and Mitchell, Barbara H.—Child Abuse—Procedure and Evidence in Juvenile Courts. [Limp, £4·25.]

Parsloe, Phyllida—Juvenile Justice in Britain and the United States. The Balance of Rights and Needs (Library of Social Work). [Cased, £7·25.]

Priestley, Philip, Fears, Denise and Fuller, Roger—Justice for Juveniles. The 1969 Children and Young Persons Act: A case for reform? (Library of Social Work). [Cased, £3·95.]

MISCELLANEOUS

Baker, John—The Neighbourhood Advice Centre. [Cased, £6·50.]

The Bar List of the United Kingdom 1978. Ed. by Stevens Editorial staff. [Limp, £10.]

Brown, W. J.—'O' Level Law (Concise College Texts). [Cased, £5·50. Paperback, £2·85.]

Bruce, Richard—Success in Law (Success Study Books). [Paperback, £2·50.]

Byles, Anthea and Morris, Pauline—Unmet Need. The case of the neighbourhood law centre. [Paperback, £2·95.]

Cohen, Steve, Green, Stephanie, et al.—The Law and Sexuality. [Cased, £3·95. Paperback, £1.]

Current Law Year Book 1977; Current Law Citator 1977. [Year Book: Cased. Citator: Limp, £22.]

Curzon L. B.—Basic Law (M & E Handbooks). [Paperback, 95p.]

Faulks, Sir Neville—A Law unto Myself. [Cased, £5·95.]

Gordon, R. J. F.—Caravans and the Law. [Paperback, £3·80.]

Honoré, Tony—Sex Law. [Cased, £8·95.]

Jackson, Stanley—The Old Bailey. [Cased, £6·25.]

Poole, J. R. and Kiers, P. G. D.—Migration—United Kingdom. [Paperback, £11·50.]

Shaw's Directory of Courts in England and Wales 1978. [Paperback, £3·50.]

MISCELLANEOUS—*continued*

Sim, R. S. and Scott, D. M. M.—A Level English Law. 5th ed. [Paperback, £3·50. Cased, £5·50.]

Squibb, G. D.—Doctor's Commons. [Bound, £10.]

Williams, Glanville—Learning the Law. 10th ed. [Cased, £3·50. Paperback, £2.]

The Year Book of World Affairs 1978. Ed. by G. W. Keeton and G. Schwarzenberger. [Cased, £9·50.]

Zander, Michael—Legal Services for the Community. [Cased, £12·50. Paperback, £5·75.]

NAME

Josling, J. F.—Change of Name. 11th ed. (Oyez Practice Notes). [Paperback, £2·50.]

NEGLIGENCE

Bingham, R.—The Modern Cases on Negligence. 3rd ed. [Cased, £28.]

NEWSPAPERS

Callender Smith, Robin—Press Law (Concise College Texts). [Cased, £5·50. Paperback, £2·75.]

PATENTS AND DESIGNS

Cawthra, B. I.—Patent Licensing in Europe. [Cased, £16.]

Johnston, Dan—Design Protection. Illustrated by Peter Kneebone. [Cased, £5.]

Myrants, George—The Protection of Industrial Designs. A practical guide for businessmen and industrialists. [Cased, £8·50.]

Patents Act 1977—Queen Mary College Patent Conference Papers. Ed. by Mary Vitoria. [Paperback, £7·25.]

The Chartered Institute of Patent Agents (Eds.)—Patent Law of the United Kingdom. 4th Cumulative Supplement. [Paperback, £3·75.]

Patent Law Review 1977 (Volume 9). Ed. by Thomas E. Costner. [Cased, £30.]

Rosenberg, Peter D.—Patent Law Fundamentals. [Cased, £20.]

Walton, A. M. and Laddie, H. I. L.—Patent Law of Europe and the United Kingdom. [Loose-leaf, £50.]

White, T. A. Blanco, Jacob, Robin and Davies, Jeremy D.—Patents, Trademarks, Copyright and Industrial Designs. 2nd ed. [Cased, £6. Paperback, £3·75.]

PENSIONS AND SUPERANNUATIONS

Palmer, Barry—Tolley's Pension Schemes. [Paperback, £3·50.]

PLANNING LAW

Heap, Sir Desmond—An Outline of Planning Law. 7th ed. [Cased, £8. Paperback, £6·75.]

Little, A. J.—The Enforcement of Planning Control. 4th ed. [Paperback, £5·60.]

POLICE

Baker and Wilkie's Police Promotion Handbooks. No. 1. Criminal Law. 5th ed. by E. R. Baker and F. B. Dodge. [Limp, £2·60.]

Calvert, Fred—Constables' Pocket Guide to Powers of Arrest and Charges. 6th ed. [Limp, £1·95.]

Powis, David—The Signs of Crime. A Field Manual for Police. [Paperback, £4·50.]

Simpson, Keith—Police: The Investigation of Violence (The Police Studies Series). [Cased, £4·95.]

Varwell, D. W. P.—Police and the Public (The Police Studies Series). [Cased, £2·95.]

PRISONS

Penal Policy and Prison Architecture. Ed. by Peter Dickens et al. [Paperback, £4·85.]

Stanfield, R. A.—The Detention Centre. [Limp, £2·15.]

REAL PROPERTY AND CONVEYANCING

Aldridge, Trevor M.—Boundaries, Walls and Fences. 4th ed. (Oyez Practice Notes). [Paperback, £3·95.]

Aldridge, Trevor M.—Guide to Enquiries before Contract. [Paperback, £1·75.]

Aldridge, Trevor M.—Guide to Enquiries of Local Authorities. [Paperback, £1·75.]

Barnsley, D. G.—Land Options. [Cased, £15.]

Denman, D. R.—The Place of Property (Studies in Land Economy). [Cased, £6·50.]

Emmet on Title. 17th ed. by J. T. Farrand and J. Gilchrist Smith. [Cased, £45.]

Garner, J. F.—Local Land Charges. 8th ed. [Paperback, £4·50.]

George, E. F. and George, A.—The Sale of Flats. 4th ed. [Cased, £11.]

Giles, Marjorie—Buying & Selling a House in England & Wales. [Paperback, £1·95.]

BOOKS AND ARTICLES

REAL PROPERTY AND CONVEYANCING—*continued*

Steele, Robert T.—Do-it-Yourself Conveyancing. [Cased, £4·95.]

Watson, J. J.—How to Buy Your Property Without a Solicitor. [Paperback, £4·95.]

Williams on Title. Second Cumulative Supplement to the 4th ed. by G. Battersby. [Paperback, £10·80.]

REVENUE LAW

Butterworths 1978 Budget Tax Tables. 14th ed. Ed. by Leslie Livens, David Bertram and Neil Thomas. [Paperback, £1·25.]

Butterworth's Orange Tax Handbook 1977–78. 2nd ed. (Butterworth Taxbook Annual). [Limp, £7·50.]

Butterworth's Orange Tax Handbook 1978–79. Ed. by Moiz Sadikali and David Roberts. [Paperback, £7·95.]

Butterworth's Yellow Tax Handbook 1977–78. 16th ed. (Butterworth Taxbook Annual). [Limp, £8·95.]

Butterworth's Yellow Tax Handbook 1978–79. 17th ed. Ed. by David Roberts and Moiz Sadikali. [Paperback, £9·95].

Dymond's Capital Transfer Tax. First Supplement by Reginald K. Jones and Roy R. Greenfield. [Paperback, £5.]

Frommel, S. N.—Taxation of Branches and Subsidiaries in Western Europe, Canada and the U.S.A. 2nd ed. [Paperback, £13·50.]

Goodman, Wolfe, D.—International Double Taxation of Estates and Inheritances. [Paperback, £13·50.]

The Hambro Tax Guide 1978–79 by A. A. Silke and W. I. Sinclair. [Cased, £5·50.]

Harvey, Eric L.—Tolley's Income Tax 1978–79. [Paperback, £6.]

Harvey, Eric and Young, David—Tolley's Corporation Tax 1978–79. [Paperback, £3·50.]

Hayton and Tiley—Capital Transfer Tax. 2nd ed. [Cased, £14·90.]

Institute for Fiscal Studies—The Structure and Reform of Direct Taxation. [Paperback, £6·95.]

Kay, J. A. and King, M. A.—The British Tax System. [Paperback, £2·95. Cased, £6·50.]

Mainprice, Hugh—Value Added Tax. [Paperback, £7.]

Mathew, Robin—Wheatcroft and Whiteman on Capital Gains Tax. 2nd Cumulative Supplement to the 2nd ed. [Paperback, £2·25.]

Mellows, Anthony R.—Taxation of Land Transactions. 2nd ed. [Cased, £18].

Potter & Monroe's Tax Planning with Precedents. 8th ed. by D. C. Potter and A. R. Thornhill. [Cased, £16.]

Pritchard, W. E.—Capital Gains Tax. 4th ed. [Paperback, £2·90.]

Pritchard, W. E.—Income Tax. 7th ed. 1978–79. [Paperback, £3.]

Rowland's Guide to the Taxes Acts & C.T.T. Ed. by Nigel Eastaway with David Trill. [Limp, £8·50.]

Tiley, John—Revenue Law. 2nd ed. [Cased, £22. Paperback, £14.]

Tiley, John—Revenue Law. Supplement to 2nd ed. [Paperback, £2.]

Toby, R. A.—The Theory and Practice of Income Tax. [Cased, £13.]

Toch, Henry—Income Tax. 10th ed. (M & E Handbooks). [Paperback, £2·25.]

Tolley's Tax Tables 1978–79. [Paperback, £1·20.]

Walters, R. M.—Capital Transfer Tax. 3rd ed. [Paperback, £2·50.]

Whillan's Tax Tables 1978–79. 31st ed. by Leslie Livens. [Paperback, £1·75.]

Williams, Donald B.—A Guide to Tax on Maintenance Payments. 2nd ed. [Paperback, £2·50.]

ROAD TRAFFIC

Bingham's Motor Claims Cases. Second supplement to 7th ed. by J. A. Taylor. [Paperback, £4·50.]

Bretten, G. R.—"Special Reasons." 4th ed. [Paperback, £3.]

Kitchin's Road Transport Law 1978. 19th ed. by James Duckworth. [Limp, £6·95.]

Wilkinson's Road Traffic Offences. 9th ed. by Patrick Halnan. [Cased, £18.]

SALE OF GOODS

Cranson, Ross—Consumers and the Law (Law in Context). [Cased, £15. Paperback, £7·95.]

Harries, John—Consumers: Know your rights (It's your law series). [Paperback, £3·95.]

Newsome, Eric L.—The Trade Descriptions Acts and the Motor Vehicle. [Limp, £2·70.]

SCOTLAND

Wilson, W. A.—Introductory Essays on Scots Law. [Paperback, £4.]

BOOKS

SHIPPING AND MARINE INSURANCE

Abecassis, David W.—The Law and Practice relating to Oil Pollution from Ships. [Cased, £27·50.]

Brown R. H.—Marine Insurance. Vol. 1—Principles. 4th ed. [Cased, £4·50.]

Diamond, Anthony—The Hague—Visby Rules. [Paperback, £1·50.]

Geen, G. K.—The Law of Pilotage. [Paperback, £4·50.]

Grime, Robert—Shipping Law (Concise College Texts). [Cased, £8·65. Paperback, £5·25.]

Hardy Ivamy, E. R.—Casebook on Shipping Law. 2nd ed. [Paperback, £4·50.]

Hudson, N. G. and Milburn, D. G.—Marine Claims Handbook. 2nd ed. [Paperback, £2·95.]

Stevens, Edward P.—Shipping Practice. 10th ed. revised by C. J. S. Butterfield (Pitman International Text). [Limp, £3·95.]

Sturt, Richard H. B.—The New Collision Regulations. [Paperback, £4·50.]

Wilford, Michael, Coghlin, Terence, Healy, Nicholas—Time Charters. [Cased, £18.]

Witherby & Co.—Reference Book of Marine Insurance Clauses. 50th and Revised ed. [Paperback, £6·50.]

SOCIAL SECURITY

Calvert, Harry—Social Security Law. 2nd ed. [Paperback, £6·85.]

Ogus, A. I. and Barendt, E. M.—The Law of Social Security. [Cased, £17·50. Paperback, £11·75.]

Partington, Martin—Claim in Time. [Cased, £7·95. Paperback, £2·95.]

SOCIAL SERVICES

Byrne, Anthony and Padfield, Colin—Social Services Made Simple (Made Simple Series). [Paperback, £1·95.]

Grace, Clive and Wilkinson, Philip—Negotiating the Law: Social Work and the Legal Services (Routledge Direct Editions). [Paperback, £3·95.]

Raisbeck B. L.—Law and the Social Worker. [Cased, £7·95. Paperback, £2·95.]

Roberts, Gwyneth—Essential Law for Social Workers. [Paperback, £4·95.]

SOLICITORS

Harrowes, David—Managing the Partnership Office. [Limp, £4·50.]

Moeran, Edward—Legal Aid Summary—1978 ed. [Paperback, £1·95.]

Williams, Donald B.—Costs, A Practical Introduction. [Paperback, £2.]

SUPREME COURT PRACTICE

The Supreme Court Practice 1979 in Two Volumes with First Cumulative Supplement. General Ed.: I. H. Jacob. [Cased, £75.]

Williams, Emlyn—ABC Guide to the Practice of the Supreme Court. 39th ed. [Paperback, £6·75.]

TORTS

Abbott, Howard—Product Liability—An Exercise in Corporate Survival. [Paperback, £4·50.]

Bradbury, P. L.—Cases and Statutes on Tort. 2nd ed. (Concise College Casenotes). [Cased, £6. Paperback, £3·35.]

Clerk and Lindsell on Torts. Second Cumulative Supplement to the 14th ed. (Common Law Library). [Paperback, £3·50.]

Cracknell's Law Students' Companion. Torts. 5th ed. by M. G. Lloyd. [Paperback, £5·95.]

Fleming, John G.—The Law of Torts. 5th ed. [Cased, £17. Paperback, £14.]

Heydon, J. D.—Economic Torts. 2nd ed. (Modern Legal Studies). [Cased, £5. Paperback, £3·20.]

James, Philip S. and Brown, D. J. L.—General Principles of the Law of Torts. 4th ed. [Cased, £11·50. Paperback, £7·50.]

TRADE AND INDUSTRY

Bennion, Francis—The Consumers Credit Act Manual. [Paperback, £6.]

Cunningham, James P.—The Fair Trading Act 1973—Consumer Protection and Competition Law. First Supplement. [Paperback, £9.]

Everton, Ann R.—Trade Winds—An introduction to the U.K.'s law of competition. [Paperback, £1·95.]

Frank, W. F.—Legal Aspects of Industry and Commerce. 8th ed. revised by Kevin Williams and Colin Perkins. [Paperback, £3·95.]

Guest, A. G. and Lomnicka, Eva—An Introduction to the Law of Credit and Security. [Paperback, £8·85.]

BOOKS AND ARTICLES

TRADE AND INDUSTRY—*continued*

Harvey, Brian W.—The Law of Consumer Protection and Fair Trading. [Cased, £8·95. Paperback, £5·95.]

Marsh, S. B. and Soulsby, J.—Business Law. Revised ed. [Limp, £4·50.]

Painter, A. A.—A Guide to Consumer Protection Law. [Paperback, £4.]

Ruff, Anne R.—Commercial and Industrial Law (M & E Handbooks). [Paperback, £1·75.]

Stevens & Borrie Mercantile Law. 17th ed. by J. K. Macleod and A. T. Hudson. [Cased, £11·50. Paperback, £6·95.]

WILLS

Brighouse's Short Forms of Wills. 10th ed. by Edward F. George and Arthur George. [Cased, £8·75.]

Davies, D. T.—Will Precedents and Capital Transfer Tax. [Cased, £11.]

Distribution on Intestacy. 1977 ed. [Paperback, £1.]

Pettitt, D. M.—The Will Draftsman's Handbook. [Paperback, £6·50.]

Tristram and Cooke's Probate Practice. 25th ed. by R. B. Rowe, Edmund Heward and G. F. Dawe. Consulting Ed. D. H. Colgate. [Cased, £30.]

Williams' Law Relating to Wills. Third Supplement to 4th ed. by C. H. Sherrin and R. A. Wallington. [Paperback, £3·90.]

INDEX OF ARTICLES

BOOKS AND ARTICLES

ARTICLES

ARTICLES

BOOKS AND ARTICLES

ARTICLES

CORPORATION TAX

Domestication and financial companies (*J. Dunford*): 100 Tax. 144

Small profits—lower tax rates (*H. S. A. MacNair*): 178 Acct. 592

Some U.K. taxation considerations (*M. J. Gammie*): 100 Tax. 437

The concept of corporate residence (*M. J. Gammie*): 100 Tax. 328

Willingale *v.* International Commercial Bank Limited (*L. Blom-Cooper*): [1978] B.T.R. 229

COUNTY COURT PRACTICE

Removal of stay of proceedings in county courts: 122 S.J. 242

CRIMINAL LAW

A criminal's rights in property for committing a crime and a deprivation order (*J. K. Bentil*): 142 J.P.N. 8

A maze in law! (*K. W. Lidstone*): [1978] Crim.L.R. 332

A new aspect of EEC criminal law in U.K. courts (*D. Mulcock and D. L. Brewer*): 142 J.P.N. 568

A new look at the inquest in the light of *Brodrick* (*H. H. Pilling*): 18 Med.Sci. & Law 13

A respectable infusion of dignified crime (*D. B. Smith*): 1978 J.R. 1

A small new liberty? (*D. W. Williams*): 128 New L.J. 9

" A storm in a teacup "—and the finger-printing issue (*D. Telling*): 142 J.P.N. 219

A woman's right to choose (*D. C. Bradley*): 41 M.L.R. 365

Abortion in New South Wales—legal or illegal? (*B. Lucas*): 52 A.L.J. 327

Act of shouting and swearing as threatening or abusive behaviour (*J. K. Bentil*): 142 J.P.N. 514

Agents receipt of money from clients as deposit and the law of theft (*J. K. Bentil*): 142 J.P.N. 100

Appellate attitudes towards compensation orders (*R. Brazier*): [1977] Crim.L.R. 710

Appropriation: a single or continuous act? (*Prof. G. Williams*): [1978] Crim. L.R. 69

Arrest and detention—the conceptual maze (*D. Telling*): [1978] Crim.L.R. 320

Ascertaining whether there is something worthwhile appropriating and the criminal law (*J. K. Bentil*): 142 J.P.N. 329

Assault (*C. Bird*): [1978] 3 Court 3.

Assault on a constable (*M. Noon*): [1978] 3 Court 16

Attempting the impossible: 142 J.P.N. 396

Attempting to commit a summary offence: 142 J.P.N. 367

Attempts to pervert the course of justice (*G. Keeton*): 142 J.P.N. 412

Bail—the debate continues: 142 J.P.N. 310

CRIMINAL LAW—*cont.*

Bail—the last Act: 142 J.P.N. 141

Balancing tyrannies in the administration of criminal justice: the right to remain silent (*R. W. Harding*): 52 A.L.J. 145

Blasphemy in Scots law (*G. Maher*): 177 S.L.T. 257

Called to a police station (*B. Nash*): [1978] L.A.G.Bul. 64

Cannabis (*M. Blyth*): 142 J.P.N. 466

Capital punishment: 68 J. Crim.L. & C. 601

Cheque and credit card frauds in English law—who is deceived?: [1977] L.Exec. 115

Claiming compensation for crime (*J. Cooper*): [1978] L.A.G.Bul. 162

Community service and the tariff (*K. Pease*): [1978] Crim.L.R. 269

Community service and the tariff (*A. Wills, R. Trewartha and K. Pease*): [1978] Crim.L.R. 540

Community service: concept and practice (*G. A. Read*): 142 J.P.N. 571

Community service for fine defaulters (*J. West*): 142 J.P.N. 425

Community service—impact for change (*D. Mathieson*): 141 J.P.N. 730

Community service re-appraised: 142 J.P.N. 439

Compensation: 141 J.P.N. 758

Compensation for detention (*C. Shelbourn*): [1978] Crim.L.R. 22

Compensation for violence (*G. Keeton*): 142 J.P.N. 567

Compensation orders and custodial sentences (*P. Softley and R. Tarling*): [1977] Crim.L.R. 720

Compounding the confusion in inchoate offences (*G. Williams*): 128 New L.J. 724

Conflict of interests in multiple representation of criminal co-defendants (*H. Van Hoey*): 68 J.C.L. & Crim. 226

Conspiracy under the Criminal Law Act 1977 (*J. C. Smith*): 1977 Crim.L.R. 638

Corroboration and self-corroboration (*Dr. A. J. Ashworth*): 142 J.P.N. 266

Corroboration: the liar's snare (*A. J. Ashworth*): 142 J.P.N. 422

Crime of specific intent and those of basic interest—an unenlightening dichotomy (*J. K. Bentil*): 142 J.P.N. 611

Crime and the company (*B. Harris*): 142 J.P.N. 65

Criminal bankruptcy (*A. N. Khan*): 122 S.J. 324

Criminal bankruptcy (*A. Samuels*): 142 J.P.N. 218

Criminal compensation by an offender (*A. N. Khan*): 122 S.J. 338 and 357

Criminal injuries compensation (*E. R. Howman*): 142 J.P.N. 264

Criminal injuries compensation: some recent developments (*A. N. Khan*): 122 S.J. 548

Criminal Legal Aid in 1976 (*H. Levenson*): 128 New L.J. 52

Criminal liability for transmitting disease (*A. Lynch*): [1978] Crim.L.R. 612

BOOKS AND ARTICLES

ARTICLES

BOOKS AND ARTICLES

CRIMINAL LAW—*cont.*

The Law Commission's Report No. 83. Duress (*A. T. H. Smith*): [1978] Crim. L.R. 122

The Law Commission's Report No. 83: Entrapment (*Dr. A. J. Ashworth*): [1978] Crim.L.R. 137

The Law Commission's Report No. 83: Necessity (*G. Williams*): [1978] Crim. L.R. 128

The legal effect of certain sentences (*M. McColl*): [1977] 4 Court 31

The legal requirements of sentences and orders in criminal cases (*J. Greenhill*): [1977] 4 Court 11

The making of English criminal law: Blackstone, Foster and East (*A. J. Ashworth*): [1978] Crim.L.R. 389

The manacle of the hearsay rule: proving that goods are stolen (*Dr. A. J. Ashworth*): 141 J.P.N. 714

The mental element in crime: the Law Commission's Report No. 89 (*G. Williams and B. Hogan*): [1978] Crim. L.R. 588

The mentally abnormal offender: 128 New L.J. 967

The metamorphosis of section 6 of the Theft Act (*J. R. Spencer*): [1977] Crim.L.R. 653

The new Home Office figures on pleas and acquittals—what sense do they make? (*J. Baldwin and M. McConville*): [1978] Crim.L.R. 196

The new law of bail: 142 J.P.N. 84

The new statutory offence of conspiracy (*G. Williams*): 127 New L.J. 1164, 1188

The place of compensation in the penal system (*M. Wasik*): [1978] Crim.L.R. 599

The prostitute and the beggar (*R. Graham*): [1977] 3 Court 16

The Public Order Acts (*B. H. Parsons*): [1977] 3 Court 35

The right to remain silent (*Hon. Mr. Justice F. M. Neasey*): 51 A.L.J. 360

The suspected person (*C. Bird*): [1977] 3 Court 11.

The termination of life support measures and the law of murder (*P. D. G. Skegg*): 41 M.L.R. 423

The test of obscenity: how it actually works (*C. Lewis*): 75 L.S.Gaz. 301

The use of photographs for the purposes of identification (*D. F. Libling*): [1978] Crim.L.R. 343

Theft Act 1978 (*A. Samuels*): 122 S.J. 667

Treason (*A. Wharam*): 128 New L.J. 851

Trespassers and owners, liberties and duties (*Dr. A. J. Ashworth*): 142 J.P.N. 155 and 172

Unsilencing your hostile witness (*V. Tunkel*): 128 New L.J. 478

Voluntariness, causation and strict liability (*M. Budd and A. Lynch*): [1978] Crim.L.R. 74

CRIMINAL LAW—*cont.*

What do we know of the causes of wife battering? (*M. D. A. Freeman*): [1977] Fam. Law 196

White collar crime (*G. Hampel*): 51 A.L.J. 629

Young offenders: borstal or imprisonment (*A. N. Khan*): 122 S.J. 482

CROWN PRACTICE

Habeas corpus: 68 J.Crim.L. & C. 571

Restraint upon exercises of the royal prerogative (*R. J. C. Munday*): 75 L.S. Gaz. 293

The application of legislation to the commercial dealings of the Crown (*J. R. Peden*): 51 A.L.J. 756

The Criminal Injuries Compensation Board: the first ten years (1964–1974) (*R. W. Hodgkin*): 6 Anglo-Am. 34

The suspending power exhumed (*W. A. McKean*): [1978] P.L. 7

CUSTOMS AND EXCISE

Charges having an effect equivalent to customs duties: a review of cases (*F. Woolridge and R. Plender*): 3 E.L.Rev. 101

DAMAGES

Aspects of lawmaking: the Miliangos decision: 75 L.S.Gaz. 731

Civil Liability (Contribution) Act 1978 (*D. M. Morgan*): 128 New L.J. 1042

Compensation for personal injury: Royal Commission's report (*Mountstephen*): 122 S.J. 241

Damages: some recent developments (*R. G. Lawson*): 128 New L.J. 627

Damages under CMR: the decision of the House of Lords (*A. C. Hardingham*): [1978] Lloyd's M.C.L.Q. 51

Economic loss—an Australian solution (*M. Brazier*): 128 New L.J. 327

Fatal accidents: the calculation of awards (*K. M. Stanton*): 128 New L.J. 81

Interest on damages claims (*A. H. Mallinson*): 177 Acct. 731

Precedent and policy in accident compensation (*F. Sutcliffe*): 7 N.Z.U.L.R. 305

Punitive damages—an historical perspective (*M. M. Belli*): [1977] 12 Trial 40

The politics of reform in personal injury compensation (*T. G. Ison*): 27 U.T.L.J. 385

Waiting for Pearson: the policy choices to be made in accident compensation (*R. Lewis*): [1978] 12 Law Teach. 1

DEATH DUTIES

Historical aspects of the estate tax (*L. McKay*): 8 N.Z.U.L.R. 1

Jurisdictional limitations on Commonwealth and state death duty legislation (*J. D. Merralls*): 6 A.T.R. 215

DEEDS AND BONDS

Signed—and delivered? (*H. E. Markson*): 75 L.S.Gaz. 269

ARTICLES

BOOKS AND ARTICLES

ARTICLES

BOOKS AND ARTICLES

ARTICLES

BOOKS AND ARTICLES

ARTICLES

[27]

BOOKS AND ARTICLES

LANDLORD AND TENANT—*cont.*

Forfeiture provisos and arbitration clauses (*A. M. Pritchard*): 41 Conv. 427

Grounds for possession (*A. Arden*): [1978] L.A.G.Bul. 10

Incentives to private landlords (*R. J. Brien*): 128 New L.J. 864

Landlord and Tenant Act 1954—opposing a new tenancy (*H. W. Wilkinson*): 128 New L.J. 826

Landlord and tenant review (*T. M. Aldridge*): 122 S.J. 563, 580, 600 and 620

Non-exclusive occupation agreements (*A. Arden*): [1978] L.A.G.Bul. 138

Notice in disrepair cases (*R. Holt*): [1978] L.A.G.Bul. 13

Nuisance by landlords (*M. J. Russell*): 40 M.L.R. 651

Occupying for business purposes (*H. E. Markson*): 122 S.J. 288

Owner-occupiers and the Rent Act 1977 (*P. F. Smith*): 128 New L.J. 729

Second thoughts by business tenants (*T. M. Aldridge*): 122 S.J. 71

Service charges in leases (*B. J. Harding*): 247 E.G. 707

Service charges in leases (*R. Pryor*): 247 E.G. 799

Some business lease clauses reconsidered (*P. Freedman*): 121 S.J. 766

Tenancy for life or licence (*Prof. J. A. Hornby*): 93 L.Q.R. 561

The assignment of informal leases (*R. T. Fenton*): 7 N.Z.U.L.R. 342

The Landlord and Tenant Act 1954: Business tenancies (*H. W. Wilkinson*): 128 New L.J. 715

The landlord and tenant casebook for 1977 (*V. G. Wellings*): [1978] J.P.L. 221

The Rent Acts: whose protection? (*A. Arden*): 128 New L.J. 624

The running of covenants in equitable leases and equitable assignments of legal leases (*R. J. Smith*): 37 C.L.J. 98

The termination of council house tenancies (*J. F. Garner*): 122 S.J. 355

They exquisite reason, dear landlord—licences to assign and the Leasehold Reform Act (*R. A. Weidberg*): [1977] C.L.L.R. 19

Validity of leases (*M. J. Russell*): 75 L.S.Gaz. 123

LAW REFORM

Access to the law (*J. McMullen*): 127 New L.J. 1216

Archaism in the courts (*Mr. Justice G. H. Walters*): [1977] 2 M.L.J. lxxiv

Law reform and the legal profession (*Prof. A. L. Diamond and R. D. Nicholson*): 51 A.L.J. 396

Matrimonial law reform: 142 J.P.N. 95 and 111

New uses of computers by lawyers (*R. Morgan*): 128 New L.J. 421–4, supplement

Reform of U.K. taxes on income (*C. N. Beattie*) 178 Acct. 276

LAW REFORM—*cont.*

Reforming the illegitimacy laws (*J. Levin*): 8 Fam. Law 35

Some aspects of injuries affection: a case for reform (*P. Butt*): 52 A.L.J. 72

Tax reform on the political agenda (*Rt. Hon. D. Steel*): 178 Acct. 279

The politics of reform in personal injury compensation (*T. G. Ison*): 27 U.T.L.J. 385

The Royal Commission on legal services (*E. R. Horsman*): 142 J.P.N. 312

LEGAL HISTORY

The freeholder and feudalism today (*J. H. Spencer*): 122 S.J. 289

The law and the economy in mid-nineteenth century Ontario: a perspective (*R. C. B. Risk*): 27 U.T.L.J. 403

The state of the Bar (*H. Kennedy*): [1978] L.A.G.Bul. 107

A short legal history of Sarawak (*Tan Sri Datuk Lee Hun Hoe*): [1977] 2 M.L.J. ms. lviii

Blackstone's neglected child: the contract of employment (*Prof. Sir O. Kahn-Freund*): 93 L.Q.R. 508

Liability for animals in Roman law: an historical sketch (*B. S. Jackson*): 37 C.L.J. 122

Lincoln's Inns of the fourteenth century (*Sir R. Roxburgh*): 94 L.Q.R. 363

Old time conveyancing (*W. A. Greene*): 122 S.J. 4

On the origins of *Scienter* (*B. S. Jackson*): 95 L.Q.R. 85

Punitive damages—an historical perspective (*M. M. Belli*): [1977] 12 Trial 40

Sir William (*A. G. Salmon*): 122 S.J. 379 and 393

Strict liability: advance retreat—or advancing backwards (*G. Samuel*): 6 Anglo-Am. 99

Students of the common law 1590–1615: lives and ideas at the Inns of Court (*I. D. Aikenhead*): XXVII U.T.L.J. 243

The assize of nuisance: origins of an action at Common Law (*J. Loengard*): 37 C.L.J. 144

The concept of statehood and the acquisition of territory in the nineteenth century (*J. A. Andrews*): 94 L.Q.R. 408

The dialectical origins of Finch's *Law* (*W. Prest*): 36 C.L.J. 326

The making of English criminal law: Blackstone, Foster and East (*A. J. Ashworth*): [1978] Crim.L.R. 389

The making of English criminal law: Macaulay (*Sir R. Cross*): [1978] Crim. L.R. 519

The Munitions Appeal Reports 1916–1920: a neglected episode in modern legal history (*G. R. Rubin*): 1977 J.R. 221

The spirit of the seventies (*T. G. Watkin*): 6 Anglo-Am. 119

[28]

ARTICLES

Libel and Slander

Defamation and the work of committees (*A. H. Boulton*): [1978] L.G.C. 205

Insuring against libel and slander (*C. R. McDonald*): [1978] L.G.C. 288

Qualified privilege in a business context (*R. W. Hodgkin*): 122 S.J. 40

Limitation of Actions

" An iniquity unmatched by any requirement of society " (*Prof. D. Owles*): [1978] Lloyd's M.C.L.Q. 9

Limitation: house owners *v.* local authorities (*P. Eyre*): 121 S.J. 839

Limitation of actions before the European Court (*P. Oliver*): 3 E.L.Rev. 3

The possessory title (*D. Brahams*): 75 L.S.Gaz. 769

Local Government

Access to information for the elected member (*A. Samuels*): 142 L.G.Rev. 73

Anns v. *Merton L.B.C.* (*Prof. H. Street*): [1977] L.G.C. 1025

Councils, public and the press (*A. Harding Boulton*): [1978] L.G.C. 318

Council tenants' complaints and the local ombudsmen (*D. C. Hoath*): 128 New L.J. 672

Devolution has begun in London (*R. Freeman*): [1978] L.G.C. 314

Electing a chairman of a principal council (*H. W. Clarke*): [1978] L.G.C. 1051

Exclusion of press and public from consideration of an unfit house (*I. Brown*): 142 L.G.Rev. 275

Gypsies and local government (*F. Othick*): [1978] L.G.C. 922

Gypsy caravan sites (*I. Brown*): 142 L.G. Rev. 261

Homeless families and local authorities: the 1977 Act (*D. C. Hoath*): [1978] Fam. Law 99

Injunctions and authorities (*M. Dockray*): [1977] L.G.C. 958

Kensington and Chelsea Corporation Act 1977 (*A. Ellery*): [1978] L.G.C. 125

Local authorities' sales and purchases (*H. W. Wilkinson*): 128 New L.J. 415

Local authority matters (*Dr. R. G. Lawson*): 142 J.P.N. 428

Minister pleads for greater use of Community Land Act: 246 E.G. 1097

Rent arrears: how to get them in (*A. Samuels*): 141 L.G.Rev. 651

Some aspects of injurious affection: a case for reform (*P. Butt*): 52 A.L.J. 72

The guardian ad litem in care proceedings (*S. Maidment*): [1978] Fam. Law 156

The maintenance of urban classified roads (*P. Rogerson*): [1978] L.G.C. 472

The National Front and Manchester City Council (*Prof. J. F. Garner*): [1978] L.G.C. 778

The rights of councillors to attend meetings of committees of which they are not members: 142 L.G.Rev. 245

The use of wardship (*J. G. Miller*): [1977] L.G.C. 981

Magisterial Law

Adoption: the relevance of welfare to unreasonable refusal of consent (*C. Latham*): [1977] Fam. Law 178

Battered wives in magistrates' courts (*A. N. Khan*): 142 J.P.N. 207

Compensation: 142 J.P.N. 203

Domestic Proceedings and Magistrates' Courts Act 1978 (*R. L. Waters*): (1978) 122 S.J. 565, 582 and 603

Domestic proceedings in magistrates' courts—the new law (*M. Rutherford*): [1978] Fam. Law 164

EEC criminal law and magistrates' courts (*D. Mulcock and D. L. Brewer*): 142 J.P.N. 113

Improvements in remand procedure (*E. Lloyd Parry*): 75 L.S.Gaz. 940.

Magistrates' court costs in criminal cases (*P. Morrish and I. McLean*): 142 J.P.N. 5

Matrimonial law reform: 142 J.P.N. 95 and 111

Mental disorders and the magistrates' court (*T. Lawrence*): 75 L.S.Gaz. 317

No surrender? (*J. N. Martin*): 142 J.P.N.

Papers in each hand: the new bail procedure (*J. Mulreany*): 142 J.P.N. 556

Post committal proceedings before examining justices (*F. G. Glover*): 142 J.P.N. 236

Recent cases on sentencing—a new procedure (*N. Crampton*): 142 J.P.N. 482

Registration of children's maintenance orders (*N. E. Hickman*): 128 New L.J. 567

Revolution in the juvenile court: the juvenile justice standards project (*A. M. Morris*): [1978] Crim.L.R. 529

The Domestic Proceedings and Magistrates' Courts Act 1978 (*M. Spencer*): 128 New L.J. 750

The magistrates' court and European Community law (*D. Lasok*): 142 J.P.N. 190

Medicine

A lawyer's guide to lumbar disc-lesions (*J. Cyriax*): 128 New L.J. 103

Mental Health

Mental disorders and the magistrates' court (*T. Lawrence*): 75 L.S.Gaz. 317

Sentencing the abnormal offender (*A. Samuels*): 128 New L.J. 304

The courts, the 1959 Mental Health Act and compulsory admissions to mental hospitals (*P. Bean*): 142 J.P.N. 341

The mentally abnormal offender: 128 New L.J. 967

Mining Law

Mining lease or licence? (*H. E. Markson*): 121 S.J. 804

Opencast coal mining (*J. J. Pearlman*): [1978] J.P.L. 234

BOOKS AND ARTICLES

ARTICLES

BOOKS AND ARTICLES

POLICE—*cont.*

Is the English bobby a male chauvinist pig? (*C. L. Mitra*): 142 J.P.N. 161

Police: powers and obstruction (*G. A. Esson*): 1978 S.L.T. 89

Police powers of search (*W. T. West*): 122 S.J. 308

Police powers, professional privilege and the public interest (*G. W. Keeton*): 141 J.P.N. 656

Terrorism and police powers: 128 New L.J. 869

PRACTICE

Applying for judicial review: practical points (*H. E. Markson*): 122 S.J. 495 and 517

Barristers' immunity (*A. Kewley*): 122 S.J. 188

Barristers' immunity (*F. G. Glover*): [1978] Fam. Law 22

Civil legal aid and the shape of things to come: [1978] L.A.G.Bul. 108

Contempt of court: 75 L.S.Gaz. 329

Contempt of court and the legal profession (*P. Butt*): [1978] Crim.L.R. 463

Contempt—the need for reform (*A. Whitaker*): 128 New L.J. 1040

Contingent fees: a supplement to legal aid (*R. C. A. White*): 41 M.L.R. 286

Criminal Legal Aid in 1976 (*H. Levenson*): 128 New L.J. 52

Decrees in foreign currency (*E. A. Marshall*): 1978 S.L.T. 77

Determinations by Lands Tribunal without hearing: 17 R.V.R. 297

Dismissal of action for want of prosecution during limitation period: 122 S.J. 135

Forum non conveniens: 1978 S.L.T. 93

Forum conveniens or forum non conveniens (*R. J. Arnold*): 8 Sydney L.R. 540

Garnishee proceedings (*E. Williams*): 127 New L.J. 1251

How Crown Court cases are listed (*B. Cooke*): [1978] L.A.G.Bul. 5

Interest on damages claims (*A. H. Mallinson*): 177 Acct. 731

Judgment in foreign currency—developments since the *Milianger* case (*J. Mills*): [1977] C.L.L.R. 7

Judicial misconduct in the U.S.A. (*C. Marrick*): 128 New L.J. 400

Law reform and the legal profession (*Prof. A. L. Diamond and R. D. Nicholson*): 51 A.L.J. 396

Legal aid in care proceedings (*N. E. Hickman*): 128 New L.J. 877

Liberty to rummage—a search warrant in civil proceedings? (*M. Dockray*): [1977] P.L. 369

Refusing to follow precedents: rebellious courts and the fading comity doctrine (*L. V. Prott*): 51 A.L.J. 288

Service out of the jurisdiction (*A. C. Hutchinson*): 128 New L.J. 278

PRACTICE—*cont.*

Stare decisis in intermediate appellate courts practice in the English Court of Appeal, the Australian state full courts and the New Zealand Court of Appeal (*C .J. F. Kidd*): 52 A.L.J. 274

The dismissal of actions for want of prosecution (*J. P. Corbett*): 128 New L.J. 351

The *Mareva* injunction (*David G. Powles*): [1978] J.B.L. 11

The *Mareva* injunction (*J. Hull*): 75 L.S.Gaz. 848

The question of jurisdiction in relation to rent tribunals, rent officers and rent assessment committees (*P. H. Pettit*): 41 Conv. 379

The state of the Australian judicature (*Sir G. Barwick*): 51 A.L.J. 480

Uncertain steps towards a European legal profession (*D. B. Walters*): 3 E.L.Rev. 265

Unprecedented judicial precedents (*A. N. Khan*): 122 S.J. 721

U.S. letters rogatory and the English courts (*S. Isaacs*): [1978] Lloyd's M.C.L.Q. 464

When will a superior court overrule its own decision? (*L. V. Prott*): 52 A.L.J. 304

PRESS

Contempt—the need for reform (*A. Whitaker*): 128 New L.J. 1040

Councils, public and press (*A. Harding Boulton*): [1978] L.G.C. 318

PRISONS

Boards of visitors in H.M. prisons (*A. S. Johnston*): 142 J.P.N. 458

Penal reform and prison reform (*Rev. Dr. W. J. Bolt*): 142 J.P.N. 223

Prisoners' rights: 68 J.Crim.L.&C. 591

PRIVY COUNCIL PRACTICE

Politics and the Privy Council: special reference to the judicial committee (*D. B. Swinfen*): 1978 J.R. 126

PUBLIC AUTHORITIES AND PUBLIC OFFICERS

" Public bodies " (*J. F. Garner*): 121 S.J. 785

PUBLIC HEALTH

Control of pollution (*Prof. J. F. Garner*): [1978] L.G.C. 32

Food poisoning and infection: problems of compensation (*P. M. Walsh*): 142 L.G.Rev. 301

RAILWAYS

Hackney carriage licences—plying for hire (*W. T. West*): 75 L.S.Gaz. 819

RATING AND VALUATION

A dwelling worth nothing? (*F. Othick*): [1978] L.G.C. 786

A ratepayer's right to make a proposal to increase another's assessment (*F. A. Amies*): 17 R.V.R. 257 and 294

ARTICLES

BOOKS AND ARTICLES

ARTICLES

BOOKS AND ARTICLES

SHIPPING AND MARINE INSURANCE—*cont.*
Some NYPE time charter problems (*M. Mabbs*): [1978] Lloyd's M.C.L.Q. 456
The Carriage of Goods by Sea Act 1971 (*D. G. Powles*): [1978] J.B.L. 141
The duration of the sea-carrier's liability (*C. W. O'Hare*): 6 A.B.L.R. 65
The Hague-Visby Rules (*A. Diamond*): [1978] Lloyd's M.C.L.Q. 225
The Trade Practices Act 1974 and overseas cargo shipping (*J. C. McCorquodale*): 6 A.B.L.R. 41

SOCIAL SECURITY
Appeals from supplementary benefit appeal tribunals (*N. Warren*): [1978] L.A.G. Bul. 211
Social services law (*B. Hoggett*): [1978] L.G.C. 149
Social security and family law in Australia (*R. Sackville*): 27 I.C.L.Q. 127
Supplementary benefit—a new legal structure? (*J. Levin*): [1978] L.A.G.Bul. 202
Welfare benefit planning (*R. Kohn*): 75 L.S.Gaz. 504

SOLICITORS
Employment law affecting articled clerks (*M. J. Goodman*): 74 L.S.Gaz. 1092
Inquiries into legal services in New South Wales and in the United Kingdom (*R. D. Nicholson*): 51 A.L.J. 764
Is a legal aid practice possible? [1978] L.A.G.Bul. 205
Lawyers' services within the Common Market (*R. M. M. Wallace*): 121 S.J. 843
New uses of computers by lawyers (*R. Morgan*): 128 New L.J. 421-4, supplement
Organisation of the profession (*Prof. H. B. Connell*): 51 A.L.J. 350
Remuneration of the profession (*H. E. Peterson*): 51 A.L.J. 513
Research as a way to improve the quality of legal work (*M. Zander*): 128 New L.J. 576
Sollicitor-client privilege (*A. N. Kahn*): 142 J.P.N. 484
Solicitors' remuneration: a critique of recent developments in conveyancing (*R. Bowles and J. Phillips*): 40 M.L.R. 639
Standards of practice (*J. C. Richards*): 51 A.L.J. 423
The role of solicitors in divorce proceedings (*M. Murch*): 40 M.L.R. 625 and 41 M.L.R. 25
The roles of the lawyer in the planning system (*P. Boydell, Q.C.*): [1978] J.P.L. 590
The Royal Commission on legal services (*E. R. Horsman*): 142 J.P.N. 312
The solicitor's duty on exchange of contracts (*H. W. Wilkinson*): 128 New L.J. 191
Uncertain steps towards a European legal profession (*D. B. Walters*): 3 E.L.Rev. 265

STATUTES AND ORDERS
Interpretation sections (*J. F. Burrows*): 8 N.Z.U.L.R. 33
Interpreting statutes (*Prof. J. F. Garner*): [1978] L.G.C. 534
Taxing statutes are taxing statutes: the interpretation of revenue legislation (*D. W. Williams*): 41 M.L.R. 405
The interpretation of EEC legislation (*G. McFarlane*): 122 S.J. 463

STOCK EXCHANGE
Confidentiality and the securities industry —some recent trends: 75 L.S.Gaz. 786
Insider trading Hong Kong style (*B. A. K. Rider*): 128 New L.J. 897
The crime of insider trading (*B. A. K. Rider*): [1978] J.B.L. 19
The Swiss approach to insider dealing (*J. H. Jenckel and B. A. K. Rider*): 128 New L.J. 683

TORT
An account of a U.S. product liability claim (*Prof. D. Owles*): 128 New L.J. 91
Civil Liability (Contribution) Act 1978 (*D. M. Morgan*): 128 New L.J. 1042
Compensation for personal injury: Royal Commission's report (*Mountstephen*): 122 S.J. 241
Damage from natural causes: landowner's liability (*F. G. Glover*): 142 L.G.Rev. 287
Duty to avoid economic loss (*Hon. Mr. Justice H. H. Glass*): 51 A.L.J. 372
Economic loss an Australian solution (*M. Brazier*): 128 New L.J. 327
Expanding remedies in tort law, 1957–1977 (*D. W. Noel and J. J. Philips*): 20 A.T.L.A. L.Rep. 409
Injuries to unborn children (*P. F. Cane*): 51 A.L.J. 704
Insurance and foreign judgments (*P. M. North*): 128 New L.J. 315
Liability for defective premises (*C. Bennett*): 128 New L.J. 25
Liability for defective products (*C. J. Miller*): 122 S.J. 655
Products liability and international trade law (*D. J. Harland*): 8 Sydney L.R. 358
Products liability in maritime law (*P. S. Edelman*): (1978) 7 Trial 50
Should economic loss be recoverable? (*J. Wenden*): 75 L.S.Gaz. 96
The future of tort law (*G. Calabresi*): 20 A.T.L.A. L.Rep. 403
The plight of the rescuer (*A. Blake*): 128 New L.J. 476
The politics of reform in personal injury compensation (*T. G. Ison*): 27 U.T.L.J. 385
The Torts (Interference with Goods) Act 1977 (*C. Manchester*): 127 New L.J. 1219
Trees: a knotty branch of the law (*A. J. G. Brown*): 128 New L.J. 481

ARTICLES

BOOKS AND ARTICLES

TRADE AND INDUSTRY—*cont.*

Unfair trade practices legislation: symbolism and substance in consumer protection (*E. P. Belababa*): 15 Osgoode Hall L.J. 327

TRADE MARKS AND TRADE NAMES

Industrial property in the EEC (*L. Melville*): 75 L.S. Gaz. 567

The concept of property: property in intangibles (*D. F. Libling*): 94 L.Q.R. 103

TRADE UNIONS

A.C.A.S. and the union recognition procedure (*L. Dickens*): 7 I.L.J. 160

Advisory, Conciliation and Arbitration Service: recognition issues (*D. Newell*): 122 S.J. 392

After Bullock: co-operation not confrontation (*N. Bourne*): 128 New L.J. 874

Grunwick and trade union recognition (*K. Williams*): 12 L.Teach. 38

Judicial control of union tribunals (*D. R. Hall*): 51 A.L.J. 693

Religious freedom and the closed shop (*A. J. Gamble*): 1978 S.L.T. 103

The law relating to employers and trade unions (*O. H. Parsons*): 74 L.S.Gaz. 1035

Time off for trade union duties and activities: 74 L.S.Gaz. 1029

Trade unions and trade practices (*M. Sexton*): 5 A.B.L.R. 204

Union recognition procedure reviewed (*H. E. Markson*): 122 S.J. 39

TRANSPORT

Carriage by " combined transport "—recent developments (*J. Goldring*): 6 A.B.L.R. 151

Gold franc—replacement of unit of account (*L. Bristow*): [1978] Lloyd's M.C.L.Q. 31

Minibus Act 1977 (*A. Samuels*): 75 L.S. Gaz. 334

TRESPASS

Adverse possession: the squatter's title (*D. Brahams*): 244 E.G. 955

Squatters and the Criminal Law Act (*Prof. B. Harvey*): [1978] L.G.C. 1075

Trespassers and owners, liberties and duties (*Dr. A. J. Ashworth*): 142 J.P.N. 155 and 172

VALUE ADDED TAX

Having your cake and eating it (*H. H. Mainprice*): 178 Acct. 271

A VAT trap (*J. F. Avery Jones*): 122 S.J. 547

VENDOR AND PURCHASER

Constructive trusts of registered land (*J. Martin*): [1978] Conv. 52

Domestic house purchase transactions (*D. M. Bows and E. M. Bourne*): 122 S.J. 104

WILLS

A non-defining relative clause (*F. G. Glover*): 128 New L.J. 962

Defeating the dependants (*C. H. Sherrin*): [1978] Conv. 13

Discovering a testator's intention (*R. D. Mackay*): 127 New L.J. 1089

House in return for services (*W. T. West*): 122 S.J. 272

Passing particular property (*H. E. Markson*): 128 New L.J. 181

Provision for dependants and agreements for testamentary provision (*J. G. Miller*): 128 New L.J. 449

Succession 1977: 1978 S.L.T. 125 and 145

Testamentary conditions in restraint of religion (*P. Butt*): 8 Sydney L.R. 400

The advisability of making a will (*A. J. Creamer*): 179 Acct. 110

Wills in contemplation of marriage (*S. M. Bandali*): [1977] L.Exec. 119, and 6 Anglo-Am. 6

INDEX 1972–78

References are to the relevant Year Book and then the paragraph number, eg. 78/1122 means para. 1122 in the Current Law Year Book 1978.
For references to pre-1972 material, see the Index to the Current Law Year Book 1976.

Caravans,
gipsy encampments, 73/3241; 74/3057, 3744; 75/3353
Mobile Homes Act 1975 (c. 49)...75/3355
town and country planning, 72/3324, 3325; 73/3225-7; 75/3353, 3355; 78/2866
whether a dwelling-house, 77/1585
Care and protection, 73/2171; 74/2367; 75/2010, 2152, 2153; 76/1762-5
Careless driving, 72/2985-7; 73/2986; 75/3008, 3009
Caribbean Development Bank, 72/177
Carriage by Air Act, 1961 (c. 27)...61/458
Carriage by Air (Supplementary Provisions) Act, 1962 (c. 43)...62/146; 72/171
Carriage by Railway Act 1972 (c. 33)...72/2878, 2879
Carriage of Goods by Road Act, 1965 (c. 37)...65/406
Carriage of Goods by Sea Act, 1971 (c. 19)...71/10892; 77/2769
Carriage of Passengers by Road Act, 1974 (c. 35)...74/3880
Carriers, 72/336; 73/298-301; 74/291-8; 75/271-4; 76/228-34; 77/247-51; 78/203-7
bailment, 76/228
canals. See CANALS.
carriage by air. See AVIATION.
carriage by rail. See RAILWAYS.
carriage by road, 77/247-9, 1233; 78/203-5. See also ROAD TRAFFIC.
carriage by sea. See SHIPPING AND MARINE INSURANCE.
contract of carriage, 74/293
dangerous goods, 74/294; 75/3001a
forwarding agents, 74/296
goods vehicles. See ROAD TRAFFIC.
inherent vice of goods, 76/230
international arrangements, 76/1482
lien, 73/1961
limitation of liability, 73/300; 74/296, 3880; 75/273
loss of goods, 73/301; 74/3880; 75/3156; 76/228, 230-2
railways. See RAILWAYS.
road traffic. See ROAD TRAFFIC.
sub-contractors, 78/207
transport nationalisation and denationalisation. See TRANSPORT.
Transport Tribunal. See TRANSPORT.
Cars, 77/3109
Carrying offensive weapons, 73/582-4; 75/644, 645
Carrying with intent, 72/1550
Case stated—
income tax, 73/1645-6
magisterial law, 72/2098
originating motion, 75/2587, 2588
Catering. See FOOD AND DRUGS.
Cathedrals (Appointed Commissioners) Measure, 1951 (No. 4)...3257
Cathedrals (Grants) Measure, 1954 (No. 3)...54/1058
Cathedrals Measure, 1963 (No. 2)...63/1187
Cathedrals Measure 1976 (No. 1)...76/816
Cattle, 72/92-4; 73/84, 1228; 74/86, 314; 75/79; 78/78

Causation, 73/2281; 74/2554, 2622; 75/2287, 2288, 3222
Cautions, 72/1954; 74/326, 2038, 2044
Cayman Islands, 72/242, 243; 75/3218a
Cayman Islands and Turks and Caicos Islands Act, 1958 (c. 13)...58/257; 62/209
Cemetery, 74/290. See also BURIAL AND CREMATION.
Census, 72/2927
Cereals. See AGRICULTURE.
Cereals Marketing Act, 1965 (c. 14)...65/55
Certiorari, 77/2285; 78/3, 423, 1897, 2324, 2429
Ceylon, 72/244
Ceylon Independence Act, 1947 (11 & 12 Geo. 6, c. 7)...834, 835
Chambers, 73/2603
Chancery Division, 72/2689-95; 73/2603-9; 74/2896-901; 75/2592-5; 76/2113-4; 77/2286-94; 78/2326-9
Chancery of Lancaster, 73/2604
Change of name, 73/2212
Change of use. See TOWN AND COUNTRY PLANNING.
Channel Islands, 72/245, 280; 73/186-93; 75/1078, 1505, 3239. See also Alderney, Guernsey, Jersey.
Channel Islands (Church Legislation) Measure, 1931 (Amendment) Measure, 1957 (No. 1)...57/1149
Channel tunnel, 73/1550-1, 1714
Channel Tunnel (Initial Finance) Act, 1973 (c. 66)...73/1551
Character, evidence of. See CRIMINAL LAW.
Charging order, 73/2610; 75/2596, 2597; 77/2295
Charitable Trusts (Validation) Act, 1954 (c. 58)...54/409
Charities, 72/337-44; 73/302-13; 74/299-308; 75/275-85; 76/235-43; 77/252-64; 78/208-18
accounts, 76/235
Australia, 76/166
charitable bequest, 77/252
charitable purposes, 72/337; 73/302; 74/3096; 75/2762, 2763, 2774; 76/243; 77/253-5; 78/208-10
benefit to section of community, 72/337
company law, 72/337
employees, 75/2774
housing, 74/3096; 75/2762
Oxfam shop, 75/2763
political purposes, 75/278
recreation, 77/254, 255; 78/208
relief of poverty, 78/209
religious purposes, 73/310
showground purposes, 78/210
students' union, 76/243
charitable trusts, 73/303-4; 74/300; 75/278
amalgamation, 73/303
charitable proceedings, 73/304
class of potential beneficiaries, 74/300
Charities Act, 1960 (c. 58)...60/375
Charity Commissioner's Report, 78/211
collecting boxes, 76/237
Commissioners' scheme, 78/212

Gas and Gasworks—*cont.*
British Gas Corporation, 72/1612
calorific value, 72/1613; 74/1700
connection charges, 72/1138
consumers' council, 72/1615
Electricity and Gas Act, 1963...63/1530
Energy Act 1976...76/2744
excise duty, 72/788
finance, 78/1534
Gas Acts, 4285, 4286; 61/3754; 65/1749–51; 68/1728; 72/1619, 1620
gas board, a public body, 76/1318
Gas Council, 75/526
gas explosion, 74/1701
industrial training, 73/3285
limitation of prices, 74/1702
meters, 72/1621; 74/1703; 75/1523
natural gas, 72/2893; 76/2261
negligence, 74/2596, 2597
Northern Ireland. *See* NORTHERN IRELAND.
petroleum gas, 74/2856
pressure, 78/1536
rating, 72/2890; 73/2769
regulations, 72/1624a
rights of entry, 76/1323
safety regulations, 72/1625; 73/1540
superannuation. *See* PENSIONS AND SUPER-ANNUATION.
terminals, 73/2769
Gas (Borrowing Powers) Act, 1965 (c. 60)...65/1751
General average, 72/3203
General Commissioners, 73/1664, 2543
General Medical Council, 77/1889; 78/1941
General Rate Act, 1967 (c. 9)...67/3347–50
General Rate Act, 1970 (c. 19)...70/2405
General Rate (Public Utilities) Act 1977 (c. 11)...77/2451
Geneva Conventions Act, 1957 (c. 52)...57/1807
Genocide, 78/1452
Genocide Act, 1969 (c. 12)...657
German Conventions Act, 1955 (4 & 5 Eliz. 2, c. 2)...55/1407
Germany, 72/1829–35; 73/1760–6; 74/392, 2892; 75/1740, 2728, 2758, 3268
Ghana, 72/252; 73/135
Ghana (Consequential Provision) Act, 1960 (c. 41)...60/269
Ghana Independence Act, 1957 (c. 6)...57/287
Gibraltar, 72/2951; 74/1039, 2448, 2497; 78/165
Gifts, 74/1708; 75/1526–2; 77/1474; 78/1538
acceptance, 75/1527
advancement, 75/1400
contingent, 75/3571
death duties, 73/865; 75/937
undue influence. *See* FRAUD, MISREPRESENTATION AND UNDUE INFLUENCE.
validity, 74/1708; 77/1474; 78/1538
Gilbert and Ellice Islands, 72/253, 254; 75/1414, 2722, 3136, 3218a
Gipsies, 72/3347; 74/3744; 75/3353
Giro, 72/747
Glebe land, 75/1013
Goggles, 72/2385; 73/2325
Going equipped for stealing, 77/565

Goods vehicles, 72/3061; 75/2987–95; 76/2424; 77/687, 2611, 2612; 78/2588, 2589
Government Trading Funds Act, 1973 (c. 63)...73/3279
Governors, 72/255
Governors' Pensions Act, 1957 (c. 62)...57, 2662
Grants—
agriculture, 72/68
Grave financial hardship, 72/1038–43; 73/911; 74/1031, 1032; 75/973
Greater London Council, 72/2085, 2086; 73/995, 2057; 74/3752
Greater London Council (General Powers) Act, 1965...65/2374
Greater London Council (General Powers) Act, 1966...66/7294
Greater London Council (General Powers) Act, 1967...67/2375
Greece, 72/3050; 74/795, 3238; 75/761, 2758
Greenwich Hospital Act, 1947 (c. 5)...7191
Greenwich Hospital Act, 1967 (c. 74)...67/2458
Grenada, 73/204, 205
Ground rent, 77/1730
Guarantee and Indemnity, 72/1627–30; 73/1545, 1546; 74/1709, 1710; 75/1529–31; 76/1324; 77/1475–9; 78/1539–41
bank, 74/1691
export guarantee, 73/1708
foreign promissory note, 72/1627
guarantee, 72/1628, 1629; 73/1546; 74/1903; 75/1529, 1530; 76/1814; 77/363, 1476; 78/1539, 1540
indemnity, 72/3189; 75/1531
irrevocable letter of credit, 77/163
performance bond, 77/162
return of deposit, 78/141
sale of goods, 77/2672
Guarantee payments, 77/993–5; 78/951–3
Guardian *ad litem*, 75/2189, 3265
Guardianship, 73/2183, 2184; 74/2400–2; 76/1788
step-father, 73/2183
Guardianship Act, 1973 (c. 29)...73/2184; 74/2402
Guardianship and Maintenance of Infants Act, 1951 (c. 56)...3079
Guardianship of Minors Act, 1971 (c. 3)...71/5902
Guernsey, 72/256–8; 73/109, 187, 1013; 74/677, 1915; 75/1763, 1771, 3095
Guildford Cathedral Measure, 1959 (No. 3)...59/1073
Guinea, 75/1281
Gun Barrel Proof Act 1978 (c. 9)...78/1471, 1472
Gun licences, 73/1472–4; 74/1634
Guyana Independence Act, 1966 (c. 14)...66/866
Guyana Republic Act, 1970 (c. 18)...70/182

Habeas corpus, 75/656; 76/3; 77/566, 1393 4a; 78/6, 515, 1453, 1990. *See also* CROWN PRACTICE.
Hackney carriage, 77/2444, 2613

Indonesia, 75/1656, 1754
  driving licence, 74/334. *See also* ROAD
  TRAFFIC.
Indus Basin Development Act, 1960 (9 &
  10 Eliz. 2, c. 1)...60/295
Industrial and Provident Societies Act, 1952
  (c. 17)...52/1699
Industrial and Provident Societies Act, 1961
  (c. 28)...61/4278
Industrial and Provident Societies Act, 1965
  (c. 12)...65/1968, 1969
Industrial and Provident Societies Act, 1967
  (c. 48)...67/1986
Industrial and Provident Societies Act, 1975
  (c. 41)...75/1691
Industrial and Provident Societies Act 1978
  (c. 34)...78/1687
Industrial and Provident Societies (Amend-
  ment) Act, 1954 (c. 43)...54/1588
Industrial Arbitration Board, 72/1162
Industrial Assurance and Friendly Societies
  Act, 1948 (c. 39)...4963; 56/4426
Industrial Assurance and Friendly Societies
  Act, 1948 (Amendment) Act, 1958 (c. 27)
  58/1634
Industrial Common Ownership Act 1976 (c.
  78)...76/2748
Industrial Court, 72/2681, 2682; 73/2680-2
Industrial Development Act, 1966 (c. 34)...
  66/11860
Industrial Development (Ships) Act, 1970 (c.
  2)...70/2810
Industrial disease, 75/3594; 76/2905
  bladder, 77/2845
  byssinosis, 73/3496
  national insurance. *See* NATIONAL INSUR-
    ANCE.
  occupational deafness, 77/2846-9; 78/2786
  pneumoconiosis. *See* PNEUMOCONIOSIS.
  workmen's compensation. *See* WORKMEN'S
    COMPENSATION.
Industrial Diseases (Benefit) Act, 1954 (c.
  16)...54/2162
Industrial Expansion Act, 1968 (c. 32)...68/
  3867
Industrial Injuries and Diseases (Northern
  Ireland Old Cases) Act, 1975 (c. 17)...
  75/2402
Industrial Injuries and Diseases (Old Cases)
  Act, 1967 (c. 34)...67/2594, 2595
Industrial Injuries and Diseases (Old Cases)
  Act, 1975 (c. 16)...75/3595
Industrial injuries benefit, 72/2263-81; 73/
  2244-52; 75/2254-62; 76/2600-4; 77/2001,
  2853-5; 78/2787, 2788
Industrial law. *See* EMPLOYMENT.
Industrial Organisation and Development
  Act, 1947 (c. 40)...10247
Industrial relations. *See* EMPLOYMENT *and*
  TRADE UNIONS.
Industrial Relations Act, 1971 (c. 72)...71/
  3973, 3974
Industrial Reorganisation Corporation Act,
  1966 (c. 50)...66/11971
Industrial Societies, 74/1877, 1878; 75/1691;
  76/1448, 1449; 77/1626, 1627; 78/1686,
  1687
  fees, 76/1448, 1449

Industrial Societies—*cont.*
  industrial and provident societies, 74/
    1877; 76/1448; 77/1626; 78/1686
  Industrial and Provident Societies Acts,
    56/4287, 4288; 61/4278; 65/1968, 1969;
    67/1986; 68/1914; 75/1691; 78/1687
  industrial assurance, 74/1878; 76/1449;
    77/1627
Industrial training, 72/3394-6; 73/3285-8;
  74/3791, 3792; 75/3393
Industrial Training Act, 1964 (c. 16)...64/
  3620
Industrial tribunals, 72/1184, 1185; 74/1198-
  213; 75/1119-25; 76/907-11; 77/1008-17;
  78/961-9
Industry. *See* TRADE AND INDUSTRY.
Industry Act, 1971 (c. 17)...71/11593
Industry Act, 1972 (c. 63)...72/3398
Industry Act, 1975 (c. 68)...75/3394
Industry (Amendment) Act 1976 (c. 73)...
  76/2753
Infants, Children and Young Persons. *See*
  MINORS.
Infringement, 72/2568-74; 74/470-3, 2781-
  91, 2889, 2936; 75/439-52; 77/2170-83,
  2176, 3039; 78/342-52
Inheritance (Provision for Family and Dependants) Act, 1975 (c. 63)...75/3582
Injunction, 72/2746-51; 73/3658-63; 75/
  2637-44; 76/276, 2153-7, 2159-61; 78/
  2376-8
  against Crown, 74/3801
  against disciplinary proceedings to, 75/
    2638
  against husband, 73/2663; 74/1786
  against landlord, 74/2062
  alternative remedies, 73/2659
  computer, purchase of, 76/2153
  contempt, 78/1601
  contract of employment, threat to ter-
    minate, 75/1095
  county court, 72/551, 552; 78/379
  delay, 74/2715
  discharge of, 76/2154
  disciplinary proceedings, 75/2638
  domestic violence, 77/1538, 1567
  ex parte, 77/1567; 78/1602
  exclusion of adult child from parental
    home, 75/2637
  form of order, 74/1035
  interlocutory, 76/276, 2155-7, 2159-61;
    78/2379
  irrevocable credit, 75/163
  jurisdiction of High Court, 73/2660
  libel, 77/1784, 1786
  local authorities, 56/6781; 74/2967
  mandatory, 73/2661; 74/2966
  Mareva injunction, 78/2376
  no justiciable cause of action, 77/2344
  nuisance, 74/2715, 2721, 2723; 77/2146
  patents and designs, 72/2575
  pending appeal, 74/2965
  petition within three years of marriage,
    73/2663
  picketing, 75/2453
  principles of grant, 75/2640

Medicine—*cont.*

poisons, 72/2140, 2141; 73/2137; 74/2329; 75/2114; 76/1720; 77/1899; 78/1952
port health authorities, 74/3077, 74/2318, 2469
prescriptions, 78/1953
private practice, 76/1827
professions supplementary to medicine, 75/2115
Professions Supplementary to Medicine Act, 1960 (c. 66)...62/1904; 63/2196
public health. *See* PUBLIC HEALTH.
radioactive substances, 78/1954
safety and medicines, 75/2116; 76/1722; 77/1900
sale, 76/1723; 77/1900a; 78/1955
supply of medicines, 78/1956
therapeutic substances, 72/2143; 73/2138; 74/2333
veterinary drugs, 78/1957
veterinary surgery, 72/2143a, 2144; 73/2139, 75/2117; 78/1958
world health, 74/1973

Medicines Act, 1968 (c. 67)...68/2462; 77/1894–5
Medicines Act, 1971 (c. 69)...71/7303, 7304

Meetings, 75/2001, 3452

companies. *See* COMPANY LAW.
local authorities. *See* LOCAL GOVERNMENT.
Public Bodies (Admission to Meetings) Act, 1960 (c. 67)...60/2618
public meetings, 75/2001
members' club, 72/1740
validity, 75/3452

Memorandum in writing, 72/3540; 73/3456–8; 75/1612, 3531, 3541; 77/1975

Mens rea, 73/566–570; 74/653, 654, 657; 75/2993; 76/486, 496, 499. *See also* Intent.

Mental Health, 72/1093; 73/2140–5; 74/2335–41, 75/2120–9; 76/1724–9; 77/1901–5; 78/1959

Court of Protection, 72/2145; 73/2140, 2141; 75/2120
criminal offence, 77/511
discharge, 72/2146
divorce, 72/1093
false imprisonment, 75/2568
hospital, 75/2122
hospital order, 73/2142; 74/737; 76/1724
ill-treatment of patient, 76/1725
informal patient, 77/457
insanity. *See* CRIMINAL LAW; DIVORCE AND MATRIMONIAL CAUSES.
law reform, 76/1579
Law Reform (Miscellaneous Provisions) Act, 1949 (c. 100)...5973
Mental Health Act, 1959 (c. 72)...59/1970, 1971; 60/1892
Mental Health (Amendment) Act, 1975 (c. 29)...75/2124, 2125
mental health services, 74/2219, 2337
mental treatment, 75/715
mentally abnormal offenders, 75/1934; 76/502
mentally handicapped children, 74/1095, 2196
Northern Ireland. *See* NORTHERN IRELAND.

Mental Health—*cont.*

nurse, assault by, 75/2128
patient, assault on by nurse, 75/2128
proceedings, 72/1017
property of lunatic, 75/3577
psychiatric patients, 73/2144; 74/717
receiving order, 77/1904
residential home, 73/2145
review tribunals, 76/1729
settlement, 77/1905
Mental Health Act, 1959 (c. 72)...59/1970, 1971; 60/1892
Mental Health (Amendment) Act, 1975 (c. 29)...75/2124
Merchandise marks, 72/3422, 3423
Merchandise Marks Act, 1953 (c. 48)...53/3656
Merchant shipping. *See* SHIPPING AND MARINE INSURANCE.
Merchant Shipping Act, 1948 (c. 44)...9648 56/8313
Merchant Shipping Act, 1950 (c. 9)...9649, 9650
Merchant Shipping Act, 1952 (c. 14)...52/3264
Merchant Shipping Act, 1954 (c. 18)...54/3121, 3122
Merchant Shipping Act, 1964 (c. 47)...64/3424
Merchant Shipping Act, 1965 (c. 47)...65/3653
Merchant Shipping Act 1967 (c. 26)...67/3665
Merchant Shipping Act, 1970 (c. 36)...70/2688; 78/2750
Merchant Shipping Act, 1974 (c. 43)...74/3622; 77/2804; 78/2751
Merchant Shipping (Liability of Shipowners and Others) Act, 1958 (c. 62)...58/3183
Merchant Shipping (Load Lines) Act, 1967 (c. 27)...67/3666
Merchant Shipping (Minicoy Lighthouse) Act, 1960 (c. 42)...60/2985
Merchant Shipping (Oil Pollution) Act, 1971 (c. 59)...71/11013, 11014
Merchant Shipping (Safety Convention) Act, 1949 (c. 43)...9651; 56/8317
Merchant Shipping (Safety Convention) Act, 1977 (c. 24)...77/2805
Meteorology, 72/1865; 73/1793
Meters—
electricity, 71/3911; 75/1076
gas, 72/1621; 75/1523
Methodist Church, 78/213b
Metropolitan Magistrates' Courts Act, 1959 (c. 45)...59/2006
Metropolitan police, 72/2630
Metropolitan Police Act, 1839 (Amendment) Act, 1958 (c. 48)...58/2560
Metropolitan Police (Borrowing Powers) Act, 1952 (c. 19)...52/2595
Midwives, 77/1992
Midwives Act, 1951 (c. 53)...6211
Midwives (Amendment) Act, 1950 (c. 13)...6212
Migrant workers, 73/1306, 1307. *See also* EUROPEAN COMMUNITIES.
Milford Haven Conservancy Act, 1958 (c. 23)...58/3184

PRINTED IN GREAT BRITAIN

BY

THE EASTERN PRESS LTD.

OF LONDON AND READING